Vampires, werewolves, UFOs and ghosts, or maybe the latest report of a pterodactyl sighting?

Life after dark will never be the same once you've read *The Vampire Gallery* and the new editions of *The Vampire Book* and *Unexplained!* From fictional characters to real-life reports of strange people and mysterious events, these comprehensive guides to the unknown will leave you begging (or howling) for more.

The Vampire Gallery: A Who's Who of the Undead

Read about 300 fictional vampires from 19th- and 20th-century literature, film, music, theatre, poetry and comic books. Vampire expert Dr. J. Gordon Melton provides intriguing essays on these characters and their creators.

Dr. J. Gordon Melton • 1998 • Paperback • 600 pages
125 illustrations • ISBN 1-57589-053-1

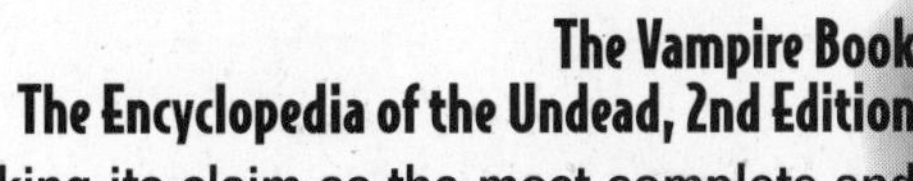

The Vampire Book
The Encyclopedia of the Undead, 2nd Edition

Re-staking its claim as the most complete and authoritative source on the subject, *The Vampire Book* is back – with more facts, photos (including a 16-page color insert) and new features guaranteed to quench the thirst of even the most die-hard fans.

Dr. J. Gordon Melton • 1998 • Paperback • 900 pages
300 illustrations • 40 color photos • ISBN 1-57859-071-X

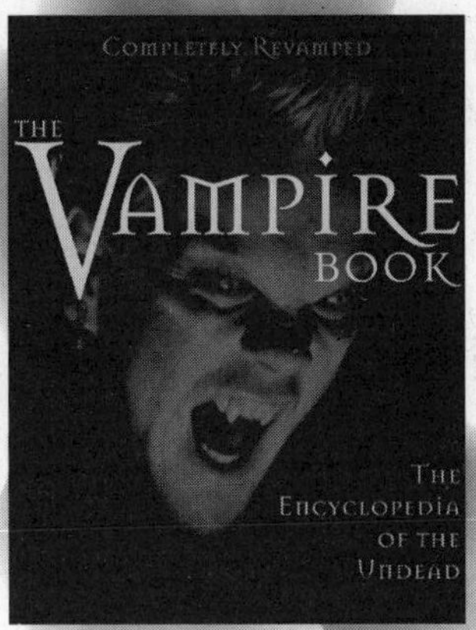

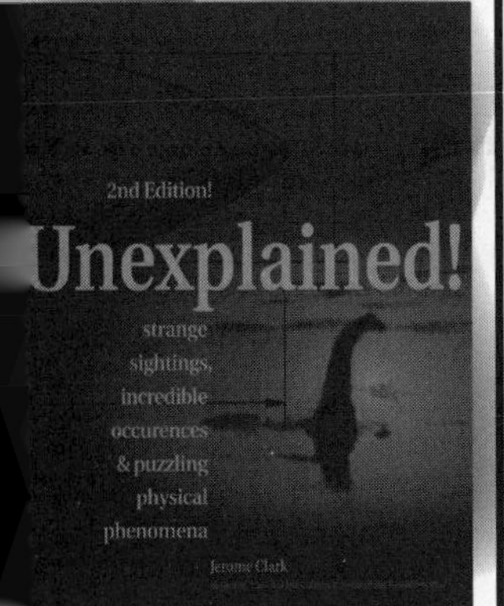

Unexplained! Strange Sightings, Incredible Occurrences, and Puzzling Physical Phenomena, 2nd Edition

This new edition of *Unexplained!* delves into the mysteries of crop circles, UFO sightings, strange creatures like the Chupacabra, a Mexican goat sucker (as featured on *The X-Files*) and much more. Arranged in easy-to-read subject chapters, fans will enjoy this updated and expanded edition.

Jerome Clark • 1998 • Paperback • 600 pages
150 photos and illustrations • ISBN 1-57859-070-1

Available at bookstores everywhere, or in the U.S. call 1-800-776-6265

ALSO AVAILABLE FROM VISIBLE INK PRESS

VideoHound's® Golden Movie Retriever®

VideoHound's Vampires on Video

VideoHound's Sci-Fi Experience: Your Quantum Guide to the Video Universe

VideoHound's Complete Guide to Cult Flicks and Trash Pics

VideoHound's Video Premieres: The Only Guide to Video Originals and Limited Releases

VideoHound's Independent Film Guide

VideoHound's Family Video Guide, 2nd Edition

VideoHound's Soundtracks: Music from the Movies, Broadway and Television

The Vampire Book, 2nd Edition: The Encyclopedia of the Undead

The Vampire Gallery: A Who's Who of the Undead

The UFO Book: Encyclopedia of the Extraterrestrial

Unexplained! 2nd Edition: Strange Sightings, Incredible Occurrences, and Puzzling Physical Phenomena

VIDEOHOUND'S HORROR SHOW

VIDEOHOUND'S HORROR SHOW

999 Hair-Raising, Hellish, and Humorous Movies

Mike Mayo

Foreword by William Lustig

Detroit London

VIDEOHOUND'S® HORROR SHOW

Published by Visible Ink Press,
a division of Gale Research
835 Penobscot Bldg.
Detroit MI 48226-4094

Address after
September 15, 1998:

Visible Ink Press
27500 Drake Rd.
Farmington Hills MI 48331-3535

Art Director: Mary Krzewinski
Photos: The Kobal Collection

Mayo, Mike, 1948-
Videohound's horror show : 999 hair-raising, hellish, and humorous movies / Mike Mayo
p. cm.
Includes index.
ISBN 1-57859-047-7 (alk. paper)
1. Horror films—Catalogs. 2. Video recordings—Catalogs.
I. Title.
PN1995.9.H6M3247 1998
016.79143'6164—dc21 98-21515
CIP

ISBN 1-57859-047-7
Printed in the United States of America

10 9 8 7 6 5 4 3 2

A Cunning Canine Production®

Table of Contents

THE REVIEWS

SIDEBARS

FOREWORD

Hi. My name is Bill and I am a horror film junkie.

If you bought this book (or if you are a cheapskate reading it in the book store) you are probably not unlike myself. You search every "mom and pop" video store—you know you'll never find them at Blockbuster—for that undiscovered gem that you haven't seen. You often travel into neighborhoods where you wouldn't normally go on a dare to find that long out-of-print video. You even have moments of despair considering the possibility that *you have seen all the horror films worth seeing.*

Horror is entertainment at its most primitive, which is why it has traditionally been embraced by the young and vilified by the establishment. As an avid video/laserdisc/DVD collector (someone recently commented that my collection is more like a video store), I have been frustrated by the indifference video companies have for their genre films (particularly low-budget ones). This indifference is surprising since the genre transcends race, gender, politics, religion, and nationality. The ugly truth is that video company executives still view horror as a disreputable genre and treat the films as such. Sure, they'll pocket the money earned from them, but will embrace instead the latest Jane Austen piece of crap.

My work as a producer/director of genre films gives me the opportunity to travel around the country and the world. Everywhere I go, I make it a point to discover THAT video store. It can be Mondo Video A-Go-Go in L.A., Scarecrow Video in Seattle, Kim's in N.Y.C., Cult Films in Amsterdam, Cinemania in Sacramento, The Cinema Store in London, or Thomas Video in Detroit. The frustration of not being able to find certain films (or if available, quality uncut, widescreen transfers) caused me to take action.

With the support of a like-minded video executive, Jay Douglas of Anchor Bay Entertainment (based, of all places, in Troy, Michigan—go figure), I have been searching for the rights and elements to restore neglected genre films. Releasing overlooked, underappreciated gems like *Brute Force, Naked City, Daughters of Darkness, Alice Sweet Alice, Girl on a Motorcycle, Zombie, Fantastic Planet, The Boogeyman, Tenderness of Wolves,* as well as Hammer Film's *Dracula, Prince of Darkness, Rasputin the Mad Monk, Plague of Zombies, The Reptile, Lost Continent, Quatermass and the Pit, The Satanic Rites of Dracula, The Legend of the Seven Golden Vampires* (with its re-edited U.S. version *Seven Brothers Meet Dracula*), *Shatter, Frankenstein Created Woman, The Mummy's Shroud, The Devil Rides Out, The Witches, Quatermass 2, X the Unknown, Four Sided Triangle, The Abominable Snowman, Prehistoric Women, The Vengeance of She, The Viking Queen,* and *A Challenge for Robin Hood* on video, laserdisc, and DVD—digitally mastered, uncut in their original theatrical aspect ratios—has been truly a labor of love.

If you are tired of watching *Scream* and/or *Friday the 13th* for the 20th time and are searching for alternatives, this is the perfect book for you.

—William Lustig
West Hollywood, CA
May, 1998

William Lustig produced and directed Maniac *(1981) and* Vigilante *(1983), and directed* Maniac Cop *(1987),* Hit List *(1988),* Relentless *(1989),* Maniac Cop 2 *(1990), and* Uncle Sam *(1996). But of all his credits, he is most proud of his appearance as a "Fake Shemp" in Sam Raimi's* Army of Darkness.

INTRODUCTION

Somewhere, a group of kids are taking their places around a television in someone's basement or in an apartment or a den. Wherever they are, no adults are close by. Not now. Not tonight.

A boy turns off the lights. The others laugh but they understand what's going on and they like it. One girl curls in a chair and hugs a pillow tight to her chest. Another sprawls across the floor, then edges closer to her friend by the sofa. A second boy makes a lame joke as he slips the tape into the VCR and the screen goes black. He throws himself onto the sofa and wonders if he could put his arm across the back where the girl is sitting. They hear the music—quick staccato notes of a piano, shrill brass or dark textured chords of a pipe organ—before the first image appears. It might be the hard grin of a lighted jack-o-lantern or headlights cutting across wet pavement at night.

They're ready to be frightened and they delight in the anticipation of it.

That's the lasting appeal of the horror movie. It can be both an individual and group experience that lets us see a stylized preview of our own mortality, then vicariously overcome it. As Stephen King puts it, when we watch a horror movie, we dare the nightmare.

I first tapped into that shared fright decades ago and can remember it as vividly and completely as any important moment in my life. It must have been sometime in the late 1950s—a Friday night when my parents finally allowed my sisters and me to stay up to watch the late show. They must not have known the title. If they had, surely we'd have been sent to bed, but the three of us wound up huddled together in a wide armchair and saw those headlights on gleaming wet asphalt.

The movie was Don Siegel's *Invasion of the Body Snatchers.* Though it contains no gore, no grotesque monsters, it frightened us to the marrow. (It still does, far more than any of the remakes.) No, we did not catch the sexual interplay woven throughout the story and we didn't understand the politics. Those elements make the film something much more than a horror movie, but they really don't matter.

Even a child can recognize the comfortable, all-too-real small town setting of Santa Mira, California, where the story is set. A child knows that half-formed creatures lurk in the shadows of every basement. A child understands adults who are suddenly and inexplicably "not themselves." Ask any kid. These things scare them every day.

And that is the simple criterion by which we judge horror movies. The good ones scare us.

The other stuff may be important—the "subtext," the symbolism, the archetypes, the levels of meaning—but if a horror movie doesn't scare us, it isn't a good horror movie. Of course, for every *Invasion of the Body Snatchers*, there's a *Night of the Lepus* about giant mutant killer bunnies terrorizing the lettuce harvest. We can't ignore those, either, now can we? They fall under the general heading of Bad Horror We Love, and they're given their due here.

But, going back to the good horror movies—how do they scare us?

The best ones share three common elements that are the building blocks of any work of popular narrative fiction—on film or in print—but they're essential to horror:

1) We empathize with the characters. Even if we don't like or identify with them, we have to invest emotion in their fate. We've got to care about them.
2) We accept and believe in the setting. It may be a little California town or the spaceship *Nostromo*, but on some level we must enter that world and understand its rules.
3) We're afraid of the monster. It can be a specific creature or thing; it can be a spirit, a concept. Whatever, it must touch an existing fear within us or create one.

Perverse beings that we humans are, we enjoy being scared. Some of the earliest projected moving images were of locomotives heading directly toward the screen. Those raw pictures were so powerful that they sent inexperienced audiences screaming for the exits. Of course, those same audiences turned right around and paid to see the locomotives again, and they still pay to be scared in other ways.

Filmmakers' sophistication has risen considerably from those first simple movies, but the reaction they're trying to provoke hasn't changed.

Fast forward to the mid-1960s.

It's Friday night on a college campus. A group of dateless guys heads out of a dormitory to the Free Flicks. They don't really care what the movie is; they just want to kill some time before they start drinking beer. They're typically rowdy, boisterous, loud, rude. When they realize that they're going to watch a silent movie fergodssake, they become even louder and ruder, making stupid jokes about the florid acting style and silly plot ideas like characters' holding up one hand to ward off the Strangler. After 20 or 30 minutes, they're hooting so hard at their own humor that they can barely contain themselves. Jeez, isn't this the funniest thing you ever saw; it's so silly; it's ridiculous...

...and then, OHMYGOD!, Mary Philbin reaches over his shoulder and snatches off Lon Chaney's mask and the whole auditorium falls silent.

The stretched-tight skull-face, the lipless mouth stretched over rotted malformed teeth, the lank hair, flattened ears, porcine snout. And those eyes bulging out of dark sockets.

That face is the stuff of nightmares and it stopped us cold in our ignorant laughter. Of course, we got over it and began mocking the screen again, but the jeers weren't the same. Chaney had scared us profoundly. He still does.

Good horror movies do not lose their power. They go in and out of fashion— styles of dress and grooming become dated—but the really good ones are built on a core of believability that remains strong and vital beneath the surface. Boris Karloff's Frankenstein monster can still stun an audience. Twenty years from now, perhaps *Scream* will do the same, or by then it may have been long forgotten. We'll see.

Fast forward again another dozen or so years. The undergraduate who watched *Phantom of the Opera* has become a film reviewer. A new low-budget horror movie is opening with no fanfare. Made by some guy named Carpenter that nobody's ever heard of.

I remember that I didn't have to see it. My colleague at the paper was taking care of the review, but it was a slow night. My wife and I had recently moved to another little college town in the mountains—a town of modest one- and two-story houses on tree-lined streets.

She was away that evening. The Lyric Theatre was close, so I decided to walk over. Bought a large popcorn; had no trouble finding a seat—like I said, it was a slow night. Then the lights went down, and that staccato piano filled the auditorium and the lighted jack-o-lantern appeared. And, for the next 92 minutes I tried to convince myself that I wasn't afraid of the monster stalking the little town of Haddonfield. No psycho stalking babysitters was going to scare me! I was, after all, a trained professional who watches films on two tracks, constantly examining his emotional reaction through the cold lens of reason, the better to understand how he is being manipulated and explain that to readers of the newspaper.

Yeah, right.

Actually, it worked while I was in the theatre. But when I got up from my seat and walked outside—outside into a town of modest one- and two-story houses on tree-lined streets much like Haddonfield—that was a different story. Then, I realized, I'd walked out of the theatre and into the movie. I got home very quickly, telling myself all the way that such things don't happen, that guy isn't really alive. And I almost believed myself but I still turned on all the lights and opened all the closets and wondered when the hell my wife was coming back.

A good horror movie makes you do that when you're alone and you don't have to hide your reaction.

Halloween was released before the home video revolution changed the way studio executives thought about horror. They had understood the "herd instinct," if you will, of horror fans in a theatrical context, but didn't believe that it would translate to home video.

"The success of horror movies on video initially baffled many people," Ed Hulse wrote in *Video Business* magazine. "Conventional wisdom held that shudder shows were most effective in theatres, where large groups of strangers huddled together in the dark, bonded by their feelings of dread. Video, it was once believed, would dilute the experience; who'd be scared watching a horror film in the living room with family and friends?

"While the wags pontificated, consumers snatched horror/sci-fi tapes from store shelves as fast as they could be stocked."

But why is that? What attracts young people to video horror in groups?

In part, it's because many horror movies are stories of initiation, of discovery, and that's what young people are in the middle of. Countless horror plots—from *Dracula* to *The Silence of the Lambs*—can be boiled down to this: An unknown force attacks a group of younger people, killing some of them. The rest are guided by an older person who shows them how to defeat the monster.

Other horror films work in exactly the opposite direction, not leading adolescents into adulthood, but allowing all audiences to revert to childhood.

Stephen King says that "the mythic, 'fairy tale' horror film intends to take away the shades of gray...; it urges us to put away our more civilized and adult penchant for analysis and to become children again, seeing things in pure blacks and pure whites. It may be that horror movies provide psychic relief on this level because this invitation to lapse into simplicity, and even outright madness is extended so rarely. We are told we may allow our emotions a free rein...or no rein at all." (*Danse Macabre*, Everest House, 1980.)

Micro-budget mogul Roger Corman expresses similar sentiments in simpler terms. "Put together correctly, the classic horror sequence is the equivalent of the sexual act. The sharp, shocking event at the end that releases the tension is the equivalent of the orgasmic climax. A comedian building tension successfully to a punch line gets a laugh at the climax. A director in a horror genre does the same but gets a scream. Either way, there is growing tension and release—all analogous to the rhythms of a sexual act." (*How I Made a Hundred Movies in Hollywood and Never Lost a Dime*, Random House, 1990.)

Poet, screenwriter, and critic R.H.W. Dillard has examined horror's most memorable creatures in more detail. He thinks, for example, that the werewolf is a symbol of urban evil, the predator who moves unseen among the masses. The Mummy is "the grave itself bursting hideously through the window, death calling in a gigantic and violently irresistible form." The vampire "insidiously steals from his victims even the peace of death and the safety of the grave.... The vampire comes closest of all these figures of evil in the horror film to representing sin itself."

Finally, the Frankenstein Monster is a "fallen and flawed thing, alone in a world of hate and misunderstanding, out of harmony with the design of his creator and an offense to himself and to nature in that creator's eyes." (*Man at the Movies*, edited by W.R. Robinson, LSU Press, 1967.)

This book looks at those characters—along with the various aliens, bugs, and serial killers who are more popular today—and is not ashamed to laugh when laughter is the appropriate reaction, as it so often is. We all claim that we want our cinematic horror fare to be a rich, well-aged cheddar, but we know that we have to settle for Cheez Doodles, and sometimes—admit it!—we *like* Cheez Doodles. To that end, the VideoHound and I have examined the field carefully and we've chosen the 999 scariest, funniest, dopiest, and most unclassifiable horror movies on tape for review herein. (Why 999? Because the VideoHound claims that is the Number of the Beast in dog years.) The changes in the field that have evolved over the decades are the subject of various sidebar articles, and so are the most important characters, studios, and people in the business.

The lines that once separated horror, s-f, suspense, and fantasy have been so blurred that the definitions don't mean much any more. So we went back to the basic criterion: Is the movie scary? Beyond that, call it whatever you like. Is *Wait Until Dark* a suspense film or a horror film? Stephen King says that it's one of the most frightening movies he's ever seen and that's good enough for me. For the purposes of this book, plot elements are less important than the telling of the tale. After all, isn't *Macbeth* a horror story?

That attitude also accounts for some of the Hound's more unusual choices. Others may not think that *Apocalypse Now, Taxi Driver,* and *The Wizard of Oz* are horror movies but they sure scared me. Simply for the record, my own top-13 horror list is:

Alien
Frankenstein
Halloween
Invasion of the Body Snatchers
Island of Lost Souls
M
Night of the Living Dead
Peeping Tom
The Phantom of the Opera
Psycho
Re-Animator
The Silence of the Lambs
The Wolf Man

When the decision was made to limit this book to 999 titles, we had to set some guidelines. First, of course, we went for the scariest and that meant that the most successful—from *The Edison Frankenstein* to *Mimic*—are here. But so are the less heralded "little" films (*Jack's Back*), video premieres (*Dark Angel: The Ascent*), and foreign films (*An Untold Story*). We've tried to avoid the lame horror-comedies and watered-down made-for-TV fare. And since this is a VideoHound guide, we've avoided features that are not available on tape or disc. When applicable, special note is made of both poor and excellent transfers from film to tape.

In many of the reviews, you'll notice references to "the opening shot," "the first reel," "the introduction." I choose that approach for two reasons. First, most good horror movies show you what they're up to from the get-go. If I can make that purpose clear in a short review, then I've helped you make a choice the next time you go to the video store. Second, I do not give away any important details. Even though this book is meant for fans who have probably seen a lot of horror movies, nobody's seen everything, and it would be unforgivable of me to spoil a film. (That rule does not apply to the junk. Perhaps it is giving away too much to reveal that the hero of *Blood Freak* is transformed into a turkey-headed monster, but that's the fun of the movie.)

As for the to **Woof!** ratings, to my mind they are the least important part of the book. They're a personal comparative judgment and with horror films, even more than with other forms, individual reactions are matters of age and timing. I hope I've illustrated that with the stories about *Invasion*, *Phantom*, and *Halloween*. When you encounter the right film at the right time in your life, other critical assessments count for little. I don't expect anyone to accept my conclusions and prejudices. Instead, I hope that when we disagree, you'll examine those differences and come to a better understanding of your own values and tastes.

Fast forward one more time to the very recent past.

As I began putting *Horror Show* together, my wife and I moved away from Virginia to a small town in New Jersey. (Appropriately for the subject, we found a house that's within sight of two cemeteries.) For me, everything that had been familiar and comfortable became strange and more than a little threatening. I was in Haddonfield, or was it Santa Mira? A block away from my new house, I was lost. All that had been real was gone. In its place was a strange world that often hurt me—toes stubbed on new stairs, fingers gashed on unexpected edges. I rediscovered an appreciation for the unexplored territory of youth, a country full of glittering threats and promises and wrong turns.

That's the world of the horror film. To quote Richard Dillard again, "We are sitting, you and I, in the plush (if somewhat worn) seats of a darkened movie house—featureless, all of us seated in rows, hearing the first dark chords of a somber score, waiting for the hard grin of death's skull to chill us all to the bone."

We've gone from the darkened movie house to the darkened den and the VCR, but our emotions and expectations of horror have not changed. All of us—young and old—want to face that bastard Death and walk away from him whole, healthy, and stronger for it.

We know that isn't the way life really ends, but this isn't life. This is the movies.

So, step right in. Have a seat on the sofa while I set up this tape. The horror show's about to begin....

—Mike Mayo
Chatham, NJ
March, 1998

ACKNOWLEDGMENTS

VideoHound's Horror Show would not have been possible without considerable help from the following people:

Jim Olenski of Thomas Video in Clawson, Michigan, and Irv Slifkin of Movies Unlimited in Philadelphia generously loaned tapes of older films.

Irv Slifkin also wrote the four sidebar interviews with Charles Band, William Friedkin, Stephen King, and Dan O'Bannon. Irv writes and edits the Movies Unlimited Video Catalog. He's also written about film and video for the *Los Angeles Times*, the *Philadelphia Enquirer*, *Video Business*, *The Hollywood Reporter*, *Empire*, and the *Chicago Tribune*.

Carol Schwartz, senior editor at Visible Ink, asked the right questions and, I hope, caught most of my mistakes.

Tom Weisser of Video Search of Miami supplied several of the Asian films and many of the Jesus Franco and Jean Rollin titles.

Bjarni Brown at Sue Procko Public Relations helped with the Anchor Bay Entertainment re-releases and restorations.

Sue Boyer introduced me to *Dark Carnival*, the fine book about Tod Browning by David J. Skal and Elias Savada.

Richard Dillard showed me many of these movies and we watched quite a few of them together for the first time.

Drew Geishecker at Voyager supplied important information on laser editions.

Johnny Schulze at Incredibly Strange Filmworks made a review copy of *The Edison Frankenstein* available.

Mike Jaworski at West Coast Video in Chatham helped out with informed advice and suggestions on some lesser-known titles.

Victoria Joyce at the Virginia Film Festival arranged the interview that is the source of the quotes in the Fay Wray sidebar.

The reference librarians at the Chatham Borough Public Library were invaluable in locating books through interlibrary loan. If I'd known earlier how efficient they were, I'd have asked for more.

Janice Clifford at Full Moon Entertainment, Josh Davidson at Avalanche Home Entertainment, Frank Djeng at Tai Seng, Fritz Friedman at Columbia Tri-Star, Gretchen Hegle at Home Vision Cinema, Mike Krause at Rhino Home Video, Mike Raso at E.I. Independent, Tony Rosen at Troma Team Video, and Pamela White at York Home Video arranged screeners of new titles and new editions.

To all—thank you, thank you, thank you.

VIDEO SOURCES

Some of the movies in this book are not currently in print, and some of them that are may be difficult to find using conventional devices such as the neighborhood video rental chain. Many independent and mail-order video outlets specialize in rare or hard-to-find movies. We have included a small list of such outlets to assist you in your search.

Thomas Video
122 S. Main St.
Clawson MI 48017
248-280-2833
fax: 248-280-4463
tomvid@mich.com

Movies Unlimited
3015 Darnell Rd.
Philadelphia PA 19154
800-4-MOVIES

Video Vision
4603 Bloomington Ave.
Minneapolis MN 55407
612-728-0000

Video Oyster
145 W. 12th St.
New York NY 10011
fax: 212-989-3533
www.videooyster.com
video@videooyster.com

Facets Video
1517 W. Fullerton Ave.
Chicago IL 60614
800-331-6197

A Million and One World-Wide Videos
PO Box 349
Orchard Hill GA 30266
800-849-7309
fax: 770-227-0873

Home Film Festival
PO Box 2032
Scranton PA 18501
800-258-3456

Video Vault
323 S. Washington St.
Alexandria VA 22314
800-VAULT66
www.videovault.com

Luminous Film & Video
PO Box 1047
Medford NY 11763
516-289-1644
fax: 516-654-3637
www.lfvw.com

Video Library
7157 Germantown Ave.
Philadelphia PA 19119
800-669-7157
www.vlibrary.com

Video Discounters
821 NE Bayberry Ct.
Jensen Beach FL 34957
videodiscounts@juno.com

Alphabetization

Titles are arranged on a word-by-word basis, including articles and prepositions. Leading articles (A, An, The) are ignored in English-language titles; the equivalent foreign articles are not ignored (because so many people—not you, of course—don't recognize them as articles); thus, *The Abominable Dr. Phibes* appears in the "A"s, but *Un Chien Andalou* appears in the "U"s. Acronyms appear alphabetically as if regular words; for example, *C.H.U.D.* is alphabetized as "CHUD." Common abbreviations in titles sort as if they were spelled out, so *The Island of Dr. Moreau* will be alphabetized as "Island of Doctor Moreau" and *Mr. Stitch* as "Mister Stitch." Movie titles with numbers, such as *2000 Maniacs*, are alphabetized as if the number were spelled out—so this title would appear in the "T"s as if it were "Two Thousand Maniacs."

(1) Halloween

(2) In 1978, John Carpenter made a "little" movie about three teenaged girls and a madman, and changed the motion picture business. In terms of return on investment, *Halloween* quickly became the most profitable independent film ever made. Its influence on virtually every horror movie that's been made since then is incalculable. The implacable stalker who kills young people (usually while they're engaged in any sexual activity) has become a cliche, but Carpenter and Debra Hill—his co-writer, producer, and even co-director in some scenes—invented the character. The plot is simple and relentless. So is Carpenter's direction. The film exists in several versions on tape and disc. The best are the 1997 Anchor Bay cassette, which is the full-length theatrical release, digitally mastered and letterboxed, and the Criterion Collection laserdisc. The disc also contains extra footage that was shot during the filming of *Halloween 2* and separate audio track commentary by Carpenter, Hill, and star Jamie Lee Curtis. For fans who know the film well, their comments are illuminating. Carpenter points out flaws, shortcuts that worked, and those that didn't. Jamie Lee Curtis is a little nostalgic and sounds completely relaxed and open about her first job (at age 19). Debra Hill has some of the best stories, but she is unusually thin-skinned and defensive about the film's sexual side.
(3) ***AKA***: *John Carpenter's Halloween.* (4)

(5) 1978 (6) (R) (7) 90m (8) /C (9) *US* (10) Jamie Lee Curtis, Donald Pleasence, Nancy Loomis, P.J. Soles, Charles Cyphers; (11) ***D:*** John Carpenter; (12) ***W:*** John Carpenter, Debra Hill; (13) ***C:*** Dean Cundey; (14) ***M:*** John Carpenter. (15) Mayo Medal '78: Best New Scream Queen (Jamie Lee Curtis). (16) **VHS, LV, letterbox** (17) *VTR, CRC*

Sample Review

Each review contains up to 17 tidbits of information, as enumerated below. Please realize that we faked a bit of info in this review for demonstration purposes.

1. Title (see also the Alternative title below, and the **Alternative Titles Index**)
2. Synopsis/review
3. Alternative title (we faked it here)
4. One- to four-bone rating (or **Woof!**), four bones being the ultimate praise
5. Year released
6. MPAA rating
7. Length in minutes
8. Black and white (B) or color (C)
9. Foreign film code (if produced outside the U.S.); see next column
10. Cast, including cameos and voiceovers (V)
11. Director(s)
12. Writer(s)
13. Cinematographer(s)
14. Music composer(s)/lyricist(s)
15. Awards, including nominations (we took some liberties here)
16. Format(s), including VHS, laser videodisc (LV), DVD, CD-I, letterboxed, and closed captioned
17. Distributor code(s), if available on video (see also **Distributor List** and **Distributor Guide**)

Foreign Film Codes

The foreign film codes indicate the country or countries in which a film was produced or financed. A listing of films by country may also be found in the **Category Index** under "Foreign" and the appropriate country.

AL Algerian
AR Argentinian
AT Austrian
AU Australian
BE Belgian
BR Brazilian
GB British
CA Canadian
CH Chinese
CL Colombian
CU Cuban
CZ Czech
DK Danish
NL Dutch
PH Filipino
FI Finnish
FR French
GE German
GR Greek
HK Hong Kong
HU Hungarian
IC Icelandic
IN Indian
IA Iranian
IR Irish
IS Israeli
IT Italian
JP Japanese
KO Korean
LI Lithuanian
MA Macedonian
MX Mexican
NZ New Zealand
NI Nicaraguan
NO Norwegian
PL Polish
PT Portuguese
RU Russian
SA South African
SP Spanish
SW Swedish
SI Swiss
TU Turkish
TW Taiwanese
VT Vietnamese
VZ Venezuelan
YU Yugoslavian

FILMS A TO Z

Abbott and Costello Meet Dr. Jekyll and Mr. Hyde

The boys are bumbling London Bobbies to Boris Karloff's Dr. Jekyll in a pedestrian entry in the comic series. The Hyde makeup, usually worn by stunt man Eddie Parker, is little more than a gorilla mask and the transformation effects are substandard. Karloff is completely comfortable with his limited role. Craig Stevens, TV's Peter Gunn, is the romantic lead. The suffragette chorus line routine will raise feminist hackles. Combining this particular horror story with comedy is handled more entertainingly by the various Warner Bros. cartoons starring Sylvester the Cat and Tweetie-Hyde.

1952 77m/B Bud Abbott, Lou Costello, Boris Karloff, Craig Stevens, Helen Westcott, Reginald Denny, John Dierkes; ***D:*** Charles Lamont; ***W:*** John Grant, Leo Loeb; ***C:*** George Robinson. **VHS** *USH*

Abbott and Costello Meet Frankenstein

Bud and Lou are railroad baggage clerks in Florida where strange crates arrive for the wax museum. Dracula (Bela Lugosi) wants to revive Frankenstein's monster (Glenn Strange) by giving him Lou's brain! Lawrence Talbot (Lon Chaney, Jr.), AKA The Wolfman, says no. It's all played for laughs, making

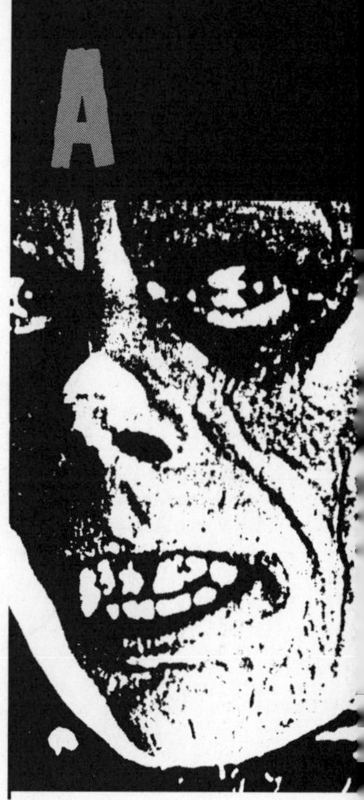

this one of the better horror comedies, with the emphasis definitely on comedy. At one point, director Charles T. Barton allows the Count's reflection to show in a mirror! For shame! Still, some of the animated effects are pretty cool. By the time this lively romp was made, the monsters had passed their prime, and so they're figures of fun. That's fine for Bud and Lou, but for the creatures, familiarity breeds complacency. ***AKA:*** Abbott and Costello Meet the Ghosts.

1948 83m/B Bud Abbott, Lou Costello, Lon Chaney Jr., Bela Lugosi, Glenn Strange, Lenore Aubert, Jane Randolph; ***D:*** Charles T. Barton; ***W:*** John Grant, Robert Lees, Frederic Rinaldo; ***C:*** Charles Van Enger; ***V:*** Vincent Price. **VHS, LV** *USH*

Abbott and Costello Meet the Invisible Man

Bud and Lou are newly graduated detectives who are hired by a boxer (Arthur Franz) falsely accused of murder to clear his name. Before they can do anything, he shoots up with Supertransparent Joy Juice. Yes, the plot is baldly lifted from *The Invisible Man Returns,* and some of the scenes are directly recycled, too, including those cute little hamsters in their leather harnesses. The special effects make for a more comfortable fit with the popular comedians' style than many of their other pairings with the Universal horror stars who were then far past their prime.

1951 82m/B Bud Abbott, Lou Costello, Nancy Guild, Adele Jergens, Sheldon Leonard, William Frawley, Gavin Muir, Arthur Franz; ***D:*** Charles Lamont; ***W:*** Frederic Rinaldo, John Grant, Robert Lees; ***C:*** George Robinson. **VHS** *USH*

Abbott and Costello Meet the Killer, Boris Karloff

As the clumsy title suggests, this is hardly the finest hour for any of the key participants. Karloff is a conman to Bud and Lou's hotel employees. The comedy is played out on the studio's familiar sets. Compared to the duo's other teamings with Universal monsters, it's average or below, and wouldn't be included here if Karloff weren't in it.

1949 84m/B Bud Abbott, Lou Costello, Boris Karloff, Lenore Aubert, Gar Moore, Donna Martell, Alan Mowbray, James Flavin, Roland Winters; ***D:*** Charles T. Barton; ***W:*** John Grant, Hugh Wedlock Jr., Howard Snyder. **VHS, LV, Closed Caption** *USH*

Abbott and Costello Meet the Mummy

The title pretty much says it all for this one. By the time Universal made the film, the studio had produced five Mummy features and had paired the comedians with four other horror stars. The bloom was far off the rose. Still, the slapstick and pratfalls are quickly paced, and though there's comparatively little actual Mummy footage, a giant iguana does pop up briefly and inexplicably, and, yes, that's Richard Deacon as the high priest Semu. This was the last for Bud and Lou with Universal.

1955 90m/B Bud Abbott, Lou Costello, Marie Windsor, Michael Ansara, Dan Seymour, Kurt Katch, Richard Deacon, Mel Welles, Edwin Parker; ***D:*** Charles Lamont; ***W:*** John Grant; ***C:*** George Robinson. **VHS** *USH, FCT*

The Abominable Dr. Phibes

In Vincent Price's long and varied work in the field, this may be his most enjoyable role. As a vengeful 1920s mad doctor, he's droll and virtually silent. More important to the film, he's got a fine, funny script and excellent co-stars to work with. Though Terry-Thomas, Hugh Griffith, and Joseph Cotten don't have as much to do, they contribute substantially. Add in grand sets,

Vincent Price as Dr. Anton Phibes in Robert Fuest's *The Abominable Dr. Phibes.*

"This *is* my costume. I'm a homicidal maniac. They look like everyone else."

—Wednesday (Christina Ricci) explains why she isn't wearing a Halloween costume in *The Addams Family*

costumes, jazzy music, props, and even some fair scares amid the laughs. Robert Fuest directs with a confident, wry tone and gives new meaning to the term "acid rain." Yes, that's Caroline Munro as the late Mrs. Phibes. Simply a delight for fans of Grand Guignol comedy. 🦴🦴🦴½

1971 (PG) 90m/C *GB* Vincent Price, Joseph Cotten, Hugh Griffith, Terry-Thomas, Virginia North, Susan Travers, Alex Scott, Caroline Munro, Peter Gilmore, Aubrey Woods, John Laurie; ***D:*** Robert Fuest; ***W:*** William Goldstein, James Whiton; ***C:*** Norman Warwick. **VHS, LV** *ORI*

The Addams Family

The original one-joke movie is short on plot, long on the delicious graveyard humor that Charles Addams created. The best moments are virtual recreations of magazine cartoons. A few scenes of manic action—a silly duel, a dance, a school play—seem out of step with the otherwise deliberately slow pace. Somehow, though, the relationship between Morticia (Anjelica Huston) and Gomez (Raul Julia) is so believably intense that it energizes the rest of the film. The rest of the casting, notably Christina Ricci as Wednesday and Christopher Lloyd as Uncle Fester, is equally inspired. Remarkably, the sequel is even better. 🦴🦴½

1991 (PG-13) 102m/C Anjelica Huston, Raul Julia, Christopher Lloyd, Dan Hedaya, Elizabeth Wilson, Judith Malina, Carel Struycken, Dana Ivey, Paul Benedict, Christina Ricci, Jimmy Workman, Christopher Hart, John Franklin; ***Cameos:*** Marc Shaiman; ***D:*** Barry Sonnenfeld; ***W:*** Caroline Thompson, Larry Thompson; ***C:*** Owen Roizman; ***M:*** Marc Shaiman. Golden Raspberry Awards '91: Worst Song ("Addams Groove"); Nominations: Academy Awards '91: Best Costume Design. **VHS, LV, Letterboxed, Closed Caption** *PAR*

Addams Family Values

As a killer blonde with the most basic instincts, Joan Cusack is a welcome addition to cartoonist Charles Addams' ghoulish clan. She joins the family as a nanny for Gomez (Raul Julia) and Morticia's (Anjelica Huston) new son Pubert, though her sights are really set on Uncle Fester (Christopher Lloyd). Young Christina Ricci almost steals the film from all of them. Even though the humor is based on grisly material, it's never offensive. As the title indicates, though, those who define "family values" narrowly will likely disagree. Paul Rudnick's script is stronger and funnier than the original, and director Barry Sonnenfeld seems more comfortable with the material. 🦴🦴🦴

1993 (PG-13) 93m/C Anjelica Huston, Raul Julia, Christopher Lloyd, Joan Cusack, Carol Kane, Christina Ricci, Jimmy Workman, Kaitlyn Hooper, Kristen Hooper, Carel Struycken, David Krumholtz, Christopher Hart, Dana Ivey, Peter MacNicol, Christine Baranski, Mercedes McNab; ***D:*** Barry Sonnenfeld; ***W:*** Paul Rudnick; ***M:*** Marc Shaiman. Golden Raspberry Awards '93: Worst Song ("WHOOMP! There It Is"); Nominations: Academy Awards '93: Best Art Direction/Set Decoration; Golden Globe Awards '94: Best Actress—Musical/Comedy (Huston). **VHS, LV, Letterboxed, Closed Caption** *PAR*

The Addiction

Totally bummed out by pictures of My Lai and a walk down a tough inner city street, philosophy grad student Catherine (Lili Taylor) is set upon by a suave exotic vampire (Annabella Sciorra) in a slinky evening dress. Catherine's progress from neophyte to card-carrying undead is a slow dreamlike black-and-white exercise in contradiction. On one hand, vampirism is presented as a logical alternative to reading Kierkegaard and Sartre. In their worst moments—and there are far too many of these—the bloodsuckers sound like refugees from a particularly windy David Mamet play—talking, talking, talking about things the audience cares absolutely nothing about. The film is stylishly staged and photographed. Long stretches appear to be thoroughly humorless, but then they're punctuated by moments of violence so bizarre they can only be seen as low comedy. With the challenging and unpredictable Abel Ferrara, it's

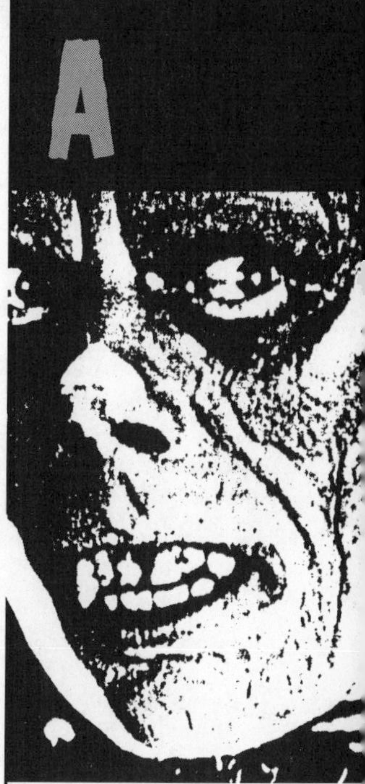

always hard to tell when he's being serious and when he's putting us on. Maybe those are the same.

1995 (R) 82m/B Lili Taylor, Christopher Walken, Annabella Sciorra, Edie Falco, Paul Calderone, Fredro Star, Kathryn Erbe, Michael Imperioli; ***D:*** Abel Ferrara; ***W:*** Nicholas St. John; ***M:*** Joe Delia. Nominations: Independent Spirit Awards '96: Best Actress (Taylor), Best Film. **VHS** *PGV*

Afraid of the Dark

It would be unfair to reveal virtually any of the plot twists in this disturbing psychological horror story. It's told almost completely from the p.o.v. of young Lucas (Ben Keyworth), a British boy who's first seen behind a pair of Coke-bottle-bottom glasses. Someone in his cozy urban neighborhood is slashing blind women with a straight razor. His own mother (Fanny Ardant) might be a victim. The real focus, though, is on Lucas as we slowly learn who and what he is. The source of the horror is childhood itself, what it's like to be small and inexperienced, and powerless in a world made for larger beings. It's complex, challenging, and unconventional. Writer Mark Peploe's (*The Passenger, The Sheltering Sky, Little Buddha*) directorial debut is a small masterpiece.

1992 (R) 91m/C *FR GB* Ben Keyworth, James Fox, Fanny Ardant, Paul McGann, Clare Holman, Robert Stephens; ***D:*** Mark Peploe; ***W:*** Mark Peploe; ***C:*** Bruno de Keyzer. **VHS, LV, Closed Caption** *COL, NLC*

After Midnight

The students taking Psych 102—the Psychology of Fear—go to their professor's house to tell scary campfire stories about a haunted house, a pack of killer dogs, and a deranged killer. For the anthology's framing device, one of their disgruntled classmates is lurking around outside with an axe. Dialogue and production values are well above average. The pace is deliberately slow, a bit too slow really, but at least the film shows some originality and it keeps the bloody special effects to a minimum.

1989 (R) 90m/C Marg Helgenberger, Marc McClure, Alan Rosenberg, Pamela Segall, Nadine Van Der Velde, Ramy Zada, Jillian McWhirter, Billy Ray Sharkey, Judie Aronson, Tracy Wells, Ed Monaghan, Monique Salcido, Penelope Sudrow; ***D:*** Jim Wheat, Ken Wheat; ***W:*** Jim Wheat, Ken Wheat. **VHS, Closed Caption** *FOX, MGM*

Alice in Wonderland

To younger viewers who are sorting out the differences between reality and fiction, this Disney fantasy is a frightening vision of insanity. (At least it was to me when I first saw it.) Even the relatively innocent moments, such as the singing flowers, are threatening, and the psychedelic characters become more and more unpredictable as Alice's journey down the rabbit hole progresses to the Red Queen with her bloody roses. When that madwoman screams, "Off with her head!" you'll believe her. No, it may not be as memorable an evocation of a nightmare as *The Wizard of Oz*, but it's close enough.

1951 (G) 75m/C ***D:*** Hamilton Luske, Wilfred Jackson, Clyde Geronimi; ***V:*** Kathryn Beaumont, Ed Wynn, Sterling Holloway, Jerry Colonna. Nominations: Academy Awards '51: Scoring of a Musical. **VHS, LV, Closed Caption** *DIS, FCT, KUI*

Alice Sweet Alice

Though this psycho-horror is hyped as the debut of a very young Brooke Shields, she has a tiny role. The film is really a complex indictment of Catholicism. Director Alfred Sole's use of middle-class New Jersey locations recalls the better work of George Romero, and he fills the screen with realistic grotesques who are every bit as frightening as walking corpses. He and co-writer Rosemary Ritvo create an interconnected series of bizarre conflicts involving Alice (Paula Sheppard), her sister Karen (Shields), her extended family, community, and church in

THE SILENT ERA

1910-1938

The first silent horror movies established themes, patterns, and conventions that are still popular in the genre today. The vampires, mad scientists, and other monsters—both human and supernatural—made their first appearances before the arrival of sound. More important, though, were the makeup effects that brought to life creatures who could exist only onscreen.

In 1910, Thomas Edison produced a 16-minute version of Mary Shelley's *Frankenstein* with horrifying monster makeup created by star Charles Ogle. For years, it was thought that all complete prints of the film had been lost, but a copy has recently been discovered and is being offered for sale by a small distributor. (It's reviewed here under the title *Edison Frankenstein.*)

In conventional feature-length horror films, one of the first important characters is Cesare, the dark-eyed Somnambulist (Conrad Veidt), who frightened 1919 audiences in *The Cabinet of Dr. Caligari*. The massive moving statue in *The Golem* (1920) can be seen as another version of the Frankenstein Monster.

In 1920, John Barrymore was both the good doctor and his stringy-haired, seedy alter-ego in *Dr. Jekyll and Mr. Hyde.* Hyde is one of horror's great villains—he would appear many times in the years to come—but he pales beside Max Schreck's *Nosferatu.* Actually, the character and the film were made by director F.W. Murnau (real name, Plumpe) under the title *Dracula.* But in a legal dispute with Bram Stoker's estate, a judge ruled that Murnau had infringed upon Stoker's copyrighted material and ordered all copies of the film destroyed. That didn't happen—thank goodness! —but Murnau did change the names of the characters and places in the film.

Max Schreck's vampire is a genuine nightmare, more rat than man, who personifies death on a massive scale. (Werner Herzog and Klaus Kinski recreated the character in 1979's *Nosferatu the Vampyre,* soon to be available on video from Anchor Bay in both English and German language versions.) The undead of the sound era would all take more recognizably human form with much stronger sexual implications.

Lon Chaney (see sidebar) was already a star when he made the first of his two horror masterpieces, *The Hunchback of Notre Dame,* in 1923. A combination of impressive sets, prosthetics that have never been equalled, and incredible athleticism made the film one of the best of its time. Two years later, under painful facial makeup, Chaney became Erik, *The Phantom of the Opera.* (That's him glaring at you from the margins.) It's another story that's often been retold on stage and screen, but his is still the definitive version.

Chaney also created an impressive-looking vampiric character who's not technically "undead" in Tod Browning's 1927 *London After Midnight.* Unfortunately, all copies of the film and the negative appear to have been lost, though rumors of its rediscovery appear often.

It's not surprising that those faces are the first images we remember from the silent horror movies. In the earliest years, filmmakers were limited by bulky equipment and relatively primitive optical effects. They had to depend on individual actors, and they quickly learned that many of the techniques of the stage couldn't be transferred to the screen. Their medium was different, and so they set about to invent new ways to scare audiences.

That happened most memorably at the end of the silent era with an eyeball and a straight razor in Luis Bunuel and Salvador Dali's *Un Chien Andalou.*

the early 1960s. The film's influence on various slasher films of following decades, particularly the Italians, is obvious. Despite a modest budget, it's aged better than many more expensive productions of the same era. The ending's terrific. ***AKA:*** Holy Terror; Communion.

1976 (R) 112m/C Linda Miller, Paula Sheppard, Mildred Clinton, Niles McMaster, Jane Lowry, Rudolph Willrich, Brooke Shields; ***D:*** Alfred Sole; ***W:*** Alfred Sole, Rosemary Ritvo; ***C:*** John Friberg, Chuck Hall. **VHS** *VTR, BTV, HHT*

Alien

The seven-member crew of the space freighter "Nostromo" is awakened from artificial sleep when the ship's computer picks up a signal from a stormy planet. They investigate and the rest is horror history. Director Ridley Scott and writer Dan O'Bannon tell a deceptively simple and completely frightening story. The importance of the magnificent sets created by Ron Cobb and H.R. Giger cannot be overemphasized. Giger's "biomechanical" creature has influenced almost every screen monster that's come since. Cobb calls the interior of the "Nostromo" a "cross between an art deco dance hall and a World War II bomber." Combine all that with letter-perfect ensemble acting led by Sigourney Weaver's career-defining Ripley and the result is an unqualified masterpiece. None of the expensive sequels has approached its intensity.

1979 (R) 116m/C Tom Skerritt, Sigourney Weaver, Veronica Cartwright, Yaphet Kotto, Harry Dean Stanton, Ian Holm, John Hurt; ***D:*** Ridley Scott; ***W:*** Dan O'Bannon; ***C:*** Derek Vanlint; ***M:*** Jerry Goldsmith. Academy Awards '79: Best Visual Effects; Nominations: Academy Awards '79: Best Art Direction/Set Decoration. **VHS, LV** *FOX*

Alien Dead

Clunky early effort from prolific low-budget auteur Fred Olen Ray is strictly amateur night, notable only for the presence of a remarkably dapper and trim Buster Crabbe in his last film role. Otherwise, the acting is on the enthusiastic non-professional level, and the direction isn't much better. Ray often loses focus and the slow action is padded with useless filler. The plot has to do with "living dead" cannibal zombies in a Florida swamp. ***AKA:*** It Fell from the Sky.

1979 (R) 75m/C Buster Crabbe, Linda Lewis, Ray Roberts, Mike Bonavia; ***D:*** Fred Olen Ray; ***W:*** Fred Olen Ray. **VHS** *NO*

Aliens

James Cameron turns Ridley Scott's deliberately paced horror-suspense classic into a hard-charging action movie. Space Marines go back to the original planet to rescue colonists and find an infestation of H.R. Giger's famous creations. Accompanying them, Ripley (Sigourney Weaver) overcomes her fear, and ends things with a thrilling confrontation with the Queen Mother Alien. Fine performances all around (particularly from Lance Henriksen who gives his android character a subtle twist of mechanical weirdness), and a roller-coaster pace. Followed by a substandard sequel.

1986 (R) 138m/C Sigourney Weaver, Michael Biehn, Lance Henriksen, Bill Paxton, Paul Reiser, Carrie Henn, Jenette Goldstein; ***D:*** James Cameron; ***W:*** James Cameron, Walter Hill; ***M:*** James Horner. Academy Awards '86: Best Sound Effects Editing, Best Visual Effects; Nominations: Academy Awards '86: Best Actress (Weaver), Best Art Direction/Set Decoration, Best Film Editing, Best Sound, Best Original Score. **VHS, LV, Letterboxed, Closed Caption** *FOX*

Alien3

By far the weakest entry in the series, *Alien3* suffers from director David Fincher's rock-video approach to the subject. Part three went through several writers and directors and emerged as a fairly unintelligible mess. It begins in standard fashion with Ripley (Sigourney Weaver) crash landing her escape vehicle on a prison planet. Of course, the critter hitched a ride, too.

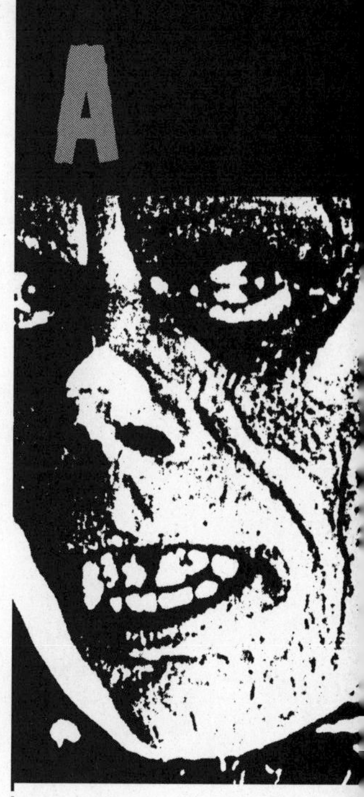

"Fear is a very strong reaction. It makes people realize that they're alive. Their hearts start to beat faster."

—John Cameron as quoted in *Film Yearbook*, 1988.

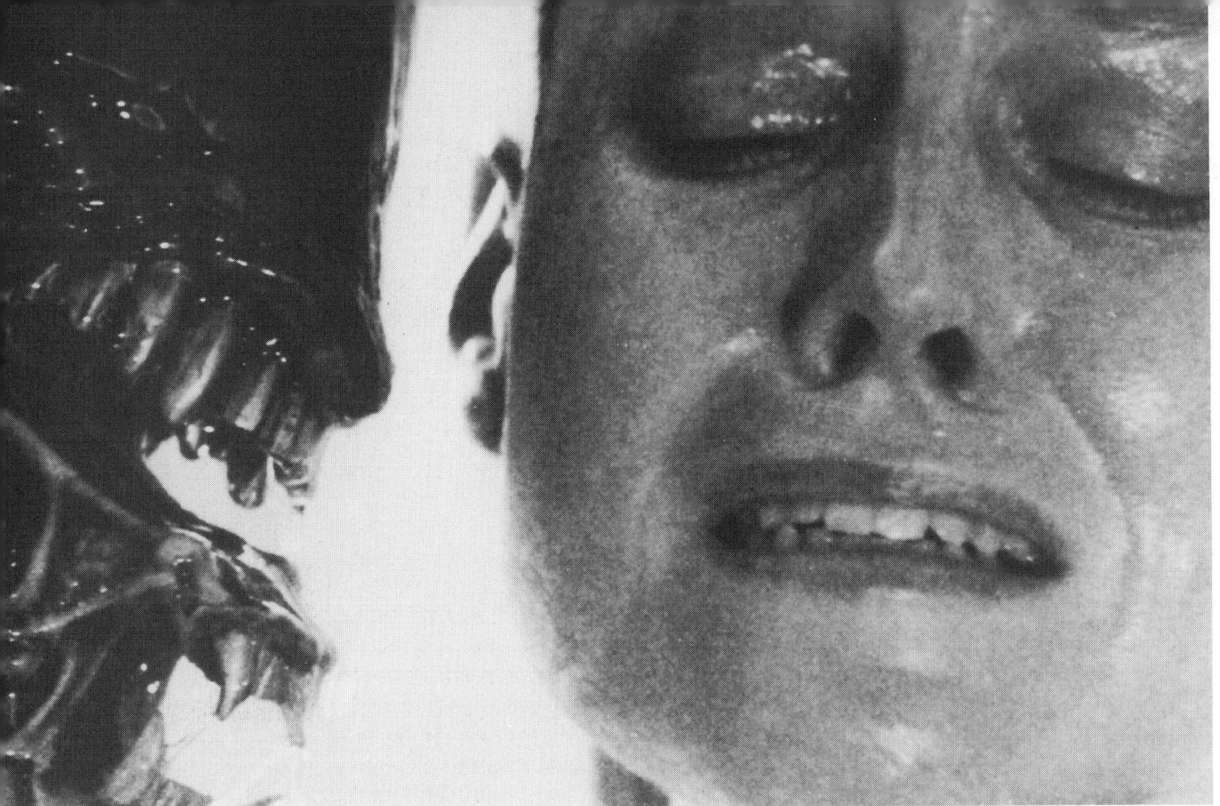

The Alien and Officer Ripley (Sigourney Weaver) in *Alien3.*

But Fincher demonstrates such disdain for the basics of narrative storytelling that most viewers will probably watch the last third of the film wondering what the hell is going on. That's a perfect way to destroy any suspense the action might generate. The creature effects don't measure up to the others, either. 🦴

1992 (R) 135m/C Sigourney Weaver, Charles S. Dutton, Charles Dance, Paul McGann, Brian Glover, Ralph Brown, Danny Webb, Christopher John Fields, Holt McCallany, Lance Henriksen; ***D:*** David Fincher; ***M:*** Elliot Goldenthal. Nominations: Academy Awards '92: Best Visual Effects. **VHS, LV, Letterboxed, Closed Caption** *FXV*

Alligator

No-frills B-movie knows exactly what it is—a rip-off of *Jaws* complete with here-comes-the-monster music—and doesn't try to be anything else. Following the big-critter formula faithfully, John Sayles' script is based on the urban legend of a 'gator that was flushed down a toilet into metropolitan sewers where it grows to monstrous proportions. Robert Forster is the cop hunting the reptile; Robin Riker is the cute herpetologist who helps him; Dean Jagger is the evil millionaire behind it all; comic Jack Carter is the mayor of Chicago. Toward the end, when the beastie appears in full sunlight, the film becomes outright comedy and Sayles lets his politics show. Throughout, it's fast-moving and fun. 🦴🦴🦴

1980 (R) 94m/C Robert Forster, Jack Carter, Henry Silva, Robin Riker, Dean Jagger, Michael V. Gazzo, Perry Lang, Bart Braverman, Angel Tompkins, Sue Lyon; ***D:*** Lewis Teague; ***W:*** John Sayles, Frank Ray Perilli. **VHS** *LIV*

Alligator 2: The Mutation

The only original element in this remake-sequel is professional wrestling. Beyond that dubious addition, the flick is a rehash of the above-average Lewis Teague/John Sayles original with Steve Railsback as the evil industrialist who dumps growth-enhancing chemicals into the sewers, Joseph Bologna as the police detective on the critter's trail, and Dee Wallace Stone as the scientist. They're abetted by a dozen or so equally stale stereotypes and some negligible monster effects.

1990 (PG-13) 92m/C Steve Railsback, Dee Wallace Stone, Joseph Bologna, Woody Brown, Bill Daily, Brock Peters, Richard Lynch, Holly Gagnier; ***D:*** Jon Hess; ***W:*** Curt Allen; ***C:*** Joseph Mangine. **VHS, LV** *COL, NLC*

An American Werewolf in London

John Landis' ambitious updating of *The Wolf Man* may be the most frightening combination of comedy and horror ever put onscreen. Knocking around England, two American college kids, David (David Naughton) and Jack (Griffin Dunne), are attacked by a creature on the moor. David survives and his problems begin with a series of terrifying visions. Initially, Landis sets a friendly, leisurely pace and the first violent scenes are carefully shrouded in darkness. The really good scares in the middle are based on the characters, and particularly on David's state of mind, giving his terror a strongly sympathetic dimension. And that's the real appeal of good werewolf stories—the mix of revulsion and sympathy that the protagonist's situation produces. At the same time, waking up to find Jenny Agutter as your nurse makes you think that maybe a little case of lycanthropy wouldn't be so bad after all. The only flaw is a relatively weak ending.

1981 (R) 97m/C David Naughton, Griffin Dunne, Jenny Agutter, Frank Oz, Brian Glover, Lila Kaye, David Schofield, John Woodvine, Don McKillop, Paul Kember, Colin Fernandes; ***D:*** John Landis; ***W:*** John Landis; ***M:*** Elmer Bernstein. Academy Awards '81: Best Makeup. **VHS, LV** *LIV*

An American Werewolf in Paris

Semi-sequel begins with a meeting on the Eiffel Tower that's so preposterous the rest ought not to work at all, but somehow it does. Young tourist Andy (Tom Everett Scott) is immediately smitten by Seraphine (Julie Delpy), and quickly learns that she's not like other French girls. The writers give credit to John Landis' *American Werewolf in London,* and they use some of the same plot devices but the tone is much lighter. The tragic aspects of the original, which came first in *The Wolf Man,* are absent. Instead, we've got good werewolves and bad werewolves. The pace is quick and director Anthony Waller's (*Mute Witness*) style is much more fluid. Even though Peter Lloyd's transformation and monster effects are more graphic, the film isn't as frightening as Landis'. That's Waller as the Metro driver.

1997 (R) ?m/C Julie Delpy, Tom Everett Scott, Julie Bowen, Pierre Cosso, Thierry Lhermitte, Vince Vieluf, Phil Buckman, Tom Novembre, Isabelle Constantini, Anthony Waller; ***D:*** Anthony Waller; ***W:*** Anthony Waller, Tim Burns, Tom Stern; ***C:*** Egon Werdin; ***M:*** Wilbert Hirsch. **VHS** *TOU*

The Amityville Horror

Stephen King argues that the success of this ridiculous story can be found in the lean economics of the time—that people were able to identify with the plight of a young couple (James Brolin and Margot Kidder) who'd sunk everything they had into a Long Island house that turned out to be a lemon. So's the movie, but it has still turned the word "Amityville" into a franchise that's generated seven (count 'em, seven!) sequels to date. The plot is standard haunted house stuff with a weak ending and Rod Steiger on hand to chew the

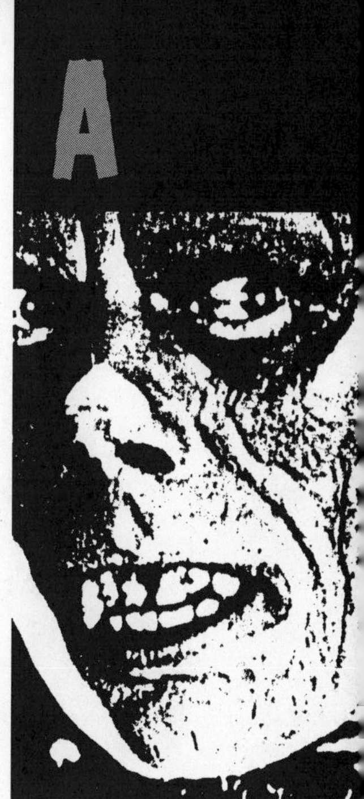

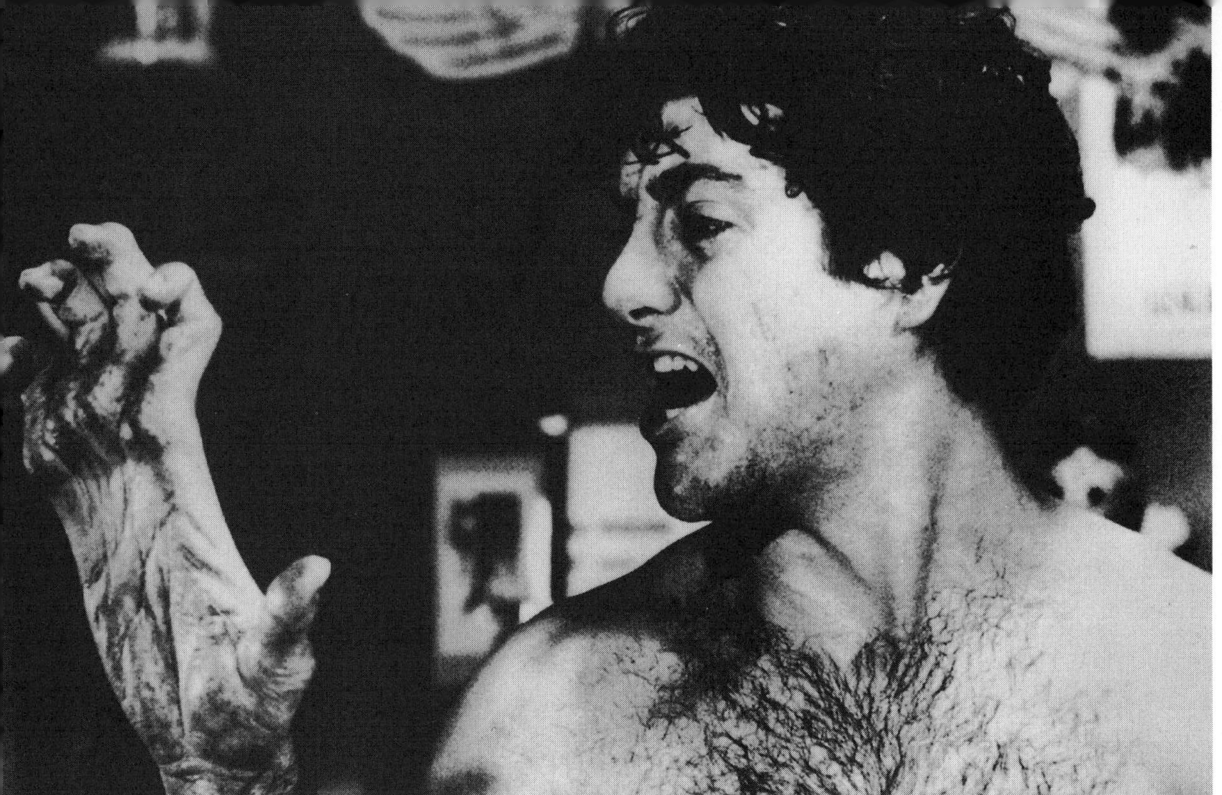

David Kessler (David Naughton) in *An American Werewolf in London.*

scenery as a priest. On the plus side, the house has a feeling of reality to it. 🦴

1979 (R) 117m/C James Brolin, Margot Kidder, Rod Steiger, Don Stroud, Murray Hamilton, Helen Shaver, Amy Wright, Val Avery; ***D:*** Stuart Rosenberg; ***W:*** Sandor Stern; ***C:*** Fred W. Koenekamp; ***M:*** Lalo Schifrin. Nominations: Academy Awards '79: Best Original Score. **VHS, LV** *WAR, OM*

Amityville 2: The Possession

Burt Young is his usual obnoxious screen self as the seedy patriarch of a family that buys the famous Long Island house. Child abuse, incest, arguments, shouting matches, telekinesis, possession, and the unspeakable horror of a damp basement are all visited upon them. Director Damiano Damiani tries gamely to punch up the low-level suspense with a restlessly mobile camera. Filmed in Jersey City and Mexico City. 🦴

1982 (R) 110m/C James Olson, Burt Young, Andrew Prine, Moses Gunn, Rutanya Alda; ***D:*** Damiano Damiani; ***W:*** Tommy Lee Wallace; ***C:*** Franco Di Giacomo; ***M:*** Howard Blake. **VHS, LV**

Amityville 3: The Demon

Like most "3"s made in 3-D, this one looks muddy and dark on the conventional small screen, and without the dubious benefit of the optical effect of the third dimension, the in-your-face camerawork is pointless. So is the table-rapping plot which begins with a big green hairball. Why—beyond the obvious motivation of a paycheck—are such a talented cast and director wasting their time on drek like this? Look for a young Meg Ryan. ***AKA:*** Amityville 3-D. 🦴

1983 (R) 98m/C Tony Roberts, Tess Harper, Robert Joy, Candy Clark, John Beal, Leora Dana, John Harkins, Lori Loughlin, Meg Ryan; ***D:*** Richard Fleischer; ***W:*** William Wales; ***C:*** Fred Schuler; ***M:*** Howard Blake. **VHS, LV** *VES, LIV*

Amityville 4

4 kicks off in high gear with the house attacking priests who come to exorcise it. According to the subtitle, the evil escapes through an electrical outlet and takes up residence in a particularly hideous lamp which then relocates to California. Many of the scares have to do with other appliances—from tea kettles to chainsaws and disposals—that turn themselves on. Stars Patty Duke and Jane Wyatt are spared the most embarrassing moments. ***AKA:*** The Amityville Horror: The Evil Escapes, Part 4.

1989 (R) 95m/C Patty Duke, Jane Wyatt, Norman Lloyd, Frederic Lehne, Brandy Gold; ***D:*** Sandor Stern; ***W:*** Sandor Stern; ***M:*** Rick Conrad. **VHS** *THV*

Amityville: A New Generation

Transplanting the questionable horrors of a Long Island single-family home and a middle-class family to a studio loft filled with boho artist types does not generate any significant increases on the scare-scale. This time, the source of the spooks or whatever is a mirror that a homeless guy claims is an old family heirloom. He gives it to photographer Keys (Ross Partridge) and terrible things happen to him and his pals. The young cast is blandly attractive. The same writers do better work with *Amityville 1992*. 

1993 (R) 92m/C Ross Partridge, Julia Nickson-Soul, David Naughton, Richard Roundtree, Terry O'Quinn; ***D:*** John Murlowski; ***W:*** Christopher DeFaria, Antonio Toro. **VHS, LV, Closed Caption** *REP*

The Amityville Curse

The fifth installment in the title-only series adds some intentional humor, but it's a wasted effort. Even judged by the low standards set by its predecessors, this one's a lackluster effort. It's about five adults who stay in a rundown house and are bothered by ghosts, dogs, tarantulas, a confessional in the basement, and that old favorite, the bathtub full of blood. Filmed in Canada, it's slow, pointless, and without scares. **Woof!**

1990 (R) 91m/C *CA* Kim Coates, Dawna Wightman, Helen Hughes, David Stein, Cassandra Gava, Jan Rubes; ***D:*** Tom Berry; ***W:*** Michael Krueger, Norvell Rose. **VHS, LV** *VTR, THV*

Amityville Dollhouse

The economic premise of the original becomes '90s pop psychological stuff with two single parents (Robin Thomas and Starr Andreeff) bringing a "blended family" into an ugly new house in California. Some time before, another house burned on the site and the titular dollhouse (with the two funny little windows) has been left in a shed. Joshua Michael Stern's plot borrows freely from *Poltergeist* and *Pet Sematary* and contains some scary stuff involving wasps and an attempt at characterization. The rest is familiar special effects, capably done and arguably no worse than the original.

1996 (R) 97m/C Robin Thomas, Starr Andreeff, Allen Cutler, Rachel Duncan, Jarrett Lennon, Clayton Murray, Frank Ross, Lenora Kardorf, Lisa Robin Kelly; ***D:*** Steve White; ***W:*** Joshua Michael Stern. **VHS, Closed Caption** *REP*

Amityville 1992: It's about Time

If truth-in-titling laws were enforced, this would have been called *The Amityville Clock*. Said timepiece is brought by Jake (Stephen Macht) from a house torn down for a tract development. Jake's an adman who's broken up with Andrea (Shawn Weatherly), but their relationship with each other and with his kids is complicated. Director Tony Randel also made one of the *Hellraiser* movies and displays more affinity for elaborate clockwork devices.

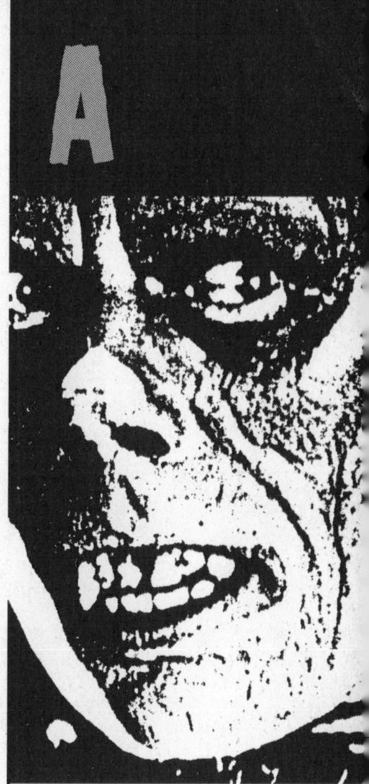

THE HOUND SALUTES

VINCENT PRICE

Though he could be as bombastic as the best of them—and often was—Vincent Price never got the credit he deserved for more low-keyed, conversational approaches to screen acting. When called upon, he was restrained, even subtle and touching.

But subtle and touching don't sell tickets in horror, and that's where this oversized talent made a fair part of his living.

Price was born in St. Louis in 1911, the son of a wealthy candy manufacturer. He graduated from Yale and studied theatre at the University of London where he was "discovered" playing Prince Albert opposite Helen Hayes in the hit play *Victoria Regina*. He went to Hollywood in 1938 and was briefly under contract to Universal where he made *The Tower of London* and *The Invisible Man Returns*.Twentieth Century Fox gave him a better offer, and for the next decade, he played it straight with key roles in *Laura*, *The Three Musketeers*, and *Champagne for Caesar*, among others. He also lectured and wrote about art. He returned to horror in 1953 with the 3-D *House of Wax* and, five years later, the big-budget hit, *The Fly*.

It wasn't until the late 1950s and early '60s that he cultivated the slightly arrogant and sneering villainous image that many associate with him now. Then he had a trio of popular black-and-white films beginning with *The House on Haunted Hill*, *The Tingler* (both made for William Castle), and *Return of the Fly*.

The Fall of the House of Usher began Price's association with Roger Corman and the several Edgar Allan Poe adaptations that were so popular in the mid-'60s. *The Conqueror Worm*, his best work in those years, is often assumed to be part of the Poe-Corman cycle. It's not. The more accurate British title is *Witchfinder General*. Unfortunately, its young British director Michael Reeves died soon after it was finished.

In the early '70s, Price shifted gears again and came up with another terrific trio of dry horror-comedies, *The Abominable Dr. Phibes*, *Dr. Phibes Rises Again*, and *Theatre of Blood*. After that, his horror career was less important than other interests, most notably hosting the long-running PBS series *Mystery*.

Luckily, he was able to end his career on a graceful note of appreciation. In 1982, he was the inspiration for a stop-motion animated short film called *Vincent*, and he also narrated it. The director was a young Tim Burton, who went on to give Price his elegiac final role as the Inventor in *Edward Scissorhands*.

SIGNIFICANT CONTRIBUTIONS TO HORROR

House of Wax **(1953)**

The Fly **(1958)**

The Tingler **(1959)**

The Fall of the House of Usher **(1960)**

The Pit and the Pendulum **(1961)**

The Raven **(1963)**

Masque of the Red Death **(1965)**

The Conqueror Worm **(1968)**

Scream and Scream Again **(1970)**

The Abominable Dr. Phibes **(1971)**

Dr. Phibes Rises Again **(1972)**

Theatre of Blood **(1973)**

Edward Scissorhands **(1990)**

Actually, this entry is the best in the weak series with top-notch production values and genuine scares, including a graphic dog attack. 🦴🦴🦴

1992 (R) 95m/C Stephen Macht, Shawn Weatherly, Megan Ward, Damon Martin, Nita Talbot, Dick Miller; ***D:*** Tony Randel; ***W:*** Christopher DeFaria, Antonio Toro. **VHS, LV, Closed Caption** *REP*

Anaconda

Gonzo tongue-in-cheek take on *Creature from the Black Lagoon* is mildly enjoyable for all the wrong reasons. The snake itself is such a blatant special effect that it's not at all frightening and that's somehow part of the fun. Documentary filmmakers are headed up the Amazon to find the lost Shimmyshamba tribe. Director Terri Flores (Jennifer Lopez), cameraman Danny Rich (Ice Cube), and Dr. Cale (Eric Stoltz) are more or less in charge until they run into Paul Sarone (Jon Voight), a half-mad snake hunter. A few others fill out the cast, and experienced horror fans can predict the order in which they'll become anaconda snack-pacs. The critter itself is big enough to bolt down a Buick, but the main attraction is Jon Voight. He has a wonderful time playing a crazed villain with a psychotic Ricky Ricardo accent and a collection of grimacing facial expressions that bear no resemblance to any known emotion. 🦴🦴🦴

1996 (PG-13) 90m/C Jon Voight, Jennifer Lopez, Ice Cube, Eric Stoltz, Owen C. Wilson, Kari Wuhrer, Jonathan Hyde, Vincent Castellanos; ***D:*** Luis Llosa; ***W:*** Jim Cash, Jack Epps Jr., Hans Bauer; ***C:*** Bill Butler; ***M:*** Randy Edelman. **VHS, LV, Closed Caption** *COL*

And Now the Screaming Starts

Handsome, slow-moving period piece begins with voiceover narration suggesting *Rebecca* but eventually becomes a town-with-a-secret Gothic as young bride Catherine (Stephanie Beacham) tries to learn what her husband Charles (Ian Ogilvy) is hiding at the Fengriffin estate. Director Roy Ward Baker overuses non-scary gimmicks—disembodied hand, face at the window, etc.—and bad music, but the story does have some suspense. Unfortunately, that suspense is overplayed and its revelation is less than compelling. The production is well acted throughout, with Peter Cushing bringing his customary grace to the proceedings. ***AKA:*** Bride of Fengriffen; Fengriffen; I Have No Mouth But I Must Scream. 🦴🦴

1973 (R) 87m/C *GB* Peter Cushing, Herbert Lom, Patrick Magee, Ian Ogilvy, Stephanie Beacham, Geoffrey Whitehead, Guy Rolfe, Rosalie Crutchley, Gillian Lind, Janet Key; ***D:*** Roy Ward Baker; ***W:*** Roger Marshall; ***C:*** Denys Coop. **VHS** *NO*

Andy Warhol's Dracula

Tongue-in-cheek comedy opens with Dracula (Udo Kier) painting his hair—yes, painting—before a mirror in which he casts no reflection but can, presumably, see himself with vampire vision or something. His butler (Arno Juerging) persuades him to leave his castle and go to Italy where he can recharge his batteries with "wirgin" blood. He ends up on a nobleman's (Vittorio De Sica) estate where a Marxist stud-muffin servant (Joe Dallesandro) spouts rhetoric and makes the Count's quest much more difficult with the family's four daughters. The whole production is much more polished than the companion *Frankenstein*, and, until the last limb-lopping reel, it's not nearly as bloody either. The ensemble histrionics are wondrous to behold, and not one frame is meant to be taken seriously. Though Paul Morrissey is credited as director, some sources claim that the film was made by Antonio Margheriti. ***AKA:*** Blood for Dracula; Young Dracula; Dracula Cerca Sangue di Vergine e...Mori de Sete; Dracula Vuole Vivere: Cerca Sangue de Vergina; Andy Warhol's Young Dracula. 🦴🦴🦴

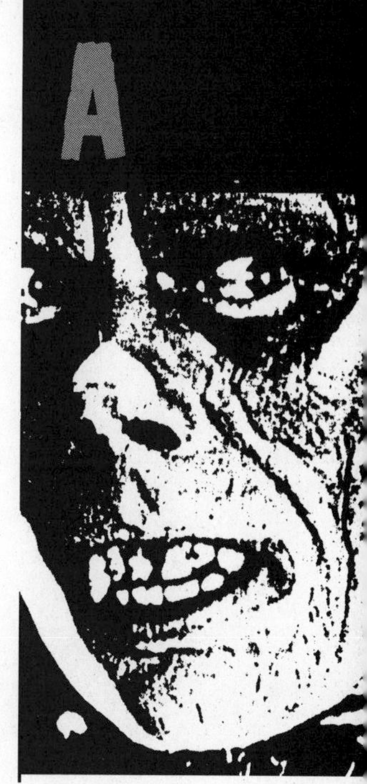

"Count Dracula may not seem like the ideal husband, though he's of a very good family."

—La Marchesa Di Fiore (Maxine McKendry) tries to marry off her daughters in *Andy Warhol's Dracula.*

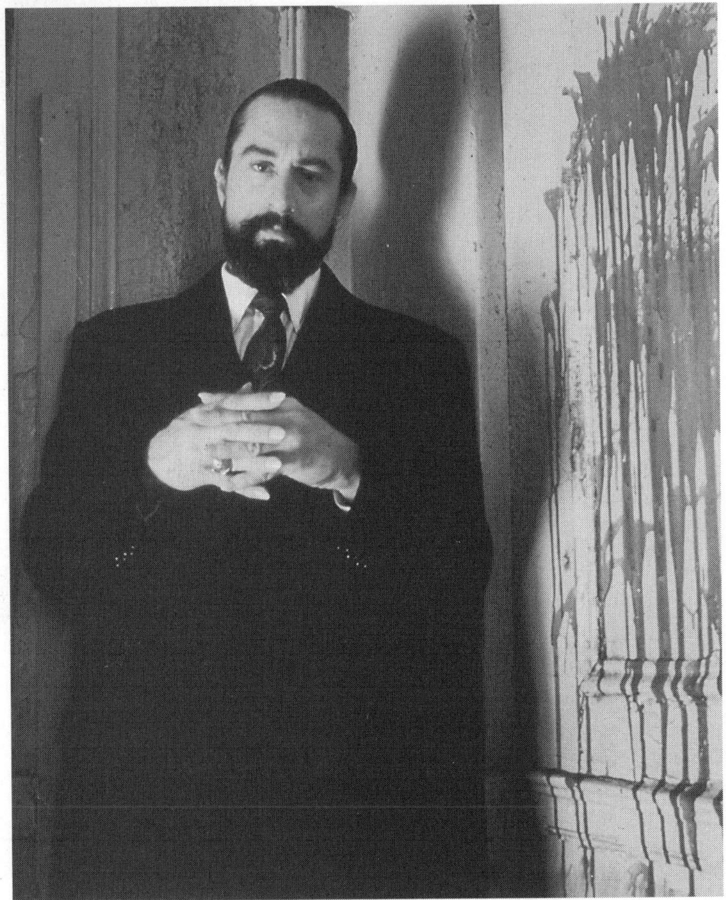

Robert De Niro as Louis Cyphre in *Angel Heart*.

1974 (R) 106m/C *IT FR* Udo Kier, Arno Juerging, Maxine McKendry, Joe Dallesandro, Vittorio De Sica, Milena Vukotic, Dominique Darel, Stefania Casini, Silvia Dionisio; ***Cameos:*** Roman Polanski; ***D:*** Paul Morrissey, Anthony (Antonio Margheriti) Dawson; ***W:*** Paul Morrissey; ***C:*** Luigi Kuveiller. **VHS** *TRI*

Andy Warhol's Frankenstein

Infamous camp classic is still properly revolting. It's also slow, too talky, poorly acted, and flat out ugly. The substandard production values don't look any better on video than they did on the big screen. The story revolves around the incestuous Baron (Udo Kier), his sister (Monique Van Vooren), her lover (Joe Dallesandro), and a couple of creations. Since the film was made for 3-D, lots of objects and bleeding organs are thrust toward the camera. The decapitation effects aren't going to scare anybody these days. For energy and imagination it compares poorly to *Rocky Horror,* which was made a year later. Though Warhol crony Paul Morrissey is credited as director, many sources say that Italian Antonio Margheriti is responsible. ***AKA:*** Flesh for Frankenstein; The Frankenstein Experiment; Up Frankenstein; The Devil and Dr. Frankenstein; Carne per Frankenstein; Frankenstein.

1974 (X) 95m/C *GE FR IT* Udo Kier, Monique Van Vooren, Joe Dallesandro, Dalia di Lazzaro, Arno Juerging, Nicoletta Elmi, Srdjan Zelenovic, Marco Liofredi, Cristina Gaioni; ***D:*** Paul Morrissey; ***W:*** Paul Morrissey; ***C:*** Luigi Kuveiller. **VHS** *TRI, MLB*

Angel Heart

Some very scary stuff is undermined (at least partially) by an odd sense of humor. Tough '50s detective Harry Angel (Mickey Rourke) receives a call from the law firm of MacIntosh and Winesap. Not long after that, he tells us that he has a problem with chickens. We're supposed to take him seriously? What begins as noir moves into dreamy, nightmarish surrealism and becomes an exercise in style for director Alan Parker, sticking close to the source material, William Hjortsberg's fine novel, *Falling Angel.* Visually striking with Rourke at his seediest.

1987 (R) 112m/C Mickey Rourke, Robert De Niro, Lisa Bonet, Charlotte Rampling, Michael Higgins, Charles Gordone, Kathleen Wilhoite, Stocker Fountelieu, Brownie McGhee; ***D:*** Alan Parker; ***W:*** Alan Parker; ***C:*** Michael Seresin; ***M:*** Trevor Jones. **VHS, LV** *LIV, FCT*

Anne Rice: Birth of the Vampire

BBC and Lifetime cable coproduction proves that the author's career is every bit as interesting as her fiction, though the film gets off to an unsteady start when it sketches in Rice's New Orleans background with a credulous parapsychologist and other mystics. Once producer/director Anand Tucker focuses on the subject, it all falls into place. Though she writes about the supernatural, Anne Rice's fiction contains a strong element of emotional autobiography. Her reaction to the death of a daughter explains some of the pain and poetry in her work. In the best part of the film, Tucker combines well-chosen voice-over quotes from *Interview with the Vampire* with the expected "up close and personal" glimpses at Rice's home life. For the author's most passionate fans, all this may be old news but it still makes for an interesting story.

1994 45m/C *D:* Anand Tucker. **VHS** *FXV*

Apocalypse Now

Call it a war movie, call it a horror movie—Francis Ford Coppola's other masterpiece is a nightmare. The story, loosely based on Joseph Conrad's *Heart of Darkness,* begins and ends as a dream, and the plot weaves its way upriver through the illogical images of a dream. The surreal opening montage of jungle, dust, helicopters, and flame merges into the alcohol-drenched fever dream of Capt. Willard (Martin Sheen) staring at the ceiling fan in his Saigon hotel. "I wanted a mission," he says, "and for my sins, they gave me one." Coppola captures the madness of that war, finding no easy answers, no clear-cut heroes and villains. It's a nightmare, and the more nightmarish it gets, the more sense it makes. The laser edition has been remastered under the supervision of cinematographer Vittorio Storaro and sound genius Walter Murch. (Both won well-deserved Oscars for their original work on the film.) The restored version ends without the final air attack on the village that was shown in some theatres, and that too seems appropriate to the story. It also makes the concluding horrors at Kurtz's (Marlon Brando) compound even more intense.

1979 (R) 153m/C Marlon Brando, Martin Sheen, Robert Duvall, Frederic Forrest, Sam Bottoms, Scott Glenn, Albert Hall, Laurence "Larry" Fishburne, Harrison Ford, G.D. Spradlin, Dennis Hopper, Colleen Camp, Tom Mason, R. Lee Ermey; ***D:*** Francis Ford Coppola; ***W:*** Francis Ford Coppola, John Milius; ***C:*** Vittorio Storaro; ***M:*** Carmine Coppola. Academy Awards '79: Best Cinematography, Best Sound; British Academy Awards '79: Best Director (Coppola), Best Supporting Actor (Duvall); Cannes Film Festival '79: Best Film; Golden Globe Awards '80: Best Director (Coppola), Best Supporting Actor (Duvall), Best Score; National Society of Film Critics Awards '79: Best Supporting Actor (Forrest); Nominations: Academy Awards '79: Best Adapted Screenplay, Best Art Direction/Set Decoration, Best Director (Coppola), Best Film Editing, Best Picture, Best Supporting Actor (Duvall). **VHS, LV, CD-I , Letterboxed** *PAR*

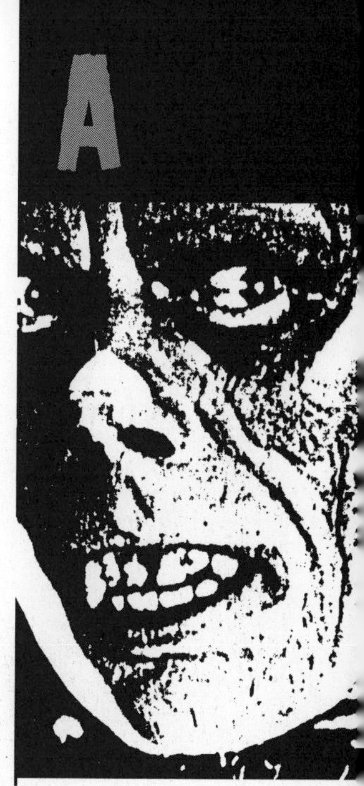

"The horror. The horror."

—Colonel Kurtz' (Marlon Brando) last line in *Apocalypse Now.*

Appointment with Fear

Dead teen flick uses Egyptian astral projection claptrap as a basis for generic stalker-slasher action. More attractive young women (Michelle Little, Kerry Remsen, Deborah Voorhees) are the target. The two main settings are a realistically cluttered Los Angeles suburb and a sterile hillside mansion. Direction by the pseudonymous Alan Smithee is remarkably sloppy with shadows of equipment clearly visible in some shots, and this is the kind of movie where you watch for that kind of stuff because it's more interesting than anything else onscreen, and that includes unintentional humor, mimes, and interpretative dance.

1985 (R) 95m/C Michael Wyle, Michelle Little, Kerry Remsen, Douglas Rowe, Garrick Dowhen, Deborah Voorhees; ***D:*** Alan Smithee, Razmi Thomas; ***W:*** Gideon Davis, Bruce Mead. **VHS, LV** *LIV*

Apprentice to Murder

In Pennsylvania, 1928, John Reese (Donald Sutherland) is a faith healer and medicine man who mixes simple Christianity, mysti-

"Respect is fine, but actually I've always wanted to be feared."

—Dr. Ross Jennings (Jeff Daniels) in *Arachnophobia.*

cism, and potions. Billy Kelly (Chad Lowe) becomes his protege, and at the same time meets Alice (Mia Sara), a bold, angelic young woman. Does Reese have supernatural powers, or is he a charlatan? When director R.L. Thomas tries to answer those questions, the action becomes choppy and fragmented. As long as it's focused on the three main characters and their setting, it's much more interesting. Give it an A for effort and a C for execution.

1988 (PG-13) 97m/C Donald Sutherland, Mia Sara, Chad Lowe, Eddie Jones; ***D:*** Ralph L. Thomas; ***W:*** Allan Scott, Wesley Moore. **VHS, LV, Closed Caption** *VTR, HHE*

April Fool's Day

Is Muffy St. John (Deborah Foreman) the perky little cutiepie she appears to be? Or is she a psycho who invites her college pals for a weekend getaway at her isolated island lodge so she can bump them off? They're all a bunch of blandly attractive white kids who look like they'd rather be on Melrose Place. How long does it take for them to start kicking the bucket? Not very. Do you care who's doing it or why? Nope, not a bit. Despite top-grade studio production values, the whole thing is an ineffective repetition of the tired dead-teenager formula.

1986 (R) 90m/C Deborah Foreman, Jay Baker, Pat Barlow, Lloyd Berry, Deborah Goodrich, Ken Olandt, Griffin O'Neal, Tom Heaton, Mike Nomad, Leah K. Pinsent, Clayton Rohner, Amy Steel, Thomas F. Wilson; ***D:*** Fred Walton; ***W:*** Danilo Bach; ***M:*** Charles Bernstein. **VHS, LV, Closed Caption** *PAR*

Arachnophobia

The Spielberg organization puts its polished spin on a cracking good monster story. The critters in questions are the lethal offspring of a Venezuelan superspider who finds its way in a particularly gruesome manner to the little town of Camaina, California. That's also where the new doctor, Ross Jennings (Jeff Daniels) has just moved with his family. He's deathly afraid of spiders; his wife (Harley Jane Kozak) isn't. The clever script is built along familiar horror conventions. Director Frank Marshall lets things move a little too slowly, and at the key moment when he could really drab the audience, he lets go. But those are quibbles. Anyone who's at all arachnophobic—and who isn't?—will get serious creeps from the second half. The production may be too slick for the subject matter, but the film is still a real treat.

1990 (PG-13) 109m/C Jeff Daniels, John Goodman, Harley Jane Kozak, Julian Sands, Roy Brocksmith, Stuart Pankin, Brian McNamara, Mark L. Taylor, Henry Jones, Peter Jason, James Handy; ***D:*** Frank Marshall; ***W:*** Wesley Strick, Don Jakoby; ***C:*** Mikael Salomon; ***M:*** Trevor Jones. **VHS, LV, Letterboxed, Closed Caption** *HPH*

Army of Darkness

From its beginning as a cult hit on video, Sam Raimi's *Evil Dead* series has evolved from low-budget horror to bizarre comedy. This third installment is a multi-genre parody of horror, action, sword-and-sorcery, and s-f, where no convention is sacred. Everything is played for laughs. A brief introduction, including a cameo appearance by Bridget Fonda, explains how Ash (Bruce Campbell) came to be hurled back through time to the 13th century, along with a chainsaw, a sawed-off 12-gauge, and a 1973 Olds Delta 88, to save the world from a host of the living dead. Imagine the physical violence of the Three Stooges combined with the absurdism of *Monty Python and the Holy Grail* and you'll see what Raimi is trying to do. ***AKA:*** Evil Dead 3; The Medieval Dead.

1992 (R) 77m/C Bruce Campbell, Embeth Davidtz, Marcus Gilbert, Ian Abercrombie, Richard Grove, Michael Earl Reid, Tim Quill, Bridget Fonda, Patricia Tallman, Theodore (Ted) Raimi, Ivan Raimi; ***D:*** Sam Raimi; ***W:*** Sam Raimi, Ivan Raimi; ***C:*** Bill Pope; ***M:*** Joseph LoDuca, Danny Elfman. **VHS, LV, Letterboxed, Closed Caption** *USH, FCT*

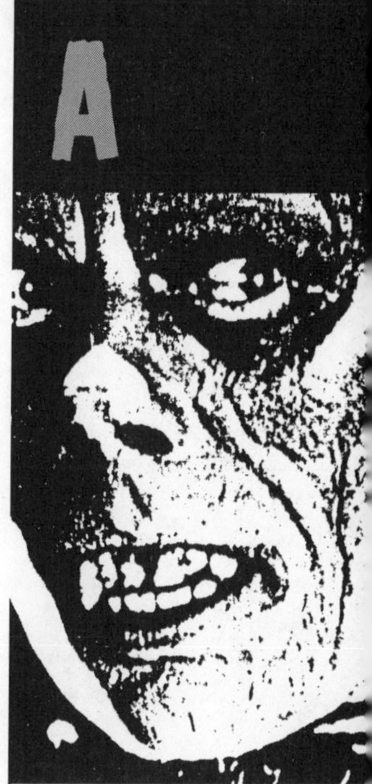

Arnold

In a bizarre wedding scene, Karen (Stella Stevens), an unapologetic gold digger, marries the title character (Norman Stuart), already a corpse, to get her hooks into his considerable estate. From that point on, this featherweight black horror spoof becomes even more outrageous with a series of creative murders. A stellar troupe of character actors does a fine job with saucy, offbeat material, particularly Stevens, who has a touch for this kind of hard-to-define comedy. Recommended for her fans.

1973 (PG) 96m/C Stella Stevens, Roddy McDowall, Elsa Lanchester, Victor Buono, Bernard Fox, Farley Granger, Shani Wallis, Jamie Farr, Patric Knowles, John McGiver, Norman Stuart; ***D:*** Georg Fenady; ***W:*** Jameson Brewer, John Fenton Murray; ***C:*** William B. Jurgensen; ***M:*** George Duning. **VHS** *NO*

The Arrival

Intense s-f horror is driven by the same paranoia that makes *The X-Files* such a hit, with some really creative special effects, good characters, and an unpredictable story. Radio astronomer Zane Zaminski (Charlie Sheen) discovers a signal from another star and is immediately downsized by his boss Gordian (Ron Silver). At the same time, environmental researcher Ilana Green (Lindsay Crouse) can't believe some of the numbers she's seeing. In many respects writer/director David Twohy's first-contact story follows an established formula, but even its most familiar developments are handled with freshness, and no review should spoil the surprises. The well-chosen effects combine models, computer-generated creatures, some neat transformations, and a deeply frightening scene involving scorpions. It's one of the most uncomfortable moments in modern horror. ***AKA:*** Shockwave.

1996 (PG-13) 109m/C Charlie Sheen, Ron Silver, Lindsay Crouse, Teri Polo; ***D:*** David N. Twohy; ***W:*** David N. Twohy; ***C:*** Hiro Narita; ***M:*** Arthur Kempel. **VHS, LV, Closed Caption, DVD** *LIV*

The Art of Dying

Wings Hauser is one of the best B-movie actors in the business and with this psycho-killer horror, he proves that he's not a bad director, either. He stars as a Hollywood cop helping runaways. The most recent threat to these kids is insane would-be film director Gary Werntz, who stages reenactments of scenes from horror movies using real bullets and chainsaws. Though the violence is graphic, it's leavened by humor and it's not excessive. The performances are much better than you find in most B-movies, or most A-movies, for that matter. Kathleen Kinmont is very good as Hauser's mysterious girlfriend, but Mitch Hara, as the psycho's flamboyant assistant, steals this sleeper from everyone else.

1990 90m/C Wings Hauser, Michael J. Pollard, Sarah Douglas, Kathleen Kinmont, Sydney Lassick, Mitch Hara, Gary Werntz; ***D:*** Wings Hauser. **VHS, LV** *PMH*

Ashes and Flames

Dreamlike independent production is a semi-plotless series of images and vignettes about death and madness, hence the title. The cast handles slow physical action and limited dialogue with deadpan lack of emotion. Imagine *Lost Highway* told in the black-and-white style of *Carnival of Souls.* Sam is a man-child morgue attendant. Dahlia is a waitress. Her dead sister may be the connection between them, but nothing, not even the names, is certain. A strange heterophobia provides suspense of a sort, and it's also the source of considerable humor, possibly intentional. One character reduces the action to "the male specimen's problems with copulation" and that seems to be writer/director Anthony Kane's overriding concern. His screen is filled with phallic symbols, the most impressive among them being a thick firehose with a shiny nozzle.

Bonnie (Barbara Parkins) in *Asylum.*

In the end, the vague surrealism may prove too arty for horror fans and not arty enough for cineastes. 🦴🦴½

1997 90m/C Aisha Prigann, Sasha DeMarino, Mark Schultz; ***D:*** Anthony Kane; ***W:*** Anthony Kane. **VHS** *EII*

Asylum

Four inmates of a mental institution tell stories about themselves to a young doctor (Robert Powell). Barbara Parkins helps her lover kill his wife; Peter Cushing commissions a tailor to make a special suit; Charlotte Rampling is a woman with emotional problems and a murderous friend (Britt Ekland); Herbert Lom has created a homunculus of himself. A sense of humor helps the anthology, but an intrusive soundtrack incongruously taken from Dvorak's "New World Symphony" sets absolutely the wrong mood. ***AKA:*** House of Crazies. 🦴🦴½

1972 (PG) 100m/C *GB* Peter Cushing, Herbert Lom, Britt Ekland, Barbara Parkins, Patrick Magee, Barry Morse, Robert Powell, Richard Todd, Charlotte Rampling, Ann Firbank, Sylvia Syms, James Villiers, Geoffrey Bayldon, Megs Jenkins; ***D:*** Roy Ward Baker; ***W:*** Robert Bloch; ***C:*** Denys Coop. **VHS, LV** *NO*

Atom Age Vampire

Despite the title, this is really a mad scientist tale with a loopy wolfman angle. Like so many nutcase surgeons in the early '60s, Albert (Alberto Lupo) wants to use his skills and great discovery—"spontaneous generation in cells"—to reconstruct a disfigured cutiepie, the weepy Jeanette (Susanne Loret). His faithful assistant Monique (Franca Parisi Strahl) is less than enchanted. Eventually, the doc turns into a beastie that looks like Michael Landon in *I Was a Teenage Werewolf.* The pace meanders; the editing's choppy; the black-and-white photography is dark; and nothing's very scary. ***AKA:*** Seddok, l'Erede di Satana.

1961 71m/B *IT* Alberto Lupo, Susanne Loret, Sergio Fantoni, Franca Parisi Strahl, Ivo Garrani, Andrea Scotti, Rina Franchetti; ***D:*** Anton Giulio Majano; ***W:*** Anton Giulio Majano, Alberto Bevilacqua, Gino De Santis; ***C:*** Aldo Giordani. **VHS** *RHI*

Attack of the Giant Leeches

It's poor white Florida swamp trash vs. giant mutant worms in this early Corman effort. (Roger's executive producer; his brother Gene is credited as producer.) The main attractions are perhaps the most comical rubber monster suits ever to grace a low-budget horror flick and Yvette Vickers, a blonde bombshell of the Mamie Van Doren school, as Liz, the wayward wife. Even for a black-and-white Corman quickie, it's pretty thin stuff—but then, it doesn't claim to be anything more. ***AKA:*** The Giant Leeches; She Demons of the Swamp.

1959 62m/B Ken Clark, Yvette Vickers, Gene Roth, Bruno Ve Sota, Michael Emmet; ***D:*** Bernard L. Kowalski; ***W:*** Leo Gordon; ***C:*** John M. Nickolaus Jr. **VHS** *RHI*

Attack of the Killer Tomatoes

Spoof of bad horror movies is arguably no funnier than its subject, but it's fine for the target audience—kids who like to watch adults acting silly. Most of the humor is pretty obvious, but some of the jokes are actually funny and nothing about the movie is mean spirited. The monsters of the title are simply refugees from the produce department. There's no blood, sex, or rough language. According to at least one source, the helicopter crash is real—it certainly looks real—and the pilot was killed. The cult following that has developed—sequels, animated series, re-released "director's cut" on video—proves that indeed, there's no accounting for taste.

1977 (PG) 100m/C George Wilson, Jack Riley, Rock Peace, Eric Christmas; ***D:*** John DeBello; ***W:*** John DeBello. **VHS, Closed Caption** *TOU*

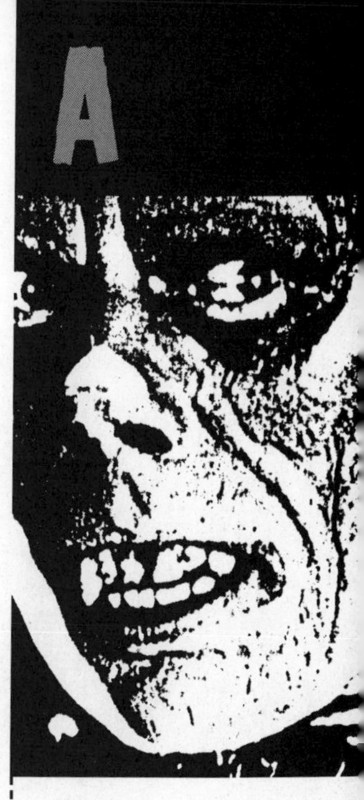

Audrey Rose

All reincarnation stories tend to be a bit loopy. Even the most skeptical viewers accept that, but this one abuses the privilege, skipping off into the farthest regions of La-La Land. Anthony Hopkins persuades John Beck and Marsha Mason that their daughter has the soul of his daughter because that little girl died a few minutes before their girl was born. How does he know this? Psychics told him and he went to India to check it out. Throughout the action is either boring or silly. Blame Frank de Felitta. He wrote the novel and the script, and he co-produced the film. **Woof!**

1977 (PG) 113m/C Marsha Mason, Anthony Hopkins, John Beck, John Hillerman, Susan Swift, Norman Lloyd; ***D:*** Robert Wise; ***W:*** Frank de Felitta; ***C:*** Victor Kemper. **VHS** *MGM*

The Awakening

A laborious introduction establishes the relationship between the mummy Kara and Margaret Corbeck (Stephanie Zimbalist). Margaret's dad Matthew (Charlton Heston) discovered Kara's tomb at the exact moment she—Margaret—was born. After that's sorted out, the pace becomes jerky and fragmented. Though a capable cast does good work, the plot is far too dependent on coincidence. The film is the second based on Bram Stoker's little-known novel, *Jewel of the Seven Stars.* (The first is *Jewel of the Mummy's Tomb.*) Director Mike Newell has had more success in the mainstream with *Four Weddings and a Funeral* and *Donnie Brasco.*

1980 (R) 101m/C *GB* Charlton Heston, Susannah York, Stephanie Zimbalist, Patrick Drury, Ian McDiarmid,

The 1930s

Dracula, Frankenstein, and the Mummy

The modern horror film was born at the beginning of the 1930s. In the first three years of the decade, six masterpieces were released and by the end of it, six more (perhaps as many as nine) had been added. Most of the characters and plots came from popular fiction and the stage.

The biggest financial hit for the Universal studio in 1931 was the Tod Browning-Bela Lugosi *Dracula,* which was filmed simultaneously with the now-famous Spanish language version by George Melford, who worked at night on the same sets. Those films solidified the studio's association with horror that had begun with the silent versions of *The Phantom of the Opera* and *The Hunchback of Notre Dame*. Some might say that Universal's horrors peaked ten months later with the James Whale-Boris Karloff *Frankenstein*; to most critics and reviewers (including this one), it is the finest horror film ever made. 1931 was also the year for Carl Dreyer's dreamy *Vampyr,* and the Frederic March version of *Dr. Jekyll and Mr. Hyde.*That same year, Peter Lorre was brilliant as the serial child murderer in Fritz Lang's *M,* paving the way for the hundreds of cinematic psychopaths who have followed.

Karloff returned a year later with his second great genre role as Im-ho-tep, *The Mummy,* loosely based on stories surrounding the 1922 Howard Carter discovery of the tomb of King Tutankhamen. Then Karloff joined a superb ensemble cast for James Whales' 1932 horror-comedy *The Old Dark House*. Charles Laughton was H.G. Wells' Dr. Moreau in *The Island of Lost Souls.* 1932 was also the year for what may be Browning's finest work, *Freaks.*

In 1933, Boris Karloff turned down the studio's request, and the title role in James Whale's *The Invisible Man* went to Claude Rains. But towering over everything else that year was horror's biggest star ever, the magnificent *King Kong.*

Karloff and Lugosi teamed up for the first time in 1934 in Edgar C. Ulmer's never-duplicated art deco-Bauhaus horror *The Black Cat.* A year later, in 1935, they did it again, less successfully, in *The Raven.* Karloff and Whale reunited to make *The Bride of Frankenstein.* Peter Lorre played yet another demented killer in *Mad Love.* Browning and Lugosi reteamed for the semi-comic *Mark of the Vampire* and Henry Hull was *The Werewolf of London.*

At the end of the decade, Karloff put on the Monster makeup for the last time, co-starring with Lugosi and Basil Rathbone in the underrated *Son of Frankenstein.* As the threat of global war became more real and immediate, Charles Laughton starred as Quasimodo to Maureen O'Hara's Esmeralda in a proudly propagandistic *The Hunchback of Notre Dame.*

Looking back at the way the films of the decade changed, the introduction of sound was the first major development. That, of course, changed the way all films were made, but sound has a special place in horror. Used properly, sound can be just as frightening as image. (Of course, it can be misused just as badly, too.) Later in the '30s, developments in technology and film stocks freed cameras from the sound equipment and the images onscreen became much brighter and clearer. At the same time, acting styles became more naturalistic. A truly cinematic style of acting was finding its way separate from the conventions of the theatre. To see all of those ideas illustrated, watch *Frankenstein* and *Son of Frankenstein* as a double feature and notice how radically different they are.

Bruce Myers, Nadim Sawalha, Jill Townsend; ***D:*** Mike Newell; ***W:*** Allan Scott, Chris Bryant, Clive Exton; ***C:*** Jack Cardiff; ***M:*** Claude Bolling. **VHS** *WAR*

The Awful Dr. Orloff

The prolific Spanish director Jess Franco got his start with this hash of elements borrowed from Dr. Jekyll, Jack the Ripper, and Frankenstein. Trying to repair his daughter's scarred face, Dr. Orloff (Howard Vernon) and his blind assistant Morpho (Riccardo Valle, whose makeup looks weirdly like a cartoon of the young Dustin Hoffman) kidnap women and operate on them. The acting is alternately hammy and understated. The rest of the film is likewise uneven with some creepy images surrounded by clumsy cliches and overlong, talky scenes. ***AKA:*** Gritos en la Noche.

1962 86m/B *SP* Howard Vernon, Diana Lorys, Frank Wolff, Riccardo Valle, Conrado San Martin, Perla Cristal, Maria Silva, Mara Laso; ***D:*** Jess (Jesus) Franco; ***W:*** Jess (Jesus) Franco; ***C:*** Godofredo Pacheco; ***M:*** Jose Pagan, Antonio Ramirez Angel. **VHS, Letterboxed** *SMW, TPV*

Axe

See *A Scream in the Streets/Axe*.

Bad Dreams

Spooky Richard Lynch is the Jim Jones-style leader of a '70s cult. He comes after survivor Cynthia (Jennifer Rubin) after she awakens from a 13-year coma. The setting for her rehabilitation is a hospital where she works with a therapy group whose members come across as refugees from a bad sitcom. Though the film was made years before the incidents at Waco, the images of fiery destruction have eerie echoes in reality. Despite a capable cast and a more than adequate budget, the scares settle into *Elm Street* familiarity with a dash of Argento gore.

1988 (R) 84m/C Bruce Abbott, Jennifer Rubin, Richard Lynch, Harris Yulin, Dean Cameron, Elizabeth Daily, Susan Ruttan, Charles Fleischer, Sy Richardson; ***D:*** Andrew Fleming; ***W:*** Andrew Fleming, Steven E. de Souza; ***C:*** Alexander Grusynski; ***M:*** Jay Michael Ferguson. **VHS, LV, Closed Caption** *FOX*

Bad Moon

Slick theatrical disappointment ought to fare better with fans on video. It's an inventive werewolf tale with a good twist—one of the main characters is a German Shepherd. That's Thor (Primo), who's owned by Marjorie (Mariel Hemingway) and her young son Brett (Mason Gamble). Marjorie invites her wayward brother Ted (Michael Pare) to stay at her Rocky Mountain home. Out in the Orient, Ted was bitten by a wolf creature. It doesn't take long for him and Thor to decide who's top dog, as it were. Director Eric Red sometimes shifts to a canine point of view with a slightly flattened blurred image. The monster transformation effects aren't very good and they're not helped by the high polish of the whole production. A grittier, rougher look would have served the story better. Can't be compared to Mike Nichols' *Wolf* but worth a look.

1996 (R) 79m/C Mariel Hemingway, Michael Pare, Mason Gamble, Ken Pogue; ***D:*** Eric Red; ***W:*** Eric Red; ***C:*** Jan Kiesser; ***M:*** Daniel Licht. **VHS, Closed Caption** *WAR*

The Bad Seed

Hollywood's most famous "evil child" horror looks dated now. It's very much a filmed play that is too limited by conventions of the stage. Patty McCormack is Rhoda, the perfect little '50s girl whose model exterior hides a prepubescent sociopath. Nancy Kelly is the increasingly suspicious and fearful mother. Though those two have their moments, the rest of the cast seems to think they're still on Broadway, playing to the last row of the balcony. For a more moving and complex treatment of the

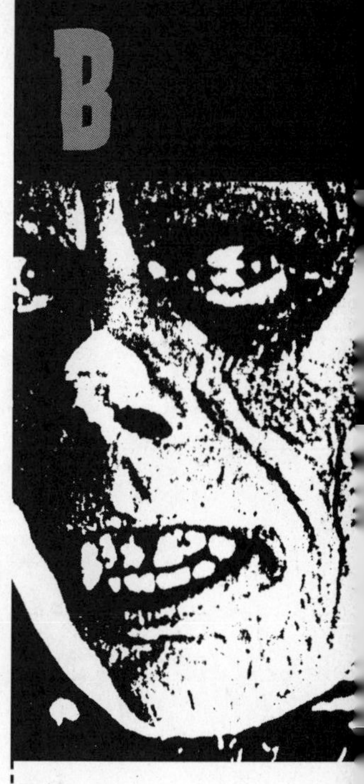

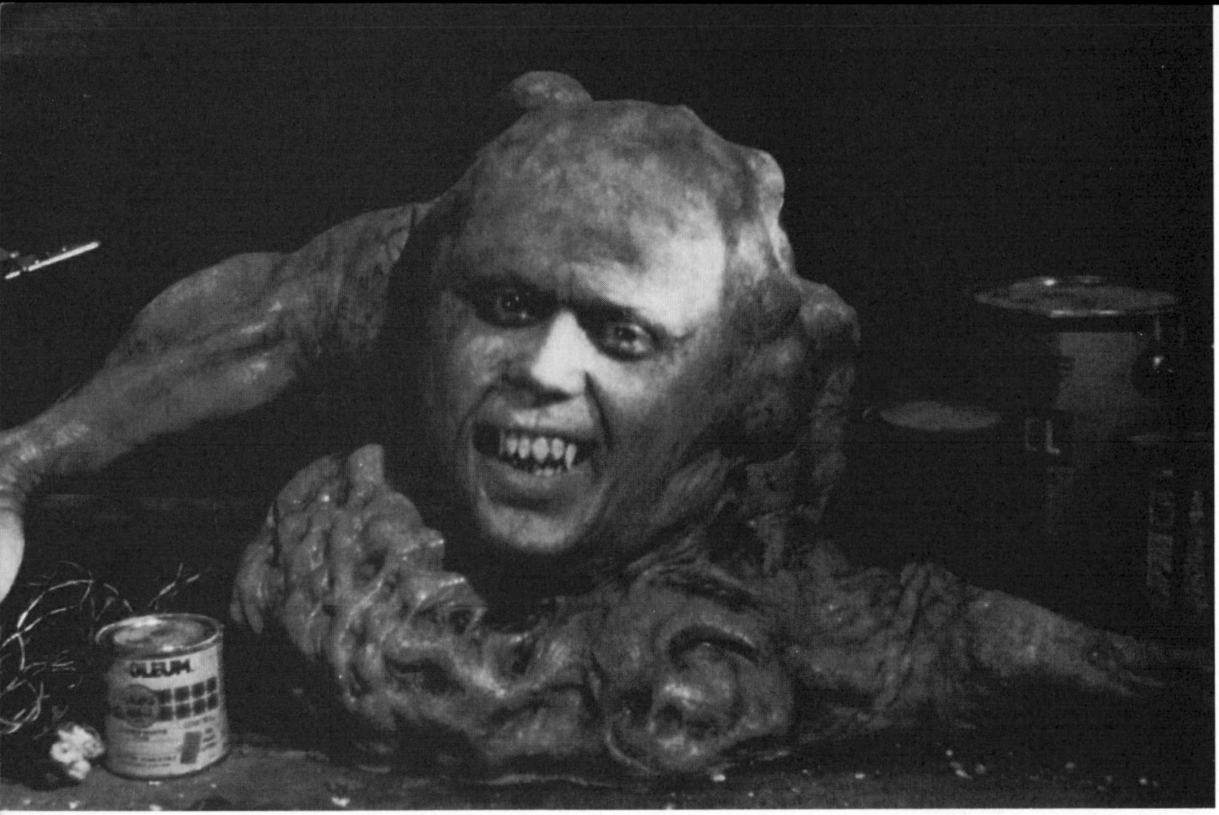

Brother Belial in *Basket Case 2.*

same subject, see *The Other.* Ignore the embarrassing coda.

1956 129m/B Patty McCormack, Nancy Kelly, Eileen Heckart, Henry Jones, Evelyn Varden, Paul Fix; ***D:*** Mervyn LeRoy; ***M:*** Alex North. Golden Globe Awards '57: Best Supporting Actress (Heckart); Nominations: Academy Awards '56: Best Actress (Kelly), Best Black and White Cinematography, Best Supporting Actress (Heckart, McCormack). **VHS** *WAR*

Bad Taste

Truth in titling! Director Peter Jackson's debut is virtually a student film—crude and grainy—with several confident directorial touches that preview what he'd do in *Heavenly Creatures* and *The Frighteners.* Carnivorous aliens take over a small town in rural New Zealand. "We've got a bunch of extraterrestrial psychopaths on our hands," says one of our silly heroes. The hit team sent to deal with them are comic figures. Their prolonged fight with the aliens is a live action Roadrunner cartoon with grotesquely exaggerated violence. Heads are split apart; brains are eaten; etc. Director Jackson also plays two of the leading roles and acts with himself in one remarkable cliff scene. It all ends with a nasty "born again" joke.

1988 90m/C *NZ* Peter Jackson, Pete O'Herne, Mike Minett, Terry Potter, Craig Smith, Doug Wren, Dean Lawrie; ***D:*** Peter Jackson; ***W:*** Peter Jackson; ***C:*** Peter Jackson. **VHS, LV** *NO*

The Banker

The title character, Spaulding Osbourne (Duncan Regehr), is a wealthy financier whose passions are primitive religions and *Snow White and the Seven Dwarfs.* The opening scene, strongly reminiscent of *Betty Blue,* is a stylish blend of eroticism and violence that sets the tone for the rest of this updating of Jack the Ripper. Robert Forster is the veteran cop with a rookie

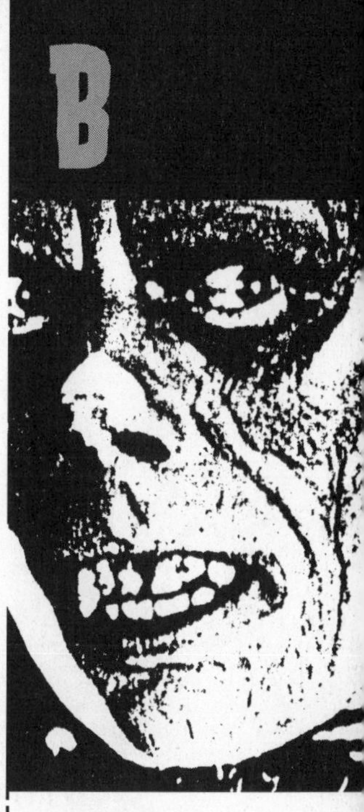

partner and an ex-girlfriend (Shanna Reed) who's a TV newswoman. These three walking cliches threaten to sink the story in predictability, but Osbourne gets crazier and crazier (and funnier) as the film goes along. You're never quite sure what he's going to do next, and so the second half pulls away from the formula. Slick music video production values and a fast pace make it a potent guilty pleasure.

1989 (R) 90m/C Robert Forster, Jeff Conaway, Leif Garrett, Duncan Regehr, Shanna Reed, Deborah Richter, Richard Roundtree, Teri Weigel, E.J. Peaker; ***D:*** William Webb. **VHS, LV** *NO*

Basic Instinct

Though this overheated commercial hit is usually thought of as a thriller, it can also be seen as horror, particularly in its unrated video version. That one opens with a scene of graphic sexual violence that few films in the genre can equal. Whatever logical lapses the story suffers—and it's filled with gaping holes from one end to the other—director Paul Verhoeven, writer Joe Ezsterhas, and star Sharon Stone make her character, bisexual author Catherine Tramell, one of the screen's most powerful femmes fatales. She may be a psycho killer; San Francisco cop Nick Curran (Michael Douglas) may not care. Stone's brassy, flashing, fearless performance turned her into a star overnight. Even so, some have dismissed the film as misogynist exploitation that denigrates women. Horror or suspense, feminism or homophobic trash, it's still a prime guilty pleasure.

1992 (R) 123m/C Michael Douglas, Sharon Stone, George Dzundza, Jeanne Tripplehorn, Denis Arndt, Leilani Sarelle Ferrer, Bruce A. Young, Chelcie Ross, Dorothy Malone, Wayne Knight, Stephen Tobolowsky; ***D:*** Paul Verhoeven; ***W:*** Joe Eszterhas; ***C:*** Jan De Bont; ***M:*** Jerry Goldsmith. MTV Movie Awards '93: Best Female Performance (Stone), Most Desirable Female (Stone); Nominations: Academy Awards '92: Best Film Editing, Best Original Score. **VHS, Closed Caption, DVD** *LIV, PMS*

Basket Case

One of the all-time great low-budget horrors is an ingeniously twisted original in every respect. After a bloody suburban opening, the scene shifts to a grainy, squalid Times Square where Duane (Kevin Van Hentenryck) carries a large wicker basket. He talks to the basket; he feeds it hamburgers and hotdogs. Inside is Belial. He's the amazing creation of Kevin Haney and John Caglione who use stop-motion animation and models to transform Belial into one of the most grotesque and believable monsters you'll ever see. Writer/director/editor Frank Henenlotter's plot is too outrageous for words, and the actors handle it masterfully. The combination of strong atmosphere and total unpredictability gives this one an overall weirdness that few horror films even attempt. Followed by two inferior titles; fans should seek out Henenlotter's *Brain Damage* instead.

1981 89m/C Kevin Van Hentenryck, Terri Susan Smith, Beverly Bonner, Robert Vogel, Diana Browne, Lloyd Pace, Bill Freeman, Joe Clarke, Ruth Neuman, Richard Pierce; ***D:*** Frank Henenlotter; ***W:*** Frank Henenlotter; ***C:*** Bruce Torbet. **VHS, LV** *NO*

Basket Case 2

With its grimy look, relatively restrained special effects, and bizarre sense of humor, the original is a solid cult hit. The disappointing sequel is a comparatively expensive production, but in this case, more is definitely less. Most of the action takes place on clean well-lighted sets with a glossy "Hollywood" look. The plot ignores key aspects of the first film. Until the conclusion, when writer/director Frank Henenlotter does manage to twist some kinks into the action, the plot ambles along without focus or the raw craziness that drove the first film. Followed by yet another.

1990 (R) 90m/C Kevin Van Hentenryck, Annie Ross, Kathryn Meisle, Heather Rattray, Jason Evers, Ted Sorel, Matt Mitler; ***D:*** Frank Henenlotter; ***W:*** Frank Henenlotter; ***C:*** Robert Baldwin; ***M:*** Joe Renzetti. **VHS, LV, Closed Caption** *VTR, IME, SGE*

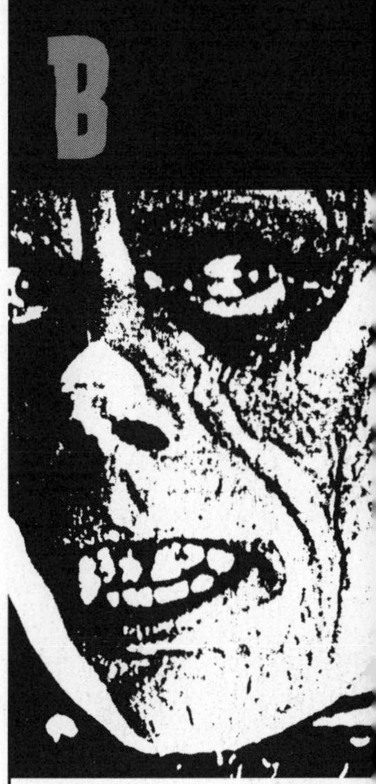

Basket Case 3: The Progeny

If the first sequel spoofed everything that was scary, sick, and wonderful in the original, the third installment is even weaker. It's a slender parody built around people in rubber masks and suits. The simple-minded plot about tolerance of differences and the unimportance of appearances would be preachy if it were meant to be taken seriously. It's not. Fans of Frank Henenlotter's brilliant low-budget original, and his underrated *Brain Damage,* should avoid both this one and *2.* **Woof!**

1992 (R) 90m/C Annie Ross, Kevin Van Hentenryck, Gil Roper, Tina Louise Hilbert, Dan Biggers, Jim O'Doherty, Jackson Faw, Jim Grimshaw; ***D:*** Frank Henenlotter; ***W:*** Frank Henenlotter, Robert Martin; ***C:*** Bob Paone; ***M:*** Joe Renzetti. **VHS, Closed Caption** *USH, SGE*

Beast of the Yellow Night

Drive-in classic from the Philippines combines a variation on the werewolf story and a sell-your-soul-to-the-devil angle. With the exception of familiar character actor Vic Diaz as a plump cheerful Satan, the cast is stiff and seems uncomfortable with the fairly demanding dialogue. But for those who see the film as an exercise in nostalgia, that's more positive than negative. Despite the silly monster makeup, complete with fright wig, this one's O.K.

1970 (R) 87m/C *PH* John Ashley, Mary Wilcox, Eddie Garcia, Vic Diaz; ***D:*** Eddie Romero. **VHS** *VCI, INC*

The Beast with Five Fingers

Despite a slow beginning and an uneven tone throughout, this is an intriguing horror based on flawed characters. At his mature creepiest, Peter Lorre is an astrologist who believes that his deceased employer's (Victor Francen) disembodied hand has escaped from the crypt. The acting ranges from J. Carrol Naish's delightfully stereotyped Italian police commisario to Robert Alda's silky conman and Charles Dingle's greedy heir. The hand effects by William McGann and H. Koenkamp are some of the best, far superior to the foolishness in Oliver Stone's *The Hand.* Director Robert Florey does fine black-and-white work and he gets a lot from Max Steiner's score.

1946 88m/B Robert Alda, Andrea King, Peter Lorre, Victor Francen, J. Carrol Naish, Charles Dingle; ***D:*** Robert Florey; ***W:*** Curt Siodmak; ***M:*** Max Steiner. **VHS, Closed Caption** *MGM*

The Beast Within

Mid-budget combination of town-with-a-secret and werewolf plotlines puts the formulas through their paces well enough. A terrible assault takes place in Nioba, Mississippi, 1964. Seventeen years later, Eli (Ronny Cox) and Caroline (Bibi Besch) MacCleary go back there to find out what's wrong with their son Michael (Paul Clemens). The southern Gothic elements have a gruff humor. A strong and slightly unusual setting—the deep South in winter—and a cast filled with seasoned character actors help considerably. The plot doesn't make as much sense as it might, but that's not a huge flaw. Careful viewers will catch a big continuity mistake in one kitchen scene before the gross-out stuff kicks in.

1982 (R) 98m/C Ronny Cox, Bibi Besch, L.Q. Jones, Paul Clemens, Don Gordon, Katherine Moffat, Ron Soble, John Dennis Johnston; ***D:*** Philippe Mora; ***W:*** Tom Holland; ***C:*** Jack L. Richards; ***M:*** Les Baxter. **VHS** *MGM*

Tom Laws (Ron Soble) and Michael MacCleary (Paul Clemens) in *The Beast Within.*

"Never trust the living."

—Juno (Sylvia Sidney), the coach, to her new ghosts Adam (Alec Baldwin) and Barbara (Geena Davis) in *Beetlejuice.*

Beauty Evil Rose

The glamorous witch Da-Chie (Usang Yeong Fang) kidnaps young women to do her evil bidding which involves..., well, evil stuff. Who cares about plot? For American audiences, the appeal of Hong Kong movies lies in their utter unpredictability. Boxing scenes, soft-core sex, motorcycle chases, snake monsters, cult doings, women raping men at gunpoint are all intercut at a furious pace. It's like watching the best parts from all your drive-in favorites from the 1970s wrapped up into a big juicy video burrito.

1994 90m/C *HK* Usang Yeong Fang, Suen Chi Wai; ***D:*** Lam Wuah Chuen. **VHS** *VSM*

Beetlejuice

Perhaps Tim Burton's most imaginative combination of horror and comedy is also one of his most enjoyable. Alec Baldwin and Geena Davis are the recently deceased young couple who can't leave their beloved rural home and want to get rid of the shallow new inhabitants (Jeffrey Jones, Catherine O'Hara, and Winona Ryder). Michael Keaton is the title character, an obnoxious supernatural used car salesman who offers to help. Burton's visual humor has never been stronger, and it benefits immeasurably from Danny Elfman's score. As usual, Burton gets perfectly pitched performances from a well-cast troupe that includes Dick Cavett, Susan Kellerman, and Robert Goulet in key support. Of the witty effects, the sandworms, the dinner party, and the snake scene are the most impressive.

1988 (PG) 92m/C Michael Keaton, Geena Davis, Alec Baldwin, Sylvia Sidney, Catherine O'Hara, Winona Ryder, Jeffrey Jones, Dick Cavett, Glenn Shadix, Susan Kellerman, Robert Goulet; ***D:*** Tim Burton; ***W:*** Michael McDowell, Warren Skaaren; ***C:*** Thomas Ackerman; ***M:*** Danny Elfman. Academy Awards '88: Best Makeup; National Society of Film Critics Awards '88: Best Actor (Keaton). **VHS, LV, 8mm, Closed Caption, DVD** *WAR, FCT, TLF*

Before I Hang

In one way, this slow-moving talky thriller is as relevant as it ever was. It begins with Dr. Garth (Boris Karloff) on trial for physician-assisted suicide. Later, with the help of Dr. Howard (Edward Van Sloan), he develops a miracle drug. It comes, of course, with a catch. Much of the "mad scientist" plot is downright silly, but Karloff's performance as an interesting, contradictory character is among his best. Otherwise, the stylized sets, lighting, and acting are very much a product of the time.

1940 60m/B Boris Karloff, Evelyn Keyes, Bruce (Herman Brix) Bennett, Edward Van Sloan, Ben Taggart, Pedro de Cordoba, Wright Kramer, Bertram Marburgh, Don Beddoe, Robert Fiske; ***D:*** Nick Grinde; ***W:*** Robert D. Andrews; ***C:*** Benjamin Kline. **VHS** *COL*

The Believers

Following the death of his wife, police psychologist Martin Sheen moves from Minneapolis to New York City, where he and his young son become the targets of a Santeria cult that sacrifices children. Director John Schlesinger handles the potentially exploitative material with a sure hand. The script by Mark Frost—a frequent collaborator with David Lynch and a fine novelist in his own right—is built on carefully drawn, sympathetic characters and horrifying conflicts that move well beyond familiar formulas. The film shares some thematic elements with *Burn Witch, Burn* and *Rosemary's Baby,* but don't make any direct comparisons. This sleeper's an original—one of the prolific director's best, but lesser-known efforts. Gary Farmer cameos as one of the movers.

1987 (R) 114m/C Martin Sheen, Helen Shaver, Malick Bowens, Harris Yulin, Robert Loggia, Jimmy Smits, Richard Masur, Harley Cross, Elizabeth Wilson, Lee Richardson, Carla Pinza; ***D:*** John Schlesinger; ***W:*** Mark Frost; ***C:*** Robby Muller; ***M:*** J. Peter Robinson. **VHS, LV, Closed Caption** *HBO*

Ben

Like the original, *Willard,* this sequel is ridiculous and poorly lit, but it's also undeniably effective at the key moments, touching that deep fear and hatred of vermin that crosses all cultural boundaries. Ben, the telepathic regent of rodents, leads his followers in more suburban mayhem and becomes pals with an insufferable kid (Lee Harcourt Montgomery). It all looks and sounds like it was made for TV with glossy but thin production values. Given the presence of Meredith Baxter, it might have been an episode of *Family Ties* that wandered into *The Twilight Zone.* Today, the film is more famous for the theme song that launched Michael Jackson's solo career. Listening to Montgomery warble that tune is doubly creepy now for all the wrong reasons. 🦴

1972 (PG) 95m/C Joseph Campanella, Lee Montgomery, Arthur O'Connell, Rosemary Murphy, Meredith Baxter, Norman Alden, Paul Carr, Kaz Garas, Kenneth Tobey, Richard Van Heet; ***D:*** Phil Karlson; ***W:*** Gilbert Ralston; ***C:*** Russell Metty. Golden Globe Awards '73: Best Song ("Ben"); Nominations: Academy Awards '72: Best Song ("Ben"). **VHS, LV** *NO*

Beyond the Door

They could have called this one "Rosemary's Exorcist." Jessica (Juliet Mills) is going to have the devil's baby—if her head doesn't unscrew itself first. On one level, the movie might be seen as pro-life horror, but forget the issue and the politics. In all technical categories the film is so bad it's barely watchable. Atrocious lighting, dubbing, editing, and acting combine to create one of the Hound's biggest WOOFS! ***AKA:*** Beyond Obsession; Chi Sei; The Devil within Her. **Woof!**

1975 (R) 97m/C *IT* Juliet Mills, Richard Johnson, David Colin Jr.; ***D:*** Richard Barrett, Oliver Hellman; ***W:*** Richard Barrett, Oliver Hellman. **VHS, LV, Closed Caption** *NO*

Beyond the Door 2

Mario Bava's story of psychic revenge and incestuous longings has nothing to do with the first *Beyond the Door.* It was retitled in this country apparently to capitalize on that film's inexplicable success. Young Marco (David Colin, Jr.) lusts for his mother Dora (Daria Nicolodi) and tells her calmly that he's going to kill her. The final part of the three-character psycho-horror is Bruno (John Steiner), her second husband. For once, Bava's vivid imagery and wild camerawork are used to describe complex emotional reality, not physical or narrative reality, and so his techniques are much more effective. Many fans consider this to be Bava's best and I agree, though *Black Sunday* is hard to top. Bava died in 1980. ***AKA:*** Shock; Shock (Transfer Suspense Hypnos); Suspense; Al 33 di Via Orologio fa Sempre Freddo. 🦴🦴🦴

1979 (R) 90m/C *IT* John Steiner, Daria Nicolodi, David Colin Jr., Ivan Rassimov, Nicola Salerno; ***D:*** Mario Bava; ***W:*** Lamberto Bava, Franco Barbieri, Dardano Sacchetti, Paolo Brigenti; ***C:*** Alberto Spagnoli. **VHS** *NO*

Big Trouble in Little China

Was trucker Jack Burton (Kurt Russell) killed when a whole block of downtown San Francisco went up in a ball of green flame? Of course not. Russell adapts an ersatz John Wayne drawl for this free-falling martial arts/fantasy/action/horror comedy. It has to do with a kidnapped bride (Suzee Pai), the evil wizard Lo Pan (James Hong), gangs, monsters, gunfights, and three magical figures who wear big lampshades on their heads. Director John Carpenter and D.P. Dean Cundey give the production more polish than Carpenter's quickly made films usually have. A cast of familiar American and Asian character

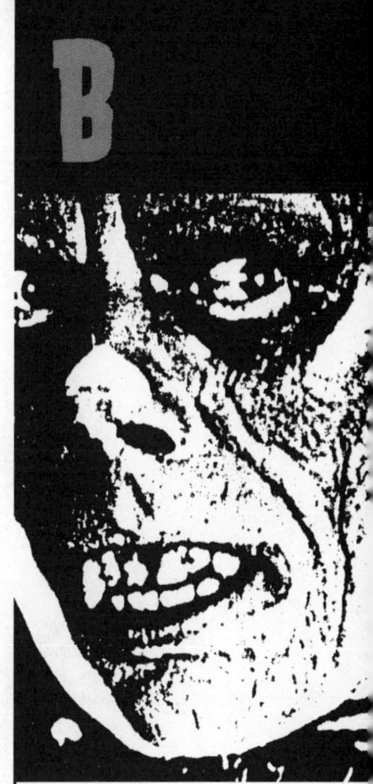

Melanie Daniels (Tippi Hedren) in Hitchcock's *The Birds.*

actors handle the silly dialogue with a snappy Hawksian pace.

1986 (PG-13) 99m/C Kurt Russell, Suzee Pai, Dennis Dun, Kim Cattrall, James Hong, Victor Wong, Kate Burton; ***D:*** John Carpenter; ***W:*** David Weinstein, Gary Goldman, W.D. Richter; ***C:*** Dean Cundey; ***M:*** John Carpenter, Alan Howarth. **VHS, LV, Letterboxed, Closed Caption** *FXV, FOX*

Billy the Kid Versus Dracula

The title is really more enjoyable than the execution of this mind-numbing genre-jumper. The title characters (Chuck Courtney and John Carradine) are both after the Barbie-esque Betty (Melinda Plowman). As an exercise in cheapjack '50s camp nostalgia, it's good for a few laughs, but nothing more. The bat effects, "transformations" (for want of a better word), and Carradine's pop-eyed hypnosis bit are the highlights...or lowlights, depending.

1966 95m/C Chuck Courtney, John Carradine, Melinda Plowman, Walter Janovitz, Harry Carey Jr., Roy Barcroft, Virginia Christine, Bing Russell, Olive Carey; ***D:*** William Beaudine; ***W:*** Carl K. Hittleman; ***C:*** Lothrop Worth. **VHS** *VYY*

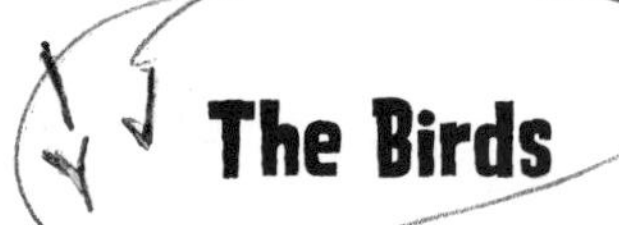

The Birds

Though incidents of avian attacks have been documented, Alfred Hitchcock has said that he views his most challenging horror film as "a speculation" with no connection to reality. In the book *Hitchcock Truffaut,* he says "With *The Birds* I made sure that the public would not be able to anticipate from one scene to another," and he certainly manages that. In the little town of Bodega Bay, flocks of birds inexplicably attack people. Non-lovebirds Mitch Brenner (Rod Taylor), an idealistic lawyer, and Melanie Daniels (Tippi Hedren), a flighty socialite, are inexorably drawn into and trapped by the situation. Reflecting the plot, all of the personal relationships defy cinematic conventions, and, more importantly, so does the ending. The big scenes—the attack on the restaurant, the schoolyard, the house, the escape—have been copied hundreds of times since. The film was a critical and commercial disappointment at the time, probably because the public that Hitchcock was trying to surprise was expecting another *Psycho*. Followed decades later by a poor TV sequel.

1963 (PG-13) 120m/C Rod Taylor, Tippi Hedren, Jessica Tandy, Veronica Cartwright, Suzanne Pleshette, Ethel Griffies, Charles McGraw, Ruth McDevitt; ***D:*** Alfred Hitchcock; ***W:*** Evan Hunter; ***C:*** Robert Burks. **VHS, LV** *USH*

The Black Cat

The collaboration of director Edgar G. Ulmer and stars Karloff and Lugosi in their first screen appearance together in the "suggestion" of a Poe story is horror's forgotten masterpiece. The deceptively complex and elegant plot isn't particularly frightening by itself. Instead, the film should be appreciated for its look. In purely visual terms, the Bauhaus/art deco sets and costumes make this one of the most striking pictures ever made, regardless of genre. Karloff and Lugosi do some of their best work in quiet roles. It's quite clear throughout that the horrors being evoked are born in modern warfare. They're shown in architecture, image, and character. Ignore the off-putting, heavy classical score and comic relief. ***AKA:*** House of Doom; Vanishing Body.

1934 65m/B Boris Karloff, Bela Lugosi, David Manners, Jacqueline Wells, Lucille Lund, Henry Armetta; ***D:*** Edgar G. Ulmer; ***W:*** Edgar G. Ulmer; ***C:*** John Mescall. **VHS, LV** *MLB, USH*

The Black Cat

Like so many Italian horrors, this one's a wacky, virtually plotless exercise in style—mediocre as it is—over substance. The titular feline is a harmless, altogether unthreatening creature, despite the filmmakers' best attempts to persuade us otherwise. Miles (the jut-jawed and always enjoyably hammy Patrick Magee) is a medium who hangs out in the cemetery of an English village. Jill (Mimsy Farmer) is a photographer. The aforementioned kitty is allegedly killing people. Yeah, right. The dark video transfer makes a hash of whatever director Lucio Fulci is trying to accomplish with his febrile camerawork. ***AKA:*** Il Gatto Nero.

1981 92m/C *IT GB* Patrick Magee, Mimsy Farmer, David Warbeck, Al Cliver, Dagmar Lassander, Geoffrey Copleston, Daniela Dorio; ***D:*** Lucio Fulci; ***W:*** Lucio Fulci, Biagio Proietti; ***C:*** Sergio Salvati; ***M:*** Pino Donaggio. **VHS** *RHI*

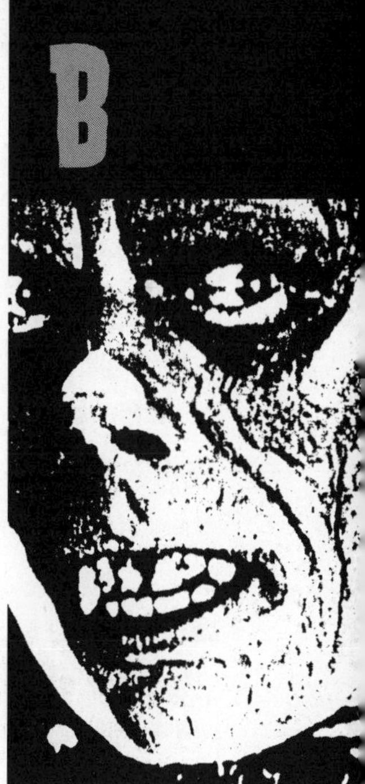

Black Friday

Karloff and Lugosi's third teaming is more watchable than *The Raven*, but nowhere close to *The Black Cat*. The illogical plot has surgeon Karloff transplanting the brain of a gangster into the skull of his professor friend (Stanley Ridges) after a car accident. The good doctor then expects his pal to be himself, though he might remember where the gangster brain left a fortune in hidden loot. The use of spinning headlines to move the story along quickly becomes irritating, but Karloff's debonair performance overcomes a lot. Lugosi fares less well in a much smaller role as a rival gangster. The characters make no more sense than the plot, which is a loco riff on *Jekyll and Hyde*. It's somehow reminiscent of those Looney Tunes cartoons where Tweetie is transformed into a monstrous killer canary who terrifies poor Sylvester.

1940 70m/B Boris Karloff, Stanley Ridges, Bela Lugosi, Anne Nagel, Anne Gwynne, Paul Fix, Virginia Brissac, James Craig; ***D:*** Arthur Lubin; ***W:*** Curt Siodmak, Eric Taylor; ***C:*** Woody Bredell. **VHS, Closed Caption** *USH*

"In the name of Satan, I place a curse upon you...my revenge will strike down you and your accursed house... I shall return to torment you and to destroy throughout the nights of time."

—Barbara Steele in *Black Sunday*.

The Black Room

Period noirish yarn has nothing to do with *Frankenstein* in terms of plot, but the two films are remarkably similar in other ways—sets, atmosphere, setting, the presence of Boris Karloff. He plays a dual role as an evil Baron and the good, foppish twin who, according to the family curse, will kill his older brother. The pace is swift and virtually all of the violence occurs off camera.

1935 70m/B Boris Karloff, Marian Marsh, Robert Allen, Katherine DeMille, John Buckler, Thurston Hall; ***D:*** Roy William Neill; ***W:*** Henry Myers, Arthur Strawn; ***C:*** Allen Siegler. **LV** *COL, MLB*

Black Sabbath

The venerable Boris Karloff introduces three short films and stars as a vampire in the last one. The pace is slow, and each tale contains at least one solid scare. Writer/director Mario Bava's horror is based on character and situation, not graphic visual effects. "The Drop of Water" comes from a Chekhov story about a nurse preparing a corpse. "The Telephone" has a contemporary—'60s—setting and makes incomplete sense. "Wurdalak," from a story by Alexei Tolstoy, is creepily atmospheric with echoes of "The Monkey's Paw." It's the most substantial of the three and is complex enough to have been expanded to feature length. ***AKA:*** I Tre Volti della Paura; Black Christmas; The Three Faces of Terror; The Three Faces of Fear.

1964 99m/C *IT* Boris Karloff, Jacqueline Pierreux, Michele Mercier, Lidia Alfonsi, Susy Anderson, Mark Damon, Rika Dialina; ***D:*** Mario Bava; ***W:*** Alberto Bevilacqua, Marcello Fondato, Mario Bava; ***C:*** Ubaldo Terzano; ***M:*** Les Baxter. **VHS** *SNC*

Black Sunday

Despite some dated dialogue, the key images in Mario Bava's masterpiece have lost none of their power. The resurrected revenge-seeking witch plot is familiar, but it's spun out at a lively pace with attention to detail. The stunning Barbara Steele is the Russian witch in question, and her twin, a potential victim. Her initial execution is still a frightening moment. So is her rebirth, complete with scorpions. The inky black-and-white atmosphere and the Gothic elements of the plot strongly influenced the generation of Hammer films that would follow. Bava would revisit the subject in the third section of *Black Sabbath*. ***AKA:*** La Maschera del Demonio; The Demon's Mask; House of Fright; Revenge of the Vampire.

1960 83m/B *IT* Barbara Steele, John Richardson, Ivo Garrani, Andrea Checchi, Arturo Dominici, Antonio Pierfederici, Tino Bianchi, Clara Bindi, Enrico Oliveri, Germana Dominici; ***D:*** Mario Bava; ***W:*** Mario Bava, Ennio de Concini, Mario Serandrei; ***C:*** Mario Bava, Ubaldo Terzano; ***M:*** Les Baxter. **VHS** *SMW, SNC, MOV*

Black Werewolf

Curious werewolf tale based on a James Blish story ("There Shall Be No Darkness") combines elements of *The Most Dangerous Game, Ten Little Indians,* and blaxploitation with a gimmick—the "werewolf break" which gives viewers 30 seconds near the end to come up with the identity of the wolfman (or wolfwoman). Multimillionaire Tom Newcliffe (Calvin Lockhart) invites houseguests—each with a nasty secret—for a weekend at his security-enhanced country estate, and claims that one of them is a monster. The mystery side of the story demands long passages of explanatory dialogue while the action side is often reduced to pointless motion. Peter Cushing stands out in the supporting cast. Lockhart's impressive in the lead. An archetypal '70s theme and score by Douglas Gamley is the finishing touch. ***AKA:*** The Beast Must Die.

1975 (PG) 93m/C *GB* Peter Cushing, Calvin Lockhart, Charles Gray, Anton Diffring, Marlene Clark, Ciaran

Madden, Tom Chadbon, Michael Gambon; ***D:*** Paul Annett; ***W:*** Michael Winder; ***C:*** Jack Hildyard; ***M:*** Douglas Gamley. **VHS, LV** *NO*

Blacula

With great early '70s music and clothes, this is more easily appreciated as blaxploitation than as horror. In 1780, an African prince (William Marshall) goes to Transylvania to enlist Dracula's (Charles MaCauley) aid in stopping the slave trade. Instead, he's vampirized by the evil Count, and locked in a coffin to reappear in present day L.A. With his rumbling bass voice and striking physical presence, Marshall invites comparison to Christopher Lee. Unfortunately, many of supporting undead look like they're on their way to the middle school Halloween party. On the whole, this one's fun and not meant to be taken seriously. Followed by *Scream Blacula Scream.* 🦴🦴🦴

1972 (PG) 92m/C William Marshall, Thalmus Rasulala, Denise Nicholas, Vonetta McGee, Gordon Pinsent, Emily Yancy, Charles Macaulay, Ted Harris; ***D:*** William Crain; ***W:*** Raymond Koenig, Joan Torres; ***C:*** John Stevens. **VHS, LV** *ORI*

Blade of the Ripper

Muddled slasher tale has to do with Julie (Edwige Fenech), an ambassador's wife, and her ex-lover who may be a serial killer. Or is it her new beau? What about hubby? Most of the scares are retreaded Hitchcock, but the real problem is the way the screen is filled with such extreme close-ups you can often see only half a face. Other scenes are either overexposed and bleached out or mired in muddy darkness. Blame goes to director Sergio Martino or the video transfer or both. Cult fav Fenech is the only reason to catch this one. ***AKA:*** The Next Victim; Next!; Lo Strano Vizio della Signora Ward. 🦴🦴

1970 90m/C George Hilton, Edwige Fenech, Alberto De Mendoza, Ivan Rassimov; ***D:*** Sergio Martino; ***W:*** Ernesto Gastaldi, Eduardo Brochero. **VHS** *NO*

The Blob

Even if it didn't have a young "Steven" McQueen in the lead, this tongue-in-cheek gem would still be on the great '50s low-budget hit list. Carnivorous snot in a meteorite flashes above Lovers Lane where Steve (McQueen) and Jane (Aneta Corsaut) are parked. The critter crashes into a farmer's field and grows to enormous size. The teens try to do all the right things but bone-headed adults pay no attention. Burt Bacharach's bouncy "Beware the Blob" theme sets exactly the right tone. The whole idea of combining *Rebel without a Cause* characters and situation with a cheap monster from outer space plot is inspired. 🦴🦴🦴

1958 83m/C Steve McQueen, Aneta Corsaut, Olin Howlin, Earl Rowe, Steve Chase, John Benson; ***D:*** Irvin S. Yeaworth Jr.; ***W:*** Kate Phillips, Theodore Simonson; ***C:*** Thomas E. Spalding; ***M:*** Burt Bacharach, Hal David. **VHS, LV, Letterboxed** *GEM, MLB, CRC*

The Blob

Remake of a perfectly good original is predictably pointless and overblown with a barfbag full of graphic effects. After a prolonged introduction of several characters who aren't going to be around very long, the titular creature crashes to earth, and straightaway commences to blobifying people. Brave young Brian (Kevin Dillon) and Meg (Shawnee Smith) try to warn everyone but the adults won't listen. Toward the end, when the Blob has achieved split-level dimensions, the special effects really aren't any better than they were in 1958. 🦴🦴

1988 (R) 92m/C Kevin Dillon, Candy Clark, Joe Seneca, Shawnee Smith, Donovan Leitch, Jeffrey DeMunn, Ricky Paull Goldin, Del Close; ***D:*** Chuck Russell; ***W:*** Chuck Russell, Frank Darabont; ***C:*** Mark Irwin. **VHS, LV, Closed Caption** *COL*

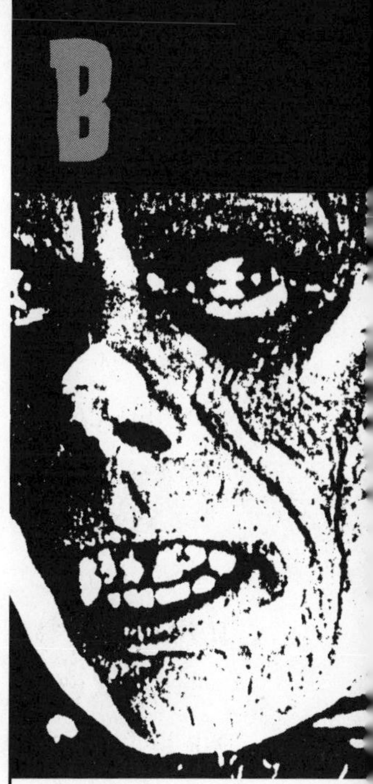

Chuck Russell's *The Blob* (1988).

Blood & Donuts

Director Holly Dale and writer Andrew Rai Berzins make full use of a limited budget in this enjoyable little Canadian comedy. Boya (Gordon Currie) is a Toronto vampire who's accidentally awakened after a 25-year-long nap. Perhaps in need of a caffeine fix, he hangs out at a rundown coffee shop where Molly (Helene Clarkson) is a waitress. He's a romantic Byronic vampire who upsets a gangster's (David Cronenberg) plans to take over the neighborhood. Considering the current excesses of the genre, the action is relatively restrained. The main irritant is Justin Louis as Earl, the cabbie. While everyone else is playing it straight, he shamelessly gnaws on the scenery. Dale has come up with neat variations on familiar themes.

1995 (R) 89m/C *CA* Gordon Currie, Justin Louis, Helene Clarkson, Fiona Reid, Frank Moore; ***Cameos:*** David Cronenberg; ***D:*** Holly Dale; ***W:*** Andrew Rai Berzins; ***C:*** Paul Sarossy. Nominations: Genie Awards '96: Best Actress (Clarkson), Best Costume Design, Best Original Screenplay. **VHS, LV, Closed Caption** *LIV*

Blood and Roses

This version of the oft-told story makes less than complete sense, and the sight of Bardot wannabe Annette Vadim strolling about lazily in a wedding dress isn't nearly as frightening as it's intended to be (or needs to be). She's Carmilla Karnstein, who's in love with her wealthy cousin Leopoldo (Mel Ferrer), who's about to marry Georgia (Elsa Martinelli). The romantic comedy aspects are particularly out of place and the film treats the whole issue of vampirism like an embarrassing relative it would rather not acknowledge. The performances are anemic. Apparently director Roger Vadim means for this to be taken as serious drama when it needs a strong shot of the cheesiness he brings to *Barbarella*. ***AKA:*** Et Mourir de Plaisir.

1961 74m/C *FR IT* Mel Ferrer, Elsa Martinelli, Annette Vadim, Marc Allegret, Jacques-Rene Chauffard; ***D:*** Roger Vadim; ***W:*** Roger Vadim, Claude Martin, Roger Vailand, Claude Brule; ***C:*** Claude Renoir. **VHS, Closed Caption** *PAR*

Blood Beach

Modest, well-photographed little B-movie seems almost embarrassed by the silliness of its own plot. Something is living under the Santa Monica beach and sucking people and animals down into the sand. In the last reel, when the monster has to make an appearance, writer/director Jeffrey Bloom keeps it in shadow and makes no attempt to explain its presence. That's probably just as well. The film is more comfortable with kitschy beach scenes, slightly overexposed and in soft focus so that the light takes on an almost tangible quality. Those have nothing to do with the alleged story, but they're pretty to watch. 🦴🦴

1981 (R) 92m/C David Huffman, Marianna Hill, John Saxon, Burt Young, Otis Young, Pamela McMyler, Bobby Bass, Darrell Fetty, Stefan Gierasch, Harriet Medin; ***D:*** Jeffrey Bloom; ***W:*** Jeffrey Bloom; ***C:*** Steven Poster. **VHS** *NO*

Blood Feast

Reportedly filmed for less than $70,000 in Miami, the first splatter movie is really a camp comedy. The silly writing and non-professional acting are actually part of the film's weird appeal. By today's standards, the gore effects in the story of an Egyptian caterer/killer (Mal Arnold) are tame. But in 1963, no one showed lopped limbs or scooped brains on the silver screen. Producer/director Herschell Gordon Lewis creates—in his own crude way—a pornography of violence. Like conventional pornography, it's about limits, about crossing lines that cannot be crossed. Because of that, the film has undeniable historical value as a milestone in the genre. ***AKA:*** Feast of Flesh. 🦴🦴

1963 70m/C Connie Mason, Thomas Wood, Mal Arnold, Scott H. Hall, Lyn Bolton, Toni Calvert, Gene Courtier; ***D:*** Herschell Gordon Lewis; ***W:*** Allison Louise Downe; ***C:*** Herschell Gordon Lewis. **VHS** *SMW, FCT*

Blood Freak

Remember what happened to David Hedison in the original *Fly*? Something similar befalls poor Hershell (Steve Hawkes), an Elvisian biker...but with a turkey. He's the hero of this drive-in wonder made in Florida. He's also involved with two sisters, devout Christian Angel who gives impromptu Bible lessons to her depraved dope-toking sister Anne and anyone else who'll listen. Topping it all off is a seedy, chain-smoking, wheezing on-camera narrator who interrupts the action at regular intervals to read a script that might have been written by Ed Wood, Jr., on a particularly festive day. It's a rambling meditation on faith, God, the nature of the universe, and health, that ends with a coughing fit. Required viewing for connoisseurs of the bizarre. Everyone else can pass. ***AKA:*** Blood Freaks. 🦴🦴½

1972 86m/C Steve Hawkes, Dana Cullivan, Randy Grinter Jr., Tina Anderson, Heather Hughes; ***D:*** Brad Grinter, Steve Hawkes. **VHS**

Blood Legacy

Standard haunted house tale has a family of spoiled heirs who all hate each other spend a week in their bitter dad's (John Carradine) mansion to claim their inheritance. Ax murders, incest, insanity, and bad flashbacks ensue. The action is slow, stiffly staged, and full of talk. An ensemble cast of familiar faces from '60s TV seems understandably embarrassed by the material. It compares poorly to the Corman and Hammer horrors of the same vintage. The one-bone rating is mostly for the clothes. ***AKA:*** Legacy of Blood. 🦴

1973 (R) 77m/C John Carradine, John Russell, Faith Domergue, Merry Anders, Richard Davalos, Jeff Mor-

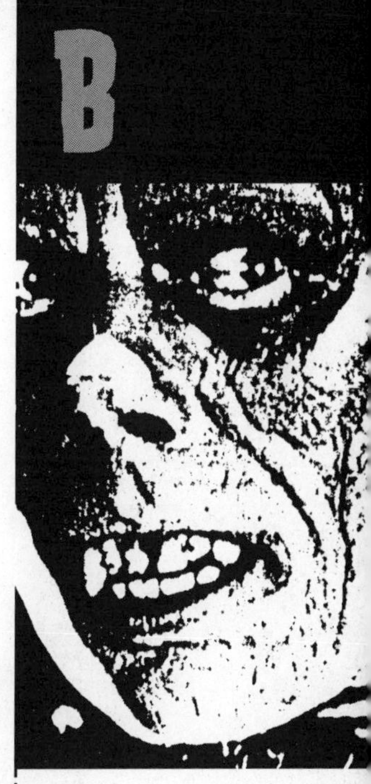

"Are you inferrin' to me?!"

—Earl the cabbie (Justin Louis) tries to emulate Travis Bickle in *Blood & Donuts*.

The 1940s

Abbott & Costello Meet the Sequels

World War II put a serious crimp in horror movies.

That really isn't as flippant as it sounds. How can people be interested in cinematic scares when they're involved in a massive conflict against barbarous evil? More directly, at the beginning of the decade, the film industry, like other American industries, put all of its energies into the war effort. Horror and propaganda are an uneasy mix. (In England, horror movies were actually banned.)

The United States was entering the war when Universal released the last of its great original horrors, *The Wolf Man* with Lon Chaney, Jr., and Claude Rains. For the rest of the decade, the studio would rely on two kinds of sequels. The first came up with various combinations of the Frankenstein monster, Dracula, and the Wolfman. The second was a series of *Mummy* movies that brought the Wrapped One to America, where he shuffled around sipping Tana tea and scaring the daylights out of the locals.

Also in 1941, Spencer Tracy played *Dr. Jekyll and Mr. Hyde* without makeup or effects-enhanced transformation scenes. He and director Victor Fleming made one of the best versions of Robert Louis Stevenson's oft-filmed story.

In 1942, producer Val Lewton and director Jacques Tourneur began a partnership at the RKO studio that resulted in some of the most critically praised horror movies to come out of Hollywood. Their first was *The Cat People*. It was followed by *I Walked with a Zombie* and *The Leopard Man*.

Universal remade Lon Chaney's *Phantom of the Opera* in 1943 with a much more sympathetic Claude Rains as Erik, though top billing went to singer Nelson Eddy. In the same year, Chaney, Jr., donned the vampire's cape in *Son of Dracula*. A year later, Bela Lugosi played another vampire named Tesla in Columbia's *Return of the Vampire*. Ray Milland starred in one of the best conventional ghost stories, *The Uninvited*.

Hollywood's "classy" horror continued in the post-war years with *Picture of Dorian Gray*, featuring George Sanders at his droll best. Also in 1945, Boris Karloff starred in the understated (and largely unknown) *Isle of the Dead*, and Robert Wise directed *The Body Snatcher*, an intelligent grave-robbing tale loosely based on the notorious exploits of Edinburgh's Burke and Hare. In England, *Dead of Night* was one of the first "anthology" horrors—short stories collected within a loose narrative structure.

As the decade came to a close, the genre was virtually lifeless. Universal admitted as much when it began teaming its horror stars with Bud Abbott and Lou Costello, two of the most popular screen comedians of the time. The old guys were good for laughs and little more. Horror was going to have to move in other directions to find a newer and younger audience.

Two other major changes were in the offing for horror and for the movie business in general. First, the Supreme Court in 1949 hit the studios with the Paramount Consent Decree, a decision that forced Warner Bros., Paramount, MGM, and Twentieth Century Fox to give up the theatre chains they owned. Second, television was on the way.

row, Roy Engle; ***D:*** Carl Monson; ***W:*** Eric Norden; ***C:*** Jack Beckett. **VHS** *CNG, MRV, GEM*

Blood of Dracula

Camp classic from 1957 is a perfect example of Mayo's First Rule of Horror—No film with a dance scene can be seriously frightening. This one has teen boarding-school debs spinning the platters and dancing with seat cushions, not to mention the "Puppy Love" production number. The other parts of the slow-moving snoozer involve pre-liberation feminism and risible vampire makeup, as the evil Miss Branding (Louise Lewis) taps into young Nancy's (Sandra Harrison) inner sources of power and turns her into a monster. Recommended for viewing by large groups who are ready to laugh. ***AKA:*** Blood Is My Heritage; Blood of the Demon. 🦴🦴

1957 71m/B Sandra Harrison, Louise Lewis, Gail Ganley, Jerry Blaine, Heather Ames, Malcolm Atterbury, Richard Devon, Thomas B. Henry; ***D:*** Herbert L. Strock; ***W:*** Ralph Thornton; ***C:*** Monroe Askins. **VHS** *COL, OM*

Blood of Dracula's Castle

Camp '60s drive-in fare actually begins at Marineland, and then heads for the desert (or is it the beach?) where Mr. and Mrs. Dracula (Alexander D'Arcy and Paula Raymond) have their titular castle. Their servant John Carradine keeps a supply of nubile young blood donors chained up in the basement. An escaped homicidal maniac (Robert Dix) and a hunchback (Ray Young) are part of the mix, too, when a young couple comes to visit the place. Director Al Adamson pushed the limits for graphic violence in those gentler times, but the whole film is still an ultra-low-budget effort of some historical and curiosity value but little else. ***AKA:*** Dracula's Castle. 🦴🦴

1969 84m/C John Carradine, Alexander D'Arcy, Paula Raymond, Ray Young, Vicki Volante, Robert Dix, John Cardos; ***D:*** Al Adamson, Jean Hewitt; ***W:*** Rex Carlton; ***C:*** Laszlo Kovacs. **VHS** *NO*

The Blood on Satan's Claw

Is the devil loose in a 17th century English village? Or are malicious teenaged girls (a la *The Crucible*) up to something, or are high-spirited kids playing, or is something else going on? That's the curious beginning of a first-class historical horror. The large cast lacks individual definition and the story is sometimes too confused, particularly toward the end, but that's O.K. Director Piers Haggard creates a strong evocation of place and time with carefully chosen locations and a restrained use of effects. His work is comparable in style and subtlety to another unorthodox film of its time, *The Wicker Man*. ***AKA:*** Satan's Skin; Satan's Claw. 🦴🦴🦴

1971 90m/C *GB* Patrick Wymark, Linda Hayden, Barry Andrews, Michele Dotrice, James Hayter, Avice Landon, Simon Williams, Tamara Ustinov; ***D:*** Piers Haggard; ***C:*** Dick Bush. **VHS** *MGM, FCT*

Blood Orgy of the She-Devils

Fans of alternative cinema are the only audience for this grandly titled, wonderfully overacted goofiness. The story of witches, zombies, past lives, interpretive dance, the Indian spirit guide Taka-Waka, and "psychometrized" objects is told with the cheesy look and cheesy mindset of an early '70s Philippine exploitation flick but without the skin, the sex, or the gore. Instead, it's got unfettered imagination to burn with wacky plot twists that other movies never even imagine, much less attempt to show. 🦴

1974 (PG) 73m/C Lila Zaborin, Tom Pace, Leslie McRae, Ray Myles, Victor Izay, William Bagdad; ***D:*** Ted V. Mikels; ***W:*** Ted V. Mikels; ***C:*** Anthony Salinas. **VHS** *NO*

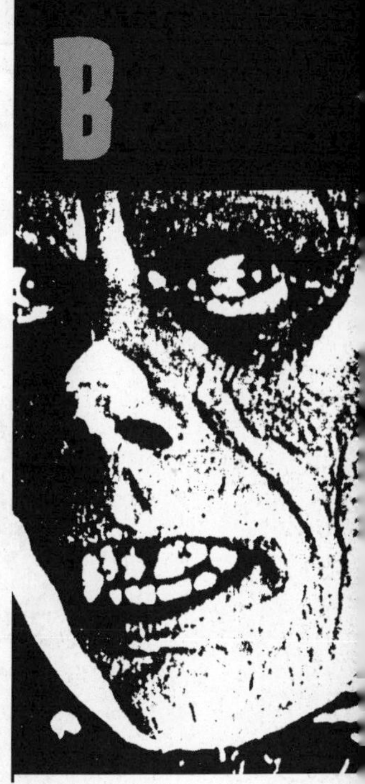

Blood Relations

In an unhappy Canadian household, even lies aren't what they seem. An egomaniacal surgeon (Jan Rubes) may have killed his wealthy wife. His unstable son (Kevin Hicks) hasn't forgiven him. The son's manipulative girlfriend (Lydie Denier) looks like the dead woman, and his dying grandfather (Ray Walston) may be the kinkiest of them all. The games they play with and against each other in a snow-covered mansion become creepier and creepier until they reach a wonderfully nasty Grand Guignol conclusion. One of the better sleepers in your favorite video store. 🦴🦴🦴½

1987 (R) 88m/C *CA* Jan Rubes, Ray Walston, Lydie Denier, Kevin Hicks, Lynne Adams, Sam Malkin, Steven Saylor, Carrie Leigh; ***D:*** Graeme Campbell. **VHS, LV** *NLC*

Blood Salvage

Horror/comedy about organ transplants is cut from the same cloth as the cult classic *Motel Hell.* Jake (Danny Nelson) uses his tow truck business as a front for an organ bank. He removes them from unwilling donors and sells them to unscrupulous doctors through middleman Ray Walston. Things are just dandy until Jake falls for April (Lori Birdsong), who's paralyzed from the waist down. Jake, a latter-day Victor Frankenstein in coveralls, decides to help her. Writing, acting, direction, and sense of place (rural Georgia) are several notches above average. The gross moments are played for laughs of the haunted house peeled-grapes-for-eyeballs variety. Also, the screen is filled with religious imagery and language that's somehow appropriate to this story of twisted love and sacrifice. ***AKA:*** Mad Jake. 🦴🦴🦴½

1990 (R) 90m/C Danny Nelson, Lori Birdsong, John Saxon, Ray Walston, Christian Hesler, Ralph Pruitt Vaughn, Laura Whyte, Evander Holyfield; ***D:*** Tucker Johnson; ***W:*** Tucker Johnson, Ken Sanders; ***C:*** Michael Karp. **VHS, LV** *TTC*

The Blood Spattered Bride

Vicente Aranda mixes exploitation and fiery no-prisoners feminism in a strange evocative update of Sheridan LeFanu's *Carmila.* Troubled newlyweds (Simon Andreu and Maribel Martin) go to his lonely, lavish provincial estate and eventually are joined by a vampiric ghost (Alexandra Bastedo), who has perhaps the weirdest introduction in the history of horror. Time has rendered some of the film's surrealistic touches and sexual notions dated and humorous. The somnambulant pace and striking locations have lost nothing, though. Simon Andreu's portrayal of the nameless self-centered husband is piggishly perfect. In theatrical release, the violent ending was severely reedited. The unrated tape is shocking. Of the three adaptations of the novel (the others are Roger Vadim's *Blood and Roses* and *The Vampire Lovers*), this is by far the best. The cliched use of a body double is a flaw. ***AKA:*** Blood Castle; La Novia Esangrentada; Bloody Fiance; Till Death Us Do Part. 🦴🦴🦴

1972 82m/C *SP* Simon Andreu, Maribel Martin, Alexandra Bastedo, Dean Selmier, Montserrat Julio, Maria Rosa Rodriguez, Angel Lombarte; ***D:*** Vicente Aranda; ***W:*** Vicente Aranda; ***C:*** Fernando Arribas. **VHS** *MPI*

Blood Ties

Cult fav director Jim McBride makes this Fox-TV pilot a combination of *The Lost Boys* and *Melrose Place.* A young man goes to L.A. to stay with relatives after his family is murdered. Christian vigilantes led by Bo Hopkins are after him, too. Though Hopkins' people think of the boy's kinfolk as "the undead," they prefer to be called "Carpathian-Americans." While some keep to the old traditions, others, including our hero Harry (Patrick Bauchau), think "it's time we came out of the coffin." But uncle Eli (Salvator Xuereb) warns that if they go public, that's "when the pogroms begin."

The rest involves conflicts between the elders and the young Carpathian-Americans who live in loft apartments, ride motorcycles, and engage in sexy dance numbers. McBride has fun with well-worn horror movie themes, tinkering with the conventions of the genre, and indulging in some timely social humor.

1992 90m/C Harley Venton, Patrick Bauchau, Kim Johnston-Ulrich, Michelle Johnson, Jason London, Bo Hopkins, Grace Zabriskie, Salvator Xuereb; ***D:*** Jim McBride; ***W:*** Richard Shapiro. **VHS** *NHO*

Bloodlust: Subspecies 3

The Transylvanian locations are about all that this sequel has going for it. *3* is the weakest of the *Subspecies* series, though the gooey effects will appeal to hardcore fans. (See reviews of *Subspecies* and *Bloodstone* for more information.) The filmmakers have continued with the similar *Vampire Journals.* ***AKA:*** Subspecies 3.

1993 (R) 83m/C Anders Hove, Kevin Blair, Denice Duff, Pamela Gordon, Ion Haiduc, Michael DellaFemina; ***D:*** Ted Nicolaou; ***W:*** Ted Nicolaou. **VHS, LV, Closed Caption** *FLL*

Bloodstone: Subspecies 2

The good-vampire/bad-vampire bit was the premise of the original *Subspecies,* and it ended with both characters temporarily out of commission. The first sequel begins with some really yucky Grand Guignol scenes wherein bad vamp Radu (Anders Hove), decapitated at the end of the first film is, as it were, recapitated. It doesn't help the long bad hair day he's having—not to mention bad face, bad hands, bad drool. We're talking serious personal hygiene problems here. Again, there's nothing too original about the plot. The good vampire's American girlfriend (Denice Duff) steals the Bloodstone, a supernatural lava light, and heads for Bucharest. The rest contains enough imaginative, grotesque effects to keep even the most jaded fan happy and nauseous. Followed by *Bloodlust.* ***AKA:*** Subspecies 2.

1992 (R) 107m/C Anders Hove, Denice Duff, Kevin Blair, Michael Denish, Pamela Gordon, Ion Haiduc; ***D:*** Ted Nicolaou; ***W:*** Ted Nicolaou. **VHS, LV, Closed Caption** *FLL*

The Bloodsuckers

Offbeat vampire tale opens with the dreaming spires of Oxford but quickly goes to Greece where Richard Fountain (Patrick Mower), a Don with a future, is seduced by Chrises (Imogen Hassell). Their drug orgy scene is really funny. When his pals, led by Patrick Macnee, try to bring him back, their search turns into several long chase scenes. Between those, the film often resorts to voiceover narration to keep things moving. That may partially explain why director Robert Hartford-Davis had his name removed from the credits. Both the alternate title, *Incense for the Damned,* and the title of the novel it's based on, *Doctors Wear Scarlet,* are more appropriate. Much of the acting is fine and the exotic settings are well utilized. Writer Julian More doesn't so much equate vampirism with drug use and sexual obsession as intermix the three. The ending is unfortunate. ***AKA:*** Incense for the Damned; Doctors Wear Scarlet.

1970 90m/C *GB* Patrick Macnee, Peter Cushing, Patrick Mower, Edward Woodward, Alex Davion, Imogen Hassall, Madeline Hinde, Johnny Sekka; ***D:*** Robert Hartford-Davis; ***W:*** Julian More; ***C:*** Desmond Dickinson. **VHS** *SNC*

Bloodsucking Nazi Zombies

The title will warm the heart of any horror fan, but the execution doesn't live up to it.

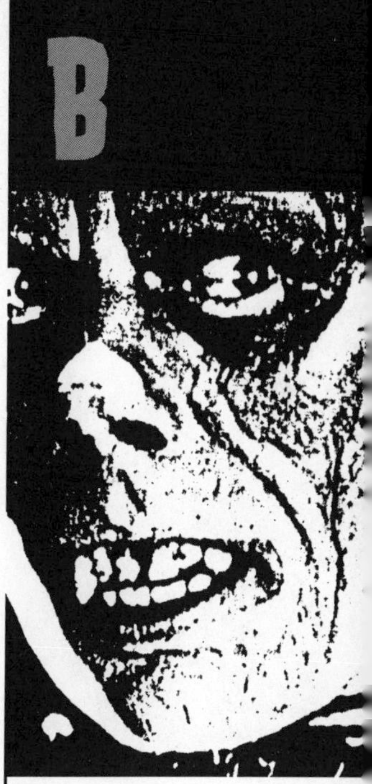

VIDEO HORROR BOOKSHELF

At the end of this book in the "Horror Connections" section, you'll find a general listing of books about horror films. It covers the field well, but when I was working on these reviews, I found that I turned to five titles more often than the others. They deserve extra attention because at least three are a little difficult to find, and every curious fan should take a look at them.

The first is the maddening *The Overlook Film Encyclopedia: Horror* edited by Phil Hardy (Overlook Press, 1995, $40, trade paper). It's a thorough collection of opinionated, sometimes overwritten reviews of horror movies made between 1896 and 1992. It's a useful, intelligent book, handsomely laid out and printed on heavy paper. It is also curiously organized. Films are listed alphabetically within the year of their release. To find an individual entry, you have to check the index to make sure you've got the right year. (As any fan knows, when you start talking release dates and copyrights, the years can be confusing.)

Even so, that's a legitimate way to organize such a book, and it's especially useful for students of the genre who are interested in larger trends. Unfortunately, the publishers did not go to the extra time and expense of a full index of the people involved. If you're interested in a particular director or actor or writer, you'll have to look elsewhere. (The complete index to this book is a good place to start.)

One other caveat is even more important. In their discussions of these films, the authors regularly synopsize the entire plot. If you haven't seen a particular title, do NOT read the *Overlook* review first. It's likely to tell you much more than you want to know.

The Universal Story (Crown, 1983, out of print) by Clive Hirschhorn is a terrific reference source for anyone who appreciates the films that Universal made in the 1930s and '40s. The book is a history of the studio from its beginnings to the mid-1980s. Hirschhorn's tone is generally complimentary, but he judges each film that the studio made and he's not a cheerleader. He organizes the reviews within a decade-by-decade history of the studio.

Japanese Cinema Encyclopedia (Vital Books, 1997, $19.95, trade paper) by Thomas Weisser and Yuko Mihara Weisser and *Asian Cult Cinema* (Boulevard Books, 1997, $14, trade paper) by Thomas Weisser are an excellent two-volume introduction to the incredible films that have been made in China and Japan in recent years. Jackie Chan is a household name; John Woo's movies make millions but they're only the beginning of what I predict will be a significant influence in American film.

The Asian filmmakers have been studying American movies for generations. They've created their own storytelling styles in horror and other genres, and they're doing some startling work. A few of the best are reviewed here. Anyone who wants to know more should see Weisser's books. He runs Video Search of Miami and has a good working knowledge of the field.

Finally, R.H.W. Dillard's *Horror Films* (Monarch/Simon & Schuster, 1976, out of print) is part of the Monarch Film Studies series. It's a thoughtful critical examination of the artistic and moral dimensions of the horror film as the author saw them in the mid-1970s. He focuses on *Frankenstein, The Wolf Man, Night of the Living Dead,* and *Fellini Satyricon.* He is a serious academic critic but his writing is completely free of the mind-numbing jargon that infects so much scholarly prose. His points are clear, well thought-out, and based on the films themselves. As I worked my way through this book, I found myself going back often to *Horror Films* to recheck key points. I recommend it to any horror fan. If you don't have a copy, find one.

No, I will not lend you mine.

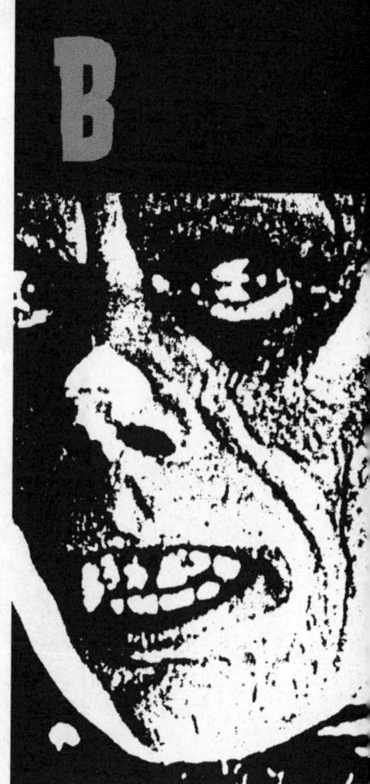

Aside from some brightly lit desert scenes, the film is so dark and hard to make out that it's virtually unwatchable. The story has to do with a World War II treasure hidden at an oasis where the titular characters are still hanging around. The zombie makeup is so lame that it makes the slow travelogue scenes look good. The obvious inspirations are George Romero's *Living Dead* movies and Armando de Ossorio's *Blind Dead,* but this doesn't measure up. ***AKA:*** Oasis of the Zombies; Treasure of the Living Dead. **Woof!**

1982 75m/C *SP FR* Manuel Gelin, France Jordan, Jeff Montgomery, Miriam Landson, Eric Saint-Just, Caroline Audret, Henry Lambert; ***D:*** Jess (Jesus) Franco, A.M. Frank; ***W:*** A. L. Mariaux. **VHS** *NO*

Bloody Birthday

Because they were born during a full solar eclipse, three angelic children (Elizabeth Hoy, Billy Jacoby, Andy Freeman) become tiny homicidal maniacs on their tenth birthday. That brain-dead premise is the dubious starting point for a substandard dead-teen horror. Beyond the underaged psychos angle, the film's only claim to fame now is a nude scene with comedienne Julie Brown. ***AKA:*** Creeps.

1980 (R) 92m/C Susan Strasberg, Jose Ferrer, Lori Lethin, Melinda Cordell, Joe Penny, Ellen Geer, Julie Brown, Michael Dudikoff, Billy Jacoby, Elizabeth Hoy, Andy Freeman; ***D:*** Edward Hunt; ***W:*** Edward Hunt, Barry Pearson. **VHS** *NO*

Bloody Moon

The ugliest moment in this ugly Grand Guignol combines an onscreen decapitation (on that old favorite, the conveyor belt and buzz saw) with the murder of a child. The whole thing is a virtually plotless Jess Franco exercise in slasher misogyny as young women are killed at a language school. It's all made even more unbearable by a disco soundtrack and woop-woop sound effects used to introduce the killer. ***AKA:*** Die Saege des Todes. **Woof!**

1983 84m/C *GE* Olivia Pascal, Christopher Brugger, Ann-Beate Engelke, Antonia Garcia, Nadja Gerganoff, Corinna Gillwald, Jasmin Losensky, Maria Rubio, Alexander Waechter; ***D:*** Jess (Jesus) Franco; ***W:*** Jess (Jesus) Franco, Rayo Casablanca; ***C:*** Juan Soler. **VHS** *TWE*

Boccaccio '70

This anthology was so scandalous when it was released in this country in 1962 that it played only at a few drive-ins, "art houses," and college campuses. Though relatively few people saw these short Italian films, two images from them were burned into the public consciousness. The first is Sophia Loren in lacy underwear; the second is Anita Ekberg as the giant temptress who steps off of a billboard in Fellini's *The Temptation of Dr. Antonio.* The doctor is a blue-nosed prude; she's his sweetest nightmare come to monstrous life. The sight of this huge buxom goddess striding through miniature sets like a blonde Godzilla is indescribable and altogether wonderful.

1962 145m/C *IT* Anita Ekberg, Romy Schneider, Tomas Milian, Sophia Loren, Peppino de Filippo; ***D:*** Vittorio De Sica, Luchino Visconti, Federico Fellini, Mario Monicelli; ***W:*** Federico Fellini, Mario Monicelli; ***M:*** Nino Rota. **VHS** *NO*

Body Bags

Producer/director John Carpenter, as a cadaverous coroner, introduces these made-for-cable short stories. His version of *Tales of the Crypt* shares the same graveyard humor and bloody gore. In the first, a young woman (Alex Datcher) working the night shift at a gas station is menaced by a serial killer. In "Hair," the best of the bunch, balding Richard (Stacy Keach) will do anything to get "the stallion look." In "Eye," a baseball player (Mark Hamill) gets an eyeball transplant donated by a murderer. As a group, these are O.K. but

John Gray (Boris Karloff) in *The Body Snatcher*.

nothing more. Fans will catch several genre directors in cameos. ***AKA:*** John Carpenter Presents Body Bags. 🦴🦴🦴

1993 (R) 95m/C Alex Datcher, Robert Carradine, Stacy Keach, David Warner, Mark Hamill, Twiggy, John Agar, Deborah Harry, Sheena Easton, David Naughton, John Carpenter; ***Cameos:*** Wes Craven, Sam Raimi, Roger Corman, Tobe Hooper; ***D:*** Tobe Hooper, John Carpenter; ***W:*** Billy Brown, Dan Angel; ***M:*** John Carpenter, Jim Lang. **VHS, LV, Closed Caption** *REP*

The Body Snatcher

Classy horror begins on an incongruously bright note with the sunny streets of Edinburgh, 1831, and Gray (Boris Karloff) the friendly cabman. But the story moves slowly into darker, more complex moral ground. Gray is a grave robber; his client, Dr. MacFarlane (Henry Daniell), is having an affair. The script, reportedly rewritten by producer Val Lewton under the name Carlos Keith from Philip MacDonald's original, is about degrees of responsibility and evil acts committed for the greater good. Director Robert Wise handles it masterfully, using sound to suggest violence and shadows to hide it. Karloff's sparkling performance is one of his most engaging, and it's a solid counterpoint to Daniell's long slow boil. In Karloff's career, all roles pale in comparison to Frankenstein's Monster, but the wily Gray is a strong second. The film's style may have fallen out of fashion, but it's still a masterpiece. 🦴🦴🦴🦴

1945 77m/B Edith Atwater, Russell Wade, Rita (Paula) Corday, Boris Karloff, Bela Lugosi, Henry Daniell, Sharyn Moffett, Donna Lee; ***D:*** Robert Wise; ***W:*** Philip MacDonald, Val Lewton, Carlos Keith; ***C:*** Robert De Grasse. **VHS, LV** *TTC*

Body Snatchers

For sheer paranoia, Abel Ferrara's take may not be as suspenseful as Don Siegel's original, but it's better than Philip Kaufman's 1978 remake. The inventive special effects are about as skin-crawly as any you'll see. They involve soft, gently probing little tendrils that do absolutely revolting things. Sullen teenaged Marti Malone (Gabrielle Anwar) hates everything about the new military base where her family has moved. She doesn't much care for her dad (Terry Kinney), stepmom (Meg Tilly), or little brother (Reilly Murphy) either. The only thing she likes is a handsome chopper pilot (Billy Wirth). Of course, they're all potential pod fodder. Initially, Ferrara uses a funereal pace to turn the ordinary into the ominous, effectively building tension until the icky effects kick in. On the minus side, he overuses the shortcut of panning his camera through walls between rooms. It's a technique that rudely reminds viewers they're watching a movie when they should be suspending their disbelief. Judged against the rest of the film, it's a minor flaw. This one really works well. 🦴🦴🦴½

1993 (R) 87m/C Gabrielle Anwar, Meg Tilly, Terry Kinney, Forest Whitaker, Billy Wirth, R. Lee Ermey, Reilly Murphy; ***D:*** Abel Ferrara; ***W:*** Stuart Gordon, Dennis Paoli, Nicholas St. John; ***C:*** Bojan Bazelli; ***M:*** Joe Delia. **VHS, LV, Closed Caption** *WAR*

The Boogens

In the years between its short theatrical release and its belated appearance on home video, this wonderful little low-budget horror developed a cult reputation. It's really nothing more than a torpidly slow variation on the dead-teenager formula, but it's still fun for fans of alternative cinema. Why? Because the title creatures are so silly. When they finally show up, having boogenized most of the cast, they look like large, toothy, tentacled frogs that have been squashed. Maybe that's why they live in abandoned Colorado mine shafts, but nothing about them is explained. Why bother? 🦴🦴½

1981 m/C John Crawford, Fred McCarren, Rebecca Balding, Anne-Marie Martin, Med Flory, Jeff Harlan; ***D:*** James L. Conway; ***W:*** David O'Malley, Bob Hunt; ***C:*** Jon Lormer, Paul Hipp. **VHS** *REP*

The Boogeyman

See *Stephen King's Nightshift Collection*.

Boxing Helena

David Lynch's daughter Jennifer makes a credible debut with a grim little black comedy about sex, dismemberment, and power. For assorted Oedipal reasons, Dr. Cavanaugh (Julian Sands) is obsessed by the mercurial Helena (Sherilyn Fenn). When fate, or something, brings her to his isolated mansion, he makes the best of it, even if he has to resort to drastic measures to make her stay. Ms. Lynch contends that her plot is a metaphor for love and that has some validity. She does sustain a surreal, dreamlike mood with an ending that's as loopy as the rest. The unrated laserdisc edition differs only slightly from the theatrical release. 🦴🦴½

1993 (R) 107m/C Julian Sands, Sherilyn Fenn, Bill Paxton, Kurtwood Smith, Betsy Clark, Nicolette Scorsese, Art Garfunkel; ***D:*** Jennifer Lynch; ***W:*** Jennifer Lynch; ***M:*** Graeme Revell. Golden Raspberry Awards '93: Worst Director (Lynch). **VHS, LV, Closed Caption** *ORI*

Brain Damage

Frank Henenlotter's second low-budget feature about a boy and his pet monster is a visceral anti-drug horror-comedy that's almost as good as *Basket Case*. The critter is a grotesque, intelligent parasite that feeds on brains (human or animal) and is capable of injecting its host with a highly addictive hallucinogen. This thing is called Aylmer, or Elmer, and in one of the film's strangest moments, it launches into an a cappella version of that old Glenn Miller favorite, "Elmer's Tune." Aylmer comes into the possession of young Brian (Rick Herbst), and, as it begins to gain control of him, Aylmer argues that it's all right to kill people, as long as Brian isn't directly involved. Or, as he puts it, "Part of my talent, Brian, is to spare you any unpleasantness." There's plenty of unpleasantness to be spared. The violence is graphic, outlandish, and comic. A strong sexual element, again reminiscent of *Basket Case,* is played mostly for laughs. Beyond the Grand Guignol horror, *Brain Damage* has some serious things to say about addiction, about how it changes a person, and about how it can kill or hurt others. For Henenlotter's fans, it's a must-see. 🦴🦴🦴

1988 (R) 89m/C Rick Herbst, Gordon MacDonald, Jennifer Lowry, Theo Barnes, Lucille Saint Peter; ***Cameos:*** Kevin Van Hentenryck, Beverly Bonner; ***D:*** Frank Henenlotter; ***W:*** Frank Henenlotter; ***C:*** Bruce Torbet; ***V:*** John Zacherle. **VHS, Closed Caption** *PAR*

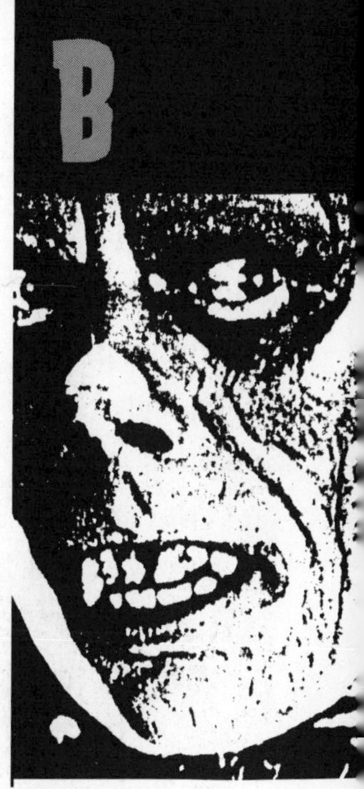

"Do not put your faith in such trinkets of deceit. We are in Transylvania, and Transylvania is not England. Our ways are not your ways, and you shall see many strange things."

—Dracula (Gary Oldman) comments on Harker's (Keanu Reeves) crucifix in *Bram Stoker's Dracula.*

Brain Dead

Dr. Martin (Bill Pullman) is engaged in theoretical brain research until his unctuous, avaricious pal Reston (Bill Paxton) persuades him to do a little primary work on Halsey (Bud Cort), a madman who knows some things that the Eunice corporation needs. A "kinder, gentler lobotomy" may be in order. As Dr. Martin becomes more deeply involved, he shares Halsey's paranoid schizophrenia. Veteran writer Charles Beaumont's script is a sharp, intelligent, hallucinatory comedy. Combine it with two terrific performances from the Bills right before they became stars, and savvy direction by Adam Simon, making the most of a modest budget. Beaumont, responsible for many of the best *Twilight Zone* episodes, brings the same fascinating unpredictability. Before it's over, the film becomes a multilayered examination of madness.

1989 (R) 85m/C Bill Pullman, Bill Paxton, Bud Cort, Patricia Charbonneau, Nicholas Pryor, George Kennedy; ***D:*** Adam Simon; ***W:*** Charles Beaumont. **VHS** *MGM*

The Brain That Wouldn't Die

This obscure little '50s' schlocker deserves a place in the Alternative Hall of Fame (or Shame). Though writer/director Joseph Green never reaches the heights that Ed Wood, Jr., achieved, it's not for lack of trying. After a painfully slow, uneventful introduction and an off-camera car crash, a mad scientist (Herb Evers) keeps his decapitated fiancee Janey's (Virginia Leith) head alive on a tray in his lab. He tenderly advises the noggin, "Sleep, my darling, rest and grow stronger," and then sets out to strip clubs and modeling agencies to find a suitable body for reattachment. Yes, this mad scientist is also a lounge lizard! Janey, meanwhile, has gone a little nutso—and who could blame her?—psychically contacting the creature who lives in the lab closet. But the film really belongs to Leslie Daniel as the henchman Kurt. He and Janey engage in such long philosophical conversations, you'd think they're Vladimir and Estragon waiting for Godot, not the closet creature. None of that—bizarre as it is—can prepare the viewer for Kurt's death. It is a full 2 minutes and 45 seconds of rabid, unfettered scenery chewing which must be seen to be appreciated. ***AKA:*** The Head that Wouldn't Die.

1963 92m/B Herb Evers, Virginia Leith, Adele Lamont, Leslie Daniel; ***D:*** Joseph Green; ***W:*** Joseph Green. **VHS** *RHI, FCT*

Brainscan

Michael (Edward Furlong), a teen with a troubled past, spends most of his time in his room playing with an elaborate computer-video-communications set-up. He also loves (and videotapes) Kimberly (Amy Hargreaves), the girl next door. When his best friend Kyle (Jamie Marsh) tells him that "Brainscan," a new interactive video game, is guaranteed to "satisfy your sickest fantasies," Michael orders a copy right away. Initially, the "virtual reality" game appears to involve the player in the commission of an incredibly realistic murder. Michael thinks it's about the neatest thing he's ever done until he turns on the news later and learns that.... You know where it's all leading. The other key characters are police detective Hayden (Frank Langella) and Trickster (T. Ryder Smith), a Freddy Kruegeresque demon who has truly disgusting eating habits. Can you believe it—mustard on bananas!

1994 (R) 96m/C Edward Furlong, Frank Langella, T. Ryder Smith, David Hemblen, Amy Hargreaves, Jamie Marsh, Victor Ertmanis; ***D:*** John Flynn; ***W:*** Andrew Kevin Walker; ***M:*** George S. Clinton. **VHS, LV, Closed Caption** *COL*

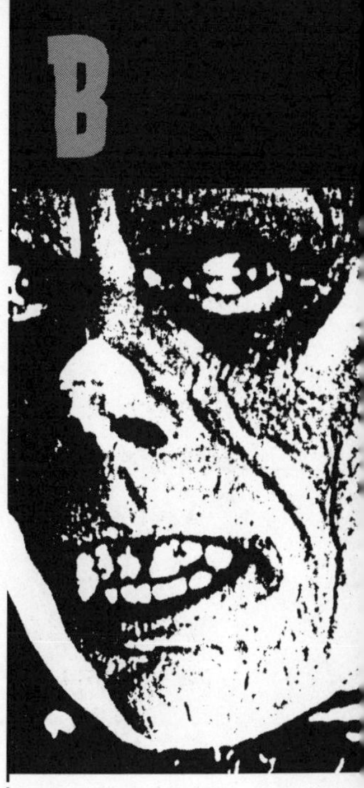

Bram Stoker's Dracula

With the exception of one backlot shot, director Francis Coppola and photographer Michael Ballhaus made their film on elaborate sets where they had full control of the frame. In almost every shot, something's going on beyond the simple narrative flow. On Coppola's densely layered, crowded screen, the background may contain an unusual twist to the action, or an odd arrangement of shapes. The simple act of stepping over a threshold may seem strange and hesitant because the action has been filmed backward, then run forward through the projector. The familiar plot is presented as a romantic love story taken to an operatic extreme. Gary Oldman is perhaps the most Byronic Dracula ever brought to the screen. Despite all the changes in makeup—many of them hideous and grotesque—he's handsome, exotic, dark, larger than life. Anthony Hopkins' Van Helsing is a masterful combination of eccentricity, authority, and almost Pythonesque humor. On a separate soundtrack on the laserdisc, Coppola, his son Roman (who worked as special effects supervisor and second-unit director), and makeup supervisor Greg Cannon talk about their work and their intentions. They reveal how many of the special effects were accomplished. (Some of them are so simple, you'll be surprised at how easily you were tricked.) Coppola also explains why he gave the film such baroque depth. He's able to analyze his own creative processes as well as any director since Hitchcock. ***AKA:*** Dracula.

1992 (R) 128m/C Gary Oldman, Winona Ryder, Anthony Hopkins, Keanu Reeves, Richard E. Grant, Cary Elwes, Bill Campbell, Sadie Frost, Tom Waits; ***D:*** Francis Ford Coppola; ***W:*** Jim V. Hart; ***C:*** Michael Ballhaus. Academy Awards '92: Best Costume Design, Best Makeup, Best Sound Effects Editing; Nominations: Academy Awards '92: Best Art Direction/Set Decoration. **VHS, LV, Letterboxed, Closed Caption, DVD** *COL*

The Bride

One dark and stormy night, Dr. Frankenstein (Sting) is fooling around up in the tower. His creation (Clancy Brown) appears to be honked off about the situation in general. And well he should be. The doc has promised him a sweetie, but when she turns out to be cute-as-a-button Jennifer Beals, he decides to keep her for himself. The story then splits, half following the Monster and his picaresque *Of Mice and Men* adventures with a dwarf (David Rappaport, who easily steals the film), and half following the humorless Sting who actually looks prettier than his newest creation. Despite the title, the focus is really on the first plot line. The Rube-Goldberg-inspired lab scenes are bright and lively but the whole thing is unfocused and far too long.

1985 (PG-13) 118m/C Sting, Jennifer Beals, Anthony Higgins, David Rappaport, Geraldine Page, Clancy Brown, Phil Daniels, Veruschka; ***D:*** Franc Roddam; ***W:*** Lloyd Fonvielle; ***C:*** Stephen Burum; ***M:*** Maurice Jarre. **VHS, LV, Closed Caption** *COL*

The Bride of Frankenstein

Though James Whale's sequel is considered superior to his original by many critics, it is at best an uneven film filled with dated humor. (The introduction remains a particular embarrassment.) Yes, it's much more polished and Whale's direction is more confident. Yes, Karloff's interpretation of the Monster is more complex and nuanced. Yes, the Bride (Elsa Lanchester) is created in the Mother of All Lab Scenes. But the famous sequence at the Hermit's cabin is so brilliantly spoofed by Mel Brooks, Peter Boyle, and Gene Hackman in *Young Frankenstein* that it's almost impossible to watch it now without unintentional laughter. Flaws notwithstanding, this is one of horror's finer, but not finest moments.

"To a new world of gods and monsters!"

—Dr. Pretorius (Ernest Thesiger) to Dr. Frankenstein (Colin Clive) in *The Bride of Frankenstein.*

Elsa Lanchester and Boris Karloff in *The Bride of Frankenstein.*

1935 75m/B Boris Karloff, Elsa Lanchester, Ernest Thesiger, Colin Clive, Una O'Connor, Valerie Hobson, Dwight Frye, John Carradine, E.E. Clive, O.P. Heggie, Gavin Gordon, Douglas Walton; ***D:*** James Whale; ***W:*** John L. Balderston, William Hurlbut; ***C:*** John Mescall. Nominations: Academy Awards '35: Best Sound. **VHS, LV** *USH, MLB*

Bride of Re-Animator

What a disappointment. Sequel to the cult masterpiece goes too far in all the wrong directions. Of course, the prosthetic special effects are graphic, but severed body parts have been so overused that they don't even have the power to shock anymore. The strong, flippant humor of the first film has become studied, though star Jeffrey Combs gives it his best. Worst of all, the filmmakers don't even pay attention to plot details from the original. Characters who were clearly dead and/or squashed are brought back without explanation. No, logic is not a prime consideration in cheap horror movies, but that kind of unimaginative sloppiness is an insult to fans. ***AKA:*** Re-Animator 2. **Woof!**

1989 99m/C Bruce Abbott, Claude Earl Jones, Fabiana Udenio, Jeffrey Combs, Kathleen Kinmont, David Gale, Mel Stewart; ***D:*** Brian Yuzna; ***W:*** Rick Fry, Woody Keith; ***C:*** Rick Fichter; ***M:*** Richard Band. **VHS, LV, Closed Caption** *AHV*

Bride of the Monster

Though *Plan 9 from Outer Space* is Ed Wood, Jr.'s, alternative masterpiece, this one is arguably more inept. Made famous in Tim Burton's *Ed Wood,* it's a silly exercise notable for Lugosi's final starring appearance—he died during the filming of *Plan 9*—and the ridiculous immobile octopus monster with which several "victims" pretend to struggle. Even Wood's fans—and I am one—must admit that he could be boring with long pointless scenes that are neither funny, suspenseful, nor goofy. They're just slow and lifeless, and *Bride* has far too many of them. ***AKA:*** Bride of the Atom.

1956 70m/B Bela Lugosi, Tor Johnson, Loretta King, Tony McCoy, Harvey B. Dunn, George Becwar, Paul Marco, Billy Benedict, Dolores Fuller; ***D:*** Edward D. Wood Jr.; ***W:*** Edward D. Wood Jr., Alex Gordon; ***C:*** William C. Thompson. **VHS** *SNC, VYY, HHT*

The Bride with White Hair

Supernatural epic is one of the most lavish and ambitious Hong Kong imports. It's a magical tale of warring clans, one led by Ye Hong (Leslie Cheung, who looks a lot like Johnny Depp), the young warrior prince who falls in love with his enemy, Wolf Girl (Bridgette Lin Ching Hsia). Their story mixes operatic overstatement with soaring Shakespearian plot turns and real emotional depth. Director Ronny Yu works with a large cast on unbelievably evocative sets. The action scenes employ flying effects and highly stylized fights and swordplay. The stuntwork owes more to dance than to conventional martial arts films. Followed by a sequel.

1993 92m/C *HK* Leslie Cheung, Brigitte Lin Ching Hsia; ***D:*** Ronny Yu. **VHS, Letterboxed** *TAI*

The Bride with White Hair 2

Absolutely wonderful sequel is simpler than the original, as the white-haired witch continues her revenge against the eight clans. A straightforward rescue-of-the-kidnapped-bride plot provides the basis for a no-holds-barred battle of the sexes fought on a cosmic scale—men against women, youth against elders, love against anger. Blood flies; passions soar; the Bride's white hair can now behead her enemies. (Have the people at Clairol been told of this?) The story works with the stuff of myth and fairy tales which is also the stuff of horror with the thematic compass needle closer to true north. Even viewers who are not familiar with the conventions of Chinese film will appreciate the power of these images and the epic scope of the story. Brigitte Lin Ching Hsia and Leslie Cheung repeat their roles, but most of the action is handled by young cast members. As the fearless Moon, Christy Chung easily steals the film.

1993 80m/C *HK* Brigitte Lin Ching Hsia, Leslie Cheung, Christy Chung; ***D:*** David Wu. **VHS, LV, Letterboxed** *TAI*

The Brides of Dracula

"Transylvania—land of dark forests, dread mountains, and unfathomed lakes! Still the home of magic and devilry as the 19th century draws to a close...." That quote sets the tone for one of Hammer's best efforts. Despite the absence of Christopher Lee—there is no character named Dracula in the film and no one gets married either—the whole production has the studio's famous high gloss and the story is carefully written. Key elements of the script would be recycled many times in other films. This may be Peter Cushing's finest portrayal of Van Helsing. Here he's an active, energetic protagonist. As the lovely young teacher Marianne and the evil Baron, Yvonne Monlaur and David Peel bear a disquieting resemblance to Barbie and Ken. The other characters are clever variations on familiar stereotypes with a proper amount of humor. The conclusion is especially suspenseful.

1960 86m/C *GB* Peter Cushing, Martita Hunt, Yvonne Monlaur, Freda Jackson, David Peel, Mona Washbourne, Miles Malleson, Henry Oscar, Michael Ripper, Andree Melly; ***D:*** Terence Fisher; ***W:*** Peter Bryan, Edward Percy, Jimmy Sangster; ***C:*** Jack Asher. **VHS, LV** *USH, FCT*

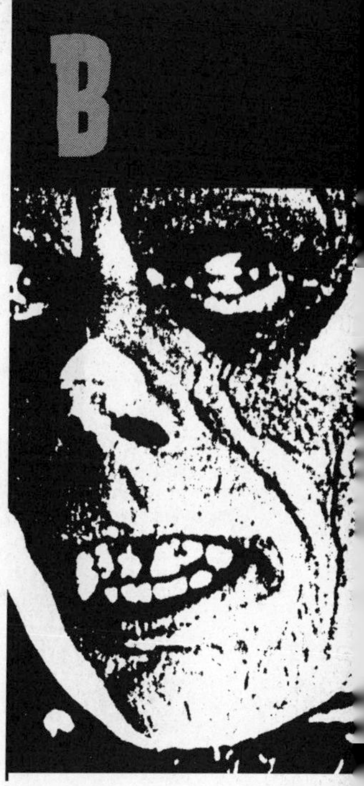

THE HOUND SALUTES

DAVID CRONENBERG

David Cronenberg is the most consistently interesting, intelligent, and challenging director making horror films today.

Even his explorations outside the genre, particularly *M. Butterfly,* contain strong elements of horror, and a distinct sensibility, expressed both visually and thematically, informs all of his work. From the cheap thrills of *Rabid* and *Shivers* to the more carefully crafted *Dead Ringers* and *Crash,* Cronenberg's concerns are obvious. He's a director who uses horror to explore serious ideas, not merely to titillate or frighten.

He's a Canadian—born in Toronto in 1943, also educated there—and many of his films have a Canadian setting. It's more useful, though, to think of him as a North American filmmaker. He has worked in Hollywood and there are no regional limitations on his work.

In his earliest films, *Shivers* and *Rabid,* horror is associated directly with sex. The parasitic creatures in *Shivers* create uncontrollable erotic rage; the star of *Rabid* is ex-porn queen Marilyn Chambers, who's inadvertently turned into a vampiric monster through surgery. The tiny monsters in *The Brood,* his fourth film, are literal "children of rage" who come from an insane mother (Samantha Eggar). In *Videodrome,* violent pornography broadcast from a satellite transforms viewers, creating "the new flesh."

In *Scanners,* the intersection of flesh and machinery begun in *Videodrome* becomes even more complex, and the theme continues into *The Fly.* Perhaps it ends in Cronenberg's most recent work, *Crash,* or perhaps it

The Brood

For straightforward horror, this may be Cronenberg's best. It's controlled, carefully focused, imaginative, and frightening. Cronenberg works with possibly repressed memories of childhood abuse as the basis for his horror, more than a decade before the subjects would become part of popular culture. Flamboyantly mad Nola (Samantha Eggar) is under the care of Dr. Raglan (Oliver Reed), possibly a charlatan, at his "Institute of Psychoplasmics." Her ex-husband Frank (Art Hindle) fears that she's abusing their little girl during their visits. The first big scene is a remarkable set piece in a kitchen where an unseen something goes to work. The scares are so unusual that any synopsis would spoil them. The only flaws are a visually weak scene explaining the physical nature of the evil involved, and a score that borrows too heavily from *Psycho.* Like many of Cronenberg's other films, it's about insanity taking on a physical manifestation. 🦴🦴🦴½

1979 (R) 92m/C *CA* Samantha Eggar, Oliver Reed, Art Hindle, Susan Hogan, Nuala Fitzgerald, Cindy Hinds, Robert A. Silverman; ***D:*** David Cronenberg; ***W:*** David Cronenberg; ***C:*** Mark Irwin; ***M:*** Howard Shore. **VHS, LV**

The Brotherhood of Satan

Actors L.Q. Jones and Alvy Moore produced this laborious low-budget town-with-a-secret tale. Ben (Charles Bateman), Nicky (Ahna Capri), and Ben's young daughter are trapped by mysterious and largely

merely reaches another level of refinement.

The one element of Cronenberg's work that's most often overlooked—even by his fans—is humor. It lurks just beneath the surface, but it can burst through, as it does so gleefully in his adaptation of William Burrough's "unfilmable" novel, *Naked Lunch*.

Throughout his career, Cronenberg has found memorable performances from actors known for their intensity: Michael Ironside in *Scanners*, Christopher Walken in *The Dead Zone*, James Woods in *Scanners*, Oliver Reed in *The Brood*, Jeff Goldblum in *The Fly*, Peter Weller in *Naked Lunch*, both James Spader and Elias Koteas in *Crash*. His best collaborative work, though, has been with Jeremy Irons, first in the dual role of mad gynecologists in *Dead Ringers*, and then as the duped French diplomat in *M. Butterfly*.

In all of those films, Cronenberg creates a dark, frightening world whose terrors come from within. As David Thomson writes in *The Biographical Dictionary of Film*:

"Horror for Cronenberg is not a game or a meal ticket; it is, rather, the natural expression for one of the best directors working today. For Cronenberg's subject is the intensity of human frailty and decay: in short, the body and its many accelerated mutations, whether out of disease, anger, dread, or hope. These are not easy films to take. But how can horror be easy? Anyone born and reckoning on dying needs to confront Cronenberg."

SIGNIFICANT CONTRIBUTIONS TO HORROR

Shivers **(1975)**
(AKA *They Came from Within, The Parasite Murders*)

Rabid **(1977)**

The Brood **(1979)**

Scanners **(1981)**

The Dead Zone **(1983)**

Videodrome **(1983)**

The Fly **(1986)**

Dead Ringers **(1988)**

Naked Lunch **(1991)**

Crash **(1995)**

unexplained forces in a remote hamlet where adults are being killed and the survivors are insane. The whole thing has an Ed Woodsian quality of enthusiastic incoherence that's irritating and endearing in about equal measures. Veteran character actor Strother Martin (who'd worked with Jones in *The Wild Bunch*) attacks the material with gusto.

1971 (PG) 92m/C Strother Martin, L.Q. Jones, Charles Bateman, Ahna Capri, Charles Robinson, Alvy Moore, Geri Reischl; ***D:*** Bernard McEveety; ***W:*** William Welch; ***C:*** John Morrill. **VHS, LV** *GKK, IME*

A Bucket of Blood

Roger Corman says that he was trying to make "a horror-type film with a hip cutting edge" and he got it. This low-budget marvel, actually a companion piece to the original *Little Shop of Horrors*, was filmed in five days. Walter Paisley (Dick Miller) is the coffee-shop busboy who becomes an overnight sensation with the realistic statues he makes of his inadvertent murder victims. The high points are Julian Burton's Allen Ginsburgian poem-performance art, and Miller's transformation into a card-carrying boho beatnik. Remade as the altogether inferior *Death Artist*.

1959 66m/B Dick Miller, Barboura Morris, Antony Carbone, Julian Burton, Ed Nelson, Bert Convy, Judy Bamber, John Brinkley; ***D:*** Roger Corman; ***W:*** Charles B. Griffith; ***C:*** Jack Marquette. **VHS** *RHI, SNC*

Joanna Miles and a few *Bugs.*

Buffy the Vampire Slayer

"Don't you get it? I don't want to be the Chosen One! I don't want to spend the rest of my life chasing after vampires. All I want to do is graduate from high school, go to Europe, marry Christian Slater, and die!" That's how Buffy (Kristy Swanson) explains things when Donald Sutherland tries to persuade her that she's the only person who can save Southern California from an infestation of the undead. The *Clueless* humor is dated and overly broad, and the situation has been used far too often in recent years. Even so, this one works because Kristy Swanson turns in such a bright sexy performance. The fact that in her prom dress, she looks like a young Grace Kelly doesn't hurt, either, and she gets considerable help from five athletic stunt doubles. For comparative purposes, this one's somewhat better than *The Lost Boys,* not as good as *Fright Night.* It's also the basis for a popular TV series. 🦴🦴🦴

1992 (PG-13) 98m/C Kristy Swanson, Donald Sutherland, Luke Perry, Paul (Pee Wee Herman) Reubens, Rutger Hauer, Michele Abrams, Randall Batinkoff, Hilary Swank, Paris Vaughan, David Arquette, Candy Clark, Natasha Gregson Wagner; ***D:*** Fran Rubel Kazui; ***W:*** Joss Whedon; ***C:*** James Hayman; ***M:*** Carter Burwell. **VHS, LV** *FXV, PMS*

Bug

An earthquake brings huge electrically charged cockroaches from the center of the earth to the surface. These bugs eat carbon, create sparks by rubbing their legs together, and ignite their own gas. (Insert the joke of your choice here.) The VideoHound thinks *Firefarter* might be a more appropriate title, and this too-serious, too-slow production from the usually reliable producer William Castle needs all the help it can get. The uninvolving plot doesn't measure up to the insect effects or to Bradford Dillman's extremely mad scientist. The gonzo second half is better than the first. ***AKA:*** The Bug.

1975 (PG) 100m/C Bradford Dillman, Joanna Miles, Richard Gilliland, Jamie Smith-Jackson, Alan Fudge, Jesse Vint, William Castle, Patty McCormack, Jesse Vint; ***D:*** Jeannot Szwarc; ***W:*** William Castle; ***C:*** Michael Hugo; ***M:*** Charles Fox. **VHS** *PAR*

Bugged!

Low-budget black-oriented horror-comedy tries to make virtues of its flaws and almost succeeds. Following a lengthy introduction, the guys at Dead & Buried Pest Removal mistakenly load their insecticide tanks with genetic juice that causes their prey to mutate into supersmart, oversized insects. When they try to debug Divine Hill's (Priscilla Basque) house, they really mess things up. Writer/director/producer/star Ronald K. Armstrong makes things much funnier in the second half, though even at its best, this is hardly sophisticated humor. It's rough and grainy, and Armstrong bucks the current trend by keeping the levels of violence and language well within the limits of his PG-13 rating.

1996 (PG-13) 90m/C Ronald K. Armstrong, Priscilla Basque, Jeff Lee, Derek C. Johnson, Billy Graham; ***D:*** Ronald K. Armstrong; ***W:*** Ronald K. Armstrong; ***C:*** S. Torriano Berry; ***M:*** Boris Elkis. **VHS** *TTV*

Burial of the Rats

Ruthless swordfighting lesbian feminist rat-worshippers in black leather thong bikinis kidnap aspiring young author Bram Stoker (Kevin Alber) and this wacky horror spoof is off and running. Madeleine (Maria Ford) and her pals serve the Queen of Vermin (Adrienne Barbeau), whose aim is to unseat the male power structure of the village of St. Cecile. Just as soon as her minions finish their topless modern dance routine. The Russian-American made-for-cable production is a throwback to Britain's Hammer Films with the same look and a cheekier attitude toward its "classic" horror source. ***AKA:*** Roger Corman Presents Burial of the Rats; Bram Stoker's Burial of the Rats.

1995 (R) 85m/C Adrienne Barbeau, Maria Ford, Kevin Alber; ***D:*** Dan Golden. **VHS** *NHO*

Burn Witch, Burn!

Two of horror's best screenwriters, Richard Matheson and Charles Beaumont, adapt one of the field's best novelists' best works—Fritz Leiber's *Conjure Wife*—with satisfying results. Despite the stupefying title, this is a keenly observed exploration of contemporary witchcraft. It's set on a college campus where the faculty wives know a lot more about the petty academic turf wars than their allegedly smarter husbands. Professor Norman Taylor (Peter Wyngarde) is in line for a big promotion. His wife Tanzie (Janet Blair) is sure that her spells and charms are responsible. The costumes, acting style, and attitudes are a cinematic primer on late '50s sexual conflicts and identities. Stereotypes of male rationality and feminine intuition are sharpened to wicked points. (In manner, dress, look, and bearing, Wyngarde is presented as an unmistakably phallic character.) Though the conflicts are a little slow to develop, the story becomes really involving about half way through and maintains that suspense until a terrific ending. ***AKA:*** Night of the Eagle.

1962 87m/B *GB* Peter Wyngarde, Janet Blair, Margaret Johnston, Anthony Nicholls, Colin Gordon, Kathleen Byron, Reginald Beckwith, Jessica Dunning, Norman Bird, Judith Scott; ***D:*** Sidney Hayers; ***W:*** Richard Matheson, Charles Beaumont, George L. Baxt; ***C:*** Reg Wyer. **VHS** *VTR*

The Burning

Summer campers play a mean prank on caretaker Cropsy (Lou David). Five years later...oh, come on, you don't need to be

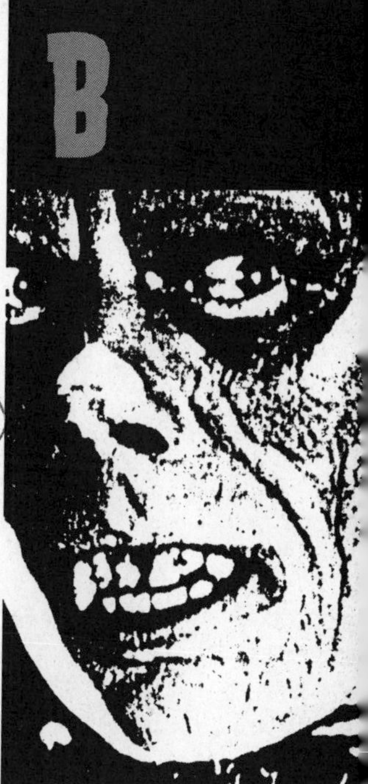

Caligari (Werner Krauss) and Cesare (Conrad Veidt) in *The Cabinet of Dr. Caligari.*

told anything about the plot. A little "T," a little "A," a lot of Tom Savini's bloody effects. The kids look and act more like real adolescents than they usually do in stalker-slasher flicks. That's an incredibly young Jason Alexander under a full head of hair, and, in a much smaller role, Holly Hunter. More importantly, the film is the debut for Miramax founders Bob and Harvey Weinstein, who share various production and writing credits.

1982 (R) 90m/C Brian Matthews, Leah Ayres, Brian Backer, Larry Joshua, Jason Alexander, Ned Eisenberg, Garrick Glenn, Carolyn Houlihan, Fisher Stevens, Lou David, Holly Hunter; ***D:*** Tony Maylam; ***W:*** Bob Weinstein, Peter Lawrence; ***C:*** Harvey Harrison; ***M:*** Rick Wakeman. **VHS** *NO*

The Cabinet of Dr. Caligari

Younger viewers will probably have trouble appreciating this early and extraordinarily influential film. With its painted-flat sets, exaggerated acting, and cartoonish costumes, it's as much a work of the 19th century as the 20th. And Cesare, the Somnambulist, can be dismissed as a guy with a funny walk and too much eye makeup. The slowly paced, grainy images are perhaps the first use of narrative film as waking dream. Along with the original *Nosferatu* and *Vampyre, Caligari* played a large part in the creation of the landscape of the horror film. ***AKA:*** Das Cabinet des Dr. Caligari.

1919 92m/B *GE* Conrad Veidt, Werner Krauss, Lil Dagover, Friedrich Feher, Hans von Twardowski, Rudolf Klein-Rogge, Rudolf Lettinger; ***D:*** Robert Wiene; ***W:*** Carl Mayer, Hans Janowitz; ***C:*** Willy Hameister. **VHS, LV** *KIV, REP, MRV*

Calling Dr. Death/ Strange Confession

The first half of this so-so Inner Sanctum double bill casts Chaney as a therapist accused of murdering his faithless wife (Ramsay Ames) during a weekend blackout. His nurse (Patricia Morison) swears he's innocent. A nosy cop (J. Carrol Naish) disagrees. Much of the story is more mystery than horror but Chaney's portrayal of a man haunted by inner demons and the hallucinatory finale lean toward the dark side. The main attraction is the sharp studio gloss that Universal gave to these modest productions. They look great with crisp black-and-white photography and sharp costumes. Morison and Ames are gorgeous. The second film begins beautifully with Chaney as a disturbed chemist arriving at a lawyer's swanky apartment with a strange story to tell and something horrible in his bag. His overwritten tale involves his beautiful wife (Brenda Joyce) and his lecherous boss (Naish), and contains dated humor and disjointed plotting. ***AKA:*** Strange Confession; The Inner Sanctum: Calling Dr. Death/Strange Confession. 🦴🦴½

1943 124m/B Lon Chaney Jr., J. Carrol Naish, Brenda Joyce, Patricia Morison, Ramsay Ames, David Bruce, Milburn Stone, Lloyd Bridges; ***D:*** Reginald LeBorg, John Hoffman; ***W:*** Edward Dein, M. Coates Webster. **VHS** *USH*

Candyman

On one level, this contradictory horror is a basic gore-fest. At the same time, it's visually sophisticated and well acted with a score by noted minimalist composer Philip Glass. More often than not, the two sides work well together. The title character (Tony Todd) is an urban legend who dwells in Cabrini Green, the notorious Chicago housing project. Graduate student Helen Lyle (Virginia Madsen) leaves the groves of academe to do some dangerous primary research into the myth. Writer/director Bernard Rose indulges his music-video taste for fast cutting in some key scenes. For the most part, though, he plays straight with the viewer and creates a palpable atmosphere of fear and dread. The conclusion is risky. 🦴🦴🦴

1992 (R) 98m/C Virginia Madsen, Tony Todd, Xander Berkeley, Kasi Lemmons, Vanessa Williams, DeJuan Guy, Michael Culkin, Gilbert Lewis, Stanley DeSantis; ***D:*** Bernard Rose; ***W:*** Bernard Rose; ***C:*** Anthony B. Richmond; ***M:*** Philip Glass. **VHS, LV, 8mm, Letterboxed, Closed Caption** *COL*

Candyman 2: Farewell to the Flesh

Totally unnecessary sequel repeats the original plot in New Orleans with the same gimmick. If anyone looks into a mirror and says the name "Candyman" five times, a towering hook-handed black man (Tony Todd) will appear and eviscerate the speaker. Guess what happens about every fifteen minutes. Two large flaws sink the film before it has a chance. First, Clive Barker's story demands that in any potentially dangerous situation, the characters involved must do the most stupid thing possible. Second, director Bill Condon lets the action ooze along at a tedious pace. Almost all of the scares come from the hook-through-the-guts routine (which isn't even very disgusting after the third or fourth time) or generic spooky stuff—one character creeping up on another, a flapping crow, swarming bees, etc. 🦴½

1994 (R) 99m/C Tony Todd, Kelly Rowan, Veronica Cartwright, Timothy Carhart, William O'Leary, Bill Nunn, Fay Hauser; ***D:*** Bill Condon; ***W:*** Rand Ravich, Mark Kruger; ***C:*** Tobias Schliessler; ***M:*** Philip Glass. **VHS** *PGV*

Cannibal! The Musical

Offbeat Troma release (offbeat even for Troma!) is adapted from a University of Colorado stage production. The subject is Alferd Packer (Juan Schwartz), who was convicted of cannibalism in 19th century Colorado. (Didn't the students at UC once vote to name the new dining hall after him?) Though this is 100 percent pure Troma with unapologetically cheesy ambiance and effects, the film is also true to its undergraduate roots with smart, irreverent,

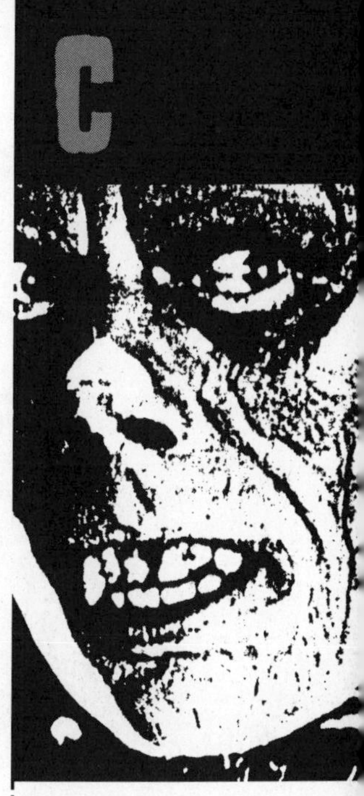

"You fools, this man is plotting our doom! We die at dawn! He is Caligari!"

—Francis (Freidrich Feher) warns his fellow asylum inmates in *The Cabinet of Dr. Caligari.*

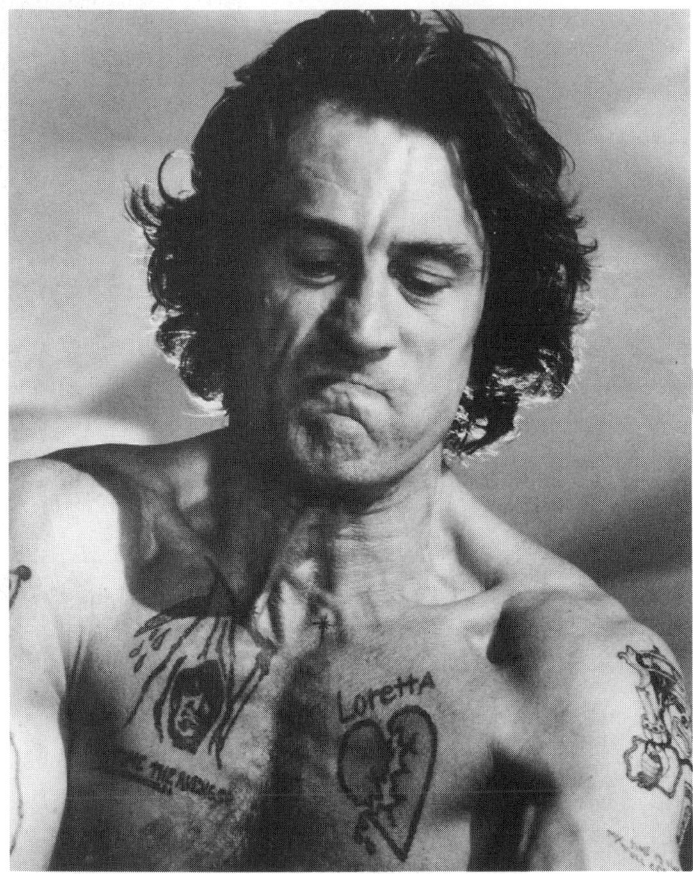

Max Cady (Robert De Niro) in Martin Scorsese's *Cape Fear* (1991).

cheerfully tasteless humor. Writer/director Trey Parker uses a cheeky attitude to compensate for an inexperienced cast and whatever-works locations and sets. More recently, Parker has created the blackly comic animated series *South Park.*

1996 (R) 105m/C Ian Hardin, Jason McHugh, Matt Stone, Trey Parker, Juan Schwartz; ***D:*** Trey Parker; ***W:*** Trey Parker. **VHS** *TTV*

Cape Fear

In *Taxi Driver,* Robert De Niro and Martin Scorsese make Travis Bickle a human monster who finds redemption. In Max Cady, they find a much more powerful monster who is angry evil incarnate. Judged by any standard, he's one of the most frightening creations of 1990s horror. From the ultraviolent "date" with Ileana Douglas to Juliette Lewis' infamous thumb-sucking scene (one of the screen's truly sick inventions) to the bloody kitchen, the horripilant moments just keep on coming. Admittedly, the filmmakers may be slumming, but they also give the manipulative story a strong moral dimension. In the end, they mean to scare you, and they certainly do. In spades. That's why this is a horror film while the 1961 Robert Mitchum-Gregory Peck version is suspense. Elmer Bernstein's score is based on Bernard Herrmann's work for the original. Director of photography Freddie Francis directed several British horror films.

1991 (R) 128m/C Robert De Niro, Nick Nolte, Jessica Lange, Juliette Lewis, Joe Don Baker, Illeana Douglas, Fred Dalton Thompson; ***Cameos:*** Robert Mitchum, Gregory Peck, Martin Balsam; ***D:*** Martin Scorsese; ***W:*** Wesley Strick; ***C:*** Freddie Francis; ***M:*** Bernard Herrmann, Elmer Bernstein. Nominations: Academy Awards '91: Best Actor (De Niro), Best Supporting Actress (Lewis). **VHS, LV, Closed Caption** *USH*

Captain Kronos: Vampire Hunter

Attempt to graft a swashbuckling hero onto a vampire tale falls victim to an unfocused script, general lack of atmosphere, weak action sequences, and—for a Hammer production—limp production values. The title character (Horst Janson) gallops about the English countryside dispatching the undead with the assistance of a hunchbacked sidekick, Prof. Grost (John Cater) and newly acquired girlfriend Carla (Caroline Munro). John Cater seems to be having a grand time, and Caroline Munro is, as always, devastating. But Horst Janson is an insubstantial dishwater blond hero. Director Brian Clemens got his start in television with *The Avengers,* and though he's looking for the same tongue-in-cheek quality, it's just not there. ***AKA:*** Kronos; Vampire Castle.

1974 (R) 91m/C *GB* Horst Janson, John Carson, Caroline Munro, Ian Hendry, Shane Briant, Wanda Ventham, John Cater, Lois Daine; ***D:*** Brian Clemens; ***W:*** Brian Clemens; ***C:*** Ian Wilson. **VHS** *NO*

Carnival of Blood

Ultra-low budget effort is a companion piece to *The Incredibly Strange Creatures Who Stopped Living...* with its sideshow setting and grainy look. But lacking the loopy musical numbers of *Incredibly,* it's left with lots of boring talk to separate the ridiculous horrors. A little bit of fake mondo stuff is no help; neither is the crackpot psychology. Burt Young is listed in the credits as John Harris. ***AKA:*** Death Rides a Carousel. **Woof!**

1971 (PG) 80m/C Earle Edgerton, Judith Resnick, Martin Barlosky, John Harris, Burt Young, Kaly Mills, Gloria Spivak; ***D:*** Leonard Kirtman; ***W:*** Leonard Kirtman. **VHS** *NO*

Carnival of Souls

A car runs off a bridge and into a deep river. One young woman (Candace Hilligoss) walks out of the water, apparently unharmed. She tries to resume her life as if nothing has happened, taking a job as a church organist in another town. At first, everything appears to be normal and dull, but then she begins to have visions of a pale figure with dark eyes. Over the course of the film, her sense of reality steadily erodes as a dreamlike atmosphere of eeriness grows stronger. Without resorting to any of the overt tricks that have become the common currency of horror films since, producer/director/actor Herk Harvey delivers the chills found in a really good episode of *The Twilight Zone.* It's easy to read deeper meanings into the plot—alienation, a descent into madness, the role of young women in a changing society—but that's not really Harvey's point. He wants to tell a good scary story that begins and ends as a mystery, without verbal explanations for the striking black-and-white images. He also presents a surprisingly realistic and detailed portrait of everyday life in this country in the early '60s. George Romero has said that he had it in mind when he made *Night of the Living Dead.*

1962 80m/B Candace Hilligoss, Sidney Berger, Frances Feist, Stan Levitt, Art Ellison, Harold (Herk) Harvey; ***D:*** Harold (Herk) Harvey; ***W:*** John Clifford; ***C:*** Maurice Prather. **VHS, LV** *EEL, MRV, SNC*

Carnosaur

The title sequence—disgusting stuff apparently filmed in a real poultry processing plant—sets the tone for your basic mad-scientist plot with several environmental twists. Out in the Nevada desert, Dr. Jane Tiptree (Diane Ladd) has created some nasty unseen critters who attack chickens, then make their way up the food chain. If the dinosaur effects created by John Buechler and Magical Media Industries aren't as realistic and convincing as Spielberg's Jurassic monsters, they're not bad at all. In fact, they're much more believable than you normally find in more expensive productions. Writer/director Adam Simon has a wicked sense of humor that gets consistently stronger and more crazed as the movie goes along. Toward the end, it becomes downright Strangelovian. Fans should seek out his other work, *Brain Dead* and *Body Chemistry 2.* Followed by two sequels to date.

1993 (R) 82m/C Diane Ladd, Raphael Sbarge, Jennifer Runyon, Harrison Page, Clint Howard, Ned Bellamy; ***D:*** Adam Simon; ***W:*** Adam Simon; ***M:*** Nigel Holton. **VHS** *NHO*

Carnosaur 2

The real inspiration for this sequel isn't *The Lost World* but James Cameron's *Aliens.* The mutant-chicken dinosaurs from the first film are back and looking for more human Happy Meals in a super-secret gov-

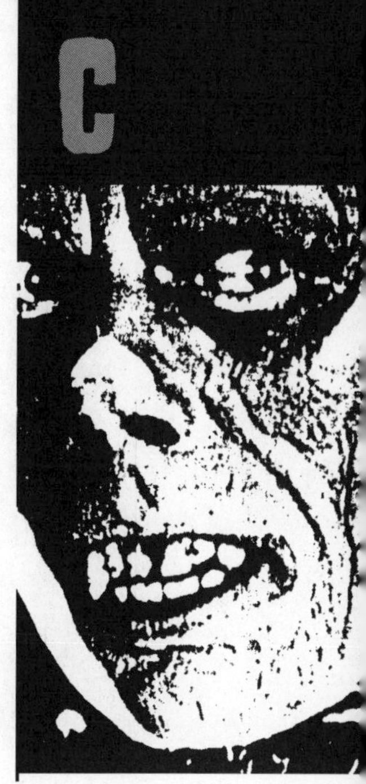

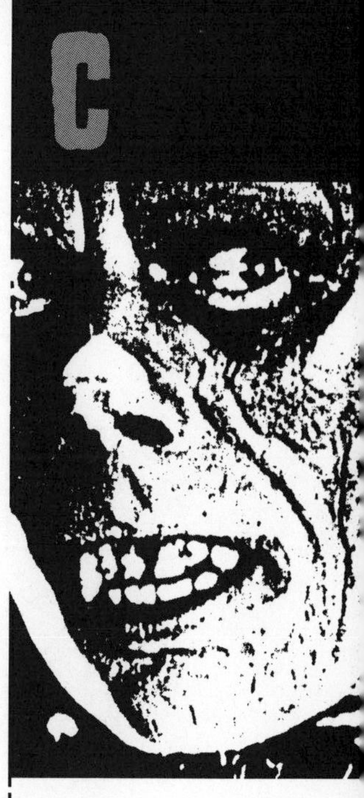

ernment installation that's about to blow up. Tick, tick, tick. Overall, the acting is better than average, and the dialogue has that gritty quality that makes Cameron's early work so much fun. Director Louis Morneau keeps things moving quickly enough that the plot lapses and less-than-stellar special effects aren't fatal.

1994 (R) 90m/C John Savage, Cliff DeYoung, Arabella Holzbog, Ryan Thomas Johnson; ***D:*** Louis Morneau. **VHS, LV** *NHO*

Carnosaur 3: Primal Species

The producers of this series have avoided the trap of repetition, coming up with fresh situations for their low-budget saurians. This time out, the government-created critters are hijacked by terrorists. Col. Higgins (Scott Valentine) leads the crack (but extremely small) military unit that's sent to get them back. Dr. Hodges (Janet Gunn) is the glamorous dinosaur expert. The basic military-academic conflict is lifted from Howard Hawks' *The Thing*. Even though the setting is your basic empty-warehouse industrial park, the whole film is arguably no sillier or more poorly plotted than *Jurassic Park: The Lost World,* but with much less impressive effects.

1996 82m/C Scott Valentine, Janet Gunn, Rick Dean, Rodger Halstead, Tony Peck; ***D:*** Jonathan Winfrey; ***M:*** Kevin Kiner. **VHS** *NHO*

The Carpenter

The scenes of gory horror are the weakest parts of this stylish Canadian production. Some of the humor is overstated, too. Otherwise, it's a sleeper of the Stephen King school with a tongue-in-cheek "all men are pigs" attitude. The film begins with a frighteningly realistic depiction of a mental breakdown. After it, Alice (Lynne Adams) and Martin (Pierce Lenoir) move to a big rural house as it's being renovated. The carpenter (Wings Hauser) is a mysterious figure who may be supernatural, or he may be a creation of Alice's imagination, or perhaps the officious Martin is up to something. For most of the running time, director David Wellington maintains that tension and uses the house to create a spooky, dreamlike atmosphere. Hauser, one of the best actors in the business, is in top form and so is Adams.

1989 (R) 85m/C *CA* Wings Hauser, Lynne Adams, Pierce Lenoir, Barbara Ann Jones, Beverly Murray; ***D:*** David Wellington; ***W:*** Doug Taylor; ***C:*** David Franco. **VHS, LV** *REP*

Carrie

Brian DePalma's adaptation of Stephen King's first published novel is one of the most influential horrors of the 1970s. The opening locker room scene so powerfully lays out the terrors of adolescence—physical, emotional, and social terrors—that the whole film plays itself out at a much higher level. Sissy Spacek's performance is so believably vulnerable and winning that it makes up for a lot later when the action shifts weakly to her fellow students' machinations. (Both she and Piper Laurie as her mother received richly deserved Academy Award nominations.) The famous pig blood scene is an extended (but mechanical) Hitchcock moment, and a key musical theme is baldly lifted from *Psycho*. Unfortunately, the cheap "surprise" finish has been copied countless times since, by DePalma among others. The film was also the basis for a notoriously short-lived Broadway musical flop.

1976 (R) 98m/C Sissy Spacek, Piper Laurie, John Travolta, William Katt, Amy Irving, Nancy Allen, Edie McClurg, Betty Buckley, P.J. Soles, Sydney Lassick, Stefan Gierasch; ***D:*** Brian DePalma; ***W:*** Lawrence D. Cohen; ***C:*** Mario Tosi; ***M:*** Pino Donaggio. National Soci-

Sissy Spacek as the title character in Brian DePalma's *Carrie*.

"I'd give my life to be dead."

—Francesco Dellamorte (Rupert Everett) in *Cemetery Man.*

ety of Film Critics Awards '76: Best Actress (Spacek); Nominations: Academy Awards '76: Best Actress (Spacek), Best Supporting Actress (Laurie). **VHS, LV** *MGM, CRC*

Castle Freak

Traditional Gothic begins with the Reillys—father John (Jeffrey Combs), mother Susan (Barbara Crampton), and blind daughter Rebecca (Jessica Dollarhide)—going to the Italian castle they've inherited. The title character, in desperate need of a manicure and a makeover, is locked in the basement. Who is he? What is he doing there? Director Stuart Gordon establishes a creepy mood and punctuates it with some sharp humor. He also comes up with a wild finale, but nothing here can match the guilty pleasures that Gordon, Combs, and Crampton created in their camp classic *Re-Animator.*

1995 (R) 90m/C Jeffrey Combs, Barbara Crampton, Jonathan Fuller, Jessica Dollarhide; ***D:*** Stuart Gordon; ***W:*** Dennis Paoli; ***C:*** Mario Vulpiani; ***M:*** Richard Band. **VHS, LV** *FLL*

The Cat and the Canary

A breathless title card sets the scene: "On a lonely, pine-clad hill overlooking the Hudson, stood the grotesque mansion of an eccentric millionaire...." Director Paul Leni uses a restlessly mobile camera to inject life into this adaptation of a play about the reading of a will 20 years after the death of the aforementioned eccentric millionaire. The story is as much comedy as horror, with verbal and slapstick humor provided mostly by Creighton Hale, a lightweight Harold Lloyd–type leading man. Leni also distorts images and plays with extreme closeups and superimposed images. As a result, the style is much more enjoyable than the substance.

1927 70m/B Laura La Plante, Creighton Hale, Tully Marshall, Gertrude Astor, Arthur Edmund Carewe, Lucien Littlefield; ***D:*** Paul Leni; ***W:*** Robert F. "Bob" Hill, Alfred A. Cohn; ***C:*** Gilbert Warrenton. **VHS** *MRV, VYY, HHT*

The Cat and the Canary

The story of a large group of people who are brought together at some remote luxurious location—usually on a dark and stormy night—and then are bumped off in inventive ways has been told many times. This is one of the more enjoyable and lively. The updating of a silent film, itself based on a play, boasts dry wit ("Between the Bolsheviks on one side and the Democrats on the other, the world will become unrecognizable.") and a solid British ensemble cast led by Wendy Hiller. The setting is Glencliffe Manor, 1934; the reason is the reading of the will. A 1939 version of the film starring Bob Hope is still unavailable on video.

1979 (PG) 96m/C *GB* Carol Lynley, Michael Callan, Wendy Hiller, Olivia Hussey, Daniel Massey, Honor Blackman, Edward Fox, Wilfrid Hyde-White, Beatrix Lehmmann, Peter McEnery; ***D:*** Radley Metzger; ***W:*** Radley Metzger; ***C:*** Alex Thomson. **VHS** *COL, OM*

Cat People

Producer Val Lewton and director Jacques Tourneur are famous for suggesting everything and showing nothing. It's an approach that's won critical praise but horror fans have always been divided. Today's younger viewers are likely to be impatient with the talky, stodgy script that's notably lacking in action. But the film does work well in the important moments—the famous stalking scene, for example, is superbly put together without a wasted frame—and the crisp black and white looks great. Irina (Simone Simon) is the mysterious Serbian woman that the clueless Oliver (Kent Smith) falls for. Their relationship is simply too coy and ill-defined

for horror or for straight drama. Perhaps the constraints of the time kept the film from dealing honestly with its sexual subject and so the approach is oblique. It becomes blatant only in such odd touches as the design of a swimming suit. Paul Schrader takes a decidedly different tack with his excellent remake. (Followed by the non-horror *Curse of the Cat People.*)

1942 73m/B Simone Simon, Kent Smith, Jane Randolph, Jack Holt, Elizabeth Russell, Alan Napier, Tom Conway; ***D:*** Jacques Tourneur; ***W:*** DeWitt Bodeen; ***C:*** Nicholas Musuraca. National Film Registry '93. **VHS, LV, Letterboxed** *BTV, TTC*

Cat People

Paul Schrader's variation on the 1942 film may be the most sexually charged film in all horror. Where the original is based on an ill-defined idea of original sin through female rebellion against male authority, this one works with more overt themes—incest, bestiality—all boiling down to the basic conservative Christian notion that sex is evil. Not that the film believes or promotes that. The keys are a feral, innocent, seductive performance by Nastassia Kinski and much more threatening work from Malcolm McDowell as her brother; a spooky hypnotic score by Giorgio Moroder; and the genteel seediness of the New Orleans setting. Schrader carefully quotes the original without really turning his film into a remake. It's on the long side, but not indulgent.

1982 (R) 118m/C Nastassia Kinski, Malcolm McDowell, John Heard, Annette O'Toole, Ruby Dee, Ed Begley Jr., John Larroquette; ***D:*** Paul Schrader; ***W:*** Alan Ormsby; ***C:*** John Bailey; ***M:*** Giorgio Moroder. **VHS, LV** *USH, FCT*

Cat's Eye

A smart grey tabby connects three Stephen King tales. In the first, James Woods takes drastic measures to quit smoking. Then Robert Hays and Kenneth McMillan are involved in a vertiginous bet, and finally Drew Barrymore is menaced by a monstrous troll. The second installment is the strongest, though the troll effects by Carlo Rambaldi are the highpoint. Director Lewis Teague gets fine performances from his felines; he's less successful with Drew Barrymore and Candy Clark. ***AKA:*** Stephen King's Cat's Eye.

1985 (PG-13) 94m/C Drew Barrymore, James Woods, Alan King, Robert Hays, Candy Clark, Kenneth McMillan, James Naughton, Charles S. Dutton; ***D:*** Lewis Teague; ***W:*** Stephen King; ***C:*** Jack Cardiff; ***M:*** Alan Silvestri. **VHS, LV, Closed Caption** *FOX, FCT*

Cemetery Man

Before he caught on with the moviegoing public in *My Best Friend's Wedding,* Rupert Everett attracted a large following among horror fans with this Italian philosophical comedy of the grotesque. He plays Francesco Delamorte, grounds keeper at the Buffalora cemetery where the dead have suddenly and for no reason begun to come back seven days after they're interred. Why? Delamorte doesn't know and doesn't care. It's just his job to keep 'em in place. In fact, he's so blase about the whole thing he hasn't even bothered to tell the authorities because there'd be too many forms to fill out. At least that's how he sees it at first, but the situation soon complicates itself in unusual ways. For example, a voluptuous woman (Anna Falchi) appears as several characters, living and dead, to tempt Delamorte. The plot doesn't follow other horror conventions, either. Director Michele Soavi is more interested in an exaggerated autumnal atmosphere and Delamorte's delicious spiritual malaise. "The living dead and the dying living are all the same," he says, "Cut from the same cloth." That's only the beginning of the nasty comments he has about today's trendily necrophilic youth culture. Balanced against that—and complementing it—is Delamorte's comic assistant Nagi (Francois Hadji-Lazaro), whose rotund body, bald head, and childish enthusiasms are clearly inspired by Curly

THE HOUND SALUTES

JACQUES TOURNEUR

Jacques Tourneur was born into the movie business. His father was French director Maurice Tourneur, who emigrated to Hollywood in 1914 when young Jacques was ten. Jacques went to Hollywood High and worked as an office boy at MGM. In 1928 he went back to Paris to edit his father's films and then to direct his own. He returned to Hollywood in 1935, working first for MGM, and then moving to RKO with his friend, producer Val Lewton.

Together, the two would become synonymous with a classy, sophisticated kind of horror. As David Thomson says in *A Biographical Dictionary of Film* (Knopf, 1994), "Time and again in these films, it is the imaginative use of light, decor, space, and movement that makes the impact of the movie." That polished style is a two-edged sword.

Their debut was *Cat People* in 1942. It remains a beautifully photographed work that still finds fans today, but it's also oddly dated in terms of content and its approach to sexual matters. Lewton and Tourneur followed it quickly with the even more atmospheric *I Walked with a Zombie* and the mystery-horror *The Leopard Man,* based on a Cornell Woolrich novel.

Though the three films share a unifying visual sense, they're completely different in terms of plot, location, and theme. That also goes for Tourneur's fourth true horror film, the underrated *Curse of the Demon* from 1957,

of the Three Stooges. Other obvious influences come from Fellini and Sam Raimi. The violence is excessive and graphic; that's part of Soavi's point and it's not meant to be taken seriously. ***AKA:*** Dellamorte Delamore; Of Death, of Love. 🦴🦴🦴½

1995 (R) 100m/C *IT* Rupert Everett, Anna Falchi, Francois Hadji-Lazaro; ***D:*** Michele (Michael) Soavi; ***W:*** Gianni Romoli; ***C:*** Mauro Marchetti; ***M:*** Manuel De Sica. **VHS, Closed Caption** *FOX*

Ceremony

Writer/director Joe Castro squeezes every penny out of an obviously strained budget and comes up with an overachieving twist on a standard exorcism/demon plot. A prologue that's unnecessarily underlined establishes a rebellious angel who is banished to earth and then is trapped in a box called The Clockwork. Centuries later, it's scheduled to open in the living room of college student Sylvia Brindisi (Emilie Talbot). She invites a group of her Christian friends over to help her get the demon back in the box. Much of the film is too talky, but the characters and their beliefs are treated seriously, and Castro's monster effects are terrific. Forrest J. Ackerman shows up as Sylvia's dad. 🦴🦴

1997 90m/C Emilie Talbot, Forrest J. Ackerman, Amy Rohren, Steven R. Diebold; ***D:*** Joe Castro; ***W:*** Joe Castro, R.E. Balli II. **VHS** *YHV*

Chamber of Horrors

Old-dark-house yarn might more accurately be classified as a thriller until the last reel when it revisits the Inquisition. It's based on an Edgar Wallace novel, but it's

which, for my money, is superior to the first three. Based on M.R. James' story, "Casting the Runes" (a terrific work irrespective of genre considerations), it has by far the strongest plot of the four, and the acting is excellent.

The truth is, though, that Tourneur will always be remembered first for his seminal film noir *Out of the Past,* with Robert Mitchum and Kirk Douglas. It's a masterpiece of its kind. None of Tourneur's work in horror quite measures up to it, and that's easy enough to understand.

Tourneur didn't seem to be completely comfortable with his subject matter in horror. He and his supporters were of the school that says the unseen, suggested horror is much more frightening than anything that could be shown. They may be right in some cases, but not all. Would *The Phantom of the Opera* have been better if we hadn't seen Lon Chaney's face? Should the producers have "suggested" that King Kong was atop the Empire State Building? Of course not.

In the end, despite their technical brilliance (which was accomplished without huge budgets), Tourneur's films don't satisfy some mainstream audiences because they're "just horror movies" and they don't satisfy many horror fans because they're not horrific enough.

Tourneur died in 1977.

SIGNIFICANT CONTRIBUTIONS TO HORROR

Cat People **(1942)**

I Walked with a Zombie **(1943)**

The Leopard Man **(1943)**

Curse of the Demon **(1957) (AKA *Night of the Demon*)**

played out as horror. A batch of conniving servants set out to bilk plucky young Canadian heiress (Lilli Palmer) out of her rightful fortune. The gimmick: seven keys to seven locks that will open a tomb. The action is dated and frivolous with strong atmosphere and engaging, funny characters. ***AKA:*** The Door with Seven Locks. 🦴🦴½

1940 80m/B *GB* Leslie Banks, Lilli Palmer; ***D:*** Norman Lee. **VHS** *MRV, SNC, VCI*

The Changeling

After the death of his wife and daughter, composer John Russell (George C. Scott) rents a spooky mansion in Seattle. He tries to resume his life but finds that the place is haunted by the loud ghost of a child. Overt scares are secondary to an understated, old-fashioned approach. The classy cast includes Melvyn Douglas as a Senator and Jean Marsh, all too briefly, as the deceased wife. Comparisons to *Ghost Story* are not out of place, though this one is probably too deliberate for some. The film is beautifully photographed and the music is well integrated into the plot. 🦴🦴½

1980 (R) 114m/C *CA* George C. Scott, Trish Van Devere, John Russell, Melvyn Douglas, Jean Marsh, John Colicos, Barry Morse, Roberta Maxwell, James B. Douglas; ***D:*** Peter Medak; ***W:*** William Gray, Diana Maddox; ***C:*** John Coquillon. Genie Awards '80: Best Film. **VHS, LV** *VES*

Children of the Corn

So-so adaptation of a fair Stephen King story has been the basis for three sequels to date. Go figure. The film begins with a familiar premise—city couple (Peter Hor-

Chucky in *Child's Play.*

ton and Linda Hamilton) stop in remote rural town and find it deserted. What happened to the inhabitants? Where did they go? Director Fritz Kiersch does a fair job of establishing his eerie atmosphere. He doesn't fare as well with a cast of child actors who are either shrill, exaggerated monsters or overly cute moppets. They can't handle writer George Goldsmith's stilted Biblical language and they shouldn't have been expected to. When the big critter finally shows up—a scene which King describes in two sentences—he doesn't work too well, either. 🦴🦴

1984 (R) 93m/C Peter Horton, Linda Hamilton, R.G. Armstrong, John Franklin, Courtney Gains, Robbie Kiger; ***D:*** Fritz Kiersch; ***W:*** George Goldsmith; ***C:*** Raoul Lomas; ***M:*** Jonathan Elias. **VHS, LV** *VTR*

Children of the Corn 2: The Final Sacrifice

Hapless little snoozer appears to have been a local production made somewhere in the Midwest with a few professional actors in the leads and enthusiastic semi-pros filling out the cast. Expect no surprises in the connect-the-dots script or the not-very-special effects. It's just a boring little horror sequel that has virtually nothing to do with Stephen King's original story. At their best, low-budget horror movies are unpredictable and bizarre. This sequel is tedious and ordinary. Amazingly, however, the title was profitable enough to generate even more entries in the uneven series. To date, *4* is the only one worth a look, and it's a real sleeper. 🦴

1992 (R) 93m/C Terence Knox, Paul Scherrer, Rosalind Allen, Christie Clark, Ned Romero, Ryan Bollman, Ted Travelstead; ***D:*** David F. Price; ***W:*** Gilbert Adler, A.L. Katz. **VHS, Closed Caption** *PAR*

Children of the Corn 3: Urban Harvest

The whole idea of vaguely Amish boys practicing voodoo is too ridiculous for words, but it's the premise of this nutty sequel that's far removed from the source material, Stephen King's story. Two farm boys, Eli (Daniel Cerney, who looks like a young Sal Mineo) and his older brother Joshua (Ron Melendez), are sent to Chicago foster parents where evil Eli conjures up monstrous corn critters in the vacant lot next door. Most of the scares are accomplished through the familiar dream-reality switch. Some of the effects by Screaming Mad George are O.K.; others are laughable. Nothing new. 🦴🦴

1995 (R) 103m/C Daniel Cerney, Ron Melendez, Mari Morrow, Duke Stroud, Jim Metzler, Nancy Lee Grahn; ***D:*** James D.R. Hickox; ***W:*** Dode Levenson; ***C:*** Gerry Lively; ***M:*** Daniel Licht. **VHS, LV, Closed Caption** *TOU*

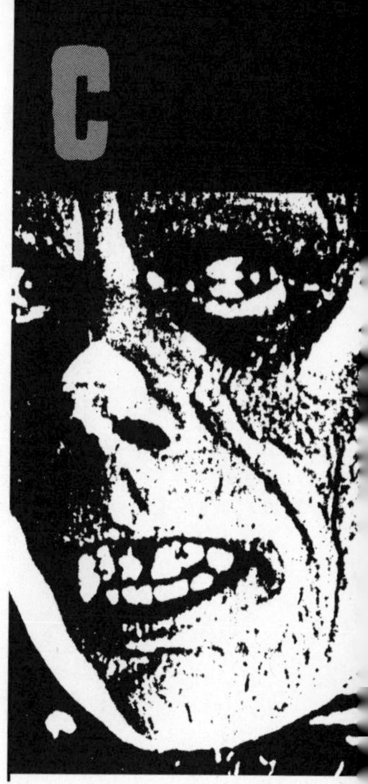

Children of the Corn 4: The Gathering

What a surprise! This sequel is easily the best in the lackluster series and a good film in its own right. Retaining Stephen King's original rural setting and villain (sort of), it really has nothing to do with the other three entries. Grace (a terrific Naomi Watts) goes back to her Nebraska hometown to take care of her ailing mother (Karen Black). Immediately, she and Doc (William Windom) are in the middle of an epidemic of an inexplicable juvenile fever. A few too many scares rely on the it's-not-real-it's-a-dream bit that's been so overused lately, but others come from the editing and the situation, and they're knockouts. The best moments involve real fears—dealing with a frail parent or a sick child. Despite some other flaws, director Greg Spence makes a fine debut. Keep a lookout for whatever he does next. ***AKA:*** Deadly Harvest. 🦴🦴🦴

1996 (R) 85m/C Naomi Watts, Brent Jennings, Jaime Renee Smith, William Windom, Karen Black; ***D:*** Greg Spence; ***W:*** Stephen Berger, Greg Spence; ***C:*** Richard Clabaugh; ***M:*** David Williams. **VHS, LV, Closed Caption** *TOU*

Children of the Night

When a horror movie opens with the words, "Allburg, U.S.A. A peaceful and unassuming township nestled in quiet woods," you know that the filmmakers have tongue firmly set in cheek. The story really gets started in an eerie flooded crypt beneath an abandoned Gothic church where Cindy (Maya McLaughlin) and Lucy (Ami Dolenz) run into some of the most imaginative cinematic undead you'll ever seen. The script is more than a little clumsy, but director Tony Randel gives the action his usual stylish touch. Since the film comes from *Fangoria* magazine, the effects are more important than the plot. This one was made by fans for fans. 🦴🦴🦴

1992 (R) 92m/C Peter DeLuise, Karen Black, Ami Dolenz, Maya McLaughlin, Evan Mackenzie, David Sawyer, Garrett Morris; ***D:*** Tony Randel; ***W:*** Nicolas Falacci; ***C:*** Richard Michalak. **VHS** *COL*

Children Shouldn't Play with Dead Things

The obvious inspiration is *Night of the Living Dead,* but these filmmakers are aiming more for laughs than for scares. Six young smart-alecks go to an island cemetery and, more than an hour later after they've tried their best to talk each other to death, they run into cannibal zombies. Some of the makeup effects (by screenwriter and star Alan Ormsby!) are O.K., but as the title indicates, nobody involved is taking this seriously. For fans of the era, it doesn't measure up to *Simon, King of the Witches.* Ormsby would go on to the script of Paul Schrader's *Cat People.* Director Bob Clark would make *Porky's* and *A Christmas Story.* ***AKA:*** Revenge of the Living Dead. 🦴

1972 85m/C Alan Ormsby, Valerie Mamches, Jeff Gillen, Anya Ormsby, Paul Cronin, Jane Daly, Roy Engelman, Robert Philip, Bruce Solomon, Alecs Baird, Seth Sklarey; ***D:*** Bob (Benjamin) Clark; ***W:*** Bob (Benjamin) Clark, Alan Ormsby; ***C:*** Jack McGowan. **VHS** *VTR*

Child's Play

Though the box art and premise make this look like a formula studio production, it's really much better. At death, the spirit of mad killer Charles Lee Ray (Brad Dourif) is transported into a Good Guys doll named Chucky. A young boy (Alex Vincent), his mother (Catherine Hicks), and a Chicago police detective (Chris Sarandon) come to realize the truth, but not before the deranged toy has run amuck. The writing is well above average, with inventive plotting and attention to character. The toy effects and Chicago locations are fine, too. Add in grim humor and an ending that just won't

"Look who's stalking."

—Ad line from *Child's Play 3.*

quit and you've got one of the best of recent years. Followed by two substandard sequels.

1988 (R) 95m/C Catherine Hicks, Alex Vincent, Chris Sarandon, Dinah Manoff, Brad Dourif, Tommy Swerdlow, Jack Colvin; ***D:*** Tom Holland; ***W:*** Don Mancini, John Lafia, Tom Holland; ***C:*** Bill Butler; ***M:*** Joe Renzetti. **VHS, LV, Closed Caption** *MGM*

Child's Play 2

Sequel actually begins well with a nice Chucky "reconstruction" scene, and young Andy (Alex Vincent) being taken in by foster parents (Jenny Agutter and Gerrit Graham) while his mom's under psychiatric observation. Unfortunately, the plot quickly collapses into all-too-familiar routines with clearly telegraphed scares. The Universal studio has a long history of franchising its most popular horror characters, and this one maintains the original's high production values and attention to detail.

1990 (R) 84m/C Alex Vincent, Jenny Agutter, Gerrit Graham, Christine Elise, Grace Zabriskie; ***D:*** John Lafia; ***W:*** Don Mancini; ***C:*** Stefan Czapsky; ***M:*** Graeme Revell; ***V:*** Brad Dourif. **VHS, LV, Closed Caption** *USH*

Child's Play 3

The subtitle could be "Chucky Goes to Military School" and the characters are now mostly teenagers. The programmed scares haven't changed; neither have the slick production values or the doll effects. They're the same combination of blood and plastic. Even for fans of the character, life is too short to watch such crappy sequels.

1991 (R) 89m/C Justin Whalin, Perrey Reeves, Jeremy Sylvers, Peter Haskell, Dakin Matthews, Travis Fine, Dean Jacobson, Matthew Walker, Andrew (Andy) Robinson; ***D:*** Jack Bender; ***W:*** Don Mancini; ***M:*** Cory Lerios, John D'Andrea; ***V:*** Brad Dourif. **VHS, LV, Closed Caption** *USH*

A Chinese Ghost Story

Once you get past the cultural differences—and there are a lot of them to be got past—you find the familiar classic horror structure. Two young lovers—Ning Tsai-shen (Leslie Cheung) and Nieh Hsiao-tsing (Joey Wong)—confront an evil force and are guided by an older man, Yen (Wu Ma), a grumpy Taoist swordsman. The special effects range from crawling desiccated corpses to a giant tongue with considerable acrobatic martial arts. Director Ching Siu Tung mixes the spooky supernatural atmosphere of a ruined temple with lyrical romanticism and some lively camerawork. In one shot, the camera appears to zoom right down a screaming man's throat. Along with John Woo's thrillers, this is one of the films that brought Hong Kong to the attention of an international audience.

1987 93m/C *HK* Leslie Cheung, Wong Tsu Hsien, Wu Ma, Joey Wong; ***D:*** Ching Siu Tung. **VHS** *FCT, VSM*

Chopper Chicks in Zombietown

When it comes to horror-comedy, the folks at Troma keep both the scares and the laughs on a primitive level, and their outrageous titles tell the truth. A female motorcycle gang tries to keep a little town from being overrun by the living dead. The general level of humor is established by jokes involving a dwarf and a busload of blind orphans. Flesh-eating zombie stuff has been done so often that the gory effects aren't particularly disgusting anymore, though this one may set a record for living-dead decapitations.

1991 (R) 86m/C Jamie Rose, Catherine Carlen, Lycia Naff, Vicki Frederick, Kristina Loggia, Gretchen Palmer, Whitney Reis, Nina Peterson, Ed Gale, David Knell, Billy Bob Thornton, Don Calfa, Martha Quinn; ***D:*** Dan Hoskins; ***W:*** Dan Hoskins; ***C:*** Tom Fraser; ***M:*** Daniel May. **VHS, LV, Closed Caption** *COL, NLC*

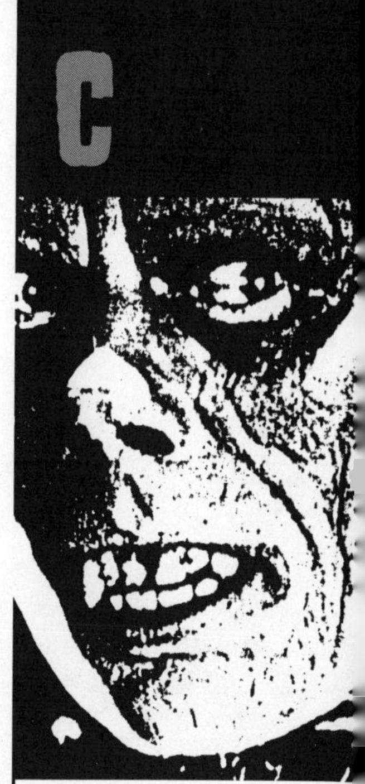

Chopping Mall

Armed robot guards in the Park Plaza Shopping Center go berserk when lightning strikes the computer. Like R2-D2 gone rogue, they attack four young couples having an after-hours party in the furniture store. B-movie favorites Paul Bartel, Mary Woronov, Gerrit Graham, and Dick Miller make cameo appearances. Exploitation vet Jim Wynorski keeps the action moving, but as a comment on materialism, his movie isn't nearly as perceptive as George Romero's *Dawn of the Dead*. ***AKA:*** Killbots.

1986 (R) 77m/C Kelli Maroney, Tony O'Dell, Suzee Slater, Russell Todd, Paul Bartel, Mary Woronov, Dick Miller, Karrie Emerson, Barbara Crampton, Nick Segal, John Terlesky, Gerrit Graham; ***D:*** Jim Wynorski; ***W:*** Jim Wynorski, Steve Mitchell; ***C:*** Tom Richmond. **VHS** *LIV*

Christine

Under John Carpenter's usual competent direction, Stephen King's automotive horror is engaging and well made, but not particularly frightening. Bookish teen Arnie (Keith Gordon) becomes the proud owner of a '58 Chrysler that's bad to the bone, and is changed by it. Dennis (John Stockwell) is his friend and protector; Leigh (Alexandra Paul) falls for the transformed Arnie. The effects are terrific, but the best part of King's novel is his understanding of teenagers and their changeable relationships. That's precisely the side of the story that's left out.

1984 (R) 110m/C Keith Gordon, John Stockwell, Alexandra Paul, Robert Prosky, Harry Dean Stanton, Kelly Preston, Christine Belford, Roberts Blossom, William Ostrander, David Spielberg, Robert Darnell; ***D:*** John Carpenter; ***W:*** Bill Phillips; ***C:*** Donald M. Morgan; ***M:*** John Carpenter, Alan Howarth. **VHS, LV, 8mm, Closed Caption** *COL*

A Christmas Carol

George C. Scott is one of the screen's finest Scrooges, both the famous "Bah, Humbug!" character and his changed or reborn self. Director Clive Donner creates an almost palpable sense of place with the historic town of Shrewsbury, England. Filled with snow and coal smoke, it captures that potent combination of horror and character revelation that makes the story so effective. Where most Christmas tales tend to be sweet and loving, Donner follows Dickens' lead and takes a more frightening path. Whatever else it may be, this is a ghost story, with Frank Finlay, Edward Woodward, and Susannah York as the spirits. All in all, a first-rate dramatization of one of the most popular works in the English language. Highly recommended.

1984 (PG) 100m/C George C. Scott, Nigel Davenport, Edward Woodward, Frank Finlay, Lucy Gutteridge, Angela Pleasence, Roger Rees, David Warner, Susannah York; ***D:*** Clive Donner; ***W:*** Roger O. Hirson. **VHS, Closed Caption** *FXV*

C.H.U.D.

Two of Hollywood's favorite political causes—homelessness and toxic waste—combine to create a so-so variation on a standard monster story. John Heard is a photographer and Daniel Stern is an activist who try to convince corrupt officials to tell the truth about a series of disappearances. The makeup effects are good, and director Douglas Cheek wisely keeps his monsters out of full sight most of the time. Watch for John Goodman and Jay Thomas briefly at the end. Followed by a sequel.

1984 (R) 90m/C John Heard, Daniel Stern, Christopher Curry, Kim Greist, John Goodman, Jay Thomas; ***D:*** Douglas Cheek; ***W:*** Parnell Hall. **VHS, LV** *VTR*

C.H.U.D. 2: Bud the Chud

Featherweight comedy really owes more to *Weekend at Bernie's* than to the origi-

The 1950s

Big Bugs, 3-D, and the Birth of Hammer

When James Nicholson walked into his partner Sam Arkoff's office at American International and announced the title he'd dreamed up—*I Was a Teenage Werewolf*—the whole business changed. It may not have been the first horror movie meant for kids who went to drive-ins, but it certainly targeted the market and declared its intentions right up front.

The 1950s, particularly the first half, are considered to be some of the worst years for "classic" horror. Yes, giant atomic bugs stomped clumsily across screens, Universal's great creations were turned into figures of fun with Abbott and Costello, and with the spread of drive-ins, unashamed exploitation (*I Was a Teenage Werewolf,* etc.) became synonymous with the genre, but anyone who takes a broader view of the field will find some of its best work.

At the beginning of the decade Charles Laughton starred in the relatively obscure but lively *The Strange Door* and then in 1955 he directed his masterpiece *The Night of the Hunter.* A year later, Don Siegel redefined cold war paranoia with *Invasion of the Body Snatchers,* and a year after that writer Richard Matheson, director Jack Arnold, and star Grant Williams spun B-movie straw into pure gold with *The Incredible Shrinking Man.*

Reacting to the explosive popularity of TV, horror tried various experiments with 3-D in *House of Wax* and *Creature from the Black Lagoon,* which work just fine without it.

At the same time, Jacques Tourneur made one of his best, *Night of the Demon.* In 1958, producer/writer James Clavell gave Vincent Price one of his finest roles in the big-budget *The Fly.*

Meanwhile in England, executives at an outfit called Hammer Pictures decided that a couple of up-and-coming young actors named Peter Cushing and Christopher Lee would be right for a remake called *The Curse of Frankenstein.* It was a huge hit and the studio quickly followed it up with Lee as the Count and Cushing as Van Helsing in *Horror of Dracula.* They teamed up for the third of many partnerships in *The Mummy* (1959).

On this side of the Atlantic, producer/director Roger Corman was turning his low-budget talents to horror with the quickie-comedy *Bucket of Blood,* which paved the way for his more ambitious explorations of Edgar Allen Poe in the 1960s. Waiting to take horror to the next level was Alfred Hitchcock.

nal. It attempts to turn generic living-dead stuff into slapstick with government-created zombies attacking suburbia. The presence of dozens of familiar faces from prime-time TV makes the whole thing look like a really bad sitcom. The material would be offensive if weren't so lame.

1989 (R) 84m/C Brian Robbins, Bill Calvert, Gerrit Graham, Tricia Leigh Fisher, Bianca Jagger, Robert Vaughn, Larry Cedar; ***D:*** David Irving. **VHS, LV** *LIV*

The Church

Considering how crazed Italian films have been recently, this Dario Argento-Michele

Soavi collaboration is downright restrained. Medieval Teutonic knights massacre peasants said to be satanists and bury them in a mass grave. Centuries later, a huge church has been built on the site. A curious librarian (Tomas Arana) thinks all cathedrals hold secrets and means to unlock them. Lotte (Asia Argento) is a caretaker's daughter there. The story begins well with some surprising visuals and intense images. Unfortunately, director Soavi and co-writers Argento and Franco Ferrini lose sight of their main characters and shift the focus in the second half to a group of largely unknown strangers who are dispatched straightaway. Who cares? Much of the music is inspired by Philip Glass. ***AKA:*** La Chiesa. 🦴🦴🦴

1990 110m/C *IT* Tomas Arana, Hugh Quarshie, Feodor Chaliapin Jr, Barbara Cupisti, Antonella Vitale, Asia Argento; ***D:*** Michele (Michael) Soavi; ***W:*** Dario Argento, Michele (Michael) Soavi, Franco Ferrini; ***C:*** Renato Tafuri; ***M:*** Keith Emerson. **VHS** *NO*

Circuit Breaker

Philip Noyce's taut nautical thriller *Dead Calm* is recast as a Gothic space opera with predictably watered-down results. Like most Gothics, it depends on people doing totally illogical things—like wandering down dark corridors in their nighties. In this version, Corbin Bernsen and Lara Harris are the spacefaring couple who come across Richard Grieco, adrift in a ruined ship. Is he an innocent victim or a slasher? The plotting leaves much to be desired. Any movie that includes the murder of a child must have a genuine reason for it. This one doesn't. It's just a low-budget horror flick that makes a serious mistake. The effects attempt things that the budget won't allow and clunky action sequences are unsuccessfully camouflaged by hyperactive overediting. The ending is the worst part of all. **Woof!**

1996 (R) 88m/C Richard Grieco, Corbin Bernsen, Lara Harris, Edie McClurg; ***D:*** Victoria Musspratt; ***W:*** Victoria Musspratt. **VHS** *NHO*

The Climax

Doctor Hohner (Boris Karloff) of the Royal Opera mourns his lost love Marselina (June Vincent), or so all of Vienna thinks. Ten years before, in a possessive rage, he strangled her. When young Angela (Susanna Foster) arrives to reprise the role that made Marselina famous, the doctor's bad thoughts come back. The film was inspired by the boxoffice success of the studio's remake of *Phantom of the Opera,* and is easily as enjoyable as the Claude Rains film. It's a lush Technicolor production that features one of Karloff's better understated performances. As the young romantic lead, Turhan Bey isn't bad, either. Judicious use of the fast-forward button makes the arias and musical numbers much easier to take. 🦴🦴🦴

1944 86m/C Boris Karloff, Susanna Foster, Turhan Bey, Gale Sondergaard, Thomas Gomez, June Vincent, Jane Farrar, Scotty Beckett; ***D:*** George Waggner; ***W:*** Curt Siodmak, Lynn Starling; ***C:*** Hal Mohr, William Howard Greene; ***M:*** Edward Ward. **VHS, Closed Caption** *USH*

A Clockwork Orange

Though Stanley Kubrick's film is unquestionably a masterpiece, it's remarkably faithful to its source material, Anthony Burgess's brilliant dystopian novel, and that debt has been largely unrecognized. The film has aged oddly. The "old ultra-violence," once so shocking, now looks—like most of Kubrick's work—too intellectual and carefully choreographed to generate a strong emotional response. (He's got to be the least passionate of modern directors.) The humor that Kubrick and star Malcolm McDowell bring is still wonderful. So is their perverse manipulation of audiences' emotions and expectations. And the strikingly sharp visuals are still remarkable. Yes, that's David Prowse, the body beneath the Darth Vader suit, as the attendant to the writer, played by Patrick Magee, a familiar face to fans of British horror. In

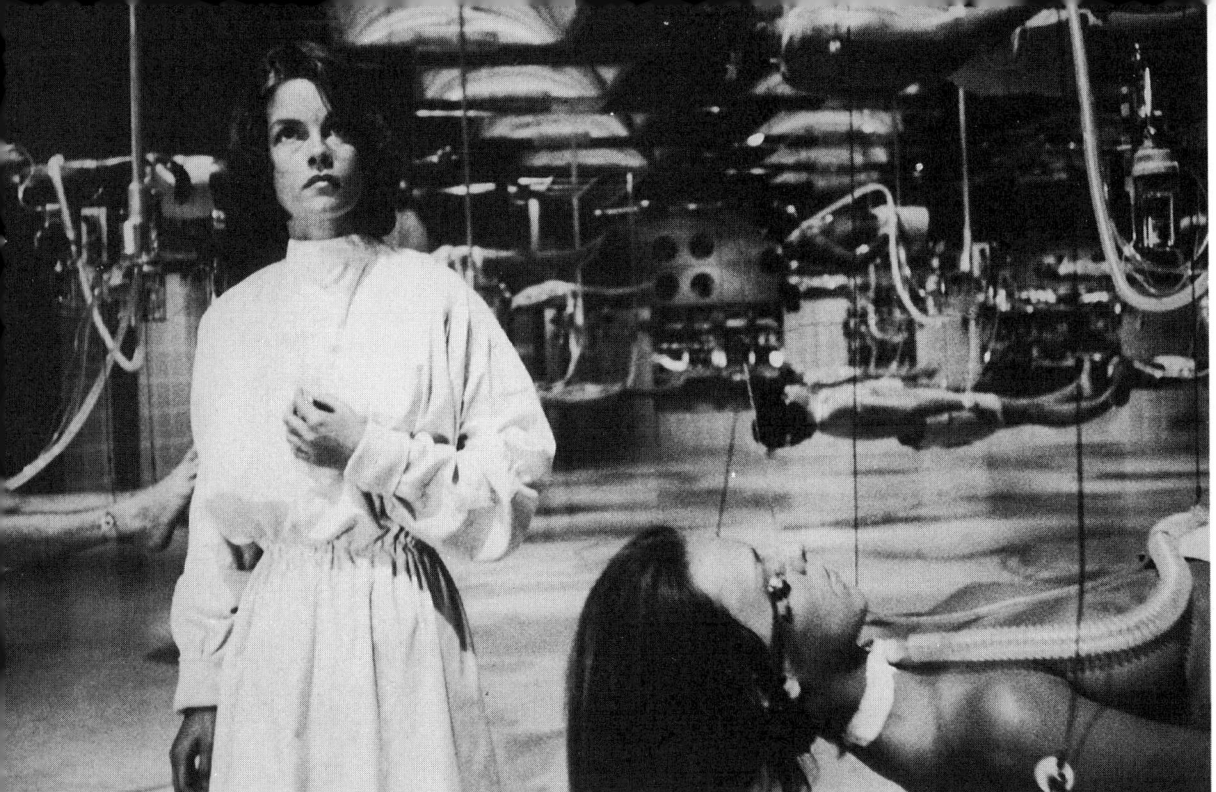

Dr. Susan Wheeler (Genevieve Bujold) in *Coma*.

1996, 90 seconds of violence were restored to the video version.

1971 (R) 137m/C *GB* Malcolm McDowell, Patrick Magee, Adrienne Corri, Michael Bates, Warren Clarke, Aubrey Morris, James Marcus, Steven Berkoff, David Prowse, John Clive, Carl Duering, Miriam Karlin; ***D:*** Stanley Kubrick; ***W:*** Stanley Kubrick; ***C:*** John Alcott. New York Film Critics Awards '71: Best Director (Kubrick), Best Film; Nominations: Academy Awards '71: Best Adapted Screenplay, Best Director (Kubrick), Best Film Editing, Best Picture. **VHS, LV, Letterboxed, Closed Caption** *WAR, FCT, FUS*

The Club

And you thought Carrie had a bad time at her high school prom! The kids at Eastern High find that one of their chaperons is a serial killer and, if that weren't enough, at the stroke of midnight, time stops. Someone on the dance committee has a lot of explaining to do. Six students and the murderous chaperon are trapped in a medieval castle. One of the students (Matthew Ferguson) is carefully made up to look like Johnny Depp, and another (Joel Wyner) is a dead ringer for Jim Carrey—and he injects a manic sense of humor to the second half of the film that almost makes up for the predictable Gothic scares. The story borrows from Sam Raimi's *Evil Dead,* but this variation on the standard dead-teenager plot lacks the out-of-control pace and crazed energy that make Raimi's films so much fun.

1994 (R) 88m/C Kim Coates, Joel Wyner, Andrea Roth, Rino Romano, Zack Ward, Kelli Taylor, Matthew Ferguson; ***D:*** Benton Spencer; ***W:*** Robert Cooper; ***M:*** Paul Zaza. **VHS, LV** *IMP*

Cobra Woman

Technically, this camp masterpiece isn't part of the genre, but several of the most famous names in Universal's horror stable, including producer George Wagner and director Robert Siodmak, are involved.

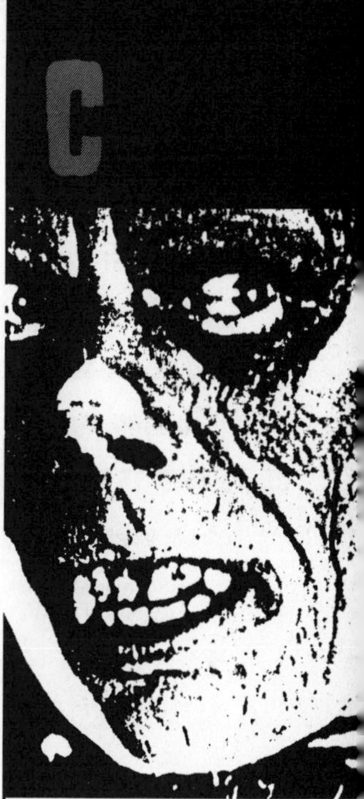

Maria Montez is the simple South Seas island village girl who's kidnapped by Lon Chaney, Jr., on the day of her wedding and taken to the island of the Cobra People where her evil twin rules. Jon Hall sets out to bring her back. The bizarre material—complete with erupting volcano, incredible costumes, and dance numbers that must be seen to be believed—is given an unusually lush Technicolor treatment.

1944 70m/C Maria Montez, Jon Hall, Sabu, Edgar Barrier, Lois Collier, Lon Chaney Jr.; ***D:*** Robert Siodmak; ***W:*** Gene Lewis, Richard Brooks; ***C:*** William Howard Greene. **VHS** *NO*

Cold Comfort

In an eerie little Canadian backwater somewhere between Lake Wobegon and Twin Peaks, a disturbed father kidnaps a lover for his daughter on her 18th birthday. As the unstable dad, Maury Chaykin looks like John Candy playing Norman Bates. He's so creepy and surprising that he dominates the film. Margaret Langrick, as his daughter, and Paul Gross, as the kidnapped travelling salesman, fade into the wallpaper when Chaykin cuts loose. The story's roots on the stage are evident in the slow stretches, but most of the time, director Vic Sarin keeps the action moving. For comparative purposes, this one is similar to an odd 1972 film, *The Strange Vengeance of Rosalie* and Stephen King's *Misery.*

1990 (R) 90m/C *CA* Margaret Langrick, Maury Chaykin, Paul Gross; ***D:*** Vic Sarin; ***W:*** Richard Beattie, Elliot L. Sims; ***C:*** Vic Sarin. **VHS** *REP*

Cold Sweat

Dark, tongue-in-cheek humor lifts this crime thriller/ghost story above the expected levels of either genre. The main players are a hitman (Ben Cross) haunted by the ghost of a recent victim, a financially strapped businessman (Dave Thomas), his faithless wife (Shannon Tweed), and their drug dealer (Adam Baldwin). The plot follows a familiar course for about an hour and then comes thoroughly unhinged in the last act. Like so many Canadian productions, the film has a bleak look. It won't be to all tastes, but horror fans in the mood for something quirky ought to give it a try.

1993 (R) 93m/C Ben Cross, Shannon Tweed, Adam Baldwin, Dave Thomas; ***D:*** Gail Harvey; ***W:*** Richard Beattie. **VHS, Closed Caption** *PAR, VTR*

Color Me Blood Red

Goremeister H.G. Lewis' 1964 answer to Roger Corman's *Bucket of Blood* isn't as snappy or as sophisticated. (This is, of course, the only context in which *Bucket of Blood* could ever be called sophisticated.) Adam Sorg (Don Joseph) decides that he prefers blood to oils or tempera for the reds in his paintings, so he murders for art supplies. Obviously, Adam's a man ahead of his time. Today he'd get a grant and be pilloried by Republicans. It's all extremely silly with gore effects, faux hip humor, and several pointless scenes on water bicycles. ***AKA:*** Model Massacre.

1964 74m/C Don Joseph, Candi Conder, Elyn Warner, Scott H. Hall, Jerome Eden, Patricia Lee, James Jackel; ***D:*** Herschell Gordon Lewis; ***W:*** Herschell Gordon Lewis; ***C:*** Herschell Gordon Lewis. **VHS** *SMW*

Coma

When a friend goes into a coma, Dr. Susan Wheeler (Genevieve Bujold) becomes interested in the idea of being alive and dead at the same time. She looks into her hospital's records and finds that it's happening there more than it should. Writer/director Michael Crichton bases his horror on the all-too-real world of the hospital. He doesn't need monsters or gallons of blood. The sight of ominous figures in green scrubs, medical machines, and tile

"Never stray from the path, never eat a windfall apple, and never trust a man whose eyebrows meet."

—Granny (Angela Lansbury) gives advice to Rosaleen (Sarah Patterson) in *The Company of Wolves.*

walls are enough to scare the pants off most viewers. Once the setting has been established, he doesn't need to do much more. The only real flaw is an overreliance on loud music at key moments. 🦴🦴🦴🦴

1978 (PG) 113m/C Genevieve Bujold, Michael Douglas, Elizabeth Ashley, Rip Torn, Richard Widmark, Lois Chiles, Hari Rhodes, Tom Selleck, Ed Harris; ***D:*** Michael Crichton; ***W:*** Michael Crichton; ***M:*** Jerry Goldsmith. **VHS, LV** *MGM*

The Comedy of Terrors

Unscrupulous undertaker Trumbull (Vincent Price) has 24 hours to come up with the back rent for Mr. Black (Basil Rathbone). After an unfunny screaming match with his wife (Joyce Jameson), he and his partner Gilly (Peter Lorre) set out to scare up new business. The pace picks up with a corpse that refuses to rest in peace. Not surprisingly, the tone owes more to the other American-International releases of the day and to the overall spirit of experimentation of the mid-'60s than to director Jacques Tourneur's more well-known work. Though Karloff has little to do as the doddering father-in-law, it's fun to see these four stars onscreen together. 🦴🦴🦴

1964 84m/C Vincent Price, Peter Lorre, Boris Karloff, Basil Rathbone, Joe E. Brown, Joyce Jameson; ***D:*** Jacques Tourneur; ***W:*** Richard Matheson; ***C:*** Floyd Crosby; ***M:*** Les Baxter. **VHS, LV** *MOV*

The Company of Wolves

Fans will be either infuriated or entranced by Angela Carter's atmospheric tale. It contains elements of horror, but its real subject is myth—fantasy, fairy tale, nursery rhyme, and archetype, all mixed and layered in a dreamlike structure with repeated images, phrases, and stories taking the place of the conventional well-made plot. Grandmother (Angela Lansbury) makes a red cloak for Rosaleen (Sarah Patterson) and fills her head with cautionary tales. But Rosaleen is making the awkward, halting transition from girl to woman and does not accept everything she hears. The setting—a foggy, nightmare combination of Disney's *Snow White* forest and Kong's Skull Island—is inseparable from the action. Like the film, it's the world of a child's fantasy seen through adult eyes. 🦴🦴🦴🦴

1985 (R) 95m/C Angela Lansbury, David Warner, Stephen Rea, Tusse Silberg, Sarah Patterson, Brian Glover, Danielle Dax, Graham Crowden, Micha Bergese, Kathryn Pogson, Georgia Slowe; ***D:*** Neil Jordan; ***W:*** Neil Jordan, Angela Carter; ***C:*** Bryan Loftus; ***M:*** George Fenton. **VHS, LV, Closed Caption** *VES, LIV*

The Conqueror Worm

The England of 1645 is torn apart by civil war and a widespread witch hunt paranoia. Matthew Hopkins (Vincent Price) leads the faithful, torturing confessions out of the accused for a price. Young Sarah (Hilary Dwyer) catches his eye. She's the fiancee of Richard (Ian Ogilvy), a soldier in Cromwell's army. Director Michael Reeves handles Hopkins' character carefully, presenting him as a conman who—to a degree—believes his own con. (The real Hopkins was involved with the prosecution and execution of more than 60 women, and was himself hanged as a sorcerer in 1647.) The pace is a bit too deliberate, but it effectively creates suspense. Though the American title comes from Poe, the film is really closer in spirit and appearance to the contemporaneous Hammer films. Also, for the times when it was made, the sexual and violent aspects of the film are groundbreakingly frank. Reeves died soon after the film was finished. ***AKA:*** Witchfinder General; Edgar Allan Poe's Conqueror Worm. 🦴🦴🦴🦴

1968 95m/C *GB* Vincent Price, Ian Ogilvy, Hilary Dwyer, Rupert Davies, Robert Russell, Patrick Wymark, Wilfrid Brambell; ***D:*** Michael Reeves; ***W:*** Michael Reeves, Louis M. Heyward, Tom Baker; ***C:*** John Coquillon. **VHS** *ORI, FCT*

Copycat

Like so many serial-killer horrors, this one somehow manages to work despite a plot that defies viewers' credulity. In terms of absolute screwiness, it's not as nutzo as *Seven,* but that's a close call. What saves it? Excellent casting and performances. Sigourney Weaver is Dr. Hudson, a terrified psychiatrist who was once attacked by a psychotic (Harry Connick, Jr.). Holly Hunter is Det. Monohan, who asks her assistance in catching another killer. Director Jon Amiel and Sigourney Weaver make Hudson's agoraphobia seem all too real, and Holly Hunter's chipper but tough detective isn't upstaged for a second. As always, the San Francisco setting helps considerably. Amiel and writers Ann Biderman and David Madsen aim their scares directly at female viewers. They play on cliches of the genre, and if it's familiar territory to anyone who's seen *Silence of the Lambs,* it's still produced with top drawer studio slickness. Manipulatively entertaining.

1995 (R) 124m/C Sigourney Weaver, Holly Hunter, Dermot Mulroney, Harry Connick Jr., William McNamara, Will Patton, John Rothman, David Michael Silverman; ***D:*** Jon Amiel; ***W:*** Ann Biderman, David Madsen; ***C:*** Laszlo Kovacs; ***M:*** Christopher Young. **VHS, Closed Caption** *WAR*

Count Dracula

Complete disappointment. Given a fine cast and an apparently adequate budget, director Jess Franco delivers perhaps the most anemic and dispirited version of the story ever put onscreen. In one short scene, Christopher Lee plays the Count as a megalomaniacal Magyar, but for the rest of his screentime, he's a pedestrian figure. Klaus Kinski's Renfield is more interesting, but not much. All of the characters are adrift in dark deep sets. Franco's use of zoom focus has seldom been more irritating, and his attempt to use stuffed animals for scares is the final insult. It will make you appreciate the Hammer Dracula films.

AKA: Bram Stoker's Count Dracula; Il Conte Dracula; Dracula 71; Nachts wenn Dracula Erwacht; The Nights of Dracula.

1971 (R) 90m/C *SP GE IT* Christopher Lee, Herbert Lom, Klaus Kinski, Frederick Williams, Maria Rohm, Soledad Miranda, Paul Mueller; ***D:*** Jess (Jesus) Franco; ***W:*** Jess (Jesus) Franco, Augusto Finochi, Peter Welbeck, Milo G. Cuccia, Carlo Fadda; ***C:*** Manuel Merino. **VHS** *REP, FCT*

Count Yorga, Vampire

Should a European vampire relocate to trendy L.A., might he not set up shop as a spiritualist? That's what Yorga (Robert Quarry) does in a nicely handled horror that's also a postcard of the late 1960s. The script and the acting are more polished than the production values, but the location work is typical of the time. Quarry is properly seductive and regal, though his harem of converts and a wardrobe that only a Vegas lounge lizard could love are more humorous than they once were. If the sight of an aristocratic vampire riding in a VW minibus is odd, the whole effort is more successful than the Hammer attempts to bring Dracula into the present. Followed by *Return of Count Yorga.*

1970 (PG) 90m/C Robert Quarry, Roger Perry, Michael Murphy, Michael Macready, Donna Anders, Judith Lang, Marsha Jordan, Julie Conners, Paul Hansen; ***D:*** Bob Kelljan; ***W:*** Bob Kelljan; ***C:*** Arch Archambault. **VHS** *NO*

Countess Dracula

Ingrid Pitt solidified her reputation as one of horror's sexiest stars with her second feature. Loosely based on legends of Countess Elizabeth Bathory, it's about a Hungarian widow (Pitt) who must bathe in the blood of virgins to retain her youth and her young beau (Sandor Eles). Compared to conventional vampire stories focused on a male figure, it's a fresh approach. Director Peter Sasdy also made the relatively unknown *Taste the Blood of Dracula*

Bonnie (Neve Campbell), Nancy (Fairuza Balk), and Sarah (Robin Tunney) levitate Rochelle (Rachel True) in ***The Craft***.

and *Hands of the Ripper* around the same time. Any horror fan who hasn't discovered these three is in for a treat.

1970 93m/C *GB* Ingrid Pitt, Nigel Green, Sandor Eles, Maurice Denham, Lesley-Anne Down, Patience Collier, Peter Jeffrey, Leon Lissek, Charles Farrell; ***D:*** Peter Sasdy; ***W:*** Jeremy Paul; ***C:*** Ken Talbot. **LV**

The Craft

Sleeper hit that might have been pure exploitation is a keenly observed, well-acted story of four teenaged girls. The supernatural elements are handled carefully, and it's not until the big gross-out conclusion that the special effects really kick in. Troubled Sarah (Robin Tunney) finds it hard to fit in at her new L.A. school. Three girls who are ostracized from the rest of the students offer friendship. With her nose ring and attitude, Nancy (Fairuza Balk) is the group's leader. Bonnie (Neve Campbell) has serious self-image problems, and Rochelle (Rachel True) is the target of racist taunts. The three have formed a frivolous coven that's all talk and silliness, but they think that having a fourth member will allow them to call up the elements or whatever. The script by Peter Filardi (*Flatliners*) and director Andrew Fleming treats magic almost as an extension of emotion. Beyond the incantations and rituals, these four girls are expressing the real fears and desires of their age—to be pretty, to be accepted, to get back at the guy who's been mean to you. Favorable comparisons to *Carrie* aren't out of place.

1996 (R) 100m/C Robin Tunney, Fairuza Balk, Neve Campbell, Rachel True, Skeet Ulrich, Helen Shaver, Cliff DeYoung, Christine Taylor, Assumpta Serna; ***D:*** Andrew Fleming; ***W:*** Andrew Fleming, Peter Filardi; ***C:*** Alexander Grusynski; ***M:*** Graeme Revell. MTV Movie Awards '97: Best Fight (Fairuza Balk/Robin Tunney). **VHS, LV, 8mm, Closed Caption, DVD** *COL*

Crash

Renowned writer and critic Anthony Boucher reportedly asked a colleague his opinion of a new novel. The man dismissed it as pornography. Still curious, Boucher pressed on and asked, "But is it good pornography?" He might have been inquiring about *Crash* and the answer would be, yes, it's good porn; slickly made and perversely enjoyable for fans of director David Cronenberg. In many ways, the film is a companion piece to his *Dead Ringers.* Both are horror films of disturbing originality. James Spader and Deborah Unger play a kinky Canadian couple who become sexually fixated on the injured victims of automobile accidents. Holly Hunter introduces them to this peculiar subculture, and Elias Koteas becomes their guide through it. That journey is essentially a series of sex scenes that emphasize broken bones, stitches, scar tissue, braces, and crutches. Cronenberg is a fine creepy director, and the first scenes are shocking. With graphic sexual material, though, acts that are at first surprising eventually become silly and finally banal. Of course, individual viewers will disagree about where those gradations occur. Throughout, only the characters' sexual sides are revealed, and those don't really change much. As a group, they begin and end with the same slack-faced expressions of jaded desire and sated fulfillment.

1995 (NC-17) 98m/C *CA* James Spader, Holly Hunter, Elias Koteas, Deborah Kara Unger, Rosanna Arquette, Peter MacNeill; ***D:*** David Cronenberg; ***W:*** David Cronenberg; ***C:*** Peter Suschitzsky; ***M:*** Howard Shore. Cannes Film Festival '96: Special Jury Prize; Genie Awards '96: Best Adapted Screenplay, Best Cinematography, Best Director (Cronenberg), Best Film Editing; Nominations: Genie Awards '96: Best Film, Best Sound. **VHS, LV, Closed Caption** *NLC, CRC*

The Craving

Though it's not meant to be funny, Paul Naschy's tale of reincarnated monsters is so wild and wooly that it's best appreciated as a comedy. Wolfman Valdemar (Naschy) is brought back to life with Elizabeth Bathory (Silvia Aquilar). He's the good monster (sort of); she's the villain. The plot whips vampirism, grave robbing, sex, and other stuff into a semi-coherent sepulchral stew. For those unfamiliar with Naschy, think of a spaghetti Western version of *Dark Shadows.* ***AKA:*** Return of the Wolfman; El Retorno del Hombre-Lobo.

1980 (R) 93m/C *SP* Paul Naschy, Julie Saly, Silvia Aquilar, Azucena Hernandez, Beatriz Elorietta, Pilar Alcon; ***D:*** Jack Molina, Paul Naschy. **VHS** *VES, LIV*

The Crawling Hand

In many ways, this is nothing more than a low-budget black-and-white teen horror from the early 1960s with a particularly loony premise. Mild-mannered student Paul (Peter Breck) turns into a raccoon-eyed homicidal zombie after he and his Swedish girlfriend Marte (Sirry Steffen) find the hand of an astronaut on the beach. With Gilligan's Skipper Alan Hale as the Sheriff and the Rivingtons' "The Bird Is the Word" on the soundtrack, the comic side is complete. But toward the end, Brock comes up with one brief moment that perfectly expresses the whole teen-angst appeal of horror to young audiences when Paul desperately tries to explain to Marte what's happening: "There are times when I'm all right and then I'm not, and then...then when I'm myself and I'm not and the periods when I'm myself are getting shorter and shorter. Do you understand?" "No." "Then don't try! I gotta get outta here. Leave me alone!"

1963 98m/B Alan Hale Jr., Rod Lauren, Richard Arlen, Peter Breck, Kent Taylor, Arline Judge, Allison Hayes, Sirry Steffen; ***D:*** Herbert L. Strock. **VHS, LV** *NOS, RHI, GEM*

The Crazies

George Romero's third film is an anti-military story about a bacteriological weapon named Trixie that gets loose, causing people to go berserk, in rural western Pennsylvania. The Army attempts to contain both

THE HOUND SALUTES

UNIVERSAL STUDIO

Of all the Hollywood studios, Universal has been the most closely identified with horror. It was founded by "Uncle" Carl Laemmle. Like so many of the people who created the American movie industry, he was an immigrant from Europe who became an accidental mogul.

In 1905, he was actually trying to get into the Chicago clothing business when he realized that moving pictures might be more profitable. One theatre led to a chain and, ten years later, after a lengthy legal battle, he opened up the Universal City production studio north of Hollywood. Thomas Edison, one of his primary competitors, and Buffalo Bill Cody were on hand.

Working with Laemmle, a young Irving Thalberg oversaw the filming of the studio's first major horror hit, *The Hunchback of Notre Dame*. Two years later, star Lon Chaney had his second screen smash with *The Phantom of the Opera*, before he followed Thalberg to MGM.

The studio's interest in horror reappeared in the early 1930s when James Whale and Tod Browning made such masterpieces as *Frankenstein*, *Dracula*, *The Mummy*, and *The Invisible Man*. The importance of those films cannot be overstated. They established standards that all other horrors are judged against. Over the years, they've been seen so often by so many people that they define the landscape of the genre.

Universal continued to make innovative horror films until 1941 when Lon Chaney, Jr., starred in *The Wolf Man*.

After that, however, it settled for sequels with a steady stream of competently made connect-the-dots *Mummy* films and various teamings of its other monsters, coming to an ignominious but fairly entertaining conclusion with the *Abbott and Costello Meet...* series of comedies in the 1940s and '50s. Made at the same time, the *Inner Sanctum* series, based on the popular radio show and starring Chaney, was much better.

the actual and P.R. damage. Remember that the film was made around the same time that the Air Force killed a flock of sheep and tried to cover it up. The references to the Vietnam War are less than subtle. Like most of Romero's work, it's rough in technical terms—harsh colors, mostly no-name cast, shot on location—but emotionally effective. In some ways, this one can be seen as a link between *Night of the Living Dead* and *Dawn of the Dead*. ***AKA:*** Code Name: Trixie. 🦴🦴🦴

1973 (R) 103m/C Lane Carroll, W.G. McMillan, Harold W. Jones, Lloyd Hollar, Lynn Lowry; ***D:*** George A. Romero; ***W:*** George A. Romero. *VTR*

Creature from the Black Lagoon

The Gill Man is certainly the most memorable guy-in-a-rubber-fish-suit monster to come out of the 1950s. That subgenre of horror is inherently lightweight, so why has this example remained so popular? It's simple. Sex. The white bathing suit scene with Julie Adams is as sensual and suggestive as Hollywood got in those days. (So that's what synchronized swimming is all about.) Beyond that indelible moment, the rubber fish suit is pretty good. The simple plot moves quickly and, somehow, that backlot

By then, the studio's production facilities and talent were an assembly line that could produce formula entertainment at a steady rate. Its films seldom rose above the level of their formulas, but they were made with solid professional competence. The sets and costumes looked good. The scripts were tight. The acting was acceptable. Perhaps most importantly, the women in front of the camera were always glamorous and they were beautifully photographed in evocative black and white.

In the 1950s, Universal's horror output diminished in quantity but not quality, with *The Incredible Shrinking Man* and *Creature from the Black Lagoon* setting standards for the decade.

In 1963, Alfred Hitchcock returned to the studio with *The Birds,* but like the rest of Hollywood then, Universal was more interested in big-budget spectaculars. Steven Spielberg came on board in 1971 with the superb made-for-TV *Duel* and then *Jaws* in '75. Since then, other smaller production companies like New Line and Dimension Films have been more important to low-budget horror, while Universal's main connection to the genre has been through Spielberg's *Jurassic Park* and *The Lost World.*

Throughout the studio's history, it has always been careful with its library. In the 1960s and '70s, it made its horror films available for local television late shows where they were rediscovered by a new generation. Then, when the home video revolution hit in the 1980s and '90s, Universal repackaged its horrors in new collections. Unlike some other studios that have slapped their films onto videotape as quickly and easily as possible, Universal has taken care to present even its most modest productions in their best form possible.

SIGNIFICANT CONTRIBUTIONS TO HORROR

***The Hunchback of Notre Dame* (1923)**

***The Phantom of the Opera* (1925)**

***Dracula* (1931)**

***Dracula* (1931) (Spanish language version)**

***Frankenstein* (1931)**

***The Mummy* (1932)**

***The Invisible Man* (1933)**

***Bride of Frankenstein* (1935)**

***Son of Frankenstein* (1939)**

***The Wolf Man* (1941)**

***Creature from the Black Lagoon* (1954)**

***The Incredible Shrinking Man* (1957)**

***The Birds* (1963)**

***Duel* (1971)**

***Jaws* (1975)**

***Jurassic Park* (1993)**

Amazon set is believable. Hans Salter's brassy score set the tone for the whole era. Originally filmed in 3-D. 🦴🦴🦴½

1954 79m/B Richard Carlson, Julie Adams, Richard Denning, Antonio Moreno, Whit Bissell, Nestor Paiva, Ricou Browning; ***D:*** Jack Arnold; ***W:*** Arthur Ross; ***M:*** Hans J. Salter. **VHS, LV** *USH*

Creature from the Haunted Sea

Legendary Roger Corman cheapie—cut from the same cloth as *Bucket of Blood* and *Little Shop of Horrors*—has a sense of humor reminiscent of the TV show *Get Smart.* The comedy was made in Puerto Rico when producer/director Corman wound up with extra time and a cast and crew from another production. A script was cranked out and Corman reportedly spent a whopping $150 for a fish monster suit, though I doubt it actually cost that much. The plot has to do with a fortune looted from the Cuban treasury, refugee soldiers, and the silly monster. Sample dialogue: "Tostada went alone into the forbidding void." Star Edward Wain is actually writer Robert Towne. 🦴🦴

THE HOUND SALUTES

CHRISTOPHER LEE

Christopher Lee's career is a result of good timing and luck, though I'm not sure those two are completely different. The simple truth is that he was able to take a role that had been completely identified with one actor for more than a generation and make it his own. Had moviegoers grown tired of Lugosi's Dracula or was Lee able invest new, more sexually charged energy into the character? Whatever the cause, in 1957, astonishingly large numbers of people flocked to theatres to see Lee in *Dracula* (AKA *Horror of Dracula*).

He was born in 1922 in London and served in the Royal Air Force during World War II. After it, he decided to try his hand at acting. In 1956, Hammer cast him as the monster in the studio's first attempt at true horror, *The Curse of Frankenstein.* In the book *House of Horror* (Lorrimer, 1973), Lee says, "I was asked to play the creature chiefly because of my size and height [6'5"] which had effectively kept me out of many pictures I might have appeared in during the preceding ten years. Most British stars flatly refused to have me anywhere near them in a film, because I was easily the tallest man around."

Reflecting the temper of the late 1950s, Lee's vampire had a more physical sexuality. Remember that the film was made at about the same time that Ian Fleming's novels were becoming best sellers. Lee's Dracula contains more than a hint of James Bond in his off-hand attitude of superiority over women.

Lee, however, kept himself from being typecast. In quick succession, he'd played the Frankenstein monster, Dracula and, in 1959, the Mummy. He drifted slowly away from horror as a roguish supporting villain in *The Two*

1960 76m/B Antony Carbone, Betsy Jones-Moreland, Beach Dickerson, Edward Wain, Edmundo Rivera Alvarez, Robert Bean, Sonya Noemi Gonzalez; ***D:*** Roger Corman; ***W:*** Charles B. Griffith; ***C:*** Jacques Marquette. **VHS** *VYY, MRV, SNC*

The Creature Walks among Us

The Gill Man's third outing is more boats, blondes, and bubbles as a quartet of doctors—and one curvy wife (Leigh Snowden)—sail into the Everglades to fetch everyone's favorite fish monster and then to surgically alter him. No, not that way; these guys want to "bring a new species into existence!" After a lot of pseudoscientific gobbledegook, they strap on the air tanks and catch him. The black-and-white photography is crystalline, both underwater and above. Though this one's more enjoyable than the second, it doesn't equal the original and it can't live up to that great title. The way the story is set up, you're rooting for the Creature all the way. The racial overtones of his eventual appearance in "human" form are unmistakable. The action's relatively slow until the conclusion, when Gill finally decides to kick ass and take names. Enjoy the movie as a period piece, and, of course, check out that great monster suit. 🦴🦴🦴

1956 79m/B Jeff Morrow, Rex Reason, Leigh Snowden, Gregg Palmer, Ricou Browning, Don Megowan, Mau-

Faces of Dr. Jekyll, a French pimp in *The Hands of Orloc*, and Sir Henry in *Hound of the Baskervilles*. Lee himself was just as comfortable in the mainstream—*The Longest Day, The Magic Christian, The Three Musketeers, Man with the Golden Gun*—but most of his paychecks involved horror in one form or another: *Horror Hotel, Rasputin the Mad Monk, Scream and Scream Again*, just to pick three of the best.

Throughout the '60s and '70s, he would return to the Dracula role, sometimes successfully but as often not. Jesus Franco's abysmal 1971 *Count Dracula* demonstrates how little control any actor has over a finished product. Though the film had an adequate budget and a script that stayed close to Stoker's source material, Franco never let Lee go after the character, and so it may be the dullest of his portrayals.

In many of those films—not *Count Dracula*—Lee co-starred with Peter Cushing, and each certainly owes some of his success to the other. They have different, complementing strengths as actors, and both have been equally successful on their own.

In recent years, Lee's best horror roles have been less conventional. He's excellent as an evil priest in *To the Devil, a Daughter* and as Lord Summerisle in *The Wicker Man*. As Hammer neared the end of its run, the *Dracula* series became so far removed from the original situation that Lee's imposing presence was all that kept the franchise from collapsing in on itself.

SIGNIFICANT CONTRIBUTIONS TO HORROR

***The Curse of Frankenstein* (1957)**

***The Horror of Dracula* (1958)**

***The Mummy* (1959)**

***Horror Hotel* (1960)**

***Rasputin the Mad Monk* (1966)**

***Dracula, Prince of Darkness* (1966)**

***Dracula Has Risen from the Grave* (1968)**

***Taste the Blood of Dracula* (1970)**

***Scream and Scream Again* (1970)**

***The Creeping Flesh* (1972)**

***The Wicker Man* (1975)**

***To the Devil, a Daughter* (1976)**

***Gremlins 2: The New Batch* (1990)**

rice Manson, Frank Chase; ***D:*** John Sherwood; ***W:*** Arthur Ross; ***M:*** Henry Mancini. **VHS, LV, Closed Caption** *USH, FCT*

Creepers

Jennifer Corvino (Jennifer Connelly) is just your average teen glamour-babe who's telepathically in tune with the insect world. Stranded in a tyrannical girl's school located in "the Swiss Transylvania," she helps John McGregor (Donald Pleasence), a crippled entomologist, and his chimpanzee assistant catch a monstrous murderer. Director Dario Argento isn't interested in normal "realistic" escapism. He exaggerates the conventions of horror in the same ways that the Italian westerns of the '60s and '70s built on their American predecessors. Some of the physical action has a cartoonish, Three Stooges quality. It's not meant to be funny, but Argento is so eager to sacrifice narrative logic for the sake of a shocking image that it's hard to say. Also, the continuity errors may be due to the film's having some 20 minutes cut from its original running time (under the title *Phenomena*). The Grand Guignol conclusion is a maggot-infested doozie. ***AKA:*** Phenomena. 🦴🦴🦴

1985 (R) 82m/C *IT* Jennifer Connelly, Donald Pleasence, Daria Nicolodi, Elenora Giorgi, Dalia di Lazzaro, Patrick Bauchau, Fiore Argento, Federica Mastroianni, Michele (Michael) Soavi, Gavin Friday; ***D:*** Dario Argento; ***W:*** Dario Argento, Franco Ferrini; ***C:*** Romano Albani; ***M:*** Simon Boswell. **VHS** *NLC*

"There are many vampires in the world today—you only have to think of the film business."

—Christopher Lee as quoted in *Films Illustrated*, August 1971.

"People used to think that when someone dies, a crow carries their soul to the land of the dead. But sometimes... only sometimes the crow brings that soul back to set the wrong things right."

—Sarah (Rochelle Davis) in *The Crow.*

The Creeping Flesh

Perhaps Cushing and Lee's most underrated work together is a complicated psychological tale that can be viewed as either supernatural horror or delusion. In 1893 Emmanuel Hildman (Peter Cushing) is an archeologist who's just found the "missing link," which in turn is the source of a phallic fossil. Emmanuel's half-brother James (Christopher Lee) runs a mental asylum. Emmanuel is obsessively overprotective of his daughter Penelope (Lorna Heilbron), and that's the real source of the story. However it's interpreted, this is a film about patriarchal power and the inability of men to understand women. Though the setting and casting make it look like a Hammer production, it's much more intricate and indirect. Also, despite the PG rating, the film contains a strong scene of sexual assault.

1972 (PG) 89m/C *GB* Peter Cushing, Christopher Lee, Lorna Heilbron, George Benson, Kenneth J. Warren, Duncan Lamont, Harry Locke, Hedger Wallace, Michael Ripper, Jenny Runacre; ***D:*** Freddie Francis; ***W:*** Peter Spenceley, Jonathan Rumbold; ***C:*** Norman Warwick. **VHS, LV** *COL, IME, MLB*

The Creeps

Librarian Anna (Rhonda Griffin) hires a detective (Justin Lauer) to get back the original manuscript of Mary Shelley's *Frankenstein,* which has been stolen by a mildly mad scientist, Berber (Bill Moynihan). He's using manuscripts and a crackpot lab to bring fictional monsters back to life. His experiment goes awry and the results are midget versions of Dracula (Phil Fondacaro), Frankenstein's Monster (Thomas Wellington), the Werewolf (Jon Simanton), and the Mummy (Joe Smith). It's a typical Full Moon production—low-budget, O.K. makeup, good effects, juvenile humor.

1997 (PG-13) 80m/C Phil Fondacaro, Rhonda Griffin, Justin Lauer, Bill Moynihan, Kristin Norton, Jon Simanton, Joe Smith, Thomas Wellington; ***D:*** Charles Band; ***W:*** Benjamin Carr. **VHS** *AFE*

Creepshow

Stephen King and George Romero pay affectionate and gory tribute to E.C. Comics with these five short films. With its use of split screens, animated frames, bright primary colors, live action that fades into and out of comic art, and even ads between the episodes, the collection is a true cinematic comic book. The best ones are "The Crate," with Adrienne Barbeau as a brassy shrew, and "Creeping up on You," with E.G. Marshall as a cheerfully wicked millionaire. King himself plays "Jordy." Fans of blood-soaked silliness won't be disappointed.

1982 (R) 120m/C Hal Holbrook, Adrienne Barbeau, Viveca Lindfors, E.G. Marshall, Stephen King, Leslie Nielsen, Carrie Nye, Fritz Weaver, Ted Danson, Ed Harris, John Amplas; ***D:*** George A. Romero; ***W:*** Stephen King; ***C:*** Michael Gornick. **VHS, LV, Closed Caption** *WAR*

Creepshow 2

Sequel anthology is second-tier material from Stephen King and screenwriter George Romero. All three stories lack interesting twists, depending instead on good production values and middling effects. The first, with George Kennedy and Dorothy Lamour as shopkeepers, is about a vengeance-seeking wooden Indian. The second puts four teenagers in the path of a lake-dwelling blob. In the third, a socialite (Lois Chiles) tries to run away from responsibility. None are as good as the better episodes of the first, or of King's *Cat's Eye* either. (King appears briefly as a truck driver in the last part.)

1987 (R) 92m/C Lois Chiles, George Kennedy, Dorothy Lamour, Tom Savini, Domenick John, Frank S. Salsedo, Holt McCallany, David Holbrook, Page Hannah, Daniel Beer, Stephen King, Paul Satterfield, Jeremy Green, Tom Wright; ***D:*** Michael Gornick; ***W:*** George A. Romero; ***C:*** Richard Hart, Tom Hurwitz. **VHS, LV, Closed Caption** *VTR*

Crocodile

Before the first image appears, the *Jaws* rip-off music tells you where you are.

Nuclear testing causes storms of Biblical proportions and unleashes a giant but only fleetingly visible crocodile that could swallow an ox, and does. The effects in this Thai-Korean production include what appears to be an upside bathroom drain for a waterspout, the occasional shots of odd pieces of the big croc, and some mondo stuff when a real crocodile is cut open. It all ends with three guys in a boat hunting the monster. Nothing new.

1981 (R) 95m/C Nat Puvanai, Tiny Tim, Angela Wells, Kirk Warren; ***D:*** Sompote Sands. **VHS** *NO*

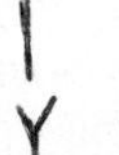

Cronos

Guillermo del Toro's elegant, haunting horror film is completely unlike any that have been produced in this country for years. It's reminiscent of David Cronenberg's early work, though del Toro's use of special effects is much more limited. Where Cronenberg might have exploded a human head onscreen, del Toro will use a glittering golden needle with fiendish delight. The bejeweled Cronos Device is a 14th century alchemist's invention that confers immortality upon the owner—immortality with a price. In present-day Mexico City, it falls into the possession of Jesus Gris (Federico Luppi), an aging antiques dealer who's devoted to his young granddaughter Aurora (Tamara Shanath). De la Guardia (Claudio Brook), a crippled and corrupt millionaire, owns the instruction manual for the gizmo and, along with his mercurial nephew (Ron Perlman), has been searching for it for years. The quirky humor has a strong Felliniesque edge, and compared to American horror movies, the pace is almost stately. There are also some genuinely tender moments, to go along with those that are utterly revolting. Writer/director del Toro tells the story through a series of slow, vivid nightmare images. More importantly, he got a winning performance from his star. Federico Luppi is the kind of actor that audiences warm to instantly, and so the film is much more involving than it sounds. Some of the scenes between him and Tamara Shanath are really touching. ***AKA:*** Chronos.

1994 (R) 92m/C *MX* Federico Luppi, Ron Perlman, Claudio Brook, Tamara Shanath, Margarita Isabel; ***D:*** Guillermo del Toro; ***W:*** Guillermo del Toro; ***C:*** Guillermo Navarro; ***M:*** Ian Deardon. **VHS, LV** *THV*

The Crow

In an unnamed, decaying inner city on Devil's Night (an excuse for arson before Halloween), Eric Draven (Brandon Lee) and his fiancee Shelly (Sofia Shinas) are murdered by four thugs. One year later, Eric rises out of the grave, literally, for revenge. Our young narrator Sarah (Rochelle Davis) explains that his love was so strong that a crow has brought him back to this world for revenge. The main villain is a Byronic gangster, Top Dollar (Michael Wincott), who lives incestuously with his half-sister Myca (Bai Ling). Eric's only ally is an honest beat cop named Albrecht (Ernie Hudson). The script, by David Schow and John Shirley from James O'Barr's comic book and strip, distills the story down to its basic elements, borrowing freely from the works of Poe and a hard-core rock sensibility. Virtually all of the action takes place at night, on rainy streets or in grimy interiors. Director Alex Proyas fills the screen with shiny blacks, deep grays, and red highlights. That dampens the film's violence while heightening the mood. The accidental death of Lee while making the film underscores its dark themes of resurrection and revenge.

1993 (R) 100m/C Brandon Lee, Ernie Hudson, Michael Wincott, David Patrick Kelly, Rochelle Davis, Angel David, Michael Massee, Bai Ling, Lawrence Mason, Bill Raymond, Marco Rodriguez, Anna Thomson, Sofia Shinas, Jon Polito, Tony Todd; ***D:*** Alex Proyas; ***W:*** David J. Schow, John Shirley; ***C:*** Darius Wolski; ***M:*** Graeme Revell. MTV Movie Awards '95: Best Song ("Big Empty"); Nominations: MTV Movie Awards '95: Best Film, Best Male Performance (Lee). **VHS, LV, Closed Caption** *TOU*

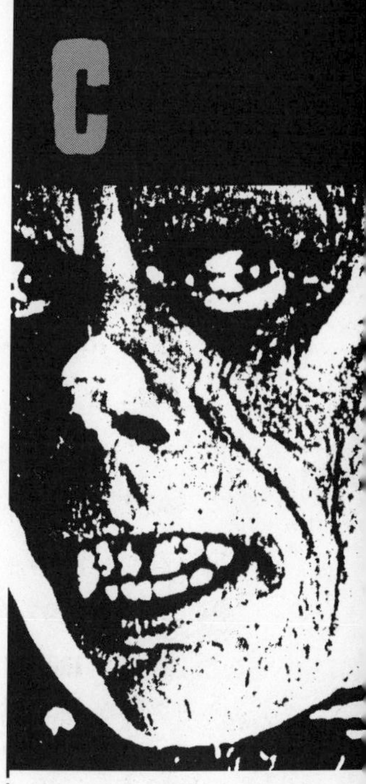

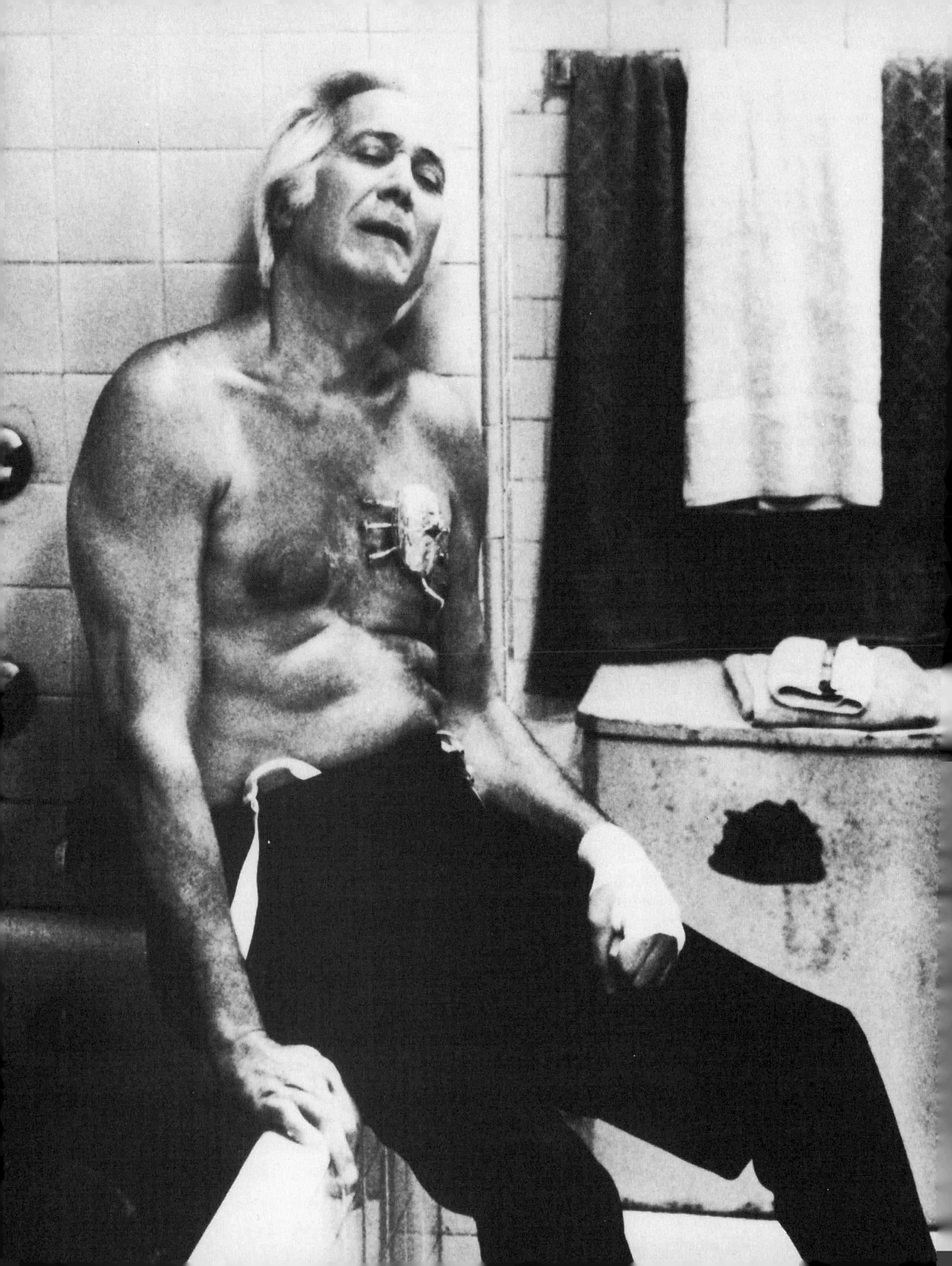

The Crow 2: City of Angels

Like most sequels, this one slavishly rehashes the most popular elements of the original. That calls for lots of inky dark atmosphere, violent special effects, and pop nihilism. The rest is nothing more than a second-rate revenge flick with a plot that lacks any complexity, and characters who have no personalities. Press notes explain that Sarah (Mia Kirshner) is a grown-up version of the character who was a child in the first film, though that's never explained onscreen. Ashe (Vincent Perez) is killed along with his young son by the sadistic drug lord Judah (Richard Brooks) and his henchmen, including Iggy Pop, and then is led back to life by a crow. Writer David Goyer tosses enough gimmicks to keep the action moving, but the script lacks the poetic flourishes that add so much to the first film. Director Tim Pope relies on computer-generated effects and models to keep the action lively in a strictly visual sense.

1996 (R) 93m/C Vincent Perez, Mia Kirshner, Iggy Pop, Richard Brooks, Ian Dury, Thuy Trang, Thomas Jane, Vincent Castellanos, Tracey Ellis; ***D:*** Tim Pope; ***W:*** David S. Goyer; ***C:*** Jean-Yves Escoffier; ***M:*** Graeme Revell. **VHS, LV, Closed Caption** *TOU*

Crucible of Horror

Michael Gough, seen more recently as Alfred the butler in the *Batman* series, plays a tyrannical suburbanite who's murdered by his wife and daughter (Yvonne Mitchell and Sharon Gurney). Gough's an excellent human monster, but they're all such unlikable characters that it's difficult to become sufficiently interested in their diabolical story. The dim lighting and faded print don't help either. As for the ending.... Writer Olaf Pooley plays the neighbor who arrives on horseback. For a grim '70s feminist double feature, watch this one with George Romero's *Season of the Witch.* ***AKA:*** Velvet House; The Corpse.

1969 91m/C *GB* Michael Gough, Yvonne Mitchell, Sharon Gurney, David Butler, Simon Gough, Nicholas Jones, Olaf Pooley, Mary Hignett; ***D:*** Viktors Ritelis; ***W:*** Olaf Pooley; ***C:*** John Mackey. **VHS** *MGM, FCT*

Crucible of Terror

Borrowing heavily from better Hammer films, this low-budget horror combines a cliched premise—mad artist (Mike Raven) who creates sculptures from living models—with a cast of unpleasant characters gathered at a depressing country house for the weekend. Thin production values and bottom-drawer acting finish it off. It's nice for American audiences to see that Brits can be just as hamfisted with this kind of exploitation as we can.

1972 95m/C *GB* Mike Raven, Mary Maude, James Bolam, John Arnatt, Ronald Lacey, Me Me Lay, Judy Matheson, Beth Morris, Melissa Stribling; ***D:*** Ted Hooker; ***W:*** Ted Hooker, Tom Parkinson; ***C:*** Peter Newbrook. **VHS** *MRV, GEM*

Cry of the Banshee

Oona (Elisabeth Bergner), a cliched and vaguely silly 16th century witch, vows vengeance on Lord Edward Whitman (Vincent Price) after his men attack and kill more of her people. Roderick (Patrick Mower) is her instrument. Compared to other witchcraft films of the era, this one is better than *Mark of the Devil,* but not nearly as complex as *The Conqueror Worm.* Also, it's not as much fun as director Gordon Kessler's *Scream and Scream Again.* Hugh Griffith has a nice cameo as a grave digger. If he's not at his best, Price is still fine.

1970 (PG) 87m/C *GB* Vincent Price, Elisabeth Bergner, Essy Persson, Hugh Griffith, Hilary Dwyer, Sally Geeson, Patrick Mower, Marshall Jones, Michael Elphick, Pamela Fairbrother, Robert Hutton; ***D:*** Gordon Hessler; ***W:*** Christopher Wicking, Tim Kelly; ***C:*** John Coquillon; ***M:*** Les Baxter. **VHS** *HBO*

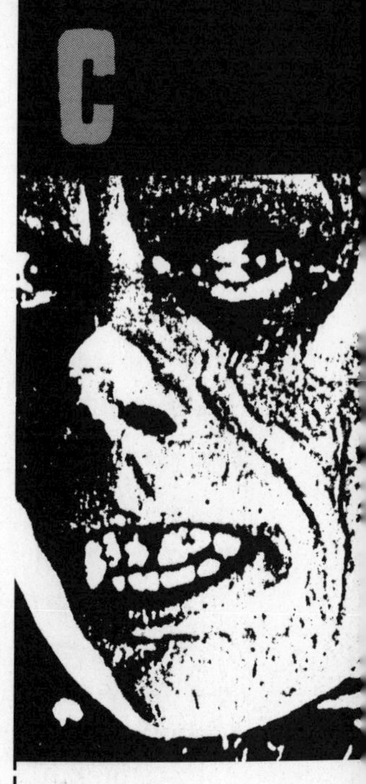

Jesus Gris (Federico Luppi) and the *Cronos* device.

"It has been written since the beginning of time, even unto these ancient stones, that evil supernatural creatures exist in a world of darkness; and that man, using the magic power of the ancient runic symbols, can call forth these powers of darkness...the demons of hell."

—Foreword to *Curse of the Demon.*

Cthulhu Mansion

This is probably the worst movie allegedly based on the works of H.P. Lovecraft. (Beyond the title, it has virtually nothing to do with HPL.) As an aging magician, Frank Finlay is far better than the weak material. His house is invaded by five of the most idiotic, poorly acted, poorly written thugs you'll ever see. It takes far too long for the forces of evil (or whatever) to rise out of the refrigerator and bump them all off. **Woof!**

1991 (R) 95m/C Frank Finlay, Marcia Layton, Brad Fisher, Melanie Shatner, Luis Fernando Alves, Kaethe Cherney, Paul Birchard, Francisco (Frank) Brana; ***D:*** J. Piquer Simon; ***W:*** J. Piquer Simon. **VHS, Closed Caption** *REP*

Cujo

Though this may not be the best adaptation of a Stephen King novel, it's certainly one of the most powerful and frightening. Like King, the filmmakers are working with both real and imagined terrors. Cujo, the rabid St. Bernard that traps a mother and her son (Dee Wallace Stone and Danny Pintauro), is a physical manifestation of the other problems the family is facing—infidelity, business catastrophe. The characters are the usual colorful, if familiar inhabitants of King's Yoknapatawpha County. The film itself is too long—director Lewis Teague's debut *Alligator* is much more economical—but the dog attacks in the second half are harrowing, and Cujo is as frightening as any of King's supernatural monsters.

1983 (R) 94m/C Dee Wallace Stone, Daniel Hugh-Kelly, Danny Pintauro, Ed Lauter, Christopher Stone, Kaiulani Lee, Mills Watson, Jerry Hardin, Billy Jacoby, Sandy Ward; ***D:*** Lewis Teague; ***W:*** Lauren Currier, Don Carlos Dunaway; ***C:*** Jan De Bont; ***M:*** Charles Bernstein. **VHS, LV** *WAR*

Cupid

Eric (Zach Galligan) has relationship problems, just like Norman Bates has mother problems and *The Stepfather* has domestic problems. That may be putting Eric in exalted company, but they are cut from the same cloth. The plot revolves around his unconventional courtship of Jennifer (Ashley Laurence). All he wants is "beauty, integrity, purity," and he'll kill anyone who gets in the way. Some of the acting is a bit too far over the top, but babyfaced Galligan is fine as psychoboy, and director Doug Campbell makes excellent use of a gaudy Gothic Victorian house for his setting, particularly in the second half.

1996 (R) 94m/C Zach Galligan, Ashley Laurence, Mary Crosby, Joseph Kell, Michael Bowen; ***D:*** Doug Campbell; ***W:*** David Benullo; ***C:*** M. David Mullen. **VHS, LV, Closed Caption** *LIV*

Curdled

As a little girl in Colombia, Gabriella (Angela Jones) develops a fascination with violent death which she takes with her to Miami. That predisposition makes her a natural for PFCS (Post Forensic Cleaning Service), Maids for Murders. At the same time, the Blueblood Killer (William Baldwin) is serially decapitating society matrons. Writers John Maass and Reb Braddock (who directs) deftly weave together Gabriella's obsessions as illustrated in her scrapbook, and the killer's acts. Joseph Julian Gonzalez's cheerful Latin score adds to the unusual and welcome humor. At times the influence of executive producer Quentin Tarantino is too obvious. (He also introduces the tape and comments at the end.) Angela Jones brings a bright, wide-eyed sexy curiosity to the macabre proceedings. The plotting is original and the satiric target is not so much violence as our national trivialization of it. For horror fans with a strong, skewed sense of humor, this is great stuff. The long "dance" scene is a high-water mark of '90s horror. Watch through the credits to see the coda.

1995 (R) 87m/C Angela Jones, William Baldwin, Mel Gorham, Barry Corbin, Bruce Ramsey, Daisy Fuentes, Lois Chiles, Carmen Lopez; ***D:*** Reb Braddock; ***W:*** John Maass, Reb Braddock; ***C:*** Steven Bernstein; ***M:*** Joseph Julian Gonzalez. **VHS, LV, Closed Caption** *TOU*

The Curse

Actor David Keith makes a credible directorial debut with a low-budget tale of environmental horror based on H.P. Lovecraft's story, "The Color out of Space." Young Zachary (Wil Wheaton) doesn't get along with his Bible-quoting stepfather (Claude Akins, who's very good). When something lands on their farm, Zach's suspicious. The effects range from excellent to ill-advised. Overall, the film is well paced and comfortable with the Tennessee locations, and it does a better job of making its subject seem real than many more expensive productions. The same story provides the source for *Die, Monster, Die* and one part of Stephen King's *Creepshow*. ***AKA:*** The Farm.

1987 (R) 92m/C Wil Wheaton, Claude Akins, Malcolm Danare, Cooper Huckabee, John Schneider, David Keith, Amy Wheaton, David Chaskin, Kathleen Jordan Gregory; ***D:*** David Keith; ***W:*** David Chaskin; ***C:*** Robert D. Forges. **VHS, LV, Closed Caption** *IME*

Curse 2: The Bite

Sequel-in-title-only finds a young fellow taking an ill-advised shortcut through a government installation in the desert. He's bitten on the hand by a nuclear serpent. Jamie Farr gives him the wrong antidote and then his whole arm turns into a snake! His girlfriend is not amused. Followed by two more sequels to date.

1988 (R) 97m/C Jill Schoelen, J. Eddie Peck, Jamie Farr, Savina Gersak, Bo Svenson, Sydney Lassick, Marianne Muellerliele, Terrence Evans; ***D:*** Fred Goodwin; ***W:*** Fred Goodwin, Susan Zelouf; ***C:*** Roberto D'Ettorre Piazzoli. **VHS** *TWE*

The Curse of Frankenstein

The Hammer organization's first foray into horror is one of its best—a fast-moving and fresh interpretation of a well-known story about the relationship between creator and creation. Peter Cushing is the brilliant young Baron who discovers the secret of life. Christopher Lee has a much smaller role as the Creature. (He and Cushing wouldn't really achieve equal footing until a year later with *The Horror of Dracula*.) Hazel Court, also familiar for her work in Roger Corman's low-budget movies, is the sexy Hammer heroine. Squeezing every penny out of a modest budget, the producers manage to create a credible mad scientist's laboratory. Cushing's approach to the role of Victor is more realistic and arrogant than Colin Clive's in 1931. Writer Jimmy Sangster compresses a complex literary work into a short, efficient screenplay with a neatly ironic ending. Terence Fisher's direction is equally economical. The humor is bleak, gory, and wry.

1957 83m/C *GB* Peter Cushing, Christopher Lee, Hazel Court, Robert Urquhart, Valerie Gaunt, Noel Hood; ***D:*** Terence Fisher; ***W:*** Jimmy Sangster; ***C:*** Jack Asher; ***M:*** James Bernard. **VHS** *WAR, MLB*

Curse of the Demon

Word has had it that producers forced director Jacques Tourneur to include explicit shots of the fire demon in his adaptation of M.R. James' great story "Casting the Runes." Though most critics decry the monster, I think this carefully made psychological horror needs those explicit moments. (Besides, hokey as the demon may be, it scared the hell out of me when I was ten years old.) Dana Andrews is excellent as the skeptical scientist who refuses to believe that Karswell (Niall MacGinnis) leads a cult of English satanists. The film's central conceit—the audience understands how important a slip of paper is

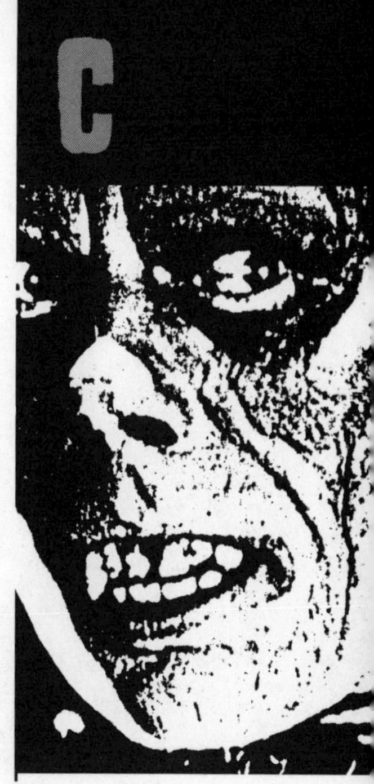

Christopher Lee in *The Curse of Frankenstein.*

while the hero treats it as a trifle—builds a unique suspense that's hard to describe. MacGinnis, perhaps more familiar to American audiences as Zeus in Ray Harryhausen's *Jason and the Argonauts,* steals the film. ***AKA:*** Night of the Demon; The Haunted.

1957 81m/B *GB* Dana Andrews, Peggy Cummins, Niall MacGinnis, Maurice Denham, Athene Seyler, Liam Redmond, Reginald Beckwith, Ewan Roberts, Peter Elliott, Brian Wilde; ***D:*** Jacques Tourneur; ***W:*** Charles Bennett, Hal E. Chester; ***C:*** Edward Scaife. **VHS, LV** *GKK, MLB*

Curse of the Mummy's Tomb

Like almost all Hammer features, this one looks and sounds great with plenty of familiar faces in the cast. Judged as a horror film though, it leaves much to be desired. The slowly developed plot concerns a love triangle and a mummy brought back to 1900 England by a crass American showman (scene-stealing character actor Fred Clark). Some suspense is created in the second half but overall, this one lacks the intensity and simplicity of the studio's 1959 *Mummy.*

1964 ?m/C Terence Morgan, Ronald Howard, Fred Clark, Jeanne Roland, George Pastell, Jack Gwillim, John Paul, Michael Ripper, Harold Goodwin, Dickie Owen; ***D:*** Michael Carreras; ***W:*** Michael Carreras, Henry Younger; ***C:*** Otto Heller.

The Curse of the Werewolf

One of Hammer's most successful horrors is second only to *The Wolfman* in its exploration of the subject. It's actually more serious in some ways and more carefully constructed. Writer/producer Anthony Hinds (whose script is based on Guy Endore's novel *Werewolf of Paris*) and director Terence Fisher see the cause of lycanthropy as human depravity, embodied in a corrupt aristocrat (Anthony Dawson). Shape-changing Leon (Oliver Reed) is the product of a series of atrocities that turn him into a genuinely tragic figure. The ambitious story is played out on a larger scale than most of the studio's efforts, and though the political element is strong, it never overpowers the personal. Religious themes are important, too. Reed, who does not appear until the midpoint, turns in a near flawless performance. Hinds reworks the material, not quite as successfully, in *Legend of the Werewolf.* 🦴🦴🦴🦴

1960 91m/C *GB* Oliver Reed, Clifford Evans, Yvonne Romain, Catherine Feller, Anthony Dawson, Michael Ripper, Peter Sallis; ***D:*** Terence Fisher; ***W:*** Anthony John Elder Hinds; ***C:*** Arthur Grant. **VHS** *USH, TLF, MLB*

Daddy's Girl

Transparently written and acted "evil child" horror has a few light scares, but the contrived plot is laid out far too predictably. Young Jody (Gabrielle Boni) loves her adoptive daddy (William Katt) so much that she knocks off anyone who threatens to separate them. Only cousin Karen (Roxana Zal) suspects what's going on. The other economic conflicts within the family are more accurate and believable. Mid-level production values give the film a brittle, shallow look. Director Martin Kitrosser vainly tries to make his pre-pubescent terror more threatening by photographing her and her pink bicycle from low angles. Judged against recent entries in the sub-genre, it's no better and no worse than *Mikey.* 🦴

1996 (R) 95m/C William Katt, Michele Greene, Roxana Zal, Mimi Craven, Whip Hubley, Gabrielle Boni; ***D:*** Martin Kitrosser; ***W:*** Steve Pesce. **VHS, LV, Closed Caption** *LIV*

Damien: Omen 2

Easily the weakest of the three *Omen* movies, this one plods along, killing off supporting characters at a predictable rate in increasingly grotesque ways. Now grown to a teenager, the son of Satan (Jonathan Scott-Taylor) goes off to military school where Lance Henriksen is the Staff Sergeant of Satan. The relative subtlety of the first film is nowhere to be found. In its place is cliched Hollywood nonsense involving a crow that apparently scares people to death. The best supernatural stories of this school use the religious element much more sparingly. The basic problem here is poor writing—in both plot and character development—so the presence of star William Holden is mostly wasted. An over-reliance on Jerry Goldsmith's hyperventilating music doesn't help either. ***AKA:*** Omen 2. 🦴

1978 (R) 110m/C William Holden, Lee Grant, Lew Ayres, Robert Foxworth, Sylvia Sidney, Lance Henriksen, Jonathan Scott-Taylor, Nicholas Pryor, Allan Arbus, Meshach Taylor; ***D:*** Don Taylor; ***W:*** Mike Hodges; ***C:*** Bill Butler; ***M:*** Jerry Goldsmith. **VHS, LV, Letterboxed** *FOX*

Dance of the Damned

Director Katt Shea Ruben makes terrific low-budget thrillers. This is one of the better romantic vampire flicks, subgenre: suicidal victim (it was an often-used formula on video in the late 1980s). He (Cyril O'Reilly) is a neck-nibbler who wants to know what the sun feels like. She (Starr Andreeff) is a stripper who wants to end it all because her life is such a mess. The exploitation elements aren't particularly strong. The story is really a two-person character study that could be more suspenseful and less sappy toward the end. Even so, some fine stylish touches make it worth a look. 🦴🦴🦴

1988 (R) 83m/C Cyril O'Reilly, Starr Andreeff; ***D:*** Katt Shea Ruben; ***W:*** Katt Shea Ruben, Andy Ruben. **VHS, LV** *NO*

Dario Argento's Trauma

Argento rounds up his usual suspects—beautiful teen heroine; threatening institu-

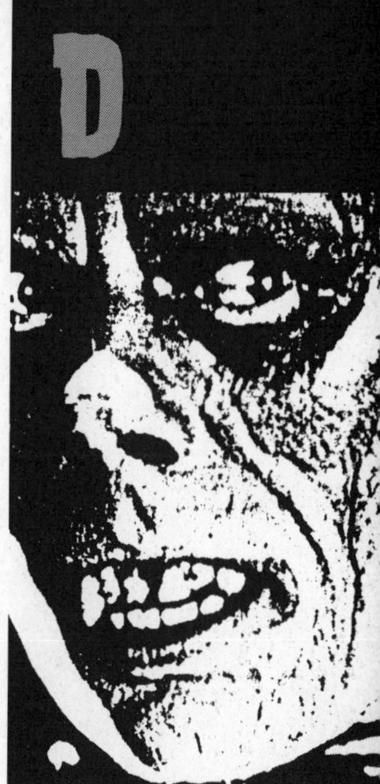

The 1960s

Hitchcock, Corman, and then Romero

Before it was over, the '60s became an unbelievably fertile, tumultuous, and creative decade for popular arts. As Jack Valenti, president of the Motion Picture Association of America, put it, "The national scene was marked by insurrection on the campus, riots in the streets, rise in women's liberation, protest of the young, questioning of church, doubts about the institution of marriage, abandonment of old guiding slogans, and the crumbling of social traditions. It would have been foolish to believe that movies, the most creative of artforms, could have remained unaffected by the change and torment in our society."

Horror was part of that change, and the first year produced one of the genuine greats, Alfred Hitchcock's *Psycho.* Hitch freely admitted that the film had been influenced by television and the rising popularity of low-budget horror films. He made it quickly, cheaply, and it became his biggest financial hit. (It was second to *Ben-Hur* at the boxoffice that year.) Every serious horror movie that's been made since acknowledges it in some way.

At the same time the Master was introducing audiences to a degree of cinematic fear they'd never experienced, in Italy, Mario Bava was reworking nightmares in *Black Sunday.* Roger Corman made both the super-quick-and-cheap *Little Shop of Horrors,* and his first exploration of Edgar Allan Poe, *The Fall of the House of Usher.*

In England, Hammer Films was at the top of its game with three of its best films, *The Brides of Dracula, The Two Faces of Dr. Jekyll,* and *The Curse of the Werewolf.*

Ironically, while Hitchcock's revolutionary work reached record numbers of moviegoers, Michael Powell's equally daring *Peeping Tom* somehow went too far. Pilloried by English critics, it was poorly distributed, often in censored versions. Until its release on video it remained, even among horror fans, a film that everybody talked about and nobody had seen.

Corman continued to work with Poe and his favorite star of the time, Vincent Price, in *The Pit and the Pendulum.* As a producer, Corman promoted the work of younger filmmakers, giving Francis Ford Coppola his first break with *Dementia 13.*

In 1962, audiences had a hard time understanding Herk Harvey's

tion, the Farraday Clinic; the psychic (Piper Laurie); the serial killer, this one called the Headhunter (who uses a mechanical decapitator); spooky empty houses, a veritable hurricane of wind and rain effects—and whips them into his usual fevered hash. Compared to other Argento Grand Guignols, the story of two young protagonists (his daughter Asia Argento and Christopher Rydell) seeking the identity of the killer as they're stalked by him (or her) makes moderately more sense than *Unsane* and *Creepers,* perhaps creditable to co-writer T.E.D. Klein. That relative coherence along with good Minnesota locations make this perhaps Argento's most accessible film for American audiences. ***AKA:*** Trauma. 🦴🦴🦴

1993 (R) 106m/C Christopher Rydell, Asia Argento, Laura Johnson, James Russo, Brad Dourif, Frederic For-

eerily nightmarish *Carnival of Souls,* and it, too, had to wait to be rediscovered by a new generation at film festivals and on video. *Burn Witch, Burn!* looked at witchcraft with unusual seriousness, and Robert Aldrich's *What Ever Happened to Baby Jane?* revived the sagging careers of Joan Crawford and Bette Davis, who both attacked difficult roles with real courage.

The audiences who'd flocked to *Psycho* didn't know what to make of Hitchcock's next work, the open-ended *The Birds,* a brilliant horror story that lacks both conventional explanations of its subject and a satisfying ending.

In 1965, Christopher Lee put on the cloak for a second time in *Dracula, Prince of Darkness.* Aldrich and Bette Davis reteamed for *Hush, Hush, Sweet Charlotte* with equally satisfying results, and Roman Polanski reached an international audience with his own low-budget shocker, *Repulsion.* Two years later, he made the comedy, *The Fearless Vampire Killers: Or Pardon Me, But Your Teeth Are in My Neck,* starring Sharon Tate, who would become his wife and later, a victim of the Manson "family." In 1968, Polanski had his biggest commercial hit with the phenomenally popular *Rosemary's Baby,* still one of the best big-budget, mainstream horrors.

Demonstrating the incredible variety of those times, '68 was also the year of Peter Bogdanovich's impressive debut, *Targets,* and Ingmar Bergman's only foray into the genre, *Hour of the Wolf.* In England, Michael Reeves' promising career was cut short by his death after he'd finished *The Conqueror Worm.*

On November 11, 1968, in reaction to the new frankness in film as seen in *Psycho* and *Rosemary,* the MPAA instituted the first "G-M-R-X" version of its rating system and effectively sidestepped government intrusion or censorship.

Finally, the decade ended with another low-budget black-and-white film that would change everything that came after it, George Romero's little zombie story, *Night of the Living Dead.*

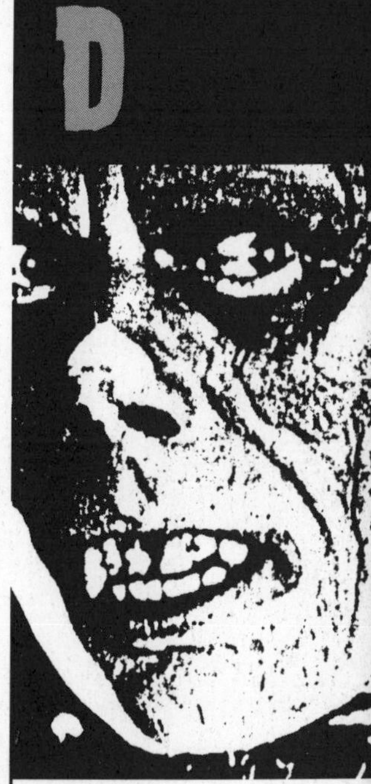

rest, Piper Laurie; ***D:*** Dario Argento; ***W:*** T.E.D. Klein, Dario Argento. **VHS, Closed Caption** *REP*

The Dark

The scares are supposed to come from a bogeyman from outer space with long hair and turn-signal eyes that emit laser beams. He also yanks people's heads off but he still isn't frightening. Neither is the loud voiceover whisper saying "the dark." The focus alternates between this critter stalking and the police standing around talking about how they can't do anything. The flat action turns funny in the last reel, stranding a competent cast without anything to do. John "Bud" Cardos reportedly replaced Tobe Hooper early in the filming. ***AKA:*** The Mutilator.

"I am everyone and no one, everything and nothing. Call me Darkman."

—Dr. Peyton Westlake (Liam Neeson) in *Darkman.*

1979 (R) 92m/C William Devane, Cathy Lee Crosby, Richard Jaeckel, Keenan Wynn, Vivian Blaine, Biff Elliot, Warren Kemmerling, Casey Kasem; ***D:*** John Cardos; ***W:*** Stanford Whitmore; ***C:*** John Morrill. **VHS** *NO*

The Dark

A creepy creepy premise, an overdeveloped sense of humor, and a deep streak of humanism make this a sleeper. The main characters are a half-mad ex-FBI agent (Brion James), a doctor (Stephen McHattie) on a mission, a sympathetic waitress (Cynthia Belliveau), an understanding gravedigger (Jaimz Woolvett), and the monstrous creature who lives under the cemetery and eats bodies. Robert C. Cooper's script follows the rules for the genre and gives fans what they want to see. But it goes a step farther and gives all of the characters—including the monster—more depth than you usually see in the genre. It's the kind of understanding that's found in stories like *Frankenstein* and *The Hunchback of Notre Dame,* but few others. By the way, the film has nothing to do with the identically titled 1979 release. 🦴🦴🦴

1994 (R) 90m/C Brion James, Jaimz Woolvett, Cynthia Belliveau, Stephen McHattie, Dennis O'Connor, Neve Campbell, Christopher Bondy, William Lynn; ***D:*** Craig Pryce; ***W:*** Robert Cooper. **VHS, LV, Closed Caption** *IMP*

Dark Angel: The Ascent

Director Linda Hassani makes a memorable debut with a horror film of humor, imagination, intelligence, and perhaps even wisdom. In the fire and brimstone hell of Hieronymus Bosch, the souls of sinners suffer eternal pain and fallen angels rule. Some of them still worship God even though they have been banished from his presence. These, after all, are rebellious angels, and none more than Veronica (Angela Featherstone), who dreams of the world above. Then she learns of an unguarded cavern that leads to the surface. Up she pops, buck naked, from a manhole cover in the middle of an unnamed city where things are just as nasty and dangerous as they are back home. Matthew Bright's script borrows bits from such diverse sources as *Splash, Death Wish,* and *The Exorcist,* but it's neither derivative nor predictable. Even the most jaded horror fan will be surprised by some of the twists. Fuzzbee Morse's score steals blatantly and effectively from Bernard Herrmann. Any fan who hasn't seen this one yet is in for a treat. 🦴🦴🦴🦴

1994 (R) 80m/C Charlotte Stewart, Daniel Markel, Michael C. Mahon, Nicholas Worth, Milton James, Angela Featherstone; ***D:*** Linda Hassani; ***W:*** Matthew Bright; ***M:*** Fuzzbee Morse. **VHS, Closed Caption** *FLL*

Dark Breed

The plot could have come straight from the 1950s, updated with creepy alien transformation effects, a *Predator*-inspired monster, and some remarkable stunt driving. Jack Scalia is the soldier in charge when a space shuttle crashes—in a nice variation on the standard lovers-lane opening—and the titular critters emerge. PM films are known for high-octane action and this one delivers, but the performances, particularly by Jonathan Banks as an infected astronaut and Robin Curtis as a pathologist, are a solid cut above average. So are the production values and the nice little riff on the famous "toast" scene from *Five Easy Pieces.* 🦴🦴🦴

1996 (R) 104m/C Jack Scalia, Jonathan Banks, Robin Curtis, Donna W. Scott; ***D:*** Richard Pepin. **VHS** *PMH*

Dark Carnival

A group of students opens a Halloween house to raise money, but their tricks and skits take on life of their own. Or is the nasty building inspector up to something? It's strictly tinfoil and papier-mache stuff

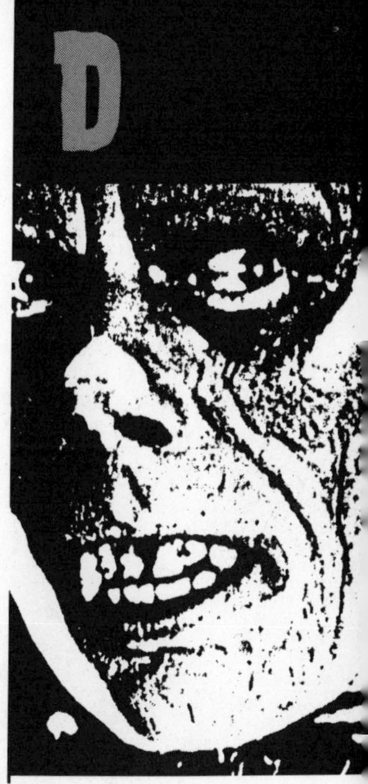

with some snotty goo, made on a bare-bones budget by a young no-name cast with more enthusiasm than expertise. In the end, it's not bad for what it is, and it doesn't pretend to be anything more.

1997 78m/C Miki Welling, Lynnie Horrigan, Micail Buse, Michael Murdock, Larry Crist; ***D:*** Eric Worthington; ***W:*** Kathleen Anne Byrnes. **VHS** *YHV*

The Dark Half

Stephen King's relationship with his nom de plume Richard Bachman provides the basis for this variation on Jekyll and Hyde. When serious novelist Thad Beaumont (Timothy Hutton) tries to kill off George Stark, the name he uses for violent potboilers, Stark appears in the flesh (Hutton again). As the greasy-haired George, Hutton looks like he's about to morph into David Keith, but he's still good in both roles. He gets excellent support from Amy Madigan, as his wife, and Michael Rooker, as the local sheriff. As always, writer/director George Romero's cluttered middle-class world adds a strong note of realism to the fantastic story. He also gives new meaning to the term "pencil neck." Perhaps the film is a little too long, but the ending justifies the length.

1991 (R) 122m/C Timothy Hutton, Amy Madigan, Michael Rooker, Julie Harris, Robert Joy, Kent Broadhurst, Beth Grant, Rutanya Alda, Tom Mardirosian, Chelsea Field, Royal Dano; ***D:*** George A. Romero; ***W:*** George A. Romero; ***M:*** Christopher Young. **VHS, Closed Caption** *ORI*

The Dark Secret of Harvest Home

In some ways, both Tom Tryon's novel and this made-for-TV adaptation can be seen as answers to *Rosemary's Baby.* The story is about the urban Constantin family (David Ackroyd, Rosanna Arquette, Joanna Miles) who move to the idyllic rural hamlet of Harvest Home. It's ruled by Widow Fortune (Bette Davis). The pace is slow and the conclusion is strong. This is Bette Davis' last major horror role and one of her best.

1978 118m/C Bette Davis, Rosanna Arquette, David Ackroyd, Rene Auberjonois, Michael O'Keefe, Joanna Miles; ***D:*** Leo Penn; ***W:*** Jennifer Miller, Jack Guss. **VHS** *USH*

Dark Tower

Barcelona architect Caroline Page (Jenny Agutter) is horrified to think that she's designed the highrise from hell. But why do people toss themselves from the 29th floor and go berserk in the lobby? A gum-snapping Michael Moriarty is the security guard troubled by visions. Director Ken Barnett (a pseudonym for Freddie Francis and his replacement, Ken Wiederhorn) relies too much on pointless shots of the building's glass-sided exterior and elevator shafts. The locations are different and the supporting cast—Carol Lynley, Kevin McCarthy, Theodore Bikel (who has a long, nutty monologue)—is strong, but the script lacks any real suspense or tension. The ending could have come from an E.C. comic.

1987 (R) 91m/C Michael Moriarty, Jenny Agutter, Theodore Bikel, Carol Lynley, Anne Lockhart, Kevin McCarthy; ***D:*** Ken Barnett, Freddie Francis, Ken Wiederhorn; ***W:*** Robert J. Avrech, Kenneth G. Blackwell. **VHS, LV** *VTR, IME*

Darkman

Writer/director Sam Raimi goes back to the Universal horror heroes of the 1930s for Dr. Peyton Westlake (Liam Neeson), "the man trapped inside the beast." He's a brilliant scientist on the verge of a huge discovery when the evil Durant (Larry Drake) tries to kill him, turning Westlake into a tortured, physically repulsive monster of great strength and uncontrollable rages. Raimi borrows bits from *The Invisible Man, The Wolf Man,* and even *Phantom*

Liam Neeson is *Darkman.*

of the Opera. The plot zooms along at a pace familiar to fans of his *Evil Dead* films, and it's punctuated with moments of crystal-clear detail. Topping off the inspired cast is Frances McDormand as a smart heroine. Danny Elfman's "cornball" score adds immeasurably. Followed by enjoyable video-premiere sequels. 🦴🦴🦴½

1990 (R) 96m/C Liam Neeson, Frances McDormand, Larry Drake, Colin Friels, Nelson Mashita, Jenny Agutter, Rafael H. Robledo, Nicholas Worth; ***D:*** Sam Raimi; ***W:*** Sam Raimi, Ivan Raimi, Daniel Goldin, Joshua Goldin, Chuck Pfarrer; ***C:*** Bill Pope; ***M:*** Danny Elfman. **VHS, LV, Closed Caption, DVD** *USH, CCB*

Darkman 2: The Return of Durant

"I choose to live on as a creature of the shadows—as Darkman!" So proclaims brilliant scientist Peyton Westlake in a sequel that harkens back to the great Universal horror series of the 1930s, most obviously *The Invisible Man*. Evil villain Durant (Larry Drake) has chosen to live on, too, even though he was turned to toast in the helicopter crash at the end of the first film. But villains that good are hard to come by, so he miraculously survived and has been in the traditional cinematic coma. Now, he's back and meaner than ever. Meanwhile, Westlake (Arnold Vosloo ably taking over for Liam Neeson) is still working on a formula for synthetic skin. Director/cinematographer Bradford May captures the energy, black humor, and comic book spirit of Sam Raimi's original, but this one lacks that extra spark, polish, and attention to small details that mark the best of Raimi's work. 🦴🦴🦴

1994 (R) 93m/C Arnold Vosloo, Larry Drake, Kim Delaney, Renee O'Connor, Rod Wilson; ***D:*** Bradford May; ***W:*** Steven McKay, Chuck Pfarrer; ***C:*** Bradford May; ***M:*** Randy Miller. **VHS, LV, Letterboxed, Closed Caption** *USH*

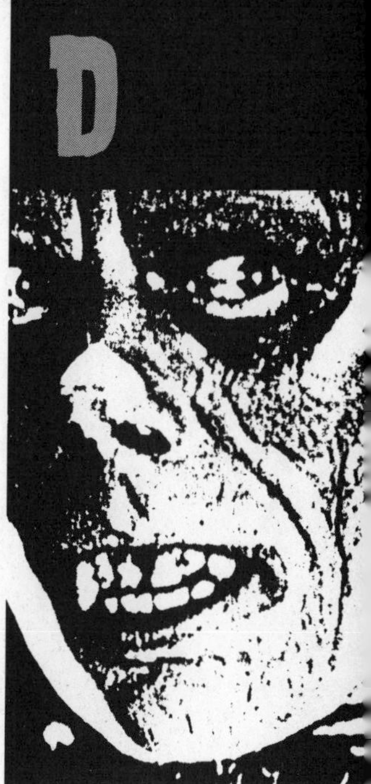

Darkman 3: Die Darkman Die

Third installment adds new characters and conflicts to the premise. Dr. Peyton Westlake (Arnold Vosloo), horribly disfigured in the first movie, is still searching for a formula for synthetic skin. The stuff he's got is temporary but it does allow him to look briefly like anyone else, including new bad guy, drug dealer Peter Rooker (Jeff Fahey, who has a grand time). Under Bradford May's direction, the pace is crisp and the action has a deliciously nasty edge, with beheadings and self-administered spinal surgery. A limited budget precludes the attention to brilliantly sharp individual detail that Sam Raimi brought to the original.

1995 (R) 87m/C Arnold Vosloo, Jeff Fahey, Darlanne Fluegel, Nigel Bennett, Roxann Biggs-Dawson; ***D:*** Bradford May; ***W:*** Mike Werb; ***M:*** Randy Miller. **VHS, LV, Letterboxed, Closed Caption** *USH*

Daughter of Darkness

Chicago schoolteacher Catherine (Mia Sara) goes to Bucharest in 1989 to search for her long-lost father (Anthony Perkins). Politics and the supernatural are combined with the emphasis too strongly on the former. Director Stuart Gordon tells a fairly pedestrian story, not nearly as innovative, interesting, or mad as *Re-Animator*. When it finally does get cranked up after almost an hour, it's too little too late. Neither star is very good, though admittedly they don't have much to work with. The Romanian locations have a grim, impoverished look.

1989 (R) 93m/C Mia Sara, Anthony Perkins, Robert Reynolds, Jack Coleman; ***D:*** Stuart Gordon. **VHS** *THV*

Daughters of Darkness

Without question, this is the most erotic lesbian vampire movie ever made. *The Hunger* pales in comparison. The opening shots establish a honeymooning couple, Stefan (John Karlen) and Valerie (Danielle Ouimet), married only a few hours, but already being divided by dishonesty and tension. After an unplanned stop at a huge, empty seaside hotel, they meet the Countess (Delphine Seyrig) and her secretary Ilona (Andrea Rau), glamorous women languid as cats. The level of sexual uncertainty among the quartet rises steadily and largely without the expected conventions. The film is beautifully written and acted on a curiously conversational level. The filmmakers approach their subject from the edges. For example, they delay the introduction of key characters and information, and they use color, pace, and camera angles to keep the viewer off balance. The Anchor Bay "collector's edition" is the full 100-minute version, more than 12 important minutes longer than the U.S. theatrical release, in a beautifully restored widescreen image. ***AKA:*** Le Rouge aux Levres; Blut an den Lippen; Erzebeth; The Promise of Red Lips; The Red Lips.

1971 (R) 87m/C *BE GE IT FR* Delphine Seyrig, John Karlen, Daniele Ouimet, Andrea Rau, Paul Esser, Georges Jamin, Joris Collet, Fons Rademakers; ***D:*** Harry Kumel; ***W:*** Harry Kumel, Pierre Drouot, Jean Ferry; ***C:*** Eddy van der Enden. **VHS, Letterboxed** *FCT, VTR*

Dawn of the Dead

Ambitious sequel actually builds on the premise of the first film and expands the original premise into more overtly political realms. After the "living dead" plague spreads into cities, four survivors (Gaylen

Ross, David Emge, Ken Foree, and Scott H. Reiniger) take refuge in a huge shopping mall and try to seal it off from the flesh-eating zombies. George Romero says that the Monroeville Shopping Center where the film was made is "a temple to consumer society." Does he then mean to drive the moneychangers from that temple? The Anchor Bay Entertainment tape contains scenes that were cut from the original theatrical release. ***AKA:*** Zombie; Zombies.

1978 126m/C David Emge, Ken Foree, Gaylen Ross, Scott H. Reiniger, David Crawford, David Early, Tom Savini, George A. Romero; ***D:*** George A. Romero; ***W:*** George A. Romero; ***C:*** Michael Gornick. **VHS, LV** *VTR, FCT*

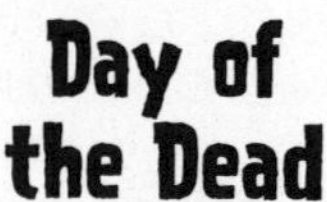

Day of the Dead

The third (and probably the final) installment of George Romero's trilogy opens inside a bare cinderblock room where Sara (Lori Cardillo) stares at a calendar on the wall. Clearly, the original situation where bodies rise up to devour the living has deteriorated. A small group of scientists and soldiers is trapped inside an underground Florida missile installation. Do they study the living dead and possibly learn how to domesticate them? Or will the military types, under the command of a martinet, screw things up even more? Romero's social criticism is even stronger than it was in *Dawn of the Dead,* making for a slow first hour. The conclusion contains some of Tom Savini's most grotesque, detailed, and sophisticated gore effects.

1985 91m/C Lori Cardille, Terry Alexander, Joe Pilato, Jarlath Conroy, Richard Liberty; ***D:*** George A. Romero; ***W:*** George A. Romero; ***C:*** Michael Gornick. **VHS, LV** *IME, VTR*

Dead Again

Kenneth Branagh follows up his bravura debut *Henry V* with this unembarrassed and unhinged reincarnation mystery. In the present, private eye Mike Church (Branagh) agrees to help amnesia victim Grace Sharp (Emma Thompson). With the help of Madison (Derek Jacobi), an antiques dealer/hypnotist, they learn that they're also Roman Strauss and his wife Margaret. The problem: Roman murdered Margaret. Are they bound to reenact their fate? Before the end, it becomes even sillier, but who cares? Branagh revels in the crazy plot details, switching between black and white and color, and he's no more subtle with that huge scissors sculpture. Fans of the older Universal horror and suspense films will really like this one.

1991 (R) 107m/C Kenneth Branagh, Emma Thompson, Andy Garcia, Lois Hall, Richard Easton, Derek Jacobi, Hanna Schygulla, Campbell Scott, Wayne Knight, Christine Ebersole; ***Cameos:*** Robin Williams; ***D:*** Kenneth Branagh; ***W:*** Scott Frank; ***C:*** Matthew F. Leonetti; ***M:*** Patrick Doyle. **VHS, LV, Letterboxed, Closed Caption** *PAR, CCB*

Dead Alive

Peter Jackson's gorefest comedy begins with a parody of *Raiders of the Lost Ark,* then shifts gears and slams into gross-out mode. The stomach-churning starts when Lionel's (Timothy Balme) mother (Elizabeth Moody) eats her own ear and it gets much, much worse. She was bitten, you see, by a Sumatran rat-monkey, causing no end of problems for Lionel and his beloved Paquita (Diana Penalver) in New Zealand, 1957. Like *Evil Dead* and *Re-Animator,* the film establishes an unhinged internal logic, then, having set its grotesque wheels in motion, it charges forward, relentlessly breaking new

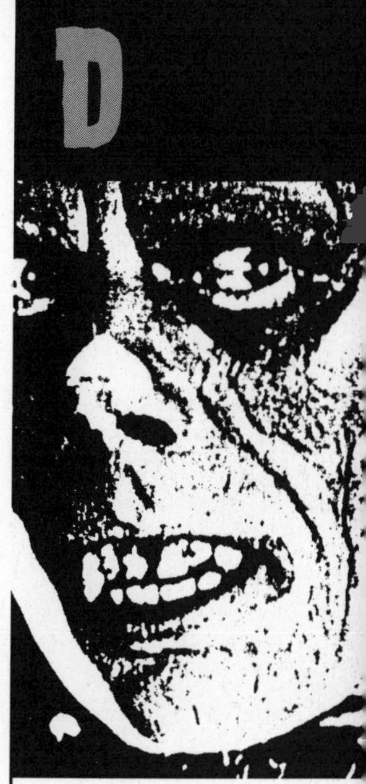

George A. Romero's *Dawn of the Dead.*

"You can try to kill me, Dan. But you can't. You can only make me dead."

—Dobbs (Jack Albertson) to Dan (James Farentino) in *Dead and Buried.*

boundaries of bad taste wherever it goes. The slapstick guts and gore are so excessive that they are no longer disgusting. Required viewing for fans of the strong stuff. ***AKA:*** Braindead. 🦴🦴🦴🦴

1993 97m/C *NZ* Timothy Balme, Elizabeth Moody, Diana Penalver, Ian Watkin, Breanda Kendall, Stuart Devenie; ***D:*** Peter Jackson; ***W:*** Peter Jackson. **VHS, LV, Closed Caption** *THV, FCT*

Dead and Buried

Anyone unfamiliar with this largely unknown shocker is in for a real treat. It's one of the best sleepers around, filled with jolts and surprises. James Farentino is the sheriff of Potters Bluff, a New England seaside town where bizarre events are taking place, and seem, somehow, to involve his sweet wife (Melody Anderson) and the garrulous undertaker/coroner (Jack Albertson). The script by Ronald Shusett and Dan O'Bannon combines a series of genuinely horrifying images with macabre humor and a cold, fog-shrouded atmosphere. Look for Robert Englund and Barry Corbin as townsfolk, and Tim Burton's squeeze Lisa Marie as a hitchhiker. 🦴🦴🦴🦴

1981 (R) 95m/C James Farentino, Jack Albertson, Melody Anderson, Lisa Blount, Bill Quinn, Michael Pataki, Robert Englund, Barry Corbin, Lisa Marie; ***D:*** Gary Sherman; ***W:*** Dan O'Bannon, Ronald Shusett. **VHS** *NO*

Dead Heat

Lame humor is tacked onto an unpleasant plot with lots of gory effects when reanimated dead cop Roger Mortis (Treat Williams) and his partner (Joe Piscopo) have 12 hours to find Roger's killer before he decomposes. Meanwhile, Vincent Price is trying to sell immortality to rich people. Most of the effects involve corpses being shot repeatedly with automatic weapons. This crap was directed by novice Mark Goldblatt and written by novice Terry Black. Inexperience is no excuse. **Woof!**

1988 (R) 86m/C Joe Piscopo, Treat Williams, Lindsay Frost, Darren McGavin, Vincent Price, Keye Luke, Clare Kirkconnell; ***D:*** Mark Goldblatt; ***W:*** Terry Black; ***C:*** Robert Yeoman; ***M:*** Ernest Troost. **VHS, LV, Closed Caption** *VTR*

Dead Man's Eyes/ Pillow of Death

Overlapping love triangles are the basis of *Dead Man's Eyes,* a poorly plotted horror-mystery. They're composed of an artist (Lon Chaney, Jr.), his fiancee (Jean Parker), his model (Acquanetta), the model's beau (Paul Kelly), and the fiancee's ex-boyfriend (George Meeker). Cornea transplants are the gimmick. The story is too talky and built on conventions that work well on radio, but not on the screen. The costumes are cooler than the characters. Acquanetta is out of her depth even in these shallow dramatic waters. The second half of the double feature, *Pillow of Death,* is much more enjoyable. It's unusually sharp with crabby humor and a tighter plot. Lawyer Chaney is accused of murdering his wife by a bunch of goony psychics. The story works through all of your basic haunted house conventions with some decent twists. Solid performances throughout. 🦴🦴

1944 130m/B Acquanetta, J. Edward Bromberg, Rosalind Ivan, Wilton Graff, Bernard B. Thomas, Lon Chaney Jr., Brenda Joyce, George Cleveland, Clara Blandick, Paul Kelly, Jean Parker, George Meeker; ***D:*** Wallace Fox, Reginald LeBorg; ***W:*** George Bricker, Dwight V. Babcock. **VHS** *USH*

Dead Men Walk

George Zucco plays the dual role of the good brother Lloyd and his evil twin Elwin who, with the aid of his assistant played by Dwight Frye, is reborn as a vampire. The low-budget effort is scratchy and dark on video. As the romantic lead David, Nedrick Young made a wise career change when he became a writer. Though he was blacklisted, he also won an Oscar for *The Defiant Ones*. ***AKA:*** Creatures of the Devil. 🦴🦴

1943 65m/B George Zucco, Mary Carlisle, Dwight Frye, Nedrick Young, Al "Fuzzy" St. John, Fern Emmett, Robert Strange; ***D:*** Sam Newfield; ***W:*** Fred Myton; ***C:*** Jack Greenhalgh. **VHS** *VCI, MRV, SNC*

Dead of Night

The premise has been reused countless times. An architect (Mervyn Johns) is invited to a country house. Upon arriving, he claims to have seen the house and the people he meets there in a recurring dream. He can almost "remember" what's going to happen. An anthology of stories follows. The subjects are a premonition, a mirror, golf, a hidden attic room, etc., and they're handled with a fine combination of humor and suspense. The segment about a ventriloquist (Michael Redgrave) and his dummy is in part a basis for William Goldman's *Magic*. Of all the older horrors waiting to be remade, this may be the best. Beware copies of the film recorded in the "EP" mode; they're grainy and barely viewable. 🦴🦴🦴½

1945 102m/B *GB* Michael Redgrave, Mervyn Johns, Sally Ann Howes, Basil Radford, Naunton Wayne, Roland Culver, Googie Withers, Frederick Valk, Antony Baird, Judy Kelly, Miles Malleson, Ralph Michael, Mary Merrall, Renee Gadd, Michael Allan, Robert Wyndham, Esme Percy, Peggy Bryan, Hartley Power, Elizabeth Welch, Magda Kun, Carry Marsh; ***D:*** Alberto Cavalcanti, Charles Crichton, Basil Dearden, Robert Hamer; ***W:*** T.E.B. Clarke, John Baines, Angus MacPhail; ***C:*** Stanley Pavey, Douglas Slocombe; ***M:*** Georges Auric. **VHS** *NO*

Dead Ringers

David Cronenberg forgoes graphic special effects for much darker psychological horrors, and makes perhaps his most accomplished and frightening film. Loosely based on truth, it's the story of twin gynecologists Bev and Elliot Mantle (both Jeremy Irons), and their relationship to an actress, Claire Niveau (Genevieve Bujold). The source of the tension is a single identity split into two bodies, but what sets this one apart is its lack of a sympathetic protagonist. There's no hero to root for, and no heroine to be placed in danger. In their place is a slowly thickening atmosphere of fear that's underlined by glossy, stylized sets and pervasive religious imagery. Cronenberg's fans will also catch the reference to *Scanners*. One of the best. 🦴🦴🦴🦴

1988 (R) 117m/C *CA* Jeremy Irons, Genevieve Bujold, Heidi von Palleske, Barbara Gordon, Shirley Douglas, Stephen Lack, Nick Nichols; ***D:*** David Cronenberg; ***W:*** David Cronenberg, Norman Snider; ***C:*** Peter Suschitzsky; ***M:*** Howard Shore. Genie Awards '89: Best Actor (Irons), Best Director (Cronenberg), Best Film; Los Angeles Film Critics Association Awards '88: Best Director (Cronenberg), Best Supporting Actress (Bujold); New York Film Critics Awards '88: Best Actor (Irons). **VHS, LV** *CCB, CRC, VTR*

Dead Waters

Mariano Baino's debut is basically an homage to the horror films of Dario Argento. He has the Argento dripping-water thing going, and the prowling camera thing and the doesn't-make-a-lick-of-sense thing. Almost 30 minutes have passed before you have the first hint of what's going on. And even then, all that's revealed is that Elizabeth (Louise Salter), a young English woman, has something to do with a remote convent. Most of the violence occurs off camera. The grossest material involves eating raw fish. Somehow, though, it all works. Despite the slow pace, the atmosphere is thick and Baino's screen is filled with grotesque faces and disturbing images. The Anglo-Russo-Italian production deserves the attention of horror fans, particularly those with a taste for European fare. 🦴🦴🦴

1997 90m/C *IT RU GB* Louise Salter, Venera Simmons, Maria Kapnist; ***D:*** Mariano Baino; ***W:*** Mariano Baino, Andrew Bark. **VHS** *YHV*

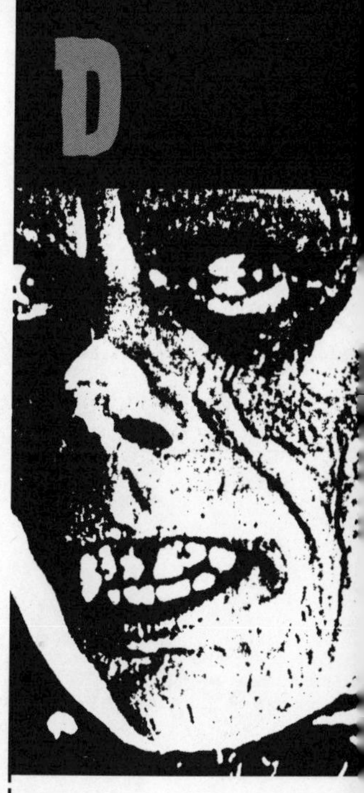

John Smith (Christopher Walken) in *Dead Zone.*

Dead Zone

David Cronenberg's thoughtful adaptation of Stephen King's novel is one of the best for both, though in many ways, it's not typical of either. John Smith (Christopher Walken) comes out of a five-year coma to find that he has unwanted psychic powers. Though Walken has gone on to create characters of much more flamboyant weirdness, this is one of the early defining roles. In Herbert Lom's long career of character parts, Dr. Weizak may be his best. Martin Sheen's chest-thumping politico is a maniacal villain. Such key details as a murderer's bedroom that reflects his madness are carefully chosen, and the film contains a suicide that is about as frightening as any put on film. Cronenberg's work has gone in different directions, but echoes of this one can be seen in *The Dark Half* and other King films and fiction.

1983 (R) 104m/C Christopher Walken, Brooke Adams, Tom Skerritt, Martin Sheen, Herbert Lom, Anthony Zerbe, Colleen Dewhurst; ***D:*** David Cronenberg; ***W:*** Jeffrey Boam; ***C:*** Mark Irwin; ***M:*** Michael Kamen. **VHS, LV, Closed Caption** *PAR*

Deadly Blessing

After Martha's (Maren Jensen) husband is killed, she finds herself alone in a rural "Hittite" community. These are not the Hittites of ancient history, but vaguely Amish folk who are obsessed by fear of the "Incubus." Even so, Ernest Borgnine and Michael Berryman are believably threatening. Some of the spider stuff involving a young Sharon Stone works well and so does the infamous snake scene. If director Wes Craven doesn't reach the imaginative commercial success that he realizes with the *Elm Street* series, he creates legitimate tension. Though he doesn't hold much back in the last reel, the overt violence is kept to a minimum, making this one of his best efforts. 🦴🦴🦴

1981 (R) 104m/C Maren Jensen, Susan Buckner, Sharon Stone, Ernest Borgnine, Jeff East, Lisa Hartman Black, Lois Nettleton, Colleen Riley, Douglas Barr, Michael Berryman; ***D:*** Wes Craven; ***W:*** Wes Craven, Glenn Benest, Matthew F. Barr; ***C:*** Robert C. Jessup; ***M:*** James Horner. **VHS**

Deadly Friend

Paul (Matthew Laborteaux) is a boy genius who invents an artificially intelligent robot, and does a little brain surgery on the side. Both skills come in handy when his pretty next-door neighbor Sam (Kristy Swanson) is hurt by her abusive father. The second half is a variation on *Frankenstein* concerning a creator's responsibility to his creation. The movie has such good intentions and good ideas that you wish it were better. The robot shouldn't be so cute; the story should be less dependent on stereotypes. It's aimed at a young audience, but kids can recognize formulas, too. Fans of director Wes Craven's *Elm Street* series will find some similarities, but they may be surprised at the film's human side. 🦴🦴🦴

1986 (R) 91m/C Matthew Laborteaux, Kristy Swanson, Michael Sharrett, Anne Twomey, Richard Marcus, Anne Ramsey; ***D:*** Wes Craven; ***W:*** Bruce Joel Rubin; ***C:*** Philip Lathrop; ***M:*** Charles Bernstein. **VHS, LV, Closed Caption** *WAR*

The Death Artist

Remake of Roger Corman's *Bucket of Blood* misses the hip, on-the-fly combination of dark humor and horror that made the original an enduring cult favorite. (He directed the first film and was executive producer on this one.) Tacky, flashy sets; lots of camp dialogue, little action. Star Anthony Michael Hall is too thick-bodied, sluggish, and charmless to generate any sympathy or interest. He's Walter Paisley, a nebbish busboy at JabberJaws coffee shop and performance studio. A wannabe who's suffering from an extreme case of artist's block, he accidentally elects to turn his models into his art, just as Vincent Price did in *House of Wax* and Boris Karloff in *Cauldron of Blood*. Shadoe Stevens steals the show as a pompous poet. In the second half, the film makes a brief, uncomfortable shift in tone from comic to serious. Attacking the contemporary art biz for being phony, shallow, and trendy is shooting fish in a barrel and this particular fish has been shot many times before. 🦴

1995 (R) 79m/C Anthony Michael Hall, Darcy Demoss, Shadoe Stevens, Paul Bartel, Mink Stole; ***D:*** Michael James McDonald; ***W:*** Michael James McDonald, Brendan Broderick; ***C:*** Christopher Baffa; ***M:*** David Wurst, Eric Wurst. **VHS** *NHO*

Death by Invitation

Early '70s rarity is worth seeking out for fans of the bizarre. The tired story is about a Colonial-era witch (Shelby Levington) who is reincarnated and seeks vengeance on the ancestors of her killer (Aaron Phillips). The opening scenes are balanced between incoherence and boredom. That part ends with an inspired monologue about militant female-chauvinist lesbian Indians. That, in turn, is matched later by a eulogy taken from the Book of Job. Though writer/director Ken Friedman has an invisible budget, the grainy black-and-white photography recalls *Carnival of Blood*. Some of the soundtrack could have come from a pinball game; other parts are acid-laced Muzak. Altogether indescribable. 🦴🦴🦴

1971 m/C Shelby Levington, Aaron Phillips, Norman Page; ***D:*** Ken Friedman; ***W:*** Ken Friedman. **VHS** *SMW*

Death Ship

This ocean-going Amityville is one of the most boring horror movies ever made. It's about the unspeakable terror of machinery operating itself. To that end, it features dozens of shots of piston rods, valves, and

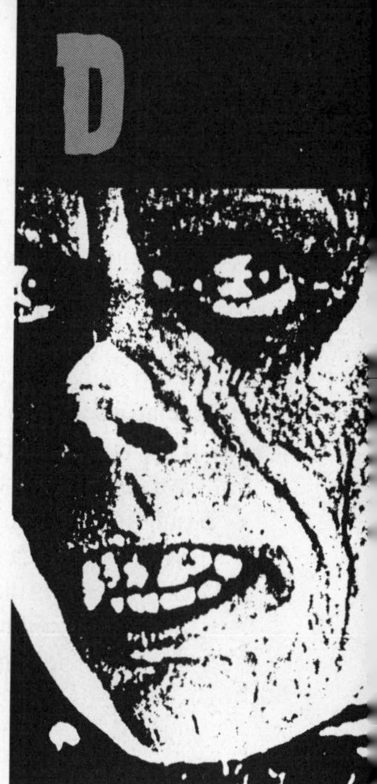

Jon Voight, Billy McKinney, and Burt Reynolds in *Deliverance.*

the like which might have been taken from those short movies they used to show in shop class. Watching George Kennedy run amuck in the last reel is no better and certainly no more frightening. The silliest moment occurs earlier when the rust bucket title character sneaks up on its victims. **Woof!**

1980 (R) 91m/C *GB CA* George Kennedy, Richard Crenna, Nick Mancuso, Sally Ann Howes, Saul Rubinek, Kate Reid, Victoria Burgoyne, Danny Higham, Jennifer McKinney; ***D:*** Alvin Rakoff; ***W:*** John Robins; ***C:*** Rene Verzier. **VHS** *NLC*

Deep Red: Hatchet Murders

Argento's excesses tend to turn comic in translation and this slasher flick is no exception. At first. For American audiences, the presence of David Hemmings, as a pianist who witnesses the first murder, helps considerably. Yes, he did the same in *Blow Up,* though that's where any useful comparison begins and ends. The interplay between him and Gianna (Daria Nicolodi, Argento's wife), a reporter, adds the right intentional humor to the violent proceedings. Many of the visual and narrative devices are repeated in *Terror at the Opera* and *Unsane*. By the middle, Argento's flowing style and relatively understandable plot make this one of his better efforts. ***AKA:*** The Hatchet Murders; Profundo Rosso; Dripping Deep Red; The Sabre Tooth Tiger; Deep Red.

1975 100m/C *IT* David Hemmings, Daria Nicolodi, Gabriele Lavia, Macha Meril, Eros Pagni, Guiliana Calandra, Erykah Badu, Clara Calamai, Nicoletta Elmi; ***D:*** Dario Argento; ***W:*** Dario Argento, Barnardino Zapponi; ***C:*** Luigi Kuveiller. **VHS** *QVD*

Deepstar Six

During the spate of low-budget underwater horrors made in the wake of *The Abyss,* this one hit bottom. It has the same plot as the others, with scientists at the seafloor upsetting a prehistoric creature. Fans will catch bits cadged from *Alien, The Beast from 20,000 Fathoms, 20,000 Leagues under the Sea, Humanoids from the Deep* and, of course, *Jaws*. The critter may be the least frightening construction of latex and foam rubber ever to be plopped in front of a camera.

1989 (R) 97m/C Taurean Blacque, Nancy Everhard, Greg Evigan, Miguel Ferrer, Matt McCoy, Nia Peeples, Cindy Pickett, Marius Weyers; ***D:*** Sean S. Cunningham; ***W:*** Lewis Abernathy, Geof Miller. **VHS, LV** *LIV*

Def by Temptation

From the beginnings of the horror film, the vampire story has been based on sexual attitudes, preconceptions, and stereotypes. And in the sexual stereotype department, no group in America carries more baggage than black men. They're the subject of James Bond III's impressive debut. The monster here is the Temptress (Cynthia Bond, no relation to JBIII), who "wants to remain in the fallen lustful state of existence...incarnate in the flesh." She picks up men in a New York bar, takes them back to her loft, and they're never seen again. Her real prey is a young divinity student undergoing a crisis of faith. Bond makes several critical observations about male sexual irresponsibility. To one degree or another, the victims deserve their fate. ("I thought I could just walk away," one character says. "Men are supposed to have it like that.") But the best part of the story is its strong traditional moral sense, so conspicuously lacking in recent horror films. Also, fans will notice that the 1990 film eerily pre-dates *The X-Files* in its approach to the subject and in Bill Nunn's character. (By the way, on the DVD version, commentary is provided by Yours Truly.)

1990 (R) 95m/C James Bond III, Kadeem Hardison, Bill Nunn, Samuel L. Jackson, Minnie Gentry, Rony Clanton, Cynthia Bond, John Canada Terrell; ***D:*** James Bond III; ***W:*** James Bond III; ***C:*** Ernest R. Dickerson. **VHS, LV, DVD** *TTV*

Deliverance

Though it's not usually considered part of the genre, John Boorman's adaptation of James Dickey's best-seller is a journey into a mythic wilderness where monsters dwell. Four suburbanites (Burt Reynolds, Jon Voight, Ned Beatty, Ronny Cox) head out for a weekend canoe trip on a river about to be dammed by the power company. They're attacked by predatory subhuman redneck sodomites in one of the most frightening and humiliating rape scenes ever put on film. The vicious act has been foreshadowed by images of inbred hillbillies and explosive large-scale destruction. A growing atmosphere of dread transforms the simple adventure into a real horror—the particulars of violent death have seldom been depicted more realistically. The conclusion has been copied by *Carrie* and countless others. Yes, that's Ed O'Neill as a deputy and James Dickey as the sheriff.

1972 (R) 109m/C Jon Voight, Burt Reynolds, Ronny Cox, Ned Beatty, James Dickey, Bill McKinney, Ed O'Neill, Charley Boorman; ***D:*** John Boorman; ***W:*** James Dickey; ***C:*** Vilmos Zsigmond; ***M:*** Eric Weissburg. **VHS, LV, Letterboxed** *WAR, FCT*

Dementia 13

Comparing Francis Ford Coppola's Gothic debut to the other low-budget Corman productions of the early 1960s, it's easy to see hints of the genius that would follow. Coppola tells a fairly simple story of ghosts and greed with pretty blonde Louise (Luana Anders) trying to pry loose some of the Haloran family fortune from the possibly demented matriarch (Ethne Dunn). At least, that's the way things begin. It's obvious that Coppola is using Hitchcock's *Psycho* as his model. A key watery moment may be the first homage to the shower

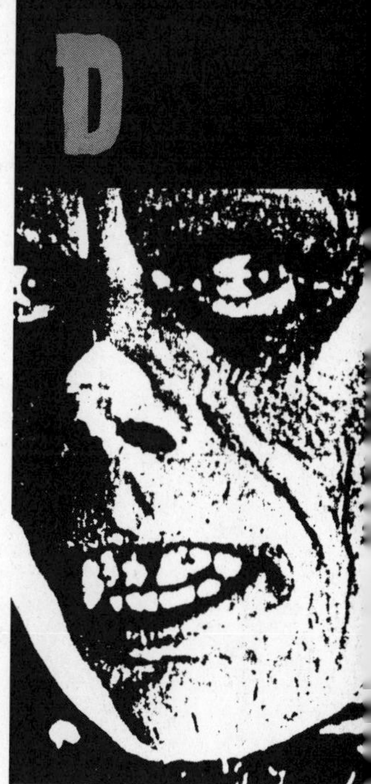

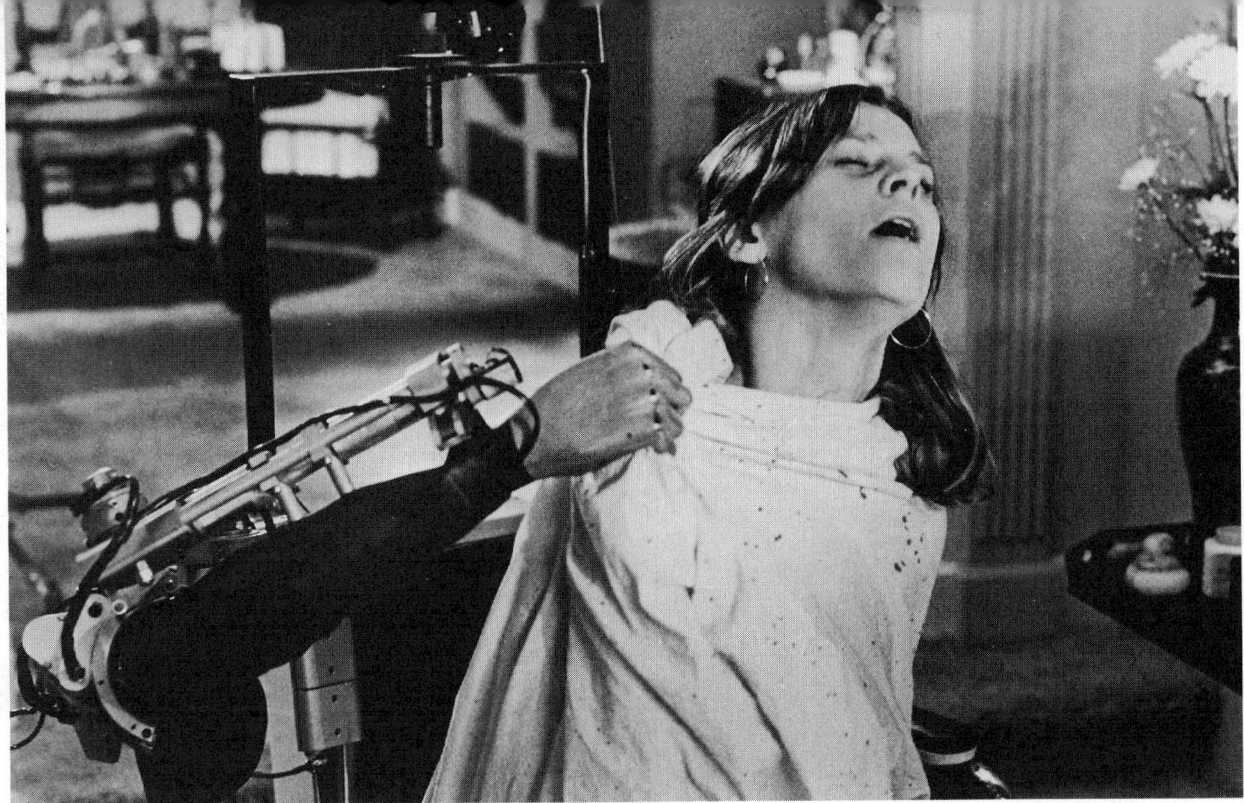

Susan Harris (Julie Christie) held hostage by Proteus IV in *Demon Seed.*

scene. More significantly, though, he shows a solid understanding of his medium—how to combine character, dialogue, sound, and image to tell a good story. And to scare an audience. Even if he'd never made another film, this one would have a following today. ***AKA:*** The Haunted and the Hunted. 🦴🦴🦴½

1963 75m/B William Campbell, Luana Anders, Bart Patton, Patrick Magee, Barbara Dowling; ***D:*** Francis Ford Coppola; ***W:*** Francis Ford Coppola; ***C:*** Ethne Dunn. **VHS** *VYY, MRV, SNC*

Demon Hunter

Bizarre Ed-Woodsian Georgia production is a hidden treasure for fans of alternative cinema. Bestoink Dooley (George Ellis) is an overweight, lank-haired Jimmy Olsen wannabe reporter who looks like a burlesque comedian with his spats, funny derby, and a big rose in his lapel. Given an opportunity to write his first story, he heads out in an old MG to find the monster of Blood Mountain, which turns out to be a guy in a goofy half-suit with a tail on each hip. The soundtrack could have been lifted from 1950s Muzak, and though the tape has a 1988 date, one license plate seems to read 1964 and that's probably right. The voice dubbing is unlike anything you've ever heard and it's matched by the beehive hair-dos, courtesy of the Decatur University of Cosmetology. The action swings back and forth between silliness and boring inanity. 🦴🦴

1988 90m/C George Ellis, Erin Fleming, Marrianne Gordon; ***D:*** Massey Cramer; ***W:*** Bob Corley. **VHS**

A Demon in My View

Anthony Perkins plays another variation on his archetypal serial killer, Norman Bates, in his last big-screen role. Arthur Johnson (Perkins) has lived for more than 20 years in an aging London apartment. He

stays on while other tenants come and go, and when the pressures of memory become too great, he strangles young women. Writer/director Petra Haffter does a fine job of adapting Ruth Rendell's novel to the screen and revealing the inner workings of Arthur's fevered psyche. She also captures the dangerous, complex moral texture of Rendell's fiction. Almost all of the violence and physical action is suggested or shown quickly. The most frightening moment—and it's a real skin crawler—involves nothing more threatening than a safety pin. Even so, this is the spookiest psychological horror film to hit the video stores since the original *The Vanishing.*

1992 (R) 98m/C Anthony Perkins, Sophie Ward, Stratford Johns; ***D:*** Petra Haffter; ***W:*** Petra Haffter. **VHS, LV, Closed Caption** *THV, MOV*

Demon Keeper

How can you not feel some affection for a monster who's obviously a guy in a scaly suit with a skull on his jockstrap? The African production is a supernatural variation on the *Ten Little Indians* plotline: isolated mansion, dark and stormy night, group of strangers who quickly become murder victims. The differences here are two psychics (Dirk Benedict and Edward Albert) and the aforementioned monster. The single bone recommendation is meant only for those in the mood for alternative entertainment.

1995 (R) 90m/C Edward Albert, Dirk Benedict, Andre Jacobs, David Sherwood, Mike Lane, Adrienne Pearce, Jennifer Steyn, Claire Marshall, Diane Nuttall, Elsa Martin, Katrina Maltby; ***D:*** Joe Tornatore. **VHS** *NHO*

Demon of Paradise

The alleged "carnivorous lizardman of the Triassic era" is another guy in a rubber fish suit. The formulaic movie is done in by a slow pace and semi-professional acting. A hazy, overcast sky and gray water make the Hawaiian locations less than inviting. In fact, the whole thing has a leaden, depressing quality, despite the obligatory hula dance.

1987 (R) 84m/C Kathryn Witt, William Steis, Leslie Huntly, Laura Banks, Frederick Bailey; ***D:*** Cirio H. Santiago; ***W:*** Frederick Bailey; ***C:*** Ricardo Remias. **VHS** *WAR*

Demon Seed

Rosemary's Baby meets Microsoft in an eerie cyber-sexual horror. Fritz Weaver has perfected artificial intelligence in his computer, Proteus IV. It's hooked up to his house via another computer named Joshua. After the workaholic Weaver separates from his wife (Julie Christie), she's alone with the machines. Proteus decides he wants a son. Director Donald Cammell tries to show Proteus' thought processes through electronic optical effects, not through the narrative line of the film, so the pace is slow and hard to follow at first. Once the "seduction" begins, the tension picks up considerably.

1977 (R) 97m/C Julie Christie, Fritz Weaver, Gerrit Graham, Berry Kroeger, Ron Hays, Lisa Lu, Larry J. Blake; ***D:*** Donald Cammell; ***W:*** Robert Jaffe, Roger O. Hirson; ***C:*** Bill Butler; ***V:*** Robert Vaughn. **VHS, LV** *MGM*

The Demons

Jess Franco's semi-soft core exploitation is a heady Italian mix of sex, religion, family, torture, and guilt. Lots of guilt. The "plot" involves the daughters (Britt Nichols and Anne Libert) of a witch who take revenge on the corrupt nobles who executed dear old mom. Much of the action is sex in a nunnery and a torture chamber. This one would be a prime guilty pleasure if Franco weren't so enamored of his zoom lens that the scandalous images are often out of focus. Give the director more credit for inspiration than execution. (The Video

"Overrated. Biochemically no different from eating large quantities of chocolate."

—John Milton (Al Pacino) defines love for Kevin Lomax (Keanu Reeves) in *The Devil's Advocate.*

Search of Miami edition is full-length and widescreen with clear subtitles beneath a blurry video transfer.) ***AKA:*** Les Demons; Los Demonios.

1974 (R) 116m/C *FR PT* Anne Libert, Britt Nichols, Doris Thomas, Howard Vernon, Karin Field, Luis Barboo; ***D:*** Jess (Jesus) Franco, Clifford Brown; ***W:*** Jess (Jesus) Franco. **VHS, Letterboxed** *UNI, VSM*

Demons

Two girls accept tickets to a Berlin Horror movie preview where they find that the cinematic monsters and the audience commingle. It's a sort of "living dead" thing where anyone who's wounded by a monster becomes one, trapping the survivors in the theatre. That idea goes back to William Castle's *The Tingler.* Like so many Italian horrors, the plot is less important than the bloody special effects and the loud rock-intensive soundtrack. ***AKA:*** Demoni.

1986 (R) 89m/C *IT* Urbano Barberini, Natasha Hovey, Paolo Cozza, Karl Zinny, Fiore Argento, Fabiola Toledo, Nicoletta Elmi; ***D:*** Lamberto Bava; ***W:*** Lamberto Bava, Dario Argento, Franco Ferrini, Dardano Sacchetti; ***C:*** Gianlorenzo Battaglia. **VHS, LV** *NO*

Demons of the Mind

Hammer's offbeat psychological horror can be seen as a companion piece to *The Wicker Man* and *The Blood on Satan's Claw,* both made around the same time. It's about a sexually troubled 19th century Baron (Paul Jones) who has decided that his teenaged children (Gillian Hills and Shane Briant) are insane and must be kept locked up in his mansion. The family's problems are reflected in the local population where someone is stalking young women. Director Peter Sykes isn't as straightforward as he could be, particularly early on, but his atmospherics are strong. The medical details are as horrifying as anything else in the film. By today's standards of sexual frankness, the premise may be hard to appreciate. ***AKA:*** Blood Evil; Blood Will Have Blood.

1972 (R) 85m/C *GB* Michael Hordern, Patrick Magee, Yvonne Mitchell, Robert Hardy, Gillian Hills, Virginia Wetherell, Shane Briant, Paul Jones, Thomas Heathcote, Kenneth J. Warren; ***D:*** Peter Sykes; ***W:*** Christopher Wicking; ***C:*** Arthur Grant. **VHS** *REP, MLB*

Demonstone

A spirit rises from the dead, possesses the body of a TV newswoman (Nancy Everhard), and tries to destroy an important Filipino family. The storyline could hardly be more far-fetched, but co-stars Jan-Michael Vincent and Lee Ermey handle the physical action well enough. Director Andrew Prowse seldom lets the pace get too slow and his use of well-chosen locations gives the film a strong sense of place. Despite the obvious weaknesses, it's lively and engaging. ***AKA:*** Heartstone.

1989 (R) 90m/C R. Lee Ermey, Jan-Michael Vincent, Nancy Everhard; ***D:*** Andrew Prowse. **VHS, LV** *NO*

The Dentist

In the thriller *Marathon Man,* William Goldman explored the horrifying potential of a man with a shrieking drill, sharp metal tools, and access to your mouth. Brian Yuzna takes the idea a ghastly step further with a variation on Hawthorne's story "Rappaccinni's Daughter." Dr. Feinstone (Corbin Bernsen) is a Beverly Hills oral surgeon driven mad by an unfaithful wife and seeking to create perfection, even if he has to kill his patients. Some of the writers and cast members worked on *Re-Animator* and the humor here is even more mordant. Bernsen's at his best, too, and the expensive look of the production makes it one of director Yuzna's best. Perhaps the personal and intimate nature of the horror explains the film's lack of popularity.

1996 (R) 93m/C Corbin Bernsen, Ken Foree, Linda Hoffman, Michael Stadvec; ***D:*** Brian Yuzna; ***W:*** Charles Finch, Stuart Gordon, Dennis Paoli; ***C:*** Levie Isaacks; ***M:*** Alan Howarth. **VHS** *THV*

Deranged

Midwestern Gothic Grand Guignol is based on the horrors of famous serial killer Ed Gein. Roberts Blossom is spookily good as Ezra, the childlike murderer who tells his unbelieving neighbors what he means to do. Directors Jeff Gillen and Alan Ormsby and makeup master Tom Savini mix graphic gore—scooping brains out of a skull with a spoon—with indescribable humor. They also make Ezra's bleak pre-psychotic life absolutely real and depressing. The dirt-cheap sets and props are somehow appropriate to the story, and the filmmakers stay closer to their source material than any of the other films Gein inspired, *Psycho, The Texas Chainsaw Massacre,* and part of *Silence of the Lambs.* On video, the feature is followed by the short 1981 documentary, *Ed Gein: American Maniac.* Producer and narrator Richard Sarno uses magazine and newspaper articles, audio clips, and fuzzy video to tell the story of Gein's crimes and arrest. He attempts to separate fact from conjecture and that's often difficult. The details described there are even sicker than any fictionalized versions and will tell you more than you really want to know. (The three-bone rating is meant only for fans of reality-based horror. Both films are very strong stuff.)

1974 (R) 82m/C *CA* Roberts Blossom, Cosette Lee, Robert Warner, Marcia Diamond, Brian Sneagle, Leslie Carlson, Marion Waldman, Micki Moore, Pat Orr, Robert McHeady; ***D:*** Jeff Gillen, Alan Ormsby; ***W:*** Jeff Gillen, Alan Ormsby. **VHS** *FRG, MRV*

Devil Doll

Though Tod Browning is best known for *Dracula* and *Freaks,* this is his most wonderfully maniacal work. Lavond (brilliantly played by Lionel Barrymore, at times in drag) is an escaped convict out for vengeance against the traitorous ex-partners who framed him. His means are miniature creatures and people manufactured by the mad bug-eyed Melita (Rafaela Ottiano, who appears to be closely related to Elsa Lanchester's *Bride of Frankenstein*). The second half is less bizarre and more sentimental than the first, but the film is still a sleeper that deserves a much larger audience.

1936 80m/B Lionel Barrymore, Maureen O'Sullivan, Frank Lawton, Rafaela Ottiano, Henry B. Walthall, Arthur Hohl, Grace Ford; ***D:*** Tod Browning; ***W:*** Tod Browning, Erich von Stroheim, Guy Endore, Garrett Fort; ***C:*** Leonard Smith. **VHS** *MGM, MLB*

Devil Doll

Entertaining if largely unknown black-and-white British horror revolves around the adversarial relationship between the Great Vorelli (Bryant Holiday) and his dummy Hugo. A devilish hypnotist-ventriloquist, Vorelli is up to no good, particularly where wealthy London socialite Maryann Horn (Yvonne Romain) is concerned. The simple effects work well, and though Ms. Romain's performance lacks complexity, the film generates some sexual tension.

1964 80m/B *GB* Bryant Holiday, William Sylvester, Yvonne Romain, Sandra Dorne, Karel Stepanek, Francis De Wolff; ***D:*** Lindsay Shonteff; ***W:*** Lance Z. Hargreaves, George Barclay; ***C:*** Gerald Gibbs. **VHS** *NO*

The Devils

Ken Russell's historical-religious-sexual-political fantasia may be the excessive director's most excessive work. Father Grandier (Oliver Reed), his mustaches curled into little devil horns, is the charismatic 17th century priest who is accused of unleashing Satan in a convent led by the

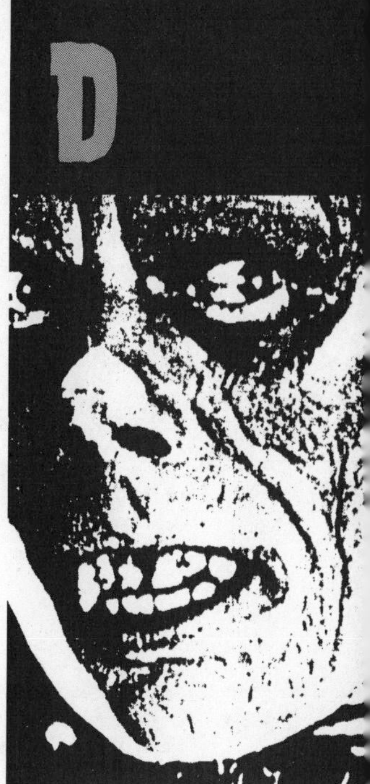

Jonathan Corbis (Ernest Borgnine) in *Devil's Rain.*

hunchbacked Sister Jeanne (Vanessa Redgrave). Father Barre (Michael Gothard) is the witch hunter who judges the matter. Though some images suggest the influence of *Fellini Satyricon,* viewers who take this nuttiness as art are on their own. The Grand Guignol torture scenes are particularly bizarre, but they're less effective than more forthrightly exploitative treatment of the same subject.

1971 (R) 109m/C *GB* Vanessa Redgrave, Oliver Reed, Dudley Sutton, Max Adrian, Gemma Jones, Murray Melvin, Michael Gothard, Georgina Hale, Christopher Logue, Andrew Faulds; ***D:*** Ken Russell; ***W:*** Ken Russell; ***C:*** David Watkin. National Board of Review Awards '71: Best Director (Russell). **VHS** *WAR*

The Devil's Advocate

Kevin Lomax (Keanu Reeves) is the best defense lawyer in Gainesville, Florida, when the wealthy and powerful John Milton (Al Pacino) invites the young man to join his international practice in New York. At first, Lomax and his wife Mary Ann (Charlize Theron) are seduced by high life in the Big Apple, but beyond the work pressure, other more frightening problems present themselves. Is Milton really Satan or is something else going on? Taylor Hackford directs with some flashy visual tricks—the first "morphing" scare is genuinely creepy—and he plays the humorous angles for all they're worth. Reeves' limitations, including an atrocious Southern accent, are glaring, but Pacino compensates with a charming, serpentine performance. Add in top-drawer production values, some relative subtle Biblical quotes, and good support from Jeffrey Jones and Judith Ivey.

1997 (R) 144m/C Al Pacino, Keanu Reeves, Charlize Theron, Judith Ivey, Craig T. Nelson, Jeffrey Jones, Connie Neilsen, Ruben Santiago-Hudson, Debra Monk, Tamara Tunie, Vyto Ruginis, Laura Harrington, Pamela Gray, Heather Matarazzo, Delroy Lindo; ***D:*** Taylor Hackford; ***W:*** Tony Gilroy, Jonathan Lemkin; ***C:*** Andrzej

Bartkowiak; ***M:*** James Newton Howard. **VHS, LV, Letterboxed, Closed Caption** *WAR*

Devil's Bride

Many consider this to be Hammer's finest achievement and I agree, though I'd hate to choose between it and *Curse of the Werewolf.* If the film isn't as well known in this country as the studio's various series featuring Dracula, Frankenstein, and the Mummy, it's a solid witchcraft tale written by Richard Matheson. In 1925, the Duc de Richleau (Christopher Lee), a "good" warlock, and the evil Mocata (Charles Gray) battle each other over Richleau's friend, Simon (Patrick Mower). Some of the effects are a little dated now, but director Terence Fisher builds suspense through a stately pace. Add in the usual excellent sets and a fleet of vintage cars. Lee's performance is one of his strongest in a conventionally heroic role. ***AKA:*** The Devil Rides Out.

1968 95m/C *GB* Christopher Lee, Charles Gray, Nike Arrighi, Leon Greene, Patrick Mower, Gwen Ffrangcon Davies, Sarah Lawson, Paul Eddington; ***D:*** Terence Fisher; ***W:*** Richard Matheson; ***C:*** Arthur Grant. *NYR*

Devil's Rain

Contemporary horror-Western ought to be better than it is; it boasts an impressive cast doing fair work and a talented director, but the light touch that Robert Fuest displayed with the *Dr. Phibes* films is buried under a leaden pace. Part of the problem is the image itself. The film was made in Todd-AO widescreen but the grubby pan-and-scan transfer effectively negates the power of the desert landscape. A lesser problem is the silly wicker cowboy hat that William Shatner wears. Ernest Borgnine is the bull-goose satanist who demands a book from Ida Lupino and her son Shatner. Brother Tom Skerritt comes to the rescue. The melting effects at the end are impressive but too late.

1975 (PG) 85m/C Ernest Borgnine, Ida Lupino, William Shatner, Eddie Albert, Keenan Wynn, John Travolta, Tom Skerritt; ***D:*** Robert Fuest; ***W:*** James Ashton, Gabe Essoe, Gerald Hopman; ***C:*** Alex Phillips Jr. **VHS, LV** *NO*

Devonsville Terror

Low-budget witchcraft story is told with a bit more inventiveness and wit than most, despite a cliche-ridden structure. Three hundred years ago the town fathers of Devonsville, in upstate New York (actually Wisconsin), brutally killed three women accused of being witches. In the present, the men's ancestors are cursed and still haven't changed their patriarchal attitudes. Enter the new teacher (Susanna Love, wife of writer/director Ulli Lommel). Donald Pleasence plays his familiar role with one bizarre and disgusting twist. The acting's uneven; some of the effects are O.K.; the rural atmosphere is strong.

1983 (R) 97m/C Suzanna Love, Donald Pleasence, Deanna Haas, Mary Walden, Robert Walker Jr., Paul Wilson; ***D:*** Ulli Lommel; ***W:*** Ulli Lommel. **VHS**

Dial Help

Over-the-top Italian production is one of the all-time alternative greats. Italian telephones are possessed by spirits and communicate with Jenny (Charlotte Lewis), an English model. The evil phones also sneak up on unsuspecting victims. Toward the end, director Ruggero Deodato creates one brilliant moment of slapstick supernatural eroticism when the telephones call Jenny and seduce her into putting on her sexiest underwear (including high heels). Then she writhes around in a tub full of sudsy green water while her phone serenades her with lush, soaring violin music. Must be seen to be appreciated. ***AKA:*** Ragno Gelido; Minaccia d'Amore.

1988 (R) 94m/C *IT* Charlotte Lewis, Marcello Modugno, Mattia Sbragia, Victor Cavallo, William Berger, Carlo Monni, Carola Stagnaro; ***D:*** Ruggero Deodato; ***C:*** Renato Tafuri. **VHS** *NO*

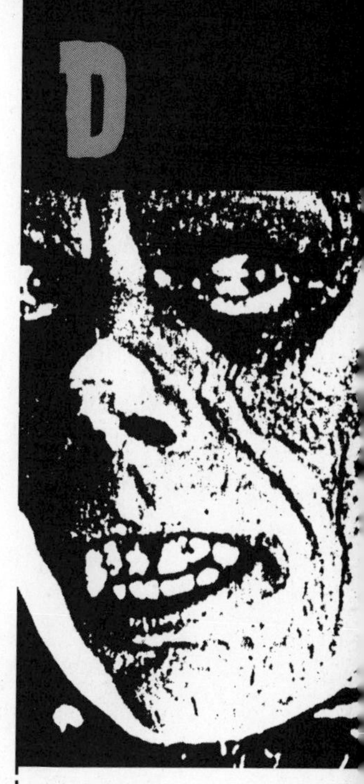

"Good and evil are so close they are chained together in the soul."

—Dr. Jekyll (Spencer Tracy) in *Dr. Jekyll and Mr. Hyde* (1941).

Diary of a Madman

Lavish production is one of Vincent Price's best but least remembered efforts. It's a lazily paced, lumbering tale by today's standards. Based on deMaupassant stories, it's about supernatural retribution, infidelity, and murder. In 1886 Paris, Price is magistrate Simon Cordier. Odette (the lovely Nancy Kovack) is an artist's model. The "Horla" is a murderous spirit that knows secrets in Cordier's past and his present weaknesses. The effects are pretty primitive and the religious symbolism is blatant, but Price's performance is comparable to his work in *The Fly,* made five years before.

1963 96m/C Vincent Price, Nancy Kovack, Chris Warfield, Ian Wolfe, Nelson Olmstead, Elaine Devry, Stephen Roberts; ***D:*** Reginald LeBorg; ***W:*** Robert Kent; ***C:*** Ellis W. Carter. **VHS** *MGM, FCT*

Die! Die! My Darling!

As the title indicates, this is Hammer's shot at *Sweet Charlotte* and *Baby Jane* territory with a slight nod to *Psycho*. American Patricia (Stefanie Powers) visits Mrs. Trefoile (Tallulah Bankhead), the British mother of her dead fiance, and finds that the older woman is a religious maniac. The tone glides from comic amusement at the Bible thumping to horror when things turn nasty. Peter Vaughan plays a similarly rapacious rube in Peckinpah's *Straw Dogs*. The gloomy country house where most of the action takes place is a constant surprise and writer Richard Matheson does his usual rock-solid work. Unfortunately, the widescreen image suffers on video. ***AKA:*** Fanatic.

1965 97m/C *GB* Tallulah Bankhead, Stefanie Powers, Peter Vaughan, Maurice Kaufman, Donald Sutherland, Gwendolyn Watts, Yootha Joyce, Winifred Dennis; ***D:*** Silvio Narizzano; ***W:*** Richard Matheson; ***C:*** Arthur Ibbetson. **VHS, Letterboxed** *COL, MLB*

Die, Monster, Die!

Typical American-International Gothic is a bit underpowered and lacking in real scares compared to A-I's best. Steve Reinhart (Nick Adams) goes to rural England to visit his sweetie Susan (Suzan Farmer). The suspicious villagers won't tell him the way to her father's (Boris Karloff) estate. He finds it to be a blighted wasteland. The pace plods, and Karloff has a relatively ineffectual role. The plot is based on H.P. Lovecraft's "The Color out of Space" (also adapted as *The Curse*). Overall, it's not as much cheesy fun as a comparable Lovecraft film of the time, *The Dunwich Horror.* ***AKA:*** Monster of Terror.

1965 80m/C *GB* Boris Karloff, Nick Adams, Suzan Farmer, Patrick Magee, Freda Jackson, Terence de Marney, Leslie Dwyer, Paul Farrell; ***D:*** Daniel Haller; ***W:*** Jerry Sohl; ***C:*** Paul Beeson; ***M:*** Don Banks. **VHS, LV** *NO*

Dinosaur Valley Girls

Filmmaker and dinosaur expert Don Glut (author of *The Dinosaur Scrapbook* and technical advisor on *Baby: Secret of the Lost Legend*) turns his interests in a more frivolous direction. A horror movie star (Ron Jeffries) is magically transported back to a prehistoric past where primordial babes with names like "Tam-Mee," "Bar-Bee," and "Tor-Ree" coexist with dinosaurs. Yes, silicone meets saurian. It's deliberately bad low-budget silliness complete with musical numbers. Sample lyric: "With rapid steps of three-toed feet, the Allosaurus prowls/ He craves a meal, perceives his prey—his hungry stomach growls!" The effects are bare-bones stuff, and the whole thing is as frivolous as its title. Curiously, the film exists in two forms—a clean, PG-rated "family" version, and an "unrated director's cut" with toplessness. Veterans William Russell and Karen Black appear in cameos.

1996 (PG) m/C Ron Jeffries; ***Cameos:*** Karen Black, William D. Russell; ***D:*** Don Glut; ***W:*** Don Glut. **VHS** *EII*

DNA

Video premiere effectively steals from *Predator, Raiders of the Lost Ark,* and *Jurassic Park* to tell an s-f/horror adventure. The story of a nasty reptilian alien beastie in the Borneo (actually Philippine) jungle makes absolutely no more sense than it has to. The characters—brave hunky Dr. Mattley (Mark Dacascos), evil scientist Wessinger (Juergen Prochnow), tough CIA babe Sommers (Robin McKee)—are lightly sketched in. The combination of guy-in-a-scaly-suit monster with some neat optical effects works well. Even if this one lacks the complexity of plot and character that really good horror needs, it's still engaging, and not too violent.

1997 (R) 94m/C Mark Dacascos, Juergen Prochnow, Robin McKee; ***D:*** William Mesa; ***W:*** Nick Davis; ***C:*** Gerry Lively; ***M:*** Christopher Stone. **VHS, Closed Caption** *CAF*

The Doctor and the Devils

Broome (Stephen Rea) and Hare (Jonathan Pryce) are 19th century grave robbers clearly based on Burke and Hare who steal bodies—the fresher the better—for Dr. Rock (Timothy Dalton). They're colorfully slimy villains and the film has the lush, crowded look of an expensive studio production. It's mostly well written—Ronald Harwood's script is based on one by Dylan Thomas—and well acted. Even so, the definitive version of this story remains Robert Wise's *The Body Snatcher.*

1985 (R) 93m/C *GB* Timothy Dalton, Julian Sands, Jonathan Pryce, Twiggy, Stephen Rea, Beryl Reid, Sian Phillips, Patrick Stewart, Phyllis Logan, T.P. McKenna; ***D:*** Freddie Francis; ***W:*** Ronald Harwood; ***M:*** John Morris. **VHS** *FOX*

Dr. Giggles

A cast of allegedly young characters lifted from a dead teenager slasher flick is transplanted to an escaped-lunatic plot. Dr. Rendell (Larry Drake) is said wacko who goes back to his hometown after the breakout to reopen his practice, killing the locals with medical devices, including a giant Band Aid. The jokes are grisly and grim. Director Manny Coto makes a limited budget look extravagant. It's solidly in the Universal tradition of slickly made, energetic horror; the good doctor deserves a place at the table with the Wolfman, Dracula, et al.

1992 (R) 96m/C Larry Drake, Holly Marie Combs, Glenn Quinn, Keith Diamond, Cliff DeYoung; ***D:*** Manny Coto; ***W:*** Manny Coto, Graeme Whifler; ***M:*** Brian May. **VHS, LV, Letterboxed, Closed Caption** *USH*

Dr. Jekyll and Mr. Hyde

Perhaps its simple-minded notions of women as frail vessels and men as depraved beasts have kept this silent version of the famous story from exerting much influence on the genre. By keeping the two sides of the character completely separate, the film never addresses the real conflict. To be fair, John Barrymore's vampiric Hyde has effective moments. In one brief shot, he creates the elongated face without makeup, and the appearance of Hyde in another scene as a huge spider is shocking. Curiously, the hideous character did not become an icon of early horror the way Chaney's Phantom or Schreck's Nosferatu did. Director John Robertson's primitive, uncinematic style has something to do with that. So does Barrymore's theatrical acting style.

1920 96m/B John Barrymore, Martha Mansfield, Brandon Hurst, Charles Lane, J. Malcolm Dunn, Nita Naldi, Louis Wolheim; ***D:*** John S. Robertson; ***W:*** Clara Beranger; ***C:*** Karl Struss, Roy F. Overbaugh. **VHS, LV** *KIV, SNC, MRV*

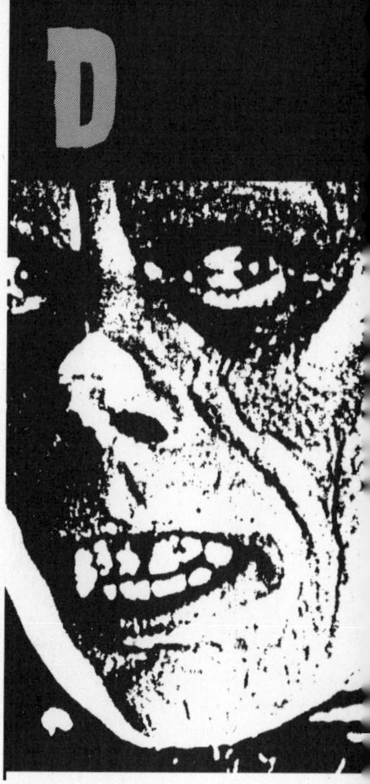

Dr. Jekyll and Mr. Hyde

Changes in filmmaking and acting styles have transformed some serious moments into comedy. Despite those, modern audiences who give this one a try will find a lot to like. Fredric March, who won an Oscar, and director Rouben Mamoulian see Jekyll as a saintly scientist who wants to be even saintlier. The transformation scenes actually aren't bad, though that can't be said of the Hyde makeup which, through no fault of its own, conjures up the image of Jerry Lewis. Miriam Hopkins is fine as the sexy floozie who brings out the beast in the Doc. The sets are wonderful and the visual symbolism plays itself out on both subtle and blatant levels. By the way, this is one of the few productions that uses the British pronunciation GEE-kul instead of JEK-ul. Some tapes restore 18 minutes, thought to have been lost, including the infamous whipping scene.

1931 96m/B Fredric March, Miriam Hopkins, Halliwell Hobbes, Rose Hobart, Holmes Herbert, Edgar Norton; ***D:*** Rouben Mamoulian; ***W:*** Samuel Hoffenstein, Percy Heath; ***C:*** Karl Struss. Academy Awards '32: Best Actor (March); Venice Film Festival '31: Best Actor (March); Nominations: Academy Awards '32: Best Adapted Screenplay, Best Cinematography. **VHS, LV** *MGM, BTV*

Dr. Jekyll and Mr. Hyde

The horror in Robert Louis Stevenson's famous story comes directly from the flawed quality of human nature. That's also what makes it so appealing to filmmakers, and that side has never been stronger than it is in the Victor Fleming-Spencer Tracy version. Their Jekyll is more lusty and forthright, and Hyde is played virtually without makeup or big transformation scenes. Yes, the casting is odd. Of the leads, only Lana Turner, whose Beatrice is a bit too beatific, seems incongruous. Somehow, Ingrid Bergman is believable as a Cockney cupcake, even without the accent. The Oscar-winning black-and-white cinematography by Joseph Ruttenberg doesn't get any better. Fleming uses darkness and spiky shadows to depict emotional turmoil, and repeats key plot points and images of the 1931 film. In that "golden age," Hollywood really understood how stories work—how to balance character, setting, and conflict to build suspense. For my money, this is the best film version of *Jekyll and Hyde*.

1941 113m/B Spencer Tracy, Ingrid Bergman, Lana Turner, Donald Crisp, Ian Hunter, Barton MacLane, Sara Allgood, Billy Bevan; ***D:*** Victor Fleming; ***W:*** John Lee Mahin; ***C:*** Joseph Ruttenberg; ***M:*** Franz Waxman. Nominations: Academy Awards '41: Best Black and White Cinematography, Best Film Editing, Best Original Dramatic/Comedy Score. **VHS, LV** *MGM*

Dr. Jekyll and Ms. Hyde

This one looks great; it's cast with attractive, funny characters; it's kinda sexy and it's as thin as dishwater. Richard Jacks (Tim Daly) is a chemist for a perfume company, who reads Dr. Jekyll's notebooks and rediscovers "a gene for all human evil." When he swallows the formula, he becomes Helen Hyde (Sean Young) in so-so transformation scenes. The rest is really an abysmal sex farce with the male-female switches occurring at inopportune moments. Though the film pretends to deplore sexual stereotypes, the first thing Helen does is to max out Richard's credit cards.

1995 (PG-13) 89m/C Timothy Daly, Sean Young, Lysette Anthony, Stephen Tobolowsky, Harvey Fierstein, Polly Bergen, Stephen Shellan; ***D:*** David F. Price; ***W:*** William Davies, William Osborne, Tim John, Oliver Butcher; ***C:*** Tom Priestley; ***M:*** Mark McKenzie. **VHS** *HBO*

Fredric March in *Dr. Jekyll and Mr. Hyde* (1931).

"Sometimes being a bitch is all a woman has to hold on to."

—Kathy Bates in *Dolores Claiborne.*

Doctor Phibes Rises Again

Ostensible sequel is really a baroque recreation of the original with humor that's even more tongue-in-cheek, if that's possible. (Sample dialogue: "I don't know about his body, but we should give his head a decent burial.") An introduction goes back over the key points of the first film wherein Dr. Phibes (Vincent Price) eludes capture by draining his blood and replacing it with embalming fluid. To rise again, he simply reverses the process. The new plot finds Phibes and Darius Biederbeck (Robert Quarry) heading for Egypt to discover the secret of eternal life at the Temple of Ibiskis, etc., etc. Amazingly, Quarry's flamboyance matches Price's. The presence of Hugh Griffith, Terry-Thomas and, all too briefly, Beryl Reid helps, too. Fiona Lewis, Valli Kemp, and Caroline Munro provide delightful window dressing. The script is filled with visual and verbal wit seldom found in horror. It's difficult to maintain such a light tone without it disintegrating into frivolity. This one manages beautifully. With grand sets and props and literary references left and right, it's every bit as enjoyable as the original.

1972 (PG) 89m/C *GB* Vincent Price, Robert Quarry, Peter Cushing, Beryl Reid, Hugh Griffith, Terry-Thomas, Fiona Lewis, Valli Kemp, Caroline Munro; ***D:*** Robert Fuest; ***W:*** Robert Fuest, Robert Blees. **VHS** *ORI*

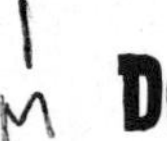

Doctor X

Dated, talky thriller is very much a filmed play. Still, to horror fans, it's well worth a look for its historical value if nothing else. For decades this early two-color Technicolor feature was lost until a print surfaced in the UCLA archives. From the opening outside the Mott Street Morgue on a foggy pier to mad scientists' labs to the gloomy mansion where the third act takes place, the atmospheric sets look great. Dr. Xavier (Lionel Atwill) and his lovely daughter Joann (Fay Wray) help the cops in their search for the serial "Moon Killer." Though the excessive comic relief and expansive acting style—both spoofed in *Young Frankenstein*—preclude any real scares, the monster makeup at the end is pretty good. Beyond director Michael Curtiz's better known mainstream work (*Casa-blanca*), his horror films also include *Mystery of the Wax Museum* and *The Walking Dead.*

1932 77m/C Lionel Atwill, Fay Wray, Lee Tracy, Preston Foster, Arthur Edmund Carewe, Leila Bennett, Mae Busch; ***D:*** Michael Curtiz; ***W:*** Earl Baldwin, Robert Tasker; ***C:*** Ray Rennahan, Richard Towers. **VHS, LV** *MGM, MLB*

Document of the Dead

In 1978, Roy Frumkes interviewed director George Romero on the set of *Dawn of the Dead*. Ten years later, he interviewed Romero again on the set of *Two Evil Eyes.* Parts of those interviews have been combined with scenes from other Romero films to create a revealing if uncritical portrait of the man and his work. When Frumkes judges Romero's movies in artistic terms, he tends to rely on film school cliches. When he turns his attention to the filmmaking process, the documentary is much better. He follows *Dawn* from the beginnings of Romero's script, through preproduction, the location filming in a huge shopping mall, and finally the editing and distribution of the film itself. Frumkes focuses on the nuts-and-bolts side of the business: lighting, makeup, special effects, and stunts. On the set of *Two Evil Eyes,* Frumkes films three takes of one seemingly simple special effects shot to show how difficult the process is. The devil really is in the details. The tape is of renewed interest with the release of the Anchor Bay "director's cut" of *Dawn.*

1990 83m/C ***D:*** Roy Frumkes. **VHS** *HTV*

Dolores Claiborne

One of the best and most handsomely produced adaptations of Stephen King's work is powered by three excellent performances and unusual conflicts. Kathy Bates is Dolores, a hard-bitten Maine woman accused of murdering her employer. Det. John Mackey (Christopher Plummer) is sure that she also killed her husband (David Strathairn) years before. Her troubled daughter Selena (Jennifer Jason Leigh) isn't sure what she believes when she comes back to the island where she grew up. Director Taylor Hackford turns the curious tale into his most satisfying work since *An Officer and a Gentleman.* Kathy Bates isn't as commanding as she was in *Misery,* but Dolores is a much more complex character. Curiously, the film never caught on in theatres, so it's a first-rate sleeper on video.

1994 (R) 132m/C Kathy Bates, Jennifer Jason Leigh, Christopher Plummer, Judy Parfitt, David Strathairn, John C. Reilly; ***D:*** Taylor Hackford; ***W:*** Tony Gilroy; ***M:*** Danny Elfman. **VHS, LV, Closed Caption** *COL*

Don't Look Now

Nicolas Roeg's non-linear approach turns what might have been a dull and conventional mystery into a harrowing horror that defies classification. In both plot and construction, the film is a constant surprise. Nothing follows expected patterns. John (Donald Sutherland) is an art historian. He and his wife Laura (Julie Christie) are in Venice working on a church restoration and getting over a devastating family loss. A series of murders have just begun, and two English sisters that they meet claim to be psychic. Those elements, combined with an unusual use of color, transform the ordinary into the ominous with remarkable effectiveness. An intensely erotic love scene may be the part that most viewers remember. It's as unconventional as all other aspects of the film, including a shocking conclusion.

1973 (R) 110m/C Donald Sutherland, Julie Christie, Hilary Mason, Clelia Matania, Massimo Serato, Leopoldo Trieste, Adelina Porrio; ***D:*** Nicolas Roeg; ***W:*** Chris Bryant, Allan Scott; ***C:*** Anthony B. Richmond; ***M:*** Pino Donaggio. **VHS, LV** *PAR*

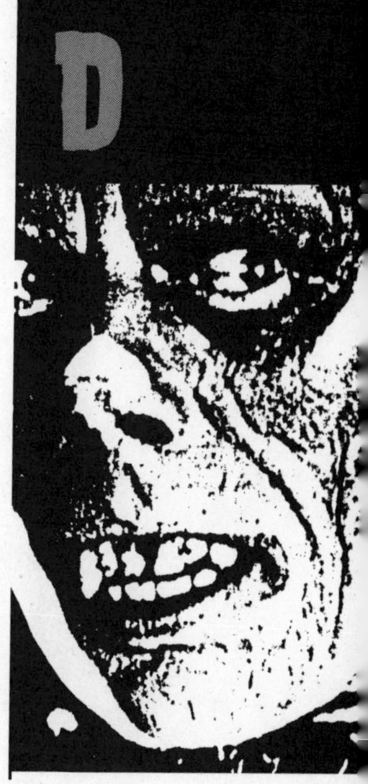

Dorian Gray

The credits admit that this one is "a modern allegory based on the work of Oscar Wilde," and the closing credits contain the final words of the novel. The rest takes Wilde's premise—a portrait that ages in place of its beautiful young subject (Helmut Berger)—and shifts the story to England in the 1950s and '60s. Most of the cinematic cliches of the time—lovers running toward each other across a field in slow motion—are trotted out, so the film isn't particularly effective as horror. It is enjoyable as a snapshot of London in gentler days. Star Berger's resemblance to Andy Warhol is remarkable but his performance as a libertine who corrupts everyone close to him is stiff and foppish. ***AKA:*** The Secret of Dorian Gray; Il Dio Chiamato a Dorian; Das Bildness des Dorian Gray; The Evils of Dorian Gray.

1970 (R) 92m/C *GE IT* Richard Todd, Helmut Berger, Herbert Lom, Marie Liljedahl, Margaret Lee, Maria Rohm, Beryl Cunningham, Isa Miranda, Eleanora Rossi-Drago, Renato Romano; ***D:*** Massimo Dallamano; ***W:*** Massimo Dallamano, Marcello Costa; ***C:*** Otello Spila. **VHS** *REP, FCT*

Double Exposure

Psychological mystery-horror is bad in about as many ways as a movie can be bad—cliched, chaotic, pretentious, confusing, and boring. The camerawork is intrusive; the characters are unbelievable and the story is senseless. It has to do with a photographer (Michael Callan) who dreams that he's killing his models, and says so to his shrink (Seymour Cassel). Meanwhile, his macho brother (James Stacy) bickers with his gay assistant (Don Potter). His girlfriend (Joanna Pettet)

THE HOUND SALUTES

BELA LUGOSI

To one generation of moviegoers, Bela Lugosi is Dracula. Beginning and end of discussion. The actor and the character are so totally identified with each other that they're indistinguishable.

To a younger generation, Lugosi's vampire is a cartoonish figure of fun, and the man himself is the person who was befriended by Ed Wood, Jr., and starred in the worst movie ever made, *Plan 9 from Outer Space*.

Those two extremes don't come close to the truth of Lugosi. He was born Bela Blasko in Hungary, 1882. After a successful career on stage and film in his home country, the handsome young heartthrob was driven by political upheaval to Germany. (In Hungary, he worked with a young director named Mihaly Kertesz, who would become Michael Curtiz later in Hollywood.) From there he immigrated to America, where he landed the title role in the stage version of *Dracula* in 1927 and was an immediate hit.

When Universal decided to film it, Lugosi was one of several candidates for the role, among them Chester Morris, Paul Muni, and Raymond Huntley, who'd played Dracula on the London stage. (Director Tod Browning's first choice was Lon Chaney, who died in 1930.) The studio went with the "safest" choice, and Bela became the Count.

But that's certainly not all he accomplished in his career, despite three serious obstacles. First, Lugosi was never comfortable or articulate in English and his lack of understanding may have hurt him in relationships with fellow actors and in business decisions. Second, when he signed on with Universal, he made a terrible business decision and went to work under a contract which never gave him the money he deserved. Third, sometime in the '30s, he became addicted to morphine, and wasn't cured of it until the 1950s when it nearly killed him.

believes he's not crazy, but two cops (Pamela Hensley and David Young) aren't so sure. You've seen it all before.

1982 (R) 95m/C Michael Callan, James Stacy, Joanna Pettet, Cleavon Little, Pamela Hensley, Seymour Cassel, David Young, Misty Rowe, Don Potter; ***D:*** William B. Hillman. **VHS** *VES*

Dracula

The years have not been kind to this seminal work. All of its flaws are glaring—stagebound script, archaic acting style, the bobbing bats, opossums apparently meant to pass for big rats (and who knows what the armadillos are doing in a Transylvanian castle?)—but the strengths are undiminished: the backgrounds and sets, the atmosphere, and, of course, Lugosi himself. Some aspects of his performance have been imitated and parodied so often that they've lost much of their power, and younger audiences will laugh at the accent and the theatrical posturing. To appreciate the film now, they should note how the various masculine-feminine conflicts are played out, with women depicted as weak-willed beings who must be protected by the male power structure and its symbol of authority—the cross.

1931 75m/B Bela Lugosi, David Manners, Dwight Frye, Helen Chandler, Edward Van Sloan, Frances Dade, Her-

Even so, between *Dracula* and *Plan 9*, several high points deserve mention. Lugosi's work with Charles Laughton in *Island of Lost Souls* is excellent, though he's hard to recognize under furry makeup. He and Karloff are superb in Edgar G. Ulmer's *The Black Cat* and in the lesser-known *The Invisible Ray*. His supporting work in *Son of Frankenstein*, *The Wolf Man*, and *The Body Snatcher* is nothing to be ashamed of, either.

Finally, as a sort of unexpected coda to Lugosi's career, in 1994, Martin Landau won a well-deserved Best Supporting Actor Academy Award for playing the aging star in Tim Burton's affectionate *Ed Wood*. It gave Lugosi at least a small measure of the respect that he never found in Hollywood.

SIGNIFICANT CONTRIBUTIONS TO HORROR

Dracula **(1931)**

The White Zombie **(1932)**

Murders in the Rue Morgue **(1932)**

Island of Lost Souls **(1933)**

The Black Cat **(1934)**

The Raven **(1935)**

Son of Frankenstein **(1939)**

The Wolf Man **(1941)**

Return of the Vampire **(1943)**

The Body Snatcher **(1945)**

Abbott and Costello Meet Frankenstein **(1948)**

Plan 9 from Outer Space **(1956)**

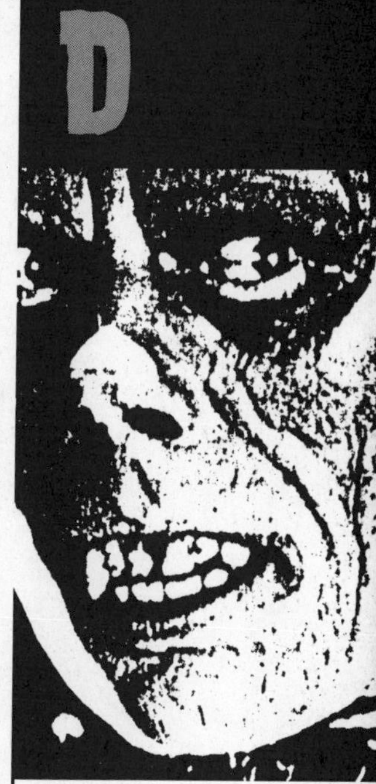

bert Bunston; ***D:*** Tod Browning; ***W:*** Garrett Fort; ***C:*** Karl Freund; ***V:*** Tod Browning. **VHS, LV** *USH, TLF, HMV*

Dracula

The famous Spanish version of the 1931 Bela Lugosi/Tod Browning classic was made simultaneously, on the same sets, at night with a Spanish-speaking cast. It shares the same flaws and strengths. By today's standards, the pace is slow but the film is so richly atmospheric—even more than the English version—that it's still a treat, particularly for those who know and love the English-language version. If Carlos Villarias lacks Bela Lugosi's presence, Lupita Tovar is a delightful (and sexy) heroine. The recently discovered print translates beautifully to video. Required viewing for the serious horror fan. 🦴🦴🦴🦴

1931 104m/B Carlos Villarias, Lupita Tovar, Eduardo Arozamena, Pablo Alvarez Rubio, Barry Norton, Carmen Guerrero; ***D:*** George Melford; ***W:*** Garrett Fort. **VHS** *USH*

Dracula

Dan Curtis, the man responsible for the original *Dark Shadows* series, produced this unusually fine version of the famous novel. If it pales beside Francis Ford Coppola's identically titled version, it still gives

"There are far worse things facing man than death."

—Dracula (Bela Lugosi) is *Dracula* (1931).

Christopher Lee is *Dracula, Prince of Darkness.*

horror fans what they want to see in the story. Richard Matheson's script is faithful to the source material, and the supporting cast, including Simon Ward, Fiona Lewis, and Nigel Davenport, is first rate. You could do much worse. ***AKA:*** Bram Stoker's Dracula.

1973 105m/C Jack Palance, Simon Ward, Fiona Lewis, Nigel Davenport, Pamela Brown, Penelope Horner, Murray Brown, Virginia Wetherell, Sarah Douglas, Barbara Lindley; ***D:*** Dan Curtis; ***W:*** Richard Matheson; ***C:*** Oswald Morris. **VHS, LV** *LIV*

Dracula

Frank Langella's Dracula isn't as menacing as Lugosi's or as powerful as Lee's. He and director John Badham interpret the Count as a Gothic hero. We see him dancing, riding a black horse with his cape flowing in the breeze, emerging dramatically from the fog, and seated for dinner surrounded by thousands of candles. Stoker's plot has been compressed and altered considerably, downplaying Van Helsing (Laurence Olivier). This version is as much a romance as pure horror, and that's certainly a valid approach. Peter Murton's sets, particularly Carfax Abbey, and John Williams' lush score are both impressive.

1979 (R) 109m/C Frank Langella, Laurence Olivier, Kate Nelligan, Donald Pleasence, Janine Duvitsky, Trevor Eve, Tony Haygarth; ***D:*** John Badham; ***W:*** W.D. Richter; ***C:*** Gilbert Taylor; ***M:*** John Williams. **VHS, LV, Letterboxed** *USH*

Dracula A.D. 1972

What an embarrassment! Lee and Cushing manage to maintain their dignity in this ill-advised update, but just barely. They play the reconstituted Count and a Van Helsing descendent who are brought together by a bunch of dope-smoking, devil-worshipping London hippies. The opening party scene looks like an out-take from TV's

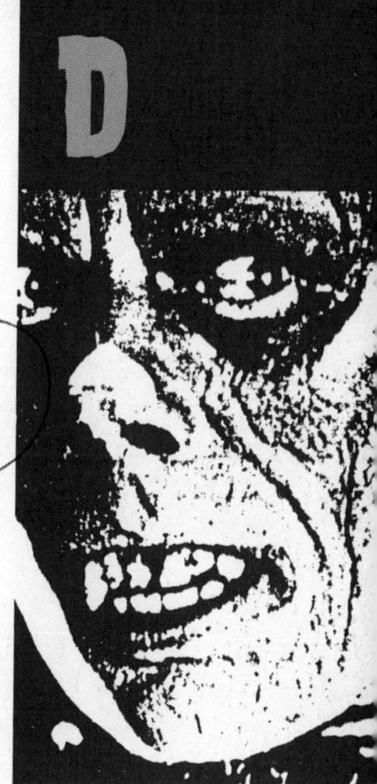

Laugh-In and the resurrection that follows is just as weak. It's all brutally dated now—the clothes, the slang, the hair, the attitude, and particularly the soundtrack that might have been borrowed from *Starsky & Hutch*. The character and intent of the "traditional" Stoker vampire story simply don't translate well to an urban environment of noisy traffic, crowded sidewalks, and construction work. That's not to say that the contemporary bloodsucker tale can't work. See *Martin, Near Dark, The Night Stalker, The Lost Boys,* etc. But Hammer films depend on period atmosphere. Without that for support, Lee and Cushing's best efforts aren't enough. ***AKA:*** Dracula Today. 🦴

1972 95m/C *GB* Christopher Lee, Peter Cushing, Christopher Neame, Stephanie Beacham, Michael Coles, Caroline Munro, Marsha Hunt, Philip Miller, Janet Key, William Ellis; ***D:*** Alan Gibson; ***W:*** Don Houghton; ***C:*** Richard Bush; ***M:*** Michael Vickers. **VHS** *WAR*

Dracula: Dead and Loving It

To place this comedy within the spectrum of Mel Brooks' films, it's much better than *Robin Hood: Men in Tights,* but not nearly as good as his masterpiece, *Young Frankenstein*. Brooks—who produced, directed, co-wrote, and starred—goes back to the original 1931 Lugosi film for most of his jokes and the plot and even for the impressive sets. He also tosses in references to England's Hammer films and Francis Ford Coppola's baroque adaptation of Stoker's story. The result is fun for horror movie fans. Leslie Nielsen is actually fairly restrained as Dracula, particularly when he's sharing the screen with Peter MacNicol as the insect-eating Renfield. MacNicol does a terrific impersonation and parody of Dwight Frye. The humor is mostly physical, with some bits involving grotesque spurts of blood. Even if Brooks' more outrageous sense of humor is missing here, his genuine affection for old movies still shows through. 🦴🦴🦴

1995 (PG-13) 90m/C Leslie Nielsen, Mel Brooks, Peter MacNicol, Lysette Anthony, Amy Yasbeck, Steven Weber, Harvey Korman, Anne Bancroft; ***D:*** Mel Brooks; ***W:*** Mel Brooks, Rudy DeLuca, Steve Haberman; ***C:*** Michael D. O'Shea; ***M:*** Hummie Mann. **VHS, LV, Closed Caption** *COL*

Dracula Has Risen from the Grave

Christopher Lee's third outing under the cape attempts to deal with questions of religious faith and doubt while, at the same time, being more sexually intense than previous Hammer vampire films...well, as sexually intense as a G-rated film can be. A hard-working Monsignor (Rupert Davies) and a priest in spiritual crisis (Ewan Hooper) split the Van Helsing role this time. Veronica Carlson, a cool blonde of the Kim Novak school, is one of Hammer's most popular heroines. She and Barry Andrews make attractive young heroes. Cinematographer-turned-director Freddie Francis moves some of the action to rooftop locations and handles it nicely. The whole film looks great. It's beautifully lit and photographed with tinting in some scenes. Though the script maintains the studio's characteristic simplicity, it moves well. And, appropriately enough for a film made in 1968, generational conflicts are important to the story. 🦴🦴🦴

1968 (G) 92m/C *GB* Christopher Lee, Rupert Davies, Veronica Carlson, Barbara Ewing, Barry Andrews, Michael Ripper, Ewan Hooper, Marion Mathie; ***D:*** Freddie Francis; ***W:*** John Elder; ***C:*** Arthur Grant; ***M:*** James Bernard. **VHS** *WAR*

Dracula, Prince of Darkness

The second film in Hammer's successful series begins with the ending of the first, wherein the good Count is reduced to a shoebox full of ashes. Flash forward ten years—about as long as it took the pro-

THE HOUND SALUTES

BRIAN DePALMA

R.I.P

SIGNIFICANT CONTRIBUTIONS TO HORROR

Sisters (1973)

Carrie (1976)

Dressed to Kill (1980)

Of all the young filmmakers who bustled onto the scene in the early 1970s, few arrived with such a flourish as Brian DePalma and then declined so dramatically. Though most of his films have been commercially successful, the comparisons that once were made to Hitchcock seem to have been totally misplaced.

The son of a surgeon, DePalma was born in Newark, New Jersey, in 1940. He went to Columbia and Sarah Lawrence and made several rough films in the raucous '60s. His break came in 1973 with *Sisters,* a crazed and bloody horror-thriller homage to Hitch, but his first real commercial hit was *Carrie* in 1976.

It's an interesting film that reflects the strengths and flaws of DePalma's career as a whole. A few important scenes work brilliantly—the most obvious is the opening in the girls' locker room—and the director gets a career-defining performance from star Sissy Spacek. Other key scenes, though, are mechanically manipulative, and DePalma's emotional detachment from the material becomes more apparent with repeated viewings. Stephen King is more charitable when he says, "DePalma's approach to the material was lighter and more deft than my own—and a good deal more artistic." (*Danse Macabre,* Everest House.)

Virtually the same observations could be made about DePalma's next commercial hit, too. *Dressed to Kill* barely holds together as a coherent narrative, but the long museum-seduction scene is nothing short of brilliant. For my money, that's DePalma's highwater mark. Everything that's come since looks pretty puny in comparison.

From that point, all of DePalma's considerable boxoffice success has been outside the genre with *The Untouchables, Carlito's Way,* and the tongue-in-cheek *Mission: Impossible.* His only return to horror is the disastrous *Raising Cain,* arguably the worst since the heyday of Ed Wood, Jr.

It's probably for the best that DePalma has left horror and gone into the mainstream. As mainstream films have become more rigidly formulaic, more dependent on effects and less on real characters, they're more suited to DePalma's icy approach.

ducers to coax Christopher Lee back into the cape. The rest follows one of the studio's favorite formulas with two couples innocently wandering into the monster's lair. An energetic abbot, Father Sandor (Andrew Keir) takes over the Van Helsing role as head vampire hunter. The best moments are the reconstitution and the imaginative ending. A grandly melodramatic score dates the film and the pace is slow by current standards, but it still stands up well to another viewing. The small cast is excellent. The women are classy and about as sexy as the 1965 screen would allow. Barbara Shelley's transformation from a proper Victorian lady into a red hot vampire mama who's ready to rumba in her negligee is a delight. Lee's silent performance is one of his strongest. ***AKA:*** The Bloody Scream of Dracula; Disciple of Dracula; Revenge of Dracula.

1965 90m/C *GB* Christopher Lee, Barbara Shelley, Andrew Keir, Francis Matthews, Suzan Farmer, Charles Tingwell, Thorley Walters, Philip Latham; ***D:*** Terence Fisher; ***W:*** John Sansom, John Elder; ***C:*** Michael Reed; ***M:*** James Bernard. **VHS** *VTR*

Dracula Rising

Art restorer Stacy Travis is commissioned to go to Europe to work on an old painting. There she finds that Christopher Atkins, the Byronic figure she met at an L.A. art show, is a vampire. But, hey, he's handsome, he's single, and he says he loves her ... could be a project. On the other hand, his brother, Doug Wert, thinks he should kill her. Does she really want this guy for an in-law? The budget is anemic; the cast is young, attractive, and stiff. Virtually identical material has been handled more entertainingly in several other recent releases.

1993 (R) ?m/C Christopher Atkins, Stacy Travis, Doug Wert, Zahari Vatahov; ***D:*** Fred Gallo. **VHS** *NHO*

Dracula vs. Frankenstein

Typically impoverished Adamson drive-in fare is notable for the final appearances of Lon Chaney, Jr., and J. Carrol Naish, trippy period clothes, and one scene of Regina Carrol's Las Vegas lounge act. The title creatures themselves have seldom looked more laughable. TV veteran Jim Davis shows up briefly as a dime-store Dirty Harry. Despite the early "GP" rating and lack of sexual activity, the film has the mindset and atmosphere of a late '60s skin flick. ***AKA:*** Blood of Frankenstein; They're Coming to Get You; Dracula Contra Frankenstein; The Revenge of Dracula; Satan's Bloody Freaks. **Woof!**

1971 (PG) 90m/C *SP* J. Carrol Naish, Lon Chaney Jr., Regina Carrol, Russ Tamblyn, Jim Davis, Anthony Eisley, Zandor Vorkov, John Joe Bob Briggs Bloom, Angelo Rossitto; ***Cameos:*** Forrest J. Ackerman; ***D:*** Al Adamson; ***W:*** William Pugsley, Sam M. Sherman; ***C:*** Paul Glickman, Gary Graver. **VHS** *NO*

Dracula's Daughter

First-rate sequel begins precisely at the end of the first with Van Helsing (Edward Van Sloan) explaining to the cops how Dracula and Renfield happen to be dead. After that bit of business and some comic relief, Countess Marya (Gloria Holden) arrives to claim the body of her dad, and the film shifts to a slow pace and somber tone. She's a complex character who wants to be "normal" and thinks that psychiatrist Dr. Garth (Otto Kruger) can cure her. The film is at best half successful with dark, beautifully staged scenes balanced against some dated overacting. Both Holden and Marguerite Churchill as Janet, the doctor's secretary and fiancee, are given the full glamour treatment.

1936 71m/B Gloria Holden, Otto Kruger, Marguerite Churchill, Irving Pichel, Edward Van Sloan, Nan Grey, Hedda Hopper; ***D:*** Lambert Hillyer; ***W:*** Garrett Fort; ***C:*** George Robinson. **VHS, Closed Caption** *USH*

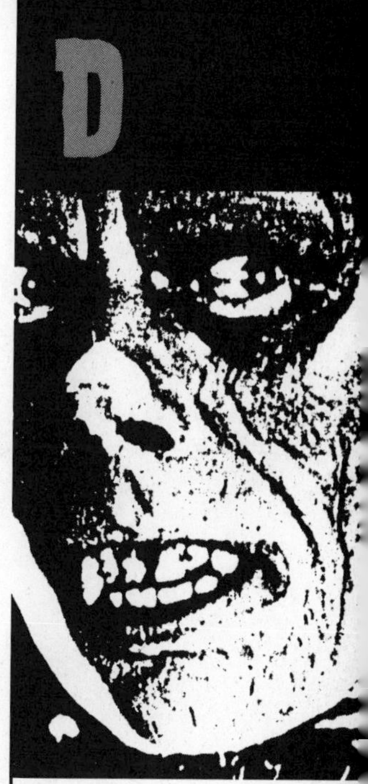

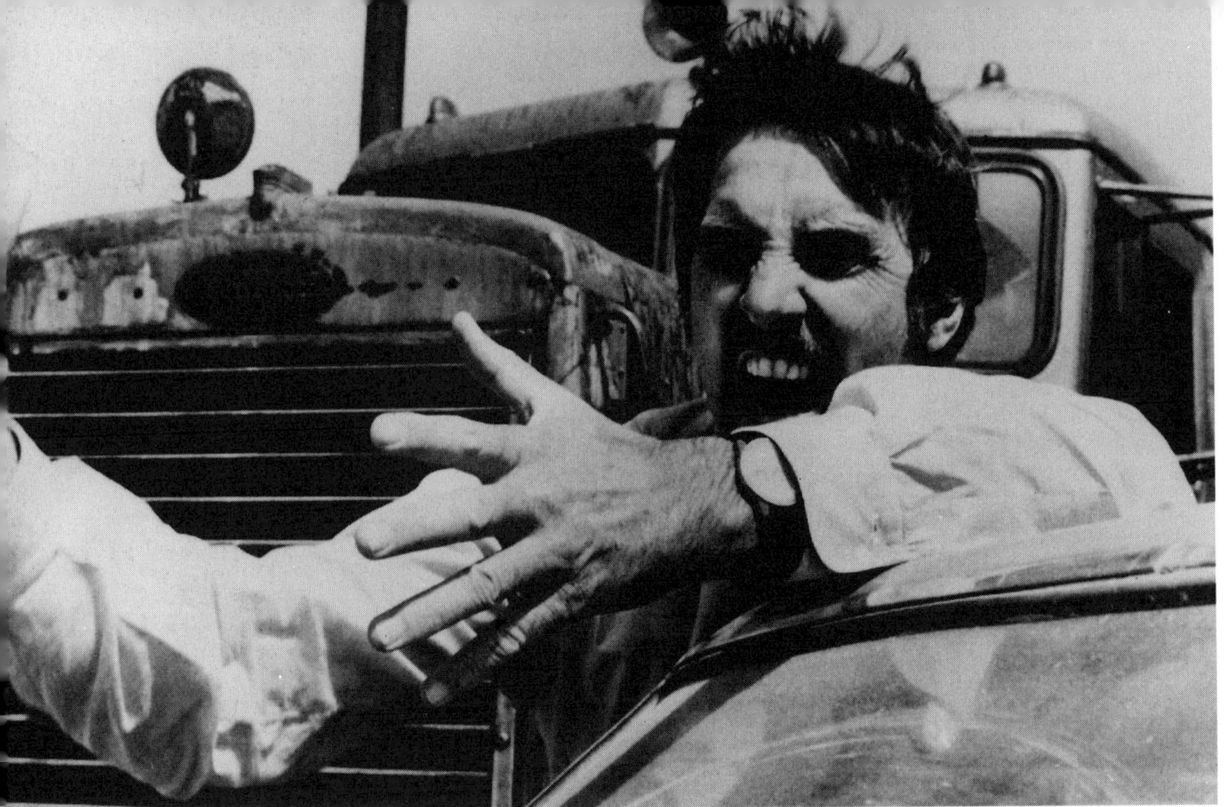

David Mann (Dennis Weaver) in *Duel.*

Dressed to Kill

Brian DePalma's *Psycho* homage/imitation begins with a soapy shower scene that paved the way for the hundreds of erotic thrillers that have come since. DePalma, star Angie Dickinson, and her body double established a new standard for mainstream films, and the scene heightens the sexual tension that's the basis for the film's horror. The real high point, though, is a brilliant, wordless 11-minute museum scene that ends with a weird joke. After it, the film never completely recovers its balance. The second half isn't nearly as intense as the first, and in the finale, DePalma copies himself with the end of *Carrie.* 🦴🦴🦴

1980 (R) 105m/C Angie Dickinson, Michael Caine, Nancy Allen, Keith Gordon, Dennis Franz, David Margulies, Brandon Maggart; ***D:*** Brian DePalma; ***W:*** Brian DePalma; ***C:*** Ralf Bode; ***M:*** Pino Donaggio. **VHS, LV, Letterboxed** *WAR, OM*

Drive-In Massacre

Somebody's using a sword to dispatch patrons who aren't paying attention to the feature. Much of the film appears to have been made at a real drive-in at night, and so it's pretty hard to make out—to make out the action, that is. The daylight scenes are talky, and the bloody effects aren't going to fool anyone. Older fans who remember "ozoners" fondly will understand the one-bone rating. Others will be less charitable. 🦴

1974 (R) 78m/C Jake Barnes, Adam Lawrence, Austin Johnson, Douglas Gudbye, Valdesta; ***D:*** Stu Segall; ***W:*** Buck Flower, John Goff. **VHS, LV** *NO*

Drop Dead Fred

Fantasy/horror tries to combine the bizarre surprises of *Beetlejuice* with an offbeat comic sensibility. Some viewers will be taken by director Ate De Jong's lively unpredictability. Others will see his story as mean-spirited and ugly. When Lizzie's (Phoebe Cates) life begins to disintegrate, her invisible childhood friend, Drop Dead Fred (Rik Mayall), returns. But is he a true fantasy figure or a product of her emotional instability? Despite script problems and an uncertain tone, Cates' strong performance earns a recommendation. One of the most underused actresses of her generation (and one of my own favorites), she makes Lizzie's predicament seem frighteningly real. Matters of madness and sanity are difficult subjects for horror. If this version isn't as successful as some—see *Brain Dead*—it's still worthwhile.

1991 (PG-13) 103m/C Phoebe Cates, Rik Mayall, Tim Matheson, Marsha Mason, Carrie Fisher, Daniel Gerroll, Ron Eldard; ***D:*** Ate De Jong; ***W:*** Carlos Davis, Anthony Fingleton; ***M:*** Randy Edelman. **VHS, LV, Closed Caption** *LIV*

Duel

Steven Spielberg had the good sense (or the good luck) to find a terrific Richard Matheson script that dovetailed with his talents as a director for his feature debut. Suburbanite David Mann (Dennis Weaver) encounters an early case of road rage writ large when he runs afoul of a psycho Peterbilt tanker truck on a rural Southern California highway. At first, it appears to be a simple misunderstanding, the kind of situation most drivers have encountered. But, as the film progresses, the semi becomes a more real and threatening monster. Note how Spielberg uses real sounds on the soundtrack at first—road noise, wind, and AM radio—and then switches to a musical score indicating a significant increase in tension and conflict. Throughout, the truck remains a believable threat because the filmmakers never resort to movie "magic" for its scares.

1971 (PG) 90m/C Dennis Weaver, Lucille Benson, Eddie Firestone, Cary Loftin; ***D:*** Steven Spielberg; ***W:*** Richard Matheson; ***M:*** Billy Goldenberg. **VHS** *USH*

The Dunwich Horror

Young warlock Wilbur Whatley (Dean Stockwell) steals a copy of the dreaded and powerful "Necronomicon" from the Miskatonic University Library and sets about to restore the Whatley family to its rightful place as rulers of the earth and the rest of the known universe. He's also got his eye on a cute co-ed (Sandra Dee). Stockwell is appropriately hammy; Dee is her inimitable blonde self, and they both get considerable help from Ed Begley and Sam Jaffe. The film is loosely based on an H. P. Lovecraft story with a strong influence of TV's *Dark Shadows*. It also foreshadows the fiction and films of Stephen King. Given the cast and the times, generational conflicts are important, too. That's Talia Coppola (Shire) as the nurse.

1970 90m/C Sandra Dee, Dean Stockwell, Lloyd Bochner, Ed Begley Sr., Sam Jaffe, Joanna Moore, Talia Shire; ***D:*** Daniel Haller; ***W:*** Curtis Hanson, Henry Rosenbaum, Ronald Silkosky; ***C:*** Richard C. Glouner; ***M:*** Les Baxter. **VHS**

Dust Devil

Like Clive Barker's *Candyman*, this tries to tell a horror story with well-developed characters in a realistic contemporary political context and an exotic setting. Chelsea Field is running away from her abusive husband when she picks up hitchhiker Robert John Burke in the Namibian desert. She should have been tipped off by his ugly sideburns; he's the title character, a spiritual creature who is endlessly rejuvenated by ritual murder. But this demon kills only people who have reached spiritual despair—those who are about to commit suicide—and he even develops an emotional attachment to them. The only person who has any understanding of what he's doing is black policeman Zakes Mokae. Writer/director Richard Stanley tends to get too tricky and inventive for his own good toward the end, and at times

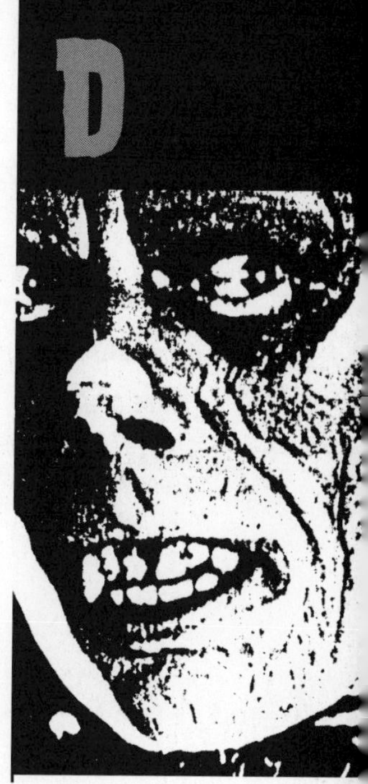

"My mother was a hardware man, and she taught me it was better to be a hammer than a nail."

—Ed Chilton (Steve Buscemi) in *Ed and His Dead Mother.*

the film threatens to become a spaghetti western. Still, it's a cut above average. Recommended. 🦴🦴🦴

1993 (R) 87m/C *GB* Robert John Burke, Chelsea Field, Zakes Mokae, Rufus Swart, John Matshikiza, William Hootkins, Marianne Saegebrecht; ***D:*** Richard Stanley; ***W:*** Richard Stanley; ***C:*** Steven Chivers; ***M:*** Simon Boswell. **VHS, Closed Caption** *PAR*

Dynasty of Fear

Psychological tale is a throwback to the earlier black-and-white thrillers that Hammer had been making about a decade before in the early '60s. Peggy Heller (Judy Geeson) impulsively marries Robert (Ralph Bates), a teacher at Michael Carmichael's (Peter Cushing) private school. Before she's even been to the place, someone attacks her. Then at the school, the attacks continue. Could the shotgun-toting Mrs. Carmichael (Joan Collins) have it in for her? Or is Peggy imagining everything? The empty school is an appropriately lonely, evocative setting, but it's overused, and this strain of horror is not the studio's real forte. ***AKA:*** Fear in the Night; Honeymoon of Fear. 🦴🦴½

1972 (PG) 93m/C *GB* Peter Cushing, Joan Collins, Ralph Bates, Judy Geeson, James Cossins, John Bown, Brian Grellis, Gillian Lind; ***D:*** Jimmy Sangster; ***W:*** Jimmy Sangster, Michael Syson; ***C:*** Arthur Grant. **VHS** *REP*

Earth Vs. the Spider

Despite so-so effects—accomplished through blown-up footage of a real spider, not stop-motion animation—this is one of the more enjoyable big-bug horrors. The script doesn't bother with explanations. No radiation or pollution causes a giant tarantula to crawl out of the Carlsbad Caverns; it just does. O.K.? The film's real purposes are revealed during the spider-attacks-the-town scene. Note the Civil Defense emblem on the rooftop siren. For those too young to remember, that siren was the sound we were expecting to hear right before the Russian missiles vaporized us. That's the real threat being addressed. Goofy dialogue helps, too. Upon first seeing the cavern, the sheriff notes, "What a place! Make a nice Elk's Hall." When old Jake ties a mattress to the roof of his car, he says, "I'm evacuatin'. That darn monster run me outta house 'n' home." ***AKA:*** The Spider. 🦴🦴

1958 72m/B Edward Kemmer, June Kennedy, Gene Persson, Gene Roth, Hal Torey, Mickey Finn; ***D:*** Bert I. Gordon; ***W:*** Laszlo Gorog, George Worthing Yates; ***C:*** Jack Marta. **VHS** *COL, MLB*

Eaten Alive

Southern Gothic is as surreal, sick, and ultra-violent as director Tobe Hooper's previous feature, *The Texas Chainsaw Massacre*. In fact, some critics see it as a continuation with a stronger correlation between sex and violence. The setting's a swamp where innkeeper Judd (Neville Brand) feeds unlucky guests (and their puppies!) to his crocodile. The low-budget effort is notable for squalid yellow light, leisure suits, and the presence of such stars as an unhealthy-looking Carolyn Jones and Mel Ferrer. The croc effects are less disgusting than the human monsters of *TCM*. Southern viewers will pick up on Hooper's regional references. Recommended only for fans of the gamiest Grand Guignol: those who "enjoy" seeing children attacked by rats, scythe-wielding maniacs, and giant reptiles. Brand is disturbingly good. ***AKA:*** Death Trap; Starlight Slaughter; Legend of the Bayou; Horror Hotel Massacre. 🦴🦴½

1976 (R) 96m/C Neville Brand, Mel Ferrer, Carolyn Jones, Marilyn Burns, Stuart Whitman, Robert Englund, William Finley, Roberta Collins, Kyle Richards; ***D:*** Tobe Hooper; ***W:*** Marti Rustam, Alvin L. Fast, Kim Henkel; ***C:*** Robert Caramico; ***M:*** Wayne Bell. **VHS** *NO*

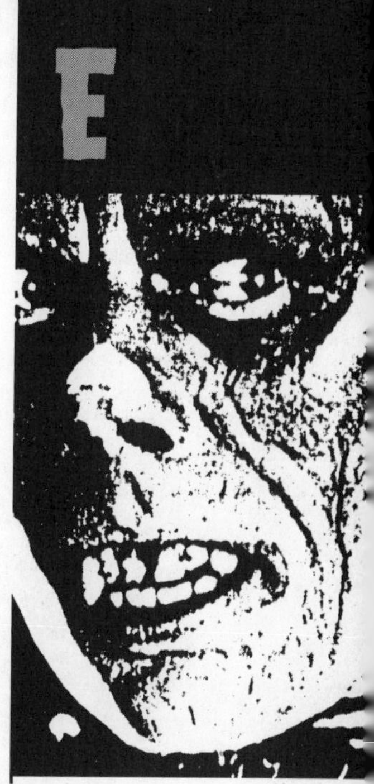

Ed and His Dead Mother

Similar material is handled with much more tastelessness (or should that be less tastefulness?) in Peter Jackson's wild and woolly *Dead Alive,* though this one has its moments. Succumbing to Mr. Powell's (John Glover) slick midwestern salesmanship, Ed (Steve Buscemi) agrees to have his departed mother (Miriam Margolyes) brought back from the dead. Uncle Benny (Ned Beatty), who'd rather be spying on the comely new neighbor (Sam Jenkins), thinks it's a bad idea. For openers, if Mom doesn't get the right food, she picks up the chainsaw and becomes cannibal. The satiric targets (family values, consumerism, corporations) are well chosen but the tone isn't quite right. Jackson's grotesque excesses are more enjoyable.

1993 (PG-13) 93m/C Ned Beatty, Steve Buscemi, John Glover, Miriam Margolyes, Sam Jenkins; ***D:*** Jonathan Wacks; ***W:*** Chuck Hughes. **VHS, LV, Closed Caption** *FXV*

Ed Gein: American Maniac

See *Deranged.*

Ed Wood

Despite its unorthodox subject matter, Tim Burton's bio-horror-comedy is a winning tale with genuine heart. Essentially, it's the true story of the first years of Ed Wood, Jr.'s (Johnny Depp) Hollywood career, and his friendship with aging horror star Bela Lugosi (Martin Landau, who won a well-deserved Oscar). Though opinions about Wood and his low-budget movies differ, two points are universally accepted. First, he was one of the worst directors ever to work behind a camera. Second, he was a terrific guy. That's what makes the movie so much fun. Depp is first rate and he gets fine support from Bill Murray, Jeffrey Jones, Sarah Jessica Parker, and Patricia Arquette. Crisp black-and-white photography makes the story less dependent on the whimsical atmosphere that underlies *Beetlejuice* and *Edward Scissorhands.* Here, Burton keeps the focus on the characters, not the sets or the special effects.

1994 (R) 127m/B Johnny Depp, Sarah Jessica Parker, Martin Landau, Bill Murray, Jim Myers, Patricia Arquette, Jeffrey Jones, Lisa Marie, Vincent D'Onofrio; ***D:*** Tim Burton; ***W:*** Scott Alexander, Larry Karaszewski; ***C:*** Stefan Czapsky. Academy Awards '94: Best Makeup, Best Supporting Actor (Landau); Golden Globe Awards '95: Best Supporting Actor (Landau); Los Angeles Film Critics Association Awards '94: Best Cinematography, Best Supporting Actor (Landau), Best Score; New York Film Critics Awards '94: Best Cinematography, Best Supporting Actor (Landau); National Society of Film Critics Awards '94: Best Cinematography, Best Supporting Actor (Landau); Screen Actors Guild Award '94: Best Supporting Actor (Landau); Nominations: British Academy Awards '95: Best Supporting Actor (Landau); Golden Globe Awards '95: Best Actor—Musical/Comedy (Depp), Best Film—Musical/Comedy; Writers Guild of America '94: Best Original Screenplay. **VHS, LV, Closed Caption** *TOU*

Edge of Sanity

Combining two famous Victorian horror tales, this Hungarian production might have been called *The Doctor and the Ripper.* Henry Jekyll (Anthony Perkins), a proper and respectable upper-class physician, first suffers a childhood sexual trauma that haunts him in nightmares. Then, while experimenting with anesthetics, he invents crack cocaine and becomes addicted. His eyes redden; his haircut goes to hell; his complexion turns white and pasty. He's transformed into the evil Jack Hyde. Yes, Jack, as in Jack the Ripper. Director Gerard Kikoine (*Buried Alive*) manages to maintain an evocative atmosphere reminiscent of the best Hammer films. Not surprisingly, Perkins' kinky performance contains echoes of Norman Bates, and so he underplays the wilder moments.

1989 (R) 85m/C *GB* Anthony Perkins, Glynis Barber, David Lodge, Sarah Maur-Thorp, Ben Cole, Lisa Davis, Jill Melford; ***D:*** Gerard Kikoine; ***W:*** J.P. Felix, Ron Raley; ***C:*** Tony Spratling. **VHS, LV, Closed Caption** *NO*

THE HOUND SALUTES

TIM BURTON

It's difficult to combine comedy and horror. In most cases, humor predominates and potentially frightening moments are part of the joke, or if the filmmakers really do mean to try to frighten their audience, then the comic moments are out of place. Changes in fashion, for example, have made the humor in older horrors from the 1930s and '40s seem far too intrusive; many producers at the time thought that comic relief was necessary to balance frightening scenes.

These days, only one director has a sensibility that's able to combine genuine scares with laughs. Tim Burton.

Though his films have been greeted with mixed commercial success, he has demonstrated a striking visual sense that grows out of his background as a cartoonist, and a macabre sense of humor that Alfred Hitchcock might have appreciated. At times, he's been less successful in controlling the free-flowing plots of his films, but that's a trade-off that many fans are willing to make.

Sources say that he was born in either 1958 or '60 in Burbank, and as a child drew cartoons based on his favorite TV shows and horror movies. A Disney fellowship sent him to the California Institute of the Arts to study animation, and at age 20, he went to work for Disney as an apprentice animator. There he made two short films—*Vincent*, about his hero Vincent Price, and *Frankenweenie*, which casts the monster as a pooch—and an episode of Faerie Tale Theater, *Aladdin and His Wonderful Lamp*, with Valerie Bertinelli, Robert Carradine, Leonard Nimoy, and James Earl Jones. Those led to his directing *Pee-Wee's Big Adventure* which, like Paul Rubens' TV show, proved to be as popular with adults as with kids.

Edison Frankenstein

One of the earliest horror films calls itself "A Liberal Adaptation from Mrs. Shelley's Famous Story for Edison Production." In a mere 14 minutes, with time left over for considerable arm flailing, it hits the high points—the mad scientist, the lab scene, the creature's birth, his creator's wedding, the confrontation. The images are flickering and indistinct—at least they are on a preview screener just going into distribution as this book is going to press. Even so, the makeup that star Charles Ogle created for himself still has shock value and the film concludes with an odd visual twist. Until a clearer print becomes available, this one's for serious students of the genre only.

1910 16m/C Charles Ogle, Augustus Phillips, Mary Fuller; ***D:*** Searle Dawley; ***W:*** Searle Dawley. **VHS** *ISF*

Edward Scissorhands

From the opening credits, it's clear that the whole story takes place within a cinematic snowglobe. Tim Burton's take on Pinocchio is a combination of fantasy, myth, fairy tale, and horror. It's also a sweet-natured companion piece to *Beetlejuice* that ought not to work at all, but does, splendidly. Vincent Price is the Inventor who creates Edward (Johnny Depp) but dies before he

After it, Burton gave his darker side more room to play in *Beetlejuice,* a light-hearted romp about an attractive young dead couple tormented by a supernatural jerk and the boorish new inhabitants of their house. Its success gave his career a big boost up the Hollywood food chain, and he turned the big-budget *Batman* into a soaring Gothic adventure.

Perhaps uncomfortable with the pressures brought on by the Bat's blockbuster profits, Burton "returned to his roots" with *Edward Scissorhands,* a charming horror-fairy tale that gave Vincent Price a graceful final role. After it, the already dark elements turned even darker with the Bat sequel, *Batman Returns.* Burton then made another artistic turn—are we sensing a pattern here?—with the sweet-natured *Ed Wood.* It's easy to speculate that the relationship in the film between the young outsider Wood (Johnny Depp) and the aging horror star Lugosi (Martin Landau) reflects Burton himself and Vincent Price.

Despite universally glowing reviews, audiences were not charmed, and they reacted the same way with *Mars Attacks!,* Burton's on-target satire of big-budget escapism. Like his best work—including the animated *The Nightmare Before Christmas,* which he co-produced and wrote—the comic elements are so tightly interlaced with the horror that audiences don't know how to react. So far, moviegoers have been most responsive when Burton is more whimsical. Hard-core horror fans, I suspect, disagree. For my part, I hope Burton continues to explore new ideas. At a time when the film industry slavishly recycles tired old formulas, Tim Burton is a rare original.

SIGNIFICANT CONTRIBUTIONS TO HORROR

***Beetlejuice* (1988)**

***Edward Scissorhands* (1990)**

***The Nightmare Before Christmas* (1993)**

***Ed Wood* (1994)**

***Mars Attacks!* (1996)**

can give the boy human hands, leaving him with blades for fingers. (Stan Winston created those effects.) The Avon lady (Dianne Wiest) brings Edward down from his black hilltop castle to the pastel 'burbs below where he falls in love with her daughter Kim (Winona Ryder). The brief role, virtually a cameo, is a fitting coda to Price's career in the field. Danny Elfman's score is one of his best.

1990 (PG-13) 100m/C Johnny Depp, Winona Ryder, Dianne Wiest, Vincent Price, Anthony Michael Hall, Alan Arkin, Kathy Baker, Conchata Ferrell, Caroline Aaron, Dick Anthony Williams, Robert Oliveri, John Davidson; ***D:*** Tim Burton; ***W:*** Tim Burton, Caroline Thompson; ***C:*** Stefan Czapsky; ***M:*** Danny Elfman. Nominations: Academy Awards '90: Best Makeup. **VHS, LV, Closed Caption** *FOX, FCT*

Elves

Christmas horror movie is perhaps not as offensive as some slasher Santa flicks, but it's close. The title critters (unconvincing, stiff models who don't measure up to Chucky or the Leprechaun) are the result of experiments by aging Nazis living in America. The PG-13 rating is problematic; despite considerable profanity, a sick sexual angle involving incest and rape, graphic violence, and full nudity in a scene where a woman is electrocuted, the MPAA ratings board says that it's O.K. for older kids. Without question, it should have been an R. Definitely not for the whole family.

"Hell is only a word. The reality is much, much worse."

—Dr. William Weir (Sam Neill) in *Event Horizon.*

1989 (PG-13) 95m/C Dan Haggerty, Deanna Lund, Julie Austin, Borah Silver; ***D:*** Jeffrey Mandel. **VHS** *NO*

Elvira, Mistress of the Dark

Cassandra Peterson takes her brand of camp humor and plugs it into a standard B-movie plot that has the buxom TV hostess heading off to the little town of Fallwell, Massachusetts, in a '58 T-bird to find out what her Aunt Morgana left her in the will. Local bluenose Chastity Pariah (Edie McClurg) is not amused. The action could move more quickly and the story could rely less on well-worn gimmicks, but Elvira's flippant feminist irreverence goes a long way. 🦴🦴

1988 (PG-13) 96m/C Cassandra Peterson, Jeff Conaway, Susan Kellerman, Edie McClurg, Daniel Greene, W. Morgan Shepherd, Kurt Fuller; ***D:*** James Signorelli; ***W:*** John Paragon, Sam Egan, Cassandra Peterson; ***C:*** Hanania Baer. **VHS, LV, Closed Caption** *VTR*

Embrace of the Vampire

Virginal college student Charlotte (Alyssa Milano) is pursued by a vampire (Martin Kemp) who, for reasons never explained, needs her to recharge his batteries. Though the same plot device was used in the frantic *Andy Warhol's Dracula,* director Anne Goursaud handles it more seriously. She certainly knows how to steam things up, making this one of the more intense "erotic" horrors. Her approach ranges from bodice-ripper romanticism to *90210* stereotypes to artfully posed Gothic seduction. Forget about coherence or logic. 🦴🦴🦴

1995 (R) 92m/C Alyssa Milano, Martin Kemp, Harrison Pruett, Charlotte Lewis, Jordan Ladd, Rachel True, Jennifer Tilly; ***D:*** Anne Goursaud; ***W:*** Halle Eaton, Nicole Coady, Rick Bitzelberger; ***M:*** Joseph Williams. **VHS, LV, Closed Caption** *TTC, IME*

Emerald Jungle

Any movie that begins with blow-gun murders in midtown Manhattan and Niagara Falls at Christmas can't be all bad, and this one lives up to its exploitative promise. The thin story of a Jim Jones-type cult is full of gratuitous mondo touches—giant hooks pierced through skin, firewalking, animal slaughter, a mongoose-cobra fight, people eating lizard guts—along with conventional cannibalism and sex. It ought to be seen through a bug-spotted windshield on a hot summer night at the drive-in, but video will do. This version's pretty sick and under the title *Eaten Alive by Cannibals* it's even longer. ***AKA:*** Eaten Alive by Cannibals; Eaten Alive; Mangiati Vivi; Mangiati Vivi dai Cannibali. 🦴🦴

1980 92m/C *IT* Robert Kerman, Janet Agren, Mel Ferrer, Luciano Martino, Mino Loy, Ivan Rassimov, Paola Senatore, Me Me Lay, Meg Fleming, Franco Fantasia; ***D:*** Umberto Lenzi; ***W:*** Umberto Lenzi; ***C:*** Frederico Zanni. **VHS** *NO*

Event Horizon

In 2047, a rescue ship travels to the orbit of Jupiter to find out what happened to the "Event Horizon," an experimental vessel that vanished there seven years before. It's just reappeared and Sam Neill, who built it, wants to know what happened. A completely capable cast, led by Laurence Fishburne and Joely Richardson, is given little to do amid some impressive sets and computer effects. The story is essentially a haunted house in outer space with one blatant reference to Clive Barker's *Hellraiser* series. The film also borrows from Frederick Pohl's *Gateway* s-f novels, but he's not credited. 🦴🦴½

1997 (R) 97m/C Laurence "Larry" Fishburne, Sam Neill, Kathleen Quinlan, Joely Richardson, Richard T. Jones, Jack Noseworthy, Sean Pertwee, Jason Isaacs; ***D:*** Paul Anderson; ***W:*** Philip Eisner; ***C:*** Adrian Biddle; ***M:*** Michael Kamen. **VHS, Closed Caption** *PAR*

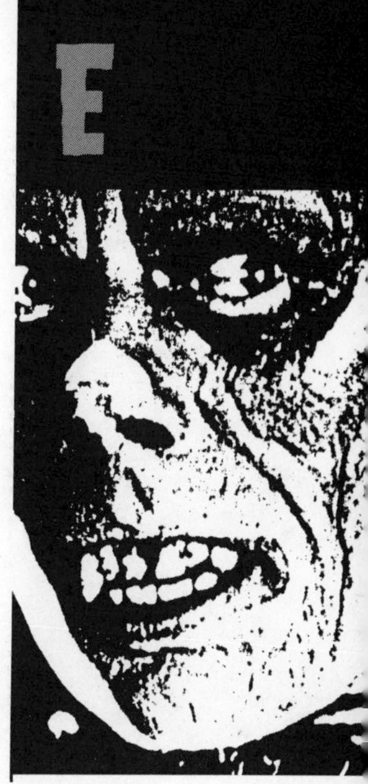

The Evil

Though it appears to be in the *Exorcist-Omen* school, this one is really more like *The Shining*. A group of researchers inadvertently lets the devil himself loose, and then tries to put him back where he belongs. With a solid cast of character actors, the result is better than you might expect and the film does have some moments that are frightening and surprising. Since the plot depends on those surprises, the less said about it, the better.

1978 (R) 80m/C Richard Crenna, Joanna Pettet, Andrew Prine, Victor Buono, Cassie Yates, George O'Hanlon Jr., Lynne Moody, Mary Louise Weller, Milton Selzer; ***D:*** Gus Trikonis; ***W:*** Donald G. Thompson; ***C:*** Mario DiLeo. **VHS**

Evil Dead

Director Sam Raimi and actor Bruce Campbell produced this cult favorite in 1983, right when the "slasher" trend in horror movies was ending. The film was lumped in with that bad lot and had only a limited theatrical release. But when home video appeared a few years later, it found its audience and became a bona fide cult hit. The story involves a group of young people who go off to a cabin in the woods and accidentally read from the Sumerian *Book of the Dead,* calling up all sorts of murderous spirits. Raimi's inventive camerawork is the real star though. Like New Zealander Peter Jackson, his approach to violence is so extreme that it's comic.

1983 (NC-17) 126m/C Bruce Campbell, Ellen Sandweiss, Betsy Baker, Hal Delrich, Sarah York; ***D:*** Sam Raimi; ***W:*** Sam Raimi; ***C:*** Tim Philo. **VHS, LV** *NO*

Evil Dead 2: Dead by Dawn

Rare sequel is actually superior to the original in some senses. Sam Raimi creates a special effects tour de force using stop-motion animation, prosthetics, reverse motion, and long dizzying tracking shots. Bruce Campbell (also a producer) being attacked by his own hand is a grand moment. The graphic violence is so removed from any reality that it has no emotional content, and that heightens the film's strong humor.

1987 (R) 84m/C Bruce Campbell, Sarah Berry, Dan Hicks, Kassie Wesley, Theodore (Ted) Raimi, Denise Bixler, Richard Domeier; ***D:*** Sam Raimi; ***W:*** Sam Raimi, Scott Spiegel; ***C:*** Peter Deming; ***M:*** Joseph LoDuca. **VHS, LV** *VTR, LIV*

Evil Dead Trap

Nami (Miyuki Ono), a Japanese late-night TV show host, is sent a tape that appears to show a brutal murder. Her cheap boss refuses to do anything, but she and her female crew decide to follow up on the tape and find the location where it was made. What follows in an abandoned factory owes much to Argento with even more visceral sex and violence. Director Toshiharu Ikeda's camera is almost never still. Takashi Ishii's script combines supernatural elements with a realistic setting and believable characters. Fans of the more grotesque Italian horror who are looking for the next big thing—here it is. The Video Search of Miami tape is letterboxed and conversationally subtitled.

1988 90m/C *JP* Miyuki Ono, Fumi Katsuragi, Hitomi Kobayashi, Eriko Nakagawa; ***D:*** Toshiharu Ikeda; ***W:*** Takashi Ishii. **VHS, Letterboxed** *VSM*

The Evil of Frankenstein

Like all Hammer films—and most films of any genre or type—this one's no better than its script. As long as Anthony Hinds' story sticks to the Baron (Peter Cushing) and his attempts to recreate his earlier work, the film is on firm ground with grand

SAM RAIMI

Sam Raimi started fooling around with 8mm. movie cameras when he was a little boy in Franklin, Michigan. (He was born in nearby Royal Oak in 1959.) From that inauspicious beginning half a continent away from the heart of the film industry, Raimi has eased his way into the business, and now seems to be ready to enter the mainstream.

His professional career began at Michigan State University where he, his brother Ivan, and their friend Robert Tapert created a short version of a goofy little horror film to entice investors into bankrolling the finished product. It became *Evil Dead,* a hit at the 1983 Cannes Festival and then a cult favorite at midnight screenings. Most fans, though, didn't discover Raimi and his movie until the home video revolution a few years later. By then, word had spread and so when *Evil Dead 2: Dead by Dawn* was released in 1987, it found a more appreciative audience.

Its boxoffice clout gave Raimi entree to the studio system. His first project was an imaginative amalgam of his favorite Universal monsters and series characters. In *Darkman,* you can find strains of *Phantom of the Opera, The Invisible Man, Frankenstein,* and *The Shadow* all whipped together at a frantic pace. In his first big-budget project, Raimi refined his flashy visual style, and he was able to add an attention to minute detail that had been absent before. Notice, for example, how carefully the story is set in an anonymous place. Even the license plates on cars and trucks have no identifying words.

With others directing, *Darkman* has been expanded into an excellent direct-to-video series. Raimi himself has turned some of his creative energies into television production with *M.A.N.T.I.S., Her-*

gizmo-intensive lab scenes and another strong performance by the star. But when it wanders afield with revisionist flashbacks to the Monster (Kiwi Kingston), a crude caricature of makeup man Jack Pierce's original, and such tired gimmicks as said Monster being preserved in a glacier (Please!), it's in trouble.

1964 84m/C *GB* Peter Cushing, Duncan Lamont, Peter Woodthorpe, Sandor Eles, Kiwi Kingston, Katy Wild; ***D:*** Freddie Francis; ***W:*** Anthony John Elder Hinds; ***C:*** John Wilcox; ***M:*** Don Banks. **VHS** *USH, MLB*

Evil Spawn

Star Bobbie Bresee, who was transformed into a monstrous critter in *Mausoleum,* suffers a similar fate after she injects herself with microbes from Venus. She plays Lynn Roman, an aging starlet who believes the juice will rejuvenate her looks and her career. It takes considerable throat clearing for writer/director Kenneth Hall to get around to that part of his cheerfully screwloose little B-flick. The real spark is Donna Shock (AKA Dawn Wildsmith) as mad Evelyn. The film has tons of grainily graphic gore and nudity, and not one ounce of seriousness. Curiously, the film was re-edited with added footage by Fred Olen Ray under the title *Alien Within.* ***AKA:*** Deadly Sting; Alive by Night; Alien Within.

1987 70m/C Bobbie Bresee, John Carradine, Drew Godderis, John Terrance, Dawn Wildsmith, Jerry Fox, Pamela Gilbert, Forrest J. Ackerman; ***D:*** Kenneth J. Hall; ***W:*** Kenneth J. Hall; ***C:*** Christopher Condon. **VHS** *NO*

cules, and *Xena: Warrior Princess* to his credit. He has also worked in various producing and acting capacities on projects by his friends Joel and Ethan Coen and John Woo.

For the moment, his interests seem to lie outside of pure horror. He directed Sharon Stone in the spaghetti-Western spoof *The Quick and the Dead,* and, as this book was going to press, he was at work on the film version of the best-selling novel *A Simple Plan.*

In whatever genre he chooses to work, Raimi ought to do well. Given his track record on TV, his instincts as a producer are right on target. His skills as a director—restless, inventive camerawork; strong rapport with actors—should serve him well with any good story. He doesn't seem to have had much trouble finding those, either.

SIGNIFICANT CONTRIBUTIONS TO HORROR

The Evil Dead **(1983)**

Evil Dead 2: Dead by Dawn **(1987)**

Darkman **(1990)**

Army of Darkness **(1992)**

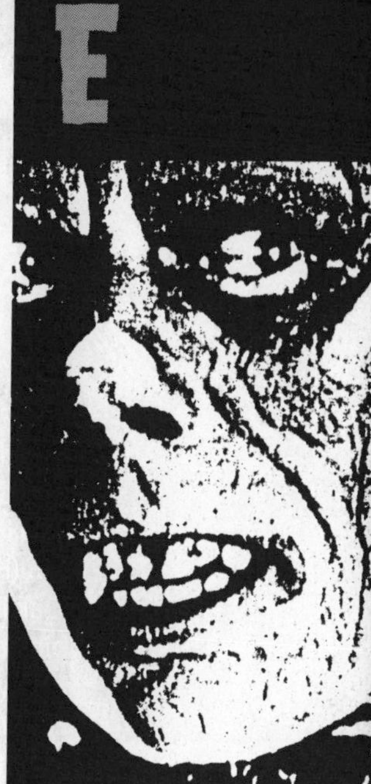

Evils of the Night

Combine a 1950s premise (vampires from outer space) with a 1970s dead teenager plot and 1980s exploitation and what do you get? Grade-Z schlock. Alas, it's not good grade-Z schlock, though the opening scene is really funny. The presence of such stalwarts as Aldo Ray, Neville Brand, Tina Louise, Julie Newmar, and John Carradine helps, but not enough. **Woof!**

1985 85m/C John Carradine, Julie Newmar, Tina Louise, Neville Brand, Aldo Ray, Karrie Emerson, Bridget Hollman; ***D:*** Marti Rustam; ***W:*** Marti Rustam, Phillip D. Connors. **VHS** *LIV*

The Ex

Yancy Butler plays the title role to a fare-thee-well, bringing a welcome tongue-in-cheek humor to wild-eyed psycho-babe Diedre Kenyon. Years ago, Diedre and David (Nick Mancuso) had a tempestuous marriage marked by rough sex and drug use. He saw the light; she had to be institutionalized. Now he's a success with a new wife, Molly (Suzy Amis), and five-year-old son. Diedre has gone off her medication and wants her old life back. Director Mark L. Lester (*Firestarter*) keeps the pot boiling nicely. That's a very good thing because if the pace slowed for one moment, viewers might start asking questions that writers Larry Cohen (*God Told Me To*) and John Lutz

(*Single White Female*) don't answer. It's acceptable to leave one murder victim unaccounted for at the end of a psycho-killer horror. But to have two central characters killed without anyone (including the cops!) noticing? That's just sloppy. 🦴🦴

1996 (R) 87m/C Yancy Butler, Nick Mancuso, Suzy Amis; ***D:*** Mark L. Lester; ***W:*** John Lutz, Larry Cohen; ***C:*** Richard Letterman; ***M:*** Paul Zaza. **VHS, LV** *LIV*

The Exorcist

The big special effects—projectile pea soup, swivelling head—aren't particularly impressive any more, but the important aspects still shine. Director William Friedkin's spare, no-frills style is as powerful as ever. He and writer/producer William Peter Blatty balance the supernatural elements with an almost documentary realism in the locations and personal relationships of the characters. They also wisely break unwritten "rules" by having important events take place off-camera. The performances and the rigorous religious aspects of the story also elevate the potentially ridiculous material. Unlike so many films in the genre, this one doesn't attempt to answer all its questions. The essential mystery remains. Stephen King has written that the source of the film's popularity lies in the generational conflicts of its time, and they are important, both explicitly and thematically. Followed by an embarrassing sequel. 🦴🦴🦴🦴

1973 (R) 120m/C Ellen Burstyn, Linda Blair, Jason Miller, Max von Sydow, Jack MacGowran, Lee J. Cobb, Kitty Winn; ***D:*** William Friedkin; ***W:*** William Peter Blatty; ***C:*** Owen Roizman; ***M:*** Jack Nitzsche; ***V:*** Mercedes McCambridge. Academy Awards '73: Best Adapted Screenplay, Best Sound; Golden Globe Awards '74: Best Director (Friedkin), Best Film—Drama, Best Screenplay, Best Supporting Actress (Blair); Nominations: Academy Awards '73: Best Actress (Burstyn), Best Art Direction/Set Decoration, Best Cinematography, Best Director (Friedkin), Best Film Editing, Best Picture, Best Supporting Actor (Miller), Best Supporting Actress (Blair). **VHS, LV, DVD** *WAR*

Regan (Linda Blair) in *The Exorcist*.

The Exorcist 2: The Heretic

In the annals of horror, this sequel can make a legitimate claim for worst major motion picture of all time. Admittedly, it's enjoyable as an alternative so-bad-it's-fun classic, but that's all. Fans of the original should never never see it. Richard Burton plays a priest (and protege of Max von Sydow's character) who's brought in to tidy things up with the teenaged Linda Blair. What is the most embarrassing moment? Could it be Burton telling his Cardinal (Paul Henreid) "I am not worthy"? Or the dual hypnosis machine that could have come straight from a bad s-f flick? How about the penthouse apartment made of polished steel? My own vote would go to Blair's "Lullaby of Broadway" softshoe routine which rivals Peter Boyle's "Putting on the Ritz" from *Young Frankenstein,* but that, of course, is meant to be funny. Inexplicably followed by another sequel. **Woof!**

1977 (R) 118m/C Richard Burton, Linda Blair, Louise Fletcher, Kitty Winn, James Earl Jones, Ned Beatty, Max von Sydow, Paul Henreid; ***D:*** John Boorman; ***W:*** William Goodhart; ***C:*** William A. Fraker; ***M:*** Ennio Morricone. **VHS** *NO*

Exorcist 3: Legion

In the wacky world of sequels, this one barely qualifies. Perhaps writer/director William Peter Blatty was trying to make up for the humiliation of *2* and so he turned his novel *Legion* into a talky serial killer-reincarnation-exorcism tale. Taking over for Lee J. Cobb as a Jewish D.C. detective, George C. Scott has a fine time with some delicious dialogue. (His "carp" speech is a joy.) The problem is that there is far too much of that dialogue. Blatty manages to create a few interesting visuals, but the true scares are few. Virtually all of the violence and much of the important physical

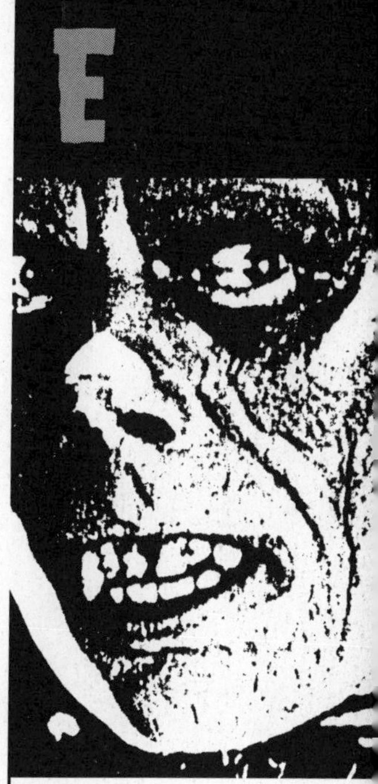

"Especially important is the warning to avoid conversations with the demon. We may ask what is relevant, but anything beyond that is dangerous.... He will lie to confuse us, but he will also mix lies with the truth to attack us."

—Father Merrin (Max von Sydow) to Father Karras (Jason Miller) in *The Exorcist*.

Eric Binford (Dennis Christopher) in *Fade to Black.*

action take place off camera. They're described, not shown. Yes, Fabio and Patrick Ewing appear briefly.

1990 (R) 105m/C George C. Scott, Ed Flanders, Jason Miller, Nicol Williamson, Scott Wilson, Brad Dourif, Nancy Fish, George DiCenzo, Viveca Lindfors, Patrick Ewing, Fabio; ***D:*** William Peter Blatty; ***W:*** William Peter Blatty; ***C:*** Gerry Fisher. **VHS, LV, Closed Caption** *FOX, CCB*

Eyes of Laura Mars

Exploitative, dull, and finally predictable psychic horror tale is all gloss and no substance. Laura Mars (Faye Dunaway) photographs kinky high-fashion layouts, and defends her work by claiming that she's actually making a statement against all this weird sex and violence. In a pig's eye. The movie constantly leers at its subject while Ms. Mars has psychic visions of real killings and becomes involved with a cop (Tommy Lee Jones). Throughout, Faye Dunaway uses two expressions to express any emotion: wide-eyed lip-quivering fear and wide-eyed stoned trance. **Woof!**

1978 (R) 104m/C Faye Dunaway, Tommy Lee Jones, Brad Dourif, Rene Auberjonois, Raul Julia, Darlanne Fluegel, Michael Tucker; ***D:*** Irvin Kershner; ***W:*** John Carpenter, David Zelag Goodman. **VHS, LV, Closed Caption** *NO*

Faceless

Give Jess (Jesus) Franco credit for some consistency. He keeps telling the same story over and over again, putting essentially the same characters through the same conflicts and complications, while making each incarnation as violent and sexual as the times will allow. This one is another version of 1961's *The Awful Dr. Orloff.* (Howard Vernon, who played the character, appears as Orloff in a cameo.) Helmut Berger is the surgeon who's trying to restore his acid-scarred sister's beauty. He's willing to resort to anything—kidnapping, torture, disco—to accomplish his fiendish scheme. The big-budget cast includes Telly Savalas, Stephane Audrane, Caroline Munro, and Anton Diffring as a Nazi doctor who worked with Mengele. (The three-bone rating is mostly for Franco fans.) ***AKA:*** Les Predateurs de la Nuit. 🦴🦴🦴

1988 98m/C Helmut Berger, Brigitte Lahaie, Chris Mitchum, Telly Savalas, Stephane Audran, Anton Diffring, Caroline Munro, Howard Vernon; ***D:*** Jess (Jesus) Franco; ***W:*** Fred Castle, Pierre Ripert, Jean Mazarain, Michele Lebrun. **VHS** *VSM*

Fade to Black

Undervalued character study can almost be seen as a West Coast *Taxi Driver* with Hollywood Boulevard standing in for the mean streets of New York. Toss in strong nods to *Targets* and *Whatever Happened to Baby Jane.* Eric Binford (Dennis Christopher) is a delivery boy who has trouble separating his encyclopedic knowledge of old movies from everyday reality. A young Marilyn wannabe (Linda Kerridge) further blurs his perceptual problems until Eric begins to take on his favorite screen identities—Dracula, the Mummy, Cody Jarrett from *White Heat*—to get even with an uncaring world. The attractions are Christopher's flamboyant but believable performance and dozens of clips and quotes from old films. 🦴🦴🦴

1980 (R) 100m/C Dennis Christopher, Tim Thomerson, Linda Kerridge, Mickey Rourke, Melinda Fee, Gwynne Gilford, Norman Burton, Morgan Paull, James Luisi, John Steadman, Marcie Barkin, Eve Brent Ashe; ***D:*** Vernon Zimmerman; ***W:*** Vernon Zimmerman; ***C:*** Alex Phillips Jr. **VHS** *MLB*

The Fall of the House of Usher

Roger Corman's first adaptation of Poe is creaky—literally. It's a three-character drama set in a mansion that is slowly and groaningly collapsing. Roderick Usher (Vincent Price) refuses to let his sister (Myrna Fahey) marry her fiance (Mark Damon) because of an undefined "family curse." Price is excellent in one of his most restrained and quiet roles. Corman and writer Richard Matheson conceive the story as a product of Roderick's imagination, and it certainly works that way. Unfortunately, early video editions are made from an imperfect print. Like so much of Corman's early work, it's due for restoration and—in this case—a widescreen, letterboxed transfer. By the way, the tape claims that it's 85 minutes long; my VCR clocks it at 78 minutes. ***AKA:*** House of Usher. 🦴🦴🦴

1960 85m/C Vincent Price, Myrna Fahey, Mark Damon, Harry Ellerbe; ***D:*** Roger Corman; ***W:*** Richard Matheson; ***C:*** Floyd Crosby; ***M:*** Les Baxter. **VHS** *WAR, OM*

Fangs! A History of Vampires in the Movies

Introduction to the cinematic undead is a series of clips, many taken from hyperventilating trailers, loosely strung together with narration by Hammer heroine Veronica Carlson. Director Bruce Hallenbeck touches lightly on the high spots, from *Nosferatu* and *Vampyr* to the Hammer films. The tone is so hokey that it will remind you of the old late-show creature features where a local guy dressed up in a cape and made bad jokes on a cardboard graveyard set. Ms. Carlson is fairly stiff and she's served poorly by some atrocious editing. Several of the snippets of film are faded and grainy, but they may spark more interest in younger viewers who haven't seen the originals. 🦴🦴

1992 60m/C ***D:*** Bruce G. Hallenbeck; ***W:*** Bruce G. Hallenbeck. **VHS** *EII*

Fascination

In 1916, well-to-do Frenchwomen (Franca Mai and Brigitte Lahaie) meet at a slaughterhouse to drink bull's blood for their health. They're up to something else, too.

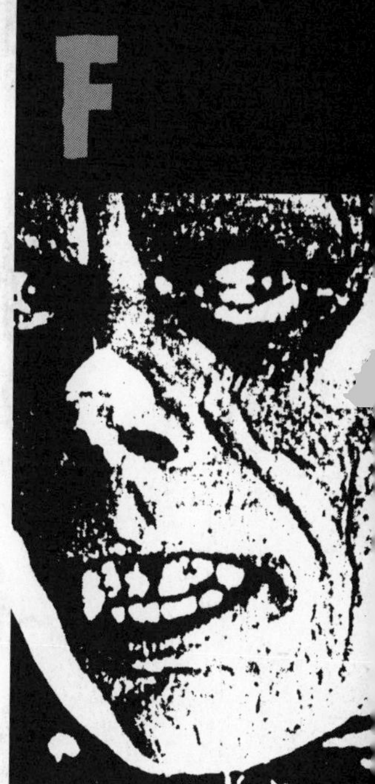

THE HOUND SALUTES

WILLIAM FRIEDKIN

William Friedkin sent shock-waves across the world in 1973 with *The Exorcist*, his horrific, special effects-filled version of William Peter Blatty's best-seller.

Following his Oscar-winning cop movie, *The French Connection*, and cinematic translation of the gay-themed play, *The Boys in the Band*, Friedkin's first foray into the fright field was both an event and an anomaly: a big-budget studio horror effort that spooked audiences with its tale of demonic possession, brought in a smashing $89 million in theatres, and garnered 10 Academy Award nominations.

But Friedkin, a Chicago native who got his start in films by directing documentaries for local television, always looked at *The Exorcist* differently than everyone else.

"*The Exorcist*, to me, was never a horror film," he says. "It was a story about fate—inexplicable things, but not a horror film. It certainly had elements of the supernatural and the bizarre, but it is, after all, based on a true story."

Although people still talk about the powerful experience of seeing *The Exorcist* for the first time, Friedkin claims he never intended to shock audiences. "I never though about this stuff when I was making *The Exorcist*," he says. "Its impact never occurred to me. There was the novel, which was a best-seller, and the paperback, which sold 12 million copies. But I had no idea of its [the film's] popularity, and the studio didn't either. They released it in only 26 theatres for the first six months. After that, it was anyone's guess what was going to happen."

And it was anyone's guess how Friedkin, perhaps the hottest director in the world, would follow the international success of that film. He decided to avoid its sequels, *Exorcist 2: The Heretic*, which John Boorman handled, and *The Exorcist 3: Legion*, which Blatty himself helmed.

"[I knew] *Exorcist 3* was not for me," says Friedkin. "It isn't a true sequel in any way—it just capitalizes on the notoriety of the first film. It was based on a book Bill [Blatty] wrote called *Legion*, but couldn't get off the ground [as a movie] until he called it *Exorcist 3*."

Instead, Friedkin followed with *Sorcerer*, an intense reworking of the 1952 French adventure classic *Wages of Fear*, about a group of

When a small-time thief (Jean-Marie Lemaire) who has betrayed his gang takes up refuge in their chateau, he thinks he's in charge. The first half is essentially soft-core exploitation that turns to fairly graphic violence in the second, with some interesting ideas about sexual power. Rollin's work—one of his best—compares favorably to American low-budget work of the same era, though it would be better if Lemaire were able to project a stronger screen presence. 🦴🦴🦴

1979 80m/C *FR* Franca Mai, Brigitte Lahaie, Jean-Marie Lemaire, Fanny Magier, Muriel Montosse, Alain Plumey; ***D:*** Jean Rollin; ***W:*** Jean Rollin; ***C:*** Georges Fromentin. **VHS** *VSM*

Fatal Attraction

A line of small print in the credits reads "screenplay by James Dearden based on his original screenplay." That curious dis-troubled men hired to drive explosives over a rugged mountain terrain. The spectral-sounding title may have been willing, but the movie audiences' spirits weren't, as *Sorcerer* received disappointing boxoffice results.

"The title has been criticized for not having much significance, but it does to me," says Friedkin. "The studio suggested other titles, but I stayed with it. To me, 'Sorcerer' means 'evil wizard,' and I think that's appropriate because it's [unexplainable] fate that drives its characters' lives."

In 1990, Friedkin returned to turf similar to his biggest hit with *The Guardian,* a stylish but muddled fable about a young couple who entrust their infant to a mysterious nanny who happens to be tree-worshipping Druid. *Mary Poppins* this isn't.

"I liked the story of *The Guardian*. It had potential to be a Brothers Grimm-styled story in a contemporary setting. That's what attracted me to it. I never thought it would be compared to *The Exorcist* as a horror film."

At one time, Friedkin was set to take another stab at the horror genre with *The Secret Diaries of Jack-the-Ripper,* but the project fell apart after the Hughes Brothers (*Menace II Society*) signed on to make a Ripper-themed film for the same company.

Whether the versatile Friedkin is tackling the gravity-defying terror of *The Exorcist,* the erotic thrills of *Jade,* the serial killer-on-trial dramatics of *Rampage,* or a reworking of the courtroom classic *12 Angry Men* for cable TV, he sees similar themes in all of his work.

"There's a kind of desperation to the characters I'm interested in," he says. "They're all in extremely heightened states in a heightened situation. And in the course of my films, we're exploring all of their fears—the rational and the irrational."

—Irv Slifkin

SIGNIFICANT CONTRIBUTIONS TO HORROR

***The Exorcist* (1973)**

***The Guardian* (1990)**

claimer explains the screwy nature of this boxoffice hit. For most of its running time, the story of an affair (between Michael Douglas and Glenn Close) that goes bad is another version of Clint Eastwood's excellent *Play Misty for Me*. But in the last reel, it changes completely when her character becomes an unapologetic, bunny-boiling female Jason Voorhees who's never dead when you think she's dead. Why? Preview audiences didn't like the more complex and downbeat original ending. (That version is now available on video, along with the theatrical release.) 🦴🦴

1987 (R) 120m/C Michael Douglas, Glenn Close, Anne Archer, Stuart Pankin, Ellen Hamilton-Latzen, Ellen Foley, Fred Gwynne, Meg Mundy, J.J. Johnston; ***D:*** Adrian Lyne; ***W:*** James Dearden; ***C:*** Howard Atherton; ***M:*** Maurice Jarre. Nominations: Academy Awards '87: Best Actress (Close), Best Adapted Screenplay, Best Director (Lyne), Best Film Editing, Best Picture, Best Supporting Actress (Archer). **VHS, LV, 8mm, Letterboxed, Closed Caption** *PAR, FCT, CCB*

"**Happiness is plaguing me.**"

—Eumolpus (Salvo Randone) in *Fellini Satyricon.*

Fatal Love

Debbie Fung (Ellen Chan) is a rookie Hong Kong cop who's talked into going undercover to catch a possible serial killer, the wealthy, handsome, and charming Fuk Tin (Michael Wong). Their relationship quickly turns into a seductive game of lies, possessions, violence, and sex. The manipulative misogynist element is undeniable, and the film works through shocking images. The characters' relative power is unbalanced throughout, and director Chan Chi Suen explores areas of horror that most American movies wouldn't go near. Scorsese's *Cape Fear* and the original *The Vanishing* come close. 🦴🦴🦴

1995 90m/C *HK* Ellen Chan, Michael Wong; ***D:*** Chan Chi Suen. **VHS** *VSM*

The Fear Chamber

At the end of his career, Boris Karloff appeared briefly in four Mexican horror films. (The footage was shot in Los Angeles.) His presence in this pitiful, disjointed piece of junk is limited to a few static scenes. The rest is grade-Z nonsense that begins with people in silver suits discovering a creature in a volcano. Sample dialogue: "I found the source of the signal. It's a rock formation that seems to have an interior life." Despite the participation of a voyeuristic dwarf, nubile babes in their underwear, one stripper, and some incredibly cheap effects, the rest isn't nearly as much fun as it sounds. The one-bone rating is meant only for fans of alternative cinema. ***AKA:*** Torture Zone; Chamber of Fear; La Camara Del Terror; Torture Chamber. 🦴

1968 88m/C *MX* Boris Karloff, Yerye Beirut, Julissa, Carlos East, Sandra Chavez, Eva Muller, Pamela Rosas, Santanon, Isela Vega; ***D:*** Juan Ibanez, Jack Hill; ***W:*** Jack Hill, Luis Enrique Vergara; ***C:*** Austin McKinney, Raul Dominguez. **VHS** *SNC, MPI*

The Fearless Vampire Killers

Taking another look at Hammer's *Kiss of the Vampire,* it's easy to see where Roman Polanski got most of the inspiration for his 1967 horror-comedy. The video edition is a full-length "director's version" that doesn't appear to be noticeably different from the theatrical release. Longer doesn't necessarily mean better, either. Like the other stylish Hammer horrors of the period, the sets and costumes are lavish. So are the camerawork and acting. Today's audiences will find the pace a little slow and Polanski's humor sometimes forced. The film has its moments—Ferdy Mayne is an excellent vampire and Sharon Tate, a lovely heroine—but it's no *Young Frankenstein.* ***AKA:*** Pardon Me, Your Teeth Are in My Neck; Dance of the Vampires. 🦴🦴½

1967 98m/C *GB* Jack MacGowran, Roman Polanski, Alfie Bass, Jessie Robbins, Sharon Tate, Ferdinand "Ferdy" Mayne, Iain Quarrier, Terry Downes, Fiona Lewis, Ronald Lacey; ***D:*** Roman Polanski; ***W:*** Gerard Brach, Roman Polanski; ***C:*** Douglas Slocombe. **VHS, LV, Letterboxed** *MGM*

Fellini Satyricon

Federico Fellini's "free adaptation of the Petronius classic" is an autobiographical horror film of pre-Christian pagan decadence. It's an episodic journey through a surreal hell that's fetid, swollen, and about to burst. "What caused the decadence?" the film's Felliniesque poet asks. "Lust of money," he answers. But a literal reading of the plot—difficult if not impossible—means less than the images, and those are some of the strongest in a body of work filled with indelible images. The underground human hive destroyed by an earthquake, a huge seafaring barge in the snow, the temple of the hermaphrodite, the Minotaur's city. On one level, it's a journey from darkness to light in a world filled with grotesques, suicide, dismemberment, impotence, and fart jokes. The videotape is a full widescreen transfer with clear subtitles beneath the image, but see the film in a theatre, if you ever get the chance. Though this hideous masterpiece has never been a commercial hit, it's one that people will be watching a hundred years from now. ***AKA:*** Satyricon.

1969 (R) 129m/C *IT* Martin Potter, Capucine, Hiram Keller, Salvo Randone, Max Born; ***D:*** Federico Fellini; ***W:*** Federico Fellini; ***C:*** Giuseppe Rotunno; ***M:*** Nino Rota. Nominations: Academy Awards '70: Best Director (Fellini). **VHS, LV, Letterboxed** *MGM, FCT, TVC*

The Fiance

Faith Moore (Lysette Anthony, also producer) and her workaholic husband Richard (Patrick Cassidy) are going through a rough time when she meets the seductive but slightly psycho Walter (William R. Moses), who insinuates his way into their lives. Moses' performance is a shade too tightly wound, but he's still a chilling figure, and the script by Greg Walker and Frank Rehwaldt is cleverly developed. In the end, it's an interesting variation on the familiar attack-on-the-family plot.

1996 (R) 94m/C William R. Moses, Lysette Anthony, Patrick Cassidy, Alina Thompson, Wanda Acuna, Gordon Thomson; ***D:*** Martin Kitrosser; ***W:*** Greg Walker, Frank Rehwaldt; ***C:*** M. David Mullen; ***M:*** Richard Bowers. **VHS, Closed Caption** *LIV*

The Final Conflict

The *Omen* series returns to something like its former level of quality for the conclusion. Perhaps the presence of Richard Donner, director of the original, as executive producer has something to do with it. Star Sam Neill, one of the best character actors in the business, makes the most of a well-written role. He carries off potentially hilarious dialogue with absolute conviction and believability, giving the adult Damien a strong streak of Nixonian bravado. The gruesome effects and stunts are better, too, particularly a long fox hunt scene. The plot is strong and the trilogy ends on a note of religio-cinematic excess worthy of Cecil B. DeMille. ***AKA:*** The Omen 3.

1981 (R) 108m/C Sam Neill, Lisa Harrow, Barnaby Holm, Rossano Brazzi, Don Gordon, Marc Boyle, Tommy Duggan, Richard Oldfield, Mason Adams, Robert Arden; ***D:*** Graham Baker; ***W:*** Andrew Birkin; ***C:*** Phil Meheux, Bob Paynter; ***M:*** Jerry Goldsmith. **VHS, LV, Letterboxed** *FOX*

Firestarter

Stephen King's story of psychic powers, government spooks, and violent effects is comparable to *The Fury,* but it's much more enjoyable. The difference—veteran B-movie director Mark L. Lester (*Truck Stop Women*) understands the pulp roots of the material and doesn't try to make the film more than it is. He keeps the plot moving swiftly, but not at the expense of believably middle-class protagonists. No matter what has happened since, Drew Barrymore certainly was a cute chubby-cheeked little rascal, even when she's flaming feds, turning them into shiskabobs in suits. George C. Scott and Martin Sheen are good villains, too.

1984 (R) 115m/C David Keith, Drew Barrymore, Freddie Jones, Martin Sheen, George C. Scott, Heather Locklear, Louise Fletcher, Moses Gunn, Art Carney, Antonio Fargas, Drew Snyder; ***D:*** Mark L. Lester; ***W:*** Stanley Mann; ***C:*** Giuseppe Ruzzolini; ***M:*** Tangerine Dream. **VHS, LV, Closed Caption** *USH*

Flesh and Blood Show

There's actually precious little of either flesh or blood in this mistitled snoozer. A troupe of young British actors is sent out to a seaside theatre to rehearse an improvisational play. It's a dark place where, decades before, murders took place. A prankster in the group stages grisly prac-

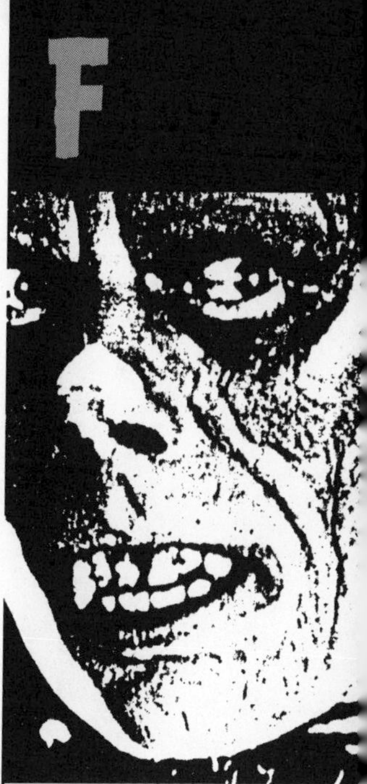

Charlie McGee (Drew Barrymore) in Stephen King's *Firestarter.*

tical jokes which become the real thing. It's a good idea and the theatrical context is interesting. The problem is that the film is too murky. The key interior scenes are impenetrable; so are some of the accents. ***AKA:*** Asylum of the Insane. 🦴🦴

1973 (R) 93m/C *GB* Robin Askwith, Candace Glendenning, Tristan Rogers, Ray Brooks, Jenny Hanley, Luan Peters, Patrick Barr, Judy Matheson, Penny Meredith; ***D:*** Pete Walker; ***W:*** Alfred Shaughnessy; ***C:*** Peter Jessop. **VHS** *SMW*

The Fly

One of the most famous '50s horror movies is also one of the most lavish. The story of a scientist (David Hedison) whose teleportation experiment goes horribly awry is remembered for its make-up effects, still shocking despite massive advances in the field. More impressive today are the strong characters who react realistically to a fantastic situation, a complex script by James Clavell (who'd go on to write the best-selling novels *Shogun* and *Tai Pan*), and a really sumptuous production. Vincent Price is excellent in a serious dramatic role. The key emotional moments are genuinely poignant, and the "Help me, please, help me!" ending is a cinematic touchstone. Followed by two sequels and a strong remake. 🦴🦴🦴🦴

1958 94m/C Vincent Price, David Hedison, Herbert Marshall, Patricia Owens; ***D:*** Kurt Neumann; ***W:*** James Clavell; ***C:*** Karl Struss. **VHS, LV** *FOX*

The Fly

David Cronenberg and Jeff Goldblum take a fantastic premise (teleportation) and treat it matter-of-factly. Their remake of the 1958 original is, in many ways, better. As the scientist Brundle, Goldblum mixes humor, horror, and pathos so effectively that his performance merits comparison to Boris

Karloff in *Frankenstein.* As he is progressively transformed into something more and more monstrous, he becomes a creature that we still care about and sympathize with. The Oscar-winning effects may lose something in transition to the small screen, but that personal element is even stronger in the more intimate medium of home video.

1986 (R) 96m/C Jeff Goldblum, Geena Davis, John Getz, Joy Boushel, Les Carlson; ***D:*** David Cronenberg; ***W:*** David Cronenberg, Charles Edward Pogue; ***C:*** Mark Irwin; ***M:*** Howard Shore. Academy Awards '86: Best Makeup. **VHS, LV, Closed Caption** *FOX*

The Fog

An old sailor (John Houseman) sits with a group of wide-eyed kids around a campfire on a beach and tells them how a ship was wrecked by a false signal fire in the fog 100 years before. If the fog ever returns, so will the sailors' ghosts, looking for revenge. They do, attacking the local radio DJ (Adrienne Barbeau), a drunken priest (Hal Holbrook), hitchhiker (Jamie Lee Curtis), and several others. No, the film isn't as taut as John Carpenter's previous effort, *Halloween,* but it's a fine spooky ghost story.

1978 (R) 91m/C Hal Holbrook, Adrienne Barbeau, Jamie Lee Curtis, Janet Leigh, John Houseman, Tom Atkins; ***D:*** John Carpenter; ***W:*** John Carpenter, Debra Hill; ***C:*** Dean Cundey; ***M:*** John Carpenter. **VHS, LV, 8mm** *COL*

The Forgotten One

Searching for inspiration, a widowed novelist (Terry O'Quinn) moves to Denver and buys an old Victorian house that's haunted by a fetching, mysterious ghost (Blair Parker). His neighbor (Kristy McNichol) helps him find answers. Admittedly, this one suffers from the logic problems that plague most supernatural stories, but beyond that, it's a spooky, sexy ghost movie. O'Quinn brings the same tightly wrapped unpredictability to this role that makes *The Stepfather* so memorable. Throughout, the formula aspects of the genre are kept to a minimum, and the special effects are atmospheric and effective. One of the best and least appreciated sleepers around.

1989 (R) 89m/C Kristy McNichol, Terry O'Quinn, Blair Parker, Elisabeth Brooks; ***D:*** Phillip Badger; ***W:*** Phillip Badger; ***C:*** James Mathers. **VHS, LV** *NO*

Frankenhooker

"Bioelectrotechnician" Jeffrey Franken's (James Lorinz) fiancee (Patty Mullen) is killed in a tragic lawn mower accident, but he manages to salvage a few key body parts. If he can just find donors for the rest, he's sure he can recreate her, so late one night he heads for Times Square. Like director Frank Henenlotter's overlooked *Brain Damage,* this one is strongly, even violently anti-drug. Though parts of the story are every bit as grotesque as his most famous cult hit *Basket Case,* they're exaggerated for a more comic effect. The real surprise here is Patty Mullen, an ex-*Penthouse* model who turns out to be an accomplished comedienne.

1990 (R) 90m/C James Lorinz, Patty Mullen, Charlotte J. Helmkamp, Louise Lasser, Shirley Stoler; ***D:*** Frank Henenlotter. **VHS, LV, Closed Caption** *SGE, FCT*

Frankenstein

The trappings—clothes, sets, makeup, acting—are all dated now, and the plot, based on a stage play, has some glaring lapses that don't completely work on the screen. All of those will probably seem funny to young audiences. But when Boris Karloff makes his big entrance as the Monster, the laughter will stop. At heart, James Whale's adaptation of Mary Shelley's novel remains the model for most of the horror films that have followed. (It's also one of the most deceptively complex films ever made.) The mad scientist ("I have discov-

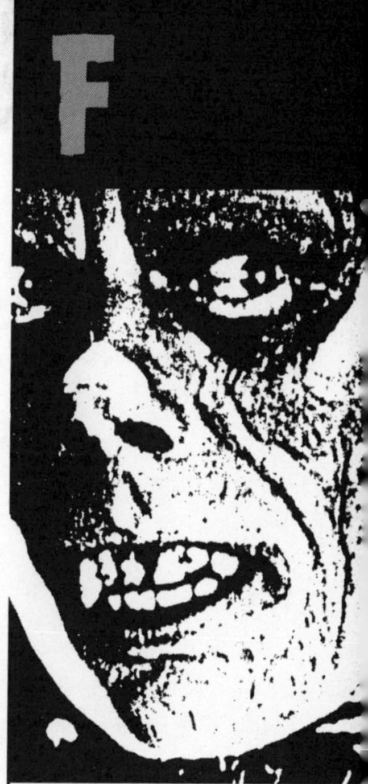

"Now I know what it feels like to be God."

—Dr. Frankenstein (Colin Clive) in *Frankenstein.*

ered the great ray that first brought life into the world!") with his lab full of crackling electricity, the peasant mob, the stylized cemetery—they've all become instantly recognizable parts of the language of film. More importantly, so is the Monster, a combination of Jack Pierce's makeup and Boris Karloff's genius as an actor. With his expressive hands, a face often filled with tortured confusion, and ungainly physical presence, he is one of horror's immortal figures. Many critics prefer the sequel, *Bride of Frankenstein,* to the original, but the films really should be seen as two parts of one story. Newer tapes include the famous "missing" scene at the lake, though a controversial line of dialogue—"Now I know what it feels like to be God!"—is still distorted.

1931 71m/B Boris Karloff, Colin Clive, Mae Clarke, John Boles, Dwight Frye, Edward Van Sloan, Frederick Kerr, Lionel Belman; ***D:*** James Whale; ***W:*** Francis Edwards Faragoh, Garrett Fort, John Balderston, Robert Florey; ***C:*** Arthur Edeson; ***M:*** David Broeckman. **VHS, LV** *USH, TLF, HMV*

Frankenstein and the Monster from Hell

Hammer's final entry in the *Frankenstein* series isn't its best, but the film still manages to find a few new angles to play with. The grave-robbing Dr. Helder (Shane Briant) is committed to an asylum run by the Baron (Peter Cushing), who's still up to his old experiments with a hulking, hairy creature (Dave Prowse). Cushing's Frankenstein remains an energetic if somewhat remote character, and Prowse finds real pathos beneath heavy makeup. Beyond simple gross-out props like a jar full of eyeballs, the lab scenes are lacking.

1974 (R) 93m/C *GB* Peter Cushing, Shane Briant, Madeleine Smith, David Prowse, John Stratton, Bernard Lee, Patrick Troughton, Sydney Bromley; ***D:*** Terence Fisher; ***W:*** Anthony John Elder Hinds; ***C:*** Brian Probyn; ***M:*** James Bernard. **VHS, Closed Caption** *PAR*

Frankenstein Created Woman

Hammer's fourth take on the Frankenstein story is a departure from most sequels. The traditional mad scientist scenes with crackling electrodes and lightning are largely absent. In their place are less expensive "soul" translocations from one body to another. To satisfy horror fans, the film has an ongoing fascination with decapitation that begins with the first scene. Peter Cushing is a bit abrupt and curt as the Baron, leaving most of the dramatic work to his co-stars Susan Denberg, Robert Morris, and particularly Thorley Walters as a sidekick whose bumbling is reminiscent of Sherlock Holmes' Dr. Watson. The story has a warm, honestly emotional basis that's often lacking in horror. The plot moves away from the traditional structure of earlier Hammer films. It's more openly geared toward a younger audience, reflecting the changes that were going on in the mid-1960s. ***AKA:*** Frankenstein Made Woman.

1966 86m/C *GB* Peter Cushing, Susan Denberg, Thorley Walters, Robert Morris, Duncan Lamont, Peter Blythe, Alan McNaughton, Peter Madden, Barry Warren, Derek Fowlds; ***D:*** Terence Fisher; ***W:*** Anthony John Elder Hinds; ***C:*** Arthur Grant.

Frankenstein Meets the Wolfman

Technically a sequel to *The Wolf Man,* this is the first Universal feature to bring two of the studio's monsters together. The formula worked well enough for a dozen or so lower-budget films that are entertaining enough, even if they don't approach the 1930s originals. Lawrence Talbot (Lon Chaney, Jr.) is resurrected by grave robbers and then cannot persuade anyone that he's a werewolf. Maleeva (Maria Ous-

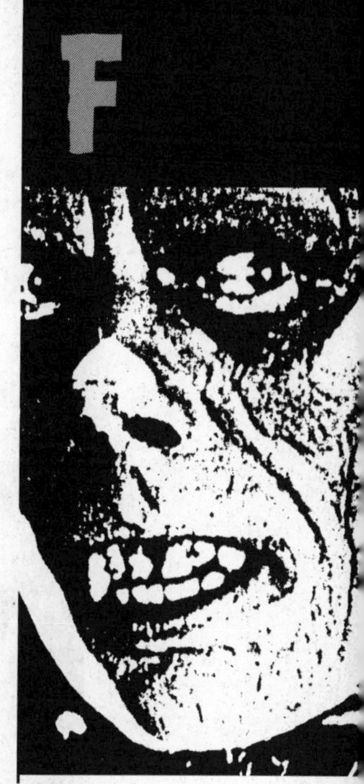

Boris Karloff is Universal's *Frankenstein* (1931).

THE HOUND SALUTES

THE FRANKENSTEIN MONSTER

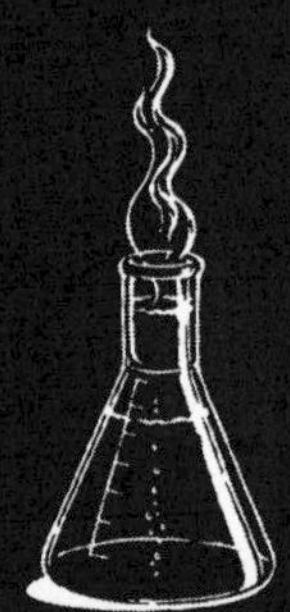

By now, everyone must be familiar with the story of how Mary Shelley, her husband Percy Shelley, Lord Byron, and Dr. Polidori kicked back one night in 1816 at the Villa Diodati near Vienna. They decided to have a little contest to see who could come up with the scariest story. She won with *Frankenstein*. The scene was inappropriately lampooned at the beginning of *Bride of Frankenstein* and it's also been dramatized in the films *Gothic* and *Haunted Summer*.

Mary Shelley's novel has been a perennial top seller from the moment it was published. It's probably been adapted to stage and screen as often as any work of popular fiction in any genre. Audiences were already familiar with the story in 1910 when the *Edison Frankenstein* was made. Like all versions, that one hits the key points in the plot: driven young scientist, monster made of body parts, creation, girlfriend, conflict.

All right, given those loose narrative restrictions, which could be applied to any number of variations on the story from *Re-Animator* to Kenneth Branagh's *Mary Shelley's Frankenstein*, the central question for audiences can be boiled down to this:

What does the monster look like?

Will he be the silly papier-mache bad-hair day of *Dracula Vs. Frankenstein*? Johnny Depp's teenaged misfit in whiteface from *Edward Scissorhands*? The guy with the cup handles above his ears in *Frankenstein Unbound*?

All of them provoke different degrees of laughter, pathos, and incredulity, and, like it or not, they all have to be compared to the 1931 *Frankenstein*. When Hammer Films decided to remake the film, one of the first things the producers learned was that though the story was in public domain, the original makeup was protected by copyright. Hammer's make-up man Phil Leakey gave Christopher Lee a suitably frightening, disfigured look, but it doesn't match that archetypal creation of director James Whale, make-up artist Jack Pierce, and actor Boris Karloff.

Details of their various contributions vary from teller to teller, but, as David Skal puts it in *The Monster Show* (Penguin, 1993), Pierce created the basic design working from sketches that Whale, who'd been a cartoonist, had made of Karloff's face. They'd agreed on certain features—the oversized forehead, the electrodes in the neck—and Karloff suggested the addition of putty on his eyelids. Their collaboration is one of the screen's most frightening figures. But if Whale and Pierce gave the monster his face, Karloff gave him a soul, and that's what brings people back to the story time and again.

A horror that the viewer comes to understand and perhaps even to love is the genre's most difficult story to construct. Botched versions are a penny a pound. The good ones never die.

penskaya) persuades him to see Dr. Frankenstein. Instead, they find his creation. As the Monster, Bela Lugosi is a parody of Karloff, though that's not entirely his fault. His character is supposed to be blind, though pre-release cuts eliminated that information. Look for Dwight Frye in a cameo. 🦴🦴🦴

1942 73m/C Lon Chaney Jr., Bela Lugosi, Patric Knowles, Lionel Atwill, Maria Ouspenskaya, Ilona Massey, Dwight Frye; ***D:*** Roy William Neill; ***W:*** Curt Siodmak; ***C:*** George Robinson. **VHS, LV** *USH, MLB*

Frankenstein Must Be Destroyed

The fifth of Hammer's Frankenstein series was meant to be the final installment. There's a coldness to the sleek production—almost a bitterness—much stronger and more obvious than it had been two years before in *Frankenstein Created Woman.* Dapper in spats, Peter Cushing is "a mad and highly dangerous medical adventurer," as the clueless authorities put it. He ruthlessly blackmails a young couple (Simon Ward and Veronica Carlson) into helping him with an oddly baroque scheme. They and the other supporting characters are colorful and well defined. In place of the conventional (and expensive) lab scenes, the monster business is accomplished through creative surgery. The simplicity of the early Hammer films has been replaced by strange plotting that includes a strong rape scene. The crazed final act is still emotionally moving. 🦴🦴🦴

1969 97m/C *GB* Peter Cushing, Veronica Carlson, Freddie Jones, Maxine Audley, Simon Ward, Thorley Walters, George Pravda, Colette O'Neil; ***D:*** Terence Fisher; ***W:*** Bert Batt; ***C:*** Arthur Grant.

Frankenstein Unbound

Curious s-f/horror (based on a Brian Aldiss novel) begins in L.A., 2031, where Joseph Buchanan (John Hurt) invents a particle weapon that creates "time slips" which transport him and his computer-enhanced sports car to Switzerland, 1817, where he meets Victor Frankenstein (Raul Julia). Mary (Bridget Fonda) and Percy Shelley (Michael Hutchence) and Lord Byron (Jason Patric) are hanging around, too, though they take smaller supporting roles. It's every bit as screwy as it sounds but not as much fun. Roger Corman, behind the camera for the first time in 20 years, gives the film a glowing look that partially makes up for the thin period details. The special effects are limited to lightshow stuff and forgettable monster makeup for Nick Brimble. In the end, the film is more interesting than good, and that's unusual for Corman, who usually works within a stronger narrative structure. ***AKA:*** Roger Corman's Frankenstein Unbound. 🦴🦴

1990 (R) 86m/C John Hurt, Raul Julia, Bridget Fonda, Jason Patric, Michael Hutchence, Catherine Rabett, Nick Brimble, Catherine Corman, Mickey Knox; ***D:*** Roger Corman; ***W:*** Roger Corman, F.X. Feeney; ***M:*** Carl Davis; ***V:*** Terri Treas. **VHS, LV, Closed Caption** *FOX*

Freaks

After a lengthy and defensive onscreen written introduction, Tod Browning's curious little thriller literally rips into action. Trapeze artiste Cleo (Olga Baclanova) flirts with the midget Hans (Harry Earles), though she and her strongman lover Hercules (Henry Victor) are mocking the little man. When they learn that Hans is rich, she schemes to marry and murder him. Browning's none-too-subtle point is that humanity has nothing to do with appearance. While the "normal" people plot to kill, the Bearded Woman has a baby and the Siamese twins work through their marital and dating problems. In their fine book, *Dark Carnival,* David Skal and Elias Savada write that the famously troubled production so shocked preview audiences that the studio cut almost a third of the running time. An attack on Cleopatra and Hercules was lost. Even so, the rainy con-

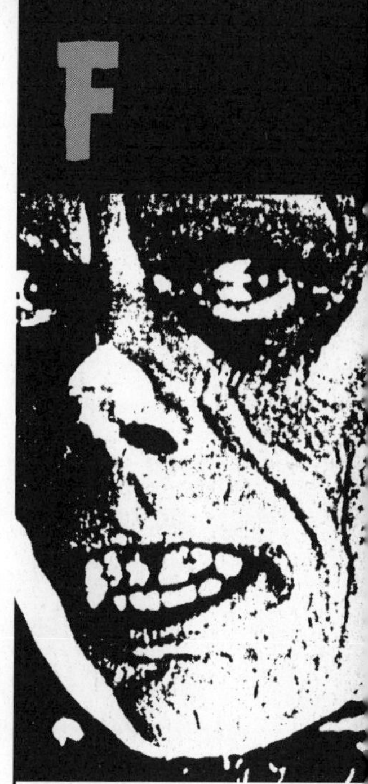

"...With humility for the many injustices done to such people (they have no power to control their lot), we present the most startling story of the *abnormal* and the *unwanted*."

—From MGM's foreword to its controversial *Freaks.*

clusion is brilliant. But some of the acting, notably by Baclanova, is crazily overwrought and much of the dialogue is impossible to understand. A surprising amount of humor still shines through. ***AKA:*** Nature's Mistakes; Forbidden Love; The Monster Show.

1932 66m/B Wallace Ford, Olga Baclanova, Leila Hyams, Roscoe Ates, Harry Earles, Henry Victor, Daisy Earles, Rose Dione, Daisy Hilton, Violet Hilton; ***D:*** Tod Browning; ***W:*** Al Boasberg, Willis Goldbeck, Leon Gordon, Edgar Allen Woolf; ***C:*** Merritt B. Gerstad. National Film Registry '94. **VHS, LV** *MGM*

Freakshow

Anthology of short South Carolina horror films uses a carnival sideshow as a framing device. That's where two teens listen to scary stories told by Gunnar Hansen (without his "Leatherface" mask from *The Texas Chainsaw Massacre*). They're fairly graphic tales about revenge, cannibalism, and such with a grisly sense of humor along the lines of the old E.C. Comics. The production values are a bit on the thin side and the pace is slow, but the films get better. "The Mummy" has a slight Poe quality, and it stars Veronica Carlson, familiar to fans for her work in Hammer horror films of the 1960s and still looking terrific. Co-director Paul Talbot is also responsible for *Hellblock 13*.

1995 (R) 102m/C Gunnar Hansen, Veronica Carlson, Brian D. Kelly, Shannon Michelle Parsons; ***D:*** William Cooke, Paul Talbot. **VHS** *AVI*

Freddy's Dead: The Final Nightmare

If nothing else, this unnumbered *6* proves that women can make horror sequels just as poorly as men. Director Rachel Talalay quotes the *Twilight Zone*'s "Nightmare at 10,000 Feet" and *The Wizard of Oz* early on, and her substantial budget allows for a barrelful of crackerjack visual effects. So what? The rest is more of the same bad acting from another bland young cast. In Ms. Talalay's favor, it should be noted that the violence is handled with cartoonish exaggeration and so it's not particularly sadistic. ***AKA:*** Nightmare on Elm Street 6: Freddy's Dead.

1991 (R) 96m/C Robert Englund, Lisa Zane, Shon Greenblatt, Leslie Deane, Ricky Dean Logan, Breckin Majer, Yaphet Kotto, Elinor Donahue, Roseanne, Johnny Depp, Alice Cooper, Tom Arnold; ***D:*** Rachel Talalay; ***W:*** Michael De Luca; ***C:*** Declan Quinn. **VHS, LV, Closed Caption** *COL, NLC*

Friday the 13th

The first entry in one of the genre's most successful franchises is a long variation on that old campfire favorite, The Hook. Judged as a low-budget horror flick, it's not bad, and not particularly original, either. The plot and direction rip off *Halloween,* and the score rips off Bernard Herrmann. Tom Savini's bloody effects are well done and have been repeated many many times since. So has the story of camp counselors being preyed on by a slasher.

1980 (R) 95m/C Betsy Palmer, Adrienne King, Harry Crosby, Laurie Bartram, Mark Nelson, Kevin Bacon, Jeannine Taylor, Robbi Morgan, Peter Brouwer, Walt Gorney; ***D:*** Sean S. Cunningham; ***W:*** Victor Miller; ***C:*** Barry Abrams. **VHS, LV, Closed Caption** *PAR*

Friday the 13th, Part 2

The series really doesn't get started until this entry, which establishes the ground rules. Like *Halloween*'s Michael Myers and all the Universal studio monsters before him, Jason is an unstoppable monster of ill-defined superpowers. Shoot him, stab him, burn him, blow him up—it doesn't matter. Every time you're really and truly sure that he's dead, he pops back up for more. Sex is the trigger; violent death is the result. That's the ongoing message of the films.

1981 (R) 87m/C Amy Steel, John Furey, Adrienne King, Betsy Palmer, Kirsten Baker, Stu Charno, Warrington Gillette, Walt Gorney, Marta Kober, Bill Randolph, Jack Marks; ***D:*** Steve Miner; ***W:*** Ron Kurz; ***C:*** Peter Stein. **VHS, LV** *PAR*

Friday the 13th, Part 3

Theatrically released in 3-D, this one features objects being thrust toward the camera. The 3-D process may also account for the picture's graininess on video. The film simply looks ugly. The producers daringly expand the original concept by having Jason kill middle-aged people along with teens, and the film is notable for Jason's acquisition of his trademark hockey goalie's mask. Beyond that, it's the same old slash-o. It's arguably the worst of the series, though personally, I'd vote for *8.* **Woof!**

1982 (R) 96m/C Dana Kimmell, Paul Kratka, Richard Brooker, Catherine Parks, Jeffrey Rogers, Tracie Savage, Larry Zerner; ***D:*** Steve Miner; ***W:*** Martin Kitrosser, Carol Watson; ***C:*** Gerald Feil. **VHS, LV** *PAR*

Friday the 13th, Part 4: The Final Chapter

It has long been my belief that this title carries with it an implied guarantee. At the very least, anyone who watches it has permission never to look at another installment. At best, the producers would have been prohibited from making any more sequels. All that *4* really has to offer is a pubescent Corey Feldman. (The horror! The horror!) The intentionally comic elements are stronger, too. And then there was *5.* **Woof!**

1984 (R) 90m/C Erich Anderson, Judie Aronson, Kimberly Beck, Peter Barton, Tom Everett, Corey Feldman, Crispin Glover, Richard Brooker; ***D:*** Joseph Zito; ***W:*** Barney Cohen; ***C:*** Joao Fernandes. **VHS, LV, Closed Caption** *PAR*

Friday the 13th, Part 5: A New Beginning

The effects, the story and the pace of the murders slavishly follow the pattern set in the earlier films. Relatively strong production values are the only virtue of this otherwise derivative effort. 🦴

1985 (R) 92m/C John Shepherd, Melanie Kinnaman, Shavar Ross, Richard Young, Juliette Cummins, Corey Feldman, Carol Lacatell, Vernon Washington; ***D:*** Danny Steinmann; ***W:*** Danny Steinmann, David M. Cohen, Martin Kitrosser; ***C:*** Stephen Posey. **VHS, LV, Closed Caption** *PAR*

Friday the 13th, Part 6: Jason Lives

6 deserves some credit for a fresh beginning, albeit one borrowed from *Ghost of Frankenstein,* wherein Jason's batteries are recharged. But that introduction uses up all the energy in this pointless sequel to a sequel to a.... **Woof!**

1986 (R) 87m/C Thom Mathews, Jennifer Cooke, David Kagen, Kerry Noonan, Renee Jones, Tom Fridley, C.J. Graham, Darcy Demoss; ***D:*** Tom McLoughlin; ***W:*** Tom McLoughlin; ***C:*** Jon Kranhouse. **VHS, LV, Closed Caption** *PAR*

Friday the 13th, Part 7: The New Blood

This entry is solidly in the tradition of the Universal ensemble horrors like *Frankenstein Meets the Wolfman* and *House of Dracula,* wherein all of the studio's fading monsters were brought together. It might have been called *Jason Meets Carrie,* with the hockey-masked cliche set against

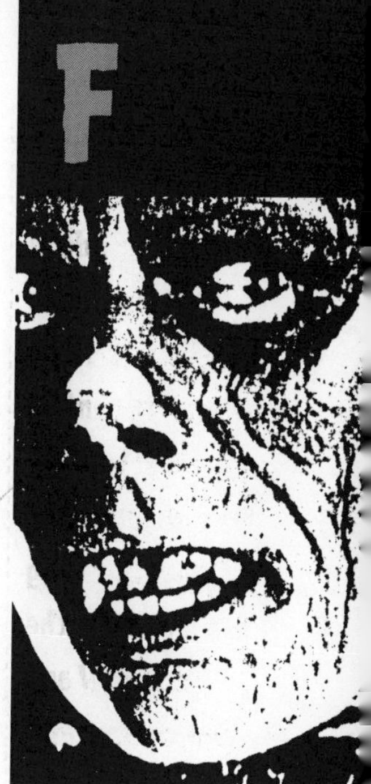

The 1970s

Exploitation, *The Exorcist*, and *Halloween*

In the 1970s, with the MPAA rating board effectively eliminating governmental and religious strictures against content, filmmakers were free to do pretty much anything they wanted onscreen. Horror charged headlong into the most profitable depths of exploitation. Having been moving in that direction anyway, England's Hammer Studios led the pack with *Countess Dracula*, *Vampire Lovers*, and *Lust for a Vampire*.

In America at the beginning of the decade, TV producer Dan Curtis was arguably the most influential voice in the genre. His popular horror soap opera hit the big screen as *House of Dark Shadows*, and he was also responsible for *The Night Stalker*, which, in 1971, was considered the best movie ever made for television.

Vincent Price turned his talents to comedy with *The Abominable Dr. Phibes*. The surprise hit of the year, though, was a story about a boy and his pet rats. *Willard* was actually number 8 of the top moneymakers of 1971. (But revealing what a nutty year that was, a softcore skin flick, *The Stewardesses*, was number 11.)

Meanwhile, in Italy, Armando de Ossorio set loose his resurrected Knights Templar in *Tombs of the Blind Dead*, establishing themes and visual motifs that would dominate European horror for years to come. The vagaries of film distribution being what they are, most American fans wouldn't be able to see de Ossorio's work as it was meant to be shown until it was restored and released on video more than 20 years later. The same can be said of Mario Bava's *Lisa and the Devil* made around the same time and radically recut from the director's original intention.

In 1972, Stanley Kubrick's adaptation of Anthony Burgess' *A Clockwork Orange* initially received an "X" rating and had to be trimmed slightly to qualify for an "R." Though arguably just as violent, John Boorman's adaptation of another literary novel, James Dickey's *Deliverance*, didn't have any trouble with the MPAA and became one of the year's commercial and critical hits.

Working at the other end of the budgetary spectrum, Sean Cunningham and Wes Craven made the inflammatory *Last House on the Left* and George Romero shifted gears after the success of *Night of the Living Dead* with his sympathetic treatment of witchcraft, *Season of the Witch*. That same year, two young directors made their debuts with studio-produced features. Brian

psychokenetic teen Tina (Lar Park Lincoln). Given the excesses of the series, the violence is relatively tame, and the action never even pretends to make sense.

1988 (R) 90m/C Lar Park Lincoln, Kevin Blair, Susan Blu, Terry Kiser, Kane Hodder, Elizabeth Kaitan, John Otrin, Heidi Kozak; ***D:*** John Carl Buechler; ***W:*** Daryl Haney; ***C:*** Paul Elliott. **VHS, LV, Closed Caption** *PAR*

Friday the 13th, Part 8: Jason Takes Manhattan

This loser ought to have been subtitled *Jason Takes a Boat Ride* because Mr.

DePalma's was the Hitchcock homage, *Sisters.* Steven Spielberg's version of Richard Matheson's short story, *Duel,* about a monstrous truck, was so popular on television that it earned a European theatrical run. Since then, Mr. Spielberg has made a fair name for himself with a few other films.

In 1973, William Friedkin redefined the genre with his thoughtful adaptation of William Peter Blatty's massive best-seller, *The Exorcist.* Though the groundbreaking special effects gave the film an undeniable shock value (and accounted for much of its popularity), its strong characters and serious religious foundation remain fresh. Also that year, Nicolas Roeg made the challenging *Don't Look Now,* and the Robin Hardy-Anthony Shaffer collaboration *The Wicker Man* began a sporadic theatrical release in this country, often in a cut version.

Once again, in 1974, the genre redefined itself with Tobe Hooper's gut-wrenching independent "meat movie," *The Texas Chainsaw Massacre.* Though it was loosely based on the exploits of serial killer Ed Gein (as was *Psycho*), a more accurate depiction of his crimes, *Deranged,* did not attract the same kind of following.

Made in the same year, Mel Brooks' *Young Frankenstein* manages to be both a laugh-out-loud horror-comedy and a lovingly accurate tribute to the Universal films of the 1930s. At the box-office, though, it and everything else trailed behind Steven Spielberg's second monster movie. With *Jaws,* he and Bruce the mechanical shark created the big summer blockbuster and Hollywood hasn't been the same since.

In 1975, two movies showed up without attracting much attention—at least initially. The first was *Shivers* (AKA *They Came from Within*), Canadian David Cronenberg's impressive debut. The second was *The Rocky Horror Picture Show.* In conventional release it caused barely a ripple, but when it resurfaced at late-night screenings, the "cult" horror hit was born.

Kubrick returned to horror in 1976 with his version of Stephen King's *Carrie,* while Romero continued to work that narrow band that lies between realism and the supernatural with *Martin.* Big-budget studio horror was represented by the absurdly entertaining *The Omen.* Wes Craven and Sean Cunningham stayed defiantly out of the mainstream with their ultra-violent *The Hills Have Eyes.*

The most influential horror film of the late '70s was certainly *Halloween.* Director John Carpenter and his partner (and co-writer) producer Debra Hill were hired to make a little suspense movie about babysitters. As Hitchcock and Romero had done before, they recreated the low-budget horror movie, and the 1980s were filled with knock-offs of wildly varying quality.

The decade ended with two haunted house horrors that could hardly have been more different. *The Amityville Horror,* based on an alleged "non-fiction" best-seller, was aimed at the fears of young families in tough economic times. Ridley Scott moved the house into outer space and H.R. Giger created one of the screen's most frightening spooks to haunt it in *Alien.* In the decade that would follow, sequel after sequel would march into suburban multiplexes.

Hockey Mask doesn't hit the Big Apple until the last reel. Why? Because it costs less to shoot film on a passenger ship than in Times Square at night. The only other difference here is more overt sadism. Writer/director Rob Hedden often pauses for several seconds while the various victims scream before Jason stabs, crushes, electrocutes, decapitates, drowns, or spears them. **Woof!**

1989 (R) 96m/C Jensen Daggett, Scott Reeves, Peter Mark Richman, Barbara Bingham, Kane Hodder, Martin Cummins, Sharlene Martin, Vincent Craig Dupree; ***D:*** Rob Hedden; ***W:*** Rob Hedden; ***C:*** Bryan England. **VHS, LV, Closed Caption** *PAR*

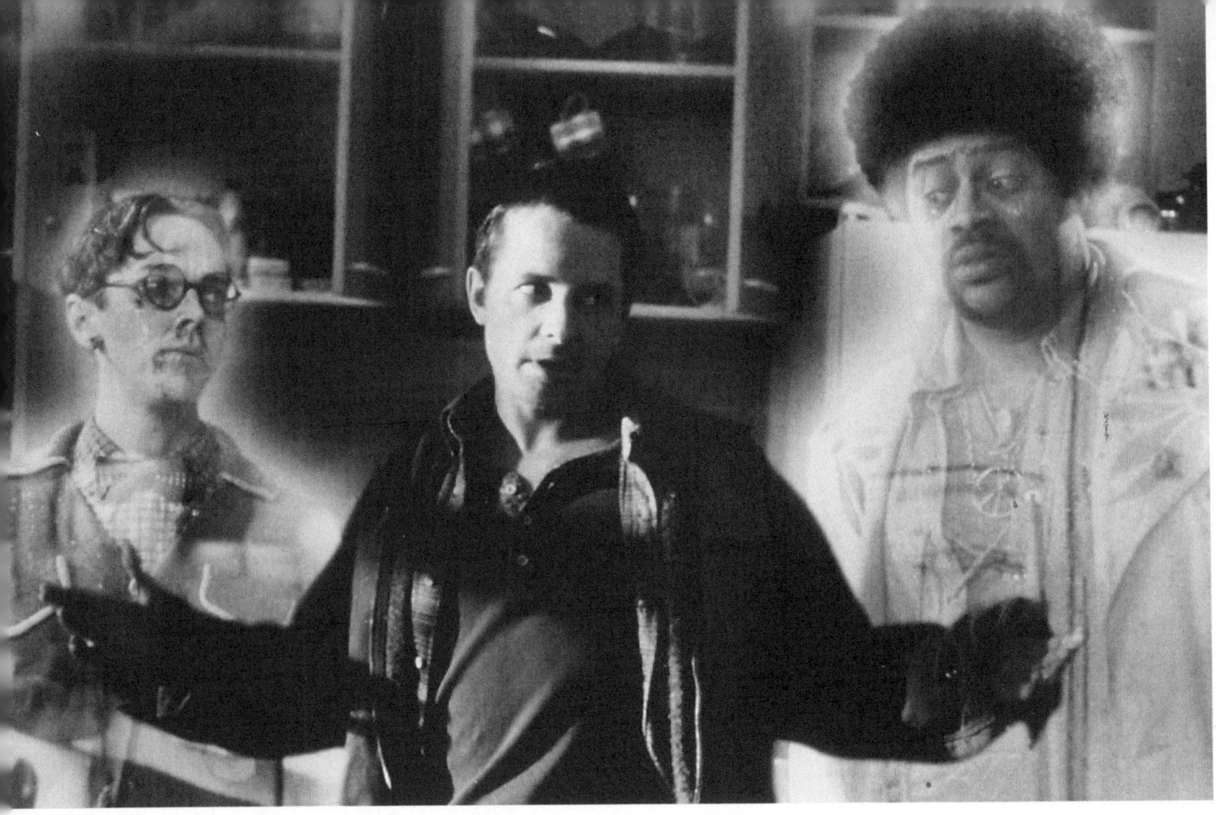

Stuart (Jim Fyfe), Frank Bannister (Michael J. Fox), and Cyrus (Chi McBride) in *The Frighteners.*

Fright House

The spirit of legendary master Ed Wood, Jr., lives on in these two short horrors that make absolutely no sense. The first, "Fright House," has something to do with a coven of chubby topless witches, a guy who does stand-up comedy on a picnic table, a monster that lives in a fireplace, and an abandoned school. The second, "Abadon," examines the horrors of bad plumbing, art school, and moldy bathrooms. Several of the characters look so much alike that it's hard to tell what's going on, but who cares? The amateurish acting and the relentless parade of horror cliches are the real attractions here. Fans of micro-budget alternative cinema will savor them.

1989 (R) 110m/C Al Lewis, Duane Jones; ***D:*** Len Anthony. **VHS** *NO*

Fright Night

Perhaps the best of the recent spate of vampires-in-the-'burbs flicks makes fine use of all the conventions of the sub-genre and combines them with first rate effects. Teenaged Charlie (William Ragsdale) can't persuade anyone that his new neighbor Jerry Dandridge (Chris Sarandon) is undead. His girlfriend Amy (Amanda Bearse) thinks Charlie's being a jerk. Making his debut, director Holland treats his young characters more honestly than many "serious" filmmakers. The nightclub scene is a brilliant set piece, but note the neat smaller touches. Dandridge makes his entrance drinking a Bloody Mary. Before an attack he whistles an offhand bar of *Strangers in the Night*. Stephen Geoffrey's Beavis & Butthead-inspired Evil Ed is terrific. So is Roddy McDowall as the hambone horror host, but the film belongs to Sarandon.

1985 (R) 106m/C William Ragsdale, Chris Sarandon, Amanda Bearse, Roddy McDowall, Stephen Geoffreys, Jonathan Stark, Dorothy Fielding, Art Evans; ***D:*** Tom Holland; ***W:*** Tom Holland; ***C:*** Jan Kiesser; ***M:*** Brad Fiedel. **VHS, LV, Closed Caption** *COL*

Fright Night 2

Therapy has convinced Charlie (William Ragsdale) that he really didn't fight a vampire in the first movie. But isn't someone moving another coffin into the horror host's (Roddy McDowall) building? As Regine, who puts the vamp back in vampire, Julie Carmen is good, but she's not nearly as impressive as Chris Sarandon in the original. Again, the inventive and often changing monster effects are impressive. The tone is not. No matter how gruesome, vampires on roller skates are not frightening. Admittedly the film is as interested in laughs as it is in screams. 🦴🦴

1988 (R) 108m/C Roddy McDowall, William Ragsdale, Traci Lind, Julie Carmen, Jonathan Gries, Russ Clark, Brian Thompson; ***D:*** Tommy Lee Wallace; ***W:*** Tommy Lee Wallace, Tim Metcalfe, Miguel Tejada-Flores; ***C:*** Mark Irwin; ***M:*** Brad Fiedel. **VHS, LV** *LIV*

The Frighteners

Ghost meets *Re-Animator* as director Peter Jackson stirs wild special effects, laughs, swooping camerawork, scares, and a breakneck pace into a zesty mix. Psychic exterminator Frank Bannister (Michael J. Fox) is a conman with ESP. Working with his ghost pals Cyrus (Chi McBride), Stuart (Jim Fyfe), and the Judge (John Astin), Bannister "haunts" houses and then charges the owners to exorcize the spirits. Despite his powers, Bannister doesn't know what to do when a more malevolent spirit appears, killing innocent victims at random. Without giving too much away, the other key ingredients are a young woman (Trini Alvarado) who believes in Bannister, a paranoid FBI agent (an inspired Jeffrey Combs), a serial murderer (Jake Busey, son of Gary), and his possibly innocent accomplice (Dee Wallace Stone). Don't worry about the plot details in the script by Jackson and collaborator Frances Walsh; they're explained as fully as they need to be. The special effects deserve as much attention as the cast. Jackson uses some impressive computer-generated scenes to tell the story. The combination of "real" and "supernatural" has never been presented more seamlessly. 🦴🦴🦴½

1996 (R) 106m/C Michael J. Fox, Trini Alvarado, Peter Dobson, Dee Wallace Stone, John Astin, Jeffrey Combs, Troy Evans, Chi McBride, Jake Busey, R. Lee Ermey, Jim Fyfe; ***D:*** Peter Jackson; ***W:*** Peter Jackson, Frances Walsh; ***C:*** Alun Bollinger, John Blick; ***M:*** Danny Elfman. **VHS, LV, Letterboxed, Closed Caption** *USH*

Frogs

How frightening would Hitchcock's *The Birds* have been if he'd had only a dozen seagulls and crows to work with? Not very. That's the restriction director George McCowan faces in this underpowered eco-horror. Pickett Smith (Sam Elliott) is a photographer who's stranded at aging zillionaire Crockett's (Ray Milland) low-country estate at the edge of an amphibian-infested swamp. Crockett says, "Man is master of the world!" Smith answers, "What if nature is trying to get back at us?" Yawn. Crockett's surrounded by greedy sycophantic children and relatives, but *Cat on a Hot Tin Roof* this is not. The real problem is that a few frogs simply are not scary. Neither is Spanish Moss. 🦴

1972 (PG) 91m/C Ray Milland, Sam Elliott, Joan Van Ark, Adam Roarke, Judy Pace, Lynn Borden, Mae Mercer, David Gilliam, George Skaff, Holly Irving; ***D:*** George McCowan; ***W:*** Robert Blees, Robert Hutchison; ***C:*** Mario Tosi; ***M:*** Les Baxter. **VHS** *WAR, OM*

From Beyond

Reteaming of the director and stars of *Re-Animator* isn't as successful because it doesn't go as far. Very loosely based on another H.P. Lovecraft story, it involves

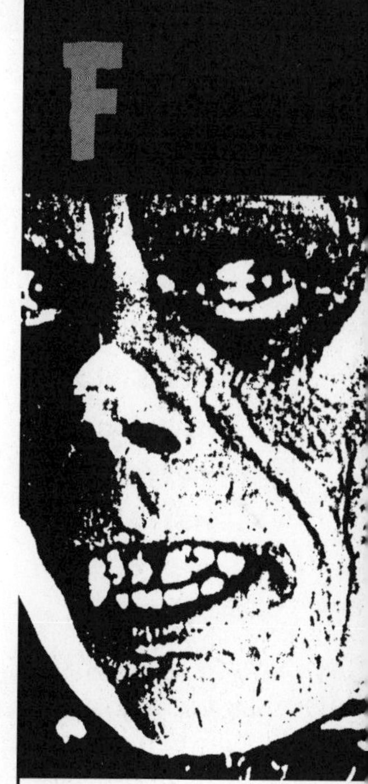

"I'm not gonna drain you completely. You're gonna turn for me, you'll be my slave. You'll live for me. You'll eat bugs because I order it. Because I don't think you're worthy of human blood, you'll feed on the blood of stray dogs. You'll be my foot stool. And at my command, you'll lick the dog shit from my boot heel. Since you'll be my dog, your new name will be 'Spot.' Welcome to slavery."

—Santanico Pandemonium (Salma Hayek) in *From Dusk Till Dawn.*

interdimensional travel via the "Praetorius Resonator" which stimulates the pineal gland. To be sure, it has its moments and the film is funny, but star Barbara Crampton never gets the chance to top her infamous "head" scene. Too bad. 🦴🦴½

1986 (R) 90m/C Jeffrey Combs, Barbara Crampton, Ted Sorel, Ken Foree, Carolyn Purdy-Gordon, Bunny Summers, Bruce McGuire; ***D:*** Stuart Gordon; ***W:*** Dennis Paoli, Brian Yuzna; ***C:*** Mac Ahlberg; ***M:*** Richard Band. **VHS, LV, Closed Caption** *LIV, VES*

From Dusk Till Dawn

Guilty-pleasure escapee from the drive-in is so violent, bloody, and grimly funny that even the most devoted fans of low-budget horror may be surprised at how far it goes. Decapitations, amputations, and burning bodies are just the beginning. After a couple of graphic killings and a rape-murder that thankfully occurs off-screen, bankrobbers Seth (George Clooney) and Richard Gecko (writer Quentin Tarantino) kidnap a family (Harvey Keitel, Juliette Lewis, and Ernest Liu). They drive their RV across the border to a Mexican strip bar, the Titty Twister, which turns out to be full of vampires. Director Robert Rodriguez keeps the action zipping right along with a quirky visual humor that gives a cartoonish quality to the most graphic moments. Tarantino's script is much closer in tone and intention to his *True Romance*. The complexity of *Pulp Fiction* is notably absent. Keitel plays the only sympathetic adult protagonist with an easy grace that leaves his younger and flashier co-stars in the shadows. 🦴🦴½

1995 (R) 108m/C George Clooney, Quentin Tarantino, Harvey Keitel, Juliette Lewis, Ernest Liu, Fred Williamson, Richard "Cheech" Marin, Salma Hayek, Michael Parks, Tom Savini, Kelly Preston, John Saxon, Danny Trejo; ***D:*** Robert Rodriguez; ***W:*** Quentin Tarantino; ***C:*** Guillermo Navarro; ***M:*** Graeme Revell. MTV Movie Awards '96: Breakthrough Performance (Clooney); Nominations: Golden Raspberry Awards '96: Worst Supporting Actor (Tarantino). **VHS, LV, Closed Caption** *TOU*

Frozen Ghost

See *Weird Woman/Frozen Ghost.*

The Funhouse

Tobe Hooper pays tribute to some of horror's best with this original and grimly funny tale. Fans will catch references to *Psycho, Halloween,* and, significantly, James Whale's *Frankenstein.* The premise traps four young people (Elizabeth Berridge, Cooper Huckabee, Largo Woodruff, and Miles Chapin) in a carnival funhouse with a hideously deformed freak (Wayne Doba) and his father (Kevin Conway). But...who are the good guys and who are the bad guys? That's the point of Larry Block's script. John Beal's music and makeup by Rick Baker and Craig Reardon add a lot. No, it's not as intense as *Texas Chainsaw*—few movies are—but it does just about everything you could ask of a good fright flick. 🦴🦴🦴

1981 (R) 96m/C Elizabeth Berridge, Shawn Carson, Cooper Huckabee, Largo Woodruff, Sylvia Miles, Miles Chapin, Kevin Conway, William Finley, Wayne Doba; ***D:*** Tobe Hooper; ***W:*** Larry Block; ***C:*** Andrew Laszlo; ***M:*** John Beal. **VHS, LV, Letterboxed** *USH*

The Fury

Wildly plotted mix of horror, Cold War espionage, action, and psychic piffle never quite comes together as well as it ought. John Cassavetes creates a well-shaded villain, and Kirk Douglas is easily his equal as the hero. Youngsters Andrew Stevens and Amy Irving frown a lot and make ookey things happen with their brains. John Williams' music helps considerably, as it always does. Look for Dennis Franz as Bob, proud owner of the new Caddy. You'll also see Daryl Hannah and James Belushi in small roles. 🦴🦴

1978 (R) 117m/C Kirk Douglas, John Cassavetes, Carrie Snodgress, Andrew Stevens, Amy Irving, Charles Durning, Carol Rossen, Rutanya Alda, William Finley, Jane Lambert, Joyce Easton, Daryl Hannah, Dennis Franz, James Belushi; ***D:*** Brian DePalma; ***W:*** John Farris; ***C:*** Richard Kline; ***M:*** John Williams. **VHS** *FOX*

Future Shock

Vivian Schilling, one of the leading voices in independent s-f/horror, writes and stars in the first installment of this anthology. She plays a wealthy woman who is either paranoid or well informed. When her husband leaves her alone overnight in their huge house, she fantasizes about a pack of wolves lurking outside. Is she delusional? Is someone trying to frighten her? Or is she reacting to the violence and horror that she sees on the evening news? In part, the film is a nice combination of elements; the traditional Gothic heroine in her nightgown caught up in an odd comic thriller. The second part, "The Roommate," is fast-forward material. The third, "Mr. Petrified Forest," is less ambitious than the first but it may be more successful. It's a wry, offbeat story of a man who appears to be having a near-death experience. Despite the flaws, director Eric Parkinson shows that he knows what he's doing and can juggle different tones.

1993 (PG-13) 93m/C Bill Paxton, Vivian Schilling, Brion James, Martin Kove; ***D:*** Eric Parkinson, Matt Reeves, Oley Sassone; ***W:*** Vivian Schilling. **VHS** *NO*

Galaxy of Terror

One demented scene has elevated this otherwise forgettable s-f/horror to true cult status. That moment comes when a ten-foot-long maggot monster attacks Technical Chief Dameia (Taaffe O'Connell), rips off all her clothes, and "licks" her to ecstasy, or something to that effect. Director Bruce Clark is understandably vague on details here. The rest is a fairly witless rip-off of *Alien* and *Star Wars* with some interesting but often gory effects and a nonsensical script. ***AKA:*** Mindwarp: An Infinity of Terror; Planet of Horrors.

1981 (R) 85m/C Erin Moran, Edward Albert, Ray Walston, Grace Zabriskie, Zalman King, Taaffe O'Connell, Robert Englund; ***D:*** B.D. Clark; ***W:*** B.D. Clark, Mark Siegler; ***C:*** Jacques Haitkin. **VHS, LV**

Gamera, Guardian of the Universe

This remake of an early Japanese giant city-stomper monster flick retains all the energy and humor of the original, and adds better special effects, acting, and production values including more expressive voice dubbing. Our hero is a big green flying turtle with a bad attitude and a desperate need for orthodontics. In this incarnation, the reason behind his resurrection isn't simple nuclear weapons but a veritable grab-bag of environmental issues from global warming to littering. Gamera appears at the same time as the Gaos show up. They're big flying creatures who eat people and poop all over the place. The movie is pure fun for kids and adults. Matt Greenfield takes particular care with the English-language version, translating signs and headlines pertinent to the action.

1995 96m/C *JP* Tsuyoski Ihara, Akira Onodera, Shinobu Nakayama, Avako Fujitani, Yukihiro Hotaru, Hatsunori Hasegawa, Hirotora Honda; ***D:*** Shusuke Kaneko, Matt Greenfield; ***W:*** Kazunori Ito. *ADF*

The Gate

A cliched but passable nightmare sequence introduces another hell-comes-to-suburbia story. When his parents leave young Glen (pudgy-cheeked pre-pubescent Stephen Dorff) unsupervised for the weekend, he opens up a doorway to another dimension in the backyard and demons pour through. (And you thought things got crazy for Tom Cruise in *Risky Business*!) It all bears some similarity to *Scream,* though for a slightly younger

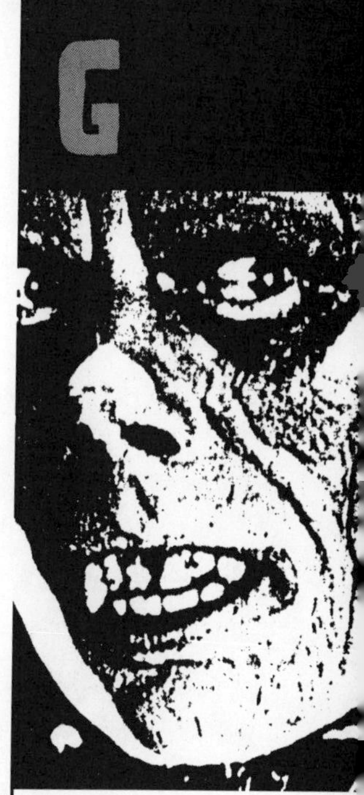

Bill Murray as Dr. Peter Venkman and Dan Aykroyd as Dr. Raymond Stantz in *Ghostbusters*.

audience, with a nod to Lovecraft's Chtulhu mythos. The stop-motion and animation effects are excellent. Followed by a sequel.

1987 (PG-13) 85m/C Christa Denton, Stephen Dorff, Louis Tripp, Kelly Rowan, Jennifer Irwin; ***D:*** Tibor Takacs; ***W:*** Michael Nankin; ***C:*** Thomas Vamos. **VHS, LV** *LIV, VES*

Gate 2

That doorway to another dimension that opened up in a suburban back yard in the first film is still there. Like people who leave their Christmas lights up all year, the folks in this neighborhood haven't done anything about this supernatural nuisance that lets in demons, devils, and stuff like that. It's just sitting there so teen Terrence (Louis Tripp) can sneak over and sacrifice a hamster to call up the forces of darkness. Any movie showing teenaged characters involved in animal sacrifice is dealing with dangerous material, but this one's so inept and formulaic that it's probably harmless.

1992 (R) 90m/C Louis Tripp, Simon Reynolds, Pamela Segall, James Villemaire, Neil Munro, James Kidnie, Andrea Ladanyi; ***D:*** Tibor Takacs; ***W:*** Michael Nankin; ***C:*** Bryan England; ***M:*** George Blondheim. **VHS, LV, Closed Caption** *COL*

Generation X-Tinct

Defying an ultra-low budget, filmmaker Michele Pacitto makes an impressive debut with a grim social satire. Set in suburbs, it's the story of Robert Tilton (Michael Passion), a true loser's loser, or, as his favorite bartender says, "a pathetic little chimp." Vain, self-pitying, manipulative, lazy, and none-too-bright, Robert is a blithe and obvious liar who deserves everything that happens to him. He's also a

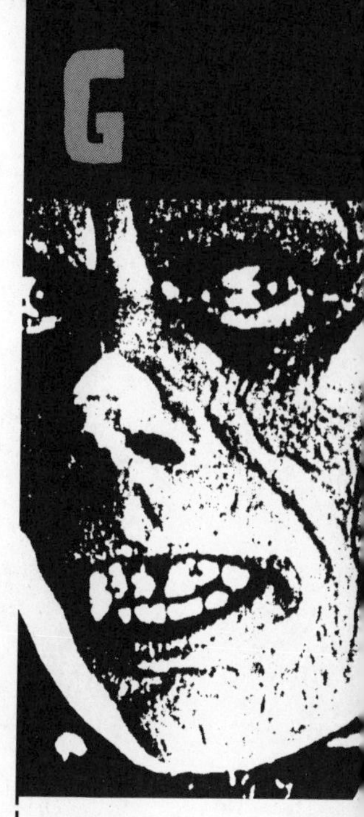

would-be psycho killer. In their quest for weed, he and his slacker pals entangle themselves in the lives of a non-nonsense drug dealer, a real estate salesman with the gonzo name Thunder Goldberg, and a hapless homicide detective. The plot is so quick and unpredictable that any synopsis would spoil the fun. And the film *is* fun, despite or perhaps because all of the main characters are so unsympathetic. Writer/director/editor Pacitto has borrowed bits from *Pulp Fiction, Trees Lounge,* and *True Romance,* but he has created a genuine original. The film rolls right along from one unexpected jolt to another and finally to a dead right, downbeat ending. Some of the acting is amateurish; some of the props and sets won't stand up to close inspection. But so what; *Generation X-Tinct* is a tough, smart, risky movie aimed at audiences looking for substance with a difference.

1997 m/C Michael Passion; ***D:*** Michele Pacitto. **VHS** *EII*

The Ghost Breakers

It's another dark and stormy night in New York. Radio gossip monger Larry Lawrence (Bob Hope) jumps out of the frying pan and into the fire when he offends a local mobster and stumbles into a conspiracy against Mary Carter (Paulette Goddard). She has just inherited Castillo Maldito on Black Island off the coast of Cuba, but someone is trying to drive her off. The last third takes place in the castle where all the traditional spooky elements of an "old dark house" tale are trotted out: secret passageways, hidden panels, zombies, ghosts, etc. Some viewers will have problems with the character of Alex (Willie Best), the stereotyped and subservient black family retainer. But it's really not fair to judge this light comedy too harshly by today's standards. No, the film is not particularly enlightened; it's just a product of its time.

1940 83m/B Bob Hope, Paulette Goddard, Richard Carlson, Paul Lukas, Willie Best, Pedro de Cordoba, Noble Johnson, Anthony Quinn; ***D:*** George Marshall; ***W:*** Walter DeLeon; ***C:*** Charles B(ryant) Lang. **VHS, LV, Closed Caption** *USH, BTV*

Ghost in the Machine

Fair little low-budget s-f/horror works with some of the same concepts that were used in *The Lawnmower Man* and *Shocker,* and like those two, it has some interesting special effects, but it's never very involving or frightening. When a serial killer's soul or spirit or whatever is zapped into a hospital's mainframe computer, he finds that he can go wherever electricity can go. Director Rachel Talalay, who also made one of the *Elm Street* sequels, handles the material competently enough without any flash.

1993 (R) 104m/C Karen Allen, Chris Mulkey, Ted Marcoux, Jessica Walter, Rick Ducommun, Wil Horneff, Nancy Fish, Brandon Adams; ***D:*** Rachel Talalay; ***W:*** William Davies, William Osborne; ***M:*** Graeme Revell. **VHS, LV, Closed Caption** *FXV*

The Ghost of Frankenstein

The fourth installment in the Universal series begins with the torch-bearing villagers attacking the Baron's castle, a scene usually reserved for the last reel. They blow up the joint, freeing the Monster (Lon Chaney, Jr.) trapped in dried sulphur...hunchbacked Ygor (Bela Lugosi) helps him out...lightning strike to the neck bolts...Dr. Ludwig (Cedric Hardwicke), the "second son of Frankenstein".... You can fill in the rest of the blanks. Chaney actually acquits himself well and he's backed up by several members of the studio's stock troupe. Followed by *Frankenstein Meets the Wolfman.*

Dr. Jenny Langer (Barbara Hale) in *The Giant Spider Invasion.*

1942 68m/B Cedric Hardwicke, Lon Chaney Jr., Lionel Atwill, Ralph Bellamy, Bela Lugosi, Evelyn Ankers, Dwight Frye; ***D:*** Erle C. Kenton; ***W:*** W. Scott Darling; ***C:*** Milton Krasner. **VHS, Closed Caption** *USH, FCT*

Ghost Story

Though it's generally dismissed by critics for the "stunt" casting of veterans Fred Astaire, Melvyn Douglas, John Houseman, and Douglas Fairbanks, Jr., I'm partial to this unconventional story of old men remembering the worst thing that ever happened to them 50 years in the past, and its supernatural consequences in the present. Besides the presence of four canny pros and Alice Krige's complex, sexy performance, the evocation of small-town New England in winter is so strong that it makes up for the flaws. Most of the literary recreations in Peter Straub's novel are missing, however.

1981 (R) 110m/C Fred Astaire, Melvyn Douglas, Douglas Fairbanks Jr., John Houseman, Craig Wasson, Alice Krige, Patricia Neal; ***D:*** John Irvin; ***W:*** Lawrence D. Cohen; ***C:*** Jack Cardiff. **VHS, LV** *USH*

Ghostbusters

Admittedly, this big-budget spoof is more comedy than horror, but the special effects are so good and often so startling that it deserves inclusion here. First there's Sigourney Weaver's possession and transformation from classical musician to lust-crazed demonbabe, and then there are Randall William Cook's terrific stop-motion animation creatures. Of course, Bill Murray and the giant Marshmallow Boy upstage them all, and the whole thing is a tongue-in-cheek romp. Worth another look on a rainy afternoon.

1984 (PG) 103m/C Bill Murray, Dan Aykroyd, Harold Ramis, Rick Moranis, Sigourney Weaver, Annie Potts, Ernie Hudson, William Atherton, David Margulies,

Steven Tash; ***D:*** Ivan Reitman; ***W:*** Dan Aykroyd, Harold Ramis; ***C:*** Laszlo Kovacs; ***M:*** Elmer Bernstein. Nominations: Academy Awards '84: Best Song ("Ghostbusters"). **VHS, LV, Closed Caption, Letterboxed, DVD** *COL, CRC*

Ghostbusters 2

A river of "psychomagnetheric" slime is running through an abandoned subway tunnel under First Avenue, and New York is suffering another supernatural psychic attack. Alas, the Ghostbusters were broken up after they were sued for all the damage they caused at the end of the original. The villainous Janosz Poha (Peter MacNichol), with a fractured accent and quirky performance, almost steals the film from the good guys, but Bill Murray's Venkman is still the center of attention. Even so, it's a sequel and lacks originality.

1989 (PG) 102m/C Bill Murray, Dan Aykroyd, Sigourney Weaver, Harold Ramis, Rick Moranis, Ernie Hudson, Peter MacNicol, David Margulies, Wilhelm von Homburg, Harris Yulin, Annie Potts, Ben Stein, Richard "Cheech" Marin, Brian Doyle-Murray, Janet Margolin; ***D:*** Ivan Reitman; ***W:*** Dan Aykroyd, Harold Ramis; ***C:*** Michael Chapman; ***M:*** Randy Edelman. **VHS, LV, Letterboxed, 8mm, Closed Caption** *COL*

The Ghoul

A dying Egyptologist (Boris Karloff) believes that the "Jewel of Eternal Light" will bring him immortality if he's buried with it clasped in his hand. His squabbling heirs and an assortment of greedy colleagues would rather keep said gem in the realm of the living. Karloff's makeup and performance display hints of his work in *Frankenstein* and *The Mummy.* But the pace is slow and so this one is enjoyable now mostly for the cast and its historical value. It was lost for years until a Czech print was discovered and restored by the Museum of Modern Art and Janus Films.

1933 73m/B *GB* Boris Karloff, Cedric Hardwicke, Ernest Thesiger, Dorothy Hyson, Ralph Richardson, Anthony Bushell, Kathleen Harrison, Harold Huth, D. A. Clarke-Smith, Jack Raine; ***D:*** T. Hayes Hunter; ***W:*** Roland Pertwee, John Hastings Turner, Rupert Downing; ***C:*** Gunther Krampf. **VHS** *VYY, SNC, DVT*

The Giant Spider Invasion

A meteorite crashes in rural Wisconsin, and, given the title, you can easily connect the rest of the dots in this formula effort. Notoriously bad special effects are the main attraction. The title critter may be the funniest ever to grace the screen. It bears a striking resemblance—particularly around the eyes—to Kermit the Frog, but it's clearly a Volkswagen. Best moment is the unforgettable spider-in-the-blender scene. A familiar "B" cast led by Steve Brodie, Alan Hale (the Skipper, whose first line is "Hi, little buddy!"), Barbara Hale (Della Street), and Bill Williams has a grand time.

1975 (PG) 76m/C Steve Brodie, Barbara Hale, Leslie Parrish, Robert Easton, Alan Hale Jr., Dianne Lee Hart, Bill Williams, Christianne Schmidtmer; ***D:*** Bill Rebane; ***W:*** Bill Rebane, Richard L. Huff, Robert Easton; ***C:*** Jack Willoughby. **VHS** *MOV*

The Girl in Room 2A

Fresh from the slammer, young Margaret (Daniela Giordano) immediately runs into trouble in her rooming house. It could be that someone is torturing and murdering young women, or it could be that Maggie's delusional. Whatever, somebody's running around in a red-hooded mask and cassock that makes him look like the Archbishop of the Mexican Wrestling Association. Raf Vallone is a Nietzsche-quoting bad guy. O.K. Gothic atmosphere is undercut by crude exploitative torture scenes. The story is often imaginative and often silly with considerable overlap.

1976 (R) 90m/C Raf Vallone, Daniela Giordano; ***D:*** William Rose. **VHS** *NO*

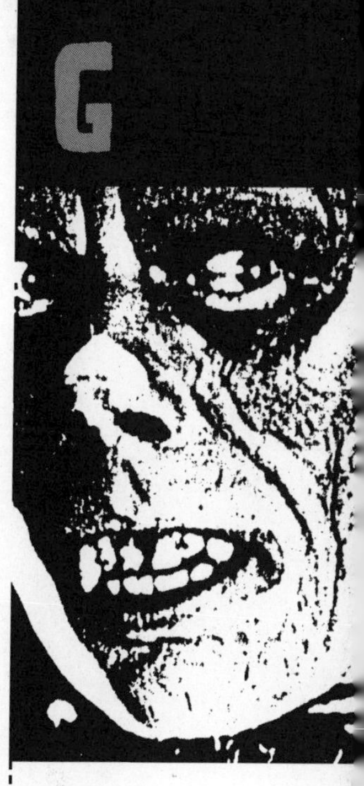

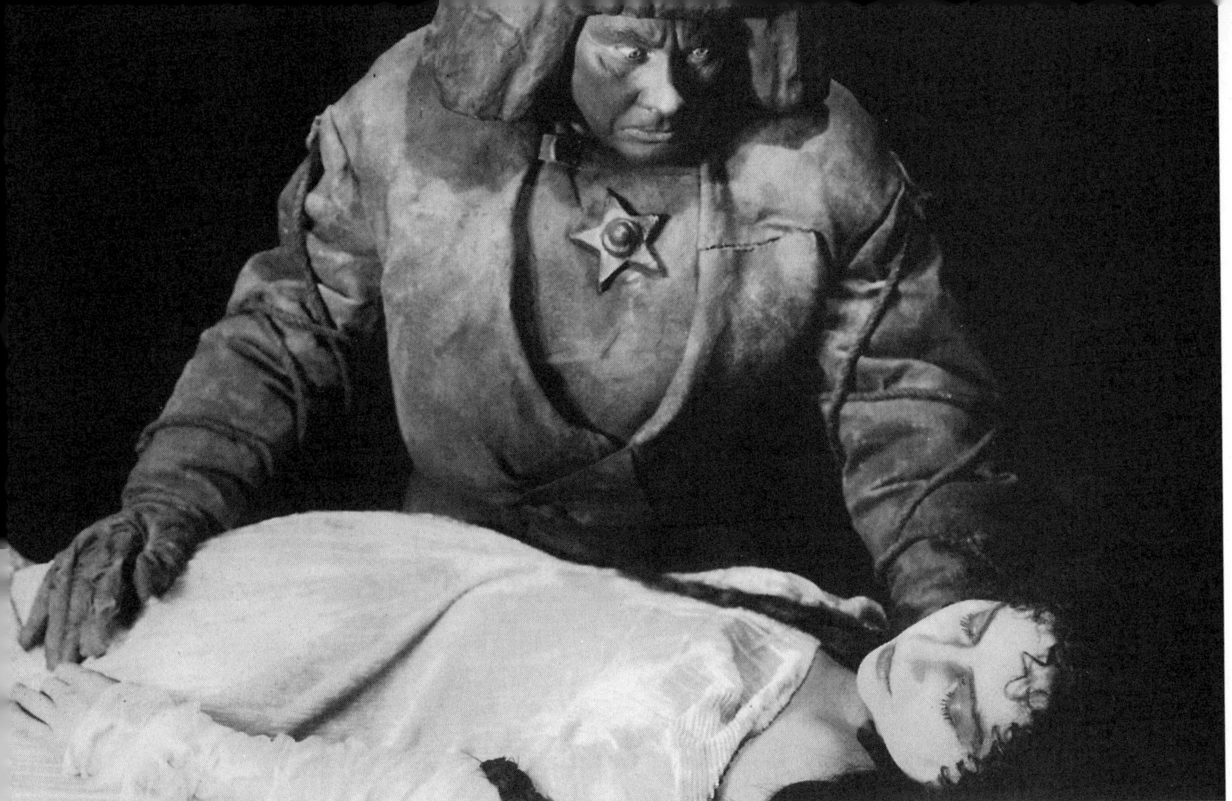

Paul Wegener as the vengeful statue in *The Golem* (1920).

The Girl with the Hungry Eyes

Loosely based on Fritz Leiber's famous short story, Jon Jacobs' unhinged adaptation concerns a Miami vampire (Christina Fulton) who's brought back to life by a South Beach hotel which commands her to find a key and a deed so that it will not be demolished to make room for a parking lot. In the process, she meets Carlos (Isaac Turner), a photographer who's in trouble with drug thugs. With her eyes wildly rolling like speed-crazed pinballs, Fulton makes Elvira, Mistress of the Dark, look like Meryl Streep. Jacobs uses simple reverse motion camera tricks to complement her excesses, though in some scenes, the quality of both lighting and sound are so poor as to make the proceedings unintelligible. 🦴🦴½

1994 (R) 84m/C Christina Fulton, Isaac Turner, Leon Herbert, Bret Carr, Susan Rhodes; ***D:*** Jon Jacobs; ***W:*** Jon Jacobs; ***M:*** Paul Inder. **VHS** *COL*

God Told Me To

Almost 20 years before the first episode of *The X-Files* aired, Larry Cohen made the prototype. All the key elements of the series are there—alien abduction, religion, troubled cop who refuses to let go the case, his suspect superiors, a powerful cabal, several bizarre inexplicable twists. A hymn-like theme (by Frank Cordell) sets the mood and it's followed by a stunning opening scene. NYPD detective Peter Nicholas (Tony LoBianco) discovers links between several apparently unrelated killings and becomes involved on the most personal level. Despite a relatively modest budget, writer/producer/director Larry Cohen has created a richly complex film that makes extensive use of New York locations. The garish colors, quick pace, and unpredictability are the stuff of a truly great B-movie. If you've missed it, find this off-kilter masterpiece. Two postscripts: That is the late Andy Kaufman as a policeman and the film is dedicated to the memory of composer Bernard Herrmann, so famous for his work with Hitchcock, Harryhausen, and Cohen's own *It's Alive*. **AKA:** Demon.

1976 (R) 89m/C Tony LoBianco, Deborah Raffin, Sylvia Sidney, Sandy Dennis, Richard Lynch, Sam Levene, Andy Kaufman; ***D:*** Larry Cohen; ***W:*** Larry Cohen; ***C:*** Paul Glickman; ***M:*** Frank Cordell. **VHS, LV, Letterboxed** *VTR, IME*

The Golem

Dated conventions have robbed the film of many of its horrific qualities, though it remains one of the most ambitious productions of the silent era, with impressive sets and a large cast. The inventive use of extreme camera angles is years ahead of its time. The story of a clay creature (played by co-director Paul Wegener) who's brought to life by a Rabbi to defend his community has strong political implications, and the subplots involving young lovers and the monster's emotions are still in use today. So is the central theme of a creator who loses control of his creation. The Video Yesteryear tape recreates the accurate silent projection speed and has an organ soundtrack. ***AKA:*** Der Golem, wie er in die Welt kam.

1920 80m/B *GE* Paul Wegener, Albert Steinruck, Ernst Deutsch, Lyda Salmonava, Otto Gebuehr, Max Kronert, Loni Nest, Greta Schroder, Hans Sturm; ***D:*** Carl Boese, Paul Wegener; ***W:*** Henrik Galeen, Paul Wegener; ***C:*** Karl Freund. **VHS** *VYY, FCS, MRV*

The Good Son

Macaulay Culkin is believable enough as an evil "Bad Seed" child, but director Joseph Ruben isn't nearly as successful here as he was in the cult favorite *The Stepfather*. Young Mark (Elijah Wood), still not over the death of his mother, leaves his western home to spend two weeks with his uncle's family in Maine. He and his cousin Henry (M.C.) become great pals right away. Before long, Henry reveals a darker, murderous side. The script by English novelist Ian McEwan is deliberate and focused on the central conflict to a fault. Experienced fans are going to be one step ahead all the way through. Elmer Bernstein's sappy, cliched score is another problem, and Ruben shows a weakness for postcard pretty pictures. Though they're meant to add dramatic weight and psychological significance to the story, they're just silly, and, in at least one case, downright laughable.

1993 (R) 87m/C Macaulay Culkin, Elijah Wood, Wendy Crewson, David Morse, Daniel Hugh-Kelly, Quinn Culkin; ***D:*** Joseph Ruben; ***W:*** Ian McEwan; ***C:*** John Lindley; ***M:*** Elmer Bernstein. Nominations: MTV Movie Awards '94: Best Villain (Culkin). **VHS, LV, Closed Caption** *FXV*

The Gorgon

"Overshadowing the village of Vandorf stands the Castle Borski. From the turn of the century a monster from an ancient age came to live here. No living thing survived and the specter of death hovered in waiting for her next victim." That foreword sets the tone for one of Hammer's most unclassifiable horrors. It's probably best not to ask why or how Megara (Prudence Hyman), sister of the Greek mythological monster Medusa, came to take up residence in Castle Borski. Just accept the fact and appreciate the intense autumnal Gothic atmosphere of the place. Peter Cushing plays a doctor who's part of a local effort to cover up the fact that people are being turned to stone. The role is out of the ordinary for him. Christopher Lee's visiting professor is the Van Helsing character.

1964 83m/C *GB* Peter Cushing, Christopher Lee, Richard Pasco, Barbara Shelley, Michael Goodliffe, Patrick Troughton, Jack Watson, Jeremy Longhurst, Toni Gilpin,

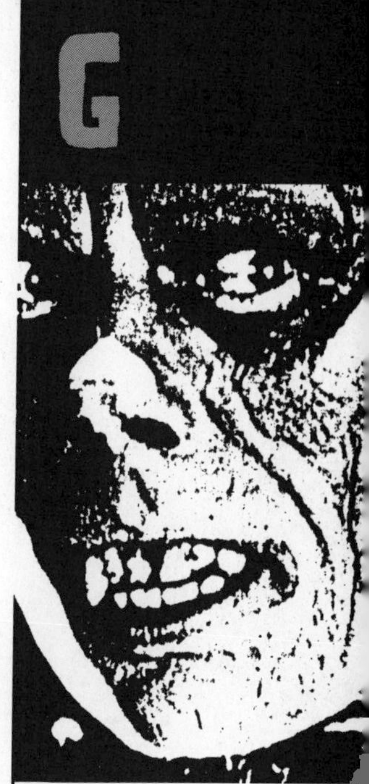

THE HOUND SALUTES

JOHN CARPENTER

When *Halloween* became the massive sleeper hit of 1978, critics took another look at John Carpenter's earlier film, *Assault on Precinct 13,* and promptly declared him to be the next John Ford, the next Howard Hawks. They were wrong.

What they did not realize is that with *Halloween,* Carpenter was making exactly the kind of film he wanted to make—quick, violent, inexpensive, entertaining.

Carpenter was born in Bowling Green, Kentucky, in 1948, and studied filmmaking at the University of Southern California. In 1970, he won an Academy Award for his short film, *The Resurrection of Bronco Billy.* He made his feature debut with writer Dan O'Bannon on the science-fiction film *Dark Star,* but *Halloween* was his breakthrough.

Since then, he's worked steadily in television and theatrical films. (His 1978 made-for-TV thriller *Someone's Watching Me!* is a terrific piece of suspense that's inexplicably unavailable on tape.) His most enjoyable works tend to blur genre definitions. While *The Fog* is definitely horror, *Escape from New York* and *Escape from L.A.* might best be described as apocalyptic comedy.

When Carpenter is off the mark, his work is virtually unwatchable. His remake of *Village of the Damned* and *Memoirs of an Invisible Man* come immediately to mind. But when he gets the right cast and the right story, he's excellent. His 1984 s-f film, *Starman,* for example, earned Jeff Bridges a Best Actor Oscar nomination. In *They Live,*—an underrated film that's become a cult favorite on video—Carpenter got an excellent, touching performance from wrestler Roddy Piper. Of his more recent work, *In the Mouth of Madness* is an ambitious, challenging

Prudence Hyman; ***D:*** Terence Fisher; ***W:*** John Gilling; ***C:*** Michael Reed; ***M:*** James Bernard. **VHS, LV** *NO*

Gothic

Ken Russell twists real historical and literary events into a wild psycho-sexual fantasy about Lord Byron (Gabriel Byrne), Percy Shelley (Julian Sands), his wife Mary (Natasha Richardson), and her stepsister Clair (Myriam Cyr) on a dark and stormy night. The film is filled with naked poets on the roof, women throwing fits and foaming at the mouth, bodies in bathtubs, laudanum and leeches, mucus and mud, perversions and phallic symbols, mechanical strippers and self-mutilation—the whole nine yards. Stephen Volk's script owes as much to Poe as it does to Mary Shelley. The same historical material provides the basis for *Haunted Summer.* 🦴🦴🦴

1987 (R) 87m/C Julian Sands, Gabriel Byrne, Timothy Spall, Natasha Richardson, Myriam Cyr; ***D:*** Ken Russell; ***W:*** Stephen Volk; ***C:*** Mike Southon; ***M:*** Thomas Dolby. **VHS, LV** *LIV, VES*

Grandma's House

As the title indicates, this horror film has a solid premise based on the primal fears that give fairy tales their power. After the loss of their parents, a brother and sister (Eric Foster and Kim Valentine) go to live

addition to the Lovecraft mythos, built around another fine performance by character actor Sam Neill.

It's also worth noting that even though *Halloween* spawned the whole "slasher" school of the 1980s, Carpenter's work lacks the misogyny that's found so often in horror. Women in his films tend to be strong characters who may be placed in jeopardy but seldom depend on a man to rescue them. Also, despite its reputation, *Halloween* is not a graphically violent film. You think you see more than Carpenter actually shows.

As this book goes to press, Carpenter his making his first vampire film, simply titled *Vampires*. If the publicity material is accurate, it will be action-oriented, along the lines of *Near Dark* and *From Dusk Till Dawn*. No surprise there.

SIGNIFICANT CONTRIBUTIONS TO HORROR

Halloween **(1978)**

The Fog **(1978)**

Christine **(1984)**

Prince of Darkness **(1987)**

They Live **(1988)**

In the Mouth of Madness **(1995)**

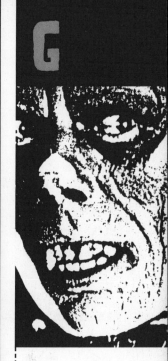

with their grandparents in a rural California town. When odd things begin to happen in and around the house, they suspect that the two older people are hiding something. Loose ends abound and the story won't stand up to any serious examination, but the pace is so quick that the cliches and flaws aren't too obvious. Similar material is handled in Bob Balaban's *Parents*, but this one's not as crazed. More importantly, it's suspenseful without being overly violent. When the protagonists are children, that's a significant distinction.

1988 (R) 90m/C Eric Foster, Kim Valentine, Brinke Stevens, Ida Lee, Len Lesser; ***D:*** Peter Rader; ***W:*** Peter C. Jensen; ***C:*** Peter C. Jensen. **VHS, LV** *NO*

The Grave

Screwball southern-Gothic comedy is made of equal parts faux-Faulkner and bad Stephen King. When convicts Tyn (Josh Charles) and King (Craig Sheffer) learn of a buried treasure, they break out of prison camp to find it. Familiar character actor John Diehl is a sadistic drug-frazzled guard; Anthony Michael Hall is a pudgy, creepy mortician; Gabrielle Anwar is the girlfriend who figures things out; and Eric Roberts, doing his best Jim Varney imitation, is a helpful redneck with a story to tell. Director Jonas Pate and his co-writer Joshua Pate try to give their film a Coen-brothers spin with

"So if your air conditioner goes on the fritz or your washing machine blows up or your video recorder conks out, before you call the repairman, turn on all the lights, check all the closets and cupboards, look under all the beds. Because you never can tell, there just might be a gremlin in your house."

—Ad line from *Gremlins.*

unexpected plot twists and cheerfully skewed dialogue ("Wish on a star long enough and you're bound to think the world owes you a twinkle for your trouble"). They haven't yet achieved that sublime Coen sensibility, but it ought to be interesting to see what they do next. 🦴🦴🦴

1995 (R) 90m/C Craig Sheffer, Josh Charles, Gabrielle Anwar, Donal Logue, John Diehl, Anthony Michael Hall, Eric Roberts; ***D:*** Jonas Pate; ***W:*** Jonas Pate, Josh Pate; ***C:*** Frank Prinzi. **VHS** *REP*

Graveyard Shift

Stephen Tsepses (Silvio Oliviero) is a vampire who works as a New York cabbie. That's how he meets his prey, people who are about to die. He's a sympathetic sort who bites only people who want to be bitten. Enter Michelle (Helen Papas), a filmmaker with a host of problems. Though the action seems serious at first, director Gerard Ciccoritti is stylish to a fault, willing to sacrifice anything for flashy rock music visuals. The performances are well above average, and the film is one of the better exercises in undead romanticism. Followed by a sequel. 🦴🦴½

1987 (R) 89m/C *IT* Silvio Oliviero, Helen Papas, Cliff Stoker; ***D:*** Gerard Ciccoritti. **VHS** *VTR*

The Great Alligator

Made years before *Jurassic Park,* this eco-horror arrives at essentially the same point. Mel Ferrer is a millionaire who creates a theme park in the jungle only to have his grand opening ruined by a giant reptile. Of course, in this micro-budgeted variation, the T-rex duties are handled by "Crooner," a big 'gator who wisely stays out of sight most of the time. In this case, the "great" in the title refers only to size, not to quality or power. The treatment of black characters as chanting primitives is casually offensive. ***AKA:*** Il Fiume del Grande Caimano; Alligators. 🦴½

1981 89m/C *IT* Barbara Bach, Mel Ferrer, Richard Johnson, Claudio Cassinelli, Romano Puppo; ***D:*** Sergio Martino; ***W:*** Sergio Martino, Ernesto Gastaldi, Luigi Montefiore, Maria Chiaretta; ***C:*** Giancarlo Ferrando. **VHS** *MPI*

Gremlins

The combination of executive producer Steven Spielberg's schmaltzy vision of small-town life with monsters who are never quite as horrible as they ought to be just doesn't work. At first, the title critters are cute little hand puppets, but if they're fed after midnight, they become grotesque creatures. Of course, our feckless hero Billy (Zach Galligan) does just that. Kids may be able to ignore the inherent contradictions in the film's two halves, but what will they make of the blackly humorous scene where Billy's girlfriend Kate (Phoebe Cates) explains why she hates Christmas? Followed by a superior sequel. 🦴

1984 (PG) 106m/C Zach Galligan, Phoebe Cates, Hoyt Axton, Polly Holliday, Frances Lee McCain, Keye Luke, Dick Miller, Corey Feldman, Judge Reinhold, Glynn Turman, Scott Brady, Jackie Joseph; ***D:*** Joe Dante; ***W:*** Chris Columbus; ***C:*** John Hora; ***M:*** Jerry Goldsmith; ***V:*** Howie Mandel. **VHS, LV, 8mm, Letterboxed, Closed Caption** *WAR, TLF*

Gremlins 2: The New Batch

At first, the little critters from the original are even more insipid and obnoxious than they were before. But about midway through, everything changes and a streak of nasty humor makes this one better than the first film. Billy (Zach Galligan) and Kate (Phoebe Cates) now work in New York for Daniel Clamp (John Glover), a zillionaire of the Trump-Turner-Murdoch school. When the Gremlins multiply into reptilian multitudes, they take over his high-tech corporate headquarters in Manhattan. The satiric jabs are right on target until writer Charlie Haas and director Joe Dante attack video reviewers in the person of Leonard

Maltin, the Hound's favorite competitor. Terrific Jerry Goldsmith score.

1990 (PG-13) 107m/C Zach Galligan, Phoebe Cates, John Glover, Christopher Lee, Robert Prosky, Robert Picardo, Haviland Morris, Dick Miller, Jackie Joseph, Keye Luke, Belinda Balaski, Paul Bartel, Kenneth Tobey, John Astin, Henry Gibson, Leonard Maltin, Hulk Hogan; ***Cameos:*** Jerry Goldsmith; ***D:*** Joe Dante; ***W:*** Charles Haas; ***C:*** John Hora; ***M:*** Jerry Goldsmith; ***V:*** Howie Mandel, Tony Randall. **VHS, LV, 8mm, Letterboxed, Closed Caption** *WAR, HHE*

Grim

Average low-budget horror suffers from a ludicrous premise and a soundtrack filled with melodramatic organ music. The title character, a guy in a silly monster suit, lives in caverns beneath a new subdivision and communicates telepathically—or something to that effect—with certain residents before he chops them up and worships the devil. The characters have no depth, and the whole thing becomes far too gory for my taste. Again, though, it's too ridiculous to be offensive.

1995 (R) 86m/C Emmanuel Xuereb, Tres Handley, Peter Tregloan; ***D:*** Paul Matthews; ***W:*** Paul Matthews. **VHS, LV** *APX*

The Guardian

If Stephen King and Mel Brooks teamed up to make a version of *Three Men and a Baby,* they couldn't come up with as many real laughs as the unintentional variety generated in this misfire. Actually, director William Friedkin begins well, with an eerie dreamlike evocation of the archetypal stuff of fairy tales: abandonment by parents, the loss of children, ancient secrets hidden deep in the forest. But that mood soon evaporates when Phil (Dwier Brown) and Kate (Carey Lowell) move to L.A. and hire Camilla (Jenny Seagrove), the nanny who's too good to be true. The laughs start when Phil dreams that a tree is growing in his living room, and the film never recovers.

1990 (R) 92m/C Jenny Seagrove, Dwier Brown, Carey Lowell, Brad Hall, Miguel Ferrer, Natalija Nogulich, Pamela Brull, Gary Swanson; ***D:*** William Friedkin; ***W:*** William Friedkin, Stephen Volk, Dan Greenberg; ***C:*** John A. Alonzo. **VHS, LV, Closed Caption** *USH*

Habitat

Despite a half-baked stereotyped premise and an uneven script, this offbeat s-f/eco-horror is really ambitious and more successful than not. In a near future when the ozone layer has disappeared, Hank Symes (Tcheky Karyo), a renegade mad scientist who's madder than most, turns the interior of his house into a fertile Garden of Eden. It's a lush jungle in a sun-blasted suburban wasteland where everything grows. His not-quite-so-mad wife Clarissa (Alice Krige) thinks it's neat. Their teenaged son Andreas (Balthazar Getty) is horribly embarrassed. That conflict between the freaky parents and the kid who wants to fit in is the most interesting part of the film, along with the computer effects. The cardboard villains and the less than successful sets get in the way. Some of the one-with-nature dialogue comes off as bad Walt Whitman—"I swim with the plankton and frolic with the sperm!"—but the intentional comic touches are fine. Writer/director Renee Daalder also made *Massacre at Central High.*

1997 (R) 103m/C Alice Krige, Balthazar Getty, Tcheky Karyo, Kenneth Welsh; ***D:*** Renee Daalder; ***W:*** Renee Daalder. **VHS** *APX*

Halloween

In 1978, John Carpenter made a "little" movie about three teenaged girls and a madman, and changed the motion picture business. In terms of return on investment, *Halloween* quickly became the most profitable independent film ever made. Its influence on virtually every horror movie that's been made since then is incalculable. The implacable stalker who kills young

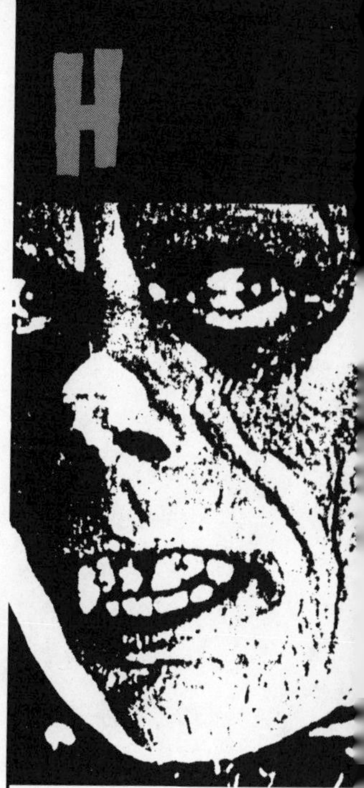

John Carpenter's *Halloween.*

people (usually while they're engaged in any sexual activity) has become a cliche, but Carpenter and Debra Hill—his co-writer, producer, and even co-director in some scenes—invented the character. The plot is simple and relentless. So is Carpenter's direction. The film exists in several versions on tape and disc. The best are the 1997 Anchor Bay cassette, which is the full-length theatrical release, digitally mastered and letterboxed, and the Criterion Collection laserdisc. The disc also contains extra footage that was shot during the filming of *Halloween 2* and separate audio track commentary by Carpenter, Hill, and star Jamie Lee Curtis. For fans who know the film well, their comments are illuminating. Carpenter points out flaws, shortcuts that worked and those that didn't. Jamie Lee Curtis is a little nostalgic and sounds completely relaxed and open about her first job (at age 19). Debra Hill has some of the best stories, but she is unusually thin-skinned and defensive about the film's sexual side. 🦴🦴🦴🦴

1978 (R) 90m/C Jamie Lee Curtis, Donald Pleasence, Nancy Loomis, P.J. Soles, Charles Cyphers; ***D:*** John Carpenter; ***W:*** John Carpenter, Debra Hill; ***C:*** Dean Cundey; ***M:*** John Carpenter. **VHS, LV, Letterboxed** *VTR, CRC*

Halloween 2: The Nightmare Isn't Over!

Earnest, uninspired sequel is set directly after the original. Apparently unfazed by the second-story fall and the six slugs Dr. Loomis (Donald Pleasence) pumped into him at the end of the first film, Michael Myers wanders about collecting sharp instruments while Laurie (Jamie Lee Curtis) heads off to the hospital where most of the second half is set. Director Rick Rosenthal repeats the same scare gimmicks of the first film and they simply can't stand up to repetition. The various plot revelations actually diminish the raw power of Carpenter's original concept and put the series on a downward spiral that has continued through several increasingly needless sequels.

1981 (R) 92m/C Jamie Lee Curtis, Donald Pleasence, Jeffrey Kramer, Charles Cyphers, Lance Guest; ***D:*** Rick Rosenthal; ***W:*** John Carpenter, Debra Hill; ***C:*** Dean Cundey; ***M:*** John Carpenter. **VHS, LV** *USH*

Halloween 3: Season of the Witch

Unusual sequel has nothing to do with the others in the series. Instead it's a town-with-a-secret story that borrows freely from *Invasion of the Bodysnatchers, The Stepford Wives,* and even *Alien*. Dr. Challis (Tom Atkins) and Ellie (Stacey Nelkin) try to find out what happened to her father in the little town of Santa Mira. Yes, that's the home of the pod people, but something else is going on at the Silver Shamrock Novelty Co. there. Unfortunately, the script by director Tommy Lee Wallace works itself into a corner and can't find its way out. Reportedly, writer Nigel Kneale (*Quatermass and the Pit*) had his name removed. The effects are bloody and imaginative.

1982 (R) 98m/C Tom Atkins, Stacey Nelkin, Dan O'Herlihy, Ralph Strait, Michael Currie; ***D:*** Tommy Lee Wallace; ***W:*** Tommy Lee Wallace; ***C:*** Dean Cundey; ***M:*** John Carpenter. **VHS, LV** *USH*

Halloween 4: The Return of Michael Myers

Eagle-eyed viewers will remember that at the end of *2*, Michael Myers isn't merely dead, he's really most sincerely dead—morally, ethically, spiritually, physically, positively, absolutely, undeniably, and reliably DEAD. But, sensing a profit, accountants decreed that he lives, hence this connect-the-dots installment. The plot contains nothing new, but several scenes have the supernatural psychopath stalking a young child (Danielle Harris) and that's offensive. The trend continues in a downward spiral of sequels. **Woof!**

1988 (R) 88m/C Donald Pleasence, Ellie Cornell, Danielle Harris, Michael Pataki, George P. Wilbur, Beau Starr, Kathleen Kinmont, Sasha Jenson, Gene Ross; ***D:*** Dwight Little; ***W:*** Alan B. McElroy; ***C:*** Peter Collister. **VHS, LV, Closed Caption** *FOX*

Halloween 5: The Revenge of Michael Myers

At the time it was made, *5* set a low-water mark for the series. It has, of course, been eclipsed by the most recent entry, but for overall lack of originality—not to mention contempt for its audience—this one remains hard to top. Beyond a few curious attempts to treat the material as comedy, the plot is the same old same old, presented with needlessly slick production values. Involving a psychic little girl (Michael Myers' niece) is inexcusable. The film performed so poorly in theatrical release that six years passed before *6* infected the multiplexes. **Woof!**

1989 (R) 96m/C Donald Pleasence, Ellie Cornell, Danielle Harris, Don Shanks, Betty Carvalho, Beau Starr, Wendy Kaplan, Jeffrey Landman; ***D:*** Dominique Othenin-Girard; ***W:*** Dominique Othenin-Girard, Shem Bitterman, Michael Jacobs; ***C:*** Rob Draper. **VHS, LV, Closed Caption** *FOX*

Halloween 6: The Curse of Michael Myers

Putrid little movie opens with shots of a pseudo-satanic ritual where a black-robed figure threatens a naked infant with a large knife. But after the repugnant beginning, it quickly disintegrates into a virtually plotless series of predictable murders. The victims include an abusive father, his nearsighted wife, and an obnoxious radio

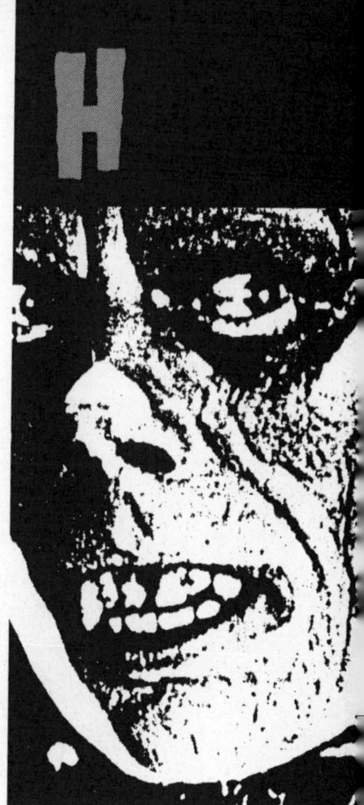

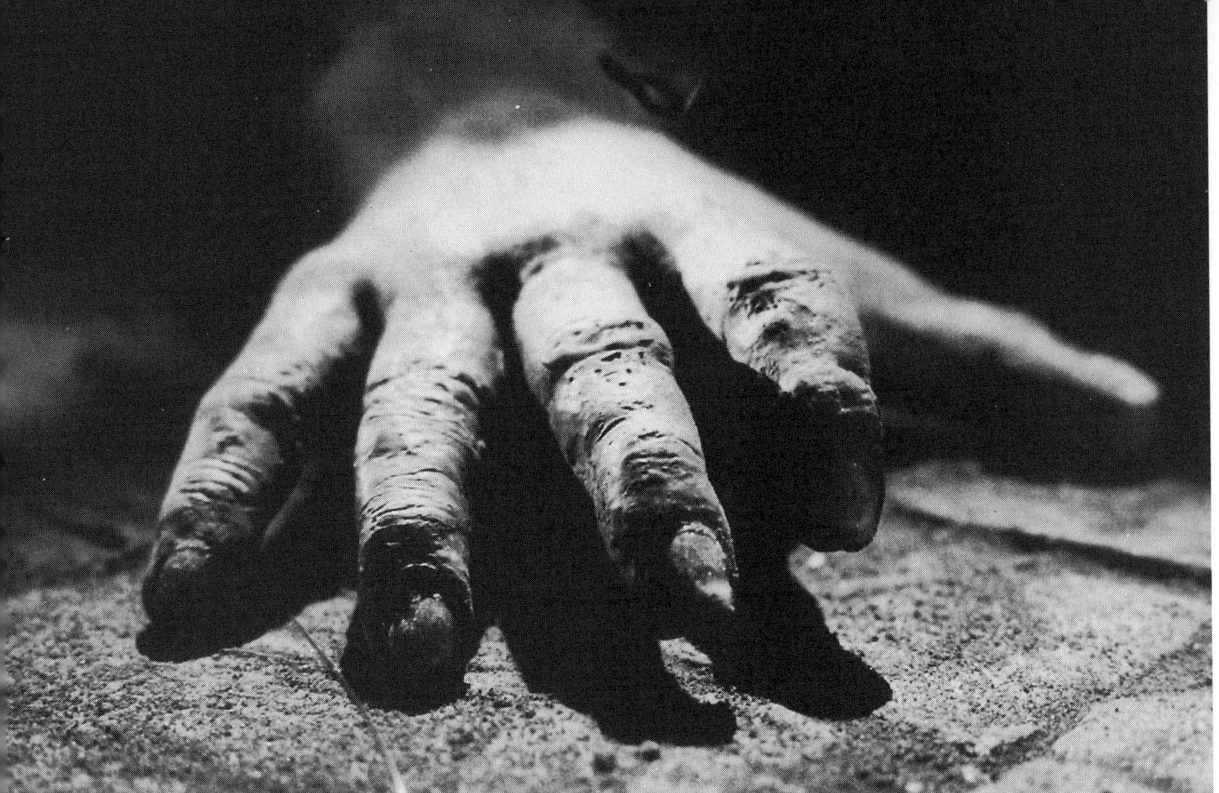

Oliver Stone's *The Hand.*

talk-show host. Veteran character actor Donald Pleasence returns as Dr. Loomis. This was his final role, completed just before he died, and he appears to have realized how abysmal the material was. Still, the entire *Halloween* franchise has a combined budget of $20 million and has grossed more than $200 million, so it probably isn't over. ***AKA:*** Halloween: The Origin of Michael Myers. **Woof!**

1995 (R) 88m/C Donald Pleasence, Mitchell Ryan, Marianne Hagan, Leo Geter, George P. Wilbur, Kim Darby, Bradford English, Devin Gardner; ***D:*** Joe Chappelle; ***W:*** Daniel Farrands; ***C:*** Billy Dickson; ***M:*** Alan Howarth. **VHS, LV, Closed Caption** *TOU*

The Hand

Director Oliver Stone screws things up grandly with this abysmal exercise in psychological horror. After a troubled cartoonist (Michael Caine) loses his hand in an auto accident, his various marital, professional, and personal problems expand to monstrous proportions. Meanwhile, the missing appendage is crawling around and killing people. Is it real or is it his fevered imagination? By turns, the action is too literal and too abstract. Unlike Stone's later work, the film lacks the stylistic flourishes or narrative drive to haul it over the long rough stretches. Stone cameos as the one-handed tramp. Caine's haircut is more frightening than the silly effects. 🦴

1981 (R) 105m/C *GB* Michael Caine, Andrea Marcovicci, Annie McEnroe, Bruce McGill, Viveca Lindfors; ***Cameos:*** Oliver Stone; ***D:*** Oliver Stone; ***W:*** Oliver Stone; ***C:*** King Baggot; ***M:*** James Horner. **VHS** *WAR*

The Hands of Orlac

Concert pianist (Mel Ferrer) injured in an accident is given an executed murderer's hands and comes to believe that they have a mind of their own. The whole idea is more than a little silly and never rings true in a psychological sense, either. Yeah, it's the hands that make the respectable newlywed check into a seedy Marseilles hotel where he runs into an equally seedy Christopher Lee. Sample dialogue: "If he's got something to hide, he'll pay through the nose 'til his eyes fall out!" Claude Bolling's jazzy score is more enjoyable. Some tapes are of less than perfect quality, with scenes alternately muddy and bleached out. ***AKA:*** Hands of the Strangler; Hands of a Strangler.

1960 95m/B *GB FR* Mel Ferrer, Christopher Lee, Felix Aylmer, Basil Sydney, Donald Wolfit, Donald Pleasence, Danny Carrel, Lucile Saint-Simon, Peter Reynolds, Campbell Singer, David Peel; ***D:*** Edmond T. Greville; ***W:*** Edmond T. Greville, John Baines, Donald Taylor; ***C:*** Desmond Dickinson; ***M:*** Claude Bolling. **VHS** *SNC*

Hands of the Ripper

As a child, Anna (Angharad Rees) watches her father, Jack the Ripper, murder her mother. Not surprisingly then, she grows up to be a troubled, lethal young woman. Dr. Pritchard (Eric Porter), a pioneering Freudian psychoanalyst, wants to study and help her, though his motives are as much ambitious as altruistic. Director Peter Sasdy makes the violence an important and inventive aspect of the story, and he handles it with some facile camera work. Writer L.W. Davidson also adds political and social dimensions to the believable characters. Though the cast is relatively unknown in the U.S., the acting is exemplary in both the leads and secondary characters. Hammer fans who have missed this sleeper are in for a treat.

1971 (R) 85m/C *GB* Eric Porter, Angharad Rees, Jane Merrow, Keith Bell, Derek Godfrey, Dora Bryan, Marjorie Rhodes, Norman Bird; ***D:*** Peter Sasdy; ***W:*** L.W. Davidson; ***C:*** Ken Talbot; ***M:*** Christopher Gunning. **VHS** *MLB*

The Hanging Woman

Truly crazed Italian-Spanish production begins with a strong, rainy funeral scene that could have introduced a good Hammer film. Within minutes, the plot sails off to the farthest shores of exploitation with necrophilia, grave robbing, and the like. Serge (Stan Cooper, with an impressive early '70s helmet of blond hair) goes to a small town to collect an inheritance from his departed uncle, the Count. He also finds a seductive Countess (Dianik Zurakowska), Igor (Paul Naschy) the lecherous gravedigger, and humor beyond description. The hyperbolic plot twists are often ridiculous and always unpredictable. In many ways, the film can be seen as a precursor to the even more unhinged Italian "living dead" movies of the 1990s. The alternative lunacy is also available in a longer "uncut" version from Video Search of Miami. ***AKA:*** Return of the Zombies; Beyond the Living Dead; La Orgia de los Muertos; Dracula, the Terror of the Living Dead; Orgy of the Dead; House of Terror.

1972 (R) 91m/C *SP IT* Stan Cooper, Vickie Nesbitt, Marcella Wright, Catherine Gilbert, Gerard Tichy, Paul Naschy, Dianik Zurakowska, Maria Pia Conte, Carlos Quiney; ***D:*** Jose Luis Merino; ***W:*** Jose Luis Merino. **VHS** *NO*

Happy Birthday to Me

Halloween Goes Preppy might have been the title of this unimaginative dead-teen flick. Virginia (Melissa Sue Anderson) barely notices that her friends and classmates are disappearing as the plot plods from one murder to another. A brain surgery sequence is the only part that isn't petrified by imitation. Some clever effects make it pretty disgusting, but a single yucky scene is hardly enough to recommend this turkey. Even taken on its own limited terms, the film never makes sense and the ridiculous "twist" ending is the final insult to viewers' intelligence.

1981 (R) 108m/C *CA* Melissa Sue Anderson, Glenn Ford, Tracy Bregman, Jack Blum, Matt Craven, Lawrence Dane, Lenore Zann, Sharon Acker, Frances Hyland, Earl Pennington; ***D:*** J. Lee Thompson; ***W:*** Timothy Bond, Peter Jobin, John C.W. Saxton; ***C:*** Miklos Lente. **VHS, LV** *COL*

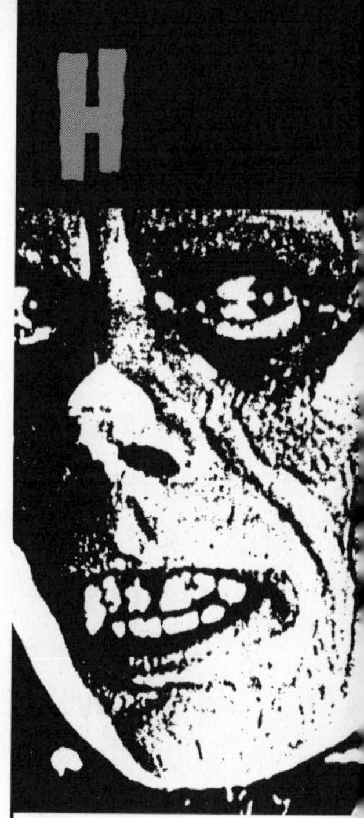

"Haven't you noticed how nothing in this house seems to move until you look away and then you just...catch something out of the corner of your eye?"

—Theodora (Claire Bloom) in *The Haunting.*

The Harvest

Variations on a popular urban myth posit a middle-class man on a trip who meets a sexy girl, gets drunk, and wakes up the next day minus a kidney or some other major organ. Charlie Pope (Miguel Ferrer) is a screenwriter who goes to Mexico to research a murder. Natalie (Leilani Sarelle Ferrer) is the very sexy girl he meets. If he's not completely successful with the resolution of that premise, director David Marconi gives the film a fever dream quality that carries it over the rough spots. Recommended. 🦴🦴🦴

1992 (R) 97m/C Miguel Ferrer, Leilani Sarelle Ferrer, Harvey Fierstein, Anthony John Denison, Tim Thomerson, Matt Clark, Henry Silva; ***D:*** David Marconi; ***W:*** David Marconi; ***M:*** Dave Allen, Rick Boston. **VHS, LV, Closed Caption** *COL*

Hatchet for the Honeymoon

John Herrington (Stephen Forsyth) tells us in a voiceover narration that he's a lunatic murderer who specializes in brides. He spends the next 90 minutes proving it. The crazed, defiantly unrealistic plot might have set the standard for the most popular Italian horrors of the following decades. The key images—birds, running water, dripping blood, etc.—all make appearances. It's less a film about a murderer than an extended illustration of insanity. Grotesque scenes and an overwrought atmosphere are far more important than the conventional, well-made plot. Like so many Eurohorrors, this one is interesting to watch but, for American audiences, emotionally uninvolving and not particularly frightening. ***AKA:*** Blood Brides; Una Hacha para la Luna de Miel; Il Rosso Segmo della Follia; An Axe for the Honeymoon; The Red Sign of Madness. 🦴🦴½

1970 90m/C *SP IT* Stephen Forsyth, Dagmar Lassander, Laura Betti, Gerard Tichy, Femi Benussi, Luciano Pigozzi, Jesus Puente; ***D:*** Mario Bava; ***W:*** Mario Bava, Santiago Moncada, Mario Musy; ***C:*** Mario Bava. **VHS** *HEG, FCT*

Haunted

Handsome, classy ghost story harkens back to such atmospheric productions as *The Uninvited*. In 1928, professor and spiritualist debunker David Ash (Aidan Quinn) goes to a country estate in answer to an old woman's cry for help. Something terrible is going on, she says. But, upon arriving, Ash is more interested in Christina (Kate Beckinsale), an uninhibited young woman who admires his book. Ash isn't so sure about her brother (Anthony Andrews), who claims, "We're all mad, you know." Based on James Herbert's novel, the script combines a nostalgic evocation of the period with various sexy undercurrents and a teasing attitude toward the supernatural. Director Lewis Gilbert (*Alfie, Educating Rita, Shirley Valentine*) handles it all with a sure hand throughout, and tosses in several surprises toward the end when many fans will think that they've got everything figured out. 🦴🦴🦴½

1995 (R) 108m/C *GB* Aidan Quinn, Kate Beckinsale, Anthony Andrews, Alex Lowe, Anna Massey, Geraldine Somerville, Victoria Shalet; ***Cameos:*** John Gielgud; ***D:*** Lewis Gilbert; ***W:*** Lewis Gilbert, Bob Kellett, Tim Prager; ***C:*** Tony Pierce-Roberts; ***M:*** Debbie Wiseman. **VHS** *HMK*

Haunted Honeymoon

Lame horror-comedy is built around Edward G. Bulwer-Lytton's famous opening line, "It was a dark and stormy night." In fact, that's all there is to the movie. The few genuine laughs it contains could have been handled in a TV skit. 1930s radio star Larry Abbot (Gene Wilder, who also wrote and directed) and his fiancee (Gilda Radner) must spend a week with his family in a castle where it is always dark and stormy. The plotless action includes some business about a werewolf, dead bodies that pop up, and Dom DeLuise in drag. What a sad, thin cinematic exit for Gilda Radner. **Woof!**

1986 (PG) 82m/C Gene Wilder, Gilda Radner, Dom DeLuise, Jonathan Pryce, Paul Smith, Peter Vaughan, Bryan Pringle, Roger Ashton-Griffiths, Jim Carter, Eve Ferret; ***D:*** Gene Wilder; ***W:*** Terence Marsh, Gene Wilder; ***C:*** Fred Schuler. **VHS, LV** *ORI*

The Haunted Strangler

Mid-level Karloff horror opens with a rowdy Dickensian execution scene at Newgate Prison, 1860. Flash forward 20 years; novelist John Rankin (Boris Karloff) attempts to reopen the investigation of the murder of a character named Martha Stewart by a mysterious one-armed man. He sees a miscarriage of justice. As it unfolds, the odd but finally archetypal story deserves more complex treatment. It's padded with Folies Bergere-style dance numbers when it ought to be more deeply involved with the characters. For Karloff fans only. ***AKA:*** The Grip of the Strangler.

1958 78m/B *GB* Boris Karloff, Anthony Dawson, Elizabeth Allan, Timothy Turner, Diane Aubrey, Dorothy Gordon, Jean Kent, Vera Day; ***D:*** Robert Day; ***W:*** John C. Cooper, Jan Read; ***C:*** Lionel Banes. **VHS** *MPI*

Haunted Summer

Historical horror based on a real event tries to turn its famous characters—the great Romantic poets, Shelley and Byron, and Mary Shelley, author of *Frankenstein*—into real, flesh-and-blood human beings. The year is 1816 when all of them lived together for a time in Byron's Swiss villa. Shelley (Eric Stoltz) is fond of morphine cocktails, skinny-dipping, and spitballs. Byron (Philip Anglim) prefers smoking opium. He's also a sexual tyrant who carries on overlapping affairs with partners of both sexes. It's all just too too decadent. It's also too too slow and oddly comic when it may not mean to be. If all of this seems more than a little familiar, it's because Ken Russell handled exactly the same material in his wonderfully weird horror comedy *Gothic.*

1988 (R) 106m/C Alice Krige, Eric Stoltz, Philip Anglim, Laura Dern, Alex Winter; ***D:*** Ivan Passer; ***W:*** Lewis John Carlino. **VHS, LV** *NO*

The Haunting

Director Robert Wise has a mixed track record in horror. *The Bodysnatcher* is brilliant, while *Audrey Rose* is an embarrassment. Though this effort has been widely praised by mainstream critics, it remains seriously flawed. The story of psychics (Julie Harris and Claire Bloom) and a scientist (Richard Johnson) investigating a haunted house is famous for its restraint; there are no graphic visual scares. The same can't be said of the ponderous, oppressive music and the overstated dialogue. Some of the breathless acting has aged poorly, too. Though the film is based on Shirley Jackson's novel, it feels like a play with the claustrophobic house substituting for the proscenium. To be fair, the story is more effective and enjoyable if it's seen as a character study of a complex, emotionally damaged woman.

1963 113m/B Julie Harris, Claire Bloom, Russ Tamblyn, Richard Johnson, Fay Compton, Rosalie Crutchley, Lois Maxwell, Valentine Dyall, Diane Clare; ***D:*** Robert Wise; ***W:*** Nelson Gidding; ***C:*** David Boulton. **VHS, LV** *MGM, FCT*

He Knows You're Alone

Not content to rip off John Carpenter's plot for *Halloween,* the brazen makers of this by-the-numbers slasher flick also lifted his music! Caitlin O'Heaney screams well and loudly in the lead. Scott Parker's script has a few bright moments that survive Armand Mastroianni's ham-fisted direction. In one

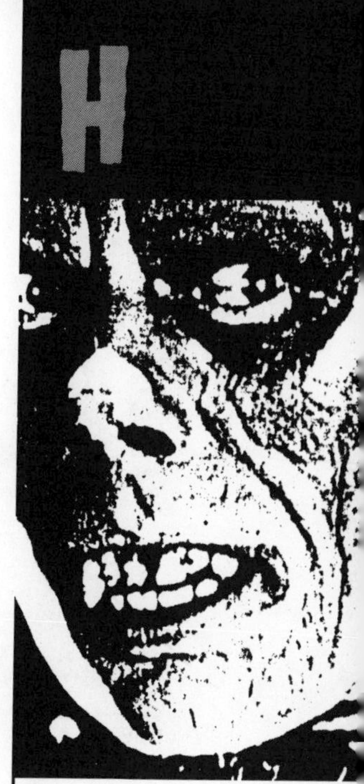

Tom Rolfing and Caitlin O'Heaney in *He Knows You're Alone.*

key scene, he does everything but superimpose an arrow on the screen to call your attention to a missing knife. Fans of the genre will hoot with derision.

1980 (R) 94m/C Don Scardino, Caitlin (Kathleen Heaney) O'Heaney, Tom Rolfing, Paul Gleason, Elizabeth Kemp, Tom Hanks, Patsy Pease, Lewis Arlt, James Rebhorn, Joseph Leon, James Carroll; ***D:*** Armand Mastroianni; ***W:*** Scott Parker; ***C:*** Gerald Feil. **VHS** *MGM*

Head of the Family

If this one were a little quicker out of the gate, it might have been a tongue-in-cheek horror-comedy hit. Unfortunately, it doesn't get really weird until the second half. The title character, Myron (J.W. Perra), is literally the "head" of the Stackpool family. In fact, he's nothing but an oversized head on a tiny wizened body, and he's psychically linked with his three subnormal siblings. They live in the faux-southern Gothic hamlet of Nob Hollow. When Lance (Blake Bailey) learns the Stackpool family secrets (there are others), he and his lover Lorretta (Jacqueline Lovell) decide to put the squeeze on the head. Not a good idea. Toward the end, producer/director Robert Talbot (actually Charles Band) comes close to his model—the wonderful cult favorite *Motel Hell*—but this one isn't quite as kinky.

1996 (R) 82m/C Blake Bailey, Jacqueline Lovell, Bob Schott, J.W. Perra; ***D:*** Robert Talbot; ***W:*** Benjamin Carr; ***C:*** Adolfo Bartoli; ***M:*** Richard Band. **VHS** *AFE*

Heathers

Bleak, black satire is as bracing and energetic as a thunderstorm. It uses a serious subject—teen suicide—as a springboard to savage every subject and group it encounters: kids, adults, cops, murderers, teachers, new-agers, conservatives, and beautiful people. J.D. (Christian Slater)

shows young Veronica (Winona Ryder) how to free herself from the conventions of suburbia. If a few people have to die in the process, that's the price we pay. Director Michael Lehmann and writer Daniel Waters aren't able to sustain their outrageous sensibility all the way, but that's a quibble.

1989 (R) 102m/C Winona Ryder, Christian Slater, Kim Walker, Shannen Doherty, Lisanne Falk, Penelope Milford, Glenn Shadix, Lance Fenton, Patrick Laborteaux, Jeremy Applegate, Renee Estevez; ***D:*** Michael Lehmann; ***W:*** Daniel Waters; ***C:*** Francis Kenny; ***M:*** David Newman. Independent Spirit Awards '90: Best First Feature. **VHS, LV, Closed Caption** *VTR, FCT*

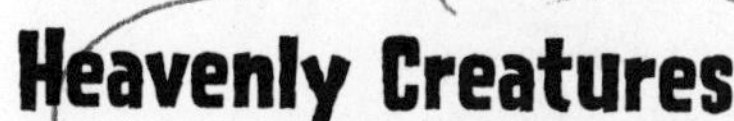

Heavenly Creatures

The only monsters in Peter Jackson's most accomplished film to date are creations of youthful imagination. They're the basis of a true horror story, and like so many true stories, it's much harder to believe than any fiction. In 1950s New Zealand, schoolmates Pauline Parker (Melanie Lynskey) and Juliette Hulme (Kate Winslet) appear to be thorough opposites. Pauline is dark-haired, thick, and shy; Juliette is blonde, slim, and completely full of herself. The two have nothing in common, save childhood ailments and hyperactive imaginations. Of course they become inseparable—two girls in constant motion, overflowing with energy, never still, never quiet, who create an elaborate fantasy "fourth world" for themselves. Jackson and co-writer Frances Walsh utilize a few impressive special effects to take viewers into the girls' fantasy life. It's a powerful creation of emerging sexuality, romance, and desire. If anyone doubts the validity of the story, much of it is based on Pauline's own diary entries, which provide occasional voiceover narration. That combination of reportage and psychological fantasy makes this a constantly surprising film, particularly toward the end. In an ironic postscript, it has been revealed since the film's release that Juliette has grown up to become mystery writer Anne Perry.

1994 (R) 110m/C *NZ* Melanie Lynskey, Kate Winslet, Sarah Pierse, Diana Kent, Clive Merrison, Simon O'Connor; ***D:*** Peter Jackson; ***W:*** Peter Jackson, Frances Walsh; ***C:*** Alun Bollinger. Nominations: Academy Awards '94: Best Original Screenplay; Australian Film Institute '95: Best Foreign Film; Writers Guild of America '94: Best Original Screenplay. **VHS, LV, Closed Caption** *TOU*

Hell Night

Four college pledges, including Marti (Linda Blair), must spend the night in haunted Garth Manor for their initiation. Their friends mean to scare them but the ghostly murderer may still be alive. Cast, plot, and setting make this one a combination of *The Exorcist, Halloween,* and *Animal House.* Actually, the setting is strong and this is one of the better dead-teen flicks, coming as it does near the beginning of the cycle.

1981 (R) 100m/C Linda Blair, Vincent Van Patten, Kevin Brophy, Peter Barton, Jenny Neumann; ***D:*** Tom De Simone; ***W:*** Randy Feldman; ***C:*** Mac Ahlberg. **VHS**

Hellblock 13

Anthology of low-budget short horror tales is told with grainy, raw-edged energy and a distinct regional flavor. Tara (Debbie Rochon) writes stories while she's on Death Row and shows them to her stolid guard (Gunnar Hansen, Leatherface from *The Texas Chainsaw Massacre*). The first of those might have been the E.C. Comics version of the horrible child murders committed by Susan Smith in South Carolina. The second is a crazy white-trash trailer-park horror-comedy wherein Heidi Mae (Jennifer Peluso) turns to a witch to get rid of abusive hubby Joe Mark (David G. Holland). In the third story, a biker gang makes its annual pilgrimage to the grave of Big Rhonda (J.J. North) to receive her blessings on the eve of a drug run. Then Tara herself really cuts loose and the film ends on a wonderfully

Tony Randel's *Hellbound: Hellraiser 2.*

loony Grand Guignol note. Debbie Rochon has the strongest role, and she brings a welcome note of humor to what might have been your basic madwoman stereotype. The individual films get better and funnier as they go along. Director Paul Talbot is also responsible for the similar *Campfire Tales* and *Freakshow.* 🦴🦴🦴

1997 91m/C Debbie Rochon, Gunnar Hansen, J.J. North, Jennifer Peluso, David G. Holland; ***D:*** Paul Talbot; ***W:*** Paul Talbot, Jeff Miller, Michael R. Smith. *NYR*

Hellbound: Hellraiser 2

Following the rules for sequels, this one amplifies the most popular elements of the first (*Hellraiser*) and omits the less-than-successful aspects. It can't replace the originality. Kirstie (Ashley Laurence) is recovering in a sanitorium. Her psychiatrist, Dr. Channard (creepily underplayed by Kenneth Cranham) knows more about her strange experiences than he should. Despite a preposterous plot and a weak ending, the film still has its moments, particularly for fans of Clive Barker, who is executive producer. Followed by more. ***AKA:*** Hellraiser 2. 🦴🦴

1988 (R) 96m/C *GB* Ashley Laurence, Clare Higgins, Kenneth Cranham, Imogen Boorman, William Hope, Oliver Smith, Sean Chapman, Doug Bradley; ***D:*** Tony Randel; ***W:*** Peter Atkins; ***C:*** Robin Vidgeon. **VHS, LV, Closed Caption** *VTR*

Hellgate

Unintentionally funny low-budget horror is a variation on the old ghostly hitchhiker story—the one that ends "and he found his sweater on her tombstone." The seductive spook lives in a ghost town full of refugees from one of George Romero's *Living Dead* movies. The plot is nothing more than an excuse to trot out unconvincing but gory

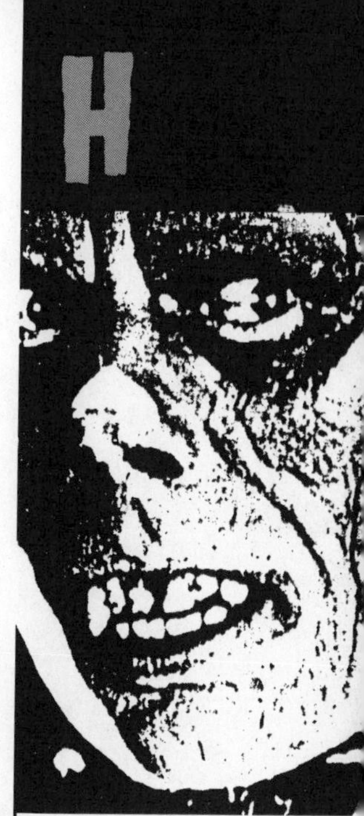

special effects. On the positive side, the bad ensemble acting from a no-name cast is inspired, and any movie with a monster goldfish can't be all bad. Fun for an appreciative crowd that's ready to laugh.

1989 (R) 96m/C Abigail Wolcott, Ron Palillo, Carel Trichardt, Petrea Curran, Evan J. Klisser, Joanne Ward; ***D:*** William A. Levey; ***W:*** Michael O'Rourke; ***C:*** Peter Palmer. **VHS, LV** *THV*

Hello Mary Lou: Prom Night 2

Forget the subtitle. This isn't a sequel. It really owes more to *A Nightmare on Elm Street.* Thirty years after she was burned to death on the bandstand as she accepted her crown, Mary Lou's (Lisa Schrage) spirit rises from the grave and tries to inhabit Vicki's body. The thing is, Vicki (Wendy Lyon) is a good girl, while Mary Lou, alive or dead, is an unrepentant temptress, who wants vengeance on the people (including Michael Ironside) responsible for her death. Think Freddy Krueger with PMS. Some of the hallucinatory scares are unexpected. So is the serious religious element. ***AKA:*** The Haunting of Hamilton High; Prom Night 2.

1987 (R) 97m/C *CA* Michael Ironside, Wendy Lyon, Justin Louis, Lisa Schrage, Richard Monette; ***D:*** Bruce Pittman; ***W:*** Ron Oliver; ***C:*** John Herzog. **VHS, LV, Closed Caption** *NO*

Hellraiser

Author Clive Barker makes a credible directorial debut in this tale of ultimate pleasure and pain. Those come from the Cenobites, five creatures who are conjured up by an intricate puzzle box, and who descend upon a damaged family (Andrew Robinson, Clare Higgins, Ashley Laurence). Though the tricky story is bloody, it doesn't wallow in gore. Four of the Cenobites are genuinely frightening figures, but the fifth, and allegedly the most terrifying, is a guy who's got his head where his butt ought to be. Followed by sequels.

1987 (R) 94m/C *GB* Andrew (Andy) Robinson, Clare Higgins, Ashley Laurence, Sean Chapman, Oliver Smith, Robert Hines, Doug Bradley, Nicholas Vince; ***D:*** Clive Barker; ***W:*** Clive Barker; ***C:*** Robin Vidgeon; ***M:*** Christopher Young. **LV, Closed Caption** *VTR*

Hellraiser 3: Hell on Earth

Clive Barker's series follows a predictably smooth downward curve in originality and quality. Too-familiar exploding heads and rattling chains have replaced the Cenobites. When variations of them finally do show up, they're almost tongue-in-cheek (or at least camera-in-cheek). TV reporter Joey (Terry Farrell) tracks down the story behind an emergency room death and eventually finds Pinhead (Doug Bradley). The film is fairly well acted, but like virtually all sequels these days, it over-relies on elaborate sets, slick visuals, and a conventional plot.

1992 (R) 91m/C Doug Bradley, Terry Farrell, Kevin Bernhardt, Paula Marshall, Ken Carpenter, Peter Boynton, Ashley Laurence; ***D:*** Anthony Hickox; ***W:*** Peter Atkins; ***C:*** Gerry Lively. **VHS, LV, Closed Caption** *PAR*

Hellraiser 4: Bloodline

In the long and infamous career of Alan Smithee, this may be his most despicable film. Smithee is the pseudonym used by directors when they're so dissatisfied or embarrassed by the fruit of their labors that they choose not to sign their real names. Who can blame special effects expert Kevin Yeagher for disowning this one? The fourth in author/producer Clive Barker's series is a century-hopping tale of torture and mutilation told with a creepy affinity for its subjects. It depends on sharp objects graphically penetrating or

Michael Berryman in *The Hills Have Eyes.*

slicing flesh for its horror. Some scenes involve a child and though they're not explicit, they add a queasy note to an already rancid, distasteful effort. Though the film is only 81 minutes long, it's not nearly short enough. **Woof!**

1995 (R) 81m/C Bruce Ramsey, Valentina Vargas, Doug Bradley, Kim Myers, Christina Harnos, Charlotte Chatton, Paul Perri, Mickey Cotrell; ***D:*** Alan Smithee, Kevin Yagher; ***W:*** Peter Atkins; ***C:*** Gerry Lively; ***M:*** Daniel Licht. **VHS, LV, Closed Caption** *PAR*

Helter Skelter Murders

This slow curiosity looks like a poorly done re-enactment of the Sharon Tate murders (without narration), not a true feature. It's mostly black and white, about nameless characters who seldom speak. Location footage was filmed in courtrooms and what appears to be the real Spahn's Movie Ranch where the Manson "family" lived for a time. The physical details of the crimes may be accurate, as far as they go, but the emotions of the characters never ring true and the action is forgettable.

1971 (R) 83m/B Brian Klinknett, Debbie Duff, Phyllis Estes; ***D:*** Frank Howard; ***W:*** J.J. Wilkie, Duke Howze; ***C:*** Frank Howard. **VHS** *EEL*

Henry: Portrait of a Serial Killer

John McNaughton's fact-based chiller is simply one of the most disturbing and frightening horror films anyone has ever made. Henry (grimly underplayed by Michael Rooker) is an illiterate drifter who moves from job to job, and kills at random. Though Henry claims to have been abused as a child, that doesn't explain him. Neither does the sexual element that some of the murders contain. Killing is simply something he does without emotion or

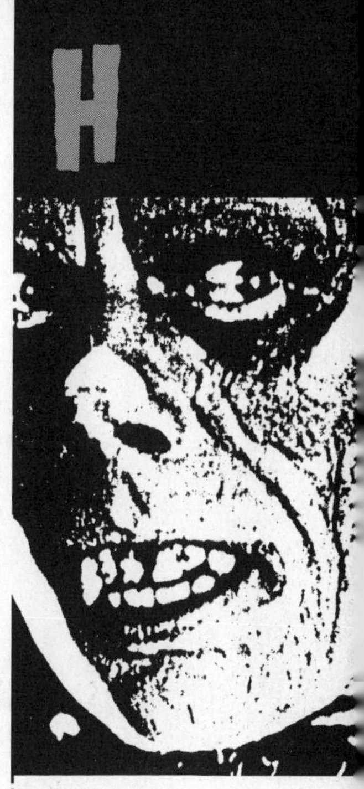

pleasure. McNaughton tells the story with a deliberately flat, documentary style: stark naturalistic lighting and acting, Midwest locations, grainy color, limited music. The film was rated X for violence and subject matter, but has been released on tape without a rating. It is definitely not for kids, and older audiences looking for titillating violence or elaborate effects will be disappointed. In terms of onscreen acts of violence, *Henry* contains only a tiny fraction of the average *Friday the 13th* or *Elm Street* flick. But this is a real nightmare and these suggested horrors—including an unexpected ending—are much more terrifying than graphic cinematic schlock. Followed by a lesser 1996 sequel. 🦴🦴🦴🦴

1990 (X) 90m/C Michael Rooker, Tom Towles, Tracy Arnold; ***D:*** John McNaughton; ***W:*** John McNaughton, Richard Fire; ***C:*** Charlie Lieberman. **VHS, LV** *MPI*

Hideous

Charles Band's Full Moon label specializes in low-budget horror and s-f with big-budget polish. This one's a comedy about four little psychic snot-covered little freaks, or "goobers," as our nominal hero calls them. Said goobers are locked up in a castle with a motley group of humans who mostly deserve anything that happens to them. We've got the competing greedy collectors of medical abnormalities, their broker, the ballsy moll, the not-so-tough detective, and the dumb blonde. Most of the humor's pretty sharp, but it degenerates into perhaps the most pitiful swordfight ever perpetrated on videotape. The spark is Jacqueline Lovell's Sheila. Her swaggering performance easily upstages her co-stars. Given the right roles, she could be another Pam Grier or Claudia Jennings. 🦴🦴🦴

1997 (R) m/C Jacqueline Lovell, Rhonda Griffin, Mel Johnson Jr., Michael Citrinti, Traci May, Jerry O'Donnell; ***D:*** Charles Band; ***W:*** Benjamin Carr; ***M:*** Richard Band. **VHS** *AFE*

Hideous Sun Demon

Archetypal monster-created-by-nuclear-radiation story begins with this ominous voiceover narration: "Immediately after the launching of U.S. satellites number one and number three into outer space, newspaper headlines across the country told the world of a new radiation hazard from the sun, far more deadly than cosmic rays. An obscure scientist, my colleague Dr. Gilbert MacKenna, had already discovered this danger from the sun. This is his story." The unlucky Gilbert (producer/director Robert Clarke) is exposed to a new isotope—pesky things, those isotopes—and comes to realize that every time he goes out in the sun, he turns into the title character and commits unspeakable acts. Does Gil put up the convertible top on his MG? Of course not. ***AKA:*** Blood on His Lips; Terror from the Sun; The Sun Demon. 🦴🦴🦴

1959 75m/B Robert Clarke, Patricia Manning, Nan Peterson, Patrick Whyte, Peter Similuk, Fred La Porta, Robert Garry; ***D:*** Robert Clarke; ***W:*** Doane R. Hoag, E. S. Seeley Jr.; ***C:*** Vilis Lapenieks, John Morrill, Stan Follis. **VHS** *EEL, MRV, RHI*

Highway to Hell

Made-for-cable horror comedy is notable mostly for its relatively high-powered cast, including Patrick Bergin as the devil who kidnaps young bride Kristy Swanson. Even though the plot is a crackpot variation on the myth of Orpheus and Eurydice—with Chad Lowe in the Orpheus role—this one's too sloppy and too studied to be a prime guilty pleasure. Toward the end it does have a few moments, and strong support from the likes of Richard Farnsworth and Pamela Gidley helps, too. 🦴🦴🦴

1992 (R) 93m/C Patrick Bergin, Adam Storke, Chad Lowe, Kristy Swanson, Richard Farnsworth, C.J. Graham, Lita Ford, Kevin Peter Hall, Pamela Gidley, Brian Helgeland; ***Cameos:*** Gilbert Gottfried; ***D:*** Ate De Jong. **VHS, Closed Caption** *HBO*

"Baby's fat. You fat. Fat juicy."

—Cannibal Mars (Lance Gordon) sizes up his dinner—an adult and a baby—in *The Hills Have Eyes.*

Conde Petrovski (Jorge Rigaud) in *Horror Express.*

The Hills Have Eyes

Wes Craven's companion piece to *The Texas Chainsaw Massacre* deals with subject matter that's actually more revolting, but it isn't presented with the same unrelenting intensity. Three generations of a Midwestern family head out into the desert in a station wagon towing a camper trailer (complete with air freshener) and run smack into a degenerate clan of subhuman cannibal savages. In the end, though, it's hard to say who is the more savage. That's Craven's unsubtle point, and for low-budget violent exploitation it certainly delivers the goods. The villains are a full evolutionary step down from the drug dealers in Craven's *Last House on the Left*. The VideoHound applauds the two brave and resourceful German Shepherds. Followed by a poor sequel.

1977 (R) 83m/C Susan Lanier, Robert Houston, Martin Speer, Dee Wallace Stone, Russ Grieve, John Steadman, James Whitworth, Michael Berryman, Virginia Vincent, Lance Gordon, Janus Blythe; ***D:*** Wes Craven; ***W:*** Wes Craven; ***C:*** Eric Saarinen. **VHS, LV** *NO*

The Hills Have Eyes, Part 2

Like most sequels, this one's a transparent attempt to milk a title for a few more bucks. Motorcycle-racing teens—who happen to have a drum of highly explosive "superfuel" in their bus—go back out into the desert. A couple of cannibals from the first film, including bald Michael Berryman, are still hanging around, etc., etc. More sophisticated production values are not necessarily an improvement. The whole thing lacks the raw reptilian manipulative power of the original.

1984 86m/C Michael Berryman, Kevin Blair, John Joe Bob Briggs Bloom, Janus Blythe, John Laughlin, Tamara Stafford, Peter Frechette; ***D:*** Wes Craven; ***W:*** Wes Craven; ***C:*** David Lewis. **VHS** *REP*

The Hitcher

Cult favorite is a rare horror that makes a virtue of its low budget. Jim Halsey (C. Thomas Howell) is an innocent young man driving across a lonely desert highway where he picks up Ryder (Rutger Hauer), one of the most believably terrifying psychos ever to ooze onto the screen. Or is he something else? Eric Red's (*Near Dark*) script is properly vague. For a time. You don't want to know anything more about the plot. Director Robert Harmon sets the story against a sun-blasted, dusty Western landscape. If he can't maintain complete intensity to the end, he comes close enough. Jazzman Mark Isham gives him a subdued haunted score to set the mood. This one would make a great triple bill with *Nature of the Beast* and *Duel.*

1986 (R) 98m/C Rutger Hauer, C. Thomas Howell, Jennifer Jason Leigh, Jeffrey DeMunn, John M. Jackson, Billy Green Bush; ***D:*** Robert Harmon; ***W:*** Eric Red; ***C:*** John Seale; ***M:*** Mark Isham. **VHS, LV, Closed Caption** *HBO, OM*

Hocus Pocus

Horror-comedy tries to capture the gentle humor and strong visuals of *Beetlejuice,* but director Kenny Ortega doesn't have Tim Burton's natural affinity for the material. Apparently, he didn't have much control over his three stars, either. The Sanderson sisters (Bette Midler, Sarah Jessica Parker, Kathy Najimy) are practicing witches in 17th century Salem. After they kill a child and turn another into a cat, they're executed and return 300 years later to raise a little hell on Halloween. Though they look fairly grotesque, the most frightening thing about them is the ferocity with which they attack their roles, the scenery, their co-stars, and each other. Nothing is safe when they cut loose.

1993 (PG) 95m/C Bette Midler, Kathy Najimy, Sarah Jessica Parker, Thora Birch, Doug Jones, Omri Katz, Vinessa Shaw, Stephanie Faracy, Charles Rocket; ***Cameos:*** Penny Marshall, Garry Marshall; ***D:*** Kenny Ortega; ***W:*** Neil Cuthbert, Mick Garris; ***M:*** John Debney. **VHS, LV, Closed Caption** *DIS, BTV*

The Horror Chamber of Dr. Faustus

It's difficult to overestimate the influence of Georges Franju's film, particularly on the European horrors of the 1960s and '70s. The story of a doctor—in this case played by Pierre Brasseur—trying to restore a young woman's beauty (Edith Scob) with the help of another woman (Alida Valli), is one that would be revisited often, particularly by Jesus Franco. Franju handles it much more subtly, though his explicit surgery scenes pave the way for the bloody excesses to come. The film bears some similarities to *Psycho* too, with an equally strong conclusion. ***AKA:*** Eyes Without a Face; Les Yeux Sans Visage; Occhi Senza Volto.

1959 84m/B *FR* Alida Valli, Pierre Brasseur, Edith Scob, Francois Guerin; ***D:*** Georges Franju; ***C:*** Eugene (Eugen Shufftan) Shuftan; ***M:*** Maurice Jarre. **VHS, LV** *SNC, TPV, INT*

Horror Express

Spanish production is set in pre-revolutionary Russia. Imagine *The Thing* on the Trans-Siberian Express. Archeologist Christopher Lee has found a critter frozen in the ice and is taking it to England for study. Rival Peter Cushing is jealous and wants to find out what's happening, but said critter has no intention of going to England or anywhere else. Then toss in Telly Savalas as a crazed cossack and a mad monk. The railway setting works well, too, making this one classy fun with a slight satiric edge. ***AKA:*** Panic on the Trans-Siberian Express; Panico en el Transiberiano; Panic in the Trans-Siberian Train.

1972 (R) 88m/C *SP GB* Christopher Lee, Peter Cushing, Telly Savalas, Alberto De Mendoza, Sylvia Tortosa, Julio

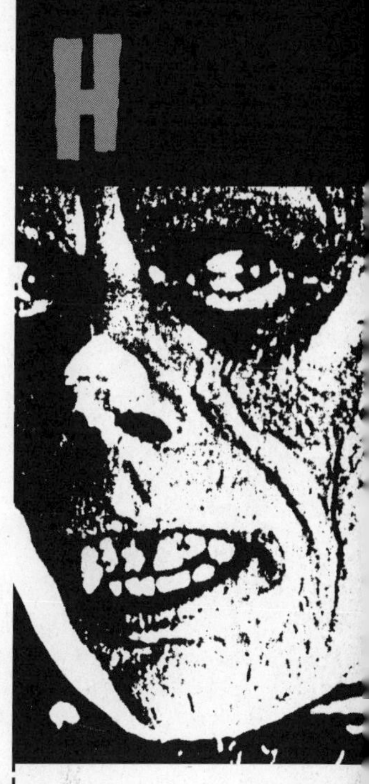

"There's the stink of hell on this train—even the dog can smell it."

—Conde Petrovski (Jorge Rigaud) in *Horror Express.*

PETER CUSHING

Notice the way Peter Cushing could concentrate and use his hands during complicated bits of stagecraft. Apparently simple acts—preparing a slide to view under a microscope or packing up his stakes, mallets, and holy water in a bag—become acts that reveal shadings of character. The mad scientist may indeed be mad, but he's also an experienced, careful technician. The vampire hunter is prepared and grimly determined.

Cushing's teachers at the Guildhall School of Music and Drama in London must have instructed him well. Born in 1913, in Kenley, England, Cushing said that from the time he was a child, he knew he wanted to be an actor. After he'd finished with school, he worked with a repertory company until he'd saved enough money for a one-way ticket to Hollywood. He found work there, including, curiously, a small role in Laurel and Hardy's *A Chump at Oxford*, but with the outbreak of World War II he went back to England where he served in the Entertainments National Service Association.

After the war, he went back into movies with another small role, this one in Olivier's *Hamlet*. He was appearing regularly on television in those days, too, and had already been contacted by the people at Hammer Studio about working for them when he learned about their new project. It was 1956. "I heard they were considering a remake of *Frankenstein*. I remember liking the earlier version very much, which had Boris Karloff playing the monster and Colin Clive playing Frankenstein. So I rang up my agent, who told Hammer I was still keen to work for them. And that's how it all happened." (*House of Horrors*, Lorrimer, 1973).

The result was *Curse of Frankenstein*; he would play the Baron four more times. That film also marked the beginning of his long association with co-star Christopher Lee, who played the monster. In 1958, they had an even bigger hit with *Horror of Dracula*.

In the years that followed, Cushing seldom strayed far

Pena, Angel Del Pozo, Helga Line, Jorge Rigaud, Jose Jaspe; ***D:*** Gene Martin; ***W:*** Julian Zimet, Arnaud d'Usseau; ***C:*** Alejandro Ulloa. **VHS** *SNC, MRV, HHT*

Horror Hotel

In an early role, Christopher Lee firmly establishes his horror credentials as Professor Driscoll, who sends young Nan Barlow (Venetia Stevenson) off for some primary research in Whitewood, Massachusetts, where a witch was burned centuries before. George Baxt's script owes a bit to *Burn Witch, Burn!* and can be seen as a precursor to *Psycho*. With its lovely black-and-white photography and fog-shrouded atmosphere, the film really is a "lost" milestone of the 1960s. Its influence on such films as *Salem's Lot, Carnival of Souls*, and many of the Italian horrors of the '80s and '90s is not hard to spot. The Anchor Bay tape has been lovingly restored. ***AKA:*** The City of the Dead. 🦴🦴🦴

1960 76m/B *GB* Christopher Lee, Patricia Jessel, Betta St. John, Dennis Lotis, Venetia Stevenson, Valentine Dyall; ***D:*** John Llewellyn Moxey; ***W:*** George L. Baxt; ***C:*** Desmond Dickinson. **VHS, LV** *VTR, JEF*

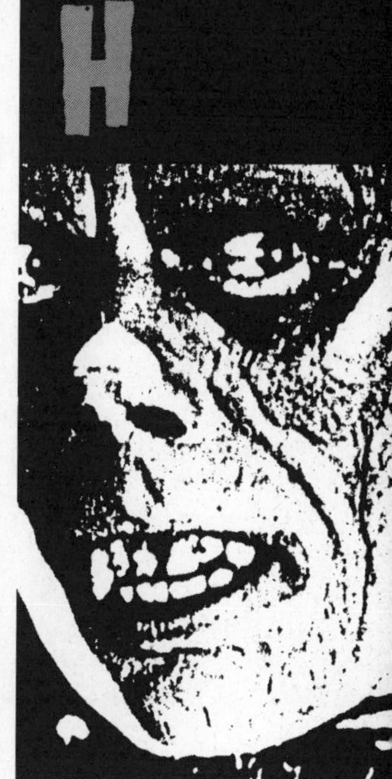

from horror, mystery, and s-f. He was Holmes in *Hound of the Baskervilles,* an unscrupulous doctor in *The Gorgon,* and an archeologist in *The Mummy.* He reached his largest audience as Darth Vader's general in *Star Wars.*

In most of those roles, his intense concentration is based on an element of sympathetic humanism. That quality is, however, conspicuous in its absence in the later Frankenstein films, where he played the Baron as a bloodless intellectual who has lost his soul. It was, I think, a conscious decision he made about the character, not a lack of interest on his part. At the same time, he found the complexities of a Puritan witchhunter in *Twins of Evil,* and an investigative pathologist in *Legend of the Werewolf.*

On screen and off, he always appeared to be a gentleman, and in that regard, he's in good company with Boris Karloff.

SIGNIFICANT CONTRIBUTIONS TO HORROR

Curse of Frankenstein **(1957)**

Horror of Dracula **(1958)**

Revenge of Frankenstein **(1958)**

The Mummy **(1959)**

Brides of Dracula **(1960)**

The Gorgon **(1964)**

Vampire Lovers **(1970)**

Twins of Evil **(1971)**

Frankenstein and the Monster from Hell **(1974)**

Legend of the Werewolf **(1975)**

The Horror of Dracula

Hammer's second horror film (after *The Curse of Frankenstein*) opens with the spiral columns which would become a virtual signature for the studio. The shot is followed by blood spattering on a closed coffin, setting an appropriate mood. Screenwriter Jimmy Sangster's telling of the story owes more to Bram Stoker's novel than to the stageplay which had launched Bela Lugosi's career. This one is also more streamlined and cinematic than earlier versions. But the real key to the film's enduring success is the teaming of Christopher Lee and Peter Cushing—horror's answer to Lemmon and Matthau—as the Count and Van Helsing. They play the roles with absolute conviction. Lee's interpretation of the familiar character is fresh and sexually charged; Cushing's Van Helsing is equally energetic. They complement each other well and make perfectly matched antagonists. The unsubtle message of many early Hammer films—men's domination of women and fear of female sexuality—is in full flower here. Followed by a fine sequel, *Dracula, Prince of Darkness*. ***AKA:*** Dracula.

1958 82m/C *GB* Peter Cushing, Christopher Lee, Michael Gough, Melissa Stribling, Carol Marsh, John Van Eyssen, Valerie Gaunt, Charles Lloyd Pack, Miles Malleson; ***D:*** Terence Fisher; ***W:*** Jimmy Sangster; ***C:*** Jack Asher; ***M:*** James Bernard. **VHS, LV** *WAR, FCT, MLB*

"I see glimpses of a strange world...a world of people who are dead and yet alive."

—Rita Hussman (Anne Gwynne) in *House of Frankenstein.*

The Horror of Frankenstein

In one of Hammer's last variations on the famous tale, it's obvious that everyone involved was more interested in having fun with the material than in telling a serious story. This Victor Frankenstein (Ralph Bates) is an amoral libertine who blithely kills his father and then moves in with Dad's mistress (Kate O'Mara). When he gets around to his "experiments," he hires a comic bodysnatcher (Dennis Price) who steals the movie. The monster is played by David Prowse, who went on to be Darth Vader in the *Star Wars* trilogy. Writer/director Jimmy Sangster is an old hand at this kind of material. It's enjoyable if you're in the mood for fairly heavy-handed gallows humor, particularly in the last reel. But it's far from Hammer's best work. Two caveats: (1) Sources list the running time of this title at 95 and 93 minutes. The Republic edition is 91 minutes long, though there are no obvious deletions. (2) It's recorded at the slower EP speed, under the trademarked QEP mode, and the clarity of the picture isn't as sharp as conventional SP tapes.

1970 93m/C *GB* Ralph Bates, Kate O'Mara, Dennis Price, David Prowse, Veronica Carlson, Joan Rice, Bernard Archard, Graham James; ***D:*** Jimmy Sangster; ***W:*** Jimmy Sangster, Jeremy Burnham; ***C:*** Moray Grant. **VHS** *MLB*

Horror Planet

Vile, repulsive, dimwitted imitation of *Alien* manages to disgust and bore in almost equal measures. On an archeological expedition to a distant planet, archeo-astronaut Judy Geeson is impregnated by a creature with glowing green liquid. As her stomach swells, she bumps off her companions, who are easy prey. In any given situation, if there's something stupid that these one-dimensional characters can do, rest assured they will. The special effects aren't, and the general level of sets and props is marked by the motorcycle helmets meant to pass for space helmets. ***AKA:*** Inseminoid. **Woof!**

1980 (R) 93m/C *GB* Robin Clarke, Jennifer Ashley, Stephanie Beacham, Judy Geeson, Stephen Grives, Victoria Tennant; ***D:*** Norman J. Warren; ***W:*** Gloria Maley, Nick Maley. **VHS, LV**

The Horror Show

Standard criminal-comes-back-from-execution-to-get-cop tale boasts genre stars Brion James and Lance Henriksen in the leads, but that's about all. It has no internal logic, and instead recycles elements from *Elm Street, Halloween, The Terminator,* etc. Reportedly it was meant to be part of the forgettable *House* series but turned out too violent. ***AKA:*** House 3.

1989 (R) 95m/C Brion James, Lance Henriksen, Rita Taggart, Dedee Pfeiffer, Aron Eisenberg, Matt Clark, Thom Bray; ***D:*** James Isaac; ***W:*** Alan Smithee, Leslie Bohem; ***C:*** Mac Ahlberg. **VHS** *MGM*

Hour of the Wolf

Ingmar Bergman's foray into horror is an unconventional story that ignores conventional narrative structure for a more dreamlike surrealism. Johan Borg (Max von Sydow) and his wife (Liv Ullmann) live in a cottage on an isolated island. Their supposedly simple life is complicated by a

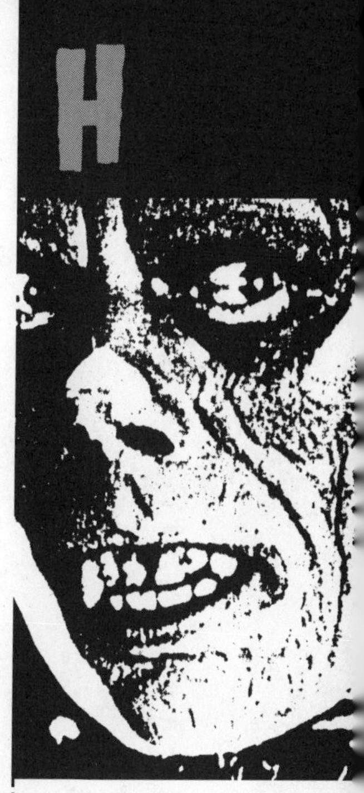

gaggle of bizarre neighbors. Or are they ghosts? Visions? One is a Lugosi-like figure and the others are grotesques of various stripes. They constantly crowd and threaten Johan, making key scenes intensely claustrophobic. Sven Nykvist's black-and-white photography is striking, but despite the strength of the images and tightly wrapped performances from the leads, Bergman is very much an acquired taste. ***AKA:*** Vargtimmen.

1968 89m/B *SW* Max von Sydow, Liv Ullmann, Ingrid Thulin, Erland Josephson, Gertrud Fridh, Gudrun Brost, Georg Rydeberg, Naima Wifstrand, Bertil Anderberg, Ulf Johansson; ***D:*** Ingmar Bergman; ***W:*** Ingmar Bergman; ***C:*** Sven Nykvist. National Board of Review Awards '68: Best Actress (Ullmann); National Society of Film Critics Awards '68: Best Director (Bergman). **VHS** *MGM, FCT, BTV*

House

Roger Cobb (William Katt) is a horror novelist suffering from writer's block. You'd think that inheriting the haunted house where he grew up would be just the thing for him, but no. Instead of inspiration, he gets some of the cheesiest Vietnam flashbacks ever put on film. A few of the effects have a little shock value, but that's about all. The attempts at humor undercut the horror and the story disintegrates in the last third, becoming a "lite" version of Sam Raimi's *Evil Dead* movies. The basic problem is that the house itself is too obviously a set. Followed by a sequel.

1986 (R) 93m/C William Katt, George Wendt, Richard Moll, Kay Lenz, Michael Ensign, Mary Stavin, Susan French; ***D:*** Steve Miner; ***W:*** Ethan Wiley; ***C:*** Mac Ahlberg; ***M:*** Harry Manfredini. **VHS, LV, Closed Caption** *VTR*

House 2: The Second Story

In the last scene, our hero Jesse (Arye Gross) straps on his six-shooter, gets into a horse-drawn wagon, and rides off into the sunset with his best friend (Jonathan Stark), a sacrificial virgin (Devin Devasquez), a baby pterodactyl, and a critter that's a cross between a puppy and a caterpillar. Unfortunately, the road to that lunatic conclusion isn't much fun. The slow sequel follows no internal logic. Anything can happen at any time. The humor seems to be aimed at a pre-teen audience but the violence involves lots of blood and exploding heads. Why bother?

1987 (PG-13) 88m/C John Ratzenberger, Arye Gross, Royal Dano, Bill Maher, Jonathan Stark, Lar Park Lincoln, Amy Yasbeck, Devin Devasquez; ***D:*** Ethan Wiley; ***W:*** Ethan Wiley; ***C:*** Mac Ahlberg. **VHS, LV, Closed Caption** *VTR*

House of Dark Shadows

The first feature taken from the popular TV series isn't taken quite far enough. It hurriedly introduces a large cast of characters without fully explaining their relationships or the setting—all of which were familiar to viewers in the early 1970s—and then lets the story drag along at a lugubrious pace. That's part of the suspense of an episodic soap opera but it's completely wrong for a film. This one has also aged poorly with a raw, grainy look on video that compares poorly to the Hammer and Corman films of the same era. Barnabas Collins (Jonathan Frid) predates the "good" Byronic vampire popularized by Anne Rice. Here, he's revived in the present, finds a double of his lost love (Kathryn Leigh Scott), etc., etc. Once things get cranked up, they run more smoothly, but the movie is still too slow with an overwrought score that doesn't help.

1970 (PG) 97m/C Jonathan Frid, Joan Bennett, Grayson Hall, Kathryn Leigh Scott, Roger Davis, Nancy Barrett, John Karlen, Thayer David, Louis Edmonds; ***D:*** Dan Curtis; ***W:*** Sam Hall, Gordon Russell; ***C:*** Arthur Ornitz. **VHS** *MGM, FUS*

THE HOUND SALUTES

JOHN CARRADINE

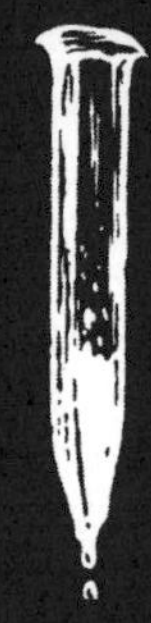

Various sources claim that the peripatetic character actor's parents were an Associated Press correspondent, noted attorney, poet, painter, and surgeon. Perhaps they were all of those and much much more, and that explains why their son Richmond Reed Carradine, born in 1906 in Greenwich Village, was famous for walking the streets of Hollywood and reciting long speeches from Shakespeare.

In any case, the man who may have appeared in more movies (220) than anyone else got his start on stage in New Orleans in 1925. A couple of years later, he hitchhiked to Hollywood but didn't appear on screen until 1930.

In 1935, he signed a contract with Fox and changed his name to John Carradine. Without question, his two best roles came from John Ford, who directed him in *Stagecoach* (1939) and *The Grapes of Wrath* (1940). Throughout his career, though, whether he was in fashion or out, Carradine was a journeyman whatever-it-takes-to-pay-the-bills actor. From *Around the World in 80 Days* to *Hillbillys in a Haunted House*, he showed up and read his lines and he was seldom shy about it. In his prime, his big booming voice, natural theatricality, and intense expressions made him a first choice for showy supporting roles in all sorts of films. Later, when he worked with less elevated material, he was able to appear menacing and vital.

Within the genre, he had a small role in *Bride of Frankenstein*, but made a larger impression as a dapper vampire in *House of Frankenstein* and *House of Dracula*.

Like so many actors of his generation, toward the end of his life, he was forced to accept roles in some pretty shabby low-budget movies, but he was also seen in good films then, too. He's excellent in both *The Sentinel* (1976) and *The Howling* (1981). His sons Keith, David, and Robert carry on the family tradition, working regularly in theatre, film, and television.

SIGNIFICANT CONTRIBUTIONS TO HORROR

Bride of Frankenstein **(1935)**

House of Frankenstein **(1944)**

House of Dracula **(1945)**

Billy the Kid Vs. Dracula **(1966)**

The Sentinel **(1976)**

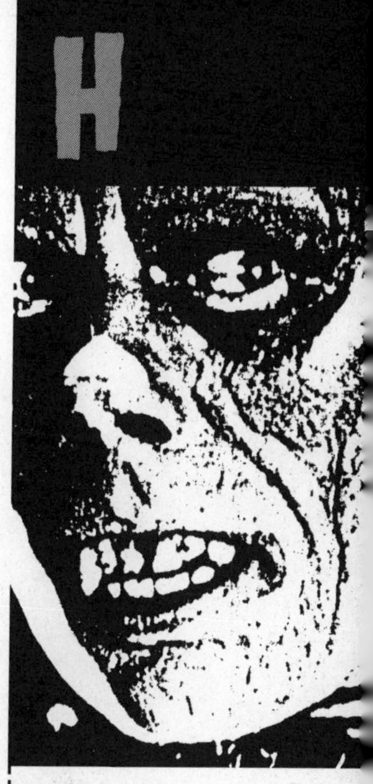

House of Dracula

Sequel to *House of Frankenstein* brings Universal's most popular characters—Dracula (John Carradine), the Wolfman (Lon Chaney, Jr.), Frankenstein's Monster (Glenn Strange)—back for a second ensemble effort. Nothing's particularly scary. In the opening shot, the strings holding up the bat are clearly visible. Dr. Edelman (Onslow Stevens) tries to "cure" the various monsters, until Drac puts his moves on the doc's glamorous nurse (Martha O'Driscoll). Except for that bat, the production values and sets are up to the studio's standard, and it's fun to watch a veteran cast going through familiar paces. 🦴🦴🦴

1945 67m/B Lon Chaney Jr., Martha O'Driscoll, John Carradine, Lionel Atwill, Onslow Stevens, Glenn Strange, Jane Adams, Ludwig Stossel; ***D:*** Erle C. Kenton; ***W:*** Edward T. Lowe; ***C:*** George Robinson. **VHS, LV, Closed Caption** *USH, FCT*

House of Frankenstein

One dark and stormy night, Professor Lampini's (George Zucco) Chamber of Horrors sideshow is passing by Newstadt Prison, where Dr. Neiman (Boris Karloff) and his hunchback Daniel (J. Carrol Naish) escape. The fifth in Universal's series isn't the equal of the first three, but it's thoroughly enjoyable formula entertainment from a studio that knew exactly what it was doing. The story is divided into two halves, both moving rapidly and with a remarkable amount of physical action. The ice cave set (used a year before in *Frankenstein Meets the Wolfman*) is grand. John Carradine fits right in as Dracula. Once again, the Monster (Glenn Strange) and the Wolfman (Lon Chaney, Jr.) have issues. 🦴🦴🦴

1944 71m/B Boris Karloff, J. Carrol Naish, Lon Chaney Jr., John Carradine, Elena Verdugo, Anne Gwynne, Lionel Atwill, Peter Coe, George Zucco, Glenn Strange, Sig Rumann; ***D:*** Erle C. Kenton; ***W:*** Edward T. Lowe; ***C:*** George Robinson. **VHS, LV** *USH*

House of the Long Shadows

American author Kenneth McGee (Desi Arnaz, Jr.) bets his British publisher (Richard Todd) that he can knock off a Gothic novel in 24 hours if he has isolation and atmosphere. The publisher arranges for him to go to Baldpate Manor in Wales, where he's visited by veteran horror stars Peter Cushing (with a lisp), Vincent Price, Christopher Lee, and John Carradine. This is the only time the four post-war horror greats appeared together, and they don't break a sweat with the lightweight, semi-comic material. Variations of the Edgar Wallace story have been filmed several times. This is one of the tightest, recommended for fans of the cast. 🦴🦴🦴

1982 (PG) 96m/C *GB* Vincent Price, Christopher Lee, Peter Cushing, John Carradine, Desi Arnaz Jr., Sheila Keith, Richard Todd; ***D:*** Pete Walker; ***W:*** Michael Armstrong; ***C:*** Norman G. Langley. **VHS** *MGM*

The House of Usher

South African howler bears only a passing resemblance to the master's short story and deserves no comparison to the Roger Corman 1960 version. Until the overly violent conclusion, it's a Gothic romance complete with a big spooky house (riddled with hidden passages) and the plucky heroine (Romy Windsor) who's prone to wandering the halls late on dark and stormy nights, while dressed in her peignoir and carrying a candle. Filling out the dance card are the dark, brooding older guy (Oliver Reed) who owns the joint, and the mysterious figure locked in the attic. Whenever the action flags, the scenery falls down as the house allegedly collapses. ***AKA:*** Edgar Allan Poe's House of Usher; The Fall of the House of Usher. 🦴🦴

1988 (R) 92m/C *SA* Oliver Reed, Donald Pleasence, Romy Windsor, Rufus Swart, Norman Coombes, Anne Stradi; ***D:*** Alan Birkinshaw; ***W:*** Michael J. Murray; ***M:*** Gary Chang. **VHS, LV** *COL*

"Never do anything you wouldn't want to be caught dead doing."

—John Carradine to son David, as quoted in *Film Yearbook*, 1985.

Sue Allen (Phyllis Kirk) in *House of Wax.*

House of Wax

Vincent Price is Professor Jared, a wax sculptor who refuses to do a chamber of horrors because his devotion to "art" is so pure. His unscrupulous business partner suggests they torch the place and cash in. The ensuing fire is a grand set piece. After it, a mad killer (clearly based on Erik, the Phantom of the Opera) stalks turn-of-the-century New York. Made in 3-D, the action is often ponderously slow, hokey, and lavishly staged, like most big-budget studio films of the time. The grandly mad character who talks to his creations is perfectly suited to Price's penchant for ham. Yes, that's a very young and hunky Charles Bronson, as well as a very blonde and slim Carolyn Jones. 🦴🦴🦴

1953 (PG) 88m/C Vincent Price, Frank Lovejoy, Carolyn Jones, Phyllis Kirk, Paul Cavanagh, Charles Bronson, Paul Picerni; ***D:*** Andre de Toth; ***W:*** Crane Wilbur; ***C:*** Bert Glennon. **VHS, LV** *WAR, MLB*

House of Whipcord

A disingenuous preface ("This film is dedicated to those who are disturbed by today's lax moral codes and who eagerly await the return of corporal punishment....") sets the tone for a grim, oppressively dark British variation on *The Story of O* with torture (mostly offscreen) replacing sex. The plot revolves around a French model who's kidnapped and locked up in a private prison run by feeble, demented aristocracy. The reasons why are too silly to mention. Producer/director Pete Walker is more interested in a blunt-object attack on the ruling power structure—"the establishment" as it was called at the time—with more anger than subtlety. 🦴🦴

1975 102m/C *GB* Barbara Markham, Patrick Barr, Ray Brooks, Penny Irving, Anne Michelle; ***D:*** Pete Walker. **VHS** *MON, LIV*

House on Haunted Hill

Secret passages, the vat of acid in the basement, walking skeletons, ghosts in the hallway, even the proverbial dark and stormy night—they're all part of William Castle's good-natured collection of cliches. Eccentric millionaire Vincent Price offers a disparate group—test pilot, shop girl, columnist, doctor—$10,000 apiece to spend the night in a house where gruesome murders have been committed. You don't need three guesses to figure out the rest, and you get the feeling, right or wrong, that everybody had fun on the sets of Castle productions. Nobody had any illusions about art; this is unapologetic cinematic popcorn with lots of salt and butter. For those who don't know, Castle was affectionately spoofed in *Matinee*. 🦴🦴🦴

1958 75m/B Vincent Price, Carol Ohmart, Richard Long, Alan Marshal, Carolyn Craig, Elisha Cook Jr.; ***D:*** William Castle; ***W:*** Robb White; ***C:*** Carl Guthrie. **VHS, LV, Closed Caption** *FOX, FCT, MLB*

The House on Sorority Row

Filmed near Baltimore, this tepid little time-waster came near the end of the first wave of "dead-teenager" movies and helped to send the genre into welcome oblivion for several years. Some of the sisters think that they've killed their strict housemother, but since they're about to throw a big party, they decide to chuck the old gal into the swimming pool and proceed as planned. Before long, sorority sisters are being stabbed, slashed, and gored, and writer/director Mark Rosman abandons any pretense at logic. ***AKA:*** House of Evil; Seven Sisters. **Woof!**

1983 90m/C Eileen Davidson, Kate McNeil, Robin Meloy, Lois Kelso Hunt, Christopher Lawrence, Janis Zido; ***D:*** Mark Rosman; ***W:*** Mark Rosman; ***C:*** Tim Suhrstedt; ***M:*** Richard Band. **VHS, LV** *VES*

The House on Straw Hill

Offbeat exploitation mixes inventive softcore sex (some of it quite funny) with bloody psycho-revenge elements. The key characters are a successful novelist (Udo Kier), his girlfriend (Fiona Richmond), and his new secretary (Linda Hayden). Each has secrets to keep. A couple of rapacious rubes fill out the cast. Sources claim that censors cut 30 minutes from the running time, which might account for the uncertain shifts in tone. Even so, this one deserves its cult following. ***AKA:*** Expose; Trauma. 🦴🦴🦴

1976 (R) 84m/C *GB* Udo Kier, Linda Hayden, Fiona Richmond, Karl Howman, Patsy Smart; ***D:*** James Kenelm Clarke; ***W:*** James Kenelm Clarke; ***C:*** Denis Lewiston. **VHS** *NO*

The House That Vanished

Flighty English model Valerie (Andrea Allan) wanders out into the country with her beau Terry (Alex Leppard) on a foggy night. In a grim dark house, they witness a murder. The next day, it doesn't seem so real, but other questions remain. The rest is about half exploitation and half solid horror. A scruffy, realistically middle-class milieu serves the story well and balances the Gothic aspects. Though she's not a particularly versatile actress, Andrea Allan is an attractive heroine. The most effective moments contain twisted echoes of *Psycho*. Director Joseph Larraz takes a similarly evocative approach in his cult favorite, *Vampyres*. ***AKA:*** Scream and Die; Psycho Sex Fiend. 🦴🦴🦴

1973 (R) 84m/C *GB* Andrea Allan, Karl Lanchbury, Judy Matheson, Maggie Walker, Alex Leppard; ***D:*** Joseph (Jose Ramon) Larraz. **VHS** *LIV*

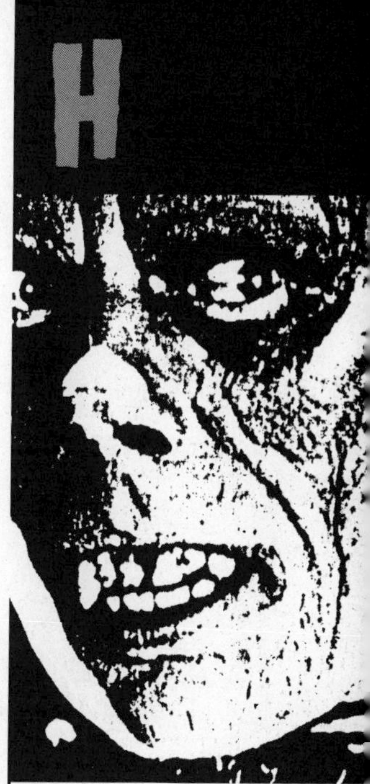

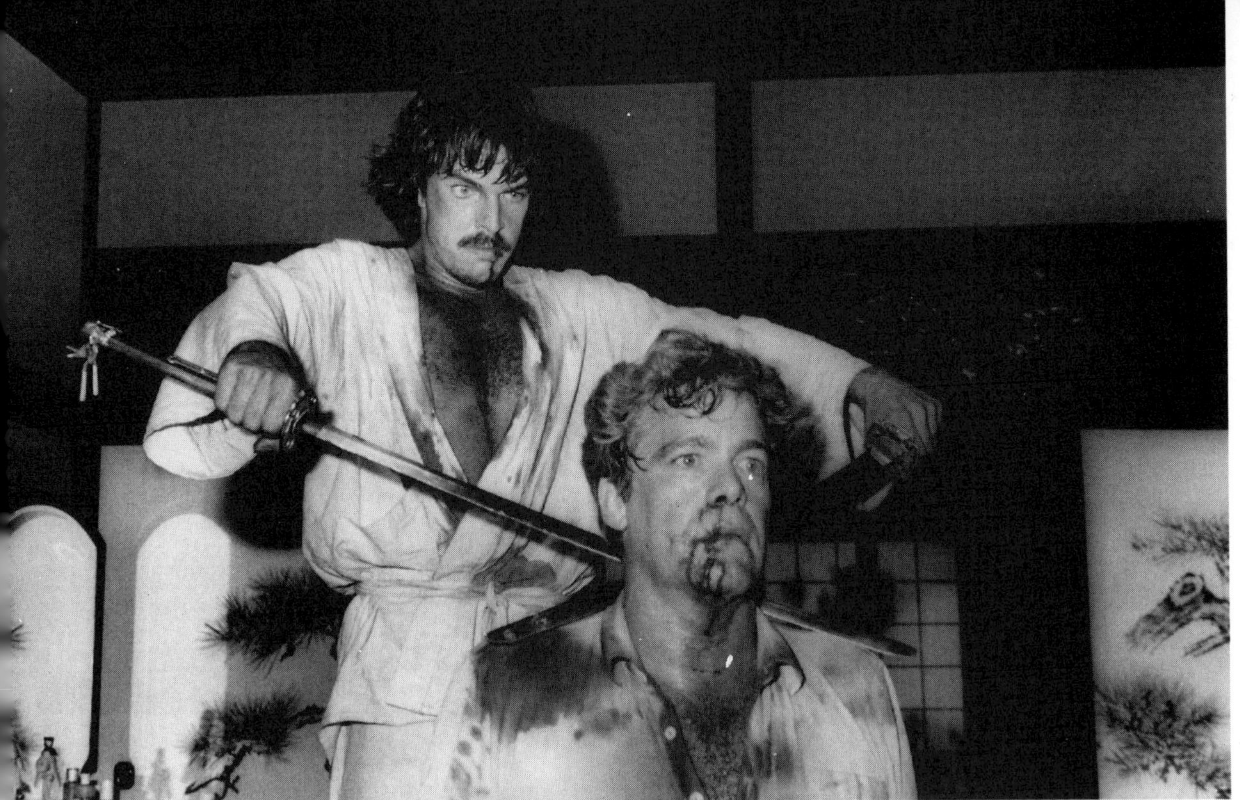

Ted Fletcher (Edward Albert) and Alex Curtis (Doug McClure) in *House Where Evil Dwells.*

House Where Evil Dwells

Embassy worker Alex (Doug McClure) finds a Kyoto house for his American friends Ted (Edward Albert) and Laura (Susan George). But the place is haunted by the ghosts of a faithless wife and two samurai warriors who died there in an 1840 love triangle/murder-suicide. The spirits are shown as translucent figures who sometimes occupy the bodies of the contemporary characters. Those overlaid images are never anything more than obvious photographic tricks and so that side isn't at all frightening. And though nudity and hanky-panky abound, the sexual aspects are mostly lukewarm. Director Kevin Connor seems more comfortable with postcard scenic shots of picturesque Japanese landscapes. Some crab critters and one witch are briefly spooky; the big finish is unintentionally funny. Virtually the same story is told in the thriller *Fatal Past.* 🦴🦴

1982 (R) 88m/C Edward Albert, Susan George, Doug McClure, Amy Barett, Mako Hattori, Toshiya Maruyama, Henry Mitowa, Tsuyako Okajima, Tsuiyuki Sasaki; ***D:*** Kevin Connor; ***W:*** Robert Subotsky; ***C:*** Jacques Haitkin. **VHS** *MGM*

The Howling

Director Joe Dante and writer John Sayles have created one of the smartest and funniest werewolf movies ever, and Rob Bottin's make-up is the equal of their story. The film is a particular treat for horror fans because it's filled with jokes and appearances by some of the most familiar faces in the genre. (Yes, that's Roger Corman as the man fishing for change in the phone booth, and Sayles himself as the morgue attendant.) The plot successfully combines realistic contemporary horror—in the form of a serial murderer-rapist (Robert Picardo) who's fixated on a TV newswoman (Dee Wallace)—with semi-traditional lycanthropy. More importantly, the story has an emotional realism which is, admittedly, sometimes overplayed by Wallace. The conclusion is as strong as the rest of the story, making this one required viewing. By the way, it has virtually nothing to do with the several sequels that have followed. 🦴🦴🦴🦴

1981 (R) 91m/C Dee Wallace Stone, Patrick Macnee, Dennis Dugan, Christopher Stone, Belinda Balaski, Kevin McCarthy, John Carradine, Slim Pickens, Elisabeth Brooks, Robert Picardo, Dick Miller, Kenneth Tobey; ***Cameos:*** John Sayles, Roger Corman; ***D:*** Joe Dante; ***W:*** John Sayles, Terence H. Winkless; ***C:*** John Hora; ***M:*** Pino Donaggio. **VHS, LV** *COL*

Howling 2: Your Sister Is a Werewolf

Real and unintentional humor commingle to create a genuinely bizarre alternative classic which has nothing to do with Joe Dante's original. Christopher Lee appears to be justifiably embarrassed to find himself in this nonsense. Though Sybil Danning is only onscreen briefly and has to play her big love scene while sprouting fur, the producers make the most of her presence. They were so enamored of the moment where she rips her dress off that they repeat it not once, not twice, but ten—count 'em, ten—times during the closing credits. Followed by many more sequels. ***AKA:*** Howling 2: Stirba—Werewolf Bitch. 🦴🦴🦴

1985 (R) 91m/C *FR IT* Sybil Danning, Christopher Lee, Annie McEnroe, Marsha Hunt, Reb Brown, Ferdinand "Ferdy" Mayne, Judd Omen, Jimmy Nail; ***D:*** Philippe Mora; ***W:*** Gary Brandner, Robert Sarner; ***C:*** Geoffrey Stephenson. **VHS, LV** *REP*

Howling 3: The Marsupials

Director Philippe Mora, also responsible for the semi-uproarious adaptation of Whitley Strieber's *Communion,* attempts to mix scares and laughs, but completely misses the sly humor of the original. Jerboa (Imogen Annseley) is a psychic Australian werewolf who leaves the country for the big city and immediately lands a role in a cheap horror flick. Curiously, a defecting Russian ballerina suffers a similar telepathic-lycanthropic condition. The writing, acting, and editing suggest that the humor is meant to be parody, but can a bad movie really spoof other bad movies? And even if it can, do you want to watch that? 🦴🦴

1987 (PG-13) 94m/C *AU* Barry Otto, Imogen Annesley, Dasha Blahova, Max Fairchild, Ralph Cotterill, Leigh Biolos, Frank Thring Jr., Michael Pate; ***D:*** Philippe Mora. **VHS, LV** *LIV*

Howling 4: The Original Nightmare

The title is the only link to the sharp 1981 Joe Dante/John Sayles horror-comedy. The plot contains all the right ingredients for a decent cheap thrill: novelist (Romy Windsor) recovering from nervous breakdown goes to the country to relax and hears strange animal noises at night. Why are the locals so strange? Is her husband part of their conspiracy? Is he fooling around with the sultry shopkeeper in town? Why is she having visions of a short nun? Alas, these goofy goings-on generate no suspense. The whole thing is almost saved by some really bad acting, but fans have seen better. 🦴🦴

1988 (R) 94m/C Romy Windsor, Michael T. Weiss, Antony Hamilton, Susanne Severeid, Lamya Derval, Dennis Folbigge; ***D:*** John Hough. **VHS, LV** *LIV*

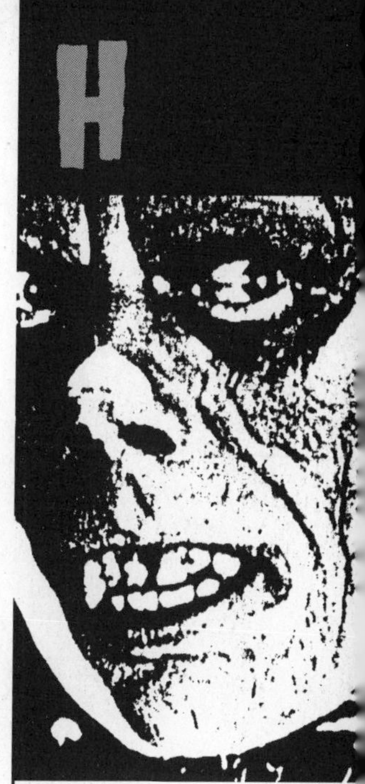

Lon Chaney is *The Hunchback of Notre Dame* (1923).

The Howling: New Moon Rising

In the long and sorry history of multiple sequels, this vanity project may well be the most egregious and inexcusable. Redneck humor and amateur acting make the horror-comedy look (and sound) like the *Hee-Haw* version of *The Wolfman*. Australian writer/producer/star/director/editor and post-production supervisor Clive Turner is the man responsible. When his characters aren't engaged in endless boring conversations or telling penis jokes, they're playing "Deep in the Heart of Texas" on their zippers or—worse yet!—line dancing. This is one of those rare movies that you watch with a growing sense of wonder as you tell yourself that it cannot possibly get any worse and then it does—over and over again. The negligible effects are a short step up from home movies. If the Hound had such a rating, this one would get four WOOFS! ***AKA:*** Howling 7. **Woof!**

1995 (R) 92m/C Clive Turner, John Ramsden, Ernest Kester, Elizabeth She, Jacqueline Armitage, Romy Windsor; ***D:*** Clive Turner; ***W:*** Clive Turner. **VHS, LV, Closed Caption** *NLC*

H.P. Lovecraft's Necronomicon: Book of the Dead

This collection of three short horror films loosely based on the master's stories is notable for high production values and some deliciously nasty special effects. The first entry, with Bruce Payne, is virtually a vignette about drowning; the second features David Warner as a man with a peculiar affliction involving cold temperatures; the third (and best) is an ambitious Grand

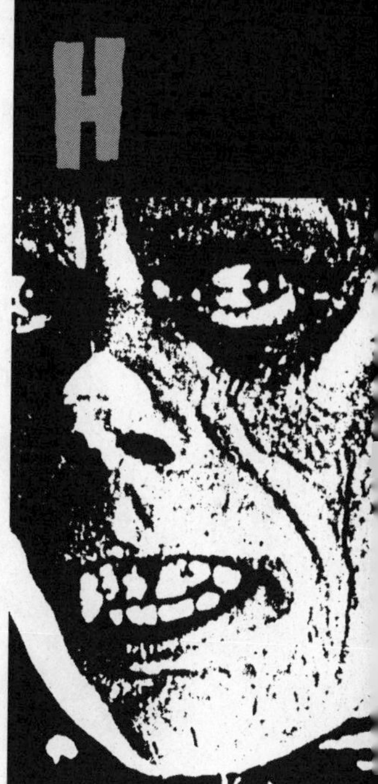

Guignol so bizarre it defies description. As a group, the three—and the framing device with Jeffrey Combs as Lovecraft—avoid the graphic sadism that infects so much contemporary horror while delivering the gruesome excesses that fans of the genre delight in. ***AKA:*** Necronomicon.

1993 (R) 96m/C Bruce Payne, Belinda Bauer, Bess Meyer, David Warner, Signy Coleman, Richard Lynch, Dennis Christopher, Jeffrey Combs, Maria Ford, Don Calfa; ***D:*** Brian Yuzna, Shusuke Kaneko, Christophe Gans; ***W:*** Brian Yuzna, Christophe Gans, Brent Friedman, Kazunori Ito; ***C:*** Gerry Lively, Russ Brandt; ***M:*** Joseph LoDuca, Daniel Light. **VHS, LV, Closed Caption** *NLC*

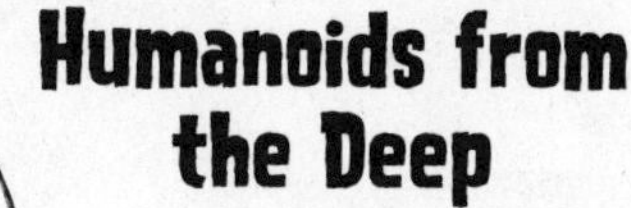

Humanoids from the Deep

The 1980 original lives up to its title as one of the genuinely great drive-in exploitation flicks. In the first shots, veteran B-movie director Barbara Peeters establishes a strong Pacific Northwest locale, and then proceeds to tell an unembarrassed story of giant mutant salmon monsters (i.e. guys in drippy, long-armed rubber suits created by Rob Bottin) whose accelerated evolutionary drive forces them out of the ocean and onto the shore to mate with human women! It ends with a grand nighttime attack on a waterfront fair. The new edition of the tape has been digitally remastered to crystalline clarity and begins with a nice introductory interview between Leonard Maltin and producer Roger Corman. ***AKA:*** Monster.

1980 (R) 81m/C Doug McClure, Ann Turkel, Vic Morrow, Cindy Weintraub, Anthony Penya, Denise Balik; ***D:*** Barbara Peeters; ***W:*** Frank Arnold, Frederick James; ***C:*** Daniel Lacambre; ***M:*** James Horner. **VHS** *NHO*

Humanoids from the Deep

Producer Roger Corman continues to plow familiar fields with another remake of a drive-in alternative classic. Evil executives at the Canco fishery have been dumping a green growth hormone that looks like industrial-strength creme de menthe into the bay to increase their catch. Instead, they create giant mutant salmon monsters. Before you can say "Sushi!" guys in rubber suits are chowing down on beach parties and skinny dippers. This low-budget effort lacks the sense of place and unashamed cheesiness of the 1980 film, not to mention its originality. In their place is a too-ridiculous-for-words sexual angle. A couple of O.K. explosions and flaming fishmen are all this one's got to offer. Rent the first film. ***AKA:*** Roger Corman Presents: Humanoids from the Deep.

1996 (R) 90m/C Robert Carradine, Emma Samms, Mark Rolston; ***D:*** Jeff Yonis. **VHS** *NHO*

Humongous

From the opening scene where a woman avoids a drunken bully at a party by running out into the darkness and away from any help, this is one of those movies where characters usually do the most stupid thing possible in any dangerous situation. The body of the film is standard dead-teenager stuff, Canadian style, with five snotty kids taking a boat trip to a remote island inhabited by wild dogs and a murderous cannibal. It takes far too long for the kids to be bumped off. Production values range from fairly refined to night scenes of impenetrable darkness. The same people are responsible for *Prom Night.*

1982 (R) 93m/C *CA* Janet Julian, David Wallace, Janet Baldwin, Joy Boushel, Page Fletcher; ***D:*** Paul Lynch; ***W:*** William Gray; ***C:*** Brian R.R. Hebb. **VHS** *NLC*

The Hunchback of Notre Dame

The first filmed version of Victor Hugo's enduring potboiler is really more a big-

LON CHANEY, SR.

Lon Chaney's parents were deaf mutes and so he learned early on how to communicate without words. Later, after he'd worked in an opera house and experimented with makeup and prosthetics, he became "The Man of a Thousand Faces." Multiple amputee, ape-man, vampire, Chinese villain—Chaney played them all and early movie audiences loved him.

He was born Alonzo Chaney in Colorado Springs on April Fool's Day, 1883. He left home as a teenager to act in travelling troupes. In 1912, he settled down in Hollywood at the new Universal Studio where he made his reputation with director Tod Browning. They worked often together in *The Black Bird, Outside the Law, The Road to Mandalay, The Unholy Three,* and *West of Zanzibar.* For horror fans, their most famous silent collaboration is the lost film, *London After Midnight,* with Chaney decked out in grotesque vampire makeup. That film, like several others, is not a true part of the genre. For various reasons, early Hollywood producers were reluctant to make supernatural stories. They were willing to include vampires and other monsters, but only if they were revealed to be false in the last reel.

That reservation does not apply to Chaney's masterpieces. Judged by any standard, they're two of horror's greatest achievements.

The first is *The Hunchback of Notre Dame.* To play Victor Hugo's heroic monster Quasimodo, Chaney created perhaps his most elaborate disguise. Various sources claim that Chaney's Hunchback makeup weighed 20, 50, or 72 pounds. The whole film, with its elaborate facade of the cathedral of Notre Dame, is one of the silent era's most impressive productions, and absolutely nothing about it diminishes Chaney's performance.

He managed to top it two years later when he played Erik the Opera Ghost in *The Phantom of the Opera.* With that film, he set a standard for human-monster makeup that has never been surpassed. The effects were created, Chaney claimed, mostly through paints and lighting, though others involved in the production have said that he wore painful wire device to distort his nose. Whatever the truth, it's one of the most famous faces in all film.

budget melodrama than true horror. It's dated, grainy, and overblown. Still, Lon Chaney, Sr.'s makeup and athletic performance set standards for the genre. More important, Chaney's Quasimodo is one of the earliest and more influential examples of the character whose monstrous appearance belies a sympathetic human soul. Despite Chaney's pioneering work, this version ranks third behind the 1939 Charles Laughton production and the 1982 TV movie with Anthony Hopkins. 🦴🦴🦴

1923 100m/B Lon Chaney Sr., Patsy Ruth Miller, Norman Kerry, Ernest Torrence, Kate Lester, Brandon Hurst; ***D:*** Wallace Worsley; ***W:*** Edward T. Lowe; ***C:*** Tony Kornman, Robert S. Newhard. **VHS, LV** *KIV, MRV, NOS*

The Hunchback of Notre Dame

Today, the anti-fascist propaganda aspects of this masterpiece are obvious—and what's wrong with that? Even though

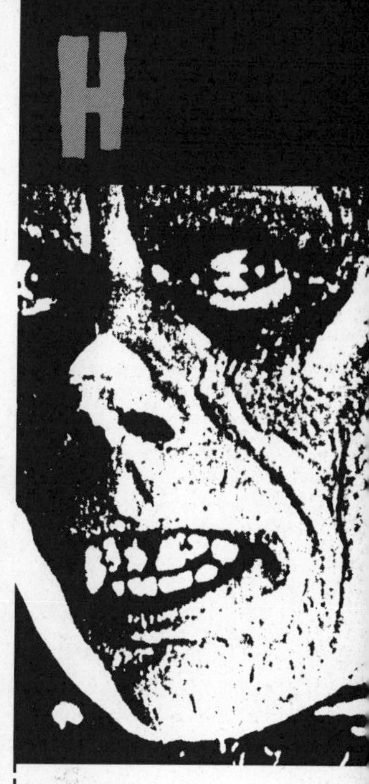

Unfortunately, it was also Chaney's last great role. He did re-create his silent hit *The Unholy Three* with sound to equally strong audience response, but before he could take the lead in Tod Browning's *Dracula,* he died of throat cancer.

In his fine book, *Heroes of the Horrors* (Collier, 1975), Calvin Thomas Beck writes, "Lon Chaney made the most indelible impression in America, not so much because of his roles but because of what he *did* with them. His understanding of pathos and his ability to humanize even the most bizarre characterization emblazoned portrayals upon the screen that were among the most unique of their time; to this date, nearly all remain unforgettable."

Chaney was played by James Cagney in the 1957 film *Man of a Thousand Faces.* His son, Lon Chaney, Jr., also starred in many horror films.

SIGNIFICANT CONTRIBUTIONS TO HORROR

***Hunchback of Notre Dame* (1923)**

***Phantom of the Opera* (1927)**

Charles Laughton's makeup doesn't equal Lon Chaney's, he's such a marvelous actor that he's a more sympathetic and moving Quasimodo. Teaming him with Maureen O'Hara's Esmeralda is the magical chemistry that Hollywood creates every decade or so. (If you don't mist up when she gives him water and then when he stumbles back into the cathedral, something's wrong.) Cedric Hardwicke's Claude Frollo is a complex and sinister villain. The gigantic cathedral facade, the bell tower sets, and the proverbial cast of thousands are just terrific. Also, since the black-and-white film was made for a conventional-sized screen, it looks grand on video. The big finish, complete with molten lead spewing from the mouths of gargoyles, is about as good as it gets.

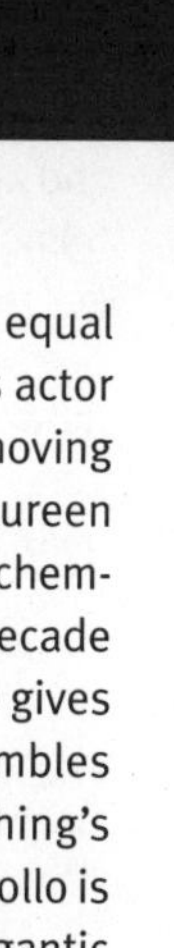

1939 117m/B Charles Laughton, Maureen O'Hara, Edmond O'Brien, Cedric Hardwicke, Thomas Mitchell, George Zucco, Alan Marshal, Walter Hampden, Harry Davenport, Curt Bois, George Tobias, Rod La Rocque; ***D:*** William Dieterle; ***W:*** Sonya Levien, Bruno Frank;

"Why was I not made of stone like thee?"

—Quasimodo (Charles Laughton) speaks to the gargoyles atop Notre Dame in *The Hunchback of Notre Dame* (1939).

C: Joseph August; *M:* Alfred Newman. Nominations: Academy Awards '39: Best Sound, Best Score. **VHS, LV** *TTC, CCB, VCN*

The Hunchback of Notre Dame

Like the other costume dramas of its time, this one is slow, showy, long, and overacted. In terms of plot, it is fairly faithful to Hugo's novel. Gina Lollobrigida is a spirited Esmeralda, the sultry gypsy who catches the eye of bell-ringer Quasimodo (Anthony Quinn) and his boss at the cathedral, Claude Frollo (Alain Cuny). The main attraction is La Lollo at the height of the mid-'50s cheesecake phase of her career, and there's a lot to be said for that. To show off his star, director Jean Delannoy often stops the action cold—her dance in a very red, very tight dress, for example. Alas, the rest can't match that moment. Quinn is trapped under heavy, stiff prosthetic makeup and Cuny is a mopey villain. This version runs a distant fourth behind Lon Chaney's 1923 silent film, the brilliant 1939 William Dieterle-Charles Laughton picture, and the underrated 1982 made-for-TV movie with Anthony Hopkins, Lesley Anne Down, and Derek Jacobi. ***AKA:*** Notre Dame de Paris. 🦴🦴

1957 (PG) 104m/C *FR* Anthony Quinn, Gina Lollobrigida, Alain Cuny, Jean Danet, Robert Hirsch, Jean Tissier; ***D:*** Jean Delannoy; ***W:*** Jacques Prevert, Jean Aurenche; ***C:*** Michel Kelber; ***M:*** Georges Auric. **VHS, LV, Closed Caption** *TOU*

The Hunchback of Notre Dame

This made-for-TV production isn't as lavish as the 1939 film, but it's still one of the most enjoyable screen adaptations. The key is the casting. Lesley-Anne Down is at her loveliest as the gypsy Esmeralda. Derek Jacobi's Dom Claude Frollo has the right combination of villainy and love. Anthony Hopkins, nearly unrecognizable under the makeup, deserves comparison to Charles Laughton and Lon Chaney, Sr. Quasimodo is one of horror's great characters—the monster we fear but come to love—and Hopkins wrings every drop of emotion out of him. (For comparative purposes, notice how differently he handles Dr. Hannibal Lecter in *Silence of the Lambs.*) The story of love and adventure in an exotic medieval setting is probably too complicated for very young viewers, but horror fans of any age who enjoy spectacle and can understand the emotions involved will be fascinated. ***AKA:*** Hunchback. 🦴🦴🦴½

1982 (PG) 102m/C Anthony Hopkins, Derek Jacobi, Lesley-Anne Down, John Gielgud, Tim Pigott-Smith, Rosalie Crutchley, Robert Powell; ***D:*** Michael Tuchner. **VHS** *THV*

The Hunger

Miriam (Catherine Deneuve), a beautiful 2000-year-old vampire, needs help when she realizes that John (David Bowie), her current lover, is aging fast. Enter Sarah Roberts (Susan Sarandon), a blood specialist whose research involves geriatrics. Tony Scott's visually sumptuous tale is spun out at an appropriately languid pace, complete with relatively tame soft-focus lesbian love scenes between Deneuve and Sarandon, and an understated mix of violence and sly humor. Bowie adds the right element of sexual mystery to the proceedings. This one paves the way for a generation of MTV-influenced escapist films emphasizing glossy style over story. It's also the titular source for a cable-TV horror series. A laserdisc edition features a letterboxed screen and original movie trailer. 🦴🦴🦴½

1983 (R) 100m/C Catherine Deneuve, David Bowie, Susan Sarandon, Cliff DeYoung, Ann Magnuson, Dan Hedaya, Willem Dafoe, Beth Ehlers, Suzanne Bertish, Rufus Collins, James Aubrey; ***D:*** Tony Scott; ***W:*** Michael Thomas, Ian Davis; ***C:*** Stephen Goldblatt, Tom Mangravite. **VHS, LV, Letterboxed** *MGM*

Huntress: Spirit of the Night

This awkward Gothic is rough, grainy, and energetic. When Tara (Jenna Bodnar) returns to the old homestead in Wales (actually Romania), she experiences certain changes involving sex and possible transformations. The atmosphere is effective, but this one's less a horror movie than a soft-core skin flick. And in that regard, it's a darn good one; note the bench scene.

1995 m/C Jenna Bodnar, Charles Cooper, Michael Wiseman, Blair Valk, David Starzyk, Constantin Cotimanis; ***D:*** Mark Manos; ***W:*** James Sealskin; ***M:*** Fuzzbee Morse. **VHS** *AFE*

Hush, Hush, Sweet Charlotte

Let's get past the flaws first: It's long, slow by today's standards, and most of the Southern accents and idioms are as phony as they come. Forgot those. This is a terrific faux Faulkner Gothic with Grand Guignol flourishes. Did the young Charlotte (Bette Davis) really kill her lover (Bruce Dern) back in 1927? Thirty-seven years later, is she insane, or, as the sheriff says, "She's not really crazy. She just acts that way because other people seem to expect it of her." That's the center of the film. The performances by Davis and her co-stars Olivia de Havilland, Joseph Cotten, and Agnes Moorehead are some of their most delightful (and nasty). The last reels show how much can be done with black-and-white cinematography. Director of photography Joseph Biroc was nominated for an Academy Award. (So was Agnes Moorehead.)

1965 134m/B Bette Davis, Olivia de Havilland, Joseph Cotten, Agnes Moorehead, Mary Astor, Bruce Dern, Cecil Kellaway, Victor Buono; ***D:*** Robert Aldrich; ***W:*** Lukas Heller, Henry Farrell; ***C:*** Joseph Biroc. Golden Globe Awards '65: Best Supporting Actress (Moorehead); Nominations: Academy Awards '64: Best Art Direction/Set Decoration (B & W), Best Black and White Cinematography, Best Costume Design (B & W), Best Film Editing, Best Song ("Hush, Hush, Sweet Charlotte"), Best Supporting Actress (Moorehead), Best Original Score. **VHS, LV, Closed Caption** *FOX*

I Dismember Mama

Albert (Zooey Hall) is convincingly unbalanced, an individual so out of touch with reality that he needs to be institutionalized. Anyone forced to wear his hideous wig would need professional help. And that hairpiece sets the standard for a slice of low-budget misogyny. The film's tension is derived from this murderous lunatic being on the loose with a little girl, and that is not entertainment. ***AKA:*** Poor Albert and Little Annie.

1974 (R) 81m/C Zooey Hall, Joanne Moore Jordan, Greg Mullavey, Marlene Tracy, Geri Reischl, Marlene Tracy; ***D:*** Paul Leder; ***W:*** William W. Norton Sr.; ***C:*** William Swenning. **VHS** *GEM*

I Know What You Did Last Summer

Writer Kevin Williamson's follow-up to *Scream* is loosely based on Lois Duncan's young adult novel. The small-town quarterback (Ryan Phillippe), the beauty queen (Sarah Michelle Gellar), the brainy girl (Jennifer Love Hewitt), and the ambitious poor boy (Freddie Prinze, Jr.) are the protagonists of the self-aware horror. In the middle of their last summer of irresponsibility after they've graduated from high school, they're involved in an accident, perhaps a murder. They cover it up, but a year later, it's not over. Yes, there's more than a little Hitchcock in the premise, and, for a time, Williamson and Scottish director Jim Gillespie follow the master's lead with a tricky, unpredictable tale. The second half becomes more conventional stalker stuff. The young characters are attractive, though the girls are in constant danger of

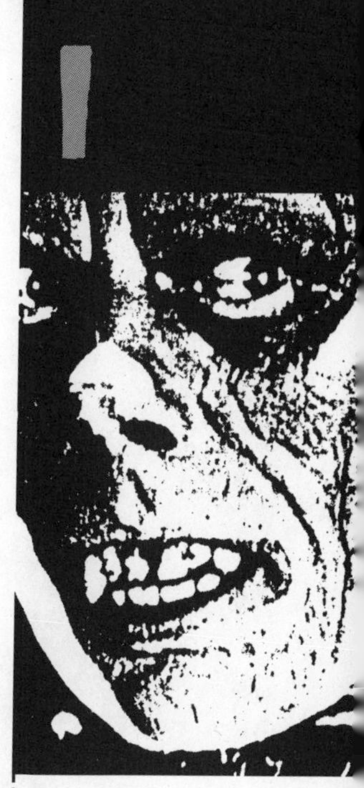

Betsy Connell (Frances Dee) and Paul Holland (Tom Conway) in *I Walked with a Zombie.*

falling out of their Wonderbras. What the film really lacks is a convincing sense of place. In North Carolina, the mountains and the beach are opposite ends of the state. At press time, something to the effect of *I Still Know What You Did Last Summer* was in the works. 🦴🦴½

1997 (R) 101m/C Jennifer Love Hewitt, Sarah Michelle Gellar, Ryan Phillippe, Freddie Prinze Jr., Muse Watson, Anne Heche, Bridgette Wilson, Johnny Galecki, Dan Albright; ***D:*** Jim Gillespie; ***W:*** Kevin Williamson; ***C:*** Denis Crossan; ***M:*** John Debney. **VHS, LV, Closed Caption, DVD** *COL*

I Spit on Your Grave

The infamous title is accurate enough for this feminist revenge fantasy. Jennifer (Camille Keaton) is brutally raped in her upstate New York vacation home, and gets even with the four attackers. The crimes, quoting John Boorman's *Deliverance,* are shown with unflinching horror. At first, the male characters are one-dimensional monsters. Later they're revealed to be two-dimensional monsters. Throughout, the viewer is squarely on Jenny's side, though some critics have attacked the film as misogynistic. Anyone who makes it through the first half will get that visceral, atavistic jolt that a good revenge flick—even one as crude and single-minded as this—can deliver. Similar material was handled in Abel Ferrara's *Ms. 45*. ***AKA:*** Day of the Woman. 🦴🦴

1977 (R) 98m/C Camille Keaton, Eron Tabor, Richard Pace, Anthony Nichols, Gunter Kleeman; ***D:*** Mier Zarchi; ***W:*** Mier Zarchi; ***C:*** Yuri Haviv. **VHS, LV** *VES*

I Walked with a Zombie

Curious variation on *Jane Eyre* (with a hint of *Rebecca*) is widely considered to be Val

Lewton and Jacques Tourneur's masterpiece. Like their other collaborations, it's more well-mannered talk than action, beautifully staged and photographed in evocative black and white. Nurse Connell (Frances Dee) goes to the island of St. Sebastian, West Indies, to look after a plantation owner's (Tom Conway) catatonic wife. Though the film's racial attitudes can be seen as paternalistic, it at least presents black characters, which, at that time, did not exist in most Hollywood releases. Conway's caddish performance is similar to his work in *The Cat People.* Frances Dee has a simpler role; the camera gives her an elegant glamour. The big voodoo ceremony is an impressive set piece.

1943 69m/B Frances Dee, Tom Conway, James Ellison, Christine Gordon, Edith Barrett, Darby Jones, Sir Lancelot; ***D:*** Jacques Tourneur; ***W:*** Curt Siodmak, Ardel Wray; ***C:*** J. Roy Hunt. **VHS, LV** *FCT, MLB, TTC*

I Was a Teenage Frankenstein

Made to cash in on the popularity of *Teenage Werewolf,* this even sillier sequel is most famous now for Professor Frankenstein's (Whit Bissell) one-liner about "a civil tongue in your head." Let's not spoil it for anyone who might have missed this oft-broadcast cult favorite. Gary Conway is the bad doctor's creation. In the end, the film delivers the nostalgic thrills the title promises, with considerable humor and a few genuine scares.

1957 m/B Gary Conway, Whit Bissell, Robert Burton, Phyllis Coates, George Lynn; ***D:*** Herbert L. Strock; ***W:*** Aben Kandel; ***C:*** Lothrop Worth. *COL, OM*

I Was a Teenage Werewolf

"That's a million dollar title on a hundred thousand dollar picture." So said producer Sam Arkoff when his partner James Nicholson came into the office with this one, and he's right. Though the film is a typical piece of American-International mid-'50s youth exploitation, it's also the debut of Michael Landon. He's Tony, a violent, troubled teen. Dr. Brandon (Whit Bissell) is the semi-mad psychiatrist who leads Tony on a drug-induced journey to his past lives, conjuring up a hairy-faced, slobbering monster. The parallel bars scene has a place in the Alternative Hall of Fame. Bissell would reprise his role in the even more tongue-in-cheek *Teenage Frankenstein.*

1957 70m/B Michael Landon, Yvonne Lime, Whit Bissell, Tony Marshall, Dawn Richard, Barney Phillips, Ken Miller, Cindy Robbins, Michael Rougas, Robert Griffin, Joseph Mell, Malcolm Atterbury, Eddie Marr, Vladimir Sokoloff, Louise Lewis, S. John Launer, Guy Williams, Dorothy Crehan; ***D:*** Gene Fowler Jr.; ***W:*** Ralph Thornton; ***C:*** Joseph LaShelle. **VHS** *COL, FCT, MLB*

I'm Dangerous Tonight

Entertaining supernatural hokum is loosely based on a Cornell Woolrich story. A magical Aztec ceremonial cloak releases the darker side of anyone who wears it, initially causing a few offscreen murders and such. But then the cloak falls into the hands of a mousy college student (Madchen Amick); she tailors it into a slinky red party dress, and PRESTO!, the innocent undergrad becomes a femme fatale reincarnation of Rita Hayworth in *Gilda.* That's the finest moment, though the rest of the movie benefits considerably from fine supporting work. This one was made for the USA cable network and so Tobe Hooper's approach to violence and gore is relatively tame.

1990 (R) 92m/C Madchen Amick, Corey Parker, R. Lee Ermey, Mary Frann, Dee Wallace Stone, Anthony Perkins, Natalie Schafer, William Berger; ***D:*** Tobe Hooper; ***W:*** Alice Wilson. **VHS** *USH*

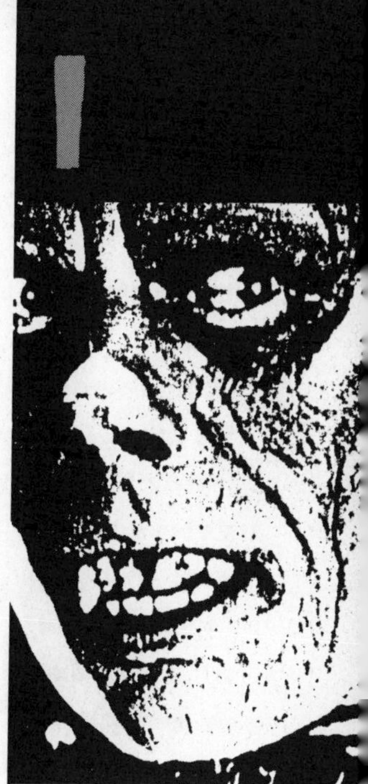

"And in that moment, I knew the answer to the riddle of the infinite. I had thought in terms of man's own limited dimension. I had presumed upon nature. That existence begins and ends is man's conception, not nature's. And I felt my body dwindling, melting, becoming nothing. My fears melted away. And in their place came acceptance. All this vast majesty of creation, it had to mean something. And then I meant something, too. Yes, smaller than the smallest, I meant something, too. To God, there is no zero. I still exist!"

—Scott Carey (Grant Williams) closing soliloquy in *The Incredible Shrinking Man.*

Impulse

Who would ever imagine Captain Kirk to be a psycho-killer stud muffin? It is difficult, but that's exactly what his character Matt Sloan is in this Florida-produced embarrassment. If nothing else, the film is a reminder of just how monstrous a fashion disaster the mid-'70s were. His wardrobe combines the most egregious elements of *Superfly* and a cheap Vegas lounge act. An Ed Wood-ish ineptitude gives the action a so-bad-it's-fun quality for fans of such, but that's hardly a recommendation. Should not be confused with the 1984 s-f film and the 1990 cop thriller of the same title. ***AKA:*** Want a Ride, Little Girl?; I Love to Kill.

1974 (PG) 85m/C William Shatner, Ruth Roman, Harold Sakata, Kim Nicholas, Jennifer Bishop, James Dobson; ***D:*** William Grefe. **VHS** *LIV*

In the Mouth of Madness

Like *Wes Craven's New Nightmare,* this is a horror film about imagination, the source of all horror. But writer Michael De Luca and director John Carpenter are telling a more traditional story that's firmly rooted in the H.P. Lovecraft mythos. As no-nonsense investigator John Trent (Sam Neill) searches for missing horror author Sutter Cane (Juergen Prochnow), he finds that the novels have an odd effect on him. Be patient with the complex structure. This is a well-made film with some genuinely creepy moments. Sam Neill is a fine hero. The subtle special effects created by Industrial Light and Magic and KNB EFX Group are excellent.

1995 (R) 95m/C Sam Neill, Juergen Prochnow, Julie Carmen, Charlton Heston, David Warner, John Glover, Bernie Casey, Peter Jason, Frances Bay; ***D:*** John Carpenter; ***W:*** Michael De Luca; ***M:*** John Carpenter, Jim Lang. **VHS, LV, Closed Caption** *TTC, NLC*

In the Realm of the Senses

Based on incidents that occurred in Tokyo in 1936, this is the story of the terrifying sexual relationship that develops between a young businessman, Kichi-San (Eiko Matsuda), and Sada (Tatsuya Fuji), an ex-prostitute. Their affair moves from simple sex to a virtual exchange of identities and finally to a sort of mutual death wish. It is difficult to describe the intense, unsettling atmosphere that director Nagisa Oshima creates. The film contains graphic sexual acts and explicit violence that makes "splatter" horror films seem as childish and silly as they really are. *Realm* is a sensual horror story. The foreign setting—white-painted geishas, the droning atonal music that sounds so harsh to western tastes, the flowing robes and stark sets—gives the story a vivid, nightmarish surrealism. It's a demanding, overly long work that is so extreme it's recommended to videophiles with strong stomachs and a taste for the truly unusual.

1976 (NC-17) 105m/C *JP FR* Tatsuya Fuji, Eiko Matsuda, Aio Nakajima, Meika Seri; ***D:*** Nagisa Oshima. **VHS** *FXL, CVC*

The Incredible Shrinking Man

By today's standards, the special effects would hardly rate a raised eyebrow, though the fight with the spider still scares me. And the idea of shrinking humans, or enlarging their surroundings, has been used often enough in movies before and since. The real difference here is Richard Matheson's intelligent and serious script, based on his novel. It takes the stuff of pulp horror and refines it into something that approaches poetry at the conclusion, and raises the archetypal material far above the B-level. Add to that veteran Jack

Arnold's sure-handed direction and a surprisingly effective performance by Grant Williams in the lead.

1957 81m/B Grant Williams, Randy Stuart, April Kent, Paul Langton, Raymond Bailey, William Schallert, Frank Scanell, Billy Curtis; ***D:*** Jack Arnold; ***W:*** Richard Matheson; ***C:*** Ellis W. Carter. **VHS, LV** *USH, MLB*

Incredibly Strange Creatures Who Stopped Living and Became Mixed-Up Zombies

Ultra-low budget horror is famous for three things, none of which have anything to do with horror: 1) the title; 2) director Ray Dennis Steckler's guerilla documentary technique; 3) early '60s nostalgia in a series of bad cocktail lounge acts. Under the name Cash Flagg, Steckler plays the hipster hero Jerry, who's hypnotized by sideshow gypsy Madam Estrella (Brett O'Hara) to do her murderous bidding. The grainy action is solidly in the Ed Woods/Roger Corman vein, and the three-bone rating is only for those who appreciate the period. ***AKA:*** The Teenage Psycho Meets Bloody Mary; The Incredibly Strange Creatures.

1963 90m/C Cash Flagg, Carolyn Brandt, Brett O'Hara, Atlas King, Sharon Walsh, Toni Camel, Erina Enyo; ***D:*** Ray Dennis Steckler; ***W:*** Gene Pollock, Robert Silliphant; ***C:*** Laszlo Kovacs, Vilmos Zsigmond, Joseph Mascelli. **VHS** *NO*

Incubus

Without question, this is the first movie John Cassavetes would have had removed from his resume. He plays a Dr. Cordell, recently arrived in a small town with his daughter, when a series of rape-murders begins. Cassavetes mumbles and slouches his way through a performance that has all the sparkle of dry mud, and his work is the best in the movie! Director John Hough indulges his penchant for pointlessly weird camera angles—under the wheelchair, over the bathroom stall—and it's all backed up by Stanley Myers' score that steals blatantly from *Jaws* and *Psycho*. The dead-teenager plot has a supernatural angle but the whole thing is more revolting than scary. **Woof!**

1982 (R) 90m/C *CA* John Cassavetes, Kerrie Keane, Helen Hughes, Erin Flannery, John Ireland, Duncan McIntosh; ***D:*** John Hough; ***W:*** George Franklin; ***C:*** Conrad Hall, Albert J. Dunk; ***M:*** Stanley Myers. **VHS, LV** *VES*

The Indestructible Man

Curious low-budget horror places veteran Chaney, near the end of his career, in a *Dragnet*-style crime tale complete with voiceover narration, unemotional dialogue, and immobile camera work. A not-particularly mad scientist accidentally revives "Butcher" Benton (Chaney) after he's been executed. Now invulnerable and superhumanly strong, the gangster lumbers off for revenge upon his cronies and his traitorous lawyer. Looking old and tired, Chaney is far past his prime. The best moments are L.A. street scenes with trolley cars, and welcome stock footage of squad cars and motorcycles screaming out of the basement of the police station. Enjoyable mostly as period nostalgia or as an early prototype for *The Terminator.*

1956 70m/B Lon Chaney Jr., Marian Carr, Max Casey Adams Showalter; ***D:*** Jack Pollexfen. **VHS** *NOS, MRV, SNC*

The Inner Sanctum

See *Dead Man's Eyes/Pillow of Death*; *Calling Dr. Death/Strange Confession*; *Weird Woman/Frozen Ghost*.

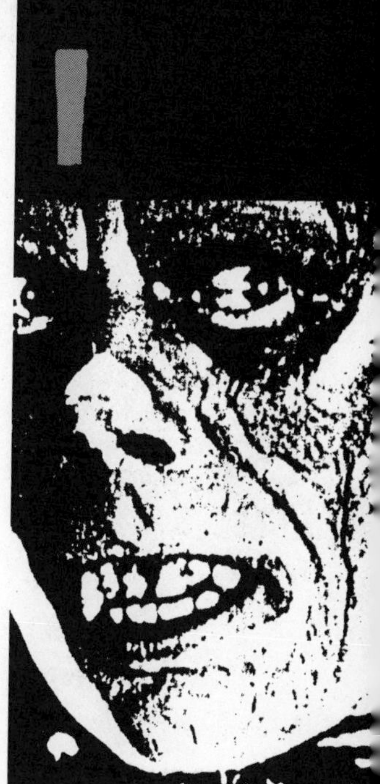

Benton (Lon Chaney, Jr.) in *The Indestructible Man.*

Innocent Blood

John Landis' guilty-pleasure companion piece to *An American Werewolf in London* might have been called *A French Vampire in Pittsburgh.* Marie (Anne Parillaud) finds herself in the middle of a Mafia gang war and decides to indulge in a little Italian food. Joe Gennaro (Anthony LaPaglia) is a cop who has infiltrated Sal Macelli's (Robert Loggia) family. Don Rickles has a nice cameo as a mob lawyer. Fans will also spot genre luminaries Forrest J. Ackerman, Dario Argento, and Sam Raimi in bit parts. Landis is trying to be as irreverent and provocative as possible, and he's generally successful. 🦴🦴🦴

1992 (R) 112m/C Anne Parillaud, Anthony LaPaglia, Robert Loggia, David Proval, Don Rickles, Rocco Sisto, Kim Coates, Chazz Palminteri, Angela Bassett, Tom Savini, Frank Oz, Forrest J. Ackerman, Sam Raimi, Dario Argento, Linnea Quigley; ***D:*** John Landis; ***W:*** Michael Wolk; ***C:*** Mac Ahlberg; ***M:*** Ira Newborn. **VHS, LV, Letterboxed, Closed Caption** *WAR, PMS*

Interview with the Vampire

The Anne Rice-Neil Jordan adaptation of her famous novel is the *Gone with the Wind* of vampire movies. Like *GWTW,* it's long, romantic, and wildly overstated. Unlike *GWTW,* it's gruesomely bloody, disgusting and, at the right times, very funny. Louis (Brad Pitt), a centuries-old undead, recounts his story to a reporter (Christian Slater), telling how he was transformed in 18th century New Orleans by Lestat (Tom Cruise), and came to transform young Claudia (Kirsten Dunst). Director Jordan lets the tone tack between opulence and outright horror without ever losing control of the story. He also generates the intensity that any real horror film needs. The gay subtext, so important to Rice's work, is remarkably strong for a mainstream film. Her script is talky and often poetic, and the cast is up to it, though Cruise's fey performance is initially off-putting. Stan Winston's effects are among his best. Fans should also see *Anne Rice: Birth of the Vampire.* 🦴🦴🦴

1994 (R) 123m/C Tom Cruise, Brad Pitt, Kirsten Dunst, Christian Slater, Antonio Banderas, Stephen Rea, Domiziana Giordano; ***D:*** Neil Jordan; ***W:*** Anne Rice; ***C:*** Philippe Rousselot; ***M:*** Elliot Goldenthal. MTV Movie Awards '95: Best Male Performance (Pitt), Breakthrough Performance (Dunst), Most Desirable Male (Pitt); Nominations: Academy Awards '94: Best Art Direction/Set Decoration, Best Original Score; Golden Globe Awards '95: Best Supporting Actress (Dunst), Best Score; MTV Movie Awards '95: Best Film, Most Desirable Male (Slater, Cruise), Best On-Screen Duo (Tom Cruise/Brad Pitt), Best Villain (Cruise). **VHS, LV, Closed Caption, DVD** *WAR*

Into the Badlands

Collection of three short supernatural tales (based on stories by Will Henry, Marcia Muller, and Bryce Walton) has the look and slow pace of a spaghetti western with cliched dialogue and grotesque characters. Bounty hunter Barstow (Bruce Dern) is the narrator. The first story concerns an outlaw (Dylan McDermott) who falls in love with a prostitute (Helen Hunt). In the second, two women (Mariel Hemingway and Lisa Pelikan) are trapped in a cabin by a snow storm and a pack of wolves. In the third, Barstow finds his prey. The middle story, potentially the strongest, fails because the two characters are unpleasant, boring, and insipid. You'll be pulling for the wolves all the way. More troubling is the way director Sam Pillsbury handles the graphic violence. He seems to take sadistic delight in some scenes and that makes the film more than a little sickening for non-gore fans. 🦴🦴

1992 (R) 89m/C Bruce Dern, Mariel Hemingway, Helen Hunt, Dylan McDermott, Lisa Pelikan, Andrew (Andy) Robinson; ***D:*** Sam Pillsbury; ***W:*** Dick Beebe, Marjorie David, Gordon Dawson. **VHS** *USH*

Invasion of the Body Snatchers

"In my practice I've seen how people have allowed their humanity to drain away—only it happens slowly, instead of all at once. They didn't seem to mind." That's how Dr. Miles Bennell (Kevin McCarthy) eventually describes the strange things that are going on in the little town of Santa Mira. How he comes to that understanding is one of the most suspenseful and frightening movies ever made. By now, the story of the pod people is familiar, and the film's dead-on assessment of the '50s political and social paranoia has been thoroughly discussed. (But consider, for a moment, the religious implications of altogether ordinary-looking monsters who claim to be "reborn into an untroubled world.") The Daniel Mainwaring-Don Siegel film works so well on so many levels that its power as a pure thriller is often overlooked. It's beautifully constructed—steadily, inexorably ratcheting up the pressure. Notice how Siegel changes the lighting from bright sun to tightening shadows that reflect the characters' growing awareness. McCarthy's performance builds from blase self-satisfaction to raving dementia without a false move. (By the way, that is director Sam Peckinpah—who helped with the script—as Charlie, the gas man.) If possible, see the widescreen edition. Siegel uses the whole frame and the missing action is all too obvious on conventional tapes. A shorter alternative version of the film eliminates the framing device. Remade in 1978 and 1994. 🦴🦴🦴🦴

1956 80m/B Kevin McCarthy, Dana Wynter, Carolyn Jones, King Donovan, Larry Gates, Jean Willes, Whit Bissell, Sam Peckinpah, Donald Siegel; ***D:*** Donald Siegel; ***W:*** Daniel Mainwaring, Sam Peckinpah; ***C:*** Ellsworth Fredericks. **VHS, LV, Letterboxed, Closed Caption** *REP, CRC, MLB*

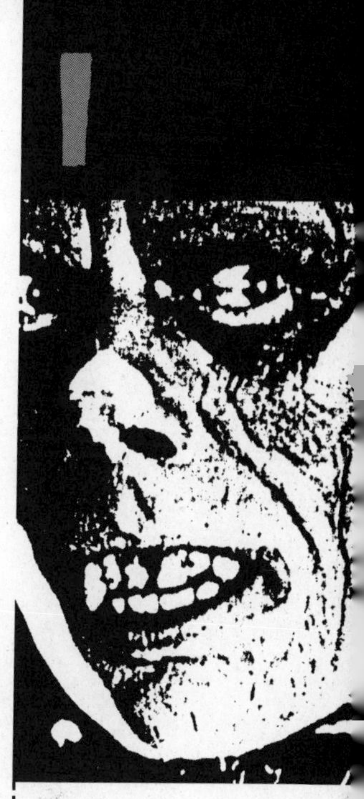

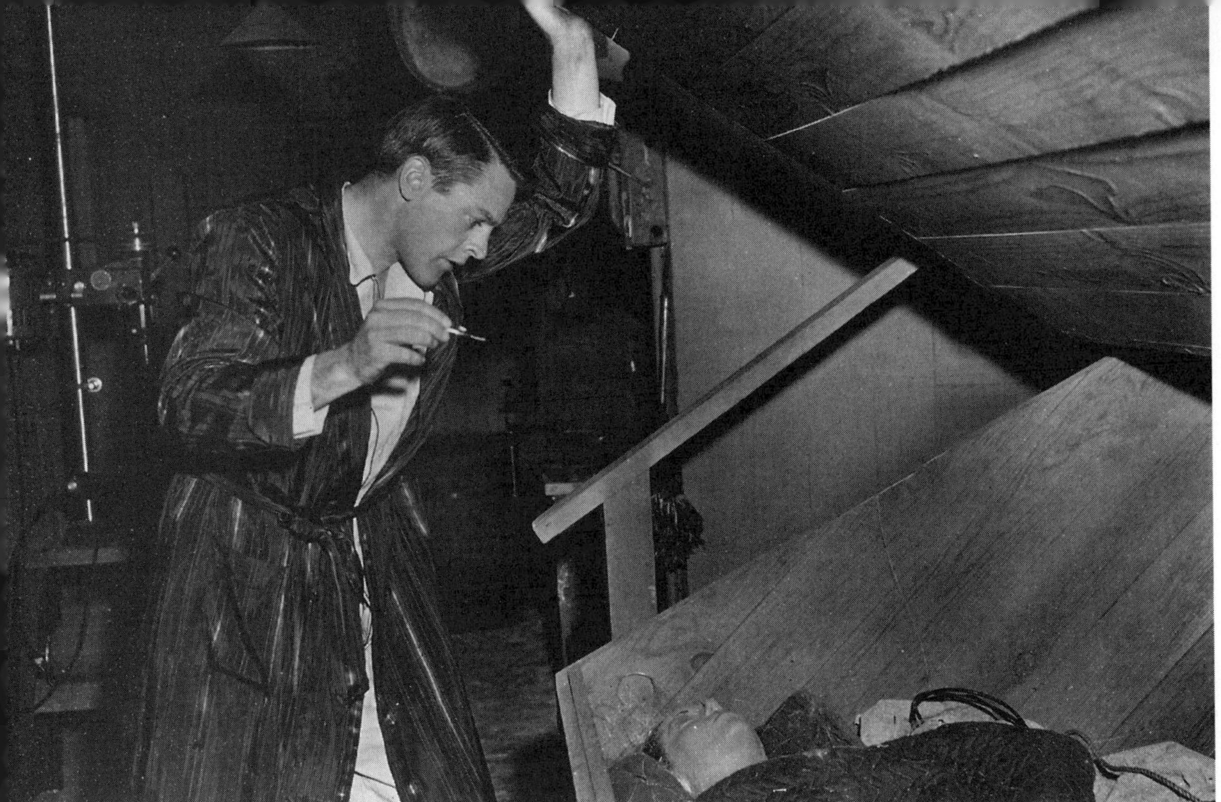

Dr. Miles Bennell (Kevin McCarthy) in *Invasion of the Body Snatchers* (1956).

Invasion of the Body Snatchers

Philip Kaufman's remake of Don Siegel's masterpiece is livelier, more graphic and violent—but it doesn't replace the original. Kaufman moves the setting from a small town to San Francisco where public health inspector Donald Sutherland slowly comes to discover the pod people. The film is too long with unresolved plotlines, and Kaufman's tendency to show off behind the camera with weird angles becomes obtrusive. Still, it's a good suspenseful story, well acted by an excellent cast. Remade again in 1994 by Abel Ferrara as *Body Snatchers*.

1978 (PG) 115m/C Donald Sutherland, Brooke Adams, Veronica Cartwright, Leonard Nimoy, Jeff Goldblum, Kevin McCarthy, Donald Siegel, Art Hindle, Robert Duvall; ***D:*** Philip Kaufman; ***W:*** W.D. Richter; ***C:*** Michael Chapman. **VHS, LV, Letterboxed** *MGM*

The Invisible Ghost

Mr. Kessler (Bela Lugosi) sits down to dinner and orders his servant Evans (Clarence Muse) to serve an empty chair where he addresses his wife. The rest of the situation involving mysterious murders is much much wackier, so wacky that any synopsis would spoil the cheap thrills. In many ways, this one's cut from the same cloth as the short Universal features of the same era, but without the crystalline production values. It's also notable for its respectful treatment of the sole black character, almost unknown in mainstream Hollywood films then.

1941 70m/B Bela Lugosi, Polly Ann Young, John McGuire, Clarence Muse, Betty Compson; ***D:*** Joseph H. Lewis; ***W:*** Helen Martin, Al Martin; ***C:*** Marcel Le Picard. **VHS** *VYY, MRV, SNC*

The Invisible Man

"Power! Power to walk into the gold vaults of the nations, into the secrets of kings, into the holy of holies! Power to make the multitudes run squealing in terror at the touch of my little invisible finger!" That's how mad scientist Jack Griffin (Claude Rains) proclaims his newly acquired transparency. Director James Whale takes H.G. Welles' "scientific romance" on a universal fantasy and turns it into a study of megalomania. (Remember that the film was made at a time when real megalomaniacs were on the rise in Germany and Italy.) Though the effects are dated now, the film zips right along with real energy and the sets are terrific. James Whale's talents as a film director had increased considerably since his horror debut with *Frankenstein.* Deprived of most of an actor's tools, Rains gives his voice a harsh, raspy quality that suits a character who's maddened by the side effects of the drug—monocaine—that renders him pigmentationally challenged. The only flaw is a relatively weak, undramatic conclusion. 🦴🦴🦴½

1933 71m/B Claude Rains, Gloria Stuart, Dudley Digges, William Harrigan, Una O'Connor, E.E. Clive, Dwight Frye, Henry Travers, Holmes Herbert, John Carradine, Walter Brennan; ***D:*** James Whale; ***W:*** R.C. Sherriff; ***C:*** Arthur Edeson. **VHS, LV** *USH, MLB*

The Invisible Man Returns

Sequel doesn't come close to the original, but it's not bad, with important comic elements. Ratcliffe (Vincent Price) is an innocent man who's given a dose of super-Clearasil by the brother of the original *Invisible Man* to spring him from the slammer where he's about to hang for murder. A youthful Price is uncharacteristically restrained while almost everyone else in the cast is shameless broad. The effects are the point anyway, and the VideoHound loves the invisible hamsters in their little leather harnesses. 🦴🦴🦴

1940 81m/B Cedric Hardwicke, Vincent Price, John Sutton, Nan Grey; ***D:*** Joe May; ***W:*** Lester Cole, Curt Siodmak; ***C:*** Milton Krasner. **VHS** *USH, MLB*

The Invisible Maniac

Ultra-low budget, leering exploitation combines elements of *The Invisible Man* with *Dr. Jekyll and Mr. Hyde,* but the main inspiration, clearly, is *Porky's.* Mad scientist Kevin Dornwinkle (Noel Peters) is already a psycho killer (of the escaped-from-the-asylum variety) when he invents his invisibility drug. By then he's teaching high school physics in summer school, and finds that the bugjuice "has the inexplicable side effect" of drawing him to the girl's locker room. A sense of humor, Peters' silly performance, and the thankful lack of a sequel earn this one a single guilty bone. 🦴

1990 (R) 87m/C Noel Peters, Shannon Wilsey, Melissa Moore, Robert Ross, Rod Sweitzer, Eric Champnella, Kalei Shellabarger, Gail Lyon, Debra Lamb; ***D:*** Rif (Adam Rifkin) Coogan; ***W:*** Rif (Adam Rifkin) Coogan; ***C:*** James Bay; ***M:*** Marc David Decker. **VHS** *REP*

The Invisible Man's Revenge

By the fifth installment, Universal has strayed so far from the source that the credits claim only "suggested by H.G. Wells." That's appropriate for a bizarre socio-political tale of evil gentry exploiting the common man, sort of. Robert Griffin (Jon Hall) is a semi-psychotic recovered amnesiac who goes from South Africa to England to track down the aristocrats

"Operator, get me the Federal Bureau of Investigation. Yes, it's an emergency."

—Dr. Hall (Whit Bissell) in the last line to *Invasion of the Body Snatchers* (1956).

THE HOUND SALUTES

JAMES WHALE

On the evening of May 29, 1957, James Whale drowned in his swimming pool. He'd been in poor health and he couldn't swim. The circumstances were, as they say, mysterious, until his suicide note was revealed some time later. The ending is not inappropriate for a director whose star burned brightly and briefly.

Whale was a Brit, born July 22, 1896, in Dudley, England. Before he came to America, he was a newspaper cartoonist, prisoner of war (where he first acted), and then a theatre director. His success with the stage hit *Journey's End* brought him to Hollywood for the film version, but he will always be remembered for a quartet of horror films, three acknowledged masterpieces and one that's very good.

The first is *Frankenstein,* and though it's a film with problems—an ungainly script based on a play, limited camera movement due to the newness of sound technology—its strengths remain undimmed, and they can be traced directly to Whale and his work with his star Boris Karloff and their makeup wizard Jack Pierce. They understood that the core of the story is the audience's mixed emotional reaction to the Monster. Initial fear and revulsion must turn to pity and finally to understanding. They do. Brilliantly.

Karloff said no to the lead in Whale's second hit, *The Invisible Man,* and he was probably right to do it. It's a role for an actor with a strong, richly textured voice and in that respect few were ever silkier than Claude Rains. He and Whale turned what might have been nothing more than an exercise in tricky effects into a hugely entertaining story. (Despite the advances in those effects, the universal fantasy of the premise has yet to be handled so well.)

Karloff and Whale were reunited on *Bride of Frankenstein,* which is generally considered the

(Lester Matthews and an under-used Gale Sondergaard) who bilked him out of his diamond mine. (I am not making this up; writer Bertram Millhauser gets the credit.) After the rich folks slip him a mickey and sic their lawyer on him, Griffin comes across mad doctor John Carradine, who's been experimenting with an invisibility drug. The film is slow and so clunky that it's almost a comedy, but it was made on the studio's backlot with the customary attention to detail and some fine black-and-white effects that predate James Cameron's *The Abyss.* 🦴🦴½

1944 78m/B Jon Hall, John Carradine, Gale Sondergaard, Lester Matthews, Evelyn Ankers, Alan Curtis, Leon Errol, Doris Lloyd; ***D:*** Ford Beebe; ***W:*** Bertram Millhauser; ***C:*** Milton Krasner. **VHS, Closed Caption** *USH*

The Invisible Ray

It's a dark and stormy night out at the lab where Dr. Rukh (Boris Karloff) invites the sleek, dapper, and skeptical Dr. Benet (Bela Lugosi) to see his Andromeda Ray, which reveals the past. When the scene shifts to Africa, the ugly racism of the 1930s becomes blatant. Otherwise, the story is pure s-f nonsense. Lugosi has the more sympathetic role, but neither star can do much with the less than stellar material. As Rukh's young wife, Frances Drake is a knockout. 🦴🦴½

1936 82m/B Boris Karloff, Bela Lugosi, Frances Drake, Frank Lawton, Beulah Bondi, Walter Kingsford; ***D:*** Lambert Hillyer; ***W:*** John Colton; ***C:*** George Robinson. **VHS, LV** *USH, MLB*

better of the two treatments of Mary Shelley's novel, but I disagree. The bizarre introduction is inexcusable, and throughout the film, the humor—always important to Whale's work—intrudes on the horror. That said, the second half is about as good as horror ever gets.

Whale's fourth film, the very good one, is *The Old Dark House,* perhaps the ultimate "dark and stormy night" yarn.

Probably because Whale made his Big Three within a four-year period for the same studio (Universal), they're often lumped together by critics and fans. That's wrong. The three films are different in all important ways, save the intelligence behind them. They were all successful too, but Whale chose not to be associated with horror after *Bride,* and his career sputtered to an early end by 1939.

SIGNIFICANT CONTRIBUTIONS TO HORROR

Frankenstein **(1931)**

The Old Dark House **(1932)**

The Invisible Man **(1933)**

The Bride of Frankenstein **(1935)**

Invitation to Hell

Made-for-TV thriller is a transitional work for director Wes Craven. It lacks the subversive excesses of his early films and the polish of his more expensive *Swamp Thing* and the *Elm Street* series. Aerospace engineer Matt Winslow (Robert Urich) moves with wife Patricia (Joanna Cassidy) and kids (Barret Oliver and Soleil Moon Frye) to a new job and a new town. Jessica Jones (Susan Lucci) runs the Steaming Springs Country Club. The transparent script makes it clear from the opening scene that she's a demon and before long we learn that the club is a cover for a supernatural conspiracy. A capable cast can't compete with goofy plot revelations that lead to a camp conclusion. The presence of Kevin McCarthy suggests a connection with *Invasion of the Body Snatchers,* but don't expect to find it. 🦴🦴

1984 100m/C Susan Lucci, Robert Urich, Joanna Cassidy, Kevin McCarthy, Patty McCormack, Joe Regalbuto, Soleil Moon Frye, Barret Oliver; ***D:*** Wes Craven. **VHS** *COL, OM*

Island of Dr. Moreau

Updating of *Island of Lost Souls* lacks the frightening intensity of that film, but it's not without winning moments. Those are provided mostly by Burt Lancaster, who's

Mutant creation, David Thewlis, and Fairuza Balk in John Frankenheimer's *The Island of Dr. Moreau* (1996).

conducting bizarre experiments on a remote island. Michael York is the young hero who's stranded there. When the doc goes to work on him, it's a horrifying scene. The human-animal makeup isn't as successful. When the creations are shown in full-color sunlight, as they often are, it's pretty obvious that these are people in rubber masks. Some of the dialogue is equally unpersuasive.

1977 (PG) 99m/C Burt Lancaster, Michael York, Nigel Davenport, Barbara Carrera, Richard Basehart, Nick Cravat; ***D:*** Don Taylor; ***W:*** John Herman Shaner, Al Ramrus; ***C:*** Gerry Fisher. **VHS** *WAR, OM*

The Island of Dr. Moreau

Seen strictly as a horror-comedy, this one's hard to top. Marlon Brando's mountainous Moreau is the *Mad Magazine* version of his Col. Kurtz from *Apocalypse Now.* He makes his first entrance in white makeup, an umbrella hat, and a Popemobile. He also adopts a lisping Boris Karloff British accent. Val Kilmer, as his assistant Montgomery, and David Thewlis, as the castaway Douglas, give their characters a curious gay spin. (The fact that top-billed Kilmer plays a supporting role and character actor Thewlis is the protagonist says a lot about the unbalanced dramatic weight.) The story doesn't differ significantly from the original. Director John Frankenheimer (who took over from writer Richard Stanley after the traditional "creative differences") and D.P. William Fraker keep the action quick and bright. Some of Stan Winston's makeup effects are excellent, but the overall tone is wrong for horror. Still, the entire production is so bizarre that it deserves a look for curiosity value, if nothing else.

1996 (PG-13) 91m/C Marlon Brando, Val Kilmer, David Thewlis, Fairuza Balk, Marco Hofschneider, Temuera

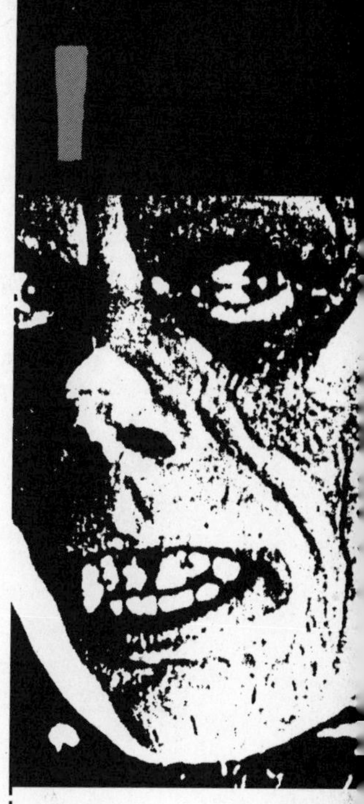

Morrison, Ron Perlman; ***D:*** John Frankenheimer; ***W:*** Richard Stanley, Ron Hutchinson; ***C:*** William A. Fraker. Nominations: Golden Raspberry Awards '96: Worst Picture, Worst Supporting Actor (Kilmer, Brando), Worst Director (Frankenheimer), Worst Screenplay. **VHS, LV, Closed Caption** *NLC*

Island of Lost Souls

Like Stevenson's *Dr. Jekyll and Mr. Hyde,* H.G. Wells' *The Island of Dr. Moreau* finds its horror in the most basic elements of humanity—the nature of good and evil, society, sex, and religious belief. The 1932 film adaptation is by far the most successful and frightening, though Wells himself is said to have disliked it. The main reasons are Charles Laughton's silky performance as the doctor whose experiments attempt to turn animals into men and women; inventive work by director Erle C. Kenton and cinematographer Karl Struss; and simple yet effective makeup. In appearance and attitude, the film resembles *King Kong.* The "are we not men" ritual is terrific, and several of the nocturnal jungle scenes have nightmarish intensity. For a perplexing double feature, watch this one with Tod Browning's *Freaks,* made the same year.

1932 71m/B Charles Laughton, Bela Lugosi, Richard Arlen, Leila Hyams, Kathleen Burke, Stanley Fields, Robert F. (Bob) Kortman, Arthur Hohl; ***Cameos:*** Alan Ladd, Randolph Scott, Buster Crabbe; ***D:*** Erle C. Kenton; ***W:*** Philip Wylie, Waldemar Young; ***C:*** Karl Struss. **VHS, Closed Caption** *USH, FCT, BTV*

Isle of the Dead

This dark, graceful film is virtually motionless. During the Balkan war, a Greek general (Boris Karloff at his best) is trapped on an island cemetery with seven other people. One old woman believes that a vampiric spirit is loose. The others calmly debate faith vs. reason until the end when one of the spookiest shocks you'll ever experience takes place. It's really no more overt than the rest, but it's been so carefully set up that it's a hard jolt. Particularly recommended for older fans. Kids probably won't have the patience for it.

1945 72m/B Boris Karloff, Ellen Drew, Marc Cramer, Katherine Emery, Helen Thimig, Alan Napier, Jason Robards Sr.; ***D:*** Mark Robson; ***W:*** Josef Mischel, Ardel Wray; ***C:*** Jack MacKenzie. **VHS, LV** *TTC, FCT, IME*

It!

Arthur Pimm (Roddy McDowall) is a British Norman Batesian mamma's boy who's already up to no-good when he comes into possession of the legendary Golem, a massive Hebrew statue that can come to life and do its master's bidding. Will it help him get a promotion at the museum or perhaps to win the lovely Ellen (Jill Haworth)? Filmmaker Herbert J. Leder gives the material semi-serious treatment. The action gets off to a slow, stiff, talky start and never moves very quickly. With his trademarked light touch, McDowall is fine. The creature looks suspiciously like a stone Conehead. ***AKA:*** Anger of the Golem; Curse of the Golem.

1967 95m/C *GB* Roddy McDowall, Paul Maxwell, Jill Haworth, Noel Trevarthen, Ernest Clark, Ian McCulloch; ***D:*** Herbert J. Leder; ***W:*** Herbert J. Leder; ***C:*** David Boulton.

It's Alive

Versatile and inventive director Larry Cohen uses horror's most famous line of dialogue as a descriptive title for a monstrous mutant baby. Said infant comes equipped with vampire-like fangs and the leg muscles and jumping power of a mature kangaroo. The little fiend attacks the milkman and, in true B-movie fashion, hides out in the Los Angeles sewers. Bernard Herrmann's score—one of his last—helps to raise this one to genuine cult status. Followed by sequels.

1974 (PG) 91m/C John P. Ryan, Sharon Farrell, Andrew Duggan, Guy Stockwell, James Dixon, Michael Ansara; ***D:*** Larry Cohen; ***W:*** Larry Cohen; ***C:*** Fenton Hamilton; ***M:*** Bernard Herrman. **VHS** *WAR, FCT*

Larry Cohen's *It's Alive.*

It's Alive 2: It Lives Again

At his best, Larry Cohen is one of horror's true originals, a writer who comes up with fresh ideas and a director who makes small budgets a virtue in his energetic stories. But he can't do much more with sequels than anyone else can. Although this one begins with a paranoid premise of government surveillance of pregnant women, the atmosphere and acting are too laid back to sustain it. Like the first, it's about giant mutant killer babies. The central question here is: are they good giant mutant killer babies or bad giant mutant killer babies? Do you really care?

1978 (R) 91m/C Frederic Forrest, Kathleen Lloyd, John P. Ryan, Andrew Duggan, John Marley, Eddie Constantine; ***D:*** Larry Cohen; ***W:*** Larry Cohen; ***C:*** Fenton Hamilton. **VHS** *WAR, FCT*

It's Alive 3: Island of the Alive

Third *Alive* feature boasts the best cast and highest production values of the trilogy. It also maintains the series' most significant contribution to the genre—the combination of revulsion, fear, and parental love that the mutant infants inspire. Michael Moriarty, writer/director Larry Cohen's frequent star and collaborator, is the father who stands up for his kid after many misgivings. Some of the creatures are handled with stop-motion animation. The free-flowing story wanders into some odd political and narrative areas as the children grow. For a sequel, this one's interesting enough, but it's far from Cohen's best.

1987 (R) 94m/C Michael Moriarty, Karen Black, Laurene Landon, Gerrit Graham, James Dixon, Neal Israel, MacDonald Carey; ***D:*** Larry Cohen; ***W:*** Larry Cohen; ***C:*** Daniel Pearl. **VHS** *WAR*

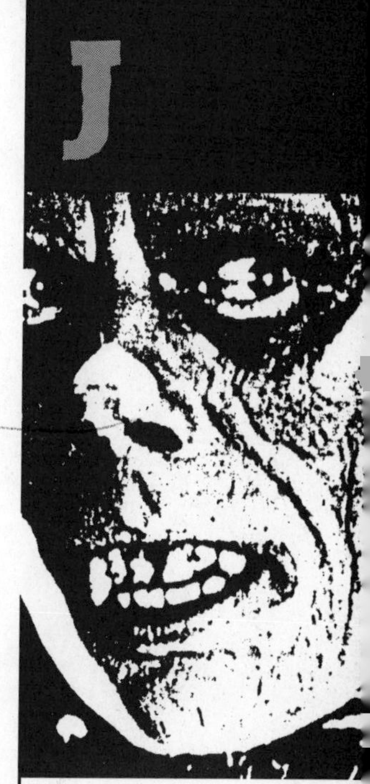

Jack Be Nimble

New Zealand Gothic horror has been properly compared to Stephen King's work and to Peter Jackson's *Heavenly Creatures,* though it's much darker and more frightening. Jack (Alexis Arquette) and his sister Dora (Sarah Kennedy) are taken from their parents as children and raised in separate homes. She goes to middle-class suburbia; he winds up in a rural hellhole. His tortured upbringing there turns him into a rebellious, unstable young man who's driven to find his lost sister. By then she has begun an affair with Teddy (Bruno Lawrence), who understands her on an unusually sympathetic level. And that is all anyone should know about the plot. Writer/director Garth Maxwell is an imaginative filmmaker who really knows what he's doing with grim, grainy images. Despite its obviously limited budget, the film is strong stuff, building to an unpredictable finish that's not for everyone.

1994 (R) 93m/C *NZ* Alexis Arquette, Sarah Kennedy, Bruno Lawrence; ***D:*** Garth Maxwell; ***W:*** Garth Maxwell; ***M:*** Chris Neal. **VHS** *TRI*

Jack-O

The equivalent of a suburban Halloween spook house is a low-budget horror comedy emphasizing laughs over scares. Like any good spook house, it's also a loving evocation of the season. The opening nursery rhyme, "Mr. Jack will break your back and cut off your head with a whack, whack, whack," sets the tone. The bloody effects that follow are about the least realistic you'll ever see, and the hoary plot revolves around a warlock who's resurrected as a pumpkin-headed slasher. Young Ryan Latshaw is fine as the trick-or-treating hero who shares the screen with a host of horror veterans led by John Carradine, Cameron Mitchell, Dawn Wildsmith, Linnea Quigley, and Brinke Stevens, who ham it up happily. If it weren't for one shower scene, this one would be recommended for kids. Instead, it's aimed more at nostalgic drive-in fans.

1995 (R) 90m/C Linnea Quigley, Ryan Latshaw, Cameron Mitchell, John Carradine, Dawn Wildsmith, Brinke Stevens; ***D:*** Steve Latshaw. **VHS, LV** *TRI, IME*

Jack the Ripper

Jesus Franco's take on the famous story is just as much a remake of *The Awful Dr. Orlof* (1962) as it is a dramatization of real events, though it is faithful to a few of the nastiest details of the Whitechapel murders. Twitchy Klaus Kinski is the insane doctor who's obsessed with a ballet dancer and takes out his madness on prostitutes. For the most part, Franco, who's known for his fast and loose work, sticks to the first rule of Hollywood—keep the camera on the star. Long stretches of Kinski close-ups and talky exposition are punctuated by graphic sexual violence. ***AKA:*** Der Dirnenmoerder von London.

1976 (R) 82m/C *SI GE* Klaus Kinski, Josephine Chaplin, Herbert Fux, Ursula von Wiese, Lina Romay, Andreas Mannkopff; ***D:*** Jess (Jesus) Franco; ***W:*** Jess (Jesus) Franco; ***C:*** Peter Baumgartner. **VHS** *VES*

Jack's Back

Rowdy Herrington's underpublicized sleeper is one of the rare treats on the horror shelves of your local video store. The premise—100 years later, to the day, someone is recreating Jack the Ripper's crimes in L.A.—sounds like the derivative flapdoodle of a bad made-for-cable feature. But writer/director Herrington fills the screen with evocatively lit compositions and surprising plot twists. The first act conclusion is a corker and so's the tricky ending. Star James Spader's sleepy-eyed diffidence cuts against the grain of his character—a dedicated young doctor—but it still works.

Steven Spielberg's *Jaws.*

Ignore the formulaic sound of the synopsis and take a look. 🦴🦴🦴½

1987 (R) 97m/C James Spader, Cynthia Gibb, Rod Loomis, Rex Ryon, Robert Picardo, Jim Haynie, Chris Mulkey, Danitza Kingsley, Wendell Wright; ***D:*** Rowdy Herrington; ***W:*** Rowdy Herrington; ***C:*** Shelly Johnson. **VHS, LV, Closed Caption** *PAR*

Jacob's Ladder

The opening scene in Vietnam—featuring a strong early appearance by Ving Rhames—is as shocking a slice of wartime horror as you're likely to see. Flash forward to New York where Jacob (Tim Robbins) is a possibly delusional postman living with Jezebel (Elizabeth Pena). The rest of the plot is virtually review-proof. To reveal any of it would spoil all of it. Director Adrian Lyne's polished visual style mixes the mundane and the nightmarish with frightening originality. Jake may be mad or he may have been driven mad or, as Jezzy puts it, "New York is full of creatures." The performances couldn't be better. The second half is more problematic. 🦴🦴🦴

1990 (R) 116m/C Tim Robbins, Elizabeth Pena, Danny Aiello, Matt Craven, Pruitt Taylor Vince, Jason Alexander, Patricia Kalember, Eriq La Salle, Ving Rhames, Macaulay Culkin; ***D:*** Adrian Lyne; ***W:*** Bruce Joel Rubin; ***C:*** Jeffrey L. Kimball; ***M:*** Maurice Jarre. **VHS, LV, Closed Caption** *LIV, FCT*

The Jar

Writer George Bradley and director Bruce Toscano try to tell a serious psychological horror story modeled on Polanski's *Repulsion* with a microscopic budget. It's dark and boring. Paul (Gary Wallace) has an off-screen car accident that brings a jar in a brown paper bag into his possession. Paul thinks that the ugly little creature inside it is taking over his life. Most of the non-action is set in his dimly lit apartment. The film may well be an accurate portrayal of

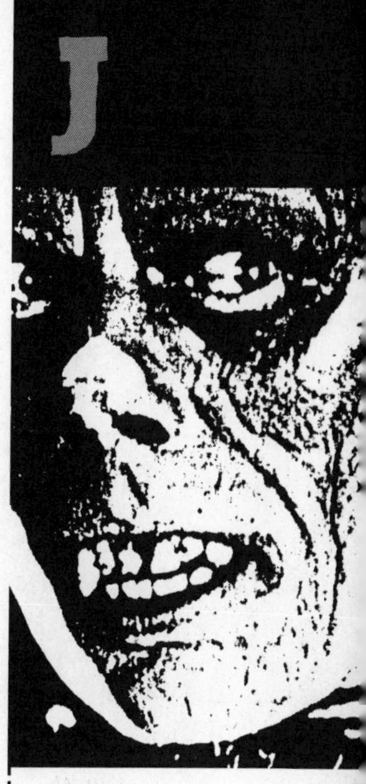

an emotional breakdown, but it's also so tortuously slow that you'll think your VCR has been packed with glue. By the way, the Ray Bradbury story with the same title and a similar plot is the basis for a memorable episode of *The Twilight Zone*.

1984 90m/C Gary Wallace, Karen Sjoberg; ***D:*** Bruce Toscano; ***W:*** George Bradley. **VHS** *NO*

Jason Goes to Hell: The Final Friday

This is the second time that the producers have used the word "final" in the title, so, clearly, they cannot be trusted. As for the film itself, it's pretty much the same old same old verging on self parody, except for the plot elements blatantly stolen from *The Hidden* and a pervasive casual sadism. After Mr. Hockey Mask has been blown into hundreds of pieces in the first reel, he comes back. Why? Because his heart—"filled with a black viscous fluid," according to the coroner—is still alive! Ironically, the changes in film technology and moviegoers' appetite for gore have made these later sequels more technically proficient than the low-budget original.

1993 (R) 89m/C Kane Hodder, John D. LeMay, Kari Keegan, Steven Williams, Steven Culp, Erin Gray, Richard Gant, Leslie Jordan, Billy Green Bush, Rusty Schwimmer, Allison Smith, Julie Michaels; ***D:*** Adam Marcus; ***W:*** Dean Lorey, Jay Huguely-Cass; ***M:*** Harry Manfredini. **VHS, LV, Closed Caption** *NLC, IME*

Jaws

Technical problems turned what might have been nothing more than another monster movie into one of horror's best. The tales about the difficulties with "Bruce," the mechanical shark, are the stuff of Hollywood legend. (According to one version, the producers initially thought that real sharks could be trained to perform.) When Bruce didn't work, young director Spielberg was forced to shoot around it and to suggest what he couldn't show. In the process, every scene set on or near the ocean became doubly suspenseful. Even in bright daylight, the surface of the water is hiding a creature that comes straight from our collective nightmares. The two main settings—the island village of Amity and the fishing boat—are well realized. The script wisely jettisons the needless subplots from Peter Benchley's novel and focuses on the three protagonists—the sheriff (Roy Scheider), the scientist (Richard Dreyfuss), and the salt (Robert Shaw)—as they hunt for the shark. If the telling of the story is a bit stilted and formal, it was good enough to keep thousands of people out of the ocean during the summer of '75. John Williams' ominous here-comes-the-shark theme and soaring score add immeasurably. Take another look.

1975 (PG) 124m/C Roy Scheider, Robert Shaw, Richard Dreyfuss, Lorraine Gary, Murray Hamilton, Carl Gottlieb; ***Cameos:*** Peter Benchley; ***D:*** Steven Spielberg; ***W:*** Peter Benchley, Carl Gottlieb; ***C:*** Bill Butler; ***M:*** John Williams. Academy Awards '75: Best Film Editing, Best Sound, Best Original Score; Golden Globe Awards '76: Best Score; Nominations: Academy Awards '75: Best Picture. **VHS, LV, Letterboxed** *USH*

Jaws 2

Pale shadow has almost all of the gimmicks of the original but none of the punch. No surprise there; it was a troubled production with original director John Hancock replaced by Jeannot Szwarc three weeks into shooting and the script by Hancock's wife Dorothy Tristan rewritten by Carl Gottlieb. Star Roy Scheider was contractually obligated to make the movie, and the lack of originality and enthusiasm is obvious everywhere. If there were truth-in-titling laws, this would have been called *Jaws $*. **Woof!**

1978 (PG) 116m/C Roy Scheider, Lorraine Gary, Murray Hamilton, Joseph Mascolo, Jeffrey Kramer, Collin

THE HOUND SALUTES

STEVEN SPIELBERG

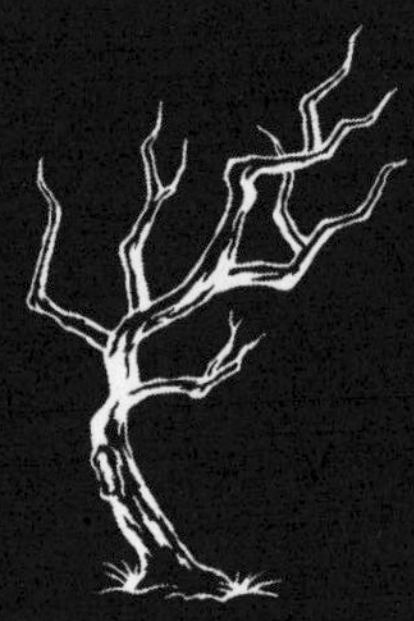

Hollywood's most successful filmmaker is also one of its best horror directors. Steven Spielberg got his start in the business with a superbly crafted monster story and he returns to the genre regularly.

In fact, looking back at his career, you can draw a straight line connecting the truck in *Duel,* the shark in *Jaws,* and the T-rex in *Jurassic Park.* They're all variations on the same terrifyingly powerful, single-minded predator who will stop at nothing to get you.

Spielberg's rich and diverse career hasn't been limited by genre considerations. In their own ways, both *Raiders of the Lost Ark* and *Schindler's List* are masterpieces. One is light-hearted escapism while the other is an epic of sacrifice and redemption. Spielberg is such a gifted cinematic storyteller that he can succeed at both extremes.

His fascination with film came early. Born in Cincinnati in 1947, he began making home movies as a boy, studied film at California State College, Long Beach, and signed a contract to direct for Universal at age 21. His early work was done for television in both series and feature-length films. He first came to the attention of horror fans in 1971 with *Duel,* based on Richard Matheson's story of a salesman who's threatened by a tractor-trailer truck. It was followed in 1972 by *Something Evil,* a haunted house story starring Darren McGavin and Sandy Dennis. Remarkably, it is unavailable on tape, though if memory serves, it's a subtle work,

Wilcox; ***D:*** Jeannot Szwarc; ***W:*** Carl Gottlieb, Howard Sackler; ***C:*** Michael C. Butler; ***M:*** John Williams. **VHS, LV, Letterboxed** *USH*

Jaws 3

What a shame that the long-rumored National Lampoon's *Jaws 3—People 0* project never found its way to the screen. Instead, we've got this waterlogged mess, originally made in 3-D. Perhaps it's that 3-D process that makes it look so cheap and rough on video, with really poor effects. The lame action is set in an aquatic amusement park owned by Calvin Buchard (Louis Gossett, Jr.). It's so poor that the film really is a legitimate contender for Worst Sequel ever, and it's certainly the most embarrassing entry on writer Richard Matheson's resume. ***AKA:*** Jaws 3-D.

1983 (PG) 98m/C Dennis Quaid, Bess Armstrong, Louis Gossett Jr., Simon MacCorkindale, Lea Thompson, John Putch; ***D:*** Joe Alves; ***W:*** Richard Matheson, Carl Gottlieb; ***C:*** James A. Contner; ***M:*** John Williams. **VHS, LV** *USH*

Jekyll and Hyde

Tepid retelling never really gets to the heart of the matter. Michael Caine plays the good doctor and his brutal alter-ego. The first part follows the familiar plot until Jekyll falls in love with his sister-in-law (Cheryl Ladd). Then, for a time, the focus is on Victorian values and mores, complete with egregious overacting from all concerned. When it returns to Mr. Hyde, the film becomes a standard mid-budget monster flick with a surprise ending that's no surprise. The transformation effects are

akin in setting and atmosphere to *The Other.*

When *Jaws* became a massive commercial hit in 1975—after months of public speculation that it was going over budget and would be a disaster—the summer blockbuster was born and the economics of the industry were fundamentally changed. Spielberg wisely chose to dissociate himself with the sequels that followed.

Instead, his next foray into horror was *Poltergeist* in 1982. Though the extravagant haunted house story was directed by Tobe Hooper, it was produced, co-written and, some said, co-directed by Spielberg.

Then in 1993, Spielberg had his biggest hit to that time with his thunderous adaptation of Michael Crichton's best-seller, *Jurassic Park.* It is, quite simply, the best dinosaur movie anyone has ever made. Take another look and notice how the opening scenes depend so much on sound and inference. It works in the same way that *Jaws* did. The shark was introduced by showing the effects of the attack on the victim while the attacking monster remains hidden. I vividly remember being in a benefit preview screening for *Jurassic Park* and watching dozens of crying children being led up the aisle and out of the theatre before the first dinosaur had shown up.

A horror movie that can do that is a great horror movie!

SIGNIFICANT CONTRIBUTIONS TO HORROR

Duel **(1971)**

Jaws **(1975)**

Poltergeist **(1982)**

Jurassic Park **(1993)**

nothing special, and the Hyde makeup looks like a lumpy onion with a bad attitude. In her own way, Cheryl Ladd doesn't fare much better. She has to wear a bustle that is truly remarkable. Hit the pause button when that astonishing appendage appears. 🦴🦴

1990 100m/C Michael Caine, Cheryl Ladd, Joss Ackland, Ronald Pickup, Kim Thomson, Lionel Jeffries, Kevin McNally, Lee Montague, Diane Keen, David Schofield; ***D:*** David Wickes; ***W:*** David Wickes; ***C:*** Norman G. Langley. **VHS** *THV*

Jennifer

In setting and storyline, this is an unabashed copy of *Carrie.* The only real difference is that unlike the telekinetic Carrie, Jennifer (Lisa Pelikan) has magical powers over snakes. She then uses that to get back at her snippy classmates. The film never tries to be more than it is, and Lisa Pelikan is fine in the lead with help from a supporting cast of seasoned pros. ***AKA:*** Jennifer (The Snake Goddess). 🦴🦴

1978 (PG) 90m/C Lisa Pelikan, Bert Convy, Nina Foch, John Gavin, Wesley Eure, Jeff Corey; ***D:*** Brice Mack; ***W:*** Kay Cousins Johnson, Steve Krantz. **VHS** *LIV, VES*

Judge & Jury

Joey Meeker (David Keith) is another of those mad killers who is resurrected after he's electrocuted. Or are his various incarnations (some involving orange hair and black nail polish) a product of Michael's (Martin Kove) imagination because he was involved with Joey's wife's death? The

"He was king in the world he knew, but now he comes to civilization merely a captive, a show to gratify your curiosity. Ladies and gentlemen, look at Kong."

—Carl Denham (Robert Armstrong) introduces his ape in *King Kong.*

derivative material is handled with more wit and style than it really deserves. The key participants—Keith, Kove, and veteran video director John Eyres—are old hands with this level of well-made low-budget *Elm Street* material. 🦴🦴½

1996 (R) 98m/C David Keith, Martin Kove, Laura Johnson, Thomas Ian Nichols, Paul Koslo; ***D:*** John Eyres; ***W:*** John Eyres, John Cianetti, Amanda I. Kirpaul; ***C:*** Bob Paone; ***M:*** Johnathon Flood. **VHS, LV** *APX*

Jugular Wine: A Vampire Odyssey

In Alaska, footloose college professor James Grace (Shaun Irons) is bitten by a vampire. Maybe. He might also discover inklings of a larger conspiracy involving a monstrous figure named Legion. Back home in Philadelphia, Grace feels that he's changing or perhaps dying. Whatever, he sets off on a journey to learn what has happened. Young filmmaker Blair Murphy attempts to do more than his meager budget (and probably his experience) will allow. The result is wildly uneven but consistently entertaining and intelligent, combining exploitation with serious literary and philosophical ideas in a tenuous balance. The bloody effects are much more believable than you often see in more sophisticated productions. The rough, picaresque road-movie quality makes virtues of most flaws though it all could make more sense than it does. It's still more enjoyable than *Nadja* or *The Addiction*. That's Murphy as the blond Nickadeamous. 🦴🦴🦴½

1994 95m/C Shaun Irons, Rachelle Parker, Gordon Capps, Aki Aleong, Henry Rollins, Stan Lee, Frank Miller, Michael Colyar, Lisa Malkiewicz; ***D:*** Blair Murphy; ***W:*** Blair Murphy; ***C:*** Baird Bryant; ***M:*** John Butler. **VHS** *EII*

Julia and Julia

Kathleen Turner plays Julia in two parallel worlds. In one, she marries Paolo (Gabriel Byrne) and he's killed immediately after the ceremony. In the second, he lives and they have a six-year-old son. But when Julia-1 finds her way into Julia-2's life, she finds that Julia-2 also has a lover (Sting). Julia's initial reaction of joy, confusion, disbelief, and hope is completely convincing and moving. Director Peter Del Monte is also able to generate considerable erotic tension. But the plot, credited to no less than four writers, becomes more and more complex, and runs out of gas before it's over. If the ending had lived up to the body of the film, this would have been a must-see. But many viewers will feel cheated. 🦴🦴½

1987 (R) 98m/C Kathleen Turner, Sting, Gabriel Byrne, Gabriele Ferzetti, Angela Goodwin; ***D:*** Peter Del Monte; ***W:*** Silvia Napolitano, Joe Minion, Sandro Petraglia, Peter Del Monte; ***C:*** Giuseppe Rotunno; ***M:*** Maurice Jarre. **VHS, LV, Closed Caption** *FOX*

Jurassic Park

In making an absolutely spectacular dinosaur film, that elusive Hollywood "chemistry" works to perfection...well, near perfection. First, the monsters created by Dennis Muren, Stan Winston, and Michael Lantieri with live action, stop-motion animation, and computer-generated digital images are magnificent. Even on the small screen, T-Rex and Velociraptor are completely frightening. Second, the script by novelist Michael Crichton and David Koepp puts a cast of interesting stock figures through a series of adrenaline-pumping adventures. Finally, director Steven Spielberg mixes image and sound deftly, and keeps the whole thing zipping right along at a potboiler pace. At the same time, his tendency toward over-sweetness bubbles close to the surface a time or two. Even so, for some younger horror fans, this movie will generate nightmares that might last for years. To date, followed by one less-successful sequel. 🦴🦴🦴½

1993 (PG-13) 127m/C Sam Neill, Laura Dern, Jeff Goldblum, Richard Attenborough, Bob Peck, Martin Ferrero,

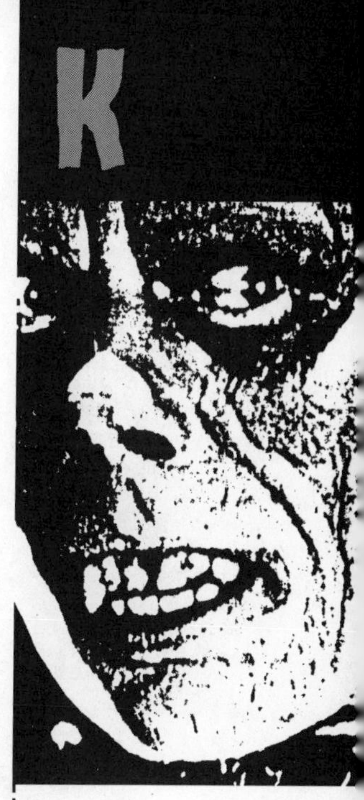

B.D. Wong, Joseph Mazzello, Ariana Richards, Samuel L. Jackson, Wayne Knight; ***D:*** Steven Spielberg; ***W:*** David Koepp, Michael Crichton; ***C:*** Dean Cundey; ***M:*** John Williams; ***V:*** Richard Kiley. Academy Awards '93: Best Sound, Best Sound Effects Editing, Best Visual Effects; Nominations: MTV Movie Awards '94: Best Film, Best Villain (T-Rex), Best Action Sequence. **VHS, LV, Closed Caption, DVD** *USH*

The Keep

Like all of Michael Mann's work, this variation on the Golem legend is so sophisticated in visual terms that it borders on genius. Mann can replace conventional dialogue with image, sound, and music as well as anyone ever has. (If possible, the film should be seen on the best video equipment with headphones.) That also makes for an emotional coolness in the attempt to equate Nazism with a sort of Lovecraftian supernatural evil. In 1941, Germans led by Juergen Prochnow and Gabriel Byrne let some huge, powerful force loose in a Romanian castle. Ian MacKellan, as a Jewish scholar, and Scott Glenn, as a mysterious partisan who's been transformed, are fine, but Mann is more interested in smoky light, an elegantly composed screen, and bizarre effects. The elaborate style justifies a deliberate pace.

1984 (R) 96m/C Scott Glenn, Alberta Watson, Juergen Prochnow, Robert Prosky, Gabriel Byrne, Ian McKellen; ***D:*** Michael Mann; ***W:*** Michael Mann, Dennis Lynton Clark; ***C:*** Alex Thomson; ***M:*** Tangerine Dream. **VHS, LV, Letterboxed** *PAR, OM*

The Kindred

A multi-tentacled, slime-oozing, ultra-yucky monster is easily upstaged by Rod Steiger's eye-rolling, scenery-munching, where-did-he-get-that-toupee? overacting. The clumsy story has to do with your basic mad scientist and a group of young people in an isolated house with said critter. In the big scare scenes, one woman is killed by a watermelon, another turns into a fish (sort of), and a third is attacked by a clogged kitchen drain. We've all had days like that, haven't we?

1987 (R) 92m/C Rod Steiger, Kim Hunter, David Allan Brooks, Timothy Gibbs, Amanda Pays, Talia Balsam, Jeffrey Obrow, Peter Frechette, Julia Montgomery; ***D:*** Stephen Carpenter, Jeffrey Obrow; ***W:*** Stephen Carpenter, Joseph Stefano, John Penney, Earl Ghaffari, Jeffrey Obrow; ***M:*** David Newman. **VHS, LV** *LIV*

King Kong

One of Hollywood's true masterpieces is so richly layered and enjoyable that its simple core is often overlooked. This is the story of an innocent guy from the sticks who's on his own in New York and looking for a girl. Everything about the film fits together perfectly. It begins when Robert Armstrong's gruff Carl Denham says, "All right, the public wants a girl and this time I'm going to give 'em what they want!" and then finds Ann Darrow (Fay Wray, one of the sweetest, sexiest heroines ever and the original Scream Queen) who steals the heart of the King himself, and I don't mean Elvis. The combination of Willis O'Brien's effects, Max Steiner's thunderous score, and the terrific sets create the black-and-white reality of a remembered dream. For an unapologetic piece of popular entertainment, the film has been subjected to academic and political analyses of every stripe. It remains, however, stubbornly critic-proof. And because the movie was made before widescreen processes, it looks beautiful on video. Most editions are of the original 101-minute 1933 version, not the bowdlerized 1938 re-release that eliminated most of the film's still shocking violence. The Criterion Collection laserdisc contains extra material and separate commentary by film preservationist and historian Ronald Haver.

1933 101m/B Fay Wray, Bruce Cabot, Robert Armstrong, Frank Reicher, Noble Johnson, Sam Hardy, James Flavin; ***D:*** Ernest B. Schoedsack, Merian C. Cooper; ***W:*** James A. Creelman, Ruth Rose, Edgar Wallace; ***C:*** Edward Linden; ***M:*** Max Steiner. National Film Registry '91. **VHS, LV, 8mm, Closed Caption** *TTC, FUS, CRC*

Beauty (Fay Wray) and the Beast in *King Kong* (1933).

King Kong

Producer Dino De Laurentiis' remake adds absolutely nothing to the original. All right, it does mark the debut of Jessica Lange, but she has long since lived it down. The special effects, though more advanced in some respects, are not as believable as Willis O'Brien's stop-motion work. Not one moment in this film even comes close to the Kong vs. T-Rex fight. Other elements of the original—the protagonist's innocence, the implied sexuality—have been heightened to the point that they smack of parody. About the best that can be said is that this one's better than the lamentable sequel. 🦴🦴

1976 (PG) 135m/C Jeff Bridges, Charles Grodin, Jessica Lange, Rene Auberjonois, John Randolph, Ed Lauter, Jack O'Halloran, Dennis Fimple, John Agar, Rick Baker; ***D:*** John Guillermin; ***W:*** Lorenzo Semple Jr.; ***C:*** Richard Kline; ***M:*** John Barry. Academy Awards '76: Best Visual Effects; Nominations: Academy Awards '76: Best Cinematography, Best Sound. **VHS, LV, 8mm** *PAR, HMV*

King Kong Lives

This inept sequel to a bad remake is worse than I can describe, worse than you can imagine. For starters, Kong has been in a coma since his fall from the World Trade Center ten years before. Dr. Franklin (Linda Hamilton) is about to implant a jumbo-sized artificial heart, but she needs blood, lots of it, for a transfusion. That's when Hank (Brian Kerwin) shows up with Lady Kong. The rest is even more insulting to your intelligence, with gobs of gooey sentimentality at the end and not the first trace of intentional humor. Too simple-minded for adults, too graphically violent for kids, and all the way through, it has a leering sexual subtext. **Woof!**

1986 (PG-13) 105m/C Brian Kerwin, Linda Hamilton, John Ashton, Peter Michael Goetz; ***D:*** John Guillermin; ***W:*** Steven Pressfield, Ronald Shusett. **VHS, LV, Closed Caption** *WAR*

Kingdom of the Spiders

Overachieving B-movie is solidly in the tradition of the underrated Jack Arnold films of the 1950s. In rural Arizona, farm animals are dying. Vet William Shatner is baffled; Tiffany Bolling is the obligatory science-babe who deduces that the animals were killed by spider venom. In one neat sequence, the sexual conventions of the genre are turned upside down, and the ending is a nice turn on *Night of the Living Dead*. Writers Alan Caillou and Richard Robinson and director John "Bud" Cardos don't make any apologies for what they're doing and handle things with the right combination of seriousness and humor. 🦴🦴🦴

1977 (PG) 90m/C William Shatner, Tiffany Bolling, Woody Strode; ***D:*** John Cardos; ***W:*** Alan Caillou, Richard Robinson; ***C:*** John Morrill. **VHS** *NO*

Kiss Me, Kill Me

Valentina (Isabelle DeFunes) is a swinging photographer who's set upon by Baba Yaga (Carroll Baker), a sort of vampiric witch. She's aided by an evil, sexy S&M doll that comes to life. In many ways, this oddity is an archetypal '60s movie with funky jazzy music, coy sex, radical politics, and hallucinatory dream sequences. Though director Corrado Farina's film is based on a comic book character created by Crepax, the influences of Fellini and Antonioni are just as obvious. Exploitation with several odd twists is recommended mostly to fans of the era. ***AKA:*** Devil's Witch; Baba Yaga; So Sweet, So Perverse; Cosi dolce...cosi perversa; Baby Yaga—Devil Witch. 🦴🦴🦴

1969 (R) 91m/C Carroll Baker, George Eastman, Isabelle DeFunes, Ely Gallo; ***D:*** Corrado Farina; ***W:*** Corrado Farina. **VHS** *NO*

Kiss of the Vampire

Hammer's third vampire film (after *Horror of Dracula* and *Brides of Dracula*) is one of its best, despite the absence of Cushing and Lee. They're replaced by Clifford Evans as the drunken, remorseful vampire hunter Zimmer, and Noel Willman as the aristocratic Ravna. Writer Anthony Hind's script is a simple variation on Stoker's story that the studio would rework time and again over the next decade. Young couple (Edward De Souza and Jennifer Daniel) comes across vampire's castle and is entrapped. Though there's barely a plunging neckline, the sexual aspects are strong, with a faint hint of lesbianism. The introductory burial scene is a tremendous shocker; the effects at the end are comparatively weak. Clearly, the film is a strong influence on Roman Polanksi's *The Fearless Vampire Killers*. ***AKA:*** Kiss of Evil. 🦴🦴🦴🦴

1962 88m/C *GB* Clifford Evans, Noel Willman, Edward De Souza, Jennifer Daniel, Barry Warren, Jacqueline Wallis, Peter Madden, Isobel Black, Vera Cook, Olga Dickie; ***D:*** Don Sharp; ***W:*** Anthony John Elder Hinds; ***C:*** Alan Hume; ***M:*** James Bernard. **VHS, Closed Caption** *USH*

Labyrinth

When self-centered Sarah (Jennifer Connelly) foolishly invites the King of the Goblins (David Bowie) to take the little brother she has to babysit, he accepts. Her suburban neighborhood is transformed into a labyrinth filled with magical creatures; she has 13 hours to find a castle at the center and rescue the tot. Director Jim Henson quotes Salvadore Dali, Walt Disney, Maurice Sendak, and M.C. Escher in the creation of his frightening, gritty wonderland. In this world of fairy tales, beauty and wonder are never far from ugliness, and they are often all part of the same thing. In the end, the story is about growing up, maturing, accepting responsibility—in short, all of the things that most movies, even those aimed at kids, are not about. 🦴🦴🦴

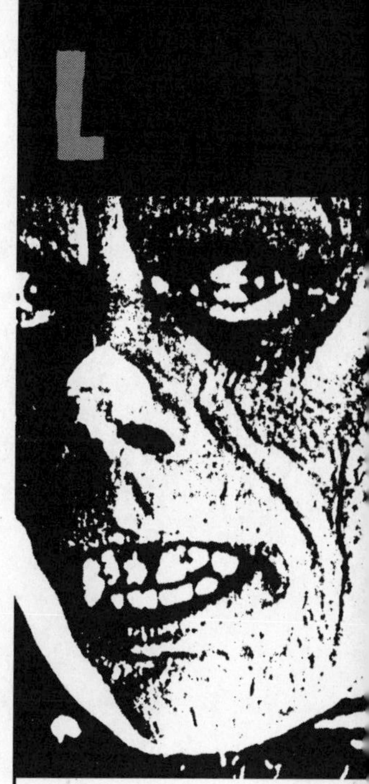

THE HOUND SALUTES

FAY WRAY

The term has fallen into general disfavor these days, and Fay Wray has hated it for decades, but she is still the original "scream queen" in the most literal sense. Even before she sees King Kong, she has a famous rehearsal scene on the deck of a ship. She imagines the horror and reacts to it with a full-throated trumpet that sets the stage for the adventurous second act.

More importantly, her vocal blasts provide an outlet for audiences' reactions. When she first spots the King as he knocks down trees to meet his blind date, she does exactly what we want to do.

She was born in Canada in 1907, but soon moved to America. In a 1995 interview, she said that one of her earliest memories—and the one that made her want to become an actress—was of seeing her first movie in a Salt Lake City theatre. She couldn't recall the title of the film, but the experience was still strong. She remembered the dust motes floating overhead in the light of the projector's beam, and the emotions of the crowd around her. "I was probably about six years old, and I sensed that the people in the audience were very happy. It was sweet enchantment."

Ten years later in Los Angeles, she was working in Hal Roach short comedies and Hoot Gibson Westerns. Her first break was in Erich von Stroheim's *The Wedding March.* After that, she worked in more prestigious productions with Emil Jannings, Gary Cooper, William Wellman, and Josef von Sternberg. Her appearance in *The Four Feathers* (1929) introduced her to Merian C. Cooper and Ernest Schoedsack, who would cast her in *King Kong.*

In those days before the Screen Actors Guild, her schedule could be grueling. On *Kong,* she once worked for 22 hours straight, spending much of the time suspended six feet above the floor in the unsteady grip of a huge fake gorilla hand. She was supposed to be trying to escape from it, but the more she wriggled, the looser the fingers became.

Because *Kong* took so long to make, her other important appearances in horror were produced at the same time with over-

1986 (PG) 90m/C David Bowie, Jennifer Connelly, Toby Froud, Shelley Thompson, Dave Goelz, Karen Prell, Steve Whitmire; ***D:*** Jim Henson; ***W:*** Jim Henson, Terry Jones; ***C:*** Alex Thomson; ***M:*** Trevor Jones, David Bowie. **VHS, LV, 8mm, Closed Caption** *NLC*

Lady Frankenstein

Italian import begins as a fairly straightforward variation on the standard themes with the venerable Joseph Cotton playing our man Frank not so much as a mad scientist but more as an aggressive humanist. "Here on earth, Man is God," he says, and "Let man's will be done." Cotton has the presence to bring off such hokum. But he exits at the end of the first act, turning things over to his daughter (Sara Bay), who follows in daddy's experimental footsteps. Meanwhile, his creation ravages the countryside. With the addition of familiar voice dubbing, the whole thing sounds and looks a little like a gladiator flick. It ends up being fair to middling exploitation. ***AKA:*** La Figlia di Frankenstein; The Daughter of Frankenstein; Madame Frankenstein. 🦴🦴

lapping shooting schedules. She co-starred with Lionel Atwill in two early two-color Technicolor horrors for director Michael Curtiz, *Doctor X* and *Mystery of the Wax Museum*. Her role in *The Vampire Bat*, with Melvyn Douglas, is far too small. *The Most Dangerous Game* was made with much of the same cast, on the *Kong* sets at night.

All of those films, and the work she'd do later, fade into the woodwork when compared to *King Kong*. Despite the incredible special effects created by Willis O'Brien, the film wouldn't be the masterpiece it is without Fay Wray's sweet, sexy, lovable presence. As the Carl Denham character says, "All right, the public wants a girl and this time, I'm going to give 'em what they want." He certainly did. Fay Wray is the right actress in the right role at the right time. You don't argue when that kind of lightening strikes. You accept it and you enjoy it.

SIGNIFICANT CONTRIBUTIONS TO HORROR

The Most Dangerous Game **(1932)**

Doctor X **(1932)**

King Kong **(1933)**

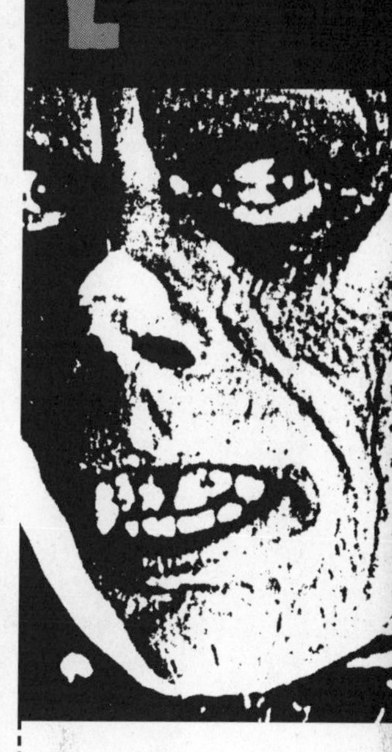

1972 (R) 84m/C *IT* Joseph Cotten, Rosalba (Sara Bay) Neri, Mickey Hargitay, Paul Muller, Herbert Fux, Renate Kasche, Ada Pometti, Lorenzo Terzon, Paul Whiteman; ***D:*** Mel Welles; ***W:*** Edward Di Lorenzo; ***C:*** Riccardo Pallton Pallottini. **VHS** *SNC, HEG*

The Lair of the White Worm

Ken Russell pits paganism (in the form of snake worship) against Christianity in a wonderfully screwy adaptation of Bram Stoker's last novel, AKA *The Garden of Evil*. When Lady Sylvia (Amanda Donohoe), "the fanged princess of darkness," arrives in contemporary England, no boy scout is safe. Our four heroes are the Trent sisters (Catherine Oxenberg and Sammi Davis), whose parents disappeared a year before, archeologist Angus Flint (Peter Capaldi), who finds a huge skull in their backyard, and Lord James (Hugh Grant), the local Pooh-Bah who's still investigating the disappearances. The plot quickly succumbs to Russell's trademark flamboyance. 🦴🦴🦴

Lady Sylvia (Amanda Donohoe) in *The Lair of the White Worm.*

1988 (R) 93m/C *GB* Amanda Donohoe, Sammi Davis, Catherine Oxenberg, Hugh Grant, Peter Capaldi, Stratford Johns, Paul Brooke, Christopher Gable; ***D:*** Ken Russell; ***W:*** Ken Russell; ***C:*** Dick Bush; ***M:*** Stanislas Syrewicz. **VHS, LV** *VES, LIV, TPV*

Last Days of Planet Earth

Japanese interpretation of the predictions of Nostradamus with a soundtrack that might have come from an Italian spy flick is every bit as gonzo as you might imagine. The film uses so much stock footage that it often looks like a documentary. But then there are the giant sea slugs and the weed-choked subway tunnels and the groovy, drug-crazed hippie love-in and the incredible exploding traffic jam. Excessive voiceover narration vainly attempts to impose logic and continuity on the plotless cataclysmic action. Virtually every line of dialogue is preachy and pedantic, finally endorsing an environmentally based totalitarianism. With so much hysterical energy in play, this craziness is seldom dull. Personally, I think the whole problem can be traced back to the heroine's thigh-high white vinyl zipper platform boots. ***AKA:*** Prophecies of Nostradamus; Catastrophe 1999; Nostradamus No Daiyogen.

1974 88m/C *JP* Tetsuro Tamba, So Yamamura, Takashi Shimura; ***D:*** Toshio Masuda. **VHS, Closed Caption** *PAR*

The Last Horror Film

Location filming at the Cannes festival and a gossipy peek at the business side of the industry are the main attractions here. Cabbie Vinny Durand (Joe Spinell) is a semi-crazed fan of Jana Bates (Caroline Munro) and a would-be filmmaker. Does he go to France to stalk the star or to make a movie deal? Whichever, someone is slicing and dicing Jana's associates. Spinell's sweaty, voyeuristic obsession seems quite real and sick, but the ideas and the writing are better than the overall execution. The film never really rises above the level of the genre. ***AKA:*** The Fanatic.

1982 (R) 87m/C Caroline Munro, Joe Spinell, Judd Hamilton, Devin Goldenberg, David Winters; ***D:*** David Winters; ***W:*** Tom Klassen, Judd Hamilton, David Winters. **VHS** *NO*

Last House on the Left

Judged by the standards of violence that it helped to establish, this early '70s psycho/revenge cheapie looks fairly tame today. Two not-so-innocent teenaged girls (Sandra Cassel and Lucy Grantham) are brutalized by a semi-comic gang of dimwits who then take refuge in the wrong place. The combination of sadistic horror, generational conflict, and "dumb" comedy is still strong stuff, however crudely made. Filmmakers Wes Craven and Sean Cunningham mean to be provocative. Their work would be more effective with less comic relief—note the goofy deputy played by video stalwart Martin Kove—but the film's influence on the low-budget horrors that would follow is undeniable. ***AKA:*** Krug and Company; Sex Crime of the Century. 🦴🦴½

1972 (R) 83m/C David Hess, Lucy Grantham, Sandra Cassel, Mark Sheffler, Fred J. Lincoln, Jeramie Rain, Gaylord St. James, Cynthia Carr, Ada Washington, Martin Kove; ***D:*** Wes Craven; ***W:*** Wes Craven; ***C:*** Victor Hurwitz. **VHS, LV** *LIV, VES, HHE*

The Lawnmower Man

In a loose retelling of *Frankenstein,* Jobe Smith (Jeff Fahey) is a slow-witted handyman whose brain power is boosted by exposure to Dr. Angelo's (Pierce Brosnan) experiments in virtual reality. The plot has almost nothing to do with Stephen King's short story—he had his name removed from the title—but the tone is faithful to his fictional territory of small towns, bullies, kids, cruelty, abuse, ominous government agencies and, of course, a big pyrotechnic finale. The video version is 30 minutes longer than the theatrical release, with more special effects and a fully developed, coherent story. Its well-deserved popularity on tape has elevated the film above cult status and into the realm of a solid mainstream hit. Followed by a sequel that's more s-f than horror, and has even less to do with King's ideas. 🦴🦴🦴½

1992 (R) 108m/C Jeff Fahey, Pierce Brosnan, Jenny Wright, Mark Bringleson, Geoffrey Lewis, Jeremy Slate, Dean Norris, Troy Evans, John Laughlin; ***D:*** Brett Leonard; ***W:*** Brett Leonard, Gimel Everett; ***C:*** Russell Carpenter. **VHS, LV, Closed Caption** *COL, FCT, MOV*

Leatherface: The Texas Chainsaw Massacre 3

Californians Michelle (Kate Hodge) and Ryan (William Butler) stop at the wrong Texas gas station and wind up in the clutches of the Sawyer family. Though the violence is just as graphic as the original with even more sophisticated production values, it's still a conventional *3*. The intentional humor further diminishes the aura of palpable dread created by the original. Spirited performances from Kate Hodge and Ken Foree are all that keep the single bone rating from being a WOOF! 🦴

1989 (R) 81m/C Kate Hodge, William Butler, Ken Foree, Tom Hudson, R.A. Mihailoff; ***D:*** Jeff Burr; ***W:*** David J. Schow; ***C:*** James L. Carter. **VHS, LV** *COL*

Legend of Boggy Creek

This semi-documentary approach to an Arkansas version of the Bigfoot legend was a hugely popular regional drive-in hit in theatrical release. It has the rough appeal of a good folktale, despite the fact that the Fouke monster, as it's called, is a guy in a gorilla suit who never does anything particularly threatening. Most of the cast appear to be nonprofessional actors playing themselves or telling what they saw over travelogue footage of a southern swamp. The local color—bottle trees, dirt roads, and doublewides—is absolutely accurate. The horror is a joke. 🦴½

1975 (G) 87m/C Willie E. Smith, John P. Nixon, John W. Gates, Jeff Crabtree, Buddy Crabtree; ***D:*** Charles B. Pierce; ***W:*** Earl E. Smith; ***C:*** Charles B. Pierce. **VHS** *LIV, MRV*

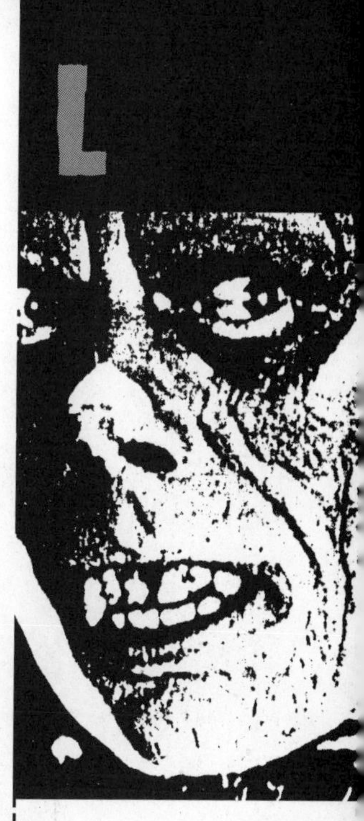

Ben Fisher (Roddy McDowall), Ann Barrett (Gayle Hunnicutt), and Dr. Chris Barrett (Clive Revill) in *The Legend of Hell House.*

The Legend of Hell House

A dying rich man hires a team of investigators to prove the existence of the afterlife in "the Mt. Everest of haunted houses." A credulous physicist (Clive Revill), his wife (Gayle Hunnicutt), a medium (Pamela Franklin), and a survivor (Roddy McDowall) of a previous examination of the house go there for a week. Richard Matheson's script is a model of efficiency, setting up characters and conflict in the first few minutes without a wasted motion. Once the group's inside the house—a marvelously well-realized place—director John Hough creates a dark, threatening atmosphere. By standards of the time set by *The Exorcist,* the action is comparatively inoffensive, but this is top-drawer, well-acted stuff. The electronic score by Brian Hodgson and Delia Derbyshire adds a lot. Two caveats: some scares resort to table-thumping, and the tape comes from a faded print. 🦴🦴🦴

1973 (PG) 94m/C Roddy McDowall, Pamela Franklin, Clive Revill, Gayle Hunnicutt, Peter Bowles, Roland Culver, Michael Gough; ***D:*** John Hough; ***W:*** Richard Matheson; ***C:*** Alan Hume; ***M:*** Brian Hodgson, Delia Derbyshire. **VHS, LV, Closed Caption** *FOX*

Legend of the Werewolf

Despite transformation and monster effects that aren't all they could be, this interpretation of the wolfman story is worth a look. As he did in *Curse of the Werewolf,* writer Anthony Hinds approaches the story realistically. Young Etoile's (David Rintoul) doomed parents are poor European political refugees. He's raised by wolves and as a boy, is taken in by a carnival barker (Hugh Griffith). The emotional upheavals of puberty spark his murderous changes. Those, of course, bring a curious pathologist (Peter Cushing) into the picture. With that strong cast, including Ron Moody, the acting is excellent and so is the story. The 19th century French settings and characters recall the paintings of Toulouse Lautrec. Unfortunately, some of the video prints look rough and faded. 🦴🦴🦴

1975 (R) 90m/C *GB* Peter Cushing, Hugh Griffith, Ron Moody, David Rintoul, Lynn Dalby, Stefan Gryff, Renee Houston, Norman Mitchell, Marjorie Yates, Roy Castle; ***D:*** Freddie Francis; ***W:*** Anthony John Elder Hinds. **VHS** *MRV*

Lemora: A Child's Tale of the Supernatural

Obscure drive-in horror is obviously made by people with more enthusiasm than experience or resources. (In an interview accompanying the film on tape, director Richard Blackburn admits as much when he describes the making of the film and its distribution in the early 1970s.) The 1930s story of devout young Christian Lila Lee's (Rainbeaux Smith) search for her gangster father is essentially a classic voyage to the underworld with a seedy bus driver serving as the Charon figure who takes her on the first steps to the title character (a memorable Leslie Gilb). Despite crude production values, the film creates an frightening, hallucinatory mood. It also skirts the exploitation elements so common in the genre (note the subtitle) and deserves its strong cult following. ***AKA:*** The Lady Dracula; The Legendary Curse of Lemora; Lemora, Lady Dracula. 🦴🦴🦴

1973 (PG) 80m/C Leslie Gilb, Cheryl "Rainbeaux" Smith, William Whitton, Steve Johnson, Hy Pyke, Maxine Ballantyne, Parker West, Richard Blackburn; ***D:*** Richard Blackburn; ***W:*** Robert Fern, Richard Blackburn; ***C:*** Robert Caramico. **VHS** *FRG*

The Leopard Man

Though many consider this Lewton-Tourneur collaboration to be less successful than either *The Cat People* or *I Walked with a Zombie,* it's cut from the same highly stylized cloth and it isn't derivative of the other two. The story—based on Cornell Woolrich's novel *Black Alibi* and more mystery than true horror—concerns murders in a New Mexico town that are blamed on an escaped leopard. A threatening aura of the unknown is strong, particularly in the famous street scenes. But the film's attempts at social criticism—"The poor don't cheat one another," a character ponderously states, "they're all poor together"—are forced, naive, and out of place. Today, the lack of location exteriors doesn't help either. 🦴🦴🦴

1943 66m/B Jean Brooks, Isabel Jewell, James Bell, Margaret Landry, Dennis O'Keefe, Margo, Rita (Paula) Corday, Abner Biberman; ***D:*** Jacques Tourneur; ***W:*** Ardel Wray; ***C:*** Robert De Grasse. **VHS, LV**

Leprechaun

Formulaic little video premiere has been the source of three sequels to date, with the threat of more to come. The poorly written story lurches into gear with a clumsy introduction and then moves to a back-lot North Dakota setting. The main attraction is the presence of cute-as-a-junebug Jennifer Aniston as Tori, the California teeny-babe trapped for the summer up there in the Northern Tier. As the title character, Warwick Davis is a nasty-looking thing. The gore is played mostly for attempted laughs; the pace is fast and fitful; and what's this shoe fetish that the little gremlin has? 🦴½

1993 (R) 92m/C Warwick Davis, Jennifer Aniston, Ken Olandt, Mark Holton, John Sanderford, Robert Gorman, Shay Duffin, John Voldstad; ***D:*** Mark Jones; ***W:*** Mark Jones; ***C:*** Levie Isaacks. **VHS, LV** *THV*

Leprechaun 2

Low-budget sequel is a definite step down from the none-too-wonderful original. On

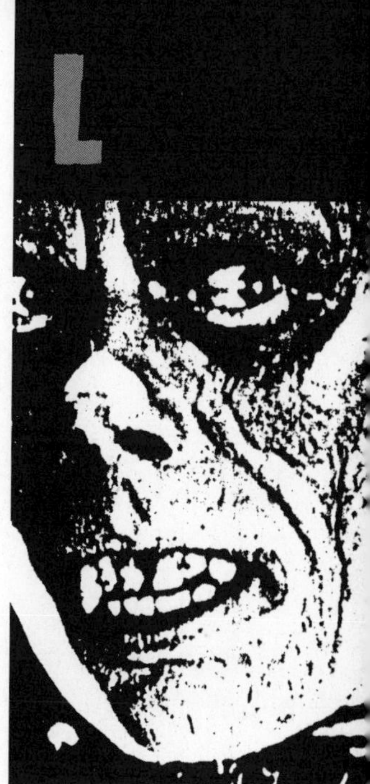

his 2,000th birthday, the grody little critter (Warwick Davis) gets "to claim his bride" if she sneezes three times. L.A. babe Bridget (Shevonne Durkin) is the lucky gal. The nasty makeup and the ridiculous fake Irish legends are the same; the sadistic sexual angle is new and unneeded. One scene directly quotes Tod Browning's *Freaks.* 🦴

1994 (R) 85m/C Warwick Davis, Sandy Baron, Adam Biesk, James Lancaster, Clint Howard, Kimmy Robertson, Charlie Heath, Shevonne Durkin; ***D:*** Rodman Flender; ***W:*** Turi Meyer, Al Septien; ***M:*** Jonathan Elias. **VHS, LV, Closed Caption** *THV*

Leprechaun 3

Third time lucky and the lame series comes up with a winner. A smart, funny script by Brian Dubos pays virtually no attention to the predecessors and moves the setting to Las Vegas where innocent student Scott (John Gatins) and magician Tammy (Lee Armstrong) come up against the short green guy (Warwick Davis). While director Brian Trenchard-Smith does a fine job with the characters and the Vegas exteriors, his budget is too meager to recreate the frenzied, full-frontal electronic assault of a casino floor. Veteran Michael Callan almost steals the show as the casino owner. 🦴🦴½

1995 (R) 93m/C Warwick Davis, John Gatins, Michael Callan, Caroline Williams, Lee Armstrong; ***D:*** Brian Trenchard-Smith; ***W:*** Brian Dubos. **VHS, LV, Closed Caption** *THV*

Leprechaun 4: In Space

Slapdash entry has virtually nothing to do with the others in the equally slapdash series. Sometime in an unspecified future, on the planet Ithacon, our short, ugly villain persuades a buxom blonde princess (Rebecca Cross) to marry him by promising to make her wealthy. (Hey, he's not the first.) Actually, the whole concept is an excuse for humor, intentional but not very funny, and O.K. effects, some involving penises and big bugs. The cast includes *Home Improvement*'s Debbe Dunning. 🦴½

1996 (R) 98m/C Warwick Davis, Rebekah Carlton, Brent Jasmer, Debbe Dunning, Rebecca Cross, Tim Colceri; ***D:*** Brian Trenchard-Smith; ***W:*** Dennis Pratt. **VHS** *THV*

Les Raisins de la Mort

Attacked by a man whose face rots before her eyes, Elizabeth (Marie-Georges Pascal) flees across a barren French countryside where she encounters more predatory zombies. Actually, this is one of the prolific Jean Rollin's better efforts, though it is squarely in the Euro-gore tradition of the 1970s. The opening scenes on an almost empty train are particularly good, and the plot recalls *Night of the Living Dead* without being imitative. In an onscreen introduction, Rollin remembers how bitterly cold it was when the film was made and that fits the bleak tone. The title refers to the wine grapes that cause the zombie plague. 🦴🦴🦴

1978 87m/C *FR* Marie-Georges Pascal, Jean Pierre Bouyou, Christian Meunier, Brigitte Lahaie, Serge Marquand, Felix Marten; ***D:*** Jean Rollin; ***W:*** Jean Rollin. **VHS** *VSM*

Leviathan

Influenced by James Cameron's *The Abyss,* a spate of underwater horror movies were released in the late 1980s. This is one of the better attempts, despite a familiar story—huge monster attacks undersea mining camp, killing the crew. Director George Cosmatos builds suspense through misdirection and downplays graphic special effects. He got good performances from a troupe of fine character actors in stock roles: competent captain (Peter Weller), joker (Daniel Stern), grumbler (Ernie Hudson), his sidekick (Michael

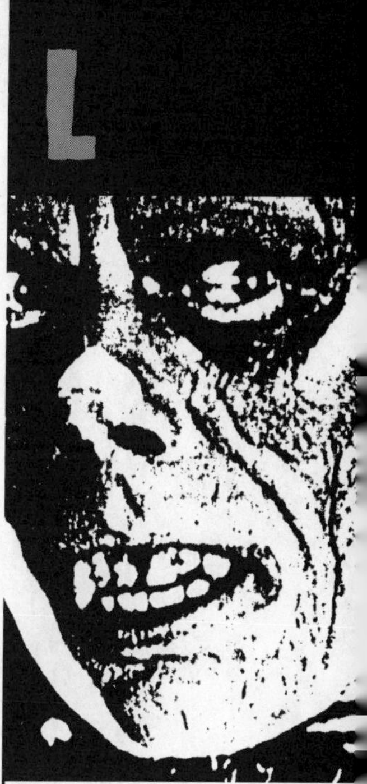

Carmine), fitness freak (Amanda Pays), Doc (Richard Crenna), worrier (Hector Elizondo), bright babe (Lisa Eilbacher), and, of course, the critter who owes a debt to *Alien*.

1989 (R) 98m/C Peter Weller, Ernie Hudson, Hector Elizondo, Amanda Pays, Richard Crenna, Daniel Stern, Lisa Eilbacher, Michael Carmine, Meg Foster; ***D:*** George P. Cosmatos; ***W:*** David Peoples, Jeb Stuart; ***C:*** Alex Thomson; ***M:*** Jerry Goldsmith. **VHS, LV, Letterboxed, Closed Caption** *MGM*

Lifeforce

Using only the bare bones of Colin Wilson's fine novel, *The Space Vampires*, screenwriters Dan O'Bannon and Don Jakoby add lots of fancy effects and a bizarre senseless ending. Capt. Carlsen (a manic Steve Railsback), of the space shuttle Churchill, discovers a huge ship with dead bat-like creatures and three bodies preserved in plastic. Back on earth, the humans reawaken and zap people. The sequence where a buck-naked Mathilda May stalks several security guards must be seen to be believed. For an hour and 40 minutes of cheap thrills, you could do worse.

1985 (R) 100m/C Steve Railsback, Peter Firth, Frank Finlay, Patrick Stewart, Michael Gothard, Nicholas Ball, Aubrey Morris, Nancy Paul, Mathilda May, John Hallam; ***D:*** Tobe Hooper; ***W:*** Dan O'Bannon, Don Jakoby; ***C:*** Alan Hume; ***M:*** Henry Mancini, Michael Kamen. **VHS, LV** *MGM*

Lifespan

Cerebral s-f/horror is too slow and talky, particularly at first, but stick with it. The story of a conspiracy and a search for an immortality drug—or "death control pill," as one character puts it—is rewarding and different. Young Dr. Benjamin Lamb (Hiram Keller) is an American in Amsterdam who tries to find the results of a dead colleague's missing research. In the process, he becomes kinkily involved with the man's mistress, Anna (Tina Aumont), and a suave menacing stranger (Klaus Kinski) from Switzerland. With his images of death, aging, Nazi atrocities, and grave robbing, director Alexander Whitelaw creates a growing atmosphere of menace. It builds a bit too deliberately to a properly unconventional ending. Whitelaw is also responsible for the unusual *Vicious Circles*.

1975 85m/C *GB* Klaus Kinski, Hiram Keller, Tina Aumont; ***D:*** Alexander Whitelaw. **VHS** *VES*

Link

In the opening scene of this English horror, producer/director Richard Franklin shows off with some flashy camera moves. And while the VideoHound isn't against chasing cats in general, he cannot condone the way the carnivorous chimp treats felines in the film. And when it does the same with dogs! Dr. Phillip (Terence Stamp) hires Jane Chase (Elisabeth Shue) to be his assistant. Guess what happens with their primate experiments at a remote seaside mansion. Even the excellent casting combined with a few good effects aren't enough to overcome the limits of the script, which calls for the human characters to aim most of their dialogue at chimps and orangutans. Stamp seems vaguely contemptuous of the material, and not without reason. For a much deeper and frightening examination of similar ideas, see George Romero's *Monkey Shines*.

1986 (R) 103m/C *GB* Elisabeth Shue, Terence Stamp, Steven Pinner, Richard Garnett; ***D:*** Richard Franklin; ***W:*** Everett DeRoche; ***C:*** Mike Molloy; ***M:*** Jerry Goldsmith. **VHS, Closed Caption** *REP*

Lisa and the Devil

Lisa Reiner (Elke Sommer), a tourist, sees a medieval fresco of a bald devil. Moments later in an antique store, she meets Telly Savalas. They're the same guy! A long dark night of discovery at an ornate mansion

Rick Moranis as Seymour Krelborn with Audrey II in Frank Oz's *Little Shop of Horrors* (1986).

ensues, and the action takes on a finely tuned surrealistic edge. According to various reports, soon after it was finished, the film was re-edited to cash in on the popularity of *The Exorcist* and has been seen only rarely in its intended form. That's a real shame because this is one of Mario Bava's most controlled, beautifully photographed, and sumptuous works. Savalas is sardonically superb. Though the film was fairly daring in its day, now the coy nudity is almost charming. At the end of the Anchor Bay edition, three key scenes of sex and violence have been salvaged. They provide an interesting look at the filmmaking process, but the end result is actually better without them. (The four-bone rating applies only to the Anchor Bay *Lisa and the Devil,* not to the *House of Exorcism* version.) ***AKA:*** The House of Exorcism; La Casa Dell' Exorcismo; The Devil and the Dead; The Devil in the House of Exorcism; El Diablo se Lleva a los Muertos; Il Diavolo e i Morti; Lisa e il Diavolo. 🦴🦴🦴🦴

1975 (R) 93m/C *IT SP* Telly Savalas, Elke Sommer, Sylva Koscina, Robert Alda, Alessio Orano, Gabriele Tinti, Eduardo Fajardo, Espartaco Santoni, Alida Valli; ***D:*** Mario Bava; ***W:*** Mario Bava, Alfred Leone; ***C:*** Cecilio Paniagua. **VHS** *VTR*

Listen

Sarah's (Brooke Langton) best pal, the slinky Krista (Sarah Buxton), expects more from their relationship, even though Sarah has just moved into her boyfriend Jake's (Gordon Currie from *Blood and Donuts*) San Francisco apartment building. At the same time, another of those pesky psycho serial killers is preying on prostitutes. Canadian director Gavin Wilding and writers Jonas Quastel and Michael Bafaro understand that the serial killer has become such a stock character that the details of that side are merely sketched in. The ending is particularly good with a "it's him—no, it's him—no, it's her—no, it's the

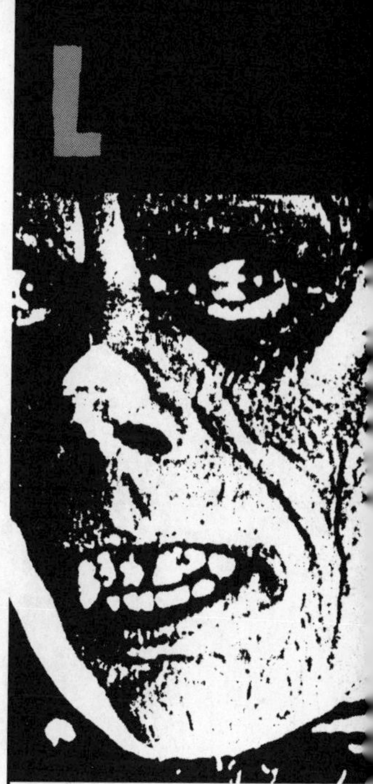

first guy!" series of twists. *Scream* fans have seen worse.

1996 (R) 104m/C Brooke Langton, Sarah Buxton, Gordon Currie, Andy Romano, Joel Wyner; ***D:*** Gavin Wilding; ***W:*** Jonas Quastel, Michael Bafaro; ***C:*** Brian Pearson; ***M:*** David Davidson. **VHS, LV** *ORI*

Little Shop of Horrors

Producer/director Roger Corman brags that he made his most famous cult hit in only two days on a leftover sound stage for a budget somewhere between $22 and $100,000. Today it's still enjoyable, with some genuinely funny gems surrounded by wall-to-wall hambone overacting. The carnivorous flower Audrey Jr. is a fair special effect that's easily upstaged by Dick Miller as a florivorous man. Beyond that—and a kinetic last reel—the action is all talk, including a fine *Dragnet* parody. The story is the basis for a hugely popular stage musical that was filmed in 1986.

1960 70m/B Jackie Joseph, Jonathan Haze, Mel Welles, Jack Nicholson, Dick Miller, Myrtle Vail; ***D:*** Roger Corman; ***W:*** Charles B. Griffith; ***C:*** Arch R. Dalzell. **VHS, LV** *VTR, NOS, HHT*

Little Shop of Horrors

This lively, funny, snappy, scary, bizarre, and surprising musical horror strikes a strange edgy tone in the first scene and maintains it all the way through. Somehow, Frank Oz is able to remain true to the double roots of his story—Roger Corman's famous cult hit and the off-Broadway play based on it—without letting a large budget and high-powered cast ruin things. As the star-crossed lovers Seymour and Audrey, Rick Moranis and Ellen Greene are very good, though they're upstaged by Steve Martin as a sadistic Elvisian dentist and, of course, Audrey II, the carnivorous houseplant that begins looking like a brussels sprout with lips and ends as a huge, tentacled monster. Great songs. (A planned DVD release may restore the original "dark" ending.)

1986 (PG-13) 94m/C Rick Moranis, Ellen Greene, Vincent Gardenia, Steve Martin, James Belushi, Christopher Guest, Bill Murray, John Candy, Tisha Campbell, Tichina Arnold, Michelle Weeks; ***D:*** Frank Oz; ***W:*** Howard Ashman; ***C:*** Bob Paynter; ***M:*** Miles Goodman, Alan Menken, Howard Ashman; ***V:*** Levi Stubbs Jr. Nominations: Academy Awards '86: Best Song ("Mean Green Mother from Outer Space"). **VHS, LV, Closed Caption** *WAR, HMV, MVD*

Little Witches

Low-budget overachiever unashamedly rips off the sleeper hit *The Craft*. The stories are essentially identical and so are the filmmakers' mostly non-exploitative approaches to the material. Finding themselves with time on their hands over Easter break, Catholic schoolgirls led by the naughty Jamie (Sheeri Rappaport) and the nice Faith (Mimi Reichenmeister) unearth an ancient demon and form a coven. With a few exceptions, the young actresses are pretty good. As she proved with *Number One Fan,* director Jane Simpson is able to invest low-budget material with style and spirit. Some of the effects are laughable, and the ending is weak, but for a genre piece, it's O.K.

1996 (R) 91m/C Mimi Reichmeister, Jack Nance, Jennifer Rubin, Sheeri Rappaport, Melissa Taub, Zoe Alexander, Zelda Rubinstein, Eric Pierpont; ***D:*** Jane Simpson; ***W:*** Brian DiMuccio, Dino Vindeni; ***M:*** Nicholas Rivera. **VHS** *APX*

The Lodger

Like so much of Hitchcock's work, this early silent thriller blurs the lines between horror and mystery. Loosely based on Jack the Ripper, it's a serial killer tale. The title

THE HOUND SALUTES

ANCHOR BAY

Though it's certainly not the VideoHound's policy to give one studio or distributor preference over another, when it comes to vintage horror on video, one label stands out—Anchor Bay Entertainment.

In 1995, the organization began searching out the rights for older "cult" titles, many of them horror, to restore to their finest quality. The first was George Romero's *Night of the Living Dead*. The copyright is in public domain and so different editions now fill the bargain bins at tape stores, but the Anchor Bay edition is the only one made from the original negative.

Among the company's current restorations are Lucio Fulci's *Zombie*, *Daughters of Darkness*, Hammer's *Plague of the Zombies*, *Dracula, Prince of Darkness*, and *The Reptile*. They all look great, and that's the point.

Horror fans, by nature, tend to venture out of the mainstream, to search out those offbeat titles that promise the seldom-seen. And most fans have been disappointed, if not by the content of the films, then by the overall grubbiness of the image. It doesn't matter whether the movie in question is seen on tape or at a midnight screening. Prints get scratched and banged up, and they're often transferred to video with less-than-perfect attention to detail.

Through the efforts of vice president Jay Douglas and producer/director/preservationist William Lustig, Anchor Bay is fighting that tide. They're trying to save their favorites where they can acquire the rights. It often means chasing down different prints and negatives, and putting together the best "elements" of each to make a complete version.

In an interview, Lustig said, "The major distributors are unaware of the cult following of

character (Ivor Novello) may be "The Avenger" who murders blonde women. He has a strongly vampiric appearance, both ominous and seductive. The familiar Hitchcock themes emerge—fear of police, the blonde heroine, the man who wants to control her, the innocent on the run from the law—and his simple, effective methods of building suspense are already in place. Note the what's-in-the-box scene. Interestingly, at one point, the Lodger wears what appears to be a Freddy Krueger sweater. Hitch shows up in a newsroom and in a crowd scene on a bridge. ***AKA:*** The Case of Jonathan Drew; The Lodger: A Case of London Fog. 🦴🦴🦴

1926 91m/B *GB* Ivor Novello, Marie Ault, Arthur Chesney, Malcolm Keen, June; ***Cameos:*** Alfred Hitchcock; ***D:*** Alfred Hitchcock; ***W:*** Alfred Hitchcock, Eliot Stannard. **VHS** *VYY, NOS, GPV*

Lord of Illusions

Clive Barker delivers the particular kind of horror that his fans seem to love in this supernatural tale of sadomasochism, torture, and self-mutilation, with a strong undercurrent of kinky homosexuality. Nix (Daniel von Bargen) is a Mansonesque cult leader with unattractive followers in 1982. Flash forward a dozen or so years to the film's present where Harry D'Amour (Scott Bakula), a private detective with a bent for

many of the films that they own. Or because the films were licensed prior to video, the rights are in a cloudy area. It becomes a stalemate between the distributor and many times, the now-defunct production company or the no-longer-existing licensors. I've been trying to license films that have fallen through the cracks, and seeking out the problems for each of these films."

He has found some good ones, and there are more out there to be found.

Anchor Bay titles are usually packaged in a modified light plastic clamshell box with a removable paper sleeve. Many of them contain extra elements—deleted scenes, trailers, etc.—and they're priced for sale.

Fans may well disagree with all of the choices the company has made, but they won't deny the value of its efforts.

As this book was going to print, Anchor Bay had just announced new editions of *The Night Stalker* and *The Night Strangler*, widescreen versions of *Q, the Winged Serpent*, Hammer's *Satanic Rites of Dracula, Legend of the Seven Golden Brothers* and *The Seven Brothers Meet Dracula, The Devil Rides Out, Frankenstein Created Woman*, Jess Franco's *Succubus* and *Kiss Me, Monster*, George Romero's *The Crazies* and *Season of the Witch*, Cronenberg's *Shivers*, Herzog's *Nosferatu* (in both German and English), and a special 20th anniversary two-tape edition of *Halloween*.

For fans, these tapes are worth extra effort to find.

SIGNIFICANT CONTRIBUTIONS TO HORROR

Dracula, Prince of Darkness **(1966)**

The Lost Continent **(1968)**

Night of the Living Dead **(1968)**

Daughters of Darkness **(1971)**

Lisa and the Devil **(1975)**

Halloween **(1978)**

Zombie **(1980)**

the supernatural, is recovering from an exorcism he assisted. A flimsy pretext involves him with a magician (Kevin J. O'Connor) and his wife (Famke Janssen). Several other folks are killed in the course of Harry's "investigation," but that's really too strong a word to apply to the plot. Though there's virtually no intentional humor in the film, one of the main bad guys runs around in skintight gold lame pants, and the big finish is a drawn-out affair with about a dozen you-think-he's-dead-but-he's-not cinematic cliches. Barker's characters are thin and the dialogue is pedestrian. ***AKA:*** Clive Barker's Lord of Illusions. 🦴

1995 (R) 109m/C Scott Bakula, Famke Janssen, Kevin J. O'Connor, Daniel von Bargen, Joel Swetow, Barry Sherman, Jordan Marder, Joseph Latimore, Vincent Schiavelli; ***D:*** Clive Barker; ***W:*** Clive Barker; ***C:*** Ronn Schmidt. **VHS, LV, Closed Caption** *MGM*

The Lost Boys

Joel Schumacher says, "My fear was that I'd wake up in the middle of the night and thinking, My God, you wanted to make *Lawrence of Arabia* and *Grand Illusion* and you're making a teenage vampire movie. Now, can we make the greatest teenage vampire in the history of the world?" He may not have accomplished that goal—*Near Dark* comes to mind—but this one's

"**One thing about living in Santa Carla I could never stomach was all the damn vampires.**"

—Grandpa's (Barnard Hughes) coda in *The Lost Boys.*

O.K. Michael (Jason Patric) and Sam (Corey Haim) move with their divorced mom (Dianne Wiest) to Santa Carla, California—"the murder capital of the world"—and discover a gang of undead adolescents led by David (Kiefer Sutherland). Schumacher and d.p. Michael Chapman make the flimsy material look much better than it actually is with some dandy visual tricks, and the young cast isn't bad, either. Still, the story relies so much on Hollywood conventions that it's easy to predict what's going to happen, and the big finish is equally stereotyped stuff.

1987 (R) 97m/C Jason Patric, Kiefer Sutherland, Corey Haim, Jami Gertz, Dianne Wiest, Corey Feldman, Barnard Hughes, Edward Herrmann, Billy Wirth, Jamison Newlander, Brooke McCarter, Alex Winter; ***D:*** Joel Schumacher; ***W:*** Jeffrey Boam, Janice Fischer, James Jeremias; ***C:*** Michael Chapman; ***M:*** Thomas Newman. **VHS, LV, 8mm, Letterboxed, Closed Caption** *WAR, FUS*

Lost Continent

Hammer's most bizarre production is impossible to describe. It begins with a wildly inappropriate theme song and electric organ score that could have come from Happy Hour at a motel cocktail lounge. That introduces a group of characters from a Graham Greene novel inexplicably transplanted into a seagoing Edgar Rice Burroughs plot. A leaky freighter is en route to Caracas with a dangerous explosive cargo, five desperate passengers with secrets of their own, a troubled, cynical captain (Eric Porter), and a mutinous crew. On the horizon lie a hurricane, carnivorous seaweed, religious persecution, and giant man-eating mollusks. The whole thing is every bit as strange, screwy, and wonderful as it sounds. No, it's not completely successful but it's never dull. The Anchor Bay transfer to tape is absolutely clear and slightly letterboxed. The print also contains eight minutes that were too "adult" for American audiences in 1968.

1968 97m/C Eric Porter, Hildegarde Knef, Suzanna Leigh, Tony Beckley, Nigel Stock, Neil McCallum, Ben Carruthers, Jimmy Hanley, Dana Gillespie; ***D:*** Michael Carreras; ***W:*** Michael Nash; ***C:*** Paul Beeson. **VHS, Letterboxed** *VTR*

Lost Highway

David Lynch's surreal horror is a noirish mystery without answers, told through the "logic" of a nightmare. To enjoy the film, if that's possible, viewers must forget about narrative conventions and accept Lynch's dreamy evocation of 3:00 a.m. nightworld delirium where nothing is certain. In the opening scene, a voice over an intercom tells saxophonist Fred Madison (Bill Pullman) "Dick Laurent is dead." Fred suspects that his sultry brunette wife Renee (Patricia Arquette) is unfaithful. A spooky pop-eyed pasty-faced Mystery Man (Robert Blake) further muddies the waters before Fred is inexplicably transformed into young mechanic Pete Dayton (Balthazar Getty), who falls for Alice (Patricia Arquette again), platinum blonde moll of the vicious mobster Mr. Eddy (Robert Loggia who, according to the credits, is also the aforementioned Dick Laurent). Throughout, the sex is hot and graphic, and so is the violence. Those, of course, are Lynch's stock and trade. This one may please his most rabid fans, but it's unlikely to win many converts to the cause.

1996 (R) 135m/C Bill Pullman, Patricia Arquette, Balthazar Getty, Robert Loggia, Robert (Bobby) Blake, Gary Busey, Jack Nance, Richard Pryor, Natasha Gregson Wagner, Lisa Boyle, Michael Massee, Jack Kehler, Henry Rollins, Gene Ross, Scott Coffey; ***D:*** David Lynch; ***W:*** David Lynch, Barry Gifford; ***C:*** Peter Deming; ***M:*** Angelo Badalamenti. **VHS, LV, Closed Caption** *PGV*

The Lost World: Jurassic Park 2

This clumsily plotted sequel has more dinosaurs, tinier dinosaurs, faster dinosaurs, cuter dinosaurs, and hungrier dinosaurs than the first film. It also has a ridiculous ending that falls apart completely. Two competing groups—noble scientists and nasty hunters—go to another island where dinosaurs flourish. The first bunch is led by a reluctant Ian Malcolm (Jeff Goldblum) and Kelly, his 12-year-old black daughter (Vanessa Lee Chester). With them are Sarah (Julianne Moore), his socio-paleontologist girlfriend; brave Greenpeace video-documentarian Nick (Vince Vaughn); and "equipment systems specialist" Eddie (Richard Schiff). (That cockamamie collection of cinematic diversity says a lot about the film's lapses.) The human characters aren't as interesting as the dinosaurs created by Dennis Muren, Stan Winston, and Michael Lantieri. They were responsible for the critters in the original, and their new work is even more lifelike, complex, and believable. Regarding the film's violence, younger children who could handle the original will be fine with this one. Will they be scared? Sure they will. It's a monster movie; they're supposed to be scared. They'll see one guy turned into T-Rex toejam, and several others are eaten. But Spielberg never dwells on the harsher moments or stages them too vividly. ***AKA:*** Jurassic Park 2. 🦴🦴½

1997 (PG-13) 129m/C Jeff Goldblum, Julianne Moore, Vince Vaughn, Arliss Howard, Pete Postlethwaite, Peter Stormare, Vanessa Lee Chester, Richard Schiff; ***D:*** Steven Spielberg; ***W:*** David Koepp; ***C:*** Janusz Kaminski; ***M:*** John Williams. **VHS, LV, Letterboxed, Closed Caption, DVD** *USH*

Lurkers

The first part of this repulsive little movie is focused on the emotional and psychological abuses that cause horrible nightmares in a little girl. When she grows up, she's haunted. Childhood fears are the source of almost all horror stories, but this presentation is unnecessarily brutal and ugly. Your VCR has a fast-forward button. Use it. **Woof!**

1988 (R) 90m/C Christine Moore, Gary Warner, Marina Taylor, Carissa Channing, Tom Billett; ***D:*** Roberta Findlay; ***W:*** Ed Kelleher, Hariette Vidal; ***C:*** Roberta Findlay. **VHS** *NO*

Lurking Fear

Transylvanian locations don't really work for an adaptation of one of horror master H.P. Lovecraft's better stories. The setting is supposed to be America, and several scenes just don't look right. Also, Lovecraftians will be appalled at the liberties that were taken. His frightening tale has been turned it into a crime movie, with lots of shoot-'em-up violence and grotesque special effects, along the lines of Robert Rodriguez's *From Dusk Till Dawn*. It's about a group of less-than-completely sympathetic characters trapped underground by zombie-like creatures. That is not what HPL had in mind. Still, for today's horror fans who like lots of gore, the production values are solid. 🦴🦴

1994 (R) 78m/C Jon Finch, Blake Bailey, Ashley Lauren, Jeffrey Combs, Paul Mantee, Allison Mackie, Joe Leavengood, Vincent Schiavelli; ***D:*** C. Courtney Joyner; ***W:*** C. Courtney Joyner; ***M:*** Jim Manzie. **VHS, LV** *PAR*

Lust for a Vampire

Hammer's follow up to the lesbo-erotic *Vampire Lovers* is a weak vehicle made without the studio's usually solid plotting. The initial reconstitution of a dead vampire has been done before and much more elaborately. Most of the action is set in a girl's school, giving the producers license to have the young ladies indulge in assorted toplessness, back rubs, and one wrongheaded bit of interpretive dance. Seductress Carmilla (Yutte Stensgaard) is blandly, blondly pretty, and she tends to cross her eyes when feigning ecstasy which is kind of cute. It's obvious throughout that the filmmakers are going through familiar motions. Not Hammer's finest hour, but one of its sexier. ***AKA:*** To Love a Vampire. 🦴🦴

1971 (R) 95m/C *GB* Ralph Bates, Barbara Jefford, Suzanna Leigh, Michael Johnson, Yutte Stensgaard, Pippa Steele, Helen Christie, David Healy, Mike Raven;

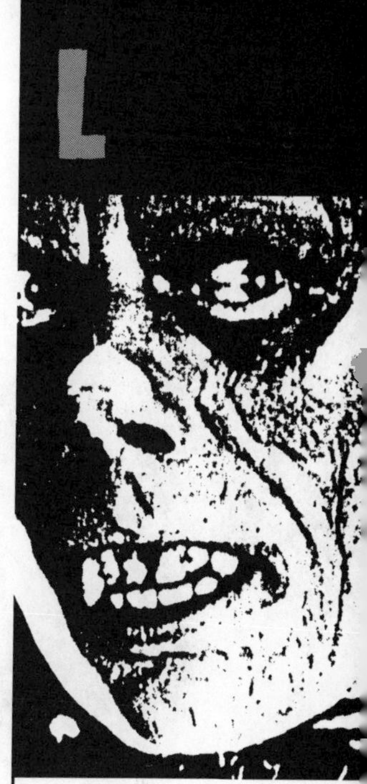

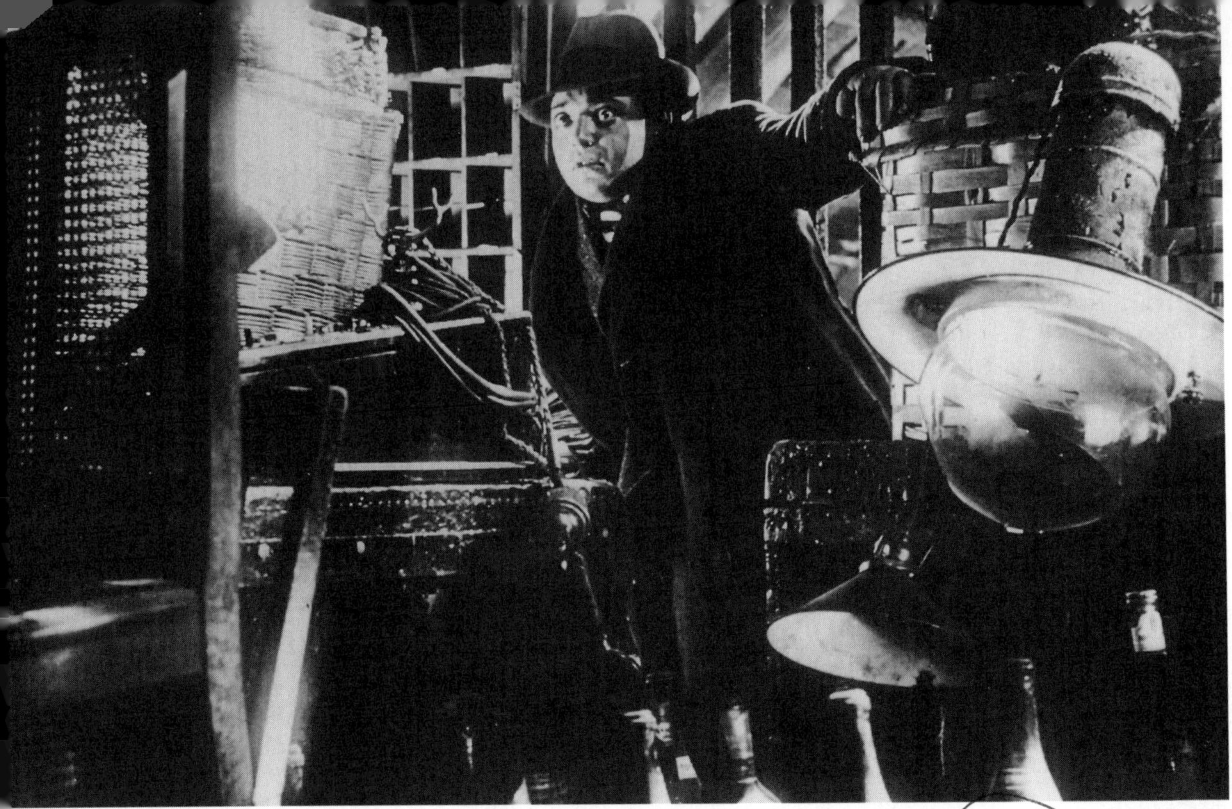

Franz Beckert (Peter Lorre) in *M*.

D: Jimmy Sangster; ***W:*** Tudor Gates; ***C:*** David Muir. **VHS, LV** *MLB*

Luther the Geek

Bizarre little 1990 production has earned itself a strong underground reputation. Here, the word "geek" is used in its original meaning. Forget nerds; it actually refers to carnival performers who bite the heads off of live animals, usually chickens. That's what the title character does. He's also a homicidal maniac who sets his sights on a rural midwestern farm house. The result might have been titled *The Chainsaw Massacres of Madison County.* Director Carlton Albright aims for that same Grand Guignol combination of sex and violence. The presence of Stacy Haiduk doesn't hurt a bit.

1990 90m/C Edward Terry, Joan Roth, J. Jerome Clarke, Tom Mills, Stacy Haiduk; ***D:*** Carlton J. Albright; ***W:*** Whitey Styles; ***C:*** David Knox. **VHS** *DAP*

M

With a fact-based story, Fritz Lang set the formula for the serial killer crime-horror film in 1931. Franz Beckert (Peter Lorre) is a compulsive child murderer whose crimes paralyze a city. When the cops clamp down on the local underworld, the crooks decide to catch the killer themselves. Lang tells the story by intercutting between the various forces involved, but at the horrific heart of it is Lorre's brilliant performance as a human monster. Though the film was released in the same year as Lugosi's *Dracula,* it's by far the more frightening of the two today. Lorre embodies many of the evils that Lugosi symbolizes. At the beginning, Lang uses starkly simple images—a ball, a balloon, an empty dinner plate—to convey the enormity of the crimes. Then Lang turns things around with Lorre's haunted confession. At the end, when various parties comment on the terrible crimes, they frame a debate that's still going on today. *M* is simply one of the world's great films, not to mention how suspenseful and entertaining it is. Several labels carry the title and they vary in quality. In 1997, the film was restored with an extra scene replaced at the end. The Home Vision Cinema edition of that version has been beautifully remastered, and is the best available on tape. 🦴🦴🦴🦴

1931 111m/B *GE* Peter Lorre, Ellen Widmann, Inge Landgut, Gustav Grundgens, Otto Wernicke, Ernest Stahl-Nachbaur, Franz Stein, Theodore Loos, Fritz Gnass, Fritz Odemar, Paul Kemp, Theo Lingen, Georg John, Karl Platen, Rosa Valetti, Hertha von Walther, Rudolf Blumner; ***D:*** Fritz Lang; ***W:*** Fritz Lang, Thea von Harbou; ***C:*** Fritz Arno Wagner, Gustav Rathje; ***M:*** Edvard Grieg. **VHS** *HMV, NOS, HHT*

Macbeth

The Scottish accents lay it on a bit thick, but Orson Welles' *Macbeth* is a horror film from the first image of witches mixing "hellbroth" and producing a crude statue of Macbeth (Welles), and then Macbeth's admitting his own "deep black desires." Welles emphasizes the supernatural aspects of the story as graphically as the times would allow. Both he and Jeanette Nolan, as the sexy Lady Macbeth, play their characters as creatures of monstrous ambition. The wet, rough, labyrinthine sets are inspired. On tape, the 45th anniversary edition was restored by the UCLA Film Archives and the Folger Shakespeare Library in Washington to the sharp but inky clarity that Welles intended. 🦴🦴🦴

1948 111m/B Orson Welles, Jeanette Nolan, Dan O'Herlihy, Roddy McDowall, Robert Coote; ***D:*** Orson Welles. **VHS, LV** *REP, TVC*

Macbeth

Roman Polanski chooses a striking variation on the standard view of the witches to begin his version of "The Scottish Play." The rest of his telling is more realistic than Orson Welles' dark, stylized interpretation. The muddy, cold, rain-soaked look of the Middle Ages has rarely been realized more believably. The violence is presented in all its stark horror. Polanski and co-writer Kenneth Tynan have the murder of Duncan appear onscreen. At the same time, hallucinations and images of blindness occur throughout. Jon Finch and Francesca Annis are excellent in the leads, though at almost two and a half hours, this is a long hike. Also, the film was made in Todd-AO 35 widescreen and key scenes suffer in the pan-and-scan transfer. 🦴🦴🦴

1971 (R) 139m/C Jon Finch, Nicholas Selby, Martin Shaw, Francesca Annis, Terence Baylor; ***D:*** Roman Polanski; ***W:*** Roman Polanski, Kenneth Tynan. **VHS, LV** *COL, HMV*

Mad at the Moon

Irritating attempt at "serious" horror sinks under a leaden pace. It takes more than 10 minutes for the first action of any consequence to take place; 50 minutes for the putative subject to appear. For a plot, combine *Madame Bovary* with *The Wolf Man* in an Old West setting. Does Jenny's (Mary Stuart Masterson) husband James (Stephen Blake) become a wolf? If so, should she leave him for the hunky Miller (Hart Bochner), a dubious prairie Fabio? To show that these characters are caught in the grip of seismic emotions, director Martin Donovan (who also made the riveting *Apartment Zero*) indulges in long non-riveting static shots where they stare moodily at nothing in particular. Despite noble intentions, it's boring, boring, boring. 🦴

1992 (R) 98m/C Mary Stuart Masterson, Hart Bochner, Fionnula Flanagan, Cec Verrell, Stephen Blake; ***D:*** Martin Donovan; ***W:*** Martin Donovan, Richard Pelusi. **VHS, LV, Closed Caption** *REP*

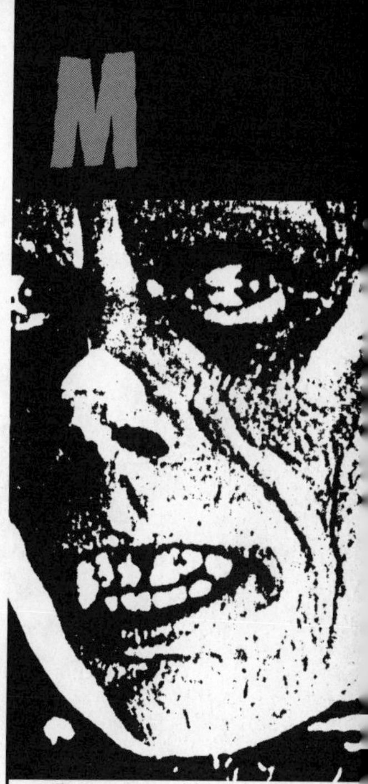

THE HOUND SALUTES

PETER LORRE

Given his immediately identifiable appearance, voice, and accent, it's odd that Peter Lorre didn't do more work in horror. But in his busy career, he really had only a handful of films in the genre. They were of uniformly high quality, from his masterful debut to the concluding comedies.

He was born Laszlo Lowenstein on June 26, 1904, in the Carpathian Mountains of Hungary. As a teenager he left home hoping to find work in the Vienna theatre, but the crushing economic conditions of the time made it difficult. Still, he got a job at a bank and founded a small improvisational group that gave him some experience. By the late 1920s, he was married and working regularly on the Berlin stage. In 1930, as he was preparing a Bertolt Brecht play, he was approached by Fritz Lang who gave him the script for *M*, written by Lang's wife Thea von Harbou.

The film, powered by Lorre's brilliant performance as a serial child murderer, remains one of the greats. Lorre is a terrifying, tortured villain. He and Lang slyly manipulate the audience's emotions and expectations by first making the horror of the crimes so tangible and then subtly forcing us at least to recognize the killer's helpless motivations. In many ways, *M* was decades ahead of its time. The serial killer has become a much more recognizable stereotype in recent years, but he's never been examined with such care.

Lorre, however, was caught up in the politics of the time, and as Nazism came to power in Germany, he left. He went first to France, then to England where he worked with Alfred Hitchcock on the first version of *The Man Who Knew Too Much*, and finally to Hollywood.

Mad Doctor of Blood Island

"Now the Mad Doctor of Blood Island invites YOU to join him in taking the OATH of GREEN BLOOD... I, a living breathing creature of the cosmic entity, am now ready to enter the realm of those chosen to be allowed to drink of the Mystic Emerald fluids herein offered. I join the Order of Green Blood with an open mind and through this liquid's powers am now prepared to safely view the unnatural green-blooded ones without fear of contamination." Unfortunately, that onscreen introduction is the best part of this campy, politically incorrect Philippine import. It's a standard mad scientist story with a guy in a cheap monster mask and gloves. The directors are fond of an unwatchable pulsing in and out zoom to introduce the critter. The film is also an early appearance of cult favorite Angelique Pettyjohn, who died in 1992. ***AKA:*** Tomb of the Living Dead; Blood Doctor.

1969 110m/C *PH* John Ashley, Ronald Remy, Alicia Alonzo, Alfonso Carvajal, Angelique Pettyjohn; ***D:*** Gerardo (Gerry) De Leon, Eddie Romero; ***C:*** Justo Paulino. **VHS** *NO*

Mad Love

Yvonne Orlac (Frances Drake) is the reigning "scream queen" of the Parisian Grand Guignol stage. The ominous Dr. Gogol

His first studio film was the wonderful *Mad Love,* where he played the unhinged surgeon Dr. Gogol—with a smoothly shaved, egg-shaped head and memorable makeup (including mechanical hands)—who gives pianist Colin Clive a new pair of hands. After it, perhaps resisting the industry's inevitable type-casting, he became the Japanese detective Mr. Moto in a series of films. In 1941, he returned to horror of a sort in Robert Florey's *The Face Behind the Mask,* unavailable on video. That same year, he had his best American role as the lispingly lethal fop Joel Cairo in *The Maltese Falcon.* Then he had a small part in a little movie that nobody ever watches called *Casablanca.*

He and Florey returned to the perennially popular crazy-pianist-with-evil-hands plot for *The Beast with Five Fingers* in 1946. Throughout the '50s, he was seen in bigger budget films like *20,000 Leagues under the Sea,* and he didn't do any more work in horror until the mid-'60s with the American International comedies *The Raven, Tales of Terror,* and *Comedy of Terrors.* They are at best acceptable light entertainment, and, near the end of his career, a tired-looking Lorre seemed to be having fun with them.

In Roger Corman's book *How I Made 100 Movies in Hollywood and Never Lost a Dime* (Random House, 1990), he and Jack Nicholson recall that during the making of *The Raven,* Lorre's improvisational skills were still sharp. He and Nicholson played fast and loose with the script, much to the displeasure of their co-star, Boris Karloff.

SIGNIFICANT CONTRIBUTIONS TO HORROR

M **(1931)**

Mad Love **(1935)**

The Beast with Five Fingers **(1946)**

The Raven **(1963)**

(Peter Lorre in perhaps his most impressive and commanding role after *M*) is her biggest fan and his devotion is, indeed, mad love. Though the oft-filmed plot involves Gogol's transplanting hands onto her pianist husband Stephen (Colin Clive), the film belongs to Lorre. The main flaw is the comic relief of the period. The black-and-white photography is superb, and some of the sets are impressive, but nothing onscreen tops Lorre's eggshell-smooth bald dome, and the makeup he wears toward the end. ***AKA:*** The Hands of Orlac.

1935 70m/B Peter Lorre, Colin Clive, Frances Drake, Ted Healy, Edward Brophy, Sara Haden, Henry Kolker; ***D:*** Karl Freund; ***W:*** P.J. Wolfson, John L. Balderston, Guy Endore; ***C:*** Gregg Toland, Chester Lyons. **VHS** *MGM*

The Maddening

Wretched little suspense/horror movie is more distasteful than frightening. At core, it's a hostage story about a delusional couple (Burt Reynolds and Angie Dickinson at their all-time hammiest) who kidnap a young woman (Mia Sara) and her little girl. Though the material isn't handled as pure exploitation, it contains some out-of-place humor and graphic violence specifically aimed at women and children. That is not entertainment. Fortunately, the whole thing is so inept that it's not as offensive as it might have been. Director Danny Huston is the son of John. **Woof!**

1995 (R) 97m/C Burt Reynolds, Angie Dickinson, Mia Sara, Brian Wimmer, Josh Mostel, William Hickey;

Fats the dummy and Corky Withers (Anthony Hopkins) in *Magic*.

D: Danny Huston; ***W:*** Leslie Greif. **VHS, LV, Closed Caption** *THV*

Madhouse Mansion

Curiously mannered horror/comedy is so British, with indecipherable accents and customs, that the beginning makes virtually no sense. In the 1920s, three snotty young aristocratic twits—Talbot (Larry Dann), Duller (Vivian Mackerell), and McFayden (Murray Melvin)—go to stay at a strange house in Wales where ghosts, or something, appear. Initially, one of them, Miss Sophie (Marianne Faithful), is in danger of falling out of her decolletage. But once she changes clothes even that limited suspense disappears. The script refers to the stories of M.R. James, and the film has a little of that intellectual spookiness, but not enough. In fact, several scenes look like Monty Python skits without the humor. Barbara Shelley, familiar from Hammer films, plays two small roles. ***AKA:*** Ghost Story. 🦴🦴🦴

1974 (PG) 86m/C *GB* Marianne Faithfull, Leigh Lawson, Anthony Bate, Larry Dann, Sally Grace, Penelope Keith, Vivian Mackerell, Murray Melvin, Barbara Shelley; ***D:*** Stephen Weeks; ***C:*** Peter Hurst. **VHS** *NO*

Magic

The strengths of this psychological horror are writer William Goldman's solid knowledge of the working side of show business and his typically well-constructed plot. On the other side of the camera are three terrific performances by Anthony Hopkins as Corky Withers, the magician with deep problems; Ann-Margret as Peg Snow, the girl from his past; and Burgess Meredith as Ben Greene, his caring agent. If Richard Attenborough's direction is a bit too studied, the story is compelling, and the whole film has that rough unpolished quality that makes good '70s movies so rewatchable.

The upstate New York locations are fine, and the emotional underpinnings of the story are unusual but accurate. 🦴🦴🦴

1978 (R) 106m/C Anthony Hopkins, Ann-Margret, Burgess Meredith, Ed Lauter, Jerry Houser, David Ogden Stiers, Lillian Randolph; ***D:*** Richard Attenborough; ***W:*** William Goldman; ***C:*** Victor Kemper; ***M:*** Jerry Goldsmith. **VHS, LV** *NO*

The Majorettes

As the title indicates, this is an unashamed slasher flick notable only for its large cast of unknowns and the cliched killer's p.o.v. Seconds after the opening credits have rolled, the girls hit the showers. Minutes later, the first throat is slashed. The young actresses seem so obviously uncomfortable and embarrassed by the nudity that the film's voyeurism has a sick edge. The ending with the killer gazing ominously at prepubescent girls underscores that side. The plot doesn't depart from the formula until the last act. The rest is too slow and too talky. That's director John Russo as the coroner. **Woof!**

1987 (R) 93m/C Kevin Kindlan, Terrie Godfrey, Mark V. Jevicky, Sueanne Seamans, John Russo, Bill Hinzman, Russell Streiner; ***D:*** Bill Hinzman; ***W:*** John Russo. **VHS** *LIV, VES, TEM*

Man Beast

Though he's not as famous as Ed Wood, Jr., back in the '50s, Jerry Warren made low-budget horror/s-f flicks that were just as silly as the master's. In this Abominable Snowman tale, the heroine (Virginia Maynor) sits around a Tibetan hut in a sleeveless dress; people climb the Himalayas in windbreakers; and the Yetis are guys in exceptionally shaggy suits. The scant physical action is clunky. The Acme Video edition is recorded in the substandard EP mode which, in this case, is appropriate. **Woof!**

1955 65m/B Rock Madison, Virginia Maynor, George Skaff, Lloyd Nelson, Tom Maruzzi; ***D:*** Jerry Warren. **VHS** *NOS, MRV, RHI*

Man Made Monster

"Dynamo Dan" McCormick (Lon Chaney, Jr.) is already a carnival star when he survives a bus crash into a high tension power pole. The evil "electrobiologist" Dr. Rigas (Lionel Atwill) subjects him to experiments that make Dan a voltage junkie of enormous strength. The result is a crazed variation on *Frankenstein* with indescribable effects. The whole idea of a character invulnerable to electrocution was popular in the early days of cinematic horror. This is neither the best nor the worst example, made with the studio's usual high standards and tightfisted budget. ***AKA:*** Atomic Monster; The Electric Man. 🦴🦴½

1941 61m/B Lon Chaney Jr., Lionel Atwill, Anne Nagel, Frank Albertson, Samuel S. Hinds; ***D:*** George Waggner; ***W:*** Joseph West; ***C:*** Elwood Bredell. **VHS, Closed Caption** *USH*

The Mangler

Big-budget horror from director Tobe Hooper is remarkably incompetent. Almost everything about the film is a mistake, so it's hard to know where to begin. Why not start with the accents? The dubbing is so goofy that somehow, all the characters sound like refugees from an Italian gladiator movie. The aimless plot, loosely based on a Stephen King short story, has to do with a laundry machine possessed by demons, and its sidekick, an old icebox. Nasal cop Ted Levine knows that laundry owner Robert Englund is somehow causing people to be chewed up by the thing. Near the end, when the heroes are spouting Latin to exorcize the demons from the mangler, it sounds for all the world like one of them says, "In Excelsis Fats Domino." Also available in an unrated version. **Woof!**

1994 (R) 106m/C Robert Englund, Ted Levine, Daniel Matmor, Vanessa Pike, Demetre Phillips, Lisa Morris, Ashley Hayden, Vera Blacker; ***D:*** Tobe Hooper; ***W:*** Tobe Hooper, Peter Welbeck, Stephen Brooks; ***C:*** Amnon Salomon; ***M:*** Barrington Pheloung. **VHS, LV, Closed Caption** *NLC, TTC, IME*

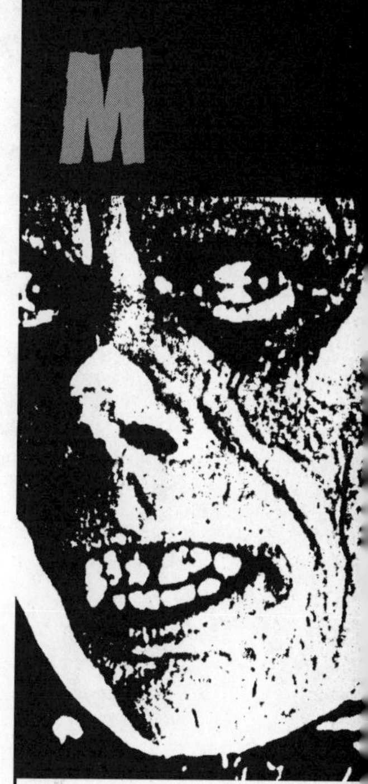

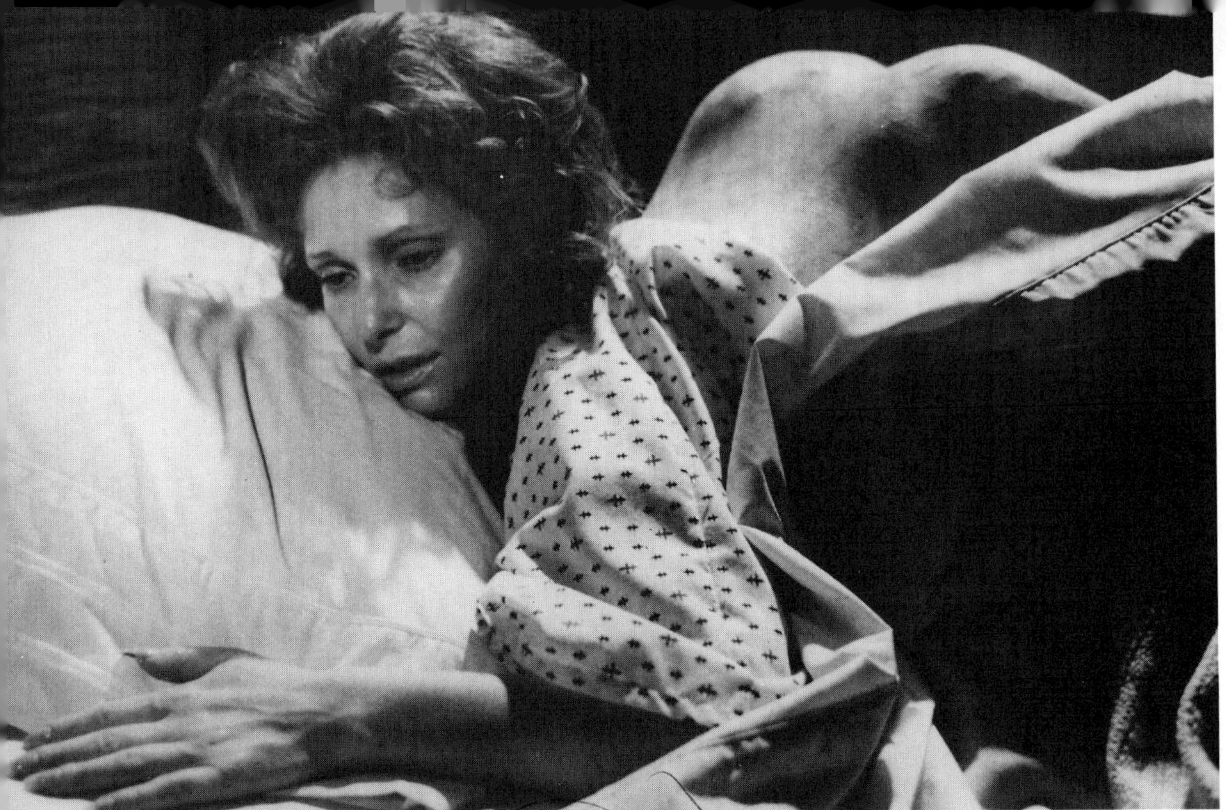

Karen (Susan Strasberg) agonizes over the mysterious growth on her back in *The Manitou.*

Manhunter

Michael Mann's slick psycho-killer film wasn't the huge popular hit that Jonathan Demme's *Silence of the Lambs* became, but it's still a well-made crime/horror tale. Both films tell the same story—FBI agent (William Petersen) enlists the help of jailed psychotic genius Hannibal Lecktor (sic) (deftly underplayed by Brian Cox) in nabbing another psycho. Both films also attempt to get inside the mind of today's most popular stock villain, the serial killer. And, of course, both are based on Thomas Harris' fine novels. (*Silence* is the sequel to *Red Dragon,* the source for *Manhunter.*) Mann is an inventive stylist who can pump up ordinary scenes with pastel light, odd camera angles, and the like. But those same tricks keep him from getting to the emotional core that Jodie Foster, Anthony Hopkins, and Demme found in *Silence.* The supporting characters—including Cox, Tom Noonan as the killer, and Joan Allen as the woman who might save him from his madness—are as interesting as the leads. The offbeat rock score has aged poorly. ***AKA:*** Red Dragon. 🦴🦴🦴½

1986 (R) 100m/C William L. Petersen, Kim Greist, Joan Allen, Brian Cox, Dennis Farina, Stephen Lang, Tom Noonan; ***D:*** Michael Mann; ***W:*** Michael Mann; ***C:*** Dante Spinotti. **VHS, LV, Letterboxed, Closed Caption** *WAR*

Maniac

This early black-and-white Hammer entry gets off to a quick start with an offscreen rape and immediate, imaginative vengeance for it. But once the hero (Kerwin Mathews) makes his entrance, the pace drops off. He becomes involved with a cafe owner (Nadia Gray) and her Bardot-like daughter (Liliane Brousse). The rural French setting is refreshingly different and the women are sexy. The contrived plot is more problematic. 🦴🦴

1963 86m/B *GB* Kerwin Mathews, Nadia Gray, Donald Houston, Liliane Brousse; ***D:*** Michael Carreras; ***W:*** Jimmy Sangster; ***C:*** Wilkie Cooper; ***M:*** Stanley Black. **VHS** *COL, MLB*

Maniac

On the box copy of the remastered Anchor Bay tape, director William Lustig explains his collaboration with writer/star Joe Spinell and effects wizard Tom Savini in the production of this above-average psycho-killer tale. The plot is loosely based, in part, on the New York Son of Sam murders. Frank Zito (Spinell) is a fat, pathetic loner who murders and scalps women. Some of the physical details of his life and crimes ring true, but the psychological side is a collection of pop cliches, all based on another bad mommy. In the end, it's one of the best examples of a limited and distasteful genre. Spinell and co-star Caroline Munro would play similar characters in *The Last Horror Movie.*

1980 91m/C Joe Spinell, Caroline Munro, Gail Lawrence, Kelly Piper, Tom Savini, Rita Montone, Hyla Marrow; ***D:*** William Lustig; ***W:*** C.A. Rosenberg, Joe Spinell; ***C:*** Robert Lindsay. **VHS** *VTR*

Maniac Cop

First-rate action/horror benefits enormously from an all-star B-movie cast turning in unusually energetic performances. Between them, producer/writer Larry Cohen and director William Lustig have been responsible for some of the best low-budget entertainment (and a few clunkers). This slightly overplotted variation on the slasher stereotype makes good use of New York locations, and it's got a nice sense of humor. The main flaw is supposedly tough vice cop Laurene Landon, who shrieks like a schoolgirl at any hint of violence. Yes, that's director Sam Raimi as the TV reporter at the St. Patrick's Day parade. Followed by two sequels.

1988 (R) 92m/C Tom Atkins, Bruce Campbell, Laurene Landon, Richard Roundtree, William Smith, Robert Z'Dar, Sheree North, Sam Raimi; ***D:*** William Lustig; ***W:*** Larry Cohen; ***C:*** Vincent Rabe. **VHS** *TWE, HHE*

Maniac Cop 2

For those who missed the first film or have forgotten it, *2* begins with the big finish wherein the title character (Robert Z'Dar) is impaled through the chest by a large wooden beam. Is that enough to keep a potentially profitable psycho-monster down? You know it's not. Writer/producer Larry Cohen and director William Lustig create realistically nasty urban squalor. The Hollywood gunplay is standard issue, with shotgunned bodies flying through plate-glass windows; so are the other cop cliches. Outlandish chases with superb stuntwork are better. Only the last third approaches the filmmakers' better work.

1990 (R) 90m/C Robert Davi, Claudia Christian, Michael Lerner, Bruce Campbell, Laurene Landon, Robert Z'Dar, Clarence Williams III, Leo Rossi; ***D:*** William Lustig; ***W:*** Larry Cohen; ***C:*** James Lemmo. **VHS, LV, Letterboxed, Closed Caption** *LIV*

Maniac Cop 3: Badge of Silence

Though begun by Larry Cohen and William Lustig, creators of the first two films, this one has since been disowned by them, according to Lustig. It opens with a voodoo ritual reviving the oft-deceased psycho-patrolman (Robert Z'Dar). According to co-director Lustig, the people who financed the film were trying, inexplicably, to make a *Maniac Cop* movie for people who don't like *Maniac Cop* movies. The relatively "realistic" urban environment becomes a caricature, and the tone of moral superiority that the film takes to tabloid journalism is thoroughly hypocritical. Like Jason and Freddy, MC gets weaker and more heavily padded with recycled material from the earlier films with each outing.

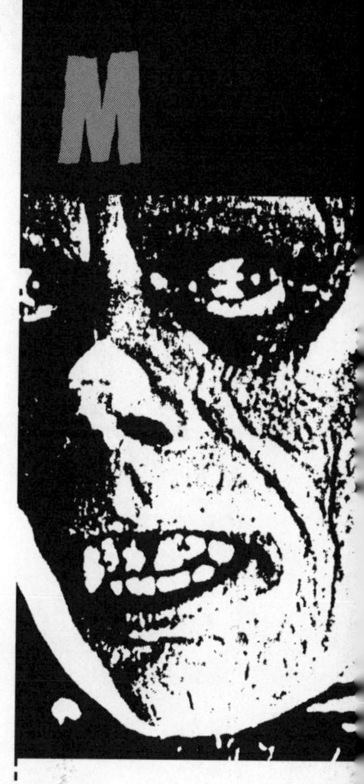

"You have the right to remain silent...forever!"

—Ad line from ***Maniac Cop.***

"Did you watch me— I was greater than any *real* vampire!"

—Count Mora (Bela Lugosi) in *Mark of the Vampire.*

1993 (R) 85m/C Robert Z'Dar, Robert Davi, Gretchen Becker, Paul Gleason, Doug Savant, Caitlin Dulany, Jackie Earle Haley, Robert Forster; ***D:*** William Lustig, Joel Soisson; ***W:*** Larry Cohen; ***M:*** Jerry Goldsmith. **VHS, Closed Caption** *NO*

The Manitou

Pure hokum at least has the courage of its hokey convictions. It's working in a narrow range between supernatural horror and light comedy, and manages to carry it off entertainingly because the production values are unusually high—the film looks much more polished than many of the period—and because Tony Curtis turns in a canny performance in a role perfectly suited to his skills. He's Erskin, a bogus medium ("Harry's the name, Tarot's the game.") whose ex-girlfriend Karen (Susan Strasberg) has developed a tumor on her neck. The growth eventually becomes a monster that takes over a hospital. Stella Stevens, Ann Sothern, Burgess Meredith, and Michael Ansara provide better support than their stereotyped characters deserve. Director William Girdler also made *Grizzly* and *Abby* before he was killed in a helicopter crash. 🦴🦴🦴

1978 (PG) 104m/C Susan Strasberg, Tony Curtis, Stella Stevens, Ann Sothern, Burgess Meredith, Michael Ansara, Jon Cedar, Paul Mantee, Lurene Tuttle, Jeanette Nolan; ***D:*** William Girdler; ***W:*** William Girdler, Tom Pope, Jon Cedar; ***C:*** Michael Hugo; ***M:*** Lalo Schifrin. **VHS, LV** *COL, NLC*

Man's Best Friend

The producers of the *Child's Play* series turn their attention to monstrous dogs and the VideoHound is not amused. Lori Tanner (Ally Sheedy), a TV reporter long on ambition and short on brains, rescues Max from Dr. Jarret's (Lance Henriksen) lab. The doc has spliced Max's genes so that he has all sorts of powers, including the ability to disguise himself as a box of old clothes. That is not a joke, and it's not the silliest thing about the movie, either. Beyond the immediate shock value of a few scenes, there's nothing to this formula flick. 🦴

1993 (R) 87m/C Ally Sheedy, Lance Henriksen, Frederic Lehne, Robert Costanzo, John Cassisi, J.D. Daniels; ***D:*** John Lafia; ***W:*** John Lafia; ***M:*** Joel Goldsmith. **VHS, LV, Closed Caption** *NLC*

Mark of the Devil

German production covers similar territory to *The Conqueror Worm,* but treats it much more exploitatively, with prolonged scenes of torture aimed mostly at women. Pockfaced Reggie Nalder, known best as the assassin in Hitchcock's *The Man Who Knew Too Much,* is fine as the rapacious witchfinder Albino. Though the script is said to be based on true stories, the film is slow and talky between gore scenes. The incongruous soundtrack adds nothing, and the violence is handled with such relish that the film leaves a bad taste. The Anchor Bay tape has been restored to remarkable, if lamentable clarity. Followed by a sequel. ***AKA:*** Burn, Witch, Burn; Brenn, Hexe, Brenn; Austria 1700; Satan; Hexen bis aufs Blut Gequaelt. 🦴🦴

1969 (R) 96m/C *GB GE* Herbert Lom, Olivera Vuco, Udo Kier, Reggie Nalder, Herbert Fux, Michael Maien, Ingeborg Schoener, Johannes Buzalski, Gaby Fuchs, Adrian Hoven; ***D:*** Michael Armstrong; ***W:*** Sergio Casstner, Adrian Hoven; ***C:*** Ernst W. Kalinke. **VHS** *VTR, TPV, VDM*

Mark of the Vampire

Even though the supernatural elements are discounted in the end, and despite egregious comic relief, the strong images, better acting, and graveyard atmospherics make this one of the '30s finest moments. Lionel Barrymore, as the investigating Professor, is almost as impressive as Bela Lugosi's virtually mute Count Mora and his daughter Luna (Caroll Borland), who makes one grand airborne entrance. Until the unfortunate denouement, director Tod Browning and cinematographer James

Wong Howe create beautiful and spooky black-and-white images that rival *Frankenstein* and *Dracula*. Recommended. ***AKA:*** Vampires of Prague.

1935 61m/B Lionel Barrymore, Bela Lugosi, Elizabeth Allan, Lionel Atwill, Jean Hersholt, Donald Meek, Carroll Borland; ***D:*** Tod Browning; ***W:*** Tod Browning, Guy Endore, Bernard Schubert; ***C:*** James Wong Howe. **VHS** *MGM, MLB*

Martin

Is Martin (John Amplas) a very disturbed young man, or is he an 84-year-old vampire? His older cousin (Lincoln Maazel) from the old country believes the latter and wants to save Martin's soul and then to destroy him. Whatever the truth, Martin is killing people. So what if he uses drugs and razor blades instead of hypnotic gazes and fangs—the results are the same. In the end, George Romero's story is about being human. With its grainy color and closely observed Pittsburgh locations, the film is reminiscent of another often-overlooked Romero gem, *Monkey Shines*. The characters have been so thoroughly stripped of conventional movie glamour that the picture is much more realistic than 99 percent of the movies that come out of Hollywood. (That's Romero as Father Howard.) *Martin* is one of horror's most accomplished sleepers.

1976 (R) 96m/C John Amplas, Lincoln Maazel, Christine Forrest, Elayne Nadeau, Tom Savini, Sarah Venable, George A. Romero, Fran Middleton; ***D:*** George A. Romero; ***W:*** George A. Romero; ***C:*** Michael Gornick; ***M:*** Donald Rubinstein. **VHS, LV** *VTR*

Mary, Mary, Bloody Mary

It's a dark and stormy Mexican night—so dark and stormy that the opening scenes appear to be submerged within your TV. Once the action brightens—the movie runs for 15 minutes before the opening credits roll—you realize how pitiful the acting is. Mary Gilmore (Christina Ferrare) is a vampiric painter who stabs her victims with a hair pin and drinks their blood. Director Juan Moctezuma is really more interested in the exploitation angles of the story. The suspenseless stretches between the arty softcore scenes are interminable, and John Carradine's caped character adds a note of unneeded and unintentional comedy.

1976 (R) 85m/C Christina Ferrare, David Young, Helena Rojo, John Carradine; ***D:*** Juan Lopez Moctezuma; ***W:*** Malcolm Marmorstein; ***M:*** Tom Bahler. **VHS** *NO*

Mary Reilly

Director Stephen Frears makes a mistake in his first shot by opening with Julia Roberts on her knees scrubbing a stoop, and the camera focused squarely on her butt. Nobody looks good from that angle. (For comparative purposes only, see the much more flattering Roberts rearview as she climbs the steps in *Dying Young*.) After it, though, Frears settles down to tell the story (based on Valerie Martin's novel) of Dr. Jekyll (John Malkovich) from the point of view of one of his servants, Mary Reilly (Roberts). It's a dark tale made more so by Mary's memories of childhood abuse. The flaws are obvious—slow pace, Roberts' on-and-off Irish accent—and so are the positives—Malkovich's performance, great sets, strong Gothic atmosphere. Each generation reinterprets the Jekyll and Hyde story, and this version makes legitimate and thoughtful contributions, albeit somewhat laboriously and obviously. Recommended to students of Stevenson's original and to those who are curious about the proper method of skinning a live eel.

1995 (R) 108m/C Julia Roberts, John Malkovich, George Cole, Michael Gambon, Kathy Staff, Glenn Close, Michael Sheen, Bronagh Gallagher, Linda Bassett, Henry Goodman, Ciaran Hinds, Sasha Hanav; ***D:*** Stephen Frears; ***W:*** Christopher Hampton; ***C:*** Philippe Rousselot; ***M:*** George Fenton. Nominations: Golden Raspberry Awards '96: Worst Actress (Roberts), Worst Director (Frears). **VHS, LV, Closed Caption** *COL*

"Guaranteed to upset your stomach!"

—Ad line from *Mark of the Devil.*

THE HOUND SALUTES

TOD BROWNING

Of all the pioneers who worked in horror's "golden age," Tod Browning is the most problematic. Studio interference with his work was so severe that you've got to wonder what the films would have been like if he'd been able to get what he wanted on the screen. It's easy to speculate that he'd be considered a much more important filmmaker now.

Browning certainly led an interesting life. Born in 1882 in Louisville, Kentucky, he ran away from home at 16 and joined the circus. He worked on both sides of the camera with D.W. Griffith on *Intolerance* (1916) and eventually became a director, making several silent films with Lon Chaney, Sr. In fact, Chaney had been scheduled to star in *Dracula* but he died, too soon, in 1930. (Think for a moment about what a Lon Chaney *Dracula* might have been. Wow!)

That didn't happen. Instead, Browning went with Bela Lugosi, who was already familiar to audiences in the role from his work on the stage, and the image of the vampire was set in cinematic concrete. The film was a huge commercial success and was responsible, at least in part, for the first important wave of sound horror films. (Browning, by the way, "appears" in the film as the voice of the harbormaster who discovers Renfield in the hold of the "Vesta.")

Browning used the clout that *Dracula* gave him to jump from Universal to MGM, where he'd made silent films with Chaney, and where Louis B. Mayer and Irving Thalberg hoped that he'd bring in another winner. They got *Freaks,* a strange, violent story set in the sideshow world Browning knew. Though the film is well respected now, it was a disaster in 1932, and it's hard to understand why they didn't see it coming. As it was written, the film was to end with sideshow freaks attacking and mutilating the "normal" couple who had threatened them. The man is castrated and the woman is disfigured. Preview audiences were so grossed out that nearly a third of the film was

Mary Shelley's Frankenstein

Director/star Kenneth Branagh's take on the famous novel is a glorious mess of a movie—energetic to a fault, handsomely produced, and often visually astonishing. A stilted, creaky script by Steph Lady and Frank Darabont and an unbalanced pace lie at the heart of the film's problems. Victor's (Branagh) childhood and family life are laboriously detailed. The centerpiece lab scenes are real lu-lus involving assorted fluids, industrial-strength acupuncture, and a Rube Goldberg contraption that looks like an old-fashioned copper bathtub. The result is the Creature (Robert De Niro), scarred, innocent, frightened, and strong. Some of the early scenes are staged on huge but virtually empty sets that leave the viewer wondering where all the furniture is. In the middle section, where several important events take place, the pace is so hurried that the plot makes little sense. As both actor and director, Branagh seems barely under control. He and Helena Bonham Carter might have found their characters on the cover of a paperback bodice-ripper. Co-producer Francis Ford Coppola was much more successful with a similar

cut. It fared poorly in the larger markets, and was more successful in the Northeast and Midwest. Unfortunately for the studio, it also became a lightning rod for various "reform" groups who wanted to rein in Hollywood.

Browning went on to make two more interesting works, *Mark of the Vampire* and *Devil Doll,* but by then, his career was over. Perhaps the saddest thing about it—at least for now—is the apparent disappearance of one of his great silent films, *London After Midnight,* with Lon Chaney in a false vampire role. Stills of Chaney abound but all prints and negatives of the film appear to have been lost. Rumors of a copy persist, but nothing has come of them.

For more on Browning, see *Dark Carnival* (Anchor Books, 1995), by David S. Skal and Elias Savada, an excellent examination of the man and his films.

SIGNIFICANT CONTRIBUTIONS TO HORROR

***Dracula* (1931)**

***Freaks* (1932)**

***Mark of the Vampire* (1935)**

***Devil Doll* (1936)**

approach to *Bram Stoker's Dracula.* ***AKA:*** Frankenstein.

1994 (R) 123m/C Kenneth Branagh, Robert De Niro, Helena Bonham Carter, Tom Hulce, Aidan Quinn, John Cleese, Ian Holm, Richard Briers, Robert Hardy, Cherie Lunghi, Celia Imrie, Trevyn McDowell; ***D:*** Kenneth Branagh; ***W:*** Frank Darabont, Steph Lady; ***M:*** Patrick Doyle. Nominations: Academy Awards '94: Best Makeup. **VHS, LV, 8mm, Closed Caption** *COL*

The Mask

Typical low-budget black-and-white effort of the early '60s is filled with overblown music and equally overblown bad acting. The mask is a mosaic skull-like thing that gives the wearer hallucinations. Those scenes were filmed in 3-D. Whenever the ponderous voiceover commands "Put the Mask on Now!" audiences were supposed to put on 3-D glasses. Without them, the weird effects have little more than immediate shock value. The Rhino edition, hosted by Elvira, contains the 3-D scenes, and is sold with the glasses. ***AKA:*** Eyes of Hell; The Spooky Movie Show.

1961 85m/B *CA* Paul Stevens, Claudette Nevins, Bill Walker, Anne Collings, Martin Lavut, Leo Leyden, Bill Bryden, Eleanor Beecroft, Steven Appleby; ***D:*** Julian Roffman; ***W:*** Slavko Vorkapich, Franklin Delessert, Sandy Haver, Frank Taubes; ***C:*** Herbert S. Alpert. **VHS, LV** *RHI, MLB*

Prince Prospero (Vincent Price) in *Masque of the Red Death* (1965).

The Mask

Even star Jim Carrey's broad physical comedy is overshadowed by special effects created at George Lucas' International Light & Magic (ILM) in this combination of live-action and animation. Stanley Ipkiss (Carrey) is a mild-mannered bank clerk who's everyone's stepping stone, until he finds "The Mask." Once he puts it on, he becomes a green-faced, zoot-suited caricature of himself with super powers, the sort of character who might have been created by renowned animators Tex Avery or Chuck Jones. (References to both of them appear prominently.) What plot there is involves gangsters, a sexy singer (Cameron Diaz), and supernatural stuff, but the effects are the real stars here. Despite heavy gun violence, this one's O.K. for kids. 🦴🦴🦴

1994 (PG-13) 100m/C Jim Carrey, Cameron Diaz, Peter Greene, Peter Riegert, Amy Yasbeck, Orestes Matacena, Richard Jeni, Ben Stein; ***D:*** Chuck Russell; ***W:*** Mike Werb; ***C:*** John R. Leonetti; ***M:*** Randy Edelman. Blockbuster Entertainment Awards '95: Comedy Actor, Theatrical (Carrey), Female Newcomer, Theatrical (Diaz); Blockbuster Entertainment Awards '96: Comedy Actor, Video (Carrey); Nominations: Academy Awards '94: Best Visual Effects; Golden Globe Awards '95: Best Actor—Musical/Comedy (Carrey); MTV Movie Awards '95: Breakthrough Performance (Diaz), Most Desirable Female (Diaz), Best Comedic Performance (Carrey), Best Dance Sequence (Jim Carrey/Cameron Diaz). **VHS, Closed Caption** *NLC*

Masque of the Red Death

In terms of budget, this is Roger Corman's most lavish and expensive Poe adaptation. Vincent Price attacks his role as the evil Prince Prospero with obvious delight, but he's still almost upstaged by Hazel Court at her loveliest. Charles Beaumont's script borrows from other Poe stories, most obviously "Hop-Frog," and the film is fleshed out with moderate doses of '60s sin, sex, and psychedelia. The result, photographed by Nicholas Roeg, has aged well. As producer, Corman remade the film in 1989, and the title showed up again in 1990. 🦴🦴🦴½

1965 88m/C *GB* Vincent Price, Hazel Court, Jane Asher, Patrick Magee, David Weston, Nigel Green, Julian Burton, Skip Martin, Gaye Brown, John Westbrook; ***D:*** Roger Corman; ***W:*** Charles Beaumont, R. Wright Campbell; ***C:*** Nicolas Roeg. **VHS** *ORI, MLB*

Masque of the Red Death

This Corman-produced remake of his own 1964 original is curiously slow and dispirited though fairly faithful to Poe's story. Prince Prospero (Adrian Paul) tries to defeat the plague of the Red Death by bringing all of his noble pals inside and sealing the gates of the city. He imports a few comely peasant wenches for entertainment and also invites his old teacher, Machiavel (Patrick Macnee). Prospero is a dark, brooding sort who's prone to sophomoric philosophical reflection when he's not paying more attention than he should to his sister Lucretia (Tracy Reiner). He worries about Life and Death and the Duty of the Prince and stuff like that. Despite atmospheric sets; silly costumes, wigs, and dialogue; swordfights; and boiling oil to pour on the peasants, the film lacks the two key ingredients that made the Corman movies so enjoyable: speed and lack of self-consciousness. 🦴🦴

1989 (R) 90m/C Patrick Macnee, Jeffery Osterhage, Adrian Paul, Tracy Reiner, Maria Ford, Clare Hoak; ***D:*** Larry Brand; ***W:*** Larry Brand, Daryl Haney. **VHS, LV** *MGM, IME*

Massacre at Central High

Though it's not technically horror, this cult favorite fits neatly into the dead-teenager cycle of the mid-1970s. New student David (Derrel Maury) takes matters into his own hands when a gang harasses his fellow high-school students and gets rid of the gang members, one by one. Despite some silly dialogue, the low-budget production is above average. The violence is sometimes ridiculous, sometimes surprising and shocking. One brief but effective love scene probably has something to do with the film's enduring popularity on video. So does a strong political element to the story. Co-star Andrew Stevens has gone on to produce, direct, and star in many low-budget films on video. Writer/director Renee Daalder has also made the equally curious and difficult-to-pigeonhole *Habitat.* ***AKA:*** Blackboard Massacre. 🦴🦴🦴

1976 (R) 85m/C Derrel Maury, Andrew Stevens, Kimberly Beck, Robert Carradine, Roy Underwood, Steve Bond, Steve Sikes, Lani O'Grady, Damon Douglas, Cheryl "Rainbeaux" Smith; ***D:*** Renee Daalder; ***W:*** Renee Daalder; ***C:*** Bert Van Munster. **VHS** *MPI*

Mausoleum

Traumatized as a young girl by the death of her mother, Susan (Bobbie Bresee) sees visions in a haunted cemetery. Ten years later, the Nomed family curse strikes. Her eyeballs are tinted green, fog floats down the hallway of her palatial home, and she turns into a monstrous hairy demon with carnivorous breasts. The mix of too-familiar lighting and sound effects generates no real scares, though some of John Buechler's makeup has shock value. The plot is a silly mish-mash of *Carrie* and *The Exorcist* with more exploitation elements, though Bobbie Bresee and Marjoe Gortner, as her worried husband, handle the material fairly seriously. Fans of cheap thrills have seen worse and much better. 🦴🦴

1983 (R) 96m/C Marjoe Gortner, Bobbie Bresee, Norman Burton, LaWanda Page, Shari Mann, Julie Christy Murray, Laura Hippe, Maurice Sherbanee; ***D:*** Michael Dugan; ***W:*** Robert Madero, Robert Barich; ***C:*** Robert Barich. **VHS, LV**

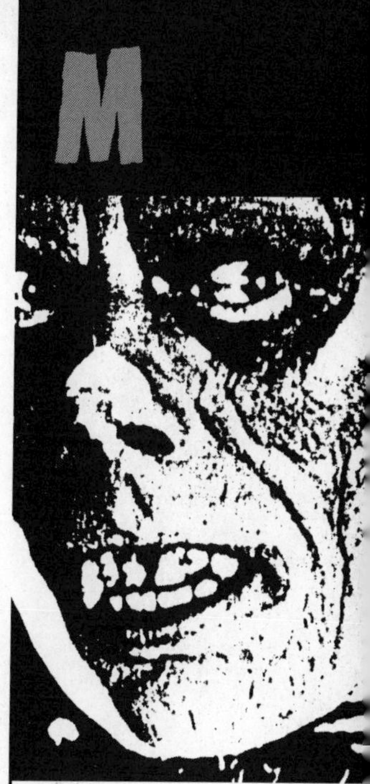

HOUND OF HORROR

People often ask if there really is a VideoHound and the answer is, of course, yes.

He lives in a luxurious penthouse kennel high atop the Penobscot Building in downtown Detroit. If you read the credits page carefully, you'll see that Marty Connors is the publisher of Visible Ink Press, but the VideoHound oversees production of all of the books. His picture's on the cover, isn't it?

The cinematic canine's interest in film and video goes back several generations. His family has been in the movie business since the early 1930s. The VideoHound is related to both Lassie and Rin Tin Tin on his father's side, and as a pup, he was virtually raised by his aunt Asta. It was the family's association with the European ARF conglomerate that brought the Hound into publishing.

It is true that the VideoHound has turned many of his daily duties over to the editors at Visible Ink Press. These days, the Hound devotes much of his time to his work on the board of governors of the ASPCA and to the Clinique Canine Cosmetics Scholarship program. He remains a dedicated movie fan. Of more importance to this book, he is a serious student of the horror film.

The Hound has an extensive personal collection of tapes and discs. He generally prefers older, black-and-white horrors of the 1940s and '50s and watches several each week. When pressed, he will admit to a slightly guilty predilection for the more garish Philippine horror movies. His input in that area was invaluable for this book.

Some readers are probably wondering how a dog can operate a TV and VCR. At one time, it was difficult, but now with an extra-large remote, he has no trouble.

Of course, no one except Ted Turner (a close personal friend of the Hound) can own every movie,

Maximum Overdrive

Writer/director Stephen King isn't wrong when he calls this a "moron movie," but that doesn't mean that it's not fun in its own garish, grease-stained, merrily destructive way. Machines take on a life of their own and become the mechanical equivalent of George Romero's zombies to a group of people trapped in the Dixie Boy truck stop by circling semis. Emilio Estevez and Laura Harrington are O.K. in the leads. Remade for TV in 1997 as *Trucks.*

1986 (R) 97m/C Emilio Estevez, Pat Hingle, Laura Harrington, Christopher Murney, Yeardley Smith, Stephen King; ***D:*** Stephen King; ***W:*** Stephen King; ***M:*** AC/DC. **VHS, LV** *ORI, WAR*

Meridian: Kiss of the Beast

Erotic videos are a dime a dozen, but this Gothic variation on *Beauty and the Beast* is one of the best. American Catherine Bomarzini (Sherilyn Fenn) has just returned to the family estate in Italy, a palatial spread filled with oversized sculptures. (It's actually the family estate of director Charles Band.) In short order, she and her best friend Gina (Charlie Spradling) fall in with a traveling carnival led by a dark magician (Malcolm Jamieson). After a wild night of carousing, a fearsome lion-like critter shows up in the

so sometimes he gets an itch to see something else. When that happens—and it often seems to happen on warm sunny afternoons—he instructs the staff to have one of the Visible Ink interns bring his limousine around and drive him to one of the local video stores. With his smiling face upraised through the open sunroof, he has become a familiar sight on Griswold Street.

Then in the evening, with an icy bone-dry gin martini at his side, the Hound will settle down to enjoy a double feature. He usually watches something new first—perhaps the latest hot Hollywood horror—followed by another look at one of the older Universal features, often starring Karloff, Lugosi, or the Hound's personal favorite, the Wolfman.

He suggests that you give it a try. At the end of the day, you could do worse.

SIGNIFICANT CONTRIBUTIONS TO HORROR

VideoHound's Horror Show

VideoHound's Golden Movie Retriever

VideoHound's Vampires on Video

VideoHound's Cult Flicks and Trash Pics

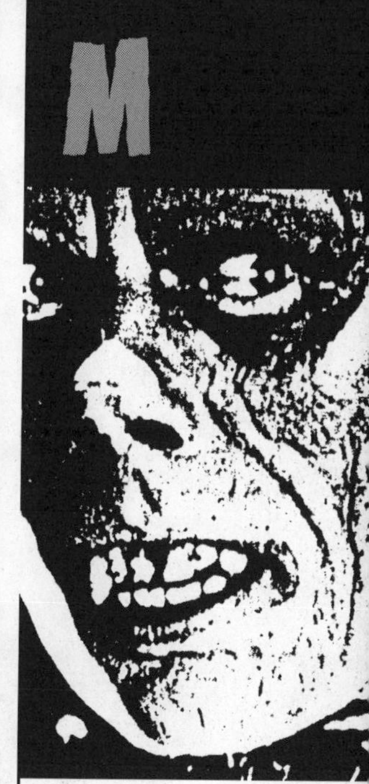

boudoir. Before it's all over, an evil dwarf, a ghost or two, a legend, and a Renaissance painting have been tossed into the mix. Sherilyn Fenn handles the lead with the right combination of seriousness and flippancy. Staying true to the spirit of the genre, she gets dolled up in antique dresses (complete with several pounds of jewelry), wanders through miles and miles of eerie corridors, and swoons at all the appropriate moments. 🦴🦴🦴

1990 (R) 90m/C Sherilyn Fenn, Malcom Jamieson, Hilary Mason, Alex Daniels, Phil Fondacaro, Charlie Spradling; ***D:*** Charles Band; ***W:*** Dennis Paoli; ***M:*** Pino Donaggio. **VHS, LV, Closed Caption** *PAR*

Midnight Kiss

Director Joel Bender combines topical elements—date rape, sexual harassment—with cop cliches and vampire cliches. LAPD Det. Carrie Blass (Michelle Owens) wants to nab a rapist-murderer who drains his victims of blood. The effete blond vampire (Gregory A. Greer) looks like a junkie refugee from a glam rock band and sports a crucifix earring. Why? Apparently, he's some kind of secular neck nosher. All the men in the movie are either pigs, undead, or both. The action is unnecessarily violent and may or may not appeal to gore fans. Owens is better than the material, and the action takes one fair twist, but those really

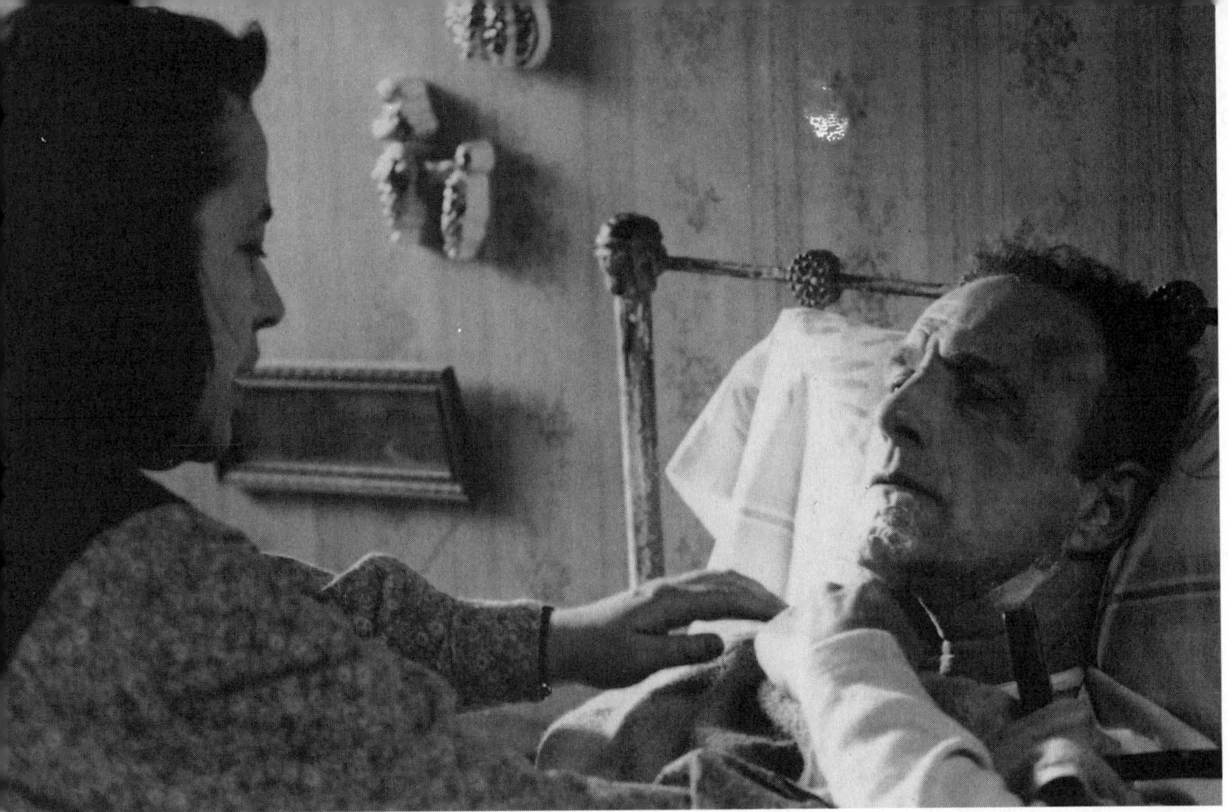

Annie Wilkes (Kathy Bates) is novelist Paul Sheldon's (James Caan) "number one fan" in Stephen King's *Misery*.

aren't recommendations. Yes, that's Celeste Yarnall, *The Velvet Vampire* herself, as Sheila, the first victim. 🦴🦴

1993 (R) 85m/C Michelle Owens, Gregory A. Greer, Celeste Yarnall; ***D:*** Joel Bender; ***W:*** John Weidner, Ken Lamplugh. **VHS** *NO*

Mikey

In the evil-child sub-genre, this is a relatively weak but expensively staged entry. It lacks the emotional power of *The Other* and the strong performance of Patty McCormack in *The Bad Seed*. Even though he's offed his entire family before the first ten minutes, Mikey (Brian Bonsall) isn't believably threatening. He's a troubled, manipulative psychoboy who's a young version of *The Stepfather*. But director Dennis Dimster can't elevate his nightmare world to the same level of believability that *Stepfather* writer Donald Westlake and director Joseph Ruben create. The adult cast of character actors do well with the unsurprising script. 🦴

1992 (R) 92m/C Brian Bonsall, John Diehl, Lyman Ward, Josie Bissett, Ashley Laurence, Mimi Craven, Whitby Hertford; ***D:*** Dennis Dimster. **VHS, Closed Caption** *IMP*

Mimic

Guillermo del Toro's *Cronos* is the most innovative and original take on the traditional vampire that anyone's made in decades. With the help of writers John Sayles, Steven Soderbergh, and Matthew Robbins, he does the same with big-bug s-f/horror here, combining humanism with bizarre effects. A snowy New York City introduction establishes Dr. Susan Tyler (Mira Sorvino) as the science babe who inadvertently creates the creatures in question when she cures a devastating cockroach-borne children's plague. Three years later, giant mutant bugs decide it's payback time. Compared to *Cronos,* these scares and jolts are more conventionally telegraphed—not surprising in a big-budget studio release—and the influence of TV's *The X-Files* is all too evident. Otherwise, the film boasts great sets, a high-octane third act, and nasty bug effects (and bug guts effects) from Rob Bottin and Tyruben Ellingson.

1997 (R) 105m/C Jeremy Northam, Mira Sorvino, Josh Brolin, Charles S. Dutton, Giancarlo Giannini, F. Murray Abraham; ***D:*** Guillermo del Toro; ***W:*** John Sayles, Steven Soderbergh, Matthew Robbins; ***M:*** Marco Beltrami. **VHS, Closed Caption** *TOU*

Mirror, Mirror

Curious feminist horror is based on a huge old supernatural mirror that bridges generations and dimensions (or something to that effect; the details aren't spelled out). The setting is a small town where oddball newcomer Megan (Rainbow Harvest) has a hard time adjusting to high school. She finds herself captivated by the antique mirror left in the bedroom of her new house. As she spends more time with it, terrible things happen to those who torment her at school. The script written by four women—one of them director Marina Sargenti—borrows liberally from *Beetlejuice, The Amityville Horror, Carrie,* and several other Stephen King works. Throughout, the male characters are either well-meaning oafs or pawns to be manipulated by their evil girlfriends. At its best, the film avoids blatant violence and instead uses blood as a metaphor. Toward the end, the action degenerates into hand-in-the-disposal special effects. Even so, it's more ambitious than most low-budget horror movies. Fans should definitely take a look. Followed by so-so sequels.

1990 (R) 105m/C Karen Black, Rainbow Harvest, Kristin Datillo, Ricky Paull Goldin, Yvonne De Carlo, William Sanderson, Charlie Spradling, Ann Hearn, Stephen Tobolowsky; ***D:*** Marina Sargenti; ***W:*** Marina Sargenti. **VHS, LV** *NO*

Mirror, Mirror 2: Raven Dance

When a movie opens with a tattooed skinhead band playing at a Catholic orphanage for no audience, you know that plot doesn't count for much. The effects are all that this one has going for itself. They range from a guy in a silly rubber suit to some really good, inventive work done with lights and computers. The violence is too outlandish to be offensive. A cast of horror vets including Roddy McDowall, Sally Kellerman, William Sanderson, Veronica Cartwright, and several continuity errors are part of the fun, too. Followed by *3.*

1994 (R) 91m/C Tracy Wells, Roddy McDowall, Sally Kellerman, Veronica Cartwright, William Sanderson, Lois Nettleton; ***D:*** Jimmy Lifton; ***W:*** Jimmy Lifton, Virginia Perfili. **VHS, LV** *ORP*

Mirror, Mirror 3: The Voyeur

This video premiere opens with some computer-enhanced stuff that's pretty fancy for a low-budget effort and continues to attempt more than it can deliver. The semi-hysterical plot launches into ritual suicide (sort of) by Cassandra (Monique Parent) because she can't be with her lover Anthony (Billy Drago), while her drug-dealing husband has stashed a briefcase full of cash in the living room of the empty mansion where they live. Really poor sound is the most obvious corner that the filmmakers cut. Cheapjack action sequences don't add anything. The recurring image of two rotisserie chickens—apparently meant to represent the lovers—is an appropriately daft touch. The two directors may well have made two separate but tangential movies—one about the drug business involving David Naughton as a cop, the other an erotic reincarnation tale with a fair special effects finish—and chopped them together.

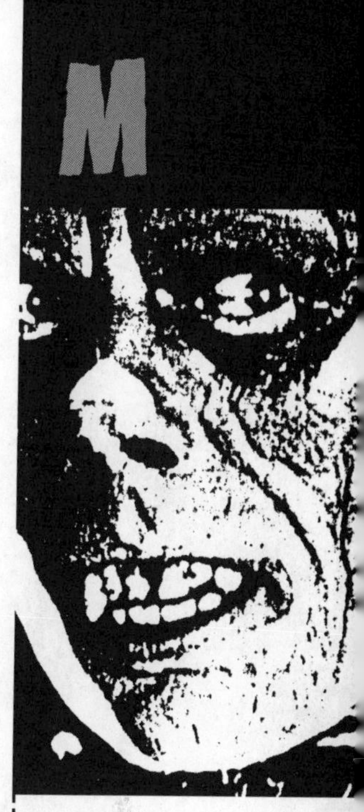

Farmer Vincent (Rory Calhoun) and his sister Ida (Nancy Parsons) are the hosts in *Motel Hell.*

1996 91m/C Billy Drago, Monique Parent, David Naughton, Mark Ruffalo, Elizabeth Baldwin, Richard Cansino; ***D:*** Rachel Gordon, Virginia Perfili; ***W:*** Steve Tymon; ***C:*** Nils Erickson. **VHS** *MTH*

Misery

Annie Wilkes (Kathy Bates) is perhaps Stephen King's most impressive and memorable human monster. She's a madwoman whose obsession with the fictional Misery Chastain is transformed into a fantasy-come-true when she rescues Misery's creator (James Caan) from a car accident and imprisons him in her cluttered, claustrophobic Rocky Mountain cabin. William Goldman's script is airtight. The best scares are intense and shocking. Some of King's ideas about the relationship between popular artist and fan are lost in translation to the screen. Bates' Oscar-winning performance is unforgettable and overshadows Caan's more controlled work.

1990 (R) 107m/C James Caan, Kathy Bates, Lauren Bacall, Richard Farnsworth, Frances Sternhagen, Graham Jarvis; ***D:*** Rob Reiner; ***W:*** William Goldman; ***C:*** Barry Sonnenfeld; ***M:*** Marc Shaiman. Academy Awards '90: Best Actress (Bates); Golden Globe Awards '91: Best Actress—Drama (Bates). **VHS, LV, Closed Caption** *COL, BTV*

Mr. Stitch

Troubled, stylized update of *Frankenstein* starts slow and never generates any real energy. Much of it takes place on a nearly empty white set where the proverbial mad scientist (Rutger Hauer) has created a sexless patchwork man (Wil Wheaton) who combines all races and genders—a sort of off-the-shelf Michael Jackson. Following lengthy discussions of innocence and religion, the plot finally makes an entrance. That has to do with sinister government plots, half-hearted chases, and a sympathetic psychologist (Nia Peeples). Producer/director/writer Roger Avary also co-wrote *Pulp Fiction* but you'd hardly guess it on the basis of this Frano-American effort. It's really more akin to George Lucas' student film-turned-feature *THX-1138.*

1995 (R) 98m/C Rutger Hauer, Wil Wheaton, Nia Peeples, Taylor Negron, Ron Perlman, Michael Harris; ***Cameos:*** Tom Savini; ***D:*** Roger Roberts Avary; ***W:*** Roger Roberts Avary. **VHS** *AVE*

Monkey Shines

George Romero uses Pittsburgh as a setting for a story firmly based in reality. When an accident leaves law student Allan Mann (Jason Beghe) a quadriplegic, his friend Geoffrey (John Pankow) arranges for a special monkey, Ella (Boo), to be trained to help him with the tasks most people take for granted. Also on hand when Allan and Ella become psychically linked are an overprotective mother (Joyce Van Patten) and an ill-tempered nurse (Christine Forrest). The real strength of the film is the way it depicts everyday horror, claustrophobia, and helpless anger. At its worst, an enraged supermonkey is much less frightening than well-intentioned, manipulative friends and relatives. ***AKA:*** Monkey Shines: An Experiment in Fear; Ella.

1988 (R) 108m/C Jason Beghe, John Pankow, Kate McNeil, Christine Forrest, Stephen Root, Joyce Van Patten, Stanley Tucci, Janine Turner; ***D:*** George A. Romero; ***W:*** George A. Romero; ***C:*** James A. Contner; ***M:*** David Shire. **VHS, LV, Closed Caption** *ORI*

The Monster of Piedras Blancas

Unintentional horror/comedy is a blatant rip-off of *Creature from the Black Lagoon,* but the funniest moment is a parody (maybe) of the famous surf scene from *From Here to Eternity.* Here though, our hero has a skin diver's mask on top of his head. The movie is also noteworthy for having perhaps the least convincing man-in-a-rubber-suit monster of the 1950s. Compared to this critter, the original Godzilla is Lon Chaney.

1957 72m/B Les Tremayne, Jeanne Carmen, Forrest Lewis, John Harmon, Don Sullivan; ***D:*** Irvin Berwick; ***W:*** H. Haile Chace; ***C:*** Philip Lathrop. **VHS** *REP, MRV, VDM*

Mosquito

Mutant mosquitoes from outer space are bigger than buzzards. Following the formula right down the line, they attack a campground filled with semi-professional actors. The redneck comedy is broad, dim, and aimed at horror fans. Gunnar Hansen, the original "Leatherface," has a major chainsaw scene. The special effects are a mix of real insects, models, and computer creations. The pace begins slowly and picks up later.

1995 (R) 92m/C Gunnar Hansen, Ron Asheton, Steve Dixon, Rachel Loiselle, Tim Loveface; ***D:*** Gary Jones; ***W:*** Gary Jones, Steve Hodge, Tom Chaney; ***C:*** Tom Chaney; ***M:*** Allen Lynch, Randall Lynch. **VHS** *NO*

The Most Dangerous Game

Perhaps more adventure than horror, this Gothic is a companion piece to *King Kong,* made by the same people on some of the same sets with overlapping casts and similar atmosphere. The famous plot involves a hunter (Joel McCrea) who becomes the hunted when he's shipwrecked on Count Zaroff's (Leslie Banks) South Pacific island. Robert Armstrong's comic drunk has nothing to do with his Carl Denham character from *Kong,* but Fay Wray's sexy heroine is in the Ann Darrow mold. Zaroff is a properly satanic villain, and the zippy pace makes this a particularly entertaining version of the oft-filmed story. ***AKA:*** The Hounds of Zaroff.

1932 78m/B Joel McCrea, Fay Wray, Leslie Banks, Robert Armstrong, Noble Johnson; ***D:*** Ernest B. Schoedsack, Irving Pichel; ***W:*** James A. Creelman; ***C:*** Henry W. Gerrard; ***M:*** Max Steiner. **VHS** *SNC, NOS, VYY*

Motel Hell

"There's all kinds of critters in Farmer Vincent's fritters!" So says the proprietor (Rory Calhoun), famous for his preservative-free, 100-percent natural smoked sausages. But what does he have to do with the automobile accidents that happen nightly near his motel? And what's going on in that walled garden out back? The answers are graphically (but not too graphically) provided in this blackly comic version of *The Texas Chainsaw Massacre*. Before it's over, virtually every melodramatic cliche imaginable—including heroine Nina Axelrod on the buzz saw—has been brought into play. British director Kevin Connor makes good use of stark lighting and gurgling sound effects to create creepy atmosphere. In many ways, this laid the groundwork for *Re-Animator* and the works of Sam Raimi and New Zealand's Peter Jackson.

1980 (R) 102m/C Rory Calhoun, Nancy Parsons, Paul Linke, Nina Axelrod, Wolfman Jack, Elaine Joyce, Dick Curtis, Rosanne Katon, Monique St. Pierre; ***D:*** Kevin Connor; ***W:*** Robert Jaffe, Steven-Charles Jaffe; ***C:*** Thomas Del Ruth. **VHS, LV** *MGM*

The Mummy

Karloff appears in the famous Mummy makeup only briefly in the memorable first few minutes of this seminal work, made between his initial appearances as the Frankenstein monster. The bandaged image is so memorable, though, that it provides the inspiration for the sequels and remakes that have followed. For most of the film, Karloff is Ardeth Bey, the cold-eyed, glacially slow, resurrected Egyptian. In that role, he's really more of a Dracula figure. Helen Grovner (Zita Johann) is his long-lost love. Karl Freund's stylized direction and the whole art-deco look of the production have aged beautifully. (Some stilted dialogue has not.) Those who know the film only from old creature-feature late shows owe themselves another look at the tape. The crisp black and white has been carefully restored to its original clarity, and Karloff's performance may be the best-kept secret of his long career. For those planning a Mummy-thon, the chronological order of the Universal series is *Mummy's Hand* (1940), ...*Tomb* (1942), ...*Ghost* (1944), and ...*Curse* (1944).

1932 72m/B Boris Karloff, Zita Johann, David Manners, Edward Van Sloan, Arthur Byron, Bramwell Fletcher, Noble Johnson, Leonard Mudie, Henry Victor; ***D:*** Karl Freund; ***W:*** John L. Balderston; ***C:*** Charles Stumar. **VHS, LV** *USH, TLF*

The Mummy

Following the success of its versions of *Frankenstein* and *Dracula,* Hammer's third foray into horror is one of the studio's most lavish productions. The screen is filled with lush sets, costumes, and make-up. (The ancient Egyptians wear enough mascara to supply a dozen New York hookers.) Despite an outfit that virtually immobilizes his face, Christopher Lee makes the title character a creature of impressive strength and size—a 4,000-year-old fool for love. Even though most of his dialogue is wonderful Egyptological hokum, he maintains a straight face. (It couldn't have been easy.) As always, Peter Cushing is excellent as the doughty hero who does the right thing. Recommended.

1959 88m/C *GB* Peter Cushing, Christopher Lee, Felix Aylmer, Yvonne Furneaux, Eddie Byrne, Raymond Huntley, George Pastell, Michael Ripper, John Stuart; ***D:*** Terence Fisher; ***W:*** Jimmy Sangster; ***C:*** Jack Asher. **VHS, LV** *WAR, MLB*

The Mummy's Curse

Attentive videophiles will remember that at the end of *Mummy's Ghost,* Kharis (Lon

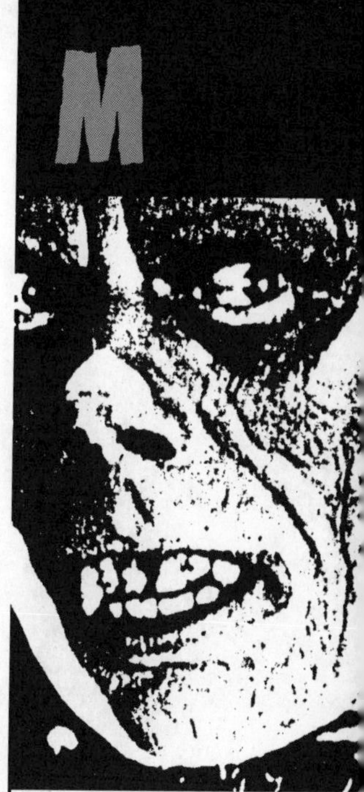

Ardeth Bey (Boris Karloff) is *The Mummy* (1932).

THE HOUND SALUTES

HAMMER FILMS

Hammer Films was born out of a partnership between Enrique Carreras and Will Hinds, who sometimes performed on stage as Will Hammer. Carreras bought his first theatre in Hammersmith, London, in 1913. In 1935, he and Hammer formed Exclusive Films, Ltd. Eventually, Enrique's son James came into the business, as did his son Michael. So did Will Hind's son Anthony. It was Michael Carreras and Anthony Hinds who actually started Hammer Films in 1947.

Their first international hit was *The Quatermass Xperiment* (AKA *The Creeping Unknown*), a 1955 science-fiction film. When the studio turned to horror in 1957, it struck the vein of boxoffice gold that Universal found in the 1930s. It was a result of the same combination of planning and luck.

First, Hammer chose the right stories to tell, and then it found the right people to put on both sides of the camera. The first two films were *The Curse of Frankenstein* and *The Horror of Dracula,* both written by Jimmy Sangster, who took a fresh approach to the novels, and both directed by Terence Fisher. Both co-starred Christopher Lee (as the Monster and as Dracula) and Peter Cushing (as Baron Frankenstein and van Helsing). Over the next several years, that core team—with contributions from writer Wolf Mankowitz, producer Anthony Hinds (who often wrote as John Elder), and actor Oliver Reed—would make *Brides of Dracula, The Mummy, Revenge of Frankenstein, The Two Faces of Dr. Jekyll,* and *The Curse of the Werewolf.* Judged by any standard, they're seven of the finest post-war horrors.

Once the studio had its team in place, it recycled a few sets and supported the guys onscreen with glamorous women—Hazel Court, Melissa Stribling, Carol Marsh, Yvonne Furneaux, Yvonne Romain, Yvonne Monlaur, Dawn Addams—in dresses as diaphanous and daringly decollete as the times would allow.

Again, like Universal, Hammer would manage to remain innovative and vigorous within the genre for more than a decade. Even

Chaney, Jr.) shuffled under the surface of the water in a swamp in Mapleton, Massachusetts, with his princess sweetie in his arms. At the beginning of this one, he emerges from a Louisiana swamp that the government is draining. With equally blithe inexplicability, he has become a part of Cajun lore. A few minutes later, up pops Mrs. Mummy (Virginia Christine) from the muddy tracks of a bulldozer. About the best that can be said of this unapologetically screwloose material is that it's fast, short, and really no worse than you ought to expect for the fifth entry in a series that was always made on parsimonious budgets. The use of the lone black character for comic relief reflects the socially acceptable racism of the 1940s. 🦴🦴

1944 61m/B Lon Chaney Jr., Peter Coe, Virginia Christine, Kay Harding, Dennis Moore, Martin Kosleck, Kurt Katch; ***D:*** Leslie Goodwins; ***W:*** Bernard Schubert; ***C:*** Virgil Miller. **VHS, Closed Caption** *USH, FCT*

The Mummy's Ghost

An uncharacteristically low-keyed John Carradine is the new priest who's called

when the sequels became derivative, the films looked good. The studio made a wide range of non-horror films, too, and remained active until the mid 1970s when the trend toward bloodier horror (*Night of the Living Dead*) and other market pressures forced Hammer out of the business. It tried to compete with its own brand of classy vampire exploitation (*Lust for a Vampire, Twins of Evil,* etc.), but the edge was gone.

The truth is that the studio did more with the "classic" horror themes than anyone could have reasonably expected. Much of the credit has to go to Lee and Cushing, who always took their characters seriously, even when they were placed in creaky vehicles.

Today, Hammer's best work is still extremely popular with older nostalgic fans and with a younger generation that appreciates top-drawer production values, solidly constructed stories, good performances, and restrained sexiness.

SIGNIFICANT CONTRIBUTIONS TO HORROR

***The Curse of Frankenstein* (1957)**

***The Horror of Dracula* (1958)**

***The Mummy* (1959)**

***The Curse of the Werewolf* (1960)**

***Brides of Dracula* (1960)**

***The Two Faces of Dr. Jekyll* (1960)**

***Kiss of the Vampire* (1962)**

***Dracula, Prince of Darkness* (1966)**

***Plague of the Zombies* (1966)**

***The Reptile* (1966)**

***Lost Continent* (1968)**

***Hands of the Ripper* (1971)**

upon to feed Tana-leaf tea to the loosely wrapped Lon Chaney, Jr. Even though this entry is marginally less formulaic than the one before (*Mummy's Tomb*), it's just as silly and even more unevenly acted by a cast of the studio's stock troupe. The day-for-night effects are noticeably weak. Ramsay Ames does continue the tradition of striking *Mummy* heroines.

1944 61m/B Lon Chaney Jr., John Carradine, Ramsay Ames, Robert Lowery, Barton MacLane, George Zucco; ***D:*** Reginald LeBorg; ***W:*** Griffin Jay, Henry Sucher, Brenda Weisberg; ***C:*** William Sickner. **VHS, Closed Caption** *USH, FCT*

The Mummy's Hand

Universal's pot-boiling series gets off to a lighthearted start with this second entry, which really establishes the ground rules—Tana leaves, high priests of Carnac, princess, etc. Never has southern California looked less like Egypt than it does here, and when the old priest says "Kharis rests on de udder side ub dis mountain," you know you're not dealing with completely serious material. George Zucco is properly malevolent with Wallace Ford and Cecil Kellaway providing comic relief. Ele-

THE HOUND SALUTES

LIONEL ATWILL

If Erich von Stroheim hadn't already been tagged "the man you love to hate," Lionel Atwill could have used it. In dozens of films, many of them horror, he was the cold, erudite, pitiless villain who did dreadful, dastardly deeds and got what was coming to him in the last reel.

But one of his best roles—and my own favorite—is as the one-armed Police Chief Krogh in *Son of Frankenstein*. The character has charm and humor. He provides unexpected irony at the conclusion and Atwill is thoroughly winning. That's not what he's remembered for, though. His bad guys are too good.

Atwill was born into a wealthy family in Croydon, England, 1885. After a successful career on the British stage, he came to America where he married well, to Louise Cromwell, and continued acting and touring in plays. When he got to Los Angeles, he stopped and was discovered. The Warner studio tried to equal Universal's success with horror in 1932's *Dr. X* and then the next year with *Mystery of the Wax Museum*, both directed by Michael Curtiz. With those two, Atwill's sinister screen persona was firmly established.

Though he played character roles in many different kinds of films—*Captain Blood, The Three Musketeers, To Be or Not to Be*—he kept coming back to horror in the various Universal sequels of the early 1940s, and he was always good at it. Most of his

ments of *Dracula* and *The Wolfman* creep in, too.

1940 70m/B Dick Foran, Wallace Ford, Peggy Moran, Cecil Kellaway, George Zucco, Tom Tyler, Eduardo Ciannelli, Charles Trowbridge; ***D:*** Christy Cabanne; ***W:*** Griffin Jay, Maxwell Shane; ***C:*** Elwood Bredell. **VHS, Closed Caption** *USH*

The Mummy's Tomb

Lon Chaney, Jr., dons the Ace bandages for Mr. M's third outing, and Turhan Bey takes over the priestly skulking duties. A condensed ten-minute version of *Mummy's Hand* sets the scene. After that, the high priest moves to Mapleton, Massachusetts, where he's arranged a job as cemetery caretaker. The dishwater-thin revenge plot depends on the back-lot atmospherics that the studio used so effectively in those days. Chaney's makeup and hum-drum acting are both second rate.

1942 71m/B Lon Chaney Jr., Dick Foran, John Hubbard, Elyse Knox, George Zucco, Wallace Ford, Turhan Bey; ***D:*** Harold Young; ***W:*** Griffin Jay, Henry Sucher; ***C:*** George Robinson. **VHS, Closed Caption** *USH, FCT*

Murder Weapon

Legendary low-budget horror reverses all of the conventions of the slasher flick. In this one, the heavy-breathing killer is stalking young guys. Recently released from a psychiatric institution, our heroines Dawn (Linnea Quigley) and Amy (Karen Russell) have, perhaps unadvisedly, gone off their medications. They invite several guys over to their house for an afternoon of beer and whatever. In flashback scenes, their psychiatrist (*Carol Burnett Show* veteran Lyle Waggoner) tries to explain the root of their problems, while, one by one, the guys disappear. There's no real suspense, and the imaginative killings are so

success was due to sharp facial features that photographed extremely well with the expressive black-and-white lighting techniques of the day. His impatient, clipped accent and line readings reinforced his physical appearance.

At the height of his professional popularity, he found himself involved in a sex scandal. It grew from a reported orgy at his 1940 Christmas party and eventually wound up with perjury charges leveled at Atwill. After the usual legal tapdancing, he was given a brief probation, but his career in big-budget films was over. He died of pneumonia in 1946 while working on a serial.

SIGNIFICANT CONTRIBUTIONS TO HORROR

Dr. X (1932)

Mystery in the Wax Museum (1933)

Son of Frankenstein (1939)

Man Made Monster (1941)

Ghost of Frankenstein (1942)

illogical and unrealistic that the graphic prosthetic special effects don't even have much immediate shock value. They're just bloody and silly. The film never tries to be anything more than low-budget escapism and it succeeds at that quite admirably. It's an early effort from the prolific Dave DeCoteau made under his nom de video Ellen Cabot.

1990 (R) 90m/C Linnea Quigley, Karen Russell, Lyle Waggoner; ***D:*** David DeCoteau, Ellen Cabot; ***W:*** Ross A. Perron. **VHS, LV** *NO*

Murders in the Rue Morgue

Bela Lugosi's trademark histrionics are given full rein in this uneven and very loose adaptation of Poe's famous story. He's Dr. Mirakle, a Caligarian figure who wants to mix human and ape blood, though his actions are much more explicitly sexual. The Expressionistic lighting and setting are more interesting than the story. The main problems are that the young lovers Pierre (Leon Ames) and Camille (Sidney Fox) are so saccharine that they'll set your teeth on edge, and the "ape"—at various times played by a chimp, a guy in a chubby suit, and something else—is never very frightening.

1932 61m/B Bela Lugosi, Sidney Fox, Leon Ames, Brandon Hurst, Arlene Francis, Noble Johnson; ***D:*** Robert Florey; ***W:*** John Huston, Tom Reed, Dale Van Every; ***C:*** Karl Freund. **VHS, Closed Caption** *USH*

Mute Witness

The first half is about as suspenseful as anything that's been put on film in recent years. Writer/director Anthony Waller sets

"Exterminate all rational thought. That is the conclusion I have come to."

—Bill Lee (Peter Weller) in *Naked Lunch.*

the scene quickly. Billy Hughes (Marina Sudina) is a mute American special effects technician working on a cheap horror flick in Moscow. Mistakenly locked in the huge studio one night after filming has finished for the day, she sees something she shouldn't. That act leads to an extended white-knuckle chase through the building. It's a brilliant set piece, told with almost no dialogue. Unfortunately, the second half begins with an emotional misstep that's necessary to keep the plot moving and the rest of the film isn't nearly as strong as the beginning. Throughout, however, Waller mixes suspense and humor effectively, and he gets fine performances from an unknown cast. (Don't miss a surprising uncredited guest star as the villain.) He also manages to add some fresh twists to the is-it-real-or-is-it-a-movie gimmick that's so popular these days in films-within-films. 🦴🦴🦴🦴

1995 (R) 100m/C *GB* Marina Sudina, Fay Ripley, Evan Richards, Oleg Jankowsky, Igor Volkow, Sergei Karlenkov; ***Cameos:*** Alec Guinness; ***D:*** Anthony Waller; ***W:*** Anthony Waller; ***C:*** Egon Werdin; ***M:*** Wilbert Hirsch. **VHS, LV, Closed Caption** *COL*

My Bloody Valentine

In one daring burst of originality, the slasher killer in this holiday-themed horror uses a pickax instead of a knife. Wow! Beyond that, the rest is a dull repetition of the formula that John Carpenter created in *Halloween,* with a no-name cast of young characters being killed off by a faceless psycho. This is one of the least impressive in an undistinguished lot of imitators. **Woof!**

1981 (R) 91m/C *CA* Paul Kelman, Lori Hallier, Neil Affleck, Keith Knight, Alf Humphreys, Cynthia Dale, Terry Waterland, Peter Cowper, Don Francks, Jack Van Evera; ***D:*** George Mihalka; ***W:*** John Beaird; ***C:*** Rodney Gibbons. **VHS, LV** *PAR*

Mystery of the Wax Museum

Early two-color Technicolor horror is a companion piece to director Michael Curtiz's *Doctor X* (1932). Lionel Atwill is the wax sculptor who's driven mad by an unscrupulous partner; Glenda Farrell is the sassy reporter on the trail of a story about missing bodies; Fay Wray is her innocent roommate. The story, remade in 3-D as *House of Wax* with Vincent Price, is never very frightening, but the cast and the impressive sets are excellent. 🦴🦴🦴

1933 77m/C Lionel Atwill, Fay Wray, Glenda Farrell, Frank McHugh, Allen Vincent, Holmes Herbert; ***D:*** Michael Curtiz; ***W:*** Carl Erickson, Don Mullaly; ***C:*** Ray Rennahan. **VHS, LV** *MGM, MLB*

Nadja

Any contemporary vampire story that casts Peter Fonda as a long-haired, bicycle-riding, vodka-swilling Van Helsing has a sense of humor. This one does, but not quite enough. Nadja (Elina Lowensohn) is the jaded daughter of Dracula. She and her brother Edgar (Jared Harris) live in New York, where they become involved with Lucy (Galaxy Craze) and her husband Jim (Martin Donovan), Van Helsing's nephew. The younger characters are such shallow, self-absorbed sorts that it's hard to work up much interest in them. With the notable exception of some irritatingly fuzzy Pixel sequences, the black-and-white photography is ultra-crisp. Virtually the same material was given similar but more pretentious treatment in *The Addiction*. O.K. for fans. 🦴🦴

1995 (R) 92m/B Elina Lowensohn, Suzy Amis, Galaxy Craze, Martin Donovan, Peter Fonda, Karl Geary, Jared Harris; ***Cameos:*** David Lynch; ***D:*** Michael Almereyda; ***W:*** Michael Almereyda; ***C:*** Jim Denault; ***M:*** Simon Fisher Turner. Nominations: Independent Spirit Awards '96: Best Actress (Lowensohn), Best Cinematography, Best Director (Almereyda). **VHS** *HMK*

Naked Lunch

Bizarre drug comedy is more polished than *Trainspotting*, but, in its way, just as demented, funny, and disgusting. William Lee (Peter Weller) is a brown-suited exterminator and sometimes writer whose various addictions and compulsions coalesce into a phantasmagoric hallucination. The material is so strong that even some of Cronenberg's fans may have trouble getting with it. Weller's dazed, not-quite-earthbound performance is pretty extreme, even for him, and it matches the rest of the story. Inanimate objects sprout sexual organs and indescribable perversions are tossed out like jokes when William ingests "black meat," a drug made from "the flesh of the giant aquatic Brazilian centipede." As the introductory quote states, "Nothing is true; everything is permitted." Not surprisingly, the material loses its edge before the film is over. 🦴🦴🦴

1991 (R) 117m/C Peter Weller, Judy Davis, Ian Holm, Julian Sands, Roy Scheider, Monique Mercure, Nicholas Campbell, Michael Zelniker, Robert A. Silverman, Joseph Scorsiani; ***D:*** David Cronenberg; ***W:*** David Cronenberg; ***M:*** Howard Shore. Genie Awards '92: Best Adapted Screenplay, Best Art Direction/Set Decoration, Best Cinematography, Best Director (Cronenberg), Best Film, Best Sound, Best Supporting Actress (Mercure); New York Film Critics Awards '91: Best Screenplay, Best Supporting Actress (Davis); National Society of Film Critics Awards '91: Best Director (Cronenberg), Best Screenplay. **VHS, Closed Caption** *FXV*

Natural Born Killers

Told with the aggressive pace and look of a rock video, Oliver Stone's two-hour hallucination of violence is *A Clockwork Orange* taken to the nth degree. Though he means for the work to be a horrific parody of contemporary attitudes toward celebrity criminals, it's at best only partially successful. At worst, it's a victim of its own excesses. Stone uses several different film stocks and tricks to keep viewers off balance—black and white, grainy color, negative images, rear projections, odd captions, crazy angles, tilted cameras, tinting. His nominal heroes are Mickey (Woody Harrelson) and Mallory (Juliette Lewis), young lovers and mass murderers who become media darlings. Why do they kill? Child abuse presented as a TV sitcom. Perhaps Stone means them to be the dark side of Forrest Gump, pure American evil as opposed to his pure goodness. Or perhaps they are merely extensions of our national love of romantic criminals that goes back to Billy the Kid and Bonnie and Clyde. But how serious can Stone's criticism of media "glorification" be when he casts a popular magazine coverboy like Harrelson in the lead? In the end, after all the impressive visual wizardry has worn off, what's left is a bitter aftertaste of hypocrisy. The "director's cut" available on video is presumably even more violent. 🦴🦴

1994 (R) 119m/C Woody Harrelson, Robert Downey Jr., Juliette Lewis, Tommy Lee Jones, Ashley Judd, Tom Sizemore, Rodney Dangerfield, Rachel Ticotin, Arliss Howard, Russell Means, Denis Leary, Steven Wright, Pruitt Taylor Vince; ***D:*** Oliver Stone; ***W:*** Oliver Stone; ***C:*** Robert Richardson; ***M:*** Trent Reznor. Nominations: Golden Globe Awards '95: Best Director (Stone); MTV Movie Awards '95: Best On-Screen Duo (Woody Harrelson/Juliette Lewis), Best Kiss (Woody Harrelson/Juliette Lewis). **VHS, LV, Closed Caption** *WAR, THV*

Nature of the Beast

Jack (Lance Henriksen) is a paunchy traveling salesman. Adrian (Eric Roberts) is a spooky hitchhiker. They meet on the road in a remote California desert, miles away from the interstate. We also know that a serial killer is chopping up people, and a million bucks-plus is missing from a Las Vegas casino. What does Adrian have in his daypack? Why is Jack so protective of his locked briefcase? Writer/director Victor Salva uses a deliberately slow pace and edgy characterizations to maintain suspense. Henriksen and Roberts have built their careers on quirky, colorful roles and these are two of their best. Henriksen is particularly strong—he also gets credit as "creative consultant"—and his perfor-

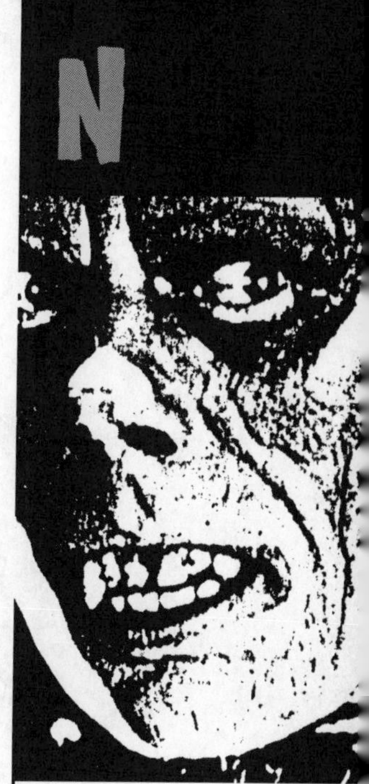

The 1980s

Violence, Special Effects, and VCRs

In the first half of the 1980s, things got bloody, really bloody. As fans demanded realistic violence, special effects became much more graphic and sophisticated, though the tricks filmmakers employed were simple. At first. As the decade went on, models and stop-motion animation took on a life of their own.

Brian DePalma decided to mix eroticism and horror and to let the plot take care of itself in *Dressed to Kill.* It was such a potent combination that hardly anybody noticed that the movie didn't make any sense. Stanley Kubrick got bravura performances out of Jack Nicholson and Shelley Duvall in his adaptation of Stephen King's *The Shining*, but his showy directorial style got in the way of really good scares. That was certainly not the case with the first of the many *Halloween* imitators. Probably the most successful—if we measure success by sheer quantity—was the *Friday the 13th* series, which got its start in 1980.

A year later, John Landis made *An American Werewolf in London*, almost a companion piece to the Joe Dante-John Sayles take on the same subject, *The Howling.*

At the same time, Frank Henenlotter created a micro-budget masterpiece mixing the supernatural with the all-too real horrors of New York's Times Square in *Basket Case.* In 1983, Sam Raimi created some remarkable visual effects on a shoestring budget, combined them with indescribable humor and took the dead-teen formula into uncharted areas with the first of his *Evil Dead* comedies.

Meanwhile, Tobe Hooper, with the strong influence of producer Steven Spielberg, went for big-budget scares in *Poltergeist.* In Italy, Dario Argento continued to craft wildly plotted exercises in excessive violence with *Tenebrae.*

Director Tony Scott, whose name would become synonymous with the most polished lightweight escapism, got his start with a high-gloss lesbian vampire picture, *The Hunger.*

Harold Ramis spoofed expensive supernatural summer movies with *Ghostbusters*, though it was an expensive supernatural summer movie (and an exceptionally profitable one). A few months later, Spielberg and Dante teamed up for the similar *Gremlins.*

In 1984, Michael Mann, who'd carve out a name for himself a few years later with the TV series *Miami Vice*, made the visually stunning World War II horror, *The Keep.*

The first *Nightmare on Elm Street* hit theatres then, too. A year later Stuart Gordon released his gore comedy *Re-Animator* on an unsuspecting world. Not coincidentally for the enduring popularity of both, that's when the home video revolution began. In a very few years, VCRs became commonplace in American homes and video stores popped up in every neighborhood. The movie-viewing habits of horror fans would change so profoundly that by the early 1990s, people would be seeing more movies on tape than they'd see in theatres.

In 1986, Mann would return to horror with *Manhunter*, an adaptation of Thomas Harris' novel *Red Dragon* that brought the first screen incarnation of Hannibal Lecter.

In 1986 author Clive Barker was able to translate his unique sense of terror to the screen with *Hellraiser.* A year later, Adrian Lyne blurred the lines between horror and suspense with the retooled thriller *Fatal Attraction.* George Sluizer took a much more realistic approach in 1988 with his bone-chilling *The Vanishing* and viewers in America got their first taste of the Grand Guignol excesses of Japanese animation in *Urotsukidoji.*

By the end of the decade, home video was firmly established as an important economic force in entertainment, and though the overall quality of horror films didn't increase, the quantity certainly did.

mance carries the spooky story over several rough spots.

1994 (R) 91m/C Eric Roberts, Lance Henriksen, Brion James; ***D:*** Victor Salva; ***W:*** Victor Salva. **VHS, LV, Closed Caption** *NLC*

Near Dark

Kathryn Bigelow's directorial debut is just your basic contemporary Western/vampire/Peckinpah-homage. It's a frightening, violent, erotic story told with a sly touch of black humor. Young Caleb (Adrian Pasdar) is seduced by Mae (Jenny Wright) and kidnapped by a gang of vampires (though that word is never used) who travel around the Southwest in stolen cars at night. Then-unknown Lance Henriksen, Bill Paxton, and Tim Thomerson do fine work. The best parts are a grotesque bloody set-piece in a roadhouse and a shootout with the cops at a seedy motel. The only flaw is a weak ending. Bigelow's flair for action gives the film a gritty texture that helps it past the lapses.

1987 (R) 95m/C Adrian Pasdar, Jenny Wright, Bill Paxton, Jenette Goldstein, Lance Henriksen, Tim Thomerson, Joshua Miller; ***D:*** Kathryn Bigelow; ***W:*** Kathryn Bigelow, Eric Red; ***C:*** Adam Greenberg; ***M:*** Tangerine Dream. **VHS, LV** *HBO, IME*

Needful Things

In style and appearance, this Stephen King adaptation is similar to Kubrick's *The Shining*. Both are visually impressive, slow moving, and brightened by mordant, dry wit. Neither is particularly frightening. The devil (Max von Sydow) opens an antique store in Castle Rock, Maine, and touches the townspeople's deepest desires. Writer W.D. Richter does a good job of compressing the long novel, but some of the subplots may not make sense to those who haven't read it. Director Fraser Heston gets journeyman work from a cast of first-rate character actors (Ed Harris, Bonnie Bedelia, Amanda Plummer, J.T. Walsh), but the film belongs to von Sydow's affable, persuasive Satan.

1993 (R) 120m/C Ed Harris, Bonnie Bedelia, Max von Sydow, Amanda Plummer, J.T. Walsh; ***D:*** Fraser Heston; ***W:*** W.D. Richter; ***M:*** Patrick Doyle. **VHS, LV, Closed Caption** *COL*

Neighbors

Though it's not normally viewed as a horror film, this dark uncomfortable fantasy defies any easy classification. Earl Kleese (John Belushi) returns to his grubby, nightmarish suburban home—conveniently located beneath crackling high power lines, and between a vacant house and a swamp—to discover weird and possibly mad new neighbors Vic (Dan Aykroyd) and Ramona (Cathy Moriarty), who proceed to invade his life. As their actions become increasingly more strange, Earl suspects that his wife (Kathryn Walker) may be in league with these weirdos. But neither Earl nor the audience knows what's real and what comes from his imagination. Writer Larry Gelbart and director John Avildsen keep viewers guessing all the way through. Yes, it's too offbeat and original to appeal to all tastes, but for the right audiences, a genuine sleeper.

1981 (R) 90m/C John Belushi, Dan Aykroyd, Kathryn Walker, Cathy Moriarty; ***D:*** John G. Avildsen; ***W:*** Larry Gelbart; ***M:*** Bill Conti. **VHS, LV** *NO*

The Nest

Killer mutant cockroaches take over a small resort island, resulting in deliciously nasty special effects and lots of creepy crawly critters. The cast is better than you'd expect, too, especially Terri Treas, as the scientist who turns out to be a little kinky for her insects. The story gets funnier and grosser as it goes along, giving bug-monster fans everything they could ask for.

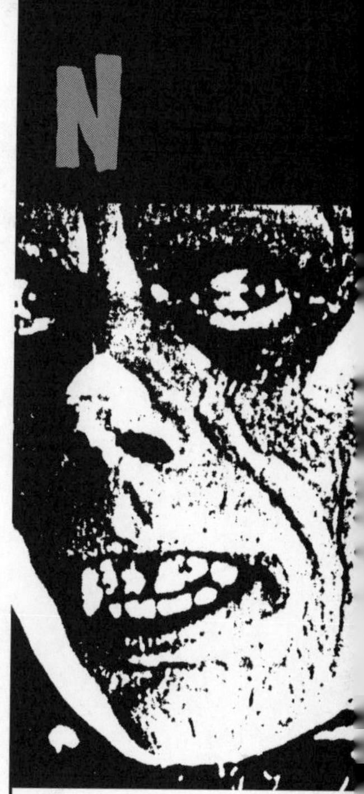

"Daddy would have gotten us Uzis."

—Samantha (Kelli Maroney) laments her inadequate weapons in *Night of the Comet*.

1988 (R) 89m/C Robert Lansing, Lisa Langlois, Franc Luz, Terri Treas, Stephen Davies, Diana Bellamy, Nancy Morgan; ***D:*** Terence H. Winkless; ***W:*** Robert King; ***M:*** Rick Conrad. **VHS** *MGM*

Netherworld

Curiously, this slick Full Moon production has never caught on with fans the way that some of its lesser efforts have. The story has to do with reincarnation, magic, and such on a plantation in the Louisiana backwater. Director David Schmoeller creates an odd waking-nightmare quality that's really chilling in its best moments. Some of the effects are ingenious, but the show is stolen by character actor Robert Burr as a deliciously decadent, Edsel-driving lawyer. Also, the Edgar Winter blues score is terrific. Watch all the way through the end of the credits for a nice final joke.

1990 (R) 87m/C Michael C. Bendetti, Denise Gentile, Anjanette Comer, Holly Floria, Robert Burr, Robert Sampson; ***D:*** David Schmoeller; ***W:*** Billy Chicago; ***C:*** Adolfo Bartoli; ***M:*** Edgar Winter. **VHS, LV, Closed Caption** *FLL*

Night Angel

The setting is a fashion magazine. Lilith (Isa Andersen) is a female demon who returns to seduce and destroy. Most of the time she looks like any other skinny fashion model, but when she turns up the heat, she changes. Her mascara looks like it was applied with a pallet knife and she grows shiny black fingernails about three inches long. When she goes after her victims, she's so trashy she makes Madonna look like Martha Stewart. Director Dominique Othenin-Girard keeps it all campy, flashy, and slick. The action peaks in the long phantasmagorical dream sequence.

1990 (R) 90m/C Isa Anderson, Linda Ashby, Debra Feuer, Helen Martin, Karen Black, Doug Jones, Gary Hudson, Sam Hennings; ***D:*** Dominique Othenin-Girard; ***W:*** Joe Augustyn. **VHS, LV** *NO*

Night Gallery

Anthology of three Rod Serling stories is famous for providing Steven Spielberg his first directorial work. His episode is the story of a ruthless blind rich woman (Joan Crawford) who wants to "buy" someone else's eyes for a few hours of sight. It's a lesser variation on the same theme Serling explored with Burgess Meredith in the memorable "Time Enough at Last" episode of *The Twilight Zone*. As usual with Serling, the stories are openly emotional and on the slow side. Beyond a couple of neat touches, Spielberg's segment is nothing special. But he showed the right people in Hollywood that he could handle a major star and the rest is boxoffice history. His next work, *Duel*, shows what he would become.

1969 95m/C Joan Crawford, Roddy McDowall, Tom Bosley, Barry Sullivan, Ossie Davis, Sam Jaffe, Kate Greenfield, Richard Kiley, George Macready, Norma Crane, Barry Atwater; ***D:*** Steven Spielberg, Boris Sagal, Boris Shear; ***W:*** Rod Serling. **VHS** *USH*

Night Hunter

Attempt to combine martial arts with horror relies too heavily on the former. Perhaps that's to be expected with Don Wilson as Jack Cutter, vampire hunter. He gets help from *World Inquisitor* tabloid reporter Raimy Baker (Melanie Smith) as he goes after Jacqueline Tournier (Maria Ford) and her undead pals. (Older horror fans will catch the joke with the name.) Wilson has the presence to carry the simple story, and, of course, he handles the physical action gracefully. This one's an energetic low-budget effort, though the contemporary vampire concept has been handled much more imaginatively in recent years.

1995 (R) 86m/C Don "The Dragon" Wilson, Melanie Smith, Nicholas Guest, Maria Ford; ***D:*** Rick Jacobson. **VHS** *NHO*

Night Monster

Clunky formula picture from the Universal back lot is fun for fans of the '40s. It's an "old dark house" tale complete with secret passages and clearly telegraphed killings. Bela Lugosi is the secretive butler. Other stereotypes include the lecherous chauffeur, the wise-cracking maid, the paralyzed millionaire, the doctors who paralyzed him, a mystic from the East, and a chain-smoking mystery writer. Sample dialogue: "Dick, you're always writing about things like this. Who do you think this homicidal maniac is?" The featherweight stuff is solidly acted by a troupe of veteran character actors who make the constant cliches fun. ***AKA:*** House of Mystery.

1942 80m/B Bela Lugosi, Ralph Morgan, Lionel Atwill, Leif Erickson, Don Porter, Irene Hervey, Nils Asther; ***D:*** Ford Beebe; ***W:*** Clarence Upson Young; ***C:*** Charles Van Enger. **VHS, Closed Caption** *USH*

Night of a Thousand Cats

Hugo (Hugo Stiglitz) flies around Mexico City in his helicopter and picks up girls. Really! (Don't ask how.) He takes them to his remote monastery where, with the help of his mute bald servant Dargo (Zulma Faiad), he kills them and feeds them to a bunch of house cats he keeps locked in the basement. With wild early '70s clothes, music, and glorious incompetence—one flashback stops midway, then starts over—it's hard to say exactly how much of the comedy is intentional, but who cares? This time, the Hound is firmly on the felines' side. ***AKA:*** La Noche de los Mil Gatos; Blood Feast; Cats.

1972 (R) 83m/C *MX* Anjanette Comer, Zulma Faiad, Hugo Stiglitz, Christa Linder, Teresa Velasquez, Barbara Ange; ***D:*** Rene Cardona Jr. **VHS** *JEF*

Night of the Cobra Woman

Incoherent almost to the point of unwatchability, this lesser Philippine drive-in cheapie doesn't fare well on video. Marlene Clark is the nurse who is granted semi-immortality with a catch after she's bitten by a snake who really has her best interests at heart. The human-to-serpent transformations aren't the least bit believable or scary (though the real snakes are). The high point is what appears to be a real fight between an eagle and a cobra. (This film does NOT contain one of those "No animals were harmed, etc." disclaimers.) Co-star Joy Bang does have astonishingly long prehensile toes, clearly displayed in a couple of barefoot scenes.

1972 (R) 85m/C *PH* Joy Bang, Marlene Clark, Roger Garrett, Slash Marks, Vic Diaz; ***D:*** Andrew Meyer; ***W:*** Andrew Meyer. **VHS** *NLC, OM*

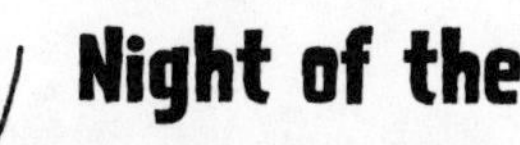

Night of the Comet

After a comet zaps the world, wiping out most of the people but leaving the material goods intact, tough-minded Valley Girls Reggie (Catherine Mary Stewart) and Samantha (Kelli Maroney) Belmont don't even need credit cards to clean out the mall. If only there weren't all these darn zombies wandering around, not to mention the mad scientists (Geoffrey Lewis and Mary Woronov). Writer/director Thom Eberhardt makes his heroines appealing young women, but toward the end, the story takes on a tired, almost nihilistic cast which, like the zombies, seems to have been borrowed from a *Living Dead* film. By the way, the premise is lifted from one of Conan Doyle's Prof. Challenger stories.

1984 (PG-13) 90m/C Catherine Mary Stewart, Kelli Maroney, Robert Beltran, Geoffrey Lewis, Mary Woronov, Sharon Farrell, Michael Bowen; ***D:*** Thom Eberhardt; ***W:*** Thom Eberhardt; ***C:*** Arthur Albert. **VHS, Closed Caption** *FOX*

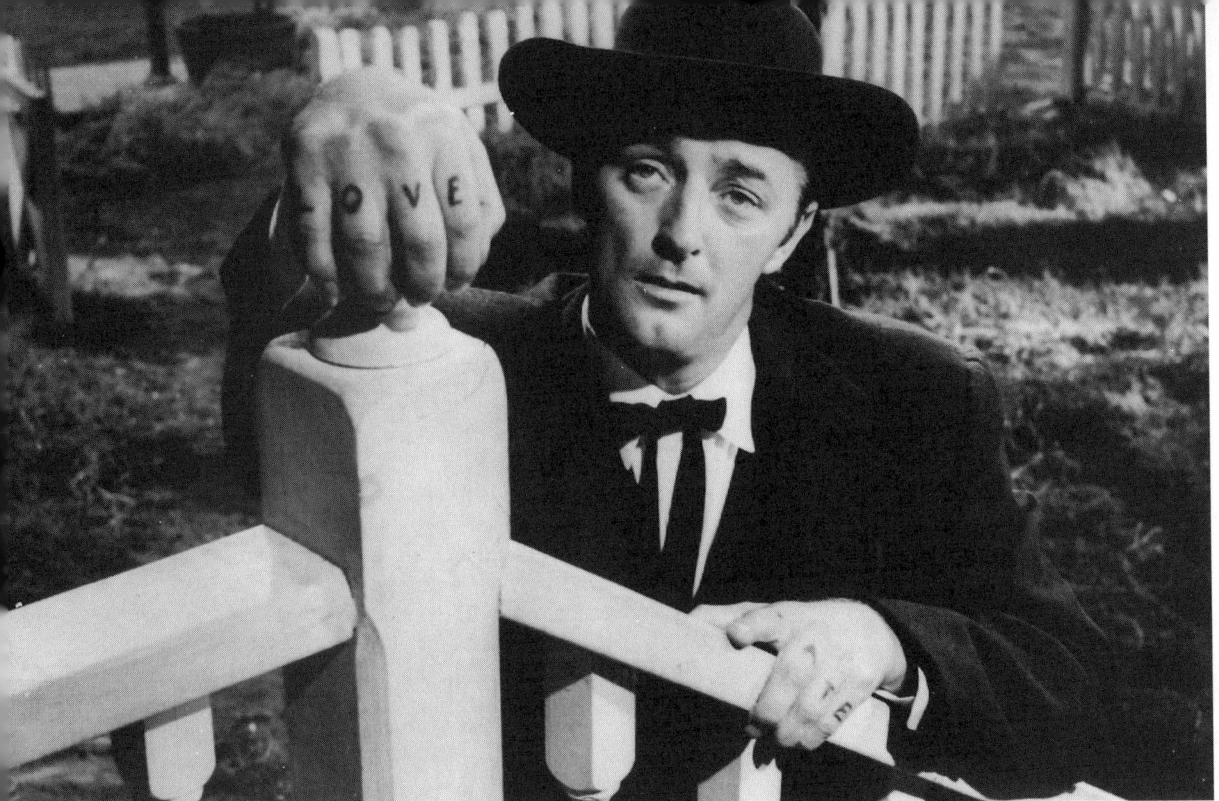

Rev. Harry Powell (Robert Mitchum) in *The Night of the Hunter.*

Night of the Creeps

Schlocky little B-horror revels in its own schlock. The plot is standard stuff involving parasitic slugs from outer space that infect a college town and turn the kids into living-dead zombies. Writer/director Fred Dekker keeps the pace zipping right along and he collected a troupe of seasoned professionals, including Tom Atkins, Dick Miller, and Kenneth Tobey. For once, the scares and the humor—much of it aimed at fans, with Corman University as the setting and characters named Cameron, Landis, and Raimi—complement each other well. ***AKA:*** Creeps; Homecoming Night.

1986 (R) 89m/C Jason Lively, Jill Whitlow, Tom Atkins, Steve Marshall, Wally Taylor, Bruce Solomon, Kenneth Tobey, Dick Miller; ***D:*** Fred Dekker; ***W:*** Fred Dekker; ***C:*** Robert New. **VHS, LV, Closed Caption** *NO*

The Night of the Hunter

Charles Laughton's only turn in the director's chair defies easy categorization. Though it's usually considered film noir, of sorts, it's really more psycho-killer Gothic, with Robert Mitchum in perhaps his most frightening role. Historians and critics are divided on where the credit should go, so give equal shares to Laughton, screenwriter James Agee, and novelist Davis Grubb. The plot is simple. A homicidal preacher (Robert Mitchum) worms his way into the Harper family's affections. He means to steal the $10,000 that Ben Harper (Peter Graves) stole and hid before he was executed. Widow Willa (Shelley Winters) is an easy mark, but her son John (Billy Chapin) isn't fooled. When Preacher becomes more insane and vicious, John and his sister Pearl (Sally Jane Bruce) have to turn to Rachel Cooper (Lillian Gish) for help. Casting Robert Mitchum as the charismatic villain and Lillian Gish as a resourceful rescuer was a masterstroke. Though the roles go directly against their images, both stars are at their best. As director, Laughton took some extraordinary chances with odd angles and overt symbolism. Even judged by today's standards, some moments are so bizarre, startling, and unpredictable that they defy description. One of the best.

1955 93m/B Robert Mitchum, Shelley Winters, Lillian Gish, Don Beddoe, Evelyn Varden, Peter Graves, James Gleason, Billy Chapin, Sally Jane Bruce; ***D:*** Charles Laughton; ***W:*** James Agee. National Film Registry '92. **VHS, LV** *MGM*

Night of the Lepus

"They're as big as wolves—and just as vicious!" says Dr. Clark (DeForest Kelley). They're...they're giant mutant carnivorous bunny rabbits! The earth trembles beneath the thunder of their mighty paws! Grown men weep at the sight of their twitching noses! Well, actually, they don't weep and the earth doesn't tremble, but you will giggle when you see these little critters hopping around HO-scale sets in slow motion to make them appear large and powerful. If the filmmakers had only embraced the humor of their subject and coaxed their cast into the same spirit, this might have been a cult classic. Instead, they brought together a group of so-so character actors—and one genuine star, Janet Leigh—who turn in wooden performances that match the lame script. It's interesting to compare this laugher with *Ben* and *Willard,* all three about small furry mammals and all produced at about the same time. Rats are scary; rabbits are not. Even a bad movie about rats will have a few frightening moments, but not even Steven Spielberg could invest bunnies with credible ferocity.

1972 (PG) 88m/C Stuart Whitman, Janet Leigh, Rory Calhoun, DeForest Kelley, Paul Fix, Minnie Fullerton; ***D:*** William Claxton; ***W:*** Don Holliday, Gene R. Kearney; ***C:*** Ted Voightlander; ***M:*** Jimmie Haskell. *NYR*

Night of the Living Dead

Raymond Chandler said that hard-boiled mystery writer Dashiell Hammett gave murder back to the people who were good at it by setting his stories in a real world populated by believable characters. In 1968, George Romero did the same thing for horror. At that time, Roger Corman's low-budget Poe adaptations were pretty well played out, and on the other end of the spectrum, Roman Polanski's baroque *Rosemary's Baby* was the kind of movie that could come only from a big studio. Romero and a group of his friends who were also investors decided to make a "little" black-and-white movie where they lived, in Pittsburgh. After considerable squabbling (which is reflected in the film itself), they settled upon a simple story about the recently deceased rising up to eat the flesh of the non-deceased. Several people—with nary a stereotype in the bunch—are trapped in a farmhouse by these stumbling zombies. Over the course of a day and a night, they try to survive, making one wrong decision after another as the horror and suspense steadily increase. Romero found uniformly good and natural performances from an unknown cast. As the sheriff, George Kosana is outstanding, and his most famous line—"They're dead; they're all messed up."—was an improvisation. Though the film has been copied, imitated, and parodied countless times, it remains an intense experience. Since the title is in public domain, tapes vary widely in quality. The Anchor Bay edition, made from the original negative, is by far the best. ***AKA:*** Night of the Flesh Eaters; Night of the Anubis.

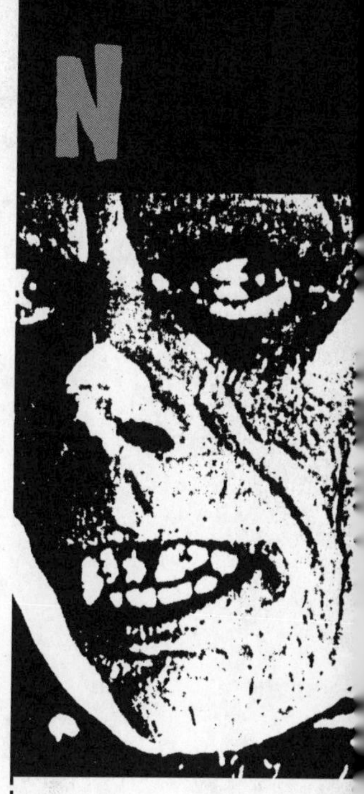

"Kill the brain and you kill the ghoul."

—A TV announcer advising on zombie defense in *Night of the Living Dead* (1968).

THE HOUND SALUTES

GEORGE ROMERO

Every decade or so the horror film is reinvented, and in 1968, it was George Romero's turn with *Night of the Living Dead*. The film has been championed and pilloried on artistic, moral, and political grounds. It remains a significant influence on the horror that has come since and it's still a huge favorite with fans. As Robin Wood wrote, *Night of the Living Dead* "is a landmark of the American horror film. It proved decisively that significant and commercially successful work in that genre could be produced outside Hollywood, on a low budget, independent of major studios." (*International Dictionary of Films & Filmmakers, V. II*, Putnam/Perigee, 1984.)

The film's genesis and creation were true collaborative efforts, though. Romero almost didn't direct it.

Born in 1940 in New York, he had come to Pittsburgh as a student at the Carnegie Institute of Technology (now Carnegie-Mellon University), fallen in love with the city, and stayed there. In 1963, he and some friends started Latent Image, a production company that made local TV commercials. It developed a reputation for doing good work on modest budgets. A job doing an innovative spot for Calgon laundry detergent gave the fledgling filmmakers the money and the confidence to try their hands at a feature.

Horror was not their first choice. They'd already tried to get several more serious and high-minded projects off the ground but they settled for a black-and-white fright flick on purely commercial grounds. So, they put up some of their own money, attracted investors for the rest, and set out to make a movie. The original ideas came from Romero. He and John Russo wrote most of the script with help from at least three others. The group decision-making process continued with egos getting in the way, until

1968 90m/B Judith O'Dea, Duane Jones, Karl Hardman, Marilyn Eastman, Keith Wayne, Judith Ridley, Russell Streiner, George Kosana, Bill "Chilly Billy" Cardille; ***D:*** George A. Romero; ***W:*** John A. Russo; ***C:*** George A. Romero. **VHS, LV** *VTR, NOS, HHT*

Night of the Living Dead

Offbeat remake may not be completely necessary but it's not altogether bad, either. The main strengths are commanding performances by Tony Todd and Patricia Tallman in the leads. (Her Barbara is a much more active and assertive character than she was before.) The main weakness is lack of originality. The story doesn't vary significantly from the first version, and how many "living dead" zombies have stumbled across the screen in the past decades? The technical advances in effects and a more generous budget actually work against the claustrophobic intensity that made the first film a cult hit.

1990 (R) 92m/C Tony Todd, Patricia Tallman, Tom Towles, William Butler, Bill Moseley, McKee Anderson, Kate Finneran; ***D:*** Tom Savini; ***W:*** George A. Romero; ***C:*** Frank Prinzi. **VHS, LV** *COL*

Romero was chosen to be the man behind the camera and the editing machine.

The rest is horror history, well if uncritically detailed in Paul R. Gagne's *The Zombies that Ate Pittsburgh* (Dodd Mead, 1987).

In all that has been written about the film, though, one simple fact tends to be lost. Like Hitchcock in *Psycho,* Romero found his horror in everyday human beings. Forget the silly little radiation-from-the-returning-Venus-probe explanation that's lamely mentioned. The zombies are not exotic vampires or monsters from outer space or the black lagoon. They're us.

Romero expands the concept in the *Dead* sequels. He also plays with it in his underrated *Season of the Witch* and *Martin.* Completely human evil without mystic trappings has always been the source of his best work.

Over the years, Romero has built his reputation with more expensive projects, often involving Stephen King. Recently, his output has dropped off as he's become entangled in what industry insiders call "development hell," where studios are momentarily enthusiastic about projects but then, somehow, change their collective minds. The most enticing of those was a remake of Universal's *The Mummy,* which at this writing seems to be on again with another director. There's also still talk of a fourth *Dead* film, though the trilogy has been brought to a satisfactory conclusion.

Romero himself has been quoted as saying that if he has five lights and a few good actors, they can do something scary, and he's proved that he can. Working within the studio system, it's doubtful that they'll come up with anything as scary as *Night of the Living Dead.* Not many have.

SIGNIFICANT CONTRIBUTIONS TO HORROR

Night of the Living Dead **(1968)**

Season of the Witch **(1973)**

Martin **(1977)**

Dawn of the Dead **(1978)**

Day of the Dead **(1985)**

Monkey Shines **(1988)**

The Dark Half **(1991)**

Night of the Scarecrow

O.K. '90s formula horror flick is nicely photographed with a few bloody good touches as the titular boogieman cuts his swatch through the cornfields and into the rural hamlet of Hanford. The religious imagery is overused and poorly understood. Director Jeff Burr breaks no new ground. Elizabeth Barondes is a fine independent heroine and '60s veteran Martine Beswick shows up as the preacher's wife. 🦴🦴🦴

1995 (R) 90m/C Elizabeth Barondes, John Mese, Stephen Root, Bruce Glover, Dirk Blocker, Howard Swain, Gary Lockwood, John Lazar, John Hawkes, Martine Beswick; ***D:*** Jeff Burr; ***W:*** Reed Steiner, Dan Mazur; ***C:*** Thomas Callaway; ***M:*** Jim Manzie. **VHS, Closed Caption** *REP*

Night School

The presence of Rachel Ward, who's gone on to much better things, is the only redeeming feature of this otherwise disposable stab & slasher. Hot on the trail of a serial decapitator, Harvard-educated Lt. Austin (Leonard Mann) bops around Boston in a BMW with his comic sidekick

"Just because I'm showing somebody being disemboweled doesn't mean that I have to get heavy and put a message behind it."

—George Romero as quoted in *Film Yearbook,* 1983.

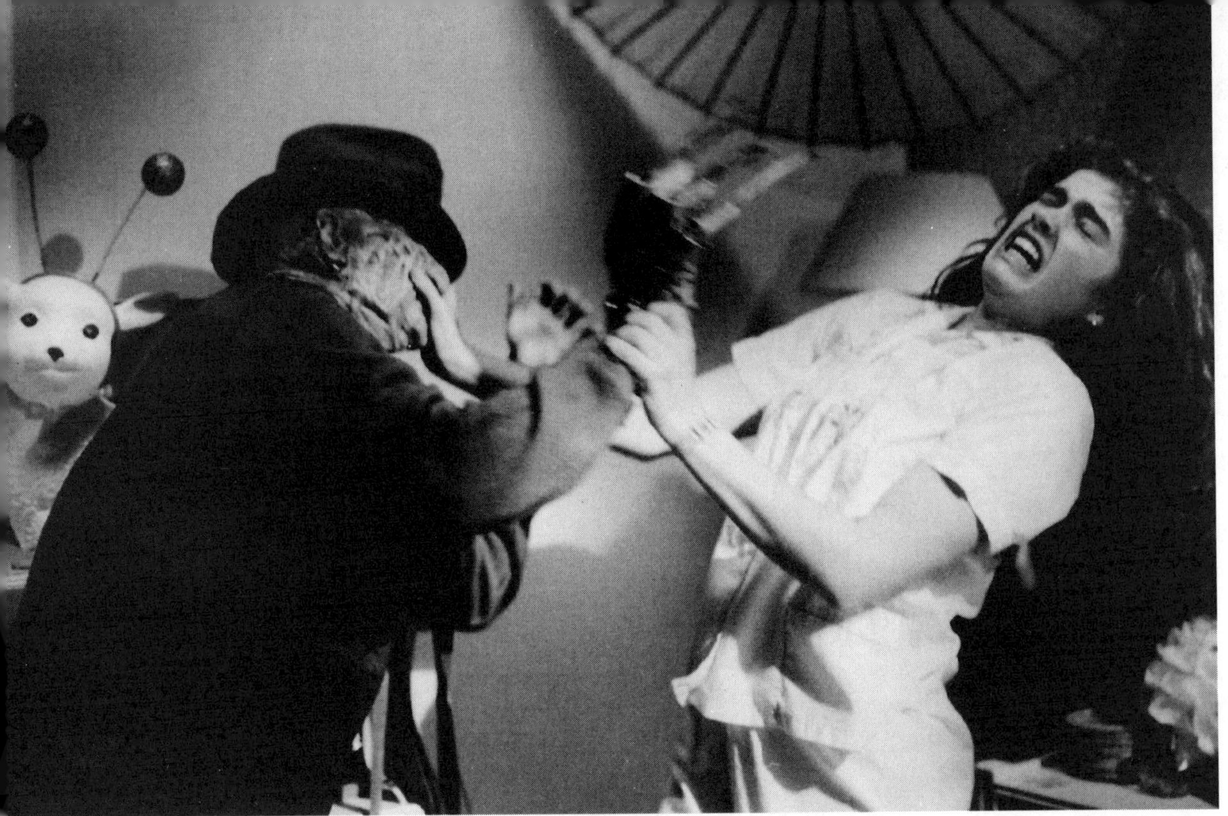

Freddy Krueger (Robert Englund) and Nancy Thompson (Heather Langenkamp) in Wes Craven's *A Nightmare on Elm Street*.

Sgt. Taj (Joseph R. Sicari). They suspect Prof. Snyder (Drew Snyder), who's carrying on, as they say, with his assistant Eleanor (Ward). Ruth Avergon's script is transparent and Ken Hughes' direction is slow. You have been warned. ***AKA:*** Terror Eyes. 🦴

1981 (R) 89m/C Leonard Mann, Rachel Ward, Drew Snyder, Joseph R. Sicari, Nicholas Cairis, Bill McCann, Margo Skinner; ***D:*** Ken Hughes; ***W:*** Ruth Avergon; ***C:*** Mark Irwin; ***M:*** Brad Fiedel. **VHS** *FOX*

The Night Stalker

When it aired in 1971, this was generally regarded as the best movie ever made for television, and it's aged more gracefully than many of its theatrical contemporaries. It was one of the first horror films to combine realistic police procedural details and a contemporary setting with vampire lore. Add in solid characters based on familiar stereotypes—wisecracking reporter, tough editor, weasely politico—and a winning off-the-cuff comic performance by Darren McGavin in the lead. Both Richard Matheson's script and the photography are rock solid. Journeyman director John Llewellyn Moxey never lets the pace flag. Followed by a sequel, *The Night Strangler,* and a TV series. 🦴🦴🦴

1971 73m/C Darren McGavin, Carol Lynley, Simon Oakland, Ralph Meeker, Claude Akins, Kent Smith, Larry Linville, Barry Atwater; ***D:*** John Llewellyn Moxey; ***W:*** Richard Matheson. *FOX*

The Nightcomers

Michael Winner's "prequel" to Henry James' *Turn of the Screw* is much trashier and more enjoyable than the source material. Screenwriter Michael Hastings' (*Tom & Viv*) interpretation of the characters and

their story is just as transparent as James' is opaque. Quint (Marlon Brando) is carrying on an overheated, kinky S&M affair with Miss Jessel (Stephanie Beacham) under the curious eyes of two watchful children. Brando's animated performance as a cheerful, conniving manchild is a delight and can be seen in some ways as a dry run for *Last Tango in Paris*. The film benefits from Robert Paynter's handsome photography, excellent locations, and a fine Jerry Fielding score. The conclusion's a shock.

1972 (R) 96m/C *GB* Marlon Brando, Stephanie Beacham, Thora Hird, Harry Andrews, Christopher Ellis, Verna Harvey, Anna Palk; ***D:*** Michael Winner; ***W:*** Michael Hastings; ***C:*** Bob Paynter; ***M:*** Jerry Fielding. **VHS, LV** *COL, NLC*

Nightmare

Is wealthy teenager Janet (Jennie Linden) really insane, or is someone—perhaps her guardian Henry Baxter (David Knight) or nurse Grace Maddox (Moira Redmond)—trying to drive her mad? This black-and-white Hammer entry lacks the studio's best-known stars but, as is almost always the case, it's a rock-solid story told by professionals who know what they're doing. It's comparable to the more restrained William Castle efforts of the same time, but not another *Psycho*.

1963 83m/B *GB* Jennie Linden, David Knight, Moira Redmond, Brenda Bruce; ***D:*** Freddie Francis; ***W:*** Jimmy Sangster; ***C:*** John Wilcox; ***M:*** Don Banks. **VHS, Closed Caption** *USH*

The Nightmare Before Christmas

Producer Tim Burton and director Henry Selick sustain a dark, charmed mood in this stop-motion animation feature. When Jack Skellington, the King of Halloween, discovers Christmastown, he decides that the two holidays should be combined. The filmmakers are trying to create another variation on the whimsical atmosphere that was so important to *Edward Scissorhands* and *Beetlejuice*, a mixture of childlike wonder and horror that isn't truly frightening. Danny Elfman's songs carry much of the action. Only "What's This?" really cuts loose, but Elfman's instrumental score is terrific. In the end, the film is so unusual that animation fans are the real audience. ***AKA:*** Tim Burton's The Nightmare Before Christmas.

1993 (PG) 75m/C ***D:*** Henry Selick; ***W:*** Caroline Thompson, Tim Burton; ***M:*** Danny Elfman; ***V:*** Danny Elfman, Chris Sarandon, Catherine O'Hara, William Hickey, Ken Page, Ed Ivory, Paul (Pee Wee Herman) Reubens, Glenn Shadix. Nominations: Academy Awards '93: Best Visual Effects; Golden Globe Awards '94: Best Score. **VHS, LV, Closed Caption** *TOU*

A Nightmare on Elm Street

Consider for a moment the marketing genius behind Freddy Krueger and the *Elm Street* series. Freddy (Robert Englund) is a ghost, in the loosest sense of the term—the spirit of a child molester who was burned to death by the parents of his victims. Now he can come back with his razor-fingered glove-thingy. He can appear and disappear at will. He can pop from here to there instantaneously. He can do terrible things in either the visible or invisible mode, in either the dream world or the real world. And he has no real motivation; he's just mean, hates everything and everybody. Because his powers are so elastic, this little moneymaker can be killed and resurrected as long as he stays in the black. See the following sequels and *Wes Craven's New Nightmare*.

1984 (R) 92m/C John Saxon, Heather Langenkamp, Ronee Blakley, Robert Englund, Amanda Wyss, Nick Corri, Johnny Depp, Charles Fleischer; ***D:*** Wes Craven; ***W:*** Wes Craven; ***C:*** Jacques Haitkin; ***M:*** Charles Bernstein. **VHS, LV, Closed Caption** *VTR, CDV, IME*

ROBERT ENGLUND

Who'd have ever thought that an old fedora, moth-eaten sweater, second-rate scar makeup, and a glove with hedge trimmer fingers would be the ticket to the top of the horror heap?

They certainly did the trick for Robert Englund.

He and writer/director Wes Craven (who left the series after the first installment) used those simple props—and several million dollars' worth of special effects—to create Freddy Krueger, a reincarnated child molester who's at the center of the six *Nightmare on Elm Street* movies and *Wes Craven's New Nightmare*.

Before Freddy found him, Englund was a boyish-looking character actor—born in 1949 in Glendale, California—who got his start acting on stage in New York and Michigan. He appeared sporadically in all sorts of films. One early appearance is in the drive-in favorite *Buster and Billie* with Jan Michael Vincent. He was also in Bob Rafelson's *Stay Hungry* and Barbra Streisand's *A Star Is Born*. Much of his early work was on television, and in the post-Freddy years, he has continued to be a sought-after guest on many series.

For horror fans, his first major appearance is in Tobe Hooper's *Eaten Alive*, where he's a dissatisfied customer at a rural whorehouse. One of his early films, *Sunburst*, has been retitled *Slashed Dreams* on video, and Englund appeared in the cult favorite *Dead and Buried*. He was also in *V*, both the TV series and the movie about alien Nazi lizards from outer space. In 1989, between *Elm Street 4* and

A Nightmare on Elm Street 2: Freddy's Revenge

Fans of this popular but overrated series have long held that the even-numbered entries are the worst, and *2* certainly bears them out. Some of the sillier effects involve flying tennis balls, exploding hotdogs, and a possessed parakeet, not to mention the boy who talks with his mouth full. Everything about this one, from the opening dream sequence to the slaughtered teens to the cliched ending, strictly follows the formula. The unintentional humor is a relief from the numbing routine. **Woof!**

1985 (R) 87m/C Mark Patton, Hope Lange, Clu Gulager, Robert Englund, Kim Myers, Robert Rusler, Marshall Bell, Sydney Walsh; ***D:*** Jack Sholder; ***W:*** David Chaskin; ***C:*** Jacques Haitkin. **VHS, LV, Closed Caption** *VTR, CDV, IME*

A Nightmare on Elm Street 3: Dream Warriors

Sheer inventiveness alone does not make a good horror movie. Neither do special effects involving tongues, and this is the virtual *Gone with the Wind* of tongue-effect movies. Other than those, it's more of the same as the ubiquitous Freddy (Robert Englund) shows up everywhere, even on *The Dick Cavett Show*, and preys on insti-

5, he turned in an effective interpretation of the title character in an updated *Phantom of the Opera*. He played both himself and Freddy in *Wes Craven's New Nightmare*. Due for tentative release on November 13, 1999, is *Freddy Vs. Jason*, wherein, presumably, Krueger and his cut-rate competition will appear together, making good on the implied threat at the conclusion of *Jason Goes to Hell*.

Beyond Englund's ability to keep the character fresh (with the considerable help of those aforementioned effects), he and the producers have handled their franchise player wisely, turning Freddy into a new version of the E.C. Comics Cryptkeeper.

Englund's one foray into directing is the forgettable *976-EVIL*.

SIGNIFICANT CONTRIBUTIONS TO HORROR

Eaten Alive **(1976)**

A Nightmare on Elm Street **(1984)**

Phantom of the Opera **(1986)**

Wes Craven's New Nightmare **(1994)**

tutionalized kids, including the then almost-famous Patricia Arquette, as well as Laurence (then Larry) Fishburne, whose resume already included *Apocalypse Now* and the TV soap *One Life to Live*. Original heroine Heather Langenkamp returns (she also plays herself in the final installment, *Wes Craven's New Nightmare*). Throughout, the pace is quick and director Charles Russell (*The Mask*) never seems to take this dumb stuff seriously. Though fans praise this one highly, it's still got a "3" in the title.

1987 (R) 96m/C Patricia Arquette, Robert Englund, Heather Langenkamp, Craig Wasson, Laurence "Larry" Fishburne, Priscilla Pointer, John Saxon, Brooke Bundy, Jennifer Rubin, Rodney Eastman, Nan Martin, Dick Cavett, Zsa Zsa Gabor; ***D:*** Chuck Russell; ***W:*** Chuck Russell, Bruce Wagner, Wes Craven, Frank Darabont; ***C:*** Roy Wagner; ***M:*** Angelo Badalamenti. **VHS, LV, Closed Caption** *VTR, CDV, IME*

A Nightmare on Elm Street 4: Dream Master

Since, as the subtitle indicates, the movie is essentially a dream from the first shot, it contains no real scares—just shocks and surprises on some remarkable sets. As you ought to expect from any sequel with a *4* in the title, the plot is familiar. The main characters are blandly, generically attractive. Director Renny Harlin shows off with flashy overdirection whenever he can. He gives the production such a high gloss that it's the most glittering piece of eye-candy in the series.

1988 (R) 99m/C Robert Englund, Rodney Eastman, Danny Hassel, Andras Jones, Tuesday Knight, Lisa

Wilcox, Ken Sagoes, Toy Newkirk, Brooke Theiss, Brooke Bundy; ***D:*** Renny Harlin; ***W:*** Brian Helgeland, Scott Pierce; ***C:*** Steven Fierberg; ***M:*** Craig Safan. **VHS, LV, Closed Caption** *VTR, CDV, IME*

"One, two, Freddy's comin' for you. Three, four, better lock your door. Five, six, grab a crucifix. Seven, eight, gonna stay up late. Nine, ten, never sleep again...."

—A child's chant in *A Nightmare on Elm Street.*

A Nightmare on Elm Street 5: Dream Child

Freddy (Robert Englund) attacks Alice's (Lisa Wilcox) unborn fetus. (No, the film has nothing to add to the abortion debate.) Again, the dream structure eliminates real scares, so the filmmakers concentrate on imaginative effects. Also, since so much of the horror is based on pregnancy, childbirth, and monster infants, women may react to the story on a more fundamental level; credit writer Leslie Bohem.

1989 (R) 90m/C Robert Englund, Lisa Wilcox, Kelly Jo Minter, Danny Hassel, Erika Anderson, Nicholas Mele, Beatrice Boepple, Christopher Ellis; ***D:*** Stephen Hopkins; ***W:*** Leslie Bohem; ***C:*** Peter Levy; ***M:*** Jay Michael Ferguson. Golden Raspberry Awards '89: Worst Song ("Bring Your Daughter to the Slaughter"). **VHS, LV, Closed Caption** *VTR, IME*

Nightmares

So-so anthology benefits from the presence of stars on the verge of fame. In the first story, Lisa (Christina Raines) goes out for smokes while a homicidal maniac is on the loose. JJ (Emilio Estevez) plays a video game for very high stakes. Suffering a crisis of faith, desert priest Father Frank (Lance Henriksen) battles a four-wheel-drive devil in the best episode. Finally, Stephen (Richard Masur) and Claire's (Veronica Cartwright) house is attacked by giant supernatural polter-rats. Veteran film and TV director Joseph Sargent handles things briskly.

1983 (PG) 99m/C Christina Raines, Emilio Estevez, Moon Zappa, Lance Henriksen, Richard Masur, Veronica Cartwright; ***D:*** Joseph Sargent; ***W:*** Jeffrey Bloom, Christopher Crowe. **VHS** *USH*

Nightscare

Rare horror/comedy actually manages to be frightening, funny, and original. It's obvious from the first shot—an extreme close-up of a hypodermic needle entering flesh—that director Vadim Jean is trying to work on a primal level. Gilmore (Keith Allen) is an insane murderer. Dr. Lyell (Elizabeth Hurley) is the neurologist who's treating him with an experimental drug, which she's also testing herself. Detective Hamilton (Craig Fairbrass) is the cop who arrested Gilmore and still has reason to hate him. The drug brings the three of them together. Jean does a fine job of depicting different states of perception—dream, drugged, memory, sobriety—and making them equally "real" onscreen. Whenever the film threatens to take itself too seriously, a dry, mordant humor shows up. Don't miss the last little visual joke that's tossed in at the end of the closing credits. ***AKA:*** Night Scare; Beyond Bedlam.

1993 (R) 89m/C *GB* Craig Fairbrass, Elizabeth Hurley, Keith Allen, Jesse Birdsall, Craig Kelly; ***D:*** Vadim Jean; ***W:*** Vadim Jean. **VHS, LV, Closed Caption** *LIV*

Nightwing

Well-intentioned adaptation really doesn't do justice to Martin Cruz Smith's fine novel, despite its faithfulness to the plot. Duran (Nick Mancuso) is an Indian deputy who discovers a flock of vampire bats carrying a plague. The main problem is the bats—they're never remotely believable or frightening. The script isn't much better. The flaky characters from Smith's novel have been replaced by a series of cliches. The rest of the cast, including Kathryn Harrold, Stephen Macht, and David Warner, are capable, but they have nothing to work with. Coulda been a contender.

1979 (PG) 103m/C Nick Mancuso, David Warner, Kathryn Harrold, Strother Martin, Stephen Macht, Pat Corley, Charles Hallahan, Ben Piazza, George Clutesi; ***D:*** Arthur Hiller; ***W:*** Steve Shagan, Bud Shrake, Martin

Cruz Smith; ***C:*** Charles Rosher Jr.; ***M:*** Henry Mancini. **VHS, LV** *COL*

Nightwish

What is the creepy professor (Jack Starrett) up to with his grad students (Clayton Rohner, Elizabeth Kaitan, Alisha Das) and their dream research? Writer/director Bruce Cook comes up with some nice scares (particularly toward the end) amid the usual supernatural cliches in a fair parapsychological horror. O.K. for fans but nothing new. Also available in an unrated version.

1989 (R) 96m/C Jack Starrett, Robert Tessier, Clayton Rohner, Elizabeth Kaitan, Alisha Das, Tom Dugan, Brian Thompson, Artur Cybulski; ***D:*** Bruce Cook Jr.; ***W:*** Bruce Cook Jr. **VHS, LV** *NO*

976-EVIL

Actor Robert Englund (of Freddy Krueger fame) makes an unspectacular directorial debut with a variation on the standard dead-teen formula. The gimmick is a telephone "horrorscope" that turns against its young callers. The most frightening thing onscreen is an out-of-control Sandy Dennis doing her best Shelly Winters imitation. Englund treats the material with a light sense of humor, but beyond the big finish, the production values are rough—even for such a low-budget effort—and the characters are virtual cartoons. Also, the movie has far too many cats for the Hound's taste.

1988 (R) 102m/C Stephen Geoffreys, Jim Metzler, Maria Rubell, Sandy Dennis, Robert Picardo, Leslie Deane, Pat O'Bryan, J.J. Cohen; ***D:*** Robert Englund; ***W:*** Brian Helgeland, Rhet Topham; ***C:*** Paul Elliott; ***M:*** Tom Chase, Steve Rucker. **VHS, LV, Closed Caption** *COL*

Nomads

It's difficult to believe that director John McTiernan (*Die Hard, Predator*) made his debut with this impressively cast but weak horror flick. Lesley-Anne Down is an L.A. doctor; Pierce Brosnan is a French anthropologist who comes raving into her emergency room, whispers something in her ear, and dies. He then returns in her visions of his past. The titular creatures dress like refugees from a heavy metal concert, play loud rock music, and spray paint garage doors. The film dithers confusingly between two time lines, and never really defines its villains.

1986 (R) 91m/C Pierce Brosnan, Lesley-Anne Down, Adam Ant, Anna Maria Monticelli, Mary Woronov, Hector Mercado; ***D:*** John McTiernan; ***W:*** John McTiernan; ***C:*** Stephen Ramsey; ***M:*** Bill Conti. **VHS, LV** *IME, PAR*

Normal Life

In *Henry: Portrait of a Serial Killer,* John McNaughton took an uncomfortably perceptive look inside the mind of a psychotic. His subject in this midwestern Gothic is another unusual individual based on a real killer. Pam Anderson (Ashley Judd) is a case study in abnormality, a woman whose "normal life" is anything but. A combination of self-absorbed obsessive love, drug abuse, and mood swings have virtually destroyed her marriage to Chris (Luke Perry), a cop. McNaughton and writers Peg Haller and Bob Schneider go straight to the dark heart of this couple. Even those who appreciate the trip will find that some of the more bizarre emotional moments go too far and others don't go far enough. And even if the ending is accurate and appropriate, it's less than completely right. Even so, the film is an ambitious, challenging, and mostly successful examination of the American dream gone sour.

1996 (R) 108m/C Luke Perry, Ashley Judd, Bruce A. Young, Jim True, Dawn Maxey, Penelope Milford, Tom Towles; ***D:*** John McNaughton; ***W:*** Bob Schneider, Peg Haller; ***C:*** Jean De Segonzac. **VHS, LV, Closed Caption** *NLC*

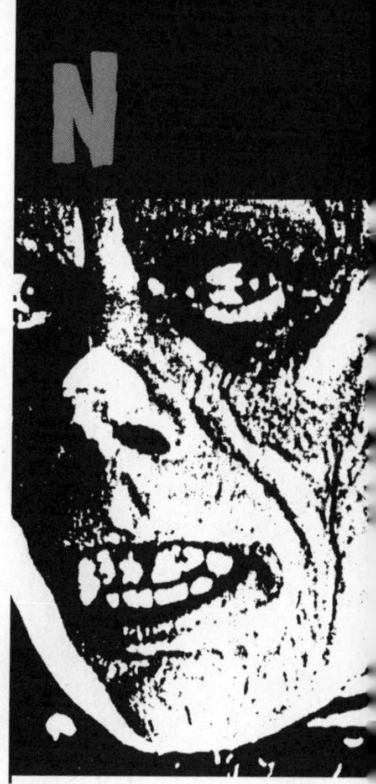

THE HOUND SALUTES

BORIS KARLOFF

In his book *The Monster Show: A Cultural History of Horror* (Penguin, 1993), David Skal quotes Boris Karloff's memories of the creation of the Frankenstein monster. He and makeup genius Jack Pierce had worked with several concepts. When they finally had something that was ready for a screen test, they didn't know whether it would frighten people or make them laugh.

"I was thinking this," Karloff said, "practicing my walk as I rounded a bend in the corridor and came *face-to-face* with this prop man.

"He was the first person to see the monster—I watched to study his reaction. It was quick to come. He turned white—gurgled—and lunged out of sight down the corridor. Never saw him again. Poor chap, I would have liked to thank him—he was the audience that first made me *feel* like the monster."

Though some embellishment probably went into that little story, it's certainly got enough emotional truth to warrant retelling. Karloff's monster is a universally recognized icon of movie horror, but audiences seeing the film for the first time still get a chill in that moment when Karloff steps into the light.

Karloff was born William Henry Pratt in England, 1887, the youngest of nine children. He was educated at Merchant Taylors' School, Uppingham, and King's College, and tried his hand at various trades and occupations before he set off in May, 1909, to seek his fortune in Canada. Finding himself doing day labor in Vancouver, he managed to land a job with a travelling theatrical company and spent the next eight years acting throughout the western United States and Canada until, like so many others, he wound up in Los Angeles.

Between 1917 and 1931 when he made *Frankenstein,* Karloff appeared in more than 90 films, most of them now lost or forgotten. When he couldn't find work in the movies, Karloff drove trucks. So, by the time he tried to turn himself into the monster, Karloff was 43 years old, spectacularly unsuccessful at his chosen craft, and experienced in the ways of the world. You can see it in photographs taken at the time. Karloff had a few miles on him, and because of it, he had the kind of real "character" that a younger actor couldn't have given the monster—no matter what the makeup.

Variations on the story say that Bela Lugosi, already a horror star for *Dracula,* either turned down the role or suggested Karloff for it.

Nosferatu

The first feature-length adaptation of Bram Stoker's *Dracula* is still one of the best horror films ever made—complex, serious, and frightening. The famous makeup has lost none of its power. Note how Renfield's (Alexander Granach) appearance foreshadows Dracula's (Max Schreck). That creature with the elongated fingers and ratlike fangs and face is an indelible part of horror cinema, as much as Chaney's Phantom and Karloff's Monster. Famous copyright infringement legal questions caused English-language versions of the film to change the name *Dracula* to *Orlok,* but it's been restored in some video editions. If some devices don't work now—using fast motion to indicate power; having Dracula rise

Karloff himself said that director James Whale approached him at lunch in the Universal commissary and asked him to test for the part. In any case, Karloff was able to give the character the combination of violence and pathos that keeps bringing viewers back to the story.

Though none of his other work in the field equalled *Frankenstein* and its sequel, his career is one of the most successful in horror. To be sure, there are embarrassments on his resume, but Karloff was always active, not only in films but also on stage—two years on Broadway with *Arsenic and Old Lace*—and on television where he's perennially popular in the Dr. Seuss/Chuck Jones *How the Grinch Stole Christmas*. And he was able to end his horror career on an honorable, appreciative note playing himself in Peter Bogdanovich's *Targets*.

Finally, the one thing that makes his story so unusual in the entertainment business is the complete lack of bitter, back-biting tales about him. He appears to have been a true gentleman in the best sense of the word.

SIGNIFICANT CONTRIBUTIONS TO HORROR

Frankenstein **(1931)**

The Mummy **(1932)**

The Old Dark House **(1932)**

The Ghoul **(1933)**

The Black Cat **(1934)**

The Bride of Frankenstein **(1935)**

The Raven **(1935)**

The Invisible Ray **(1936)**

The Walking Dead **(1936)**

Son of Frankenstein **(1939)**

The Body Snatcher **(1945)**

Isle of the Dead **(1945)**

The Strange Door **(1951)**

Corridors of Blood **(1958)**

The Raven **(1963)**

Black Sabbath **(1964)**

Targets **(1968)**

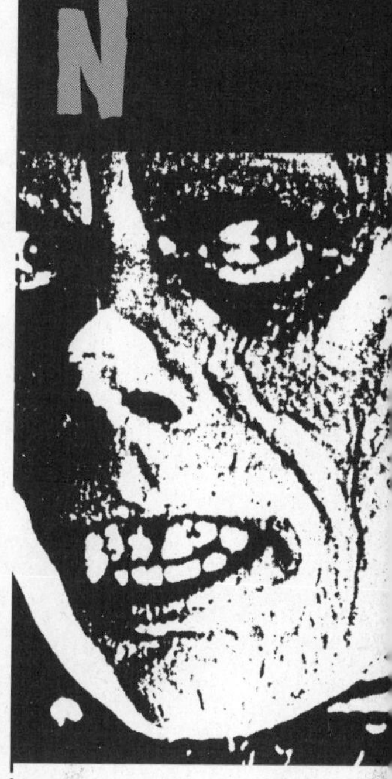

"And at that moment, as if by a miracle, the sick no longer died, and the stifling shadow of the vampire vanished with the morning sun."

—Max Schreck dissolves in the sunlight at the conclusion of *Nosferatu* (1922).

rigidly from his coffin as if on hinged feet—director F.W. Murnau's miasmic dreamlike atmosphere is a remarkable creation. Also, the relationship between Dracula and Nina (Greta Schroeder) is much more complicated. The Kino on Video edition, reproduced with bright tinting and a Timothy Howard score, is probably the clearest. It uses the English-language names. The Video Film Classics is sometimes bleached out black and white with the more familiar German names and an appropriate but simple music soundtrack. Required viewing, particularly for younger fans. ***AKA:*** Nosferatu, Eine Symphonie des Grauens; Nosferatu, A Symphony of Terror; Nosferatu, A Symphony of Horror; Nosferatu, the Vampire; Terror of Dracula; Die Zwolfte Stunde. 🦴🦴🦴🦴

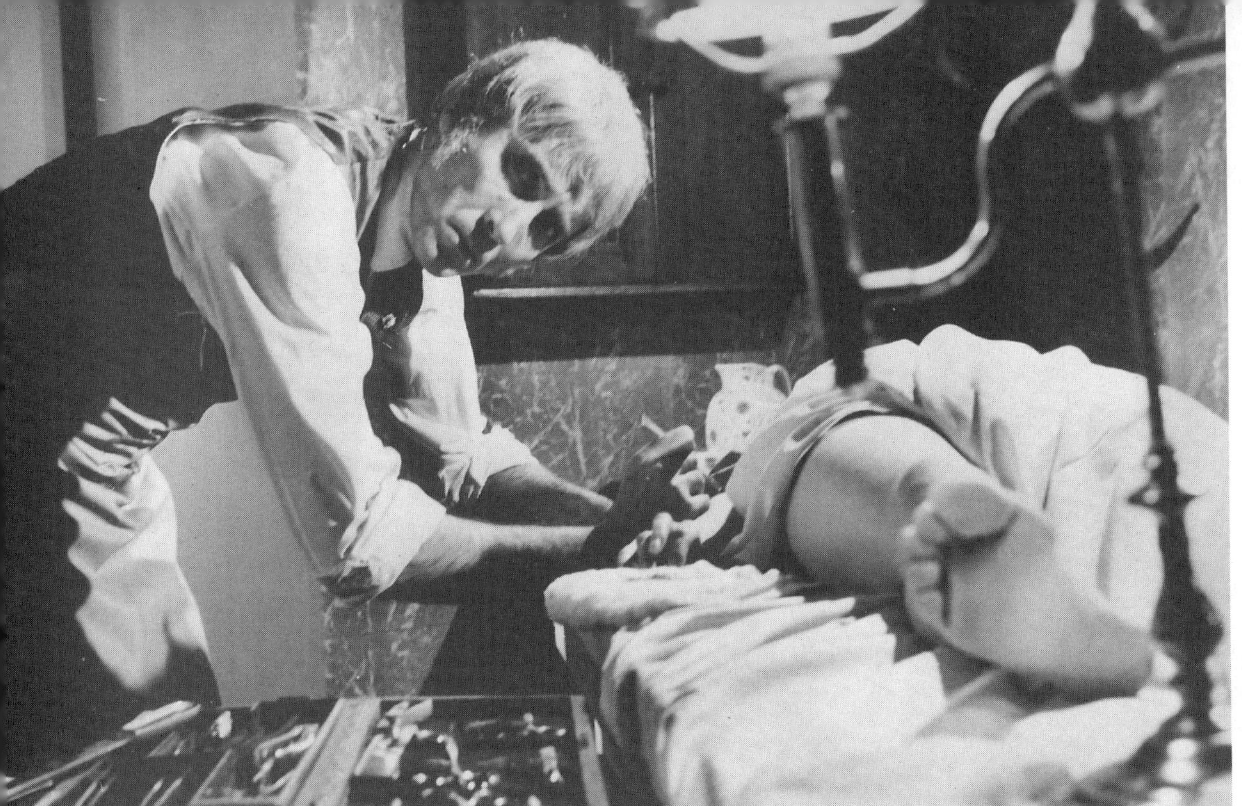

Dr. Neuhart (Christopher Lee) in *The Oblong Box.*

1922 63m/B *GE* Max Schreck, Alexander Granach, Gustav von Wagenheim, Greta Schroeder, John Gottowt, Ruth Landshoff, G.H. Schnell; ***D:*** F.W. Murnau; ***W:*** Henrik Galeen; ***C:*** Fritz Arno Wagner. **VHS, LV** *KIV, MRV, NOS*

Nosferatu the Vampyre

Werner Herzog's remake is faithful to the original, most importantly in the makeup for Klaus Kinski, which reproduces Max Schreck's terrifying devil-rat face. Isabelle Adjani, an actress who's seen far too seldom in this country, is very good, too, but the whole production somehow lacks energy and passion. In 1999, two versions will be available from Anchor Bay: an English-language tape, and a two-tape set that includes the English-language version and a subtitled German-language version with 15 minutes of added footage. 🦴🦴

1979 107m/C *FR GE* Klaus Kinski, Isabelle Adjani, Bruno Ganz, Roland Topor, Walter Ladengast; ***D:*** Werner Herzog; ***W:*** Werner Herzog; ***C:*** Jorg Schmidt-Reitwein. **VHS** *VTR*

Not Like Us

This offbeat comedy is one of the neatest sleepers in your favorite video store. The opening scene combines ominous music with idealized pictures of a bucolic small town named Tranquility. That juxtaposition of sound and image continues as mysterious deaths accumulate. The local coroner attributes them to "multiple purple rash wounds of the epidermis." Another "expert" suspects insufficient fiber in the victims' diet. Could newcomers John (Morgan Englund) and Janet Jones (Rainer Grant) have anything to do with it? Anita (Joanna Pacula) says no. She likes Janet but her suspicious, insular neighbors disagree. If that weren't enough, homewrecker Vicki (Annabelle Gurwitch) is trying to steal Anita's hubby (Peter Onorati). Writer Daniella Purcelli and director Dave

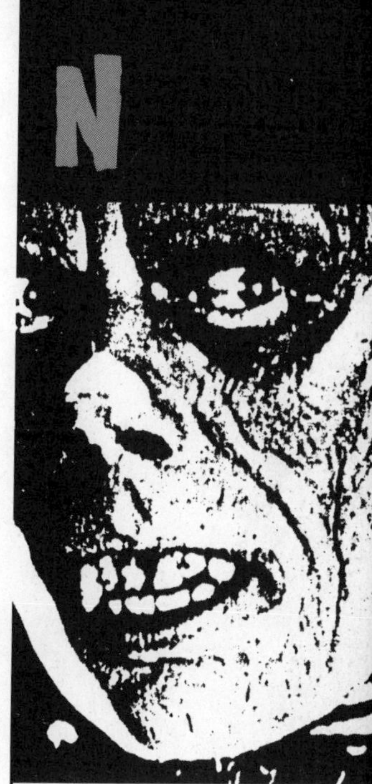

Payne have drawn inspiration from a host of sources—*Motel Hell, Parents, Meet the Hollowheads, Not of This Earth*. The humor is cheeky, gory, and light. Pacula is a little too serious as the heroine who tends to overlook important information. Grant steals the show as the ballbreaker from another world. It all ends with wicked red-meat special effects.

1996 (R) 87m/C Joanna Pacula, Annabelle Gurwitch, Peter Onorati, Morgan Englund, Rainer Grant; ***D:*** Dave Payne; ***W:*** Daniella Purcelli. **VHS** *NHO*

Not of This Earth

The first remake of Roger Corman's original (still unavailable on tape) has virtually everything that a B-movie fan could ask for: total lack of seriousness, zippy plot, cheesy special effects, and oodles of gratuitous nudity. Arthur Roberts is a vampire from the planet Davonna who collects human blood and sends it to the folks back home. Traci Lords is the nurse who unwittingly helps him by providing transfusions. But why is smoke coming from the furnace when the temperature is close to 100 outside? Is someone getting rid of the remains of an unlucky door-to-door vacuum cleaner salesman?

1988 (R) 92m/C Traci Lords, Arthur Roberts, Lenny Juliano, Rebecca Perle, Ace Mask, Roger Lodge; ***D:*** Jim Wynorski; ***W:*** Jim Wynorski, R.J. Robertson. **VHS** *MGM*

Not of This Earth

How many times can producer Roger Corman make *Not of This Earth*? He did it in 1957, then in 1988, and again in 1996. Well, why not? The story of a vampire from another planet is archetypally simple and perfect for a low budget. It's essentially a comedy and this version, like the others, doesn't take itself seriously. The effects range from amateurish to innovative. Michael York is a fine alien. As Nurse Amanda, Elizabeth Barondes is easily the equal of Beverly Garland and Traci Lords, and director Terry Winkless might follow in the footsteps of Corman himself (who directed the original) and schlockmeister Jim Wynorski, who handled the first remake.

1996 (R) 92m/C Michael York, Elizabeth Barondes, Richard Belzer, Parker Stevenson; ***D:*** Terence H. Winkless; ***W:*** Charles Philip Moore. **VHS** *NHO*

Nowhere

Gregg Araki's too-hip-for-its-own-good nihilistic horror/comedy opens with a male version of the shower scene from *Dressed to Kill*. But teenaged Dark (James Duval) isn't sure whether he wants to fantasize about girls or boys. That's really the least of his problems. A dimwit Clive Barker wannabe, he has a "predomination" of his impending death and obsessively videotapes his own vapid life. Then there's the alien who's killing his equally empty-headed classmates. Despite the ugly *Natural Born Killers* look and all the posturing, the film is neither as funny nor as smart as it's trying to be. The social commentary is particularly thin and sophomoric. Araki does manage to be simultaneously toadying and contemptuous toward his young subjects.

1996 (R) 82m/C James Duval, Rachel True, Kathleen Robertson, Nathan Bexton, Guillermo Diaz, Alan Boyce, Christina Applegate, Jeremy Jordan, Chiara Mastroianni, Debi Mazar, Jordan Ladd, Thyme Lewis, Sarah Lassez, Ryan Phillippe, Heather Graham, Scott Caan; ***Cameos:*** John Ritter, Beverly D'Angelo, David Leisure, Traci Lords, Shannen Doherty; ***D:*** Gregg Araki; ***W:*** Gregg Araki; ***C:*** Arturo Smith. **VHS** *NLC*

The Nurse

Like so many video premieres, this one's slickly made for the small screen with an attractive cast and a script that follows the formula for the girlfriend/fiancee/whatever-from-hell who threatens a family from within. The film doesn't add anything new,

Ambassador Thorn (Gregory Peck) in *The Omen.*

but it does run through the paces efficiently. Laura Harriman (Liza Zane) goes after the Martins because she thinks they're responsible for the disaster that struck her family. Her main target is immobilized stroke victim Bob (John Stockwell), and she wants him to see her destroy his loved ones. Liza Zane takes the right fiendish glee in the role of the she-devil. John Stockwell is a good character actor who can convey a lot without most of his craft's physical tools. 🦴🦴

1997 (R) 94m/C Lisa Zane, John Stockwell, Janet Gunn, William R. Moses, Nancy Dussault, Sherrie Rose, Jay Underwood, Michael Fairman; ***D:*** Rob Malenfant; ***W:*** Richard Brandes; ***C:*** Feliks Parnell; ***M:*** Richard Bowers. **VHS, LV, Closed Caption** *LIV*

The Oblong Box

In 19th century England, Julian Markham (Vincent Price) keeps his brother Edward (Alastair Williamson) chained and locked up in the family mansion. The reasons why go back to a gruesome crucifixion ritual that took place some time before in Africa. Christopher Lee is a grave-robbing doctor who becomes embroiled in the Markhams' problems. The source of the horror is upper-class hypocrisy and arrogance. In both the expensive look and neatly written script, the film is comparable to the Hammer productions of the late 1960s. ***AKA:*** Edgar Allan Poe's The Oblong Box. 🦴🦴🦴

1969 (PG) 91m/C *GB* Vincent Price, Christopher Lee, Alastair Williamson, Hilary Dwyer, Peter Arne, Harry Baird, Carl Rigg, Sally Geeson, Maxwell Shaw; ***D:*** Gordon Hessler; ***W:*** Lawrence Huntington; ***C:*** John Coquillon. **VHS** *NO*

Of Unknown Origin

Slickly made Canadian production is actually one of the better rat-themed horrors. With his wife (Shannon Tweed) and young son gone on vacation, hard-working busi-

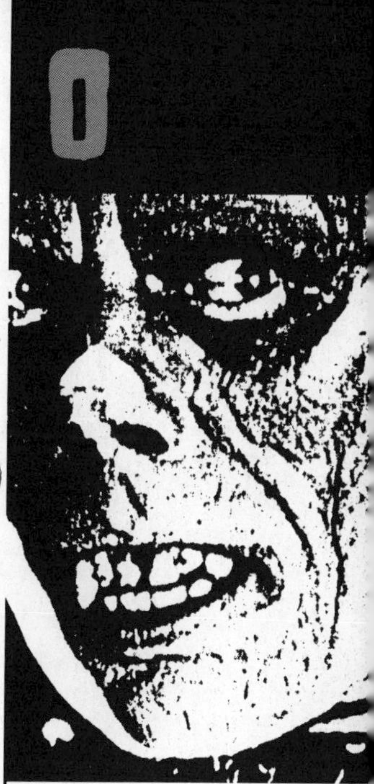

nessman Bart Hughs (Peter Weller) finds his brownstone under attack by an oversized mama rat. Gradually, his obsession with work is transferred to the vermin. His tactics steadily escalate. The rat's tactics escalate right back. Weller brings his usual intensity to the role, and the various interiors become an integral part of the story. The rat's first big appearance is a real flesh-crawling shocker. Toward the end, it goes too far and the physical action meant to be tragic becomes comic, but this one's still worth a look.

1983 (R) 88m/C *CA* Peter Weller, Jennifer Dale, Lawrence Dane, Kenneth Welsh, Louis Del Grande, Shannon Tweed; ***D:*** George P. Cosmatos; ***W:*** Brian Taggert; ***C:*** Rene Verzier. **VHS** *WAR*

The Old Dark House

Three travelers (Raymond Massey, Gloria Stuart, Melvyn Douglas) are trapped by a storm at a nasty country manse inhabited by Femm (Ernest Thesiger), his deaf sister (Eva Moore), and his hideously scarred butler (Boris Karloff), "an uncivilized brute." Soon Porterhouse (Charles Laughton) and Gladys (Lillian Bond) join the bedraggled band. The film is remarkably sexy and frank for the '30s, and the sardonic humor is still fresh. The acting is theatrically broad. In the expansive troupe, Laughton is the most flamboyant. All in all, a treat.

1932 71m/B Boris Karloff, Melvyn Douglas, Charles Laughton, Gloria Stuart, Ernest Thesiger, Raymond Massey, Lillian Bond, Eva Moore, Brember Wills, John Dudgeon; ***D:*** James Whale; ***W:*** Benn W. Levy, R.C. Sherriff; ***C:*** Arthur Edeson. **VHS** *KIV, FCT*

Omega Man

Richard Matheson's brilliant post-apocalypse vampire novel becomes an allegory for the societal conflicts of the late 1960s. After Sino-Russian germ warfare starts a plague, Neville (Charlton Heston) is the only "normal" human in a Los Angeles overrun by an insane cult of albino neo-Luddite barbarians. He happily slaughters them until he finds more survivors. From the opening scene—where he pops in an 8-track tape and plays the theme to *A Summer Place,* to the trenchant comments on consumerism and responsibility, the film is a series of surprises with a remarkable sense of desolation and dour deadpan humor. In many ways, it can be seen as a companion piece to *Night of the Living Dead.* Both are about things falling apart. The main difference is an excellent, though undervalued performance by a major star in an unorthodox role.

1971 (PG) 98m/C Charlton Heston, Anthony Zerbe, Rosalind Cash, Paul Koslo, Eric Laneuville, Lincoln Kilpatrick; ***D:*** Boris Sagal; ***W:*** John W. Corrington, Joyce H. Corrington; ***C:*** Russell Metty. **VHS, LV** *WAR*

The Omen

The first part of what must be Hollywood's most successful supernatural trilogy has aged gracefully. Director Richard Donner, known best for the *Lethal Weapon* series, turns David Seltzer's preview-to-Armageddon story into a first-rate potboiler. Evil is incarnated in a rosy-cheeked little cherub. His spooky nanny—effectively underplayed by Billie Whitelaw—is a lethal Mary Poppins who's given in to the dark side of the force. The plot is filled with inventive twists and shocks and a welcome restraint in the effects department. Unfortunately, those shocks are diluted on video by a poor pan-and-scan transfer. (The widescreen laser edition is a must for fans.) Followed by two theatrical sequels and one made for TV. ***AKA:*** Birthmark.

1976 (R) 111m/C Gregory Peck, Lee Remick, Harvey Stephens, Billie Whitelaw, David Warner, Holly Palance, Robert Rietty, Patrick Troughton, Martin Benson, Leo McKern, Richard Donner; ***D:*** Richard Donner; ***W:*** David Seltzer; ***C:*** Gilbert Taylor; ***M:*** Jerry Goldsmith. Academy Awards '76: Best Original Score; Nominations: Academy Awards '76: Best Song ("Ave Satani"). **VHS, LV, Letterboxed** *FOX*

Loretta Leversee, John Ritter, and the clan in ***The Other***.

Once Bitten

The Countess (Lauren Hutton) is a centuries-old vampire who must have virgin blood three times before Halloween. Mark (Jim Carrey) is her target. She easily cuts him out of the pack at a singles bar and takes him back to her palatial hilltop home. The bite marks she leaves aren't on his neck. Most of the visual and verbal humor is uninspired, with only short flashes of Carrey's trademark shtick. The sexual jokes should either have been made more explicit or eliminated. At a PG-13 level, they're either embarrassed or smirky.

1985 (PG-13) 94m/C Lauren Hutton, Jim Carrey, Cleavon Little, Karen Kopins, Thomas Balltore, Skip Lackey; ***D:*** Howard Storm; ***W:*** Jonathan Roberts, David Hines, Jeffrey Hause; ***C:*** Adam Greenberg; ***M:*** John Du Prez. **VHS, LV, Closed Caption** *LIV*

One Dark Night

Competent little horror begins well but fizzles quickly. To join Carol's (Robin Evans) sorority, Julie (Meg Tilly) has to spend the night in a mausoleum where the evil and powerful psychic Raymar is entombed. The pace slows to a crawl after Julie enters the building, and once it picks up again, all the scares are supposed to come from rotting corpses, a device that wears thin quickly. Before it's over, the whole business has become downright silly instead of frightening. It's not meant to be a comedy. ***AKA:*** Entity Force; Mausoleum.

1982 (R) 94m/C Meg Tilly, Adam West, David Mason Daniels, Robin Evans, Elizabeth Daily; ***D:*** Tom McLoughlin. **VHS** *NO*

Opera

See *Terror at the Opera.*

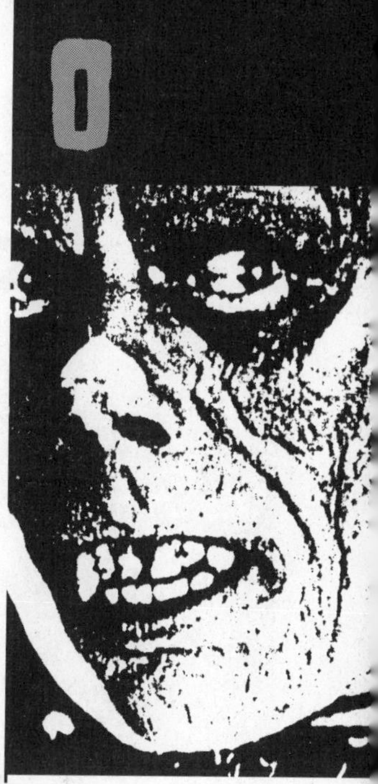

Orca

Legitimate contender for the coveted Worst Movie Ever is based on the goony premise that a killer whale is so upset by Nolan's (Richard Harris) killing his pregnant mate that he becomes a vengeance-obsessed psycho-whale. It was widely reported when the film was released that to create the famous scene where the whale bites off a leg, the filmmakers had to fill a prosthetic limb with shrimp. The real whale footage is O.K., but that's what National Geographic specials are for. Richard Harris' fearless overacting in the face of such atrocious material earns the film its single bone. ***AKA:*** Orca—Killer Whale; The Killer Whale.

1977 (PG) 92m/C Richard Harris, Charlotte Rampling, Bo Derek, Keenan Wynn, Will Sampson, Robert Carradine; ***D:*** Michael Anderson Sr.; ***W:*** Sergio Donati, Luciano Vincenzoni; ***C:*** Ted Moore; ***M:*** Ennio Morricone. **VHS, LV** *PAR*

Orson Welles' Ghost Story

Under the title *Return to Glennascaul,* this restrained tale was nominated for an Oscar in the best short subject category in 1953. In a commendably succinct introduction to the restored tape, Peter Bogdanovich explains how the film came to be made. Welles and his Irish friends Hilton Edwards and Micheal Mac Liammoir were involved in other projects, and took advantage of gaps in their production schedules to film an elegantly simple little ghost story. In plot and construction, it's a cinematic adaptation of a campfire tale. Welles, playing himself, tells how he picked up a man (Michael Laurence) stranded near Dublin late one night. He then retells the man's story about the two women he'd met in similar circumstances years before. Imagine a low-keyed episode of *The Twilight Zone* and you'll understand what Welles and the others are up to. It's a nicely atmospheric yarn that's helped immeasurably by Welles' rich narration. ***AKA:*** Return to Glennascaul: A Story That Is Told.

195? 30m/C Orson Welles, Michael Laurence; ***D:*** Hilton Edwards; ***W:*** Hilton Edwards. **VHS** *MPI*

The Other

Writer/producer Tom Tryon's adaptation of his best-selling novel is one of the most gripping evil child tales ever put onscreen. Most viewers will probably figure out one part of the story a little early, but that's not a real problem. Holland and Niles Perry (Martin and Chris Udvarnoky) are good and evil young twins. The "accidents" that happen around them are suspenseful and shocking, and built on real insights into the world of children. The combination of rural setting and '30s nostalgia creates a strong sense of place. Director Robert Mulligan is restrained in the violence he chooses to show and the film is all the creepier and more frightening for that restraint.

1972 (PG) 100m/C Martin Udvarnoky, Chris Udvarnoky, Uta Hagen, Diana Muldaur, Norma Connolly, Victor French, John Ritter, Loretta Leversee, Lou Frizzell, Portia Nelson, Jenny Sullivan; ***D:*** Robert Mulligan; ***W:*** Tom Tryon; ***C:*** Robert L. Surtees; ***M:*** Jerry Goldsmith. **VHS** *FOX*

The Outing

The theme music, blatantly stolen from *Halloween,* is the tip-off to another dead-teenager flick. The only difference here is that the killer is a genie and the genie is in Houston. Three delinquents kill an old gypsy woman who has a lamp. Within seconds they're dead, and the lamp has been sent to Dr. Wallace (James Huston) and his girlfriend Eve (Deborah Winters, who's also the old gypsy woman, the associate producer, and, clearly, a woman who knows how to save money on production costs). The film is dark, grainy, and seldom in

Helen (Anna Massey) in *Peeping Tom.*

sharp focus, muting the violence and cheap effects. ***AKA:*** The Lamp.

1987 (R) 87m/C Deborah Winters, James Huston, Andra St. Ivanyi, Scott Bankston, Mark Mitchell, Andre Chimene, Damon Merrill, Barry Coffing; ***D:*** Tom Daley; ***W:*** Warren Chaney; ***C:*** Herbert Raditschnig. **VHS** *LIV*

Pale Blood

The idea of a European vampire in a modern American city is nothing new, but director V.V. Dachin Hsu gives it a fresh spin. A serial murderer is draining young women's blood in L.A. Romanian Michael Fury (George Chakiris from *West Side Story*) is so interested that he's hired a detective (Pamela Ludwig) to keep him informed. Van (Wings Hauser), a video artist with several loose screws, is obsessed with the killings. Hsu seems more comfortable with stylistic touches and a strong dreamy atmosphere than with plot and so the pace is slow. Genre veteran Hauser has a high time with the material and injects some real energy, especially at the end. Good location work, too.

1991 (R) 93m/C George Chakiris, Wings Hauser, Pamela Ludwig, Diana Frank, Darcy Demoss, Earl Garnes; ***D:*** V.V. Dachin Hsu; ***W:*** V.V. Dachin Hsu, Takashi Matsuoka. **VHS, LV** *COL, OM*

The Para Psychics

Obscure drive-in exploitation begins as a comedy with a gigolo and a conman getting hooked up with a telepathic blonde and her mother. Then it turns into a low-budget variation on *The Fury* and *Firestarter* with a nod to *Carrie* and a Greek setting. The whole thing has the lunatic unpredictability of a Hong Kong movie. How else to explain the moment when the scene abruptly and inexplicably shifts from a hotel hallway to a bowling alley?

1986 77m/C Jessica Dublin, Maria Aliferi, Peter Winter, Chris Nomicos; ***D:*** Nico Mastorakis; ***W:*** Nico Mastorakis. **VHS** *NO*

Paradise Lost: The Child Murders at Robin Hood Hills

This non-fiction southern Gothic is as chilling as any conventional horror film, and in the end all the more frightening for its unanswered questions. In May 1993, three eight-year-old Arkansas boys are mutilated and murdered. Police suspect "occult" activity, and soon three teenagers—Jessie Misskelley, Jr., Damien Echols, and Jason Baldwin—are arrested. Jessie, with an IQ of 72, confesses but gets key details wrong and quickly recants. Still, it's enough for the authorities and the trial proceeds. That's the story Joe Berlinger and Bruce Sinofsky (*Brother's Keeper*) tell in a long, unpredictable, and admittedly biased documentary. At the end, few viewers will think that they know what really happened, and most will fear that whoever killed those boys is still out there. 🦴🦴🦴

1995 150m/C ***D:*** Joe Berlinger, Bruce Sinofsky; ***C:*** Robert Richman. **VHS, Closed Caption** *CAF*

Paranoiac

Eleanor (Janette Scott) thinks that she sees her dead brother Anthony (Alexander Davion) at church, but it's obvious from the first scene that her other brother, the no-good rotten Simon (Oliver Reed), is up to something. Like Hammer's other black-and-white horror/thrillers of the early '60s, this one is built on such a shaky psychological foundation that it's never particularly frightening. It's still sharply photographed and well acted by all concerned, particularly Reed. 🦴🦴½

1962 80m/B *GB* Oliver Reed, Janette Scott, Alex Davion, Liliane Brousse, Sheila Burell, Maurice Denham; ***D:*** Freddie Francis; ***W:*** Jimmy Sangster; ***C:*** Arthur Grant; ***M:*** Elisabeth Lutyens. **VHS, Closed Caption** *USH*

Parents

In a deeply distorted vision of the 1950s, young Michael (Bryan Madorsky), Mom (Mary Beth Hurt), and Dad (Randy Quaid) move to a new town and a split-level filled with coral and turquoise furniture and appliances. The shy, silent, and basically unlikable boy is troubled by visions of his parents with bloodstained mouths. When they give evasive answers about the main course at dinner, he comes to believe that they are cannibals. Is that the truth, or is he a very disturbed child? The script presents no easy answers or escapes. For the most part, actor-turned-director Bob Balaban succeeds in making this a disturbing, unnerving piece of work. All of the colors are slightly off, too intense. Food has seldom been so revoltingly photographed. The characters are just a notch or two off dead center, and a soundtrack of syrupy big band hits has been poured over these disquieting visual images. Though there is a grimly humorous angle to the story, this is not a comedy. It's the stuff of nightmares. 🦴🦴🦴½

1989 (R) 81m/C Randy Quaid, Mary Beth Hurt, Bryan Madorsky, Sandy Dennis, Kathryn Grody, Deborah Rush, Graham Jarvis, Juno Mills-Cockell; ***D:*** Bob Balaban; ***W:*** Christopher Hawthorne; ***C:*** Robin Vidgeon; ***M:*** Angelo Badalamenti, Jonathan Elias. **VHS, LV** *LIV, VES, HHE*

Peeping Tom

It's impossible to overestimate the influence of Michael Powell's brilliant but rarely screened 1960 masterpiece. It can be seen as the missing link between Fritz Lang's *M* and *Psycho* in the realistic school of horror. Essentially, it's the story of Mark (Karl-Heinz Boehm), a twisted young film technician driven to murder women as he photographs them. He falls in love with Helen (Anna Massey), but her blind mother (Maxine Audley) seems to know everything about him. Voyeurism is a prime subject, but Powell is also concerned with the nature of film itself, from the perspective of both the creator and the viewer. Seen simply as a thriller, it's Hitchcockian in the very best sense of the term—complex, witty, suspenseful, unpredictable. Even though the violence is not explicit by today's standards, it's still a deeply disturbing piece of work. The Criterion laserdisc version recreates Powell's vivid use of color, and also the sound that's remarkably clear and important to the film. Required viewing for any serious student of horror. 🦴🦴🦴🦴

1960 88m/C Karl-Heinz Boehm, Moira Shearer, Anna Massey, Maxine Audley, Esmond Knight, Shirley Anne

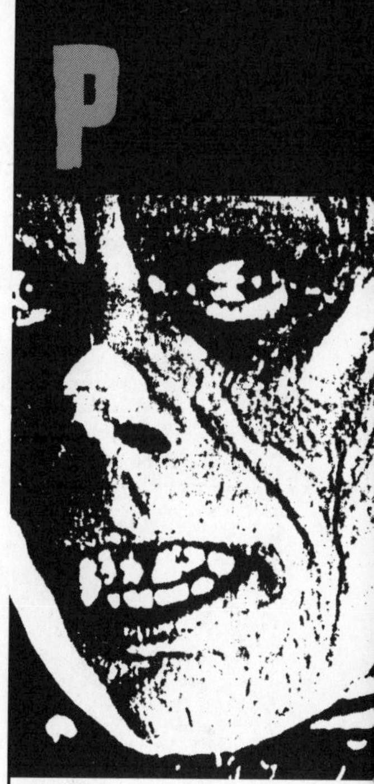

"Feast your eyes, glut your soul on my accursed ugliness."

—Erik (Lon Chaney, Sr.) to Christine Daae (Mary Philbin) in *The Phantom of the Opera* (1925).

Field, Brenda Bruce, Pamela Green, Jack Watson, Nigel Davenport, Susan Travers, Veronica Hurst, Martin Miller, Miles Malleson; ***Cameos:*** Michael Powell; ***D:*** Michael Powell; ***W:*** Leo Marks; ***C:*** Otto Heller. **VHS, LV** *HMV*

The People under the Stairs

Wes Craven addresses capitalism and the nuclear family in a subversive Grand Guignol horror. Evil is represented by seemingly "normal" white adults. Poor black kids, burglars, and horribly deformed "freaks" are the heroes. Using the tarot cards as a structure, the film follows young Fool (Brandon Adams) on his journey of discovery in the world of two slumlords (Everett McGill and Wendy Robie). The core of the story is the eternal rebellion of children against parents, and a teenaged audience will probably appreciate it more than parents think they should.

1991 (R) 102m/C Everett McGill, Wendy Robie, Brandon Adams, Ving Rhames, A.J. Langer, Sean Whalen, Kelly Jo Minter; ***D:*** Wes Craven; ***W:*** Wes Craven; ***C:*** Sandi Sissel; ***M:*** Don Peake. **VHS, LV, Closed Caption** *USH*

Pet Sematary

Stephen King's version of "The Monkey's Paw" is one of his most frightening novels, and Mary Lambert's film, made from his script, is one of the best adaptations of his work. Lewis and Rachel Creed (Dale Midkiff and Denise Crosby) and their two kids move into a Maine country house on a busy road. Jud (Fred Gwynne) warns them that it won't be safe for the family cat. The road has claimed so many animals that there's a "Pet Sematary" in the forest. Deeper in the forest, there's another pet cemetery with a darker purpose. Toward the end, some comic relief is dubious, and the film lasts 30 seconds too long, but it's still a potent chiller about the destructive, possessive side of love. Followed by a lamentable sequel.

1989 (R) 103m/C Dale Midkiff, Fred Gwynne, Denise Crosby, Blaze Berdahl, Brad Greenquist, Miko Hughes, Stephen King; ***D:*** Mary Lambert; ***W:*** Stephen King; ***C:*** Peter Stein; ***M:*** Elliot Goldenthal. **VHS, LV, 8mm, Closed Caption** *PAR*

Pet Sematary 2

Nasty little sequel is notable only for the sadistic quality of its graphic violence. It's one thing for a film to depict children and animals in life-threatening situations. It's another to show the perpetrators of the violence taking such glee in the torture they inflict. But the film is so ineptly made that it will never attract a large audience. Richard Outten's script blunders from one contrived confrontation to the next and director Mary Lambert proves that women can make ugly, violent exploitation as poorly as men can. Where the original film is about familial love gone bad, *2* is about special effects. **Woof!**

1992 (R) 102m/C Anthony Edwards, Edward Furlong, Clancy Brown, Jared Rushton, Darlanne Fluegel, Lisa Waltz, Jason McGuire, Sarah Trigger; ***D:*** Mary Lambert; ***W:*** Richard Outten; ***C:*** Russell Carpenter. **VHS, LV, Closed Caption** *PAR*

Phantasm

The ads call this one "a truly bizarre science-fiction horror fantasy," and for once they aren't exaggerating. The senseless plot concerns two parentless brothers who discover weird goings-on at the local funeral parlor, including the infamous airborne, brain-drilling chrome ball; malevolent hooded midgets in monk's robes; and the Tall Man (Angus Scrimm). Creepy, unpredictable nightmare fashioned on a shoestring by young independent producer/writer/director Don A. Coscarelli contains enough wildly imaginative twists and inventions for a dozen horror movies, but not enough logic for one. The plot and sensibility could have come straight from a Roadrunner cartoon, with about as much attention paid to the laws of physics.

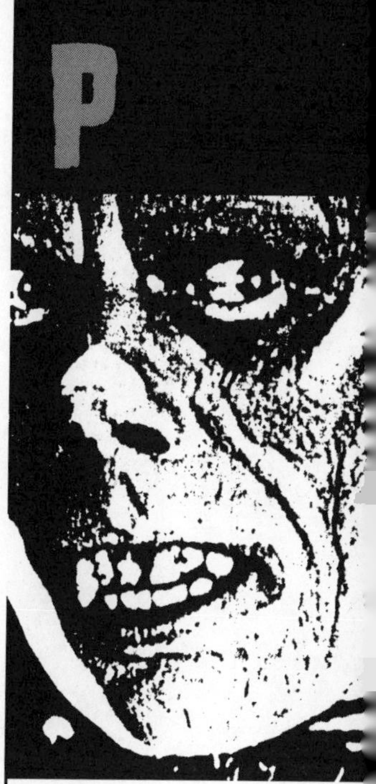

Scenes were cut out of the original film to avoid an "X" rating. Followed by obligatory sequels.

1979 (R) 90m/C Michael Baldwin, Bill Thornbury, Reggie Bannister, Kathy Lester, Terrie Kalbus, Ken Jones, Susan Harper, Lynn Eastman, David Arntzen, Angus Scrimm, Bill Cone; ***D:*** Don A. Coscarelli; ***W:*** Don A. Coscarelli; ***C:*** Don A. Coscarelli. **VHS, LV** *COL*

Phantasm II

Don Coscarelli's sequel is almost as screwy and weird as his 1979 original, a horror/s-f/fantasy/comedy with lots of gruesome special effects. For those who came in late, it's about the Tall Man (Angus Scrimm), a mortician with yellow goop for blood, a bunch of reanimated corpses that have been turned into monster midgets who run around in little monk's robes, and a chrome baseball that does really nasty things. Do not expect the plot to make sense; Coscarelli's not interested. His story just rolls along from one bizarre event to the next, finally arriving at a predictable ending.

1988 (R) 97m/C James LeGros, Reggie Bannister, Angus Scrimm, Paula Irvine, Samantha Phillips, Ken Tigar; ***D:*** Don A. Coscarelli; ***W:*** Don A. Coscarelli; ***C:*** Daryn Okada. **VHS, LV** *USH*

Phantasm III: Lord of the Dead

Don Coscarelli's horror-comedies actually predate the *Friday the 13th* and *Elm Street* series, and, like them, they don't follow any internal logic. A character who's killed in one scene, reappears in the next without explanation; dream and reality are constantly confused; etc.—you know the drill. The events onscreen are nothing more than Coscarelli's excuse to trot out special effects of amputations, decapitations, lobotomies, and the like involving the now-familiar Tall Man and flying chrome balls. For better or worse, the gory stuff is played strictly for laughs. Even though the effects have become much more polished, that's not necessarily an improvement.

1994 (R) 91m/C Reggie Bannister, A. Michael Baldwin, Bill Thornbury, Gloria Henry, Kevin Connor, Angus Scrimm; ***D:*** Don A. Coscarelli; ***W:*** Don A. Coscarelli. **VHS, LV, Closed Caption** *USH*

Phantom Empire

Producer/director Fred Olen Ray boasts that he made this tribute to serials in six days and that's easy to believe. The movie is about treasure hunters running through caves away from silly monsters that look like dime-store Morlocks. The cast of genre veterans—including Robby the Robot with a modified gumball machine head—doesn't sweat the frivolous comic material.

1987 (R) 85m/C Ross Hagen, Jeffrey Combs, Dawn Wildsmith, Robert Quarry, Susan Stokey, Michelle (McClellan) Bauer, Russ Tamblyn, Sybil Danning; ***D:*** Fred Olen Ray; ***W:*** Fred Olen Ray, T.T. Lankford. **VHS** *NO*

The Phantom of the Opera

Gaston LeRoux's tale is one of the most popular potboilers of all time—on stage, page, or screen. Chaney's version is the most famous and rightly so. The big scenes—the falling chandelier, the underground lake, the masked ball, the final chase, and, of course, the unmasking—are still terrific. Despite changes in dramatic style, this is one of Chaney's most impressive acting jobs. If you can take your eyes off his makeup, notice how expressively he uses his hands. Since the title is in public domain, the film is available from several labels. The versions vary widely in quality. Look for one that has a musical soundtrack, the tinted scenes, and, more importantly, be sure that the transfer has been made from a print projected at silent speed (16 frames per second), not sound speed

(24 frames per second), which gives normal motion the fast, jerky quality mistakenly associated with early films. The laserdisc version is best.

1925 101m/B Lon Chaney Sr., Norman Kerry, Mary Philbin, Gibson Gowland, Arthur Edmund Carewe, Snitz Edwards; ***D:*** Rupert Julian; ***W:*** Elliot J. Clawson, Raymond L. Schrock; ***C:*** Virgil Miller. **VHS, LV** *KIV, NOS, FUS*

The Phantom of the Opera

Claude Rains, one of the most versatile and effortless actors ever to grace the screen, is a thoroughly sympathetic Phantom, but this expensive production is a failure as a horror film. Far too much time is spent on the trivial romantic triangle and light opera performances. Tellingly, in the credits, Rains gets third billing after Nelson Eddy and Susanna Foster. The allegedly frightening elements are largely reduced to silliness involving a cape and a broad-brimmed hat. Even the chandelier, unmasking, and sewer scenes are disappointing.

1943 92m/C Nelson Eddy, Susanna Foster, Claude Rains, Edgar Barrier, Leo Carrillo, Hume Cronyn, J. Edward Bromberg; ***D:*** Arthur Lubin; ***W:*** Samuel Hoffenstein, Eric Taylor; ***C:*** Hal Mohr, William Howard Greene. Academy Awards '43: Best Color Cinematography, Best Interior Decoration; Nominations: Academy Awards '43: Best Sound, Scoring of a Musical. **VHS, LV** *USH*

The Phantom of the Opera

Robert Englund won't make anyone forget Lon Chaney, but his full-bore Phantom is nothing to be ashamed of. In fact, director Dwight Little and writer Duke Sandefur's interpretation of the story is underrated and surprisingly well crafted. In this gory version, made in Hungary, Erik is equal parts Faust and Jack the Ripper. As the aspiring opera star Christine, Jill Schoelen's studied girlishness is irritating but in character. The whole film might have been better with a little less gore and a good falling chandelier scene.

1989 (R) 93m/C Robert Englund, Jill Schoelen, Alex Hyde-White, Bill Nighy, Terence Harvey, Stephanie Lawrence; ***D:*** Dwight Little; ***W:*** Duke Sandefur; ***C:*** Elemer Ragaly. **VHS, LV, Closed Caption** *COL*

Picture of Dorian Gray

Pandro Berman, the producer who was responsible for so many of the best RKO and MGM films, is also behind the most opulent version of Oscar Wilde's famous story of youth and corruption. Though expressionless, Hurd Hatfield is fine as the far-too-handsome Victorian aristocrat, and although Angela Lansbury received an Oscar nomination for her performance as his first victim, the film belongs to George Sanders. His Lord Henry Wootten is the epigrammatic voice of the author ("Most people die of a sort of creeping common sense and discover too late that the only things one never regrets are one's mistakes.") The portrait itself—"the emblem of his own conscience...that would teach him to loathe his own soul"—is shown in Technicolor, but Harry Stradling's Oscar-winning black-and-white cinematography is lush.

1945 110m/B Hurd Hatfield, George Sanders, Donna Reed, Angela Lansbury, Peter Lawford, Lowell Gilmore, Miles Mander; ***D:*** Albert Lewin; ***W:*** Albert Lewin; ***C:*** Harry Stradling. Academy Awards '45: Best Black and White Cinematography; Golden Globe Awards '46: Best Supporting Actress (Lansbury); Nominations: Academy Awards '45: Best Interior Decoration, Best Supporting Actress (Lansbury). **VHS, LV** *MGM, FHE, TVC*

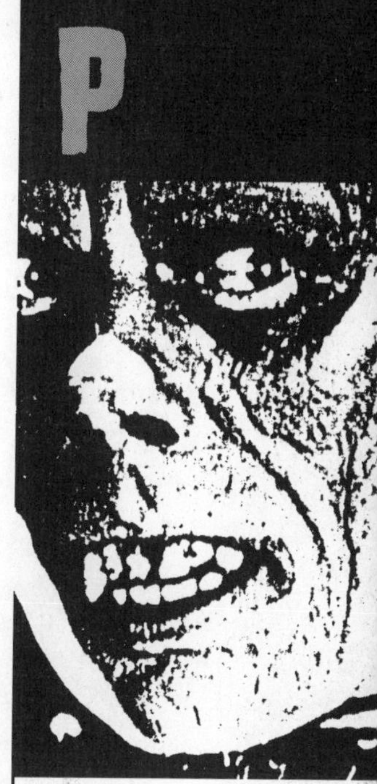

"If I'd get back my youth, I'd do anything in the world—except get up early, take exercise, or be respectable."

—George Sanders in *Picture of Dorian Gray.*

Lon Chaney is *The Phantom of the Opera* (1925).

THE HOUND SALUTES

PHANTOM OF THE OPERA

Gaston Leroux began his novel *The Phantom of the Opera* by boldly stating, "The Opera Ghost really existed. He was not, as was long believed, a creature of the imagination of the artists, the superstition of the managers, or the absurd and impressionable brains of the young ladies of the ballet, their mothers, the box-keepers, the cloak-room attendants, or the concierge. No, he existed in flesh and blood, though he assumed all the outward characteristics of a real phantom, that is to say, of a shade."

Of course, Leroux was lying; that's what fiction writers do, but a certain amount of his story is based on fact.

Leroux (1868-1927) himself was a grand character. He was a bon vivant who inherited a considerable fortune as a young man. In what must have been six glorious months in Paris, 1889, he spent most of his inheritance on women, wine, and gambling, and wasted the rest. After that, he became an investigative reporter and then a novelist. Like any good writer, he could recognize the elements of an interesting story when he found them, and he never let the facts get in the way when the plot needed a little help. The best tales come from a subtle mix of truth, exaggeration, and outright invention.

In a foreword to the 1985 75th Anniversary edition of the novel, Peter Haining outlines the actual construction of the Paris Opera House. He says that when the site was being excavated in the 1860s, the workers discovered a large body of water that had to be drained before the foundation could be built. Once that had been accomplished, they let the water drain back in. So, yes, one key detail which seems totally unbelievable is true. The whole place is built over a subterranean lake!

It is also true that the construction of the Opera House was interrupted by the 1871 uprising known as the Paris Commune. It ended with 20,000 dead when the French government retook the city. But was a mass grave of massacre victims really discovered beneath the Opera House? I don't know. It could be whole cloth or it could be the kind of grisly detail that made the rest of the story more plausible to French readers of the early 20th century. Another key moment in the story apparently comes from a real event, too. In 1896, a chandelier's counterweight fell on an audience. It shouldn't have taken Leroux long to figure out how to switch that bit of business around to make it more exciting.

In a long epilogue to the novel, Leroux goes into detailed but properly vague explanations of how all of the Opera Ghost's feats within the building could have been accomplished.

They make for curious reading now because the novelist is answering questions that moviegoers don't bother to ask. Does it matter that a particular marble pillar is really hollow and wide enough to accommodate two men where the Opera Ghost might have ventriloquistically whispered his instructions? No, We've come to accept "movie magic" for the details, as long as the film itself is doing what we want it to do.

Besides, Lon Chaney broke the code on the *Phantom* when he created his makeup. That horror is the real "truth" behind Leroux's story.

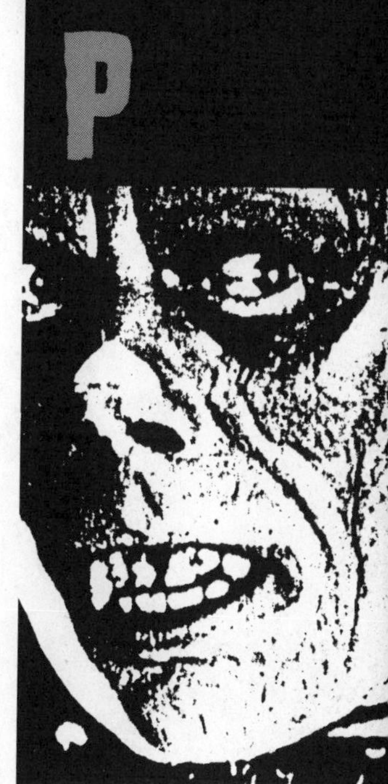

Pillow of Death

See *Dead Man's Eyes/Pillow of Death.*

Pin ...

Disturbed young Leon (played successively by Jacob Tierney, Steven Bednarski, and David Hewlett) is an apple who hasn't fallen from the tree. His father, Dr. Linden (Terry O'Quinn), is a strange disciplinarian while his mother (Bronwen Mantel) keeps clear plastic slipcovers on all the furniture and thinks that Leon's friends are germ-ridden disease carriers. His younger sister Ursula (Michelle Anderson, Katie Shingler, and Cyndy Preston) has survived relatively unscathed. Pin is the transparent dummy in dad's office with which Leon develops an obsessive attachment. Few mainstream films deal with the changes in childhood and adolescence as well as this one. Writer/director Sandor Stern also delivers the goods with surprising scares that are developed through the characters. One of the best and least-recognized recent sleepers.

1988 (R) 103m/C Cyndy Preston, David Hewlett, Terry O'Quinn, Bronwen Mantel, Helene Udy, Patricia Collins, Steven Bednarski, Katie Shingler, Jacob Tierney, Michelle Anderson; ***D:*** Sandor Stern; ***W:*** Sandor Stern; ***C:*** Guy Defaux. **VHS, LV** *VTR, IME*

Pinocchio's Revenge

Almost any horror movie involving kids and toys is going to get to parents where they live, and despite the formula nature of its plot this one does. After its maker is labeled a serial killer, the murderous marionette becomes the property of his public defender (Rosalind Allen) and her young daughter (Brittany Alyse Smith). Writer/director Kevin Tenney tries to combine conventional cinematic scares with more "real" evil. The puppet effects by Gabe Bartalos are alright, but the Wood Boy is no Chucky. For that matter, neither of them would be a match for Richard Matheson's Zuni fetish doll in *Trilogy of Terror.*

1996 (R) 96m/C Rosalind Allen, Brittany Alyse Smith, Todd Allen, Lewis Van Bergen, Aaron Lustig, Ron Canada; ***D:*** Kevin S. Tenney; ***W:*** Kevin S. Tenney; ***M:*** Dennis Michael Tenney. **VHS** *THV*

Piranha

A rural Texas resort area is plagued by attacks from ferocious man-eating fishies created by a scientist to be used as a secret weapon in the Vietnam War. Spoofy horror film—the title monsters are little more than bubbles and red dye in the water—follows the familiar quick-and-dirty Corman formula, and features director Joe Dante's signature in-jokes in the background. One tiny stop-motion critter appears in an all-too-brief cameo. This was the first script by novelist/filmmaker John Sayles to be produced; he also appears as the Army sentry. Followed by a sequel (James Cameron's feature debut) in 1981, and remade but not improved upon in 1996.

1978 (R) 90m/C Bradford Dillman, Heather Menzies, Kevin McCarthy, Keenan Wynn, Barbara Steele, Dick Miller, Paul Bartel, John Sayles; ***D:*** Joe Dante; ***W:*** John Sayles; ***C:*** Jamie Anderson; ***M:*** Pino Donaggio. **VHS** *WAR, OM*

Piranha

New version adds nothing to the early effort from director Joe Dante, writer John Sayles, and producer Roger Corman, who's also behind this one. In fact, it lacks that nice flourish of stop-motion animation and it may even reuse some of the silly little two-dimensional fish "monsters" from the original. The rest of the effects are accomplished, as they were before, with red dye and a submerged bubble machine. Alexandra Paul and William Katt are the less-than-dynamic duo who must save the summer camp and the new lakefront development

from the titular carnivorous fishies, created by the government as a secret weapon. If you have the choice, give this one a pass and find the real thing. 🦴🦴

1995 (R) 81m/C Alexandra Paul, William Katt, Soleil Moon Frye, Monte Markham, Darlene Carr, James Karen, Lincoln Kilpatrick; ***D:*** Scott Levy. **VHS** *NHO*

Piranha 2: The Spawning

James Cameron's directorial debut stinks. The whole idea of carnivorous flying fish zipping up out of the ocean and going for people's jugulars is just so damn silly that there's nothing anyone could have done with it. Because of that, the fact that nothing much happens in the first half isn't that serious. Give Cameron and writer H.A. Milton credit for trying to take their main characters beyond stereotypes. In the leads, Tricia O'Neil and the ever-reliable Lance Henriksen are fine, but conventional special effects simply cannot create believable flying creatures—not bats and certainly not fish. ***AKA:*** Piranha 2: Flying Killers. 🦴

1982 (R) 88m/C Tricia O'Neil, Steve Marachuk, Lance Henriksen, Ricky Paul; ***D:*** James Cameron; ***W:*** H.A. Milton; ***C:*** Roberto D'Ettorre Piazzoli. **VHS, LV** *NLC*

The Pit and the Pendulum

Roger Corman's second foray into Poe territory takes a more active approach. The relative restraint of *Fall of the House of Usher* is replaced by some hammy overacting and a Richard Matheson script that's unusually stilted at first. "The point seems of vital import to you," one character orates without an ounce of believability. Vincent Price is Nicholas, the son of an inquisitor who isn't over the death of his wife Elizabeth (Barbara Steele). If you can put up with the talky first half, the second pays off with a spirited conclusion. The torture sequence may be Roger Corman's finest combination of sets, sound, action, and editing. 🦴🦴🦴

1961 80m/C Vincent Price, John Kerr, Barbara Steele, Luana Anders, Antony Carbone; ***D:*** Roger Corman; ***W:*** Richard Matheson; ***C:*** Floyd Crosby; ***M:*** Les Baxter. **VHS** *WAR, OM*

The Pit & the Pendulum

Told in the spirit of Corman, this one is a tongue-in-cheek version of several of Poe's stories, with a small tip of the hat to Mel Brooks' *History of the World—Part 1*. The mad inquisitor Torquemada (Lance Henriksen) is attracted to a baker's wife (Rona De Ricci) who's mistakenly imprisoned for witchcraft. An Italian Cardinal (Oliver Reed) has come to town to restrain the excesses of the Spanish Inquisition, but Torquemada, a slave to his obsession, tries to torture a confession, and perhaps more, from the woman. The Grand Guignol torture scenes are inventive and repulsive, though, doubtless, not as inventive and repulsive as the real thing. A shocking streak of sardonic humor keeps the action from becoming too sadistic. Director Stuart Gordon (*Re-Animator*) does fine work, even if he can't match the conclusion of Corman's original. 🦴🦴🦴🦴

1991 (R) 97m/C Lance Henriksen, Rona De Ricci, Jonathan Fuller, Jeffrey Combs, Tom Towles, Stephen Lee, Frances Bay, Oliver Reed; ***D:*** Stuart Gordon; ***W:*** Dennis Paoli; ***M:*** Richard Band. **VHS, LV, Closed Caption** *FLL*

Plague of the Zombies

One of Hammer's best was late to arrive on video, but it's worth the wait. The Anchor Bay Entertainment transfer is excellent

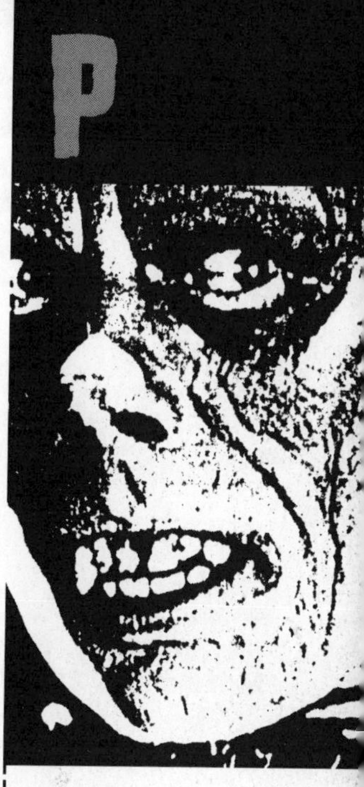

Squire Hamilton (John Carson) in Hammer's *Plague of the Zombies.*

THE HOUND SALUTES

ROGER CORMAN

Even though his name is virtually synonymous with low-budget, entertaining horror (and exploitation and s-f and motorcycles and...), Roger Corman will probably be remembered best for the other filmmakers whose careers he advanced. That list includes Francis Ford Coppola, Martin Scorsese, John Sayles, Ron Howard, Jonathan Demme, Joe Dante, James Cameron, Paul Bartel, and Peter Bogdanovich.

Corman's own career as producer and director is worth noting, too, because he was so instrumental in keeping the horror film alive at a time when the larger studios were ignoring it.

Born in Detroit in 1926, Corman studied engineering at Stanford and literature at Oxford before he broke into the bottom floor of the movie business reading scripts, and then writing them. In the early 1950s, when the industry began to feel the effects of the Paramount Consent Decree that had broken up the studio ownership of theatres, Corman teamed up with James Nicholson and Sam Arkoff at American International Pictures.

In those years, Corman cranked out low-budget westerns, s-f, and horror at a furious pace, ending with two horror-comedies that are enduring cult favorites, *A Bucket of Blood* and *Little Shop of Horrors*. After them, Corman turned his attention to Edgar Allan Poe and made more expensive and lavish-looking horrors. Beginning with *The Fall of the House of Usher* and ending with *Masque of the Red Death*, Corman made eight Poe-inspired period horrors, most of them starring Vincent Price. Those pretty much ended Corman's direct involvement with horror, though he continues to produce, and directed the uneven *Frankenstein Unbound* in 1990.

In recent years, the names of his production company has changed several times, and Corman has been content to have others remake his older titles for the second or third time. Where his works once appeared first at drive-ins, they now go straight to video or cable. Despite the different media, they're the same competently made genre escapism that he directed and produced in the 1960s—neither much better nor worse.

SIGNIFICANT CONTRIBUTIONS TO HORROR

The Wasp Woman **(1959)**

A Bucket of Blood **(1959)**

Little Shop of Horrors **(1960)**

The Fall of the House of Usher **(1960)**

The Pit and the Pendulum **(1961)**

Premature Burial **(1962)**

The Raven **(1963)**

Masque of the Red Death **(1965)**

with a slightly letterboxed, crystalline image. O.K., the title is silly and the plot does revolve around zombies in 19th century Cornwall, England—not the usual setting—but that's not a problem. This is essentially a vampire story with a twist. Relative unknowns Andre Morell, as the Van Helsing character, and John Carson as the villainous Squire, are every bit as good as Cushing and Lee. Jacqueline Pearce and Diane Clare are demurely sexy Hammer heroines. The presence of familiar character actor Michael Ripper doesn't hurt either. The makeup is easily the equal of more recent living dead movies. And let's not overlook the political aspects of a story about the relationship between the upper class and workers. Zombies of the world, unite! You have nothing to lose but your shrouds!

1966 90m/C *GB* Andre Morell, John Carson, Diane Clare, Alex Davion, Jacqueline Pearce, Brook Williams, Michael Ripper, Marcus Hammond, Roy Royston; ***D:*** John Gilling; ***W:*** Peter Bryan, John Elder; ***C:*** Arthur Grant; ***M:*** James Bernard. **VHS, Letterboxed** *VTR*

Plan 9 from Outer Space

In his famous and sad final role, Bela Lugosi's screen time is less than two minutes. (See Tim Burton's *Ed Wood* for the full version of the relationship between Lugosi and the young director.) Wood's wife's chiropractor replaced the star and kept himself hidden behind cape and hat. The rest of Wood's alternative masterpiece—almost universally acknowledged to be the "worst" film ever made—is the stuff of Hollywood legend. Aliens in silk pajamas conspire to resurrect several slow-moving zombies from a cardboard graveyard and to conquer the Earth before we warlike humans destroy the rest of the universe with "solarite bombs." Spaceships that look suspiciously like paper plates blaze across the sky, and Wood's famous penchant for rambling philosophical dialogue is given free rein. ***AKA:*** Grave Robbers from Outer Space.

1956 78m/B Bela Lugosi, Tor Johnson, Lyle Talbot, Vampira, Gregory Walcott, Tom George Duryea Keene, Dudley Manlove, Mona McKinnon, Duke Moore, Joanna Lee, Bunny Breckinridge, Criswell, Carl Anthony, Paul Marco, Norma McCarty, David DeMering, Bill Ash, Conrad Brooks, Edward D. Wood Jr.; ***D:*** Edward D. Wood Jr.; ***W:*** Edward D. Wood Jr.; ***C:*** William C. Thompson. **VHS, LV** *RHI, EEL, SNC*

Poltergeist

Though Tobe Hooper directed this hugely popular horror hit, it was produced and cowritten by Steven Spielberg. In some ways, then, it can be seen as the dark side of *E.T.,* also released in the summer of 1982. The Freelings (JoBeth Williams and Craig T. Nelson) learn why they got such a good deal on their suburban tract house when it attacks them and their kids. Most of the scares are original and frightening. Structurally, the film is sound, with careful preparation establishing place and mood. The main flaw is the conclusion, which ought to be more solidly connected to the earlier action. At the end, the characters simply need a better reason to spend more time in the place. Critics have floated many theories about the film's success—it's about the destruction of suburbia, Reagan-era politics, etc.,—but it's simply a good, well-acted, spooky movie. Followed by lesser sequels.

1982 (PG) 114m/C JoBeth Williams, Craig T. Nelson, Beatrice Straight, Heather O'Rourke, Zelda Rubinstein, Dominique Dunne, Oliver Robbins, Richard Lawson, James Karen, Michael McManus; ***D:*** Tobe Hooper; ***W:*** Steven Spielberg, Michael Grais, Mark Victor; ***C:*** Matthew F. Leonetti; ***M:*** Jerry Goldsmith. Nominations: Academy Awards '82: Best Original Score. **VHS, LV, DVD, Letterboxed** *MGM*

Poltergeist 2: The Other Side

The humor and homey sense of the first film here seems forced. That suburban

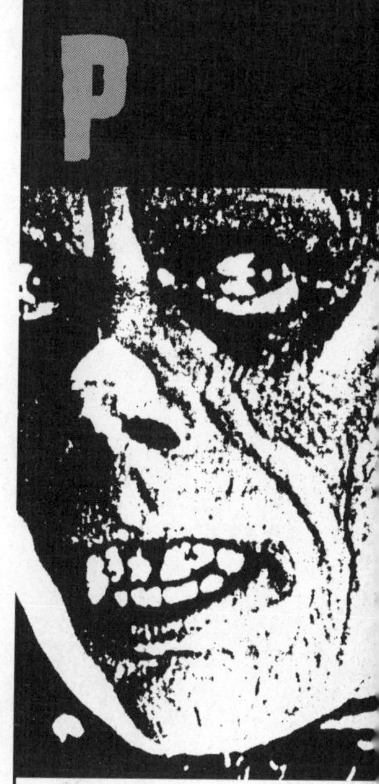

"This house is clean."

—Tangina's (Zelda Rubenstein) premature proclamation in *Poltergeist*.

THE HOUND SALUTES

ALFRED HITCHCOCK

Alfred Hitchcock is commonly referred to as "the Master of Suspense," and that's a reasonably accurate sobriquet. But he also made a great horror film—one that still scares people more than 30 years after it was first released on an unsuspecting public, and so any book about the subject must include at least a brief tribute to him.

Besides, the truth is that, as he readily admitted, Hitchcock liked to scare people. Whether his films are classified as suspense, mystery, thriller, or horror, he wanted to involve his audience in the story and then to frighten them. "Fear in the cinema is my special field," Hitchcock wrote in 1949, "and I have, perhaps dogmatically, but I think with good cause, split cinematic fear into two broad categories—terror and suspense."

Psycho works with both of those categories.

About ten years later, around the time he was making it, Hitchcock wrote, "Without wanting to seem immodest, I can't help but compare what I try to put in my films with what Poe put in his stories: a perfectly unbelievable story recounted to readers with such a hallucinatory logic that one has the impression that this same story can happen to you tomorrow."

That is precisely what Hitchcock did. Time after time he was able to create the "hallucinatory logic" that moviegoers love to experience. It began with what he considered to be the first true "Hitchcock film," *The Lodger,* in 1926. Loosely based on a Jack the Ripper character, it's an early serial killer story which, along with Fritz Lang's *M* (1931), influenced the more "realistic" strain of horror.

It would be almost 30 years before Hitchcock returned to true horror with *Psycho,* and then he really did create the impression that the things that happened at the Bates Motel could happen to you tomorrow.

The most famous moment is the shower scene. It's been spoofed, honored, and quoted

"realism" has been replaced by dopey special effects. Geraldine Fitzgerald's kindly old grandma and Heather O'Rourke's psychic cherub are cloyingly sweet. A few of the scares work well—notably the cadaverous Julian Beck's first appearance and a worm monster created by H.R. Giger—but most of the action is a rerun of the first film and lightning does not strike twice. 🦴🦴

1986 (PG-13) 92m/C Craig T. Nelson, JoBeth Williams, Heather O'Rourke, Will Sampson, Julian Beck, Geraldine Fitzgerald, Oliver Robbins, Zelda Rubinstein; ***D:*** Brian Gibson; ***W:*** Mark Victor, Michael Grais; ***C:*** Andrew Laszlo; ***M:*** Jerry Goldsmith. **VHS, LV, Letterboxed, Closed Caption** *MGM*

Poltergeist 3

3 finds young Carol Anne (Heather O'Rourke, who died before the film's release) staying with her aunt and uncle (Nancy Allen and Tom Skerritt) in a ritzy Chicago highrise. Watered down versions of those silly spooks from the first two show up again. Slick production values can't cover up a lack of originality. Many of the effects involve mirrors and ice. Overall, it's a solid step down from the disappointing *2*. Followed by a cable TV series. 🦴

1988 (PG-13) 97m/C Tom Skerritt, Nancy Allen, Heather O'Rourke, Lara Flynn Boyle, Zelda Rubinstein;

more than any other moment in movies, regardless of genre, and I'd bet that most moviegoers can remember the time and the circumstances when they first experienced it. They should. It is pure filmmaking at its best. Depending on how you choose to measure it, the scene is about a minute long and it contains more than 90 pieces of film. Bernard Herrmann's jagged violins are a dead solid perfect musical accompaniment to the wordless action.

What many people often overlook is the fact that the scene comes at a crucial point in the story after our expectations have been led in several different directions. By then, we're not sure exactly what's going to happen, but we certainly aren't expecting anything like that.

Astonishingly, Hitchcock follows the scene with two more almost as memorable—Detective Arbogast's going back downstairs and the revelation of Norman's mother.

Hitchcock followed his masterpiece with another "pure" horror film. But where *Psycho* was exactly the right film at the right time, *The Birds* was just a few years ahead of its time. Audiences simply weren't ready for a story that contains no explanation and an unsatisfactory ending. (That story would come in 1968 with *Night of the Living Dead*.) It's a shame because *The Birds* is brilliant, and despite the huge leaps that have been made in special effects, it remains fresh and less dated than many films of the early 1960s. It's also, I think, Hitchcock's last great film, though cases can be made for *Marnie* as a companion piece to *Vertigo*, and *Frenzy*.

That's a subject for further debate, perhaps over a bottle of wine after a Hitchcock double feature. Now, there's a good idea!

SIGNIFICANT CONTRIBUTIONS TO HORROR

***The Lodger* (1926)**

***Psycho* (1960)**

***The Birds* (1963)**

D: Gary Sherman; *W:* Gary Sherman, Brian Taggert; *C:* Alex Nepomniaschy. **VHS, LV, Closed Caption** *MGM*

Polymorph

Horror/s-f/comedy begins with standard elements: teen campers, house in the Ohio woods, monster from outer space that inhabits bodies and pops from person to person. Fans have been there before many times. Writer/producer/director J.R. Bookwalter tweaks the formula with a strung-out cokehead (Sasha Graham) who's guarding a significant stash for her gangster pals. At times, the action is a little too talky, but the actors do very good work for non- and semi-professionals. Bookwalter also makes excellent use of animated title cards at transitions. The violence isn't excessive and the characters have some depth. 🦴🦴🦴

1996 86m/C Ariauna Albright, James Edwards, Jennifer Huss, Sasha Graham; *D:* J.R. Bookwalter; *W:* J.R. Bookwalter. **VHS** *EI*

Popcorn

The slice-and-dice plot of this horror/comedy is too ridiculous to dignify with synop-

"Blondes are the best victims. They're like virgin snow which shows up the bloody footprints."

—Alfred Hitchcock as quoted in *Sunday Times*, September 1, 1973.

"Buy a bag...go home in a box."

—Ad line from *Popcorn.*

sis. It involves the destruction of an old movie palace and an all-night "horrorthon" where a generic slasher is at work. The parodic black-and-white clips from fictional '50s movies are the point and they're terrific. *Mosquito* is a 3-D big-bug micro-epic complete with stock footage of Air Force jet fighters, and *The Stench* features "aromarama." First-time director Mark Herrier began his career by appearing in all three *Porky's* movies, and he brings that same unsophisticated approach to this one.

1989 (R) 93m/C Jill Schoelen, Tom Villard, Dee Wallace Stone, Derek Rydell, Elliott Hurst, Kelly Jo Minter, Malcolm Danare, Ray Walston, Tony Roberts, Karen Witter; ***D:*** Mark Herrier, Alan Ormsby; ***W:*** Alan Ormsby. **VHS, LV, 8mm** *COL*

Premature Burial

Guy Carrell (Ray Milland) is certain he'll be interred before he's completely inert. His fiancee Emily (Hazel Court) tut-tuts his obsession. Justifiably famous for his budgetary tight-fistedness, producer/director Roger Corman makes the fullest possible use of a few richly decorated and fog-shrouded Gothic sets, including a crypt with an escape route. Veteran writers Charles Beaumont and Ray Russell use Poe's morbid fear as the premise for a cracking good yarn. Like Shakespeare, they leave the stage littered with bodies.

1962 81m/C Ray Milland, Richard Ney, Hazel Court, Heather Angel, Alan Napier, John Dierkes, Dick Miller; ***D:*** Roger Corman; ***W:*** Charles Beaumont, Ray Russell; ***C:*** Floyd Crosby. **VHS, LV** *LIV, MLB*

Prince of Darkness

One of John Carpenter's best and most underrated films works through intelligent dialogue, carefully measured special effects, and excellent performances from an ensemble cast. When a priest (Donald Pleasence) learns that the last member of an odd order, the Brotherhood of Sleep, has died, he inspects the church that the brothers guarded. Why are street people so attracted to it, and what is that big jar of goop that looks like molten lime Jell-O in the basement? Theoretical physics and ultimate evil are involved. Fans will catch echoes of *Poltergeist* and Carpenter's own *Assault on Precinct 13*.

1987 (R) 102m/C Donald Pleasence, Lisa Blount, Victor Wong, Jameson Parker, Dennis Dun, Susan Blanchard, Anne Howard, Ken Wright, Dirk Blocker; ***Cameos:*** Alice Cooper; ***D:*** John Carpenter; ***W:*** John Carpenter; ***C:*** Gary B. Kibbe; ***M:*** John Carpenter. **VHS, LV** *USH*

Prom Night

Good acting and above-average production values are put in service of a plot that doesn't deviate a millimeter from the standard dead-teenager slasher/stalker formula. It borrows most blatantly from *Halloween* with the "six years before" prologue, and from *Carrie* in the second half. Jamie Lee Curtis and four of her high school friends are the prey of a killer out to avenge an earlier murder. But much more terrifying than that plot is the "Disco Madness" theme of the titular dance. Flashing lights, raised arms, pointing fingers, polyester—the horror, the horror.

1980 (R) 91m/C *CA* Jamie Lee Curtis, Leslie Nielsen, Casey Stevens, Eddie Benton, Antoinette Bower, Michael Tough, Pita Oliver, David Mucci, Joy Thompson, Mary Beth Rubens; ***D:*** Paul Lynch; ***W:*** William Gray; ***C:*** Robert New. **VHS, LV** *NLC*

Prom Night 3: The Last Kiss

3 is a sequel to *Hello Mary Lou: Prom Night 2* and has nothing to do with the first film. As it opens, Mary Lou Maloney (Courtney Taylor), the unrepentant party girl and murderess, breaks out of her shackles in hell with a nail file and returns to high school. She sets her sights on struggling student Alex (Tim Conlon) and does everything in her devilish powers to further his academic career. This time out, the recycled plot is treated as comedy. Despite fair effects and production values, it remains pretty wrapping around an empty box. Followed by an even less necessary *4.* 🦴

1989 (R) 97m/C Tim Conlon, Cyndy Preston, Courtney Taylor, David Stratton, Dylan Neal, Jeremy Ratchford; ***D:*** Ron Oliver, Peter Simpson; ***W:*** Ron Oliver; ***C:*** Rhett Morita. **VHS, LV** *LIV*

Prom Night 4: Deliver Us from Evil

Father Jonas (James Carver) prays to "save sluts and whores" as the stigmata bleed on his palms. Moments later, the psycho-priest is killing kids at the prom and indulging in self flagellation. About the best that can be said of this tedious Canadian production is that it appears to be the last in a poor series. 🦴

1991 (R) 95m/C *CA* Nikki DeBoer, Alden Kane, Joy Tanner, Alle Ghadban, James Carver; ***D:*** Clay Borris; ***W:*** Richard Beattie. **VHS, Closed Caption** *LIV*

Prophecy

One of the first eco-horrors about pollution-generated mutant critters has aged gracelessly. The story is solid, if too familiar, with EPA doctor (Robert Foxworth) and his pregnant wife (Talia Shire) discovering evil doings out in the woods at the paper plant. Director John Frankenheimer knows how to keep action moving well. The main problem is a monster that's obviously a creation of the effects department. Writer David Seltzer hits much closer to home with *The Omen.* 🦴🦴

1979 (PG) 102m/C Talia Shire, Robert Foxworth, Armand Assante, Victoria Racimo, Richard Dysart, George Clutesi; ***D:*** John Frankenheimer; ***W:*** David Seltzer; ***C:*** Harry Stradling Jr. **VHS** *NO*

The Prophecy

Enjoyable and surprisingly witty religious horror goes beyond the traditional structure of Good vs. Evil as represented by God and Satan. The key combatants are angels involved in an eons-long war with each other. These angels are not halo-topped sweetie-pies who float around performing the odd miracle here and there. To these creatures, humans are "talking monkeys" who have usurped their favored place in the presence of God. It's hard for Harry (Elias Koteas), a priest-turned-cop, to know which side to take in the conflict. On one hand, Gabriel (Christopher Walken, at his dead-pan creepiest) is willing to kill anyone who gets in his way. But since he can't drive, his mobility is limited. His opposite number Timothy (Eric Stoltz) seems to be looking for a soul to steal. They're after a young Arizona Indian girl whose only protection is her elementary school teacher (Virginia Madsen). First-time writer/director Gregory Widen gets excellent performances from a seasoned cast, and he gives the whole film a gritty, intense look that fits the subject. He also avoids most of the genre's cliches, and the film's intelligent black humor keeps it from being too heavy. Followed by a sequel. 🦴🦴🦴½

1995 (R) 97m/C Christopher Walken, Eric Stoltz, Elias Koteas, Virginia Madsen, Amanda Plummer, Viggo Mortensen; ***D:*** Gregory Widen; ***W:*** Gregory Widen; ***C:*** Bruce Douglas Johnson, Richard Clabaugh; ***M:*** David Williams. **VHS, LV, Closed Caption** *MAX*

The Prophecy 2: Ashtown

Rare sequel is just as good, just as offbeat as the original, and even funnier. The first film establishes two warring factions of angels—those faithful to god and those who are jealous of humans, "talking monkeys," as they call us. None of them are miracle-making altruists. They're heavenly Terminators, and Gabriel (Christopher

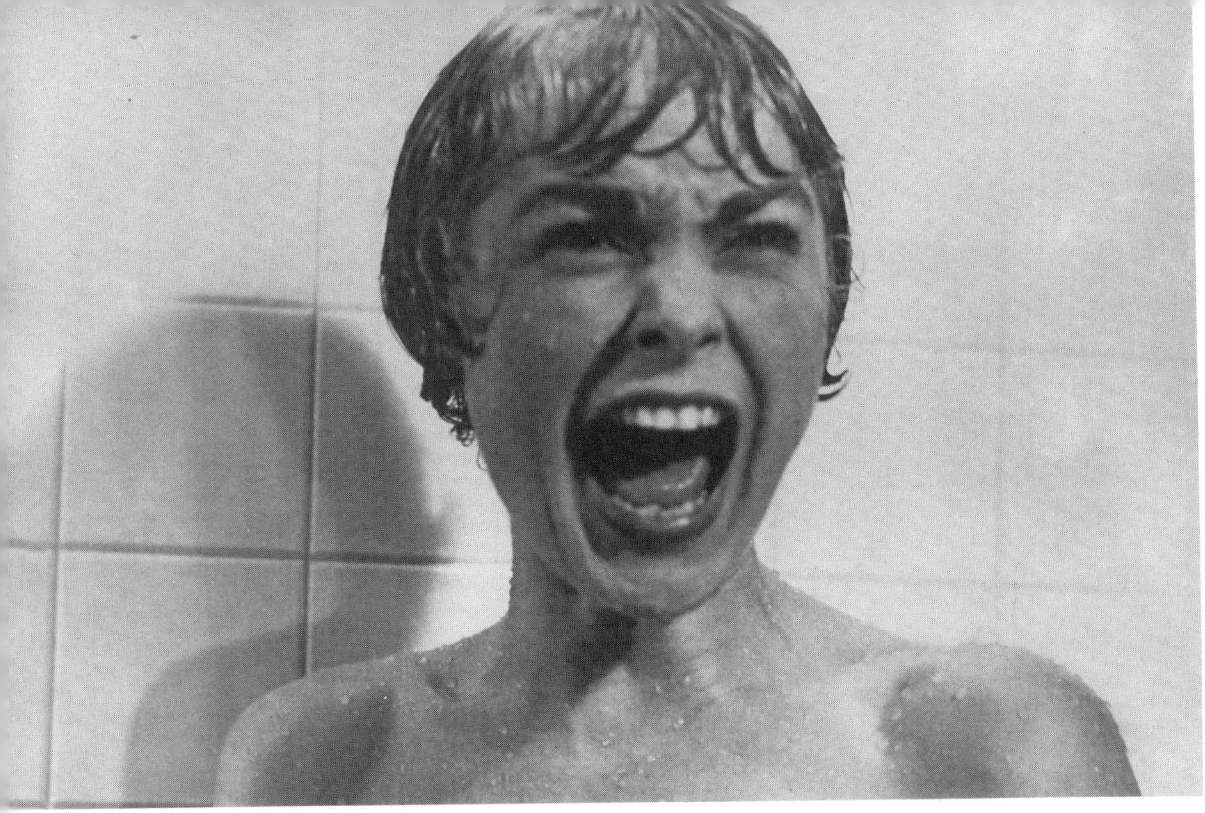

Marion Crane (Janet Leigh) in Hitchcock's *Psycho.*

Walken) is the baddest of the bunch. He's after Valerie Rosales (Jennifer Beals), a nurse who's been impregnated by angel Daniel. Director Greg Spence, also responsible for the surprise sleeper *Children of the Corn 4,* brings real wit and innovation to the story. Gabriel's entrance is a terrific set piece and the ending is even better. Some of the plotting is a tad too elaborate but that's not a real problem. Inexplicably, this gem made its debut on video.

1997 (R) 83m/C Christopher Walken, Russell Wong, Eric Roberts, Jennifer Beals, Bruce Abbott, Brittany Murphy, Steve Hytner, Glenn Danzig; ***D:*** Greg Spence; ***W:*** Greg Spence, Matt Greenberg; ***M:*** David Williams. **VHS, LV, Closed Caption** *TOU*

Proteus

Brit monster movie shows a strong influence of TV's *The X-Files.* Both use the same simple, proven tricks to build suspense: remote isolated location, dark smoky rooms and hallways, flashlights, slimy monsters. The setting is a deserted offshore oil rig-turned-genetics lab. That's where a gang of young drug dealers find themselves when their boat blows up and where they uncover some nasty surprises. When the monster finally appears, it's something of a disappointment. For the most part, though, director Bob Keen uses nasty-looking mucous and makeup effects borrowed from Japanese animated films to conjure up scares. In the leads, Craig Fairbrass and Toni Barry aren't bad.

1995 (R) 97m/C *GB* Doug Bradley, Craig Fairbrass, Toni Barry; ***D:*** Bob Keen. **VHS, Closed Caption** *THV*

Psycho

In 1960, Alfred Hitchcock invented the modern horror film with a modest masterpiece that has influenced virtually everything in the field that's been made since.

Loosely inspired by infamous killer Ed Gein, the movie deliberately and constantly misleads audiences. Today, everybody knows the story and the big scenes are built on images that have become cinematic archetypes. But that's hindsight. In 1960, no one expected the leading lady (Janet Leigh) to make such an early and shocking exit, and no one expected a murderer to look like the boy next door. Co-star Tony Perkins had been known for serious, generally "nice" roles. More to the point, the whole idea of an opportunistic serial killer was unheard of. Today, the only part of the film that's at all dated is Simon Oakland's lengthy concluding explanation. The film itself is so craftily constructed that even Hitchcock's fans will find something new when they see it again. In his interviews with Francois Truffaut, Hitchcock said that he didn't consciously recreate "an old-fashioned Universal horror-picture" but that's precisely what the Bates Motel is. He also said that he was consciously working within the economic limits of a television production (except for the shower scene), and so now the film plays beautifully on home video. Followed by lesser sequels.

1960 109m/B Anthony Perkins, Janet Leigh, Vera Miles, John Gavin, John McIntire, Martin Balsam, Simon Oakland, Ted Knight, John Anderson, Frank Albertson, Patricia Hitchcock; ***D:*** Alfred Hitchcock; ***W:*** Joseph Stefano; ***C:*** John L. Russell; ***M:*** Bernard Herrmann. Golden Globe Awards '61: Best Supporting Actress (Leigh); Nominations: Academy Awards '60: Best Art Direction/Set Decoration (B & W), Best Black and White Cinematography, Best Director (Hitchcock), Best Supporting Actress (Leigh). **VHS, LV** *USH, TLF*

Psycho 2

No, this one doesn't come close to the original, but it's not a bad horror movie, either. And it is a true sequel, a logical continuation of the characters and story of Hitchcock's low-budget masterpiece with several genuinely suspenseful moments. More importantly, Tom Holland's script has a wickedly funny sense of black humor. After being institutionalized for 22 years, Norman Bates (Anthony Perkins) is declared sane, over the loud objections of Lila Loomis (Vera Miles, continuing her role from the first film). Back at the old motel, the first thing Norman sees is a shape in the upper left window of the house on the hill. Then his mother calls. Is someone trying to drive him mad again, or is Norman just doing what comes naturally?

1983 (R) 113m/C Claudia Bryar, Anthony Perkins, Vera Miles, Meg Tilly, Robert Loggia, Dennis Franz; ***D:*** Richard Franklin; ***W:*** Tom Holland; ***C:*** Dean Cundey; ***M:*** Jerry Goldsmith. **VHS, LV** *USH*

Psycho 3

Beyond a few references to other Hitchcock films, this sequel is just another slasher flick. After a reprise of the ending to *2*, a young nun, Maureen (Diana Scarwid) leaves her convent under horrible (and funny) circumstances borrowed from *Vertigo*. Eventually, she and Duane (Jeff Fahey) find themselves as the only guests at the Bates Motel, where Norman (director Anthony Perkins) is still having conversations with Mom up in the house on the hill. Though the violence is handled with some care, the action is poorly written and poorly paced.

1986 (R) 93m/C Anthony Perkins, Diana Scarwid, Jeff Fahey, Roberta Maxwell, Robert Alan Browne, Hugh Gillin, Lee Garlington; ***D:*** Anthony Perkins; ***W:*** Charles Edward Pogue; ***C:*** Bruce Surtees; ***M:*** Carter Burwell. **VHS, LV, Closed Caption** *USH*

Psycho 4: The Beginning

Fran Ambrose's (CCH Pounder) radio talk show is focused on "boys who kill their mothers." Naturally, Norman (Anthony Perkins) calls in to share his experiences. In flashback, young Norman (Henry

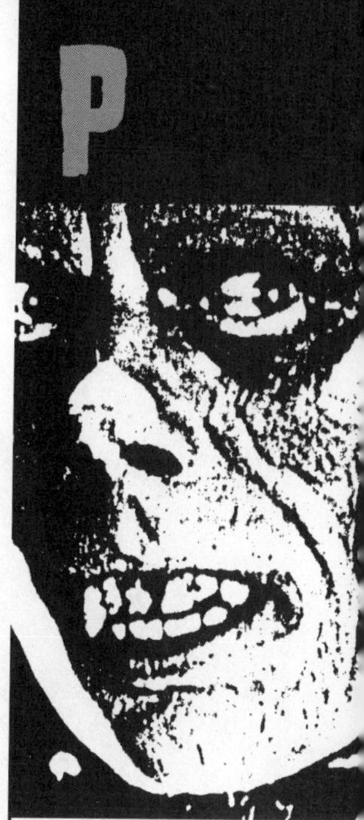

"They're probably watching me. Well, let them. Let them see what kind of person I am. I'm not even going to swat that fly. I hope they are watching. They'll see. They'll see and they'll know and they'll say, 'Why, she wouldn't even harm a fly.'"

—Mrs. Bates' voice in *Psycho.*

Haggis (Florence Schauffler) in *Pumpkinhead.*

Pumpkinhead

TV host and drive-in movie critic emeritus Joe Bob Briggs has said that this is the most requested title among his incarcerated fans. It's easy to see why. At the beginning, special effects master Stan Winston's directorial debut hammers on emotional buttons without wasting a single motion. Grotesque monster (Tom Woodruff, Jr., in terrific makeup), loving widowed father (Lance Henriksen), his young son, thoughtless rich city kids ripping up the rural setting on their dirt-bikes—that's the set-up. But once the conflicts are being engaged, Winston gives the story a serious twist, refusing to take the easy, expected path. Throughout, his direction is sure-handed; just notice the way he uses light and smoke. In Henriksen's long career, this is one of his most complex roles and the whole film is one of the unrecognized greats. ***AKA:*** Vengeance: The Demon.

1988 (R) 89m/C Lance Henriksen, John DiAquino, Kerry Remsen, Matthew Hurley, Jeff East, Kimberly Ross, Cynthia Bain, Joel Hoffman, Florence Schauffler, Buck Flower, Tom Woodruff Jr.; ***D:*** Stan Winston; ***W:*** Gary Gerani, Mark Patrick Carducci; ***C:*** Bojan Bazelli; ***M:*** Richard Stone. **VHS, LV, Closed Caption** *MGM*

Thomas, from *E.T.*) remembers dear old mom (Olivia Hussey). Like the other entries in the series, it's partially tongue-in-cheek and enjoyable enough if you don't compare it to the original. Thomas is eerily reminiscent of Perkins as he was in 1960. Graeme Revell's score is built around Bernard Herrmann's original music. Director Mick Garris also did *Stephen King's The Stand.* This one was made for cable with exceptionally high production values.

1990 (R) 96m/C Anthony Perkins, Henry Thomas, Olivia Hussey, CCH Pounder, Warren Frost, Donna Mitchell; ***D:*** Mick Garris; ***W:*** Joseph Stefano; ***C:*** Rodney Charters; ***M:*** Bernard Herrmann, Graeme Revell. **VHS, LV** *USH*

Pumpkinhead 2: Blood Wings

The elements that were combined so gracefully in the original—the memorable atmosphere, strong characters, intelligent twists on the revenge formula—come back as hollow cliches in a story that's really a remake, not a sequel. Obnoxious teens in an Arkansas backlot resurrect the son of the first title character. Some of the effects are excellent, and it's good to see Andy Robinson (the psycho killer in *Dirty Harry,* who almost always plays villains) cast as the hero. He's a New York cop who becomes a rural sheriff. Beyond that, the film is a competently made, polished slasher flick with Bill Clinton's brother Roger as the mayor. 🦴🦴½

1994 (R) 88m/C Ami Dolenz, Andrew (Andy) Robinson, Kane Hodder, R.A. Mihailoff, Linnea Quigley, Steve Kanaly, Caren Kaye, Gloria Hendry, Soleil Moon Frye, Mark McCracken, Roger Clinton; ***D:*** Jeff Burr; ***W:*** Ivan Chachornia, Constantin Chachornia. **VHS, LV** *LIV*

Puppet Master

The first installment in the Band organization's most popular series is a slickly made, Stephen King sort of story about a haunted hotel filled with psychics and murderous marionettes. The action begins well with a suspenseful opening sequence but slides downhill. The special effects are acceptable and the production values are high throughout, but the plot is uninvolving and the characters are flat. Even so, it has been followed by four more to date. 🦴🦴½

1989 (R) 90m/C Paul LeMat, Jimmie F. Skaggs, Irene Miracle, Robyn Frates, Barbara Crampton, William Hickey, Matt Roe, Kathryn O'Reilly; ***D:*** David Schmoeller; ***W:*** Joseph G. Collodi; ***C:*** Sergio Salvati; ***M:*** Richard Band. **VHS, LV, Closed Caption** *FLL*

Quatermass and the Pit

The only flaws in this intelligent and consistently surprising British horror/s-f are thin effects and a relatively weak conclusion to a strong story. Professor Quatermass (Andrew Kier) is a prickly scientist who counters military thick-headedness, in the person of Col. Breen (Julian Glover), with skeptical humanism. Their point of contention is an object uncovered during the renovation of a London subway stop. Dr. Roney (James Donald), an anthropologist, suspects it may be extraterrestrial. But what about the humanoid skeletons buried around it? Echoes of Nigel Kneale's script can be seen in *2001* and Stephen King's *The Tommyknockers*. Director Roy Ward Baker keeps the offbeat action on track throughout. Beyond the limited effects, it's a remarkably beautiful film that makes good use of color and light. Though it makes a belated arrival on home video, the Anchor Bay digitally mastered transfer is sparkling clear and slightly letterboxed. The remake of a 1958 BBC original is one of Hammer's best and that's very good, indeed. ***AKA:*** Five Million Years to Earth. 🦴🦴🦴½

1967 97m/C *GB* James Donald, Andrew Keir, Barbara Shelley, Julian Glover, Duncan Lamont, Bryan Marshall; ***D:*** Roy Ward Baker; ***W:*** Nigel Kneale; ***C:*** Arthur Grant; ***M:*** Tristam Carey. **VHS, Letterboxed** *VTR*

Rabid

Though it's not David Cronenberg's best, by any means, this combination of medical, sexual, and mechanical horrors provides an early look at some of the themes he would explore more fully in other films. In a triumph of casting, porn star Marilyn Chambers is Rose, a motorcycle accident victim whose skin grafts mutate, turning her into a vampiric carrier of a new strain of rabies. In the first half, the horror is based on intimate surgical fears which turn into larger and less frightening "Living Dead" excesses later. Cronenberg's fans will spot the thematic and symbolic links to the later, more serious work. ***AKA:*** Rage. 🦴🦴🦴

1977 (R) 90m/C *CA* Marilyn Chambers, Frank Moore, Joe Silver, Howard Ryshpan, Patricia Gage, Susan Roman; ***D:*** David Cronenberg; ***W:*** David Cronenberg; ***C:*** Rene Verzier. **VHS** *WAR*

Rabid Grannies

What a title! Two aging sisters (Catherine Aymerie and Caroline Brackman) receive a surprise birthday present from their devil-worshiping nephew. The gift turns their party into a gorefest as they rip into various family members—literally. The bloody effects are laughably amateurish, but that's appropriate for this wicked (and sometimes too talky) satire. The good

Christopher Lee is *Rasputin the Mad Monk.*

folks at Troma Team Video imported the schlock from Belgium. Recommended for fans of bad movies only. 🦴🦴🦴

1989 (R) 89m/C *BE* Catherine Aymerie, Caroline Brackman, Danielle Daven, Raymond Lescot, Anne Marie Fox, Richard Cotica, Patricia Davie; ***D:*** Emmanuel Kervyn; ***W:*** Emmanuel Kervyn. **VHS, LV** *VTR*

Race with the Devil

A doctoral thesis could be written about the social and cinematic implications of stars Peter Fonda, from *Easy Rider* (1969), and Warren Oates, from *Two Lane Blacktop* (1971), trading in their hot wheels for an RV land yacht to take on vacation with their wives, Loretta Swit and Lara Parker. They run into an (unintentionally) semi-comic coven of Texas satanists. Can local sheriff R.G. Armstrong be trusted? The veteran cast handles the confused paint-by-numbers script more seriously than they need to. The snake scene is pretty scary. 🦴🦴

1975 (PG) 88m/C Peter Fonda, Warren Oates, Loretta Swit, Lara Parker, R.G. Armstrong; ***D:*** Jack Starrett; ***W:*** Wes Bishop, Lee Frost; ***C:*** Robert C. Jessup. **VHS, Closed Caption** *FOX, FCT*

Raging Angels

Alan Smithee—the pseudonym that directors use when they're too embarrassed by the fruit of their labor—adds another alternative notch to his belt with this nutsy horror. The crackpot plot might have come from a right-wing religious wacko's fantasy—one world government led by Antichrist Michael Pare. Allied against him are a drunken young rocker (Sean Patrick Flanery), his bland blonde girlfriend (Monet Mazur), and his nutty grandmother Shelley Winters...yes, Shelley Winters at her blowzy, scenery-gnawing worst. (Her death scene is a real corker, one of the true lowlights in her distinguished career.) As a goofy psychic, veteran co-star Diane Ladd gives the redoubtable Ms.

Winters a run for her money with some inspired histrionics.

1995 (R) 97m/C Sean Patrick Flanery, Monet Mazur, Michael Pare, Diane Ladd, Shelley Winters, Arielle Dombasle; ***D:*** Alan Smithee; ***W:*** Kevin Rock, David Markov, Chris Bittler; ***C:*** Bryan England; ***M:*** Terry Plumeri. **VHS, Closed Caption** *THV*

Raising Cain

This howler was the final nail in the coffin of Brian DePalma's reputation. In essence, he has created an homage to himself, cobbling together bits from his own *Sisters, Carrie, Blow Out,* and *Dressed to Kill.* Then he adds a touch of *Psycho* plus assorted fruits and nuts. The result is simply silly. It has to do with Carter Nix (John Lithgow), who may be hallucinating a twin named Cain. For most of the film, the viewer isn't supposed to know what's real, with dream sequences within dream sequences, lots of slow motion, and long long tracking shots where DePalma vainly attempts to show what a hotshot director he is. For group viewing as an unintentional comedy, it rates four meaty bones; on its own merits it deserves the Hound's biggest **Woof!**

1992 (R) 95m/C John Lithgow, Lolita Davidovich, Steven Bauer, Frances Sternhagen, Cindy Girard, Tom Bower, Mel Harris, Gabrielle Carteris, Barton Heyman; ***D:*** Brian DePalma; ***W:*** Brian DePalma; ***C:*** Stephen Burum; ***M:*** Pino Donaggio. **VHS, LV, Letterboxed, Closed Caption** *USH*

The Rape After

Thomas Weisser's book *Asian Cult Cinema* explains that the disfigured child at the beginning of this unsettling film is the result of his father's syphilis. The rest of the story amplifies the concept of horrors that are based on real human failings (drug use, madness, hatred) mixed with supernatural scares. It's a confusing tale connected by strange coincidence about a vengeful spirit that lives in a stolen statue. The story is marred by poor subtitling, but some of the images are really hideous. Perhaps the strongest is an attack on a priest by rats and birds. Director Ho Meng Hua works well with dark atmosphere and even darker emotions.

1986 88m/C *HK* Chang Ching Yu, Tsui Sui; ***D:*** Ho Meng Hua. **VHS** *VSM*

The Rapture

Too original, daring, and unsettling for a timid theatrical market, this controversial religious horror has become a cult favorite on video. Though it's far from a perfect film, Michael Tolkin's story of conversion treats charismatic Christianity with a seriousness that's almost never seen in popular entertainment. Mimi Rogers plays a woman who renounces an empty life of sexual experimentation and becomes devoutly religious, only to be betrayed by God. Perhaps. Whatever beliefs viewers bring to the film, it's a disturbing, thought-provoking experience. Recommended.

1991 (R) 100m/C Mimi Rogers, David Duchovny, Patrick Bauchau, Will Patton; ***D:*** Michael Tolkin; ***W:*** Michael Tolkin; ***C:*** Bojan Bazelli. **VHS, LV** *COL*

Rasputin the Mad Monk

Hammer recycles both the principal sets and cast members from *Dracula, Prince of Darkness* for this full-blown melodrama. Naturally, the key is Christopher Lee's energetic portrayal of the famous character—though for American audiences there is some unintentional humor in the pronunciation of his name as Ras-POOTIN. Barbara Shelley is excellent as the royal lady-in-waiting he seduces. Lee interprets the monk as a charismatic combination of Jesus, Dracula, and Walt Whitman. Ignore the beard and wig; listen to his rough loud voice, and notice the way he uses his hands. Though the film lacks a persuasive Russian setting, it's still a lot of fun for

THE HOUND SALUTES

CHARLES BAND

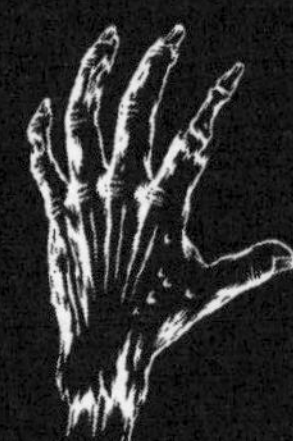

Charles Band is a name brand in the world of video.

When the prolific producer/director/studio head's name appears on a film, audiences pretty much know what to expect: a low-budget, high concept movie with lots of special effects, macho heroes, sexy (and sometimes, naked) heroines, and a fair degree of action.

He's been a pioneer in the video world, starting Media Home Entertainment in the late 1970s, distributing such cult items as *Flesh Gordon* and *The Groove Tube*, and, later, being involved with a host of other video-related enterprises, including Empire Entertainment, Wizard Video, Full Moon Pictures, the family-oriented Moonbeam label, Amazing Fantasy Video, and Surrender Cinema. And among the films he has been involved with are *Dollman, Meridian,* the *Puppet Master* series, *Troll, Subspecies, Dragonworld,* and *Prehysteria.*

Not bad for a guy in his mid 40s whose first efforts were the soft porn film *Cinderella* and *Mansion of the Doomed,* an *Eyes Without a Face* wannabe with Richard Basehart and Gloria Grahame.

The son of Albert Band—veteran director of the classic creeper, *I Bury the Living* and many spaghetti westerns and gladiator movies—Charles Band thinks his twenty-plus years of success has to do "inherently with its content, the artwork, and at least the promise that there's something entertaining."

Always a supporter of the video market, Band has had a few of his productions get into movie theatres, most notably *Re-Animator,* Stuart Gordon's Lovecraft camp-out; *Parasite,* a 3-D film Band directed with a young Demi Moore; and *Trancers* (AKA *Future Cop*) with Band regular Tim Thomerson and Helen Hunt. But Band seems perfectly content cranking out films for video viewers.

Hammer fans. The Anchor Bay letterboxed restoration—newly arrived on tape—is flawless. The liner notes claim that a nine-year-old Lee actually met Prince Yusupoff, one of the assassins. 🦴🦴🦴

1966 90m/B *GB* Christopher Lee, Barbara Shelley, Richard Pasco, Francis Matthews, Suzan Farmer, Nicholas Pennell, Renee Asherson, Derek Francis; ***D:*** Don Sharp; ***W:*** John Elder; ***C:*** Michael Reed; ***M:*** Don Banks. **VHS, Letterboxed** *VTR*

The Raven

Lugosi and Karloff's second teaming is a real disappointment following the brilliant *Black Cat,* though it is closer to Poe's themes. Bela Lugosi is a half-mad surgeon who thinks that he's a god "with the taint of human emotion." He enlists a criminal (Karloff) to help him get rid of an inconvenient judge. The main problem is unintentional humor, nowhere more evident than in the modern dance interpretation of Poe's poem, "The Raven." Karloff's make-up and one strong mirror scene are the best moments. 🦴🦴

1935 62m/B Boris Karloff, Bela Lugosi, Irene Ware, Lester Matthews, Samuel S. Hinds; ***D:*** Lew (Louis Friedlander) Landers; ***W:*** David Boehm, Jim Tully; ***C:*** Charles Stumar. **VHS, LV** *USH*

"I never made a picture that I felt deserves this current market, where you have a big event film or something personal or very special," he says. "Of the films I've made (about 150), maybe 20-25 have had any theatrical exposure. I really make movies for video, television, and foreign markets."

The Band brand name has helped his direct-to-video empire through strong marketing efforts. Band has a fan club with thousands of members. He has put out trading cards, comic books, and CD soundtracks for his films in the past. Occasionally, he'd take to the road with a cross-country promotion, showing clips from upcoming projects and some of the creatures that have appeared in his films.

Band believes these efforts have helped strengthen his following over the years, even though video renters are not always an easy sell. "They are very discerning," he says. "Once they've looked at two 'A' films, they may have patience for one other film. And 'B' movies have to jump off a shelf. If not, you're stuck in the morass of 'B' movies that are released each month that never go anywhere."

Although Band seems to have everything figured out, with his slick box covers, stop-motion and computer-generated beasts, and occasional boobs, he claims there's no sure thing in this business.

"There's no formula for making a good genre film," he says. "Everybody seems to come up with one, but you really can't create anything that's going to have value four or five years from now. This is a business that changes every year. Everybody is looking for the next trend, but nobody can predict it."

—Irv Slifkin

SIGNIFICANT CONTRIBUTIONS TO HORROR

Re-Animator **(1984)**

Puppet Master **series (1989-94)**

Subspecies **series (1990-93)**

Netherworld **(1990)**

Dark Angel: The Ascent **(1994)**

Meridian: Kiss of the Beast **(1990)**

The Raven

Egged on by the pixilated Dr. Bedlo (Peter Lorre), Dr. Erasmus Craven (Vincent Price) confronts the powerful sorcerer Scarabus (Boris Karloff) to find his lost Lenore (Hazel Court). Along for the ride are Bedlo's son (Jack Nicholson) and Craven's daughter (Olive Sturgess). The picture was filmed in three weeks with considerable comic improvisation by Lorre and Nicholson which, according to producer/director Roger Corman, Karloff disliked. The three veterans have a wonderful time with the material, particularly Lorre. He's really funny with some of his best light physical comedy. The duelling sorcerers finale is fine, too. Despite a typically penurious Corman budget, the film looks so good that it ought to be a candidate for restoration of its faded colors. 🦴🦴🦴

1963 86m/C Vincent Price, Boris Karloff, Peter Lorre, Jack Nicholson, Hazel Court, Olive Sturgess; ***D:*** Roger Corman; ***W:*** Richard Matheson; ***C:*** Floyd Crosby; ***M:*** Les Baxter. **VHS, LV** *MLB*

Razorback

A beautifully photographed introduction establishes a desolate setting in the Australian wilderness. The creature in ques-

"Pot's a misdemeanor. Decapitation seems a bit severe."

—Lt. D'Agost (Tom Sizemore) reflects on a murder victim in *The Relic.*

tion is a giant pig, a sort of Outback Jaws that can attack without warning from anywhere. The titanic tusker can crash through houses and rip apart cars. Both the fast-moving kinetic action and the grotesque characters owe a lot to the *Mad Max* films. Gregory Harrison is the American who goes looking for his wife (Judy Morris), a reporter, in the desert. The film really belongs to Bill Kerr as the grizzled boar hunter. Slaughterhouse sets are more frightening than the seldom-seen creature. Director Russel Mulcahy has gone on to make the first two *Highlander* movies and *The Shadow.* 🦴🦴½

1984 (R) 95m/C *AU* Gregory Harrison, Bill Kerr, Arkie Whiteley, Judy Morris, Chris Haywood, David Argue; ***D:*** Russell Mulcahy; ***W:*** Everett De Roche; ***C:*** Dean Semler. **VHS** *WAR*

Re-Animator

Few if any horror films mix strong sexual humor and equally strong effects as well as this cult favorite. H.P. Lovecraft's serial novella, *Herbert West, Re-animator,* about a serum that revives the dead (sort of), is brought to the screen with all the grotesque inventiveness that the special effects folk can provide. Richard Band's music shamelessly "borrows" from Bernard Herrmann's scores for *The Trouble with Harry* and *North by Northwest.* The famous "head" scene has never been duplicated. On home video, the film exists in three editions. The R-rated theatrical release is the tamest of three. The unrated tape is more popular, and the 1995 videodisc is the definitive version. It contains outtakes, a key deleted scene, and commentary by cast and crew. 🦴🦴🦴½

1985 86m/C Jeffrey Combs, Bruce Abbott, Barbara Crampton, David Gale, Robert Sampson, Gerry Black, Carolyn Purdy-Gordon; ***D:*** Stuart Gordon; ***W:*** Stuart Gordon, Dennis Paoli, William J. Norris; ***C:*** Mac Ahlberg; ***M:*** Richard Band. **VHS, LV** *LIV, VES*

The Refrigerator

Newlyweds (David Simonds and Julia McNeal) move from Ohio to the Big Apple and find that the titular appliance is possessed by the devil. Yes, they've got an ancient Norge from hell, and there's not much that the flamenco-dancing Bolivian super (Angel Caban) can do about it. The horror and comedy mix is successful about half the time. Some moments have an Ira Levinsort of creepiness while others are just dumb. The lived-in, made-on-location look of the production is a plus. 🦴🦴½

1991 86m/C David Simonds, Julia McNeal, Angel Caban, Nena Segal, Jaime Rojo, Michelle DeCosta, Phyllis Sanz; ***D:*** Nicholas A.E. Jacobs; ***W:*** Nicholas A.E. Jacobs; ***C:*** Paul Gibson. **VHS** *NO*

The Reincarnation of Peter Proud

Considering that the title character (Michael Sarrazin) is the reincarnation of a compulsive philanderer, the title is a weak joke, and neither the script nor the acting is much better. Peter has dreams of his murder years before at the hands of his jealous wife (Margot Kidder). At considerable length, he digs up the details of his earlier self and goofily reenacts them. The expensive production looks great, with dated '70s fashions, but remains resolutely silly. It would make a fine nonsensical past-life double feature with *Audrey Rose.* 🦴½

1975 (R) 105m/C Michael Sarrazin, Jennifer O'Neill, Margot Kidder, Cornelia Sharpe, Paul Hecht; ***D:*** J. Lee Thompson; ***W:*** Max Ehrlich; ***C:*** Victor Kemper; ***M:*** Jerry Goldsmith. **VHS, LV** *LIV, VES*

Relentless

Buck (Judd Nelson), the victim of an abusive father (and an incompetent barber who gave him the worst bowl haircut since

Moe Howard), is a psychotic serial killer. Malloy (Robert Loggia) and Dietz (Leo Rossi) are the cops after him. At his best, director William Lustig has an excellent touch with Los Angeles locations and he handles violence well. Nelson is a legitimate heir to Anthony Perkins' Norman Bates. We're not asked to sympathize with him, but we are asked to understand the forces that have made him what he is, and that's an unusual level of complexity in popular entertainment. Despite a predictable plot, this one works well within the genre. To my tastes, it's far superior to the overrated *Seven.*

1989 (R) 92m/C Judd Nelson, Robert Loggia, Meg Foster, Leo Rossi, Pat O'Bryan, Mindy Seeger, Angel Tompkins, Ken Lerner, George Flower; ***D:*** William Lustig. **VHS, LV, Closed Caption** *COL*

The Relic

A slickly produced, by-the-numbers variation on the *Alien* formula became something of a surprise hit in theatrical release, and has been even more popular with audiences on video. Following an exposition-packed introduction, the scene shifts to a Chicago natural history museum and the labyrinth of sewers and tunnels beneath it where a South American mutant monster decapitates supporting characters and eats their hypothalamuses (hypothalami?). Tough cop Tom Sizemore and tough evolutionary biologist Penelope Ann Miller set things right. Clayton Rohner, Linda Hunt, and James Whitmore make the most of their tissue-thin backup roles. Journeyman filmmaker Peter Hyams is an excellent director of photography and a so-so director. He creates an effective sense of place and wisely keeps his monster under wraps until the third act, when he reveals just enough of Stan Winston's beastie. Somehow, the whole thing is much more entertaining than it ought to be.

1996 (R) 110m/C Penelope Ann Miller, Tom Sizemore, Linda Hunt, James Whitmore, Clayton Rohner, Thomas Ryan, Lewis Van Bergen, Chi Muoi Lo, Robert Lesser; ***D:*** Peter Hyams; ***W:*** Amy Holden Jones, John Raffo, Rick Jaffa, Amanda Silver; ***C:*** Peter Hyams; ***M:*** John Debney. **VHS, Closed Caption** *PAR*

The Reptile

Lesser-known Hammer entry follows the studio's proven formula with snake monsters filling in for the traditional vampires. Following the death of his brother Charles (David Baron), Harry (Ray Barrett) and Valerie (Jennifer Daniel) move into the departed's English country cottage. They find sullen, frightened villagers, a disagreeable aristocrat (Noel Willman), his beautiful daughter (Jacqueline Pearce), and secrets that are revealed at a tortuously languid pace. But Hammer films are about atmosphere and this one's got oodles. It also features perhaps the first use of a sitar in the score of an English film. The underlying message—the inability of rational white males to understand the larger world, much less to control it—is widely accepted as gospel now. The weakest part of the film is the faintly ridiculous monster makeup.

1966 90m/C *GB* Jacqueline Pearce, Ray Barrett, Noel Willman, Jennifer Daniel, Michael Ripper, John Laurie, Marne Maitland, Charles Lloyd Pack, George Woodbridge, David Baron; ***D:*** John Gilling; ***W:*** John Elder; ***C:*** Arthur Grant; ***M:*** Don Banks. **VHS** *VTR*

Repulsion

Carol (Catherine Deneuve) is a young beautician who descends into madness when her sister (Yvonne Furneaux) leaves her in their London apartment. "She's a bit strung up, isn't she?" sis' beau (Ian Hendry) observes. Deneuve's virtually mute and expressionless performance is somehow right for a character whose emotional collapse goes back to her childhood, though sexual explanations are strongly suggested, too. Younger viewers should understand the sexual relationship in the

film was fairly scandalous in its time. Roman Polanski finds horror in the most mundane details of everyday life—a wall, a crack in the sidewalk, and of course that famous rabbit. The apartment itself becomes a reflection of deliberately paced and deeply personal terrors. On the Criterion Collection laserdisc, Polanski explains the purely commercial roots of the film's production. For whatever reason it was made, this remains one of the most excruciating films of the 1960s. 🦴🦴🦴🦴

1965 105m/B *GB* Catherine Deneuve, Yvonne Furneaux, Ian Hendry, John Fraser, Patrick Wymark, James Villiers, Renee Houston, Helen Fraser, Mike Pratt, Valerie Taylor; ***D:*** Roman Polanski; ***W:*** Roman Polanski, Gerard Brach, David Stone; ***C:*** Gilbert Taylor. **VHS, LV** *COL, CRC*

The Resurrected

A good eerie plot—slightly similar to director Dan O'Bannon's script for *Dead and Buried* and based on an H. P. Lovecraft story—loses focus through some little mistakes. Clair Ward (Jane Sibbett) hires detective John March (John Terry) to discover the reason behind her husband Charles Dexter's (Chris Sarandon) obsession. He claims to be involved in "the interrogation of matter," but why have the cops found body parts in his riverfront Rhode Island lab? Like a supernatural *Double Indemnity,* the film is built around March's tape-recorded narration. Small scenes—getting a phone number, changing a shirt—needlessly call attention to themselves, and the impressive ending isn't all it could be. On the other hand, a long subterranean finale is excellent and Todd Master's monster effects are unsettling. 🦴🦴🦴

1991 (R) 108m/C John Terry, Jane Sibbett, Chris Sarandon, Robert Romanus; ***D:*** Dan O'Bannon; ***M:*** Richard Band. **VHS** *LIV*

Vincent D'Agosta (Tom Sizemore) in *The Relic.*

The Return of Count Yorga

Uneven but more polished sequel begins with a spooky vampires-erupting-from-the-grave scene. It's followed by an attack on a house taken from *Night of the Living Dead.* The scene also recalls the Manson family's Tate-LaBianco murders that were still fresh in the public mind when the film was made. Robert Quarry is an imposing European vampire who seems totally out of place in the tackiness of early 1970s California. Mariette Hartley is an attractive, mostly passive heroine, but too much of the action is frantic, pointless running down dark hallways and stairs. Look for Craig T. Nelson is a small supporting role as a cop. 🦴🦴

1971 (R) 97m/C Robert Quarry, Mariette Hartley, Roger Perry, Yvonne Wilder, Rudy DeLuca, George Macready, Walter Brooke, Tom Toner, Karen Huston, Paul Hansen, Craig T. Nelson; ***D:*** Bob Kelljan; ***W:*** Bob Kelljan, Yvonne Wilder; ***C:*** Bill Butler. **VHS** *ORI*

The Return of Dr. X

Despite the title, this one has virtually nothing to do with Michael Curtiz's *Doctor X,* made seven years before. It's a campy B horror-comedy that gets off to a rocky start when wise-cracking reporter Walt Barnett (Wayne Morris) discovers a disappearing body. It doesn't really kick into gear until Humphrey Bogart (in his only horror role) shows up as Dr. Quesne, a twitchy, lispy, vampiric medico who's up to no good. Not one frame is meant to be taken seriously, and so it's a lot of fun. 🦴🦴½

1939 ?m/B Wayne Morris, Humphrey Bogart, Rosemary Lane, Dennis (Stanley Morner) Morgan, John Litel, Lya Lys, Huntz Hall; ***D:*** Vincent Sherman; ***W:*** Lee Katz; ***C:*** Sid Hickox. *NYR*

THE HOUND SALUTES

DAN O'BANNON

Dan O'Bannon's name has been synonymous with some of the most ambitious horror and science-fiction films ever made. He worked on screenplays for *Alien, Total Recall, Dark Star, Screamers,* and *Heavy Metal,* while directing credits include the screamingly funny *Return of the Living Dead* and *The Resurrected,* based on a story by H.P. Lovecraft.

A native of St. Louis, Missouri, O'Bannon has an interest in genre films that can be traced back to his childhood. "My old man took me to sci-fi and horror films at the local theatre," he recalls. "They just sunk in. If he would have taken me ice-skating I may have been an Olympic skater."

With high regard for *The Thing, Invasion of the Body Snatchers,* and *Forbidden Planet,* O'Bannon went to the prominent University of Southern California (USC) film school, where he befriended John Carpenter, another horror and sci-fi fan. At school, they worked on *Dark Star,* a space movie spoof, which drew the money and attention of Hollywood producers, who bankrolled the student project for a theatrical release.

The film became a cult favorite, inspiring Carpenter to go his own way, writing other projects and eventually directing *Halloween.* O'Bannon landed in Paris where he was set to oversee the special effects of an ill-fated version of *Dune,* to be directed by Alejandro Jodorowsky (*Santa Sangre*). While in France, O'Bannon met conceptual artists H.R. Giger and Mobius, whose otherworldly work inspired him to write the screenplay for *Alien.*

Sometimes in Hollywood—like space—no one can hear you scream.

But O'Bannon did do a lot of screaming—and battling—before, during, and after the making of *Alien.* While it became a big hit and spawned three sequels, disputes over script changes and writing credits with producers David Giler and Walter Hill have left O'Bannon philosophical about how the film business works.

"I would have been happy having my name on the film first, then have Giler and Hill's name [on the script], because I think they did some of the bad things in the script and it would be nice to share the blame," says O'Bannon. "Because they made me fight to the death [over screen credit], we had to go to the Writer's Guild and they were sympathetic to me as an underdog.

"It's nice to have sole credit on a big film like that and it helped my career, but it made me look like not such a hot writer. There's some bum writing in the film which I have to live with to this day and it still grinds at me."

Alien is not the only film that brings mixed emotions to the writer/director. He labored on and now detests *Lifeforce* and *Invaders from Mars,* two Cannon

Return of Dracula

Director Paul Landres blatantly steals the story and structure of Hitchcock's masterpiece *Shadow of a Doubt* for this tale of a European vampire in 1950s American suburbia. Impersonating an immigrant relative, Dracula (Francis Lederer) comes to stay with Cora Mayberry (Greta Granstedt) and her teenaged daughter Rachel (Norma Eberhardt) in Carleton, California. The acting is prissy, and the pace is slow. Interestingly, the film was produced the same year that Christopher Lee made his

Productions directed by Tobe Hooper. He helped retool *Dead and Buried* only to have his work abandoned, but sees the film advertised upon release as "from the creators of *Alien.*" Other projects have included *Blue Thunder,* the helicopter actioner he co-scripted, and adaptations of two Philip K. Dick stories which eventually became *Total Recall* and *Screamers.*

O'Bannon finally got an opportunity to take some control of his writing in 1985 when he directed *Return of the Living Dead,* a wild zombie satire based loosely on George A. Romero's classic *Night of the Living Dead.*

Rewriting a script by *Night* collaborator John A. Russo, O'Bannon fused grotesque imagery, pitch black humor, a pulsating punk-heavy metal soundtrack, and an unlikely cast of character actors like Clu Gulager and James Karen and "Scream Queens" Linnea Quigley and Jewel Shepard to tell the tale of ghouls rising from the dead when a poisonous gas from a military base is unleashed in the atmosphere.

O'Bannon is a big fan of *Night of the Living Dead.* "It scared me," he says. "It has a definite cumulative horror you could not escape. It was powerful."

Originally, Tobe Hooper was going to direct *Return* in 3-D, but shortly after O'Bannon took over the project, the 3-D was scrapped. "Luckily, we abandoned the idea," says O'Bannon. "That's all I needed after dealing with all of those rain machines."

Return of the Living Dead was shot for a paltry $3 million (with another $1.5 million used for legal fees involving Romero who, according to O'Bannon, tried unsuccessfully to block its production). It has returned a nice profit, inspired two sequels and led to another directorial assignment for O'Bannon: 1991's *The Resurrected,* an atmospheric adaptation of H.P. Lovecraft's "The Case of Charles Dexter Ward," which has gained an enthusiastic following among video fright aficionados. Also in the works is *Hemoglobin,* a horror tale with Rutger Hauer, directed by Canadian Peter Svatek.

—*Irv Slifkin*

SIGNIFICANT CONTRIBUTIONS TO HORROR

(as screenwriter)

Alien **(1979)**

Dead and Buried **(1989)**

(as director)

Return of the Living Dead **(1985)**

The Resurrected **(1991)**

debut as the character in *Horror of Dracula.* In this interpretation, the sexual charge of Lee's portrayal is conspicuously absent. For the most serious fans, this one has some curiosity value—note the way Landres uses one spot of color in the black and white—but little more. ***AKA:*** The Curse of Dracula; The Fantastic Disappearing Man. 🦴🦴

1958 77m/C Francis Lederer, Norma Eberhardt, Ray Stricklyn, Jimmie Baird, John Wengraf, Virginia Vincent, Greta Granstedt; ***D:*** Paul Landres; ***W:*** Pat Fielder; ***C:*** Jack MacKenzie. **VHS** *MGM, FCT*

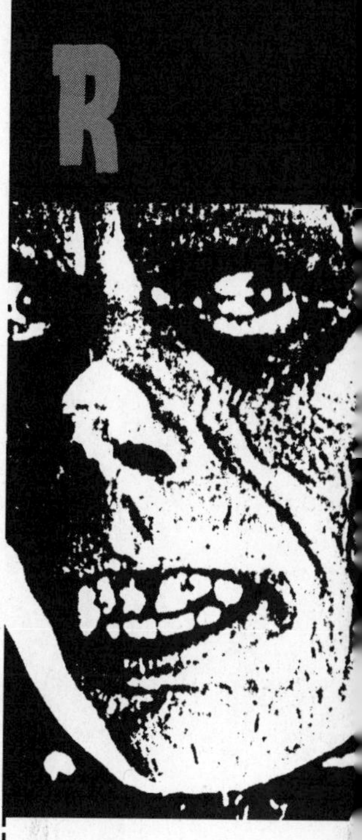

Return of the Evil Dead

Armando de Ossorio's second *Blind Dead* effort is a strong sequel, much more tightly plotted than the original. Resurrected cannibalistic Medieval knights have become something of a cottage industry in European horror. These Templars pop back up for the 500th anniversary of their execution, and, in *Night of the Living Dead* fashion, trap a diverse group of squabbling people in a building. The Knights themselves look like Klansmen in dirty sheets. But when they're riding their hooded horses in slow motion, they make a memorable impression. The Anchor Bay edition of the tape has been restored to a degree of clarity that's really astonishing. ***AKA:*** Return of the Blind Dead; El Ataque de los Muertos Sin Ojos.

1975 85m/C *SP PT* Tony Kendall, Esther Roy, Frank Blake, Fernando Sancho, Lone Fleming, Loreta Tovar, Jose Canalejas; ***D:*** Armando de Ossorio; ***W:*** Armando de Ossorio; ***C:*** Miguel Mila. **VHS** *VTR*

Return of the Fly

Black-and-white sequel begins with the funeral of the original Fly's widow, attended by her brother-in-law Delambre (Vincent Price) and son Philippe (Brett Halsey), who has yet to learn the truth about dear old dad's experiments. Once he does, you know what's going to happen. The film isn't as expensively produced as the original. The cheesy pulp plot and makeup effects really owe more to the lower-budget Universal productions of the 1940s and the American International horrors of the '50s. Price is at his most theatrical. This one's followed by a third, *Curse of the Fly,* as yet unavailable on video.

1959 80m/B Vincent Price, Brett Halsey, John Sutton, Dan Seymour, David Frankham, Danielle De Metz, Ed Wolff; ***D:*** Edward L. Bernds; ***W:*** Edward L. Bernds, Brydon Baker. **VHS, LV** *FOX, FCT*

Return of the Living Dead

Comic sequel, of sorts, begins with the idea that George Romero's cult hit is based on a real incident, but the truth behind it is that a combination of hazardous-waste spill and military cover-up created the carnivorous corpses. A series of Three-Stoogian blunders reignites the plague, setting a graveyard full of fresh bodies loose on a bunch of teens. Director Dan O'Bannon keeps things popping right along, and the yuck-factor goes right off the scale with some impressively staged bloody effects. It's all so far-fetched and outrageous that this one's recommended to gore fans only.

1985 (R) 90m/C Clu Gulager, James Karen, Linnea Quigley, Don Calfa, Jewel Shepard, Beverly Randolph, Miguel Nunez, Brian Peck; ***D:*** Dan O'Bannon; ***W:*** Dan O'Bannon; ***C:*** Jules Brenner. **VHS, LV** *NO*

Return of the Living Dead 2

As sequels to horror-comedies go, this one's O.K., but it's no *Evil Dead 2.* It simply takes the premise of the first *Return* —that George Romero's *NotLD* was based on a real incident—and treats it even more frivolously. The Army spills a can of gas that recharges corpses who then set upon teenagers. Heads are lopped off; limbs are hacked; blood cascades. Ho-humm. Seen it a hundred times.

1988 (R) 89m/C Dana Ashbrook, Marsha Dietlein, Philip Bruns, James Karen, Thom Mathews, Suzanne Snyder, Michael Kenworthy, Thor Van Lingen; ***D:*** Ken Wiederhorn; ***W:*** Ken Wiederhorn; ***C:*** Robert Elswit. **VHS, LV, Closed Caption** *ORI, WAR*

Dan O'Bannon's *Return of the Living Dead.*

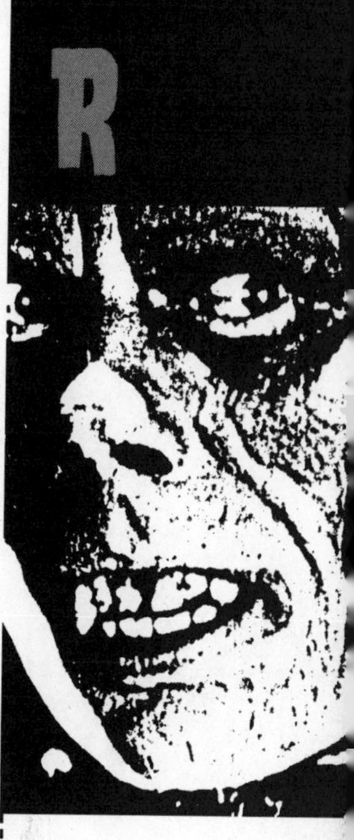

Return of the Living Dead 3

Love-smitten teen Curt (J. Trevor Edmond) uses the government's secret Trioxin gas to reanimate his girlfriend Julie (Mindy Clarke) after she's a little bit killed in a motorcycle accident. The result is another gore comedy with gross effects and a predilection for self-mutilation. The third time around, this one-joke wonder is wearing paper thin. As the Colonel in charge, Kent McCord ("One Adam-12, see the zombie") is his usual ramrod stolid self. The imaginative corpse effects are the point. 🦴½

1993 (R) 97m/C Mindy Clarke, J. Trevor Edmond, Kent McCord, Basil Wallace, Fabio Urena; ***D:*** Brian Yuzna; ***W:*** John Penney; ***M:*** Barry Goldberg. **VHS, LV, Closed Caption** *THV*

Return of the Vampire

The Columbia studio attempts to recreate the successful Universal formula, whipping together several elements in a lumpy half-baked loaf. The story begins in 1918 with the vampire Armand Tesla (Bela Lugosi) being guarded by a werewolf (Matt Willis). Flash forward to the London Blitz of World War II, where Tesla is resurrected and goes after the family who staked him years before. The wolf transformation effects aren't much, and Lugosi's first return to the role of a vampire after *Dracula* is a bit of a letdown, too. He has some very smooth scenes and energetic flashes, but the wartime setting is a distraction. So is the werewolf angle, and why is the hairy-faced fellow always wandering around with brown paper packages? The basic problem is a silly script. Sample dialogue: "Poor Andreas...what a tragedy to lose his soul again." 🦴🦴

1944 69m/B Bela Lugosi, Nina Foch, Miles Mander, Matt Willis, Frieda Inescort, Roland Varno, Gilbert Emery, Ottola Nesmith; ***D:*** Lew (Louis Friedlander) Landers; ***W:*** Griffin Jay; ***C:*** L.W. O'Connell, John Stumar. **VHS, LV** *NO*

Return to Salem's Lot

Larry Cohen's semi-comic vampire tale is not really a sequel to Tobe Hooper's miniseries. Instead, he uses Stephen King's premise of a small town overrun by bloodsuckers as a platform from which he can satirize conservative American smugness. Under the leadership of Judge Axel (Andrew Duggan), the undead inhabitants of 'Salem's Lot are afraid of change, drugs, and AIDS. They have their own version of history that casts them as outsiders who came to this country seeking freedom from unjust persecution. It wouldn't be fair to reveal what they want of anthropologist Joe Weber (Michael Moriarty) and the cigar-chomping Van Meer (actor/director Sam Fuller). At best, Cohen is half successful; the snappy, sexy moments aren't consistent. The whole film has an unfinished, hurried feeling and not very impressive effects. Recommended more to Cohen's fans than to King's. 🦴🦴½

1987 (R) 101m/C Michael Moriarty, Ricky Addison Reed, Samuel Fuller, Andrew Duggan, Evelyn Keyes, Jill Gatsby, June Havoc, Ronee Blakley, James Dixon, David Holbrook; ***D:*** Larry Cohen; ***W:*** Larry Cohen, James Dixon; ***C:*** Daniel Pearl. **VHS, Closed Caption** *WAR*

Revenge of the Creature

Insipid sequel largely ignores the elements that made the original so good. The Gill Man spends most of the running time chained to the bottom of a tank at Marineland pining away for flashy ichthyology grad student Lori Nelson. (Yes, Mr. G still has a thing for bleached blondes.) As

Revenge of the Creature.

an example of '50s kitsch nostalgia, it earns full marks; as a horror film, it's a joke. Yes, that's a young Clint Eastwood as the comic lab assistant.

1955 82m/B John Agar, Lori Nelson, John Bromfield, John Wood, Nestor Paiva, Clint Eastwood, Robert B. Williams, Grandon Rhodes; ***D:*** Jack Arnold; ***W:*** Martin Berkeley; ***C:*** Charles S. Welbourne. **VHS, LV, Closed Caption** *USH, FCT*

Reversal of Fortune

This is a cold, analytical examination of unlikable characters caught in an intriguing situation. By now, the story of Claus von Bulow and his wife Sunny is fairly familiar, but director Barbet Schroeder tells this true-crime tale with some of the techniques of horror. His sense of place, for example, is really strong, and part of the film is narrated by a comatose Sunny (Glenn Close). Jeremy Irons' mordant, haughty portrayal of Claus won an unexpected Oscar.

1990 (R) 112m/C Jeremy Irons, Glenn Close, Ron Silver, Annabella Sciorra, Uta Hagen, Fisher Stevens, Julie Hagerty, Jack Gilpin, Christine Baranski; ***D:*** Barbet Schroeder; ***W:*** Nicholas Kazan. Academy Awards '90: Best Actor (Irons); Golden Globe Awards '91: Best Actor—Drama (Irons); Los Angeles Film Critics Association Awards '90: Best Actor (Irons), Best Screenplay; National Society of Film Critics Awards '90: Best Actor (Irons); Nominations: Academy Awards '90: Best Adapted Screenplay, Best Director (Schroeder). **VHS, LV, 8mm, Closed Caption** *WAR, FCT, BTV*

The Rocky Horror Picture Show

On video, the audience-participation element of the Mother of All Midnight Screenings is lost, though what you and your friends want to do and wear in the privacy of your own place is none of the Hound's business. So, what about the movie itself? As a kinky musical send-up of old horror movies, it's campy, vampy, and not bad at all. The rock score is loud and energetic; the lyrics surprisingly witty. Susan Sarandon and Barry Bostwick are fine as the innocent heroine and hero, but the film belongs to Tim Curry's Dr. Frank-N-Furter. He redefines outrageous excess as the mad scientist who favors mascara, high heels, and fishnet hose. Curry wrings every drop of humor from the role—and there's a lot to wring. In the process, he shows how a talented stage actor can overpower a screen production, either on film or video.

1975 (R) 105m/C Tim Curry, Susan Sarandon, Barry Bostwick, Little Nell, Richard O'Brien, Patricia Quinn, Jonathan Adams, Peter Hinwood, Meat Loaf; ***D:*** Jim Sharman; ***W:*** Jim Sharman, Richard O'Brien; ***C:*** Peter Suschitzsky; ***M:*** Richard O'Brien. **VHS, LV, Closed Caption** *FOX, FCT, PMS*

Rosemary's Baby

Few works of fiction or film can succeed both as horror and as mainstream entertainment. This one does, and it's as suspenseful and enjoyable today as it was when it was made. The solidly plotted story revolves around an innocent midwestern girl (Mia Farrow) married to an ambitious young New York actor (John Cassavetes) who'll do almost anything to advance his career. Ruth Gordon won an Oscar for her scene-stealing performance as a nosy neighbor in a spooky apartment building. Not to take anything away from writer/director Roman Polanski—countless good novels have been screwed up on their way to the screen—but both the dramatic structure and the characters come straight from Ira Levin's novel. Polanski did bring a sexual frankness to the story that was unknown in popular film of the time.

1968 (R) 134m/C Mia Farrow, John Cassavetes, Ruth Gordon, Sidney Blackmer, Maurice Evans, Patsy Kelly, Elisha Cook Jr., Charles Grodin, William Castle, Ralph

Mia Farrow as Rosemary Woodhouse in Roman Polanski's *Rosemary's Baby*.

"I'm not into politics. I'm into survival."

—Ben Richards (Arnold Schwarzenegger) in *The Running Man.*

Bellamy; ***D:*** Roman Polanski; ***W:*** Roman Polanski; ***C:*** William A. Fraker; ***M:*** Krzysztof Komeda. Academy Awards '68: Best Supporting Actress (Gordon); Golden Globe Awards '69: Best Supporting Actress (Gordon); Nominations: Academy Awards '68: Best Adapted Screenplay. **VHS, LV** *PAR, MLB, BTV*

Rumpelstiltskin

Really good horror movies set up certain rules—the monster can be killed by silver, is afraid of fire, cannot cross water, etc.—and use them to create suspense. This one doesn't, though the action scenes are all right, the characters are colorful, and the title character is properly grotesque. There's something inherently frightening about squat, quick critters, and as played by Max Grodenchik, this creepster bears a distinct resemblance to Ross Perot. The story has to do with a young widow (Kim Johnston-Ulrich) and her baby, but it really doesn't stick to the basic elements of the fairy tale—social advancement, greed, deal-making, fate. Instead, it's a relatively standard chase/horror movie that makes the most of a low budget. Comedian Tommy Blaze provides scene-stealing support. Director Mark Jones has also made the similar *Leprechaun* series. To date we've been spared a sequel to this one. 🦴🦴

1996 (R) 91m/C Kim Johnston-Ulrich, Tommy Blaze, Max Grodenchik, Allyce Beasley; ***D:*** Mark Jones; ***W:*** Mark Jones; ***C:*** Doug Milsome; ***M:*** Charles Bernstein. **VHS, Closed Caption** *REP*

The Running Man

A look at Arnold Schwarzenegger's resume reveals that this is the last film he made before he became a brand-name star. He's Ben Richards, a cop unjustly convicted of murder, who's forced to take part in a dangerous futuristic TV game show hosted by the nasty Killian (scene-stealing Richard Dawson). Richards battles colorful bad guys with names like Buzzsaw, Subzero, and Dynamo. Director Paul Michael Glaser keeps the action clipping right along. Arnold and Maria Conchita Alonso are fine as battling protagonists. It's based on a Stephen King novel, written as Richard Bachman. The result may be more easily categorized as action, compared to horror, but it's still fun for those who think light escapism suffers from overinflated budgets. 🦴🦴🦴

1987 (R) 101m/C Arnold Schwarzenegger, Richard Dawson, Maria Conchita Alonso, Yaphet Kotto, Mick Fleetwood, Dweezil Zappa, Jesse Ventura, Jim Brown; ***D:*** Paul Michael Glaser; ***W:*** Steven E. de Souza; ***C:*** Thomas Del Ruth; ***M:*** Harold Faltermeyer. **VHS, LV** *LIV*

Salem's Lot

This mini-series cut to feature length is rather abruptly edited at the beginning. Introductory material involving key characters was left on the cutting room floor, and the obvious commercial breaks are intrusive. The made-for-TV production values haven't improved with age, either, but James Mason's dapper, effortless performance as the villainous Straker is still superb. Nobody else in the cast comes close to him. The scares work fairly well, too, though the vampire effects have been eclipsed in several theatrical films that have been made since. The Barlow vampire makeup is based on the original *Nosferatu*. ***AKA:*** Blood Thirst. 🦴🦴½

1979 (PG) 112m/C David Soul, James Mason, Lance Kerwin, Bonnie Bedelia, Lew Ayres, Ed Flanders, Elisha Cook Jr., Reggie Nalder, Fred Willard, Kenneth McMillan, Marie Windsor; ***D:*** Tobe Hooper; ***W:*** Paul Monash; ***C:*** Jules Brenner. **VHS, LV** *WAR*

Santa Sangre

Felliniesque fantasy opens with a naked man (Axel Jodorowsky) on a perch in a cell, and immediately flashes back to a Mexico City circus filled with grotesques. Director Alejandro Jodorowsky (father of Axel) tackles organized religion, greed, castration, sex, and various Oedipal relationships with

bucketsful of symbolism. It's difficult to tell how much of this is meant to be taken seriously in any respect—very little, I suspect—because the violence and sex are cartoonishly broad, and chickens figure prominently. Some of the graveyard images, however, are hauntingly lovely and at the end, the story somehow becomes touching. Wonderful soundtrack.

1990 (R) 123m/C *IT MX* Axel Jodorowsky, Sabrina Dennison, Guy Stockwell, Blanca Guerra, Thelma Tixou, Adan Jodorowsky, Faviola Tapia, Jesus Juarez; ***D:*** Alejandro Jodorowsky; ***W:*** Robert Leoni, Claudio Argento, Alejandro Jodorowsky; ***C:*** Danielle Nannuzzi; ***M:*** Simon Boswell. **VHS, LV, Closed Caption** *REP, FCT*

The Satanic Rites of Dracula

Hammer films always fare better with a period setting. This ludicrously plotted, disjointed effort concerns a coven of witches, vampirism, espionage, Nobel Prize winners and finally, Armageddon. Christopher Lee and Peter Cushing manage to bring their usual strength to the familiar roles of the Count and Van Helsing, but the rest is so much claptrap, overdirected with too many extreme camera angles, and poorly written. Still, it's all marginally better than the previous entry in the series, the dreadful *Dracula, A.D. 1972.* ***AKA:*** Count Dracula and His Vampire Bride; Dracula Is Dead and Well and Living in London.

1973 88m/C *GB* Christopher Lee, Peter Cushing, Michael Coles, William Franklyn, Freddie Jones, Joanna Lumley, Richard Vernon, Patrick Barr, Barbara Yo Ling; ***D:*** Alan Gibson; ***W:*** Don Houghton; ***C:*** Brian Probyn. **VHS** *MLB*

Satan's Princess

After an introduction in 17th century Barcelona (where comedian Jack Carter plays a monk), the scene shifts to the present where Cherney (Robert Forster), a burnt-out ex-cop, agrees to find a runaway daughter. The girl has fallen under the spell of Nicole St. James (Lydie Denier), an immortal sorceress or something. Stephen Katz's plot mixes action scenes and the supernatural with partial success, at best. The sexual side of the story reaches its strangest point when a sizzling love scene is intercut with a family Christmas reunion that's so saccharine it would nauseate Martha Stewart. Luckily, the ending is the nuttiest part of a very nutty guilty pleasure.

1990 90m/C Robert Forster, Caren Kaye, Lydie Denier, Phillip Glasser, Michael Harris, Ellen Geer, Jack Carter; ***D:*** Bert I. Gordon; ***W:*** Stephen Katz. **VHS, Closed Caption** *PAR*

Savage Weekend

Top-drawer soft-core exploitation is only so-so horror. Stereotyped Manhattanites go upstate for a weekend on the farm. Their various fantasies get full play while the stereotyped locals lurk about threateningly. The highpoints are William Sanderson's nutty backwoods rube, a character he would perfect on TV's *Bob Newhart Show,* and the barn scene, a memorable moment of raw sleaze. Some sources claim the film was made in 1976 and released in 1980 at the height of the "dead-teenager" craze. It has become something of a cult hit on video. No director is listed on the tape; some sources credit David Paulsen, and some list John Mason Kirby. ***AKA:*** The Killer Behind the Mask; The Upstate Murders.

1980 (R) 88m/C Christopher Allport, James Doerr, Marilyn Hamlin, Caitlin (Kathleen Heaney) O'Heaney, David Gale, William Sanderson; ***D:*** David Paulsen, John Mason Kirby; ***W:*** David Paulsen. **VHS**

Scalpel

Often-surprising southern Gothic sleeper involves a plastic surgeon (Robert Lans-

THE HOUND SALUTES

WES CRAVEN

Unless he does something truly spectacular in the latter stages of his career, Wes Craven will go down in the annals of horror as the creator of Freddy Krueger. That's really a bum rap.

Craven is an academic who turned to horror in the early 1970s. He was born in 1939 in Cleveland, Ohio, and has degrees from Wheaton College and Johns Hopkins. He was a college professor before he went to work with Sean Cunningham (*Friday the 13th*) on the infamously violent *Last House on the Left.* (The film's proponents have given it a figleaf of respectability by claiming that it's loosely based on Bergman's *Virgin Spring.*)

Five years later, Craven topped *Last House* with *The Hills Have Eyes,* an even more violent tale of desert-dwelling cannibals that rivals *The Texas Chainsaw Massacre* in its overall atmosphere of inhumanity.

After that, Craven began to split his time between feature films and television. The TV work, *Summer of Fear* and *Invitation to Hell,* is featherweight fluff, but both comic book-inspired *Swamp Thing* and the more autobiographical *Deadly Blessing* are worth a look. They're well-crafted stories that are built on interesting settings.

Then in 1984, Craven came up with *A Nightmare on Elm Street.* The irony is that even though the series and the character of Freddy Krueger are now solidly identified with Craven, he sold his rights to the sequels so he could direct the first one. Actually, it's doubly ironic because now Craven can boast that he's been associated with only the best elements of *Elm Street*—the first film and the last, *Wes Craven's New Nightmare,* an intelligent meditation on the powers and responsibilities of storytelling.

After *Elm Street,* Craven's work has varied in quality from the disjointed *The Serpent and the Rainbow* to the underrated *The People under the Stairs* to the Eddie Murphy vehicle *Vampire in Brooklyn.*

ing) who's been cut out of his father-in-law's will because the granddaughter (the surgeon's daughter) has disappeared. Why? Because she saw her father drown her boyfriend. Soon after grandad's demise, the surgeon finds a girl (Judith Chapman) with a disfigured face which he can transform into the image of his missing daughter. Yes, it's contrived and convoluted, but writer/director John Grissmer twists his tale in unexpected directions. ***AKA:*** False Face.

1976 (R) 95m/C Robert Lansing, Judith Chapman, Arlen Dean Snyder, Sandy Martin, David Scarroll; ***D:*** John Grissmer; ***W:*** John Grissmer. **VHS** *NLC*

Scanners

Exploding head effects burst onto the screen with David Cronenberg's story of dueling telepaths and government agents. (Yes, it's a lot like *Firestarter* and *The Fury.*) At its best, the film makes the experience of telepathy seem real as an uncontrollable babble of interior voices, and, as Cronenberg carefully points out, isn't that what madness is? At its worst, the special effects take over, and they're still pretty good. Michael Ironsides' insane Revok steals the show. The wild plot is pretty tame compared to Cronenberg's more recent work.

When it appeared that Craven might have played out his hand in the field, he directed the surprise boxoffice smash, *Scream,* and once again he was acclaimed as a genius.

In the end, though, Craven's real place in horror will be more difficult to judge. He's certainly not a dazzling visual stylist, and sometimes he seems to let his material get away from him. (With the interference and intrusions that ignorant studio executives tend to make on horror films, it's hard to place all of the blame in that area on Craven's shoulders.) On the other hand, he has tried to test himself, to tell different kinds of stories. (We'll ignore the lamentable *The Hills Have Eyes, Part 2.*)

Who knows? Given the spectacular success of *Scream* and its sequel, Wes Craven might have some more aces that he hasn't played.

SIGNIFICANT CONTRIBUTIONS TO HORROR

Last House on the Left **(1972)**

The Hills Have Eyes **(1977)**

A Nightmare on Elm Street **(1984)**

Wes Craven's New Nightmare **(1994)**

Scream **(1996)**

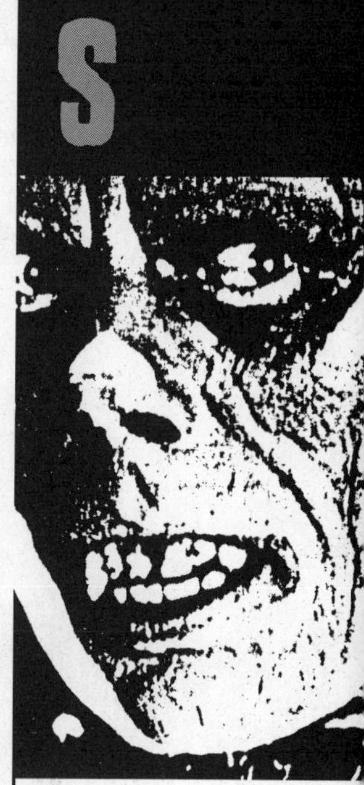

1981 (R) 102m/C *CA* Stephen Lack, Jennifer O'Neill, Patrick McGoohan, Lawrence Dane, Michael Ironside, Robert A. Silverman; ***D:*** David Cronenberg; ***W:*** David Cronenberg; ***C:*** Mark Irwin; ***M:*** Howard Shore. **VHS, LV** *COL*

The Scars of Dracula

By the fifth installment, Hammer's Dracula franchise is getting (ahem) long in the tooth. The compact simplicity and strong structure of the earlier films are missing. Instead, the weak script recycles the most popular elements without generating any energy of its own. Various folks find increasingly silly reasons to traipse up to Dracula's (Christopher Lee) castle. The comic opera touches are no help and the fake bat bobbing on a string is an insult to the studio's fans. As usual, the women are fetching, but on balance, the bad far outweighs the good. 

1970 (R) 96m/C *GB* Christopher Lee, Jenny Hanley, Dennis Waterman, Wendy Hamilton, Patrick Troughton, Michael Gwynn, Anouska Hempel, Michael Ripper, Christopher Matthews, Delta Lindsay; ***D:*** Roy Ward Baker; ***W:*** Anthony John Elder Hinds; ***M:*** James Bernard. **VHS, LV** *REP, MLB*

Schizo

A solid opening focused on a working-class British world of work and claustro-

"Schizophrenia... when the left hand doesn't know who the right hand is killing!!"

—Ad line from *Schizo.*

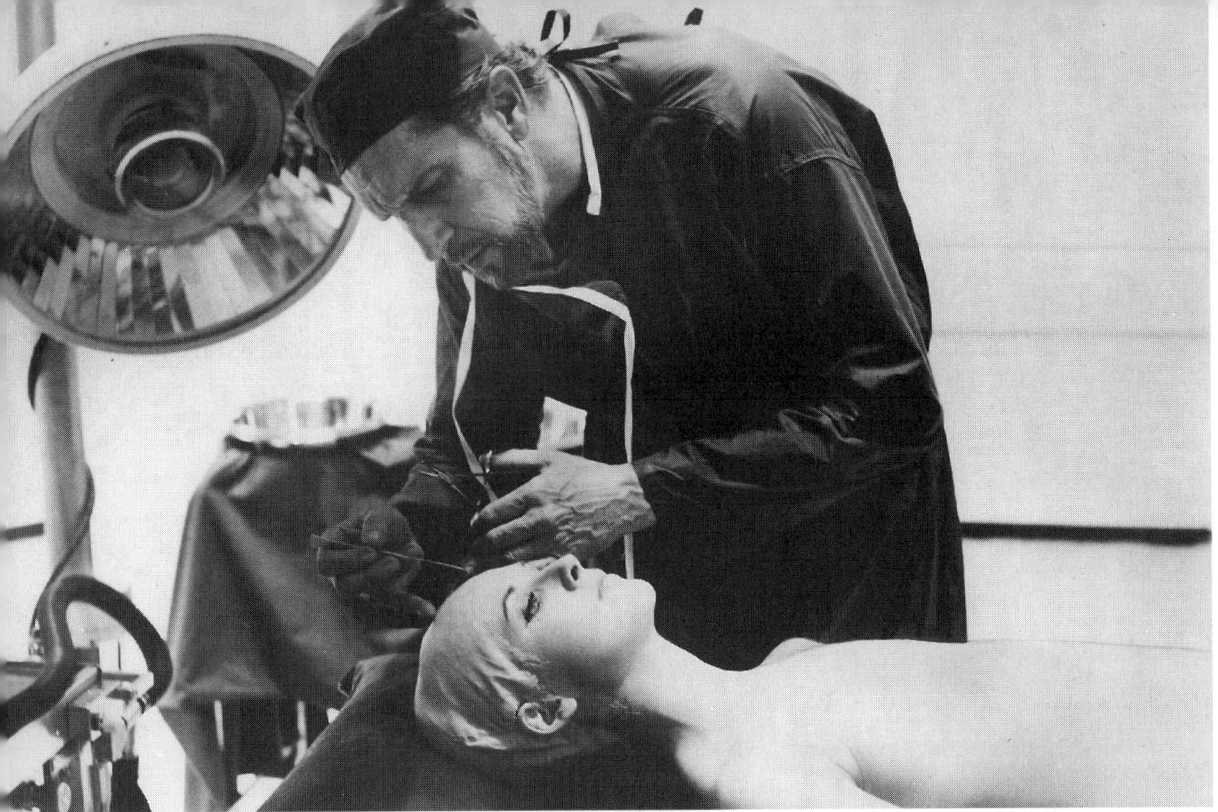

Dr. Browning (Vincent Price) in *Scream and Scream Again.*

phobic rooms eventually gives way to a so-so psycho killer story. Samantha (Lynne Frederick) is a newly married ice skater; William Haskin (John Leyton) is a troubled man with a machete who's stalking her. Some of the scares are trickily worked out and the location work is excellent throughout. On the other hand, killers hide in the back seats of small cars, shadows lurk on stairways, etc. The ending is right. ***AKA:*** Amok; Blood of the Undead. 🦴🦴½

1977 (R) 109m/C *GB* Lynne Frederick, John Leyton, Stephanie Beacham, John Fraser, Jack Watson, John McEnery; ***D:*** Pete Walker; ***W:*** John M. Watson Sr.; ***C:*** Peter Jessop. **VHS**

Scream

Wes Craven understands his audience as well as any filmmaker in the business. He aims this one at kids who have seen every movie in the horror section of their local video store, and assumes that they understand the rules and conventions of slasher flicks. Then he and writer Kevin Williamson base their scares and twists on those assumptions, making references to virtually every major American horror film from *Frankenstein* to *Elm Street*. At the end, after they've laughingly described and demonstrated all of the genre's cliches, they twist them around to a satisfying and unusual conclusion. Clearly, it's the kind of movie that could be too self-aware and self-referential for its own good, but it strikes the right note with young viewers who have made it a huge hit in theatrical release and on video. Followed by one sequel to date. ***AKA:*** Scary Movie. 🦴🦴🦴

1996 (R) 111m/C Drew Barrymore, Neve Campbell, Courteney Cox, David Arquette, Skeet Ulrich, Rose McGowan, Henry Winkler, Liev Schreiber, W. Earl Brown, Jamie Kennedy, Lawrence Hecht; ***Cameos:*** Wes Craven, Linda Blair; ***D:*** Wes Craven; ***W:*** Kevin Williamson; ***C:*** Mark Irwin; ***M:*** Marco Beltrami. MTV Movie Awards '97: Best Film; Nominations: MTV Movie Awards '97: Best Female Performance (Campbell). **VHS, LV, Closed Caption** *TOU*

Scream 2

Sidney (Neve Campbell) trades psychotherapy for college, only to be harassed by a lunatic willing to duplicate her nightmares from the original. All the cast that survived the first film are back: tabloid TV reporter Gale Weathers (Courtney Cox), who has turned a best-seller about the murders into a movie called *Stab*; lovable, huggable sheriff Dewey (David Arquette); and horror film fanatic Randy (Jamie Kennedy). Jerry O'Connell is Sidney's new beau. Director Wes Craven and writer Kevin Williamson add more of the satirical spark that propelled its predecessor into boxoffice success. By following the rules of sequels, they increase the suspense—everyone is a suspect—and gore, making this entry to the popular franchise a hard one to top. Those who prefer horror films that are not constantly examining themselves in their own mirrors will have trouble. *3* is on the way. ***AKA:*** Scream Again. 🦴🦴🦴

1997 (R) 120m/C Courteney Cox, Neve Campbell, Jerry O'Connell, David Arquette, Jada Pinkett, Jamie Kennedy, Liev Schreiber, Sarah Michelle Gellar, Laurie Metcalf, Elise Neal, Lewis Arquette, Duane Martin, Omar Epps, David Warner; ***Cameos:*** Tori Spelling; ***D:*** Wes Craven; ***W:*** Kevin Williamson; ***C:*** Peter Deming; ***M:*** Marco Beltrami. **VHS** *TOU*

Scream and Scream Again

Horror, s-f, spies, and archetypal '60s music are whipped into a semi-coherent froth. Dr. Browning's (Vincent Price) nurse is murdered in a vampire-like sexual attack, and a hardcase cop (Alfred Marks) investigates. At the same time, a totalitarian spy is up to something, and a guy in the hospital finds that he's missing a new extremity every time he wakes up. (His reaction is apparently the source of the title.) Peter Cushing's appearance is a cameo; Christopher Lee is an intelligence officer who's only tangentially involved. A long chase scene filled with surprising twists is the highpoint. ***AKA:*** Screamer. 🦴🦴🦴

1970 (PG) 95m/C *GB* Vincent Price, Christopher Lee, Peter Cushing, Judy Huxtable, Alfred Marks, Anthony Newlands, Uta Levka, Judi Bloom, Yutte Stensgaard; ***D:*** Gordon Hessler; ***W:*** Christopher Wicking; ***C:*** John Coquillon. **VHS** *LIV, ORI*

Scream Dream

The spirit of murdered satanic rocker Michelle Shock takes over the body of her replacement (Melissa Moore) and goes after everybody who did her dirt. If the film had two consecutive seconds of believability, it would be offensive and repulsive. But director Donald Farmer shows just how little can be done with meager money and talent. It's strictly amateur night in Cookeville, Tennessee, where this shot-on-video alternative epic was made. That's also why it's so much fun. The tone is established early when Michelle seduces a button-down-collar kid from the suburbs. His facial expression, meant to convey blissful heights of sexual ecstasy, is worth the price of a rental all by itself. Then there's the evil monster that's so obviously a hand puppet. 🦴🦴½

1989 (R) 80m/C Melissa Moore, Carole Carr, Nikki Riggins, Jesse Ray; ***D:*** Donald Farmer; ***W:*** Donald Farmer. **VHS** *NO*

Scream for Help

"My name is Christina Ruth Cromwell. I'm 17 and I live in New Rochelle. I think my stepfather is trying to murder my mother." That diary entry is the beginning of a variation on the *Scream* and *Heavenly Creatures* formula with a little *Wait until Dark* tossed in for the third act. Is young Christina (Rachael Kelly) right about her slimy stepdad (David Brooks) or are the raging hormones and insecurities of adolescence

> **"I tell you I saw blood on the bottom of her shoes; not exactly blood—it was gore, hanging there like a runny nose."**
>
> —Rosemary Ackerman (Mary Jo Catlett) accuses the *Serial Mom.*

having their way with her? Not enough is done with that angle and the story quickly settles into familiar patterns that aren't without humor. Another diary entry reads: "Not only is he an incompetent murderer, he's a total asshole." The suburban landscape is handled well. Both the acting and the music are substandard but the film certainly deserves some credit for the exploding bathroom and overall sleaziness.

1986 (R) 95m/C Rachael Kelly, David Brooks, Marie Masters; ***D:*** Michael Winner; ***W:*** Tom Holland. **VHS, LV** *ORI, WAR*

A Scream in the Streets/Axe

Ultra-crude drive-in double feature from the early '70s doesn't really get cranked up until the second half. The first is a cop story about a cross-dressing serial rapist. It's Ed-Woodsian stuff with one fairly explicit scene. The second, "Axe," about a trio of sadistic hitmen hiding out in a North Carolina farmhouse with a girl and her grandfather, is just as roughly made (one short step above home movies) but more effectively weird. It's a combination of Hemingway's *The Killers* and *Psycho,* with realistic, gritty locations.

197? (R) 137m/C Frank Bannon, Linda York, John Kirkpatrick, Con Covert, Brandy Lyman, Rosie Stone, Jack Canon, Frederick Friedel, Leslie Lee; ***D:*** Carl Monson, Frederick Friedel; ***W:*** Eric Norden, Frederick Friedel. **VHS** *BFV*

Screamers

In their first incarnation, Screamers are little mechanical buzzsaw beasties that rip through the sand the way Bugs Bunny burrows his way to the Carrot Festival at Pismo Beach. But these critters shred the human inhabitants of Sirius 6B in 2078. Why? It has to do with a war that has burned out Commander Joe Hendrikssen (Peter Weller). Director Christian Duguay draws out the plot at a methodical pace, the better to appreciate the frozen Canadian landscapes, grim industrial interiors, and the above-average effects. Jennifer Rubin is fine as the tough Hawksian heroine. She and Weller handle the naturalistic dialogue more comfortably than their co-stars. Horror fans will catch references to *Alien* and Cronenberg's *The Brood.*

1996 (R) 107m/C Peter Weller, Jennifer Rubin, Andrew Lauer, Charles Powell, Ron White, Michael Caloz; ***D:*** Christian Duguay; ***W:*** Dan O'Bannon, Miguel Tejada-Flores; ***C:*** Rodney Gibbons; ***M:*** Normand Corbeil. Nominations: Genie Awards '96: Best Art Direction/Set Decoration, Best Supporting Actor (White), Best Score. **VHS, LV, 8mm, Closed Caption** *COL*

Season of the Witch

When it was produced in 1973, George Romero's self-described "feminist film" may have had more social relevance than it does now. Today its sexual politics are obvious and off-putting. It's more successful as a portrait of a middle-aged woman's emotional disintegration. As Joan Mitchell (Jan White) approaches the big 4-0, she experiences dreams or hallucinations that portray her life as surreal fantasies. The "empty nest syndrome" is taken to new heights when Joan becomes interested in a neighborhood witch and her coven. Like most of Romero's work, it's made mostly on suburban locations and subtly acted by a de-glamorized unknown cast. The too-talky story can be seen as strict realism without any supernatural elements. In that respect, it's a companion piece to Romero's *Martin,* though not nearly as suspenseful or engrossing. ***AKA:*** Hungry Wives; Jack's Wife.

1973 (R) 89m/C Jan White, Ray Laine, Bill Thunhurst, Joedda McClain, Virginia Greenwald, Ann Muffly, Neil Fisher, Esther Lapidus, Dan Mallinger, Ken Peters; ***D:*** George A. Romero; ***W:*** George A. Romero; ***C:*** George A. Romero. **VHS** *VTR*

Seeding of a Ghost

This bizarre morality play moves so swiftly in so many unexpected directions that it's difficult to describe. It's been called THE Hong Kong gore flick and that's accurate as far as it goes. Elements of exploitation and crime drama are also important. A cabbie (Philip Ko) hits a grave-robbing warlock. Later, the cabbie returns to the warlock for help punishing men who have committed a terrible crime against him and his faithless wife (Chuan Chi Hui). He gets his revenge. Big time. In a few important moments, director Yang Chuan's wild Argento camera angles are inspired. Asian Grand Guignol at its grandest. ☠☠☠

1986 90m/C *HK* Philip Ko, Chuan Chi Hui; ***D:*** Yang Chuan. **VHS** *VSM*

Seizure

Oliver Stone's debut is a variation on *Dead of the Night.* Horror author Edmund (Jonathan Frid) invites a group of friends and associates to his country house for a weekend visit after recurring dreams of the horrors that will befall them. Cult favorites Mary Woronov, Martine Beswick, Troy Donahue, and Herve Villechaize are among them. Inexpertly made on a low budget—you can see shadows of cameras in some scenes—the film has aged poorly, but like so many of Stone's works, its excesses (like the three escaped lunatics, one a female Harvard professor!) are perversely enjoyable. The cast handles the bizarre material rather well, particularly Frid. ☠☠½

1974 (PG) 93m/C *CA* Jonathan Frid, Herve Villechaize, Christina Pickles, Martine Beswick, Joseph Sirola, Troy Donahue, Mary Woronov, Anne Meacham; ***D:*** Oliver Stone; ***W:*** Oliver Stone, Edward Andrew Mann; ***C:*** Roger Racine. **VHS** *NO*

The Sender

Is John Doe 83 (Zeljko Ivanek) insane, or can he project his dreams into everyday reality? That's what psychiatrist Dr. Gail Farmer (Kathryn Harrold) has to figure out about her patient. Some of the effects go too far, provoking unintentional laughter, but Thomas Baum's script makes the institutional setting real, and the characters are so well drawn that the weak spots are easy to overlook. Director Roger Christian handles action well and at the end, he borrows one of Hitchcock's favorite tricks to build suspense. Not bad. ☠☠½

1982 (R) 92m/C *GB* Kathryn Harrold, Zeljko Ivanek, Shirley Knight, Paul Freeman, Sean Hewitt, Harry Ditson, Marsha Hunt, Al Matthews, Angus MacInnes, Olivier Pierre; ***D:*** Roger Christian; ***W:*** Thomas Baum; ***M:*** Trevor Jones. **VHS, LV** *PAR*

The Sentinel

Big-budget horror borrows freely from *Rosemary's Baby* and *The Exorcist*—too freely, really—but it's still entertaining in a mainstream vein with a few solid scares. Supermodel Alison Parker (Christina Raines) is going through serious personal problems, which are revealed in hamfisted flashback when she moves into a new Brooklyn brownstone and meets her "very strange" neighbors. For openers, they may be ghosts, but cops Eli Wallach and Christopher Walken suspect that all may not be kosher with Alison and her fiance Michael (Chris Sarandon). The apartment building's sense of reality helps considerably. The big spooky finish directly quotes Tod Browning's *Freaks.* ☠☠☠

1976 (R) 92m/C Chris Sarandon, Christina Raines, Ava Gardner, Jose Ferrer, Sylvia Miles, John Carradine, Burgess Meredith, Tom Berenger, Beverly D'Angelo, Jeff Goldblum, Arthur Kennedy, Deborah Raffin, Eli Wallach, Christopher Walken; ***D:*** Michael Winner; ***W:*** Michael Winner, Jeffrey Konvitz; ***C:*** Richard Kratina. **VHS** *USH*

Serial Mom

Beneath the June Cleaver facade of Beverly Sutphin's (Kathleen Turner) life, a Charles Manson is ready to leap into action at the

Christina Raines and Ava Gardner in ***The Sentinel.***

slightest provocation. She keeps a lovely home for her dentist husband Eugene (Sam Waterston), and teenaged children Misty (Ricki Lake) and Chip (Matthew Lillard), but when anything disrupts her perfect world, she flies into a murderous rage. This sort of satiric comedy calls for a light touch and John Waters is near perfect. His script balances humor and horror without going too far in either direction. Given this material, many directors might have turned the film into a real stomach-turning wallow in graphic effects. Waters does indulge his taste for the unsettling in some scenes, but he wants viewers to see what motivates Beverly, even if they don't sympathize with her, and, to understand their own fascination with this raw subject matter. That's the point in the last third, where the popularity of the criminal as media star is given the Waters treatment. 🦴🦴🦴🦴

1994 (R) 93m/C Kathleen Turner, Sam Waterston, Ricki Lake, Matthew Lillard, Mink Stole, Traci Lords, Justin Whalin, Mary Jo Catlett, Susan Lowe, Mary Vivian Pearce; ***Cameos:*** Suzanne Somers, Joan Rivers, Patty Hearst; ***D:*** John Waters; ***W:*** John Waters; ***M:*** Basil Poledouris. **VHS, LV, Letterboxed, Closed Caption** *HBO*

The Serpent and the Rainbow

Ambitious Wes Craven effort is far from his best. It's a handsome production—too handsome in ways. Out in the Amazon jungle, a shaman gives credulous Harvard don Dennis Allan (Bill Pullman) some magic mushroom juice. He has visions and seven years later pops down to Haiti to investigate "zombification" drugs. The rest wanders through grotesque horror, gauzy romanticism, political terror, and hallucinations. The acting is mannered, and though some of the shocks are really jolting, the whole unfocused thing takes itself far too seriously. Zakes Mokae steals the film as the Ton Ton Macute villain. The credits claim "based on a true story." That's no excuse. 🦴

1987 (R) 98m/C Bill Pullman, Cathy Tyson, Zakes Mokae, Paul Winfield, Conrad Roberts, Badja Djola, Theresa Merritt, Brent Jennings, Michael Gough; ***D:*** Wes Craven; ***W:*** Richard Maxwell, A.R. Simoun; ***C:*** John Lindley; ***M:*** Brad Fiedel. **VHS, LV** *USH*

Serpent's Lair

Young marrieds Tom and Alex (Jeff Fahey and Heather Medway) move into a new apartment with an unsavory past and a recently deceased tenant. The neighbor (Patrick Bauchau) is a strange, friendly old coot, but soon, upsetting sexual dreams intrude. Can you say *Rosemary*? Don't bother. This is a male version, with Lilith (Lisa B) slinking straight out of a Victoria's Secret catalog to seduce Tom. But her vamping is a caricature. Director Jeff Reiner doesn't seem to understand that with this particular kind of sexual material, a little goes a long way. The scares are sparse, and since Lilith is so closely identified with felines, a better title might have been *Cat Box*. Filmed in Romania. 🦴½

1995 (R) 90m/C Jeff Fahey, Heather Medway, Lisa B, Anthony Palermo, Kathleen Noone, Taylor Nichols, Patrick Bauchau; ***D:*** Jeff Reiner; ***W:*** Marc Rosenberg; ***C:*** Feliks Parnell; ***M:*** Vinnie Golia. **VHS** *REP*

Seven

Stuck with a collection of cliched characters and a story that makes absolutely no sense (just try to figure out how the concluding actions are planned and executed), director David Fincher and production designer Arthur Max wrestle the film into submission with sheer style. The plot involving a serial killer working his way through the seven deadly sins means nothing compared to the overall texture of depravity and palpable horror. The story is carefully removed from any hint of reality. It takes place in a rainy city without name or location. The keys to the film's popularity are a terrifically understated performance by Morgan Freeman as Somerset, the cop a week from retirement, and very good work from Brad Pitt whose star was on the rise. Though the ending makes no rational sense, it is undeniably suspenseful. ***AKA:*** Se7en. 🦴🦴🦴

1995 (R) 127m/C Brad Pitt, Morgan Freeman, Gwyneth Paltrow, Kevin Spacey, R. Lee Ermey, Richard Roundtree, John C. McGinley, Julie Araskog, Reg E. Cathey, Peter Crombie; ***D:*** David Fincher; ***W:*** Andrew Kevin Walker; ***C:*** Darius Khondji; ***M:*** Howard Shore. MTV Movie Awards '96: Best Film, Most Desirable Male (Pitt), Best Villain (Spacey); National Board of Review Awards '95: Best Supporting Actor (Spacey); New York Film Critics Awards '95: Best Supporting Actor (Spacey); Broadcast Film Critics Association Awards '95: Best Supporting Actor (Spacey); Nominations: Academy Awards '95: Best Film Editing; British Academy Awards '95: Best Original Screenplay; MTV Movie Awards '96: Best On-Screen Duo (Brad Pitt/Morgan Freeman). **VHS, LV, Closed Caption, DVD** *NLC*

The Seventh Sign

Relatively effective apocalyptic thriller based on the Book of Revelation shares the basic credibility problem that plagues any work of the genre. To some viewers, it's dealing with the literal word of God; to others it's the pure baloney of tabloid headlines. Though the VideoHound tends toward the luncheon meat school of criticism, he's willing to give these movies a look. This one revolves around a troubled pregnant woman (Demi Moore) and a taciturn stranger (Juergen Prochnow). She gives a good, convincing performance reminiscent of Mia Farrow in *Rosemary's Baby*, and Australian director Carl Schultz keeps the special effects to a minimum. 🦴🦴

1988 (R) 105m/C Demi Moore, Juergen Prochnow, Michael Biehn, John Heard, Peter Friedman, Manny Jacobs, John Taylor, Lee Garlington, Akosua Busia; ***D:*** Carl Schultz; ***W:*** W.W. Wicket; ***C:*** Juan Ruiz-Anchia; ***M:*** Jack Nitzsche. **VHS, LV, Closed Caption** *COL*

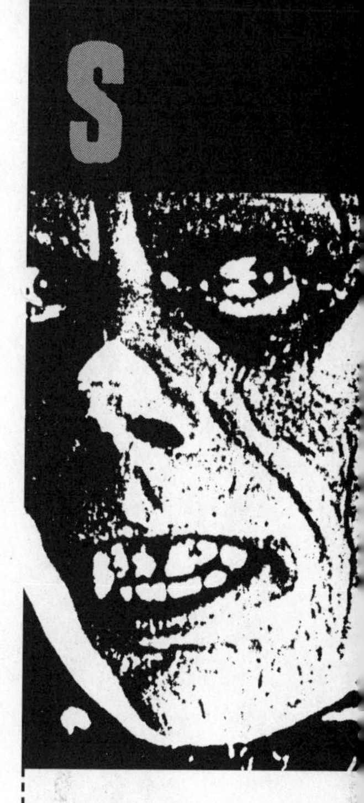

"This isn't going to have a happy ending."

—Det. William Somerset (Morgan Freeman) in *Seven*.

Jack Torrance (Jack Nicholson) in *The Shining* (1980).

Shallow Grave

Fiercely original exercise in suspense/comedy/horror is so consistently surprising that potential viewers should know as little as possible about the plot. In Glasgow, Scotland, narrator David (Christopher Eccleston) shares a large apartment with Alex (Ewan McGregor), a smart-alecky reporter, and Juliet (Kerry Fox), a doctor. The search for a fourth roommate leads them into uncharted psychological territory. Writer John Hodge (a doctor by profession) and director Danny Boyle take Hitchcockian delight in setting up audience expectations, then twisting them a few unsettling degrees and adding a strong dash of black humor. Judged by the standards of most American films, the depiction of violence is so restrained as to be almost polite. But in a couple of significant moments, Boyle's approach is nauseatingly effective. Almost all of the action takes place within the apartment but the pace moves so quickly—the film is never dull—that it doesn't feel constrained. Though Boyle isn't above showing off with his camera, the tricks are always in service of the story and are usually employed to avoid slow spots.

1994 (R) 91m/C *GB* Kerry Fox, Christopher Eccleston, Ewan McGregor, Keith Allen, Ken Stott, Colin McCredie, John Hodge; ***D:*** Danny Boyle; ***W:*** John Hodge; ***C:*** Brian Tufano; ***M:*** Simon Boswell. **VHS** *PGV*

The Shining

Director Stanley Kubrick boasted during production that his adaptation of Stephen King's novel of a haunted hotel would be the most terrifying film ever made. It's not. It is handsome and well acted, but it's almost more a suspense film in the traditional sense than a horror film. Kubrick makes full use of his intricate, grandiose sets and caresses them with his constantly

moving camera. In the big finish, when Jack Nicholson is chasing his son through snow-covered topiary, the sheer beauty of the scene is more impressive than its menace. And the famous moment with the spectral bartender, where Nicholson is having his first drink in five months, is so evocatively lit and carefully crafted that you can almost taste the bourbon. In 1997, the film was remade as a television miniseries.

1980 (R) 143m/C Jack Nicholson, Shelley Duvall, Danny Lloyd, Scatman Crothers, Joe Turkel, Barry Nelson, Philip Stone, Lia Beldam, Billie Gibson, Barry Dennan, David Baxt, Lisa Burns, Alison Coleridge, Kate Phelps, Anne Jackson, Tony Burton; ***D:*** Stanley Kubrick; ***W:*** Stanley Kubrick, Diane Johnson; ***C:*** John Alcott. **VHS, LV, Closed Caption** *WAR*

Shock Chamber

As the subtitle admits, this Canadian anthology is an impoverished imitation of Dan Curtis' *Trilogy of Terror* with less than satisfactory results. The connecting gimmick is the three surviving brothers (Doug Stone) of identical quadruplets who are all involved with criminal activities. Their stories have to do with love potions, ghoulish rubes, and grave robbing. The weak plots are brightened by grim humor and a realistic sense of place, notably in the second installment, but they're not enough to recommend this disappointment to fans of the short form. ***AKA:*** Shock Chamber: A Trilogy of Terror.

1996 96m/C *CA* Doug Stone, Karen Cannata, Jackie Samuda, Russell Ferrier; ***D:*** Steve DiMarco; ***W:*** Steve DiMarco. *NYR*

Shock 'Em Dead

Rock 'n' roll horror collects an impressive lack of talent for a terrific unintentional comedy. When a wannabe musician (Stephen Quadros) sells his soul to the devil, he is immediately transformed into a rock star, complete with long black wig, leather britches, excessive jewelry, mascara, mansion, and groupies (including the lovely Karen Russell). The downside is that he's a vampire. Then he falls for a band manager (Traci Lords). Admittedly, some of the jokes are intentional and many of them are funny, but it's still very silly stuff.

1990 (R) 94m/C Traci Lords, Aldo Ray, Troy Donahue, Stephen Quadros, Tim Moffett, Karen Russell, Gina Parks, Laurel Wiley, Tyger Sodipe; ***D:*** Mark Freed; ***W:*** Andrew Cross, Mark Freed, Dave Tedder; ***C:*** Ron Chapman. **VHS, LV** *NO*

Shock Waves

This is arguably the best example of a curious subgenre of horror—the underwater Nazi zombie movie. Rose (Brooke Adams) tells the flashback story of a Caribbean excursion boat, captained by John Carradine, that lands on an island inhabited by a mad German doctor (Peter Cushing). You do not need three guesses to figure out what he's up to. Some of the locations, notably an old hotel, are spooky, and director Ken Wiederhorn is able to give the fascist creatures their moments, too. ***AKA:*** Death Corps; Almost Human.

1977 (PG) 90m/C Peter Cushing, Brooke Adams, John Carradine, Luke Halpin, Jack Davidson, Fred Buch; ***D:*** Ken Wiederhorn; ***W:*** Ken Wiederhorn, John Kent Harrison; ***C:*** Reuben Trane; ***M:*** Richard Einhorn. **VHS**

Shocker

On one hand, Wes Craven creates a fierce satire on television and the way the medium distorts our view of reality. On the other, he panders to his young male target audience by presenting the horror—yet another psychotic mass murderer, Horace Pinker (Mitch Pileggi)—as a heroic villain, and violence becomes a thoughtless end in itself. Most of the time, though, the film is just another derivative exercise in obvious special effects, borrowing liberally from Craven's own work, as well as *The Hidden* and *Horror Show*. After he's elec-

THE HOUND SALUTES

HANNIBAL LECTER

and Other Serial Killers

The random or "serial" killer has become one of the most popular stereotypes in horror and crime stories. His numbers have increased exponentially in books and films over the past decade or so, due in large part to novelist Thomas Harris' brilliant creation, Dr. Hannibal Lecter.

(The various slashers and stalkers of countless dead-teenager flicks are not included in this consideration of serial killers for two reasons. 1) They're a representation of adolescent sexual anxiety and 2) producers' infinite capacity to exploit that anxiety with bad movies.)

In most of the important ways, the first appearance of the serial killer in Fritz Lang's *M* is still the most complex and believable. The script by Lang's wife, Thea von Harbou, was based on a real series of child murders that had occurred in Germany. Peter Lorre plays the nameless killer with understated but wholly believable menace. One look at him and you believe that he's the kind of predatory monster who could commit unspeakable acts. Then, by the end of the story, the filmmakers force you to look at him again and to understand how little control he has over his actions. They do not ask for forgiveness, but, unlike most of today's filmmakers, they refuse to allow the audience a comfortably superior reaction to their story.

Hannibal Lecter first appeared on screen in Michael Mann's stylish-to-a-fault *Manhunter,* an adaptation of Harris' *Red Dragon*. Several factors can be cited to explain *Manhunter*'s lack of box-office success compared to *The Silence of the Lambs*. They're noted in the reviews, but the real reason (or at least an important one) is that Michael Mann told an essentially conventional serial killer story with one man slaughtering innocents and another man bringing him to justice.

In *Silence,* both Harris and director Jonathan Demme bring the conflict into much sharper focus by casting a believably strong and competent young woman (Jodie Foster) as the protagonist. If the serial killer as a character represents the threatening power of white male authority figures—and it clearly does—then you don't solve the dramatic problem by defeating him with another white male authority figure.

trocuted, Pinker, who has literally worshipped at the feet of the god of TV, becomes a channel-surfing Freddy Krueger who returns to attack his enemies. 🦴🦴

1989 (R) 111m/C Michael Murphy, Peter Berg, Cami Cooper, Mitch Pileggi, Richard Price, Timothy Leary, Heather Langenkamp, Theodore (Ted) Raimi, Richard Brooks, Sam Scarber; ***D:*** Wes Craven; ***W:*** Wes Craven; ***C:*** Jacques Haitkin; ***M:*** William Goldstein. **VHS, LV, Closed Caption** *USH*

The Silence of the Lambs

Three filmmakers—director Jonathan Demme and stars Jodie Foster and Anthony Hopkins—at the top of their form have created a rare hit that's both a mainstream Oscar-winning success and a first-rate horror film. Foster is Clarice Starling, ambitious

Those three films are all superbly constructed melodramas. Though they're serious to different degrees, their primary purpose is to entertain. The modern serial killer film that tries hardest to examine the phenomenon accurately is John McNaughton's *Henry: Portrait of a Serial Killer.*

It's loosely based on the confessions of convicted murderer and habitual liar Henry Lee Lucas. Accurate or not, it's the most harrowing glimpse inside the world of a psychopath ever put on film. As Henry, Michael Rooker is as frightening as Lorre in *M,* but McNaughton's film intentionally lacks the dramatic revelations and changes of Lang's. Henry kills people at the beginning; Henry's going to kill more people as he drives off at the end. He's the same implacable, inexplicable figure let loose on the world.

To my mind, he's the most frightening and disturbing example of his type. The film was originally given an "X" rating by the MPAA, not for the graphic nature of the violence but for the suffocating atmosphere of dread that McNaughton creates. Henry is simply so believable and realistic that he repels more viewers than he attracts.

Too much reality carries horror into territory where only a few of the heartiest hard-core fans will follow.

Hannibal Lecter, on the other hand, is seductive, attractive, urbane, and perceptive to such an absurd degree that he's a psychopathic Sherlock Holmes. Both Brian Cox and Anthony Hopkins have a wonderful time with him, and, like Henry, at the end of his most recent screen appearance, Lecter, in full command of his considerable resources, is let loose on the world. As Harris sets the scene at the end of *Silence,* Lecter is being served his room service dinner in a posh hotel: "He did not want the waiter handing him wine to taste—he found the smell of the man's watchband objectionable."

That kind of humor puts the murderous doctor in another realm entirely.

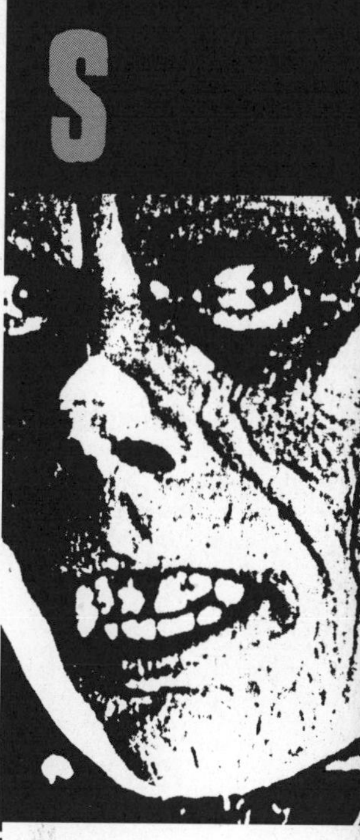

young FBI trainee who's sent to interview imprisoned serial killer Hannibal Lecter (Hopkins) to catch another murderer (Ted Levine, whose carefully shaded performance is easy to overlook). Writer Ted Tally deftly compresses Thomas Harris' fiction, and Demme handles the action with a sure touch, mixing character, complex plotting, and locations that have a feeling of absolute authenticity. Repeated viewings reveal what a careful craftsman Demme is, and even the most superficial glance reveals how much TV's *The X-Files* has lifted from the film. The conclusion cries out for a sequel which has been rumored for years but, to date, has not been announced. Yes, that is producer Roger Corman, who gave Demme his start, as the FBI director. The Criterion Collection laserdisc contains commentary by Demme,

"I do wish we could chat longer, but I'm having an old friend for dinner."

—Dr. Hannibal "the Cannibal" Lecter (Anthony Hopkins) means exactly what he says in *The Silence of the Lambs.*

Foster, Hopkins, Tally, and FBI agent John Douglas. It's also letterboxed to present the full widescreen image. 🦴🦴🦴🦴

1991 (R) 118m/C Jodie Foster, Anthony Hopkins, Scott Glenn, Ted Levine, Brooke Smith, Charles Napier, Roger Corman, Anthony Heald, Diane Baker, Chris Isaak; ***D:*** Jonathan Demme; ***W:*** Ted Tally; ***C:*** Tak Fujimoto; ***M:*** Howard Shore. Academy Awards '91: Best Actor (Hopkins), Best Actress (Foster), Best Adapted Screenplay, Best Director (Demme), Best Picture; British Academy Awards '91: Best Actor (Hopkins), Best Actress (Foster); Directors Guild of America Awards '91: Best Director (Demme); Golden Globe Awards '92: Best Actress—Drama (Foster); National Board of Review Awards '91: Best Director (Demme), Best Film, Best Supporting Actor (Hopkins); New York Film Critics Awards '91: Best Actor (Hopkins), Best Actress (Foster), Best Director (Demme), Best Film; Writers Guild of America '91: Best Adapted Screenplay; Nominations: Academy Awards '91: Best Film Editing, Best Sound. **VHS, LV, Letterboxed, Closed Caption** *ORI, FCT, IME, CRC*

Silent Scream

Scotty Parker (Rebecca Balding) arrives late at a southern California college and has to scrounge up off-campus living arrangements. The clifftop place she finds bears a certain resemblance to the Bates residence, but she's desperate. Though at first the film appears to be just another stalker tale, it's carefully constructed with believable, sympathetic characters who avoid cliches. The younger cast members are fine and their elders—particularly Yvonne DeCarlo, Barbara Steele, Cameron Mitchell, and comedian Avery Schreiber in a serious role—are even better. Director Denny Harris makes inventive use of the house's interior spaces to create suspense. For horror fans, the levels of graphic violence and titillation may be too low, but the Hitchcockian story is tightly written with a strong ending. 🦴🦴🦴½

1980 (R) 87m/C Rebecca Balding, Cameron Mitchell, Avery Schreiber, Barbara Steele, Steve Doubet, Brad Reardon, Yvonne De Carlo; ***D:*** Denny Harris; ***W:*** Wallace C. Bennett, Jim Wheat, Ken Wheat; ***C:*** Michael D. Murphy, David Shore. **VHS** *NO*

Silver Bullet

The first half of Stephen King's no-frills werewolf story focuses on the daylight side of the creature and its nighttime activities. Then in the second, the action focuses on Marty (Corey Haim), a wheelchair-bound boy who has discovered that identity. He persuades his sister (Megan Follows) and uncle (Gary Busey) to believe him, and they have to face the beast. King's script doesn't fool around much and novice director Daniel Attias handles his job the same way. The only real flaw is a lack of sense of place. ***AKA:*** Stephen King's Silver Bullet. 🦴🦴½

1985 (R) 95m/C Corey Haim, Gary Busey, Megan Follows, Everett McGill, Robin Groves, Leon Russom, Terry O'Quinn, Bill Smitrovich, Kent Broadhurst, Lawrence Tierney; ***D:*** Daniel Attias; ***W:*** Stephen King; ***C:*** Armando Nannuzzi. **VHS, LV, Closed Caption** *PAR*

Simon, King of the Witches

"My name is Simon and I live in the storm drain," our hero (Andrew Prine) states, leading even the slowest viewer to wonder just how powerful this would-be regent really is. Actually, Prine isn't bad at all and the late-'60s hippy-dippy milieu is a trip. Both the humor and the loose plot involving Simon's episodic encounters with corrupt officials, bogus witches, and drug dealers are reminiscent of Russ Meyers' *Beyond the Valley of the Dolls,* but without the crazier excesses. Magic itself is treated in a mostly matter-of-fact manner with low-tech effects. 🦴🦴🦴

1971 (R) 90m/C Andrew Prine, Brenda Scott, George Paulsin, Norman Burton, Ultra Violet; ***D:*** Bruce Kessler; ***W:*** Robert Phippeny; ***C:*** David L. Butler. **VHS** *UNI*

Single White Female

One of the best of the early '90s psycho-femme horrors casts Jennifer Jason Leigh

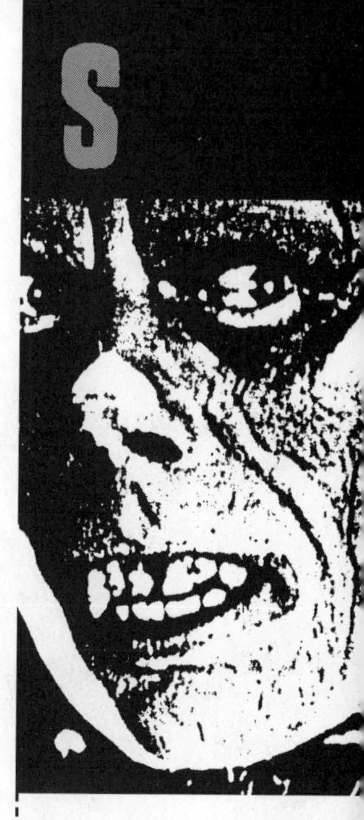

as Hedra, the roommate from hell who takes over Allie's (Bridget Fonda) life. The motivation is a rent-controlled apartment and director Barbet Schroeder gives even the weirdest plot turn a sense of grim New York reality. The gradual revelation of Hedra's personality makes the story, based on John Lutz's novel, fascinating and frightening. Comparisons to Polanski's *Repulsion* and the cult hit *Apartment Zero* are in order. Fonda and Leigh turn in remarkable performances. Their strong, unbalanced relationship rings consistently true. Leigh has made her career on chancy roles, but this is as close to the edge as she has ever worked.

1992 (R) 107m/C Bridget Fonda, Jennifer Jason Leigh, Steven Weber, Peter Friedman, Stephen Tobolowsky, Frances Bay, Renee Estevez, Kenneth Tobey; ***D:*** Barbet Schroeder; ***W:*** Don Roos; ***M:*** Howard Shore. MTV Movie Awards '93: Best Villain (Leigh). **VHS, LV, 8mm, Closed Caption** *COL, BTV*

Sister My Sister

Despite a story that sounds like exploitation, this is a serious psychological horror along the lines of Polanski's *Repulsion*. It's based on the same true story that inspired Jean Genet's play, *The Maids*. In France, 1932, the impoverished Christine (Joely Richardson) and her younger sister Lea (Jodhi May) work for Madame Danzard (Julie Walters) and her daughter Isabelle (Sophie Thursfield). From the opening moments, the viewer knows that the story ends in violence. But how does it come to that? What drives two women to murder two other women? Director Nancy Meckler handles the action deftly, creating tension and suspense in small moments. An excellent cast handles the claustrophobic, emotionally wrenching material without a single misstep.

1994 (R) 89m/C *GB* Julie Walters, Joely Richardson, Jodhi May, Sophie Thursfield; ***D:*** Nancy Meckler; ***W:*** Wendy Kellelman; ***C:*** Ashley Ropwe; ***M:*** Stephen Warbeck. **VHS** *APX*

Sisters

Brian DePalma's first mainstream film is arguably his best. In fact, some might say it's his only really good, original work. From the opening notes of Bernard Herrmann's vertiginous score (one of his finest), DePalma's debt/homage to Hitchcock is obvious. It's about a crazy woman (Margot Kidder with an incredibly irritating accent) whose separated Siamese twin maniacally murders her lovers (maybe). The story contains all the elements that recur in DePalma's later, more derivative work—voyeurism, obsession, the equation of sex and violence. The use of split screen to show simultaneous action from two points of view is excellent. The stratospheric weirdness of the third act is wonderful, and the ending is unlike anything you're likely to see. ***AKA:*** Blood Sisters.

1973 (R) 93m/C Margot Kidder, Charles Durning, Barnard Hughes, Jennifer Salt, William Finley, Lisle Wilson, Mary Davenport, Dolph Sweet; ***D:*** Brian DePalma; ***W:*** Brian DePalma, Louisa Rose; ***C:*** Gregory Sandor; ***M:*** Bernard Herrmann. **VHS** *WAR, OM*

Skeeter

Updated version of a '50s atomic horror isn't quite as enjoyable as the similarly derivative *Mosquito*. Something strange is going on in the little mountain town of Clear Sky and horror fans know that the illegal toxic waste dump is responsible, even if the heroes don't. The presence of Charles Napier as the corrupt sheriff and Michael J. Pollard as the town's mad fool do a lot to perk things up. The effects are more silly than scary because it's almost impossible to make flying monsters believable. One interesting change has taken place over the last 40 years. In '50s big-bug flicks, the culprit almost always has something to do with nuclear power. The government, working with scientists and/or the military, is able to overcome it. Today, that same government is almost

"C'mon, you comin', or are you just gonna stand there and make lemonade in ya pants?"

—Eloquent werewolf chasers in *Silver Bullet*.

Danielle Breton (Margot Kidder) in *Sisters.*

always in cahoots with evil capitalists to cause the environmental damage that creates the monster. In pop culture shorthand, government has become the problem, not the solution. 🦴🦴

1993 (R) 95m/C Tracy Griffith, Jim Youngs, Charles Napier, Michael J. Pollard; ***D:*** Clark Brandon; ***W:*** Clark Brandon, Lanny Horn; ***M:*** David Lawrence. **VHS, LV** *COL*

Skinner

Flawed examination of a repellant subject—serial murder and torture—has moments that approach *Henry: Portrait of a Serial Killer,* though they're not nearly as powerful or frightening. The quirky casting—Ricki Lake as an unsuspecting landlady, Ted Raimi (brother of Sam) as the killer, and particularly Traci Lords as a woman with several secrets and a mission—helps to counter an ultra-low budget. Director Ivan Nagy (a key participant in the infamous *Heidi Fleiss, Hollywood Madame* business) creates a midwestern Gothic atmosphere of dread and horror, particularly at the beginning. When he gets more graphic, the story becomes bloody, sickening, and predictable. The really gory moments are so excessive they're almost comic. 🦴🦴

1993 (R) 89m/C Theodore (Ted) Raimi, Traci Lords, Ricki Lake; ***D:*** Ivan Nagy. **VHS, LV** *APX*

Sleepwalkers

Arguably King's worst film work is about shape-shifting monsters who feed on the life force of virgins and are vulnerable only to cat scratches. The incestuous mother Mary (Alice Krige) and son Charles (Brian Krause) set their sights on young Tanya (Madchen Amick). King's script meanders through pointless chitchat scenes. Unless something is blowing up or bleeding right in front of director Mick Garris' camera, he doesn't know how to photograph it. At one point, he tosses in close-ups of knees. The only cast member who doesn't shame him- or herself is Sparks, who plays Clovis, the brave cat. ***AKA:*** Stephen King's Sleepwalkers. **Woof!**

1992 (R) 91m/C Brian Krause, Madchen Amick, Alice Krige, Jim Haynie, Cindy Pickett, Lyman Ward, Ron Perlman; ***Cameos:*** Stephen King, Tobe Hooper, Mark Hamill, Glenn Shadix, Joe Dante, Clive Barker, John Landis, Dan Martin; ***D:*** Mick Garris; ***W:*** Stephen King; ***C:*** Rodney Charters. **VHS, LV, Closed Caption** *COL*

Slipping into Darkness

A young retarded man is killed, and his brother (John DiAquino) thinks that three rich girls (led by Michelle Johnson) were responsible. He enlists two biker pals to find the truth. The first half is by turns clumsy and sharp. Writer/director Eleanor Gaver mixes laughably bad dialogue with some interesting, original visuals. But then in the second half, when we begin to learn who these characters really are, and why they're doing what they're doing, the action becomes much weirder and is filled with warped surprises. Finally, the film lives up to its title and transforms itself into a spooky Nebraska Gothic.

1988 (R) 86m/C Belle Mitchell, Laslo Papas, Beverly Ross, T.J. McFadden, Michelle Johnson, John DiAquino; ***D:*** Eleanor Gaver; ***W:*** Eleanor Gaver. **VHS, LV** *HHE*

The Slumber Party Massacre

Noted feminist author Rita Mae Brown has said that she meant for this script to be a parody of dead-teen slasher flicks. That's easy to believe, but the movie sure didn't turn out that way, despite some intentional humor and an understanding of adolescent girls' behavior. A killer (Michael Villela) with an electric drill and a long bit is loose on the weekend that Trish's (Michele Michaels) parents leave her home alone and she invites some girlfriends over. A surfeit of T&A, including a Brinke Stevens cameo, is really all this pedestrian entry has going for it. And, at 78 minutes, it is short. Two sequels have followed.

1982 (R) 78m/C Michele Michaels, Robin Stille, Andre Honore, Michael Villela, Debra Deliso, Gina Mari, Brinke Stevens, Jean Vargas, Rigg Kennedy; ***D:*** Amy Holden Jones; ***W:*** Rita Mae Brown; ***C:*** Stephen Posey. **VHS**

Snow White: A Tale of Terror

Michael Cohn's made-for-cable interpretation of the Grimm fairy tale is more imaginative, thoughtful, and insightful than 99 per cent of the horror movies that go to theatres. The visual influences range from Vermeer to Cocteau's *Beauty and the Beast* to *Night of the Living Dead.* The changes in story and character are unsettlingly perceptive. In this version, the conflict between Snow White (played by Taryn Davis as a child and Monica Keena as a teen) and the Queen (Sigourney Weaver) is much more complicated and competitive. The girl isn't completely innocent and the older woman has reason to feel threatened. Sam Neill is the father and husband who's caught in the middle. A bleak, wintry-autumnal medieval atmosphere bolsters some excellent acting from all concerned. Give writers Thomas Szollosi and Deborah Serra considerable credit for going back to the Grimm Brothers' archetypal roots and weaving them into new patterns. Fans should make an extra effort to find this one. ***AKA:*** Snow White in the Black Forest; Grimm Brothers' Snow White.

1997 (R) 101m/C Sigourney Weaver, Sam Neill, Monica Keena, Gil Bellows, Taryn Davis; ***D:*** Michael Cohn; ***W:*** Thomas Szollosi, Deborah Serra; ***C:*** Mike Southon; ***M:*** John Ottman. **VHS, LV** *PGV*

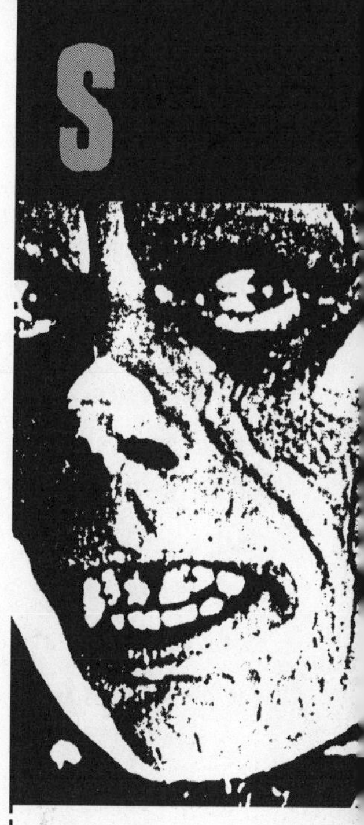

"The first Stephen King story written expressly for the scream."

—Ad line from *Sleepwalkers.*

"The Monster had escaped and was ravaging the countryside—maiming, killing, terrorizing. One night he burst into our house. My father took a gun and fired at him, but the savage brute sent him crashing to a corner. Then, he grabbed me by the arm.... One doesn't easily forget, Herr Baron, an arm torn out by the roots!"

—Krogh (Lionel Atwill) recounting to the Baron Frankenstein (Basil Rathbone) how he lost his arm in *Son of Frankenstein.*

Sole Survivor

At first the plot and the eerie alienated atmosphere are straight from *Carnival of Souls.* Denise Watson (Anita Skinner) is the sole survivor of an airplane crash that unstable psychic actress Karla Davis (Caren Larkey) somehow predicts. Strange visions plague Denise, or is she seeing real dead people? Some of the acting isn't all it could be, but Thom Eberhardt's dialogue is offhandedly realistic. Given the nature of the supernatural material, it's realistic, too, and the plot manages to maintain its trickiness all the way through. This is one of the best hidden treasures tucked away in the back of your favorite video store. Look for Brinke Stevens in a small role and Leon (credited as Leon Robinson) in a cameo.

1984 (R) 85m/C Anita Skinner, Kurt Johnson, Caren Larkey, Brinke Stevens, Leon Robinson; ***D:*** Thom Eberhardt; ***C:*** Russell Carpenter. **VHS** *LIV, VES*

Something Wicked This Way Comes

"First of all, it was October...." That's the way both Ray Bradbury's famous novel and his adaptation begin. It's a lyrical, unashamedly nostalgic horror film that remains strictly faithful to the magical tone of the fiction. Will Halloway (Vidal Peterson) and Jim Nightshade (Shawn Carson) are 12 years old and about to learn "the fearful needs of the human heart" when Dark's Pandemonium Carnival arrives in their small town. It's an evil, seductive entertainment where wishes are granted at a terrible price. Dark (Jonathan Pryce) and the mute Dust Witch (Pam Grier) know those wishes and are ready to accommodate them. Will's father (Jason Robards, Jr.), the town librarian, is the boys' guide. Director Jack Clayton creates some truly frightening moments—particularly for those bothered by spiders—but he's more successful in evoking Bradbury's unique vision of youth and magic and things that cannot be explained.

1983 (PG) 94m/C Jason Robards Jr., Jonathan Pryce, Diane Ladd, Pam Grier, Richard Davalos, James Stacy, Royal Dano, Vidal Peterson, Shawn Carson; ***D:*** Jack Clayton; ***W:*** Ray Bradbury; ***C:*** Stephen Burum; ***M:*** James Horner. **VHS, LV** *DIS*

Sometimes They Come Back

Jim Norman (Tim Matheson) and his wife Sally (Brooke Adams) move back to the small town his parents left 27 years before. Jim finds that the horrors of his past haven't diminished and the ghosts are still there. Writers Lawrence Konner and Mark Rosenthal and director Tom McLoughlin effectively flesh out King's short story while retaining his weathered small-town atmosphere and his understanding of the enduring power of childhood bullies. Matheson's very good in a straight dramatic role. On video, the made-for-TV feature contains extra footage of violence and grotesque special effects.

1991 (R) 97m/C Tim Matheson, Brooke Adams, Robert Rusler, William Sanderson; ***D:*** Tom McLoughlin; ***W:*** Lawrence Konner, Mark Rosenthal. **VHS, LV, Closed Caption** *THV*

Sometimes They Come Back ... Again

The plot to this sequel-remake is nothing special. It cannibalizes several other Stephen King works and tosses in a ton of witchcraft hokum. That said, the story of resurrected satanic teen bullies who terrorize John Porter (Michael Gross) and his daughter Michelle (Hilary Swank) is not without style and polish. A few of the effects are really striking. Alexis Arquette is very good as the lead bad guy, and so are Gross and Swank.

1996 (R) 98m/C Michael Gross, Hilary Swank, Alexis Arquette, Jennifer Elise Cox; ***D:*** Adam Grossman; ***W:*** Adam Grossman; ***C:*** Christopher Baffa; ***M:*** Peter Manning Robinson. **VHS** *THV*

Son of Dracula

The first use of "Alucard" for "Dracula" is underlined for slow learners as the Count (Lon Chaney, Jr.) makes a less-than-spectacular debut in America. He arrives by train at Dark Oaks plantation at the invitation of Kay (Louise Albritton), a credulous Southern belle who believes in the occult. Chaney isn't completely comfortable with the role. Perhaps that's why he's largely absent in the opening reels. The film really owes more to the carefully crafted mid-budget horrors that Universal was cranking out at a steady pace during those years than it does to the original *Dracula* or to the sequel *Dracula's Daughter.* It does contain some neat scenes, like the coffin rising up out of the swamp, and the second half is stronger with inventive plot twists and a spookier atmosphere. ***AKA:*** Young Dracula.

1943 80m/B Lon Chaney Jr., Evelyn Ankers, Frank Craven, Robert Paige, Louise Allbritton, J. Edward Bromberg, Samuel S. Hinds; ***D:*** Robert Siodmak; ***W:*** Eric Taylor; ***C:*** George Robinson. **VHS, LV** *USH*

Son of Frankenstein

Though it's generally considered to be the weakest of the three films in which Boris Karloff played the Creature, in many ways, this one is more enjoyable today. Under the direction of veteran Rowland V. Lee, it's certainly less fantastic and overwrought than James Whale's work. Wolf Frankenstein (Basil Rathbone) returns to the ancestral castle, only to find that the villagers still haven't forgiven him for what his daddy did. He's trying to make amends when old Ygor (Bela Lugosi) tells him that the monster still lives. But it seems that he left his headlights on and needs a little recharge. The sets and the sharp black-and-white cinematography are first rate, but the acting carries the film. Lugosi was never more restrained and seldom better than he is here. Karloff, as always, is excellent. (This was the last time he played the role.) Even facing that kind of competition, Rathbone and Lionel Atwill (as Krogh, the sympathetic local cop) are never upstaged.

1939 99m/C Basil Rathbone, Bela Lugosi, Boris Karloff, Lionel Atwill, Josephine Hutchinson, Donnie Dunagan, Emma Dunn, Edgar Norton, Lawrence Grant, Lionel Belmore; ***D:*** Rowland V. Lee; ***W:*** Willis Cooper; ***C:*** George Robinson. **VHS, LV** *USH*

Sorceress

Wildly complicated, fast-paced and cheesy horror is notable for a veteran cast and some not-so-special effects. It's about a couple of witches (Julie Strain and Linda Blair) competing over the career of a young executive. One wants to advance it; the other wants to hurt him. The filmmakers are professionals in the field. Director Jim Wynorski knows how to do a lot on a limited budget and doesn't try to do things he shouldn't. He doesn't exactly stretch the limits of the genre, either.

1994 (R) 93m/C Julie Strain, Larry Poindexter, Linda Blair, Edward Albert; ***D:*** Jim Wynorski. **VHS** *TRI*

Soultaker

This over-achieving little B-movie has become a solid cult hit. Made in Alabama and written by star Vivian Schilling, it's the story of four young people who are killed in a car wreck. Their spirits are thrown clear and the title character (Joe Estevez), a spooky guy in a long black raincoat, is dispatched to take them to the other side, or wherever. Details and tricky special effects aren't too important here. The film charges along with the senseless energy of a live-action cartoon.

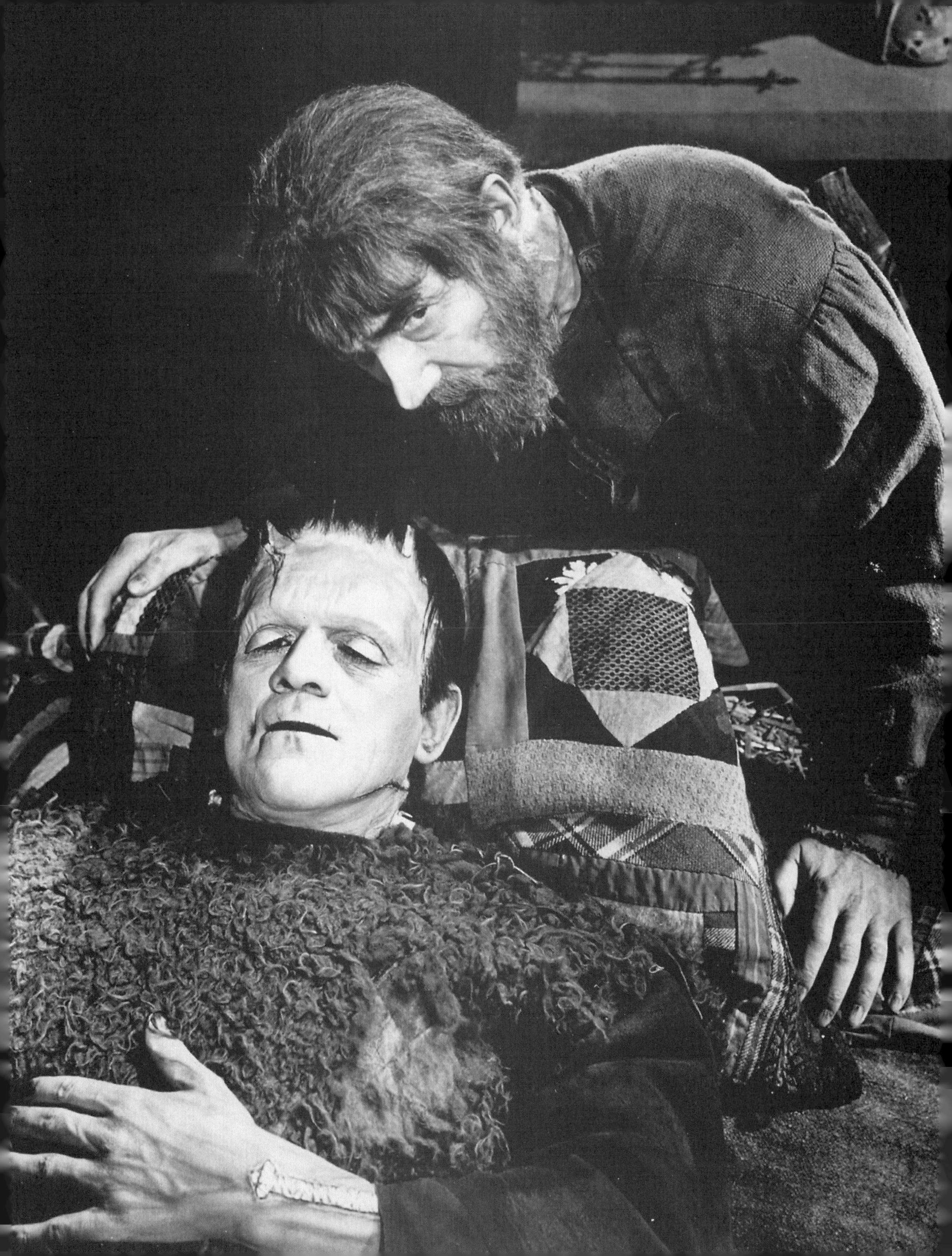

1990 (R) 94m/C Joe Estevez, Vivian Schilling, Gregg Thomsen, David Shark, Jean Reiner, Chuck Williams, Robert Z'Dar; ***D:*** Michael Rissi; ***W:*** Vivian Schilling; ***C:*** James Rosenthal. **VHS, LV** *NO*

Spasms

Canadian production is actually one of the better giant snake movies, though, admittedly, that is a small subgenre. This one's at least as enjoyable as the tongue-in-cheek excesses of *Anaconda.* The serpent in question once bit wealthy hunter Jason Kincaid (Oliver Reed), so now he and it are psychically linked through "viral telepathy," or so claims Dr. Brazilian (Peter Fonda). Then a snake cult (don't ask) lets the beastie loose in San Diego. Many of the effects have been eclipsed in recent years, and the snake p.o.v. shots are cliches, and, with the exception of Reed, the cast is only O.K. But the snake, created by Raymond A. Mendez, is not bad. ***AKA:*** Death Bite.

1982 (R) 92m/C *CA* Peter Fonda, Oliver Reed, Kerrie Keane, Al Waxman, Miguel Fernandez, Marilyn Lightstone, Laurie Brown, Gerard Parkes; ***D:*** William Fruet; ***W:*** Don Enright. **VHS** *NO*

Spawn

Todd McFarlane's popular comic book makes a semi-successful live-action feature. Long stretches of complicated overplotting are balanced unsteadily against long effects-intensive fight and chase scenes with little overlap or interaction. Special agent Ed Simmons (Michael Jai White) becomes Spawn, a hellish superhero who battles the Clown (John Leguizamo, looking and sounding like *The Simpsons'* Krusty on bad acid). Calisotro (Nicol Williamson) tries to guide our hero to the paths of righteousness. The hardware, pyrotechnics, and monsters are all fine. Director Mark A.Z. Dippe also sustains a pulp Gothic sensibility not unlike *The Crow* and *Darkman*. What's lacking is a clear human element. The children are handled with particular clumsiness. Released theatrically in a PG-13 rating; also available R-rated on video.

1997 (PG-13) 97m/C Michael Jai White, John Leguizamo, Martin Sheen, Theresa Randle, D.B. Sweeney, Nicol Williamson, Melinda Clarke; ***D:*** Mark Dippe; ***W:*** Alan B. McElroy; ***C:*** Guillermo Navarro; ***M:*** Graeme Revell. **VHS, LV, Closed Caption** *WAR*

Species

At heart, this is an *X-Files* -inspired B-horror that's been pumped up with a classy cast and expensive effects, and is trying to pass itself off as serious escapism. Sil (Natasha Henstridge), created from outer-space DNA, can be an icy blonde babe one moment and a disgusting alien creature (created by H.R. Giger) the next. She's loose in L.A. and her biological clock is ticking. A government team (Marg Helgenberger, Alfred Molina, Forest Whitaker, Michael Madsen) is on her trail. The plot tends to ramble pointlessly for long stretches of time, and in key scenes, the dialogue states the obvious with unintentionally hilarious results. Some of the bits of business there are funny and surprising. Others—including a weak conclusion—are strictly formula. Throughout, the thrills are slick and cheap.

1995 (R) 108m/C Ben Kingsley, Michael Madsen, Alfred Molina, Forest Whitaker, Marg Helgenberger, Natasha Henstridge; ***D:*** Roger Donaldson; ***W:*** Dennis Feldman; ***C:*** Andrzej Bartkowiak; ***M:*** Christopher Young. MTV Movie Awards '96: Best Kiss (Natasha Henstridge/Anthony Guidera); Nominations: MTV Movie Awards '96: Breakthrough Performance (Henstridge). **VHS, LV, Closed Caption, DVD** *MGM*

Specters

Subway work uncovers the entrance to Demetiano's Tomb off the Roman cata-

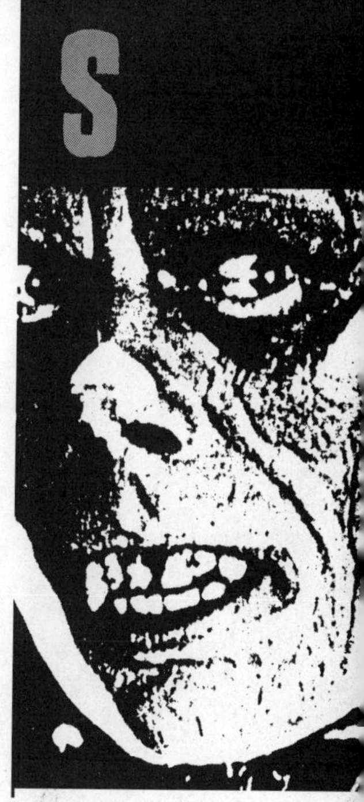

The Monster (Boris Karloff) and Ygor (Bela Lugosi) in *Son of Frankenstein.*

THE HOUND SALUTES

✓LON CHANEY, JR.

When Lon Chaney divorced his wife Cleva, he took their eight-year-old son Creighton to live with him and he told the boy that his mother had died. A few years later, Creighton learned the truth and was understandably upset. How much did that affect the young man who years later would change his name to Lon Chaney, Jr.? It's impossible to say. In interviews, he often spoke fondly of his father, but that's what most interviewers wanted to hear, and successful Hollywood careers are not built on uncomfortable truths. Also, everyone who knew the senior Chaney seems to have agreed that his career was much more important to him than his family.

Lon, Jr., must have understood that. After all, he literally grew up in the theatre, and by the time he was an adolescent, his dad was an established character actor and then a star at Universal. He strongly dissuaded his son from following his profession, but two years after he died in 1930, Lon, Jr., took the plunge.

Initially, he struggled through small roles the way any young actor—even one with a famous father—has to do. He had no association with horror, either. His first break was a moment of inspired casting. With his bulky body and broad face, Chaney was a near perfect Lenny in the 1939 *Of Mice and Men*. A year after that, though, he won the lead in *The Wolf Man*, Universal's last great horror film, and the path for the rest of his career was firmly set.

As Ed Naha writes in *Horrors: From Screen to Scream* (Flair/Avon, 1975), "Chaney delved into the realm of horror with a gusto usually greater than the films he appeared in war-

combs. Prof. Lasky (Donald Pleasence), an archeologist, thinks that an ancient evil lies beneath the Christian crypt. Yes, the influence of *Five Million Years to Earth* is obvious in plot details, but this one stands on its own. The subterranean atmosphere is well realized, and, despite contributions by four writers, the story is strong. So are the acting, dubbing, and pace. Though the film isn't as graphically violent as many recent Italian horrors, it compares favorably to the best of de Ossorio and Argento, making clearly defined parallels between supernatural evil and more recognizable human evil—greed, lust, covetousness. The ending's weak. ***AKA:*** Spettri. 🦴🦴🦴

1987 95m/C *IT* Donald Pleasence, John Pepper, Erna Schurer, Katrine Michelsen; ***D:*** Marcello Avallone; ***W:*** Marcello Avallone, Andrea Purgatori, Dardano Sacchetti, Maurizio Tedesco. **VHS** *IMP*

Spectre

Combine the first half of *Poltergeist* with the end of *The Shining* in an Irish setting and you've got this almost-good/almost-bad video premiere. Will (Greg Evigan), Maura (Alexandra Paul), and their young daughter Audrey (Briana Evigan) move to Maura's ancestral home in the Auld Sod and find that it's haunted. Some of the scenes work—the computer-generated

ranted." That's true. It's also true that the genre was in decline when Chaney was in his prime. Instead of trying to find new creations and situations, Universal was content to recycle its older ones in competently made but relatively uninspired sequels. Chaney shared top billing in a long series of them. At various times, he portrayed the Frankenstein monster, and even the *Son of Dracula*, but he was always at his best as the lupine Lawrence Talbot. He also delivered fine, polished performances in the studio's Inner Sanctum series, now available on tape as double features.

By the end of his career, plagued by health problems and heavy drinking, he was reduced to some truly inferior junk. Even then, however, he could create sympathetic characters from shopworn material.

SIGNIFICANT CONTRIBUTIONS TO HORROR

The Wolf Man **(1941)**

Frankenstein Meets the Wolfman **(1942)**

Son of Dracula **(1943)**

Weird Woman **(1944)**

Spider Baby **(1964)**

critter and the cleaver-wielding parent, for example. Others—the roast turkey that attacks the dinner guests—aren't so hot. Overall the film suffers from a lack of attention to detail. Midway through, a character is beheaded. After the initial reaction, he's forgotten. The setting isn't as evocative as it could be, either, and the exploitation angle is needlessly strong. ***AKA:*** House of the Damned; Roger Corman Presents: House of the Damned. 

1996 (R) 82m/C Greg Evigan, Alexandra Paul, Briana Evigan, Eamon Draper, Dick Donaghue; ***D:*** Scott Levy; ***W:*** Brendan Broderick; ***C:*** Christopher Baffa; ***M:*** Christopher Lennertz. **VHS** *NHO*

The Spellbinder

Rosemary's Baby meets *L.A. Law* as a slickly produced video premiere. In a slowly paced introduction, L.A. lawyer Jeff Mills (Timothy Daly) meets and rescues sexy young Miranda (Kelly Preston) from a spooky guy with a knife. At length, she tells him that she's trying to escape a coven of witches. He invites her to move in with him anyway. Things don't really get cranked up until the second half and even then, director Janet Greek paces the action fitfully. The special effects are inventive. The conclusion generates a fair amount of suspense too.

Terry O'Quinn is *The Stepfather.*

1988 (R) 96m/C Timothy Daly, Kelly Preston, Rick Rossovich, Audra Lindley; ***D:*** Janet Greek; ***W:*** Tracy Torme; ***M:*** Basil Poledouris. **VHS, Closed Caption** *FOX*

Spider Baby

The mad Merrye family lives in a remote decaying mansion somewhere between the *Little Shop of Horrors* and the Bates Motel. Chauffeur Lon Chaney, Jr., protects the kids—Virginia (Jill Banner), a Leatherface Lolita; Elizabeth (Beverly Washburn); and Ralph (Sid Haig), their doglike brother—from lawyers, greedy relatives, and other predators. Veteran exploitation director Jack Hill cranked this comic quickie out in record time. It's cut from the same cloth as *Little Shop* and *Bucket of Blood,* but it's more twisted than either of them. *Spider Baby* enjoyed a theatrical re-release 30 years after its 1964 run, and has earned an understandably strong cult following. ***AKA:*** The Liver Eaters; Spider Baby, or the Maddest Story Ever Told; Cannibal Orgy, or the Maddest Story Ever Told.

1964 86m/B Lon Chaney Jr., Mantan Moreland, Carol Ohmart, Sid Haig, Beverly Washburn, Jill Banner, Quinn Redeker, Mary Mitchell; ***D:*** Jack Hill. **VHS** *VTR, MLB, HEG*

Spontaneous Combustion

The title refers to spontaneous "human" combustion, an occurrence fairly widely reported by 19th century paranormal investigators, but somewhat declasse among today's believers. David (Brad Dourif) is the child of parents who took part in a strange 1955 nuclear experiment. The opening contrast of feel-good newsreel images of the '50s with the realities is handled nicely, if a little too slowly. Dourif does some of his best and most sympathetic work as the grown child who's become an anti-nuclear activist with a great vintage Studebaker. The rest is a companion piece to *Firestarter* and thoroughly enjoyable in its own crazed way. Dick Butkus and director John Landis have cameos.

1989 (R) 97m/C Brad Dourif, Jon Cypher, Melinda Dillon, Cynthia Bain, William Prince, Dey Young, Dick Butkus, John Landis; ***D:*** Tobe Hooper; ***W:*** Tobe Hooper, Howard Goldberg; ***C:*** Levie Isaacks; ***M:*** Graeme Revell. **VHS, LV** *VTR*

Star Time

Henry (Michael St. Gerard) is a disturbed young man who's ready to kill himself because his favorite TV show has been canceled. Sam Bones (John P. Ryan), a Mephistophelian creation of Henry's imagination, suggests that he kill people instead. Writer/director Alexander Cassini works with more intelligence and imagination than money in this exploration of the horror of loneliness. He also gets a terrific performance from John Ryan, a character actor whose face is more familiar than his name to most viewers. The dim, undernourished look of the film is a distraction. 🦴🦴🦴

1992 85m/C Michael St. Gerard, John P. Ryan, Maureen Teefy; ***D:*** Alexander Cassini; ***W:*** Alexander Cassini; ***C:*** Fernando Arguelles. **VHS** *MNC*

Starship Troopers

Robert Heinlein's novel is one of the great young adult s-f adventures. Paul Verhoeven's screen version is a virtual live-action cartoon with a sculpted young cast charging through a series of self-aware war movie cliches. The setting is a fascist future where bugs from another galaxy engage humans in interstellar war. Johnny Rico (Caspar Van Dien) and Dizzy Flores (Dina Meyer) are gung-ho Mobile Infantry soldiers who do battle against the critters on a desert world (Wyoming and South Dakota). The whole film is perversely entertaining as it savages its own politics while delivering a rip-roaring shoot-'em-up. It ventures into horror when the giant bugs start sucking brains. 🦴🦴🦴

1997 (R) 129m/C Caspar Van Dien, Michael Ironside, Neil Patrick Harris, Clancy Brown, Denise Richards, Dina Meyer, Jake Busey, Patrick Muldoon, Seth Gilliam, Rue McClanahan, Marshall Bell, Eric Bruskotter, Blake Lindsley, Anthony Michael Ruivivar, Dean Norris; ***D:*** Paul Verhoeven; ***W:*** Edward Neumeier; ***C:*** Jost Vacano; ***M:*** Basil Poledouris. Nominations: Academy Awards '97: Best Visual Effects. **VHS, LV, Closed Caption, DVD** *COL*

Stay Tuned

Could Satan (Jeffrey Jones) be the program director of a satellite dish company who lures unsuspecting couch potatoes to sell their souls? Ray Knable (John Ritter) is the ultimate spud who, along with his wife Helen (Pam Dawber), is sucked into the electronic universe of multi-channel programming. The best bit is a cartoon from famed Warner Bros. animator Chuck Jones. Other parodies, like *Three Men and Rosemary's Baby* are little more than cute titles. In the end, this is a formula film with an insincere message: turn off the TV and do something. Yeah, right. Gimme the remote. 🦴🦴½

1992 (PG-13) 90m/C John Ritter, Pam Dawber, Jeffrey Jones, Eugene Levy, David Tom, Heather McComb; ***D:*** Peter Hyams; ***W:*** Tom S. Parker; ***M:*** Bruce Broughton. **VHS, LV, Closed Caption** *WAR*

The Stepfather

In the opening scene, we learn that a man (Terry O'Quinn, in a career-defining role) has savagely murdered his suburban family, altered his identity, and escaped. Then we meet the new family he has gathered around himself a year later. The teen daughter (Jill Schoelen) thinks he's creepy, but she can't make her mother (Shelley Hack) or anyone else believe her. The rest is a combination of brutal surprises, the blackest of black humor, and terrific suspense. Writer Donald Westlake makes this guy a combination of Ward Cleaver and Norman Bates. For any horror fan who's missed this brilliant independent production, it's required viewing. Followed by two lesser sequels. 🦴🦴🦴🦴

1987 (R) 89m/C Terry O'Quinn, Shelley Hack, Jill Schoelen, Stephen Shellan, Charles Lanyer, Stephen E. Miller; ***D:*** Joseph Ruben; ***W:*** Donald E. Westlake; ***C:*** John Lindley; ***M:*** Patrick Moraz. **VHS, LV, Closed Caption** *COL*

Stepfather 2: Make Room for Daddy

This is not so much a true sequel as a recycling of the plot of the first film, one of the finest cult hits of recent years. As the title

"What kind of man changes names like other people change their clothes and then marries into fatherless families? And how can such a man be a loving father, a devoted husband, right up until the time he decides to come and *wipe* that family off the face of this planet?"

—*The Stepfather*, that's who.

character who uses any handy alias, Terry O'Quinn is the homicidal maniac who survived the shooting, stabbing, and whatall that ended the original and is locked up in a psychiatric hospital. John Auerbach's script is faithful to the character and it has a few good one-liners, but it's still predictable. So is Jeff Burr's direction. Altogether unnecessary.

1989 (R) 93m/C Terry O'Quinn, Meg Foster, Caroline Williams, Jonathan Brandis, Henry Brown, Mitchell Laurance; ***D:*** Jeff Burr; ***W:*** John P. Auerbach; ***C:*** Jacek Laskus. **VHS, LV** *NO*

The Stepford Wives

Few films—and even fewer horror films—become part of the language, but "Stepford" is an all-purpose adjective for robotic mindlessness. It should be. Ira Levin's tale is one of the defining works of late-20th century American horror. His novel and William Goldman's screen adaptation are companion pieces to *Rosemary's Baby*, sharing the same respectable affluent villains and, more importantly, perfectly tuned paranoia. Director Bryan Forbes effectively creates menace out of the commonplace and ordinary. In the lead, Katherine Ross may be too restrained, but that's all right; the supporting cast (Paula Prentiss, Nanette Newman, Tina Louise) picks up the slack. Beyond the obvious feminist message, the film is really about the horror of bland comfortable suburban conformity. And in a way, the passage of time has proved the truth of Levin's central idea. Today, successful middle-aged corporate executives don't have "Stepford Wives"; they have "trophy wives." Some might say that's a distinction without a difference. Followed by three made-for-TV sequels: *Revenge of the Stepford Wives* (1980), *The Stepford Children* (1987), and *The Stepford Husbands* (1996).

1975 115m/C Katharine Ross, Paula Prentiss, Peter Masterson, Nanette Newman, Patrick O'Neal, Tina Louise, Dee Wallace Stone, William Prince, Mary Stuart Masterson, Carol Rossen; ***D:*** Bryan Forbes; ***W:*** William Goldman; ***C:*** Owen Roizman; ***M:*** Michael Small. **VHS** *VTR*

Stephen King's Golden Years

After an explosion at a secret military research facility, 70-year-old janitor Harlan Williams (Keith Szarabajka) stops aging and starts growing younger. His evil superiors fall upon each other in an internecine turf war that catches him and his wife Gina (Frances Sternhagen) in the middle. The result is a combination of *Firestarter*—one reference is made to it—and the myth of Baucis and Philemon. The main problems are a lethargic pace, poor production values most obvious in the tacky sets, and a general lack of tension. The tape contains an ending that didn't make it to TV because the ratings for the mini-series were so justifiably low. That's King as the bus driver.

1991 232m/C Keith Szarabajka, Frances Sternhagen, Ed Lauter, R.D. Call, Stephen King; ***D:*** Kenneth Fink, Stephen Tolkin, Allen Coulter, Michael G. Gerrick; ***W:*** Stephen King, Josef Anderson. **VHS, LV, Closed Caption** *WOV*

Stephen King's It

Stephen King's huge novel fared better than many of his works when it was transformed into a mini-series. The lengthy plot is still simplified, but even at three hours-plus, the pace zips right along. The story concerns a group of childhood friends who, in their youth, overcame a hazily defined, protean critter. It often appears as Pennywise (Tim Curry), the evil clown, but it can assume other incarnations, many involving inventive special effects. Years later, when the kids have grown up, the boogie man comes back. An ensemble cast of TV veterans including Harry Anderson, Dennis Christopher, Richard Masur, Annette O'Toole, Tim Reid, John Ritter, and

Richard Thomas does commendable work. Director Tommy Lee Wallace doesn't let the effects overpower the story. 🦴🦴½

1990 193m/C Tim Reid, Richard Thomas, John Ritter, Annette O'Toole, Richard Masur, Dennis Christopher, Harry Anderson, Olivia Hussey, Tim Curry, Jonathan Brandis, Michael Cole; ***D:*** Tommy Lee Wallace; ***W:*** Stephen King; ***M:*** Richard Bellis. **VHS, LV** *WAR*

Stephen King's Nightshift Collection

In the first of these two short films, "The Woman in the Room," a lawyer (Michael Cornelison) must make important decisions about his mother's (Dee Croxton) dying. With the addition of a prisoner (Brian Libby), it's a three-character meditation on the morality of assisted suicide. Like writer/director Frank Darabont's more famous adaptation of King, *The Shawshank Redemption,* it's less true horror than honest humanism with a definite *Twilight Zone* moment. The second, "The Boogeyman" (which appears to be a student film), deals with adult fears and accusations of child abuse. Both were made on bare-bones budgets. ***AKA:*** The Woman in the Room; The Boogeyman. 🦴🦴½

1983 60m/C Michael Cornelison, Dee Croxton, Brian Libby, Michael Read, Bert Linder; ***D:*** Frank Darabont, Jeffrey C. Schiro; ***W:*** Frank Darabont, Jeffrey C. Schiro. **VHS** *KAR, HHE, GEG*

Stephen King's The Langoliers

At three hours, this adaptation of Stephen King's novella is much too long. The length may have been fine for a mini-series, but for unpretentious home video escapism—which is all it means to be—the running time is excessive. Scenes that add little to the story are overinflated to ridiculous dramatic heights, and too much time is spent in group gum-flapping about the *Twilight Zone*-ish situation. That involves mysterious goings-on aboard a Los Angeles to Boston night flight and creatures that "eat" time. The critters and several aerial exteriors are created by computer-generated effects that are far too obvious and far too cheap. The characters are the usual mix of King folk with Bronson Pinchot's untethered psycho at center stage. (That's King as the chairman of the fantasy sequence.) ***AKA:*** The Langoliers. 🦴🦴

1995 (PG-13) 180m/C David Morse, Bronson Pinchot, Patricia Wettig, Dean Stockwell, Kate Maberly, Christopher Collet, Kimber Riddle, Mark Lindsay Chapman, Frankie Faison, Baxter Harris; ***Cameos:*** Stephen King, Tom Holland; ***D:*** Tom Holland; ***W:*** Tom Holland; ***C:*** Paul Maibaum; ***M:*** Vladimir Horunzhy. **VHS, LV, Closed Caption** *REP*

Stephen King's The Night Flier

You'd think that a vampire (Michael H. Moss) who learns to fly a Cessna would update his wardrobe, but this one wears the full-length satin-lined cape. Though this made-for-cable feature is based on a King short story, it owes almost as much to *Kolchak, the Night Stalker.* Richard Dees (Miguel Ferrer) is a supermarket tabloid reporter who, after baring his burnt-out soul at length, goes on the trail of a bloodsucker who finds his victims at small airports. Dees' more enthusiastic competition is Katherine Blair (Julie Entwisle, who looks like a perky young Phoebe Cates). The effects are graphic enough to satisfy gore fans, but some of the early physical action is stiffly choreographed. The film has a bright polish, clever structure, acting's that well above average, and a bang-up finish. It did so well on cable that it earned a theatrical release. ***AKA:*** The Night Flier. 🦴🦴🦴

1996 (R) ?m/C Michael H. Moss, Miguel Ferrer, Julie Entwisle; ***D:*** Mark Pavia; ***W:*** Mark Pavia, Jack O'Donnell. *NYR*

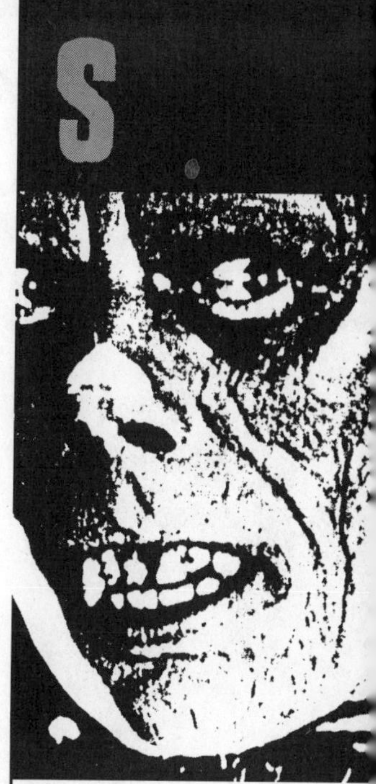

THE HOUND SALUTES

STEPHEN KING

Stephen King, the one-man master of the macabre, doesn't rest on his laurels. Just when you think the reigning "King" of horror has slowed down, along comes another novel, short story collection, movie, or TV mini-series. It's been going this way since 1976, when his *Carrie* was turned into a hot movie, starring Sissy Spacek and directed by Brian DePalma.

In fact, that first book-to-film project is one of the Maine native's favorite Hollywood experiences. He also counts *The Dead Zone, Stand by Me, Creepshow,* and *Misery* among strong translations of his written work.

Surprisingly, another film he has high regard for is 1989's critically reviled *Pet Sematary.* Directed by music video specialist Mary Lambert, the film told of a father dealing with the death of his young son who has close encounters of a spiritual kind on an ancient Indian burial ground.

"I like the film a lot," King admits. "Most of the reviews were negative, but that's a good sign with a horror picture. It shows you did something right. It means you certainly offended somebody."

The story, King says, hits close to home. "A lot of this actually happened," he recalls. "When my son, Owen, was two, we lived in a house similar to the one in the movie. I was the writer-in-residence at the University of Maine. He was discovering how fast his little legs could run. He ran towards the road where a truck was coming. I just ran out to get him, but the incident stayed with me.

"*Pet Sematary* was this object lesson in how close we are to dying. And how great parents' responsibilities are, and how easy it is for attention to lapse long enough for something to happen. That was the impetus to write the book."

King's decision to script *Pet Sematary* came after being disappointed with the cinematic treatments of *Firestarter, Silver Bullet,* and *The Running Man,* among others. "I felt that if I could keep some control of the screenplay myself, maybe we could come up with a picture that had the same hard edge of the book. I didn't want it softened or turned into *Cujo,* where the little boy lives in the end—surprise! I wanted the value of the book kept intact."

At one time, King wanted to be as far away from the film business as possible. "I don't feel any urge to control after I sign a piece of paper," King said in a 1979 interview. "I say 'See you later. You have what you need and I have what I want. As long as the check doesn't bounce, you and I are quits.'"

Stephen King's The Stand

Since King's huge novel has been a best-seller twice, everyone must be familiar with the story of an America decimated by "superflu" and turned into a battleground between Good and Evil. This adaptation, written by King and directed by Mick Garris, is faithful in tone and form to the fiction. Even at six hours, though, it still leaves out some material. Fans of the novel will also see where it cuts some corners in the big scenes, most notably those in the corn fields. The film is well cast with Gary Sinise, Jamey Sheridan, Molly Ringwald, Laura San Giacomo, Ruby Dee, Ossie Davis, Rob Lowe, and Ray Walston han-

In recent years, however, King has taken a more active role in getting his works turned into TV and movie projects. For example, King was quite distraught over Stanley Kubrick's 1980 version of *The Shining,* so he played executive producer on a 1997 miniseries of the same book, as yet unavailable on tape.

"If I had to do that all over again," King said in 1989, "I'd cast anybody but Jack Nicholson—even Shirley MacLaine! This is supposed to be about a guy who is driven crazy. The minute Jack comes on the screen, you say 'This guy is crazy.' I'd like to recast that. Kubrick's idea was that the guy had lost it already. That takes some of the tragedy out of the story for me." As promised, King recast Nicholson's maniacal writer with a calmer Timothy Daly of TV's *Wings.*

King also had an opportunity to rework 1986's disastrous *Maximum Overdrive,* his directorial debut, into *Trucks,* a cable movie starring Timothy Busfield (*thirtysomething*). Of the tale featuring Emilio Estevez battling a convoy of killer trucks, Kings says: "I didn't get the job because I went to film school. I got the job because I'm Stephen King. If you become famous enough, they'll let you hang yourself in Times Square with live TV coverage."

Well, King is certainly famous enough—and rich enough—to retire, but that's just not going to happen. The indefatigable wordsmith has no less than five new projects slated to appear in some form in 1998, including the long-delayed film of *Apt Pupil,* helmed by Bryan Singer, director of *The Usual Suspects*; a television version of his novel *Rose Madder*; the video and limited theatrical release of *The Night Flier,* a film about a tabloid journalist (Miguel Ferrer) and a serial killer; and *Storm of the Century,* a miniseries detailing a horrific storm and its aftermath, which he wrote and is producing.

One wonders if there's any subject that frightens the undisputable King of creepiness that he hasn't explored yet.

"Hmmm. How about constipation. Now that scares me."

—Irv Slifkin

SIGNIFICANT CONTRIBUTIONS TO HORROR

(as screenwriter)

***Pet Sematary* (1989)**

***Stephen King's It* (1990)**

***Stephen King's The Stand* (1994)**

(as novelist)

Carrie

'Salem's Lot

The Shining

The Stand

The Dead Zone

Cujo

Misery

The Dark Half

Dolores Claiborne

Desperation

dling most of the dramatic action. And that's John Bloom (AKA drive-in critic Joe Bob Briggs) as the Texas highway patrolman and director Sam Raimi as a road guard. All in all, this is one of the more successful adaptations of King's longer fiction, which tends to suffer when forced into the length of a conventional theatrical feature. ***AKA:*** The Stand. 🦴🦴🦴

1994 360m/C Jamey Sheridan, Ruby Dee, Gary Sinise, Molly Ringwald, Miguel Ferrer, Laura San Giacomo, Rob Lowe, Adam Storke, Matt Frewer, Corin "Corky" Nemec, Ray Walston, Bill Fagerbakke, Ossie Davis, Shawnee Smith, Rick Aviles, John Joe Bob Briggs Bloom, Michael Lookinland; ***Cameos:*** Ed Harris, Kathy Bates, Kareem Abdul-Jabbar, Stephen King, Sam Raimi; ***D:*** Mick Garris; ***W:*** Stephen King; ***C:*** Edward Pei. **VHS, LV, Closed Caption** *REP*

"**More terror. Less filling.**"

—Ad line from *Stephen King's Thinner.*

Stephen King's The Tommyknockers

One of King's better evil-underground-monster tales translates well to video. A writer (Marg Helgenberger) uncovers something on her farm that gives various inhabitants of Haven, Maine, strange new creativity and intelligence, among other powers. Condensed from a longer TV miniseries, the video version flows smoothly with some good non-spectacular effects and the usual assortment of familiar types portrayed by a troupe of first-rate character actors. Unfortunately, the best inventions of King's fiction don't make it to the screen. Structurally, this one's similar to *Needful Things* and *It* with a strong touch of *Invasion of the Body Snatchers*. For those unfamiliar with the story, the ending's a terrific payoff. ***AKA:*** The Tommyknockers. 🦴🦴🦴

1993 (R) 120m/C Jimmy Smits, Marg Helgenberger, Joanna Cassidy, E.G. Marshall, Traci Lords, John Ashton, Allyce Beasley, Cliff DeYoung, Robert Carradine, Leon Woods, Paul McIver; ***D:*** John Power; ***W:*** Lawrence D. Cohen. **VHS, LV, Closed Caption** *THV, TWV*

Stephen King's Thinner

Fair little B-horror is a faithful adaptation of its source, a novel written under King's Richard Bachman pseudonym. It's sluggishly paced, and the acting ranges from understatement to shameless histrionics. Overweight, prosperous lawyer Billy Halleck (Robert John Burke) accidentally kills an old gypsy woman. The gypsy leader Tadzu (Michael Constantine) curses him with the single word, "Thinner," and leaves town. Miraculously, Billy's new diet seems to be working. The pounds melt away and he can eat anything he wants. But delight turns to fear. Sudden weight loss? Writer/director Tom Holland (*The Langoliers*) maintains King's uneasy balance of social observation and cheap pulp thrills. But the comfortable ease of suburbia is at odds with the gypsies, who are virtual cartoon cliches, none more than the slingshot-wielding Gina (former MTV veejay Kari Wuhrer). ***AKA:*** Thinner. 🦴🦴

1996 (R) 92m/C Robert John Burke, Joe Mantegna, Lucinda Jenney, Michael Constantine, Kari Wuhrer, John Horton, Sam Freed, Daniel von Bargen, Elizabeth Franz, Joy Lentz, Jeff Ware; ***Cameos:*** Stephen King; ***D:*** Tom Holland; ***W:*** Michael McDowell, Tom Holland; ***C:*** Kees Van Oostrum; ***M:*** Daniel Licht. **VHS, LV, Closed Caption** *REP*

Stormswept

Soft-core southern Gothic horror comedy begins on a familiar note with six crew members of a film production company trapped by a thunderstorm in a haunted Louisiana mansion. An unspeakable crime occurred there years before. Now, an evil, sexually charged spirit pervades the place and a mysterious blonde (Kathleen Kinmont) has set up housekeeping in the basement. An early establishing shot of a spider walking through an ornate chandelier sets the mood, and the rest of the film pretty much lives up to it. Some of writer/director David Marsh's scares are conventional dark-and-stormy-night stuff, but there are enough inventive moments to keep your interest. Fans have seen much worse. 🦴🦴

1995 94m/C Julie Hughes, Melissa Moore, Kathleen Kinmont, Justin Carroll, Lorissa McComas, Ed Wasser, Kim Kopf, Hunt Scarritt; ***D:*** David Marsh; ***W:*** David Marsh. **VHS** *MTH*

Strait-Jacket

William Castle's attempt to cash in on the success of Robert Aldrich's *Whatever Happened to Baby Jane?* opens with a scream, shattering glass and lurid headline. Lucy Harbin (Joan Crawford)—"very much a woman and very much aware of the fact," our narrator claims—uses an ax to knock off her two-timing hubby and his girlfriend.

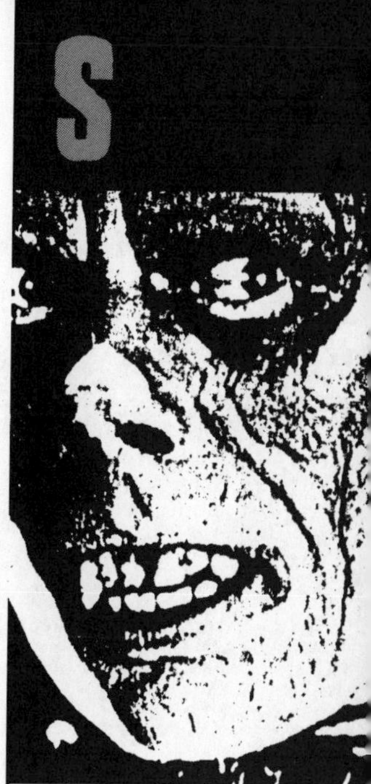

Twenty years later, her daughter Carol (Diane Baker) who witnessed the whole thing is waiting when Mommie Dearest is released from the asylum, and, to nobody's surprise, more chop-chop murders ensue. The plotting isn't as tight as it is in Aldrich's films. If the black-and-white photography isn't as sparkling, the work is still an effective period piece that's not without its moments. Robert Bloch's script is not another *Psycho.*

1964 89m/B Joan Crawford, Leif Erickson, Diane Baker, George Kennedy, Howard St. John, Rochelle Hudson, Edith Atwater, Lee Majors; ***D:*** William Castle; ***W:*** Robert Bloch; ***C:*** Arthur E. Arling; ***M:*** Van Alexander. **VHS** *COL*

Strange Behavior

Writer Bill Condon and director Michael Laughlin try their hands at a Stephen King-like tale of a small town where teens are transformed into murderous zombies. Could Dr. Parkinson's (Fiona Lewis) drug-based behavior modification experiments with students have anything to do with it? The filmmakers use a few simple tricks well enough, and they treat the characters seriously, but the pace is pokey and some of the violent effects don't measure up to the level of believability that the story demands. The old needle-in-the-eyeball routine still works, though. Made in New Zealand with a good cast, including Michael Murphy, Scott Brady, Louise Fletcher, and Charles Lane. ***AKA:*** Dead Kids; Small Town Massacre.

1981 (R) 105m/C Michael Murphy, Louise Fletcher, Dan Shor, Fiona Lewis, Arthur Dignam, Marc McClure, Scott Brady, Dey Young, Charles Lane; ***D:*** Michael Laughlin; ***W:*** Michael Laughlin, Bill Condon; ***C:*** Louis Horvath. **VHS** *COL, RHI, FCT*

Strange Confession

See *Calling Dr. Death/Strange Confession.*

The Strange Door

Charles Laughton is at his mischievous best as the evil Sire de Maletroit, a 17th century aristocrat who has a nasty plan in mind for his niece, Blanche (Sally Forrest). ("I'll feed your liver to the swine," he threatens a cohort.) With its impressive dungeons and secret passages, and Boris Karloff in support as Voltan, the film looks as good as the best Universal horrors of the '30s and '40s. Throughout, the physical action is lively and the ending's a doozy. The main attraction, though, is Laughton's zesty performance.

1951 81m/B Charles Laughton, Boris Karloff, Paul Cavanagh, Sally Forrest, Richard Stapley, Michael Pate, Alan Napier; ***D:*** Joseph Pevney; ***W:*** Jerry Sackheim; ***C:*** Irving Glassberg. **VHS, Closed Caption** *USH*

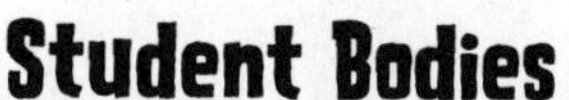

Student Bodies

Parody of bad slasher movies falls victim to the excesses of its subject. In yet another story of a heavy-breathing psycho killing teenagers, writer/director Mickey Rose identifies the conventions of the genre and mocks them, but that's all. A few nice touches like cheerleaders carrying black pom-poms to a fellow student's funeral aren't enough. Similar material is given much more enjoyable and intelligent treatment in *Heathers* and *Scream.*

1981 (R) 86m/C Kristen Riter, Matthew Goldsby, Richard Brando, Joe Flood, Joe Talarowski, Mimi Weddell; ***D:*** Mickey Rose; ***W:*** Mickey Rose. **VHS, LV** *PAR*

The Stuff

In *God Told Me To* and *Q,* Larry Cohen has made two of the best low-budget horrors of recent years. Despite some sharp moments, this horror-satire doesn't measure up to them. Cohen's subject is American materialism and our tendency to overindulge in anything pleasurable. His "stuff" is yogurt-looking goo that bub-

THE HOUND SALUTES

BERNARD HERRMANN

Though his rich, diverse career began with a universally acknowledged masterpiece and encompassed every kind of film from epics to mystery to period piece before it was over, Bernard Herrmann also wrote some of the most evocative, frightening music that ever graced the horror screen.

He was born in 1911 in New York, and studied at New York University and the Juilliard School. He was a member of Aaron Copland's Young Composers' Group and by 1934, he was a radio conductor for the Columbia Broadcasting System. He'd already worked with Orson Welles' Mercury Theater of the Air before he went to Hollywood to score his first film, *Citizen Kane*. After it, he worked steadily and became closely associated with Alfred Hitchcock. Curiously, both men were known as demanding perfectionists but they were able to maintain a working relationship for more than a decade. In professional terms, they certainly found the best in each other. (Try to imagine *Psycho* without those stabbing strings.)

Herrmann's biographer Steven Smith (*A Fire at the Center*) suggests that the irascibility came from his not being taken as a "serious" composer. If that's the case, music-lovers' loss is filmgoers' gain. Herrmann's score for *Vertigo* may be the most successful combination of image, plot, and music ever assembled. His soaring, dizzy romantic orchestrations fill the gaps in the psychologically sound but logically challenged plot.

Herrmann and Hitchcock went their separate ways after Hitchcock rejected his score for *Marnie*. Hitchcock was said to have been looking for a more "youthful" sound then to attract new audi-

bles up out of the ground and quickly becomes the nation's favorite dessert. But what is it doing to the people who eat it and why is it crawling around in the refrigerator at night? An industrial spy (Michael Moriarty), a cookie magnate (Garrett Morris), and a P.R. whiz (Andrea Marcovicci) set out to discover the secret. Their efforts are ruined by ham-fisted editing. Important scenes are chopped off prematurely and transitions are jarringly rough.

1985 (R) 93m/C Michael Moriarty, Andrea Marcovicci, Garrett Morris, Paul Sorvino, Danny Aiello, Brooke Adams, Patrick O'Neal, Alexander Scourby, Scott Bloom; ***D:*** Larry Cohen; ***W:*** Larry Cohen. **VHS, Closed Caption** *VTR*

Subspecies

With this video premiere, producer Charles Band and director Ted Nicolaou began a partnership that has become a virtual mini-studio in Romania. The no-frills vampire story is an updated Hammer film. The terrific opening scene takes place inside a castle where two really hideous guys (one of whom has a serious problem with drooling) are doing absolutely disgusting stuff. Throughout, the Gothic sets and locations are properly atmospheric with creaking doors and heavy organ music. The plot, revolving around good and bad vampire brothers, is acceptable. The evil Radu's (Anders Hove) makeup is based on the original *Nosferatu* and if the whole thing

ences to his films. That didn't work. All of his post-Herrmann pictures are lesser efforts. At the same time, Herrmann was discovered (and employed) by the next generation of filmmakers who, it ought to be said, revered Hitch, too.

Brian DePalma was lucky enough to get some of Herrmann's best music in *Sisters.* Herrmann also added considerably to Larry Cohen's low-budget *It's Alive,* and Cohen wisely had the music reworked for the two sequels. Herrmann's final score was for Martin Scorsese's *Taxi Driver.* It's one of his most haunted and not really like any of the other work he did in the last decades of his life.

As Alex Ross writes in the conclusion to his liner notes for the CD *Bernard Herrmann: The Film Scores* (Esa-Pekka Salonen/Los Angeles Philharmonic, Sony Classical, 1996): "What distinguishes Herrmann from most Hollywood composers is that his work can be heard very much on its own terms. The films for which he wrote seem to mirror his own concerns, rather than the other way round. How much of the emotional intensity we feel in these greatest achievements of Welles and Hitchcock—directors not noted for their romantic touch—comes from the dark passion of Benny Herrmann? Huge longings worked their way out of this man's soul: most of all the longing for greatness, for a symphonic and operatic breadth just out of reach. Transmuting his thoughts into the world of film, he achieved a different kind of immortality. Herrmann will haunt a vast, captive audience into the far future."

SIGNIFICANT CONTRIBUTIONS TO HORROR

***Psycho* (1960)**

***The Birds* (1963)—as sound consultant**

***Sisters* (1973)**

***It's Alive* (1974)**

***Taxi Driver* (1976)**

***Cape Fear* (1991)—Elmer Bernstein score based on Herrmann's 1962 original**

seems more than a little overdone, that's what the material calls for. It isn't meant to be subtle. Followed by sequels *Bloodstone* and *Bloodlust.* 🦴🦴🦴

1990 (R) 90m/C Laura Tate, Michael Watson, Anders Hove, Michelle McBride, Irina Movila, Angus Scrimm; ***D:*** Ted Nicolaou. **VHS, LV, 8mm, Closed Caption** *FLL*

Summer of Fear

When young Julia's (Lee Purcell) parents are killed in a wreck, she moves in with Rachel (Linda Blair) and her family. Rachel comes to believe that the standoffish newcomer is a witch who's out to steal her boyfriend, her father, and her new party dress. The story, based on Lois Duncan's well-regarded young adult novel, is similar to Fritz Lieber's *Conjure Wife,* filmed as *Weird Woman* and *Burn Witch, Burn!* For Linda Blair, the role marks a transition between her prepubescent *Exorcist* character and the flashy sexpots she'd play a few years later. In the same way, for director Wes Craven the film is a large step away from his early exploitation and toward mainstream respectability. Look for a young Fran Drescher as Rachel's friend. ***AKA:*** Stranger in Our House. 🦴🦴

1978 94m/C Linda Blair, Lee Purcell, Jeremy Slate, Carol Lawrence, MacDonald Carey, Jeff McCracken, Jeff East, Fran Drescher; ***D:*** Wes Craven; ***M:*** Tom D'Andrea. **VHS** *NO*

"Bad luck isn't brought by broken mirrors, but by broken minds."

—Dr. Frank Mandel (Udo Kier) in *Suspiria.*

The Surgeon

Think *E.R.* meets *Re-Animator* in a dandy little medical horror/comedy with a first-rate ensemble cast. The title character (Sean Haberle) is the proverbial mad scientist—actually he's a little madder than most—who's out to get everyone who has thwarted his research in "pituitary extract." Those include Malcolm McDowell and Charles Dance. Isabel Glasser and James Remar are the good doctors. Peter Boyle is the cop on the case. Director Carl Schenkel and special effects coordinator Steve Johnson have come up with some genuinely creepy moments, most of them infused with strong humor. It's difficult to maintain an effective ratio of laughs and scares, but they manage. ***AKA:*** Exquisite Tenderness. 🦴🦴🦴

1994 (R) 100m/C *GE* Isabel Glasser, James Remar, Sean Haberle, Charles Dance, Peter Boyle, Malcolm McDowell, Charles Bailey-Gates, Gregory West, Mother Love; ***D:*** Carl Schenkel; ***W:*** Patrick Cirillo; ***C:*** Thomas Burstyn; ***M:*** Christopher Franke. **VHS** *APX*

Suspiria

On the darkest and stormiest night of them all, a young American dancer (Jessica Harper) goes to a new school in Germany. Before she can set foot inside the door, her fellow students are being killed. Director Dario Argento introduces some of the same characters, ideas, and motifs he works with in later films, notably *Creepers.* They share the same flaws, too. Plot coherence is flimsy at best, and realistic motivations for some of the excesses are hard to find. To my taste, Argento is also overdependent on loud sound effects and music to make the visuals more upsetting. The acting varies from understated realism, despite often ludicrous dialogue, to a crazed Teutonic caricature. That said, Argento can create striking images, and he tosses in Hitchcock quotes from such odd sources as *North by Northwest* and *The Birds.* Like so much of Argento's work, this is easier to admire than to like. 🦴🦴½

1977 (R) 92m/C *IT* Jessica Harper, Joan Bennett, Alida Valli, Udo Kier, Stefania Casini, Flavio Bucci, Barbara Magnolfi, Rudolf Schuendler; ***D:*** Dario Argento; ***W:*** Dario Argento, Daria Nicolodi; ***C:*** Luciano Tovoli. **VHS, LV, Letterboxed, Closed Caption** *FXL, HHE, QVD*

Tales from the Crypt Presents Bordello of Blood

In an uninspired follow up to *Demon Knight,* both the bloody special effects and the humor are based on overly familiar cliches. Despite the expensive polish of the production, the film has a careless, thrown-together quality. A half-hearted prologue introduces supervampire Lilith (Angie Everhart). The scene abruptly shifts to Los Angeles where she runs the titular establishment out of a mortuary. Katherine (Erika Eleniak) hires comic detective Rafe Guttman (Dennis Miller) to find her brother (Corey Feldman) after the wayward sibling visits Lilith. A TV preacher (Chris Sarandon) is involved, too, but exactly what he's doing is never clear. Not that it matters. Writer/director Gilbert Adler is more interested in exploding bodies and bad one-liners. ***AKA:*** Bordello of Blood. 🦴

1996 (R) 87m/C Dennis Miller, Angie Everhart, Chris Sarandon, Corey Feldman, Erika Eleniak; ***D:*** Gilbert Adler; ***W:*** Gilbert Adler, A.L. Katz; ***C:*** Tom Priestley; ***M:*** Chris Boardman. **VHS, LV, Closed Caption** *USH*

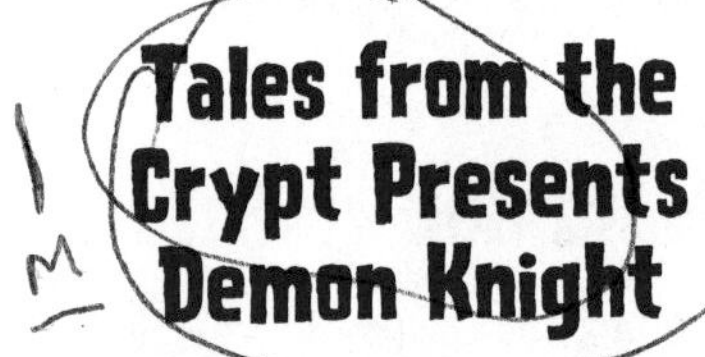

Tales from the Crypt Presents Demon Knight

First-rate little horror comedy based on the popular cable TV series—and before that, the lurid E.C. Comics from the 1950s—boasts excellent production values, a smart script, and a talented cast. In terms of plot, this is your basic Good vs. Evil, End of the World As We Know It story. (Pay no attention to the framing device with the Crypt Keeper.) Outside a little New Mexico town on a dark and stormy night, the Collector (Billy Zane) chases a mysterious stranger, Brayker (William Sadler), and traps a doughty group of characters in a hotel. It's not giving anything away to reveal that the Collector is a cheerful demon who conjures up a host of disgusting monsters. Director Ernest R. Dickerson (*Juice, Surviving the Game*) made his reputation as Spike Lee's cinematographer, and is particularly careful with lighting, using shadows to dampen the more grotesque special effects—beheadings, arms being ripped off, etc. The horror is also leavened with a generous streak of saucy wit. ***AKA:*** Demon Knight; Demon Keeper. 🦴🦴🦴

1994 (R) 93m/C Billy Zane, William Sadler, Jada Pinkett, Brenda Bakke, CCH Pounder, Dick Miller, Thomas Haden Church, John Schuck, Gary Farmer, Charles Fleischer; ***D:*** Ernest R. Dickerson; ***W:*** Ethan Reiff, Cyrus Voris, Mark Bishop; ***C:*** Rick Bota; ***M:*** Ed Shearmur; ***V:*** John Kassir. **VHS, LV, Closed Caption** *USH*

Tales from the Darkside: The Movie

Four-part anthology of three comedies and an odd love story varies in quality, though it is well made. For those whose taste runs to visceral black humor, the film is funny and even enjoyable. In the wraparound story, Deborah Harry is a society matron planning a dinner party. "Lot 249" is a Mummy tale with Christian Slater. The strongest segment is "The Cat from Hell," written by George Romero from a Stephen King story. "Lover's Vow" is a predictable entry about an artist (James Remar) and a mystery woman (Rae Dawn Chong). The "yuck" factor is high, with inventively bloody effects, but the sly, gleeful tone keeps these stories from becoming oppressive. 🦴🦴🦴

1990 (R) 93m/C Deborah Harry, Christian Slater, David Johansen, William Hickey, James Remar, Rae Dawn Chong, Julianne Moore, Robert Klein, Steve Buscemi, Matthew Lawrence; ***D:*** John Harrison; ***W:*** George A. Romero, Michael McDowell. **VHS, LV, Closed Caption** *PAR*

Targets

Not on the National Rifle Association's top-ten list, Peter Bogdanovich's debut is a fine, economically made horror film that neatly brings the conventions of the past into the violent present of 1968. In those days, America was just getting used to the idea that someone might take a rifle onto a tower and shoot people for no reason. Boris Karloff plays Byron Orlok, an aging horror star; Bogdanovich is Sammy Michaels, a young director trying to persuade Orlok to act in his film. Tim O'Kelly is Bobby Thompson, a conservative young man filled with family values who's about to go over the edge. How those three and a few others converge at a drive-in theatre makes for a grim, fascinating tale. 🦴🦴🦴½

1968 (PG) 90m/C Boris Karloff, James Brown, Tim O'Kelly, Peter Bogdanovich, Mary Jackson, Sandy Baron, Monte Landis, Mike Farrell, Nancy Hsueh, Arthur Peterson, Tanya Morgan; ***D:*** Peter Bogdanovich; ***W:*** Peter Bogdanovich; ***C:*** Laszlo Kovacs. **VHS** *PAR*

Taste the Blood of Dracula

A debauched British Lord (Ralph Bates) takes the title literally and puts a curse on his cowardly associates—three outwardly proper gentlemen who have secretly formed a hellfire club. The development turns Dracula (Christopher Lee) into a partially sympathetic figure. Shifting the scene to Victorian England further distances the film from earlier entries in the then 12-year-old series. A strong autumnal atmosphere helps considerably, but the film isn't as tightly structured as its predecessors. Key characters tend to pass out

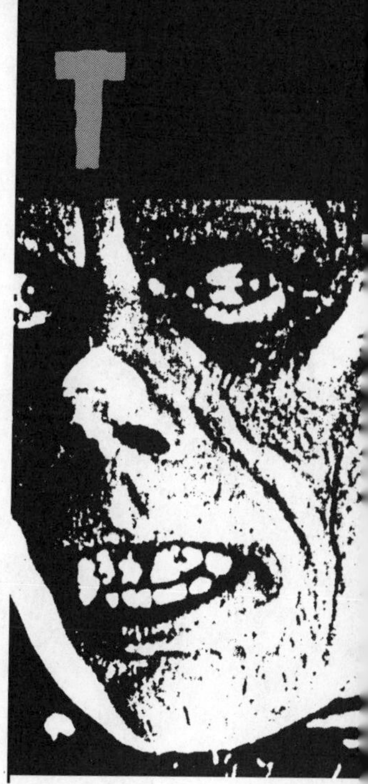

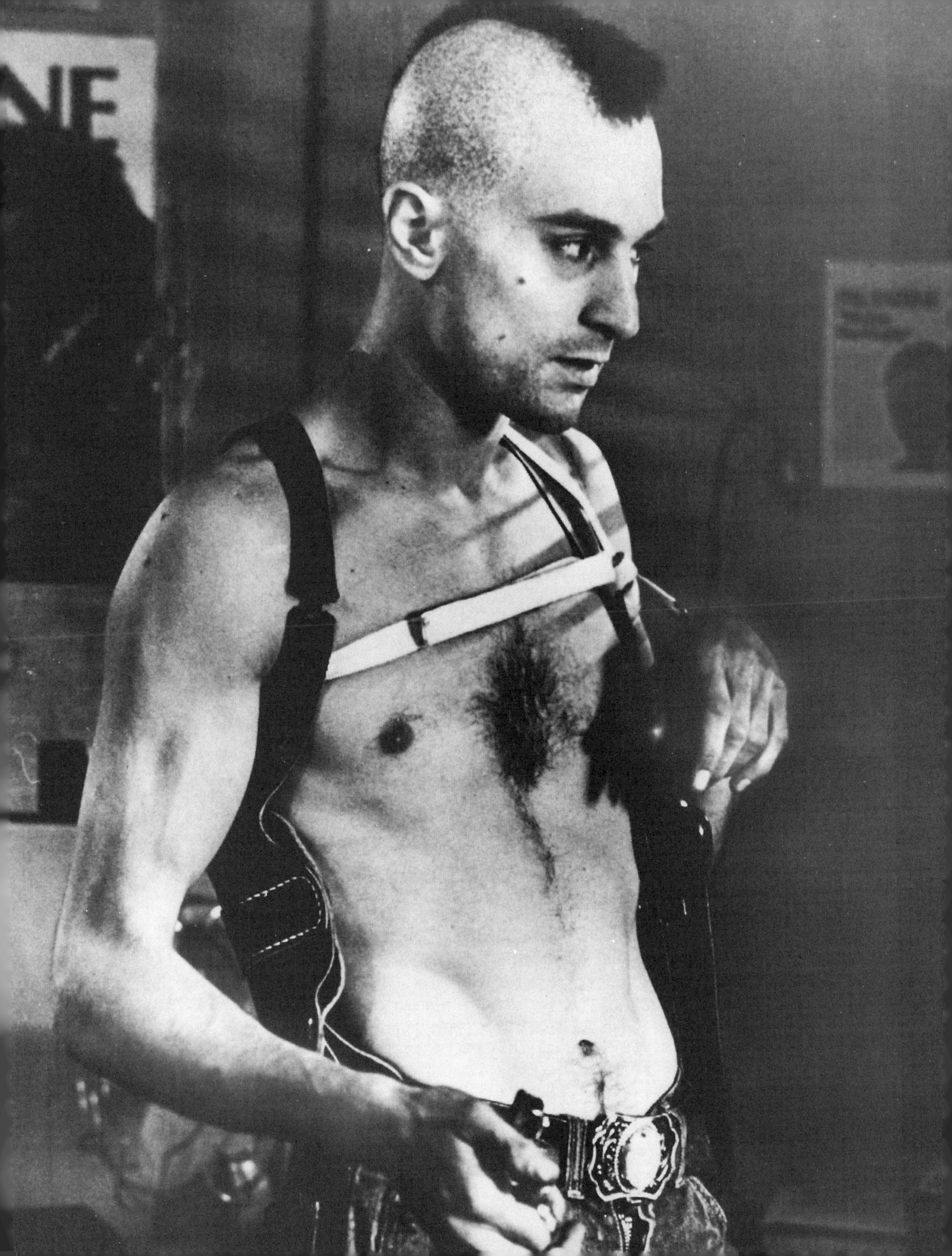

and regain consciousness at convenient moments. The generational conflicts that had been subplots are central here.

1970 (PG) 91m/C *GB* Christopher Lee, Ralph Bates, Geoffrey Keen, Gwen Watford, Linda Hayden, John Carson, Peter Sallis, Isla Blair, Martin Jarvis, Roy Kinnear, Anthony Higgins, Anthony Corlan, Michael Ripper; ***D:*** Peter Sasdy; ***W:*** Anthony John Elder Hinds; ***C:*** Arthur Grant; ***M:*** James Bernard. **VHS** *WAR*

Taxi Driver

Many critics and viewers have tried to turn Travis Bickle (Robert De Niro) into either a hero or a villain. He's neither. He's a sympathetic monster, like Karloff's Creature in *Frankenstein,* who's driven deeper and deeper into madness by the surreal nightside city surrounding him. Writer Paul Schrader, director Martin Scorsese, and composer Bernard Herrmann make that world indelibly real. Though the film isn't often considered a work of horror, it's told through the conventions of the genre. Bickle's slow transformation from stoic loner to insane assassin, and his essentially accidental redemption are deeply frightening. The laserdisc version is slightly longer than the tape, with commentary by Scorsese and Schrader, storyboards, complete screenplay, and Scorsese's production photos.

1976 (R) 112m/C Robert De Niro, Jodie Foster, Harvey Keitel, Cybill Shepherd, Peter Boyle, Albert Brooks; ***D:*** Martin Scorsese; ***W:*** Paul Schrader; ***C:*** Michael Chapman; ***M:*** Bernard Herrmann. British Academy Awards '76: Best Supporting Actress (Foster); Cannes Film Festival '76: Best Film; Los Angeles Film Critics Association Awards '76: Best Actor (De Niro), National Film Registry '94;; New York Film Critics Awards '76: Best Actor (De Niro); National Society of Film Critics Awards '76: Best Actor (De Niro), Best Director (Scorsese), Best Supporting Actress (Foster); Nominations: Academy Awards '76: Best Original Score. **VHS, LV, 8mm, DVD, Letterboxed** *NO*

Temptress

Photographer Karin Swann (Kim Delaney) returns from India with a suggestive new tattoo to remind her of the "spiritual reawakening" that she found when she tapped into her "goddess energy." Actually, she tapped into a little more than she realized and her goddess is one mean mother. Her live-in boyfriend (Chris Sarandon) is not amused. A mysterious stranger (Ben Cross) says that he understands. The possession story that follows is extremely well told. Writer Melissa Mitchell and director Lawrence Lanoff manage to combine the supernatural with everyday reality and psychological reality remarkably well. They also use the conventions of the genre to show both the creative and destructive aspects of sex. A sleeper.

1995 (R) 93m/C Kim Delaney, Chris Sarandon, Corbin Bernsen, Dee Wallace Stone, Jessica Walter, Ben Cross; ***D:*** Lawrence Lanoff; ***W:*** Melissa Mitchell; ***M:*** Michael Stearns. **VHS, Closed Caption** *PAR*

The Tenant

Roman Polanski's bizarre horror-comedy can be seen as a remake (of sorts) of his brilliant *Repulsion.* He quotes several key moments and even casts himself as Tronofski, a strange little guy who becomes obsessed by the previous occupant of his grim little Paris apartment—a woman who attempted suicide. It's a slowly paced and uninvolving story, notable mostly for the casting of veterans Melvyn Douglas as the building owner and a restrained Shelley Winters as the concierge. Isabelle Adjani is given far too little to do as the near-sighted Stella. Polanski's off-center humor is not to all tastes (certainly not to mine), and the sight of him in

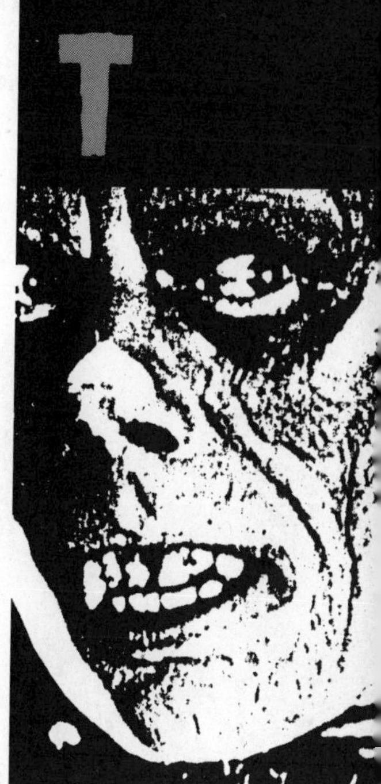

Travis Bickle (Robert De Niro) in *Taxi Driver.*

Madame Dioz (Jo Van Fleet) and Madame Gaderian (Lila Kedrova) in *The Tenant.*

drag will not remind anyone of Catherine Deneuve. ***AKA:*** Le Locataire.

1976 (R) 126m/C *FR* Roman Polanski, Isabelle Adjani, Melvyn Douglas, Jo Van Fleet, Bernard Fresson, Shelley Winters, Lila Kedrova; ***D:*** Roman Polanski; ***W:*** Gerard Brach, Roman Polanski; ***C:*** Sven Nykvist. **VHS** *NO*

Tenebrae

See *Unsane*.

Terrified

Quirky suspense film defies easy categorization or review. It's a guessing game. The audience knows that Olive (Heather Graham) is a troubled young woman. With good reason. But when she claims that she's being stalked by a stranger and is attacked in her apartment, is she fantasizing or is she telling the truth? Are director James Merendino and co-writer Megan Heath taking *Repulsion* as their model? Or is it *Psycho* ? Or are they up to something else entirely? Balancing that elliptical uncertainty, much of the dialogue seems absolutely authentic and Heather Graham's performance is fine. Despite some narrative lapses and a conclusion that won't sit well with all viewers, this one still earns a strong recommendation for fans of psychological puzzles.

1994 (R) 90m/C Heather Graham, Lisa Zane, Rustam Branaman, Tom Breznahan; ***Cameos:*** Max Perlich, Balthazar Getty, Richard Lynch, Don Calfa; ***D:*** James Merendino; ***W:*** James Merendino, Megan Heath. **VHS** *APX*

The Terror

Legendary Roger Corman production boasts no less than five directors. Corman has written that he began the film hoping to crank out another Poe-inspired Gothic quickie. As various complications ensued, he had young Francis Ford Coppola shoot some footage in Big Sur; and co-writer Jack Hill also took a shot. So did Monte Hellman and finally star Jack Nicholson got behind the camera. Why not? He was then married to his pregnant co-star Sandra Knight. This serial collaboration begins as a hallucination with a delirious Napoleonic officer (Nicholson) riding down a beach. Then it becomes a turgid period piece when he reaches Boris Karloff's castle, and finally the oft-revised plot virtually disintegrates. In the end, it's mostly about characters wandering down dark hallways and paths for no discernible reason. ***AKA:*** Lady of the Shadows.

1963 81m/C Boris Karloff, Jack Nicholson, Sandra Knight, Dick Miller, Dorothy Neumann, Jonathan Haze; ***D:*** Roger Corman, Jack Hill, Francis Ford Coppola, Monte Hellman, Dennis Jacob, Jack Nicholson; ***W:*** Leo Gordon, Jack Hill; ***C:*** John M. Nickolaus Jr. **VHS** *NOS, SNC, HHT*

The Terror

It's a dark and stormy English night when a young director (John Nolan) and his actress cousin (Carolyn Courage) decide to make a movie about an ancestor who was burned at the stake as a witch. The ghost doesn't take kindly to the notion of having her life dramatized and does something about it. Her weapons include the amazing collapsing movie set, the incredible flying Land Rover, and the dreaded flaming bathtub! None of them is meant to be funny, but they are. At least this one isn't as disgusting as director Norman J. Warren's wretched *Inseminoid.*

1979 (R) 86m/C John Nolan, Carolyn Courage, James Aubrey, Glynis Barber, Sarah Keller, Tricia Walsh; ***D:*** Norman J. Warren. **VHS** *VCI, VCD, HHE*

Terror at Red Wolf Inn

Upside—impoverished college student Regina (Linda Gillin) wins a free vacation at Red Wolf Inn. Downside—the owners (Mary Jackson and Arthur Space) may be cannibals. That's not to say they aren't nice people, and their grandson (John Neilson) is really cute. The humor avoids the excesses typical to this kind of horror-comedy in favor of a kinder, gentler *Arsenic and Old Lace* tone. Mostly. The ending is very much in keeping with the rest. ***AKA:*** Club Dead; Terror House; The Folks at Red Wolf Inn.

1972 (R) 90m/C Linda Gillin, Arthur Space, John Neilson, Mary Jackson, Janet Wood, Margaret Avery; ***D:*** Bud Townsend; ***W:*** Allen Actor. **VHS**

Terror at the Opera

Dario Argento translates the familiar *Phantom of the Opera* plot into a baroque slasher tale. The sumptuous production is visually fascinating eye-candy with a strange humor which often appears to be intentional, though where both opera and horror are concerned, the line between intentional and un- is often hard to distinguish. Argento begins with crisp editing and flowing camerawork, but as the story goes on, it loses focus and the director indulges his love for visual flourishes. Happily, even eagerly, he sacrifices logic and coherence to flashy images, no matter how pointless. (In a typical moment, Argento flips the camera over for no reason.) That said, he also gives fans what they want to see in the bloody scenes. In his best bits, sharp metal meets soft tissue in graphic close-up. It all arrives at a grand nutball conclusion with a "ravencam" point of view and finally—so help me—a quote from *The Sound of Music.* The full-length widescreen version, titled *Opera,* captures all of Argento's wild, lyrical camerawork and more of his Grand Guignol excesses. But this version, available from Video Search of Miami, lacks the sharp clarity of the American edition. Both tapes make full use of the setting and the music. ***AKA:*** Opera.

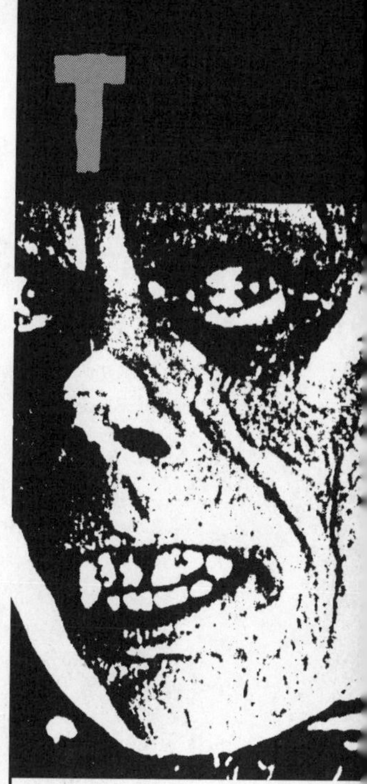

Lt. Duvalier (Jack Nicholson) in *The Terror* (1963).

1988 (R) 107m/C *IT* Christina Marsillach, Ian Charleson, Urbano Barberini, William McNamara, Antonella Vitale, Barbara Cupisti, Coralina Cataldi Tassoni, Daria Nicolodi; ***D:*** Dario Argento; ***W:*** Dario Argento, Franco Ferrini; ***C:*** Ronnie Taylor. **VHS** *FCT*

Terror in the Haunted House

A slow introduction unsubtly establishes that newlywed Sheila (Cathy O'Donnell) is being somehow tricked by her husband Justin (Gerald Mohr) with dreams of a haunted house. The "Psycho-Rama" gimmick is micro-second flashes of ugly images and words superimposed over the conventional image. You can see these "subliminal messages" clearly if you slow the tape, but why would anyone want to make this laborious black-and-white clunker any longer than it already is? It's all talk and virtually no action. ***AKA:*** My World Dies Screaming.

1958 90m/C Gerald Mohr, Cathy O'Donnell, William Ching, John Qualen, Barry Bernard; ***D:*** Harold Daniels; ***W:*** Robert C. Dennis; ***C:*** Frederick E. West. **VHS** *RHI, MLB, CCB*

Terror in Toyland

Sexually traumatized by seeing Mom and Santa together when he was a child in 1947, Harry (Brandon Maggart) grows up to be a Christmas-obsessed psycho who knows who's been naughty and nice. Of all the holiday-themed horrors that have become a staple of low-budget video, this may be the cheapest looking but it has inspired moments—like Santa's speech to a group of kids telling them to be good and to obey their parents, or suffer the consequences. Producer Edward Pressman is better known for his work with Oliver Stone. ***AKA:*** Christmas Evil; You Better Watch Out.

1985 90m/C Brandon Maggart, Jeffrey DeMunn, Dianne Hull, Scott McKay, Peter Friedman, Joe Jamrog; ***D:*** Lewis Jackson; ***W:*** Lewis Jackson. **VHS**

Terror Train

A first-rate cast does fair work with imitative material. It's *Halloween on Amtrak* as someone knocks off masked partygoers on a train. Jamie Lee Curtis is our full-throated heroine. Ben Johnson is the conductor. Writer T.Y. Drake and director Roger Spottiswoode let the pace drag, even toward the end, though they are somewhat restrained with the graphic violence. Director of photography John Alcott makes the interior of the train a vivid setting with his inventive use of light and gauze filters. Fans may not be disappointed, but they won't find much they haven't seen before. ***AKA:*** Train of Terror.

1980 (R) 97m/C Jamie Lee Curtis, Ben Johnson, Hart Bochner, David Copperfield, Vanity, Howard Busgang, Michael Shanks, Amanda Tapping, Troy Kennedy Martin, Anthony Sherwood, Timothy Webber; ***D:*** Roger Spottiswoode; ***W:*** T. Y. Drake; ***C:*** John Alcott. **VHS, LV** *FOX*

Tetsuo: The Iron Man

One morning, a Japanese fellow looks in the mirror and finds an aluminum zit on his cheek. He pops it and blood spurts everywhere; then he's being chased around a subway station by a woman who's got metal goop on her forehead and hand, which she may have got by touching a second guy, and when guy number one goes back home to his girlfriend, more metallic accoutrements pop up, and unless you're into some very kinky fetishes, that's all you want to know. The rest is more comic than shocking. Yes, it's all grotesque, violent, and sexual, but it's handled as an exaggerated black-and-white silent comedy with so-so effects. Imagine a fast-paced MTV version of that alternative classic *Robot Monster,* the B-movie featuring a guy in a gorilla suit and a diving helmet, and you're close to the mark. Followed by a sequel.

1992 67m/B *JP* Tomoroh Taguchi, Kei Fujiwara, Shinya Tsukamoto; ***D:*** Shinya Tsukamoto; ***W:*** Shinya Tsukamoto. **VHS** *FXL*

The Texas Chainsaw Massacre

The purity of Tobe Hooper's low-budget psychotic vision has often been copied—by him and by others—but the inescapable, fully realized insanity of the film has never been equaled. It's an essentially plotless story of kids who wander off the main road and into a rural house full of cannibals. The story moves with the free association "logic" of a nightmare. Horror piles upon horror ignoring conventional narrative structure. It's the repetitive nature of the events that has earned the film its undimmed reputation. Decades after its debut, *TCM* is still the ultimate "meat movie." If anyone has surpassed it, I don't want to know.

1974 (R) 86m/C Marilyn Burns, Allen Danzinger, Paul A. Partain, William Vail, Teri McMinn, Edwin Neal, Jim Siedow, Gunnar Hansen, John Dugan, Jerry Lorenz; ***D:*** Tobe Hooper; ***W:*** Tobe Hooper, Ken Henkel; ***C:*** Daniel Pearl; ***M:*** Wayne Bell. **VHS, LV, Closed Caption** *MPI*

Texas Chainsaw Massacre 2

A breathless voiceover narrator claims that the Lonestar cannibals of the first film simply disappeared despite the best efforts of the cops to find them for 13 years. It turns out that the Sawyer family has been winning chili cook-offs and living under an amusement park. The intensity of the original has been replaced with outrageous

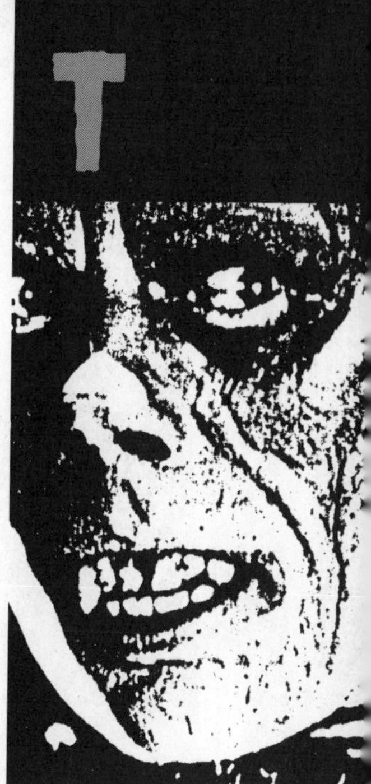

The masked killer in *Terror Train.*

stunts and jokes. Dwarfed beneath a huge cowboy hat, Dennis Hopper is a vengeance-seeking Texas Ranger. Tom Savini's bloody effects are more sophisticated than the first film's, but more is definitely not better. Followed by two more equally negligible sequels to date. **Woof!**

1986 (R) 90m/C Dennis Hopper, Caroline Williams, Bill Johnson, Jim Siedow, Bill Moseley, Lou Perry; ***D:*** Tobe Hooper; ***W:*** L.M. Kit Carson; ***C:*** Richard Kooris; ***M:*** Tobe Hooper. **VHS, LV, Closed Caption** *VTR*

The Texas Chainsaw Massacre 4: The Next Generation

Four promgoers—including Jennie (Renee Zellweger)—who are so obnoxious that they deserve anything that happens to them wander out into the boonies where they're attacked by the familiar family of maniacs led by Vilmer (Matthew McConaughey), who has a mechanical leg. The plot is essentially a slightly comic parody of the original. The production values are the highest of the four films, but so what? Curiosity value from the pre-fame presence of the two stars is all the derivative flick has to offer. ***AKA:*** Return of the Texas Chainsaw Massacre.

1995 (R) 94m/C Renee Zellweger, Matthew McConaughey, Tony Perenski, Robert Jacks, Lisa Newmyer; ***D:*** Kim Henkel; ***W:*** Kim Henkel; ***C:*** Levie Isaacks. **VHS, Closed Caption** *COL*

Theatre of Blood

In a companion piece to *The Abominable Dr. Phibes,* Vincent Price is Edward Lionheart, a hammy Shakespearian actor who takes vengeance on anyone who has written an unfavorable review of his work. With

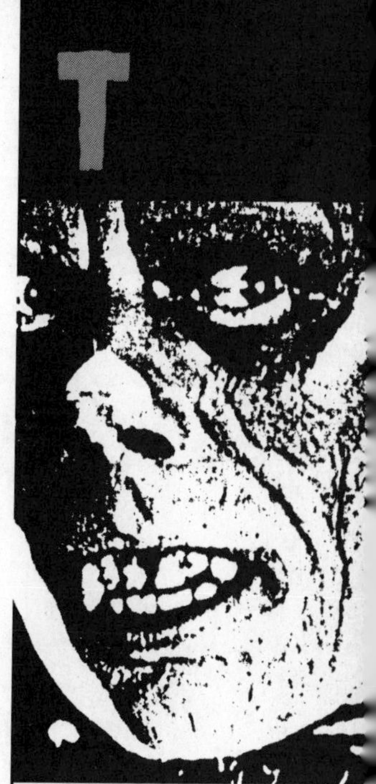

the help of a mob of crazies and his daughter Edwina (Diana Rigg), he concocts baroque schemes to get rid of London's drama critics, each murder quoting a bloody moment from the Bard. Like so many films of its time, it's also about the establishment under siege by the rabble. The wit is sharp and the whole film plays to Price's strengths as an actor. (It ends with his literally attacking the scenery.) Douglas Hickcox's energetic, swiftly paced direction keeps the theatrical aspects from ruining the film. Note Lionheart's "suicide" scene. One quibble: Diana Rigg spends far too much time in disguise. ***AKA:*** Much Ado about Murder.

1973 (R) 104m/C *GB* Vincent Price, Diana Rigg, Ian Hendry, Robert Morley, Dennis Price, Diana Dors, Milo O'Shea, Harry Andrews, Coral Browne, Robert Coote, Jack Hawkins, Michael Hordern, Arthur Lowe; ***D:*** Douglas Hickox; ***W:*** Anthony Greville-Bell; ***C:*** Wolfgang Suschitzky. **VHS, LV** *MGM*

Them!

Mutated giant ants wreak havoc on a New Mexico town in the first of the big-bug horrors. It far surpasses the rest, mostly because the formula hadn't been set in cinematic stone yet. The script contains several human touches, and the whole production benefits from neat WWII hardware—flame throwers, Tommy guns, B-24s. Throughout, the focus is more on the characters' reactions to the situation than on the critters themselves. That's fine, because these ants are not particularly convincing and the real point is audiences' fears concerning the then-new "atomic age." See how many names you can spot among the supporting cast.

1954 93m/B James Whitmore, Edmund Gwenn, Fess Parker, James Arness, Onslow Stevens, Jack Perrin, Joan Weldon, Sean McClory, Sandy Descher, Dub Taylor, William Schallert, Leonard Nimoy; ***D:*** Gordon Douglas; ***W:*** Ted Sherdeman; ***C:*** Sid Hickox. **VHS, LV** *WAR*

They Bite

Excellent low-budget horror satire works hard to make virtues of its obvious limitations. The setting is Florida and the subject, appropriately, is the making of a low-budget horror movie. While the schlockmeisters (including porn star Ron Jeremy) are creating their flick, real fish monsters and other weird guys are invading the beaches. Ichthyologist Melody Duncan (Donna Frotscher) is on the case. It's obvious that writer/director Brett Piper loves his subject matter. (True cognoscenti will catch his arcane reference to another low-budget epic, *The Boogens.*) The effects range from intentionally silly rubber suits to good model work. The acting (both professional and non-) is fine but it's the humor that makes this one so much fun for drive-in fans.

1995 (R) 96m/C Donna Frotscher, Nick Baldasare, Charlie Barnett, Ron Jeremy; ***D:*** Bret Piper; ***W:*** Bret Piper. **VHS** *MTH*

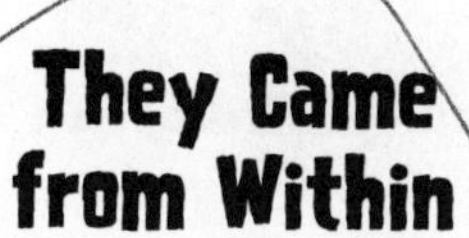

They Came from Within

In the spirit of the times, David Cronenberg's debut combines elements of *Night of the Living Dead* and *Deep Throat.* From the bizarre opening shots, Cronenberg's trademark combination of outrageous violence, medicine, and sex is right up front. The setting is a luxurious Montreal high-rise apartment where turdlike parasitic creatures infect human hosts. Though the prosthetic effects aren't as blatant as they are today, they're every bit as revolting. Visually and thematically, the film sets the tone for Cronenberg's later work, from *Rabid* to *Crash.* The aphrodisiacal horror isn't sustained all the way through, and toward the end, some of the sexual material comes across as comic. The Avalanchie edition has been digitally remastered and

THE HOUND SALUTES

TOBE HOOPER

Tobe Hooper landed on the horror scene with a big wet splat.

In 1974, he took the new permissiveness in popular entertainment to limits nobody had imagined. It's true that his work was preceded by Hershell Gordon Lewis' early '60s gore movies, but with *The Texas Chainsaw Massacre* Hooper did something different. He didn't treat the blood and guts as a joke; he placed his horror in the same world of rural American reality that George Romero's "living dead" occupied. His approach was just as simple.

As Lew Brighton wrote in *The Film Journal* (vol. 2, no. 4) "*Chainsaw* is a meat movie. It is, in fact, the *Gone with the Wind* of meat movies—a grossly colorful celebration of violence for its own sake, with no redeeming social value or enlightening message whatever. There is not even any sex to adulterate the experience."

Brighton got it right. Even though the amounts of graphic violence and gore have increased substantially, few films can match *Chainsaw* in sheer intensity. Once Hooper sets his simple plot in motion, it doesn't stop and the atmosphere of dread builds in measured increments until the last frame. Hooper, who was born in Texas in 1943, loosely based his story on Ed Gein, the Wisconsin man who was also the model for Hitchcock's *Psycho*. But Hooper turned the individual into a family of cannibals and made a second family of unlucky travellers their prey.

The film immediately became a notorious and profitable independent production, and Hooper went to Hollywood. Nothing he has made working within the studio system comes close to *Chainsaw*, though his second independent feature, *Eaten Alive*, is a strong companion piece. Of his

looks great. ***AKA:*** Shivers; The Parasite Murders. 🦴🦴🦴

1975 (R) 87m/C *CA* Paul Hampton, Joe Silver, Lynn Lowry, Barbara Steele, Susan Petrie, Allan Magicovsky; ***D:*** David Cronenberg; ***W:*** David Cronenberg; ***C:*** Robert Saad. **VHS** *LIV, VES*

They Live

Nada (Roddy Piper) is a drifter who tumbles to an alien mind-control conspiracy. Special sunglasses reveal their insidious propaganda and skeletal faces. The s-f/horror is an unsubtle criticism of conservative economic and social policies, but director John Carpenter spins things out with his usual sure touch for escapism, and wrestler Piper is a fine hero. As for the plot, it's pretty easy to accept, particularly for those who've always had their doubts about Newt Gingrich. Though the film is based on a short story by Ray Nelson, many of the film's ideas are also used in the great *Illuminatus* cult novels of Robert Shea and Robert Anton Wilson. (The clip in the film is from *The Monolith Monsters*.) 🦴🦴🦴½

1988 (R) 88m/C Roddy Piper, Keith David, Meg Foster, George Flower, Peter Jason, Raymond St. Jacques, John Lawrence, Sy Richardson, Jason Robards III, Larry Franco; ***D:*** John Carpenter; ***W:*** Frank Armitage, John Carpenter; ***M:*** Alan Howarth, John Carpenter. **VHS, LV** *USH*

studio work, the underrated *The Funhouse* isn't bad at all, and *Spontaneous Combustion* benefits from one of Brad Dourif's better performances. Certainly his most commercially successful picture is *Poltergeist,* but that looks and feels more like producer Steven Spielberg's work than Hooper's.

Both *Lifeforce* and *I'm Dangerous Tonight* are silly but energetically entertaining. Hooper's adaptation of Stephen King's short story, *The Mangler,* is a travesty.

To be fair, no filmmaker could consistently recreate the uncompromising visceral power of *Chainsaw,* and if anyone did, audiences wouldn't respond. Note the lack of response to any of the three even more distasteful sequels. Fans have ignored them and so have conservative critics.

SIGNIFICANT CONTRIBUTIONS TO HORROR

The Texas Chainsaw Massacre **(1974)**

Eaten Alive **(1976)**

The Funhouse **(1981)**

Poltergeist **(1982)**

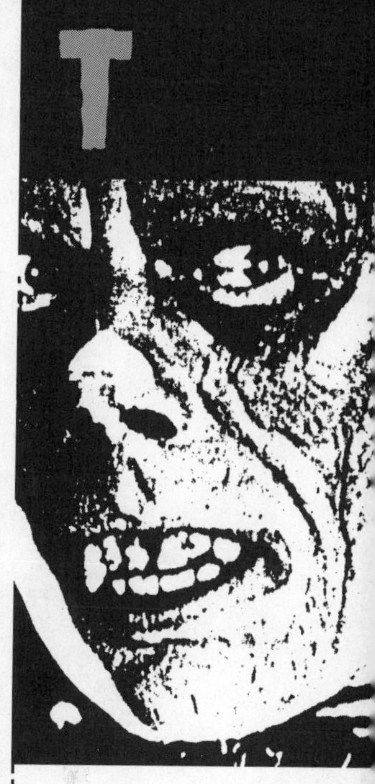

The Thing

A vampire vegetableman (James Arness) from outer space crashes his saucer into the arctic ice. Soldiers and scientists, led by Kenneth Tobey and Robert Cornthwaite, thaw him out, then do a lot of squabbling among themselves. The Killer Carrot is a giant, hungry, seed-dispersing creature run amuck, unaffected by missing body parts, bullets, or cold. Director Christian Nyby—with considerable help from producer Howard Hawks, writers Charles Lederer, and an uncredited Ben Hecht—makes this one of the most tightly constructed stories of the 1950s. Equally important is the film's atmosphere of frozen claustrophobia and isolation. In every respect, save faithfulness to John Campbell's original story "Who Goes There?," this one is superior to John Carpenter's remake. ***AKA:*** The Thing from Another World. 🦴🦴🦴🦴

1951 87m/B James Arness, Kenneth Tobey, Margaret Sheridan, Dewey Martin, Robert Cornthwaite; ***D:*** Christian Nyby, Howard Hawks; ***W:*** Charles Lederer, Ben Hecht; ***C:*** Russell Harlan; ***M:*** Dimitri Tiomkin. **VHS, LV, Letterboxed** *NO*

The Thing

Writer Bill Lancaster goes back to John Campbell's famous short story "Who Goes There?" for John Carpenter's version. It's

"It thaws out...wakes up...probably not in the best of moods."

—McCready (Kurt Russell) describes *The Thing* (1982).

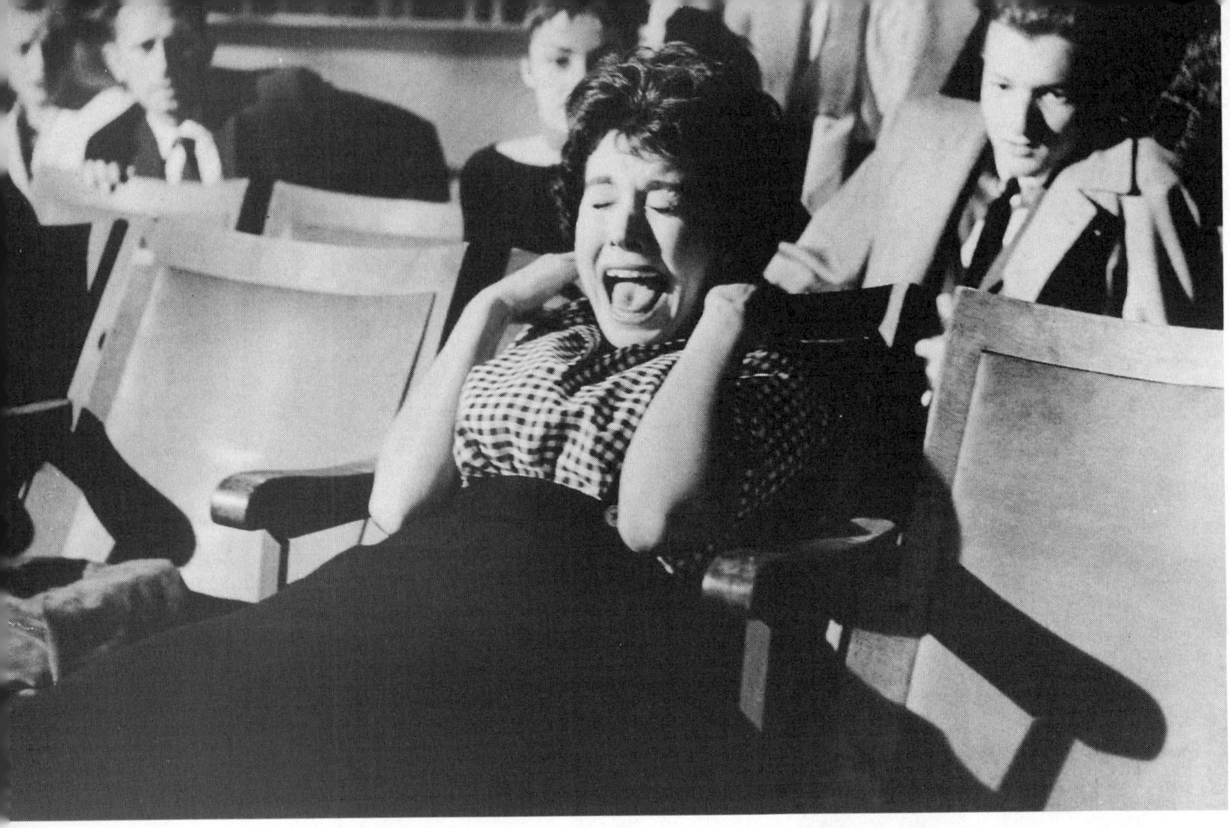

William Castle's *The Tingler.*

more graphic than the first (which is really more s-f than horror) with the premise of a shape-changing alien whose ship crashes in Antarctica. The British Columbian and Alaskan locations are convincingly cold and bleak, but the characters are generally unsympathetic, led by Kurt Russell's sombrero-topped McCready. The real point of the film is Albert Whitlock's baroque monster effects, which lose their shock value well before the film's over.

1982 (R) 109m/C Kurt Russell, Wilford Brimley, T.K. Carter, Richard Masur, Keith David, Richard Dysart, David Clennon, Donald Moffat, Thomas G. Waites, Charles Hallahan; ***D:*** John Carpenter; ***W:*** Bill Lancaster; ***C:*** Dean Cundey; ***M:*** Ennio Morricone. **VHS, LV** *USH*

The Thirsty Dead

Silly Philippine vampire tale is really a campy, kitschy rip-off of *She* made on a shoestring. Jennifer Billingsley and three pals are kidnapped and taken to a jungle Shangri-La ruled by a priestess who dances a slow-motion hokey-pokey and worships Ra-Oom, a head in a red plastic cube. He thinks Jennifer is the reincarnated goddess, yadda yadda yadda. For a Philippine production, this one's awfully tame. ***AKA:*** The Blood Cult of Shangri-La; Blood Hunt.

1974 (PG) 90m/C *PH* John Considine, Jennifer Billingsley, Judith McConnell, Fredricka Meyers, Tani Phelps Guthrie; ***D:*** Terry Becker. **VHS** *NO*

301, 302

The woman in apartment 301 (Eun-Jin Bang) is a recently divorced chef. The woman across the hall in 302 (Sin-Hye Hwang) is a shy, self-loathing, bulimic writer. In the opening scenes, we learn that 302 has disappeared. 301's flashbacks slowly reveal their relationship from the day she moved into the building. Writer Suh-Goon Lee and director Chul-Soo Park set much of the story

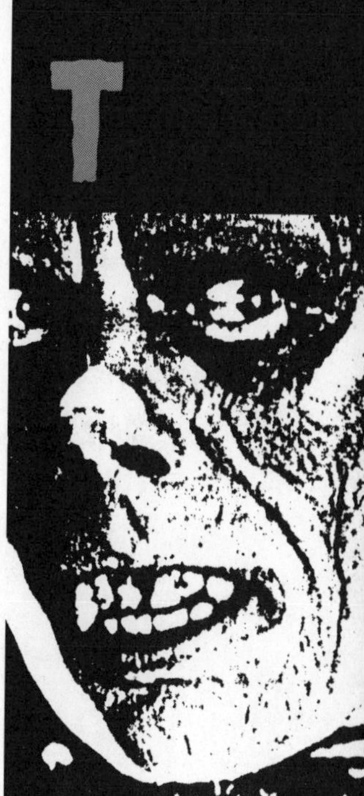

within the apartment building and the other homes that have made the two women who and what they are. The most obvious influence is Polanski's *Repulsion,* but you can also see hints of *Heavenly Creatures, An Untold Story,* and other more recent works. If some of the revelations are trite, others are shocking, and the film's humor is sharply edged and hard to define. The story is beautifully constructed with rare intelligence. An award winner in Korea and at several festivals.

1994 99m/C *KO* Eun-Jin Bang, Sin-Hye Hwang, Chu-Ryun Kim; ***D:*** Chul-Soo Park; ***W:*** Suh-Goon Lee. **VHS** *EVE*

Thrill of the Vampire

Of all the tacky '60s exploitation horror flicks, this is probably the tackiest and most exploitative. Though the synopsis—honeymooners (Sandra Julien and Jean Durand) stop by a castle to visit her cousins and are seduced by hippie vampires (Michel Delahaye, Jacques Robiolles, and Dominique, who's the spitting image of Olive Oyl)—sounds like *Daughters of Darkness,* the films could not be more different. In an introduction, director Jean Rollin admits that he was making a parody, something "between a comedy and a vampire film." His combination of the mundane and the surreal might have served as an example for TV perfume commercials of the 1990s. The soundtrack contains some of the worst garage rock ever recorded. ***AKA:*** Le Frisson des Vampires; Sex and the Vampire; The Terror of the Vampires; Vampire Thrills.

1970 ?m/C Michel Delahaye, Dominique, Jean Durand, Sandra Julien, Nicole Nancel, Jacques Robiolles, Kuelan Herce, Marie-Pierre Tricot; ***D:*** Jean Rollin; ***W:*** Jean Rollin. **VHS** *VSM*

Time Walker

A mummy wanders about a southern California college campus (apparently being pulled on a skateboard that's kept just below the frame of the camera) and does a *Halloween* number on unsuspecting undergraduates. Why? Because his crystals have been stolen, of course. The violence isn't graphic enough to be distracting and the whole thing is so earnest in its ineptitude that nobody could take it seriously. For *Plan 9* laughs, it's fun, but nothing more.

1982 (PG) 86m/C Ben Murphy, Nina Axelrod, Kevin Brophy, James Karen, Austin Stoker; ***D:*** Tom Kennedy; ***W:*** Tom Friedman, Karen Levitt; ***M:*** Richard Band. **VHS** *NLC*

The Tingler

Producer/director William Castle's onscreen introductory warning about the "tingling sensation" that some viewers may experience refers to the famous gimmick he'd planned for the film's theatrical release. Some theatre seats were to be wired to give audience members a mild shock in key scenes. The Tingler is an insect-like creature created in the spine by "the force of fear." It's all as hokey and silly as it sounds. Vincent Price's conversational, understated performance as a curious coroner with a faithless frau (Pamela Lincoln) is one of his best. Beyond the loopy horror aspects, which are a ton of fun, the film's subtext of male-female sexual and economic competition in the 1950s is fascinating.

1959 82m/B Vincent Price, Darryl Hickman, Judith Evelyn, Philip Coolidge, Patricia Cutts, Pamela Lincoln; ***D:*** William Castle; ***W:*** Robb White; ***C:*** Wilfred M. Kline. **VHS** *COL*

To Die For

What might have been just another tale of a vampire in contemporary L.A. is elevated by solid production values, good acting, and relatively restrained effects. What really sets this one apart, though, is the feminine point of view. Leslie King's script

"They're the Blind Dead, but that will be no handicap, for they can still *hear* their victims."

—Ad line from *Tombs of the Blind Dead.*

could have been called *Designing Women Meet Dracula.* Realtor Kate Wooten (Sydney Walsh) runs into Vlad (Brendan Hughes) at a party and is immediately smitten. He's one of those dark, passionate, Byronic vampires who could have come straight from the cover of a paperback bodice-ripper. Most of the rest is familiar good vampire vs. bad vampire stuff. Followed by a sequel. (Not to be confused with the 1995 Nicole Kidman comic mystery.) ***AKA:*** Dracula: The Love Story. 🦴🦴🦴

1989 (R) 99m/C Brendan Hughes, Scott Jacoby, Duane Jones, Steve Bond, Sydney Walsh, Amanda Wyss, Ava Fabian; ***D:*** Deran Sarafian; ***W:*** Leslie King; ***C:*** Jacques Haitkin; ***M:*** Cliff Eidelman. **VHS, LV** *NO*

To Die For 2: Son of Darkness

In the first film, a pretty L.A. realtor fell in love with a "good" Byronic vampire and ran afoul of his "bad" brother. In *2,* the situation remains the same but the location has moved to the rural Lake Serenity. When Nina's (Rosalind Allen) adopted baby becomes mysteriously ill, she takes him to Dr. Max Schreck (Max Praed). He "cures" the boy by increasing his red cell count. Soon, she's visiting Max's estate for dinner and whatever while Max's evil, cigar-smoking brother Tom (Steve Bond) and Celia (Amanda Wyss) are terrorizing the local population. The sheriff (Vince Edwards) blames coyote attacks. The sensual and romantic aspects of the story can be traced to Anne Rice's vampire novels, and the names recall *Nosferatu.* The humor, acting, stunt work, and special effects are first rate. In the end, this one's much more enjoyable than most theatrical sequels. ***AKA:*** Son of Darkness: To Die For 2. 🦴🦴🦴

1991 (R) 95m/C Rosalind Allen, Steve Bond, Scott Jacoby, Michael Praed, Jay Underwood, Amanda Wyss, Remy O'Neill, Vince Edwards; ***D:*** David F. Price. **VHS, Closed Caption** *THV*

To Sleep with a Vampire

Intelligent two-character vampire story is a remake of *Dance of the Damned.* The protagonists are a sensitive, nameless vampire (Scott Valentine) and Nina (Charlie Spradling), a suicidal stripper. She desperately wants to see her estranged young son before she ends her life; he wants to know what the sun feels like. In Patricia Harrington's script (based on the original by Katt Shea and Andy Ruben), they come to an understanding. Director Adam Friedman makes the most of limited special effects (including switchblade fingernails) and he gets moving performances from his leads. Though they sound like cliches, these two become sympathetic, fully believable characters before it's over. Recommended. 🦴🦴🦴🦴

1992 (R) 90m/C Scott Valentine, Charlie Spradling, Richard Zobel, Ingrid Vold, Stephanie Hardy; ***D:*** Adam Friedman; ***W:*** Patricia Harrington. **VHS** *NHO*

To the Devil, a Daughter

In the opening scene, Father Michael (Christopher Lee) questions his faith, perhaps even actively renouncing it. Twenty years later, he leads a young nun, Catherine (Nastassia Kinski) out of a convent and into some form of vague danger. That uncertainty is the point. The other key player is John Verney (Richard Widmark), an occult writer. Chris Wicking's script—based on a Dennis Wheatley novel—avoids cliches and, at the risk of confusing the viewer, creates real suspense. The presence of a veteran ensemble cast (including Honor Blackman and Denholm Elliott) not normally associated with horror adds to that quality. Comparisons to *The Devil's Bride* and *The Exorcist* are not out of place. Though the tape is advertised as exploitation, it's really more serious and more entertaining. ***AKA:*** Child of Satan.

1976 (R) 93m/C Richard Widmark, Christopher Lee, Nastassia Kinski, Honor Blackman, Denholm Elliott, Michael Goodliffe; ***D:*** Peter Sykes; ***W:*** Christopher Wicking; ***C:*** David Watkin. **VHS** *REP, MLB*

Todd McFarlane's Spawn

The influences of Japanese "anime" is obvious in artistic style, subject matter, and its treatment. The graphic violence isn't really justified by the lightweight story. Despite creator Todd McFarlane's claims of a serious purpose, the story of Al Simmons, a reincarnated black spy who becomes a reluctant warrior for Hell is standard adolescent comic book stuff. That's the way this feature, taken from the HBO animated series, treats it, too. ***AKA:*** Spawn.

1997 147m/C ***D:*** Eric Rademski; ***W:*** Alan B. McElroy, Gary Hardwick; ***V:*** Keith David, Richard Dysart, Ronny Cox. **VHS** *HBO*

Tomb

Prolific exploitation auteur Fred Olen Ray's second feature revived a fledgling company in the early days of home video. This low-budget effort is an unlikely savior. It starts off with an action sequence (featuring Sybil Danning, who makes an early exit) then takes a brief pass at an Indiana Jones-style adventure before the Egyptian vampire princess Nefratis (Michelle Bauer) shows up. She hops a jet to L.A. to go after the airhead who opened her sarcophagus and the guys he sold her stuff to. You know the drill. What the film lacks in coherence and suspense (and it lacks a lot), it tries to make up for with mindless energy in a few funny scenes. Mostly, it's silly and slow.

1986 106m/C Cameron Mitchell, John Carradine, Sybil Danning, Richard Hench, Michelle (McClellan) Bauer, Susan Stokey, David Pearson, Francesca "Kitten" Natividad; ***D:*** Fred Olen Ray; ***C:*** Paul Elliott. **VHS** *TWE*

Tombs of the Blind Dead

Armando de Ossorio's first use of the resurrected Knights Templar is one of the most influential horrors of the early 1970s. Though the film is clumsily plotted, it sets the stage for several sequels and the more general trend, particularly in European films, of mixing sex (exploitative and otherwise) and graphic horror. De Ossorio's Templars are 13th century Portugese knights who torture young women and drink their blood to gain immortality. They're executed and blinded by crows that peck out their eyes, but rise up out of their graves centuries later whenever young women are nearby. Though they cannot see, they locate their victims by sound and, like American "living dead," eat them. (Later films would correct the illogical nature of the Templars' condition by changing the backstory to have them blinded before they're executed.) Questions of sexual politics aside (and the film does raise many issues in that area), the Templars are memorable, nightmarish figures. Followed by *Return of the Blind Dead, Horror of the Zombies,* and *Night of the Seagulls* (not available on video). The remastered Anchor Bay Entertainment tapes of *Tombs* and *Return* are incredibly sharp and clear. ***AKA:*** The Blind Dead; La Noche dell Terror Ciego; La Noche de la Muerta Ciega; Crypt of the Blind Dead; Night of the Blind Dead.

1972 (PG) 102m/C *SP PT* Caesar Burner, Lone Fleming, Helen Harp, Joseph Thelman, Rufino Ingles, Maria Silva; ***D:*** Armando de Ossorio; ***W:*** Armando de Ossorio; ***C:*** Pablo Ripoll. **VHS** *VTR*

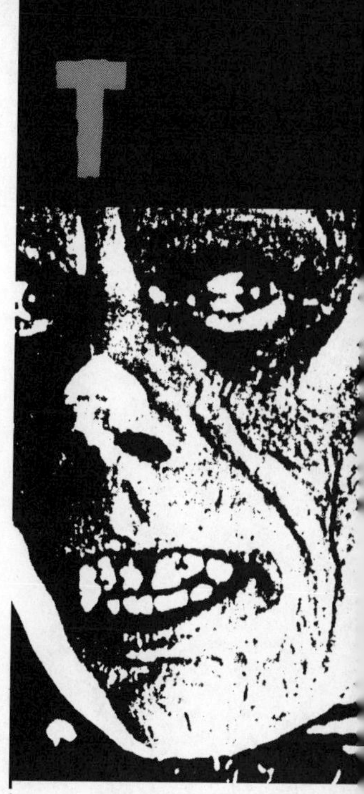

Holmes Herbert, Leo G. Carroll, Barbara O'Neil, and Nan Grey in *The Tower of London* (1939).

Torture Chamber of Baron Blood

Peter Kleist (Antonia Cantafora), a young American, goes to Austria to discover his family roots. He's the ancestor of a particularly vicious Baron and ignorantly resurrects the guy. Most of the action is set in a castle where director Mario Bava makes full use of the towers, dungeons, and secret passageways. The film has a strange and more ominous atmosphere than Bava's previous effort, *Lisa and the Devil.* He also revisits some of the images he first used in *Black Sunday.* The highpoint is a long strikingly lit night chase scene. In the big torture sequence at the end, the participants are less than completely persuasive. ***AKA:*** Baron Blood; Gli Orrori del Castello di Norimberga; The Blood Baron; Chamber of Tortures; The Thirst of Baron Blood.

1972 (PG) 90m/C *IT* Joseph Cotten, Elke Sommer, Massimo Girotti, Rada Rassimov, Antonio Cantafora; ***D:*** Mario Bava; ***W:*** Vincent Fotre, William Bairn; ***M:*** Les Baxter. **VHS** *VTR*

Tourist Trap

Solid little B-picture makes the most of its budget and tells a scary yarn solidly in the *Psycho/Halloween/Texas Chainsaw Massacre* tradition. A group of kids searching for their missing friend are stranded at the remote Slausen's Desert Oasis motel. Slausen (Chuck Connors) is an affable sort who helps them with their car trouble, but tells them to stay away from the house down the hill where "Davey" lives. You know what they're going to do, but so what? Director David Schmoeller frightens you when he means to and that's enough. Good ending, too.

1979 (PG) 90m/C Tanya Roberts, Chuck Connors, Robin Sherwood, Jocelyn Jones, Jon Van Ness, Dawn Jeffory,

Keith McDermott; ***D:*** David Schmoeller; ***W:*** David Schmoeller; ***M:*** Pino Donaggio. **VHS, LV, Closed Caption** *PAR*

The Tower of London

If the VideoHound were rigidly literal, this one might not be included. It's really more costume drama than horror, but the cast and the studio (Universal) have such strong ties to the genre that strict definitions count for little. Basil Rathbone is the sly, treacherous hunchback Richard III. As the bald, club-footed executioner Mord, an ominous Boris Karloff looks like Michael Berryman's grandfather. (His role is far too small.) A young Vincent Price makes his debut in support; he stars in Roger Corman's 1962 remake.

1939 93m/B Basil Rathbone, Boris Karloff, Barbara O'Neil, Ian Hunter, Vincent Price, Nan Grey, John Sutton, Leo G. Carroll, Holmes Herbert, Miles Mander; ***D:*** Rowland V. Lee; ***W:*** Robert N. Lee; ***C:*** George Robinson. **VHS** *USH*

Tower of London

At first, this is more historical drama than horror, but it becomes a comfortable companion piece to the Poe adaptations made by director Roger Corman and star Vincent Price, who's at his villainous best as the mad hunchbacked Richard III. Writers Leo V. Gordon, Amos Powell, and James B. Gordon borrow many ideas and scenes from *Macbeth*. As he'd do so many other times, Corman uses a few good sets and costumes to make a low-budget effort look much more expensive. The action vacillates between stodgy portentous speeches and more lively scenes of gleeful torture, murder, and ghosts created by guilt. It's a remake of a 1939 Basil Rathbone film, not really horror, in which Price had a smaller role.

1962 79m/B Vincent Price, Michael Pate, Joan Freeman, Robert Brown, Sandra Knight, Justice Watson; ***D:*** Roger Corman; ***W:*** Leo Gordon, F. Amos Powell, James B. Gordon; ***C:*** Arch R. Dalzell. **VHS** *MGM, FCT*

Town that Dreaded Sundown

Early serial killer story is supposedly based on truth and is told as a documentary with lots of local (Texas, Arkansas) color and non-professionals as extras. In Texarkana, 1946, a masked man is attacking couples in lovers lane. Top Texas Ranger Ben Johnson is brought in to head up the task force. The attacks are presented mostly with grim, grainy naturalism. Set at night, they're hard to make out. Director Charles B. Pierce depends more on sound and atmosphere than visuals. Considerable cornball redneck humor doesn't help much. Careful viewers will see a cameraman in the train sequence.

1976 (R) 90m/C Ben Johnson, Andrew Prine, Dawn Wells, Jimmy Clem, Charles B. Pierce; ***D:*** Charles B. Pierce; ***W:*** Earl E. Smith; ***C:*** Jim Roberson. **VHS** *WAR, OM*

The Toxic Avenger

Troma's alternative superhero is a *Mad* magazine/Three Stooges sort of horror comedy. Melvin is a weakling who's dumped into an open vat of toxic waste and emerges as "Toxie," the monstrous Avenger, a rough cross between Arnold Schwarzenegger and Mr. PotatoHead, who fights injustice wherever he finds it. That includes bad guys (and bad girls) who like to go out and drive drunk and run down kids on bikes. We're not talking subtlety here. And if you think those guys are bad, wait till you see what Toxie does to the thieves who try to rob Tromaville's finest Mexican restaurant. Followed by sequels and a TV cartoon series. Toxie has become so popular that he's now the unofficial Troma spokesman.

1986 (R) 90m/C Mitchell Cohen, Andree Maranda, Jennifer Baptist, Robert Prichard, Cindy Manion; ***D:*** Michael Herz, Lloyd (Samuel Weil) Kaufman; ***W:*** Joe Ritter. **VHS, LV, DVD** *TRO, TTV*

"We called him Mother Superior on account of the length of his habit."

—Renton (Ewan McGregor) in *Trainspotting.*

The Toxic Avenger, Part 2

Tromaville's favorite superhero goes off to Japan to find his long-lost father while an evil corporation tries to turn his town into a nuclear waste dump and to strip Toxie of his Tromatic superpowers. It's vintage Troma—cheap, violent, funny, gross, and unashamed. Accordion-playing celebrity Phoebe Legere fits in comfortably as Toxie's blind girlfriend. Any movie that makes jokes about tattooed black midget bodybuilders can't be all bad. Followed by a third. (By the way, on the DVD version, commentary is provided by Yours Truly.)

1989 (R) 90m/C Ron Fazio, Phoebe Legere, Rick Collins, John Altamura; ***D:*** Michael Herz, Lloyd (Samuel Weil) Kaufman; ***W:*** Lloyd (Samuel Weil) Kaufman, Gay Partington Terry. **VHS, LV, Closed Caption, DVD** *TTV, TRO*

The Toxic Avenger, Part 3: The Last Temptation of Toxie

The fiendish boss (Rick Collins) of Apocalypse Inc. is still trying to take over Tromaville, and Toxie is still trying to get new eyes for his blind girlfriend (Phoebe Legere). But, if she can see, what will she think of New Jersey's only superhero, misshapen as he is? "The plot was thickening," Toxie says, "and I was to be the cornstarch!" Heads are torn off; guts are ripped out—all in the inimitable Troma fashion.

1989 (R) 102m/C Ron Fazio, Phoebe Legere, John Altamura, Rick Collins, Lisa Gaye, Jessica Dublin; ***D:*** Michael Herz, Lloyd (Samuel Weil) Kaufman; ***W:*** Lloyd (Samuel Weil) Kaufman, Gay Partington Terry. **VHS** *TTV, TRO*

Trainspotting

Director Danny Boyle's grim comedy is a horror film about heroin. Boyle uses his considerable skills to translate the sensations of drug use into visual terms, at one point even going inside a hypodermic needle. The surreal world of addiction that he creates is much more vivid than the weirdness of his first film, *Shallow Grave.* A few months in the fractured lives of Renton (Ewan McGregor) and his junkie friends are revealed in a series of episodic vignettes and scenes that coalesce into a single plotline toward the end. The humorous moments deal mostly with repulsive bodily functions and they are bizarre beyond description. But John Hodge's script can turn tragic in a second, and it does so with dreadful, terrifying power. Whatever else it may be—social commentary, surrealism, character study—this is one of the most frightening films of the 1990s.

1995 (R) 94m/C *GB* Ewan McGregor, Ewen Bremmer, Jonny Lee Miller, Robert Carlyle, Kevin McKidd, Kelly Macdonald, Shirley Henderson, Pauline Lynch; ***D:*** Danny Boyle; ***W:*** John Hodge; ***C:*** Brian Tufano. British Academy Awards '95: Best Adapted Screenplay; Nominations: Academy Awards '96: Best Adapted Screenplay; Australian Film Institute '96: Best Foreign Film; British Academy Awards '95: Best Film; Independent Spirit Awards '97: Best Foreign Film; MTV Movie Awards '97: Breakthrough Performance (McGregor); Writers Guild of America '96: Best Adapted Screenplay. **VHS, LV, Closed Caption** *TOU*

Transformations

Bargain basement knock-off of *Alien3* is poorly written, slow, and badly acted. Space pilot John Wolf (Rex Smith) crashes on the penal mining colony of Hephaestous IV after a snot-covered monster transforms itself into a naked babe and gives him a really bad rash. Patrick Macnee is a priest who thinks that unspeakable apocalyptic evil is loose on the planet. Actually the most frightening things are the ticky-tacky sets. **Woof!**

1988 (R) 84m/C Rex Smith, Patrick Macnee, Lisa Langlois, Christopher Neame; ***D:*** Jay Kamen; ***W:*** Mitch Brian. **VHS, LV** *VTR*

Transmutations

Genre-bender begins well with lots of action setting up the conflict virtually without dialogue. Based on a Clive Barker story, the film mixes detection and horror fairly well, but the ending is a letdown. A solid cast of character actors does good work. The special effects are relatively restrained because the aim is a certain thoughtfulness. The result is similar to *Hellraiser* in some ways, though not as impressive. ***AKA:*** Underworld.

1985 (R) 103m/C *GB* Denholm Elliott, Steven Berkoff, Miranda Richardson, Nicola Cowper, Larry Lamb, Art Malik, Ingrid Pitt, Irina Brook, Paul Brown; ***D:*** George Pavlou; ***W:*** Clive Barker, James Caplin; ***C:*** Syd Macartney. **VHS, LV** *LIV*

Tremors

Universal has always been known for its horror films, and this updated version of such grand '50s big-creature features as *Them* and *The Beast from 20,000 Fathoms* is one of the studio's better recent efforts. It's told with excellent production values—even on the small screen, the picture is remarkably crisp—a solid ensemble cast (Kevin Bacon, Fred Ward, Michael Gross, singer Reba McEntire), no-nonsense direction, and a script that manages to combine laughs and scares in the right ratio. The plot revolves around a race of carnivorous super-worms who live underground and surface in the desert town of Perfection, Nevada, where they decide to have lunch. Given that premise, you might expect the effects to be on the humorous side, but they're actually quite good. The film has developed a strong following on video. The sequel's not bad either.

1989 (PG-13) 96m/C Kevin Bacon, Fred Ward, Finn Carter, Michael Gross, Reba McEntire, Bibi Besch, Bobby Jacoby, Charlotte Stewart, Victor Wong, Tony Genaros, Ariana Richards; ***D:*** Ron Underwood; ***W:*** S.S. Wilson, Brent Maddock; ***C:*** Alexander Grusynski; ***M:*** Ernest Troost. **VHS, LV, Closed Caption** *USH*

Tremors 2: Aftershocks

Above-average sequel recreates the original's sense of humor and builds on the inventive special effects that were so much fun before. Fred Ward and Michael Gross reprise their roles as cowboy and survivalist. Writer/director S.S. Wilson co-wrote the first film, so this one retains its offbeat sensibility. Monster earthworms, called "Graboids," have returned to the oilfields of Chiapis, Mexico. Since Earl Bassett (Ward) has frittered away the wealth and fame that came from his earlier triumph over the monsters, he accepts an offer from the Mexican government to hunt down this infestation. Off he goes with new sidekick Grady (Christopher Gartin). Not surprisingly, this one isn't as lively or as explosive as the first film—sequels almost never are—but it's still enjoyable because the characters are treated seriously, and the violence isn't excessive. Fine fare for younger horror fans.

1996 (PG-13) 100m/C Fred Ward, Michael Gross, Helen Shaver, Christopher Gartin, Marcelo Tubert; ***D:*** S.S. Wilson; ***W:*** S.S. Wilson, Brent Maddock. **VHS, LV, Closed Caption** *USH*

Trick or Treat

In this low-budget *Carrie*, geekish Eddie (Marc Price) finds refuge from the torment of his classmates in head-banger heavy metal, and so he's distraught when his hero Sammi Curr (Tony Fields) is killed in a motel fire and won't be biting off the heads of any more live snakes. When Eddie electronically resurrects Curr, he gets revenge. Rhet Topham's script neither condemns nor blindly accepts the music business, and director Charlie Martin Smith (Terry the Toad in *American Graffiti*) gets fine work from a young cast, and he makes good use of some surprising effects. Definitely a sleeper.

THE HOUND SALUTES

RICHARD MATHESON

His range is astonishing.

Think of it: The same man wrote *The Incredible Shrinking Man* in 1957 and *Duel* in 1971, and between those, he also created *Kolchak: The Night Stalker* and the Zuni Fetish Doll from *Trilogy of Terror.* The horror film wouldn't be what it is today without the many contributions of Richard Matheson.

He was born in 1926 in Allendale, New Jersey. He was wounded in action during World War II, and after it studied journalism at the University of Missouri. The laconic, understated emotions of non-fiction can be found in much of his best screenwriting. Matheson got his start with short fiction. Two of his early novels, *I Am Legend,* from 1954, and *The Shrinking Man,* from 1956, have been filmed, though Matheson was so dissatisfied with the first version of *Legend,* entitled *The Last Man on Earth,* that he had his name removed from the credits. It was more successfully remade as *The Omega Man* with Charlton Heston.

He also contributed many episodes to television's *Twilight Zone,* perhaps most memorably with the unforgettable *Nightmare at 20,000 Feet* and *The Invaders,* where Agnes Moorhead fights off tiny spacemen. He's also worked with producer/director Dan Curtis, of *Dark Shadows* fame, on several other projects for the small screen.

During the 1960s, much of Matheson's work was done with Roger Corman's adaptations of Edgar Allan Poe stories. Despite Poe's reputation as a master of the macabre, very few of his terrors are external, and so in turning psychological horror into screen horror, Matheson wandered far from the texts of *The Fall of the House of Usher* and *The Raven.* With the livelier *The Pit and the Pendulum,* he was able to build a plot that arrives at something like the scene Poe envisioned, and it may well be the finest screen moment for both Poe and Corman.

1986 (R) 97m/C Tony Fields, Marc Price, Ozzy Osbourne, Gene Simmons, Elaine Joyce, Glenn Morgan, Lisa Orgolini, Doug Savant; ***D:*** Charles Martin Smith; ***W:*** Joel Soisson, Michael S. Murphy, Rhet Topham; ***C:*** Robert Elswit. **VHS, Closed Caption** *ORI, WAR*

Trick or Treats

A pudgy brat (Chris Graver, son of director Gary) torments his babysitter (Jackie Giroux) on Halloween night, while his nutty father Malcolm (Peter Jason) escapes from a mental institution. (The execution is even more idiotic than the synopsis.) The intentional humor isn't even remotely funny. For a cinematographer with a good reputation (he's worked with Orson Welles), director Gary Graver can't use light very well. The whole film is muddy and dim. Worse, it's boring. Welles is credited as "Magical Advisor." **Woof!**

1982 (R) 90m/C Carrie Snodgress, David Carradine, Jackie Giroux, Steve Railsback, Chris Graver, Peter Jason, Jillian Kesner, Paul Bartel; ***D:*** Gary Graver. **VHS** *LIV, VES*

Trilogy of Terror

Anyone who's wondered about the source of the band name "The Voluptuous Horror of Karen Black" hasn't seen this video masterpiece. She stars in three Richard Mathe-

Around the same time, several of his screenplays were produced in England. The best of those are *Burn Witch, Burn,* and *The Devil's Bride* (AKA *The Devil Rides Out*), two early examples of witchcraft stories that reject the convenient stereotypes, and *Die! Die! My Darling!*

In many ways though, the Poe adaptations are out of character for Matheson. He's one of the first post-war writers, who took horror out of crypts and graveyards and put it in apartments and kitchens. Matheson has said that the central theme in all of his work is "The individual isolated in a threatening world, attempting to survive." He is able to make the ordinary very threatening, indeed.

Perhaps the finest example of that side of his work is *Duel,* the over-achieving made-for-TV Steven Spielberg film.

SIGNIFICANT CONTRIBUTIONS TO HORROR

The Incredible Shrinking Man **(1957)**

The Fall of the House of Usher **(1960)**

The Pit and the Pendulum **(1961)**

Burn Witch, Burn! **(1962)**

Duel **(1971)**

Trilogy of Terror **(1975)**

The Night Stalker **(1971)**

Trilogy of Terror 2 **(1996)**

son stories directed by Dan Curtis of *Dark Shadows* fame. "Julie" is a nice reversal on an adolescent male fantasy. "Millicent and Therese" is a transparent sisters story. "Amelia" brings Matheson's famous Zuni Fetish Doll from the story "Prey" to the screen. It's simply one of the scariest mini-monster yarns ever written and this adaptation is terrific. It's perfectly constructed with a final image that comes straight from a nightmare. Followed by an above average sequel. 🦴🦴🦴

1975 78m/C Karen Black, Robert Burton, John Karlen, Gregory Harrison, George Gaynes, James Storm, Kathryn Reynolds, Tracy Curtis; ***D:*** Dan Curtis; ***W:*** Richard Matheson. **VHS** *NO*

Trilogy of Terror 2

The three video campfire tales in this collection are told by old pros who know exactly what they're doing. The title says it all with "Graveyard Rats." "Bobby" is a neat variation on "The Monkey's Paw," and "He Who Kills" is a sequel to Richard Matheson's modern classic story "Prey" about a murderous Zuni Fetish Doll. Lysette Anthony is a spirited protagonist in all three. Dan Curtis, creator of the original *Dark Shadows,* directs with the same appreciation for the material. Forget the self-consciousness of *Scream.* These are unashamedly old-fashioned stories

> **"Lon Chaney and Boris Karloff didn't like the word 'horror.' They, like I, went for the French description: 'the theatre of the *fantastique*.'"**
>
> —Christopher Lee as quoted in the *Daily Mail*, August 25, 1976.

meant to frighten. Turn out the lights and enjoy. 🦴🦴🦴

1996 (R) 90m/C Lysette Anthony, Richard Fitzpatrick, Geraint Wyn Davies, Matt Clark, Geoffrey Lewis, Blake Heron; ***D:*** Dan Curtis; ***W:*** Dan Curtis, William F. Nolan, Richard Matheson; ***M:*** Robert Cobert. **VHS, Closed Caption** *PAR*

Troll

Italian-American production isn't completely successful, but it has its moments. When a troll sets out to take over an apartment building, only young Harry (Noah Hathaway) realizes it. Eunice St. Clair (played at various times by June Lockhart and her daughter Anne) seems to know what's going on. The other key character is a dwarf named Mallory (Phil Fondacaro). When they're at the center of the action, Ed Naha's script is as good as it's trying to be. At other times, though, director John Buechler's elaborate troll creatures and makeup effects are transparent camera tricks. You can almost see the wires. Overall, though, the good outweighs the bad. 🦴🦴½

1986 (PG-13) 86m/C Noah Hathaway, Gary Sandy, Anne Lockhart, Sonny Bono, Shelley Hack, June Lockhart, Michael Moriarty, Jennifer Beck, Phil Fondacaro, Brad Hall, Julia Louis-Dreyfus; ***D:*** John Carl Buechler; ***W:*** Ed Naha; ***C:*** Romano Albani; ***M:*** Richard Band. **VHS, LV** *LIV, VES*

Tromeo & Juliet

The studio that brought us the Toxic Avenger now turns the Bard's tragic romance into a gross horror satire that's told with unbelievably poor taste. Any moviegoer who can't find something to be offended by really isn't trying. Excessive body piercing, child abuse, monstrous transformations, sexual proclivities of every stripe—all of them are part of the story of Tromeo Que (Will Keenan) and Juliet Capulet (Jane Jensen). They're a couple of New York teens whose fathers hate each other. Why? It all has to do with a film studio scam and other betrayals hidden deep in the past. As for the rest of the plot, it's about as faithful to the Bard as it needs to be, but that's not the point with Troma. Writer/director Lloyd Kaufman (also the studio boss) is trying to be funny and provocative. It's a telling comment on our time that it takes a close-up nipple-piercing to shock today's audiences. I, for one, was truly Tromatized. By the way, be sure to watch the closing credits. That's where some of the best jokes are. 🦴🦴🦴½

1995 (R) 95m/C Will Keenan, Jane Jensen, Debbie Rochon, Lemmy; ***D:*** Lloyd (Samuel Weil) Kaufman; ***W:*** James Gunn; ***C:*** Brendan Flynt. **VHS, DVD** *TTV*

Twilight People

"You are to participate in the single most important scientific event in the history of life on this planet!" the mad Nazi scientist pretentiously declaims. Yeah, right. This forgettable Philippine quickie about people surgically turned into animals is really a mix of *The Island of Dr. Moreau, The Most Dangerous Game,* and *Freaks*. Makeup and effects are jokes. Pam Grier is wasted in an early role as the Cat Woman. ***AKA:*** Beasts. **Woof!**

1972 (PG) 84m/C *PH* John Ashley, Pat Woodell, Jan Merlin, Pam Grier, Eddie Garcia; ***D:*** Eddie Romero. **VHS** *VCI*

Twins of Evil

Hammer adds two interesting new wrinkles to the vampire story with this late entry. First, having a misogynist Puritan witch hunter, Gustav Weil (Peter Cushing), in opposition to the Countess Mircalla (Katya Wyeth) and Count Karnstein (Damien Thomas), places the viewer on uncertain ground. Whose side are you on? Second, casting Madeleine and Mary Collinson (twin *Playboy* models of limited acting abilities) as the heroines is less edifying. Writer Tudor Gates and director John

Hough create a few memorable scenes, but the exploitation elements are so strong that they unbalance the film, and many of the conventions of the genre are treated with casual, almost comic lightness. In the third act, the generational and political conflicts of the early '70s take center stage. ***AKA:*** The Gemini Twins; Twins of Dracula; The Virgin Vampires. 🦴🦴🦴

1971 86m/C *GB* Madeleine Collinson, Mary Collinson, Peter Cushing, Kathleen Byron, Dennis Price, Damien Thomas, David Warbeck, Katya Wyeth, Maggie Wright, Luan Peters, Kristen Lindholm, Judy Matheson; ***D:*** John Hough; ***W:*** Tudor Gates. **VHS** *MLB*

Two Evil Eyes

Two of horror's best—George Romero and Dario Argento—take inventive approaches to Poe stories with the advantage of fine casts and production values. Adrienne Barbeau and her lover (Ramy Zada) loot her rich dying husband's bank accounts in "The Facts in the Case of Mr. Valdemar." Romero treats the story as an exercise in Hitchcockian suspense with some terrific visual shocks at the end. In "The Black Cat," Dario Argento transforms Poe's tale of retribution into a nightmare. Tequila-swilling photographer Harvey Keitel has a fondness—or is it an obsession?—with gory crime scenes. He also has a poor relationship with his weird lover Annabelle's (Madeleine Potter) cat. It becomes a blood-stained slice of Grand Guignol grotesquery with Keitel giving another full bore performance. The two films share intense claustrophobia and crazed endings. ***AKA:*** Due Occhi Diabolici. 🦴🦴🦴

1990 (R) 121m/C *IT* Adrienne Barbeau, Ramy Zada, Harvey Keitel, Madeleine Potter, Bingo O'Malley, E.G. Marshall, John Amos, Sally Kirkland, Kim Hunter, Martin Balsam, Tom Atkins; ***D:*** George A. Romero, Dario Argento; ***W:*** George A. Romero, Dario Argento, Franco Ferrini; ***C:*** Giuseppe Maccari, Peter Reniers; ***M:*** Pino Donaggio. **VHS, LV** *FXV, VTR*

The Two Faces of Dr. Jekyll

Dr. Jekyll (Paul Massie) divides individual personality into two parts, "an inner man beyond good and evil" and "man as he would be, free of the restrictions society places upon us, subject only to his own will." Director Terence Fisher takes a tack that others have used, and with equal success, making Hyde the smoother, more calculating and sophisticated side of the tweedy, brusque Jekyll. The various parallels at work in Wolf Mankowitz's adaptation of Stevenson have seldom been drawn so blatantly. Here, for example, Jekyll's wife Kitty (Dawn Addams) has her own conflicting natures. As her lover, Christopher Lee almost steals the film. Unfortunately, the film's colors have lost vibrancy on the video transfer and the widescreen image suffers. A letterboxed restoration would be welcome. ***AKA:*** House of Fright; Jekyll's Inferno. 🦴🦴🦴

1960 87m/C *GB* Paul Massie, Dawn Addams, Christopher Lee, David Kossoff, Francis De Wolff, Oliver Reed, Norma Marla, Terry Quinn; ***D:*** Terence Fisher; ***W:*** Wolf Mankowitz; ***C:*** Jack Asher. **VHS, Closed Caption** *COL*

2000 Maniacs

To contemporary audiences, accustomed to hyper-realistic violent effects, Herschell Gordon Lewis' pioneering effort in gore is almost pure comedy. The giggling rednecks of Pleasant Valley, Georgia, trick vacationing Yankees into their small town, planning to make the visitors the guests of honor at the centennial barbecue. The hayseed humor and the soundtrack of folk music and cheap electric organ make it resemble an episode of *Hee-Haw* that's given in to the dark side of the force. 🦴½

1964 75m/C Thomas Wood, Connie Mason, Jeffrey Allen, Ben Moore, Gary Bakeman, Jerome Eden, Shelby Livingston, Michael Korb, Yvonne Gilbert, Mark Douglas, Linda Cochran, Vincent Santo, Andy Wilson;

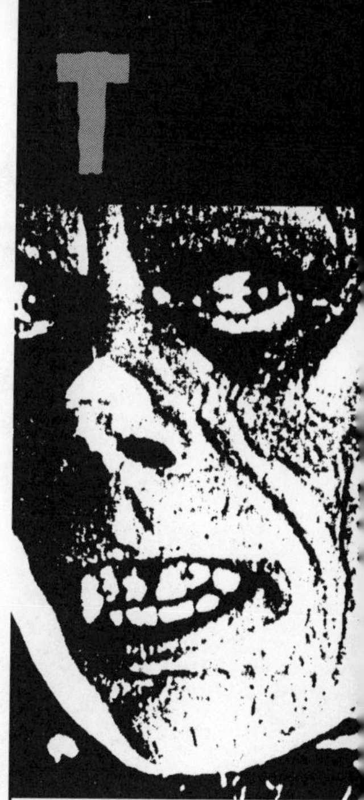

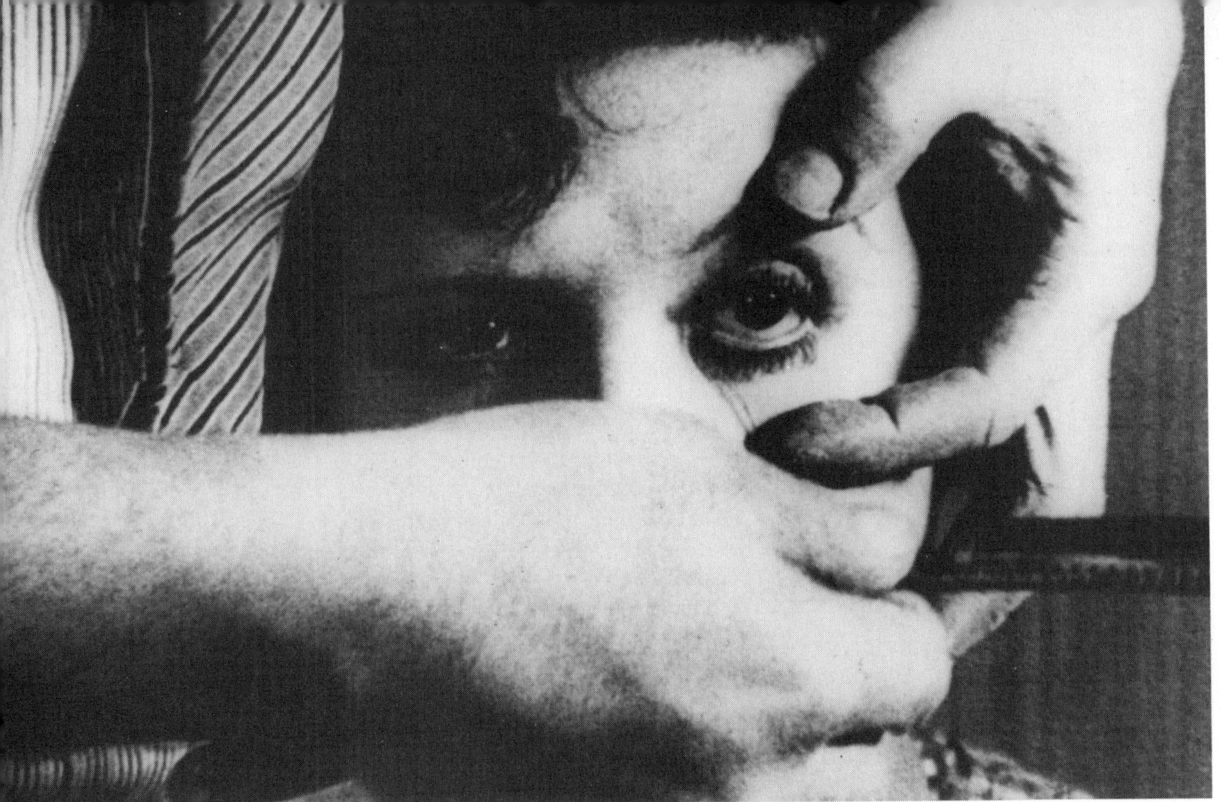

An eye-popping moment in *Un Chien Andalou.*

D: Herschell Gordon Lewis; ***W:*** Herschell Gordon Lewis; *C:* Herschell Gordon Lewis. **VHS** *SMW*

Un Chien Andalou

From the opening images of a man sharpening a straight razor, then slicing open a woman's eyeball, this short film from director Luis Bunuel and Salvador Dali has set standards of shock value that few of today's horrors can match. It's 16 minutes of surrealistic sex, violence, comedy, disembodied hands, dead horses, and hairy armpits. The VideoHound is somewhat miffed that even though the title translates "Andalusian Dog," there are no canines in the film! Is this fair? Is it a cruel hoax or more surrealist humor? Echoes and quotes can be seen in *Naked Lunch, Silence of the Lambs,* and even TV's *Laugh-In.* ***AKA:*** An Andalusian Dog. 🦴🦴🦴

1928 16m/B *FR* Pierre Batcheff, Simone Marevil, Jaime Miravilles, Luis Bunuel, Salvador Dali; ***D:*** Luis Bunuel, Salvador Dali; ***W:*** Luis Bunuel, Salvador Dali. **VHS** *HHT, GVV*

Understudy: The Graveyard Shift 2

In a sequel to the cult hit video premiere, vampire Oliviero returns to the set of a horror film that's in production and becomes the star. Writer/director Gerard Ciccoritti has a genuine flair for this kind of story. He treats the genre seriously, avoiding campy outrageousness on one side and artiness on the other. The film doesn't hold up all the way through—toward the end, plot is sacrificed to stylishness—but it's much better than *Friday the 13th* or the other formula series. 🦴🦴🦴

1988 (R) 88m/C *CA* Wendy Gazelle, Mark Soper, Silvio Oliviero, Ilse von Glatz, Tim Kelleher; ***D:*** Gerard Ciccoritti; ***C:*** Barry Stone. **VHS, LV** *NO*

The Uninvited

One of Hollywood's best love/ghost stories is old-fashioned in the best sense of the term. It's deftly plotted and atmospheric with well-developed characters. In 1937, London music critic Rick Fitzgerald (Ray Milland) and his sister Pamela (Ruth Hussey) impulsively buy an old house in Cornwall on a cliff overlooking the Atlantic. The initially cozy tone turns chilly as Rick falls for the daughter (Gail Russell) of the deceased owner. Crisp black-and-white photography was nominated for an Oscar. Victor Young's music's not bad either. The weak link is the visible "ghosts" which reportedly do not exist in British prints of the film.

1944 99m/B Ray Milland, Ruth Hussey, Donald Crisp, Cornelia Otis Skinner, Gail Russell, Alan Napier, Dorothy Stickney; ***D:*** Lewis Allen; ***W:*** Dodie Smith; ***C:*** Charles B(ryant) Lang; ***M:*** Victor Young. Nominations: Academy Awards '44: Best Black and White Cinematography. **VHS, LV** *USH*

The Unnamable

Though the film as little to do with H.P. Lovecraft's lightly plotted short story, writer/director Jean-Paul Ouellette is mostly faithful to the master's heightened sense of horror. At least he is at first when Randolph Carter (Mark Kinsey Stephenson) challenges his fellow Miskatonic University students to spend a night in a house where a wizard was killed. The middle is uninspired and repetitious things-that-go-bump-in-the-night stuff when two couples go to the house. Curiously, the creature is portrayed by a woman, Katrin Alexandre, inside a fairly impressive monster suit.

1988 87m/C Charles King, Mark Kinsey Stephenson, Alexandra Durrell, Laura Albert, Eben Ham, Blane Wheatley, Mark Parra, Katrin Alexandre; ***D:*** Jean-Paul Ouellette; ***W:*** Jean-Paul Ouellette; ***C:*** Tom Fraser. **VHS, LV** *VTR, THV*

The Unnamable 2: The Statement of Randolph Carter

As undergraduate writer Randolph Carter, Mark Kinsey Stephenson is a poised, intelligent Lovecraftian figure. In this sequel, he pores over the copy of the "Necronomicon" he found in the first film. The monster—B-diva Julie Strain in an even better suit—is ready to cut loose in the little college town of Arkham. Prof. Warren (John Rhys-Davies) helps Carter figure out what's in the caverns beneath the graveyard. The hokum is no closer to the source material than the first film. Alyda (Maria Ford) wandering around naked beneath a long Lady Godiva wig sets the semicomic tone. ***AKA:*** H.P. Lovecraft's The Unnamable Returns; The Unnamable Returns.

1992 (R) 104m/C Mark Kinsey Stephenson, John Rhys-Davies, David Warner, Julie Strain, Maria Ford, Charles Klausmeyer; ***D:*** Jean-Paul Ouellette; ***W:*** Jean-Paul Ouellette; ***C:*** Greg Gardiner. **VHS, LV, Closed Caption** *NO*

Unsane

As is usually the case with Dario Argento movies, the plot is complicated and pretty much dispensable. It serves merely as a clunky, coincidence-driven device to string together a series of sexual and violent images that often involve beautiful women in some stage of undress. In Rome, American horror novelist Peter Neal (Anthony Franciosa) finds that someone is copying passages from his book *Tenebrae* in real razor murders. The silliness of that side of the film is balanced against Argento's inventive camerawork, which alternates between careful attention to extreme close-up detail and long, complex tracking and crane shots. Argento deserves full credit for his stylish visuals, but the material so flamboyantly ignores the conventions of cinematic "realism" that many viewers won't appreciate it. The widescreen "direc-

THE HOUND SALUTES

DWIGHT FRYE

Dwight Frye occupies a unique place in the history of movie horror. He is, without question, the genre's most popular henchman. In that role, he henched for some of the best—Colin Clive, Bela Lugosi, Lionel Atwill, George Zucco.

He was born Dwight Fry in Kansas, 1899. According to Jan Garfield, writing in *Famous Monsters of Filmland* #219, Dwight added the "e" to make the name look better when he joined a theatre company in Spokane, Washington. Like so many of the actors in the 1930s, he learned his craft in small theatre companies, and eventually made it to Broadway where he seems to have been most successful with lighter comedies and melodramas.

He joined many of his fellow stage actors heading west for Hollywood as a result of a curious bit of synchronicity. In 1927, sound came to the movies, and in 1929, the bottom fell out of the stock market, crippling theatre business in New York. Actors with good voices who could memorize lines were suddenly in demand. Frye found a few roles—in the original *Maltese Falcon* he was Wilmer, the part that would be made famous a decade later by another fine supporting actor, Elisha Cook, Jr.—before Tod Browning cast him as Renfield in *Dracula*.

Though most fans' initial image of Renfield is the giggling, fly-munching lunatic, remember that he also introduces the story as the sane, fastidious solicitor who brings the legal documents to Castle Dracula. His reactions to those glorious Gothic sets mirror our own. Later, when the plot bogs down in the middle, Frye's over-the-top antics are the most enjoyable part of the film, despite the fact that some last-minute cuts make his character's actions more confusing than they actually are.

A year later, Frye reprised and considerably refined the character when he played Fritz in James Whale's *Frankenstein*. Again, most viewers immediately think of Fritz in relation to his semi-comic brain switching scene, but his character is actually part of

tor's cut," titled *Tenebrae,* is about ten minutes longer than the R-rated version. The additional footage, containing a few bits of more graphic gore, is really less important than the full-sized image. The long central chase scene with the doberman makes sense when you can see all the action. Argento's signature camerawork really requires the full theatrical ratio to be appreciated. ***AKA:*** Tenebrae; Sotto gli Occhi dell'Assassino. 🦴🦴½

1982 91m/C *IT* Anthony (Tony) Franciosa, John Saxon, Daria Nicolodi, Giuliano Gemma, Christian Borromeo, Mirella D'Angelo, Veronica Lario, Ania Pieroni, Carola Stagnaro, John Steiner, Lara Wendell; ***D:*** Dario Argento; ***W:*** Dario Argento; ***C:*** Luciano Tovoli. **VHS** *NO*

The Untold Story

Gamy Hong Kong horror/crime/gross-out comedy is guaranteed to offend just about everyone. The plot, based on a true story, revolves around a mass murderer. The mildest elements are cannibalism and rape. The rest is so graphic, revolting, and grotesque that it's almost impossible to watch without the fast-forward button. That said, star Anthony Wong's offhand

the film's main themes. In his essay, "Frankenstein: What Changes Darkness into Light?," from *Horror Films* (Simon & Schuster/Monarch, 1976), R.H.W. Dillard examines that angle much more fully. Fritz's character is essential to any understanding of the film.

Those, of course, are Frye's two brightest moments, though he made several other appearances in the genre. Apparently his role as Karl in *The Bride of Frankenstein* was meant to be much larger, and extra footage of him is said to have been discovered in the 1960s, but, as of this writing, it is still missing.

For the rest of his career, Frye's fortunes followed the genre. He found work retracing familiar patterns. During World War II he was too old to enlist and so he worked at the Douglas Aircraft plant. In 1943, when he'd just signed on for a role in his first major film in years, he died from a heart attack.

SIGNIFICANT CONTRIBUTIONS TO HORROR

Dracula **(1931)**

Frankenstein **(1931)**

The Vampire Bat **(1932)**

The Bride of Frankenstein **(1935)**

Dead Men Walk **(1943)**

portrayal of a murderous sociopath is every bit as authentic as Michael Rooker in *Henry: Portrait of a Serial Killer* and Anthony Perkins in *Psycho*. *The Untold Story* goes much farther than either of them, mixing horrific violence with broad humor in a manner that most western viewers have never seen. Jaded horror fans who yawn through the silly special effects of Jason, Freddie, et al, will get a real jolt out of this one. ***AKA:*** The Untold Story: Human Meat Roast Pork Buns. 🦴🦴🦴🦴

1993 95m/C *HK* Anthony Wong, Danny Lee; ***D:*** Herman Yau. **VHS, LV, Letterboxed** *TAI*

Urotsukidoji Perfect Collection

The most well-known Japanese erotic-horror "anime" is a grotesque phantasmagoria of sexual violence and blood-drenched gore involving humans, angelic beings, and huge Lovecraftian monsters. The plot revolves around scenes that attempt to recreate the hellish nightmares of Hieronymous Bosch, and often succeed in stomach-churning fashion. Director Hideki Takayama spins it all out with the fast pace

"Ha! You shudder in horror. So did I the first time...but what are a few lives when weighed in the balance against the achievement of biological science? Think of it! I have lifted the veil! I have created life."

—Dr. Otto von Niemann (Lionel Atwill) defends his "art" to Ruth Bertin (Fay Wray) in *The Vampire Bat.*

and raw energy of an early Godzilla film. If the whole thing didn't go so far beyond the bounds of good taste, it could be dismissed as misogynist porn. But this is Grand Guignol on an epic scale. Intentionally offensive and provocative, it will shock many viewers, including this one, and that's its point. The umbrella title *Urotsukidoji* refers to a long-running series and the various installments and compilations exist in several versions. The mildest of them are definitely not meant for children and the most explicit cross over into hardcore animation.

1988 240m/C *JP* ***D:*** Hideki Takayama. **VHS** *CPM*

Vamp

Three college boys (Chris Makepeace, Robert Rusler, and Gedde Watanabe) go to the city to find an ecdysiast for a frat party and wind up in the strip joint of the undead. Grace Jones is the lead dancer. Her "chair" routine in white face and adhesive tape is too bizarre for words, and, in one incarnation, her makeup is based on the original *Nosferatu.* The story takes place over one long night, and the joke wears thin early. In the narrow subgenre of teen/vampire/comedy, this ranks third behind *Fright Night* and *The Lost Boys.* Body builder Lisa Lyons appears briefly as a dominatrix vampire.

1986 (R) 93m/C Grace Jones, Chris Makepeace, Robert Rusler, Gedde Watanabe, Sandy Baron, Dedee Pfeiffer, Billy Drago, Lisa Lyons; ***D:*** Richard Wenk; ***W:*** Richard Wenk; ***C:*** Elliot Davis; ***M:*** Jonathan Elias. **VHS, LV, Closed Caption** *VTR*

The Vampire Bat

Bats infest a small town and a series of vampiric murders ensue. The cast is the main reason to see this otherwise stodgy tale. Melvyn Douglas is at his suave best as the skeptical hero. Lionel Atwill is fine as the villainous mad scientist. Dwight Frye's character is a caricature of Renfield. Fay Wray isn't given nearly enough to do. Too much comic chit-chat doesn't help the short film, though it does have a few eerie moments.

1932 69m/B Lionel Atwill, Fay Wray, Melvyn Douglas, Dwight Frye, Maude Eburne, George E. Stone; ***D:*** Frank Strayer; ***W:*** Edward T. Lowe; ***C:*** Ira Morgan. **VHS** *VYY, SNC, WFV*

Vampire Circus

Relatively obscure Hammer entry lacks the tight plotting of the studio's early work. Director Robert Young replaces it with some above-average transformation effects and soft-core sex scenes. It's about a troupe of creatures who perform as a circus and go to a remote village to avenge a vampire who was killed there years before. Though the cast lacks star power, they do acceptable work with the material.

1971 (R) 84m/C *GB* Adrienne Corri, Laurence Payne, Thorley Walters, John Moulder-Brown, Lynne Frederick, Elizabeth Seal, Anthony Corlan, Richard Owens, Domini Blythe, David Prowse; ***D:*** Robert W. Young; ***W:*** Judson Kinberg; ***C:*** Moray Grant. **VHS, LV** *IME, MLB*

The Vampire Hookers

Ultra-cheap Philippine softcore horror-comedy is about two sailors (Bruce Fairbairn and Trey Wilson) on shore leave who are picked up by undead babes. With farts-in-the-coffin jokes, the emphasis is on laughs over scares. In fact, the most frightening image is of John Carradine's painfully twisted arthritic hands. Even so, he's a delightfully hammy old vampire in an ice-cream suit. Prolific director Cirio H. Santiago has a long track record in exploitation. Perhaps he was trying to pad his resume with all the alternate titles that the film also exists under. ***AKA:*** Cemetery Girls; Sensuous Vampires; Night of the Bloodsuckers; Twice Bitten.

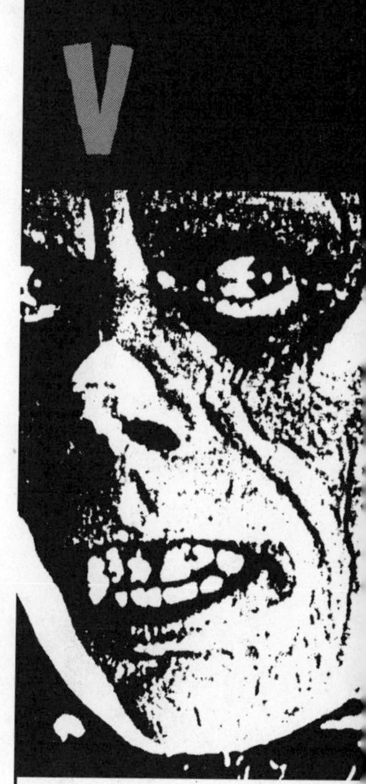

1978 (R) 82m/C *PH* John Carradine, Bruce Fairbairn, Trey Wilson, Karen Stride, Lenka Novak, Katie Dolan, Lex Winter; ***D:*** Cirio H. Santiago. **VHS** *NO*

Vampire Hunter D

From a foreword that says the film is set "in a distant future when mutants and demons slither through a world of darkness," fans of Japanese anime know what to expect—grotesque transformations, characters who can suddenly fly, bloody violence. With his cape and hat, the title character looks like The Shadow, but the story borrows freely from other sources, including *Yojimbo* and conventional horror films. The plot is simplicity itself with the laconic D taking on the vampire Magnus Lee and his monstrous gang. The visual inventions are wildly imaginative and some of the artwork is stylized.

1985 80m/C *JP* ***D:*** Toyoo Ashida. **VHS** *STP, TPV*

Vampire in Brooklyn

Yucky laughs, fairly inventive special effects, and Eddie Murphy doing another star-turn are the main attractions. Not so evident is the offbeat innovation that director Wes Craven brings to his better work—*Nightmare on Elm Street, People Under the Stairs, Shocker.* As the title suggests, the story bears a strong resemblance to *An American Werewolf in London.* The humor is virtually identical, and so is the serious/spoofy approach to horror. Maximillian (Murphy) arrives in Brooklyn looking for the only other surviving member of his race, policewoman Rita Veder (Angela Bassett). He enlists the assistance of a new "ghoul," Julius (scene-stealing Kadeem Hardison), who gives new meaning to the old druggie phrase "eat the roach." Craven keeps the pace moving right along and he gives the production an appropriately rough, gritty look.

1995 (R) 103m/C Eddie Murphy, Angela Bassett, Kadeem Hardison, Allen Payne, Zakes Mokae, John Witherspoon; ***D:*** Wes Craven; ***W:*** Charles Murphy, Christopher Parker, Michael Lucker; ***C:*** Mark Irwin; ***M:*** J. Peter Robinson. **VHS** *PAR*

Vampire Journals

Ted Nicolaou, director of the *Subspecies* movies, is slightly more serious with this good vamp vs. bad vamp tale. Zachary (David Gunn) wanders the world getting rid of pesky bloodsuckers, even though he is one himself. Ash (Jonathan Morris) runs a trendy nightclub where he recruits Eastern bloc bigwigs into the ranks of the undead for fun and profit. Perky Sofia (Kirsten Cerre) is the pianist they're both interested in. A nice introduction in a snowy graveyard sets an appropriately cold bleak tone, and Nicolaou maintains it with bleached out colors and Romanian locations. Neither the plot nor the bloody effects are anything remarkable, but the whole affair is carried off with enough style to earn it a recommendation for fans. Like all Full Moon productions, this one—probably the first of a series—makes the most of limited resources.

1996 (R) 82m/C David Gunn, Jonathan Morris, Kirsten Cerre, Starr Andreeff; ***D:*** Ted Nicolaou. **VHS** *FLL*

The Vampire Lovers

Beyond the nudity that was the film's drawing card when it was first released, this one's a mixed bag. The production values are top-notch and the key images are memorable. But the script is weak with several scenes needlessly repeated to pad it out to feature length, and though it dispenses with some of the vampiric conventions—sunlight, mirrors, coffins—it doesn't replace or explain them. As Carmilla, the predatory lesbian vampire, Ingrid Pitt radiates eroticism. As her antagonist, the General, Peter Cushing is curiously removed from most of the action. In fact, he's absent

THE HOUND SALUTES

INGRID PITT

Though her screen appearances are limited, and her true genre appearances even fewer, Ingrid Pitt deserves special mention in any examination of horror video.

Why?

She was the first actress to make a name for herself in openly erotic horror films. But distribution patterns being what they were when her career was most active, many horror fans didn't actually see her films until decades later when they appeared on tape. They saw lots of sexy stills and they knew that those films she'd made in England had appeared in larger markets. But in those days before the expansion of multi-screen theatre complexes, offbeat titles—particularly offbeat English titles—didn't find their way into the hinterlands very often.

Various sources claim that Ingrid Pitt was born either Ingoushka Petrov or Natasha Petrovana in either Poland or Germany in either 1943 or 1945. One biographer says that she worked in theatre in East Germany and escaped to the West in 1962. She had bit parts in Orson Welles' *Chimes at Midnight* and *A Funny Thing Happened on the Way to the Forum,* and larger roles in the Spanish *Sound of Horror* and the Filipino *The Omegans.* She landed a small window-dressing role in the crackerjack World War II thriller *Where Eagles Dare* with Richard Burton and Clint Eastwood.

After it came *The Vampire Lovers,* the first high-quality softcore horror film from England's Hammer studio, which had spent the 1960s testing the limits of sex and nudity on screen. Over the next decades, hundreds more would be made, but that film was the first where the camera didn't cut away for the sex scenes and the women took their clothes off. It's still top-drawer, combustible exploitation, and Ingrid Pitt leads

for most of the picture. The film never really goes into the various male-female conflicts inherent to the subject matter, so it's not as compelling as it could be. 🦴🦴½

1970 (R) 91m/C *GB* Ingrid Pitt, Pippa Steele, Madeleine Smith, Peter Cushing, George Cole, Dawn Addams, Kate O'Mara, Ferdinand "Ferdy" Mayne, Douglas Wilmer, Harvey Hall; ***D:*** Roy Ward Baker; ***W:*** Tudor Gates; ***C:*** Moray Grant. **VHS** *ORI, MLB*

Vampirella

The heroine who has enjoyed an off-and-on existence in comic books since the early 1970s makes a belated and inauspicious debut in this made-for-cable feature. Imagine a combination of cliches from a Tom Clancy techno-thriller, the origin of Superman, and an episode of the old Flash Gordon serial featuring Ming the Merciless. Hash it all together with a microscopic budget and you've got the story of a good girl (Talisa Soto) from the planet Drakulon who chases to Earth the bad guy (Roger Daltrey) who killed her daddy. The script is so slapdash it can't even deliver the guilty pleasures of good trash. Everyone involved seems to have realized how atrocious the material is and so they simply go through the motions. Vampy doesn't even wear the outrageously skimpy outfit that is her trademark in print. ***AKA:*** Roger Corman Presents: Vampirella. **Woof!**

an attractive cast. In that film, she has that extra something beyond the nudity and feigned ecstasy—the spark that separates eroticism from mere exhibitionism. It's the same indefinable quality that separates a Bettie Page from other pin-ups, a Pam Grier from other babes-behind-bars.

Hammer followed it up with *Countess Dracula*, another variation on the new explicitness. For Ingrid Pitt and horror, the third time was the charm when she played the seductive school teacher in Robin Hardy's brilliant *The Wicker Man*.

Ingrid Pitt has appeared sporadically in film (*The Final Option*) and on television (*Smiley's People*), but nothing she's done since has come close to the lasting impact she made with horror fans—all right, male horror fans—in the early 1970s.

SIGNIFICANT CONTRIBUTIONS TO HORROR

The Vampire Lovers **(1970)**

Countess Dracula **(1970)**

The Wicker Man **(1975)**

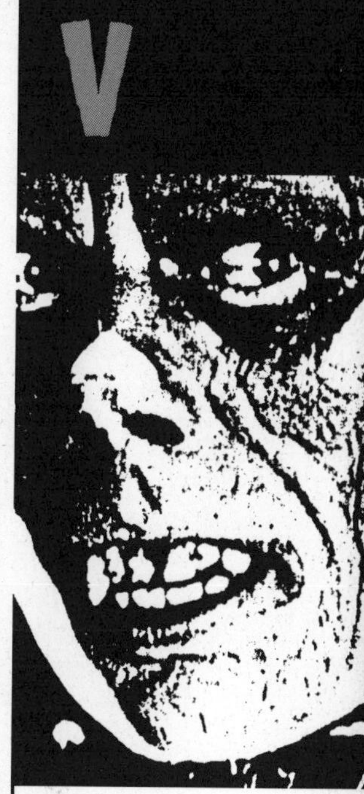

1996 (R) 90m/C Talisa Soto, Roger Daltrey, Richard Joseph Paul, Angus Scrimm, Tom Deters, Cirnna Harney, Brian Bloom; ***D:*** Jim Wynorski. **VHS** *NHO*

Vampire's Kiss

Nicolas Cage is a talented, versatile actor, but his fey performance here is so snotty and off-putting that only his most ardent admirers will stick with the story. And, for horror fans, the film is curiously embarrassed by its subject. Literary agent Peter Loew (Cage) has already confessed to his therapist (Elizabeth Ashley) that he has "issues" concerning bats when he picks up Rachel (Jennifer Beals) who bites his neck. Is she real or is she a product of his loneliness? Cage's bug-eyed (and bug-eating!) excesses render the point moot.

1988 (R) 103m/C Nicolas Cage, Elizabeth Ashley, Jennifer Beals, Maria Conchita Alonso, Kasi Lemmons, Bob Lujan, David Hyde Pierce; ***D:*** Robert Bierman; ***W:*** Joe Minion; ***C:*** Stefan Czapsky; ***M:*** Colin Towns. **VHS, LV** *NO*

Vampyr

Carl Dreyer's seminal horror film admits that it's a dream in the opening scenes and never pretends to have a formal "realistic" plot structure or a reliable protagonist. David Grey (Julian West) may well halluci-

"The television screen is the retina of the mind's eye."

—Brian O'Blivion (Jack Creley) in *Videodrome.*

nate the whole slow-moving tale for all the logical sense it makes. Barely connected images of death, sickness, and burial hint at a vampire story, and all of the key moments have been copied countless times since. By today's standards of sound and image, the film is very rough—tapes vary in quality—but any serious fan has to see it. ***AKA:*** Vampyr, Ou L'Etrange Aventure de David Gray; Vampyr, Der Traum des David Gray; Not Against the Flesh; Castle of Doom; The Strange Adventure of David Gray; The Vampire. 🦴🦴🦴🦴

1931 75m/B *GE FR* Julian West, Sybille Schmitz, Henriette Gerard, Maurice Schutz, Rena Mandel, Jan Hieronimko, Albert Bras; ***D:*** Carl Theodor Dreyer; ***W:*** Carl Theodor Dreyer, Christen Jul; ***C:*** Rudolph Mate; ***M:*** Wolfgang Zeller. **VHS** *KIV, NOS, SNC*

Vampyres

Considered by many to be Joseph Larraz's best film, this one has gained a reputation for its erotic, exploitative angle, but also works well as a grim Gothic horror. In plot and appearance, it's a companion piece to Larraz's other low-budget work of the period, *The House That Vanished.* Ted (Murray Brown) picks up Fran (Marianne Morris), an attractive hitchhiker. At her moldering country estate, he allows himself to be seduced by her and her lover Miriam (Anulka). The look is grainy, and the sex is athletic and bawdy with a fevered edge that creates a specific equation between vampirism and desire. Larraz uses a constant moaning wind and other heightened natural sound effects to accentuate the cold, autumnal feeling. The main flaws are a muddy video image and some ungainly physical action, notably in the outdoor scenes. A prime candidate for restoration. ***AKA:*** Vampyres, Daughters of Dracula; Blood Hunger; Satan's Daughters; Daughters of Dracula. 🦴🦴🦴½

1974 (R) 90m/C *GB* Marianne Morris, Anulka, Murray Brown, Brian Deacon, Sally Faulkner, Michael Byrne, Karl Lanchbury, Bessie Love, Elliott Sullivan; ***D:*** Joseph (Jose Ramon) Larraz; ***W:*** Diane Daubeney; ***C:*** Harry Waxman. **VHS** *VTR*

The Velvet Vampire

In this archetype of early '70s exploitation, vampire Diane (Celeste Yarnall) invites young Los Angelenos Lee (Michael Blodgett) and Susan (Sherry Miles) out to her desert house where she sets out to seduce them both. Most conventions of the genre—aversions to sunlight, reflections, etc.—are replaced by surreal touches and soft-core sex. That's pretty tame stuff. Blodgett has gone on to write screenplays and the horror-tinged novels *Captain Blood* and *Hero and the Terror.* ***AKA:*** Cemetary Girls; Through the Looking Glass; The Waking Hour. 🦴🦴

1971 (R) 82m/C Michael Blodgett, Sherry Miles, Celeste Yarnall, Gene Shane, Jerry Daniels, Sandy Ward, Paul Prokop, Chris Woodley, Robert Tessier; ***D:*** Stephanie Rothman; ***W:*** Stephanie Rothman, Maurice Jules, Charles S. Swartz; ***C:*** Daniel Lacambre. **VHS, LV**

Videodrome

"The battle for the mind of North America will be fought in the video arena—the videodrome." That's one aspect of David Cronenberg's perverse, challenging, unnerving exploration of violence, both real and vicarious. Max Wren (James Woods) is a cable programmer who wants to challenge the limits of his medium—a fledgling operation in the early '80s. On a pirated satellite signal, he discovers "Videodrome," ultraviolent stuff masking an even darker purpose. In some ways, the film can be seen as a transition between Cronenberg's early, relatively conventional works (*Scanners, Rabid*) and his more ambitious recent work (*Dead Ringers, Naked Lunch*). It's also a companion piece to *Crash* with its explicit, hypnotic connections between sexual arousal and pain. Though it's certainly not to all tastes, this is one of the most fiercely original horror movies ever made. Is it completely successful? No, it doesn't really make sense and it goes too far. Appropriately, the video version is slightly longer and more grotesque than the theatrical release. 🦴🦴🦴½

1983 87m/C *CA* James Woods, Deborah Harry, Sonja Smits, Peter Dvorsky, Jack Creley; ***D:*** David Cronenberg; ***W:*** David Cronenberg; ***C:*** Mark Irwin; ***M:*** Howard Shore. Genie Awards '84: Best Director (Cronenberg). **VHS, LV** *USH*

Village of the Damned

What a yawner. This flat horror film completely lacks suspense or surprises. Veteran filmmaker John Carpenter might have phoned in his remake of the excellent 1960 original. (Both that film and the sequel, *Children of the Damned,* are really more s-f than horror in their approach to the subject.) An unexplained force causes the inhabitants of a small town to pass out for several hours. When they awaken, several of the women—including Linda Kozlowski, Meredith Salenger, and Karen Kahn—are pregnant. Neither the local doctor (Christopher Reeve) nor the government scientist (Kirstie Alley) who happens to drop by know what to make of the phenomenon. Years later, the babies grow to be little kids with silvery wigs, psychic powers, and bad attitudes. In this telling, the characters have no personalities, the dialogue is sloppy and stilted, and the plot comes to a slapdash conclusion. The pedestrian special effects appear to have been tailored for the small screen. **Woof!**

1995 (R) 98m/C Christopher Reeve, Kirstie Alley, Linda Kozlowski, Mark Hamill, Meredith Salenger, Michael Pare, Peter Jason, Constance Forslund, Karen Kahn; ***D:*** John Carpenter; ***W:*** John Carpenter, David Himmelstein; ***C:*** Gary B. Kibbe; ***M:*** John Carpenter, Dave Davies. **VHS, LV, Closed Caption** *USH*

Voodoo

When young Andy (Corey Feldman) transfers to a new college, he decides to join a frat. He could've gone with the local party boys or the computer geeks, but no, Andy innocently opts for the fraternity of the walking dead. Zombie House! Bummer! The chapter prez (Joel J. Edwards) has a scheme for eternal life. He needs just one more human sacrifice...er, pledge. Director Rene Eram creates a few good atmospheric scenes, but the pace drags too often. O.K. low-budget genre piece. 🦴🦴

1995 (R) 91m/C Corey Feldman, Sarah Douglas, Jack Nance, Joel J. Edwards; ***D:*** Rene Eram; ***W:*** Brian DiMuccio, Dino Vindeni; ***M:*** Keith Bilderbeck. **VHS, LV, Closed Caption** *APX*

Wait until Dark

Few plays make the transition to the screen as smoothly as this one because the limitations of the stage play to the film's strengths: claustrophobic basement set, flamboyant characters, brick solid storyline. Combine those with ideal casting and you've got one of Hollywood's best. The basic conflict—placing a blind woman, Suzy (Audrey Hepburn), and a girl against three murderous thugs—is still as compelling as ever with deftly timed shocks and revelations. Yes, it's dated for good and for ill. The opening is a fine snapshot of mid-'60s New York, but Suzy's attitude toward her husband will set feminist teeth on edge. It's supposed to. That's part of the film's subtle take on the balance of power between women and men. Audrey Hepburn was nominated for an Oscar, and Alan Arkin as Harry Roat, Jr., from Scarsdale, who "wants to do evil things," is an unforgettable villain. The last reel is about as good as horror gets. One complaint: the color is faded on the print that the current tape was made from. A prime candidate for restoration. 🦴🦴🦴🦴

1967 105m/C Audrey Hepburn, Alan Arkin, Richard Crenna, Efrem Zimbalist Jr., Jack Weston; ***D:*** Terence Young; ***W:*** Robert B. Carrington; ***C:*** Charles B(ryant) Lang; ***M:*** Henry Mancini. Nominations: Academy Awards '67: Best Actress (Hepburn). **VHS, LV** *WAR*

SCAPEGOA
George

The Walking Dead

Karloff stars as an ex-con framed for murder, executed, and resurrected in a neatly done lab scene that deliberately recalls his creation as The Monster in *Frankenstein.* Photography, music, and even dialogue are an affectionate tip of the cinematic hat to Whale's film, made five years before. Director Michael Curtiz's film is an impressive and compact piece of work with a touching performance by the star and a fine turn by Ricardo Cortez as the sleek villain. Pay no attention to the details of the almost tongue-in-cheek plot. This fine, largely unknown entertainment ought to be a prime candidate for a remake.

1936 66m/B Boris Karloff, Ricardo Cortez, Edmund Gwenn, Marguerite Churchill, Warren Hull, Barton MacLane, Henry O'Neill, Joseph King, Addison Richards, Paul Harvey; ***D:*** Michael Curtiz; ***W:*** Ewart Adamson, Lillie Hayward, Robert D. Andrews, Peter Milne; ***C:*** Hal Mohr. *NYR*

Warlock

Passable little supernatural thriller mixes a comic book plot with unpersuasive special effects, above average acting, and a strong sense of humor. Back in 1691, a warlock (Julian Sands) escapes execution by conjuring up some kind of timestorm. He and witchhunter Redfern (Richard E. Grant) whisk forward 300 years to the living room of Kassandra (Lori Singer), a plucky Los Angeles airhead. Before long, they're all hunting for the three parts of the Grand Grimgroir, a book that will bring about the "uncreation" of the universe. The pace is quick, the laughs intentional, and the plot avoids cliches. Followed by a sequel.

1991 (R) 103m/C Richard E. Grant, Julian Sands, Lori Singer, Mary Woronov, Richard Kuss, Kevin O'Brien, Anna Levine, Allan Miller, David Carpenter; ***D:*** Steve Miner; ***W:*** David N. Twohy; ***C:*** David Eggby; ***M:*** Jerry Goldsmith. **VHS, Closed Caption** *THV*

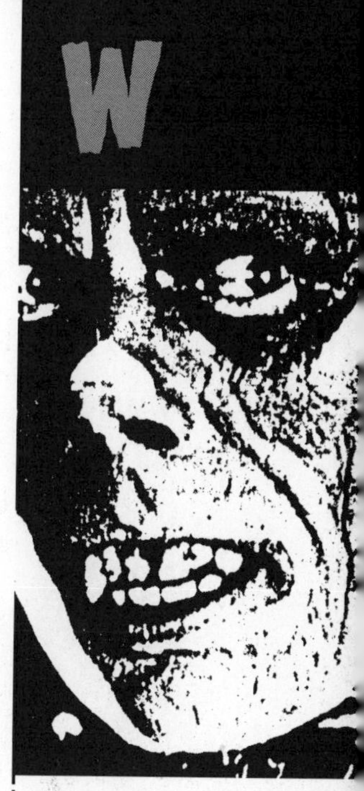

Warlock Moon

College kids Jenny (Laurie Walters) and John (Joe Spano) go to an abandoned spa and, at tortuous length, discover evil-doings. It's standard late-'70s drive-in fare—big bellbottoms, straight hair, grainy color, poor acting, and too dependent on the empty hotel locations. Those aren't necessarily fatal flaws; the pokey pace is. Jenny spends the whole movie wandering into threatening situations when she could easily walk away. The rest is padded with filler.

1973 75m/C *MX* Laurie Walters, Joe Spano, Edna Macafee, Ray Goman, Steve Solinsky, Charles Raino; ***D:*** Bill Herbert. **VHS** *UNI*

Warlock: The Armageddon

Sequel boasts better effects than the original and a plot that's just as nonsensical. The titular supernatural creature (Julian Sands) tries to collect special runestones to bring his daddy Satan into the world, etc., etc. Smalltown teens Kenny (Chris Young) and Samantha (Paula Marshall) must stop him. The inventive, graphic violence is leavened with equally bloody humor. Similar stuff is found in the 1995 *Prophecy* and *Buffy, the Vampire Slayer.*

1993 (R) 93m/C Julian Sands, Chris Young, Paula Marshall, Steve Kahan, Charles Hallahan, R.G. Armstrong, Bruce Glover, Zach Galligan, Dawn Ann Billings, Joanna Pacula; ***D:*** Anthony Hickox; ***W:*** Kevin Rock, Sam Bernard. **VHS** *THV*

Suzy Hendrix (Audrey Hepburn) in *Wait until Dark.*

"Thanks...thanks for the bullet. It was the only way. In a few moments now I'll know why all this had to be."

—A dying Dr. Wilfred Glendon (Henry Hull), after being shot by a lead (not silver!) bullet in *Werewolf of London.*

The Wasp Woman

Today, the most interesting aspect of this early Roger Corman effort is the fact that its protagonist, Janice Starlin (Susan Cabot), is the boss of her own company. Much of the conflict has to do with corporate infighting. In fact, it takes almost an hour for the first monster to appear and when it does, it leaves something to be desired. As the model and spokeswoman for her company, Janice relies on her looks. Age is taking its toll, until a scientist cooks up some supercharged royal wasp jelly for her. The side effects—psychopathic rage, murder—are unpleasant, but...for a world-class, semi-permanent makeover, they may be worth it. For an offbeat feminist triple bill, run it with *The Blood Spattered Bride* and *Invasion of the Bee Girls*. Remade for cable in 1996.

1959 84m/B Susan Cabot, Fred Eisley, Barboura Morris, Michael Marks, William Roerick, Frank Gerstle, Bruno Ve Sota, Frank Wolff; ***D:*** Roger Corman; ***W:*** Leo Gordon; ***C:*** Harry Neumann. **VHS** *NOS, RHI, SNC*

Wasp Woman

When she sees the first sign of aging in the mirror, model and cosmetics executive Janice Starlin (Jennifer Rubin) refuses to go gentle into that good night. Instead, she takes an experimental wasp hormone—"It's going to be bigger than silicone implants!" claims its maker—and looks like she's 25 again. A side effect occasionally turns her into a six-legged insect monster with a huge butt. Bummer. Director Jim Wynorski makes movies fast and cheap and this one's no exception. The more you see of the silly makeup, the less effective it is. Note to co-star Maria Ford—lose the nipple ring.

1996 (R) 81m/C Jennifer Rubin, Daniel J. Travanti, Maria Ford; ***D:*** Jim Wynorski. **VHS** *NHO*

Watchers

Extremely violent horror/s-f based on Dean R. Koontz's novel is your basic science-run-amok material. A miraculously intelligent dog and a mean, nasty, slobbering monster escape from the proverbial Top Secret Government Lab. Both were created through genetic engineering. The toothy critter is trying to kill the dog and anyone else he meets. Corey Haim is the kid who befriends Superpooch. He's played by Sandy, possibly the world's most photogenic Golden Retriever who, singlepawedly earns the films one-bone rating. (Otherwise, it would be a definite WOOF!) Michael Ironside, who's never looked more like Jack Nicholson's twin, is the evil government agent. Even judged by the relaxed standards of the genre, some of the overacting is excessive and so is the violence. It borders on sadism at times and it's often aimed at children. Followed by two inexplicable sequels.

1988 (R) 99m/C Barbara Williams, Michael Ironside, Corey Haim, Duncan Fraser, Blu Mankuma, Dale Wilson, Colleen Winton; ***D:*** Jon Hess; ***W:*** Bill Freed, Damien Lee; ***C:*** Richard Leiterman; ***M:*** Joel Goldsmith. **VHS, LV** *LIV*

Waxwork

Bizarre horror/comedy is almost an anthology of stories set in a wax museum and involving exhibits that come to life (what other kind are there?): werewolves, cannibal vampires, mummies, and such. The film has a few good moments, but as often as not, the ultra-gory special effects undercut the humor, and the big finale is very poorly edited. For no apparent reason, it ends with Leslie Gore singing "It's My Party and I'll Cry If I Want To" over the closing credits. Recommended for hardcore fans only. Followed by a sequel.

1988 (R) 97m/C Zach Galligan, Deborah Foreman, Michelle Johnson, Dana Ashbrook, Miles O'Keeffe, Patrick Macnee, David Warner, John Rhys-Davies; ***D:***

Anthony Hickox; ***W:*** Anthony Hickox; ***C:*** Gerry Lively; ***M:*** Roger Bellon. **VHS, LV** *LIV*

Waxwork 2: Lost in Time

A murderous hand escapes from the burning wax museum and follows Mark (Zach Galligan) and Sarah (Monika Schnarre). Patrick Macnee, from the first film, reappears to lead the non-dynamic duo through the Cartaglian Time Door in their ongoing fight against the forces of evil. Both the bloody violence and the looseygoosey plot are played for laughs. The film is a collage of homages to other horrors from *Frankenstein,* to *Alien, Dr. Jekyll and Mr. Hyde, Nosferatu, Dawn of the Dead,* and even *Godzilla.* Look for Bruce Campbell, David Carradine, Marina Sirtis, Sophie Ward, John Ireland, and Maxwell Caulfield in small roles, and Drew Barrymore in a cameo. ***AKA:*** Lost in Time. 🦴🦴

1991 (R) 104m/C Zach Galligan, Alexander Godunov, Bruce Campbell, Michael Des Barres, Monika Schnarre, Martin Kemp, Sophie Ward, Marina Sirtis, Juliet Mills, John Ireland, Patrick Macnee, David Carradine, Drew Barrymore; ***D:*** Anthony Hickox; ***W:*** Anthony Hickox; ***C:*** Gerry Lively. **VHS, Closed Caption** *LIV*

Weird Woman/ Frozen Ghost

Take the beginning of the first "Inner Sanctum" feature with a large grain of salt. It's a typical Hollywood mishmash that presents ersatz Hawaiians practicing voodoo. The scene then shifts to a college campus where anthropologist Lon Chaney, Jr., brings his new island bride (Anne Gwynne). His venomous ex-girlfriend Ilona (Evelyn Ankers) wants him back and spins a web of intrigue involving others. The result turns into a conflict among three women with two more providing strong support. An outclassed Chaney is caught in the middle. The story, based on a Fritz Leiber novel, was also filmed as *Burn Witch, Burn!* and it cries out to be remade again with the focus shifted to the women and the addition of another level of complexity. The humor, conflict, and characters are already there. In *Frozen Ghost,* Chaney is Gregor the Great, a mentalist who believes that he can kill psychically and so he takes a few weeks of R&R at a wax museum. Like the first half of the double feature, it revolves around jealousy, with the dapper Chaney as the object of several women's affections. Screwy plot twists bog down in tedious police investigations. It's still fun, but by far the weaker of the two. ***AKA:*** Frozen Ghost; The Inner Sanctum: Weird Woman/Frozen Ghost. 🦴🦴🦴

1944 125m/B Lon Chaney Jr., Evelyn Ankers, Ralph Morgan, Lois Collier, Douglass Dumbrille, Elena Verdugo, Anne Gwynne, Milburn Stone, Martin Kosleck; ***D:*** Harold Young, Reginald LeBorg; ***W:*** Brenda Weisberg, Bernard Schubert, Lucille Ward. **VHS** *USH*

Werewolf

This howler may well be the funniest flick of its kind since Michael Landon glued on the whiskers in *I Was a Teenage Werewolf.* Even for low-budget horror, it's bad in all the wrong ways—inept acting, cliched script, bargain-basement makeup. Though the setting is the Southwest, and some mention is made of American Indian "shapeshifters," nothing is really done with that angle. It's just a standard lycanthropy tale with little to recommend it. The lenticular "morphing" box art has better transformation effects than the movie. With the right imaginative approach, the legends of the American Indians could provide fertile ground for future horror films, but not here. 🦴

1995 (R) 99m/C George Rivero, Fred Cavalli, Adrianna Miles, Richard Lynch, Joe Estevez, R.C. Bates, Heidi Bjorn, Randall Oliver, Nena Belini, Tony Zarindast; ***D:*** Tony Zarindast; ***W:*** Tony Zarindast; ***C:*** Robert Hayes, Dan Gilman. **VHS, LV** *APX*

Sisters Blanche (Joan Crawford) and Jane (Bette Davis) in *What Ever Happened to Baby Jane?*

Werewolf of London

Wild and wooly semi sci-fi shape-shifting tale begins in Tibet where botanist Dr. Glendon (Henry Hull) is bitten by a man-beast as he finds the rare *Marifasa lumina lupina,* which blooms only under the full moon. Zipping back to England, the ominous Dr. Yogami (Warner Oland) appears to warn of "werewolfery; lycanthraphobia is the medical term." Neither Jack Pierce's makeup nor the unfocused script filled with comic relief equal the Chaney *Wolf Man,* though the big fight scene isn't bad and Valerie Hobson is one of the most glamorous Universal heroines. The main problem is that Glendon is such a cold protagonist that it's difficult to muster up much sympathy for his predicament. 🦴🦴½

1935 75m/B Henry Hull, Warner Oland, Valerie Hobson, Lester Matthews, Spring Byington, Lawrence Grant, Zeffie Tilbury; ***D:*** Stuart Walker; ***W:*** Robert Harris, John Colton; ***C:*** Charles Stumar. **VHS** *USH*

Werewolf of Washington

Tongue-in-cheek horror was made at the height of the Watergate scandal. Jack Whittier (Dean Stockwell) is the reporter-turned-White House assistant press secretary who's bitten by a wolf in Budapest. Jack is a such a political animal that when he's told about the sign of the Pentagram, he thinks it has something to do with the military. Unfortunately, the dark interiors and grainy night scenes fare poorly on the small screen, and the broad humor lacks the sharp edge that political comedy needs, though as the president, Biff McGuire is presciently Reaganesque. Both the transformation scenes and the makeup effects are on a par with the Chaney *Wolfman.* 🦴🦴

1973 (PG) 90m/C Dean Stockwell, Biff McGuire, Clifton James, Jane House, Beeson Carroll, Michael Dunn; ***D:***

Milton Moses Ginsberg; ***W:*** Milton Moses Ginsberg; ***C:*** Bob Baldwin. **VHS** *NO*

Wes Craven's New Nightmare

The *Elm Street* series takes an unexpected intellectual turn and becomes a surprisingly entertaining exercise in horror. Most of the characters play themselves. They are the actors, filmmakers, and studio executives who are involved in a work in progress, *Wes Craven's New Nightmare*. Craven has not finished the script yet but Robert Englund is definitely interested in the project. So are producers Marianne Maddalena and Sara Risher and New Line Cinema chairman Robert Shaye. Star Heather Langenkamp needs to be persuaded. When she learns that her husband (David Newsom) is secretly working on new special effects for Craven's project, she's really scared. Upon that premise, Craven builds an intricate construction about the act of storytelling and the power that some stories have. References to Hansel and Gretel are well taken. They bring up the responsibility of storytellers to their audience, particularly when children are involved. In the last reels, Craven returns to the simple, effective thrills of a good horror movie, from a harrowing freeway scene to the wild finale. 🦴🦴🦴

1994 (R) 112m/C Robert Englund, Heather Langenkamp, Miko Hughes, David Newsom, Tracy Middendorf, Fran Bennett, John Saxon, Wes Craven, Robert Shaye, Sara Risher, Marianne Maddalena; ***D:*** Wes Craven; ***W:*** Wes Craven; ***C:*** Mark Irwin; ***M:*** J. Peter Robinson. Nominations: Independent Spirit Awards '95: Best Film. **VHS, LV, Closed Caption** *NLC*

What Ever Happened to Baby Jane?

Bette Davis' fearless, Oscar-nominated performance is the spark that drives this remarkable noir horror. For those who have missed it, think *Sunset Boulevard* with an even more twisted pathology. Baby Jane (Davis) and her sister Blanche (Joan Crawford) are aging, mostly forgotten stars. Blanche is crippled and Jane is insane, though that's putting it much too lightly. Compared to Glenn Close's bunny boiler in *Fatal Attraction,* Jane is the Queen Mother psychobitch. Her first appearance as a raddled harridan is a real jaw-dropper, and the rest of the film lives up to it. Though the pace is slow by current standards, it generates considerable suspense. Note the way director Robert Aldrich and writer Lukas Heller use parallel images to tighten the various elements of the story. The brightly lit conclusion is still chilling. 🦴🦴🦴🦴

1962 132m/B Bette Davis, Joan Crawford, Victor Buono, Anna Lee, B.D. Merrill, Maidie Norman; ***D:*** Robert Aldrich; ***W:*** Lukas Heller; ***C:*** Ernest Haller. Nominations: Academy Awards '62: Best Actress (Davis), Best Black and White Cinematography, Best Costume Design (B & W), Best Sound, Best Supporting Actor (Buono). **VHS, LV, Letterboxed, Closed Caption** *WAR*

When a Stranger Calls

As proven by the homage paid to it in *Scream,* this film's influence has spread far beyond its theatrical release. The amplification of an urban legend about the threatened babysitter—"the phone calls are coming from inside the house!"—has been one of the most enduring cult favorites on home video. Part of the popularity comes from the casting. As the babysitter, Carol Kane is excellent, and so is Charles Durning as the cop obsessed with an insane killer (Tony Beckley), who turns out to be an unusually complex figure. Add in unconventional plotting that hits all the right emotional buttons and a solid feel for the suburbs and mean streets of L.A. Favorable comparisons to the original *Halloween* are not out of place. 🦴🦴🦴

1979 (R) 97m/C Carol Kane, Charles Durning, Colleen Dewhurst, Rachel Roberts, Rutanya Alda, Carmen Argenziano, Kirsten Larkin, Ron O'Neal, Tony Beckley;

D: Fred Walton; ***W:*** Fred Walton, Steve Feke; ***C:*** Don Peterman. **VHS, LV** *COL*

When a Stranger Calls Back

It took the producers more than a decade to come up with this above-average sequel, and it's easy to see why. The first film is so curiously but well constructed that it rules out standard follow-up stuff. The original villain is a fully realized individual, not a cliched movie psycho. The main characters grow during the film and the bad guy is definitely dead at the end. Still, the stalker-vs.-babysitter plot is repeated so often because it works, and writer/director Fred Walton handles it with real care. He treats the whole subject of violence against women seriously, and he comes up with an inventive (if not too believable) twist on the formula. It's also well acted, with Jill Schoelen taking over as protagonist and Carol Kane and Charles Durning repeating their famous roles.

1993 (R) 94m/C Carol Kane, Charles Durning, Jill Schoelen, Gene Lythgow, Karen Austin; ***D:*** Fred Walton; ***W:*** Fred Walton. **VHS, LV, Closed Caption** *USH*

The Whispering

Often interesting but unfocused effort wanders all over the genre landscape and never fully resolves its vague premise. The story seems to be about a mysterious pale woman who may be the incarnation of Death or perhaps some sort of spirit who encourages potential suicides. A cop turned insurance investigator (Leif Garrett) involves himself in a series of suicides after he meets a pretty girl (writer Leslie Danon) who has even less to do with the matter than he does. Some effective tricks and atmospherics don't make up for long pointless philosophical discussions and other loud scenes that go nowhere. The conclusion is equally unsatisfactory.

1994 (R) 88m/C Leif Garrett, Leslie Danon, Tom Patton, Maxwell Rutherford, Mette Holt; ***D:*** Gregory Gieras; ***W:*** Leslie Danon. **VHS** *APX*

The White Zombie

Though it's terribly dated, Lugosi's follow-up to *Dracula* is still important as the first of its kind and the progenitor of today's *Living Dead* horrors. In a backlot Haiti, a rich lecher engages Lugosi to zombiefy a young bride he lusts for. The main flaws now are a florid acting style and Lugosi's silly makeup with its exaggerated widow's peak, caterpillar eyebrows, and bald-chinned beard. Some older tapes have a scratchy soundtrack and a muddy black-and-white image that lessens the power of impressive sets.

1932 73m/B Bela Lugosi, Madge Bellamy, John Harron, Joseph Cawthorn, Robert Frazer, Brandon Hurst, George Burr Macannan, John Peters, Dan Crimmins, Clarence Muse; ***D:*** Victor Halperin; ***W:*** Garnett Weston; ***C:*** Arthur Martinelli; ***M:*** Xavier Cugat. **VHS** *NOS, VYY, CAB*

The Wicked

Campy, micro-budget Australian horror comedy is *The Rocky Horror Picture Show* without the songs (or the wit). The obligatory plot has to do with two lamebrained guys and a girl who are trapped first in a spooky little desert town and then in a spooky house. The film does have a few imaginative special effects and some nice jokes on such movie cliches as the heroine on the conveyor belt, but those wear thin quickly. Even the most devoted horror fans won't find much to hold their interest. ***AKA:*** Outback Vampires.

1989 87m/C Brett Cumo, Richard Morgan, Angela Kennedy, Maggie Blinco, John Doyle; ***D:*** Colin Eggleston. **VHS** *NO*

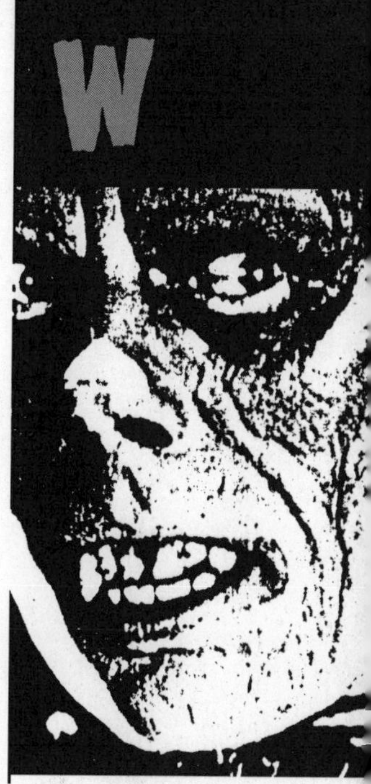

Bela Lugosi in *The White Zombie.*

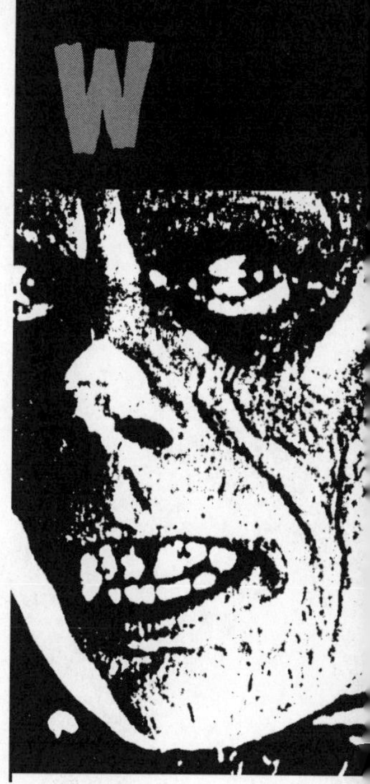

The Wicker Man

Playwright Anthony Shaffer's deftly plotted town-with-a-secret plot is genuinely intelligent and suspenseful. It's built on solid philosophical conflicts—Christianity vs. paganism, piety vs. lust, reason vs. revelry. Scottish policeman Sgt. Howie (Edward Woodward) flies to remote Summerisle to investigate the reported disappearance of a young girl. Modishly coifed Christopher Lee is the laird of the island. Everything Howie finds challenges his strong religious beliefs in ways that neither he (nor the viewer) could have anticipated. Director Robin Hardy combines plain everyday realism with dreamlike hallucinatory images. Woodward's stiff-backed performance gives his role the gravity and authority that the film needs to work. And it does work. Wonderfully. The spotty American theatrical release was chopped down to 85 minutes. The tape version is the full 103 minutes.

1975 103m/C Edward Woodward, Christopher Lee, Britt Ekland, Diane Cilento, Ingrid Pitt, Lindsay Kemp, Irene Sunters, Walter Carr, Geraldine Cowper, Lesley Mackie; ***D:*** Robin Hardy; ***W:*** Anthony Shaffer. **VHS** *REP*

Willard

Though this tepid horror became an unlikely commercial hit for its vengeful rats, its real subject is more Oedipal. Willard (Bruce Davison) still lives with his daft mother (Elsa Lanchester) while working for Martin (Ernest Borgnine), who stole the company from Willard's dead father. Though the pace is slow, journeyman director Daniel Mann gets effective performances from his leads, particularly Borgnine and Davison, and the rats are inherently creepy. Followed by the sequel *Ben.*

1971 (PG) 95m/C Bruce Davison, Ernest Borgnine, Elsa Lanchester, Sondra Locke, Michael Dante, J. Pat O'Malley; ***D:*** Daniel Mann; ***W:*** Gilbert Ralston; ***C:*** Robert B. Hauser; ***M:*** Alex North. **VHS, LV** *PAR*

Wishmaster

One of the first big effects shows a skeleton ripping itself out of a body and that's just the beginning. The story involves an ancient Persian demon-genie called a Djinn (Andrew Divoff) who's trapped in a jewel. Brought back to present-day Los Angeles, he becomes psychically connected to gem appraiser Alex Amberson (Tammy Lauren) and does a Freddy Krueger number on her and her friends. The effects rival those in the *Elm Street* series. (Robert Englund has a key supporting role, and Wes Craven is executive producer.) Like those movies, it's an exercise in bloody style over substance. ***AKA:*** Wes Craven Presents Wishmaster.

1997 (R) 90m/C Tammy Lauren, Andrew Divoff, Robert Englund, Chris Lemmon, Theodore (Ted) Raimi, John Byner, Jenny O'Hara; ***Cameos:*** Tony Todd, Kane Hodder; ***D:*** Robert Kurtzman; ***W:*** Peter Atkins; ***C:*** Jacques Haitkin; ***M:*** Harry Manfredini. **VHS, Closed Caption** *LIV*

Witchboard

For the first third or so, this low-budget effort overachieves. Jim (Todd Allen) and Brandon (Stephen Nichols) are both interested in Linda (Tawny Kitaen), but she's just met a ghost through her Ouija board. When the gum-snapping psychic Sarah (Kathleen Wilhoite) shows up, things get really interesting, but her appearance is all too brief and after it, the action settles into standard bump-in-the-night tricks. Even so, this one has enough going for it to earn a qualified recommendation for fans.

1987 (R) 98m/C Todd Allen, Tawny Kitaen, Stephen Nichols, Kathleen Wilhoite, Burke Byrnes, Rose Marie, James W. Quinn, Judy Tatum, Gloria Hayes, J.P. Luebsen, Susan Nickerson; ***D:*** Kevin S. Tenney; ***W:*** Kevin S. Tenney; ***C:*** Roy Wagner; ***M:*** Dennis Michael Tenney. **VHS, LV** *NO*

Robin Hardy's *The Wicker Man.*

The 1990s

and into the Future

In the '90s, three unrelated but important developments occurred in horror.

First, low-budget horror movies became a staple of the video market; Charles Band's Full Moon Entertainment set up a studio in Romania and began cranking out movies aimed at children and adults at a steady rate. Others were doing the same thing in less structured systems. Second, women came into their own with much more assertive roles, both as characters and as filmmakers. Third, advances in computer-generated animation began to change special effects profoundly.

In the theatrical arena, the MPAA didn't know what to do with two important releases. Director John McNaughton refused to accept the "X" rating that was given to *Henry: Portrait of a Serial Killer,* loosely based on the suspect confessions of Henry Lee Lucas. Because of that, he had trouble finding distribution and most fans discovered that disturbing film on video. When Peter Greenaway's tonier *The Cook, the Thief, His Wife and Her Lover* gave the MPAA similar problems, the organization created the NC-17 category to handle films whose content couldn't be described with the traditional "R" and "X." It was truly a case of closing the barn door after the horse had escaped since filmmakers were already bypassing the MPAA with "unrated director's cuts" on video whenever they felt like it.

Also in 1990, Sam Raimi fondly recalled the glory days of Universal with his *Darkman,* and Tim Burton combined horror, comedy, and pathos in *Edward Scissorhands.*

In many ways, 1991 may be considered the high-water mark of modern horror. At least it's the year in which the genre was embraced by the mainstream and the Academy of Motion Picture Arts and Sciences gave its top awards to one of horror's best, Jonathan Demme's *The Silence of the Lambs.* That same year, Martin Scorsese and Robert De Niro applied their considerable efforts to a remake of *Cape Fear.* De Niro was nominated for an Oscar but it went to Anthony Hopkins for his portrayal of Hannibal Lecter. Jodie Foster also took home a statue for her work in the film, and a year before, Kathy Bates won Best Actress for *Misery.*

In 1992, Sharon Stone redefined the horror/thriller femme fatale in *Basic Instinct.* So, to a lesser degree, did Kristy Swanson as *Buffy the Vampire Slayer.* Epic horror soared with Francis Ford

Witchboard 2: The Devil's Doorway

Young accountant Paige (Ami Dolenz) moves into a loft to discover her artistic side. A Ouija board left in a closet introduces her to a spirit named Susan who seems to have an agenda. Supporting characters soon drop like flies. Director Kevin Tenney shows off with some interesting but often pointless Argento-inspired camera swoopery, at one point even seeming to go through a moving car. Ami Dolenz isn't accomplished or experienced enough to be much more than a cute, clueless heroine. *3* is much better. 🦴🦴

1993 (R) 98m/C Ami Dolenz, Laraine Newman, Timothy Gibbs, John Gatins, Julie Michaels, Marvin Kaplan; ***D:*** Kevin S. Tenney; ***W:*** Kevin S. Tenney; ***C:*** David Lewis; ***M:*** Dennis Michael Tenney. **VHS, LV, Closed Caption** *REP*

Coppola's baroque *Bram Stoker's Dracula* and Steven Spielberg's chart-topping dinosaur adventure, *Jurassic Park*. It fared less well a year later with Kenneth Branagh's *Mary Shelley's Frankenstein*.

Toward the middle of the decade, violence became even more graphic and central to storylines. Oliver Stone claimed that his highly stylized *Natural Born Killers* was meant to criticize America's tendency to glamorize violence, but at the same time, he seemed to enjoy his wallow in gore. The equally arty *Seven* was more restrained and made a larger impression with fans.

Several of the most imaginative works were imports. Both *Shallow Grave* and *Trainspotting* came from Scotland's Danny Boyle, while Peter Jackson, from New Zealand, stayed within more recognizable limits of the genre with his brilliant *Heavenly Creatures* and *The Frighteners*. Italian Michele Soavi twisted the Romero/Fulci "living dead" subgenre into a sharp intellectual comedy with *Cemetery Man*.

David Lynch and David Cronenberg continued to explore their own dark obsessions with *Lost Highway* and *Crash*, respectively. But the biggest hits were found when horror, once again, was aimed at young audiences.

The trend was started in 1996 with a sleeper about schoolgirl witches, *The Craft*. It caught everyone by surprise. So did *Scream* later that year, and a year later boxoffice lightning struck again with *I Know What You Did Last Summer*. As this book went to print, sequels had been released and more were in the works.

It seems logical to predict, then, that the combination of an attractive young cast with a hip, self-conscious story is the direction that horror will take in the next century. I doubt it. *Scream* and ...*Last Summer* have done so well because they invite their audience to share the joke, to laugh knowingly at the conventions and cliches of the genre as they're experiencing those conventions and cliches. It's a "postmodern" attitude that cannot be repeated very often. Even when it works perfectly, it's not all that frightening. And that is still the point. Horror fans want to be frightened.

I, for one, don't know what form the next *Psycho* or *Night of the Living Dead* or *Halloween* will take. Horror pushes the envelope. It tests the limits of what society deems acceptable—what can and cannot be shown; which stories can be told, which cannot; are some ideas too dangerous to discuss? As long as it's a vital form, horror will find new ways to challenge and offend. But again, what form will it take?

I know that some fine, innovative horror movies have been made recently in Japan, Hong Kong, and Korea. As American audiences discover them on tape, the Asian influence is going to increase. I also suspect that as women play a more important role in all films, they'll do the same in horror.

For a fan though, such distinctions don't mean much. American, Japanese, Chinese, male, female—if somebody makes a good horror movie, I want to see it.

Witchboard 3: The Possession

This is what low-budget horror is supposed to be: inventive, spooky, well made, and with a nasty little sense of humor. The story begins with a tip of the hat to *Rosemary's Baby* and then goes on to tell a story of demonic possession via Ouija board (the only slender connection with the other entries in the series). It lures newlywed stockbroker Brian Fields (David Nerman) into all sorts of nastiness. His wife Julie (Locky Lambert) doesn't know what Brian and their creepy landlord (Cedric Smith) are up to, but when Brian brings home a new Miata, she doesn't ask too many questions. The script by Kevin S. Tenney and Jon Ezrine has little to do with

"So what do you think? Women—a mistake? Or did He do it to us on purpose?"

—Devilish Daryl Van Horne (Jack Nicholson) anguishes over the opposite sex in *The Witches of Eastwick.*

the first two *Witchboard* films, and director Peter Svatek moves things along at a nice clip. Though he's not above a few moments of Grand Guignol yuckiness, he doesn't over-rely on effects. Great stuff. 🦴🦴🦴

1995 (R) 93m/C David Nerman, Locky Lambert, Cedric Smith, Donna Sarrasin; ***D:*** Peter Svatek; ***W:*** Kevin S. Tenney, Jon Ezrine; ***C:*** Barry Gravelle. **VHS, Closed Caption** *REP*

Witchcraft

The first entry in an astonishingly popular series of video premieres borrows from *Rosemary's Baby, The Exorcist,* and *The Amityville Horror.* It lacks the grotesque special effects and overall nastiness so prevalent in many theatrical horrors. The plot concerns a young woman's worries about her husband and creepy mother-in-law after the birth of her first child. A weird opening juxtaposes the LaMaze method with burning at the stake. Horror fans have seen better and much, much worse. Over the past decade, the series has changed considerably, but it's always stayed true to its low-budget roots. 🦴🦴

1988 (R) 90m/C Anat "Topol" Barzilai, Gary Sloan, Lee Kisman, Deborah Scott; ***D:*** Robert Spera. **VHS, LV** *VSE*

Witchcraft 2: The Temptress

Exploitative fluff is an odd mixture of the very good and the very bad. The small-town setting and characters are believably realistic. The erotic elements, concerning a witch's attempt to seduce a teenager, produce unintentional laughs, and if overacting were a crime, most of the cast would be in jail. But it would be unfair to leave it at that; the film has some unsettling moments. Part of the credit goes to the makeup and costume people who dolled up the witch (Delia Sheppard) to look like a combination of Madonna and Brigitte Nielsen. Now, that is frightening. After this entry, the series found its footing. 🦴🦴½

1990 (R) 88m/C Charles Solomon, Mia Ruiz, Delia Sheppard; ***D:*** Mark Woods. **VHS, LV** *VSE*

Witchcraft 3: The Kiss of Death

Now, the formula for the series is set—lawyers vs. vampires. The plot is really silly, and so is the acting, but then, *3* is one those B-movies that's better served by bad acting than by good. What might have been just another goofy horror flick is brightened considerably by the presence of Lisa Toothman, who looks like a busty Julia Roberts. 🦴🦴½

1990 (R) 85m/C Charles Solomon, Lisa Toothman, William L. Baker, Lena Hall; ***D:*** R.L. Tillmanns. **VHS** *VSE*

Witchcraft 4: Virgin Heart

Series star Will Spanner (Charles Solomon), the son of Satan, is a California lawyer by day, warlock by night. Hopeless cynics might say there's no difference. But that premise, like the Little Engine That Could, has chugged along for more installments than Jason has managed, and one could argue that these are no worse than any of the recycled *Friday the 13th*s. 🦴

1992 (R) 92m/C Charles Solomon, Julie Strain, Clive Pearson, Jason O'Gulihar, Lisa Jay Harrington, Barbara Dow; ***D:*** James Merendino. **VHS, LV, Closed Caption** *VSE*

Witchcraft 5: Dance with the Devil

Marklen Kennedy takes over the none-too-demanding role of Will Spanner, lawyer, son of Satan, and all-around good guy. The bad guy is Cain (David Huffman), some sort of evil angel who looks like Richard Simmons and slaps people on the head like TV faith healer Ernest Aingley. When he really turns it on, no piece of scenery is safe. For alternative horror fans, though, the memorable combination of bad writing and overemoting makes this a first-rate exercise in unintentional humor.

1992 (R) 94m/C Marklen Kennedy, Carolyn Taye-Loren, Nicole Sassaman, Aysha Hauer, David Huffman; ***D:*** Talun Hsu. **VHS** *VSE*

Witchcraft 6: The Devil's Mistress

By this number, hero Spanner's character has evolved into Los Angeles divorce lawyer by day, supernatural troubleshooter by night. Someone is sacrificing young women up in the hills, so the police call on him for help. There's nothing unusual in the off-the-shelf plot or in the various love scenes that move this one into the "erotic horror" subgenre. But co-writer/director Julie Davis handles things with a fair sense of humor and she got a terrific performance from Bryan Nutter as Savanti, the bad guy with heavy-duty press-on nails. She also made the most of a small budget and limited special effects.

1994 (R) 86m/C Kurt Alan, John E. Holiday, Bryan Nutter, Jerry Spicer, Shannon Lead; ***D:*** Julie Davis; ***W:*** Julie Davis. **VHS** *VSE*

Witchcraft 7: Judgement Hour

This installment is a softcore vampire story that begins with a party for the Undead out at the Polytechnic Institute. Somebody in the casting or makeup department must have had a wicked sense of humor because a key supporting character belongs to the Kato Kaelin Hair Club, and our hero's (David Byrnes) girlfriend (April Breneman) is a ringer for Hilary Clinton.

1995 (R) 91m/C David Byrnes, April Breneman, Alisa Christensen, John Cragen, Loren Schmalle; ***D:*** Michael Paul Girard; ***W:*** Peter Fleming; ***C:*** Denis Maloney; ***M:*** Miriam Cutler. **VHS** *APX*

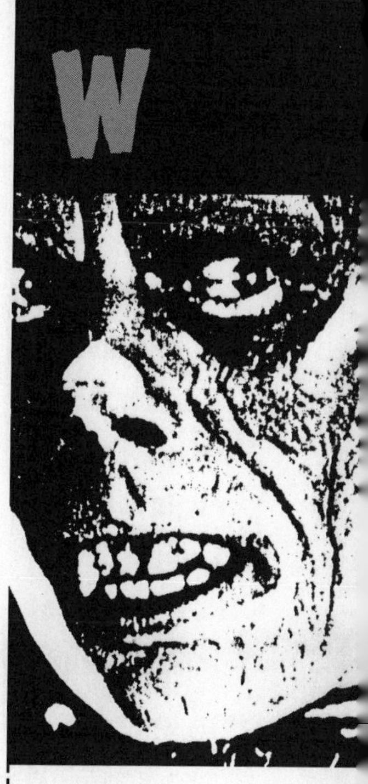

Witchcraft 8: Salem's Ghost

Sequel in name only is so cheap that you can actually see the wires in one special effects scene. The deranged dialogue contains lines like these: "A vile warlock, a wretched and evil man by the name of Simon Renfro, accused of murdering and ingesting countless children and raping more than a dozen women and forcing them into black witchery, was desecrated on this very ground and buried in what you know to be the room off your basement!" ***AKA:*** Salem's Ghost.

1995 (R) 90m/C Lee Grober, Kim Kopf, Tom Overmyer, Jack Van Landingham, David Weills, Anthoni Stuart; ***D:*** Joseph John Barmettler Jr.; ***W:*** Joseph John Barmettler Jr.; ***C:*** Denis Maloney. **VHS** *APX*

Witchcraft 9: Bitter Flesh

Will Spanner (David Byrnes), who was killed in *7*, comes back just like Patrick Swayze in *Ghost*. The only person who can hear him is Sheila (Landon Hall), a prostitute. (All the women, even the ones who are supposed to be cops and college professors, dress like hookers in this one.) The filmmakers are much more interested in the exploitation angles than in horror. This video series has never aimed very high and this entry is no exception, though it is sleazier than the others. **Woof!**

1996 (R) 90m/C Landon Hall, David Byrnes, Stephanie Beaton, Mikul Robins; ***D:*** Michael Paul Girard; ***W:*** Stephen J. Downing; ***C:*** Jeff Gateman; ***M:*** Michael Paul Girard. **VHS** *VSE*

"It's an old legend. You'll find something like it in the folklore of nearly every nation. The scientific name for it is lycanthropy. It's a variety of schizophrenia."

—Sir John Talbot (Claude Rains) lectures his son Lawrence (Lon Chaney, Jr.) in *The Wolf Man.*

Witchcraft through the Ages

One video version of the famous 1922 silent film is a 1969 condensation with narration by William Burroughs and a Jean-Luc Ponty soundtrack. It's a mix of medieval book illustrations and vignettes that dramatize the black arts—witches nibbling on corpse fingers, putting frogs and snakes into the stewpot, that sort of thing. Spooky scenes, including director Benjamin Christensen as a long-fingered Devil, are mixed with comedy in a pseudo-documentary format that often looks and sounds like an instructional film. Despite the inescapably dated quality of the material, it's so unusual that it's recommended, particularly for group viewing by horror fans. ***AKA:*** Haxan.

1922 74m/B *SW* Maren Pedersen, Clara Pontoppidan, Oscar Stribolt, Benjamin Christiansen, Tora Teje, Elith Pio, Karen Winther, Emmy Schonfeld, John Andersen; ***D:*** Benjamin Christiansen; ***C:*** Johan Ankerstjerne. **VHS** *MPI, GPV, WFV*

Witchery

Pregnant Jane (Linda Blair) dreams that she's being chased by dark figures. Whiney Leslie (Leslie Cumming) is convinced that retaining her virginity will help her understand the "witch's light" she's writing a book about. Her beau Gary (David Hasselhoff) disagrees. A pasty-faced witch (Hildegard Knef) is responsible. Most of the torpid inaction takes place in an old beach hotel. The alleged scares—a projector that runs without electricity, a bottomless bathtub—stink. The gore effects are better, but not enough. ***AKA:*** Witchcraft.

1988 96m/C David Hasselhoff, Linda Blair, Catherine Hickland, Hildegarde Knef, Leslie Cumming, Bob Champagne, Richard Farnsworth, Michael Manches; ***D:*** Fabrizio Laurenti, Martin Newlin. **VHS** *THV*

The Witches of Eastwick

Think a literate, raunchy feminist *Ghostbusters* with Jack Nicholson at his absolute wildest. One night after a few too many martinis, Jane (Susan Sarandon, who's excellent), Sukie (Michelle Pfeiffer, who's very good), and Alexandra (Cher, who's blah) concentrate on the perfect man. He appears as Daryl Van Horne (Nicholson), the devil himself. He writhes, he wriggles, he slithers, he lolls, he seduces each of them. After that...director George Miller surrenders to every excess imaginable. You may be delighted or you may be offended. You will not be bored.

1987 (R) 118m/C Jack Nicholson, Cher, Susan Sarandon, Michelle Pfeiffer, Veronica Cartwright, Richard Jenkins, Keith Joakum, Carel Struycken; ***D:*** George Miller; ***W:*** Michael Cristofer; ***C:*** Vilmos Zsigmond; ***M:*** John Williams. Los Angeles Film Critics Association Awards '87: Best Actor (Nicholson); New York Film Critics Awards '87: Best Actor (Nicholson); Nominations: Academy Awards '87: Best Sound, Best Original Score. **VHS, LV, 8mm, Closed Caption** *WAR*

The Witching

In his long and checkered career, Orson Welles was forced to take work in many less than sterling pictures, but this is probably the one he'd most like to be lost and forgotten. It's a halfbaked exploitative ripoff of *Rosemary's Baby* with Welles, effecting an Anglo-Irish accent, as Mr. Cato, boss of a coven in the small town of Lilith, California. Lori (Pamela Franklin) is the object of their transparent ambitions. Welles' performance is limited to a few short, unembarrassing scenes. ***AKA:*** Necromancy.

1972 90m/C Orson Welles, Pamela Franklin, Michael Ontkean, Lee Purcell, Lisa James, Harvey Jason, Terry Quinn; ***D:*** Bert I. Gordon; ***W:*** Bert I. Gordon, Gail March; ***C:*** Winton C. Hoch. **VHS** *NO*

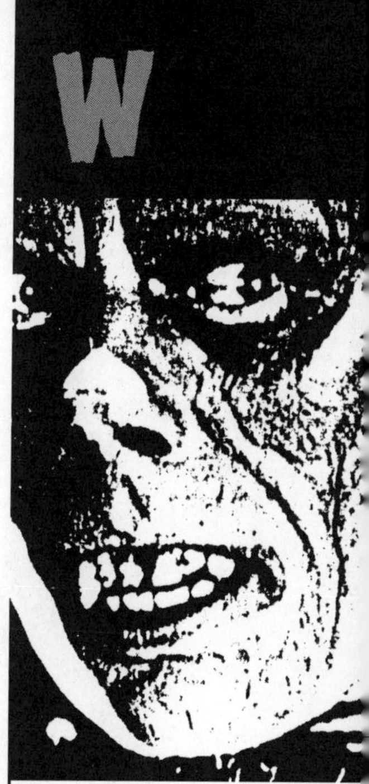

The Wizard of Gore

Both the hammy overacting and the gore effects are slightly more sophisticated here than they were in Herschell Gordon Lewis' early work. The disposable story concerns Montag the Magnificent (Ray Sagar), whose bloody stage illusions are so real that TV host Sherry Carson (Judy Cler) looks for the truth behind them. With Lewis' work, though, sophistication isn't really a virtue. This one's too slow, too talky, and lacking the hokey shock value of his first films.

1970 (R) 96m/C Ray Sager, Judy Cler, Wayne Ratay, Phil Lauenson, Jim Rau, Don Alexander, Monika Blackwell, Corinne Kirkin; ***D:*** Herschell Gordon Lewis; ***W:*** Allen Kahn; ***C:*** Alex Ameri, Daniel Krogh. **VHS** *SMW*

The Wizard of Oz

The line between fairy tale and horror lies in the eye of the beholder, and for this beholder, Margaret Hamilton crosses that line. As the sepia Almira Gulch, she's scary, but in color—green!—as the Wicked Witch of the West, she comes straight out of a nightmare. Add in her shock troops of flying chimps and those grotesque apple trees. They're all enough to be profoundly frightening for young audiences—profoundly frightening in the most wonderful, thrilling ways. In all other aspects, this milestone is beyond criticism. Considering its constant exposure on national television over the decades, it may well be the world's most-watched film.

1939 101m/C Judy Garland, Margaret Hamilton, Ray Bolger, Jack Haley, Bert Lahr, Frank Morgan, Charley Grapewin, Clara Blandick, Mitchell Lewis, Billie Burke; ***D:*** Victor Fleming; ***W:*** Noel Langley; ***M:*** Herbert Stothart. Academy Awards '39: Best Song ("Over the Rainbow"), Best Original Score, National Film Registry '89;; Nominations: Academy Awards '39: Best Color Cinematography, Best Interior Decoration, Best Picture, Best Special Effects. **VHS, LV, Closed Caption, DVD** *MGM, TLF, RDG*

Wolf

Judged strictly as an old-fashioned horror movie, *Wolf* is better than some of star Jack Nicholson's other work in the genre, particularly *The Shining*. With a solid script by novelist Jim Harrison and Wesley Strick and equally capable direction from Mike Nichols, it's scary, smart, and funny. Nicholson is fine as a book editor who's bitten by a wolf on a snowy road. Co-star Michelle Pfeiffer plays a curiously unsympathetic heroine. She and Nicholson never develop any screen "chemistry," but the last reel is terrific. The wolf makeup owes more to Lon Chaney's *The Wolf Man* than to recent work like *The Howling*. The transfer from big screen to video was done with an "image enhancing technology" that improves the clarity of the image. The difference is not dramatic, but it's certainly noticeable. Particularly in the night scenes and the big finish, the picture is extremely sharp and vivid, approaching the quality of a good laserdisc.

1994 (R) 125m/C Jack Nicholson, Michelle Pfeiffer, James Spader, Kate Nelligan, Christopher Plummer, Richard Jenkins, Om Puri, Eileen Atkins, David Hyde Pierce, Ron Rifkin, Prunella Scales; ***D:*** Mike Nichols; ***W:*** Wesley Strick, Jim Harrison; ***C:*** Giuseppe Rotunno; ***M:*** Ennio Morricone. **VHS, LV, 8mm, Closed Caption** *COL*

The Wolf Man

"The way you walk is thorny through no fault of your own, but as the rain enters the soil, the river enters the sea, so tears run to a predestined end. Find peace for a moment, my son." They don't write them like that any more, and Maria Ouspenskaya delivers the lines beautifully, describing Lawrence Talbot's (Lon Chaney, Jr.) transformation into an unwilling monster. Though he's usually ranked below the Frankenstein Monster and Dracula in Universal's roster of horror stars, the Wolf Man is one of the studio's most sympathetic creations, and he's always been popular

with audiences. The key is the way the role of Lawrence Talbot plays to Chaney's strengths as an actor. He combines physical power with vulnerability in both Talbot's guilt-ridden human side and his nocturnal, lunatic, bestial self. He shares that mixture of pathos and horror with Karloff's Monster. In one of his rare appearances in the genre, Claude Rains is excellent as the elder Talbot. To my mind, the poetic script and the lavish sets make the film much more successful and less dated than others of its time. It's a masterpiece that's been more often overlooked by critics than by fans.

1941 70m/B Lon Chaney Jr., Claude Rains, Maria Ouspenskaya, Ralph Bellamy, Bela Lugosi, Warren William, Patric Knowles, Evelyn Ankers; ***D:*** George Waggner; ***W:*** Curt Siodmak; ***C:*** Joseph Valentine. **VHS, LV** *USH*

Wolfen

Some good ideas are mixed with murky intentions for a very mixed bag. Albert Finney and Gregory Hines are the cop and the coroner trying to find the connection between the murders of a New York socialite and South Bronx derelicts. The titular creatures are responsible and given the film's screwball enviro-political sensibility, they're good guys, sort of. Still, the gory effects and deadpan humor deliver what fans expect. When you consider that director Michael Wadleigh's previous experience was the documentary *Woodstock,* and novelist Whitley Strieber would go on to popularize the alien-abduction foolishness with *Communion,* maybe this one's not so strange after all.

1981 (R) 115m/C Albert Finney, Gregory Hines, Tom Noonan, Diane Venora, Edward James Olmos, Dick O'Neill, Dehl Berti, Peter Michael Goetz, Sam Gray, Ralph Bell; ***D:*** Michael Wadleigh; ***W:*** Michael Wadleigh, David Eyre; ***C:*** Gerry Fisher; ***M:*** James Horner. **VHS, LV, Letterboxed** *WAR*

The Woman in the Room

See *Stephen King's Nightshift Collection.*

The Wraith

Amazingly, this ambitious teen-horror-car flick manages to hit on all cylinders. Can Jake (Charlie Sheen), the new kid in town, rescue sexy Keri (Sherilyn Fenn) from the unwanted advances of the nasty Packard (Nick Cassavetes), leader of a pack of young car thieves? With names like Skank, Rughead, and Gutterboy, they are wonderfully nasty and funny villains. Writer/director Mike Marvin doesn't waste much time on explanations for this brainless nonsense; he just lets it rip. If it becomes a little predictable by the last reel, the trip is still fun.

1987 (PG-13) 92m/C Charlie Sheen, Nick Cassavetes, Sherilyn Fenn, Randy Quaid, Matthew Barry, Clint Howard, Griffin O'Neal; ***D:*** Mike Marvin; ***W:*** Mike Marvin. **VHS, LV** *LIV*

XX: Beautiful Prey

Stylishly directed crime-horror story is about the appeal of violent pornography to both men and women. It opens with a shocking attack on a beautiful socialite (Kei Marimura). When police investigate, they learn that she may have invited the attack. Soon she has a female detective (Makiko Watanabe) involved in her fascination with sado-masochism. Director Toshiharu Ikeda shows real flair with one long tracking shot, a wildly mobile camera, and extreme close-ups used to emphasize key moments. One scene is a direct quote from *Body Heat,* but DePalma's *Dressed to Kill* would seem to be Ikeda's real model. The *XX* in the title refers to a series of

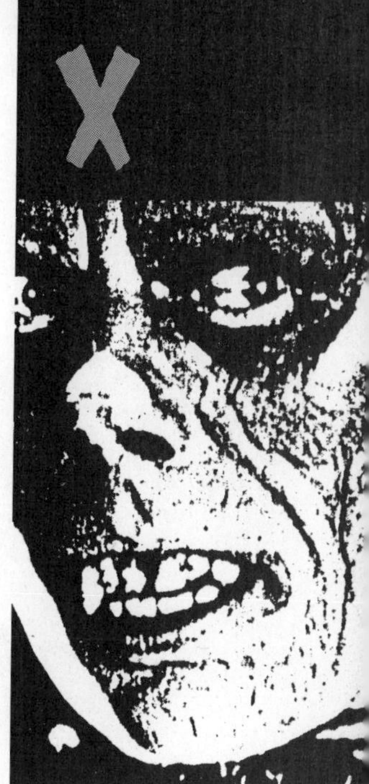

Margaret Hamilton and Judy Garland in *The Wizard of Oz.*

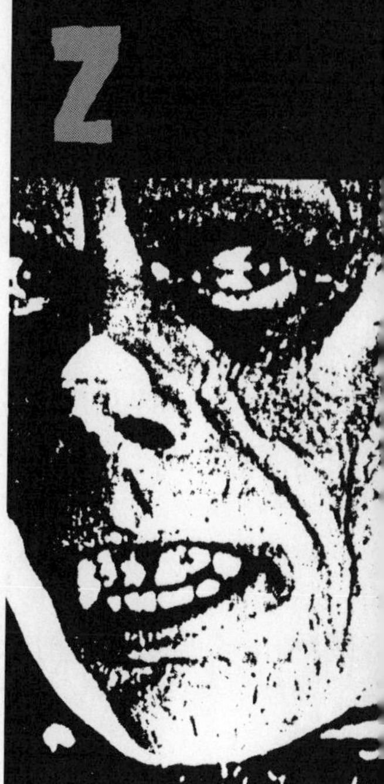

Japanese films revolving around strong female characters. Despite the strong sexual content, it would probably get an "R" rating. The film is well subtitled in colloquial English.

1996 90m/C *JP* Kei Marimura, Makiko Watanabe; ***D:*** Toshiharu Ikeda. **VHS** *VSM*

Young Frankenstein

Unlike virtually all horror-comedies, Mel Brooks' affectionate tribute works as both a parody and horror film. Note the wonderful opening shot and the superb lab scenes. (The credits thank Kenneth Strickfaden for the "original Frankenstein laboratory equipment.") Brooks is also true to the original "Golden Age" films to a remarkable degree with lavish sets, costumes, Gerald Hirschfeld's superb black-and-white photography, and a first-rate comic cast doing inspired work. As the Monster, Peter Boyle is worthy of Karloff. Madeline Kahn, Terri Garr, and Cloris Leachman are never upstaged by their co-stars; but the film belongs to Gene Wilder. No surprise there; he wrote the script with Brooks. Most of their fans would agree that this is their finest work, still as fresh, funny, and as worthy of another look as it's always been. One of horrors finest moments, and certainly the funniest.

1974 (PG) 108m/B Peter Boyle, Gene Wilder, Marty Feldman, Madeline Kahn, Cloris Leachman, Teri Garr, Kenneth Mars, Richard Haydn, Gene Hackman; ***D:*** Mel Brooks; ***W:*** Mel Brooks, Gene Wilder; ***C:*** Gerald Hirschfeld; ***M:*** John Morris. Nominations: Academy Awards '74: Best Adapted Screenplay, Best Sound. **VHS, LV, Closed Caption** *FOX, HMV*

Zombie

Italian gore-epic—perhaps the best of its kind—opens with a sailboat adrift in New York harbor and a zombie attack. After it, reporter Peter West (Ian McCulloch) and Ann Bowles (Tisa Farrow), daughter of the missing boat owner, head for the Caribbean where they find dozens of the living dead. Lucio Fulci's film was promoted as a sequel to Romero's *Dawn of the Dead,* and thematically and structurally, it is. Gianetto De Rossi's makeup effects are certainly the equal of Tom Savini's, and such key moments as the infamous splinter through the eyeball are as visceral as any in the genre. A few little continuity glitches don't detract from the bloody excesses and, to a lesser degree, the sexual exploitation. The film is available on tape under several titles with widely variable levels of image clarity. The letterboxed Anchor Bay edition is by far the best. ***AKA:*** Zombie Flesh-Eaters; Island of the Living Dead; Zombi 2.

1980 91m/C *IT* Tisa Farrow, Ian McCulloch, Richard Johnson, Al Cliver, Auretta Gay, Olga Karlatos, Stefania D'Amario, Ugo Bologna, Monica Zanchi; ***D:*** Lucio Fulci; ***W:*** Elisa Briganti; ***C:*** Sergio Salvati. **VHS, LV, Letterboxed** *VTR*

Zombie Island Massacre

Rita Jenrette was married to a congressman who was caught in the Washington Abscam scandal. She posed for *Playboy* magazine, wrote a sexy novel, and, at the end of her 15 minutes, starred in this low-budget exploitation specifically designed to show off her bod. That it does, big time. The Caribbean horror aspects are considerably less successful.

Lawrence Talbot (Lon Chaney, Jr.) is *The Wolf Man.*

1984 (R) 89m/C Rita Jenrette, David Broadnax; ***D:*** John N. Carter. **VHS** *TTV*

Zombie Lake

A skinny-dipping babe jump-starts underwater Nazi vampire zombies. After extended exposition explaining how the Nazis were killed, a girl's basketball team stops at the lake and one of the zombies pays a visit to his daughter. (I swear I am not making this up.) Under the name J.A. Lazer, Jean Rollin replaced Jesus Franco on this low-budget exploitation quickie. Amazingly, it is not the worst Nazi zombie movie. ***AKA:*** El Lago de los Muertos Vivientes; The Lake of the Living Dead. 🦴

1980 90m/C *FR SP* Howard Vernon, Pierre Escourrou, Anouchka, Anthony Mayans, Nadine Pascale, Jean Rollin; ***D:*** J.A. Laser, Jean Rollin; ***W:*** A. L. Mariaux, Julian Esteban. **VHS** *VCI*

HORROR CONNECTIONS

VideoHound's "Horror Connections" is intended to provide you, the fiendish fan, with other avenues to pursue your horror habit. We've compiled a list of web sites (warning—these come and go on a regular basis), magazines and newsletters, organizations, and books on your favorite movies, directors, stars, and other topics related to horror film. Be our guest.

WEB SITES

Absolute Horror
www.smackem.com

Alternative Cinema (Magazine)
members.aol.com/acmagazine

The Astounding B Monster (Magazine)
www.bmonster.com/

The Books of Cyber-Blood (Clive Barker)
www.afu.org/~afn15301/bocb.html

Brinke Stevens Fan Club
web.jadeinc.com/brinke/

The Cabinet of Dr. Casey
www.drcasey.com
(This site contains an extensive list of horror movie links.)

Cinefantastique (Magazine)
www.cfq.com/

Clive Barker
kspace.com/KM/spot.sys/Barker/pages/piece1.html

Clive Barker Lost Souls
www.clivebarker.com

Clive Barker Tribute Page
users.aol.com/barnabas01/barker1.htm

Clive Barker: Writer, Artist, Filmmaker
www.webcom.com/tby/cbarker.html

Clive Barker's Imajica
www.zephrapushu.com/imajica.htm

Dario Argento
www.astro.uu.se/~marcus/private/argento.html

Dario Argento
www.darioargento.org

Dario Argento: Master of Horror
www.houseofhorrors.com/argento.htm

Dario Argento: World of Horror
home2.swipnet.se/~w-20851/hemsida/dario.htm

Dark Gallery Online
www.b-movie.com/dghome.html

Dark Waters
superzippo.com/~drkwatrs

David Cronenberg
www.actlab.utexas.edu/~wolf/cronen.html

David Cronenberg
netlink.co.uk/users/zappa/cronen.html

David Cronenberg
www.chollian.net/~cynicult/cronen.html

David Cronenberg: Long Live the New Flesh
www.kgbmedia.com/WSV/cronen.html

David Cronenberg's Cinemadrome
cinemania.msn.com/cinemania/features/YouHave-BeenWarned.htm

Dawn of the Dead Rules
www.angelfire.com/il/dawnofthedeadrules

Day of the Dead
www.primenet.com/~buddy/movies/day/day.html

Draculina Online (Magazine)
www.b-movie.com/draculina.html

The Evil Dead Homepage
members.aol.com/roysteeth/edindex.html

Famous Monsters of Filmland (Magazine)
www.ktb.net/~fmof/

A Fistful of Dario (Argento)
www.en.com/users/tmr/argento.html

Gaz's Dawn of the Dead
www.users.globalnet.co.uk/~gazy/dawn/mian.htm

Hammer Horror
www.firstlevel.com/homepages/hammer/

Hammer Horror Collector's Network
www.hammerhorror.com

Hammer House of Horror
www.leba.net/~jrodkey/hammer01.html

Horror Films: A Bibliographic Guide
slaughter.net/horror/

Horror Haven
www.radzone.org/tkearns/horror.html

Horror Hotel
www.HorrorHotel.com

Horror Movies
www.horrormovies.com

House of Horrors
www.houseofhorrors.com

International Wes Craven Society
members.aol.com/IWCFS

Interview: David Cronenberg
www.filmscouts.com/intervws/dav-cro.html

Jesus Franco
users.aol.com/timothyp2/francofolder/francofile.html

Joe Sena's Dungeon of Darkness
www.dungeonofdarkness.com

Losman's Lair of Horror
www.losman.com

Lucio Fulci: Godfather of Gore
www.houseofhorrors.com/fulci.htm

Matthew Head's Friday the 13th and Stuff
www.arches.uga.edu/~friday13/

Mondo Hell (Faces of Death)
www.losman.com/fod

Monsterscene Web of Horror (Magazine)
www.monsterscene.com/

Mortado's Movie Page
www.nwlink.com/~mortado/movie.htm

Night of the Living Dead and the Morning After
www.jersey.net/~sjbcrb/sb/slasher

Page of the Dead (Night/Dawn/Day of the Dead)
home.unicom.net/~durowm

Pulsing Cinema
www.pcola.gulf.net/~kubrick

Quatermass (Hammer)
pine.shu.ac.uk/~lfmarm/quaterma/qhome.htm

The Ralston Interface: Scream Queens and Femme Fatales
www.parrett.net/~rralston/screamq.html

Realm of Darknysse
members.aol.com/darknysse/darkrelm.html

Scary Women
www.cinema.ucla.edu/women/

ScaryMann's Scary Movie Shrine
members.aol.com/ScaryMann

Scream Queens Illustrated (Magazine)
www.screamqueen.com

Shock Cinema (Magazine)
members.aol.com/shockcin

Shocking Images (Magazine)
www.apexonline.com/si

The Splatter Room
www.nw.com.au/~sabre/

Touched by the Hand of Goth
www.student.oulu.fi/~sairwas/frameX/horror/

The Unofficial Dawn of the Dead WWW Page
www.in-design.com/~flyboy/Dawn.html

The Vault
www.dct.com/~profundorosso/vault.html

Video Eyeball Magazine
www.tiac.net/users/videoeye/

Wes Craven's World
www.wescraven.com

A Whisper from Beyond (Clive Barker)
www.geocities.com/Area51/Cavern/2762/

Zombie Farm: Dawn of the Dead Preservation Page
www2.gol.com/users/noman/

MAGAZINES/NEWSLETTERS

Alternative Cinema
E.I. Independent Cinema
PO Box 371
Glenwood NJ 07418
201-509-9352
e-mail: eicinema@aol.com
web: members.aol.com/acmagazine/index.html
Quarterly. $18/year.

Chiller Theatre
PO Box 23
Rutherford NJ 07070
$23/4 issues; $5.95/issue.

Cinefantastique
Box 270
Oak Park IL 60303
708-366-5566
800-798-6515
fax: 708-366-1441
web: www.cfq.com
Bimonthly. $48/12 issues ($55 outside the U.S.).

Cinefex...The Journal of Cinematic Illusions
PO Box 20227
Riverside CA 92516
909-781-1917
Quarterly. $28/year.

Draculina
PO Box 587, Dept. BMT
Glen Carbon IL 62034
618-659-1293
e-mail: draculina@aol.com
web: www.b-movie.com/draculina.html
$24/4 issues.

Famous Monsters of Filmland
Dynacomm
Subscription Dept.
16161 Nordoff St., Crypt 480
North Hills CA 91343
web: www.ktb.net/~fmof
Bimonthly. $29.95/year ($45 in Canada and Mexico; $60 elsewhere).

Fangoria
475 Park Ave. S.
New York NY 10016
800-877-5549
10/year. $37.97/year ($46.97 outside the U.S.).

Horror Biz
PO Box 15
Demarest NJ 07627

Midnight Marquee
9721 Britinay Ln.
Baltimore MD 21234
410-665-9207
$5/issue.

Monster Scene
GOGO Entertainment Group, Inc.
1036 S. Ahrens Ave.
Lombard IL 60148
e-mail: webmaster@monsterscene.com
web: www.monsterscene.com
$24/4 issues ($36 in Canada and Mexico).

Movie Club
Movie Club Magazine
4504 Hershey Way
Baltimore MD 21236
Quarterly. $18/year ($34 outside the U.S.).

Phantom of the Movies' Videoscope
PhanMedia, Inc.
77 Franklin Ave.
Ocean Grove NJ 07756
Quarterly. $22/6 issues ($28 in Canada; $38 elsewhere).

Pitt of Horror
Chiller Theatre
PO Box 23, Dept. IP
Rutherford NJ 07070
Newsletter of the Ingrid Pitt International Fan Club (included in $19.95 membership).

Psychotronic
Michael J. Weldon
3309 Rt. 97
Narrowsburg NJ 12764-6126
914-252-6803
fax: 914-252-3905
Quarterly. $25/6 issues ($28 in Canada; $35 in South America); $5/issue.

Scarlet Street
Scarlet Street, Inc.
247 Boulevard
Glen Rock NJ 07452
201-445-0034
fax: 201-445-1496
e-mail: reditor@aol.com
Bimonthly. $35/year; $6.95/issue.

Scary Monsters
Dennis Druktenis Publishing & Mail Order, Inc.
348 Jocelyn Pl.

Highwood IL 60040
Quarterly. $5.95/issue ($8.50 in Canada).

Scream Queens Illustrated
Market Square Productions, Inc.
20 Market Sq.
Pittsburgh PA 15222
800-926-6653
web: www.screamqueen.com
Bimonthly. $36/year.

Screem Magazine
490 S. Franklin St.
Wilkes-Barre PA 18702
$5.95/issue.

Shock Cinema
Steve Puchalski
PO Box 518, Peter Stuyvesant Sta.
New York NY 10009
web: members.aol.com/shockcin/index.html
$5/issue.

Shocking Images
PO Box 601972
Sacramento CA 95860
916-974-0175
web: www.apexonline.com/si

Video Eyeball
122 Montclair Ave.
Boston MA 02131-1344
web: www.tiac.net/users/videoye
Bimonthly. $15/year in the U.S. ($18 in Canada).

Video WatchDog
PO Box 5283
Cincinnati OH 45205-0283
800-275-8395
513-471-8989
fax: 513-471-8248
Bimonthly. $24/year ($33 outside the U.S.).

ORGANIZATIONS

Academy of Science Fiction, Fantasy, and Horror Films
334 W. 54th St.
Los Angeles CA 90037
213-752-5811

Beverly Garland Club
Carl Del Vecchio
115 Prospect Ave.
Westwood NJ 07675-2113

Brinke Stevens Fan Club
8033 Sunset Blvd., Ste. 556
Hollywood CA 90046
web: web.jadeinc.com/brinke

Caroline Munro Fan Club
5 Paddington St.
London W1M 3LA England

Elvira Fan Club
14755 Ventura Blvd., 1-710
Sherman Oaks CA 91403
818-995-3461

Hammer Horror Collector's Network
909 Kara Way
Campbell CA 95008
web: www.hammerhorror.com

Ingrid Pitt International Fan Club
Chiller Theatre
PO Box 23, Dept. IP
Rutherford NJ 07070

Realm of the Vampire
c/o Sharida Rizzuto
577 Central Ave.
Jefferson LA 70121-1400

Rocky Horror Official Fan Club
204 W. 20th St.
New York NY 10011

Zacherley Fans at Large
c/o Lynda Bramberger
PO Box 434
Vails Gate NY 12584

BOOKS

The A to Z of Horror Films
Howard Maxford. 1997. Indiana University Press. $29.95 (paper).

Bela Lugosi: Master of the Macabre
Larry Edwards. 1997. McGuinn & McGuire. $17.95 (paper).

The BFI Companion to Horror
Kim Newman. 1997. Cassell Academic. $24.95 (paper).

Bright Darkness: The Lost Art of the Supernatural Horror Film
Jeremy Dyson, Pete Crowther. 1997. Cassell Academic. $21.95 (paper).

Broken Mirrors, Broken Minds: The Dark Dreams of Dario Argento
Maitland McDonaugh. 1994. Carol Publishing. $18.95.

Burton on Burton
Tim Burton. 1995. Faber & Faber. $22.95.

Christopher Lee and Peter Cushing and Horror Cinema: A Filmography of Their 22 Collaborations
Mark A. Miller. 1995. McFarland. $45.

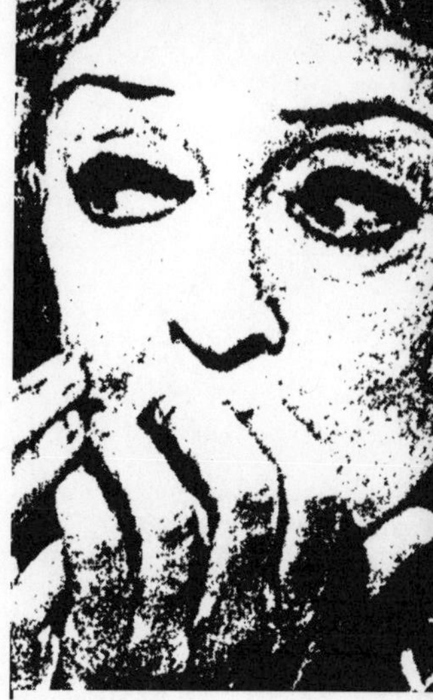

Clive Barker's A-Z of Horror
Clive Barker, Stephen Jones. 1997. Harper Prism. $29.95.

The Complete Films of Alfred Hitchcock
Robert A. Harris, Michael S. Lasky. 1993. Citadel Press. $17.95 (paper).

Creature Feature Movie Guide Strikes Again, 4th Ed.
John Stanley. 1994. Creatures at Large Press. $20 (paper).

Creature Features: The Science Fiction, Fantasy, and Horror Movie Guide
John Stanley. 1997. Berkley Publishing Group. $7.99 (paper).

Cronenberg on Cronenberg
David Cronenberg. Rev. ed., 1997. Faber & Faber. $15.95.

Cult Horror Films: From Attack of the 50 Foot Woman to Zombies of Mora Tau
Welch Everman. 1993. Citadel Press. $17.95 (paper).

Dark Carnival: The Secret World of Tod Browning, Hollywood's Master of the Macabre
David J. Skal, Elias Savada. 1995. Anchor. $23.

David Cronenberg: A Delicate Balance
Peter Morris. 1994. Eclipse Books. $9.95 (paper).

Dear Boris: The Life of William Henry Pratt A.K.A. Boris Karloff
Cynthia Lindsay. 1995. Limelight Editions. $20 (paper).

Do You Want It Good or by Tuesday? From Hammer Films to Hollywood!
Jimmy Sangster. Midnight Marquee Press. $20.

Fearing the Dark: The Val Lewton Career
Edmund G. Bansak. 1995. McFarland. $45.

The Fearmakers: The Screen's Directorial Masters of Suspense and Terror
John McCarty. 1994. St. Martin's. $14.95 (paper).

The Films of Lon Chaney
Michael F. Blake. 1998. Vestal Press. $35.

The Films of Stephen King
Ann Lloyd. 1994. St. Martin's. $14.95 (paper).

The Frankenstein Scrapbook: The Complete Movie Guide to the World's Most Famous Monster
Stephen Jones, Boris Karloff. 1995. Citadel. $15.95 (paper).

Ghoulardi—Inside Cleveland's Wildest Ride
Tom Feran, R.D. Heldenfels. 1997. Gray & Co. $17.95 (paper).

Giant Monster Movies
Robert Marrero. Fantasma Books. 1994. $17.95 (paper).

Giger's Alien
H.R.Giger, Timothy Leary. 1991. Morpheus International. $39.95.

Hammer Films: An Exhaustive Filmography
Tom Johnson, Deborah Del Vecchio. 1996. McFarland. $65.

Hammer, House of Horror: Behind the Screams
Howard Maxford. 1996. Overlook Press. $27.95.

A History of Horrors: The Rise and Fall of the House of Hammer
Denis Meikle, Christopher T. Koetting. 1996. Scarecrow Press. $55.

Horror Film Stars
Michael R. Pitts. 2nd ed., 1991. McFarland & Co.

House of Horror: The Hammer Films Story
Jack Hunter. 1996. Creation House. $19.95.

How I Made a Hundred Movies in Hollywood and Never Lost a Dime
Roger Corman with Jim Jerome. 1990. Delta. Out of print.

Immoral Tales: European Sex and Horror Movies, 1956-1984
Cathal Tohill, Pete Tombs. 1995. St. Martin's. $18.95 (paper).

Jacques Tourneur: The Cinema of Nightfall
Chris Fujiwara. 1998. McFarland. $42.50.

James Whale: A New World of Gods and Monsters
James Curtis, Kevin Brownlow. 1998. Faber & Faber. $24.95 (paper).

John Stanley's Creature Feature Movie Guide Strikes Again: An A to Z Encyclopedia to the Cinema of the Fantastic, or Is There a Mad Doctor/Dentist in the House
John Stanley. 4th ed., 1995. Creatures at Large Press. $20 (paper).

Legendary Horror Films: Essential Genre History, Offscreen Anecdotes, Special Effects Secrets, Ghoulish Facts and Photographs
Peter Guttmacher. 1995. Metro Books. $17.98.

Lon Chaney, Jr.: Horror Film Star, 1906-1993
Don G. Smith. 1996. McFarland. $32.50.

The Monster Show: A Cultural History of Horror
David J. Skal. 1993. Penguin. $14.95 (paper).

Monsters in the Closet: Homosexuality and the Horror Film
Harry M. Benshoff. 1997. Manchester University Press. $69.95.

More Things Than Are Dreamt Of: Masterpieces of Supernatural Horror—From Mary Shelley to Stephen King—in Literature and Film
James Ursini, Alain Silver, William Peter Blatty. 1994. Limelight Editions. $20 (paper).

The Nightmare Never Ends: The Official History of Freddy Krueger and the Nightmare on Elm Street Films
William Schoell, James Spencer. 1992. Citadel Press. $17.95 (paper).

Nightmare of Ecstasy: The Life and Art of Edward D. Wood, Jr.
Rudolph Grey. 1994. Feral House. $14.95 (paper).

Nightwalkers: Gothic Horror Movies—The Modern Era
Bruce Lanier Wright. 1995. Taylor. $17.95 (paper).

Of Gods and Monsters: A Critical Guide to Universal Studios' Science Fiction, Horror, and Mystery Films, 1929-1939
John T. Soister. 1998. McFarland. $65.

The Official Splatter Movie Guide
John McCarty. 1989. St. Martin's Press. $10.95 (paper).

The Official Splatter Movie Guide Vol. 2
John McCarty. 1992. St. Martin's Press. $12.95 (paper).

Order in the Universe: The Films of John Carpenter
Robert C. Cumbow. 1990. Scarecrow Press. $31.

The Overlook Film Encyclopedia: Horror
Phil Hardy. 1995. Penguin. $40 (paper); $50.

Peter Cushing: The Gentle Man of Horror and His 91 Films
Deborah Del Vecchio, Tom Johnson. 1992. McFarland. $49.95.

The Psychotronic Encyclopedia of Film
Michael Weldon. 1989. Ballantine Books. $20 (paper).

The Psychotronic Video Guide
Michael Weldon. 1996. St. Martin's Press. $29.95 (paper).

Rational Fears: American Horror in the 1950s
Mark Jancovich. 1996. Manchester University Press. $24.95 (paper).

Roger Corman: The Best of the Cheap Acts
Mark McGee. Rev. ed., 1997. McFarland. $20 (paper).

Split Image: The Life of Anthony Perkins
Charles Winecoff. 1997. Plume. $14.95 (paper).

Step Right Up! I'm Going to Scare the Pants Off America: Memoirs of a B-Movie Mogul
William Castle; intro by John Waters. 2nd ed., 1992. Pharos. $12.95 (paper).

The Stephen King Companion
George Beahm, ed. Rev. ed., 1995. Andrews & McMeel. $12.95 (paper).

Tell Me When to Look: Modern Horror Films from The Curse of Frankenstein to The Craft
John McCarty. 1997. Citadel Press. $19.95 (paper).

Terror on Tape
James O'Neill. 1994. Billboard Books. $16.95 (paper).

The Vampire Book: The Encyclopedia of the Undead
Gordon Melton. 2nd ed., 1998. Visible Ink. $24.95 (paper).

The Vampire Film: From Nosferatu to Interview with the Vampire
Alain Silver, James Ursini. 3rd ed., 1997. Limelight Editions. $25 (paper).

The Vampire Gallery
Gordon Melton. 1998. Visible Ink. $19.95 (paper).

VideoHound's Complete Guide to Cult Flicks and Trash Pics
Carol Schwartz, ed. 1996. Visible Ink. $16.95 (paper).

VideoHound's Vampires on Video
Gordon Melton. 1997. Visible Ink. $17.95 (paper).

Vintage Monster Movies
Robert Marrero. Fantasma Books. 1993. $12.95 (paper).

Weirdsville USA: The Obsessive Universe of David Lynch
Paul A. Woods. 1997. Plexus. $19.95 (paper).

Alternative Titles

Don't be scared if you think we didn't include your favorite movie. Videos like to lurk under various names in the video store, especially those flicks whose titles have been translated umpteen times. Our "Alternative Titles Index" is your key to tracking down those elusive movies, by offering an alphabetical listing of, yes, alternative titles, with cross references to the appropriate entries in our main review section. Beware—initial articles in foreign titles are not ignored in the alpha sort, so *El Diablo* will be found in the "E"s, and *Les Yeux sans Visage* in the "L"s.

Blood Brides *See* Hatchet for the Honeymoon (1970)

Blood Castle *See* The Blood Spattered Bride (1972)

The Blood Cult of Shangri-La *See* The Thirsty Dead (1974)

Blood Doctor *See* Mad Doctor of Blood Island (1969)

Blood Evil *See* Demons of the Mind (1972)

Blood Feast *See* Night of a Thousand Cats (1972)

Blood for Dracula *See* Andy Warhol's Dracula (1974)

Blood Freaks *See* Blood Freak (1972)

Blood Hunger *See* Vampyres (1974)

Blood Hunt *See* The Thirsty Dead (1974)

Blood Is My Heritage *See* Blood of Dracula (1957)

Blood of Frankenstein *See* Dracula vs. Frankenstein (1971)

Blood of the Demon *See* Blood of Dracula (1957)

Blood of the Undead *See* Schizo (1977)

Blood on His Lips *See* Hideous Sun Demon (1959)

Blood Sisters *See* Sisters (1973)

Blood Thirst *See* Salem's Lot (1979)

Blood Will Have Blood *See* Demons of the Mind (1972)

Bloody Fiance *See* The Blood Spattered Bride (1972)

The Bloody Scream of Dracula *See* Dracula, Prince of Darkness (1965)

Blut an den Lippen *See* Daughters of Darkness (1971)

The Boogeyman *See* Stephen King's Nightshift Collection (1983)

Bordello of Blood *See* Tales from the Crypt Presents Bordello of Blood (1996)

Braindead *See* Dead Alive (1993)

Bram Stoker's Burial of the Rats *See* Burial of the Rats (1995)

Bram Stoker's Count Dracula *See* Count Dracula (1971)

Bram Stoker's Dracula *See* Dracula (1973)

Brenn, Hexe, Brenn *See* Mark of the Devil (1969)

Bride of Fengriffen *See* And Now the Screaming Starts (1973)

Bride of the Atom *See* Bride of the Monster (1956)

The Bug *See* Bug (1975)

Burn, Witch, Burn *See* Mark of the Devil (1969)

Cannibal Orgy, or the Maddest Story Ever Told *See* Spider Baby (1964)

Carne per Frankenstein *See* Andy Warhol's Frankenstein (1974)

The Case of Jonathan Drew *See* The Lodger (1926)

Castle of Doom *See* Vampyr (1931)

Catastrophe 1999 *See* Last Days of Planet Earth (1974)

Cats *See* Night of a Thousand Cats (1972)

Cemetery Girls *See* The Vampire Hookers (1978)

Cemetery Girls *See* The Velvet Vampire (1971)

Chamber of Fear *See* The Fear Chamber (1968)

Chamber of Tortures *See* Torture Chamber of Baron Blood (1972)

Chi Sei *See* Beyond the Door (1975)

Child of Satan *See* To the Devil, a Daughter (1976)

Christmas Evil *See* Terror in Toyland (1985)

Chronos *See* Cronos (1994)

The City of the Dead *See* Horror Hotel (1960)

Clive Barker's Lord of Illusions *See* Lord of Illusions (1995)

Club Dead *See* Terror at Red Wolf Inn (1972)

Code Name: Trixie *See* The Crazies (1973)

Communion *See* Alice Sweet Alice (1976)

The Corpse *See* Crucible of Horror (1969)

Cosi Dolce...Cosi Perversa *See* Kiss Me, Kill Me (1969)

Count Dracula and His Vampire Bride *See* The Satanic Rites of Dracula (1973)

Creatures of the Devil *See* Dead Men Walk (1943)

Creeps *See* Bloody Birthday (1980)

Creeps *See* Night of the Creeps (1986)

Crypt of the Blind Dead *See* Tombs of the Blind Dead (1972)

The Curse of Dracula *See* Return of Dracula (1958)

Curse of the Golem *See* It! (1967)

Dance of the Vampires *See* The Fearless Vampire Killers (1967)

Das Bildness des Dorian Gray *See* Dorian Gray (1970)

Das Cabinet des Dr. Caligari *See* The Cabinet of Dr. Caligari (1919)

The Daughter of Frankenstein *See* Lady Frankenstein (1972)

Daughters of Dracula *See* Vampyres (1974)

Day of the Woman *See* I Spit on Your Grave (1977)

Dead Kids *See* Strange Behavior (1981)

Deadly Harvest *See* Children of the Corn 4: The Gathering (1996)

Deadly Sting *See* Evil Spawn (1987)

Death Bite *See* Spasms (1982)

Death Corps *See* Shock Waves (1977)

Death Rides a Carousel *See* Carnival of Blood (1971)

Death Trap *See* Eaten Alive (1976)

Deep Red *See* Deep Red: Hatchet Murders (1975)

Dellamorte Delamore *See* Cemetery Man (1995)

Demon *See* God Told Me To (1976)

Demon Keeper *See* Tales from the Crypt Presents Demon Knight (1994)

Demon Knight *See* Tales from the Crypt Presents Demon Knight (1994)

Demoni *See* Demons (1986)

The Demon's Mask *See* Black Sunday (1960)

Der Dirnenmoerder von London *See* Jack the Ripper (1976)

Der Golem, wie er in die Welt kam *See* The Golem (1920)

The Devil and Dr. Frankenstein *See* Andy Warhol's Frankenstein (1974)

The Devil and the Dead *See* Lisa and the Devil (1975)

The Devil in the House of Exorcism *See* Lisa and the Devil (1975)

The Devil Rides Out *See* Devil's Bride (1968)

The Devil within Her *See* Beyond the Door (1975)

Devil's Witch *See* Kiss Me, Kill Me (1969)

Die Saege des Todes *See* Bloody Moon (1983)

Die Zwolfte Stunde *See* Nosferatu (1922)

Disciple of Dracula *See* Dracula, Prince of Darkness (1965)

Doctors Wear Scarlet *See* The Bloodsuckers (1970)

The Door with Seven Locks *See* Chamber of Horrors (1940)

Dracula *See* Bram Stoker's Dracula (1992)

Dracula *See* The Horror of Dracula (1958)

Dracula 71 *See* Count Dracula (1971)

Dracula Cerca Sangue di Vergine e...Mori de Sete *See* Andy Warhol's Dracula (1974)

Dracula Contra Frankenstein *See* Dracula vs. Frankenstein (1971)

Dracula Is Dead and Well and Living in London *See* The Satanic Rites of Dracula (1973)

Dracula: The Love Story *See* To Die For (1989)

Dracula, the Terror of the Living Dead *See* The Hanging Woman (1972)

Dracula Today *See* Dracula A.D. 1972 (1972)

Dracula Vuole Vivere: Cerca Sangue de Vergina *See* Andy Warhol's Dracula (1974)

Dracula's Castle *See* Blood of Dracula's Castle (1969)

Dripping Deep Red *See* Deep Red: Hatchet Murders (1975)

Due Occhi Diabolici *See* Two Evil Eyes (1990)

Eaten Alive *See* Emerald Jungle (1980)

Eaten Alive by Cannibals *See* Emerald Jungle (1980)

Edgar Allan Poe's Conqueror Worm *See* The Conqueror Worm (1968)

Edgar Allan Poe's House of Usher *See* The House of Usher (1988)

Edgar Allan Poe's The Oblong Box *See* The Oblong Box (1969)

El Ataque de los Muertos Sin Ojos *See* Return of the Evil Dead (1975)

El Diablo se Lleva a los Muertos *See* Lisa and the Devil (1975)

El Lago de los Muertos Vivientes *See* Zombie Lake (1980)

El Retorno del Hombre-Lobo *See* The Craving (1980)

The Electric Man *See* Man Made Monster (1941)

Ella *See* Monkey Shines (1988)

Entity Force *See* One Dark Night (1982)

Erzebeth *See* Daughters of Darkness (1971)

Et Mourir de Plaisir *See* Blood and Roses (1961)

Evil Dead 3 *See* Army of Darkness (1992)

The Evils of Dorian Gray *See* Dorian Gray (1970)

Expose *See* The House on Straw Hill (1976)

Exquisite Tenderness *See* The Surgeon (1994)

Eyes of Hell *See* The Mask (1961)

Eyes without a Face *See* The Horror Chamber of Dr. Faustus (1959)

The Fall of the House of Usher *See* The House of Usher (1988)

False Face *See* Scalpel (1976)

Fanatic *See* Die! Die! My Darling! (1965)

The Fanatic *See* The Last Horror Film (1982)

The Fantastic Disappearing Man *See* Return of Dracula (1958)

The Farm *See* The Curse (1987)

Fear in the Night *See* Dynasty of Fear (1972)

Feast of Flesh *See* Blood Feast (1963)

Fengriffen *See* And Now the Screaming Starts (1973)

Five Million Years to Earth *See* Quatermass and the Pit (1967)

Flesh for Frankenstein *See* Andy Warhol's Frankenstein (1974)

The Folks at Red Wolf Inn *See* Terror at Red Wolf Inn (1972)

Forbidden Love *See* Freaks (1932)

Frankenstein *See* Andy Warhol's Frankenstein (1974)

Frankenstein *See* Mary Shelley's Frankenstein (1994)

The Frankenstein Experiment *See* Andy Warhol's Frankenstein (1974)

Frankenstein Made Woman *See* Frankenstein Created Woman (1966)

Frozen Ghost *See* Weird Woman/Frozen Ghost (1944)

The Gemini Twins *See* Twins of Evil (1971)

Ghost Story *See* Madhouse Mansion (1974)

The Giant Leeches *See* Attack of the Giant Leeches (1959)

Gli Orrori del Castello di Norimberga *See* Torture Chamber of Baron Blood (1972)

Grave Robbers from Outer Space *See* Plan 9 from Outer Space (1956)

Grimm Brothers' Snow White *See* Snow White: A Tale of Terror (1997)

The Grip of the Strangler *See* The Haunted Strangler (1958)

Gritos en la Noche *See* The Awful Dr. Orloff (1962)

Halloween: The Origin of Michael Myers *See* Halloween 6: The Curse of Michael Myers (1995)

Hands of a Strangler *See* The Hands of Orlac (1960)

The Hands of Orlac *See* Mad Love (1935)

Hands of the Strangler *See* The Hands of Orlac (1960)

The Hatchet Murders *See* Deep Red: Hatchet Murders (1975)

The Haunted *See* Curse of the Demon (1957)

The Haunted and the Hunted *See* Dementia 13 (1963)

The Haunting of Hamilton High *See* Hello Mary Lou: Prom Night 2 (1987)

Haxan *See* Witchcraft through the Ages (1922)

The Head That Wouldn't Die *See* The Brain that Wouldn't Die (1963)

Heartstone *See* Demonstone (1989)

Hellraiser 2 *See* Hellbound: Hellraiser 2 (1988)

Hexen bis aufs Blut Gequaelt *See* Mark of the Devil (1969)

Holy Terror *See* Alice Sweet Alice (1976)

Homecoming Night *See* Night of the Creeps (1986)

Honeymoon of Fear *See* Dynasty of Fear (1972)

Horror Hotel Massacre *See* Eaten Alive (1976)

The Hounds of Zaroff *See* The Most Dangerous Game (1932)

House 3 *See* The Horror Show (1989)

House of Crazies *See* Asylum (1972)

House of Doom *See* The Black Cat (1934)

House of Evil *See* The House on Sorority Row (1983)

The House of Exorcism *See* Lisa and the Devil (1975)

House of Fright *See* Black Sunday (1960)

House of Fright *See* The Two Faces of Dr. Jekyll (1960)

House of Mystery *See* Night Monster (1942)

House of Terror *See* The Hanging Woman (1972)

House of the Damned *See* Spectre (1996)

House of Usher *See* The Fall of the House of Usher (1960)

Howling 2: Stirba—Werewolf Bitch *See* Howling 2: Your Sister Is a Werewolf (1985)

Howling 7 *See* The Howling: New Moon Rising (1995)

H.P. Lovecraft's The Unnamable Returns *See* The Unnamable 2: The Statement of Randolph Carter (1992)

Hunchback *See* The Hunchback of Notre Dame (1982)

Hungry Wives *See* Season of the Witch (1973)

I Have No Mouth But I Must Scream *See* And Now the Screaming Starts (1973)

I Love to Kill *See* Impulse (1974)

I Tre Volti della Paura *See* Black Sabbath (1964)

Il Conte Dracula *See* Count Dracula (1971)

Il Diavolo e i Morti *See* Lisa and the Devil (1975)

Il Dio Chiamato a Dorian *See* Dorian Gray (1970)

Il Fiume del Grande Caimano *See* The Great Alligator (1981)

Il Gatto Nero *See* The Black Cat (1981)

Il Rosso Segmo della Follia *See* Hatchet for the Honeymoon (1970)

Incense for the Damned *See* The Bloodsuckers (1970)

The Incredibly Strange Creatures *See* Incredibly Strange Creatures Who Stopped Living and Became Mixed-Up Zombies (1963)

The Inner Sanctum: Calling Dr. Death/Strange Confession *See* Calling Dr. Death/Strange Confession (1943)

The Inner Sanctum: Weird Woman/Frozen Ghost *See* Weird Woman/Frozen Ghost (1944)

Inseminoid *See* Horror Planet (1980)

Island of the Living Dead *See* Zombie (1980)

It Fell from the Sky *See* Alien Dead (1979)

Jack's Wife *See* Season of the Witch (1973)

Jaws 3-D *See* Jaws 3 (1983)

Jekyll's Inferno *See* The Two Faces of Dr. Jekyll (1960)

Jennifer (The Snake Goddess) *See* Jennifer (1978)

John Carpenter Presents Body Bags *See* Body Bags (1993)

Jurassic Park 2 *See* The Lost World: Jurassic Park 2 (1997)

Killbots *See* Chopping Mall (1986)

The Killer Behind the Mask *See* Savage Weekend (1980)

The Killer Whale *See* Orca (1977)

Kiss of Evil *See* Kiss of the Vampire (1962)

Kronos *See* Captain Kronos: Vampire Hunter (1974)

Krug and Company *See* Last House on the Left (1972)

La Camara del Terror *See* The Fear Chamber (1968)

La Casa Dell' Exorcismo *See* Lisa and the Devil (1975)

La Chiesa *See* The Church (1990)

La Figlia di Frankenstein *See* Lady Frankenstein (1972)

La Maschera del Demonio *See* Black Sunday (1960)

La Noche de la Muerta Ciega *See* Tombs of the Blind Dead (1972)

La Noche de los Mil Gatos *See* Night of a Thousand Cats (1972)

La Noche dell Terror Ciego *See* Tombs of the Blind Dead (1972)

La Novia Esangrentada *See* The Blood Spattered Bride (1972)

La Orgia de los Muertos *See* The Hanging Woman (1972)

The Lady Dracula *See* Lemora: A Child's Tale of the Supernatural (1973)

Lady of the Shadows *See* The Terror (1963)

The Lake of the Living Dead *See* Zombie Lake (1980)

The Lamp *See* The Outing (1987)

The Langoliers *See* Stephen King's The Langoliers (1995)

Le Frisson des Vampires *See* Thrill of the Vampire (1970)

Le Locataire *See* The Tenant (1976)

Le Rouge aux Levres *See* Daughters of Darkness (1971)

Legacy of Blood *See* Blood Legacy (1973)

Legend of the Bayou *See* Eaten Alive (1976)

The Legendary Curse of Lemora *See* Lemora: A Child's Tale of the Supernatural (1973)

Lemora, Lady Dracula *See* Lemora: A Child's Tale of the Supernatural (1973)

Les Demons *See* The Demons (1974)

Les Predateurs de la Nuit *See* Faceless (1988)

Les Yeux sans Visage *See* The Horror Chamber of Dr. Faustus (1959)

Lisa e il Diavolo *See* Lisa and the Devil (1975)

The Liver Eaters *See* Spider Baby (1964)

Lo Strano Vizio della Signora Ward *See* Blade of the Ripper (1970)

The Lodger: A Case of London Fog *See* The Lodger (1926)

Los Demonios *See* The Demons (1974)

Lost in Time *See* Waxwork 2: Lost in Time (1991)

Mad Jake *See* Blood Salvage (1990)

Madame Frankenstein *See* Lady Frankenstein (1972)

Mangiati Vivi *See* Emerald Jungle (1980)

Mangiati Vivi dai Cannibali *See* Emerald Jungle (1980)

Mausoleum *See* One Dark Night (1982)

The Medieval Dead *See* Army of Darkness (1992)

Minaccia d'Amore *See* Dial Help (1988)

Mindwarp: An Infinity of Terror *See* Galaxy of Terror (1981)

Model Massacre *See* Color Me Blood Red (1964)

Monkey Shines: An Experiment in Fear *See* Monkey Shines (1988)

Monster *See* Humanoids from the Deep (1980)

Monster of Terror *See* Die, Monster, Die! (1965)

The Monster Show *See* Freaks (1932)

Much Ado about Murder *See* Theatre of Blood (1973)

The Mutilator *See* The Dark (1979)

My World Dies Screaming *See* Terror in the Haunted House (1958)

Nachts wenn Dracula Erwacht *See* Count Dracula (1971)

Nature's Mistakes *See* Freaks (1932)

Necromancy *See* The Witching (1972)

Necronomicon *See* H.P. Lovecraft's Necronomicon: Book of the Dead (1993)

Next! *See* Blade of the Ripper (1970)

The Next Victim *See* Blade of the Ripper (1970)

The Night Flier *See* Stephen King's The Night Flier (1996)

Night of the Anubis *See* Night of the Living Dead (1968)

Night of the Blind Dead *See* Tombs of the Blind Dead (1972)

Night of the Bloodsuckers *See* The Vampire Hookers (1978)

Night of the Demon *See* Curse of the Demon (1957)

Night of the Eagle *See* Burn Witch, Burn! (1962)

Night of the Flesh Eaters *See* Night of the Living Dead (1968)

Night Scare *See* Nightscare (1993)

Nightmare on Elm Street 6: Freddy's Dead *See* Freddy's Dead: The Final Nightmare (1991)

The Nights of Dracula *See* Count Dracula (1971)

Nosferatu, A Symphony of Horror *See* Nosferatu (1922)

Nosferatu, A Symphony of Terror *See* Nosferatu (1922)

Nosferatu, Eine Symphonie des Grauens *See* Nosferatu (1922)

Nosferatu, the Vampire *See* Nosferatu (1922)

Nostradamus No Daiyogen *See* Last Days of Planet Earth (1974)

Not Against the Flesh *See* Vampyr (1931)

Notre Dame de Paris *See* The Hunchback of Notre Dame (1957)

Oasis of the Zombies *See* Bloodsucking Nazi Zombies (1982)

Occhi Senza Volto *See* The Horror Chamber of Dr. Faustus (1959)

Of Death, of Love *See* Cemetery Man (1995)

Omen 2 *See* Damien: Omen 2 (1978)

The Omen 3 *See* The Final Conflict (1981)

Opera *See* Terror at the Opera (1988)

Orca—Killer Whale *See* Orca (1977)

Orgy of the Dead *See* The Hanging Woman (1972)

Outback Vampires *See* The Wicked (1989)

Panic in the Trans-Siberian Train *See* Horror Express (1972)

Panic on the Trans-Siberian Express *See* Horror Express (1972)

Panico en el Transiberiano *See* Horror Express (1972)

The Parasite Murders *See* They Came from Within (1975)

Pardon Me, Your Teeth Are in My Neck *See* The Fearless Vampire Killers (1967)

Phenomena *See* Creepers (1985)

Pillow of Death *See* Dead Man's Eyes/Pillow of Death (1944)

Piranha 2: Flying Killers *See* Piranha 2: The Spawning (1982)

Planet of Horrors *See* Galaxy of Terror (1981)

Poor Albert and Little Annie *See* I Dismember Mama (1974)

Profundo Rosso *See* Deep Red: Hatchet Murders (1975)

Prom Night 2 *See* Hello Mary Lou: Prom Night 2 (1987)

The Promise of Red Lips *See* Daughters of Darkness (1971)

Prophecies of Nostradamus *See* Last Days of Planet Earth (1974)

Psycho Sex Fiend *See* The House that Vanished (1973)

Rage *See* Rabid (1977)

Ragno Gelido *See* Dial Help (1988)

Re-Animator 2 *See* Bride of Re-Animator (1989)

Red Dragon *See* Manhunter (1986)

The Red Lips *See* Daughters of Darkness (1971)

The Red Sign of Madness *See* Hatchet for the Honeymoon (1970)

Return of the Blind Dead *See* Return of the Evil Dead (1975)

Return of the Texas Chainsaw Massacre *See* The Texas Chainsaw Massacre 4: The Next Generation (1995)

Return of the Wolfman *See* The Craving (1980)

Return of the Zombies *See* The Hanging Woman (1972)

Return to Glennascaul: A Story That Is Told *See* Orson Welles' Ghost Story (195?)

Revenge of Dracula *See* Dracula, Prince of Darkness (1965)

The Revenge of Dracula *See* Dracula vs. Frankenstein (1971)

Revenge of the Living Dead *See* Children Shouldn't Play with Dead Things (1972)

Revenge of the Vampire *See* Black Sunday (1960)

Roger Corman Presents Burial of the Rats *See* Burial of the Rats (1995)

Roger Corman Presents: House of the Damned *See* Spectre (1996)

Roger Corman Presents: Humanoids from the Deep *See* Humanoids from the Deep (1996)

Roger Corman Presents: Vampirella *See* Vampirella (1996)

Roger Corman's Frankenstein Unbound *See* Frankenstein Unbound (1990)

The Sabre Tooth Tiger *See* Deep Red: Hatchet Murders (1975)

Salem's Ghost *See* Witchcraft 8: Salem's Ghost (1995)

Satan *See* Mark of the Devil (1969)

Satan's Bloody Freaks *See* Dracula vs. Frankenstein (1971)

Satan's Claw *See* The Blood on Satan's Claw (1971)

Satan's Daughters *See* Vampyres (1974)

Satan's Skin *See* The Blood on Satan's Claw (1971)

Satyricon *See* Fellini Satyricon (1969)

Scary Movie *See* Scream (1996)

Scream Again *See* Scream 2 (1997)

Scream and Die *See* The House that Vanished (1973)

Screamer *See* Scream and Scream Again (1970)

The Secret of Dorian Gray *See* Dorian Gray (1970)

Seddok, l'Erede di Satana *See* Atom Age Vampire (1961)

Sensuous Vampires *See* The Vampire Hookers (1978)

Se7en *See* Seven (1995)

Seven Sisters *See* The House on Sorority Row (1983)

Sex and the Vampire *See* Thrill of the Vampire (1970)

Sex Crime of the Century *See* Last House on the Left (1972)

She Demons of the Swamp *See* Attack of the Giant Leeches (1959)

Shivers *See* They Came from Within (1975)

Shock *See* Beyond the Door 2 (1979)

Shock (Transfer Suspense Hypnos) *See* Beyond the Door 2 (1979)
Shockwave *See* The Arrival (1996)
Small Town Massacre *See* Strange Behavior (1981)
Snow White in the Black Forest *See* Snow White: A Tale of Terror (1997)
So Sweet, So Perverse *See* Kiss Me, Kill Me (1969)
Son of Darkness: To Die For 2 *See* To Die For 2: Son of Darkness (1991)
Sotto gli Occhi dell'Assassino *See* Unsane (1982)
Spawn *See* Todd McFarlane's Spawn (1997)
Spettri *See* Specters (1987)
The Spider *See* Earth Vs. the Spider (1958)
Spider Baby, or the Maddest Story Ever Told *See* Spider Baby (1964)
The Spooky Movie Show *See* The Mask (1961)
The Stand *See* Stephen King's The Stand (1994)
Starlight Slaughter *See* Eaten Alive (1976)
Stephen King's Cat's Eye *See* Cat's Eye (1985)
Stephen King's Silver Bullet *See* Silver Bullet (1985)
Stephen King's Sleepwalkers *See* Sleepwalkers (1992)
The Strange Adventure of David Gray *See* Vampyr (1931)
Strange Confession *See* Calling Dr. Death /Strange Confession (1943)
Stranger in Our House *See* Summer of Fear (1978)
Subspecies 2 *See* Bloodstone: Subspecies 2 (1992)
Subspecies 3 *See* Bloodlust: Subspecies 3 (1993)
The Sun Demon *See* Hideous Sun Demon (1959)
Suspense *See* Beyond the Door 2 (1979)
The Teenage Psycho Meets Bloody Mary *See* Incredibly Strange Creatures Who Stopped Living and Became Mixed-Up Zombies (1963)
Tenebrae *See* Unsane (1982)
Terror Eyes *See* Night School (1981)
Terror from the Sun *See* Hideous Sun Demon (1959)
Terror House *See* Terror at Red Wolf Inn (1972)
Terror of Dracula *See* Nosferatu (1922)
The Terror of the Vampires *See* Thrill of the Vampire (1970)
They're Coming to Get You *See* Dracula vs. Frankenstein (1971)
The Thing from Another World *See* The Thing (1951)
Thinner *See* Stephen King's Thinner (1996)
The Thirst of Baron Blood *See* Torture Chamber of Baron Blood (1972)
The Three Faces of Fear *See* Black Sabbath (1964)
The Three Faces of Terror *See* Black Sabbath (1964)
Through the Looking Glass *See* The Velvet Vampire (1971)
Till Death Us Do Part *See* The Blood Spattered Bride (1972)
Tim Burton's The Nightmare Before Christmas *See* The Nightmare Before Christmas (1993)
To Love a Vampire *See* Lust for a Vampire (1971)
Tomb of the Living Dead *See* Mad Doctor of Blood Island (1969)
The Tommyknockers *See* Stephen King's The Tommyknockers (1993)
Torture Chamber *See* The Fear Chamber (1968)
Torture Zone *See* The Fear Chamber (1968)
Train of Terror *See* Terror Train (1980)
Trauma *See* Dario Argento's Trauma (1993)
Trauma *See* The House on Straw Hill (1976)
Treasure of the Living Dead *See* Bloodsucking Nazi Zombies (1982)
Twice Bitten *See* The Vampire Hookers (1978)
Twins of Dracula *See* Twins of Evil (1971)
Una Hacha para la Luna de Miel *See* Hatchet for the Honeymoon (1970)
Underworld *See* Transmutations (1985)
The Unnamable Returns *See* The Unnamable 2: The Statement of Randolph Carter (1992)
The Untold Story: Human Meat Roast Pork Buns *See* The Untold Story (1993)
Up Frankenstein *See* Andy Warhol's Frankenstein (1974)
The Upstate Murders *See* Savage Weekend (1980)
The Vampire *See* Vampyr (1931)
Vampire Castle *See* Captain Kronos: Vampire Hunter (1974)
Vampire Thrills *See* Thrill of the Vampire (1970)
Vampires of Prague *See* Mark of the Vampire (1935)
Vampyr, Der Traum des David Gray *See* Vampyr (1931)
Vampyr, Ou L'Etrange Aventure de David Gray *See* Vampyr (1931)
Vampyres, Daughters of Dracula *See* Vampyres (1974)
Vanishing Body *See* The Black Cat (1934)
Vargtimmen *See* Hour of the Wolf (1968)
Velvet House *See* Crucible of Horror (1969)
Vengeance: The Demon *See* Pumpkinhead (1988)
The Virgin Vampires *See* Twins of Evil (1971)
The Waking Hour *See* The Velvet Vampire (1971)
Want a Ride, Little Girl? *See* Impulse (1974)
Wes Craven Presents Wishmaster *See* Wishmaster (1997)

CAST INDEX

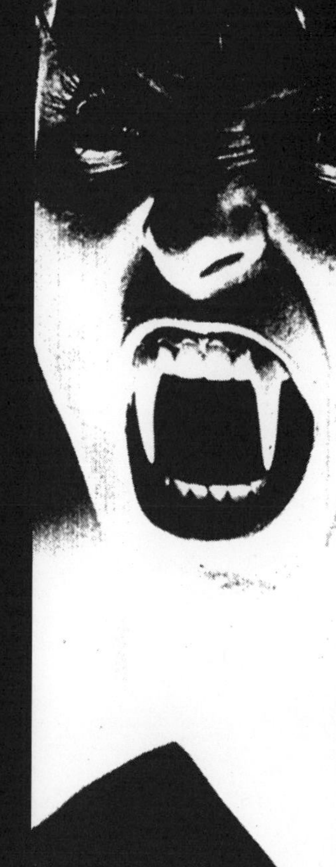

"What was that Vincent Price movie where...." Want help? The "Cast Index" provides a complete listing of cast members cited within the reviews. The actors' names are listed alphabetically by last name, and the films they appeared in are cited chronologically, from most recent film to the oldest (note that only the films reviewed in this book are included). Directors get the same treatment in the "Director Index," in case you were wondering, "What was that Roger Corman movie where...."

Neil Affleck
My Bloody Valentine '81
John Agar
Body Bags '93
King Kong '76
Revenge of the Creature '55
Janet Agren
Emerald Jungle '80
Jenny Agutter
Child's Play 2 '90
Darkman '90
Dark Tower '87
An American Werewolf in London '81
Danny Aiello
Jacob's Ladder '90
The Stuff '85
Claude Akins
The Curse '87
The Night Stalker '71
Kurt Alan
Witchcraft 6: The Devil's Mistress '94
Kevin Alber
Burial of the Rats '95
Eddie Albert
Devil's Rain '75
Edward Albert
Demon Keeper '95
Sorceress '94
House Where Evil Dwells '82
Galaxy of Terror '81
Laura Albert
The Unnamable '88
Frank Albertson
Psycho '60
Man Made Monster '41
Jack Albertson
Dead and Buried '81
Ariauna Albright
Polymorph '96
Dan Albright
I Know What You Did Last Summer '97
Pilar Alcon
The Craving '80
Robert Alda
Lisa and the Devil '75
The Beast with Five Fingers '46
Rutanya Alda
The Dark Half '91
Amityville 2: The Possession '82
When a Stranger Calls '79
The Fury '78
Norman Alden
Ben '72
Aki Aleong
Jugular Wine: A Vampire Odyssey '94
Don Alexander
The Wizard of Gore '70
Jason Alexander
Jacob's Ladder '90
The Burning '82
Terry Alexander
Day of the Dead '85
Zoe Alexander
Little Witches '96
Katrin Alexandre
The Unnamable '88
Lidia Alfonsi
Black Sabbath '64
Maria Aliferi
The Para Psychics '86
Andrea Allan
The House that Vanished '73
Elizabeth Allan
The Haunted Strangler '58
Mark of the Vampire '35
Michael Allan
Dead of Night '45
Louise Allbritton
Son of Dracula '43
Marc Allegret
Blood and Roses '61
Jeffrey Allen
2000 Maniacs '64
Joan Allen
Manhunter '86
Karen Allen
Ghost in the Machine '93
Keith Allen
Shallow Grave '94
Nightscare '93
Nancy Allen
Poltergeist 3 '88
Dressed to Kill '80
Carrie '76
Robert Allen
The Black Room '35
Rosalind Allen
Pinocchio's Revenge '96
Children of the Corn 2: The Final Sacrifice '92
To Die For 2: Son of Darkness '91
Todd Allen
Pinocchio's Revenge '96
Witchboard '87
Kirstie Alley
Village of the Damned '95
Sara Allgood
Dr. Jekyll and Mr. Hyde '41
Christopher Allport
Savage Weekend '80
Maria Conchita Alonso
Vampire's Kiss '88
The Running Man '87
Alicia Alonzo
Mad Doctor of Blood Island '69
John Altamura
The Toxic Avenger, Part 3: The Last Temptation of Toxie '89
The Toxic Avenger, Part 2 '89
Trini Alvarado
The Frighteners '96
Edmundo Rivera Alvarez
Creature from the Haunted Sea '60
Luis Fernando Alves
Cthulhu Mansion '91
Heather Ames
Blood of Dracula '57
Leon Ames
Murders in the Rue Morgue '32
Ramsay Ames
The Mummy's Ghost '44
Calling Dr. Death/Strange Confession '43
Madchen Amick
Sleepwalkers '92
I'm Dangerous Tonight '90
Suzy Amis
The Ex '96
Nadja '95
John Amos
Two Evil Eyes '90
John Amplas
Creepshow '82
Martin '76
Bertil Anderberg
Hour of the Wolf '68
Donna Anders
Count Yorga, Vampire '70
Luana Anders
Dementia 13 '63
The Pit and the Pendulum '61
Merry Anders
Blood Legacy '73
John Andersen
Witchcraft through the Ages '22
Erich Anderson
Friday the 13th, Part 4: The Final Chapter '84
Erika Anderson
A Nightmare on Elm Street 5: Dream Child '89
Harry Anderson
Stephen King's It '90
Isa Anderson
Night Angel '90
John Anderson
Psycho '60
McKee Anderson
Night of the Living Dead '90
Melissa Sue Anderson
Happy Birthday to Me '81
Melody Anderson
Dead and Buried '81
Michelle Anderson
Pin ... '88
Susy Anderson
Black Sabbath '64
Tina Anderson
Blood Freak '72
Starr Andreeff
Amityville Dollhouse '96
Vampire Journals '96
Dance of the Damned '88
Simon Andreu
The Blood Spattered Bride '72
Anthony Andrews
Haunted '95
Barry Andrews
The Blood on Satan's Claw '71
Dracula Has Risen from the Grave '68
Dana Andrews
Curse of the Demon '57
Harry Andrews
Theatre of Blood '73
The Nightcomers '72
Barbara Ange
Night of a Thousand Cats '72

CAST
INDEX

Richard Attenborough
Jurassic Park *'93*
Malcolm Atterbury
Blood of Dracula *'57*
I Was a Teenage Werewolf *'57*
Barry Atwater
The Night Stalker *'71*
Night Gallery *'69*
Edith Atwater
Strait-Jacket *'64*
The Body Snatcher *'45*
Lionel Atwill
House of Dracula *'45*
House of Frankenstein *'44*
Frankenstein Meets the Wolfman *'42*
The Ghost of Frankenstein *'42*
Night Monster *'42*
Man Made Monster *'41*
Son of Frankenstein *'39*
Mark of the Vampire *'35*
Mystery of the Wax Museum *'33*
Doctor X *'32*
The Vampire Bat *'32*
Rene Auberjonois
The Dark Secret of Harvest Home *'78*
Eyes of Laura Mars *'78*
King Kong *'76*
Lenore Aubert
Abbott and Costello Meet the Killer, Boris Karloff *'49*
Abbott and Costello Meet Frankenstein *'48*
Diane Aubrey
The Haunted Strangler *'58*
James Aubrey
The Hunger *'83*
The Terror *'79*
Maxine Audley
Frankenstein Must Be Destroyed *'69*
Peeping Tom *'60*
Stephane Audran
Faceless *'88*
Caroline Audret
Bloodsucking Nazi Zombies *'82*
Marie Ault
The Lodger *'26*
Tina Aumont
Lifespan *'75*
Julie Austin
Elves *'89*
Karen Austin
When a Stranger Calls Back *'93*
Margaret Avery
Terror at Red Wolf Inn *'72*
Val Avery
The Amityville Horror *'79*
Rick Aviles
Stephen King's The Stand *'94*
Nina Axelrod
Time Walker *'82*
Motel Hell *'80*
Hoyt Axton
Gremlins *'84*
Dan Aykroyd
Ghostbusters 2 *'89*
Ghostbusters *'84*
Neighbors *'81*
Felix Aylmer
The Hands of Orlac *'60*
The Mummy *'59*
Catherine Aymerie
Rabid Grannies *'89*
Leah Ayres
The Burning *'82*
Lew Ayres
Salem's Lot *'79*
Damien: Omen 2 *'78*
Lisa B
Serpent's Lair *'95*
Lauren Bacall
Misery *'90*
Barbara Bach
The Great Alligator *'81*
Brian Backer
The Burning *'82*
Olga Baclanova
Freaks *'32*
Kevin Bacon
Tremors *'89*
Friday the 13th *'80*
Erykah Badu
Deep Red: Hatchet Murders *'75*
William Bagdad
Blood Orgy of the She-Devils *'74*
Blake Bailey
Head of the Family *'96*
Lurking Fear *'94*
Frederick Bailey
Demon of Paradise *'87*
Raymond Bailey
The Incredible Shrinking Man *'57*
Charles Bailey-Gates
The Surgeon *'94*
Cynthia Bain
Spontaneous Combustion *'89*
Pumpkinhead *'88*
Alecs Baird
Children Shouldn't Play with Dead Things *'72*
Antony Baird
Dead of Night *'45*
Harry Baird
The Oblong Box *'69*
Jimmie Baird
Return of Dracula *'58*
Gary Bakeman
2000 Maniacs *'64*
Betsy Baker
Evil Dead *'83*
Carroll Baker
Kiss Me, Kill Me *'69*
Diane Baker
The Silence of the Lambs *'91*
Strait-Jacket *'64*
Jay Baker
April Fool's Day *'86*
Joe Don Baker
Cape Fear *'91*
Kathy Baker
Edward Scissorhands *'90*
Kirsten Baker
Friday the 13th, Part 2 *'81*
Rick Baker
King Kong *'76*
William L. Baker
Witchcraft 3: The Kiss of Death *'90*
Brenda Bakke
Tales from the Crypt Presents Demon Knight *'94*
Scott Bakula
Lord of Illusions *'95*
Belinda Balaski
Gremlins 2: The New Batch *'90*
The Howling *'81*
Nick Baldasare
They Bite *'95*
Rebecca Balding
The Boogens *'81*
Silent Scream *'80*
A. Michael Baldwin
Phantasm III: Lord of the Dead *'94*
Adam Baldwin
Cold Sweat *'93*
Alec Baldwin
Beetlejuice *'88*
Elizabeth Baldwin
Mirror, Mirror 3: The Voyeur *'96*
Janet Baldwin
Humongous *'82*
Michael Baldwin
Phantasm *'79*
William Baldwin
Curdled *'95*
Denise Balik
Humanoids from the Deep *'80*
Fairuza Balk
The Craft *'96*
The Island of Dr. Moreau *'96*
Nicholas Ball
Lifeforce *'85*
Maxine Ballantyne
Lemora: A Child's Tale of the Supernatural *'73*
Thomas Balltore
Once Bitten *'85*
Timothy Balme
Dead Alive *'93*
Martin Balsam
Two Evil Eyes *'90*
Psycho *'60*
Talia Balsam
The Kindred *'87*
Judy Bamber
A Bucket of Blood *'59*
Anne Bancroft
Dracula: Dead and Loving It *'95*
Antonio Banderas
Interview with the Vampire *'94*
Eun-Jin Bang
301, 302 *'94*
Joy Bang
Night of the Cobra Woman *'72*
Tallulah Bankhead
Die! Die! My Darling! *'65*
Jonathan Banks
Dark Breed *'96*
Laura Banks
Demon of Paradise *'87*
Leslie Banks
Chamber of Horrors *'40*
The Most Dangerous Game *'32*

Scott Bankston
The Outing '87
Jill Banner
Spider Baby '64
Reggie Bannister
Phantasm III: Lord of the Dead '94
Phantasm II '88
Phantasm '79
Frank Bannon
A Scream in the Streets/Axe '70s
Jennifer Baptist
The Toxic Avenger '86
Christine Baranski
Addams Family Values '93
Reversal of Fortune '90
Adrienne Barbeau
Burial of the Rats '95
Two Evil Eyes '90
Creepshow '82
The Fog '78
Glynis Barber
Edge of Sanity '89
The Terror '79
Urbano Barberini
Terror at the Opera '88
Demons '86
Luis Barboo
The Demons '74
Roy Barcroft
Billy the Kid Versus Dracula '66
Amy Barett
House Where Evil Dwells '82
Marcie Barkin
Fade to Black '80
Martin Barlosky
Carnival of Blood '71
Pat Barlow
April Fool's Day '86
Jake Barnes
Drive-In Massacre '74
Theo Barnes
Brain Damage '88
Charlie Barnett
They Bite '95
David Baron
The Reptile '66
Sandy Baron
Leprechaun 2 '94
Vamp '86
Targets '68
Elizabeth Barondes
Not of This Earth '96
Night of the Scarecrow '95
Douglas Barr
Deadly Blessing '81
Patrick Barr
House of Whipcord '75
Flesh and Blood Show '73
The Satanic Rites of Dracula '73
Edith Barrett
I Walked with a Zombie '43
Nancy Barrett
House of Dark Shadows '70
Ray Barrett
The Reptile '66
Edgar Barrier
Cobra Woman '44
The Phantom of the Opera '43
Matthew Barry
The Wraith '87
Toni Barry
Proteus '95
Drew Barrymore
Scream '96
Waxwork 2: Lost in Time '91
Cat's Eye '85
Firestarter '84
John Barrymore
Dr. Jekyll and Mr. Hyde '20
Lionel Barrymore
Devil Doll '36
Mark of the Vampire '35
Paul Bartel
The Death Artist '95
Gremlins 2: The New Batch '90
Chopping Mall '86
Trick or Treats '82
Piranha '78
Peter Barton
Friday the 13th, Part 4: The Final Chapter '84
Hell Night '81
Laurie Bartram
Friday the 13th '80
Anat "Topol" Barzilai
Witchcraft '88
Richard Basehart
Island of Dr. Moreau '77
Priscilla Basque
Bugged! '96
Alfie Bass
The Fearless Vampire Killers '67
Bobby Bass
Blood Beach '81
Angela Bassett
Vampire in Brooklyn '95
Innocent Blood '92
Linda Bassett
Mary Reilly '95
Alexandra Bastedo
The Blood Spattered Bride '72
Pierre Batcheff
Un Chien Andalou '28
Anthony Bate
Madhouse Mansion '74
Charles Bateman
The Brotherhood of Satan '71
Kathy Bates
Dolores Claiborne '94
Misery '90
Michael Bates
A Clockwork Orange '71
R.C. Bates
Werewolf '95
Ralph Bates
Dynasty of Fear '72
Lust for a Vampire '71
The Horror of Frankenstein '70
Taste the Blood of Dracula '70
Randall Batinkoff
Buffy the Vampire Slayer '92
Patrick Bauchau
Serpent's Lair '95
Blood Ties '92
The Rapture '91
Creepers '85
Belinda Bauer
H.P. Lovecraft's Necronomicon: Book of the Dead '93
Michelle (McClellan) Bauer
Phantom Empire '87
Tomb '86
Steven Bauer
Raising Cain '92
David Baxt
The Shining '80
Meredith Baxter
Ben '72
Frances Bay
In the Mouth of Madness '95
Single White Female '92
The Pit & the Pendulum '91
Geoffrey Bayldon
Asylum '72
Terence Baylor
Macbeth '71
Stephanie Beacham
Horror Planet '80
Schizo '77
And Now the Screaming Starts '73
Dracula A.D. 1972 '72
The Nightcomers '72
John Beal
Amityville 3: The Demon '83
Jennifer Beals
The Prophecy 2: Ashtown '97
Vampire's Kiss '88
The Bride '85
Robert Bean
Creature from the Haunted Sea '60
Amanda Bearse
Fright Night '85
Allyce Beasley
Rumpelstiltskin '96
Stephen King's The Tommyknockers '93
Stephanie Beaton
Witchcraft 9: Bitter Flesh '96
Ned Beatty
Ed and His Dead Mother '93
The Exorcist 2: The Heretic '77
Deliverance '72
Jennifer Beck
Troll '86
John Beck
Audrey Rose '77
Julian Beck
Poltergeist 2: The Other Side '86
Kimberly Beck
Friday the 13th, Part 4: The Final Chapter '84
Massacre at Central High '76
Gretchen Becker
Maniac Cop 3: Badge of Silence '93
Scotty Beckett
The Climax '44
Kate Beckinsale
Haunted '95

Tony Beckley
When a Stranger Calls '79
Lost Continent '68
Reginald Beckwith
Burn Witch, Burn! '62
Curse of the Demon '57
George Becwar
Bride of the Monster '56
Don Beddoe
The Night of the Hunter '55
Before I Hang '40
Bonnie Bedelia
Needful Things '93
Salem's Lot '79
Steven Bednarski
Pin ... '88
Eleanor Beecroft
The Mask '61
Daniel Beer
Creepshow 2 '87
Jason Beghe
Monkey Shines '88
Ed Begley, Jr.
Cat People '82
Ed Begley, Sr.
The Dunwich Horror '70
Yerye Beirut
The Fear Chamber '68
Lia Beldam
The Shining '80
Christine Belford
Christine '84
Nena Belini
Werewolf '95
James Bell
The Leopard Man '43
Keith Bell
Hands of the Ripper '71
Marshall Bell
Starship Troopers '97
A Nightmare on Elm Street 2: Freddy's Revenge '85
Ralph Bell
Wolfen '81
Diana Bellamy
The Nest '88
Madge Bellamy
The White Zombie '32
Ned Bellamy
Carnosaur '93
Ralph Bellamy
Rosemary's Baby '68
The Ghost of Frankenstein '42
The Wolf Man '41
Cynthia Belliveau
The Dark '94
Gil Bellows
Snow White: A Tale of Terror '97
Lionel Belman
Frankenstein '31
Lionel Belmore
Son of Frankenstein '39
Robert Beltran
Night of the Comet '84
James Belushi
Little Shop of Horrors '86
The Fury '78
John Belushi
Neighbors '81
Richard Belzer
Not of This Earth '96
Michael C. Bendetti
Netherworld '90
Billy Benedict
Bride of the Monster '56
Dirk Benedict
Demon Keeper '95
Paul Benedict
The Addams Family '91
Bruce (Herman Brix) Bennett
Before I Hang '40
Fran Bennett
Wes Craven's New Nightmare '94
Joan Bennett
Suspiria '77
House of Dark Shadows '70
Leila Bennett
Doctor X '32
Nigel Bennett
Darkman 3: Die Darkman Die '95
George Benson
The Creeping Flesh '72
John Benson
The Blob '58
Lucille Benson
Duel '71
Martin Benson
The Omen '76
Eddie Benton
Prom Night '80
Femi Benussi
Hatchet for the Honeymoon '70
Blaze Berdahl
Pet Sematary '89
Tom Berenger
The Sentinel '76
Peter Berg
Shocker '89
Polly Bergen
Dr. Jekyll and Ms. Hyde '95
Helmut Berger
Faceless '88
Dorian Gray '70
Sidney Berger
Carnival of Souls '62
William Berger
I'm Dangerous Tonight '90
Dial Help '88
Micha Bergese
The Company of Wolves '85
Patrick Bergin
Highway to Hell '92
Ingrid Bergman
Dr. Jekyll and Mr. Hyde '41
Elisabeth Bergner
Cry of the Banshee '70
Xander Berkeley
Candyman '92
Steven Berkoff
Transmutations '85
A Clockwork Orange '71
Barry Bernard
Terror in the Haunted House '58
Kevin Bernhardt
Hellraiser 3: Hell on Earth '92
Corbin Bernsen
Circuit Breaker '96
The Dentist '96
Temptress '95
Elizabeth Berridge
The Funhouse '81
Lloyd Berry
April Fool's Day '86
Sarah Berry
Evil Dead 2: Dead by Dawn '87
Michael Berryman
The Hills Have Eyes, Part 2 '84
Deadly Blessing '81
The Hills Have Eyes '77
Dehl Berti
Wolfen '81
Suzanne Bertish
The Hunger '83
Bibi Besch
Tremors '89
The Beast Within '82
Willie Best
The Ghost Breakers '40
Martine Beswick
Night of the Scarecrow '95
Seizure '74
Laura Betti
Hatchet for the Honeymoon '70
Billy Bevan
Dr. Jekyll and Mr. Hyde '41
Nathan Bexton
Nowhere '96
Turhan Bey
The Climax '44
The Mummy's Tomb '42
Tino Bianchi
Black Sunday '60
Abner Biberman
The Leopard Man '43
Michael Biehn
The Seventh Sign '88
Aliens '86
Adam Biesk
Leprechaun 2 '94
Dan Biggers
Basket Case 3: The Progeny '92
Roxann Biggs-Dawson
Darkman 3: Die Darkman Die '95
Theodore Bikel
Dark Tower '87
Tom Billett
Lurkers '88
Dawn Ann Billings
Warlock: The Armageddon '93
Jennifer Billingsley
The Thirsty Dead '74
Clara Bindi
Black Sunday '60
Barbara Bingham
Friday the 13th, Part 8: Jason Takes Manhattan '89
Leigh Biolos
Howling 3: The Marsupials '87
Thora Birch
Hocus Pocus '93
Paul Birchard
Cthulhu Mansion '91
Norman Bird
Hands of the Ripper '71
Burn Witch, Burn! '62
Jesse Birdsall
Nightscare '93

Carroll Borland
Mark of the Vampire '35
Max Born
Fellini Satyricon '69
Christian Borromeo
Unsane '82
Tom Bosley
Night Gallery '69
Barry Bostwick
The Rocky Horror Picture Show '75
Sam Bottoms
Apocalypse Now '79
Joy Boushel
The Fly '86
Humongous '82
Jean Pierre Bouyou
Les Raisins de la Mort '78
Julie Bowen
An American Werewolf in Paris '97
Michael Bowen
Cupid '96
Night of the Comet '84
Malick Bowens
The Believers '87
Antoinette Bower
Prom Night '80
Tom Bower
Raising Cain '92
David Bowie
Labyrinth '86
The Hunger '83
Peter Bowles
The Legend of Hell House '73
John Bown
Dynasty of Fear '72
Alan Boyce
Nowhere '96
Lara Flynn Boyle
Poltergeist 3 '88
Lisa Boyle
Lost Highway '96
Marc Boyle
The Final Conflict '81
Peter Boyle
The Surgeon '94
Taxi Driver '76
Young Frankenstein '74
Peter Boynton
Hellraiser 3: Hell on Earth '92
Caroline Brackman
Rabid Grannies '89
Doug Bradley
Hellraiser 4: Bloodline '95
Proteus '95
Hellraiser 3: Hell on Earth '92
Hellbound: Hellraiser 2 '88
Hellraiser '87
Scott Brady
Gremlins '84
Strange Behavior '81
Wilfrid Brambell
The Conqueror Worm '68
Francisco (Frank) Brana
Cthulhu Mansion '91
Kenneth Branagh
Mary Shelley's Frankenstein '94
Dead Again '91
Rustam Branaman
Terrified '94
Neville Brand
Evils of the Night '85
Eaten Alive '76
Jonathan Brandis
Stephen King's It '90
Stepfather 2: Make Room for Daddy '89
Marlon Brando
The Island of Dr. Moreau '96
Apocalypse Now '79
The Nightcomers '72
Richard Brando
Student Bodies '81
Carolyn Brandt
Incredibly Strange Creatures Who Stopped Living and Became Mixed-Up Zombies '63
Albert Bras
Vampyr '31
Pierre Brasseur
The Horror Chamber of Dr. Faustus '59
Bart Braverman
Alligator '80
Thom Bray
The Horror Show '89
Rossano Brazzi
The Final Conflict '81
Peter Breck
The Crawling Hand '63
Bunny Breckinridge
Plan 9 from Outer Space '56
Tracy Bregman
Happy Birthday to Me '81
Ewen Bremmer
Trainspotting '95
April Breneman
Witchcraft 7: Judgement Hour '95
Walter Brennan
The Invisible Man '33
Bobbie Bresee
Evil Spawn '87
Mausoleum '83
Tom Breznahan
Terrified '94
Shane Briant
Captain Kronos: Vampire Hunter '74
Frankenstein and the Monster from Hell '74
Demons of the Mind '72
Jeff Bridges
King Kong '76
Lloyd Bridges
Calling Dr. Death/Strange Confession '43
Richard Briers
Mary Shelley's Frankenstein '94
Nick Brimble
Frankenstein Unbound '90
Wilford Brimley
The Thing '82
Mark Bringleson
The Lawnmower Man '92
John Brinkley
A Bucket of Blood '59
Virginia Brissac
Black Friday '40
Kent Broadhurst
The Dark Half '91
Silver Bullet '85
David Broadnax
Zombie Island Massacre '84
Roy Brocksmith
Arachnophobia '90
Steve Brodie
The Giant Spider Invasion '75
James Brolin
The Amityville Horror '79
Josh Brolin
Mimic '97
J. Edward Bromberg
Dead Man's Eyes/Pillow of Death '44
The Phantom of the Opera '43
Son of Dracula '43
John Bromfield
Revenge of the Creature '55
Sydney Bromley
Frankenstein and the Monster from Hell '74
Charles Bronson
House of Wax '53
Claudio Brook
Cronos '94
Irina Brook
Transmutations '85
Paul Brooke
The Lair of the White Worm '88
Walter Brooke
The Return of Count Yorga '71
Richard Brooker
Friday the 13th, Part 4: The Final Chapter '84
Friday the 13th, Part 3 '82
Albert Brooks
Taxi Driver '76
Conrad Brooks
Plan 9 from Outer Space '56
David Brooks
Scream for Help '86
David Allan Brooks
The Kindred '87
Elisabeth Brooks
The Forgotten One '89
The Howling '81
Jean Brooks
The Leopard Man '43
Mel Brooks
Dracula: Dead and Loving It '95
Ray Brooks
House of Whipcord '75
Flesh and Blood Show '73
Richard Brooks
The Crow 2: City of Angels '96
Shocker '89
Edward Brophy
Mad Love '35
Kevin Brophy
Time Walker '82
Hell Night '81

CAST INDEX

Kathleen Byron
Twins of Evil *'71*
Burn Witch, Burn! *'62*
James Caan
Misery *'90*
Scott Caan
Nowhere *'96*
Angel Caban
The Refrigerator *'91*
Bruce Cabot
King Kong *'33*
Susan Cabot
The Wasp Woman *'59*
Nicolas Cage
Vampire's Kiss *'88*
Michael Caine
Jekyll and Hyde *'90*
The Hand *'81*
Dressed to Kill *'80*
Nicholas Cairis
Night School *'81*
Clara Calamai
Deep Red: Hatchet Murders *'75*
Guiliana Calandra
Deep Red: Hatchet Murders *'75*
Paul Calderone
The Addiction *'95*
Don Calfa
H.P. Lovecraft's Necronomicon: Book of the Dead *'93*
Chopper Chicks in Zombietown *'91*
Return of the Living Dead *'85*
Rory Calhoun
Motel Hell *'80*
Night of the Lepus *'72*
R.D. Call
Stephen King's Golden Years *'91*
Michael Callan
Leprechaun 3 *'95*
Double Exposure *'82*
The Cat and the Canary *'79*
Michael Caloz
Screamers *'96*
Bill Calvert
C.H.U.D. 2: Bud the Chud *'89*
Toni Calvert
Blood Feast *'63*
Toni Camel
Incredibly Strange Creatures Who Stopped Living and Became Mixed-Up Zombies *'63*
Dean Cameron
Bad Dreams *'88*
Colleen Camp
Apocalypse Now *'79*
Joseph Campanella
Ben *'72*
Bill Campbell
Bram Stoker's Dracula *'92*
Bruce Campbell
Army of Darkness *'92*
Waxwork 2: Lost in Time *'91*
Maniac Cop 2 *'90*
Maniac Cop *'88*
Evil Dead 2: Dead by Dawn *'87*
Evil Dead *'83*
Neve Campbell
Scream 2 *'97*
The Craft *'96*
Scream *'96*
The Dark *'94*
Nicholas Campbell
Naked Lunch *'91*
Tisha Campbell
Little Shop of Horrors *'86*
William Campbell
Dementia 13 *'63*
Ron Canada
Pinocchio's Revenge *'96*
Jose Canalejas
Return of the Evil Dead *'75*
John Candy
Little Shop of Horrors *'86*
Karen Cannata
Shock Chamber *'96*
Jack Canon
A Scream in the Streets/Axe *'70s*
Richard Cansino
Mirror, Mirror 3: The Voyeur *'96*
Antonio Cantafora
Torture Chamber of Baron Blood *'72*
Peter Capaldi
The Lair of the White Worm *'88*
Gordon Capps
Jugular Wine: A Vampire Odyssey *'94*
Ahna Capri
The Brotherhood of Satan *'71*
Capucine
Fellini Satyricon *'69*
Antony Carbone
The Pit and the Pendulum *'61*
Creature from the Haunted Sea *'60*
A Bucket of Blood *'59*
Bill "Chilly Billy" Cardille
Night of the Living Dead *'68*
Lori Cardille
Day of the Dead *'85*
John Cardos
Blood of Dracula's Castle *'69*
Arthur Edmund Carewe
Doctor X *'32*
The Cat and the Canary *'27*
The Phantom of the Opera *'25*
Harry Carey, Jr.
Billy the Kid Versus Dracula *'66*
MacDonald Carey
It's Alive 3: Island of the Alive *'87*
Summer of Fear *'78*
Olive Carey
Billy the Kid Versus Dracula *'66*
Timothy Carhart
Candyman 2: Farewell to the Flesh *'94*
Catherine Carlen
Chopper Chicks in Zombietown *'91*
Mary Carlisle
Dead Men Walk *'43*
Les Carlson
The Fly *'86*
Leslie Carlson
Deranged *'74*
Richard Carlson
Creature from the Black Lagoon *'54*
The Ghost Breakers *'40*
Veronica Carlson
Freakshow *'95*
The Horror of Frankenstein *'70*
Frankenstein Must Be Destroyed *'69*
Dracula Has Risen from the Grave *'68*
Rebekah Carlton
Leprechaun 4: In Space *'96*
Robert Carlyle
Trainspotting *'95*
Jeanne Carmen
The Monster of Piedras Blancas *'57*
Julie Carmen
In the Mouth of Madness *'95*
Fright Night 2 *'88*
Michael Carmine
Leviathan *'89*
Art Carney
Firestarter *'84*
David Carpenter
Warlock *'91*
John Carpenter
Body Bags *'93*
Ken Carpenter
Hellraiser 3: Hell on Earth *'92*
Bret Carr
The Girl with the Hungry Eyes *'94*
Carole Carr
Scream Dream *'89*
Cynthia Carr
Last House on the Left *'72*
Darlene Carr
Piranha *'95*
Marian Carr
The Indestructible Man *'56*
Paul Carr
Ben *'72*
Walter Carr
The Wicker Man *'75*
David Carradine
Waxwork 2: Lost in Time *'91*
Trick or Treats *'82*
John Carradine
Jack-O *'95*
Evil Spawn *'87*
Tomb *'86*
Evils of the Night *'85*
House of the Long Shadows *'82*
The Howling *'81*
The Vampire Hookers *'78*
Shock Waves *'77*
Mary, Mary, Bloody Mary *'76*
The Sentinel *'76*
Blood Legacy *'73*

Josephine Chaplin
Jack the Ripper *'76*
Judith Chapman
Scalpel *'76*
Mark Lindsay Chapman
Stephen King's The Langoliers *'95*
Sean Chapman
Hellbound: Hellraiser 2 *'88*
Hellraiser *'87*
Patricia Charbonneau
Brain Dead *'89*
Josh Charles
The Grave *'95*
Ian Charleson
Terror at the Opera *'88*
Stu Charno
Friday the 13th, Part 2 *'81*
Frank Chase
The Creature Walks Among Us *'56*
Steve Chase
The Blob *'58*
David Chaskin
The Curse *'87*
Charlotte Chatton
Hellraiser 4: Bloodline *'95*
Jacques-Rene Chauffard
Blood and Roses *'61*
Sandra Chavez
The Fear Chamber *'68*
Maury Chaykin
Cold Comfort *'90*
Andrea Checchi
Black Sunday *'60*
Cher
The Witches of Eastwick *'87*
Kaethe Cherney
Cthulhu Mansion *'91*
Arthur Chesney
The Lodger *'26*
Vanessa Lee Chester
The Lost World: Jurassic Park 2 *'97*
Leslie Cheung
The Bride with White Hair 2 *'93*
The Bride with White Hair *'93*
A Chinese Ghost Story *'87*
Lois Chiles
Curdled *'95*
Creepshow 2 *'87*
Coma *'78*
Andre Chimene
The Outing *'87*
William Ching
Terror in the Haunted House *'58*
Rae Dawn Chong
Tales from the Darkside: The Movie *'90*
Alisa Christensen
Witchcraft 7: Judgement Hour *'95*
Claudia Christian
Maniac Cop 2 *'90*
Benjamin Christiansen
Witchcraft through the Ages *'22*
Helen Christie
Lust for a Vampire *'71*
Julie Christie
Demon Seed *'77*
Don't Look Now *'73*
Virginia Christine
Billy the Kid Versus Dracula *'66*
The Mummy's Curse *'44*
Eric Christmas
Attack of the Killer Tomatoes *'77*
Dennis Christopher
H.P. Lovecraft's Necronomicon: Book of the Dead *'93*
Stephen King's It *'90*
Fade to Black *'80*
Christy Chung
The Bride with White Hair 2 *'93*
Thomas Haden Church
Tales from the Crypt Presents Demon Knight *'94*
Marguerite Churchill
Dracula's Daughter *'36*
The Walking Dead *'36*
Eduardo Ciannelli
The Mummy's Hand *'40*
Diane Cilento
The Wicker Man *'75*
Michael Citrinti
Hideous *'97*
Rony Clanton
Def by Temptation *'90*
Diane Clare
Plague of the Zombies *'66*
The Haunting *'63*
Betsy Clark
Boxing Helena *'93*
Candy Clark
Buffy the Vampire Slayer *'92*
The Blob *'88*
Cat's Eye *'85*
Amityville 3: The Demon *'83*
Christie Clark
Children of the Corn 2: The Final Sacrifice *'92*
Ernest Clark
It! *'67*
Fred Clark
Curse of the Mummy's Tomb *'64*
Ken Clark
Attack of the Giant Leeches *'59*
Marlene Clark
Black Werewolf *'75*
Night of the Cobra Woman *'72*
Matt Clark
Trilogy of Terror 2 *'96*
The Harvest *'92*
The Horror Show *'89*
Russ Clark
Fright Night 2 *'88*
J. Jerome Clarke
Luther the Geek *'90*
Joe Clarke
Basket Case *'81*
Mae Clarke
Frankenstein *'31*
Melinda Clarke
Spawn *'97*
Mindy Clarke
Return of the Living Dead 3 *'93*
Robert Clarke
Hideous Sun Demon *'59*
Robin Clarke
Horror Planet *'80*
Warren Clarke
A Clockwork Orange *'71*
D. A. Clarke-Smith
The Ghoul *'33*
Helene Clarkson
Blood & Donuts *'95*
John Cleese
Mary Shelley's Frankenstein *'94*
Jimmy Clem
Town that Dreaded Sundown *'76*
Paul Clemens
The Beast Within *'82*
David Clennon
The Thing *'82*
Judy Cler
The Wizard of Gore *'70*
George Cleveland
Dead Man's Eyes/ Pillow of Death *'44*
Mildred Clinton
Alice Sweet Alice *'76*
Roger Clinton
Pumpkinhead 2: Blood Wings *'94*
Colin Clive
The Bride of Frankenstein *'35*
Mad Love *'35*
Frankenstein *'31*
E.E. Clive
The Bride of Frankenstein *'35*
The Invisible Man *'33*
John Clive
A Clockwork Orange *'71*
Al Cliver
The Black Cat *'81*
Zombie *'80*
George Clooney
From Dusk Till Dawn *'95*
Del Close
The Blob *'88*
Glenn Close
Mary Reilly *'95*
Reversal of Fortune *'90*
Fatal Attraction *'87*
George Clutesi
Nightwing *'79*
Prophecy *'79*
Kim Coates
The Club *'94*
Innocent Blood *'92*
The Amityville Curse *'90*
Phyllis Coates
I Was a Teenage Frankenstein *'57*
Lee J. Cobb
The Exorcist *'73*
Linda Cochran
2000 Maniacs *'64*
Peter Coe
House of Frankenstein *'44*
The Mummy's Curse *'44*
Scott Coffey
Lost Highway *'96*

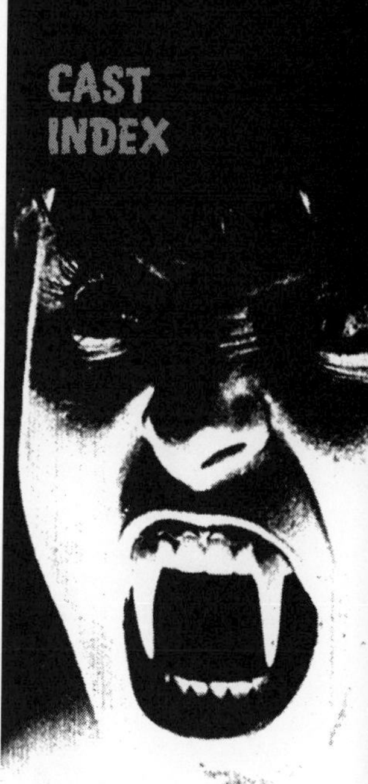

Robert Costanzo
Man's Best Friend '93
Lou Costello
Abbott and Costello Meet the Mummy '55
Abbott and Costello Meet Dr. Jekyll and Mr. Hyde '52
Abbott and Costello Meet the Invisible Man '51
Abbott and Costello Meet the Killer, Boris Karloff '49
Abbott and Costello Meet Frankenstein '48
Richard Cotica
Rabid Grannies '89
Constantin Cotimanis
Huntress: Spirit of the Night '95
Mickey Cotrell
Hellraiser 4: Bloodline '95
Joseph Cotten
Lady Frankenstein '72
Torture Chamber of Baron Blood '72
The Abominable Dr. Phibes '71
Hush, Hush, Sweet Charlotte '65
Ralph Cotterill
Howling 3: The Marsupials '87
Carolyn Courage
The Terror '79
Hazel Court
Masque of the Red Death '65
The Raven '63
Premature Burial '62
The Curse of Frankenstein '57
Gene Courtier
Blood Feast '63
Chuck Courtney
Billy the Kid Versus Dracula '66
Con Covert
A Scream in the Streets/Axe '70s
Geraldine Cowper
The Wicker Man '75
Nicola Cowper
Transmutations '85
Peter Cowper
My Bloody Valentine '81
Brian Cox
Manhunter '86
Courteney Cox
Scream 2 '97
Scream '96
Jennifer Elise Cox
Sometimes They Come Back ... Again '96
Ronny Cox
The Beast Within '82
Deliverance '72
Paolo Cozza
Demons '86
Buster Crabbe
Alien Dead '79
Buddy Crabtree
Legend of Boggy Creek '75
Jeff Crabtree
Legend of Boggy Creek '75
John Cragen
Witchcraft 7: Judgement Hour '95
Carolyn Craig
House on Haunted Hill '58
James Craig
Black Friday '40
Marc Cramer
Isle of the Dead '45
Barbara Crampton
Castle Freak '95
Puppet Master '89
Chopping Mall '86
From Beyond '86
Re-Animator '85
Norma Crane
Night Gallery '69
Kenneth Cranham
Hellbound: Hellraiser 2 '88
Nick Cravat
Island of Dr. Moreau '77
Frank Craven
Son of Dracula '43
Matt Craven
Jacob's Ladder '90
Happy Birthday to Me '81
Mimi Craven
Daddy's Girl '96
Mikey '92
Wes Craven
Wes Craven's New Nightmare '94
David Crawford
Dawn of the Dead '78
Joan Crawford
Night Gallery '69
Strait-Jacket '64
What Ever Happened to Baby Jane? '62
John Crawford
The Boogens '81
Galaxy Craze
Nadja '95
Dorothy Crehan
I Was a Teenage Werewolf '57
Richard Crenna
Leviathan '89
Death Ship '80
The Evil '78
Wait Until Dark '67
Wendy Crewson
The Good Son '93
Dan Crimmins
The White Zombie '32
Donald Crisp
The Uninvited '44
Dr. Jekyll and Mr. Hyde '41
Larry Crist
Dark Carnival '97
Perla Cristal
The Awful Dr. Orloff '62
Criswell
Plan 9 from Outer Space '56
Peter Crombie
Seven '95
Paul Cronin
Children Shouldn't Play with Dead Things '72
Hume Cronyn
The Phantom of the Opera '43
Cathy Lee Crosby
The Dark '79
Denise Crosby
Pet Sematary '89
Harry Crosby
Friday the 13th '80
Mary Crosby
Cupid '96
Ben Cross
Temptress '95
Cold Sweat '93
Harley Cross
The Believers '87
Rebecca Cross
Leprechaun 4: In Space '96
Scatman Crothers
The Shining '80
Lindsay Crouse
The Arrival '96
Graham Crowden
The Company of Wolves '85
Dee Croxton
Stephen King's Nightshift Collection '83
Tom Cruise
Interview with the Vampire '94
Rosalie Crutchley
The Hunchback of Notre Dame '82
And Now the Screaming Starts '73
The Haunting '63
Macaulay Culkin
The Good Son '93
Jacob's Ladder '90
Michael Culkin
Candyman '92
Quinn Culkin
The Good Son '93
Dana Cullivan
Blood Freak '72
Steven Culp
Jason Goes to Hell: The Final Friday '93
Roland Culver
The Legend of Hell House '73
Dead of Night '45
Leslie Cumming
Witchery '88
Juliette Cummins
Friday the 13th, Part 5: A New Beginning '85
Martin Cummins
Friday the 13th, Part 8: Jason Takes Manhattan '89
Peggy Cummins
Curse of the Demon '57
Brett Cumo
The Wicked '89
Beryl Cunningham
Dorian Gray '70
Alain Cuny
The Hunchback of Notre Dame '57
Barbara Cupisti
The Church '90
Terror at the Opera '88
Petrea Curran
Hellgate '89
Gordon Currie
Listen '96
Blood & Donuts '95

CAST
INDEX

Danielle Daven
Rabid Grannies *'89*
Harry Davenport
The Hunchback of Notre Dame *'39*
Mary Davenport
Sisters *'73*
Nigel Davenport
A Christmas Carol *'84*
Island of Dr. Moreau *'77*
Dracula *'73*
Peeping Tom *'60*
Robert Davi
Maniac Cop 3: Badge of Silence *'93*
Maniac Cop 2 *'90*
Angel David
The Crow *'93*
Keith David
They Live *'88*
The Thing *'82*
Lou David
The Burning *'82*
Thayer David
House of Dark Shadows *'70*
Lolita Davidovich
Raising Cain *'92*
Eileen Davidson
The House on Sorority Row *'83*
Jack Davidson
Shock Waves *'77*
John Davidson
Edward S cissorhands *'90*
Embeth Davidtz
Army of Darkness *'92*
Patricia Davie
Rabid Grannies *'89*
Gwen Ffrangcon Davies
Devil's Bride *'68*
Rupert Davies
The Conqueror Worm *'68*
Dracula Has Risen from the Grave *'68*
Stephen Davies
The Nest *'88*
Alex Davion
The Bloodsuckers *'70*
Plague of the Zombies *'66*
Paranoiac *'62*
Bette Davis
The Dark Secret of Harvest Home *'78*
Hush, Hush, Sweet Charlotte *'65*
What Ever Happened to Baby Jane? *'62*
Geena Davis
Beetlejuice *'88*
The Fly *'86*
Jim Davis
Dracula vs. Frankenstein *'71*
Judy Davis
Naked Lunch *'91*
Lisa Davis
Edge of Sanity *'89*
Ossie Davis
Stephen King's The Stand *'94*
Night Gallery *'69*
Rochelle Davis
The Crow *'93*
Roger Davis
House of Dark Shadows *'70*
Sammi Davis
The Lair of the White Worm *'88*
Taryn Davis
Snow White: A Tale of Terror *'97*
Warwick Davis
Leprechaun 4: In Space *'96*
Leprechaun 3 *'95*
Leprechaun 2 *'94*
Leprechaun *'93*
Bruce Davison
Willard *'71*
Pam Dawber
Stay Tuned *'92*
Anthony Dawson
The Curse of the Werewolf *'60*
The Haunted Strangler *'58*
Richard Dawson
The Running Man *'87*
Danielle Dax
The Company of Wolves *'85*
Vera Day
The Haunted S trangler *'58*
Yvonne De Carlo
Mirror, Mirror *'90*
Silent Scream *'80*
Pedro de Cordoba
Before I Hang *'40*
The Ghost Breakers *'40*
Peppino de Filippo
Boccaccio '70 *'62*
Olivia de Havilland
Hush, Hush, Sweet Charlotte *'65*
Terence de Marney
Die, Monster, Die! *'65*
Alberto De Mendoza
Horror Express *'72*
Blade of the Ripper *'70*
Danielle De Metz
Return of the Fly *'59*
Robert De Niro
Mary Shelley's Frankenstein *'94*
Cape Fear *'91*
Angel Heart *'87*
Taxi Driver *'76*
Rona De Ricci
The Pit & the Pendulum *'91*
Vittorio De Sica
Andy Warhol's Dracula *'74*
Edward De Souza
Kiss of the Vampire *'62*
Francis De Wolff
Devil Doll *'64*
The Two Faces of Dr. Jekyll *'60*
Brian Deacon
Vampyres *'74*
Richard Deacon
Abbott and Costello Meet the Mummy *'55*
Rick Dean
Carnosaur 3: Primal Species *'96*
Leslie Deane
Freddy's Dead: The Final Nightmare *'91*
976-EVIL *'88*
Nikki DeBoer
Prom Night 4: Deliver Us from Evil *'91*
Michelle DeCosta
The Refrigerator *'91*
Frances Dee
I Walked with a Zombie *'43*
Ruby Dee
Stephen King's The Stand *'94*
Cat People *'82*
Sandra Dee
The Dunwich Horror *'70*
Isabelle DeFunes
Kiss Me, Kill Me *'69*
Louis Del Grande
Of Unknown Origin *'83*
Angel Del Pozo
Horror Express *'72*
Michel Delahaye
Thrill of the Vampire *'70*
Kim Delaney
Temptress *'95*
Darkman 2: The Return of Durant *'94*
Debra Deliso
The Slumber Party Massacre *'82*
Michael DellaFemina
Bloodlust: Subspecies 3 *'93*
Julie Delpy
An American Werewolf in Paris *'97*
Hal Delrich
Evil Dead *'83*
Rudy DeLuca
The Return of Count Yorga *'71*
Dom DeLuise
Haunted Honeymoon *'86*
Peter DeLuise
Children of the Night *'92*
Sasha DeMarino
Ashes and Flames *'97*
David DeMering
Plan 9 from Outer Space *'56*
Katherine DeMille
The Black Room *'35*
Darcy Demoss
The Death Artist *'95*
Pale Blood *'91*
Friday the 13th, Part 6: Jason Lives *'86*
Jeffrey DeMunn
The Blob *'88*
The Hitcher *'86*
Terror in Toyland *'85*
Susan Denberg
Frankenstein Created Woman *'66*
Catherine Deneuve
The Hunger *'83*
Repulsion *'65*
Maurice Denham
Countess Dracula *'70*
Paranoiac *'62*
Curse of the Demon *'57*
Lydie Denier
Satan's Princess *'90*
Blood Relations *'87*

Steve Doubet
Silent Scream *'80*
Damon Douglas
Massacre at Central High *'76*
Illeana Douglas
Cape Fear *'91*
James B. Douglas
The Changeling *'80*
Kirk Douglas
The Fury *'78*
Mark Douglas
2000 Maniacs *'64*
Melvyn Douglas
Ghost Story *'81*
The Changeling *'80*
The Tenant *'76*
The Old Dark House *'32*
The Vampire Bat *'32*
Michael Douglas
Basic Instinct *'92*
Fatal Attraction *'87*
Coma *'78*
Sarah Douglas
Voodoo *'95*
The Art of Dying *'90*
Dracula *'73*
Shirley Douglas
Dead Ringers *'88*
Brad Dourif
Dario Argento's Trauma *'93*
Exorcist 3: Legion *'90*
Spontaneous Combustion *'89*
Child's Play *'88*
Eyes of Laura Mars *'78*
Barbara Dow
Witchcraft 4: Virgin Heart *'92*
Garrick Dowhen
Appointment with Fear *'85*
Barbara Dowling
Dementia 13 *'63*
Lesley-Anne Down
Nomads *'86*
The Hunchback of Notre Dame *'82*
Countess Dracula *'70*
Terry Downes
The Fearless Vampire Killers *'67*
Robert Downey, Jr.
Natural Born Killers *'94*
John Doyle
The Wicked *'89*
Brian Doyle-Murray
Ghostbusters 2 *'89*
Billy Drago
Mirror, Mirror 3: The Voyeur *'96*
Vamp *'86*
Frances Drake
The Invisible Ray *'36*
Mad Love *'35*
Larry Drake
Darkman 2: The Return of Durant *'94*
Dr. Giggles *'92*
Darkman *'90*
Eamon Draper
Spectre *'96*
Fran Drescher
Summer of Fear *'78*
Ellen Drew
Isle of the Dead *'45*
Richard Dreyfuss
Jaws *'75*
Patrick Drury
The Awakening *'80*
Jessica Dublin
The Toxic Avenger, Part 3: The Last Temptation of Toxie *'89*
The Para Psychics *'86*
David Duchovny
The Rapture *'91*
Rick Ducommun
Ghost in the Machine *'93*
John Dudgeon
The Old Dark House *'32*
Michael Dudikoff
Bloody Birthday *'80*
Carl Duering
A Clockwork Orange *'71*
Debbie Duff
Helter Skelter Murders *'71*
Denice Duff
Bloodlust: Subspecies 3 *'93*
Bloodstone: Subspecies 2 *'92*
Shay Duffin
Leprechaun *'93*
Dennis Dugan
The Howling *'81*
John Dugan
The Texas Chainsaw Massacre *'74*
Tom Dugan
Nightwish *'89*
Andrew Duggan
Return to Salem's Lot *'87*
It's Alive 2: It Lives Again *'78*
It's Alive *'74*
Tommy Duggan
The Final Conflict *'81*
Patty Duke
Amityville 4 *'89*
Caitlin Dulany
Maniac Cop 3: Badge of Silence *'93*
Douglass Dumbrille
Weird Woman/Frozen Ghost *'44*
Dennis Dun
Prince of Darkness *'87*
Big Trouble in Little China *'86*
Donnie Dunagan
Son of Frankenstein *'39*
Faye Dunaway
Eyes of Laura Mars *'78*
Rachel Duncan
Amityville Dollhouse *'96*
Emma Dunn
Son of Frankenstein *'39*
Harvey B. Dunn
Bride of the Monster *'56*
J. Malcolm Dunn
Dr. Jekyll and Mr. Hyde *'20*
Michael Dunn
Werewolf of Washington *'73*
Dominique Dunne
Poltergeist *'82*
Griffin Dunne
An American Werewolf in London *'81*
Debbe Dunning
Leprechaun 4: In Space *'96*
Jessica Dunning
Burn Witch, Burn! *'62*
Kirsten Dunst
Interview with the Vampire *'94*
Vincent Craig Dupree
Friday the 13th, Part 8: Jason Takes Manhattan *'89*
Jean Durand
Thrill of the Vampire *'70*
Shevonne Durkin
Leprechaun 2 *'94*
Charles Durning
When a Stranger Calls Back *'93*
When a Stranger Calls *'79*
The Fury *'78*
Sisters *'73*
Alexandra Durrell
The Unnamable *'88*
Ian Dury
The Crow 2: City of Angels *'96*
Nancy Dussault
The Nurse *'97*
Charles S. Dutton
Mimic *'97*
Alien3 *'92*
Cat's Eye *'85*
James Duval
Nowhere *'96*
Robert Duvall
Apocalypse Now *'79*
Invasion of the Body Snatchers *'78*
Shelley Duvall
The Shining *'80*
Janine Duvitsky
Dracula *'79*
Peter Dvorsky
Videodrome *'83*
Hilary Dwyer
Cry of the Banshee *'70*
The Oblong Box *'69*
The Conqueror Worm *'68*
Leslie Dwyer
Die, Monster, Die! *'65*
Valentine Dyall
The Haunting *'63*
Horror Hotel *'60*
Richard Dysart
The Thing *'82*
Prophecy *'79*
George Dzundza
Basic Instinct *'92*
Daisy Earles
Freaks *'32*
Harry Earles
Freaks *'32*
David Early
Dawn of the Dead *'78*
Carlos East
The Fear Chamber *'68*
Jeff East
Pumpkinhead *'88*
Deadly Blessing *'81*
Summer of Fear *'78*

Renee Estevez
Single White Female '92
Heathers '89
Wesley Eure
Jennifer '78
Art Evans
Fright Night '85
Clifford Evans
Kiss of the Vampire '62
The Curse of the Werewolf '60
Maurice Evans
Rosemary's Baby '68
Robin Evans
One Dark Night '82
Terrence Evans
Curse 2: The Bite '88
Troy Evans
The Frighteners '96
The Lawnmower Man '92
Trevor Eve
Dracula '79
Judith Evelyn
The Tingler '59
Rupert Everett
Cemetery Man '95
Tom Everett
Friday the 13th, Part 4: The Final Chapter '84
Nancy Everhard
Deepstar Six '89
Demonstone '89
Angie Everhart
Tales from the Crypt Presents Bordello of Blood '96
Herb Evers
The Brain that Wouldn't Die '63
Jason Evers
Basket Case 2 '90
Briana Evigan
Spectre '96
Greg Evigan
Spectre '96
Deepstar Six '89
Barbara Ewing
Dracula Has Risen from the Grave '68
Patrick Ewing
Exorcist 3: Legion '90
Ava Fabian
To Die For '89
Fabio
Exorcist 3: Legion '90
Bill Fagerbakke
Stephen King's The Stand '94
Jeff Fahey
Darkman 3: Die Darkman Die '95
Serpent's Lair '95
The Lawnmower Man '92
Psycho 3 '86
Myrna Fahey
The Fall of the House of Usher '60
Zulma Faiad
Night of a Thousand Cats '72
Bruce Fairbairn
The Vampire Hookers '78
Douglas Fairbanks, Jr.
Ghost Story '81
Craig Fairbrass
Proteus '95
Nightscare '93
Pamela Fairbrother
Cry of the Banshee '70
Max Fairchild
Howling 3: The Marsupials '87
Michael Fairman
The Nurse '97
Frankie Faison
Stephen King's The Langoliers '95
Marianne Faithfull
Madhouse Mansion '74
Eduardo Fajardo
Lisa and the Devil '75
Anna Falchi
Cemetery Man '95
Edie Falco
The Addiction '95
Lisanne Falk
Heathers '89
Usang Yeong Fang
Beauty Evil Rose '94
Franco Fantasia
Emerald Jungle '80
Sergio Fantoni
Atom Age Vampire '61
Stephanie Faracy
Hocus Pocus '93
James Farentino
Dead and Buried '81
Antonio Fargas
Firestarter '84
Dennis Farina
Manhunter '86
Gary Farmer
Tales from the Crypt Presents Demon Knight '94
Mimsy Farmer
The Black Cat '81
Suzan Farmer
Rasputin the Mad Monk '66
Die, Monster, Die! '65
Dracula, Prince of Darkness '65
Richard Farnsworth
Highway to Hell '92
Misery '90
Witchery '88
Jamie Farr
Curse 2: The Bite '88
Arnold '73
Jane Farrar
The Climax '44
Charles Farrell
Countess Dracula '70
Glenda Farrell
Mystery of the Wax Museum '33
Mike Farrell
Targets '68
Paul Farrell
Die, Monster, Die! '65
Sharon Farrell
Night of the Comet '84
It's Alive '74
Terry Farrell
Hellraiser 3: Hell on Earth '92
Mia Farrow
Rosemary's Baby '68
Tisa Farrow
Zombie '80
Andrew Faulds
The Devils '71
Sally Faulkner
Vampyres '74
Jackson Faw
Basket Case 3: The Progeny '92
Ron Fazio
The Toxic Avenger, Part 3: The Last Temptation of Toxie '89
The Toxic Avenger, Part 2 '89
Angela Featherstone
Dark Angel: The Ascent '94
Melinda Fee
Fade to Black '80
Friedrich Feher
The Cabinet of Dr. Caligari '19
Frances Feist
Carnival of Souls '62
Corey Feldman
Tales from the Crypt Presents Bordello of Blood '96
Voodoo '95
The Lost Boys '87
Friday the 13th, Part 5: A New Beginning '85
Friday the 13th, Part 4: The Final Chapter '84
Gremlins '84
Marty Feldman
Young Frankenstein '74
Catherine Feller
The Curse of the Werewolf '60
Edwige Fenech
Blade of the Ripper '70
Sherilyn Fenn
Boxing Helena '93
Meridian: Kiss of the Beast '90
The Wraith '87
Lance Fenton
Heathers '89
Matthew Ferguson
The Club '94
Colin Fernandes
An American Werewolf in London '81
Miguel Fernandez
Spasms '82
Christina Ferrare
Mary, Mary, Bloody Mary '76
Conchata Ferrell
Edward Scissorhands '90
Jose Ferrer
Bloody Birthday '80
The Sentinel '76
Leilani Sarelle Ferrer
Basic Instinct '92
The Harvest '92
Mel Ferrer
The Great Alligator '81
Emerald Jungle '80
Eaten Alive '76
Blood and Roses '61
The Hands of Orlac '60
Miguel Ferrer
Stephen King's The Night Flier '96
Stephen King's The Stand '94
The Harvest '92
The Guardian '90
Deepstar Six '89

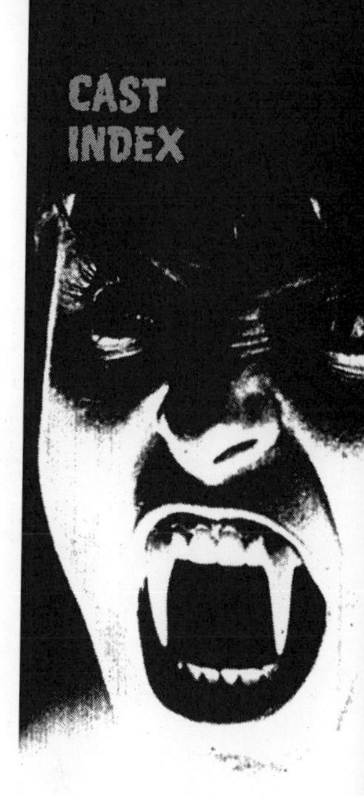

Constance Forslund
Village of the Damned '95
Robert Forster
Maniac Cop 3: Badge of Silence '93
Satan's Princess '90
The Banker '89
Alligator '80
Stephen Forsyth
Hatchet for the Honeymoon '70
Eric Foster
Grandma's House '88
Jodie Foster
The Silence of the Lambs '91
Taxi Driver '76
Meg Foster
Leviathan '89
Relentless '89
Stepfather 2: Make Room for Daddy '89
They Live '88
Preston Foster
Doctor X '32
Susanna Foster
The Climax '44
The Phantom of the Opera '43
Stocker Fountelieu
Angel Heart '87
Derek Fowlds
Frankenstein Created Woman '66
Anne Marie Fox
Rabid Grannies '89
Bernard Fox
Arnold '73
Edward Fox
The Cat and the Canary '79
James Fox
Afraid of the Dark '92
Jerry Fox
Evil Spawn '87
Kerry Fox
Shallow Grave '94
Michael J. Fox
The Frighteners '96
Sidney Fox
Murders in the Rue Morgue '32
Robert Foxworth
Prophecy '79
Damien: Omen 2 '78
Victor Francen
The Beast with Five Fingers '46
Rina Franchetti
Atom Age Vampire '61
Anthony (Tony) Franciosa
Unsane '82
Arlene Francis
Murders in the Rue Morgue '32
Derek Francis
Rasputin the Mad Monk '66
Don Francks
My Bloody Valentine '81
Larry Franco
They Live '88
Diana Frank
Pale Blood '91
David Frankham
Return of the Fly '59
John Franklin
The Addams Family '91
Children of the Corn '84
Pamela Franklin
The Legend of Hell House '73
The Witching '72
William Franklyn
The Satanic Rites of Dracula '73
Mary Frann
I'm Dangerous Tonight '90
Arthur Franz
Abbott and Costello Meet the Invisible Man '51
Dennis Franz
Psycho 2 '83
Dressed to Kill '80
The Fury '78
Elizabeth Franz
Stephen King's Thinner '96
Duncan Fraser
Watchers '88
Helen Fraser
Repulsion '65
John Fraser
Schizo '77
Repulsion '65
Robyn Frates
Puppet Master '89
William Frawley
Abbott and Costello Meet the Invisible Man '51
Robert Frazer
The White Zombie '32
Peter Frechette
The Kindred '87
The Hills Have Eyes, Part 2 '84
Lynne Frederick
Schizo '77
Vampire Circus '71
Vicki Frederick
Chopper Chicks in Zombietown '91
Sam Freed
Stephen King's Thinner '96
Andy Freeman
Bloody Birthday '80
Bill Freeman
Basket Case '81
Joan Freeman
Tower of London '62
Morgan Freeman
Seven '95
Paul Freeman
The Sender '82
Susan French
House '86
Victor French
The Other '72
Bernard Fresson
The Tenant '76
Matt Frewer
Stephen King's The Stand '94
Jonathan Frid
Seizure '74
House of Dark Shadows '70
Gavin Friday
Creepers '85
Gertrud Fridh
Hour of the Wolf '68
Tom Fridley
Friday the 13th, Part 6: Jason Lives '86
Frederick Friedel
A Scream in the Streets/Axe '70s
Peter Friedman
Single White Female '92
The Seventh Sign '88
Terror in Toyland '85
Colin Friels
Darkman '90
Lou Frizzell
The Other '72
Lindsay Frost
Dead Heat '88
Sadie Frost
Bram Stoker's Dracula '92
Warren Frost
Psycho 4: The Beginning '90
Donna Frotscher
They Bite '95
Toby Froud
Labyrinth '86
Dwight Frye
Dead Men Walk '43
Frankenstein Meets the Wolfman '42
The Ghost of Frankenstein '42
The Bride of Frankenstein '35
The Invisible Man '33
The Vampire Bat '32
Dracula '31
Frankenstein '31
Soleil Moon Frye
Piranha '95
Pumpkinhead 2: Blood Wings '94
Invitation to Hell '84
Gaby Fuchs
Mark of the Devil '69
Alan Fudge
Bug '75
Daisy Fuentes
Curdled '95
Tatsuya Fuji
In the Realm of the Senses '76
Avako Fujitani
Gamera, Guardian of the Universe '95
Kei Fujiwara
Tetsuo: The Iron Man '92
Dolores Fuller
Bride of the Monster '56
Jonathan Fuller
Castle Freak '95
The Pit & the Pendulum '91
Kurt Fuller
Elvira, Mistress of the Dark '88
Mary Fuller
Edison Frankenstein '10
Samuel Fuller
Return to Salem's Lot '87
Minnie Fullerton
Night of the Lepus '72

CAST
INDEX

Stefan Gierasch
Blood Beach *'81*
Carrie *'76*
Leslie Gilb
Lemora: A Child's Tale of the Supernatural *'73*
Catherine Gilbert
The Hanging Woman *'72*
Marcus Gilbert
Army of Darkness *'92*
Pamela Gilbert
Evil Spawn *'87*
Yvonne Gilbert
2000 Maniacs *'64*
Gwynne Gilford
Fade to Black *'80*
Jeff Gillen
Children Shouldn't Play with Dead Things *'72*
Dana Gillespie
Lost Continent *'68*
Warrington Gillette
Friday the 13th, Part 2 *'81*
David Gilliam
Frogs *'72*
Seth Gilliam
Starship Troopers *'97*
Richard Gilliland
Bug *'75*
Hugh Gillin
Psycho 3 *'86*
Linda Gillin
Terror at Red Wolf Inn *'72*
Corinna Gillwald
Bloody Moon *'83*
Lowell Gilmore
Picture of Dorian Gray *'45*
Peter Gilmore
The Abominable Dr. Phibes *'71*
Jack Gilpin
Reversal of Fortune *'90*
Toni Gilpin
The Gorgon *'64*
Daniela Giordano
The Girl in Room 2A *'76*
Domiziana Giordano
Interview with the Vampire *'94*
Elenora Giorgi
Creepers *'85*
Cindy Girard
Raising Cain *'92*
Massimo Girotti
Torture Chamber of Baron Blood *'72*
Jackie Giroux
Trick or Treats *'82*
Lillian Gish
The Night of the Hunter *'55*
Isabel Glasser
The Surgeon *'94*
Phillip Glasser
Satan's Princess *'90*
James Gleason
The Night of the Hunter *'55*
Paul Gleason
Maniac Cop 3: Badge of Silence *'93*
He Knows You're Alone *'80*
Candace Glendenning
Flesh and Blood Show *'73*
Garrick Glenn
The Burning *'82*
Scott Glenn
The Silence of the Lambs *'91*
The Keep *'84*
Apocalypse Now *'79*
Brian Glover
Alien3 *'92*
The Company of Wolves *'85*
An American Werewolf in London *'81*
Bruce Glover
Night of the Scarecrow *'95*
Warlock: The Armageddon *'93*
Crispin Glover
Friday the 13th, Part 4: The Final Chapter *'84*
John Glover
In the Mouth of Madness *'95*
Ed and His Dead Mother *'93*
Gremlins 2: The New Batch *'90*
Julian Glover
Quatermass and the Pit *'67*
Fritz Gnass
M *'33*
Paulette Goddard
The Ghost Breakers *'40*
Drew Godderis
Evil Spawn *'87*
Derek Godfrey
Hands of the Ripper *'71*
Terrie Godfrey
The Majorettes *'87*
Alexander Godunov
Waxwork 2: Lost in Time *'91*
Dave Goelz
Labyrinth *'86*
Peter Michael Goetz
King Kong Lives *'86*
Wolfen *'81*
Brandy Gold
Amityville 4 *'89*
Jeff Goldblum
The Lost World: Jurassic Park 2 *'97*
Jurassic Park *'93*
The Fly *'86*
Invasion of the Body Snatchers *'78*
The Sentinel *'76*
Devin Goldenberg
The Last Horror Film *'82*
Ricky Paull Goldin
Mirror, Mirror *'90*
The Blob *'88*
Matthew Goldsby
Student Bodies *'81*
Jenette Goldstein
Near Dark *'87*
Aliens *'86*
Ray Goman
Warlock Moon *'73*
Thomas Gomez
The Climax *'44*
Sonya Noemi Gonzalez
Creature from the Haunted Sea *'60*
Michael Goodliffe
To the Devil, a Daughter *'76*
The Gorgon *'64*
Henry Goodman
Mary Reilly *'95*
John Goodman
Arachnophobia *'90*
C.H.U.D. *'84*
Deborah Goodrich
April Fool's Day *'86*
Angela Goodwin
Julia and Julia *'87*
Harold Goodwin
Curse of the Mummy's Tomb *'64*
Barbara Gordon
Dead Ringers *'88*
Christine Gordon
I Walked with a Zombie *'43*
Colin Gordon
Burn Witch, Burn! *'62*
Don Gordon
The Beast Within *'82*
The Final Conflict *'81*
Dorothy Gordon
The Haunted Strangler *'58*
Gavin Gordon
The Bride of Frankenstein *'35*
Keith Gordon
Christine *'84*
Dressed to Kill *'80*
Marrianne Gordon
Demon Hunter *'88*
Pamela Gordon
Bloodlust: Subspecies 3 *'93*
Bloodstone: Subspecies 2 *'92*
Ruth Gordon
Rosemary's Baby *'68*
Charles Gordone
Angel Heart *'87*
Mel Gorham
Curdled *'95*
Robert Gorman
Leprechaun *'93*
Walt Gorney
Friday the 13th, Part 2 *'81*
Friday the 13th *'80*
Marjoe Gortner
Mausoleum *'83*
Louis Gossett, Jr.
Jaws 3 *'83*
Michael Gothard
Lifeforce *'85*
The Devils *'71*
Carl Gottlieb
Jaws *'75*
John Gottowt
Nosferatu *'22*
Michael Gough
The Serpent and the Rainbow *'87*
The Legend of Hell House *'73*
Crucible of Horror *'69*
The Horror of Dracula *'58*
Simon Gough
Crucible of Horror *'69*

Edmund Gwenn
Them! '54
The Walking Dead '36
Jack Gwillim
Curse of the Mummy's Tomb '64
Michael Gwynn
The Scars of Dracula '70
Anne Gwynne
House of Frankenstein '44
Weird Woman/Frozen Ghost '44
Black Friday '40
Fred Gwynne
Pet Sematary '89
Fatal Attraction '87
Deanna Haas
Devonsville Terror '83
Sean Haberle
The Surgeon '94
Shelley Hack
The Stepfather '87
Troll '86
Gene Hackman
Young Frankenstein '74
Sara Haden
Mad Love '35
Francois Hadji-Lazaro
Cemetery Man '95
Marianne Hagan
Halloween 6: The Curse of Michael Myers '95
Ross Hagen
Phantom Empire '87
Uta Hagen
Reversal of Fortune '90
The Other '72
Julie Hagerty
Reversal of Fortune '90
Dan Haggerty
Elves '89
Ion Haiduc
Bloodlust: Subspecies 3 '93
Bloodstone: Subspecies 2 '92
Stacy Haiduk
Luther the Geek '90
Sid Haig
Spider Baby '64
Corey Haim
Watchers '88
The Lost Boys '87
Silver Bullet '85
Alan Hale, Jr.
The Giant Spider Invasion '75
The Crawling Hand '63
Barbara Hale
The Giant Spider Invasion '75
Creighton Hale
The Cat and the Canary '27
Georgina Hale
The Devils '71
Jack Haley
The Wizard of Oz '39
Jackie Earle Haley
Maniac Cop 3: Badge of Silence '93
Albert Hall
Apocalypse Now '79
Anthony Michael Hall
The Death Artist '95
The Grave '95
Edward Scissorhands '90
Brad Hall
The Guardian '90
Troll '86
Grayson Hall
House of Dark Shadows '70
Harvey Hall
The Vampire Lovers '70
Huntz Hall
The Return of Dr. X '39
Jon Hall
Cobra Woman '44
The Invisible Man's Revenge '44
Kevin Peter Hall
Highway to Hell '92
Landon Hall
Witchcraft 9: Bitter Flesh '96
Lena Hall
Witchcraft 3: The Kiss of Death '90
Lois Hall
Dead Again '91
Scott H. Hall
Color Me Blood Red '64
Blood Feast '63
Thurston Hall
The Black Room '35
Zooey Hall
I Dismember Mama '74
Charles Hallahan
Warlock: The Armageddon '93
The Thing '82
Nightwing '79
John Hallam
Lifeforce '85
Lori Hallier
My Bloody Valentine '81
Luke Halpin
Shock Waves '77
Brett Halsey
Return of the Fly '59
Rodger Halstead
Carnosaur 3: Primal Species '96
Eben Ham
The Unnamable '88
Mark Hamill
Village of the Damned '95
Body Bags '93
Antony Hamilton
Howling 4: The Original Nightmare '88
Judd Hamilton
The Last Horror Film '82
Linda Hamilton
King Kong Lives '86
Children of the Corn '84
Margaret Hamilton
The Wizard of Oz '39
Murray Hamilton
The Amityville Horror '79
Jaws 2 '78
Jaws '75
Wendy Hamilton
The Scars of Dracula '70
Ellen Hamilton-Latzen
Fatal Attraction '87
Marilyn Hamlin
Savage Weekend '80
Marcus Hammond
Plague of the Zombies '66
Walter Hampden
The Hunchback of Notre Dame '39
Paul Hampton
They Came from Within '75
Sasha Hanav
Mary Reilly '95
Tres Handley
Grim '95
James Handy
Arachnophobia '90
Tom Hanks
He Knows You're Alone '80
Jenny Hanley
Flesh and Blood Show '73
The Scars of Dracula '70
Jimmy Hanley
Lost Continent '68
Daryl Hannah
The Fury '78
Page Hannah
Creepshow 2 '87
Gunnar Hansen
Hellblock 13 '97
Freakshow '95
Mosquito '95
The Texas Chainsaw Massacre '74
Paul Hansen
The Return of Count Yorga '71
Count Yorga, Vampire '70
Mitch Hara
The Art of Dying '90
Ian Hardin
Cannibal! The Musical '96
Jerry Hardin
Cujo '83
Kay Harding
The Mummy's Curse '44
Kadeem Hardison
Vampire in Brooklyn '95
Def by Temptation '90
Karl Hardman
Night of the Living Dead '68
Cedric Hardwicke
The Ghost of Frankenstein '42
The Invisible Man Returns '40
The Hunchback of Notre Dame '39
The Ghoul '33
Robert Hardy
Mary Shelley's Frankenstein '94
Demons of the Mind '72
Sam Hardy
King Kong '33
Stephanie Hardy
To Sleep with a Vampire '92
Mickey Hargitay
Lady Frankenstein '72

CAST
INDEX

David Hedison
The Fly '58
Tippi Hedren
The Birds '63
O.P. Heggie
The Bride of Frankenstein '35
Lorna Heilbron
The Creeping Flesh '72
Brian Helgeland
Highway to Hell '92
Marg Helgenberger
Species '95
Stephen King's The Tommyknockers '93
After Midnight '89
Charlotte J. Helmkamp
Frankenhooker '90
David Hemblen
Brainscan '94
Mariel Hemingway
Bad Moon '96
Into the Badlands '92
David Hemmings
Deep Red: Hatchet Murders '75
Anouska Hempel
The Scars of Dracula '70
Richard Hench
Tomb '86
Shirley Henderson
Trainspotting '95
Gloria Hendry
Pumpkinhead 2: Blood Wings '94
Ian Hendry
Captain Kronos: Vampire Hunter '74
Theatre of Blood '73
Repulsion '65
Carrie Henn
Aliens '86
Sam Hennings
Night Angel '90
Paul Henreid
The Exorcist 2: The Heretic '77
Lance Henriksen
Nature of the Beast '94
Man's Best Friend '93
Alien3 '92
The Pit & the Pendulum '91
The Horror Show '89
Pumpkinhead '88
Near Dark '87
Aliens '86
Nightmares '83
Piranha 2: The Spawning '82
Damien: Omen 2 '78
Gloria Henry
Phantasm III: Lord of the Dead '94
Thomas B. Henry
Blood of Dracula '57
Pamela Hensley
Double Exposure '82
Natasha Henstridge
Species '95
Audrey Hepburn
Wait Until Dark '67
Holmes Herbert
The Invisible Man '33
Mystery of the Wax Museum '33
Dr. Jekyll and Mr. Hyde '31
Leon Herbert
The Girl with the Hungry Eyes '94
Rick Herbst
Brain Damage '88
Kuelan Herce
Thrill of the Vampire '70
Azucena Hernandez
The Craving '80
Blake Heron
Trilogy of Terror 2 '96
Edward Herrmann
The Lost Boys '87
Jean Hersholt
Mark of the Vampire '35
Whitby Hertford
Mikey '92
Irene Hervey
Night Monster '42
Christian Hesler
Blood Salvage '90
David Hess
Last House on the Left '72
Charlton Heston
In the Mouth of Madness '95
The Awakening '80
Omega Man '71
Jennifer Love Hewitt
I Know What You Did Last Summer '97
Sean Hewitt
The Sender '82
David Hewlett
Pin ... '88
Barton Heyman
Raising Cain '92
William Hickey
The Maddening '95
Tales from the Darkside: The Movie '90
Puppet Master '89
Catherine Hickland
Witchery '88
Darryl Hickman
The Tingler '59
Catherine Hicks
Child's Play '88
Dan Hicks
Evil Dead 2: Dead by Dawn '87
Kevin Hicks
Blood Relations '87
Jan Hieronimko
Vampyr '31
Anthony Higgins
The Bride '85
Taste the Blood of Dracula '70
Clare Higgins
Hellbound: Hellraiser 2 '88
Hellraiser '87
Michael Higgins
Angel Heart '87
Danny Higham
Death Ship '80
Mary Hignett
Crucible of Horror '69
Tina Louise Hilbert
Basket Case 3: The Progeny '92
Marianna Hill
Blood Beach '81
Wendy Hiller
The Cat and the Canary '79
John Hillerman
Audrey Rose '77
Candace Hilligoss
Carnival of Souls '62
Gillian Hills
Demons of the Mind '72
Daisy Hilton
Freaks '32
George Hilton
Blade of the Ripper '70
Violet Hilton
Freaks '32
Madeline Hinde
The Bloodsuckers '70
Art Hindle
The Brood '79
Invasion of the Body Snatchers '78
Ciaran Hinds
Mary Reilly '95
Cindy Hinds
The Brood '79
Samuel S. Hinds
Son of Dracula '43
Man Made Monster '41
The Raven '35
Gregory Hines
Wolfen '81
Robert Hines
Hellraiser '87
Pat Hingle
Maximum Overdrive '86
Peter Hinwood
The Rocky Horror Picture Show '75
Bill Hinzman
The Majorettes '87
Laura Hippe
Mausoleum '83
Thora Hird
The Nightcomers '72
Robert Hirsch
The Hunchback of Notre Dame '57
Patricia Hitchcock
Psycho '60
Clare Hoak
Masque of the Red Death '89
Rose Hobart
Dr. Jekyll and Mr. Hyde '31
Halliwell Hobbes
Dr. Jekyll and Mr. Hyde '31
Valerie Hobson
The Bride of Frankenstein '35
Werewolf of London '35
Kane Hodder
Pumpkinhead 2: Blood Wings '94
Jason Goes to Hell: The Final Friday '93
Friday the 13th, Part 8: Jason Takes Manhattan '89
Friday the 13th, Part 7: The New Blood '88
John Hodge
Shallow Grave '94

CAST
INDEX

Kate Hodge
Leatherface: The Texas Chainsaw Massacre 3 '89
Joel Hoffman
Pumpkinhead '88
Linda Hoffman
The Dentist '96
Marco Hofschneider
The Island of Dr. Moreau '96
Hulk Hogan
Gremlins 2: The New Batch '90
Susan Hogan
The Brood '79
Arthur Hohl
Devil Doll '36
Island of Lost Souls '32
David Holbrook
Creepshow 2 '87
Return to Salem's Lot '87
Hal Holbrook
Creepshow '82
The Fog '78
Gloria Holden
Dracula's Daughter '36
William Holden
Damien: Omen 2 '78
Bryant Holiday
Devil Doll '64
John E. Holiday
Witchcraft 6: The Devil's Mistress '94
David G. Holland
Hellblock 13 '97
Lloyd Hollar
The Crazies '73
Polly Holliday
Gremlins '84
Bridget Hollman
Evils of the Night '85
Barnaby Holm
The Final Conflict '81
Ian Holm
Mary Shelley's Frankenstein '94
Naked Lunch '91
Alien '79
Clare Holman
Afraid of the Dark '92
Jack Holt
Cat People '42
Mette Holt
The Whispering '94
Mark Holton
Leprechaun '93
Evander Holyfield
Blood Salvage '90
Arabella Holzbog
Carnosaur 2 '94
Hirotora Honda
Gamera, Guardian of the Universe '95
James Hong
Big Trouble in Little China '86
Andre Honore
The Slumber Party Massacre '82
Noel Hood
The Curse of Frankenstein '57
Ewan Hooper
Dracula Has Risen from the Grave '68
Kaitlyn Hooper
Addams Family Values '93
Kristen Hooper
Addams Family Values '93
William Hootkins
Dust Devil '93
Bob Hope
The Ghost Breakers '40
William Hope
Hellbound: Hellraiser 2 '88
Anthony Hopkins
Bram Stoker's Dracula '92
The Silence of the Lambs '91
The Hunchback of Notre Dame '82
Magic '78
Audrey Rose '77
Bo Hopkins
Blood Ties '92
Miriam Hopkins
Dr. Jekyll and Mr. Hyde '31
Dennis Hopper
Texas Chainsaw Massacre 2 '86
Apocalypse Now '79
Hedda Hopper
Dracula's Daughter '36
Michael Hordern
Theatre of Blood '73
Demons of the Mind '72
Wil Horneff
Ghost in the Machine '93
Penelope Horner
Dracula '73
Lynnie Horrigan
Dark Carnival '97
John Horton
Stephen King's Thinner '96
Peter Horton
Children of the Corn '84
Yukihiro Hotaru
Gamera, Guardian of the Universe '95
Carolyn Houlihan
The Burning '82
Jane House
Werewolf of Washington '73
John Houseman
Ghost Story '81
The Fog '78
Jerry Houser
Magic '78
Donald Houston
Maniac '63
Renee Houston
Legend of the Werewolf '75
Repulsion '65
Robert Houston
The Hills Have Eyes '77
Anders Hove
Bloodlust: Subspecies 3 '93
Bloodstone: Subspecies 2 '92
Subspecies '90
Adrian Hoven
Mark of the Devil '69
Natasha Hovey
Demons '86
Anne Howard
Prince of Darkness '87
Arliss Howard
The Lost World: Jurassic Park 2 '97
Natural Born Killers '94
Clint Howard
Leprechaun 2 '94
Carnosaur '93
The Wraith '87
Ronald Howard
Curse of the Mummy's Tomb '64
C. Thomas Howell
The Hitcher '86
Sally Ann Howes
Death Ship '80
Dead of Night '45
Olin Howlin
The Blob '58
Karl Howman
The House on Straw Hill '76
Elizabeth Hoy
Bloody Birthday '80
Brigitte Lin Ching Hsia
The Bride with White Hair 2 '93
The Bride with White Hair '93
Wong Tsu Hsien
A Chinese Ghost Story '87
Nancy Hsueh
Targets '68
John Hubbard
The Mummy's Tomb '42
Whip Hubley
Daddy's Girl '96
Cooper Huckabee
The Curse '87
The Funhouse '81
Ernie Hudson
The Crow '93
Ghostbusters 2 '89
Leviathan '89
Ghostbusters '84
Gary Hudson
Night Angel '90
Rochelle Hudson
Strait-Jacket '64
Tom Hudson
Leatherface: The Texas Chainsaw Massacre 3 '89
David Huffman
Witchcraft 5: Dance with the Devil '92
Blood Beach '81
Daniel Hugh-Kelly
The Good Son '93
Cujo '83
Barnard Hughes
The Lost Boys '87
Sisters '73
Brendan Hughes
To Die For '89
Heather Hughes
Blood Freak '72
Helen Hughes
The Amityville Curse '90
Incubus '82
Julie Hughes
Stormswept '95

Miko Hughes
Wes Craven's New Nightmare '94
Pet Sematary '89
Chuan Chi Hui
Seeding of a Ghost '86
Tom Hulce
Mary Shelley's Frankenstein '94
Dianne Hull
Terror in Toyland '85
Henry Hull
Werewolf of London '35
Warren Hull
The Walking Dead '36
Alf Humphreys
My Bloody Valentine '81
Gayle Hunnicutt
The Legend of Hell House '73
Helen Hunt
Into the Badlands '92
Linda Hunt
The Relic '96
Lois Kelso Hunt
The House on Sorority Row '83
Marsha Hunt
Howling 2: Your Sister Is a Werewolf '85
The Sender '82
Dracula A.D. 1972 '72
Martita Hunt
The Brides of Dracula '60
Holly Hunter
Copycat '95
Crash '95
The Burning '82
Ian Hunter
Dr. Jekyll and Mr. Hyde '41
The Tower of London '39
Kim Hunter
Two Evil Eyes '90
The Kindred '87
Raymond Huntley
The Mummy '59
Leslie Huntly
Demon of Paradise '87
Elizabeth Hurley
Nightscare '93
Matthew Hurley
Pumpkinhead '88
Brandon Hurst
Murders in the Rue Morgue '32
The White Zombie '32
The Hunchback of Notre Dame '23
Dr. Jekyll and Mr. Hyde '20
Elliott Hurst
Popcorn '89
Veronica Hurst
Peeping Tom '60
John Hurt
Frankenstein Unbound '90
Alien '79
Mary Beth Hurt
Parents '89
Jennifer Huss
Polymorph '96
Olivia Hussey
Psycho 4: The Beginning '90
Stephen King's It '90
The Cat and the Canary '79
Ruth Hussey
The Uninvited '44
Anjelica Huston
Addams Family Values '93
The Addams Family '91
James Huston
The Outing '87
Karen Huston
The Return of Count Yorga '71
Michael Hutchence
Frankenstein Unbound '90
Josephine Hutchinson
Son of Frankenstein '39
Harold Huth
The Ghoul '33
Lauren Hutton
Once Bitten '85
Robert Hutton
Cry of the Banshee '70
Timothy Hutton
The Dark Half '91
Judy Huxtable
Scream and Scream Again '70
Sin-Hye Hwang
301, 302 '94
Leila Hyams
Freaks '32
Island of Lost Souls '32
Jonathan Hyde
Anaconda '96
Alex Hyde-White
The Phantom of the Opera '89
Wilfrid Hyde-White
The Cat and the Canary '79
Frances Hyland
Happy Birthday to Me '81
Prudence Hyman
The Gorgon '64
Dorothy Hyson
The Ghoul '33
Steve Hytner
The Prophecy 2: Ashtown '97
Ice Cube
Anaconda '96
Tsuyoski Ihara
Gamera, Guardian of the Universe '95
Michael Imperioli
The Addiction '95
Celia Imrie
Mary Shelley's Frankenstein '94
Frieda Inescort
Return of the Vampire '44
Rufino Ingles
Tombs of the Blind Dead '72
John Ireland
Waxwork 2: Lost in Time '91
Incubus '82
Jeremy Irons
Reversal of Fortune '90
Dead Ringers '88
Shaun Irons
Jugular Wine: A Vampire Odyssey '94
Michael Ironside
Starship Troopers '97
Watchers '88
Hello Mary Lou: Prom Night 2 '87
Scanners '81
Paula Irvine
Phantasm II '88
Amy Irving
The Fury '78
Carrie '76
Holly Irving
Frogs '72
Penny Irving
House of Whipcord '75
Jennifer Irwin
The Gate '87
Jason Isaacs
Event Horizon '97
Chris Isaak
The Silence of the Lambs '91
Margarita Isabel
Cronos '94
Neal Israel
It's Alive 3: Island of the Alive '87
Rosalind Ivan
Dead Man's Eyes/ Pillow of Death '44
Zeljko Ivanek
The Sender '82
Dana Ivey
Addams Family Values '93
The Addams Family '91
Judith Ivey
The Devil's Advocate '97
Victor Izay
Blood Orgy of the She-Devils '74
James Jackel
Color Me Blood Red '64
Robert Jacks
The Texas Chainsaw Massacre 4: The Next Generation '95
Anne Jackson
The Shining '80
Freda Jackson
Die, Monster, Die! '65
The Brides of Dracula '60
John M. Jackson
The Hitcher '86
Mary Jackson
Terror at Red Wolf Inn '72
Targets '68
Peter Jackson
Bad Taste '88
Samuel L. Jackson
Jurassic Park '93
Def by Temptation '90
Derek Jacobi
Dead Again '91
The Hunchback of Notre Dame '82
Andre Jacobs
Demon Keeper '95
Manny Jacobs
The Seventh Sign '88
Dean Jacobson
Child's Play 3 '91

Darby Jones
I Walked with a Zombie '43
Doug Jones
Hocus Pocus '93
Night Angel '90
Duane Jones
Fright House '89
To Die For '89
Night of the Living Dead '68
Eddie Jones
Apprentice to Murder '88
Freddie Jones
Firestarter '84
The Satanic Rites of Dracula '73
Frankenstein Must Be Destroyed '69
Gemma Jones
The Devils '71
Grace Jones
Vamp '86
Harold W. Jones
The Crazies '73
Henry Jones
Arachnophobia '90
The Bad Seed '56
James Earl Jones
The Exorcist 2: The Heretic '77
Jeffrey Jones
The Devil's Advocate '97
Ed Wood '94
Stay Tuned '92
Beetlejuice '88
Jocelyn Jones
Tourist Trap '79
Ken Jones
Phantasm '79
L.Q. Jones
The Beast Within '82
The Brotherhood of Satan '71
Marshall Jones
Cry of the Banshee '70
Nicholas Jones
Crucible of Horror '69
Paul Jones
Demons of the Mind '72
Renee Jones
Friday the 13th, Part 6: Jason Lives '86
Richard T. Jones
Event Horizon '97
Tommy Lee Jones
Natural Born Killers '94
Eyes of Laura Mars '78
Betsy Jones-Moreland
Creature from the Haunted Sea '60
France Jordan
Bloodsucking Nazi Zombies '82
Jeremy Jordan
Nowhere '96
Joanne Moore Jordan
I Dismember Mama '74
Leslie Jordan
Jason Goes to Hell: The Final Friday '93
Marsha Jordan
Count Yorga, Vampire '70
Don Joseph
Color Me Blood Red '64
Jackie Joseph
Gremlins 2: The New Batch '90
Gremlins '84
Little Shop of Horrors '60
Erland Josephson
Hour of the Wolf '68
Larry Joshua
The Burning '82
Robert Joy
The Dark Half '91
Amityville 3: The Demon '83
Brenda Joyce
Dead Man's Eyes/Pillow of Death '44
Calling Dr. Death/Strange Confession '43
Elaine Joyce
Trick or Treat '86
Motel Hell '80
Yootha Joyce
Die! Die! My Darling! '65
Jesus Juarez
Santa Sangre '90
Ashley Judd
Normal Life '96
Natural Born Killers '94
Arline Judge
The Crawling Hand '63
Arno Juerging
Andy Warhol's Dracula '74
Andy Warhol's Frankenstein '74
Raul Julia
Addams Family Values '93
The Addams Family '91
Frankenstein Unbound '90
Eyes of Laura Mars '78
Janet Julian
Humongous '82
Lenny Juliano
Not of This Earth '88
Sandra Julien
Thrill of the Vampire '70
Montserrat Julio
The Blood Spattered Bride '72
Julissa
The Fear Chamber '68
June
The Lodger '26
David Kagen
Friday the 13th, Part 6: Jason Lives '86
Steve Kahan
Warlock: The Armageddon '93
Karen Kahn
Village of the Damned '95
Madeline Kahn
Young Frankenstein '74
Elizabeth Kaitan
Nightwish '89
Friday the 13th, Part 7: The New Blood '88
Terrie Kalbus
Phantasm '79
Patricia Kalember
Jacob's Ladder '90
Steve Kanaly
Pumpkinhead 2: Blood Wings '94
Alden Kane
Prom Night 4: Deliver Us from Evil '91
Carol Kane
Addams Family Values '93
When a Stranger Calls Back '93
When a Stranger Calls '79
Marvin Kaplan
Witchboard 2: The Devil's Doorway '93
Wendy Kaplan
Halloween 5: The Revenge of Michael Myers '89
Maria Kapnist
Dead Waters '97
Lenora Kardorf
Amityville Dollhouse '96
James Karen
Piranha '95
Return of the Living Dead 2 '88
Return of the Living Dead '85
Poltergeist '82
Time Walker '82
Olga Karlatos
Zombie '80
John Karlen
Trilogy of Terror '75
Daughters of Darkness '71
House of Dark Shadows '70
Sergei Karlenkov
Mute Witness '95
Miriam Karlin
A Clockwork Orange '71
Boris Karloff
The Fear Chamber '68
Targets '68
Die, Monster, Die! '65
Black Sabbath '64
The Comedy of Terrors '64
The Raven '63
The Terror '63
The Haunted Strangler '58
Abbott and Costello Meet Dr. Jekyll and Mr. Hyde '52
The Strange Door '51
Abbott and Costello Meet the Killer, Boris Karloff '49
The Body Snatcher '45
Isle of the Dead '45
The Climax '44
House of Frankenstein '44
Before I Hang '40
Black Friday '40
Son of Frankenstein '39
The Tower of London '39
The Invisible Ray '36
The Walking Dead '36
The Black Room '35
The Bride of Frankenstein '35
The Raven '35

Udo Kier
Suspiria '77
The House on Straw Hill '76
Andy Warhol's Dracula '74
Andy Warhol's Frankenstein '74
Mark of the Devil '69
Robbie Kiger
Children of the Corn '84
Richard Kiley
Night Gallery '69
Val Kilmer
The Island of Dr. Moreau '96
Lincoln Kilpatrick
Piranha '95
Omega Man '71
Chu-Ryun Kim
301, 302 '94
Dana Kimmell
Friday the 13th, Part 3 '82
Kevin Kindlan
The Majorettes '87
Adrienne King
Friday the 13th, Part 2 '81
Friday the 13th '80
Alan King
Cat's Eye '85
Andrea King
The Beast with Five Fingers '46
Atlas King
Incredibly Strange Creatures Who Stopped Living and Became Mixed-Up Zombies '63
Charles King
The Unnamable '88
Joseph King
The Walking Dead '36
Loretta King
Bride of the Monster '56
Stephen King
Stephen King's Golden Years '91
Pet Sematary '89
Creepshow 2 '87
Maximum Overdrive '86
Creepshow '82
Zalman King
Galaxy of Terror '81

Walter Kingsford
The Invisible Ray '36
Ben Kingsley
Species '95
Danitza Kingsley
Jack's Back '87
Kiwi Kingston
The Evil of Frankenstein '64
Kathleen Kinmont
Stormswept '95
The Art of Dying '90
Bride of Re-Animator '89
Halloween 4: The Return of Michael Myers '88
Melanie Kinnaman
Friday the 13th, Part 5: A New Beginning '85
Roy Kinnear
Taste the Blood of Dracula '70
Terry Kinney
Body Snatchers '93
Klaus Kinski
Nosferatu the Vampyre '79
Jack the Ripper '76
Lifespan '75
Count Dracula '71
Nastassia Kinski
Cat People '82
To the Devil, a Daughter '76
Phyllis Kirk
House of Wax '53
Clare Kirkconnell
Dead Heat '88
Corinne Kirkin
The Wizard of Gore '70
Sally Kirkland
Two Evil Eyes '90
John Kirkpatrick
A Scream in the Streets/Axe '70s
Mia Kirshner
The Crow 2: City of Angels '96
Terry Kiser
Friday the 13th, Part 7: The New Blood '88
Lee Kisman
Witchcraft '88
Tawny Kitaen
Witchboard '87
Charles Klausmeyer
The Unnamable 2: The Statement of Randolph Carter '92

Gunter Kleeman
I Spit on Your Grave '77
Robert Klein
Tales from the Darkside: The Movie '90
Rudolf Klein-Rogge
The Cabinet of Dr. Caligari '19
Brian Klinknett
Helter Skelter Murders '71
Evan J. Klisser
Hellgate '89
Hildegarde Knef
Witchery '88
Lost Continent '68
David Knell
Chopper Chicks in Zombietown '91
David Knight
Nightmare '63
Esmond Knight
Peeping Tom '60
Keith Knight
My Bloody Valentine '81
Sandra Knight
The Terror '63
Tower of London '62
Shirley Knight
The Sender '82
Ted Knight
Psycho '60
Tuesday Knight
A Nightmare on Elm Street 4: Dream Master '88
Wayne Knight
Jurassic Park '93
Basic Instinct '92
Dead Again '91
Patric Knowles
Arnold '73
Frankenstein Meets the Wolfman '42
The Wolf Man '41
Elyse Knox
The Mummy's Tomb '42
Mickey Knox
Frankenstein Unbound '90
Terence Knox
Children of the Corn 2: The Final Sacrifice '92
Philip Ko
Seeding of a Ghost '86

Hitomi Kobayashi
Evil Dead Trap '88
Marta Kober
Friday the 13th, Part 2 '81
Henry Kolker
Mad Love '35
Kim Kopf
Stormswept '95
Witchcraft 8: Salem's Ghost '95
Karen Kopins
Once Bitten '85
Michael Korb
2000 Maniacs '64
Harvey Korman
Dracula: Dead and Loving It '95
Robert F. (Bob) Kortman
Island of Lost Souls '32
George Kosana
Night of the Living Dead '68
Sylva Koscina
Lisa and the Devil '75
Martin Kosleck
The Mummy's Curse '44
Weird Woman/Frozen Ghost '44
Paul Koslo
Judge & Jury '96
Omega Man '71
David Kossoff
The Two Faces of Dr. Jekyll '60
Elias Koteas
Crash '95
The Prophecy '95
Yaphet Kotto
Freddy's Dead: The Final Nightmare '91
The Running Man '87
Alien '79
Nancy Kovack
Diary of a Madman '63
Martin Kove
Judge & Jury '96
Future Shock '93
Last House on the Left '72
Harley Jane Kozak
Arachnophobia '90
Heidi Kozak
Friday the 13th, Part 7: The New Blood '88
Linda Kozlowski
Village of the Damned '95

John Larroquette
Cat People '82
Mara Laso
The Awful Dr. Orloff '62
Dagmar Lassander
The Black Cat '81
Hatchet for the Honeymoon '70
Louise Lasser
Frankenhooker '90
Sarah Lassez
Nowhere '96
Sydney Lassick
The Art of Dying '90
Curse 2: The Bite '88
Carrie '76
Philip Latham
Dracula, Prince of Darkness '65
Joseph Latimore
Lord of Illusions '95
Ryan Latshaw
Jack-O '95
Phil Lauenson
The Wizard of Gore '70
Andrew Lauer
Screamers '96
Justin Lauer
The Creeps '97
John Laughlin
The Lawnmower Man '92
The Hills Have Eyes, Part 2 '84
Charles Laughton
The Strange Door '51
The Hunchback of Notre Dame '39
Island of Lost Souls '32
The Old Dark House '32
S. John Launer
I Was a Teenage Werewolf '57
Mitchell Laurance
Stepfather 2: Make Room for Daddy '89
Ashley Lauren
Lurking Fear '94
Rod Lauren
The Crawling Hand '63
Tammy Lauren
Wishmaster '97
Ashley Laurence
Cupid '96
Hellraiser 3: Hell on Earth '92
Mikey '92
Hellbound: Hellraiser 2 '88
Hellraiser '87
Michael Laurence
Orson Welles' Ghost Story '50s
John Laurie
The Abominable Dr. Phibes '71
The Reptile '66
Piper Laurie
Dario Argento's Trauma '93
Carrie '76
Ed Lauter
Stephen King's Golden Years '91
Cujo '83
Magic '78
King Kong '76
Gabriele Lavia
Deep Red: Hatchet Murders '75
Martin Lavut
The Mask '61
Peter Lawford
Picture of Dorian Gray '45
Adam Lawrence
Drive-In Massacre '74
Bruno Lawrence
Jack Be Nimble '94
Carol Lawrence
Summer of Fear '78
Christopher Lawrence
The House on Sorority Row '83
Gail Lawrence
Maniac '80
John Lawrence
They Live '88
Matthew Lawrence
Tales from the Darkside: The Movie '90
Stephanie Lawrence
The Phantom of the Opera '89
Dean Lawrie
Bad Taste '88
Leigh Lawson
Madhouse Mansion '74
Richard Lawson
Poltergeist '82
Sarah Lawson
Devil's Bride '68
Frank Lawton
Devil Doll '36
The Invisible Ray '36
Me Me Lay
Emerald Jungle '80
Crucible of Terror '72
Marcia Layton
Cthulhu Mansion '91
John Lazar
Night of the Scarecrow '95
Cloris Leachman
Young Frankenstein '74
Shannon Lead
Witchcraft 6: The Devil's Mistress '94
Denis Leary
Natural Born Killers '94
Timothy Leary
Shocker '89
Joe Leavengood
Lurking Fear '94
Francis Lederer
Return of Dracula '58
Anna Lee
What Ever Happened to Baby Jane? '62
Bernard Lee
Frankenstein and the Monster from Hell '74
Brandon Lee
The Crow '93
Christopher Lee
Gremlins 2: The New Batch '90
Howling 2: Your Sister Is a Werewolf '85
House of the Long Shadows '82
To the Devil, a Daughter '76
The Wicker Man '75
The Satanic Rites of Dracula '73
The Creeping Flesh '72
Dracula A.D. 1972 '72
Horror Express '72
Count Dracula '71
The Scars of Dracula '70
Scream and Scream Again '70
Taste the Blood of Dracula '70
The Oblong Box '69
Devil's Bride '68
Dracula Has Risen from the Grave '68
Rasputin the Mad Monk '66
Dracula, Prince of Darkness '65
The Gorgon '64
The Hands of Orlac '60
Horror Hotel '60
The Two Faces of Dr. Jekyll '60
The Mummy '59
The Horror of Dracula '58
The Curse of Frankenstein '57
Cosette Lee
Deranged '74
Danny Lee
The Untold Story '93
Donna Lee
The Body Snatcher '45
Ida Lee
Grandma's House '88
Jeff Lee
Bugged! '96
Joanna Lee
Plan 9 from Outer Space '56
Kaiulani Lee
Cujo '83
Leslie Lee
A Scream in the Streets/Axe '70s
Margaret Lee
Dorian Gray '70
Patricia Lee
Color Me Blood Red '64
Stan Lee
Jugular Wine: A Vampire Odyssey '94
Stephen Lee
The Pit & the Pendulum '91
Phoebe Legere
The Toxic Avenger, Part 3: The Last Temptation of Toxie '89
The Toxic Avenger, Part 2 '89
James LeGros
Phantasm II '88
John Leguizamo
Spawn '97
Beatrix Lehmmann
The Cat and the Canary '79
Frederic Lehne
Man's Best Friend '93
Amityville 4 '89
Carrie Leigh
Blood Relations '87
Janet Leigh
The Fog '78
Night of the Lepus '72
Psycho '60

Jennifer Jason Leigh
Dolores Claiborne '94
Single White Female '92
The Hitcher '86
Suzanna Leigh
Lust for a Vampire '71
Lost Continent '68
Donovan Leitch
The Blob '88
Virginia Leith
The Brain that Wouldn't Die '63
Jean-Marie Lemaire
Fascination '79
Paul LeMat
Puppet Master '89
John D. LeMay
Jason Goes to Hell: The Final Friday '93
Chris Lemmon
Wishmaster '97
Kasi Lemmons
Candyman '92
Vampire's Kiss '88
Lemmy
Tromeo & Juliet '95
Jarrett Lennon
Amityville Dollhouse '96
Pierce Lenoir
The Carpenter '89
Joy Lentz
Stephen King's Thinner '96
Kay Lenz
House '86
Joseph Leon
He Knows You're Alone '80
Sheldon Leonard
Abbott and Costello Meet the Invisible Man '51
Alex Leppard
The House that Vanished '73
Ken Lerner
Relentless '89
Michael Lerner
Maniac Cop 2 '90
Raymond Lescot
Rabid Grannies '89
Len Lesser
Grandma's House '88
Robert Lesser
The Relic '96
Kate Lester
The Hunchback of Notre Dame '23
Kathy Lester
Phantasm '79
Lori Lethin
Bloody Birthday '80
Rudolf Lettinger
The Cabinet of Dr. Caligari '19
Sam Levene
God Told Me To '76
Loretta Leversee
The Other '72
Anna Levine
Warlock '91
Ted Levine
The Mangler '94
The Silence of the Lambs '91
Shelby Levington
Death by Invitation '71
Stan Levitt
Carnival of Souls '62
Uta Levka
Scream and Scream Again '70
Eugene Levy
Stay Tuned '92
Al Lewis
Fright House '89
Charlotte Lewis
Embrace of the Vampire '95
Dial Help '88
Fiona Lewis
Strange Behavior '81
Dracula '73
Dr. Phibes Rises Again '72
The Fearless Vampire Killers '67
Forrest Lewis
The Monster of Piedras Blancas '57
Geoffrey Lewis
Trilogy of Terror 2 '96
The Lawnmower Man '92
Night of the Comet '84
Gilbert Lewis
Candyman '92
Juliette Lewis
From Dusk Till D awn '95
Natural Born Killers '94
Cape Fear '91
Linda Lewis
Alien Dead '79
Louise Lewis
Blood of Dracula '57
I Was a Teenage Werewolf '57
Mitchell Lewis
The Wizard of Oz '39
Thyme Lewis
Nowhere '96
Leo Leyden
The Mask '61
John Leyton
Schizo '77
Thierry Lhermitte
An American Werewolf in Paris '97
Brian Libby
Stephen King's Nightshift Collection '83
Anne Libert
The Demons '74
Richard Liberty
Day of the Dead '85
Marilyn Lightstone
Spasms '82
Marie Liljedahl
Dorian Gray '70
Matthew Lillard
Serial Mom '94
Yvonne Lime
I Was a Teenage Werewolf '57
Fred J. Lincoln
Last House on the Left '72
Lar Park Lincoln
Friday the 13th, Part 7: The New Blood '88
House 2: The Second Story '87
Pamela Lincoln
The Tingler '59
Gillian Lind
And Now the Screaming Starts '73
Dynasty of Fear '72
Traci Lind
Fright Night 2 '88
Jennie Linden
Nightmare '63
Bert Linder
Stephen King's Nightshift Collection '83
Christa Linder
Night of a Thousand Cats '72
Viveca Lindfors
Exorcist 3: Legion '90
Creepshow '82
The Hand '81
Kristen Lindholm
Twins of Evil '71
Audra Lindley
The Spellbinder '88
Barbara Lindley
Dracula '73
Delroy Lindo
The Devil's Advocate '97
Delta Lindsay
The Scars of Dracula '70
Blake Lindsley
Starship Troopers '97
Helga Line
Horror Express '72
Bai Ling
The Crow '93
Theo Lingen
M '33
Paul Linke
Motel Hell '80
Larry Linville
The Night Stalker '71
Marco Liofredi
Andy Warhol's Frankenstein '74
Leon Lissek
Countess Dracula '70
John Litel
The Return of Dr. X '39
John Lithgow
Raising Cain '92
Cleavon Little
Once Bitten '85
Double Exposure '82
Michelle Little
Appointment with Fear '85
Little Nell
The Rocky Horror Picture Show '75
Lucien Littlefield
The Cat and the Canary '27
Ernest Liu
From Dusk Till Dawn '95
Jason Lively
Night of the Creeps '86
Shelby Livingston
2000 Maniacs '64
Christopher Lloyd
Addams Family Values '93
The Addams Family '91
Danny Lloyd
The Shining '80
Doris Lloyd
The Invisible Man's Revenge '44

Kathleen Lloyd
It's Alive 2: It Lives Again *'78*
Norman Lloyd
Amityville 4 *'89*
Audrey Rose *'77*
Chi Muoi Lo
The Relic *'96*
Tony LoBianco
God Told Me To *'76*
Harry Locke
The Creeping Flesh *'72*
Sondra Locke
Willard *'71*
Anne Lockhart
Dark Tower *'87*
Troll *'86*
Calvin Lockhart
Black Werewolf *'75*
June Lockhart
Troll *'86*
Heather Locklear
Firestarter *'84*
Gary Lockwood
Night of the Scarecrow *'95*
David Lodge
Edge of Sanity *'89*
Roger Lodge
Not of This Earth *'88*
Cary Loftin
Duel *'71*
Phyllis Logan
The Doctor and the Devils *'85*
Ricky Dean Logan
Freddy's Dead: The Final Nightmare *'91*
Kristina Loggia
Chopper Chicks in Zombietown *'91*
Robert Loggia
Lost Highway *'96*
Innocent Blood *'92*
Relentless *'89*
The Believers *'87*
Psycho 2 *'83*
Christopher Logue
The Devils *'71*
Donal Logue
The Grave *'95*
Rachel Loiselle
Mosquito *'95*
Gina Lollobrigida
The Hunchback of Notre Dame *'57*
Herbert Lom
Dead Zone *'83*
And Now the Screaming Starts *'73*
Asylum *'72*
Count Dracula *'71*
Dorian Gray *'70*
Mark of the Devil *'69*
Angel Lombarte
The Blood Spattered Bride *'72*
Jason London
Blood Ties *'92*
Richard Long
House on Haunted Hill *'58*
Jeremy Longhurst
The Gorgon *'64*
Michael Lookinland
Stephen King's The Stand *'94*
Nancy Loomis
Halloween *'78*
Rod Loomis
Jack's Back *'87*
Theodore Loos
M *'33*
Carmen Lopez
Curdled *'95*
Jennifer Lopez
Anaconda *'96*
Traci Lords
Serial Mom *'94*
Skinner *'93*
Stephen King's The Tommyknockers *'93*
Shock 'Em Dead *'90*
Not of This Earth *'88*
Sophia Loren
Boccaccio '70 *'62*
Jerry Lorenz
The Texas Chainsaw Massacre *'74*
Susanne Loret
Atom Age Vampire *'61*
James Lorinz
Frankenhooker *'90*
Peter Lorre
The Comedy of Terrors *'64*
The Raven *'63*
The Beast with Five Fingers *'46*
Mad Love *'35*
M *'33*
Diana Lorys
The Awful Dr. Orloff *'62*
Jasmin Losensky
Bloody Moon *'83*
Dennis Lotis
Horror Hotel *'60*
Lori Loughlin
Amityville 3: The Demon *'83*
Justin Louis
Blood & Donuts *'95*
Hello Mary Lou: Prom Night 2 *'87*
Julia Louis-Dreyfus
Troll *'86*
Tina Louise
Evils of the Night *'85*
The Stepford Wives *'75*
Bessie Love
Vampyres *'74*
Mother Love
The Surgeon *'94*
Suzanna Love
Devonsville Terror *'83*
Tim Loveface
Mosquito *'95*
Frank Lovejoy
House of Wax *'53*
Jacqueline Lovell
Hideous *'97*
Head of the Family *'96*
Alex Lowe
Haunted *'95*
Arthur Lowe
Theatre of Blood *'73*
Chad Lowe
Highway to Hell *'92*
Apprentice to Murder *'88*
Rob Lowe
Stephen King's The Stand *'94*
Susan Lowe
Serial Mom *'94*
Carey Lowell
The Guardian *'90*
Elina Lowensohn
Nadja *'95*
Robert Lowery
The Mummy's Ghost *'44*
Jane Lowry
Alice Sweet Alice *'76*
Jennifer Lowry
Brain Damage *'88*
Lynn Lowry
They Came from Within *'75*
The Crazies *'73*
Mino Loy
Emerald Jungle *'80*
Lisa Lu
Demon Seed *'77*
Susan Lucci
Invitation to Hell *'84*
Pamela Ludwig
Pale Blood *'91*
J.P. Luebsen
Witchboard *'87*
Bela Lugosi
Bride of the Monster *'56*
Plan 9 from Outer Space *'56*
Abbott and Costello Meet Frankenstein *'48*
The Body Snatcher *'45*
Return of the Vampire *'44*
Frankenstein Meets the Wolfman *'42*
The Ghost of Frankenstein *'42*
Night Monster *'42*
The Invisible Ghost *'41*
The Wolf Man *'41*
Black Friday *'40*
Son of Frankenstein *'39*
The Invisible Ray *'36*
Mark of the Vampire *'35*
The Raven *'35*
The Black Cat *'34*
Island of Lost Souls *'32*
Murders in the Rue Morgue *'32*
The White Zombie *'32*
Dracula *'31*
James Luisi
Fade to Black *'80*
Bob Lujan
Vampire's Kiss *'88*
Paul Lukas
The Ghost Breakers *'40*
Keye Luke
Gremlins 2: The New Batch *'90*
Dead Heat *'88*
Gremlins *'84*
Joanna Lumley
The Satanic Rites of Dracula *'73*
Deanna Lund
Elves *'89*
Lucille Lund
The Black Cat *'34*
Cherie Lunghi
Mary Shelley's Frankenstein *'94*
Ida Lupino
Devil's Rain *'75*
Alberto Lupo
Atom Age Vampire *'61*

Shari Mann
Mausoleum *'83*
David Manners
The Black Cat *'34*
The Mummy *'32*
Dracula *'31*
Patricia Manning
Hideous Sun Demon *'59*
Andreas Mannkopff
Jack the Ripper *'76*
Dinah Manoff
Child's Play *'88*
Martha Mansfield
Dr. Jekyll and Mr. Hyde *'20*
Maurice Manson
The Creature Walks Among Us *'56*
Paul Mantee
Lurking Fear *'94*
The Manitou *'78*
Joe Mantegna
Stephen King's Thinner *'96*
Bronwen Mantel
Pin ... *'88*
Steve Marachuk
Piranha 2: The Spawning *'82*
Andree Maranda
The Toxic Avenger *'86*
Bertram Marburgh
Before I Hang *'40*
Fredric March
Dr. Jekyll and Mr. Hyde *'31*
Paul Marco
Bride of the Monster *'56*
Plan 9 from Outer Space *'56*
Ted Marcoux
Ghost in the Machine *'93*
Andrea Marcovicci
The Stuff *'85*
The Hand *'81*
James Marcus
A Clockwork Orange *'71*
Richard Marcus
Deadly Friend *'86*
Jordan Marder
Lord of Illusions *'95*
Tom Mardirosian
The Dark Half *'91*
Simone Marevil
Un Chien Andalou *'28*
Margo
The Leopard Man *'43*
Janet Margolin
Ghostbusters 2 *'89*
Miriam Margolyes
Ed and His Dead Mother *'93*
David Margulies
Ghostbusters 2 *'89*
Ghostbusters *'84*
Dressed to Kill *'80*
Gina Mari
The Slumber Party Massacre *'82*
Lisa Marie
Ed Wood *'94*
Dead and Buried *'81*
Kei Marimura
XX: Beautiful Prey *'96*
Richard "Cheech" Marin
From Dusk Till Dawn *'95*
Ghostbusters 2 *'89*
Daniel Markel
Dark Angel: The Ascent *'94*
Barbara Markham
House of Whipcord *'75*
Monte Markham
Piranha *'95*
Alfred Marks
Scream and Scream Again *'70*
Jack Marks
Friday the 13th, Part 2 *'81*
Michael Marks
The Wasp Woman *'59*
Slash Marks
Night of the Cobra Woman *'72*
Norma Marla
The Two Faces of Dr. Jekyll *'60*
John Marley
It's Alive 2: It Lives Again *'78*
Kelli Maroney
Chopping Mall *'86*
Night of the Comet *'84*
Serge Marquand
Les Raisins de la Mort *'78*
Eddie Marr
I Was a Teenage Werewolf *'57*
Hyla Marrow
Maniac *'80*
Kenneth Mars
Young Frankenstein *'74*
Carol Marsh
The Horror of Dracula *'58*
Carry Marsh
Dead of Night *'45*
Jamie Marsh
Brainscan *'94*
Jean Marsh
The Changeling *'80*
Marian Marsh
The Black Room *'35*
Alan Marshal
House on Haunted Hill *'58*
The Hunchback of Notre Dame *'39*
Bryan Marshall
Quatermass and the Pit *'67*
Claire Marshall
Demon Keeper *'95*
E.G. Marshall
Stephen King's The Tommyknockers *'93*
Two Evil Eyes *'90*
Creepshow *'82*
Herbert Marshall
The Fly *'58*
Paula Marshall
Warlock: The Armageddon *'93*
Hellraiser 3: Hell on Earth *'92*
Steve Marshall
Night of the Creeps *'86*
Tony Marshall
I Was a Teenage Werewolf *'57*
Tully Marshall
The Cat and the Canary *'27*
William Marshall
Blacula *'72*
Christina Marsillach
Terror at the Opera *'88*
Donna Martell
Abbott and Costello Meet the Killer, Boris Karloff *'49*
Felix Marten
Les Raisins de la Mort *'78*
Anne-Marie Martin
The Boogens *'81*
Damon Martin
Amityville 1992: It's about Time *'92*
Dewey Martin
The Thing *'51*
Duane Martin
Scream 2 *'97*
Elsa Martin
Demon Keeper *'95*
Helen Martin
Night Angel *'90*
Maribel Martin
The Blood Spattered Bride *'72*
Nan Martin
A Nightmare on Elm Street 3: Dream Warriors *'87*
Sandy Martin
Scalpel *'76*
Sharlene Martin
Friday the 13th, Part 8: Jason Takes Manhattan *'89*
Skip Martin
Masque of the Red Death *'65*
Steve Martin
Little Shop of Horrors *'86*
Strother Martin
Nightwing *'79*
The Brotherhood of Satan *'71*
Troy Kennedy Martin
Terror Train *'80*
Elsa Martinelli
Blood and Roses *'61*
Luciano Martino
Emerald Jungle *'80*
Toshiya Maruyama
House Where Evil Dwells *'82*
Tom Maruzzi
Man Beast *'55*
Joseph Mascolo
Jaws 2 *'78*
Nelson Mashita
Darkman *'90*
Ace Mask
Not of This Earth *'88*
Connie Mason
2000 Maniacs *'64*
Blood Feast *'63*
Hilary Mason
Meridian: Kiss of the Beast *'90*
Don't Look Now *'73*
James Mason
Salem's Lot *'79*
Lawrence Mason
The Crow *'93*

The Legend of Hell House '73
Night Gallery '69
It! '67
Macbeth '48
Malcolm McDowell
The Surgeon '94
Cat People '82
A Clockwork Orange '71
Trevyn McDowell
Mary Shelley's Frankenstein '94
John McEnery
Schizo '77
Peter McEnery
The Cat and the Canary '79
Annie McEnroe
Howling 2: Your Sister Is a Werewolf '85
The Hand '81
Reba McEntire
Tremors '89
T.J. McFadden
Slipping into Darkness '88
Paul McGann
Afraid of the Dark '92
Alien3 '92
Darren McGavin
Dead Heat '88
The Night Stalker '71
Vonetta McGee
Blacula '72
Brownie McGhee
Angel Heart '87
Bruce McGill
The Hand '81
Everett McGill
The People Under the Stairs '91
Silver Bullet '85
John C. McGinley
Seven '95
John McGiver
Arnold '73
Patrick McGoohan
Scanners '81
Rose McGowan
Scream '96
Charles McGraw
The Birds '63
Ewan McGregor
Trainspotting '95
Shallow Grave '94
Biff McGuire
Werewolf of Washington '73
Bruce McGuire
From Beyond '86
Jason McGuire
Pet Sematary 2 '92
John McGuire
The Invisible Ghost '41
Stephen McHattie
The Dark '94
Robert McHeady
Deranged '74
Frank McHugh
Mystery of the Wax Museum '33
Jason McHugh
Cannibal! The Musical '96
John McIntire
Psycho '60
Duncan McIntosh
Incubus '82
Paul McIver
Stephen King's The Tommyknockers '93
Scott McKay
Terror in Toyland '85
Robin McKee
DNA '97
Ian McKellen
The Keep '84
Maxine McKendry
Andy Warhol's Dracula '74
T.P. McKenna
The Doctor and the Devils '85
Leo McKern
The Omen '76
Kevin McKidd
Trainspotting '95
Don McKillop
An American Werewolf in London '81
Bill McKinney
Deliverance '72
Jennifer McKinney
Death Ship '80
Mona McKinnon
Plan 9 from Outer Space '56
Maya McLaughlin
Children of the Night '92
Michael McManus
Poltergeist '82
Niles McMaster
Alice Sweet Alice '76
Kenneth McMillan
Cat's Eye '85
Salem's Lot '79
W.G. McMillan
The Crazies '73
Teri McMinn
The Texas Chainsaw Massacre '74
Pamela McMyler
Blood Beach '81
Mercedes McNab
Addams Family Values '93
Kevin McNally
Jekyll and Hyde '90
Brian McNamara
Arachnophobia '90
William McNamara
Copycat '95
Terror at the Opera '88
Alan McNaughton
Frankenstein Created Woman '66
Julia McNeal
The Refrigerator '91
Kate McNeil
Monkey Shines '88
The House on Sorority Row '83
Kristy McNichol
The Forgotten One '89
Steve McQueen
The Blob '58
Leslie McRae
Blood Orgy of the She-Devils '74
Jillian McWhirter
After Midnight '89
Anne Meacham
Seizure '74
Russell Means
Natural Born Killers '94
Meat Loaf
The Rocky Horror Picture Show '75
Harriet Medin
Blood Beach '81
Heather Medway
Serpent's Lair '95
Donald Meek
Mark of the Vampire '35
George Meeker
Dead Man's Eyes/ Pillow of Death '44
Ralph Meeker
The Night Stalker '71
Don Megowan
The Creature Walks Among Us '56
Kathryn Meisle
Basket Case 2 '90
Nicholas Mele
A Nightmare on Elm Street 5: Dream Child '89
Ron Melendez
Children of the Corn 3: Urban Harvest '95
Jill Melford
Edge of Sanity '89
Joseph Mell
I Was a Teenage Werewolf '57
Andree Melly
The Brides of Dracula '60
Robin Meloy
The House on Sorority Row '83
Murray Melvin
Madhouse Mansion '74
The Devils '71
Heather Menzies
Piranha '78
Hector Mercado
Nomads '86
Mae Mercer
Frogs '72
Michele Mercier
Black Sabbath '64
Monique Mercure
Naked Lunch '91
Burgess Meredith
Magic '78
The Manitou '78
The Sentinel '76
Penny Meredith
Flesh and Blood Show '73
Macha Meril
Deep Red: Hatchet Murders '75
Jan Merlin
Twilight People '72
Mary Merrall
Dead of Night '45
B.D. Merrill
What Ever Happened to Baby Jane? '62
Damon Merrill
The Outing '87
Clive Merrison
Heavenly Creatures '94
Theresa Merritt
The Serpent and the Rainbow '87
Jane Merrow
Hands of the Ripper '71
John Mese
Night of the Scarecrow '95

Elizabeth Moody
Dead Alive '93
Lynne Moody
The Evil '78
Ron Moody
Legend of the Werewolf '75
Alvy Moore
The Brotherhood of Satan '71
Ben Moore
2000 Maniacs '64
Christine Moore
Lurkers '88
Demi Moore
The Seventh Sign '88
Dennis Moore
The Mummy's Curse '44
Duke Moore
Plan 9 from Outer Space '56
Eva Moore
The Old Dark House '32
Frank Moore
Blood & Donuts '95
Rabid '77
Gar Moore
Abbott and Costello Meet the Killer, Boris Karloff '49
Joanna Moore
The Dunwich Horror '70
Julianne Moore
The Lost World: Jurassic Park 2 '97
Tales from the Darkside: The Movie '90
Melissa Moore
Stormswept '95
The Invisible Maniac '90
Scream Dream '89
Micki Moore
Deranged '74
Agnes Moorehead
Hush, Hush, Sweet Charlotte '65
Erin Moran
Galaxy of Terror '81
Peggy Moran
The Mummy's Hand '40
Rick Moranis
Ghostbusters 2 '89
Little Shop of Horrors '86
Ghostbusters '84
Mantan Moreland
Spider Baby '64
Andre Morell
Plague of the Zombies '66
Antonio Moreno
Creature from the Black Lagoon '54
Dennis (Stanley Morner) Morgan
The Return of Dr. X '39
Frank Morgan
The Wizard of Oz '39
Glenn Morgan
Trick or Treat '86
Nancy Morgan
The Nest '88
Ralph Morgan
Weird Woman/Frozen Ghost '44
Night Monster '42
Richard Morgan
The Wicked '89
Robbi Morgan
Friday the 13th '80
Tanya Morgan
Targets '68
Terence Morgan
Curse of the Mummy's Tomb '64
Cathy Moriarty
Neighbors '81
Michael Moriarty
Dark Tower '87
It's Alive 3: Island of the Alive '87
Return to Salem's Lot '87
Troll '86
The Stuff '85
Patricia Morison
Calling Dr. Death/Strange Confession '43
Robert Morley
Theatre of Blood '73
Aubrey Morris
Lifeforce '85
A Clockwork Orange '71
Barboura Morris
A Bucket of Blood '59
The Wasp Woman '59
Beth Morris
Crucible of Terror '72
Garrett Morris
Children of the Night '92
The Stuff '85
Haviland Morris
Gremlins 2: The New Batch '90
Jonathan Morris
Vampire Journals '96
Judy Morris
Razorback '84
Lisa Morris
The Mangler '94
Marianne Morris
Vampyres '74
Robert Morris
Frankenstein Created Woman '66
Wayne Morris
The Return of Dr. X '39
Temuera Morrison
The Island of Dr. Moreau '96
Jeff Morrow
Blood Legacy '73
The Creature Walks Among Us '56
Mari Morrow
Children of the Corn 3: Urban Harvest '95
Vic Morrow
Humanoids from the Deep '80
Barry Morse
The Changeling '80
Asylum '72
David Morse
Stephen King's The Langoliers '95
The Good Son '93
Viggo Mortensen
The Prophecy '95
Bill Moseley
Night of the Living Dead '90
Texas Chainsaw Massacre 2 '86
William R. Moses
The Nurse '97
The Fiance '96
Michael H. Moss
Stephen King's The Night Flier '96
Josh Mostel
The Maddening '95
John Moulder-Brown
Vampire Circus '71
Irina Movila
Subspecies '90
Alan Mowbray
Abbott and Costello Meet the Killer, Boris Karloff '49
Patrick Mower
The Bloodsuckers '70
Cry of the Banshee '70
Devil's Bride '68
Bill Moynihan
The Creeps '97
David Mucci
Prom Night '80
Leonard Mudie
The Mummy '32
Paul Mueller
Count Dracula '71
Marianne Muellerliele
Curse 2: The Bite '88
Ann Muffly
Season of the Witch '73
Gavin Muir
Abbott and Costello Meet the Invisible Man '51
Diana Muldaur
The Other '72
Patrick Muldoon
Starship Troopers '97
Chris Mulkey
Ghost in the Machine '93
Jack's Back '87
Greg Mullavey
I Dismember Mama '74
Patty Mullen
Frankenhooker '90
Eva Muller
The Fear Chamber '68
Paul Muller
Lady Frankenstein '72
Dermot Mulroney
Copycat '95
Meg Mundy
Fatal Attraction '87
Caroline Munro
Faceless '88
The Last Horror Film '82
Maniac '80
Captain Kronos: Vampire Hunter '74
Dracula A.D. 1972 '72
Dr. Phibes Rises Again '72
The Abominable Dr. Phibes '71
Neil Munro
Gate 2 '92
Michael Murdock
Dark Carnival '97
Christopher Murney
Maximum Overdrive '86

Anthony Nichols
I Spit on Your Grave '77
Britt Nichols
The Demons '74
Nick Nichols
Dead Ringers '88
Stephen Nichols
Witchboard '87
Taylor Nichols
Serpent's Lair '95
Thomas Ian Nichols
Judge & Jury '96
Jack Nicholson
Wolf '94
The Witches of Eastwick '87
The Shining '80
The Raven '63
The Terror '63
Little Shop of Horrors '60
Susan Nickerson
Witchboard '87
Julia Nickson-Soul
Amityville: A New Generation '93
Daria Nicolodi
Terror at the Opera '88
Creepers '85
Unsane '82
Beyond the Door 2 '79
Deep Red: Hatchet Murders '75
Leslie Nielsen
Dracula: Dead and Loving It '95
Creepshow '82
Prom Night '80
Bill Nighy
The Phantom of the Opera '89
Leonard Nimoy
Invasion of the Body Snatchers '78
Them! '54
John P. Nixon
Legend of Boggy Creek '75
Natalija Nogulich
The Guardian '90
Jeanette Nolan
The Manitou '78
Macbeth '48
John Nolan
The Terror '79
Nick Nolte
Cape Fear '91
Mike Nomad
April Fool's Day '86
Chris Nomicos
The Para Psychics '86
Kerry Noonan
Friday the 13th, Part 6: Jason Lives '86
Tom Noonan
Manhunter '86
Wolfen '81
Kathleen Noone
Serpent's Lair '95
Maidie Norman
What Ever Happened to Baby Jane? '62
Dean Norris
Starship Troopers '97
The Lawnmower Man '92
J.J. North
Hellblock 13 '97
Sheree North
Maniac Cop '88
Virginia North
The Abominable Dr. Phibes '71
Jeremy Northam
Mimic '97
Barry Norton
Dracula '31
Edgar Norton
Son of Frankenstein '39
Dr. Jekyll and Mr. Hyde '31
Kristin Norton
The Creeps '97
Jack Noseworthy
Event Horizon '97
Lenka Novak
The Vampire Hookers '78
Ivor Novello
The Lodger '26
Tom Novembre
An American Werewolf in Paris '97
Miguel Nunez
Return of the Living Dead '85
Bill Nunn
Candyman 2: Farewell to the Flesh '94
Def by Temptation '90
Diane Nuttall
Demon Keeper '95
Bryan Nutter
Witchcraft 6: The Devil's Mistress '94
Carrie Nye
Creepshow '82
Simon Oakland
The Night Stalker '71
Psycho '60
Warren Oates
Race with the Devil '75
Edmond O'Brien
The Hunchback of Notre Dame '39
Kevin O'Brien
Warlock '91
Richard O'Brien
The Rocky Horror Picture Show '75
Jeffrey Obrow
The Kindred '87
Pat O'Bryan
Relentless '89
976-EVIL '88
Arthur O'Connell
Ben '72
Jerry O'Connell
Scream 2 '97
Taaffe O'Connell
Galaxy of Terror '81
Dennis O'Connor
The Dark '94
Kevin J. O'Connor
Lord of Illusions '95
Renee O'Connor
Darkman 2: The Return of Durant '94
Simon O'Connor
Heavenly Creatures '94
Una O'Connor
The Bride of Frankenstein '35
The Invisible Man '33
Judith O'Dea
Night of the Living Dead '68
Tony O'Dell
Chopping Mall '86
Fritz Odemar
M '33
Jim O'Doherty
Basket Case 3: The Progeny '92
Cathy O'Donnell
Terror in the Haunted House '58
Jerry O'Donnell
Hideous '97
Martha O'Driscoll
House of Dracula '45
Ian Ogilvy
And Now the Screaming Starts '73
The Conqueror Worm '68
Charles Ogle
Edison Frankenstein '10
Lani O'Grady
Massacre at Central High '76
Jason O'Gulihar
Witchcraft 4: Virgin Heart '92
Jack O'Halloran
King Kong '76
George O'Hanlon, Jr.
The Evil '78
Brett O'Hara
Incredibly Strange Creatures Who Stopped Living and Became Mixed-Up Zombies '63
Catherine O'Hara
Beetlejuice '88
Jenny O'Hara
Wishmaster '97
Maureen O'Hara
The Hunchback of Notre Dame '39
Caitlin (Kathleen Heaney) O'Heaney
He Knows You're Alone '80
Savage Weekend '80
Dan O'Herlihy
Halloween 3: Season of the Witch '82
Macbeth '48
Pete O'Herne
Bad Taste '88
Carol Ohmart
Spider Baby '64
House on Haunted Hill '58
Tsuyako Okajima
House Where Evil Dwells '82
Dennis O'Keefe
The Leopard Man '43
Michael O'Keefe
The Dark Secret of Harvest Home '78
Miles O'Keeffe
Waxwork '88
Tim O'Kelly
Targets '68
Warner Oland
Werewolf of London '35
Ken Olandt
Leprechaun '93
April Fool's Day '86

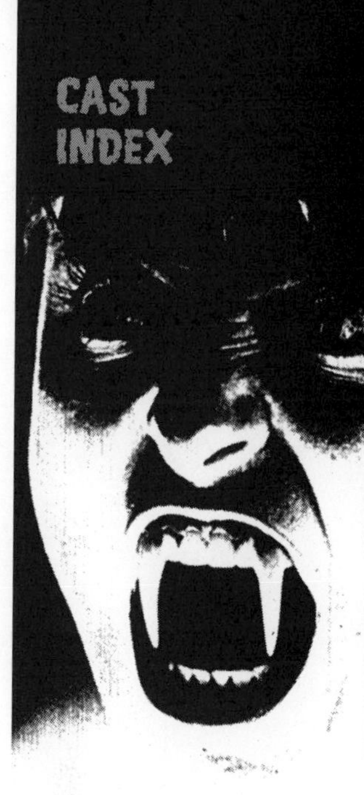

Stuart Pankin
Arachnophobia *'90*
Fatal Attraction *'87*
John Pankow
Monkey Shines *'88*
Helen Papas
Graveyard Shift *'87*
Laslo Papas
Slipping into Darkness *'88*
Michael Pare
Bad Moon *'96*
Raging Angels *'95*
Village of the Damned *'95*
Monique Parent
Mirror, Mirror 3: The Voyeur *'96*
Judy Parfitt
Dolores Claiborne *'94*
Anne Parillaud
Innocent Blood *'92*
Blair Parker
The Forgotten One *'89*
Corey Parker
I'm Dangerous Tonight *'90*
Edwin Parker
Abbott and Costello Meet the Mummy *'55*
Fess Parker
Them! *'54*
Jameson Parker
Prince of Darkness *'87*
Jean Parker
Dead Man's Eyes/ Pillow of Death *'44*
Lara Parker
Race with the Devil *'75*
Rachelle Parker
Jugular Wine: A Vampire Odyssey *'94*
Sarah Jessica Parker
Ed Wood *'94*
Hocus Pocus *'93*
Trey Parker
Cannibal! The Musical *'96*
Gerard Parkes
Spasms *'82*
Barbara Parkins
Asylum *'72*
Catherine Parks
Friday the 13th, Part 3 *'82*
Gina Parks
Shock 'Em Dead *'90*
Michael Parks
From Dusk Till Dawn *'95*

Mark Parra
The Unnamable *'88*
Leslie Parrish
The Giant Spider Invasion *'75*
Nancy Parsons
Motel Hell *'80*
Shannon Michelle Parsons
Freakshow *'95*
Paul A. Partain
The Texas Chainsaw Massacre *'74*
Ross Partridge
Amityville: A New Generation *'93*
Marie-Georges Pascal
Les Raisins de la Mort *'78*
Olivia Pascal
Bloody Moon *'83*
Nadine Pascale
Zombie Lake *'80*
Richard Pasco
Rasputin the Mad Monk *'66*
The Gorgon *'64*
Adrian Pasdar
Near Dark *'87*
Michael Passion
Generation X-Tinct *'97*
George Pastell
Curse of the Mummy's Tomb *'64*
The Mummy *'59*
Michael Pataki
Halloween 4: The Return of Michael Myers *'88*
Dead and Buried *'81*
Michael Pate
Howling 3: The Marsupials *'87*
Tower of London *'62*
The Strange Door *'51*
Jason Patric
Frankenstein Unbound *'90*
The Lost Boys *'87*
Sarah Patterson
The Company of Wolves *'85*
Bart Patton
Dementia 13 *'63*
Mark Patton
A Nightmare on Elm Street 2: Freddy's Revenge *'85*

Tom Patton
The Whispering *'94*
Will Patton
Copycat *'95*
The Rapture *'91*
Adrian Paul
Masque of the Red Death *'89*
Alexandra Paul
Spectre *'96*
Piranha *'95*
Christine *'84*
John Paul
Curse of the Mummy's Tomb *'64*
Nancy Paul
Lifeforce *'85*
Richard Joseph Paul
Vampirella *'96*
Ricky Paul
Piranha 2: The Spawning *'82*
Morgan Paull
Fade to Black *'80*
George Paulsin
Simon, King of the Witches *'71*
Bill Paxton
Boxing Helena *'93*
Future Shock *'93*
Brain Dead *'89*
Near Dark *'87*
Aliens *'86*
Allen Payne
Vampire in Brooklyn *'95*
Bruce Payne
H.P. Lovecraft's Necronomicon: Book of the Dead *'93*
Laurence Payne
Vampire Circus *'71*
Amanda Pays
Leviathan *'89*
The Kindred *'87*
Rock Peace
Attack of the Killer Tomatoes *'77*
E.J. Peaker
The Banker *'89*
Adrienne Pearce
Demon Keeper *'95*
Jacqueline Pearce
Plague of the Zombies *'66*
The Reptile *'66*
Mary Vivian Pearce
Serial Mom *'94*

Clive Pearson
Witchcraft 4: Virgin Heart *'92*
David Pearson
Tomb *'86*
Patsy Pease
He Knows You're Alone *'80*
Bob Peck
Jurassic Park *'93*
Brian Peck
Return of the Living Dead *'85*
Gregory Peck
The Omen *'76*
J. Eddie Peck
Curse 2: The Bite *'88*
Tony Peck
Carnosaur 3: Primal Species *'96*
Maren Pedersen
Witchcraft through the Ages *'22*
David Peel
The Brides of Dracula *'60*
The Hands of Orlac *'60*
Nia Peeples
Mr. Stitch *'95*
Deepstar Six *'89*
Lisa Pelikan
Into the Badlands *'92*
Jennifer *'78*
Jennifer Peluso
Hellblock 13 *'97*
Elizabeth Pena
Jacob's Ladder *'90*
Julio Pena
Horror Express *'72*
Diana Penalver
Dead Alive *'93*
Nicholas Pennell
Rasputin the Mad Monk *'66*
Earl Pennington
Happy Birthday to Me *'81*
Joe Penny
Bloody Birthday *'80*
Anthony Penya
Humanoids from the Deep *'80*
John Pepper
Specters *'87*
Esme Percy
Dead of Night *'45*
Tony Perenski
The Texas Chainsaw Massacre 4: The Next Generation *'95*

Alain Plumey
Fascination '79
Amanda Plummer
The Prophecy '95
Needful Things '93
Christopher Plummer
Dolores Claiborne '94
Wolf '94
Kathryn Pogson
The Company of Wolves '85
Ken Pogue
Bad Moon '96
Larry Poindexter
Sorceress '94
Priscilla Pointer
A Nightmare on Elm Street 3: Dream Warriors '87
Roman Polanski
The Tenant '76
The Fearless Vampire Killers '67
Jon Polito
The Crow '93
Michael J. Pollard
Skeeter '93
The Art of Dying '90
Teri Polo
The Arrival '96
Ada Pometti
Lady Frankenstein '72
Clara Pontoppidan
Witchcraft through the Ages '22
Olaf Pooley
Crucible of Horror '69
Iggy Pop
The Crow 2: City of Angels '96
Adelina Porrio
Don't Look Now '73
Don Porter
Night Monster '42
Eric Porter
Hands of the Ripper '71
Lost Continent '68
Pete Postlethwaite
The Lost World: Jurassic Park 2 '97
Don Potter
Double Exposure '82
Madeleine Potter
Two Evil Eyes '90
Martin Potter
Fellini Satyricon '69
Terry Potter
Bad Taste '88
Annie Potts
Ghostbusters 2 '89
Ghostbusters '84
CCH Pounder
Tales from the Crypt Presents Demon Knight '94
Psycho 4: The Beginning '90
Charles Powell
Screamers '96
Robert Powell
The Hunchback of Notre Dame '82
Asylum '72
Hartley Power
Dead of Night '45
Stefanie Powers
Die! Die! My Darling! '65
Michael Praed
To Die For 2: Son of Darkness '91
Mike Pratt
Repulsion '65
George Pravda
Frankenstein Must Be Destroyed '69
Karen Prell
Labyrinth '86
Paula Prentiss
The Stepford Wives '75
Cyndy Preston
Prom Night 3: The Last Kiss '89
Pin ... '88
Kelly Preston
From Dusk Till Dawn '95
The Spellbinder '88
Christine '84
Dennis Price
Theatre of Blood '73
Twins of Evil '71
The Horror of Frankenstein '70
Marc Price
Trick or Treat '86
Richard Price
Shocker '89
Vincent Price
Edward Scissorhands '90
Dead Heat '88
House of the Long Shadows '82
Theatre of Blood '73
Doctor Phibes Rises Again '72
The Abominable Dr. Phibes '71
Cry of the Banshee '70
Scream and Scream Again '70
The Oblong Box '69
The Conqueror Worm '68
Masque of the Red Death '65
The Comedy of Terrors '64
Diary of a Madman '63
The Raven '63
Tower of London '62
The Pit and the Pendulum '61
The Fall of the House of Usher '60
Return of the Fly '59
The Tingler '59
The Fly '58
House on Haunted Hill '58
House of Wax '53
The Invisible Man Returns '40
The Tower of London '39
Robert Prichard
The Toxic Avenger '86
Aisha Prigann
Ashes and Flames '97
William Prince
Spontaneous Combustion '89
The Stepford Wives '75
Andrew Prine
Amityville 2: The Possession '82
The Evil '78
Town that Dreaded Sundown '76
Simon, King of the Witches '71
Bryan Pringle
Haunted Honeymoon '86
Freddie Prinze, Jr.
I Know What You Did Last Summer '97
Juergen Prochnow
DNA '97
In the Mouth of Madness '95
The Seventh Sign '88
The Keep '84
Paul Prokop
The Velvet Vampire '71
Robert Prosky
Gremlins 2: The New Batch '90
Christine '84
The Keep '84
David Proval
Innocent Blood '92
David Prowse
Frankenstein and the Monster from Hell '74
A Clockwork Orange '71
Vampire Circus '71
The Horror of Frankenstein '70
Harrison Pruett
Embrace of the Vampire '95
Jonathan Pryce
Haunted Honeymoon '86
The Doctor and the Devils '85
Something Wicked This Way Comes '83
Nicholas Pryor
Brain Dead '89
Damien: Omen 2 '78
Richard Pryor
Lost Highway '96
Jesus Puente
Hatchet for the Honeymoon '70
Bill Pullman
Lost Highway '96
Brain Dead '89
The Serpent and the Rainbow '87
Romano Puppo
The Great Alligator '81
Lee Purcell
Summer of Fear '78
The Witching '72
Carolyn Purdy-Gordon
From Beyond '86
Re-Animator '85
Om Puri
Wolf '94
John Putch
Jaws 3 '83
Nat Puvanai
Crocodile '81
Hy Pyke
Lemora: A Child's Tale of the Supernatural '73
Stephen Quadros
Shock 'Em Dead '90
Dennis Quaid
Jaws 3 '83

CAST INDEX

The Curse of the Werewolf *'60*
The Two Faces of Dr. Jekyll *'60*

Ricky Addison Reed
Return to Salem's Lot *'87*

Shanna Reed
The Banker *'89*

Angharad Rees
Hands of the Ripper *'71*

Roger Rees
A Christmas Carol *'84*

Christopher Reeve
Village of the Damned *'95*

Keanu Reeves
The Devil's Advocate *'97*
Bram Stoker's Dracula *'92*

Perrey Reeves
Child's Play 3 *'91*

Scott Reeves
Friday the 13th, Part 8: Jason Takes Manhattan *'89*

Joe Regalbuto
Invitation to Hell *'84*

Duncan Regehr
The Banker *'89*

Frank Reicher
King Kong *'33*

Mimi Reichmeister
Little Witches *'96*

Beryl Reid
The Doctor and the Devils *'85*
Doctor Phibes Rises Again *'72*

Fiona Reid
Blood & Donuts *'95*

Kate Reid
Death Ship *'80*

Michael Earl Reid
Army of Darkness *'92*

Tim Reid
Stephen King's It *'90*

John C. Reilly
Dolores Claiborne *'94*

Jean Reiner
Soultaker *'90*

Tracy Reiner
Masque of the Red Death *'89*

Judge Reinhold
Gremlins *'84*

Scott H. Reiniger
Dawn of the Dead *'78*

Whitney Reis
Chopper Chicks in Zombietown *'91*

Geri Reischl
I Dismember Mama *'74*
The Brotherhood of Satan *'71*

Paul Reiser
Aliens *'86*

James Remar
The Surgeon *'94*
Tales from the Darkside: The Movie *'90*

Lee Remick
The Omen *'76*

Kerry Remsen
Pumpkinhead *'88*
Appointment with Fear *'85*

Ronald Remy
Mad Doctor of Blood Island *'69*

Judith Resnick
Carnival of Blood *'71*

Paul (Pee Wee Herman) Reubens
Buffy the Vampire Slayer *'92*

Clive Revill
The Legend of Hell House *'73*

Burt Reynolds
The Maddening *'95*
Deliverance *'72*

Kathryn Reynolds
Trilogy of Terror *'75*

Peter Reynolds
The Hands of Orlac *'60*

Robert Reynolds
Daughter of Darkness *'89*

Simon Reynolds
Gate 2 *'92*

Ving Rhames
The People Under the Stairs *'91*
Jacob's Ladder *'90*

Grandon Rhodes
Revenge of the Creature *'55*

Hari Rhodes
Coma *'78*

Marjorie Rhodes
Hands of the Ripper *'71*

Susan Rhodes
The Girl with the Hungry Eyes *'94*

John Rhys-Davies
The Unnamable 2: The Statement of Randolph Carter *'92*
Waxwork *'88*

Christina Ricci
Addams Family Values *'93*
The Addams Family *'91*

Joan Rice
The Horror of Frankenstein *'70*

Dawn Richard
I Was a Teenage Werewolf *'57*

Addison Richards
The Walking Dead *'36*

Ariana Richards
Jurassic Park *'93*
Tremors *'89*

Denise Richards
Starship Troopers *'97*

Evan Richards
Mute Witness *'95*

Kyle Richards
Eaten Alive *'76*

Joely Richardson
Event Horizon *'97*
Sister My Sister *'94*

John Richardson
Black Sunday *'60*

Lee Richardson
The Believers *'87*

Miranda Richardson
Transmutations *'85*

Natasha Richardson
Gothic *'87*

Ralph Richardson
The Ghoul *'33*

Sy Richardson
Bad Dreams *'88*
They Live *'88*

Peter Mark Richman
Friday the 13th, Part 8: Jason Takes Manhattan *'89*

Fiona Richmond
The House on Straw Hill *'76*

Deborah Richter
The Banker *'89*

Don Rickles
Innocent Blood *'92*

Kimber Riddle
Stephen King's The Langoliers *'95*

Stanley Ridges
Black Friday *'40*

Judith Ridley
Night of the Living Dead *'68*

Peter Riegert
The Mask *'94*

Robert Rietty
The Omen *'76*

Ron Rifkin
Wolf *'94*

Jorge Rigaud
Horror Express *'72*

Carl Rigg
The Oblong Box *'69*

Diana Rigg
Theatre of Blood *'73*

Nikki Riggins
Scream Dream *'89*

Robin Riker
Alligator *'80*

Colleen Riley
Deadly Blessing *'81*

Jack Riley
Attack of the Killer Tomatoes *'77*

Molly Ringwald
Stephen King's The Stand *'94*

David Rintoul
Legend of the Werewolf *'75*

Fay Ripley
Mute Witness *'95*

Michael Ripper
The Creeping Flesh *'72*
The Scars of Dracula *'70*
Taste the Blood of Dracula *'70*
Dracula Has Risen from the Grave *'68*
Plague of the Zombies *'66*
The Reptile *'66*
Curse of the Mummy's Tomb *'64*
The Curse of the Werewolf *'60*
The Brides of Dracula *'60*
The Mummy *'59*

Sara Risher
Wes Craven's New Nightmare *'94*

Kristen Riter
Student Bodies *'81*

John Ritter
Stay Tuned *'92*
Stephen King's It *'90*
The Other *'72*

Michael Rougas
I Was a Teenage Werewolf '57
Richard Roundtree
Seven '95
Amityville: A New Generation '93
The Banker '89
Maniac Cop '88
Mickey Rourke
Angel Heart '87
Fade to Black '80
Kelly Rowan
Candyman 2: Farewell to the Flesh '94
The Gate '87
Douglas Rowe
Appointment with Fear '85
Earl Rowe
The Blob '58
Misty Rowe
Double Exposure '82
Esther Roy
Return of the Evil Dead '75
Roy Royston
Plague of the Zombies '66
Maria Rubell
976-EVIL '88
Mary Beth Rubens
Prom Night '80
Jan Rubes
The Amityville Curse '90
Blood Relations '87
Jennifer Rubin
Little Witches '96
Screamers '96
Wasp Woman '96
Bad Dreams '88
A Nightmare on Elm Street 3: Dream Warriors '87
Saul Rubinek
Death Ship '80
Zelda Rubinstein
Little Witches '96
Poltergeist 3 '88
Poltergeist 2: The Other Side '86
Poltergeist '82
Maria Rubio
Bloody Moon '83
Pablo Alvarez Rubio
Dracula '31
Mark Ruffalo
Mirror, Mirror 3: The Voyeur '96

Vyto Ruginis
The Devil's Advocate '97
Anthony Michael Ruivivar
Starship Troopers '97
Mia Ruiz
Witchcraft 2: The Temptress '90
Sig Rumann
House of Frankenstein '44
Jenny Runacre
The Creeping Flesh '72
Jennifer Runyon
Carnosaur '93
Deborah Rush
Parents '89
Jared Rushton
Pet Sematary 2 '92
Robert Rusler
Sometimes They Come Back '91
Vamp '86
A Nightmare on Elm Street 2: Freddy's Revenge '85
Bing Russell
Billy the Kid Versus Dracula '66
Elizabeth Russell
Cat People '42
Gail Russell
The Uninvited '44
John Russell
The Changeling '80
Blood Legacy '73
Karen Russell
Murder Weapon '90
Shock 'Em Dead '90
Kurt Russell
Big Trouble in Little China '86
The Thing '82
Robert Russell
The Conqueror Worm '68
James Russo
Dario Argento's Trauma '93
John Russo
The Majorettes '87
Leon Russom
Silver Bullet '85
Maxwell Rutherford
The Whispering '94
Susan Ruttan
Bad Dreams '88

John P. Ryan
Star Time '92
It's Alive 2: It Lives Again '78
It's Alive '74
Meg Ryan
Amityville 3: The Demon '83
Mitchell Ryan
Halloween 6: The Curse of Michael Myers '95
Thomas Ryan
The Relic '96
Georg Rydeberg
Hour of the Wolf '68
Christopher Rydell
Dario Argento's Trauma '93
Derek Rydell
Popcorn '89
Winona Ryder
Bram Stoker's Dracula '92
Edward Scissorhands '90
Heathers '89
Beetlejuice '88
Rex Ryon
Jack's Back '87
Howard Ryshpan
Rabid '77
Sabu
Cobra Woman '44
William Sadler
Tales from the Crypt Presents Demon Knight '94
Marianne Saegebrecht
Dust Devil '93
Ray Sager
The Wizard of Gore '70
Ken Sagoes
A Nightmare on Elm Street 4: Dream Master '88
Michael St. Gerard
Star Time '92
Andra St. Ivanyi
The Outing '87
Raymond St. Jacques
They Live '88
Gaylord St. James
Last House on the Left '72
Al "Fuzzy" St. John
Dead Men Walk '43
Betta St. John
Horror Hotel '60

Howard St. John
Strait-Jacket '64
Eric Saint-Just
Bloodsucking Nazi Zombies '82
Lucille Saint Peter
Brain Damage '88
Monique St. Pierre
Motel Hell '80
Lucile Saint-Simon
The Hands of Orlac '60
Harold Sakata
Impulse '74
Monique Salcido
After Midnight '89
Meredith Salenger
Village of the Damned '95
Nicola Salerno
Beyond the Door 2 '79
Peter Sallis
Taste the Blood of Dracula '70
The Curse of the Werewolf '60
Lyda Salmonava
The Golem '20
Frank S. Salsedo
Creepshow 2 '87
Jennifer Salt
Sisters '73
Louise Salter
Dead Waters '97
Julie Saly
The Craving '80
Emma Samms
Humanoids from the Deep '96
Robert Sampson
Netherworld '90
Re-Animator '85
Will Sampson
Poltergeist 2: The Other Side '86
Orca '77
Jackie Samuda
Shock Chamber '96
Laura San Giacomo
Stephen King's The Stand '94
Conrado San Martin
The Awful Dr. Orloff '62
Fernando Sancho
Return of the Evil Dead '75
John Sanderford
Leprechaun '93

Joseph Scorsiani
Naked Lunch *'91*
Alex Scott
The Abominable Dr. Phibes *'71*
Brenda Scott
Simon, King of the Witches *'71*
Campbell Scott
Dead Again *'91*
Deborah Scott
Witchcraft *'88*
Donna W. Scott
Dark Breed *'96*
George C. Scott
Exorcist 3: Legion *'90*
A Christmas Carol *'84*
Firestarter *'84*
The Changeling *'80*
Janette Scott
Paranoiac *'62*
Judith Scott
Burn Witch, Burn! *'62*
Kathryn Leigh Scott
House of Dark Shadows *'70*
Tom Everett Scott
An American Werewolf in Paris *'97*
Jonathan Scott-Taylor
Damien: Omen 2 *'78*
Andrea Scotti
Atom Age Vampire *'61*
Alexander Scourby
The Stuff *'85*
Angus Scrimm
Vampirella *'96*
Phantasm III: Lord of the Dead *'94*
Subspecies *'90*
Phantasm II *'88*
Phantasm *'79*
Jenny Seagrove
The Guardian *'90*
Elizabeth Seal
Vampire Circus *'71*
Sueanne Seamans
The Majorettes *'87*
Mindy Seeger
Relentless *'89*
Nena Segal
The Refrigerator *'91*
Nick Segal
Chopping Mall *'86*
Pamela Segall
Gate 2 *'92*
After Midnight *'89*
Johnny Sekka
The Bloodsuckers *'70*
Nicholas Selby
Macbeth *'71*
Tom Selleck
Coma *'78*
Dean Selmier
The Blood Spattered Bride *'72*
Milton Selzer
The Evil *'78*
Paola Senatore
Emerald Jungle *'80*
Joe Seneca
The Blob *'88*
Massimo Serato
Don't Look Now *'73*
Meika Seri
In the Realm of the Senses *'76*
Assumpta Serna
The Craft *'96*
Susanne Severeid
Howling 4: The Original Nightmare *'88*
Athene Seyler
Curse of the Demon *'57*
Dan Seymour
Return of the Fly *'59*
Abbott and Costello Meet the Mummy *'55*
Delphine Seyrig
Daughters of Darkness *'71*
Glenn Shadix
Heathers *'89*
Beetlejuice *'88*
Victoria Shalet
Haunted *'95*
Tamara Shanath
Cronos *'94*
Gene Shane
The Velvet Vampire *'71*
Don Shanks
Halloween 5: The Revenge of Michael Myers *'89*
Michael Shanks
Terror Train *'80*
David Shark
Soultaker *'90*
Billy Ray Sharkey
After Midnight *'89*
Cornelia Sharpe
The Reincarnation of Peter Proud *'75*
Michael Sharrett
Deadly Friend *'86*
Melanie Shatner
Cthulhu Mansion *'91*
William Shatner
Kingdom of the Spiders *'77*
Devil's Rain *'75*
Impulse *'74*
Helen Shaver
The Craft *'96*
Tremors 2: Aftershocks *'96*
The Believers *'87*
The Amityville Horror *'79*
Martin Shaw
Macbeth *'71*
Maxwell Shaw
The Oblong Box *'69*
Robert Shaw
Jaws *'75*
Vinessa Shaw
Hocus Pocus *'93*
Robert Shaye
Wes Craven's New Nightmare *'94*
Elizabeth She
The Howling: New Moon Rising *'95*
Moira Shearer
Peeping Tom *'60*
Ally Sheedy
Man's Best Friend *'93*
Charlie Sheen
The Arrival *'96*
The Wraith *'87*
Martin Sheen
Spawn *'97*
The Believers *'87*
Firestarter *'84*
Dead Zone *'83*
Apocalypse Now *'79*
Michael Sheen
Mary Reilly *'95*
Craig Sheffer
The Grave *'95*
Mark Sheffler
Last House on the Left *'72*
Kalei Shellabarger
The Invisible Maniac *'90*
Stephen Shellan
Dr. Jekyll and Ms. Hyde *'95*
The Stepfather *'87*
Barbara Shelley
Madhouse Mansion *'74*
Quatermass and the Pit *'67*
Rasputin the Mad Monk *'66*
Dracula, Prince of Darkness *'65*
The Gorgon *'64*
Jewel Shepard
Return of the Living Dead *'85*
Cybill Shepherd
Taxi Driver *'76*
John Shepherd
Friday the 13th, Part 5: A New Beginning *'85*
W. Morgan Shepherd
Elvira, Mistress of the Dark *'88*
Delia Sheppard
Witchcraft 2: The Temptress *'90*
Paula Sheppard
Alice Sweet Alice *'76*
Maurice Sherbanee
Mausoleum *'83*
Jamey Sheridan
Stephen King's The Stand *'94*
Margaret Sheridan
The Thing *'51*
Barry Sherman
Lord of Illusions *'95*
Anthony Sherwood
Terror Train *'80*
David Sherwood
Demon Keeper *'95*
Robin Sherwood
Tourist Trap *'79*
Brooke Shields
Alice Sweet Alice *'76*
Takashi Shimura
Last Days of Planet Earth *'74*
Sofia Shinas
The Crow *'93*
Katie Shingler
Pin ... *'88*
Talia Shire
Prophecy *'79*
The Dunwich Horror *'70*
Dan Shor
Strange Behavior *'81*
Max (Casey Adams) Showalter
The Indestructible Man *'56*
Elisabeth Shue
Link *'86*
Jane Sibbett
The Resurrected *'91*
Joseph R. Sicari
Night School *'81*

Gale Sondergaard
The Climax *'44*
The Invisible Man's Revenge *'44*
Mark Soper
Understudy: The Graveyard Shift 2 *'88*
Ted Sorel
Basket Case 2 *'90*
From Beyond *'86*
Mira Sorvino
Mimic *'97*
Paul Sorvino
The Stuff *'85*
Ann Sothern
The Manitou *'78*
Talisa Soto
Vampirella *'96*
David Soul
Salem's Lot *'79*
Arthur Space
Terror at Red Wolf Inn *'72*
Sissy Spacek
Carrie *'76*
Kevin Spacey
Seven *'95*
James Spader
Crash *'95*
Wolf *'94*
Jack's Back *'87*
Timothy Spall
Gothic *'87*
Joe Spano
Warlock Moon *'73*
Martin Speer
The Hills Have Eyes *'77*
Jerry Spicer
Witchcraft 6: The Devil's Mistress *'94*
David Spielberg
Christine *'84*
Joe Spinell
The Last Horror Film *'82*
Maniac *'80*
Gloria Spivak
Carnival of Blood *'71*
G.D. Spradlin
Apocalypse Now *'79*
Charlie Spradling
To Sleep with a Vampire *'92*
Meridian: Kiss of the Beast *'90*
Mirror, Mirror *'90*
James Stacy
Something Wicked This Way Comes *'83*
Double Exposure *'82*
Michael Stadvec
The Dentist *'96*
Kathy Staff
Mary Reilly *'95*
Tamara Stafford
The Hills Have Eyes, Part 2 *'84*
Carola Stagnaro
Dial Help *'88*
Unsane *'82*
Ernest Stahl-Nachbaur
M *'33*
Terence Stamp
Link *'86*
Harry Dean Stanton
Christine *'84*
Alien *'79*
Richard Stapley
The Strange Door *'51*
Fredro Star
The Addiction *'95*
Jonathan Stark
House 2: The Second Story *'87*
Fright Night *'85*
Beau Starr
Halloween 5: The Revenge of Michael Myers *'89*
Halloween 4: The Return of Michael Myers *'88*
Jack Starrett
Nightwish *'89*
David Starzyk
Huntress: Spirit of the Night *'95*
Mary Stavin
House *'86*
John Steadman
Fade to Black *'80*
The Hills Have Eyes *'77*
Amy Steel
April Fool's Day *'86*
Friday the 13th, Part 2 *'81*
Barbara Steele
Silent Scream *'80*
Piranha *'78*
They Came from Within *'75*
The Pit and the Pendulum *'61*
Black Sunday *'60*
Pippa Steele
Lust for a Vampire *'71*
The Vampire Lovers *'70*
Sirry Steffen
The Crawling Hand *'63*
Rod Steiger
The Kindred *'87*
The Amityville Horror *'79*
Ben Stein
The Mask *'94*
Ghostbusters 2 *'89*
David Stein
The Amityville Curse *'90*
Franz Stein
M *'33*
John Steiner
Unsane *'82*
Beyond the Door 2 *'79*
Albert Steinruck
The Golem *'20*
William Steis
Demon of Paradise *'87*
Yutte Stensgaard
Lust for a Vampire *'71*
Scream and Scream Again *'70*
Karel Stepanek
Devil Doll *'64*
Harvey Stephens
The Omen *'76*
Robert Stephens
Afraid of the Dark *'92*
Mark Kinsey Stephenson
The Unnamable 2: The Statement of Randolph Carter *'92*
The Unnamable *'88*
Daniel Stern
Leviathan *'89*
C.H.U.D. *'84*
Frances Sternhagen
Raising Cain *'92*
Stephen King's Golden Years *'91*
Misery *'90*
Andrew Stevens
The Fury *'78*
Massacre at Central High *'76*
Brinke Stevens
Jack-O *'95*
Grandma's House *'88*
Sole Survivor *'84*
The Slumber Party Massacre *'82*
Casey Stevens
Prom Night *'80*
Craig Stevens
Abbott and Costello Meet Dr. Jekyll and Mr. Hyde *'52*
Fisher Stevens
Reversal of Fortune *'90*
The Burning *'82*
Onslow Stevens
Them! *'54*
House of Dracula *'45*
Paul Stevens
The Mask *'61*
Shadoe Stevens
The Death Artist *'95*
Stella Stevens
The Manitou *'78*
Arnold *'73*
Parker Stevenson
Not of This Earth *'96*
Venetia Stevenson
Horror Hotel *'60*
Catherine Mary Stewart
Night of the Comet *'84*
Charlotte Stewart
Dark Angel: The Ascent *'94*
Tremors *'89*
Mel Stewart
Bride of Re-Animator *'89*
Patrick Stewart
The Doctor and the Devils *'85*
Lifeforce *'85*
Jennifer Steyn
Demon Keeper *'95*
Dorothy Stickney
The Uninvited *'44*
David Ogden Stiers
Magic *'78*
Hugo Stiglitz
Night of a Thousand Cats *'72*
Robin Stille
The Slumber Party Massacre *'82*
Sting
Julia and Julia *'87*
The Bride *'85*
Nigel Stock
Lost Continent *'68*
Dean Stockwell
Stephen King's The Langoliers *'95*
Werewolf of Washington *'73*
The Dunwich Horror *'70*
Guy Stockwell
Santa Sangre *'90*
It's Alive *'74*
John Stockwell
The Nurse *'97*
Christine *'84*

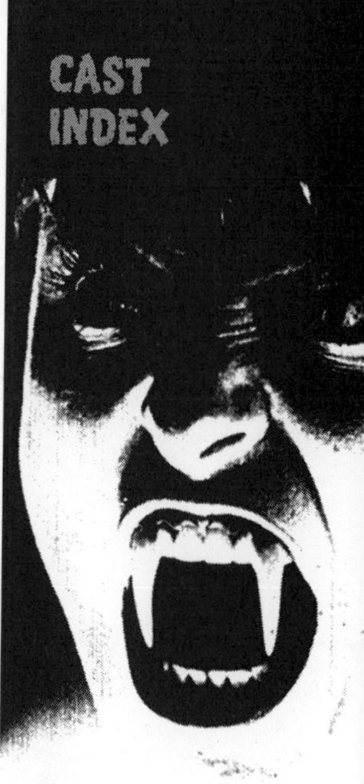

Emilie Talbot
Ceremony *'97*
Lyle Talbot
Plan 9 from Outer Space *'56*
Nita Talbot
Amityville 1992: It's about Time *'92*
Patricia Tallman
Army of Darkness *'92*
Night of the Living Dead *'90*
Tetsuro Tamba
Last Days of Planet Earth *'74*
Russ Tamblyn
Phantom Empire *'87*
Dracula vs. Frankenstein *'71*
The Haunting *'63*
Jessica Tandy
The Birds *'63*
Joy Tanner
Prom Night 4: Deliver Us from Evil *'91*
Faviola Tapia
Santa Sangre *'90*
Amanda Tapping
Terror Train *'80*
Quentin Tarantino
From Dusk Till Dawn *'95*
Steven Tash
Ghostbusters *'84*
Coralina Cataldi Tassoni
Terror at the Opera *'88*
Laura Tate
Subspecies *'90*
Sharon Tate
The Fearless Vampire Killers *'67*
Judy Tatum
Witchboard *'87*
Melissa Taub
Little Witches *'96*
Carolyn Taye-Loren
Witchcraft 5: Dance with the Devil *'92*
Christine Taylor
The Craft *'96*
Courtney Taylor
Prom Night 3: The Last Kiss *'89*
Dub Taylor
Them! *'54*
Jeannine Taylor
Friday the 13th *'80*
John Taylor
The Seventh Sign *'88*
Kelli Taylor
The Club *'94*
Kent Taylor
The Crawling Hand *'63*
Lili Taylor
The Addiction *'95*
Marina Taylor
Lurkers *'88*
Mark L. Taylor
Arachnophobia *'90*
Meshach Taylor
Damien: Omen 2 *'78*
Rod Taylor
The Birds *'63*
Valerie Taylor
Repulsion *'65*
Wally Taylor
Night of the Creeps *'86*
Maureen Teefy
Star Time *'92*
Tora Teje
Witchcraft through the Ages *'22*
Victoria Tennant
Horror Planet *'80*
John Terlesky
Chopping Mall *'86*
John Terrance
Evil Spawn *'87*
John Canada Terrell
Def by Temptation *'90*
Edward Terry
Luther the Geek *'90*
John Terry
The Resurrected *'91*
Terry-Thomas
Doctor Phibes Rises Again *'72*
The Abominable Dr. Phibes *'71*
Lorenzo Terzon
Lady Frankenstein *'72*
Robert Tessier
Nightwish *'89*
The Velvet Vampire *'71*
Brooke Theiss
A Nightmare on Elm Street 4: Dream Master *'88*
Joseph Thelman
Tombs of the Blind Dead *'72*
Charlize Theron
The Devil's Advocate *'97*
Ernest Thesiger
The Bride of Frankenstein *'35*
The Ghoul *'33*
The Old Dark House *'32*
David Thewlis
The Island of Dr. Moreau *'96*
Helen Thimig
Isle of the Dead *'45*
Bernard B. Thomas
Dead Man's Eyes/ Pillow of Death *'44*
Damien Thomas
Twins of Evil *'71*
Dave Thomas
Cold Sweat *'93*
Doris Thomas
The Demons *'74*
Henry Thomas
Psycho 4: The Beginning *'90*
Jay Thomas
C.H.U.D. *'84*
Richard Thomas
Stephen King's It *'90*
Robin Thomas
Amityville Dollhouse *'96*
Tim Thomerson
The Harvest *'92*
Near Dark *'87*
Fade to Black *'80*
Alina Thompson
The Fiance *'96*
Brian Thompson
Nightwish *'89*
Fright Night 2 *'88*
Emma Thompson
Dead Again *'91*
Fred Dalton Thompson
Cape Fear *'91*
Joy Thompson
Prom Night *'80*
Lea Thompson
Jaws 3 *'83*
Shelley Thompson
Labyrinth *'86*
Gregg Thomsen
Soultaker *'90*
Anna Thomson
The Crow *'93*
Gordon Thomson
The Fiance *'96*
Kim Thomson
Jekyll and Hyde *'90*
Bill Thornbury
Phantasm III: Lord of the Dead *'94*
Phantasm *'79*
Billy Bob Thornton
Chopper Chicks in Zombietown *'91*
Frank Thring, Jr.
Howling 3: The Marsupials *'87*
Ingrid Thulin
Hour of the Wolf *'68*
Bill Thunhurst
Season of the Witch *'73*
Sophie Thursfield
Sister My Sister *'94*
Gerard Tichy
The Hanging Woman *'72*
Hatchet for the Honeymoon *'70*
Rachel Ticotin
Natural Born Killers *'94*
Jacob Tierney
Pin ... *'88*
Lawrence Tierney
Silver Bullet *'85*
Ken Tigar
Phantasm II *'88*
Zeffie Tilbury
Werewolf of London *'35*
Jennifer Tilly
Embrace of the Vampire *'95*
Meg Tilly
Body Snatchers *'93*
Psycho 2 *'83*
One Dark Night *'82*
Charles Tingwell
Dracula, Prince of Darkness *'65*
Gabriele Tinti
Lisa and the Devil *'75*
Tiny Tim
Crocodile *'81*
Jean Tissier
The Hunchback of Notre Dame *'57*
Thelma Tixou
Santa Sangre *'90*
Kenneth Tobey
Single White Female *'92*
Gremlins 2: The New Batch *'90*
Night of the Creeps *'86*
The Howling *'81*
Ben *'72*
The Thing *'51*

Scott Valentine
Carnosaur 3: Primal Species *'96*
To Sleep with a Vampire *'92*
Rosa Valetti
M *'33*
Blair Valk
Huntress: Spirit of the Night *'95*
Frederick Valk
Dead of Night *'45*
Riccardo Valle
The Awful Dr. Orloff *'62*
Alida Valli
Suspiria *'77*
Lisa and the Devil *'75*
The Horror Chamber of Dr. Faustus *'59*
Raf Vallone
The Girl in Room 2A *'76*
Vampira
Plan 9 from Outer Space *'56*
Joan Van Ark
Frogs *'72*
Lewis Van Bergen
Pinocchio's Revenge *'96*
The Relic *'96*
Nadine Van Der Velde
After Midnight *'89*
Trish Van Devere
The Changeling *'80*
Caspar Van Dien
Starship Troopers *'97*
Jack Van Evera
My Bloody Valentine *'81*
John Van Eyssen
The Horror of Dracula *'58*
Jo Van Fleet
The Tenant *'76*
Richard Van Heet
Ben *'72*
Kevin Van Hentenryck
Basket Case 3: The Progeny *'92*
Basket Case 2 *'90*
Basket Case *'81*
Jack Van Landingham
Witchcraft 8: Salem's Ghost *'95*
Thor Van Lingen
Return of the Living Dead 2 *'88*
Jon Van Ness
Tourist Trap *'79*
Joyce Van Patten
Monkey Shines *'88*
Vincent Van Patten
Hell Night *'81*
Edward Van Sloan
Before I Hang *'40*
Dracula's Daughter *'36*
The Mummy *'32*
Dracula *'31*
Frankenstein *'31*
Monique Van Vooren
Andy Warhol's Frankenstein *'74*
Vanity
Terror Train *'80*
Evelyn Varden
The Bad Seed *'56*
The Night of the Hunter *'55*
Jean Vargas
The Slumber Party Massacre *'82*
Valentina Vargas
Hellraiser 4: Bloodline *'95*
Roland Varno
Return of the Vampire *'44*
Zahari Vatahov
Dracula Rising *'93*
Paris Vaughan
Buffy the Vampire Slayer *'92*
Peter Vaughan
Haunted Honeymoon *'86*
Die! Die! My Darling! *'65*
Ralph Pruitt Vaughn
Blood Salvage *'90*
Robert Vaughn
C.H.U.D. 2: Bud the Chud *'89*
Vince Vaughn
The Lost World: Jurassic Park 2 *'97*
Bruno Ve Sota
Attack of the Giant Leeches *'59*
The Wasp Woman *'59*
Isela Vega
The Fear Chamber *'68*
Conrad Veidt
The Cabinet of Dr. Caligari *'19*
Teresa Velasquez
Night of a Thousand Cats *'72*
Sarah Venable
Martin *'76*
Diane Venora
Wolfen *'81*
Wanda Ventham
Captain Kronos: Vampire Hunter *'74*
Harley Venton
Blood Ties *'92*
Jesse Ventura
The Running Man *'87*
Elena Verdugo
House of Frankenstein *'44*
Weird Woman/Frozen Ghost *'44*
Howard Vernon
Faceless *'88*
Zombie Lake *'80*
The Demons *'74*
The Awful Dr. Orloff *'62*
Richard Vernon
The Satanic Rites of Dracula *'73*
Cec Verrell
Mad at the Moon *'92*
Veruschka
The Bride *'85*
Yvette Vickers
Attack of the Giant Leeches *'59*
Henry Victor
Freaks *'32*
The Mummy *'32*
Vince Vieluf
An American Werewolf in Paris *'97*
Tom Villard
Popcorn *'89*
Carlos Villarias
Dracula *'31*
Herve Villechaize
Seizure *'74*
Michael Villela
The Slumber Party Massacre *'82*
James Villemaire
Gate 2 *'92*
James Villiers
Asylum *'72*
Repulsion *'65*
Nicholas Vince
Hellraiser *'87*
Pruitt Taylor Vince
Natural Born Killers *'94*
Jacob's Ladder *'90*
Alex Vincent
Child's Play 2 *'90*
Child's Play *'88*
Allen Vincent
Mystery of the Wax Museum *'33*
Jan-Michael Vincent
Demonstone *'89*
June Vincent
The Climax *'44*
Virginia Vincent
The Hills Have Eyes *'77*
Return of Dracula *'58*
Jesse Vint
Bug *'75*
Ultra Violet
Simon, King of the Witches *'71*
Antonella Vitale
The Church *'90*
Terror at the Opera *'88*
Robert Vogel
Basket Case *'81*
Jon Voight
Anaconda *'96*
Deliverance *'72*
Vicki Volante
Blood of Dracula's Castle *'69*
Ingrid Vold
To Sleep with a Vampire *'92*
John Voldstad
Leprechaun *'93*
Igor Volkow
Mute Witness *'95*
Daniel von Bargen
Stephen King's Thinner *'96*
Lord of Illusions *'95*
Ilse von Glatz
Understudy: The Graveyard Shift 2 *'88*
Wilhelm von Homburg
Ghostbusters 2 *'89*
Heidi von Palleske
Dead Ringers *'88*
Max von Sydow
Needful Things *'93*
The Exorcist 2: The Heretic *'77*
The Exorcist *'73*
Hour of the Wolf *'68*
Hans von Twardowski
The Cabinet of Dr. Caligari *'19*
Gustav von Wagenheim
Nosferatu *'22*
Hertha von Walther
M *'33*
Ursula von Wiese
Jack the Ripper *'76*

Sam Waterston
Serial Mom '94
Gwen Watford
Taste the Blood of Dracula '70
Ian Watkin
Dead Alive '93
Alberta Watson
The Keep '84
Jack Watson
Schizo '77
The Gorgon '64
Peeping Tom '60
Justice Watson
Tower of London '62
Michael Watson
Subspecies '90
Mills Watson
Cujo '83
Muse Watson
I Know What You Did Last Summer '97
Gwendolyn Watts
Die! Die! My Darling! '65
Naomi Watts
Children of the Corn 4: The Gathering '96
Al Waxman
Spasms '82
Keith Wayne
Night of the Living Dead '68
Naunton Wayne
Dead of Night '45
Shawn Weatherly
Amityville 1992: It's about Time '92
Dennis Weaver
Duel '71
Fritz Weaver
Creepshow '82
Demon Seed '77
Sigourney Weaver
Snow White: A Tale of Terror '97
Copycat '95
Alien3 '92
Ghostbusters 2 '89
Aliens '86
Ghostbusters '84
Alien '79
Danny Webb
Alien3 '92
Timothy Webber
Terror Train '80
Steven Weber
Dracula: Dead and Loving It '95
Single White Female '92
Mimi Weddell
Student Bodies '81
Michelle Weeks
Little Shop of Horrors '86
Paul Wegener
The Golem '20
Teri Weigel
The Banker '89
David Weills
Witchcraft 8: Salem's Ghost '95
Cindy Weintraub
Humanoids from the Deep '80
Michael T. Weiss
Howling 4: The Original Nightmare '88
Elizabeth Welch
Dead of Night '45
Joan Weldon
Them! '54
Mary Louise Weller
The Evil '78
Peter Weller
Screamers '96
Naked Lunch '91
Leviathan '89
Of Unknown Origin '83
Mel Welles
Little Shop of Horrors '60
Abbott and Costello Meet the Mummy '55
Orson Welles
The Witching '72
Orson Welles' Ghost Story '50s
Macbeth '48
Miki Welling
Dark Carnival '97
Thomas Wellington
The Creeps '97
Angela Wells
Crocodile '81
Dawn Wells
Town that Dreaded Sundown '76
Jacqueline Wells
The Black Cat '34
Tracy Wells
Mirror, Mirror 2: Raven Dance '94
After Midnight '89
Kenneth Welsh
Habitat '97
Of Unknown Origin '83
Lara Wendell
Unsane '82
George Wendt
House '86
John Wengraf
Return of Dracula '58
Otto Wernicke
M '33
Gary Werntz
The Art of Dying '90
Doug Wert
Dracula Rising '93
Kassie Wesley
Evil Dead 2: Dead by Dawn '87
Adam West
One Dark Night '82
Gregory West
The Surgeon '94
Julian West
Vampyr '31
Parker West
Lemora: A Child's Tale of the Supernatural '73
John Westbrook
Masque of the Red Death '65
Helen Westcott
Abbott and Costello Meet Dr. Jekyll and Mr. Hyde '52
David Weston
Masque of the Red Death '65
Jack Weston
Wait Until Dark '67
Virginia Wetherell
Dracula '73
Demons of the Mind '72
Patricia Wettig
Stephen King's The Langoliers '95
Marius Weyers
Deepstar Six '89
Sean Whalen
The People Under the Stairs '91
Justin Whalin
Serial Mom '94
Child's Play 3 '91
Blane Wheatley
The Unnamable '88
Amy Wheaton
The Curse '87
Wil Wheaton
Mr. Stitch '95
The Curse '87
Forest Whitaker
Species '95
Body Snatchers '93
Jan White
Season of the Witch '73
Michael Jai White
Spawn '97
Ron White
Screamers '96
Geoffrey Whitehead
And Now the Screaming Starts '73
Billie Whitelaw
The Omen '76
Arkie Whiteley
Razorback '84
Paul Whiteman
Lady Frankenstein '72
Jill Whitlow
Night of the Creeps '86
Stuart Whitman
Eaten Alive '76
Night of the Lepus '72
Steve Whitmire
Labyrinth '86
James Whitmore
The Relic '96
Them! '54
William Whitton
Lemora: A Child's Tale of the Supernatural '73
James Whitworth
The Hills Have Eyes '77
Laura Whyte
Blood Salvage '90
Patrick Whyte
Hideous Sun Demon '59
Ellen Widmann
M '33
Richard Widmark
Coma '78
To the Devil, a Daughter '76
Dianne Wiest
Edward Scissorhands '90
The Lost Boys '87
Naima Wifstrand
Hour of the Wolf '68
Dawna Wightman
The Amityville Curse '90
George P. Wilbur
Halloween 6: The Curse of Michael Myers '95

CAST INDEX

Michael Wong
Fatal Love '95
Russell Wong
The Prophecy 2: Ashtown '97
Victor Wong
Tremors '89
Prince of Darkness '87
Big Trouble in Little China '86
Edward D. Wood, Jr.
Plan 9 from Outer Space '56
Elijah Wood
The Good Son '93
Janet Wood
Terror at Red Wolf Inn '72
John Wood
Revenge of the Creature '55
Thomas Wood
2000 Maniacs '64
Blood Feast '63
George Woodbridge
The Reptile '66
Pat Woodell
Twilight People '72
Chris Woodley
The Velvet Vampire '71
Largo Woodruff
The Funhouse '81
Tom Woodruff, Jr.
Pumpkinhead '88
Aubrey Woods
The Abominable Dr. Phibes '71
James Woods
Cat's Eye '85
Videodrome '83
Leon Woods
Stephen King's The Tommyknockers '93
Peter Woodthorpe
The Evil of Frankenstein '64
John Woodvine
An American Werewolf in London '81
Edward Woodward
A Christmas Carol '84
The Wicker Man '75
The Bloodsuckers '70
Jaimz Woolvett
The Dark '94
Jimmy Workman
Addams Family Values '93
The Addams Family '91
Mary Woronov
Warlock '91
Chopping Mall '86
Nomads '86
Night of the Comet '84
Seizure '74
Nicholas Worth
Dark Angel: The Ascent '94
Darkman '90
Fay Wray
King Kong '33
Mystery of the Wax Museum '33
Doctor X '32
The Most Dangerous Game '32
The Vampire Bat '32
Doug Wren
Bad Taste '88
Amy Wright
The Amityville Horror '79
Jenny Wright
The Lawnmower Man '92
Near Dark '87
Ken Wright
Prince of Darkness '87
Maggie Wright
Twins of Evil '71
Marcella Wright
The Hanging Woman '72
Steven Wright
Natural Born Killers '94
Tom Wright
Creepshow 2 '87
Wendell Wright
Jack's Back '87
Kari Wuhrer
Anaconda '96
Stephen King's Thinner '96
Jane Wyatt
Amityville 4 '89
Katya Wyeth
Twins of Evil '71
Michael Wyle
Appointment with Fear '85
Patrick Wymark
The Blood on Satan's Claw '71
The Conqueror Worm '68
Repulsion '65
Geraint Wyn Davies
Trilogy of Terror 2 '96
Robert Wyndham
Dead of Night '45
Joel Wyner
Listen '96
The Club '94
Peter Wyngarde
Burn Witch, Burn! '62
Keenan Wynn
The Dark '79
Piranha '78
Orca '77
Devil's Rain '75
Dana Wynter
Invasion of the Body Snatchers '56
Amanda Wyss
To Die For 2: Son of Darkness '91
To Die For '89
A Nightmare on Elm Street '84
Emmanuel Xuereb
Grim '95
Salvator Xuereb
Blood Ties '92
So Yamamura
Last Days of Planet Earth '74
Emily Yancy
Blacula '72
Celeste Yarnall
Midnight Kiss '93
The Velvet Vampire '71
Amy Yasbeck
Dracula: Dead and Loving It '95
The Mask '94
House 2: The Second Story '87
Cassie Yates
The Evil '78
Marjorie Yates
Legend of the Werewolf '75
Barbara Yo Ling
The Satanic Rites of Dracula '73
Linda York
A Scream in the Streets/Axe '70s
Michael York
Not of This Earth '96
Island of Dr. Moreau '77
Sarah York
Evil Dead '83
Susannah York
A Christmas Carol '84
The Awakening '80
Bruce A. Young
Normal Life '96
Basic Instinct '92
Burt Young
Amityville 2: The Possession '82
Blood Beach '81
Carnival of Blood '71
Chris Young
Warlock: The Armageddon '93
David Young
Double Exposure '82
Mary, Mary, Bloody Mary '76
Dey Young
Spontaneous Combustion '89
Strange Behavior '81
Nedrick Young
Dead Men Walk '43
Otis Young
Blood Beach '81
Polly Ann Young
The Invisible Ghost '41
Ray Young
Blood of Dracula's Castle '69
Richard Young
Friday the 13th, Part 5: A New Beginning '85
Sean Young
Dr. Jekyll and Ms. Hyde '95
Jim Youngs
Skeeter '93
Chang Ching Yu
The Rape After '86
Harris Yulin
Ghostbusters 2 '89
Bad Dreams '88
The Believers '87
Lila Zaborin
Blood Orgy of the She-Devils '74
Grace Zabriskie
Blood Ties '92
Child's Play 2 '90
Galaxy of Terror '81
Ramy Zada
Two Evil Eyes '90
After Midnight '89
Roxana Zal
Daddy's Girl '96
Monica Zanchi
Zombie '80

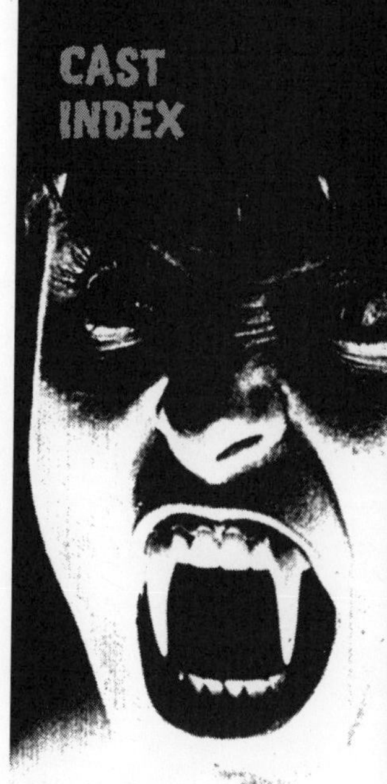

DIRECTOR INDEX

The "Director Index" lists all directors of movies reviewed in this book, presented alphabetically by last name for your perusing enjoyment. The movies they directed follow their names chronologically, with their most recent work appearing first. If you're a big fan, say, of Sam Raimi, you might also try looking up his name in the "Cast Index," because many directors make a gratuitous appearance in their own—or others'—movies.

Charles Band
The Creeps '97
Hideous '97
Meridian: Kiss of the Beast '90

Clive Barker
Lord of Illusions '95
Hellraiser '87

Joseph John Barmettler, Jr.
Witchcraft 8: Salem's Ghost '95

Ken Barnett
Dark Tower '87

Richard Barrett
Beyond the Door '75

Charles T. Barton
Abbott and Costello Meet the Killer, Boris Karloff '49
Abbott and Costello Meet Frankenstein '48

Lamberto Bava
Demons '86

Mario Bava
Beyond the Door 2 '79
Lisa and the Devil '75
Torture Chamber of Baron Blood '72
Hatchet for the Honeymoon '70
Black Sabbath '64
Black Sunday '60

William Beaudine
Billy the Kid Versus Dracula '66

Terry Becker
The Thirsty Dead '74

Ford Beebe
The Invisible Man's Revenge '44
Night Monster '42

Jack Bender
Child's Play 3 '91

Joel Bender
Midnight Kiss '93

Ingmar Bergman
Hour of the Wolf '68

Joe Berlinger
Paradise Lost: The Child Murders at Robin Hood Hills '95

Edward L. Bernds
Return of the Fly '59

Tom Berry
The Amityville Curse '90

Irvin Berwick
The Monster of Piedras Blancas '57

Robert Bierman
Vampire's Kiss '88

Kathryn Bigelow
Near Dark '87

Alan Birkinshaw
The House of Usher '88

Richard Blackburn
Lemora: A Child's Tale of the Supernatural '73

William Peter Blatty
Exorcist 3: Legion '90

Jeffrey Bloom
Blood Beach '81

Carl Boese
The Golem '20

Peter Bogdanovich
Targets '68

James Bond, III
Def by Temptation '90

J.R. Bookwalter
Polymorph '96

John Boorman
The Exorcist 2: The Heretic '77
Deliverance '72

Clay Borris
Prom Night 4: Deliver Us from Evil '91

Danny Boyle
Trainspotting '95
Shallow Grave '94

Reb Braddock
Curdled '95

Kenneth Branagh
Mary Shelley's Frankenstein '94
Dead Again '91

Larry Brand
Masque of the Red Death '89

Clark Brandon
Skeeter '93

Mel Brooks
Dracula: Dead and Loving It '95
Young Frankenstein '74

Clifford Brown
The Demons '74

Tod Browning
Devil Doll '36
Mark of the Vampire '35
Freaks '32
Dracula '31

John Carl Buechler
Friday the 13th, Part 7: The New Blood '88
Troll '86

Luis Bunuel
Un Chien Andalou '28

Jeff Burr
Night of the Scarecrow '95
Pumpkinhead 2: Blood Wings '94
Leatherface: The Texas Chainsaw Massacre 3 '89
Stepfather 2: Make Room for Daddy '89

Tim Burton
Ed Wood '94
Edward Scissorhands '90
Beetlejuice '88

Christy Cabanne
The Mummy's Hand '40

Ellen Cabot
Murder Weapon '90

James Cameron
Aliens '86
Piranha 2: The Spawning '82

Donald Cammell
Demon Seed '77

Doug Campbell
Cupid '96

Graeme Campbell
Blood Relations '87

Rene Cardona, Jr.
Night of a Thousand Cats '72

John Cardos
The Dark '79
Kingdom of the Spiders '77

John Carpenter
In the Mouth of Madness '95
Village of the Damned '95
Body Bags '93
They Live '88
Prince of Darkness '87
Big Trouble in Little China '86
Christine '84
The Thing '82
The Fog '78
Halloween '78

Stephen Carpenter
The Kindred '87

Michael Carreras
Lost Continent '68
Curse of the Mummy's Tomb '64
Maniac '63

John N. Carter
Zombie Island Massacre '84

Alexander Cassini
Star Time '92

William Castle
Strait-Jacket '64
The Tingler '59
House on Haunted Hill '58

Joe Castro
Ceremony '97

Alberto Cavalcanti
Dead of Night '45

Joe Chappelle
Halloween 6: The Curse of Michael Myers '95

Douglas Cheek
C.H.U.D. '84

Roger Christian
The Sender '82

Benjamin Christiansen
Witchcraft through the Ages '22

Yang Chuan
Seeding of a Ghost '86

Lam Wuah Chuen
Beauty Evil Rose '94

Gerard Ciccoritti
Understudy: The Graveyard Shift 2 '88
Graveyard Shift '87

B.D. Clark
Galaxy of Terror '81

Bob (Benjamin) Clark
Children Shouldn't Play with Dead Things '72

James Kenelm Clarke
The House on Straw Hill '76

Robert Clarke
Hideous Sun Demon '59

William Claxton
Night of the Lepus '72

Jack Clayton
Something Wicked This Way Comes '83

Brian Clemens
Captain Kronos: Vampire Hunter '74

Larry Cohen
It's Alive 3: Island of the Alive '87

Christian Duguay
Screamers *'96*
Thom Eberhardt
Night of the Comet *'84*
Sole Survivor *'84*
Hilton Edwards
Orson Welles' Ghost Story *'50s*
Colin Eggleston
The Wicked *'89*
Robert Englund
976-EVIL *'88*
Rene Eram
Voodoo *'95*
John Eyres
Judge & Jury *'96*
Donald Farmer
Scream Dream *'89*
Federico Fellini
Fellini Satyricon *'69*
Boccaccio *'70* '62
Georg Fenady
Arnold *'73*
Abel Ferrara
The Addiction *'95*
Body Snatchers *'93*
David Fincher
Seven *'95*
Alien3 *'92*
Roberta Findlay
Lurkers *'88*
Kenneth Fink
Stephen King's Golden Years *'91*
Terence Fisher
Frankenstein and the Monster from Hell *'74*
Frankenstein Must Be Destroyed *'69*
Devil's Bride *'68*
Frankenstein Created Woman *'66*
Dracula, Prince of Darkness *'65*
The Gorgon *'64*
The Curse of the Werewolf *'60*
The Brides of Dracula *'60*
The Two Faces of Dr. Jekyll *'60*
The Mummy *'59*
The Horror of Dracula *'58*
The Curse of Frankenstein *'57*
Richard Fleischer
Amityville 3: The Demon *'83*
Andrew Fleming
The Craft *'96*
Bad Dreams *'88*
Victor Fleming
Dr. Jekyll and Mr. Hyde *'41*
The Wizard of Oz *'39*
Rodman Flender
Leprechaun 2 *'94*
Robert Florey
The Beast with Five Fingers *'46*
Murders in the Rue Morgue *'32*
John Flynn
Brainscan *'94*
Bryan Forbes
The Stepford Wives *'75*
Gene Fowler, Jr.
I Was a Teenage Werewolf *'57*
Wallace Fox
Dead Man's Eyes/ Pillow of Death *'44*
Freddie Francis
Dark Tower *'87*
The Doctor and the Devils *'85*
Legend of the Werewolf *'75*
The Creeping Flesh *'72*
Dracula Has Risen from the Grave *'68*
The Evil of Frankenstein *'64*
Nightmare *'63*
Paranoiac *'62*
Jess (Jesus) Franco
Faceless *'88*
Bloody Moon *'83*
Bloodsucking Nazi Zombies *'82*
Jack the Ripper *'76*
The Demons *'74*
Count Dracula *'71*
The Awful Dr. Orloff *'62*
Georges Franju
The Horror Chamber of Dr. Faustus *'59*
A.M. Frank
Bloodsucking Nazi Zombies *'82*
John Frankenheimer
The Island of Dr. Moreau *'96*
Prophecy *'79*
Richard Franklin
Link *'86*
Psycho 2 *'83*
Stephen Frears
Mary Reilly *'95*
Mark Freed
Shock *'Em Dead* '90
Karl Freund
Mad Love *'35*
The Mummy *'32*
Frederick Friedel
A Scream in the Streets/Axe *'70s*
William Friedkin
The Guardian *'90*
The Exorcist *'73*
Adam Friedman
To Sleep with a Vampire *'92*
Ken Friedman
Death by Invitation *'71*
William Fruet
Spasms *'82*
Roy Frumkes
Document of the Dead *'90*
Robert Fuest
Devil's Rain *'75*
Doctor Phibes Rises Again *'72*
The Abominable Dr. Phibes *'71*
Lucio Fulci
The Black Cat *'81*
Zombie *'80*
Fred Gallo
Dracula Rising *'93*
Christophe Gans
H.P. Lovecraft's Necronomicon: Book of the Dead *'93*
Mick Garris
Stephen King's The Stand *'94*
Sleepwalkers *'92*
Psycho 4: The Beginning *'90*
Eleanor Gaver
Slipping into Darkness *'88*
Clyde Geronimi
Alice in Wonderland *'51*
Michael G. Gerrick
Stephen King's Golden Years *'91*
Alan Gibson
The Satanic Rites of Dracula *'73*
Dracula A.D. 1972 *'72*
Brian Gibson
Poltergeist 2: The Other Side *'86*
Gregory Gieras
The Whispering *'94*
Lewis Gilbert
Haunted *'95*
Jeff Gillen
Deranged *'74*
Jim Gillespie
I Know What You Did Last Summer *'97*
John Gilling
Plague of the Zombies *'66*
The Reptile *'66*
Milton Moses Ginsberg
Werewolf of Washington *'73*
Michael Paul Girard
Witchcraft 9: Bitter Flesh *'96*
Witchcraft 7: Judgement Hour *'95*
William Girdler
The Manitou *'78*
Paul Michael Glaser
The Running Man *'87*
Don Glut
Dinosaur Valley Girls *'96*
Mark Goldblatt
Dead Heat *'88*
Dan Golden
Burial of the Rats *'95*
Fred Goodwin
Curse 2: The Bite *'88*
Leslie Goodwins
The Mummy's Curse *'44*
Bert I. Gordon
Satan's Princess *'90*
The Witching *'72*
Earth Vs. the Spider *'58*
Rachel Gordon
Mirror, Mirror 3: The Voyeur *'96*
Stuart Gordon
Castle Freak *'95*
The Pit & the Pendulum *'91*
Daughter of Darkness *'89*
From Beyond *'86*
Re-Animator *'85*
Michael Gornick
Creepshow 2 *'87*
Anne Goursaud
Embrace of the Vampire *'95*
Gary Graver
Trick or Treats *'82*

James Isaac
The Horror Show '89
Lewis Jackson
Terror in Toyland '85
Peter Jackson
The Frighteners '96
Heavenly Creatures '94
Dead Alive '93
Bad Taste '88
Wilfred Jackson
Alice in Wonderland '51
Dennis Jacob
The Terror '63
Jon Jacobs
The Girl with the Hungry Eyes '94
Nicholas A.E. Jacobs
The Refrigerator '91
Rick Jacobson
Night Hunter '95
Vadim Jean
Nightscare '93
Alejandro Jodorowsky
Santa Sangre '90
Tucker Johnson
Blood Salvage '90
Amy Holden Jones
The Slumber Party Massacre '82
Gary Jones
Mosquito '95
Mark Jones
Rumpelstiltskin '96
Leprechaun '93
Neil Jordan
Interview with the Vampire '94
The Company of Wolves '85
C. Courtney Joyner
Lurking Fear '94
Rupert Julian
The Phantom of the Opera '25
Jay Kamen
Transformations '88
Anthony Kane
Ashes and Flames '97
Shusuke Kaneko
Gamera, Guardian of the Universe '95
H.P. Lovecraft's Necronomicon: Book of the Dead '93
Phil Karlson
Ben '72
Lloyd (Samuel Weil) Kaufman
Tromeo & Juliet '95
The Toxic Avenger, Part 3: The Last Temptation of Toxie '89
The Toxic Avenger, Part 2 '89
The Toxic Avenger '86
Philip Kaufman
Invasion of the Body Snatchers '78
Fran Rubel Kazui
Buffy the Vampire Slayer '92
Bob Keen
Proteus '95
David Keith
The Curse '87
Bob Kelljan
The Return of Count Yorga '71
Count Yorga, Vampire '70
Tom Kennedy
Time Walker '82
Erle C. Kenton
House of Dracula '45
House of Frankenstein '44
The Ghost of Frankenstein '42
Island of Lost Souls '32
Irvin Kershner
Eyes of Laura Mars '78
Emmanuel Kervyn
Rabid Grannies '89
Bruce Kessler
Simon, King of the Witches '71
Fritz Kiersch
Children of the Corn '84
Gerard Kikoine
Edge of Sanity '89
Stephen King
Maximum Overdrive '86
John Mason Kirby
Savage Weekend '80
Martin Kitrosser
Daddy's Girl '96
The Fiance '96
Bernard L. Kowalski
Attack of the Giant Leeches '59
Stanley Kubrick
The Shining '80
A Clockwork Orange '71
Harry Kumel
Daughters of Darkness '71
Robert Kurtzman
Wishmaster '97
John Lafia
Man's Best Friend '93
Child's Play 2 '90
Mary Lambert
Pet Sematary 2 '92
Pet Sematary '89
Charles Lamont
Abbott and Costello Meet the Mummy '55
Abbott and Costello Meet Dr. Jekyll and Mr. Hyde '52
Abbott and Costello Meet the Invisible Man '51
Lew (Louis Friedlander) Landers
Return of the Vampire '44
The Raven '35
John Landis
Innocent Blood '92
An American Werewolf in London '81
Paul Landres
Return of Dracula '58
Fritz Lang
M '33
Lawrence Lanoff
Temptress '95
Joseph (Jose Ramon) Larraz
Vampyres '74
The House that Vanished '73
J.A. (Jean Rollin) Laser
Zombie Lake '80
Steve Latshaw
Jack-O '95
Michael Laughlin
Strange Behavior '81
Charles Laughton
The Night of the Hunter '55
Fabrizio Laurenti
Witchery '88
Reginald LeBorg
Diary of a Madman '63
Dead Man's Eyes/ Pillow of Death '44
The Mummy's Ghost '44
Weird Woman/Frozen Ghost '44
Calling Dr. Death/Strange Confession '43
Herbert J. Leder
It! '67
Paul Leder
I Dismember Mama '74
Norman Lee
Chamber of Horrors '40
Rowland V. Lee
Son of Frankenstein '39
The Tower of London '39
Michael Lehmann
Heathers '89
Paul Leni
The Cat and the Canary '27
Umberto Lenzi
Emerald Jungle '80
Brett Leonard
The Lawnmower Man '92
Mervyn LeRoy
The Bad Seed '56
Mark L. Lester
The Ex '96
Firestarter '84
William A. Levey
Hellgate '89
Scott Levy
Spectre '96
Piranha '95
Albert Lewin
Picture of Dorian Gray '45
Herschell Gordon Lewis
The Wizard of Gore '70
Color Me Blood Red '64
2000 Maniacs '64
Blood Feast '63
Joseph H. Lewis
The Invisible Ghost '41
Jimmy Lifton
Mirror, Mirror 2: Raven Dance '94
Dwight Little
The Phantom of the Opera '89
Halloween 4: The Return of Michael Myers '88
Luis Llosa
Anaconda '96
Ulli Lommel
Devonsville Terror '83
Arthur Lubin
The Phantom of the Opera '43
Black Friday '40

Statement of Randolph Carter '92
The Unnamable '88
Frank Oz
Little Shop of Horrors '86
Michele Pacitto
Generation X-Tinct '97
Chul-Soo Park
301, 302 '94
Alan Parker
Angel Heart '87
Trey Parker
Cannibal! The Musical '96
Eric Parkinson
Future Shock '93
Ivan Passer
Haunted Summer '88
Jonas Pate
The Grave '95
David Paulsen
Savage Weekend '80
Mark Pavia
Stephen King's The Night Flier '96
George Pavlou
Transmutations '85
Dave Payne
Not Like Us '96
Barbara Peeters
Humanoids from the Deep '80
Leo Penn
The Dark Secret of Harvest Home '78
Richard Pepin
Dark Breed '96
Mark Peploe
Afraid of the Dark '92
Virginia Perfili
Mirror, Mirror 3: The Voyeur '96
Anthony Perkins
Psycho 3 '86
Joseph Pevney
The Strange Door '51
Irving Pichel
The Most Dangerous Game '32
Charles B. Pierce
Town that Dreaded Sundown '76
Legend of Boggy Creek '75
Sam Pillsbury
Into the Badlands '92
Bret Piper
They Bite '95
Bruce Pittman
Hello Mary Lou: Prom Night 2 '87
Roman Polanski
The Tenant '76
Macbeth '71
Rosemary's Baby '68
The Fearless Vampire Killers '67
Repulsion '65
Jack Pollexfen
The Indestructible Man '56
Tim Pope
The Crow 2: City of Angels '96
Michael Powell
Peeping Tom '60
John Power
Stephen King's The Tommyknockers '93
David F. Price
Dr. Jekyll and Ms. Hyde '95
Children of the Corn 2: The Final Sacrifice '92
To Die For 2: Son of Darkness '91
Andrew Prowse
Demonstone '89
Alex Proyas
The Crow '93
Craig Pryce
The Dark '94
Eric Rademski
Todd McFarlane's Spawn '97
Peter Rader
Grandma's House '88
Sam Raimi
Army of Darkness '92
Darkman '90
Evil Dead 2: Dead by Dawn '87
Evil Dead '83
Alvin Rakoff
Death Ship '80
Tony Randel
Amityville 1992: It's about Time '92
Children of the Night '92
Hellbound: Hellraiser 2 '88
Fred Olen Ray
Phantom Empire '87
Tomb '86
Alien Dead '79
Bill Rebane
The Giant Spider Invasion '75
Eric Red
Bad Moon '96
Matt Reeves
Future Shock '93
Michael Reeves
The Conqueror Worm '68
Jeff Reiner
Serpent's Lair '95
Rob Reiner
Misery '90
Ivan Reitman
Ghostbusters 2 '89
Ghostbusters '84
Michael Rissi
Soultaker '90
Viktors Ritelis
Crucible of Horror '69
John S. Robertson
Dr. Jekyll and Mr. Hyde '20
Mark Robson
Isle of the Dead '45
Franc Roddam
The Bride '85
Robert Rodriguez
From Dusk Till Dawn '95
Nicolas Roeg
Don't Look Now '73
Julian Roffman
The Mask '61
Jean Rollin
Zombie Lake '80
Fascination '79
Les Raisins de la Mort '78
Thrill of the Vampire '70
Eddie Romero
Twilight People '72
Beast of the Yellow Night '70
Mad Doctor of Blood Island '69
George A. Romero
The Dark Half '91
Two Evil Eyes '90
Monkey Shines '88
Day of the Dead '85
Creepshow '82
Dawn of the Dead '78
Martin '76
The Crazies '73
Season of the Witch '73
Night of the Living Dead '68
Bernard Rose
Candyman '92
Mickey Rose
Student Bodies '81
William Rose
The Girl in Room 2A '76
Stuart Rosenberg
The Amityville Horror '79
Rick Rosenthal
Halloween 2: The Nightmare Isn't Over! '81
Mark Rosman
The House on Sorority Row '83
Stephanie Rothman
The Velvet Vampire '71
Joseph Ruben
The Good Son '93
The Stepfather '87
Chuck Russell
The Mask '94
The Blob '88
A Nightmare on Elm Street 3: Dream Warriors '87
Ken Russell
The Lair of the White Worm '88
Gothic '87
The Devils '71
Marti Rustam
Evils of the Night '85
Boris Sagal
Omega Man '71
Night Gallery '69
Victor Salva
Nature of the Beast '94
Sompote Sands
Crocodile '81
Jimmy Sangster
Dynasty of Fear '72
Lust for a Vampire '71
The Horror of Frankenstein '70
Cirio H. Santiago
Demon of Paradise '87
The Vampire Hookers '78
Deran Sarafian
To Die For '89
Joseph Sargent
Nightmares '83
Marina Sargenti
Mirror, Mirror '90

The Leopard Man '43
Cat People '42

Bud Townsend
Terror at Red Wolf Inn '72

Brian Trenchard-Smith
Leprechaun 4: In Space '96
Leprechaun 3 '95

Gus Trikonis
The Evil '78

Shinya Tsukamoto
Tetsuo: The Iron Man '92

Michael Tuchner
The Hunchback of Notre Dame '82

Anand Tucker
Anne Rice: Birth of the Vampire '94

Ching Siu Tung
A Chinese Ghost Story '87

Clive Turner
The Howling: New Moon Rising '95

David N. Twohy
The Arrival '96

Edgar G. Ulmer
The Black Cat '34

Ron Underwood
Tremors '89

Roger Vadim
Blood and Roses '61

Paul Verhoeven
Starship Troopers '97
Basic Instinct '92

Luchino Visconti
Boccaccio '70 '62

Jonathan Wacks
Ed and His Dead Mother '93

Michael Wadleigh
Wolfen '81

George Waggner
The Climax '44
Man Made Monster '41
The Wolf Man '41

Pete Walker
House of the Long Shadows '82
Schizo '77
House of Whipcord '75

Flesh and Blood Show '73

Stuart Walker
Werewolf of London '35

Tommy Lee Wallace
Stephen King's It '90
Fright Night 2 '88
Halloween 3: Season of the Witch '82

Anthony Waller
An American Werewolf in Paris '97
Mute Witness '95

Fred Walton
When a Stranger Calls Back '93
April Fool's Day '86
When a Stranger Calls '79

Jerry Warren
Man Beast '55

Norman J. Warren
Horror Planet '80
The Terror '79

John Waters
Serial Mom '94

William Webb
The Banker '89

Stephen Weeks
Madhouse Mansion '74

Paul Wegener
The Golem '20

Mel Welles
Lady Frankenstein '72

Orson Welles
Macbeth '48

David Wellington
The Carpenter '89

Richard Wenk
Vamp '86

James Whale
The Bride of Frankenstein '35
The Invisible Man '33
The Old Dark House '32
Frankenstein '31

Jim Wheat
After Midnight '89

Ken Wheat
After Midnight '89

Steve White
Amityville Dollhouse '96

Alexander Whitelaw
Lifespan '75

David Wickes
Jekyll and Hyde '90

Gregory Widen
The Prophecy '95

Ken Wiederhorn
Return of the Living Dead 2 '88
Dark Tower '87
Shock Waves '77

Robert Wiene
The Cabinet of Dr. Caligari '19

Gene Wilder
Haunted Honeymoon '86

Gavin Wilding
Listen '96

Ethan Wiley
House 2: The Second Story '87

S.S. Wilson
Tremors 2: Aftershocks '96

Jonathan Winfrey
Carnosaur 3: Primal Species '96

Terence H. Winkless
Not of This Earth '96
The Nest '88

Michael Winner
Scream for Help '86
The Sentinel '76
The Nightcomers '72

Stan Winston
Pumpkinhead '88

David Winters
The Last Horror Film '82

Robert Wise
Audrey Rose '77
The Haunting '63
The Body Snatcher '45

Edward D. Wood, Jr.
Bride of the Monster '56
Plan 9 from Outer Space '56

Mark Woods
Witchcraft 2: The Temptress '90

Wallace Worsley
The Hunchback of Notre Dame '23

Eric Worthington
Dark Carnival '97

David Wu
The Bride with White Hair 2 '93

Jim Wynorski
Vampirella '96
Wasp Woman '96
Sorceress '94
Not of This Earth '88
Chopping Mall '86

Kevin Yagher
Hellraiser 4: Bloodline '95

Herman Yau
The Untold Story '93

Irvin S. Yeaworth, Jr.
The Blob '58

Jeff Yonis
Humanoids from the Deep '96

Harold Young
Weird Woman/Frozen Ghost '44
The Mummy's Tomb '42

Robert W. Young
Vampire Circus '71

Terence Young
Wait Until Dark '67

Ronny Yu
The Bride with White Hair '93

Brian Yuzna
The Dentist '96
H.P. Lovecraft's Necronomicon: Book of the Dead '93
Return of the Living Dead 3 '93
Bride of Re-Animator '89

Mier Zarchi
I Spit on Your Grave '77

Tony Zarindast
Werewolf '95

Vernon Zimmerman
Fade to Black '80

Joseph Zito
Friday the 13th, Part 4: The Final Chapter '84

CATEGORY INDEX

Okay, so it's a horror movie you're looking for, but we know you know more than that. Was it about a wax museum? Was it made in Italy? Was it based on a book by Stephen King? Our "Category Index" can help. Or are you simply wondering how many movies feature killer appliances? (We cover four.) Listed alphabetically below are seemingly endless straight genre descriptions ("Action Adventure," "Sci-Fi"), themes ("Chainsaws," "Grave Robbing,"), foreign films by country of origin (found under "Foreign" and the country in question), movies based upon the writings of an author (found alphabetically by the author's last name), plot devices (such as "Executing Revenge": movies about an executed convict who rises from the dead to seek revenge) and plot derivations (movies based upon the story "The Monkey's Paw"), or by other classifications ("Killer Apes & Monkeys," "Killer Bug & Slugs," "Killer Cars," "Killer Cats," "Killer Dogs," "Killer Dreams," "Killer Jello," etc.).

Ghost Story
The Guardian
The Hands of Orlac
Haunted
Haunted Summer
The Haunting
Hellraiser 3: Hell on Earth
The Horror of Dracula
House Where Evil Dwells
The Hunchback of Notre Dame
The Hunchback of Notre Dame
The Hunchback of Notre Dame
The Hunchback of Notre Dame
I Know What You Did Last Summer
Interview with the Vampire
Invasion of the Body Snatchers
Invasion of the Body Snatchers
The Invisible Man
Island of Dr. Moreau
The Island of Dr. Moreau
Island of Lost Souls
Jaws
Jaws 2
Jurassic Park
The Keep
The Lair of the White Worm
The Legend of Hell House
The Leopard Man
Lifeforce
The Lodger
The Lost World: Jurassic Park 2
Magic
Manhunter
Mary Reilly
Mary Shelley's Frankenstein
Misery
Monkey Shines
Naked Lunch
Needful Things
Neighbors
The Night of the Hunter
Night of the Lepus
Nightscare
Nightwing
Nosferatu
Nosferatu the Vampyre
Of Unknown Origin
The Old Dark House
Omega Man
The Omen
The Other
Pet Sematary
The Phantom of the Opera
The Phantom of the Opera
The Phantom of the Opera
Picture of Dorian Gray
Psycho
The Reincarnation of Peter Proud
The Relic
The Resurrected
Reversal of Fortune
Rosemary's Baby
The Running Man
Scream and Scream Again
The Serpent and the Rainbow
The Shining
The Silence of the Lambs
Silver Bullet
Single White Female
Something Wicked This Way Comes
Spasms
Starship Troopers
The Stepford Wives
Stephen King's It
Stephen King's The Langoliers
Stephen King's The Stand
Stephen King's The Tommyknockers
Stephen King's Thinner
Summer of Fear
The Tenant
The Thing
To the Devil, a Daughter
Tomb
Trainspotting
The Unnamable
The Vampire Lovers
Village of the Damned
Watchers
Willard
The Witches of Eastwick
The Wizard of Oz
Wolfen

Adapted from a Cartoon

The Addams Family
Addams Family Values
The Mask

Adapted from a Fairy Tale

The Company of Wolves
Pin ...
Pinocchio's Revenge
Rumpelstiltskin
Snow White: A Tale of Terror

Adapted from a Play or Musical

The Bad Seed
The Cat and the Canary
The Climax
Cold Comfort
The Devils
The Doctor and the Devils
Doctor X
Dracula
Frankenstein
The Ghost Breakers
House of the Long Shadows
Little Shop of Horrors
Macbeth
Wait Until Dark

Adapted from a Story

Alice in Wonderland
The Birds
Burial of the Rats
Candyman
Candyman 2: Farewell to the Flesh
Cat's Eye
Children of the Corn
Creature from the Black Lagoon
Creepshow
Creepshow 2
Curse of the Demon
Diary of a Madman
Die, Monster, Die!
Freaks
From Beyond
The Ghost of Frankenstein
The Girl with the Hungry Eyes
The House of Usher
H.P. Lovecraft's Necronomicon: Book of the Dead
Into the Badlands
The Lawnmower Man
Lord of Illusions
Lurking Fear
The Mangler
Masque of the Red Death
Masque of the Red Death
Maximum Overdrive
The Most Dangerous Game
The Mummy's Curse
The Mummy's Tomb
The Oblong Box
The Pit and the Pendulum
The Pit & the Pendulum
Premature Burial
Re-Animator
Revenge of the Creature
Screamers
Sometimes They Come Back ... Again
Stephen King's Nightshift Collection
The Strange Door
Tales from the Darkside: The Movie
The Thing
Transmutations
Two Evil Eyes
Vampyr

Adapted from Comics

The Crow
The Crow 2: City of Angels
The Mask
Spawn
Tales from the Crypt Presents Bordello of Blood
Tales from the Crypt Presents Demon Knight
Todd McFarlane's Spawn
Vampirella

Adapted from Television

The Addams Family
Addams Family Values
Quatermass and the Pit
Tales from the Crypt Presents Bordello of Blood
Tales from the Crypt Presents Demon Knight

Adapted from the Radio

Calling Dr. Death/Strange Confession
Dead Man's Eyes/Pillow of Death
Weird Woman/Frozen Ghost

Adolescence

See *Hell High School; Summer Camp; Teen Angst*

CATEGORY INDEX

Bad Seeds
Murderous children. See also *Childhood Visions*
Alice Sweet Alice
The Bad Seed
The Brood
Children of the Corn
Children of the Corn 2: The Final Sacrifice
Children of the Corn 3: Urban Harvest
Children of the Corn 4: The Gathering
Daddy's Girl
Damien: Omen 2
The Lost Boys
The Good Son
Mikey
The Omen
The Other
Pin...
Return to Salem's Lot
Salem's Lot
Village of the Damned

Special FX Wizards: Rick Baker
An American Werewolf in London
The Funhouse
The Fury
It's Alive
King Kong
Videodrome
Wolf

Clive Barker: Books to Film
Candyman
Candyman 2: Farewell to the Flesh
Hellbound: Hellraiser 2
Hellraiser
Hellraiser 3: Hell on Earth
Hellraiser 4: Bloodline
Lord of Illusions
Transmutations

Bathroom Scenes
An American Werewolf in London
Arachnophobia
Basic Instinct
Brain Damage
Copycat
Dressed to Kill
Fatal Attraction
Ghostbusters 2
He Knows You're Alone
Jurassic Park
Poltergeist
Poltergeist 2: The Other Side
Psycho
Psycho 2
Schizo
They Came from Within

Beatniks
A Bucket of Blood
Color Me Blood Red
The Death Artist

Behind Bars
See *Men in Prison; Women in Prison*

Behind the Scenes
See also *At the Movies*
Anaconda
Ed Wood
They Bite
Wes Craven's New Nightmare

Big Digs
The Mask
The Mummy
The Mummy's Hand
The Resurrected
Specters
Starship Troopers
Tomb

Big Rigs
See also *Motor Vehicle Dept.; Road Trip*
Big Trouble in Little China
Duel
Maximum Overdrive

Bigfoot/Yeti
Legend of Boggy Creek
Man Beast

Bikers
Blood Freak
Chopper Chicks in Zombietown
Hellblock 13
Slipping into Darkness

Biography
See *This Is Your Life*

Birds
The Birds
Blood Freak
The Crow
The Crow 2: City of Angels

Bisexuality
See also *Gays; Lesbians*
The Addiction
Basic Instinct
Mary, Mary, Bloody Mary

Black Comedy
See also *Comedy; Satire & Parody*
The Addams Family
Addams Family Values
Arnold
Curdled
Heathers
Parents
Serial Mom
Shallow Grave
Trainspotting
Vampire's Kiss
The Witches of Eastwick

Blindness
See also *Physical Problems*
Afraid of the Dark
Castle Freak
Don't Look Now
Night Gallery
Peeping Tom
Return of the Evil Dead
Tombs of the Blind Dead
The Toxic Avenger, Part 2
The Toxic Avenger, Part 3: The Last Temptation of Toxie
Wait Until Dark
Young Frankenstein

Bloody Messages
Seven
The Shining

Books
See *Necronomicon: Book of the Dead*

Special FX Wizards: Rob Bottin
The Fog
The Howling
Humanoids from the Deep
Mimic
The Thing
The Witches of Eastwick

Ray Bradbury: Books to Film
Something Wicked This Way Comes

Bringing Up Baby
See *That's a Baby?!; Parenthood; Pregnant Pauses*

Buried Alive
The House of Usher
The Oblong Box
Premature Burial

William Burroughs: Books to Film
Naked Lunch

Cabbies
Blood & Donuts
Graveyard Shift
The Last Horror Film
Seeding of a Ghost
Taxi Driver

Campus Capers
College is hell. See also *Hell High School*
Burn Witch, Burn!
Fright Night 2
Hell Night
The House on Sorority Row
Night of the Creeps
Nightwish
Scream 2
Silent Scream
Slipping into Darkness
Time Walker
The Unnamable
The Unnamable 2: The Statement of Randolph Carter
Voodoo
Weird Woman/Frozen Ghost
Witchboard

Cannibalism
Beast of the Yellow Night
Black Werewolf
Blood Feast
Cannibal! The Musical
C.H.U.D.
C.H.U.D. 2: Bud the Chud
Dawn of the Dead
Deranged
Doctor X
Emerald Jungle
Freakshow
The Hills Have Eyes
Leatherface: The Texas Chainsaw Massacre 3
Motel Hell
Night of the Living Dead
Night of the Living Dead
Parents

CATEGORY INDEX

Head of the Family
Highway to Hell
Hocus Pocus
The Horror of Frankenstein
House
House 2: The Second Story
House of the Long Shadows
Incredibly Strange Creatures Who Stopped Living and Became Mixed-Up Zombies
The Invisible Maniac
Little Shop of Horrors
The Mask
Motel Hell
Neighbors
Night of a Thousand Cats
Night of the Comet
Night of the Creeps
The Old Dark House
Once Bitten
Phantom Empire
Piranha
Piranha 2: The Spawning
Polymorph
Rabid Grannies
Re-Animator
The Refrigerator
Return of the Living Dead
Return of the Living Dead 2
Return of the Living Dead 3
Spider Baby
Student Bodies
The Stuff
Tales from the Crypt Presents Bordello of Blood
Tales from the Crypt Presents Demon Knight
Theatre of Blood
The Toxic Avenger
The Toxic Avenger, Part 2
The Toxic Avenger, Part 3: The Last Temptation of Toxie
Tremors
Tremors 2: Aftershocks
Tromeo & Juliet
Vamp
Vampire in Brooklyn

Computers

See also *Robots & Androids; Technology—Rampant*
Demon Seed
Ghost in the Machine
Jurassic Park
The Lawnmower Man

Joseph Conrad: Books to Film

Apocalypse Now

Robin Cook: Books to Film

Coma

Cops

See also *Detectives*
Apprentice to Murder
The Believers
Brainscan
Copycat
The Crow
The Dark
Dead Heat
The Exorcist
Exorcist 3: Legion
Fatal Love
God Told Me To
Innocent Blood
Manhunter
Maniac Cop
Maniac Cop 2
Maniac Cop 3: Badge of Silence
The Prophecy
Relentless
Seven
The Silence of the Lambs
They Live
The Untold Story
Vampire in Brooklyn
Witchcraft 6: The Devil's Mistress
Wolfen
XX: Beautiful Prey

Roger Corman/New World—Producer

Attack of the Giant Leeches
A Bucket of Blood
Dementia 13
The Dunwich Horror
The Fall of the House of Usher
Galaxy of Terror
Humanoids from the Deep
Little Shop of Horrors
Masque of the Red Death
Masque of the Red Death
Not of This Earth
Not of This Earth
Piranha
The Pit and the Pendulum
Premature Burial
The Raven
Targets
The Terror
To Sleep with a Vampire
Vampirella
The Wasp Woman
Wasp Woman

Corporate Shenanigans

The Devil's Advocate
Gremlins 2: The New Batch
Halloween 3: Season of the Witch
The Toxic Avenger
The Toxic Avenger, Part 2
The Toxic Avenger, P art 3: The Last Temptation of Toxie
Wolf

Creepy Houses

After Midnight
The Amityville Horror
Amityville 2: The Possession
Amityville 3: The Demon
Amityville 4
The Amityville Curse
Amityville 1992: It's About Time
Blood Legacy
Castle Freak
The Cat and the Canary
The Changeling
The Craft
Cthulhu Mansion
Dead Man's Eyes/ Pillow of Death
Demon Seed
The Evil
The Fall of the House of Usher
Fright House
Fright Night
The Ghost Breakers
Haunted
The Haunting
House
House 2: The Second Story
House of the Long Shadows
The House of Usher
House on Haunted Hill
The House that Vanished
House Where Evil Dwells
The Legend of Hell House
The Old Dark House
Paranoiac
The People Under the Stairs
Psycho
Psycho 2
Psycho 3
Psycho 4: The Beginning
The Rocky Horror Picture Show
Salem's Lot
The Shining
Silent Scream
Spectre
Stormswept
Terror in the Haunted House
The Uninvited
The Unnamable

Michael Crichton: Books to Film

Jurassic Park
The Lost World: Jurassic Park 2

Crime & Criminals

See also *Crimes of Passion; Organized Crime; Serial Killers*
Apprentice to Murder
Black Friday
Cape Fear
The Crow
The Crow 2: City of Angels
Dead Heat
Deranged
Devil Doll
The Doctor and the Devils
Drive-In Massacre
From Dusk Till Dawn
God Told Me To
The Grave
The Haunted Strangler
Henry: Portrait of a Serial Killer
The Invisible Man Returns
Jack the Ripper
Last House on the Left
M
Manhunter
Mute Witness
Natural Born Killers
Nature of the Beast
Normal Life
Psycho
Stephen King's Thinner
Seven
The Silence of the Lambs
Targets
Taxi Driver
XX: Beautiful Prey

Crimes of Passion
Basic Instinct
Fatal Attraction
Peeping Tom
Single White Female
XX: Beautiful Prey

Cult Items
An American Werewolf in London
Andy Warhol's Dracula
Andy Warhol's Frankenstein
Apocalypse Now
Army of Darkness
Attack of the Killer Tomatoes
Bad Taste
Basket Case
Billy the Kid Versus Dracula
The Blob
Blood Feast
Blood Orgy of the She-Devils
Bride of the Monster
A Bucket of Blood
The Cabinet of Dr. Caligari
Carnival of Souls
Cat People
Children Shouldn't Play with Dead Things
A Clockwork Orange
The Conqueror Worm
Dawn of the Dead
Demons
The Devils
Eaten Alive
Ed Wood
Evil Dead
Evil Dead 2: Dead by Dawn
The Fearless Vampire Killers
The Fly
Frankenstein Unbound
Freaks
God Told Me To
The Horror Chamber of Dr. Faustus
House of Wax
The Hunger
I Walked with a Zombie
I Was a Teenage Werewolf
Incredibly Strange Creatures Who Stopped Living and Became Mixed-Up Zombies
Invasion of the Body Snatchers
Little Shop of Horrors
Martin
Motel Hell
The Mummy
The Night of the Hunter
Night of the Living Dead
Peeping Tom
Phantasm
Plan 9 from Outer Space
Psycho
Re-Animator
The Rocky Horror Picture Show
The Slumber Party Massacre
Spider Baby
Them!
The Thing
The Toxic Avenger
The Toxic Avenger, Part 2
The Toxic Avenger, Part 3: The Last Temptation of Toxie
2000 Maniacs
The Wasp Woman
The Wizard of Oz

Cults
See also *Occult; Satanism*
Bad Dreams
The Believers
The Brotherhood of Satan
Burial of the Rats
Children of the Corn 2: The Final Sacrifice
Cobra Woman
The Dark Secret of Harvest Home
Dead and Buried
Deadly Blessing
Devil's Rain
From Dusk Till Dawn
Helter Skelter Murders
Lord of Illusions
Omega Man
Raging Angels
Rosemary's Baby
Shock 'Em Dead
The Spellbinder

Dance Fever
Blood of Dracula
Burial of the Rats
Cobra Woman
Curdled
Dance of the Damned
Dracula vs. Frankenstein
The Haunted Strangler
Lust for a Vampire
Prom Night
The Rocky Horror Picture Show
Suspiria
To Sleep with a Vampire
Vamp

Guy de Maupassant: Books to Film
Diary of a Madman

Death
See *Funerals; Great Death Scenes; Reincarnation; Suicide*

Death Row
See also *Executing Revenge; Men in Prison; Women in Prison*
Hellblock 13
Lost Highway
The Seventh Sign

Demons & Wizards
See also *Occult*
Army of Darkness
Bloodlust: Subspecies 3
Bloodstone: Subspecies 2
Ceremony
The Church
Cthulhu Mansion
The Demons
Demons
Demonstone
Evil Dead
Evil Dead 2: Dead by Dawn
Gate 2
Hellraiser
Hellraiser 4: Bloodline
Jack-O
Mirror, Mirror
Pumpkinhead
Pumpkinhead 2: Blood Wings
The Raven
Seizure
Tales from the Crypt Presents Demon Knight
Troll
The Unnamable 2: The Statement of Randolph Carter
Warlock
Warlock: The Armageddon
Witchcraft 5: Dance with the Devil

Dental Mayhem
See also *Evil Doctors*
The Dentist
Little Shop of Horrors
Little Shop of Horrors
Poltergeist 2: The Other Side
Serial Mom

Detectives
See also *Cops; Feds*
Abbott and Costello Meet the Invisible Man
Angel Heart
Dead Again
Lord of Illusions
Night School
Seven
Tales from the Crypt Presents Bordello of Blood

Devils
See also *Satan & Satanism*
The Craft
Dark Angel: The Ascent
The Devils
The Devil's Advocate
Highway to Hell
The Mangler
Needful Things
The Prophecy
Rosemary's Baby
Stephen King's The Stand
Witchcraft through the Ages

Phillip K. Dick: Books to Film
Screamers

Charles Dickens: Books to Film
A Christmas Carol

Dinosaurs
Carnosaur
Carnosaur 2
Carnosaur 3: Primal Species
Dinosaur Valley Girls
Jurassic Park
King Kong
The Lost World: Jurassic Park 2

Disney Animated Movies
Alice in Wonderland
The Nightmare Before Christmas

Diseases, Viruses & Plagues
Children of the Corn 4: The Gathering
C.H.U.D.
The Crazies
The Curse

Curse 2: The Bite
Isle of the Dead
Mimic
Nightwing
The Omega Man
Rabid
Stephen King's The Stand
They Came from Within
Transformations

Doctors

See *Dental Mayhem; Evil Doctors; Mad Scientists; Sanity Check; Shrinks*

Docudrama

See also *Documentary*
Deranged
Helter Skelter Murders
Henry: Portrait of a Serial Killer
Legend of Boggy Creek
Town that Dreaded Sundown

Documentary

See also *Docudrama*
Document of the Dead
Ed Gein: American Maniac *see* Deranged
Fangs! A History of Vampires in the Movies
Paradise Lost: The Child Murders at Robin Hood Hills
Witchcraft through the Ages

Dogs

See also *Killer Dogs*
Bad Moon
Cujo
The Hills Have Eyes
Man's Best Friend
The Mask
Watchers
The Wizard of Oz

Dolls That Kill

See *Killer Toys*

Sir Arthur Conan Doyle: Books to Film

Tales from the Darkside: The Movie

Dracula

See also *Vampire Babes; Vampires*
Abbott and Costello Meet Frankenstein
Blood of Dracula
Blood of Dracula's Castle
Bram Stoker's Dracula
Count Dracula
The Creeps
Dracula
Dracula
Dracula A.D. 1972
Dracula: Dead and Loving It
Dracula Has Risen from the Grave
Dracula, Prince of Darkness
Dracula Rising
Dracula vs. Frankenstein
Dracula's Daughter
The Horror of Dracula
House of Dracula
House of Frankenstein
Return of Dracula
Return of the Vampire
The Satanic Rites of Dracula
The Scars of Dracula
Son of Dracula
Taste the Blood of Dracula
Waxwork

Drama

See also *Adventure Drama; Historical Drama*
Apocalypse Now
Blood Ties
Boxing Helena
A Christmas Carol
Copycat
Crash
The Good Son
Heavenly Creatures
Helter Skelter Murders
Henry: Portrait of a Serial Killer
Hour of the Wolf
The Hunchback of Notre Dame
Impulse
In the Realm of the Senses
Jack the Ripper
Lost Highway
Macbeth
Massacre at Central High
Nadja
Naked Lunch
Natural Born Killers
Night Gallery
The Night Stalker
Normal Life
Nowhere
The Rapture
Reversal of Fortune
Santa Sangre
The Silence of the Lambs
Sister My Sister
Soultaker
Targets
Taxi Driver

Drugs

See *Pill Poppin'*

Daphne Du Maurier: Books to Film

The Birds
Don't Look Now

Lois Duncan: Books to Film

I Know What You Did Last Summer
Summer of Fear

Eco-Vengeance!

See also *Killer Bugs & Slugs*
Alligator
Anaconda
Arachnophobia
Ben
Body Snatchers
Frogs
Habitat
Jaws
Jaws 2
Jaws 3
Jurassic Park
Kingdom of the Spiders
Last Days of Planet Earth
Piranha
Piranha 2: The Spawning
Prophecy
The Toxic Avenger
The Toxic Avenger, Part 2
The Toxic Avenger, Part 3: The Last Temptation of Toxie
Willard

Elevators

Basic Instinct
Dark Tower
Fatal Attraction
The Omen
Poltergeist 3
The Silence of the Lambs

Elves

See *Leprechauns & Elves*

Erotic Thrillers

See also *Sex & Sexuality*
Basic Instinct
Cold Sweat
Dance of the Damned
Daughters of Darkness
Embrace of the Vampire
Fatal Attraction
The House that Vanished
Listen
Stormswept
Temptress
Terrified
To Sleep with a Vampire

Evil Doctors

See also *Mad Scientists*
The Abominable Dr. Phibes
The Awful Dr. Orloff
The Brood
Dead Ringers
The Dentist
The Doctor and the Devils
Dr. Giggles
Dr. Jekyll and Mr. Hyde
Dr. Jekyll and Mr. Hyde
Doctor Phibes Rises Again
Doctor X
The Island of Dr. Moreau
Island of Dr. Moreau
Island of Lost Souls
Jekyll and Hyde
Mad Doctor of Blood Island
Re-Animator
The Surgeon
The Two Faces of Dr. Jekyll

Executing Revenge

Convicts who come back for revenge after being executed. See also *Death Row; Men in Prison; Revenge*
Before I Hang
Black Friday
Exorcist 3: Legion
The Horror Show
The Indestructible Man
Judge & Jury
Maniac Cop
Shocker
The Walking Dead

Eyeballs!

See also *Hearts!*
The Birds
A Clockwork Orange
Damien: Omen 2
The Dark
Evil Dead 2: Dead by Dawn
Eyes of Laura Mars

Flesh and Blood Show
Frankenstein and the Monster from Hell
Frankenstein Created Woman
Frankenstein Must Be Destroyed
The Ghoul
The Gorgon
The Hand
The Hands of Orlac
Hands of the Ripper
Haunted
The Haunted Strangler
Hellbound: Hellraiser 2
Hellraiser
Horror Express
Horror Hotel
The Horror of Dracula
The Horror of Frankenstein
Horror Planet
House of the Long Shadows
House of Whipcord
The House on Straw Hill
The House that Vanished
It!
Kiss of the Vampire
The Lair of the White Worm
Legend of the Werewolf
Lifespan
Link
The Lodger
Lust for a Vampire
Madhouse Mansion
Maniac
Mark of the Devil
Masque of the Red Death
The Mummy
Mute Witness
The Nightcomers
Nightmare
Nightscare
The Oblong Box
Paranoiac
Plague of the Zombies
Proteus
Quatermass and the Pit
Rasputin the Mad Monk
The Reptile
Repulsion
The Satanic Rites of Dracula
The Scars of Dracula
Schizo
Scream and Scream Again
The Sender
Shallow Grave
Sister My Sister
Taste the Blood of Dracula
Theatre of Blood
Trainspotting
Transmutations
Twins of Evil
The Two Faces of Dr. Jekyll
Vampire Circus
The Vampire Lovers
Vampyres

Foreign: Canadian

The Amityville Curse
Blood & Donuts
Blood Relations
The Brood
The Carpenter
The Changeling
Cold Comfort
Crash
Dead Ringers
Death Ship
Deranged
Happy Birthday to Me
Hello Mary Lou: Prom Night 2
Humongous
Incubus
The Mask
My Bloody Valentine
Of Unknown Origin
Prom Night
Prom Night 4: Deliver Us from Evil
Rabid
Scanners
Seizure
Shock Chamber
Spasms
They Came from Within
Understudy: The Graveyard Shift 2
Videodrome

Foreign: Filipino

Beast of the Yellow Night
Mad Doctor of Blood Island
Night of the Cobra Woman
The Thirsty Dead
Twilight People
The Vampire Hookers

Foreign: French

Afraid of the Dark
Andy Warhol's Dracula
Andy Warhol's Frankenstein
Blood and Roses
Bloodsucking Nazi Zombies
Daughters of Darkness
The Demons
Fascination
The Hands of Orlac
The Horror Chamber of Dr. Faustus
Howling 2: Your Sister Is a Werewolf
The Hunchback of Notre Dame
In the Realm of the Senses
Les Raisins de la Mort
Nosferatu the Vampyre
The Tenant
Un Chien Andalou
Vampyr
Zombie Lake

Foreign: German

Andy Warhol's Frankenstein
Bloody Moon
The Cabinet of Dr. Caligari
Count Dracula
Daughters of Darkness
Dorian Gray
The Golem
Jack the Ripper
M
Mark of the Devil
Nosferatu
Nosferatu the Vampyre
The Surgeon
Vampyr

Foreign: Hong Kong

Beauty Evil Rose
The Bride with White Hair
The Bride with White Hair 2
A Chinese Ghost Story
The Rape After
Seeding of a Ghost
The Untold Story

Foreign: Italian

Andy Warhol's Dracula
Andy Warhol's Frankenstein
Atom Age Vampire
Beyond the Door
Beyond the Door 2
The Black Cat
Black Sabbath
Black Sunday
Blood and Roses
Boccaccio '70
Cemetery Man
The Church
Count Dracula
Creepers
Daughters of Darkness
Dead Waters
Deep Red: Hatchet Murders
Demons
Dial Help
Dorian Gray
Emerald Jungle
Fellini Satyricon
Graveyard Shift
The Hanging Woman
Hatchet for the Honeymoon
Howling 2: Your Sister Is a Werewolf
Lady Frankenstein
Lisa and the Devil
Santa Sangre
Specters
Suspiria
Torture Chamber of Baron Blood
Two Evil Eyes
Unsane
Zombie

Foreign: Japanese

Evil Dead Trap
Gamera, Guardian of the Universe
In the Realm of the Senses
Last Days of Planet Earth
Tetsuo: The Iron Man
Urotsukidoji Perfect Collection
Vampire Hunter D
XX: Beautiful Prey

Foreign: Korean

Crocodile
301, 302

Foreign: Mexican

Cronos
The Fear Chamber
Night of a Thousand Cats
Santa Sangre
Warlock Moon

Foreign: New Zealand

Bad Taste
Dead Alive
Heavenly Creatures
Jack Be Nimble

Foreign: Portuguese

The Demons
Return of the Evil Dead
Tombs of the Blind Dead

Foreign: Russian

Dead Waters

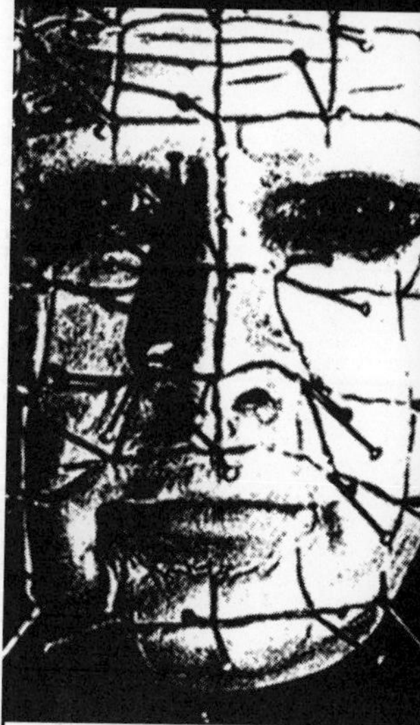

Night of the Scarecrow
Orson Welles' Ghost Story
Phantasm III: Lord of the Dead
Poltergeist
Poltergeist 2: The Other Side
Poltergeist 3
Sometimes They Come Back ... Again
Soultaker
Spectre
Stormswept
The Uninvited

Giants

Bride of the Monster
Humongous
Them!
Tremors
Tremors 2: Aftershocks

William Goldman: Books to Film

Magic

The Golem

The Golem
It!
The Keep

Grave Robbing

The Body Snatcher
Bram Stoker's Dracula
Children Shouldn't Play with Dead Things
Corridors of Blood
The Doctor and the Devils
Dracula
Dracula's Daughter
The Greed of William Hart
Kiss of the Vampire
Lifespan
Mania
Pet Sematary
Pet Sematary 2
Shock Chamber
Taste the Blood of Dracula

Great Death Scenes

See also *Funerals*
The Brain that Wouldn't Die
Buffy the Vampire Slayer
From Dusk Till Dawn
The Horror of Dracula
Jurassic Park
King Kong
The Lost World: Jurassic Park 2
Psycho
The Wizard of Oz

Growing Older

Captain Kronos: Vampire Hunter
Dorian Gray
The Hunger
Hush, Hush, Sweet Charlotte
Picture of Dorian Gray
Rabid Grannies
Stephen King's Golden Years
The Wasp Woman

Halloween

Dark Carnival
Halloween
Halloween 2: The Nightmare Isn't Over!
Halloween 3: Season of the Witch
Halloween 4: The Return of Michael Myers
Halloween 5: The Revenge of Michael Myers
Halloween 6: The Curse of Michael Myers
Hocus Pocus
Jack-O
The Nightmare Before Christmas
Trick or Treat
Trick or Treats

Hammer Films

Asylum
The Blood on Satan's Claw
The Brides of Dracula
Captain Kronos: Vampire Hunter
Countess Dracula
The Creeping Flesh
The Curse of Frankenstein
Curse of the Mummy's Tomb
The Curse of the Werewolf
Dracula A.D. 1972
Dracula Has Risen from the Grave
Dracula, Prince of Darkness
Dynasty of Fear
The Evil of Frankenstein
Frankenstein and the Monster from Hell
Frankenstein Created Woman
Frankenstein Must Be Destroyed
The Gorgon
Hands of the Ripper
The Horror of Dracula
The Horror of Frankenstein
Kiss of the Vampire
Lost Continent
Lust for a Vampire
Maniac
The Mummy
Nightmare
Paranoiac
Plague of the Zombies
Quatermass and the Pit
Rasputin the Mad Monk
The Reptile
The Satanic Rites of Dracula
The Scars of Dracula
Taste the Blood of Dracula
To the Devil, a Daughter
Twins of Evil
The Two Faces of Dr. Jekyll
Vampire Circus
The Vampire Lovers

Haunted Houses

See *Creepy Houses*

Jim Harrison: Books to Film

Wolf

Hearts!

See also *Eyeballs!*
Angel Heart
Mary Shelley's Frankenstein
The Prophecy
The Prophecy 2: Ashtown
Tales from the Crypt Presents Bordello of Blood

Hell High School

See also *Campus Capers; Teen Angst*
Blood of Dracula
Buffy the Vampire Slayer
Carrie
The Club
The Craft
Creepers
Heathers
Hello, Mary Lou: Prom Night 2
I Was a Teenage Werewolf
The Invisible Maniac
Little Witches
Lust for a Vampire
The Majorettes
Massacre at Central High
Mirror, Mirror
Prom Night
Prom Night 3: The Last Kiss
Prom Night 4: Deliver Us from Evil
Scream
Sometimes They Come Back...Again
Student Bodies
Trick or Treat

Historical Drama

See also *Period Piece*
The Climax
The Devils
Fellini Satyricon
The Hunchback of Notre Dame
The Hunchback of Notre Dame
The Hunchback of Notre Dame
The Phantom of the Opera
The Phantom of the Opera
The Phantom of the Opera
The Strange Door
The Tower of London
Tower of London

Ho-Jo's from Hell

No-exit motels and hotels.
Daughters of Darkness
Eaten Alive
The Girl with the Hungry Eyes
Motel Hell
Psycho
Psycho 2
Psycho 3
Psycho 4: The Beginning
The Shining
Terror at Red Wolf Inn
Witchery

Homosexuality

See *Bisexuality; Gays; Lesbians*

Horrible Holidays

See also *Christmas; Halloween*
April Fool's Day
Happy Birthday to Me
My Bloody Valentine

Killer Plants

Including fruits & vegetables.

Attack of the Killer Tomatoes
Body Snatchers
Invasion of the Body Snatchers
Invasion of the Body Snatchers
Little Shop of Horrors
Little Shop of Horrors
Pumpkinhead
Pumpkinhead 2: Blood Wings
The Thing

Killer Reptiles

Alligator
Alligator 2: The Mutation
Carnosaur
Carnosaur 2
Carnosaur 3: Primal Species
Creature from the Black Lagoon
The Creature Walks Among Us
Crocodile
Curse 2: The Bite
Demon of Paradise
Frogs
Jurassic Park
The Lost World: Jurassic Park 2
The Reptile
Revenge of the Creature
Spasms

Killer Rodents

The Abominable Dr. Phibes
Ben
Burial of the Rats
Nightmares
Nightwing
Of Unknown Origin
Trilogy of Terror 2
Willard

Killer Sea Creatures

Alligator
Attack of the Giant Leeches
Blood Beach
Creature from the Black Lagoon
Creature from the Haunted Sea
The Creature Walks Among Us
Deepstar Six
Demon of Paradise
Gamera, Guardian of the Universe
The Great Alligator
Humanoids from the Deep
Jaws
Jaws 2
Jaws 3
Lost Continent
The Monster of Piedras Blancas
Orca
Piranha
Piranha
Piranha 2: The Spawning
Revenge of the Creature
They Bite

Killer Statues

The Golem
It!
The Keep
Trilogy of Terror
Trilogy of Terror 2

Killer Toys

Amityville Dollhouse
Child's Play
Child's Play 2
Child's Play 3
Devil Doll
Halloween 3: Season of the Witch
Kiss Me, Kill Me
Magic
Pinocchio's Revenge
Poltergeist
Puppet Master
Trilogy of Terror
Trilogy of Terror 2

Stephen King: Books to Film

Carrie
Cat's Eye
Children of the Corn
Christine
Creepshow
Creepshow 2
Cujo
The Dark Half
Dead Zone
Dolores Claiborne
Firestarter
The Lawnmower Man
The Mangler
Maximum Overdrive
Misery
Needful Things
Pet Sematary
Return to Salem's Lot
The Running Man
Salem's Lot
The Shining
Silver Bullet
Sleepwalkers
Sometimes They Come Back
Sometimes They Come Back ... Again
Stephen King's Golden Years
Stephen King's It
Stephen King's Nightshift Collection
Stephen King's The Langoliers
Stephen King's The Night Flier
Stephen King's The Stand
Stephen King's The Tommyknockers
Stephen King's Thinner
Tales from the Darkside: The Movie

Kissin' Kin

The family that lays together.... See also *Oedipal Allegories*

Amityville 2: The Possession
Andy Warhol's Frankenstein
Blood Legacy
Cat People
The Crow
Elves
The People Under the Stairs
Sleepwalkers

Dean R. Koontz: Books to Film

Demon Seed
Watchers

Law & Lawyers

Cape Fear
The Conqueror Worm
The Devil's Advocate
The Island of Dr. Moreau
Pinocchio's Revenge
Reversal of Fortune
The Spellbinder
Stephen King's Thinner
Witchcraft 3: The Kiss of Death
Witchcraft 4: Virgin Heart
Witchcraft 5: Dance with the Devil
Witchcraft 6: The Devil's Mistress

Sheridan Le Fanu: Books to Film

Blood and Roses
The Blood Spattered Bride
The Vampire Lovers
Vampyr

Leprechauns & Elves

Elves
Leprechaun
Leprechaun 2
Leprechaun 3
Leprechaun 4: In Space

Lesbians

See also *Bisexuality; Gays; Gender Bending*

The Blood Spattered Bride
Daughters of Darkness
The Hunger
Listen
Nadja
Nowhere
The Vampire Lovers
Vampyres

Ira Levin: Books to Film

Rosemary's Baby
The Stepford Wives

Special FX Wizards: Herschell Gordon Lewis

Blood Feast
Color Me Blood Red
2000 Maniacs
The Wizard of Gore

Val Lewton—Producer

The Body Snatcher
Cat People
Isle of the Dead
The Leopard Man

The Living Dead

See *Zombies*

Loneliness

See *Only the Lonely*

H.P. Lovecraft: Books to Film

Bride of Re-Animator
Cthulhu Mansion
The Curse
Die, Monster, Die!
The Dunwich Horror
From Beyond
H.P. Lovecraft's Necronomicon: Book of the Dead

The Loving Dead

Mad Scientists

Made for Television

Magic & Magicians

Marriage

Martial Arts

Men in Prison

Metamorphosis

Meteors, Asteroids, & Comets

The Military

Mirrors

Missing Persons

Moms

The Monkey's Paw

Scripts based—some loosely—on the short story "The Monkey's Paw"

Monkeyshines

Monster Moms

Monsters

Motels & Hotels

Motor Vehicle Dept.

Mummies

Murderous Children

Musical Comedy

Musical Fantasy

Mystery & Suspense

Nanny Nightmares

Native America

Nazis & Other Paramilitary Slugs

Necronomicon—Book of the Dead

Necrophilia

Newspapers

Nuns & Priests

Obsessive Love

Occult

Edgar Allan Poe: Books to Film
The Black Cat
The Black Cat
The Fall of the House of Usher
The House of Usher
Masque of the Red Death
Masque of the Red Death
Murders in the Rue Morgue
The Oblong Box
The Pit and the Pendulum
The Pit & the Pendulum
Premature Burial
The Raven
Two Evil Eyes

Post Apocalypse
See also *Technology—Rampant*
Dawn of the Dead
Day of the Dead
Night of the Comet
Omega Man
Screamers
The Seventh Sign
Stephen King's The Stand

Pregnant Pauses
See also *That's a Baby?!*
Alien3
Demon Seed
The Fly
It's Alive
A Nightmare on Elm Street 5: Dream Child
The Prophecy 2: Ashtown
The Seventh Sign
Village of the Damned
Witchery

Prison
See *Great Escapes; Men in Prison; Women in Prison*

Prom
See also *Hell High School*
Buffy the Vampire Slayer
Carrie
The Club
Hello Mary Lou: Prom Night 2
Prom Night
Prom Night 3: The Last Kiss
Prom Night 4: Deliver Us from Evil
The Texas Chainsaw Massacre 4: The Next Generation

Prostitutes
See *Oldest Profession*

Psychiatry
See *Shrinks*

Psycho-Thriller
See also *Mystery & Suspense*
Afraid of the Dark
After Midnight
The Art of Dying
The Bad Seed
Cape Fear
Cupid
Dolores Claiborne
Dynasty of Fear
The Ex
Fatal Attraction
Haunted
Hush, Hush, Sweet Charlotte
The Invisible Ghost
Jack Be Nimble
Jacob's Ladder
Julia and Julia
M
The Maddening
Magic
Misery
The Most Dangerous Game
Nature of the Beast
Peeping Tom
Psycho 3
Raising Cain
Relentless
Repulsion
Seven
Shallow Grave
The Silence of the Lambs
Single White Female
The Stepfather
Stepfather 2: Make Room for Daddy
The Tenant
Terrified
Wait Until Dark

Psychotics/Sociopaths
See also *Roommates from Hell*
The Bad Seed
Body Bags
Boxing Helena
Cape Fear
Carrie
Copycat
Dario Argento's Trauma
Demon Hunter
The Dentist
Deranged
Dr. Giggles
Fade to Black
Fatal Attraction
The Fiance
Friday the 13th
From Dusk Till Dawn
Halloween
Helter Skelter Murders
The Hitcher
In the Mouth of Madness
M
Psycho
Psycho 2
Psycho 3
Psycho 4: The Beginning
Relentless
Repulsion
Scream
Scream 2
Seven
The Shining
The Silence of the Lambs
Single White Female
Skinner
The Stepfather
Stepfather 2: Make Room for Daddy
The Tenant
Tetsuo: The Iron Man
What Ever Happened to Baby Jane?
When a Stranger Calls Back

Puppets
See also *Killer Toys; Ventriloquists & Dummies*
Dead of Night
Devil Doll
Magic
Pinocchio's Revenge
Puppet Master

Rabbits
Alice in Wonderland
Fatal Attraction
Night of the Lepus
Repulsion

Rape
The Beast Within
The Curse of the Werewolf
Deliverance
Demon Seed
I Spit on Your Grave
It's Alive
Last House on the Left

Rebel With a Cause
See also *Rebel Without a Cause*
The Blob

Rebel Without a Cause
See also *Rebel With a Cause*
A Clockwork Orange
I Was a Teenage Werewolf

Reincarnation
Audrey Rose
Baron Blood
Dead Again
Exorcist 3: Legion
The Reincarnation of Peter Proud

Religion
See also *Judaism; Nuns & Priests*
The Addiction
Alice Sweet Alice
The Church
Def by Temptation
The Exorcist
The Exorcist 2: The Heretic
Exorcist 3: Legion
The Rapture
The Seventh Sign
Tales from the Crypt Presents Bordello of Blood
To the Devil, a Daughter

Renegade Body Parts
See also *Killer Brains*
The Addams Family
Addams Family Values
And Now the Screaming Starts
The Beast with Five Fingers
The Brain that Wouldn't Die
The Crawling Hand
Evil Dead 2: Dead by Dawn
The Hand
The Hands of Orlac
Mad Love
Waxwork 2: Lost in Time

Dracula vs. Frankenstein
The Fearless Vampire Killers
The Horror of Frankenstein
I Was a Teenage Frankenstein
Incredibly Strange Creatures Who Stopped Living and Became Mixed-Up Zombies
Little Shop of Horrors
Little Shop of Horrors
Natural Born Killers
Near Dark
Night of the Lepus
Once Bitten
The Rocky Horror Picture Show
Scream
Scream 2
Serial Mom
Stay Tuned
The Stuff
They Live
Tromeo & Juliet
Vamp
Werewolf of Washington
Young Frankenstein

Special FX Wizards: Tom Savini

The Burning
Creepshow
Dawn of the Dead
Day of the Dead
Deranged
Friday the 13th
Friday the 13th, Part 4: The Final Chapter
Maniac
Martin
Monkey Shines
Texas Chainsaw Massacre 2

Sci Fi

See also *Fantasy*
Alien
Aliens
Alien3
The Arrival
Attack of the Giant Leeches
Attack of the Killer Tomatoes
The Blob
The Blob
Body Snatchers
Bug
Circuit Breaker
The Crazies
Dark Breed
Darkman
Deepstar Six
Demon Seed
Earth Vs. the Spider
Event Horizon
The Fly
The Fly
Galaxy of Terror
Gamera, Guardian of the Universe
The Giant Spider Invasion
Habitat
Hideous Sun Demon
Horror Planet
The Incredible Shrinking Man
Invasion of the Body Snatchers
Invasion of the Body Snatchers
The Invisible Man Returns
The Lawnmower Man
Leprechaun 4: In Space
Leviathan
Lifeforce
Lost Continent
Mimic
The Monster of Piedras Blancas
Mosquito
The Nest
Night of the Lepus
Not Like Us
Not of This Earth
Not of This Earth
Omega Man
Plan 9 from Outer Space
Polymorph
Proteus
Quatermass and the Pit
Return of the Fly
The Running Man
Scream and Scream Again
Screamers
Skeeter
Species
Starship Troopers
Stephen King's The Langoliers
Tetsuo: The Iron Man
Them!
The Thing
The Thing
Time Walker
Transformations
Vampirella
Village of the Damned
Waxwork 2: Lost in Time

Science & Scientists

See also *Cloning Around; Mad Scientists*
Deadly Friend
Demon Seed
Die, Monster, Die!
The Fly
The Fly
Habitat
Jurassic Park
Link
The Lost World: Jurassic Park 2
Mimic
Phantom Empire
Return of the Fly
Species
Stephen King's Golden Years
The Thing

Sculptors

See also *Art & Artists*
A Bucket of Blood
Crucible of Terror
The Death Artist
Diary of a Madman
House of Wax
Mystery of the Wax Museum

Sea Critter Attack

See *Killer Sea Creatures*

Serial Killers

See also *Crime & Criminals; Jack the Ripper*
Addams Family Values
The Awful Dr. Orloff
The Banker
Blade of the Ripper
Body Bags
The Club
Copycat
Curdled
Dario Argento's Trauma
A Demon in My View
Deranged
Doctor X
Exorcist 3: Legion
Eyes of Laura Mars
Fatal Love
The Frighteners
Ghost in the Machine
Henry: Portrait of a Serial Killer
The Horror Show
The Howling
Impulse
Jack the Ripper
Listen
The Lodger
M
Manhunter
Maniac Cop
Natural Born Killers
Nature of the Beast
Nightscare
Normal Life
Pale Blood
Relentless
Scream
Scream 2
Serial Mom
Seven
The Silence of the Lambs
Silent Scream
Skinner
Star Time
Town that Dreaded Sundown
The Untold Story
When a Stranger Calls
When a Stranger Calls Back

Sex & Sexuality

See also *Crimes of Passion; Erotic Thrillers; Sexploitation*
Andy Warhol's Dracula
Andy Warhol's Frankenstein
Angel Heart
Boccaccio '70
Boxing Helena
Bram Stoker's Dracula
Cat People
Cold Sweat
Crash
Daughters of Darkness
The Devils
Elvira, Mistress of the Dark
Embrace of the Vampire
Evils of the Night
Fatal Attraction
Fellini Satyricon
Frankenstein Unbound
Gothic
The Hunger
In the Realm of the Senses
Lady Frankenstein
Lifeforce
Mirror, Mirror 3: The Voyeur
Murder Weapon
Naked Lunch
Peeping Tom
Raising Cain
Repulsion
The Rocky Horror Picture Show
Serpent's Lair
Stormswept
Terrified
To Sleep with a Vampire

Into the Badlands
Mad at the Moon
Near Dark

Suspense

See *Mystery & Suspense*

Technology—Rampant

See also *Computers; Killer Appliances; Robots & Androids*

Brainscan
Chopping Mall
Demon Seed
The Fly
The Fly
Ghost in the Machine
Maximum Overdrive
Screamers
Shocker
Stay Tuned

Teen Angst

See also *Hell High School*

Blood of Dracula
Body Snatchers
Brainscan
Buffy the Vampire Slayer
Carrie
Children of the Corn 2: The Final Sacrifice
Christine
The Club
The Craft
Dario Argento's Trauma
Dracula A.D. 1972
Evils of the Night
Fright Night
Gate 2
Halloween
Halloween 6: The Curse of Michael Myers
Heathers
Heavenly Creatures
I Know What You Did Last Summer
I Was a Teenage Werewolf
Jennifer
Little Witches
The Lost Boys
Mirror, Mirror
Nightmare
A Nightmare on Elm Street
A Nightmare on Elm Street 2: Freddy's Revenge
A Nightmare on Elm Street 3: Dream Warriors
A Nightmare on Elm Street 4: Dream Master
A Nightmare on Elm Street 5: Dream Child
Nowhere
One Dark Night
Paradise Lost: The Child Murders at Robin Hood Hills
Pin ...
Scream
Scream for Help
Student Bodies
The Wraith

Television

See *TV Movies; TV Pilot Movies*

That's a Baby?!

Addams Family Values
Alien
Basket Case 3: The Progeny
The Brood
Demon Seed
It's Alive
It's Alive 2: It Lives Again
It's Alive 3: Island of the Alive
A Nightmare on Elm Street 5: Dream Child
Psycho 4: The Beginning
Rosemary's Baby

This Is Your Life

Anne Rice: Birth of the Vampire
Ed Wood
Gothic
Haunted Summer
Rasputin the Mad Monk

3-D Flicks

Amityville 3: The Demon
Andy Warhol's Frankenstein
Creature from the Black Lagoon
The Creature Walks Among Us
Flesh and Blood Show
Friday the 13th, Part 3
House of Wax
Jaws 3
The Mask
Revenge of the Creature

Thrillers

See *Erotic Thrillers; Mystery & Suspense; Psycho-Thriller*

Thumbs Up

Hitchhikin' to hell. See also *Road Trips*

Creepshow 2
Dust Devil
The Fog
The Hitcher
Nature of the Beast
Orson Welles' Ghost Story

Time Travel

Army of Darkness
Frankenstein Unbound
Hocus Pocus
Warlock
Waxwork 2: Lost in Time

Torrid Love Scenes

See also *Sex & Sexuality; Sexploitation*

Angel Heart
Basic Instinct
Bram Stoker's Dracula
Daughters of Darkness
Don't Look Now
Fatal Attraction
The Harvest
In the Realm of the Senses
The Lawnmower Man
Vampyres

Trains

Horror Express
Mimic
Terror Train

Transvestites & Transsexuals

See *Gender Bending*

Trapped with a Killer!

See also *Psychotics/ Sociopaths*

Copycat
Fatal Attraction
The Maddening
Manhunter
Misery
Mute Witness
The Shining
The Silence of the Lambs
The Terror
Wait Until Dark
When a Stranger Calls
When a Stranger Calls Back

Trash

Andy Warhol's Dracula
Andy Warhol's Frankenstein
Attack of the Giant Leeches
Attack of the Killer Tomatoes
Blood Freak
Bloodsucking Nazi Zombies
Bugged!
Cannibal! The Musical
Chopper Chicks in Zombietown
Demons
Dracula vs. Frankenstein
Flesh and Blood Show
The House of Usher
I Spit on Your Grave
Impulse
Incredibly Strange Creatures Who Stopped Living and Became Mixed-Up Zombies
Motel Hell
Murder Weapon
Night of the Cobra Woman
Plan 9 from Outer Space
Rabid Grannies
The Toxic Avenger
The Toxic Avenger, Part 2
The Toxic Avenger, Part 3: The Last Temptation of Toxie
Tromeo & Juliet
2000 Maniacs
Zombie Island Massacre

Trees & Forests

Evil Dead
Evil Dead 2: Dead by Dawn
The Guardian
Poltergeist
Poltergeist 2: The Other Side
The Wizard of Oz

Troma Films

Bugged!
Cannibal! The Musical
Chopper Chicks in Zombietown
Rabid Grannies
The Toxic Avenger
The Toxic Avenger, Part 2
The Toxic Avenger, Part 3: The Last Temptation of Toxie
Tromeo & Juliet
Zombie Island Massacre

Trucks
See *Big Rigs*

True Crime
See also *Crime & Criminals; This Is Your Life; True Stories?*
Deranged
Helter Skelter Murders
Normal Life
Paradise Lost: The Child Murders at Robin Hood Hills
Sister My Sister

True Stories?
See also *This Is Your Life; True Crime*
The Amityville Horror
Apprentice to Murder
Dead Ringers
Deranged
Heavenly Creatures
Helter Skelter Murders
Henry: Portrait of a Serial Killer
Legend of Boggy Creek
Normal Life
Reversal of Fortune
Town that Dreaded Sundown
The Untold Story

Thomas Tryon: Books to Film
The Dark Secret of Harvest Home
The Other

TV Movies
Amityville 4
Blood Ties
Body Bags
Burial of the Rats
A Christmas Carol
Cold Comfort
The Dark Secret of Harvest Home
Duel
Humanoids from the Deep
The Hunchback of Notre Dame
Into the Badlands
Invitation to Hell
Jekyll and Hyde
Not of This Earth
Psycho 4: The Beginning
Sometimes They Come Back
Spectre
Stephen King's Golden Years
Stephen King's It
Stephen King's The Langoliers
Stephen King's The Night Flier
Stephen King's The Stand
Stephen King's The Tommyknockers
Summer of Fear
Trilogy of Terror
Trilogy of Terror 2
Vampirella
Wasp Woman
When a Stranger Calls Back

TV Pilot Movies
Night Gallery
The Night Stalker

Twins
See also *Family Ties*
Basket Case
Basket Case 2
Basket Case 3: The Progeny
The Black Room
Black Sunday
The Bride with White Hair
Cobra Woman
Dead Men Walk
Dead Ringers
The Other
Raising Cain
Sisters
Twins of Evil

Universal Studios
Abbott and Costello Meet Dr. Jekyll and Mr. Hyde
Abbott and Costello Meet Frankenstein
Abbott and Costello Meet the Invisible Man
Abbott and Costello Meet the Killer, Boris Karloff
Abbott and Costello Meet the Mummy
The Black Cat
The Bride of Frankenstein
Calling Dr. Death/Strange Confession
Creature from the Black Lagoon
The Creature Walks Among Us
Darkman
Darkman 2: The Return of Durant
Darkman 3: Die Darkman Die
Dead Man's Eyes/ Pillow of Death
Doctor Giggles
Dracula
Dracula's Daughter
Frankenstein
Frankenstein Meets the Wolfman
The Ghost of Frankenstein
House of Dracula
House of Frankenstein
The Hunchback of Notre Dame
The Invisible Man
The Invisible Man Returns
Island of Lost Souls
The Mummy
The Mummy's Curse
The Mummy's Ghost
The Mummy's Hand
The Mummy's Tomb
Murders in the Rue Morgue
The Phantom of the Opera
The Phantom of the Opera
The Raven
Revenge of the Creature
Son of Dracula
Son of Frankenstein
Weird Woman/ Frozen Ghost
Werewolf of London
The Wolf Man

John Updike: Books to Film
The Witches of Eastwick

Urban Legends
Alligator
Candyman
Candyman 2
C.H.U.D.
C.H.U.D. 2: Bud the Chud
The Harvest
Hellgate
I Know What You Did Last Summer
Orson Welles' Ghost Story
When a Stranger Calls

Vacations
See also *Road Trip*
An American Werewolf in London
Deliverance
Evil Dead
Evil Dead 2: Dead by Dawn
The Hills Have Eyes
I Spit on Your Grave
Race with the Devil
Terror at Red Wolf Inn
Witchery

Vampire Babes
See also *Vampires*
The Addiction
The Brides of Dracula
Buffy the Vampire Slayer
Captain Kronos: Vampire Hunter
Countess Dracula
The Craving
Daughters of Darkness
Dracula's Daughter
The Fearless Vampire Killers
Fright Night
From Dusk Till Dawn
The Girl with the Hungry Eyes
Interview with the Vampire
Lemora: A Child's Tale of the Supernatural
Lust for a Vampire
Mary, Mary, Bloody Mary
Nadja
Once Bitten
Tales from the Crypt Presents Bordello of Blood
Twins of Evil
Vamp
The Vampire Lovers
Vampire's Kiss
Vampyres
The Velvet Vampire

Vampires
See also *Dracula; Vampire Babes*
The Addiction
Anne Rice: Birth of the Vampire
Billy the Kid Versus Dracula
Black Sabbath
Blacula
Blood & Donuts
Blood and Roses
Blood Freak
Blood of Dracula's Castle
The Blood Spattered Bride
Blood Ties
Bloodlust: Subspecies 3
Bloodstone: Subspecies 2

The Bloodsuckers
Bram Stoker's Dracula
The Brides of Dracula
Buffy the Vampire Slayer
Captain Kronos: Vampire Hunter
Children of the Night
Count Dracula
Count Yorga, Vampire
The Craving
Cronos
Dance of the Damned
Daughter of Darkness
Daughters of Darkness
Dead Men Walk
Dracula
Dracula
Dracula A.D. 1972
Dracula: Dead and Loving It
Dracula Has Risen from the Grave
Dracula Rising
Dracula's Daughter
Elvira, Mistress of the Dark
Embrace of the Vampire
Evils of the Night
Fangs! A History of Vampires in the Movies
Fright Night
Fright Night 2
From Dusk Till Dawn
Graveyard Shift
The Horror of Dracula
House of Dark Shadows
House of Dracula
House of Frankenstein
The Hunger
Innocent Blood
Interview with the Vampire
Isle of the Dead
Jugular Wine: A Vampire Odyssey
Kiss of the Vampire
Lemora: A Child's Tale of the Supernatural
Lifeforce
The Lost Boys
Lust for a Vampire
Mark of the Vampire
Martin
Mary, Mary, Bloody Mary
Midnight Kiss
Nadja
Near Dark
Night Hunter
The Night Stalker
Nosferatu
Nosferatu the Vampyre
Not of This Earth
Not of This Earth
Once Bitten
Pale Blood
Rabid
The Return of Count Yorga
Return of Dracula
Return of the Vampire
Return to Salem's Lot
Salem's Lot
The Satanic Rites of Dracula
The Scars of Dracula
Sleepwalkers
Son of Dracula
Stephen King's The Night Flier
Subspecies
Tales from the Crypt Presents Bordello of Blood
Taste the Blood of Dracula
The Thirsty Dead
Thrill of the Vampire
To Die For
To Die For 2: Son of Darkness
To Sleep with a Vampire
Twins of Evil
Understudy: The Graveyard Shift 2
Vamp
The Vampire Bat
Vampire Circus
The Vampire Hookers
Vampire Hunter D
Vampire in Brooklyn
Vampire Journals
The Vampire Lovers
Vampirella
Vampire's Kiss
Vampyr
Vampyres
The Velvet Vampire
The Wicked
Witchcraft 7: Judgement Hour

Ventriloquists & Dummies

Dead of Night
Devil Doll
Magic

Vietnam War

Apocalypse Now
Jacob's Ladder

Virtual Reality

See also *Computers; Technology—Rampant*
Brainscan
Future Shock
The Lawnmower Man

Voodoo

See also *Occult*
Angel Heart
Asylum
I Walked with a Zombie
Plague of the Zombies
The Serpent and the Rainbow
Voodoo
Weird Woman/ Frozen Ghost

Edgar Wallace: Books to Film

Chamber of Horrors
King Kong
King Kong

Wax Museums

Abbott & Costello Meet Frankenstein
Crucible of Terror
House of Wax
Mystery of the Wax Museum
Waxwork
Waxwork 2: Lost in Time
Weird Woman/ Frozen Ghost

Wedding Hell

See also *Marriage*
Blood and Roses
The Blood Spattered Bride
The Bride
The Bride of Frankenstein
Bride of Re-Animator
Bride of the Monster
The Bride with White Hair
The Bride with White Hair 2
Daughters of Darkness
He Knows You're Alone
Highway to Hell
Murders in the Rue Morgue

H.G. Wells: Books to Film

The Invisible Man
The Invisible Man's Revenge
Island of Dr. Moreau
The Island of Dr. Moreau
Island of Lost Souls

Werewolves

See also *Metamorphosis; The Wolfman*
Abbott and Costello Meet Frankenstein
An American Werewolf in London
An American Werewolf in Paris
Bad Moon
Black Werewolf
Blood of Dracula's Castle
The Company of Wolves
The Craving
The Creeps
The Curse of the Werewolf
Frankenstein Meets the Wolfman
House of Dracula
House of Frankenstein
The Howling
Howling 2: Your Sister Is a Werewolf
Howling 3: The Marsupials
Howling 4: The Original Nightmare
The Howling: New Moon Rising
I Was a Teenage Werewolf
Legend of the Werewolf
Meridian: Kiss of the Beast
Return of the Vampire
Silver Bullet
Waxwork
Werewolf
Werewolf of London
Werewolf of Washington
Wolf
The Wolf Man
Wolfen

Whales

See also *Killer Sea Creatures*
Orca

Oscar Wilde: Books to Film

Dorian Gray
Picture of Dorian Gray

Witchcraft

See also *Demons & Wizards; Occult*
Beauty Evil Rose
Black Sunday
The Bride with White Hair
The Bride with White Hair 2
Burn Witch, Burn!
The Conqueror Worm
The Craft

DISTRIBUTOR LIST

The following list deciphers the three-letter distributor codes found at the end of each review. If the movie is available on video, you can look up the code here, and flip the page to the "Distributor Guide" to get the address, phone, fax, toll-free, and maybe even e-mail or web site address for the distributor. If the movie is not available on video, the codes **NO** (not currently available), **NYR** (not yet released), or **OM** (on moratorium) will appear. Please note that studio distributors do not sell to the general public; they act as wholesalers, selling only to retail outlets. Many video stores provide an ordering service; see p. xix for a list of establishments that may be able to track down your movie for you.

ADF—A.D.V. Films
AFE—Amazing Fantasy Entertainment
AHV—Avid Home Video
AOV—Admit One Video
APX—A-PIX Entertainment Inc.
AVE—WarnerVision
AVI—Arrow Video, Inc./Arrow Entertainment
BAR—Barr Films
BFV—Best Film & Video Corp.
BTV—Baker & Taylor Video
CAB—Cable Films & Video
CAF—Cabin Fever Entertainment
CCB—Critics' Choice Video, Inc.
CDV—Television International
CNG—Congress Entertainment, Inc.
CNM—Cinemacabre Video
COL—Columbia Tristar Home Video
CPM—Central Park Media/U.S. Manga Corps
CRC—Criterion Collection
CVC—Connoisseur Meridian Films
DAP—Dead Alive Productions
DIS—Walt Disney Home Video
DVT—Discount Video Tapes, Inc./Hollywood's Attic
EEL—Englewood Entertainment LLC
EII—El Independent Cinema
EVE—Evergreen Entertainment
FCS—Focus on the Family/Ministry Resources
FCT—Facets Multimedia, Inc.
FHE—Family Home Entertainment
FLL—Full Moon Pictures
FOX—CBS/Fox Video
FRG—Fright Video
FST—Festival Films
FUS—Fusion Video
FXL—Fox/Lorber Home Video
FXV—Twentieth Century Fox Home Entertainment
GEG—Granite Entertainment Group
GEM—Video Gems
GKK—Goodtimes Entertainment
GLV—German Language Video Center
GPV—Grapevine Video
GVV—Glenn Video Vistas, Ltd.
HBO—HBO Home Video
HEG—Horizon Entertainment
HHE—Hollywood Home Entertainment
HHT—Hollywood Home Theatre
HMK—Hallmark Home Entertainment
HMV—Home Vision Cinema
HPH—Hollywood Pictures Home Video
HTV—Hen's Tooth Video
IHF—International Historic Films, Inc. (IHF)
IME—Image Entertainment
IMP—Imperial Entertainment Corp.
INC—Increase/SilverMine Video
INT—Interama, Inc.
ISF—Incredibly Strange Filmworks
JEF—JEF Films, Inc.
KAR—Karol Video
KIV—Kino on Video

KUI—Knowledge Unlimited, Inc.
LIV—Live Entertainment
LSV—LSVideo, Inc.
LUM—Lumivision Corp.
MAG—Magnum Entertainment
MAX—Miramax Pictures Home Video
MGM—MGM Home Entertainment
MLB—Mike LeBell's Video
MLT—Music for Little People
MNC—Monarch Home Video
MON—Monterey Home Video
MOV—Movies Unlimited
MPI—MPI Home Video
MRV—Moore Video
MTH—MTI Home Video
MVD—Music Video Distributors
NHO—New Horizons HomeVideo
NLC—New Line Home Video
NO—*Not currently available on video*
NOS—Nostalgia Family Video
NYR—*Not yet released*
OM—*On moratorium*
ORI—Orion Home Video
ORP—Orphan Entertainment
PAR—Paramount Home Video
PGV—Polygram Video (PV)
PMH—PM Entertainment Group, Inc.
PMS—Professional Media Service Corp.
QVD—Quality Video
RDG—Reader's Digest Home Video
REP—Republic Pictures Home Video
RHI—Rhino Home Video
RXM—Rex Miller
SGE—Amsell Entertainment
SMW—Something Weird Video
SNC—Sinister Cinema
STP—Streamline Pictures
TAI—Tai Seng Video Marketing
TEM—Tempe Video
THV—Trimark Home Video
TLF—Time-Life Video and Television
TOU—Buena Vista Home Video
TPV—Tapeworm Video Distributors
TRI—Triboro Entertainment Group
TRO—Troma Inc.
TTC—Turner Home Entertainment Company
TTV—Troma Team Video
TVC—The Video Catalog
TWE—Trans-World Entertainment
TWV—Time Warner Viewer's Edge
UNI—Unicorn Video, Inc.
USH—Universal Studios Home Video
VCD—Video City Productions/Distributing
VCI—VCI Home Video
VCN—Video Connection
VDM—Video Dimensions
VEC—Valencia Entertainment Corp.
VES—Vestron Video
VHE—VCII Home Entertainment, Inc.
VSE—Vista Street Entertainment
VSM—Video Search of Miami
VTR—Anchor Bay
VYY—Video Yesteryear
WAR—Warner Home Video, Inc.
WFV—Western Media Systems
WOV—Worldvision Home Video, Inc.
YHV—York Home Video

DISTRIBUTOR GUIDE

The "Distributor Guide" provides contact information for the distributors indicated within the reviews. Each movie in the main section has at least one code located at the end of the entry. The key to these codes, preceding this guide, will lead you to the appropriate distributor (if the movie is available on video). Those titles with the code **OM** are on moratorium, and those with **NO** currently have no distributor—both meaning that they were distributed at one time, but are not currently; since they were once available, these movies may show up at your local video store. Films that have not yet made it to video (including older titles) have the designation **NYR** (not yet released). Beware: 1) Not all movies are available on video; 2) From year to year, a small minority of distributors move without telling anyone, or just plain go out of business; and 3) Studio distributors do not sell to the general public—they generally act as wholesalers, selling only to retail outlets. Many video stores provide an ordering service; check out the "Video Sources" section on p. xix for a few suggested outlets to help you track down a title.

A-PIX ENTERTAINMENT INC. *(APX)*
200 Madison Ave., 24th Fl.
New York NY 10016
206-284-4700
800-245-6472
fax: 206-286-4433

ADMIT ONE VIDEO *(AOV)*
PO Box 66, Sta. O
Toronto ON Canada M4A 2M8
416-463-5714
fax: 416-463-5714

A.D.V. FILMS *(ADF)*
5750 Bintliff, No. 217
Houston TX 77036-2123
713-977-9181

AMAZING FANTASY ENTERTAINMENT *(AFE)*
1645 N. Vine St.
Hollywood CA 90028
213-468-0599

AMSELL ENTERTAINMENT *(SGE)*
12001 Ventura Pl., 4th Fl., Ste. 404
Studio City CA 91604
818-766-8500
fax: 818-766-7873

ANCHOR BAY *(VTR)*
500 Kirts Blvd.
Troy MI 48084
248-362-4400
800-786-8777
fax: 248-362-4454

ARROW VIDEO, INC./ARROW ENTERTAINMENT *(AVI)*
135 W. 50th St., Ste. 1925
New York NY 10020
212-258-2200
fax: 212-245-1252

AVID HOME VIDEO *(AHV)*
c/o Live Home Video
15400 Sherman Way
PO Box 10124
Van Nuys CA 91406
818-908-0303
800-423-7455

BAKER & TAYLOR VIDEO *(BTV)*
700 N. Austin
Niles IL 60714
800-775-2800

BARR FILMS *(BAR)*
12801 Schabarum
Irwindale CA 91706

BEST FILM & VIDEO CORP. *(BFV)*
108 New South Rd.
PO Box 9025
Hicksville NY 11802-9025
516-931-6969
800-527-2189
fax: 516-931-5959

BUENA VISTA HOME VIDEO *(TOU)*
PO Box 908
Lakewood CA 90714-0908
310-233-3120

CABIN FEVER ENTERTAINMENT *(CAF)*
100 W. Putnam Ave.
Greenwich CT 06830
203-863-5200
fax: 203-863-5258

CABLE FILMS & VIDEO *(CAB)*
PO Box 7171, Country Club Sta.
Kansas City MO 64113
913-362-2804
800-514-2804
fax: 913-341-7365
e-mail: catchwave@sprintmail.com

CBS/FOX VIDEO *(FOX)*
PO Box 900
Beverly Hills CA 90213
562-373-4800
888-223-4FOX
fax: 562-373-4803

CENTRAL PARK MEDIA/U.S. MANGA CORPS *(CPM)*
250 W. 57th St., Ste. 317
New York NY 10107
212-977-7456
800-833-7456
fax: 212-977-8709
web: www.centralparkmedia.com

CINEMACABRE VIDEO *(CNM)*
PO Box 10005
Baltimore MD 21285-0005

COLUMBIA TRISTAR HOME VIDEO *(COL)*
Sony Pictures Plz.
10202 W. Washington Blvd.
Culver City CA 90232
310-280-5418
fax: 310-280-2485
web: www.spe.sony.com

CONGRESS ENTERTAINMENT, INC. *(CNG)*
PO Box 845
Tannersville PA 18372-0845
717-620-2333
800-847-8273
fax: 717-620-9313
e-mail: karolyn28@acx.com

CONNOISSEUR MERIDIAN FILMS *(CVC)*
1575 Westwood Blvd., Ste. 205
Los Angeles CA 90024
310-231-1350
800-529-2300
fax: 310-231-1359
web: www.meridianvideo.com

CRITERION COLLECTION *(CRC)*
c/o The Voyager Co.
578 Broadway
New York NY 10012
212-431-5199
800-446-2001
web: www.criterionco.com

CRITICS' CHOICE VIDEO, INC. *(CCB)*
PO Box 749
Itasca IL 60143
630-775-3300
800-367-7765
fax: 630-775-3340

DEAD ALIVE PRODUCTIONS *(DAP)*
111 W. Main St.
Mesa AZ 85201

DISCOUNT VIDEO TAPES, INC./HOLLYWOOD'S ATTIC *(DVT)*
PO Box 7122
Burbank CA 91510
818-843-3366
fax: 818-843-3821
web: www.discountvideotapes.com

EI INDEPENDENT CINEMA *(EII)*
68 Forest St.
Montclair NJ 07042
201-509-1616
fax: 201-746-6464
e-mail: eicinema@aol.com

ENGLEWOOD ENTERTAINMENT LLC *(EEL)*
10917 Winner Rd.
Independence MO 64052
816-252-4288
888-573-5490
fax: 816-836-3400
e-mail: moss@kenet.com
web: www.englewd.com

EVERGREEN ENTERTAINMENT *(EVE)*
6100 Wilshire Blvd., Ste. 1400
Los Angeles CA 90048

FACETS MULTIMEDIA, INC. *(FCT)*
1517 W. Fullerton Ave.
Chicago IL 60614
773-281-9075
800-331-6197
fax: 773-929-5437

FAMILY HOME ENTERTAINMENT *(FHE)*
c/o Live Home Video
15400 Sherman Way
PO Box 10124
Van Nuys CA 91410-0124
818-908-0303
800-677-0789
fax: 818-778-3259

FESTIVAL FILMS *(FST)*
6115 Chestnut Ter.
Excelsior MN 55331-8107
612-470-2172
800-798-6083
fax: 612-470-2172
e-mail: fesfilms@aol.com
web: members.aol.com/festfilms/

FOCUS ON THE FAMILY/MINISTRY RESOURCES *(FCS)*
8605 Explorer Dr.
Colorado Springs CO 80920
719-531-3400
fax: 719-548-4652

FOX/LORBER HOME VIDEO *(FXL)*
419 Park Ave. S., 20th Fl.
New York NY 10016
212-686-6777
fax: 212-685-2625

FRIGHT VIDEO *(FRG)*
PO Box 277
North Billerica MA 01862

FULL MOON PICTURES *(FLL)*
1645 N. Vine St.
Hollywood CA 90028
213-468-0599

FUSION VIDEO *(FUS)*
100 Fusion Way
Country Club Hills IL 60478
708-799-2073
fax: 708-799-8375
web: www.fusion-intl.com

GERMAN LANGUAGE VIDEO CENTER *(GLV)*
7625 Pendleton Pike
Indianapolis IN 46226-5298
317-547-1257
800-252-1957
fax: 317-547-1263
web: www.germanvideo.com

GLENN VIDEO VISTAS, LTD. *(GVV)*
6924 Canby Ave., Ste. 103
Reseda CA 91335
818-881-8110
fax: 818-981-5506
e-mail: mglass@worldnet.att.net

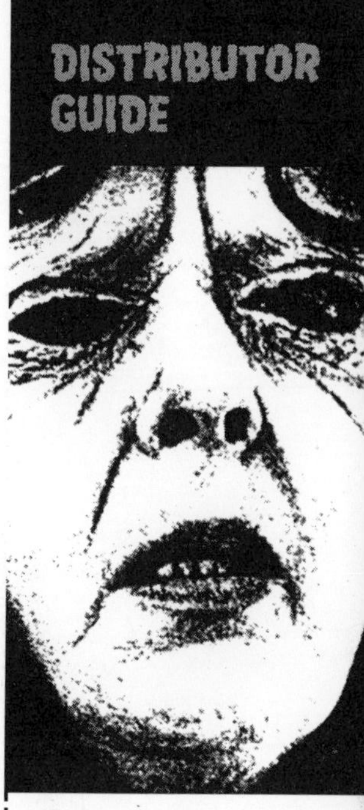

GOODTIMES ENTERTAINMENT *(GKK)*
16 E. 40th St., 8th Fl.
New York NY 10016-0113
212-951-3000
fax: 212-213-9319
e-mail: order@gtent.com
web: www.goodtimes.com

GRANITE ENTERTAINMENT GROUP *(GEG)*
22222 Sherman Way, Ste. 100
Canoga Park CA 91303

GRAPEVINE VIDEO *(GPV)*
PO Box 46161
Phoenix AZ 85063
602-973-3661
fax: 602-973-2973
web: www.grapevinevideo.com

HALLMARK HOME ENTERTAINMENT *(HMK)*
6100 Wilshire Blvd., Ste. 1400
Los Angeles CA 90048
213-634-3000
fax: 213-549-3760

HBO HOME VIDEO *(HBO)*
1100 6th Ave.
New York NY 10036
212-512-7400
fax: 212-512-7498
web: www.hbohomevideo.com

HEN'S TOOTH VIDEO *(HTV)*
2805 E. State Blvd.
Fort Wayne IN 46805
219-471-4332
fax: 219-471-4449

HOLLYWOOD HOME ENTERTAINMENT *(HHE)*
6165 Crooked Creek Rd., Ste. B
Norcross GA 30092-3105

HOLLYWOOD HOME THEATRE *(HHT)*
9830 Charlieville Blvd.
Beverly Hills CA 90212
310-203-9868

HOLLYWOOD PICTURES HOME VIDEO *(HPH)*
Fairmont Bldg. 526
500 S. Buena Vista St.
Burbank CA 91505-9842

HOME VISION CINEMA *(HMV)*
5547 N. Ravenswood Ave.
Chicago IL 60640-1199
773-878-2600
800-826-3456
fax: 773-878-8406
web: www.homevision.com

HORIZON ENTERTAINMENT *(HEG)*
45030 Trevor Ave.
Lancaster CA 93534
805-940-1040
800-323-2061
fax: 805-940-8511

IMAGE ENTERTAINMENT *(IME)*
9333 Oso Ave.
Chatsworth CA 91311
818-407-9100
800-473-3475
fax: 818-407-9111

IMPERIAL ENTERTAINMENT CORP. *(IMP)*
11846 Ventura Blvd., Ste. 300
Studio City CA 91604
818-762-0005
fax: 818-762-0006

INCREASE/SILVERMINE VIDEO *(INC)*
6860 Canby Ave., Ste. 118
Reseda CA 91335
818-342-2880
800-233-2880
fax: 818-342-4029
e-mail: quksil@aol.com

INCREDIBLY STRANGE FILMWORKS *(ISF)*
PO Box 245
Jamestown MO 65046-0245
660-849-3578
fax: 660-849-2571

INTERAMA, INC. *(INT)*
301 W. 53rd St., Ste. 19E
New York NY 10019
212-977-4830
fax: 212-581-6582
e-mail: InteramaNY@aol.com

INTERNATIONAL HISTORIC FILMS, INC. *(IHF)*
PO Box 29035
Chicago IL 60629
773-927-2900
fax: 773-927-9211
web: www.IHFfilm.com

JEF FILMS, INC. *(JEF)*
Film House
143 Hickory Hill Cir.
Osterville MA 02655-1322
508-428-7198
888-JEF-FILM
fax: 508-428-7198
e-mail: finchleyrd@aol.com

KAROL VIDEO *(KAR)*
PO Box 7600
350 N. Pennsylvania Ave.
Wilkes Barre PA 18773
717-822-8899
fax: 717-822-8226
e-mail: karolm@epix.net

KINO ON VIDEO *(KIV)*
333 W. 39th St., Ste. 503
New York NY 10018
212-629-6880
800-562-3330
fax: 212-714-0871
e-mail: kinoint@infunnse.com
web: www.kino.com

KNOWLEDGE UNLIMITED, INC. *(KUI)*
Box 52
Madison WI 53701-0052
608-836-6660
800-356-2303
fax: 608-831-1570
e-mail: ku-mail@ku.com
web: www.ku.com

LIVE ENTERTAINMENT *(LIV)*
15400 Sherman Way
PO Box 10124
Van Nuys CA 91410-0124
818-988-5060
800-677-0789
fax: 818-778-3259

LSVIDEO, INC. *(LSV)*
PO Box 415
Carmel IN 46032

LUMIVISION CORP. *(LUM)*
877 Federal Blvd.
Denver CO 80204-3212
303-446-0400
800-776-LUMI
fax: 303-446-0101

MAGNUM ENTERTAINMENT *(MAG)*
9650 De Soto Ave., Ste. M
Chatsworth CA 91311

MGM HOME ENTERTAINMENT *(MGM)*
2500 Broadway
Santa Monica CA 90404-6061
310-449-3000
fax: 310-449-3100

MIKE LEBELL'S VIDEO *(MLB)*
75 Freemont Pl.
Los Angeles CA 90005
213-938-3333
fax: 213-938-3334
e-mail: mlvideo@aol.com

REX MILLER *(RXM)*
Rte. 1, Box 457-D
East Prairie MO 63845
314-649-5048

MIRAMAX PICTURES HOME VIDEO *(MAX)*
500 S. Buena Vista St.
Burbank CA 91521
800-413-5566

MONARCH HOME VIDEO *(MNC)*
2 Ingram Blvd.
La Vergne TN 37086-7006
615-287-4632
fax: 615-287-4992
web: www.monarchvideo.com

MONTEREY HOME VIDEO *(MON)*
28038 Dorothy Dr., Ste. 1
Agoura Hills CA 91301
818-597-0047
800-424-2593
fax: 818-597-0105

MOORE VIDEO *(MRV)*
PO Box 5703
Richmond VA 23220-0703
804-745-9785
fax: 804-745-9785

MOVIES UNLIMITED *(MOV)*
3015 Darnell Rd.
Philadelphia PA 19154
215-637-4444
800-466-8437
fax: 215-637-2350
e-mail: movies@moviesunlimited.com
web: www.moviesunlimited.com

MPI HOME VIDEO *(MPI)*
16101 S. 108th Ave.
Orland Park IL 60462
708-460-0555
fax: 708-873-3177

MTI HOME VIDEO *(MTH)*
14216 SW 136th St.
Miami FL 33186
305-255-8684
800-821-7461
fax: 305-233-6943
e-mail: mti@mtivideo.com
web: www.mtivideo.com

MUSIC FOR LITTLE PEOPLE *(MLT)*
Box 1460
Redway CA 95560
707-923-3991
800-346-4445
fax: 707-923-3241

MUSIC VIDEO DISTRIBUTORS *(MVD)*
O'Neill Industrial Center
1210 Standbridge St.
Norristown PA 19401
610-272-7771
800-888-0486
fax: 610-272-6074

NEW HORIZONS HOME VIDEO *(NHO)*
2951 Flowers Rd. S., Ste. 237
Atlanta GA 30341
404-458-3488
800-854-3323
fax: 404-458-2679

NEW LINE HOME VIDEO *(NLC)*
116 N. Robertson Blvd.
Los Angeles CA 90048
310-967-6670
fax: 310-854-0602

NOSTALGIA FAMILY VIDEO *(NOS)*
PO Box 606
Baker City OR 97814
503-523-9034
800-784-8362
fax: 503-523-7115

NOT YET RELEASED *(NYR)*

ORION HOME VIDEO *(ORI)*
MGM
2500 Broadway
Santa Monica CA 90404-6061
310-449-3000
fax: 310-449-3100

ORPHAN ENTERTAINMENT *(ORP)*
6902 Sunset Blvd.
Hollywood CA 90028
213-962-6280

PARAMOUNT HOME VIDEO *(PAR)*
Bluhdorn Bldg.
5555 Melrose Ave.
Los Angeles CA 90038
213-956-3952

PM ENTERTAINMENT GROUP, INC. *(PMH)*
9450 Chivers Ave.
Sun Valley CA 91352
818-504-6332
800-934-2111
fax: 818-504-6380

POLYGRAM VIDEO (PV) *(PGV)*
825 8th Ave.
New York NY 10019
212-333-8000
800-825-7781
fax: 212-603-7960

PROFESSIONAL MEDIA SERVICE CORP. *(PMS)*
19122 S. Vermont Ave.
Gardena CA 90248
310-532-9024
800-223-7672
fax: 800-253-8853
e-mail: promedia@class.org

QUALITY VIDEO *(QVD)*
7399 Bush Lake Rd.
Minneapolis MN 55439-2027
612-893-0903
800-486-5347
fax: 612-893-1585
e-mail: email@qualitydino.com
web: www.qualitydino.com

READER'S DIGEST HOME VIDEO *(RDG)*
Reader's Digest Rd.
Pleasantville NY 10570
800-234-9000

REPUBLIC PICTURES HOME VIDEO *(REP)*
5700 Wilshire Blvd., Ste. 525 North
Los Angeles CA 90036-3659
213-965-6900
fax: 213-965-6963

RHINO HOME VIDEO *(RHI)*
10635 Santa Monica Blvd., 2nd Fl.
Los Angeles CA 90025-4900
310-828-1980
800-843-3670
fax: 310-453-5529

SINISTER CINEMA *(SNC)*
PO Box 4369
Medford OR 97501-0168
541-773-6860
fax: 541-779-8650

SOMETHING WEIRD VIDEO *(SMW)*
PO Box 33664
Seattle WA 98133
206-361-3759
fax: 206-364-7526

STREAMLINE PICTURES *(STP)*
2908 Nebraska Ave.
Santa Monica CA 90404-4109
310-998-0070
800-846-1453
fax: 310-998-1145
web: www.insv.com/streamline

TAI SENG VIDEO MARKETING *(TAI)*
170 S. Spruce Ave., Ste. 200
San Francisco CA 94080

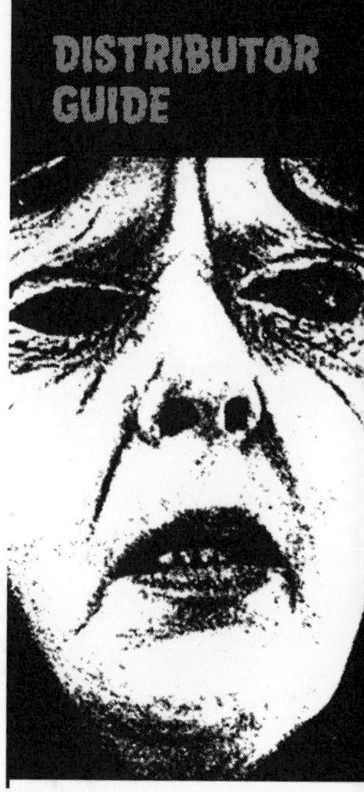

415-871-8118
800-888-3836
fax: 415-871-2392
e-mail: webstaff@taiseng.com
web: www.taiseng.com

TAPEWORM VIDEO DISTRIBUTORS *(TPV)*
27833 Hopkins Ave., Unit 6
Valencia CA 91355
805-257-4904
fax: 805-257-4820
e-mail: tapew001@interserv.com
web: www.tapeworm.com

TELEVISION INTERNATIONAL *(CDV)*
c/o Jason Films
2825 Wilcrest, Ste. 407
Houston TX 77042
713-266-3097
fax: 713-266-3148

TEMPE VIDEO *(TEM)*
Box 6573
Akron OH 44312
216-628-1950
fax: 216-628-4316

TIME-LIFE VIDEO AND TELEVISION *(TLF)*
1450 E. Parham Rd.
Richmond VA 23280
804-266-6330
800-621-7026

TIME WARNER VIEWER'S EDGE *(TWV)*
PO Box 85098
Richmond VA 23285-5098
800-947-3928
fax: 203-699-9586

TRANS-WORLD ENTERTAINMENT *(TWE)*
8899 Beverly Blvd., 8th Fl.
Los Angeles CA 90048-2412

TRIBORO ENTERTAINMENT GROUP *(TRI)*
12 W. 27th St., 15th Fl.
New York NY 10001
212-686-6116
fax: 212-686-6178

TRIMARK HOME VIDEO *(THV)*
2644 30th St.
Santa Monica CA 90405-3009
310-314-2000
fax: 310-392-0252

TROMA INC. *(TRO)*
733 9th Ave.
New York NY 10019
212-757-4555
800-83-TROMA
fax: 212-399-9885
web: www.troma.com/home

TROMA TEAM VIDEO *(TTV)*
1501 Broadway, Ste. 2605
New York NY 10036
212-997-0595
fax: 212-997-0968

TURNER HOME ENTERTAINMENT COMPANY *(TTC)*
Box 105366
Atlanta GA 35366
404-827-3066
800-523-0823
fax: 404-827-3266

TWENTIETH CENTURY FOX HOME ENTERTAINMENT *(FXV)*
PO Box 900
Beverly Hills CA 90213
310-369-3900
888-223-4FOX
fax: 310-369-5811

UNICORN VIDEO, INC. *(UNI)*
9025 Eton Ave., Ste. D.
Canoga Park CA 91304
818-407-1333
800-528-4336
fax: 818-407-8246

UNIVERSAL STUDIOS HOME VIDEO *(USH)*
100 Universal City Plz.
Universal City CA 91608-9955
818-777-1000
fax: 818-866-1483

VALENCIA ENTERTAINMENT CORP. *(VEC)*
45030 Trevor Ave.
Lancaster CA 93534-2648
805-940-1040
800-323-2061
fax: 805-940-8511

VCI HOME VIDEO *(VCI)*
11333 E. 60th Pl.
Tulsa OK 74146
918-254-6337
800-331-4077
fax: 918-254-6117
e-mail: vcihomevideo @mail.webter.com

VCII HOME ENTERTAINMENT, INC. *(VHE)*
13418 Wyandotte St.
North Hollywood CA 91605
818-764-1777
800-350-1931
fax: 818-764-0231

VESTRON VIDEO *(VES)*
c/o Live Home Video
15400 Sherman Way
PO Box 10124
Van Nuys CA 91410-0124
818-988-0303
800-367-7765
fax: 818-778-3194
e-mail: cust_serv@live-entertainment.com

THE VIDEO CATALOG *(TVC)*
7000 Westgate Dr.
St. Paul MN 55114
612-659-3700
800-733-6656
fax: 612-659-0083
e-mail: kyle@rivertrade.com

VIDEO CITY PRODUCTIONS/DISTRIBUTING *(VCD)*
4266 Broadway
Oakland CA 94611
510-428-0202
fax: 510-654-7802

VIDEO CONNECTION *(VCN)*
3123 W. Sylvania Ave.
Toledo OH 43613
419-472-7727
800-365-0449
fax: 419-472-2655

VIDEO DIMENSIONS *(VDM)*
322 8th Ave., No. 1701
New York NY 10001
212-929-6135
fax: 212-929-6135
e-mail: video@cultvideo.com
web: www.cultvideo.com/video.html

VIDEO GEMS *(GEM)*
12228 Venice Blvd., No. 504
Los Angeles CA 90066

VIDEO SEARCH OF MIAMI *(VSM)*
PO Box 161917
Miami FL 33116
305-279-9773
fax: 305-598-2665

VIDEO YESTERYEAR *(VYY)*
Box C
Sandy Hook CT 06482
800-243-0987
fax: 203-797-0819
e-mail: video@yesteryear.com

VISTA STREET ENTERTAINMENT *(VSE)*
9831 W. Pico Blvd., Ste. 4
Los Angeles CA 90035
310-556-3074
fax: 310-556-8815

WALT DISNEY HOME VIDEO *(DIS)*
500 S. Buena Vista St.
Burbank CA 91521
818-562-3560

WARNER HOME VIDEO, INC. *(WAR)*
4000 Warner Blvd.
Burbank CA 91522
818-954-6000

WARNERVISION *(AVE)*
A Time Warner Company
75 Rockefeller Plz.
New York NY 10019
212-275-2900
800-95-WARNER
fax: 212-765-0899

WESTERN MEDIA SYSTEMS *(WFV)*
30941 W. Agoura Rd., Ste. 302
Westlake Village CA 91361
818-889-7350
fax: 818-889-7350

WORLDVISION HOME VIDEO, INC. *(WOV)*
1700 Broadway
New York NY 10019-5905
212-261-2700
fax: 212-261-2950

YORK HOME VIDEO *(YHV)*
4733 Lankershim Blvd.
North Hollywood CA 91602
310-278-1034
800-84-MOVIE
fax: 818-505-8290